Collins

Collins
French
Dictionary

HarperCollins Publishers
Westerhill Road
Bishopbriggs
Glasgow
G64 2QT
Great Britain

Fifth Edition 2007

Previously published as
Collins Express French Dictionary
© HarperCollins Publishers 2006

Reprint 10 9 8 7 6

© William Collins Sons & Co. Ltd 1990
© HarperCollins Publishers 1995, 1998,
2001, 2006
© Collins Bartholomew Ltd 2005

ISBN 978-0-00-720889-0

Collins® and Bank of English® are
registered trademarks of
HarperCollins Publishers Limited

www.collinslanguage.com

A catalogue record for this book is
available from the British Library

HarperCollins Publishers,
10 East 53rd Street,
New York, NY 10022

COLLINS FRENCH POCKET DICTIONARY.
Fifth US Edition 2008

ISBN 978-0-06-143862-2

www.harpercollins.com

Typeset by Thomas Callan
'French in focus' supplement typeset by
Wordcraft, Glasgow
Verb supplement typeset by
Davidson Pre-Press, Glasgow

Printed in Italy by
Rotolito Lombarda S.p.A.

Acknowledgements
We would like to thank those authors and
publishers who kindly gave permission
for copyright material to be used in the
Collins Word Web. We would also like
to thank Times Newspapers Ltd for
providing valuable data.

TABLE DES MATIÈRES   CONTENTS

MANAGING EDITOR
Michela Clari

CONTRIBUTORS
Maree Airlie
Jean-François Allain
Gaëlle Amiot-Cadey
Cécile Aubinière-Robb
Sabine Citron
Wendy Lee
Catherine Love
Rose Rociola

SERIES EDITOR
Lorna Knight

BASED ON THE FIRST EDITION BY
Pierre-Henri Cousin
Renée Birks
Elizabeth Campbell
Hélène Lewis
Claude Nimmo
Philippe Patry
Lorna Knight

INTRODUCTION

Nous sommes très heureux que vous ayez choisi ce
dictionnaire et espérons que vous aimerez l'utiliser
et que vous en tirerez profit au lycée, à la maison, en
vacances ou au travail.

Cette introduction a pour but de vous donner quelques
conseils sur la façon d'utiliser au mieux votre dictionnaire,
en vous référant non seulement à son importante
nomenclature mais aussi aux informations contenues
dans chaque entrée. Ceci vous aidera à lire et à comprendre,
mais aussi à communiquer et à vous exprimer en
anglais contemporain.

Au début du dictionnaire, vous trouverez la liste des
abréviations utilisées dans le texte et celle de la
transcription des sons par des symboles phonétiques.
Vous y trouverez également la liste des verbes irréguliers
en anglais, suivis d'une section finale sur les nombres
et sur les expressions de temps.

COMMENT UTILISER VOTRE DICTIONNAIRE

Ce dictionnaire offre une richesse d'informations et
utilise diverses formes et tailles de caractères, symboles,
abréviations, parenthèses et crochets. Les conventions et
symboles utilisés sont expliqués dans les sections qui suivent.

ENTRÉES

Les mots que vous cherchez dans le dictionnaire - les entrées
- sont classés par ordre alphabétique. Ils sont imprimés en
couleur pour pouvoir être repérés rapidement. Les entrées
figurant en haut de page indiquent le premier (sur la page

de gauche) et le dernier mot (sur la page de droite) des deux pages en question.

Des informations sur l'usage ou sur la forme de certaines entrées sont données entre parenthèses, après la transcription phonétique. Ces indications apparaissent sous forme abrégée et en italiques (par ex. *(fam)*, *(Comm)*).

Pour plus de facilité, les mots de la même famille sont regroupés sous la même entrée (**ronger, rongeur; accept, acceptance**) et apparaissent également en couleur.

Les expressions courantes dans lesquelles apparaît l'entrée sont indiquées par des caractères romains gras différents (par exemple **retard** : [...] **avoir du ~**).

TRANSCRIPTION PHONÉTIQUE
La transcription phonétique de chaque entrée (indiquant sa prononciation) est indiquée entre crochets immédiatement après l'entrée (par ex. **fumer** [fyme]; **knee** [niː]). La liste des symboles phonétiques figure page xiii.

TRADUCTIONS
Les traductions des entrées apparaissent en caractères ordinaires ; lorsque plusieurs sens ou usages coexistent, ces traductions sont séparées par un point-virgule. Vous trouverez des synonymes de l'entrée en italiques entre parenthèses avant les traductions (par ex. **poser** *(installer : moquette, carrelage)*) ou des mots qui fournissent le contexte dans lequel l'entrée est susceptible d'être utilisée (par ex. **poser** *(question)*).

Une importance particulière est accordée à certains mots français et anglais qui sont considérés comme des « mots-clés » dans chacune des langues. Cela peut être dû à leur utilisation très fréquente ou au fait qu'ils ont divers types d'usage (par ex. **vouloir, plus; get, that**). L'utilisation de triangles et de chiffres aide à distinguer différentes catégories grammaticales et différents sens. D'autres renseignements utiles apparaissent en italiques et entre parenthèses dans la langue de l'utilisateur.

Les catégories grammaticales sont données sous forme abrégée et en italiques après la transcription phonétique (par ex. *vt, adv, conj*). Les genres des noms français sont indiqués de la manière suivante : *nm* pour un nom masculin et *nf* pour un nom féminin. Le féminin et le pluriel irréguliers de certains noms sont également indiqués (par ex. **directeur, -trice ; cheval, -aux**).

Le masculin et le féminin des adjectifs sont indiqués lorsque ces deux formes sont différentes (par ex. **noir, e**). Lorsque l'adjectif a un féminin ou un pluriel irrégulier, ces formes sont clairement indiquées (par ex. **net, nette**). Les pluriels irréguliers des noms, et les formes irrégulières des verbes anglais sont indiqués entre parenthèses, avant la catégorie grammaticale (par ex. **man** [...] (*pl* **men**) *n* ; **give** (*pt* **gave**; *pp* **~n**) *vt*).

INTRODUCTION

We are delighted that you have decided to buy this dictionary and hope you will enjoy and benefit from using it at school, at home, on holiday or at work.

This introduction gives you a few tips on how to get the most out of your dictionary – not simply from its comprehensive wordlist but also from the information provided in each entry. This will help you to read and understand modern French, as well as communicate and express yourself in the language. This dictionary begins by listing the abbreviations used in the text and illustrating the sounds shown by the phonetic symbols. You will also find French verb tables, followed by a final section on numbers and time expressions.

USING YOUR DICTIONARY
A wealth of information is presented in the dictionary, using various typefaces, sizes of type, symbols, abbreviations and brackets. The various conventions and symbols used are explained in the following sections.

HEADWORDS
The words you look up in a dictionary – 'headwords' – are listed alphabetically. They are printed in **colour** for rapid identification. The headwords appearing at the top of each page indicate the first (if it appears on a left-hand page) and last word (if it appears on a right-hand page) dealt with on the page in question.

Information about the usage or form of certain headwords is given in brackets after the phonetic spelling. This usually appears in abbreviated form and in italics (e.g. (*fam*), (*Comm*)).

Where appropriate, words related to headwords are grouped in the same entry (**ronger, rongeur; accept, acceptance**) and are also in colour. Common expressions in which the headword appears are shown in a bold roman type (e.g. **retard:** [...] **avoir du ~**).

PHONETIC SPELLINGS

The phonetic spelling of each headword (indicating its pronunciation) is given in square brackets immediately after the headword (e.g. **fumer** [fyme]; **knee** [niː]). A list of these symbols is given on page xiii.

TRANSLATIONS

Headword translations are given in ordinary type and, where more than one meaning or usage exists, these are separated by a semi-colon. You will often find other words in italics in brackets before the translations. These offer suggested contexts in which the headword might appear (e.g. **rough** (*voice*), [...] (*weather*)) or provide synonyms (e.g. **rough** (*violent*)). The gender of the translation also appears in italics immediately following the key element of the translation.

KEY WORDS

Special status is given to certain French and English words which are considered as 'key' words in each language. They may, for example, occur very frequently or have several types of usage (e.g. **vouloir, plus; get, that**). A combination of triangles and numbers helps you to distinguish different parts of speech and different meanings. Further helpful information is provided in brackets and italics.

Parts of speech are given in abbreviated form in italics after the phonetic spellings of headwords (e.g. *vt, adv, conj*). Genders of French nouns are indicated as follows: *nm* for a masculine and *nf* for a feminine noun. Feminine and irregular plural forms of nouns are also shown (**directeur, -trice; cheval, -aux**).

Adjectives are given in both masculine and feminine forms where these forms are different (e.g. **noir, e**). Clear information is provided where adjectives have an irregular feminine or plural form (e.g. **net, nette**).

ABRÉVIATIONS

ABBREVIATIONS

abréviation	*ab(b)r*	abbreviation
adjectif, locution adjectivale	*adj*	adjective, adjectival phrase
administration	*Admin*	administration
adverbe, locution adverbiale	*adv*	adverb, adverbial phrase
agriculture	*Agr*	agriculture
anatomie	*Anat*	anatomy
architecture	*Archit*	architecture
article défini	*art déf*	definite article
article indéfini	*art indéf*	indefinite article
automobile	*Aut(o)*	the motor car and motoring
aviation, voyages aériens	*Aviat*	flying, air travel
biologie	*Bio(l)*	biology
botanique	*Bot*	botany
anglais britannique	*BRIT*	British English
chimie	*Chem*	chemistry
commerce, finance, banque	*Comm*	commerce, finance, banking
informatique	*Comput*	computing
conjonction	*conj*	conjunction
construction	*Constr*	building
nom utilisé comme adjectif	*cpd*	compound element
cuisine	*Culin*	cookery
article défini	*def art*	definite article
déterminant: article; adjectif démonstratif ou indéfini *etc*	*dét*	determiner: article, demonstrative *etc*
économie	*Écon, Econ*	economics
électricité, électronique	*Élec, Elec*	electricity, electronics
en particulier	*esp*	especially
exclamation, interjection	*excl*	exclamation, interjection
féminin	*f*	feminine
langue familière (! emploi vulgaire)	*fam(!)*	colloquial usage (! particularly offensive)
emploi figuré	*fig*	figurative use
(verbe anglais) dont la particule est inséparable	*fus*	(phrasal verb) where the particle is inseparable
généralement	*gén, gen*	generally
géographie, géologie	*Géo, Geo*	geography, geology
géométrie	*Géom, Geom*	geometry
langue familière (! emploi vulgaire)	*inf(!)*	colloquial usage (! particularly offensive)
infinitif	*infin*	infinitive
informatique	*Inform*	computing
invariable	*inv*	invariable
irrégulier	*irreg*	irregular
domaine juridique	*Jur*	law

ABRÉVIATIONS		ABBREVIATIONS
grammaire, linguistique	*Ling*	grammar, linguistics
masculin	*m*	masculine
mathématiques, algèbre	*Math*	mathematics, calculus
médecine	*Méd, Med*	medical term, medicine
masculin ou féminin	*m/f*	masculine or feminine
domaine militaire, armée	*Mil*	military matters
musique	*Mus*	music
nom	*n*	noun
navigation, nautisme	*Navig, Naut*	sailing, navigation
nom ou adjectif numéral	*num*	numeral noun or adjective
	o.s.	oneself
péjoratif	*péj, pej*	derogatory, pejorative
photographie	*Phot(o)*	photography
physiologie	*Physiol*	physiology
pluriel	*pl*	plural
politique	*Pol*	politics
participe passé	*pp*	past participle
préposition	*prép, prep*	preposition
pronom	*pron*	pronoun
psychologie, psychiatrie	*Psych*	psychology, psychiatry
temps du passé	*pt*	past tense
quelque chose	*qch*	
quelqu'un	*qn*	
religion, domaine ecclésiastique	*Rel*	religion
	sb	somebody
enseignement, système scolaire et universitaire	*Scol*	schooling, schools and universities
singulier	*sg*	singular
	sth	something
subjonctif	*sub*	subjunctive
sujet (grammatical)	*su(b)j*	(grammatical) subject
superlatif	*superl*	superlative
techniques, technologie	*Tech*	technical term, technology
télécommunications	*Tél, Tel*	telecommunications
télévision	*TV*	television
typographie	*Typ(o)*	typography, printing
anglais des USA	*US*	American English
verbe (auxiliare)	*vb (aux)*	(auxiliary) verb
verbe intransitif	*vi*	intransitive verb
verbe transitif	*vt*	transitive verb
zoologie	*Zool*	zoology
marque déposée	®	registered trademark
indique une équivalence culturelle	≈	introduces a cultural equivalent

TRANSCRIPTION PHONÉTIQUE

CONSONNES		CONSONANTS
NB. **p**, **b**, **t**, **d**, **k**, **g** sont suivis d'une aspiration en anglais.		NB. **p**, **b**, **t**, **d**, **k**, **g** are not aspirated in French.
pou**p**ée	p	**p**up**p**y
bom**b**e	b	**b**a**b**y
ten**t**e **th**ermal	t	**t**en**t**
din**d**e	d	**d**a**dd**y
co**q** **qu**i **k**épi	k	**c**ork **k**iss **ch**ord
ga**g**e ba**gu**e	g	**g**a**g** **gu**ess
sale **c**e na**t**ion	s	**s**o ri**c**e ki**ss**
zéro ro**s**e	z	cou**s**in bu**zz**
ta**ch**e **ch**at	ʃ	**sh**eep **s**ugar
gilet ju**g**e	ʒ	plea**s**ure bei**g**e
	tʃ	**ch**ur**ch**
	dʒ	**j**udge **g**eneral
fer **ph**are	f	**f**arm ra**ff**le
ver**v**eine	v	**v**ery re**v**el
	θ	**th**in ma**th**s
	ð	**th**at o**th**er
lent sa**ll**e	l	**l**itt**l**e ba**ll**
rare **r**ent**r**er	ʀ	
	r	**r**at **r**a**r**e
ma**m**an fe**mm**e	m	**m**u**mm**y co**mb**
non bo**nn**e	n	**n**o ra**n**
a**gn**eau vi**gn**e	ɲ	
	ŋ	si**ng**ing ba**n**k
	h	**h**at re**h**earse
yeux pa**ill**e p**i**ed	j	**y**et
n**ou**er **ou**i	w	**w**all **w**ail
h**u**ile l**u**i	ɥ	
	x	lo**ch**

DIVERS		MISCELLANEOUS
pour l'anglais: le r final se prononce en liaison devant une voyelle	r	in English transcription: final r can be pronounced before a vowel
pour l'anglais: précède la syllabe accentuée	'	in French wordlist: no liaison before aspirate h

En règle générale, la prononciation est donnée entre crochets après chaque entrée. Toutefois, du côté anglais-français et dans le cas des expressions composées de deux ou plusieurs mots non réunis par un trait d'union et faisant l'objet d'une entrée séparée, la prononciation doit être cherchée sous chacun des mots constitutifs de l'expression en question.

PHONETIC TRANCRIPTION

VOYELLES

NB. La mise en équivalence de certains sons n'indique qu'une ressemblance approximative.

VOWELS

NB. The pairing of some vowel sounds only indicates approximate equivalence.

ici vie lyrique	i i:	heel bead
	ɪ	hit pity
jouer été	e	
lait jouet merci	ɛ	set tent
plat amour	a æ	bat apple
bas pâte	ɑ ɑ:	after car calm
	ʌ	fun cousin
le premier	ə	over above
beurre peur	œ	
peu deux	ø ə:	urgent fern work
or homme	ɔ	wash pot
mot eau gauche	o ɔ:	born cork
genou roue	u	full hook
	u:	boom shoe
rue urne	y	

DIPHTONGUES

DIPHTHONGS

	ɪə	beer tier
	ɛə	tear fair there
	eɪ	date plaice day
	aɪ	life buy cry
	au	owl foul now
	əu	low no
	ɔɪ	boil boy oily
	uə	poor tour

NASALES

NASAL VOWELS

matin plein	ɛ̃	
brun	œ̃	
sang an dans	ɑ̃	
non pont	ɔ̃	

In general, we give the pronunciation of each entry in square brackets after the word in question. However, on the English-French side, where the entry is composed of two or more unhyphenated words, each of which is given elsewhere in this dictionary, you will find the pronunciation of each word in its alphabetical position.

FRENCH VERB TABLES

1 Present participle **2** Past participle **3** Present **4** Imperfect **5** Future
6 Conditional **7** Present subjunctive

acquérir 1 acquérant **2** acquis
3 acquiers, acquérons,
acquièrent **4** acquérais
5 acquerrai **7** acquière
ALLER 1 allant **2** allé **3** vais, vas, va,
allons, allez, vont **4** allais **5** irai
6 irais **7** aille
asseoir 1 asseyant **2** assis **3** assieds,
asseyons, asseyez, asseyent
4 asseyais **5** assiérai **7** asseye
atteindre 1 atteignant **2** atteint
3 atteins, atteignons
4 atteignais **7** atteigne
AVOIR 1 ayant **2** eu **3** ai, as, a,
avons, avez, ont **4** avais **5** aurai
6 aurais **7** aie, aies, ait, ayons,
ayez, aient
battre 1 battant **2** battu **3** bats, bat,
battons **4** battais **7** batte
boire 1 buvant **2** bu **3** bois, buvons,
boivent **4** buvais **7** boive
bouillir 1 bouillant **2** bouilli **3** bous,
bouillons **4** bouillais **7** bouille
conclure 1 concluant **2** conclu
3 conclus, concluons
4 concluais **7** conclue
conduire 1 conduisant **2** conduit
3 conduis, conduisons
4 conduisais **7** conduise
connaître 1 connaissant **2** connu
3 connais, connaît, connaissons
4 connaissais **7** connaisse
coudre 1 cousant **2** cousu **3** couds,
cousons, cousez, cousent
4 cousais **7** couse
courir 1 courant **2** couru **3** cours,
courons **4** courais **5** courrai
7 coure
couvrir 1 couvrant **2** couvert
3 couvre, couvrons **4** couvrais
7 couvre

craindre 1 craignant **2** craint
3 crains, craignons **4** craignais
7 craigne
croire 1 croyant **2** cru **3** crois,
croyons, croient **4** croyais
7 croie
croître 1 croissant **2** crû, crue, crus,
crues **3** croîs, croissons
4 croissais **7** croisse
cueillir 1 cueillant **2** cueilli
3 cueille, cueillons **4** cueillais
5 cueillerai **7** cueille
devoir 1 devant **2** dû, due, dus,
dues **3** dois, devons, doivent
4 devais **5** devrai **7** doive
dire 1 disant **2** dit **3** dis, disons,
dites, **4** disais **7** dise
dormir 1 dormant **2** dormi **3** dors,
dormons **4** dormais **7** dorme
écrire 1 écrivant **2** écrit **3** écris,
écrivons, écrivent **4** écrivais **7** écrive
ÊTRE 1 étant **2** été **3** suis, es, est,
sommes, êtes, sont **4** étais
5 serai **6** serais **7** sois, sois, soit,
soyons, soyez, soient
FAIRE 1 faisant **2** fait **3** fais, fais,
fait, faisons, faites, font
4 faisais **5** ferai **6** ferais **7** fasse
falloir 2 fallu **3** faut **4** fallait
5 faudra **7** faille
FINIR 1 finissant **2** fini **3** finis,
finis, finit, finissons, finissez,
finissent **4** finissais **5** finirai
6 finirais **7** finisse
fuir 1 fuyant **2** fui **3** fuis, fuyons,
fuient **4** fuyais **7** fuie
joindre 1 joignant **2** joint **3** joins,
joignons **4** joignais **7** joigne
lire 1 lisant **2** lu **3** lis, lisons **4** lisais
7 lise
luire 1 luisant **2** lui **3** luis, luisons

4 luisais 7 luise

maudire 1 maudissant 2 maudit
3 maudis, maudissons
4 maudissait 7 maudisse

mentir 1 mentant 2 menti 3 mens,
mentons 4 mentais 7 mente

mettre 1 mettant 2 mis 3 mets,
mettons 4 mettais 7 mette

mourir 1 mourant 2 mort 3 meurs,
mourons, meurent 4 mourais
5 mourrai 7 meure

naître 1 naissant 2 né 3 nais, naît,
naissons 4 naissais 7 naisse

offrir 1 offrant 2 offert 3 offre,
offrons 4 offrais 7 offre

PARLER 1 parlant 2 parlé 3 parle,
parles, parle, parlons, parlez,
parlent 4 parlais, parlais,
parlait, parlions, parliez,
parlaient 5 parlerai, parleras,
parlera, parlerons, parlerez,
parleront 6 parlerais, parlerais,
parlerait, parlerions, parleriez,
parleraient 7 parle, parles,
parle, parlions, parliez, parlent
impératif parle! parlons! parlez!

partir 1 partant 2 parti 3 pars,
partons 4 partais 7 parte

plaire 1 plaisant 2 plu 3 plais, plaît,
plaisons 4 plaisais 7 plaise

pleuvoir 1 pleuvant 2 plu 3 pleut,
pleuvent 4 pleuvait 5 pleuvra
7 pleuve

pourvoir 1 pourvoyant 2 pourvu
3 pourvois, pourvoyons,
pourvoient 4 pourvoyais
7 pourvoie

pouvoir 1 pouvant 2 pu 3 peux,
peut, pouvons, peuvent 4
pouvais 5 pourrai 7 puisse

prendre 1 prenant 2 pris 3 prends,
prenons, prennent 4 prenais
7 prenne

prévoir like voir 5 prévoirai

RECEVOIR 1 recevant 2 reçu
3 reçois, reçois, reçoit, recevons,
recevez, rerçoivent 4 recevais

5 recevrai 6 recevrais 7 reçoive

RENDRE 1 rendant 2 rendu
3 rends, rends, rend, rendons,
rendez, rendent 4 rendais
5 rendrai 6 rendrais 7 rende

résoudre 1 résolvant 2 résolu
3 résous, résout, résolvons
4 résolvais 7 résolve

rire 1 riant 2 ri 3 ris, rions 4 riais
7 rie

savoir 1 sachant 2 su 3 sais,
savons, savent 4 savais 5 saurai
7 sache *impératif* sache! sachons!
sachez!

servir 1 servant 2 servi 3 sers,
servons 4 servais 7 serve

sortir 1 sortant 2 sorti 3 sors,
sortons 4 sortais 7 sorte

souffrir 1 souffrant 2 souffert
3 souffre, souffrons 4 souffrais
7 souffre

suffire 1 suffisant 2 suffi 3 suffis,
suffisons 4 suffisais 7 suffise

suivre 1 suivant 2 suivi 3 suis,
suivons 4 suivais 7 suive

taire 1 taisant 2 tu 3 tais, taisons
4 taisais 7 taise

tenir 1 tenant 2 tenu 3 tiens,
tenons, tiennent 4 tenais
5 tiendrai 7 tienne

vaincre 1 vainquant 2 vaincu
3 vaincs, vainc, vainquons
4 vainquais 7 vainque

valoir 1 valant 2 valu 3 vaux, vaut,
valons 4 valais 5 vaudrai 7 vaille

venir 1 venant 2 venu 3 viens,
venons, viennent 4 venais
5 viendrai 7 vienne

vivre 1 vivant 2 vécu 3 vis, vivons
4 vivais 7 vive

voir 1 voyant 2 vu 3 vois, voyons,
voient 4 voyais 5 verrai 7 voie

vouloir 1 voulant 2 voulu 3 veux,
veut, voulons, veulent 4 voulais
5 voudrai 7 veuille; *impératif*
veuillez!

VERBES IRRÉGULIERS ANGLAIS

PRÉSENT	PASSÉ	PARTICIPE	PRÉSENT	PASSÉ	PARTICIPE
arise	arose	arisen	**fight**	fought	fought
awake	awoke	awoken	**find**	found	found
be	was, were	been	**flee**	fled	fled
(am, is,			**fling**	flung	flung
are; being)			**fly**	flew	flown
bear	bore	born(e)	**forbid**	forbad(e)	forbidden
beat	beat	beaten	**forecast**	forecast	forecast
become	became	become	**forget**	forgot	forgotten
begin	began	begun	**forgive**	forgave	forgiven
bend	bent	bent	**forsake**	forsook	forsaken
bet	bet,	bet,	**freeze**	froze	frozen
	betted	betted	**get**	got	got,
bid (*at auction,*	bid	bid			(*us*)gotten
cards)			**give**	gave	given
bid (*say*)	bade	bidden	**go** (*goes*)	went	gone
bind	bound	bound	**grind**	ground	ground
bite	bit	bitten	**grow**	grew	grown
bleed	bled	bled	**hang**	hung	hung
blow	blew	blown	**hang** (*execute*)	hanged	hanged
break	broke	broken	**have**	had	had
breed	bred	bred	**hear**	heard	heard
bring	brought	brought	**hide**	hid	hidden
build	built	built	**hit**	hit	hit
burn	burnt,	burnt,	**hold**	held	held
	burned	burned	**hurt**	hurt	hurt
burst	burst	burst	**keep**	kept	kept
buy	bought	bought	**kneel**	knelt,	knelt,
can	could	(*been able*)		kneeled	kneeled
cast	cast	cast	**know**	knew	known
catch	caught	caught	**lay**	laid	laid
choose	chose	chosen	**lead**	led	led
cling	clung	clung	**lean**	leant,	leant,
come	came	come		leaned	leaned
cost	cost	cost	**leap**	leapt,	leapt,
cost (*work*	costed	costed		leaped	leaped
out price of)			**learn**	learnt,	learnt,
creep	crept	crept		learned	learned
cut	cut	cut	**leave**	left	left
deal	dealt	dealt	**lend**	lent	lent
dig	dug	dug	**let**	let	let
do (*does*)	did	done	**lie** (*lying*)	lay	lain
draw	drew	drawn	**light**	lit,	lit,
dream	dreamed,	dreamed,		lighted	lighted
	dreamt	dreamt	**lose**	lost	lost
drink	drank	drunk	**make**	made	made
drive	drove	driven	**may**	might	–
dwell	dwelt	dwelt	**mean**	meant	meant
eat	ate	eaten	**meet**	met	met
fall	fell	fallen	**mistake**	mistook	mistaken
feed	fed	fed	**mow**	mowed	mown,
feel	felt	felt			mowed

PRÉSENT	PASSÉ	PARTICIPE	PRÉSENT	PASSÉ	PARTICIPE
must	(had to)	(had to)	spend	spent	spent
pay	paid	paid	spill	spilt,	spilt,
put	put	put		spilled	spilled
quit	quit,	quit,	spin	spun	spun
	quitted	quitted	spit	spat	spat
read	read	read	spoil	spoiled,	spoiled,
rid	rid	rid		spoilt	spoilt
ride	rode	ridden	spread	spread	spread
ring	rang	rung	spring	sprang	sprung
rise	rose	risen	stand	stood	stood
run	ran	run	steal	stole	stolen
saw	sawed	sawed,	stick	stuck	stuck
		sawn	sting	stung	stung
say	said	said	stink	stank	stunk
see	saw	seen	stride	strode	stridden
seek	sought	sought	strike	struck	struck
sell	sold	sold	strive	strove	striven
send	sent	sent	swear	swore	sworn
set	set	set	sweep	swept	swept
sew	sewed	sewn	swell	swelled	swollen,
shake	shook	shaken			swelled
shear	sheared	shorn,	swim	swam	swum
		sheared	swing	swung	swung
shed	shed	shed	take	took	taken
shine	shone	shone	teach	taught	taught
shoot	shot	shot	tear	tore	torn
show	showed	shown	tell	told	told
shrink	shrank	shrunk	think	thought	thought
shut	shut	shut	throw	threw	thrown
sing	sang	sung	thrust	thrust	thrust
sink	sank	sunk	tread	trod	trodden
sit	sat	sat	wake	woke,	woken,
slay	slew	slain		waked	waked
sleep	slept	slept	wear	wore	worn
slide	slid	slid	weave	wove	woven
sling	slung	slung	weave (wind)	weaved	weaved
slit	slit	slit	wed	wedded,	wedded,
smell	smelt,	smelt,		wed	wed
	smelled	smelled	weep	wept	wept
sow	sowed	sown,	win	won	won
		sowed	wind	wound	wound
speak	spoke	spoken	wring	wrung	wrung
speed	sped,	sped,	write	wrote	written
	speeded	speeded			
spell	spelt,	spelt,			
	spelled	spelled			

LES NOMBRES

un (une)	1
deux	2
trois	3
quatre	4
cinq	5
six	6
sept	7
huit	8
neuf	9
dix	10
onze	11
douze	12
treize	13
quatorze	14
quinze	15
seize	16
dix-sept	17
dix-huit	18
dix-neuf	19
vingt	20
vingt et un (une)	21
vingt-deux	22
trente	30
quarante	40
cinquante	50
soixante	60
soixante-dix	70
soixante-et-onze	71
soixante-douze	72
quatre-vingts	80
quatre-vingt-un (-une)	81
quatre-vingt-dix	90
cent	100
cent un (une)	101
deux cents	200
deux cent un (une)	201
quatre cents	400
mille	1000
cinq mille	5000
un million	1000000

NUMBERS

one
two
three
four
five
six
seven
eight
nine
ten
eleven
twelve
thirteen
fourteen
fifteen
sixteen
seventeen
eighteen
nineteen
twenty
twenty-one
twenty-two
thirty
forty
fifty
sixty
seventy
seventy-one
seventy
eighty
eighty-one
ninety
a hundred, one hundred
a hundred and one
two hundred
two hundred and one
four hundred
a thousand
five thousand
a million

LES NOMBRES

premier (première), 1er (1ère)
deuxième, 2e or 2ème
troisième, 3e or 3ème
quatrième, 4e or 4ème
cinquième, 5e or 5ème
sixième, 6e or 6ème
septième
huitième
neuvième
dixième
onzième
douzième
treizième
quartorzième
quinzième
seizième
dix-septième
dix-huitième
dix-neuvième
vingtième
vingt-et-unième
vingt-deuxième
trentième
centième
cent-unième
millième

LES FRACTIONS ETC
un demi
un tiers
un quart
un cinquième
zéro virgule cinq, 0,5
trois virgule quatre, 3,4
dix pour cent
cent pour cent

EXEMPLES
elle habite au septième (étage)
il habite au sept
au chapitre/à la page sept
il est arrivé (le) septième

NUMBERS

first, 1st
second, 2nd
third, 3rd
fourth, 4th
fifth, 5th
sixth, 6th
seventh
eighth
ninth
tenth
eleventh
twelfth
thirteenth
fourteenth
fifteenth
sixteenth
seventeenth
eighteenth
nineteenth
twentieth
twenty-first
twenty-second
thirtieth
hundredth
hundred-and-first
thousandth

FRACTIONS ETC
a half
a third
a quarter
a fifth
(nought) point five, 0.5
three point four, 3.4
ten per cent
a hundred per cent

EXAMPLES
she lives on the 7th floor
he lives at number 7
chapter/page 7
he came in 7th

L'HEURE

quelle heure est-il?

il est ...

minuit
une heure (du matin)

une heure cinq
une heure dix
une heure et quart

une heure vingt-cinq

une heure et demie, une heure trente
deux heures moins vingt-cinq, une
    heure trente-cinq
deux heures moins vingt, une heure
    quarante
deux heures moins le quart, une heure
    quarante-cinq
deux heures moins dix, une heure
    cinquante
midi

deux heures (de l'après-midi),
    quatorze heures
sept heures (du soir), dix-sept heures

à quelle heure?

à minuit
à sept heures

dans vingt minutes
il y a un quart d'heure

THE TIME

what time is it?

it's ou it is ...

midnight, twelve p.m.
one o'clock (in the
    morning), one (a.m.)

five past one
ten past one
a quarter past one,
    one fifteen
twenty-five past one,
    one twenty-five
half-past one, one thirty
twenty-five to two,
    one thirty-five
twenty to two, one forty

a quarter to two,
    one forty-five
ten to two, one fifty

twelve o'clock, midday,
    noon
two o'clock (in the
    afternoon), two (p.m.)
seven o'clock (in the
    evening), seven (p.m.)

(at) what time?

at midnight
at seven o'clock

in twenty minutes
fifteen minutes ago

a [a] *vb voir* **avoir**

O MOT-CLÉ

à [a] (*à + le* = **au**, *à + les* = **aux**) *prép*
1 (*endroit, situation*) at, in; **être à Paris/
au Portugal** to be in Paris/Portugal;
être à la maison/à l'école to be at
home/at school; **à la campagne** in the
country; **c'est à 10 km/à 20 minutes
(d'ici)** it's 10 km/20 minutes away
2 (*direction*) to; **aller à Paris/au
Portugal** to go to Paris/Portugal; **aller
à la maison/à l'école** to go home/to
school; **à la campagne** to the country
3 (*temps*): **à 3 heures/minuit** at 3
o'clock/midnight; **au printemps/
mois de juin** in the spring/the month
of June; **à Noël/Pâques** at Christmas/
Easter; **à demain/lundi!** see you
tomorrow/on Monday!
4 (*attribution, appartenance*) to; **le livre
est à Paul/à lui/à nous** this book
is Paul's/his/ours; **un ami à moi** a
friend of mine; **donner qch à qn** to
give sth to sb
5 (*moyen*) with; **se chauffer au gaz** to
have gas heating; **à bicyclette** on a *ou*
by bicycle; **à pied** on foot; **à la main/
machine** by hand/machine
6 (*provenance*) from; **boire à la
bouteille** to drink from the bottle
7 (*caractérisation, manière*): **l'homme
aux yeux bleus** the man with the blue
eyes; **à leur grande surprise** much
to their surprise; **à ce qu'il prétend**
according to him, from what he says;
à la russe the Russian way; **à nous
deux nous n'avons pas su le faire**
we couldn't do it, even between the
two of us
8 (*but, destination*): **tasse à café** coffee
cup; **maison à vendre** house for sale;
je n'ai rien à lire I don't have anything
to read; **à bien réfléchir ...** thinking
about it ..., on reflection ...
9 (*rapport, évaluation, distribution*): **100
km/unités à l'heure** 100 km/units per
ou an hour; **payé au mois/à l'heure**
paid monthly/by the hour; **cinq à six**
five to six; **ils sont arrivés à quatre**
four of them arrived

abaisser [abese] *vt* to lower, bring
down; (*manette*) to pull down;
s'abaisser *vi* to go down; (*fig*) to
demean o.s.
abandon [abɑ̃dɔ̃] *nm* abandoning;
giving up; withdrawal; **être à l'~** to
be in a state of neglect; **laisser à l'~**
to abandon
abandonner [abɑ̃dɔne] *vt* (*personne*)
to abandon; (*projet, activité*) to
abandon, give up; (*Sport*) to retire *ou*
withdraw from; (*céder*) to surrender; **s'~
à** (*paresse, plaisirs*) to give o.s. up to
abat-jour [abaʒuʀ] *nm inv* lampshade
abats [aba] *nmpl* (*de bœuf, porc*) offal *sg*;
(*de volaille*) giblets
abattement [abatmɑ̃] *nm*:
abattement fiscal ≈ tax allowance
abattoir [abatwaʀ] *nm*

slaughterhouse

abattre [abatʀ] vt (arbre) to cut down, fell; (mur, maison) to pull down; (avion, personne) to shoot down; (animal) to shoot, kill; (fig) to wear out, tire out; to demoralize; **s'abattre** vi to crash down; **ne pas se laisser ~** to keep one's spirits up, not to let things get one down; **s'~ sur** to beat down on; (fig) to rain down on; **~ du travail** ou **de la besogne** to get through a lot of work

abbaye [abei] nf abbey

abbé [abe] nm priest; (d'une abbaye) abbot

abcès [apsɛ] nm abscess

abdiquer [abdike] vi to abdicate

abdominaux [abdɔmino] nmpl: **faire des ~** to do sit-ups

abeille [abɛj] nf bee

aberrant, e [abeʀɑ̃, ɑ̃t] adj absurd

aberration [abeʀasjɔ̃] nf aberration

abîme [abim] nm abyss, gulf

abîmer [abime] vt to spoil, damage; **s'abîmer** vi to get spoilt ou damaged

aboiement [abwamɑ̃] nm bark, barking

abolir [abɔliʀ] vt to abolish

abominable [abɔminabl] adj abominable

abondance [abɔ̃dɑ̃s] nf abundance

abondant, e [abɔ̃dɑ̃, ɑ̃t] adj plentiful, abundant, copious; **abonder** vi to abound, be plentiful; **abonder dans le sens de qn** to concur with sb

abonné, e [abɔne] nm/f subscriber; season ticket holder

abonnement [abɔnmɑ̃] nm subscription; (transports, concerts) season ticket

abonner [abɔne] vt: **s'~ à** to subscribe to, take out a subscription to

abord [abɔʀ] nm: **au premier ~** at first sight, initially; **abords** nmpl (environs) surroundings; **d'~** first

abordable [abɔʀdabl] adj (prix) reasonable; (personne) approachable

aborder [abɔʀde] vi to land ▷ vt (sujet, difficulté) to tackle; (personne) to approach; (rivage etc) to reach

aboutir [abutiʀ] vi (négociations etc) to succeed; **~ à** to end up at; **n'~ à rien** to come to nothing

aboyer [abwaje] vi to bark

abréger [abʀeʒe] vt to shorten

abreuver [abʀœve]: **s'abreuver** vi to drink; **abreuvoir** nm watering place

abréviation [abʀevjasjɔ̃] nf abbreviation

abri [abʀi] nm shelter; **être à l'~** to be under cover; **se mettre à l'~** to shelter; **à l'~ de** (vent, soleil) sheltered from; (danger) safe from

abricot [abʀiko] nm apricot

abriter [abʀite] vt to shelter; **s'abriter** vt to shelter, take cover

abrupt, e [abʀypt] adj sheer, steep; (ton) abrupt

abruti, e [abʀyti] adj stunned, dazed ▷ nm/f (fam) idiot, moron; **~ de travail** overworked

absence [apsɑ̃s] nf absence; (Méd) blackout; **avoir des ~s** to have mental blanks

absent, e [apsɑ̃, ɑ̃t] adj absent ▷ nm/f absentee; **absenter: s'absenter** vi to take time off work; (sortir) to leave, go out

absolu, e [apsɔly] adj absolute; **absolument** adv absolutely

absorbant, e [apsɔʀbɑ̃, ɑ̃t] adj absorbent

absorber [apsɔʀbe] vt to absorb; (gén Méd: manger, boire) to take

abstenir [apstəniʀ] vb: **s'~ de qch/de faire** to refrain from sth/from doing

abstrait, e [apstʀɛ, ɛt] adj abstract

absurde [apsyʀd] adj absurd

abus [aby] nm abuse; **~ de confiance** breach of trust; **il y a de l'~!** (fam) that's a bit much!; **abuser** vi to go too far, overstep the mark; **abuser de** (duper) to take advantage of; **s'abuser** vi (se méprendre) to be mistaken; **abusif, -ive** adj exorbitant; (punition) excessive

académie [akademi] nf academy; (Scol: circonscription) ≈ regional education authority

● **ACADÉMIE FRANÇAISE**
●
● The **Académie française** was
● founded by Cardinal Richelieu in
● 1635, during the reign of Louis XIII. It
● is made up of forty elected scholars
● and writers who are known as 'les
● Quarante' or 'les Immortels'. One
● of the **Académie**'s functions is to
● keep an eye on the development
● of the French language, and its
● recommendations are frequently
● the subject of lively public debate. It
● has produced several editions of its
● famous dictionary and also awards
● various literary prizes.

acajou [akaʒu] nm mahogany
acariâtre [akaʀjɑtʀ] adj cantankerous
accablant, e [akablɑ̃, ɑ̃t] adj (chaleur)
oppressive; (témoignage, preuve)
overwhelming
accabler [akable] vt to overwhelm,
overcome; ~ **qn d'injures** to heap ou
shower abuse on sb; ~ **qn de travail** to
overwork sb
accalmie [akalmi] nf lull
accaparer [akapaʀe] vt to
monopolize; (suj: travail etc) to take up
(all) the time ou attention of
accéder [aksede]: ~ **à** vt (lieu) to reach;
(accorder: requête) to grant, accede to
accélérateur [akseleʀatœʀ] nm
accelerator
accélérer [akseleʀe] vt to speed up ▷ vi
to accelerate
accent [aksɑ̃] nm accent; (Phonétique,
fig) stress; **mettre l'~ sur** (fig) to stress;
~ **aigu/grave/circonflexe** acute/
grave/circumflex accent; **accentuer**
vt (Ling) to accent; (fig) to accentuate,
emphasize; **s'accentuer** vi to become
more marked ou pronounced
acceptation [akseptasjɔ̃] nf
acceptance
accepter [aksepte] vt to accept; ~ **de**

faire to agree to do; **acceptez-vous
les cartes de crédit?** do you take
credit cards?
accès [aksɛ] nm (à un lieu) access; (Méd:
de toux) fit; (: de fièvre) bout; **d'~ facile**
easily accessible; **facile d'~** easy to
get to; **accès de colère** fit of anger;
accessible adj accessible; (livre, sujet):
accessible à qn within the reach of sb
accessoire [akseswaʀ] adj secondary;
incidental ▷ nm accessory; (Théâtre)
prop
accident [aksidɑ̃] nm accident; **par
~** by chance; **j'ai eu un ~** I've had an
accident; **accident de la route** road
accident; **accidenté, e** adj damaged;
injured; (relief, terrain) uneven; hilly;
accidentel, le adj accidental
acclamer [aklame] vt to cheer,
acclaim
acclimater [aklimate]: **s'acclimater**
vi (personne) to adapt (o.s.)
accolade [akɔlad] nf (amicale)
embrace; (signe) brace
accommoder [akɔmɔde] vt (Culin)
to prepare; **s'accommoder de** vt to
put up with; (se contenter de) to make
do with
accompagnateur, -trice
[akɔ̃paɲatœʀ, tʀis] nm/f (Mus)
accompanist; (de voyage: guide) guide;
(de voyage organisé) courier
accompagner [akɔ̃paɲe] vt to
accompany, be ou go ou come with;
(Mus) to accompany
accompli, e [akɔ̃pli] adj
accomplished; voir aussi **fait**
accomplir [akɔ̃pliʀ] vt (tâche, projet) to
carry out; (souhait) to fulfil; **s'accomplir**
vi to be fulfilled
accord [akɔʀ] nm agreement; (entre des
styles, tons etc) harmony; (Mus) chord;
d'~! OK!; **se mettre d'~** to come to an
agreement; **être d'~ (pour faire qch)**
to agree (to do sth)
accordéon [akɔʀdeɔ̃] nm (Mus)
accordion
accorder [akɔʀde] vt (faveur, délai) to

grant; (*harmoniser*) to match; (*Mus*) to tune; (*valeur, importance*) attach
accoster [akɔste] vt (*Navig*) to draw alongside ▷ vi to berth
accouchement [akuʃmɑ̃] nm delivery, (child)birth; labour
accoucher [akuʃe] vi to give birth, have a baby; **~ d'un garçon** to give birth to a boy
accouder [akude]: **s'accouder** vi: **s'~ à/contre/sur** to rest one's elbows on/ against/on; **accoudoir** nm armrest
accoupler [akuple] vt to couple; (*pour la reproduction*) to mate; **s'accoupler** vt to mate
accourir [akuRiR] vi to rush ou run up
accoutumance [akutymɑ̃s] nf (*gén*) adaptation; (*Méd*) addiction
accoutumé, e [akutyme] adj (*habituel*) customary, usual
accoutumer [akutyme] vt: **s'~ à** to get accustomed ou used to
accroc [akRo] nm (*déchirure*) tear; (*fig*) hitch, snag
accrochage [akRɔʃaʒ] nm (*Auto*) collision; (*dispute*) clash, brush
accrocher [akRɔʃe] vt (*fig*) to catch, attract; **s'accrocher** (*se disputer*) to have a clash ou brush; **~ qch à** (*suspendre*) to hang sth (up) on; (*attacher: remorque*) to hitch sth (up) to; **~ qch (à)** (*déchirer*) to catch sth (on); **il a accroché ma voiture** he bumped into my car; **s'~ à** (*rester pris à*) to catch on; (*agripper, fig*) to hang on ou cling to
accroissement [akRwasmɑ̃] nm increase
accroître [akRwatR]: **s'accroître** vi to increase
accroupir [akRupiR]: **s'accroupir** vi to squat, crouch (down)
accru, e [akRy] pp de **accroître**
accueil [akœj] nm welcome; **comité d'~** reception committee; **accueillir** vt to welcome; (*aller chercher*) to meet, collect
accumuler [akymyle] vt to accumulate, amass; **s'accumuler** vi to

accumulate; to pile up
accusation [akyzasjɔ̃] nf (*gén*) accusation; (*Jur*) charge; (*partie*): **l'~** the prosecution
accusé, e [akyze] nm/f accused; defendant; **accusé de réception** acknowledgement of receipt
accuser [akyze] vt to accuse; (*fig*) to emphasize, bring out; to show; **~ qn de** to accuse sb of; (*Jur*) to charge sb with; **~ réception de** to acknowledge receipt of
acéré, e [asere] adj sharp
acharné, e [aʃaRne] adj (*efforts*) relentless; (*lutte, adversaire*) fierce, bitter
acharner [aʃaRne] vb: **s'~ contre** to set o.s. against; (*suj: malchance*) to dog; **s'~ à faire** to try doggedly to do; (*persister*) to persist in doing; **s'~ sur qn** to hound sb
achat [aʃa] nm purchase; **faire des ~s** to do some shopping; **faire l'~ de qch** to purchase sth
acheter [aʃ(ə)te] vt to buy, purchase; (*soudoyer*) to buy; **~ qch à** (*marchand*) to buy ou purchase sth from; (*ami etc: offrir*) to buy sth for; **où est-ce que je peux ~ des cartes postales?** where can I buy (some) postcards?; **acheteur, -euse** nm/f buyer; shopper; (*Comm*) buyer
achever [aʃ(ə)ve] vt to complete, finish; (*blessé*) to finish off; **s'achever** vi to end
acide [asid] adj sour, sharp; (*Chimie*) acid(ic) ▷ nm (*Chimie*) acid; **acidulé, e** adj slightly acid; **bonbons acidulés** acid drops
acier [asje] nm steel; **aciérie** nf steelworks sg
acné [akne] nf acne
acompte [akɔ̃t] nm deposit
à-côté [akote] nm side-issue; (*argent*) extra
à-coup [aku] nm: **par ~s** by fits and starts
acoustique [akustik] nf (*d'une salle*) acoustics pl

acquéreur [akerœr] nm buyer, purchaser

acquérir [akerir] vt to acquire

acquis, e [aki, iz] pp de **acquérir** ▷ nm (accumulated) experience; **son aide nous est ~e** we can count on her help

acquitter [akite] vt (Jur) to acquit; (facture) to pay, settle; **s'acquitter de** vt (devoir) to discharge; (promesse) to fulfil

âcre [ɑkr] adj acrid, pungent

acrobate [akrɔbat] nm/f acrobat; **acrobatie** nf acrobatics sg

acte [akt] nm act, action; (Théâtre) act; **prendre ~ de** to note, take note of; **faire ~ de candidature** to apply; **faire ~ de présence** to put in an appearance; **acte de naissance** birth certificate

acteur [aktœr] nm actor

actif, -ive [aktif, iv] adj active ▷ nm (Comm) assets pl; (fig): **avoir à son ~ to** have to one's credit; **population active** working population

action [aksjɔ̃] nf (gén) action; (Comm) share; **une bonne ~** a good deed; **actionnaire** nm/f shareholder; **actionner** vt (mécanisme) to activate; (machine) to operate

activer [aktive] vt to speed up; **s'activer** vi to bustle about; to hurry up

activité [aktivite] nf activity; **en ~** (volcan) active; (fonctionnaire) in active life

actrice [aktris] nf actress

actualité [aktɥalite] nf (d'un problème) topicality; (événements): **l'~** current events; **actualités** nfpl (Cinéma, TV) the news; **d'~** topical

actuel, le [aktɥel] adj (présent) present; (d'actualité) topical; **à l'heure ~le** at the present time; **actuellement** adv at present, at the present time

    Attention à ne pas traduire *actuellement* par *actually*.

acupuncture [akypɔ̃ktyr] nf acupuncture

adaptateur [adaptatœr] nm (Élec) adapter

adapter [adapte] vt to adapt; **s'adapter (à)** (suj: personne) to adapt (to); **~ qch à** (approprier) to adapt sth to (fit); **~ qch sur/dans/à** (fixer) to fit sth on/into/to

addition [adisjɔ̃] nf addition; (au café) bill; **l'~, s'il vous plaît** could I have the bill, please?; **additionner** vt to add (up)

adepte [adɛpt] nm/f follower

adéquat, e [adekwa(t), at] adj appropriate, suitable

adhérent, e [aderɑ̃, ɑ̃t] nm/f member

adhérer [adere] **~ à** vt (coller) to adhere ou stick to; (se rallier à) to join; **adhésif, -ive** adj adhesive, sticky; **ruban adhésif** sticky ou adhesive tape

adieu, x [adjø] excl goodbye ▷ nm farewell

adjectif [adʒɛktif] nm adjective

adjoint, e [adʒwɛ̃, wɛ̃t] nm/f assistant; **adjoint au maire** deputy mayor; **directeur adjoint** assistant manager

admettre [admɛtr] vt (laisser entrer) to admit; (candidat: Scol) to pass; (tolérer) to allow, accept; (reconnaître) to admit, acknowledge

administrateur, -trice [administratœr, tris] nm/f (Comm) director; (Admin) administrator

administration [administrasjɔ̃] nf administration; **l'A~** ≈ the Civil Service

administrer [administre] vt (firme) to manage, run; (biens, remède, sacrement etc) to administer

admirable [admirabl] adj admirable, wonderful

admirateur, -trice [admiratœr, tris] nm/f admirer

admiration [admirasjɔ̃] nf admiration

admirer [admire] vt to admire

admis, e [admi, iz] pp de **admettre**

admissible [admisibl] adj (candidat) eligible; (comportement) admissible, acceptable

ADN sigle m (= acide désoxyribonucléique) DNA

adolescence [adɔlesɑ̃s] *nf*
adolescence

adolescent, e [adɔlesɑ̃, ɑ̃t] *nm/f*
adolescent, teenager

adopter [adɔpte] *vt* to adopt; **adoptif,
-ive** *adj* (*parents*) adoptive; (*fils, patrie*)
adopted

adorable [adɔrabl] *adj* delightful,
adorable

adorer [adɔre] *vt* to adore; (*Rel*) to
worship

adosser [adose] *vt*: **~ qch à** ou **contre** to
stand sth against; **s'adosser à/contre**
to lean with one's back against

adoucir [adusir] *vt* (*goût, température*)
to make milder; (*avec du sucre*) to
sweeten; (*peau, voix*) to soften;
(*caractère*) to mellow

adresse [adrɛs] *nf* (*domicile*)
address; (*dextérité*) skill, dexterity; **~
électronique** email address

adresser [adrese] *vt* (*lettre: expédier*)
to send; (: *écrire l'adresse sur*) to address;
(*injure, compliments*) to address;
s'adresser à (*parler à*) to speak to,
address; (*s'informer auprès de*) to go and
see; (: *bureau*) to inquire at; (*suj: livre,
conseil*) to be aimed at; **~ la parole à** to
speak to, address

adroit, e [adrwa, wat] *adj* skilful,
skilled

ADSL *sigle m* (= *asymmetrical digital
subscriber line*) ADSL, broadband

adulte [adylt] *nm/f* adult, grown-up
▷ *adj* (*chien, arbre*) fully-grown, mature;
(*attitude*) adult, grown-up

adverbe [advɛrb] *nm* adverb

adversaire [advɛrsɛr] *nm/f* (*Sport,
gén*) opponent, adversary

aération [aerasjɔ̃] *nf* airing; (*circulation
de l'air*) ventilation

aérer [aere] *vt* to air; (*fig*) to lighten

aérien, ne [aerjɛ̃, jɛn] *adj* (*Aviat*) air
cpd, aerial; (*câble, métro*) overhead; (*fig*)
light; **compagnie ~ne** airline

aéro... [aero] *préfixe*: **aérobic** *nm*
aerobics *sg*; **aérogare** *nf* airport
(*buildings*); (*en ville*) air terminal;

aéroglisseur *nm* hovercraft;
aérophagie *nf* (*Méd*) wind, aerophagia
(*Méd*); **aéroport** *nm* airport; **aérosol**
nm aerosol

affaiblir [afeblir]: **s'affaiblir** *vi* to
weaken

affaire [afɛr] *nf* (*problème, question*)
matter; (*criminelle, judiciaire*) case;
(*scandaleuse etc*) affair; (*entreprise*)
business; (*marché, transaction*) deal;
business *no pl*; (*occasion intéressante*)
bargain; **affaires** *nfpl* (*intérêts publics
et privés*) affairs; (*activité commerciale*)
business *sg*; (*effets personnels*) things,
belongings; **ce sont mes ~s** (*cela me
concerne*) that's my business; **occupe-
toi de tes ~s!** mind your own business!;
ça fera l'~ that will do (nicely); **se tirer
d'~** to sort it ou things out for o.s.; **avoir
~ à** (*être en contact*) to be dealing with;
les A~s étrangères Foreign Affairs;
affairer: s'affairer *vi* to busy o.s.,
bustle about

affamé, e [afame] *adj* starving

affecter [afɛkte] *vt* to affect; **~ qch
à** to allocate ou allot sth to; **~ qn à** to
appoint sb to; (*diplomate*) to post sb to

affectif, -ive [afɛktif, iv] *adj*
emotional

affection [afɛksjɔ̃] *nf* affection; (*mal*)
ailment; **affectionner** *vt* to be fond of;
affectueux, -euse *adj* affectionate

affichage [afiʃaʒ] *nm* billposting;
(*électronique*) display; **"~ interdit"** "stick
no bills"; **affichage à cristaux liquides**
liquid crystal display, LCD

affiche [afiʃ] *nf* poster; (*officielle*) notice;
(*Théâtre*) bill; **être à l'~** to be on

afficher [afiʃe] *vt* (*affiche*) to put up;
(*réunion*) to put up a notice about;
(*électroniquement*) to display; (*fig*) to
exhibit, display; **"défense d'~"** "no bill
posters"; **s'afficher** *vr* (*péj*) to flaunt
o.s.; (*électroniquement*) to be displayed

affilée [afile]: **d'~** *adv* at a stretch

affirmatif, -ive [afirmatif, iv] *adj*
affirmative

affirmer [afirme] *vt* to assert

affligé, e [aflize] *adj* distressed, grieved; **~ de** (*maladie, tare*) afflicted with

affliger [aflize] *vt* (*peiner*) to distress, grieve

affluence [aflyɑ̃s] *nf* crowds *pl*; **heures d'~** rush hours; **jours d'~** busiest days

affluent [aflyɑ̃] *nm* tributary

affolement [afɔlmɑ̃] *nm* panic

affoler [afɔle] *vt* to throw into a panic; **s'affoler** *vi* to panic

affranchir [afʀɑ̃ʃiʀ] *vt* to put a stamp *ou* stamps on; (*à la machine*) to frank (BRIT), meter (US); (*fig*) to free, liberate; **affranchissement** *nm* postage

affreux, -euse [afʀø, øz] *adj* dreadful, awful

affront [afʀɔ̃] *nm* affront; **affrontement** *nm* clash, confrontation

affronter [afʀɔ̃te] *vt* to confront, face

affût [afy] *nm*: **à l'~ (de)** (*gibier*) lying in wait (for); (*fig*) on the look-out (for)

Afghanistan [afganistɑ̃] *nm*: **l'~** Afghanistan

afin [afɛ̃]: **~ que** *conj* so that, in order that; **~ de faire** in order to do, so as to do

africain, e [afʀikɛ̃, ɛn] *adj* African ▷ *nm/f*: **A~, e** African

Afrique [afʀik] *nf*: **l'~** Africa; **l'Afrique du Nord/Sud** North/South Africa

agacer [agase] *vt* to irritate

âge [ɑʒ] *nm* age; **quel ~ as-tu?** how old are you?; **prendre de l'~** to be getting on (in years); **le troisième ~** (*période*) retirement; (*personnes âgées*) senior citizens; **âgé, e** *adj* old, elderly; **âgé de 10 ans** 10 years old

agence [aʒɑ̃s] *nf* agency, office; (*succursale*) branch; **agence de voyages** travel agency; **agence immobilière** estate agent (BRIT) *ou* real estate (US) agent's (office)

agenda [aʒɛ̃da] *nm* diary; **~ électronique** PDA

▌ Attention à ne pas traduire *agenda* par le mot anglais *agenda*.

agenouiller [aʒ(ə)nuje]: **s'agenouiller** *vi* to kneel (down)

agent, e [aʒɑ̃, ɑ̃t] *nm/f* (*aussi*: **~(e) de police**) policeman(policewoman); (*Admin*) official, officer; **agent immobilier** estate agent (BRIT), realtor (US)

agglomération [aglɔmeʀasjɔ̃] *nf* town; built-up area; **l'~ parisienne** the urban area of Paris

aggraver [agʀave]: **s'aggraver** *vi* to worsen

agile [aʒil] *adj* agile, nimble

agir [aʒiʀ] *vi* to act; **il s'agit de** (*ça traite de*) it is about; (*il est important de*) it's a matter *ou* question of; **il s'agit de faire** we (*ou* you *etc*) must do; **de quoi s'agit-il?** what is it about?

agitation [aʒitasjɔ̃] *nf* (hustle and) bustle; (*trouble*) agitation, excitement; (*politique*) unrest, agitation

agité, e [aʒite] *adj* fidgety, restless; (*troublé*) agitated, perturbed; (*mer*) rough

agiter [aʒite] *vt* (*bouteille, chiffon*) to shake; (*bras, mains*) to wave; (*préoccuper, exciter*) to perturb

agneau, x [aɲo] *nm* lamb

agonie [agɔni] *nf* mortal agony, death pangs *pl*; (*fig*) death throes *pl*

agrafe [agʀaf] *nf* (*de vêtement*) hook, fastener; (*de bureau*) staple; **agrafer** *vt* to fasten; to staple; **agrafeuse** *nf* stapler

agrandir [agʀɑ̃diʀ] *vt* to enlarge; **s'agrandir** *vi* (*ville, famille*) to grow, expand; (*trou, écart*) to get bigger; **agrandissement** *nm* (*Photo*) enlargement

agréable [agʀeabl] *adj* pleasant, nice

agréé, e [agʀee] *adj*: **concessionnaire ~** registered dealer

agréer [agʀee] *vt* (*requête*) to accept; **~ à** to please, suit; **veuillez ~, Monsieur/Madame, mes salutations distinguées** (*personne nommée*) yours sincerely; (*personne non nommée*) yours faithfully

agrégation [agʀegasjɔ̃] *nf* highest teaching diploma in France; **agrégé, e** *nm/f* holder of the *agrégation*

agrément [agʀemɑ̃] *nm* (*accord*) consent, approval; (*attraits*) charm, attractiveness; (*plaisir*) pleasure

agresser [agʀese] *vt* to attack; **agresseur** *nm* aggressor, attacker; (*Pol, Mil*) aggressor; **agressif, -ive** *adj* aggressive

agricole [agʀikɔl] *adj* agricultural; **agriculteur** *nm* farmer; **agriculture** *nf* agriculture, farming

agripper [agʀipe] *vt* to grab, clutch; **s'agripper à** to cling (on) to, clutch, grip

agro-alimentaire [agʀoalimɑ̃tɛʀ] *nm* farm-produce industry

agrumes [agʀym] *nmpl* citrus fruit(s)

aguets [agɛ] *nmpl*: **être aux ~** to be on the look out

ai [ɛ] *vb voir* **avoir**

aide [ɛd] *nm/f* assistant; carer ▷ *nf* assistance, help; (*secours financier*) aid; **à l'~ de** (*avec*) with the help *ou* aid of; **appeler (qn) à l'~** to call for help (from sb); **à l'~!** help!; **aide judiciaire** legal aid; **aide ménagère** ≈ home help (*BRIT*) *ou* helper (*US*); **aide-mémoire** *nm inv* memoranda pages *pl*; (*key facts*) handbook; **aide-soignant, e** *nm/f* auxiliary nurse

aider [ede] *vt* to help; **~ à qch** to help (towards) sth; **~ qn à faire qch** to help sb to do sth; **pouvez-vous m'~?** can you help me?; **s'aider de** (*se servir de*) to use, make use of

aïe [aj] *excl* ouch!

aie *etc* [ɛ] *vb voir* **avoir**

aigle [ɛgl] *nm* eagle

aigre [ɛgʀ] *adj* sour, sharp; (*fig*) sharp, cutting; **aigre-doux, -ce** *adj* (*sauce*) sweet and sour; **aigreur** *nf* sourness; sharpness; **aigreurs d'estomac** heartburn *sg*

aigu, ë [egy] *adj* (*objet, douleur*) sharp; (*son, voix*) high-pitched, shrill; (*note*) high(-pitched)

aiguille [egɥij] *nf* needle; (*de montre*) hand; **aiguille à tricoter** knitting needle

aiguiser [egize] *vt* to sharpen; (*fig*) to stimulate; (: *sens*) to excite

ail [aj] *nm* garlic

aile [ɛl] *nf* wing; **aileron** *nm* (*de requin*) fin; **ailier** *nm* winger

aille *etc* [aj] *vb voir* **aller**

ailleurs [ajœʀ] *adv* elsewhere, somewhere else; **partout/nulle part ~** everywhere/nowhere else; **d'~** (*du reste*) moreover, besides; **par ~** (*d'autre part*) moreover, furthermore

aimable [ɛmabl] *adj* kind, nice

aimant [ɛmɑ̃] *nm* magnet

aimer [eme] *vt* to love; (*d'amitié, affection, par goût*) to like; (*souhait*): **j'aimerais ...** I would like ...; **j'aime faire du ski** I like skiing; **je t'aime** I love you; **bien ~ qn/qch** to like sb/sth; **j'aime mieux Paul (que Pierre)** I prefer Paul (to Pierre); **j'aimerais mieux faire** I'd much rather do

aine [ɛn] *nf* groin

aîné, e [ene] *adj* elder, older; (*le plus âgé*) eldest, oldest ▷ *nm/f* oldest child *ou* one, oldest boy *ou* son/girl *ou* daughter

ainsi [ɛ̃si] *adv* (*de cette façon*) like this, in this way, thus; (*ce faisant*) thus ▷ *conj* thus; so; **~ que** (*comme*) (just) as; (*et aussi*) as well as; **pour ~ dire** so to speak; **et ~ de suite** and so on

air [ɛʀ] *nm* air; (*mélodie*) tune; (*expression*) look, air; **prendre l'~** to get some (fresh) air; **avoir l'~** (*sembler*) to look, appear; **il a l'~ triste/malade** he looks sad/ill; **avoir l'~ de** to look like; **il a l'~ de dormir** he looks as if he's sleeping; **en l'~** (*promesses*) empty

airbag [ɛʀbag] *nm* airbag

aisance [ɛzɑ̃s] *nf* ease; (*richesse*) affluence

aise [ɛz] *nf* comfort; **être à l'~** *ou* **à son ~** to be comfortable; (*pas embarrassé*) to be at ease; (*financièrement*) to be comfortably off; **se mettre à l'~** to make o.s. comfortable; **être mal à l'~**

to be uncomfortable; (*gêné*) to be ill at ease; **en faire à son ~** to do as one likes;
aisé, e *adj* easy; (*assez riche*) well-to-do, well-off

aisselle [ɛsɛl] *nf* armpit

ait [ɛ] *vb voir* **avoir**

ajonc [aʒɔ̃] *nm* gorse *no pl*

ajourner [aʒuʀne] *vt* (*réunion*) to adjourn; (*décision*) to defer, postpone

ajouter [aʒute] *vt* to add

alarme [alaʀm] *nf* alarm; **donner l'~** to give *ou* raise the alarm; **alarmer** *vt* to alarm; **s'alarmer** *vi* to become alarmed

Albanie [albani] *nf:* **l'~** Albania

album [albɔm] *nm* album

alcool [alkɔl] *nm:* **l'~** alcohol; **un ~** a spirit, a brandy; **bière sans ~** non-alcoholic *ou* alcohol-free beer; **alcool à brûler** methylated spirits (*BRIT*), wood alcohol (*US*); **alcool à 90°** surgical spirit; **alcoolique** *adj, nm/f* alcoholic; **alcoolisé, e** *adj* alcoholic; **une boisson non alcoolisée** a soft drink; **alcoolisme** *nm* alcoholism; **alco(o)test®** *nm* Breathalyser®; (*test*) breath-test

aléatoire [aleatwaʀ] *adj* uncertain; (*Inform*) random

alentour [alɑ̃tuʀ] *adv* around, round about; **alentours** *nmpl* (*environs*) surroundings; **aux ~s de** in the vicinity *ou* neighbourhood of, round about; (*temps*) round about

alerte [alɛʀt] *adj* agile, nimble; brisk, lively ▷ *nf* alert; warning; **alerte à la bombe** bomb scare; **alerter** *vt* to alert

algèbre [alʒɛbʀ] *nf* algebra

Alger [alʒe] *n* Algiers

Algérie [alʒeʀi] *nf:* **l'~** Algeria; **algérien, ne** *adj* Algerian ▷ *nm/f:* **Algérien, ne** Algerian

algue [alg] *nf* (*gén*) seaweed *no pl*; (*Bot*) alga

alibi [alibi] *nm* alibi

aligner [aline] *vt* to align, line up; (*idées, chiffres*) to string together; (*adapter*): **~ qch sur** to bring sth into

alignment with; **s'aligner** (*soldats etc*) to line up; **s'~ sur** (*Pol*) to align o.s. on

aliment [alimɑ̃] *nm* food; **alimentation** *nf* (*commerce*) food trade; (*magasin*) grocery store; (*régime*) diet; (*en eau etc, de moteur*) supplying; (*Inform*) feed; **alimenter** *vt* to feed; (*Tech*): **alimenter (en)** to supply (with); to feed (with); (*fig*) to sustain, keep going

allaiter [alete] *vt* to (breast-)feed, nurse; (*suj: animal*) to suckle

allécher [aleʃe] *vt:* **~ qn** to make sb's mouth water; to tempt *ou* entice sb

allée [ale] *nf* (*de jardin*) path; (*en ville*) avenue, drive; **~s et venues** comings and goings

allégé, e [aleʒe] *adj* (*yaourt etc*) low-fat

alléger [aleʒe] *vt* (*voiture*) to make lighter; (*chargement*) to lighten; (*souffrance*) to alleviate, soothe

Allemagne [almaɲ] *nf:* **l'~** Germany; **allemand, e** *adj* German ▷ *nm/f:* **Allemand, e** German ▷ *nm* (*Ling*) German

aller [ale] *nm* (*trajet*) outward journey; (*billet: aussi:* **~ simple**) single (*BRIT*) *ou* one-way (*US*) ticket; **~ (et) retour** return (ticket) (*BRIT*), round-trip ticket (*US*) ▷ *vi* (*gén*) to go; (*convenir*) to suit; (*suj: forme, pointure etc*) to fit; **~ (bien) avec** (*couleurs, style etc*) to go (well) with; **je vais y ~/me fâcher** I'm going to go/to get angry; **~ chercher qn** to go and get *ou* fetch (*BRIT*) sb; **~ voir** to go and see, go to see; **allez!** come on!; **allons!** come now!; **comment allez-vous?** how are you?; **comment ça va?** how are you?; (*affaires etc*) how are things?; **il va bien/mal** he's well/not well, he's fine/ill; **ça va bien/mal** (*affaires etc*) it's going well/not going well; **~ mieux** to be better; **s'en ~** (*partir*) to be off, go, leave; (*disparaître*) to go away

allergie [alɛʀʒi] *nf* allergy

allergique [alɛʀʒik] *adj:* **~ à** allergic to; **je suis ~ à la pénicilline** I'm allergic

to penicillin

alliance [aljɑ̃s] nf (Mil, Pol) alliance; (bague) wedding ring

allier [alje] vt (Pol, gén) to ally; (fig) to combine; **s'allier** to become allies; to combine

allô [alo] excl hullo, hallo

allocation [alɔkasjɔ̃] nf allowance; **allocation (de) chômage** unemployment benefit; **allocations familiales** ≈ child benefit

allonger [alɔ̃ʒe] vt to lengthen, make longer; (étendre: bras, jambe) to stretch (out); **s'allonger** vi to get longer; (se coucher) to lie down, stretch out; **~ le pas** to hasten one's step(s)

allumage [alymaʒ] nm (Auto) ignition

allume-cigare [alymsigaʀ] nm inv cigar lighter

allumer [alyme] vt (lampe, phare, radio) to put ou switch on(s); (pièce) to put ou switch the light(s) on in; (feu) to light; **s'allumer** vi (lumière, lampe) to come ou go on; **je n'arrive pas à ~ le chauffage** I can't turn the heating on

allumette [alymɛt] nf match

allure [alyʀ] nf (vitesse) speed, pace; (démarche) walk; (aspect, air) look; **avoir de l'~** to have style; **à toute ~** at top speed

allusion [a(l)lyzjɔ̃] nf allusion; (sous-entendu) hint; **faire ~ à** to allude ou refer to; to hint at

 MOT-CLÉ

alors [alɔʀ] adv **1** (à ce moment-là) then, at that time; **il habitait alors à Paris** he lived in Paris at that time
2 (par conséquent) then; **tu as fini? alors je m'en vais** have you finished? I'm going then; **et alors?** so what?
▷ conj: **alors que 1** (au moment où) when, as; **il est arrivé alors que je partais** he arrived as I was leaving
2 (tandis que) whereas, while; **alors que son frère travaillait dur, lui se reposait** while his brother was

working hard, HE would rest
3 (bien que) even though; **il a été puni alors qu'il n'a rien fait** he was punished, even though he had done nothing

alourdir [aluʀdiʀ] vt to weigh down, make heavy

Alpes [alp] nfpl: **les ~** the Alps

alphabet [alfabɛ] nm alphabet; (livre) ABC (book)

alpinisme [alpinism] nm mountaineering, climbing

Alsace [alzas] nf Alsace; **alsacien, ne** adj Alsatian ▷ nm/f: **Alsacien, ne** Alsatian

altermondialisme [altɛʀmɔ̃djalism] nm anti-globalism; **altermondialiste** adj, nm/f anti-globalist

alternatif, -ive [altɛʀnatif, iv] adj alternating; **alternative** nf (choix) alternative; **alterner** vi to alternate

altitude [altityd] nf altitude, height

alto [alto] nm (instrument) viola

aluminium [alyminjɔm] nm aluminium (BRIT), aluminum (US)

amabilité [amabilite] nf kindness

amaigrissant, e [amegʀisɑ̃, ɑ̃t] adj (régime) slimming

amande [amɑ̃d] nf (de l'amandier) almond; **amandier** nm almond (tree)

amant [amɑ̃] nm lover

amas [amɑ] nm heap, pile; **amasser** vt to amass

amateur [amatœʀ] nm amateur; **en ~** (péj) amateurishly; **amateur de musique/sport** music/sport lover

ambassade [ɑ̃basad] nf embassy; **l'~ de France** the French Embassy; **ambassadeur, -drice** nm/f ambassador(-dress)

ambiance [ɑ̃bjɑ̃s] nf atmosphere; **il y a de l'~** there's a great atmosphere

ambigu, ë [ɑ̃bigy] adj ambiguous

ambitieux, -euse [ɑ̃bisjø, jøz] adj ambitious

ambition [ɑ̃bisjɔ̃] nf ambition

ambulance [ɑ̃bylɑ̃s] nf ambulance;

appelez une ~! call an ambulance!;
ambulancier, -ière nm/f ambulance
man(-woman) (BRIT), paramedic (US)

âme [am] nf soul; **âme sœur** kindred
spirit

amélioration [ameljɔrasjɔ̃] nf
improvement

améliorer [ameljɔre] vt to improve;
s'améliorer vi to improve, get better

aménager [amenaʒe] vt (agencer,
transformer) to fit out; to lay out;
(: quartier, territoire) to develop;
(installer) to fix up, put in; **ferme
aménagée** converted farmhouse

amende [amɑ̃d] nf fine; **faire ~
honorable** to make amends

amener [am(ə)ne] vt to bring; (causer)
to bring about; **s'amener** vi to show
up (fam), turn up; **~ qn à faire qch** to
lead sb to do sth

amer, amère [amɛʀ] adj bitter

américain, e [amerikɛ̃, ɛn] adj
American ▷ nm/f: **A~, e** American

Amérique [amerik] nf: **l'~** America;
Amérique centrale/latine Central/
Latin America; **l'Amérique du Nord/
Sud** North/South America

amertume [amɛʀtym] nf bitterness

ameublement [amœbləmɑ̃] nm
furnishing; (meubles) furniture

ami, e [ami] nm/f friend; (amant/
maîtresse) boyfriend/girlfriend ▷ adj:
pays/groupe ~ friendly country/
group; **petit ~/petite ~e** boyfriend/
girlfriend

amiable [amjabl]: **à l'~** adv (Jur) out of
court; (gén) amicably

amiante [amjɑ̃t] nm asbestos

amical, e, -aux [amikal, o] adj
friendly; **amicalement** adv in a
friendly way; (dans une lettre) (with)
best wishes

amincir [amɛ̃siʀ] vt: **~ qn** to make sb
thinner ou slimmer; (suj: vêtement) to
make sb look slimmer

amincissant, e [amɛ̃sisɑ̃, ɑ̃t] adj:
régime ~ (slimming) diet; **crème ~e**
slimming cream

amiral, -aux [amiʀal, o] nm admiral

amitié [amitje] nf friendship; **prendre
en ~** to befriend; **faire ou présenter
ses ~s à qn** to send sb one's best
wishes; **"~s"** (dans une lettre) "(with)
best wishes"

amonceler [amɔ̃s(ə)le] vt to pile ou
heap up; **s'amonceler** vi to pile ou
heap up; (fig) to accumulate

amont [amɔ̃]: **en ~** adv upstream

amorce [amɔʀs] nf (sur un hameçon)
bait; (explosif) cap; primer; priming; (fig:
début) beginning(s), start

amortir [amɔʀtiʀ] vt (atténuer: choc)
to absorb, cushion; (bruit, douleur) to
deaden; (Comm: dette) to pay off; **~ un
achat** to make a purchase pay for itself;
amortisseur nm shock absorber

amour [amuʀ] nm love; **faire l'~** to
make love; **amoureux, -euse** adj
(regard, tempérament) amorous; (vie,
problèmes) love cpd; (personne): **être
amoureux (de qn)** to be in love (with
sb); **tomber amoureux (de qn)** to
fall in love (with sb) ▷ nmpl courting
couple(s); **amour-propre** nm self-
esteem, pride

ampère [ɑ̃pɛʀ] nm amp(ere)

amphithéâtre [ɑ̃fiteatʀ] nm
amphitheatre; (d'université) lecture hall
ou theatre

ample [ɑ̃pl] adj (vêtement) roomy,
ample; (gestes, mouvement) broad;
(ressources) ample; **amplement** adv:
c'est amplement suffisant that's
more than enough; **ampleur** nf (de
dégâts, problème) extent

amplificateur [ɑ̃plifikatœʀ] nm
amplifier

amplifier [ɑ̃plifje] vt (fig) to expand,
increase

ampoule [ɑ̃pul] nf (électrique) bulb;
(de médicament) phial; (aux mains, pieds)
blister

amusant, e [amyzɑ̃, ɑ̃t] adj
(divertissant, spirituel) entertaining,
amusing; (comique) funny, amusing

amuse-gueule [amyzgœl] nm inv

appetizer, snack

amusement [amyzmã] nm
(*divertissement*) amusement; (*jeu etc*)
pastime, diversion

amuser [amyze] vt (*divertir*) to
entertain, amuse; (*égayer, faire rire*) to
amuse; **s'amuser** vi (*jouer*) to play; (*se
divertir*) to enjoy o.s., have fun; (*fig*) to
mess around

amygdale [amidal] nf tonsil

an [ã] nm year; **avoir quinze ans** to be
fifteen (years old); **le jour de l'an, le
premier de l'an, le nouvel an** New
Year's Day

analphabète [analfabɛt] nm/f
illiterate

analyse [analiz] nf analysis; (*Méd*) test;
analyser vt to analyse; to test

ananas [anana(s)] nm pineapple

anatomie [anatɔmi] nf anatomy

ancêtre [ãsɛtʀ] nm/f ancestor

anchois [ãʃwa] nm anchovy

ancien, ne [ãsjɛ̃, jɛn] adj old; (*de
jadis, de l'antiquité*) ancient; (*précédent,
ex-*) former, old; (*par l'expérience*)
senior ▷ nm/f (*dans une tribu*) elder;
ancienneté nf (*Admin*) (length of)
service; (*privilèges obtenus*) seniority

ancre [ãkʀ] nf anchor; **jeter/lever l'~** to
cast/weigh anchor; **ancrer** vt (*Constr:
câble etc*) to anchor; (*fig*) to fix firmly

Andorre [ãdɔʀ] nf Andorra

andouille [ãduj] nf (*Culin*) sausage made
of chitterlings; (*fam*) clot, nit

âne [ɑn] nm donkey, ass; (*péj*) dunce

anéantir [aneãtiʀ] vt to annihilate,
wipe out; (*fig*) to obliterate, destroy

anémie [anemi] nf anaemia;
anémique adj anaemic

anesthésie [anɛstezi] nf anaesthesia;
faire une ~ locale/générale à qn to
give sb a local/general anaesthetic

ange [ãʒ] nm angel; **être aux ~s** to be
over the moon

angine [ãʒin] nf throat infection;
angine de poitrine angina

anglais, e [ãglɛ, ɛz] adj English ▷ nm/f:
A~, e Englishman(-woman) ▷ nm

(*Ling*) English; **les A~** the English; **filer à
l'~e** to take French leave

angle [ãgl] nm angle; (*coin*) corner;
angle droit right angle

Angleterre [ãglətɛʀ] nf: **l'~** England

anglo... [ãglɔ] préfixe Anglo-, anglo(-);
anglophone adj English-speaking

angoisse [ãgwas] nf anguish, distress;
angoissé, e adj (*personne*) distressed

anguille [ãgij] nf eel

animal, e, -aux [animal, o] adj, nm
animal

animateur, -trice [animatœʀ, tʀis]
nm/f (*de télévision*) host; (*de groupe*)
leader, organizer

animation [animasjõ] nf (*voir animé*)
busyness; liveliness; (*Cinéma: technique*)
animation

animé, e [anime] adj (*lieu*) busy, lively;
(*conversation, réunion*) lively, animated

animer [anime] vt (*ville, soirée*) to liven
up; (*mener*) to lead

anis [ani(s)] nm (*Culin*) aniseed; (*Bot*)
anise

ankyloser [ãkiloze]: **s'ankyloser** vi
to get stiff

anneau, x [ano] nm (*de rideau, bague*)
ring; (*de chaîne*) link

année [ane] nf year

annexe [anɛks] adj (*problème*) related;
(*document*) appended; (*salle*) adjoining
▷ nf (*bâtiment*) annex(e); (*jointe à une
lettre*) enclosure

anniversaire [anivɛʀsɛʀ] nm
birthday; (*d'un événement, bâtiment*)
anniversary

annonce [anõs] nf announcement;
(*signe, indice*) sign; (*aussi:* **~ publicitaire**)
advertisement; **les petites ~s** the
classified advertisements, the small
ads

annoncer [anõse] vt to announce; (*être
le signe de*) to herald; **s'~ bien/difficile**
to look promising/difficult

annuaire [anyɛʀ] nm yearbook,
annual; **annuaire téléphonique**
(telephone) directory, phone book

annuel, le [anyɛl] adj annual, yearly

annulation [anylasjɔ̃] nf cancellation
annuler [anyle] vt (rendez-vous, voyage) to cancel, call off; (jugement) to quash (BRIT), repeal (US); (Math, Physique) to cancel out; **je voudrais ~ ma réservation** I'd like to cancel my reservation
anonymat [anɔnima] nm anonymity; **garder l'~** to remain anonymous
anonyme [anɔnim] adj anonymous; (fig) impersonal
anorak [anɔrak] nm anorak
anorexie [anɔrɛksi] nf anorexia
anormal, e, -aux [anɔrmal, o] adj abnormal
ANPE sigle f (= Agence nationale pour l'emploi) national employment agency
antarctique [ɑ̃tarktik] adj Antarctic ▷ nm: **l'A~** the Antarctic
antenne [ɑ̃tɛn] nf (de radio) aerial; (d'insecte) antenna, feeler; (poste avancé) outpost; (petite succursale) sub-branch; **passer à l'~** to go on the air; **antenne parabolique** satellite dish
antérieur, e [ɑ̃terjœr] adj (d'avant) previous, earlier; (de devant) front
anti... [ɑ̃ti] préfixe anti...; **antialcoolique** adj anti-alcohol; **antibiotique** nm antibiotic; **antibrouillard** adj: **phare antibrouillard** fog lamp (BRIT) ou light (US)
anticipation [ɑ̃tisipasjɔ̃] nf: **livre/ film d'~** science fiction book/film
anticipé, e [ɑ̃tisipe] adj: **avec mes remerciements ~s** thanking you in advance ou anticipation
anticiper [ɑ̃tisipe] vt (événement, coup) to anticipate, foresee
anti...: **anticorps** nm antibody; **antidote** nm antidote; **antigel** nm antifreeze; **antihistaminique** nm antihistamine
antillais, e [ɑ̃tijɛ, ɛz] adj West Indian, Caribbean ▷ nm/f: **A~, e** West Indian, Caribbean
Antilles [ɑ̃tij] nfpl: **les ~** the West Indies; **les Grandes/Petites ~** the Greater/Lesser Antilles
antilope [ɑ̃tilɔp] nf antelope
anti...: **antimite(s)** adj, nm: **(produit) antimite(s)** mothproofer; moth repellent; **antimondialisation** nf anti-globalization; **antipathique** adj unpleasant, disagreeable; **antipelliculaire** adj anti-dandruff
antiquaire [ɑ̃tikɛr] nm/f antique dealer
antique [ɑ̃tik] adj antique; (très vieux) ancient, antiquated; **antiquité** nf (objet) antique; **l'Antiquité** Antiquity; **magasin d'antiquités** antique shop
anti...: **antirabique** adj rabies cpd; **antirouille** adj inv anti-rust cpd; **antisémite** adj anti-Semitic; **antiseptique** adj, nm antiseptic
antivirus [ɑ̃ti'virus] nm (Inform) antivirus; **antivol** adj, nm: **(dispositif) antivol** anti-theft device
anxieux, -euse [ɑ̃ksjø, jøz] adj anxious, worried
AOC sigle f (= appellation d'origine contrôlée) label guaranteeing the quality of wine
août [u(t)] nm August
apaiser [apeze] vt (colère, douleur) to soothe; (personne) to calm (down), pacify; **s'apaiser** vi (tempête, bruit) to die down, subside; (personne) to calm down
apercevoir [apɛrsəvwar] vt to see; **s'apercevoir de** vt to notice; **s'~ que** to notice that
aperçu [apɛrsy] nm (vue d'ensemble) general survey
apéritif [aperitif] nm (boisson) aperitif; (réunion) drinks pl
à-peu-près [apøprɛ] (péj) nm inv vague approximation
apeuré, e [apœre] adj frightened, scared
aphte [aft] nm mouth ulcer
apitoyer [apitwaje] vt to move to pity; **s'apitoyer (sur)** to feel pity (for)
aplatir [aplatir] vt to flatten; **s'aplatir** vi to become flatter; (écrasé) to be

flattened

aplomb [aplɔ̃] nm (équilibre) balance, equilibrium; (fig) self-assurance; nerve; **d'~** steady

apostrophe [apɔstʀɔf] nf (signe) apostrophe

apparaître [apaʀɛtʀ] vi to appear

appareil [apaʀɛj] nm (outil, machine) piece of apparatus, device; (électrique, ménager) appliance; (avion) (aero)plane, aircraft inv; (téléphonique) phone; (dentier) brace (BRIT), braces (US); **"qui est à l'~?"** "who's speaking?"; **dans le plus simple ~** in one's birthday suit; **appareil(-photo)** camera; **appareiller** vi (Navig) to cast off, get under way ▷ vt (assortir) to match up

apparemment [apaʀamɑ̃] adv apparently

apparence [apaʀɑ̃s] nf appearance; **en ~** apparently

apparent, e [apaʀɑ̃, ɑ̃t] adj visible; (évident) obvious; (superficiel) apparent

apparenté, e [apaʀɑ̃te] adj: **~ à** related to; (fig) similar to

apparition [apaʀisjɔ̃] nf appearance; (surnaturelle) apparition

appartement [apaʀtəmɑ̃] nm flat (BRIT), apartment (US)

appartenir [apaʀtəniʀ]: **~ à** vt to belong to; **il lui appartient de** it is his duty to

apparu, e [apaʀy] pp de **apparaître**

appât [apɑ] nm (Pêche) bait; (fig) lure, bait

appel [apɛl] nm call; (nominal) roll call; (: Scol) register; (Mil: recrutement) call-up; **faire ~ à** (invoquer) to appeal to; (avoir recours à) to call on; (nécessiter) to call for, require; **faire ou interjeter ~** (Jur) to appeal; **faire l'~** to call the roll; (Scol) to call the register; **sans ~** (fig) final, irrevocable; **faire un ~ de phares** to flash one's headlights; **appel d'offres** (Comm) invitation to tender; **appel (téléphonique)** (tele)phone call

appelé [ap(ə)le] nm (Mil) conscript

appeler [ap(ə)le] vt to call; (faire venir: médecin etc) to call, send for; **s'appeler** vi: **elle s'appelle Gabrielle** her name is Gabrielle, she's called Gabrielle; **comment vous appelez-vous?** what's your name?; **comment ça s'appelle?** what is it called?; **être appelé à** (fig) to be destined to

appendicite [apɑ̃disit] nf appendicitis

appesantir [apəzɑ̃tiʀ]: **s'appesantir** vi to grow heavier; **s'~ sur** (fig) to dwell on

appétissant, e [apetisɑ̃, ɑ̃t] adj appetizing, mouth-watering

appétit [apeti] nm appetite; **bon ~!** enjoy your meal!

applaudir [aplodiʀ] vt to applaud ▷ vi to applaud, clap; **applaudissements** nmpl applause sg, clapping sg

application [aplikasjɔ̃] nf application

appliquer [aplike] vt to apply; (loi) to enforce; **s'appliquer** vi (élève etc) to apply o.s.; **s'~ à** to apply to

appoint [apwɛ̃] nm (extra) contribution ou help; **avoir/faire l'~** to have/give the right change ou money; **chauffage d'~** extra heating

apporter [apɔʀte] vt to bring

appréciable [apʀesjabl] adj appreciable

apprécier [apʀesje] vt to appreciate; (évaluer) to estimate, assess

appréhender [apʀeɑ̃de] vt (craindre) to dread; (arrêter) to apprehend

apprendre [apʀɑ̃dʀ] vt to learn; (événement, résultats) to learn of, hear of; **~ qch à qn** (informer) to tell sb (of) sth; (enseigner) to teach sb sth; **~ à faire qch** to learn to do sth; **~ à qn à faire qch** to teach sb to do sth; **apprenti, e** nm/f apprentice; **apprentissage** nm learning; (Comm, Scol: période) apprenticeship

apprêter [apʀete] vt: **s'~ à faire qch** to get ready to do sth

appris, e [apʀi, iz] pp de **apprendre**

apprivoiser [apʀivwaze] vt to tame

approbation [apʀɔbasjɔ̃] nf approval

approcher [apʁɔʃe] vi to approach, come near ▷ vt to approach; (*rapprocher*): **~ qch (de qch)** to bring ou put sth near (to sth); **s'approcher de** to approach, go ou come near to; **~ de** (*lieu, but*) to draw near to; (*quantité, moment*) to approach

approfondir [apʁɔfɔ̃diʁ] vt to deepen; (*question*) to go further into

approprié, e [apʁɔpʁije] adj: **~ (à)** appropriate (to), suited to

approprier [apʁɔpʁije]: **s'approprier** vt to appropriate, take over; **s'~ en** to stock up with

approuver [apʁuve] vt to agree with; (*trouver louable*) to approve of

approvisionner [apʁɔvizjɔne] vt to supply; (*compte bancaire*) to pay funds into; **s'approvisionner en** to stock up with

approximatif, -ive [apʁɔksimatif, iv] adj approximate, rough; (*termes*) vague

appt abr = **appartement**

appui [apɥi] nm support; **prendre ~ sur** to lean on; (*objet*) to rest on; **l'~ de la fenêtre** the windowsill, the window ledge

appuyer [apɥije] vt (*poser*): **~ qch sur/contre** to lean ou rest sth on/against; (*soutenir: personne, demande*) to support, back (up) ▷ vi: **~ sur** (*bouton*) to press, push; (*mot, détail*) to stress, emphasize; **~ sur le frein** to brake, to apply the brakes; **s'appuyer sur** to lean on; (*fig: compter sur*) to rely on

après [apʁɛ] prép after ▷ adv afterwards; **2 heures ~** 2 hours later; **~ qu'il est** ou **soit parti** after he left; **~ avoir fait** after having done; **d'~** (*selon*) according to; **~ coup** after the event, afterwards; **~ tout** (*au fond*) after all; **et (puis) ~?** so what? **après-demain** adv the day after tomorrow; **après-midi** nm ou nf inv afternoon; **après-rasage** nm inv aftershave; **après-shampooing** nm inv conditioner; **après-ski** nm inv snow boot

après-soleil [apʁɛsɔlej] adj inv after-sun cpd ▷ nm after-sun cream ou lotion

apte [apt] adj capable; **~ à qch/faire qch** capable of sth/doing sth; **~ (au service)** (*Mil*) fit (for service)

aquarelle [akwaʁɛl] nf watercolour

aquarium [akwaʁjɔm] nm aquarium

arabe [aʁab] adj Arabic; (*désert, cheval*) Arabian; (*nation, peuple*) Arab ▷ nm/f: **A~** Arab ▷ nm (*Ling*) Arabic

Arabie [aʁabi] nf: **l'~ (Saoudite)** Saudi Arabia

arachide [aʁaʃid] nf (*plante*) groundnut (plant); (*graine*) peanut, groundnut

araignée [aʁene] nf spider

arbitraire [aʁbitʁɛʁ] adj arbitrary

arbitre [aʁbitʁ] nm (*Sport*) referee; (: *Tennis, Cricket*) umpire; (*fig*) arbiter, judge; (*Jur*) arbitrator; **arbitrer** vt to referee; to umpire; to arbitrate

arbre [aʁbʁ] nm tree; (*Tech*) shaft

arbuste [aʁbyst] nm small shrub

arc [aʁk] nm (*arme*) bow; (*Géom*) arc; (*Archit*) arch; **en ~ de cercle** semi-circular

arcade [aʁkad] nf arch(way); **arcades** nfpl (*série*) arcade sg, arches

arc-en-ciel [aʁkɑ̃sjɛl] nm rainbow

arche [aʁʃ] nf arch; **arche de Noé** Noah's Ark

archéologie [aʁkeɔlɔʒi] nf arch(a)eology; **archéologue** nm/f arch(a)eologist

archet [aʁʃɛ] nm bow

archipel [aʁʃipɛl] nm archipelago

architecte [aʁʃitɛkt] nm architect

architecture [aʁʃitɛktyʁ] nf architecture

archives [aʁʃiv] nfpl (*collection*) archives

arctique [aʁktik] adj Arctic ▷ nm: **l'A~** the Arctic

ardent, e [aʁdɑ̃, ɑ̃t] adj (*soleil*) blazing; (*amour*) ardent, passionate; (*prière*) fervent

ardoise [aʁdwaz] nf slate

ardu, e [aʁdy] adj (*travail*) arduous; (*problème*) difficult

arène [aʀɛn] *nf* arena; **arènes** *nfpl* (*amphithéâtre*) bull-ring *sg*

arête [aʀɛt] *nf* (*de poisson*) bone; (*d'une montagne*) ridge

argent [aʀʒɑ̃] *nm* (*métal*) silver; (*monnaie*) money; **argent de poche** pocket money; **argent liquide** ready money, (ready) cash; **argenterie** *nf* silverware

argentin, e [aʀʒɑ̃tɛ̃, in] *adj* Argentinian ▷ *nm/f*: **A~, e** Argentinian

Argentine [aʀʒɑ̃tin] *nf*: **l'~** Argentina

argentique [aʀʒɑ̃tik] *adj* (*appareil-photo*) film *cpd*

argile [aʀʒil] *nf* clay

argot [aʀgo] *nm* slang; **argotique** *adj* slang *cpd*; (*très familier*) slangy

argument [aʀgymɑ̃] *nm* argument

argumenter [aʀgymɑ̃te] *vi* to argue

aride [aʀid] *adj* arid

aristocratie [aʀistɔkʀasi] *nf* aristocracy; **aristocratique** *adj* aristocratic

arithmétique [aʀitmetik] *adj* arithmetic(al) ▷ *nf* arithmetic

arme [aʀm] *nf* weapon; **armes** *nfpl* (*armement*) weapons, arms; (*blason*) (coat of) arms; **~s de destruction massive** weapons of mass destruction; **arme à feu** firearm

armée [aʀme] *nf* army; **armée de l'air** Air Force; **armée de terre** Army

armer [aʀme] *vt* to arm; (*arme à feu*) to cock; (*appareil-photo*) to wind on; **~ qch de** to reinforce sth with; **s'armer de** to arm o.s. with

armistice [aʀmistis] *nm* armistice; **l'A~** ≈ Remembrance (BRIT) ou Veterans (US) Day

armoire [aʀmwaʀ] *nf* (tall) cupboard; (*penderie*) wardrobe (BRIT), closet (US)

armure [aʀmyʀ] *nf* armour *no pl*, suit of armour; **armurier** *nm* gunsmith

arnaque [aʀnak] (*fam*) *nf* swindling; **c'est de l'~** it's a rip-off; **arnaquer** (*fam*) *vt* to swindle

arobase [aʀobaz] *nf* (*symbole*) at symbol; **"paul ~ société point fr"** "paul at société dot fr"

aromates [aʀɔmat] *nmpl* seasoning *sg*, herbs (and spices)

aromathérapie [aʀɔmateʀapi] *nf* aromatherapy

aromatisé, e [aʀɔmatize] *adj* flavoured

arôme [aʀom] *nm* aroma

arracher [aʀaʃe] *vt* to pull out; (*page etc*) to tear off, tear right; (*légumes, herbe*) to pull up; (*bras etc*) to tear off; **s'arracher** *vt* (*article recherché*) to fight over; **~ qch à qn** to snatch sth from sb; (*fig*) to wring sth out of sb

arrangement [aʀɑ̃ʒmɑ̃] *nm* agreement, arrangement

arranger [aʀɑ̃ʒe] *vt* (*gén*) to arrange; (*réparer*) to fix, put right; (*régler: différend*) to settle, sort out; (*convenir à*) to suit, be convenient for; **cela m'arrange** that suits me (fine); **s'arranger** *vi* (*se mettre d'accord*) to come to an agreement; **je vais m'~** I'll manage; **ça va s'~** it'll sort itself out

arrestation [aʀɛstasjɔ̃] *nf* arrest

arrêt [aʀɛ] *nm* stopping; (*de bus etc*) stop; (*Jur*) judgment, decision; **à l'~** stationary; **tomber en ~ devant** to stop short in front of; **sans ~** (*sans interruption*) non-stop; (*très fréquemment*) continually; **arrêt de travail** stoppage (of work)

arrêter [aʀete] *vt* to stop; (*chauffage etc*) to turn off, switch off; (*fixer: date etc*) to appoint, decide on; (*criminel, suspect*) to arrest; **s'arrêter** *vi* to stop; **~ de faire** to stop doing; **arrêtez-vous ici/au coin, s'il vous plaît** could you stop here/at the corner, please?

arrhes [aʀ] *nfpl* deposit *sg*

arrière [aʀjɛʀ] *nm* back; (*Sport*) fullback ▷ *adj inv*: **siège/roue ~** back ou rear seat/wheel; **à l'~** behind, at the back; **en ~** behind; (*regarder*) back, behind; (*tomber, aller*) backwards; **arrière-goût** *nm* aftertaste; **arrière-grand-mère** *nf* great-grandmother; **arrière-grand-père** *nm* great-grandfather;

arrière-pays nm inv hinterland; **arrière-pensée** nf ulterior motive; mental reservation; **arrière-plan** nm background; **à l'arrière-plan** in the background; **arrière-saison** nf late autumn

arrimer [aʀime] vt to secure; (cargaison) to stow

arrivage [aʀivaʒ] nm consignment

arrivée [aʀive] nf arrival; (ligne d'arrivée) finish

arriver [aʀive] vi to arrive; (survenir) to happen, occur; **il arrive à Paris à 8h** he gets to ou arrives in Paris at 8; **à quelle heure arrive le train de Lyon?** what time does the train from Lyons get in?; **~ à** (atteindre) to reach; **~ à faire qch** to succeed in doing sth; **en ~ à** (finir par) to come to; **il arrive que** it happens that; **il lui arrive de faire** he sometimes does

arrobase [aʀɔbaz] nf (Inform) @, 'at' sign

arrogance [aʀɔgɑ̃s] nf arrogance

arrogant, e [aʀɔgɑ̃, ɑ̃t] adj arrogant

arrondissement [aʀɔ̃dismɑ̃] nm (Admin) ≈ district

arroser [aʀoze] vt to water; (victoire) to celebrate (over a drink); (Culin) to baste; **arrosoir** nm watering can

arsenal, -aux [aʀsənal, o] nm (Navig) naval dockyard; (Mil) arsenal; (fig) gear, paraphernalia

art [aʀ] nm art

artère [aʀtɛʀ] nf (Anat) artery; (rue) main road

arthrite [aʀtʀit] nf arthritis

artichaut [aʀtiʃo] nm artichoke

article [aʀtikl] nm article; (Comm) item, article; **à l'~ de la mort** at the point of death

articulation [aʀtikylasjɔ̃] nf articulation; (Anat) joint

articuler [aʀtikyle] vt to articulate

artificiel, le [aʀtifisjɛl] adj artificial

artisan [aʀtizɑ̃] nm artisan, (self-employed) craftsman; **artisanal, e, -aux** adj of ou made by craftsmen; (péj)

cottage industry cpd; **de fabrication artisanale** home-made; **artisanat** nm arts and crafts pl

artiste [aʀtist] nm/f artist; (de variétés) entertainer; (musicien etc) performer; **artistique** adj artistic

as¹ [a] vb voir **avoir**

as² [ɑs] nm ace

ascenseur [asɑ̃sœʀ] nm lift (BRIT), elevator (US)

ascension [asɑ̃sjɔ̃] nf ascent; (de montagne) climb; **l'A~** (Rel) the Ascension

● **ASCENSION**

●

● The **fête de l'Ascension** is a public
● holiday in France. It always falls on
● a Thursday, usually in May. Many
● French people take the following
● Friday off work too and enjoy a long
● weekend.

asiatique [azjatik] adj Asiatic, Asian
▷ nm/f: **A~** Asian

Asie [azi] nf: **l'~** Asia

asile [azil] nm (refuge) refuge, sanctuary; (Pol): **droit d'~** (political) asylum

aspect [aspɛ] nm appearance, look; (fig) aspect, side; **à l'~ de** at the sight of

asperge [aspɛʀʒ] nf asparagus no pl

asperger [aspɛʀʒe] vt to spray, sprinkle

asphalte [asfalt] nm asphalt

asphyxier [asfiksje] vt to suffocate, asphyxiate; (fig) to stifle

aspirateur [aspiʀatœʀ] nm vacuum cleaner; **passer l'~** to vacuum

aspirer [aspiʀe] vt (air) to inhale; (liquide) to suck (up); (suj: appareil) to suck up; **~ à** to aspire to

aspirine [aspiʀin] nf aspirin

assagir [asaʒiʀ]: **s'assagir** vi to quieten down, settle down

assaisonnement [asɛzɔnmɑ̃] nm seasoning

assaisonner [asɛzɔne] vt to season

assassin [asasɛ̃] nm murderer;

assassin; **assassiner** *vt* to murder; (*esp Pol*) to assassinate

assaut [aso] *nm* assault, attack; **prendre d'~** to storm, assault; **donner l'~ à** to attack

assécher [asefe] *vt* to drain

assemblage [asɑ̃blaʒ] *nm* (*action*) assembling; (*de couleurs, choses*) collection

assemblée [asɑ̃ble] *nf* (*réunion*) meeting; (*assistance*) gathering; (*Pol*) assembly; **l'A~ nationale** the National Assembly (*the lower house of the French Parliament*)

assembler [asɑ̃ble] *vt* (*joindre, monter*) to assemble, put together; (*amasser*) to gather (together), collect (together); **s'assembler** *vi* to gather

asseoir [aswaʀ] *vt* (*malade, bébé*) to sit up; (*personne debout*) to sit down; (*autorité, réputation*) to establish; **s'asseoir** *vi* to sit (o.s.) down

assez [ase] *adv* (*suffisamment*) enough, sufficiently; (*passablement*) rather, quite, fairly; **~ de pain/livres** enough *ou* sufficient bread/books; **vous en avez ~?** have you got enough?; **j'en ai ~!** I've had enough!

assidu, e [asidy] *adj* (*appliqué*) assiduous, painstaking; (*ponctuel*) regular

assied *etc* [asje] *vb voir* **asseoir**

assiérai *etc* [asjeʀe] *vb voir* **asseoir**

assiette [asjɛt] *nf* plate; (*contenu*) plate(ful); **il n'est pas dans son ~** he's not feeling quite himself; **assiette à dessert** dessert plate; **assiette anglaise** assorted cold meats; **assiette creuse** (soup) dish, soup plate; **assiette plate** (dinner) plate

assimiler [asimile] *vt* to assimilate, absorb; (*comparer*): **~ qch/qn à** to liken *ou* compare sth/sb to; **s'assimiler** *vr* (*s'intégrer*) to be assimilated, assimilate

assis, e [asi, iz] *pp de* **asseoir** ▷ *adj* sitting (down), seated

assistance [asistɑ̃s] *nf* (*public*) audience; (*aide*) assistance; **enfant de**

l'A~ **publique** child in care

assistant, e [asistɑ̃, ɑ̃t] *nm/f* assistant; (*d'université*) probationary lecturer; **assistant(e) social(e)** social worker

assisté, e [asiste] *adj* (*Auto*) power assisted; **~ par ordinateur** computer-assisted; **direction ~e** power steering

assister [asiste] *vt* (*aider*) to assist; **~ à** (*scène, événement*) to witness; (*conférence, séminaire*) to attend, be at; (*spectacle, match*) to be at, see

association [asɔsjasjɔ̃] *nf* association

associé, e [asɔsje] *nm/f* associate; (*Comm*) partner

associer [asɔsje] *vt* to associate; **s'associer** *vi* to join together; **s'~ à qn pour faire** to join (forces) with sb to do; **s'~ à** (*couleurs, qualités*) to be combined with; (*opinions, joie de qn*) to share in; **~ qn à** (*profits*) to give sb a share of; (*affaire*) to make sb a partner in; (*joie, triomphe*) to include sb in; **~ qch à** (*allier à*) to combine sth with

assoiffé, e [aswafe] *adj* thirsty

assommer [asɔme] *vt* (*étourdir, abrutir*) to knock out, stun

Assomption [asɔ̃psjɔ̃] *nf*: **l'~** the Assumption

assorti, e [asɔʀti] *adj* matched, matching; (*varié*) assorted; **~ à** matching; **assortiment** *nm* assortment, selection

assortir [asɔʀtiʀ] *vt* to match; **~ qch à** to match sth with; **~ qch de** to accompany sth with

assouplir [asupliʀ] *vt* to make supple;

(fig) to relax; **assouplissant** *nm* (fabric) softener

assumer [asyme] *vt (fonction, emploi)* to assume, take on

assurance [asyrɑ̃s] *nf (certitude)* assurance; *(confiance en soi)* (self-)confidence; *(contrat)* insurance (policy); *(secteur commercial)* insurance; **assurance au tiers** third-party insurance; **assurance maladie** health insurance; **assurance tous risques** *(Auto)* comprehensive insurance; **assurances sociales** ≈ National Insurance *(BRIT)*, ≈ Social Security *(US)*; **assurance-vie** *nf* life assurance *ou* insurance

assuré, e [asyre] *adj (certain: réussite, échec)* certain, sure; *(air)* assured; *(pas)* steady ▷ *nm/f* insured (person); **assurément** *adv* assuredly, most certainly

assurer [asyre] *vt (Finance)* to insure; *(victoire etc)* to ensure; *(frontières, pouvoir)* to make secure; *(service)* to provide, operate; **s'assurer (contre)** *(Comm)* to insure o.s. (against); **s'~ de/ que** *(vérifier)* to make sure of/that; **s'~ (de)** *(aide de qn)* to secure; **~ à qn que** to assure sb that; **~ qn de** to assure sb of

asthmatique [asmatik] *adj, nm/f* asthmatic

asthme [asm] *nm* asthma

asticot [astiko] *nm* maggot

astre [astʀ] *nm* star

astrologie [astʀɔlɔʒi] *nf* astrology

astronaute [astʀonot] *nm/f* astronaut

astronomie [astʀonɔmi] *nf* astronomy

astuce [astys] *nf* shrewdness, astuteness; *(truc)* trick, clever way; **astucieux, -euse** *adj* clever

atelier [atəlje] *nm* workshop; *(de peintre)* studio

athée [ate] *adj* atheistic ▷ *nm/f* atheist

Athènes [atɛn] *n* Athens

athlète [atlɛt] *nm/f (Sport)* athlete; **athlétisme** *nm* athletics *sg*

atlantique [atlɑ̃tik] *adj* Atlantic ▷ *nm*: **l'(océan) A~** the Atlantic (Ocean)

atlas [atlɑs] *nm* atlas

atmosphère [atmɔsfɛʀ] *nf* atmosphere

atome [atom] *nm* atom; **atomique** *adj* atomic, nuclear

atomiseur [atɔmizœʀ] *nm* atomizer

atout [atu] *nm* trump; *(fig)* asset

atroce [atʀɔs] *adj* atrocious

attachant, e [ataʃɑ̃, ɑ̃t] *adj* engaging, lovable, likeable

attache [ataʃ] *nf* clip, fastener; *(fig)* tie

attacher [ataʃe] *vt* to tie up; *(étiquette)* to attach, tie on; *(ceinture)* to fasten ▷ *vi (poêle, riz)* to stick; **s'attacher à** *(par affection)* to become attached to; **~ qch à** to tie *ou* attach sth to

attaque [atak] *nf* attack; *(cérébrale)* stroke; *(d'épilepsie)* fit

attaquer [atake] *vt* to attack ▷ *vi* to attack; **s'attaquer à** *(personne)* to attack; *(problème)* to tackle; **~ qn en justice** to bring an action against sb, sue sb

attarder [ataʀde]: **s'attarder** *vi* to linger

atteindre [atɛ̃dʀ] *vt* to reach; *(blesser)* to hit; *(émouvoir)* to affect; **atteint, e** *adj (Méd)*: **être atteint de** to be suffering from; **atteinte** *nf*: **hors d'atteinte** out of reach; **porter atteinte à** to strike a blow at

attendant [atɑ̃dɑ̃] *adv*: **en ~** meanwhile, in the meantime

attendre [atɑ̃dʀ] *vt (gén)* to wait for; *(être destiné ou réservé à)* to await, be in store for ▷ *vi* to wait; **s'attendre à (ce que)** to expect (that); **attendez-moi, s'il vous plaît** wait for me, please; **~ un enfant** to be expecting a baby; **~ de faire/d'être** to wait until one does/is; **attendez qu'il vienne** wait until he comes; **~ qch de** to expect sth of

> Attention à ne pas traduire *attendre* par *to attend*.

attendrir [atɑ̃dʀiʀ] *vt* to move (to pity); *(viande)* to tenderize

attendu, e [atɑ̃dy] adj (visiteur)
expected; (événement) long-awaited; ~
que considering that, since

attentat [atɑ̃ta] nm assassination
attempt; **attentat à la pudeur**
indecent assault no pl; **attentat
suicide** suicide bombing

attente [atɑ̃t] nf wait; (espérance)
expectation

attenter [atɑ̃te]: ~ **à** vt (liberté) to
violate; ~ **à la vie de qn** to make an
attempt on sb's life

attentif, -ive [atɑ̃tif, iv] adj (auditeur)
attentive; (examen) careful; ~ **à**
careful to

attention [atɑ̃sjɔ̃] nf attention;
(prévenance) attention, thoughtfulness
no pl; **à l'~ de** for the attention of; **faire
~ (à)** to be careful (of); **faire ~ (à ce)
que** to be ou make sure that; ~**!** careful!,
watch out!; ~ **à la voiture!** watch
out for that car!; **attentionné, e** adj
thoughtful, considerate

atténuer [atenɥe] vt (douleur) to
alleviate, ease; (couleurs) to soften;
s'atténuer vi to ease; (violence etc)
to abate

atterrir [ateʀiʀ] vi to land;
atterrissage nm landing

attestation [atɛstasjɔ̃] nf certificate

attirant, e [atiʀɑ̃, ɑ̃t] adj attractive,
appealing

attirer [atiʀe] vt to attract; (appâter) to
lure, entice; ~ **qn dans un coin/vers
soi** to draw sb into a corner/towards
one; ~ **l'attention de qn** to attract
sb's attention; ~ **l'attention de qn
sur** to draw sb's attention to; **s'~ des
ennuis** to bring trouble upon o.s., get
into trouble

attitude [atityd] nf attitude; (position
du corps) bearing

attraction [atʀaksjɔ̃] nf (gén)
attraction; (de cabaret, cirque) number

attrait [atʀɛ] nm appeal, attraction

attraper [atʀape] vt (gén) to catch;
(habitude, amende) to get, pick up;
(fam: duper) to con; **se faire ~** (fam) to

be told off

attrayant, e [atʀɛjɑ̃, ɑ̃t] adj
attractive

attribuer [atʀibɥe] vt (prix) to
award; (rôle, tâche) to allocate, assign;
(imputer): ~ **qch à** to attribute sth to;
s'attribuer vt (s'approprier) to claim
for o.s.

attrister [atʀiste] vt to sadden

attroupement [atʀupmɑ̃] nm crowd

attrouper [atʀupe]: **s'attrouper** vi
to gather

au [o] prép +dét = **à +le**

aubaine [oben] nf godsend

aube [ob] nf dawn, daybreak; **à l'~** at
dawn ou daybreak

aubépine [obepin] nf hawthorn

auberge [obɛʀʒ] nf inn; **auberge de
jeunesse** youth hostel

aubergine [obɛʀʒin] nf aubergine

aucun, e [okœ̃, yn] dét no, tournure
négative +any; (positif) any ▷ pron none,
tournure négative +any; any(one);
**sans ~
doute** without any doubt; **plus
qu'~ autre** more than any other; **il
le fera mieux qu'~ de nous** he'll do
it better than any of us; ~ **des deux**
neither of the two; ~ **d'entre eux** none
of them

audace [odas] nf daring, boldness;
(péj) audacity; **audacieux, -euse** adj
daring, bold

au-delà [od(ə)la] adv beyond ▷ nm: **l'~**
the hereafter; ~ **de** beyond

au-dessous [odsu] adv underneath;
below; ~ **de** under(neath), below;
(limite, somme etc) below, under; (dignité,
condition) below

au-dessus [odsy] adv above; ~ **de**
above

au-devant [od(ə)vɑ̃]: ~ **de** prép: **aller
~ de** (personne, danger) to go (out) and
meet; (souhaits de qn) to anticipate

audience [odjɑ̃s] nf audience; (Jur:
séance) hearing

audiovisuel, le [odjovizɥel] adj
audiovisual

audition [odisjɔ̃] nf (ouïe, écoute)

hearing; (*Jur: de témoins*) examination; (*Mus, Théâtre: épreuve*) audition
auditoire [oditwaʀ] *nm* audience
augmentation [ɔgmɑ̃tasjɔ̃] *nf* increase; **augmentation (de salaire)** rise (in salary) (*BRIT*), (pay) raise (*US*)
augmenter [ɔgmɑ̃te] *vt* (*gén*) to increase; (*salaire, prix*) to increase, raise, put up; (*employé*) to increase the salary of ▷ *vi* to increase
augure [ogyʀ] *nm*: **de bon/mauvais ~** of good/ill omen
aujourd'hui [oʒuʀdɥi] *adv* today
aumône [omon] *nf inv* alms *sg*; **aumônier** *nm* chaplain
auparavant [oparavɑ̃] *adv* before(hand)
auprès [opʀɛ]: **~ de** *prép* next to, close to; (*recourir, s'adresser*) to; (*en comparaison de*) compared with
auquel [okɛl] *prép +pron* = **à +lequel**
aurai *etc* [ɔʀe] *vb voir* **avoir**
aurons *etc* [oʀɔ̃] *vb voir* **avoir**
aurore [`ʀ] *nf* dawn, daybreak
ausculter [ɔskylte] *vt* to sound (the chest of)
aussi [osi] *adv* (*également*) also, too; (*de comparaison*) as ▷ *conj* therefore, consequently; **~ fort que** as strong as; **moi ~** me too
aussitôt [osito] *adv* straight away, immediately; **~ que** as soon as
austère [ostɛʀ] *adj* austere
austral, e [ɔstʀal] *adj* southern
Australie [ostʀali] *nf*: **l'~** Australia; **australien, ne** *adj* Australian ▷ *nm/f*: **Australien, ne** Australian
autant [otɑ̃] *adv* (*intensité*) so much; **je ne savais pas que tu la détestais ~** I didn't know you hated her so much; (*comparatif*): **~ (que)** as much (as); (*nombre*) as many (as); **~ (de)** so much (*ou* many); as much (*ou* many); **~ partir** we (*ou* you *etc*) may as well leave; **~ dire que ...** one might as well say that ...; **pour ~** for all that; **d'~ plus/mieux (que)** all the more/the

better (since)
autel [otɛl] *nm* altar
auteur [otœʀ] *nm* author
authentique [otɑ̃tik] *adj* authentic, genuine
auto [oto] *nf* car
auto...: **autobiographie** *nf* autobiography; **autobronzant** *nm* self-tanning cream (*or* lotion *etc*); **autobus** *nm* bus; **autocar** *nm* coach
autochtone [ɔtɔktɔn] *nm/f* native
auto...: **autocollant, e** *adj* self-adhesive; (*enveloppe*) self-seal ▷ *nm* sticker; **autocuiseur** *nm* pressure cooker; **autodéfense** *nf* self-defence; **autodidacte** *nm/f* self-taught person; **auto-école** *nf* driving school; **autographe** *nm* autograph
automate [ɔtɔmat] *nm* (*machine*) (automatic) machine
automatique [ɔtɔmatik] *adj* automatic ▷ *nm*: **l'~** direct dialling
automne [ɔtɔn] *nm* autumn (*BRIT*), fall (*US*)
automobile [ɔtɔmɔbil] *adj* motor *cpd*, car *cpd* ▷ *nf* (motor) car; **automobiliste** *nm/f* motorist
autonome [ɔtɔnɔm] *adj* autonomous; **autonomie** *nf* autonomy; (*Pol*) self-government, autonomy
autopsie [ɔtɔpsi] *nf* post-mortem (examination), autopsy
autoradio [otoʀadjo] *nm* car radio
autorisation [ɔtɔʀizasjɔ̃] *nf* permission, authorization; (*papiers*) permit
autorisé, e [ɔtɔʀize] *adj* (*opinion, sources*) authoritative
autoriser [ɔtɔʀize] *vt* to give permission for, authorize; (*fig*) to allow (of)
autoritaire [ɔtɔʀitɛʀ] *adj* authoritarian
autorité [ɔtɔʀite] *nf* authority; **faire ~** to be authoritative; **les ~s** the authorities
autoroute [otoʀut] *nf* motorway (*BRIT*), highway (*US*); **~ de**

l'information (*Inform*) information superhighway

● **AUTOROUTE**
●
● Motorways in France, indicated
● by blue road signs with the letter A
● followed by a number, are toll roads.
● The speed limit is 130 km/h (110 km/
● h when it is raining). At the tollgate,
● the lanes marked 'réservé' and with
● an orange 't' are reserved for people
● who subscribe to 'télépéage', an
● electronic payment system.

auto-stop [otostɔp] *nm*: **faire de l'~** to hitch-hike; **prendre qn en ~** to give sb a lift; **auto-stoppeur, -euse** *nm/f* hitch-hiker

autour [otuʀ] *adv* around; **~ de** around; **tout ~** all around

 MOT-CLÉ

autre [otʀ] *adj* **1** (*différent*) other, different; **je préférerais un autre verre** I'd prefer another *ou* a different glass
2 (*supplémentaire*) other; **je voudrais un autre verre d'eau** I'd like another glass of water
3: **autre chose** something else; **autre part** somewhere else; **d'autre part** on the other hand
▷ *pron*: **un autre** another (one); **nous/vous autres** us/you; **d'autres** others; **l'autre** the other (one); **les autres** the others; (*autrui*) others; **l'un et l'autre** both of them; **se détester l'un l'autre/les uns les autres** to hate each other *ou* one another; **d'une semaine à l'autre** from one week to the next; (*incessamment*) any week now; **entre autres** (*personnes*) among others; (*choses*) among other things

autrefois [otʀəfwa] *adv* in the past
autrement [otʀəmɑ̃] *adv* differently; (*d'une manière différente*) in another way; (*sinon*) otherwise; **~ dit** in other words
Autriche [otʀiʃ] *nf*: **l'~** Austria; **autrichien, ne** *adj* Austrian ▷ *nm/f*: **Autrichien, ne** Austrian
autruche [otʀyʃ] *nf* ostrich
aux [o] *prép +dét* = **à +les**
auxiliaire [ɔksiljɛʀ] *adj, nm/f* auxiliary
auxquelles [okɛl] *prép +pron* = **à +lesquelles**
auxquels [okɛl] *prép +pron* = **à +lesquels**
avalanche [avalɑ̃ʃ] *nf* avalanche
avaler [avale] *vt* to swallow
avance [avɑ̃s] *nf* (*de troupes etc*) advance; progress; (*d'argent*) advance; (*sur un concurrent*) lead; **avances** *nfpl* (*amoureuses*) advances; **(être) en ~** (to be) early; (*sur un programme*) (to be) ahead of schedule; **à l'~, d'~** in advance
avancé, e [avɑ̃se] *adj* advanced; (*travail*) well on, well under way
avancement [avɑ̃smɑ̃] *nm* (*professionnel*) promotion
avancer [avɑ̃se] *vi* to move forward, advance; (*projet, travail*) to make progress; (*montre, réveil*) to be fast; to gain ▷ *vt* to move forward, advance; (*argent*) to advance; (*montre, pendule*) to put forward; **s'avancer** *vi* to move forward, advance; (*fig*) to commit o.s.
avant [avɑ̃] *prép, adv* before ▷ *adj inv*: **siège/roue ~** front seat/wheel ▷ *nm* (*d'un véhicule, bâtiment*) front; (*Sport: joueur*) forward; **~ qu'il (ne) parte** before he goes *ou* leaves; **~ de partir** before leaving; **~ tout** (*surtout*) above all; **à l'~** (*dans un véhicule*) in (the) front; **en ~** (*se pencher, tomber*) forward(s); **partir en ~** to go on ahead; **en ~ de** in front of
avantage [avɑ̃taʒ] *nm* advantage; **avantages sociaux** fringe benefits; **avantager** *vt* (*favoriser*) to favour; (*embellir*) to flatter; **avantageux, -euse** *adj* (*prix*) attractive
avant...: **avant-bras** *nm inv* forearm; **avant-coureur** *adj inv*: **signe avant-**

coureur advance indication *ou* sign;
avant-dernier, -ière *adj, nm/f* next
to last, last but one; **avant-goût** *nm*
foretaste; **avant-hier** *adv* the day
before yesterday; **avant-première**
nf (*de film*) preview; **avant-veille** *nf*:
l'avant-veille two days before

avare [avaʀ] *adj* miserly, avaricious
▷ *nm/f* miser; **~ de** (*compliments etc*)
sparing of

avec [avɛk] *prép* with; (*à l'égard de*)
to(wards), with; **et ~ ça?** (*dans magasin*)
anything else?

avenir [avniʀ] *nm* future; **à l'~**
in future; **politicien/métier d'~**
politician/job with prospects *ou* a
future

aventure [avɑ̃tyʀ] *nf* adventure;
(*amoureuse*) affair; **aventureux, -euse**
adj adventurous, venturesome; (*projet*)
risky, chancy

avenue [avny] *nf* avenue

avérer [aveʀe]: **s'avérer** *vb +attrib* to
prove (to be)

averse [avɛʀs] *nf* shower

averti, e [avɛʀti] *adj* (well-)informed

avertir [avɛʀtiʀ] *vt*: **~ qn (de qch/que)**
to warn sb (of sth/that); (*renseigner*)
to inform sb (of sth/that); **avertissement**
nm warning; **avertisseur** *nm* horn,
siren

aveu, x [avø] *nm* confession

aveugle [avœgl] *adj* blind ▷ *nm/f* blind
man/woman

aviation [avjasjɔ̃] *nf* aviation; (*sport*)
flying; (*Mil*) air force

avide [avid] *adj* eager; (*péj*) greedy,
grasping

avion [avjɔ̃] *nm* (aero)plane (BRIT),
(air)plane (US); **aller (quelque part)
en ~** to go (somewhere) by plane, fly
(somewhere); **par ~** by airmail; **avion à
réaction** jet (plane)

aviron [aviʀɔ̃] *nm* oar; (*sport*): **l'~**
rowing

avis [avi] *nm* opinion; (*notification*)
notice; **à mon ~** in my opinion;
changer d'~ to change one's mind;

jusqu'à nouvel ~ until further notice

aviser [avize] *vt* (*informer*): **~ qn de/que**
to advise *ou* inform sb of/that ▷ *vi*
to think about things, assess the
situation; **nous ~ons sur place** we'll
work something out once we're there;
s'~ de qch/que to become suddenly
aware of sth/that; **s'~ de faire** to take
it into one's head to do

avocat, e [avɔka, at] *nm/f* (*Jur*)
barrister (BRIT), lawyer ▷ *nm* (*Culin*)
avocado (pear); **~ de la défense**
counsel for the defence; **avocat
général** assistant public prosecutor

avoine [avwan] *nf* oats *pl*

○ **MOT-CLÉ**

avoir [avwaʀ] *nm* assets *pl*, resources
pl; (*Comm*) credit
▷ *vt* **1** (*posséder*) to have; **elle a 2
enfants/une belle maison** she has
(got) 2 children/a lovely house; **il a les
yeux bleus** he has (got) blue eyes; **vous
avez du sel?** do you have any salt?;
avoir du courage/de la patience to
be brave/patient

2 (*âge, dimensions*) to be; **il a 3 ans** he
is 3 (years old); **le mur a 3 mètres de
haut** the wall is 3 metres high; *voir aussi*
faim; **peur** *etc*

3 (*fam: duper*) to do, have; **on vous a
eu!** (*dupé*) you've been done *ou* had!;
(*fait une plaisanterie*) we *ou* they had
you there

4: **en avoir après** *ou* **contre qn** to have
a grudge against sb; **en avoir assez** to
be fed up; **j'en ai pour une demi-heure**
it'll take me half an hour

5 (*obtenir, attraper*) to get; **j'ai réussi
à avoir mon train** I managed to
get *ou* catch my train; **j'ai réussi à
avoir le renseignement qu'il me
fallait** I managed to get (hold of) the
information I needed

6 (*éprouver*): **avoir de la peine** to be
ou feel sad

▷ *vb aux* **1** to have; **avoir mangé/dormi**

to have eaten/slept
2 (*avoir +à +infinitif*): **avoir à faire qch**
to have to do sth; **vous n'avez qu'à lui**
demander you only have to ask him
▷ *vb impers* **1**: **il y a** (*+ singulier*) there is; (*+ pluriel*) there are; **il y avait du café/des gâteaux** there was coffee/there were cakes; **qu'y-a-t-il?, qu'est-ce qu'il y a?** what's the matter?, what is it?; **il doit y avoir une explication** there must be an explanation; **il n'y a qu'à ...** we (*ou* you *etc*) will just have to ...; **il ne peut y en avoir qu'un** there can only be one
2 (*temporel*): **il y a 10 ans** 10 years ago; **il y a 10 ans/longtemps que je le sais** I've known it for 10 years/a long time; **il y a 10 ans qu'il est arrivé** it's 10 years since he arrived

avortement [avɔʀtəmɑ̃] *nm* abortion
avouer [avwe] *vt* (*crime, défaut*) to confess (to); **~ avoir fait/que** to admit *ou* confess to having done/that
avril [avʀil] *nm* April
axe [aks] *nm* axis; (*de roue etc*) axle; (*fig*) main line; **axe routier** main road, trunk road (BRIT), highway (US)
ayons *etc* [ɛjɔ̃] *vb voir* **avoir**

b

bâbord [babɔʀ] *nm*: **à ~** to port, on the port side
baby-foot [babifut] *nm* table football
bac [bak] *abr m* = **baccalauréat** ▷ *nm* (*récipient*) tub
baccalauréat [bakalɔʀea] *nm* high school diploma
bâcler [bakle] *vt* to botch (up)
baffe [baf] (*fam*) *nf* slap, clout
bafouiller [bafuje] *vi, vt* to stammer
bagage [bagaʒ] *nm* piece of luggage; (*connaissances*) background, knowledge; **nos ~s ne sont pas arrivés** our luggage hasn't arrived; **bagage à main** piece of hand-luggage
bagarre [bagaʀ] *nf* fight, brawl; **bagarrer: se bagarrer** *vi* to have a fight *ou* scuffle, fight
bagnole [baɲɔl] (*fam*) *nf* car
bague [bag] *nf* ring; **bague de fiançailles** engagement ring
baguette [baget] *nf* stick; (*cuisine chinoise*) chopstick; (*de chef d'orchestre*) baton; (*pain*) stick of (French) bread;

baguette magique magic wand
baie [bε] *nf* (*Géo*) bay; (*fruit*) berry; **baie (vitrée)** picture window
baignade [bεɲad] *nf* bathing; **"~ interdite"** "no bathing"
baigner [beɲe] *vt* (*bébé*) to bath; **se baigner** *vi* to have a swim, go swimming *ou* bathing; **baignoire** *nf* bath(tub)
bail [baj, bo] (*pl* **baux**) *nm* lease
bâiller [baje] *vi* to yawn; (*être ouvert*) to gape
bain [bε̃] *nm* bath; **prendre un ~** to have a bath; **se mettre dans le ~** (*fig*) to get into it *ou* things; **bain de bouche** mouthwash; **bain moussant** bubble bath; **bain de soleil: prendre un bain de soleil** to sunbathe; **bain-marie** *nm*: **faire chauffer au bain-marie** (*boîte etc*) to immerse in boiling water
baiser [beze] *nm* kiss ▷ *vt* (*main, front*) to kiss; (*fam!*) to screw (!)
baisse [bεs] *nf* fall, drop; **être en ~** to be falling, be declining
baisser [bese] *vt* to lower; (*radio, chauffage*) to turn down ▷ *vi* to fall, drop, go down; (*vue, santé*) to fail, dwindle; **se baisser** *vi* to bend down
bal [bal] *nm* dance; (*grande soirée*) ball; **bal costumé** fancy-dress ball
balade [balad] (*fam*) *nf* (*à pied*) walk, stroll; (*en voiture*) drive; **balader** (*fam*): **se balader** *vi* to go for a walk *ou* stroll; to go for a drive; **baladeur** *nm* personal stereo, Walkman®
balai [balε] *nm* broom, brush
balance [balɑ̃s] *nf* scales *pl*; (*signe*): **la B~** Libra; **balance commerciale** balance of trade
balancer [balɑ̃se] *vt* to swing; (*fam: lancer*) to fling, chuck; (: *jeter*) to chuck out; **se balancer** *vi* to swing, rock; **se ~ de** (*fam*) not to care about; **balançoire** *nf* swing; (*sur pivot*) seesaw
balayer [balεje] *vt* (*feuilles etc*) to sweep up, brush up; (*pièce*) to sweep; (*objections*) to sweep aside; (*suj: radar*) to scan; **balayeur, -euse** *nm/f*

roadsweeper
balbutier [balbysje] *vi, vt* to stammer
balcon [balkɔ̃] *nm* balcony; (*Théâtre*) dress circle; **avez-vous une chambre avec ~?** do you have a room with a balcony?
Bâle [bal] *n* Basle, Basel
Baléares [baleaʀ] *nfpl*: **les ~** the Balearic Islands, the Balearics
baleine [balεn] *nf* whale
balise [baliz] *nf* (*Navig*) beacon; (marker) buoy; (*Aviat*) runway light, beacon; (*Auto, Ski*) sign, marker; **baliser** *vt* to mark out (with lights *etc*)
balle [bal] *nf* (*de fusil*) bullet; (*de sport*) ball; (*fam: franc*) franc
ballerine [bal(ə)ʀin] *nf* (*danseuse*) ballet dancer; (*chaussure*) ballet shoe
ballet [balε] *nm* ballet
ballon [balɔ̃] *nm* (*de sport*) ball; (*jouet, Aviat*) balloon; **ballon de football** football
balnéaire [balneεʀ] *adj* seaside *cpd*; **station ~** seaside resort
balustrade [balystʀad] *nf* railings *pl*, handrail
bambin [bɑ̃bε̃] *nm* little child
bambou [bɑ̃bu] *nm* bamboo
banal, e [banal] *adj* banal, commonplace; (*péj*) trite; **banalité** *nf* banality
banane [banan] *nf* banana; (*sac*) waist-bag, bum-bag
banc [bɑ̃] *nm* seat, bench; (*de poissons*) shoal; **banc d'essai** (*fig*) testing ground
bancaire [bɑ̃kεʀ] *adj* banking; (*chèque, carte*) bank *cpd*
bancal, e [bɑ̃kal] *adj* wobbly
bandage [bɑ̃daʒ] *nm* bandage
bande [bɑ̃d] *nf* (*de tissu etc*) strip; (*Méd*) bandage; (*motif*) stripe; (*magnétique etc*) tape; (*groupe*) band; (: *péj*) bunch; **faire ~ à part** to keep to o.s.; **bande dessinée** comic strip; **bande sonore** sound track
bande-annonce [bɑ̃danɔ̃s] *nf* trailer
bandeau, x [bɑ̃do] *nm* headband; (*sur les yeux*) blindfold
bander [bɑ̃de] *vt* (*blessure*) to bandage;

~ les yeux à qn to blindfold sb

bandit [bɑ̃di] nm bandit

bandoulière [bɑ̃duljɛʀ] nf: **en ~** (slung ou worn) across the shoulder

Bangladesh [bɑ̃ɡladɛʃ] nm: **le ~** Bangladesh

banlieue [bɑ̃ljø] nf suburbs pl; **lignes/ quartiers de ~** suburban lines/areas; **trains de ~** commuter trains

bannir [baniʀ] vt to banish

banque [bɑ̃k] nf bank; (activités) banking; **banque de données** data bank

banquet [bɑ̃kɛ] nm dinner; (d'apparat) banquet

banquette [bɑ̃kɛt] nf seat

banquier [bɑ̃kje] nm banker

banquise [bɑ̃kiz] nf ice field

baptême [batɛm] nm christening; baptism; **baptême de l'air** first flight

baptiser [batize] vt to baptize, christen

bar [baʀ] nm bar

baraque [baʀak] nf shed; (fam) house; (dans une fête foraine) stall, booth; **baraqué, e** (fam) adj well-built, hefty

barbare [baʀbaʀ] adj barbaric

barbe [baʀb] nf beard; **la ~!** (fam) damn it!; **quelle ~!** (fam) what a drag ou bore!; **à la ~ de qn** under sb's nose; **barbe à papa** candy-floss (BRIT), cotton candy (US)

barbelé [baʀbəle] adj, nm: **(fil de fer) ~** barbed wire no pl

barbiturique [baʀbityʀik] nm barbiturate

barbouiller [baʀbuje] vt to daub; **avoir l'estomac barbouillé** to feel queasy

barbu, e [baʀby] adj bearded

barder [baʀde] (fam) vi: **ça va ~** sparks will fly, things are going to get hot

barème [baʀɛm] nm (Scol) scale; (table de référence) table

baril [baʀi(l)] nm barrel; (poudre) keg

bariolé, e [baʀjɔle] adj gaudily-coloured

baromètre [baʀɔmɛtʀ] nm barometer

baron, ne [baʀɔ̃] nm/f baron(ess)

baroque [baʀɔk] adj (Art) baroque; (fig) weird

barque [baʀk] nf small boat

barquette [baʀkɛt] nf (pour repas) tray; (pour fruits) punnet

barrage [baʀaʒ] nm dam; (sur route) roadblock, barricade

barre [baʀ] nf bar; (Navig) helm; (écrite) line, stroke

barreau, x [baʀo] nm bar; (Jur): **le ~** the Bar

barrer [baʀe] vt (route etc) to block; (mot) to cross out; (chèque) to cross (BRIT); (Navig) to steer; **se barrer** (fam) ▷ vi to clear off

barrette [baʀɛt] nf (pour cheveux) (hair) slide (BRIT) ou clip (US)

barricader [baʀikade]: **se barricader** vi to barricade o.s.

barrière [baʀjɛʀ] nf fence; (obstacle) barrier; (porte) gate

barrique [baʀik] nf barrel, cask

bar-tabac [baʀtaba] nm bar (which sells tobacco and stamps)

bas, basse [bɑ, bɑs] adj low ▷ nm bottom, lower part; (vêtement) stocking ▷ adv low; (parler) softly; **au ~ mot** at the lowest estimate; **en ~** down below; (d'une liste, d'un mur etc) at/to the bottom; (dans une maison) downstairs; **en ~ de** at the bottom of; **un enfant en ~ âge** a young child; **à ~ ...!** down with ...!

bas-côté [bɑkote] nm (de route) verge (BRIT), shoulder (US)

basculer [baskyle] vi to fall over, topple (over); (benne) to tip up ▷ vt (contenu) to tip out; (benne) to tip up

base [bɑz] nf base; (Pol) rank and file; (fondement, principe) basis; **de ~** basic; **à ~ de café** etc coffee etc -based; **base de données** database; **baser** vt to base; **se baser sur** vt (preuves) to base one's argument on

bas-fond [bɑfɔ̃] nm (Navig) shallow; **bas-fonds** nmpl (fig) dregs

basilic [bazilik] nm (Culin) basil

basket [baskɛt] nm trainer (BRIT), sneaker (US); (aussi: **~-ball**) basketball

basque [bask] adj Basque ▷ nm/f: **B~** Basque; **le Pays Basque** the Basque Country

basse [bɑs] adj voir **bas** ▷ nf (Mus) bass; **basse-cour** nf farmyard

bassin [basɛ̃] nm (pièce d'eau) pond, pool; (de fontaine;: Géo) basin; (Anat) pelvis; (portuaire) dock

bassine [basin] nf (ustensile) basin; (contenu) bowl(ful)

basson [basɔ̃] nm bassoon

bat [ba] vb voir **battre**

bataille [batɑj] nf (Mil) battle; (rixe) fight; **elle avait les cheveux en ~** her hair was a mess

bateau, x [bato] nm boat, ship; **bateau-mouche** nm passenger pleasure boat (on the Seine)

bâti, e [bɑti] adj: **bien ~** well-built; **terrain ~** piece of land that has been built on

bâtiment [bɑtimɑ̃] nm building; (Navig) ship, vessel; (industrie) building trade

bâtir [bɑtiR] vt to build

bâtisse [bɑtis] nf building

bâton [bɑtɔ̃] nm stick; **parler à ~s rompus** to chat about this and that

bats [ba] vb voir **battre**

battement [batmɑ̃] nm (de cœur) beat; (intervalle) interval; **10 minutes de ~** 10 minutes to spare

batterie [batRi] nf (Mil, Élec) battery; (Mus) drums pl, drum kit; **batterie de cuisine** pots and pans pl, kitchen utensils pl

batteur [batœR] nm (Mus) drummer; (appareil) whisk

battre [batR] vt to beat; (blé) to thresh; (passer au peigne fin) to scour; (cartes) to shuffle ▷ vi (cœur) to beat; (volets etc) to bang, rattle; **se battre** vi to fight; **~ la mesure** to beat time; **~ son plein** to be at its height, be going full swing; **~ des mains** to clap one's hands

baume [bom] nm balm

bavard, e [bavar, ard] adj (very) talkative; gossipy; **bavarder** vi to chatter; (commérer) to gossip; (divulguer un secret) to blab

baver [bave] vi to dribble; (chien) to slobber; **en ~** (fam) to have a hard time (of it)

bavoir [bavwar] nm bib

bavure [bavyr] nf smudge; (fig) hitch; (policière etc) blunder

bazar [bazar] nm general store; (fam) jumble; **bazarder** (fam) vt to chuck out

BCBG sigle adj (= bon chic bon genre) preppy, smart and trendy

BD sigle f = **bande dessinée**

bd abr = **boulevard**

béant, e [beɑ̃, ɑ̃t] adj gaping

beau, bel, belle [bo, bɛl] (mpl **~x**) adj beautiful, lovely; (homme) handsome; (femme) beautiful ▷ adv: **il fait ~** the weather's fine ▷ nm: **faire le ~** (chien) to sit up and beg; **un ~ jour** one (fine) day; **de plus belle** more than ever, even more; **on a ~ essayer** however hard we try; **bel et bien** well and truly; **le plus ~ c'est que ...** the best of it is that ...

MOT-CLÉ

beaucoup [boku] adv **1** a lot; **il boit beaucoup** he drinks a lot; **il ne boit pas beaucoup** he doesn't drink much ou a lot

2 (suivi de plus, trop etc) much, a lot; **il est beaucoup plus grand** he is much ou a lot taller; **c'est beaucoup plus cher** it's a lot ou much more expensive; **il a beaucoup plus de temps que moi** he has much ou a lot more time than me; **il y a beaucoup plus de touristes ici** there are a lot ou many more tourists here; **beaucoup trop vite** much too fast; **il fume beaucoup trop** he smokes far too much

3: **beaucoup de** (nombre) many, a lot of; (quantité) a lot of; **beaucoup d'étudiants/de touristes** a lot of ou many students/tourists; **beaucoup**

de courage a lot of courage; **il n'a pas beaucoup d'argent** he hasn't got much ou at lot of money
4: **de beaucoup** by far

beau...: **beau-fils** nm son-in-law; (remariage) stepson; **beau-frère** nm brother-in-law; **beau-père** nm father-in-law; (remariage) stepfather
beauté [bote] nf beauty; **de toute ~** beautiful; **finir qch en ~** to complete sth brilliantly
beaux-arts [bozaʀ] nmpl fine arts
beaux-parents [boparɑ̃] nmpl wife's/husband's family, in-laws
bébé [bebe] nm baby
bec [bɛk] nm beak, bill; (de théière) spout; (de casserole) lip; (fam) mouth; **bec de gaz** (street) gaslamp
bêche [bɛʃ] nf spade; **bêcher** vt to dig
bedaine [bədɛn] nf paunch
bedonnant, e [bədɔnɑ̃, ɑ̃t] adj potbellied
bée [be] adj: **bouche ~** gaping
bégayer [begeje] vt, vi to stammer
beige [bɛʒ] adj beige
beignet [bɛɲɛ] nm fritter
bel [bɛl] adj voir **beau**
bêler [bele] vi to bleat
belette [bəlɛt] nf weasel
belge [bɛlʒ] adj Belgian ▷ nm/f: **B~** Belgian
Belgique [bɛlʒik] nf: **la ~** Belgium
bélier [belje] nm ram; (signe): **le B~** Aries
belle [bɛl] adj voir **beau** ▷ nf (Sport): **la ~** the decider; **belle-fille** nf daughter-in-law; (remariage) stepdaughter; **belle-mère** nf mother-in-law; stepmother; **belle-sœur** nf sister-in-law
belvédère [bɛlvedɛʀ] nm panoramic viewpoint (or small building there)
bémol [bemɔl] nm (Mus) flat
bénédiction [benediksjɔ̃] nf blessing
bénéfice [benefis] nm (Comm) profit; (avantage) benefit; **bénéficier**; **bénéficier de** vt to enjoy; (situation) to benefit by ou from; **bénéfique** adj beneficial

Benelux [benelyks] nm: **le ~** Benelux, the Benelux countries
bénévole [benevɔl] adj voluntary, unpaid
bénin, -igne [benɛ̃, iɲ] adj minor, mild; (tumeur) benign
bénir [beniʀ] vt to bless; **bénit, e** adj consecrated; **eau bénite** holy water
benne [bɛn] nf skip; (de téléphérique) (cable) car; **benne à ordures** (amovible) skip
béquille [bekij] nf crutch; (de bicyclette) stand
berceau, x [bɛʀso] nm cradle, crib
bercer [bɛʀse] vt to rock, cradle; (suj: musique etc) to lull; **~ qn de** (promesses etc) to delude sb with; **berceuse** nf lullaby
béret [beʀe] nm (aussi: **~ basque**) beret
berge [bɛʀʒ] nf bank
berger, -ère [bɛʀʒe, ɛʀ] nm/f shepherd(-ess); **berger allemand** alsatian (BRIT), German shepherd
Berlin [bɛʀlɛ̃] n Berlin
Bermudes [bɛʀmyd] nfpl: **les (îles) ~** Bermuda
Berne [bɛʀn(ə)] n Bern
berner [bɛʀne] vt to fool
besogne [bəzɔɲ] nf work no pl, job
besoin [bəzwɛ̃] nm need; **avoir ~ de qch/faire qch** to need sth/to do sth; **au ~** if need be; **le ~** (pauvreté) need, want; **être dans le ~** to be in need ou want; **faire ses ~s** to relieve o.s.
bestiole [bɛstjɔl] nf (tiny) creature
bétail [betaj] nm livestock, cattle pl
bête [bɛt] nf animal; (bestiole) insect, creature ▷ adj stupid, silly; **il cherche la petite ~** he's being pernickety ou over fussy; **bête noire** pet hate; **bête sauvage** wild beast ou animal
bêtise [betiz] nf stupidity; (action) stupid thing (to say ou do)
béton [betɔ̃] nm concrete; **(en) ~** (alibi, argument) cast iron; **béton armé** reinforced concrete
betterave [bɛtʀav] nf beetroot (BRIT), beet (US); **betterave sucrière**

sugar beet

Beur [bœʀ] *nm/f* person of North African origin living in France

beurre [bœʀ] *nm* butter; **beurrer** *vt* to butter; **beurrier** *nm* butter dish

biais [bjɛ] *nm* (*moyen*) device, expedient; (*aspect*) angle; **en ~, de ~** (*obliquement*) at an angle; **par le ~ de** by means of

bibelot [biblo] *nm* trinket, curio

biberon [bibʀɔ̃] *nm* (feeding) bottle; **nourrir au ~** to bottle-feed

bible [bibl] *nf* bible

biblio... [biblio] *préfixe:* **bibliobus** *nm* mobile library van; **bibliothécaire** *nm/f* librarian; **bibliothèque** *nf* library; (*meuble*) bookcase

bic® [bik] *nm* Biro®

bicarbonate [bikaʀbɔnat] *nm:* **~ (de soude)** bicarbonate of soda

biceps [bisɛps] *nm* biceps

biche [biʃ] *nf* doe

bicolore [bikɔlɔʀ] *adj* two-coloured

bicoque [bikɔk] (*péj*) *nf* shack

bicyclette [bisiklɛt] *nf* bicycle

bidet [bidɛ] *nm* bidet

bidon [bidɔ̃] *nm* can ▷ *adj inv* (*fam*) phoney

bidonville [bidɔ̃vil] *nm* shanty town

bidule [bidyl] (*fam*) *nm* thingumajig

 MOT-CLÉ

bien [bjɛ̃] *nm* **1** (*avantage, profit*): **faire du bien à qn** to do sb good; **dire du bien de** to speak well of; **c'est pour son bien** it's for his own good

2 (*possession, patrimoine*) possession, property; **son bien le plus précieux** his most treasured possession; **avoir du bien** to have property; **biens (de consommation** *etc*) (consumer *etc*) goods

3 (*moral*): **le bien** good; **distinguer le bien du mal** to tell good from evil

▷ *adv* **1** (*de façon satisfaisante*) well; **elle travaille/mange bien** she works/eats well; **croyant bien faire, je/il ...** thinking I/he was doing the right thing, I/he ...; **tiens-toi bien!** (*assieds-toi correctement*) sit up straight!; (*debout*) stand up straight!; (*sois sage*) behave yourself!; (*prépare-toi*) wait for it!; **c'est bien fait!** it serves him (*ou* her *etc*) right!

2 (*valeur intensive*) quite; **bien jeune** quite young; **bien assez** quite enough; **bien mieux** (very) much better; **j'espère bien y aller** I do hope to go; **je veux bien le faire** (*concession*) I'm quite willing to do it; **il faut bien le faire** it has to be done; **Paul est bien venu, n'est-ce pas?** Paul did come, didn't he?; **où peut-il bien être passé?** where can he have got to?

3 (*beaucoup*): **bien du temps/des gens** quite a time/a number of people

4 (*au moins*) at least; **cela fait bien deux ans que je ne l'ai pas vu** I haven't seen him for at least *ou* a good two years

▷ *adj inv* **1** (*en bonne forme, à l'aise*): **je me sens bien** I feel fine; **je ne me sens pas bien** I don't feel well; **on est bien dans ce fauteuil** this chair is very comfortable

2 (*joli, beau*) good-looking; **tu es bien dans cette robe** you look good in that dress

3 (*satisfaisant*) good; **elle est bien, cette maison/secrétaire** it's a good house/she's a good secretary; **c'est bien?** is that *ou* it O.K.?; **c'est très bien (comme ça)** it's fine (like that)

4 (*moralement*) right; (: *personne*) good, nice; (*respectable*) respectable; **ce n'est pas bien de ...** it's not right to ...; **elle est bien, cette femme** she's a nice woman, she's a good sort; **des gens bien** respectable people

5 (*en bons termes*): **être bien avec qn** to be on good terms with sb

▷ *préfixe:* **bien-aimé, e** *adj, nm/f* beloved; **bien-être** *nm* well-being; **bienfaisance** *nf* charity; **bienfait** *nm* act of generosity, benefaction; (*de la science etc*) benefit; **bienfaiteur, -trice** *nm/f* benefactor/benefactress; **bien-fondé** *nm* soundness; **bien que** *conj* (al)though; **bien sûr** *adv* certainly

bientôt [bjɛ̃to] *adv* soon; **à ~** see you soon
bienveillant, e [bjɛ̃vɛjɑ̃, ɑ̃t] *adj* kindly
bienvenu, e [bjɛ̃vny] *adj* welcome; **bienvenue** *nf*: **souhaiter la bienvenue à** to welcome; **bienvenue à** welcome to
bière [bjɛR] *nf* (*boisson*) beer; (*cercueil*) bier; **bière blonde** lager; **bière brune** brown ale (*BRIT*), dark beer (*US*); **bière (à la) pression** draught beer
bifteck [biftɛk] *nm* steak
bigorneau, x [bigɔRno] *nm* winkle
bigoudi [bigudi] *nm* curler
bijou, x [biʒu] *nm* jewel; **bijouterie** *nf* jeweller's (shop); **bijoutier, -ière** *nm/f* jeweller
bikini [bikini] *nm* bikini
bilan [bilɑ̃] *nm* (*fig*) (net) outcome; (: *de victimes*) toll; (*Comm*) balance sheet(s); **un ~ de santé** a (medical) checkup; **faire le ~ de** to assess, review; **déposer son ~** to file a bankruptcy statement
bile [bil] *nf* bile; **se faire de la ~** (*fam*) to worry o.s. sick
bilieux, -euse [biljø, øz] *adj* bilious; (*fig: colérique*) testy
bilingue [bilɛ̃g] *adj* bilingual
billard [bijaR] *nm* (*jeu*) billiards *sg*; (*table*) billiard table
bille [bij] *nf* (*gén*) ball; (*du jeu de billes*) marble
billet [bijɛ] *nm* (*aussi*: **~ de banque**) (bank)note; (*de cinéma, de bus etc*) ticket; (*courte lettre*) note; **billet électronique** e-ticket; **billetterie** *nf* ticket office; (*distributeur*) ticket machine; (*Banque*) cash dispenser
billion [biljɔ̃] *nm* billion (*BRIT*), trillion (*US*)
bimensuel, le [bimɑ̃sɥɛl] *adj* bimonthly
bio [bjo] *adj inv* organic
bio... [bjo] *préfixe* bio...; **biochimie**

nf biochemistry; **biographie** *nf* biography; **biologie** *nf* biology; **biologique** *adj* biological; (*produits, aliments*) organic; **biométrie** *nf* biometrics; **biotechnologie** *nf* biotechnology; **bioterrorisme** *nm* bioterrorism
Birmanie [biRmani] *nf* Burma
bis [bis] *adv*: **12 ~** 12a ou A ▷ *excl, nm* encore
biscotte [biskɔt] *nf* toasted bread (*sold in packets*)
biscuit [biskɥi] *nm* biscuit (*BRIT*), cookie (*US*)
bise [biz] *nf* (*fam: baiser*) kiss; (*vent*) North wind; **grosses ~s (de)** (*sur lettre*) love and kisses (from)
bisexuel, le [bisɛksɥɛl] *adj* bisexual
bisou [bizu] (*fam*) *nm* kiss
bissextile [bisɛkstil] *adj*: **année ~** leap year
bistro(t) [bistRo] *nm* bistro, café
bitume [bitym] *nm* asphalt
bizarre [bizaR] *adj* strange, odd
blague [blag] *nf* (*propos*) joke; (*farce*) trick; **sans ~!** no kidding!; **blaguer** *vi* to joke
blaireau, x [blɛRo] *nm* (*Zool*) badger; (*brosse*) shaving brush
blâme [blɑm] *nm* blame; (*sanction*) reprimand; **blâmer** *vt* to blame
blanc, blanche [blɑ̃, blɑ̃ʃ] *adj* white; (*non imprimé*) blank ▷ *nm/f* white, white man(-woman) ▷ *nm* (*couleur*) white; (*espace non écrit*) blank; (*aussi*: **~ d'œuf**) (egg-)white; (*aussi*: **~ de poulet**) breast, white meat; (*aussi*: **vin ~**) white wine; **~ cassé** off-white; **chèque en ~** blank cheque; **à ~** (*chauffer*) white-hot; (*tirer, charger*) with blanks; **blanche** *nf* (*Mus*) minim (*BRIT*), half-note (*US*); **blancheur** *nf* whiteness
blanchir [blɑ̃ʃiR] *vt* (*gén*) to whiten; (*linge*) to launder; (*Culin*) to blanch; (*fig: disculper*) to clear ▷ *vi* (*cheveux*) to go white; **blanchisserie** *nf* laundry
blason [blazɔ̃] *nm* coat of arms
blasphème [blasfɛm] *nm* blasphemy

blazer [blazɛʀ] *nm* blazer

blé [ble] *nm* wheat; **blé noir** buckwheat

bled [blɛd] (*péj*) *nm* hole

blême [blɛm] *adj* pale

blessé, e [blese] *adj* injured ▷ *nm/f* injured person, casualty

blesser [blese] *vt* to injure; (*délibérément*) to wound; (*offenser*) to hurt; **se blesser** to injure o.s.; **se ~ au pied** to injure one's foot; **blessure** *nf* (*accidentelle*) injury; (*intentionnelle*) wound

bleu, e [blø] *adj* blue; (*bifteck*) very rare ▷ *nm* (*couleur*) blue; (*contusion*) bruise; (*vêtement: aussi:* **~s**) overalls *pl*; (*fromage*) blue cheese; **bleu marine** navy blue; **bleuet** *nm* cornflower

bloc [blɔk] *nm* (*de pierre etc*) block; (*de papier à lettres*) pad; (*ensemble*) group, block; **serré à ~** tightened right down; **en ~** as a whole; **bloc opératoire** operating *ou* theatre block; **blocage** *nm* (*des prix*) freezing; (*Psych*) hang-up; **bloc-notes** *nm* note pad

blog, blogue [blɔg] *nm* blog; **bloguer** *vi* to blog

blond, e [blɔ̃, blɔ̃d] *adj* fair, blond; (*sable, blés*) golden

bloquer [blɔke] *vt* (*passage*) to block; (*pièce mobile*) to jam; (*crédits, compte*) to freeze

blottir [blɔtiʀ]: **se blottir** *vi* to huddle up

blouse [bluz] *nf* overall

blouson [bluzɔ̃] *nm* blouson jacket; **blouson noir** (*fig*) ≈ rocker

bluff [blœf] *nm* bluff

bobine [bɔbin] *nf* reel; (*Élec*) coil

bobo [bobo] *abr m/f* = bourgeois bohème (*fam*) boho

bocal, -aux [bɔkal, o] *nm* jar

bock [bɔk] *nm* glass of beer

bœuf [bœf] *nm* ox; (*Culin*) beef

bof [bɔf] (*fam*) *excl* don't care!; (*pas terrible*) nothing special

bohémien, ne [bɔemjɛ̃, -ɛn] *nm/f* gipsy

boire [bwaʀ] *vt* to drink; (*s'imprégner de*) to soak up; **~ un coup** (*fam*) to have a drink

bois [bwa] *nm* wood; **de ~, en ~** wooden; **boisé, e** *adj* woody, wooded

boisson [bwasɔ̃] *nf* drink

boîte [bwat] *nf* box; (*fam: entreprise*) firm; **aliments en ~** canned *ou* tinned (BRIT) foods; **boîte à gants** glove compartment; **boîte à ordures** dustbin (BRIT), trashcan (US); **boîte aux lettres** letter box; **boîte d'allumettes** box of matches; (*vide*) matchbox; **boîte de conserves** can *ou* tin (BRIT) of food; **boîte (de nuit)** night club; **boîte de vitesses** gear box; **boîte postale** PO Box; **boîte vocale** (*Tél*) voice mail

boiter [bwate] *vi* to limp; (*fig: raisonnement*) to be shaky

boîtier [bwatje] *nm* case

boive *etc* [bwav] *vb voir* **boire**

bol [bɔl] *nm* bowl; **un ~ d'air** a breath of fresh air; **j'en ai ras le ~** (*fam*) I'm fed up with this; **avoir du ~** (*fam*) to be lucky

bombarder [bɔ̃baʀde] *vt* to bomb; **~ qn de** (*cailloux, lettres*) to bombard sb with

bombe [bɔ̃b] *nf* bomb; (*atomiseur*) (aerosol) spray

 MOT-CLÉ

bon, bonne [bɔ̃, bɔn] *adj* **1** (*agréable, satisfaisant*) good; **un bon repas/ restaurant** a good meal/restaurant; **être bon en maths** to be good at maths (BRIT) *ou* math (US)

2 (*charitable*): **être bon (envers)** to be good (to)

3 (*correct*) right; **le bon numéro/ moment** the right number/moment

4 (*souhaits*): **bon anniversaire!** happy birthday!; **bon voyage!** have a good trip!; **bonne chance!** good luck!; **bonne année!** happy New Year!; **bonne nuit!** good night!

5 (*approprié, apte*): **bon à/pour** fit to/for; **à quoi bon?** what's the use?

6: **bon enfant** *adj inv* accommodating,

easy-going; **bonne femme** (*péj*) woman; **de bonne heure** early; **bon marché** *adj inv*, *adv* cheap; **bon mot** witticism; **bon sens** common sense; **bon vivant** jovial chap; **bonnes œuvres** charitable works, charities ▷ *nm* **1** (*billet*) voucher; **bon cadeau**) gift voucher; **bon d'essence** petrol coupon; **bon du Trésor** Treasury bond
2: **avoir du bon** to have its good points; **pour de bon** for good
▷ *adv*: **il fait bon** it's *ou* the weather is fine; **sentir bon** to smell good; **tenir bon** to stand firm
▷ *excl* good!; **ah bon?** really?; **bon, je reste** right then, I'll stay; *voir aussi* **bonne**

bonbon [bɔ̃bɔ̃] *nm* (boiled) sweet
bond [bɔ̃] *nm* leap; **faire un ~** to leap in the air
bondé, e [bɔ̃de] *adj* packed (full)
bondir [bɔ̃diʀ] *vi* to leap
bonheur [bɔnœʀ] *nm* happiness; **porter ~** (à qn) to bring (sb) luck; **au petit ~** haphazardly; **par ~** fortunately
bonhomme [bɔnɔm] (*pl* **bonshommes**) *nm* fellow; **bonhomme de neige** snowman
bonjour [bɔ̃ʒuʀ] *excl*, *nm* hello; (*selon l'heure*) good morning/afternoon; **c'est simple comme ~!** it's easy as pie!
bonne [bɔn] *adj voir* **bon** ▷ *nf* (*domestique*) maid
bonnet [bɔnɛ] *nm* hat; (*de soutien-gorge*) cup; **bonnet de bain** bathing cap
bonsoir [bɔ̃swaʀ] *excl* good evening
bonté [bɔ̃te] *nf* kindness *no pl*
bonus [bɔnys] *nm* no-claims bonus; (*de DVD*) extras *pl*
bord [bɔʀ] *nm* (*de table, verre, falaise*) edge; (*de rivière, lac*) bank; (*de route*) side; **(monter) à ~** (to go) on board; **jeter par-dessus ~** to throw overboard; **le commandant de/les hommes du ~** the ship's master/crew; **au ~ de la mer** at the seaside; **au ~ de la route** at the

roadside; **être au ~ des larmes** to be on the verge of tears
bordeaux [bɔʀdo] *nm* Bordeaux (wine) ▷ *adj inv* maroon
bordel [bɔʀdɛl] *nm* brothel; (*fam!*) bloody mess (!)
border [bɔʀde] *vt* (*être le long de*) to line; (*qn dans son lit*) to tuck up; (*garnir*): **~ qch de** to edge sth with
bordure [bɔʀdyʀ] *nf* border; **en ~ de** on the edge of
borne [bɔʀn] *nf* boundary stone; (*aussi*: **~ kilométrique**) kilometre-marker, ≈ milestone; **bornes** *nfpl* (*fig*) limits; **dépasser les ~s** to go too far
borné, e [bɔʀne] *adj* (*personne*) narrow-minded
borner [bɔʀne] *vt*: **se ~ à faire** (*se contenter de*) to content o.s. with doing; (*se limiter à*) to limit o.s. to doing
bosniaque [bɔsnjak] *adj* Bosnian ▷ *nm/f*: **B~** Bosnian
Bosnie-Herzégovine [bɔsniɛʀzegɔvin] *nf* Bosnia-Herzegovina
bosquet [bɔskɛ] *nm* grove
bosse [bɔs] *nf* (*de terrain etc*) bump; (*enflure*) lump; (*du bossu, du chameau*) hump; **avoir la ~ des maths** *etc* (*fam*) to have a gift for maths *etc*; **il a roulé sa ~** (*fam*) he's been around
bosser [bɔse] (*fam*) *vi* (*travailler*) to work; (*travailler dur*) to slave (away)
bossu, e [bɔsy] *nm/f* hunchback
botanique [bɔtanik] *nf* botany ▷ *adj* botanic(al)
botte [bɔt] *nf* (*soulier*) (high) boot; (*gerbe*): **~ de paille** bundle of straw; **botte de radis/d'asperges** bunch of radishes/asparagus; **bottes de caoutchouc** wellington boots
bottin [bɔtɛ̃] *nm* directory
bottine [bɔtin] *nf* ankle boot
bouc [buk] *nm* goat; (*barbe*) goatee; **bouc émissaire** scapegoat
boucan [bukɑ̃] (*fam*) *nm* din, racket
bouche [buʃ] *nf* mouth; **faire du ~ à ~ qn** to give sb the kiss of life *ou* mouth-

to-mouth resuscitation (BRIT); **rester ~ bée** to stand open-mouthed; **bouche d'égout** manhole; **bouche d'incendie** fire hydrant; **bouche de métro** métro entrance

bouché, e [buʃe] *adj* (flacon etc) stoppered; (temps, ciel) overcast; (péj fam: personne) thick (fam); **c'est un secteur ~** there's no future in that area; **avoir le nez ~** to have a blocked(-up) nose; **l'évier est ~** the sink's blocked

bouchée [buʃe] *nf* mouthful; **bouchées à la reine** chicken vol-au-vents

boucher, -ère [buʃe] *nm/f* butcher ▷ *vt* (trou) to fill up; (obstruer) to block (up); **se boucher** *vi* (tuyau etc) to block up, get blocked up; **j'ai le nez bouché** my nose is blocked; **se ~ le nez** to hold one's nose; **boucherie** *nf* butcher's (shop); (fig) slaughter

bouchon [buʃɔ̃] *nm* stopper; (de tube) top; (en liège) cork; (fig: embouteillage) holdup; (Pêche) float

boucle [bukl] *nf* (forme, figure) loop; (objet) buckle; **boucle (de cheveux)** curl; **boucle d'oreille** earring

bouclé, e [bukle] *adj* (cheveux) curly

boucler [bukle] *vt* (fermer: ceinture etc) to fasten; (terminer) to finish off; (fam: enfermer) to shut away; (quartier) to seal off ▷ *vi* to curl

bouder [bude] *vi* to sulk ▷ *vt* to stay away from

boudin [budɛ̃] *nm*: **~ (noir)** black pudding; **boudin blanc** white pudding

boue [bu] *nf* mud

bouée [bwe] *nf* buoy; **bouée (de sauvetage)** lifebuoy

boueux, -euse [bwø, øz] *adj* muddy

bouffe [buf] (fam) *nf* grub (fam), food

bouffée [bufe] *nf* (de cigarette) puff; **une ~ d'air pur** a breath of fresh air; **bouffée de chaleur** hot flush (BRIT) *ou* flash (US)

bouffer [bufe] (fam) *vi* to eat

bouffi, e [bufi] *adj* swollen

bouger [buʒe] *vi* to move; (dent etc) to be loose; (s'activer) to get moving ▷ *vt*

to move; **les prix/les couleurs n'ont pas bougé** prices/colours haven't changed

bougie [buʒi] *nf* candle; (Auto) spark(ing) plug

bouillabaisse [bujabɛs] *nf* type of fish soup

bouillant, e [bujɑ̃, ɑ̃t] *adj* (qui bout) boiling; (très chaud) boiling (hot)

bouillie [buji] *nf* (de bébé) cereal; **en ~** (fig) crushed

bouillir [bujiʀ] *vi, vt* to boil; **~ d'impatience** to seethe with impatience

bouilloire [bujwaʀ] *nf* kettle

bouillon [bujɔ̃] *nm* (Culin) stock no pl; **bouillonner** *vi* to bubble; (fig: idées) to bubble up

bouillotte [bujɔt] *nf* hot-water bottle

boulanger, -ère [bulɑ̃ʒe, ɛʀ] *nm/f* baker; **boulangerie** *nf* bakery

boule [bul] *nf* (gén) ball; (de pétanque) bowl; **boule de neige** snowball

boulette [bulɛt] *nf* (de viande) meatball

boulevard [bulvaʀ] *nm* boulevard

bouleversement [bulvɛʀsəmɑ̃] *nm* upheaval

bouleverser [bulvɛʀse] *vt* (émouvoir) to overwhelm; (causer du chagrin) to distress; (pays, vie) to disrupt; (papiers, objets) to turn upside down

boulimie [bulimi] *nf* bulimia

boulimique [bulimik] *adj* bulimic

boulon [bulɔ̃] *nm* bolt

boulot, te [bulo, ɔt] *adj* plump, tubby ▷ *nm* (fam: travail) work

boum [bum] *nm* bang ▷ *nf* (fam) party

bouquet [bukɛ] *nm* (de fleurs) bunch (of flowers), bouquet; (de persil etc) bunch; **c'est le ~!** (fam) that takes the biscuit!

bouquin [bukɛ̃] (fam) *nm* book; **bouquiner** (fam) *vi* to read

bourdon [buʀdɔ̃] *nm* bumblebee

bourg [buʀ] *nm* small market town

bourgeois, e [buʀʒwa, waz] (péj) adj ≈ (upper) middle class; **bourgeoisie** *nf* ≈ upper middle classes pl

bourgeon [buʀʒɔ̃] *nm* bud

Bourgogne [buʀgɔɲ] nf: **la ~** Burgundy ▷ nm: **bourgogne** burgundy (wine)

bourguignon, ne [buʀgiɲɔ̃, ɔn] adj of ou from Burgundy, Burgundian

bourrasque [buʀask] nf squall

bourratif, -ive [buʀatif, iv] (fam) adj filling, stodgy (pej)

bourré, e [buʀe] adj (fam: ivre) plastered, tanked up (BRIT); (rempli): **~ de** crammed full of

bourrer [buʀe] vt (pipe) to fill; (poêle) to pack; (valise) to cram (full)

bourru, e [buʀy] adj surly, gruff

bourse [buʀs] nf (subvention) grant; (porte-monnaie) purse; **la B~** the Stock Exchange

bous [bu] vb voir **bouillir**

bousculade [buskylad] nf (hâte) rush; (cohue) crush; **bousculer** vt (heurter) to knock into; (fig) to push, rush

boussole [busɔl] nf compass

bout [bu] vb voir **bouillir** ▷ nm bit; (d'un bâton noueux) tip; (d'une ficelle, table, rue, période) end; **au ~ de** at the end of, after; **pousser qn à ~** to push sb to the limit; **venir à ~ de** to manage to finish; **à ~ portant** (at) point-blank (range)

bouteille [butɛj] nf bottle; (de gaz butane) cylinder

boutique [butik] nf shop

bouton [butɔ̃] nm button; (sur la peau) spot; (Bot) bud; **boutonner** vt to button up; **boutonnière** nf buttonhole; **bouton-pression** nm press stud

bovin, e [bɔvɛ̃, in] adj bovine; **bovins** nmpl cattle pl

bowling [buliŋ] nm (tenpin) bowling; (salle) bowling alley

boxe [bɔks] nf boxing

BP abr = **boîte postale**

bracelet [braslɛ] nm bracelet

braconnier [brakɔnje] nm poacher

brader [brade] vt to sell off; **braderie** nf cut-price shop/stall

braguette [bragɛt] nf fly ou flies pl (BRIT), zipper (US)

braise [brɛz] nf embers pl

brancard [brɑ̃kaʀ] nm (civière) stretcher; **brancardier** nm stretcher-bearer

branche [brɑ̃ʃ] nf branch

branché, e [brɑ̃ʃe] (fam) adj trendy

brancher [brɑ̃ʃe] vt to connect (up); (en mettant la prise) to plug in

brandir [brɑ̃diʀ] vt to brandish

braquer [brake] vi (Auto) to turn (the wheel) ▷ vt (revolver etc): **~ qch sur** to aim sth at, point sth at; (mettre en colère): **~ qn** to put sb's back up

bras [brɑ] nm arm; **~ dessus, ~ dessous** arm in arm; **se retrouver avec qch sur les ~** (fam) to be landed with sth; **bras droit** (fig) right hand man

brassard [brasaʀ] nm armband

brasse [bras] nf (nage) breast-stroke; **brasse papillon** butterfly (stroke)

brassée [brase] nf armful

brasser [brase] vt to mix; **~ l'argent/ les affaires** to handle a lot of money/ business

brasserie [brasʀi] nf (restaurant) café-restaurant; (usine) brewery

brave [brav] adj (courageux) brave; (bon, gentil) good, kind

braver [brave] vt to defy

bravo [bravo] excl bravo ▷ nm cheer

bravoure [bravuʀ] nf bravery

break [brɛk] nm (Auto) estate car

brebis [bʀəbi] nf ewe; **brebis galeuse** black sheep

bredouiller [bʀəduje] vi, vt to mumble, stammer

bref, brève [bʀɛf, ɛv] adj short, brief ▷ adv in short; **d'un ton ~** sharply, curtly; **en ~** in short, in brief

Brésil [bʀezil] nm Brazil

Bretagne [bʀətaɲ] nf Brittany

bretelle [bʀətɛl] nf (de vêtement, de sac) strap; (d'autoroute) slip road (BRIT), entrance/exit ramp (US); **bretelles** nfpl (pour pantalon) braces (BRIT), suspenders (US)

breton, ne [bʀətɔ̃, ɔn] adj Breton ▷ nm/f: **B~, ne** Breton

brève [bʀɛv] adj voir **bref**

brevet [bʀəvɛ] *nm* diploma, certificate; **brevet des collèges** exam taken at the age of 15; **brevet (d'invention)** patent; **breveté, e** *adj* patented

bricolage [bʀikɔlaʒ] *nm*: **le ~** do-it-yourself

bricoler [bʀikɔle] *vi* (*petits travaux*) to do DIY jobs; (*passe-temps*) to potter about ▷ *vt* (*réparer*) to fix up; **bricoleur, -euse** *nm/f* handyman(-woman), DIY enthusiast

bridge [bʀidʒ] *nm* (*Cartes*) bridge

brièvement [bʀijɛvmɑ̃] *adv* briefly

brigade [bʀigad] *nf* (*Police*) squad; (*Mil*) brigade; **brigadier** *nm* sergeant

brillamment [bʀijamɑ̃] *adv* brilliantly

brillant, e [bʀijɑ̃, ɑ̃t] *adj* (*remarquable*) bright; (*luisant*) shiny, shining

briller [bʀije] *vi* to shine

brin [bʀɛ̃] *nm* (*de laine, ficelle etc*) strand; (*fig*): **un ~ de** a bit of

brindille [bʀɛ̃dij] *nf* twig

brioche [bʀijɔʃ] *nf* brioche (bun); (*fam: ventre*) paunch

brique [bʀik] *nf* brick; (*de lait*) carton

briquet [bʀikɛ] *nm* (*cigarette*) lighter

brise [bʀiz] *nf* breeze

briser [bʀize] *vt* to break; **se briser** *vi* to break

britannique [bʀitanik] *adj* British ▷ *nm/f*: **B~** British person, Briton; **les B~s** the British

brocante [bʀɔkɑ̃t] *nf* junk, second-hand goods *pl*; **brocanteur, -euse** *nm/f* junkshop owner; junk dealer

broche [bʀɔʃ] *nf* brooch; (*Culin*) spit; (*Méd*) pin; **à la ~** spit-roasted

broché, e [bʀɔʃe] *adj* (*livre*) paper-backed

brochet [bʀɔʃɛ] *nm* pike *inv*

brochette [bʀɔʃɛt] *nf* (*ustensile*) skewer; (*plat*) kebab

brochure [bʀɔʃyʀ] *nf* pamphlet, brochure, booklet

broder [bʀɔde] *vt* to embroider ▷ *vi*: **~ (sur les faits** *ou* **une histoire)** to embroider the facts; **broderie** *nf* embroidery

bronches [bʀɔ̃ʃ] *nfpl* bronchial tubes; **bronchite** *nf* bronchitis

bronze [bʀɔ̃z] *nm* bronze

bronzer [bʀɔ̃ze] *vi* to get a tan; **se bronzer** to sunbathe

brosse [bʀɔs] *nf* brush; **coiffé en ~** with a crewcut; **brosse à cheveux** hairbrush; **brosse à dents** toothbrush; **brosse à habits** clothesbrush; **brosser** *vt* (*nettoyer*) to brush; (*fig: tableau etc*) to paint; **se brosser les dents** to brush one's teeth

brouette [bʀuɛt] *nf* wheelbarrow

brouillard [bʀujaʀ] *nm* fog

brouiller [bʀuje] *vt* (*œufs, message*) to scramble; (*idées*) to mix up; (*rendre trouble*) to cloud; (*désunir: amis*) to set at odds; **se brouiller** *vi* (*vue*) to cloud over; (*gens*): **se ~ (avec)** to fall out (with)

brouillon, ne [bʀujɔ̃, ɔn] *adj* (*sans soin*) untidy; (*qui manque d'organisation*) disorganized ▷ *nm* draft; **(papier) ~** rough paper

broussailles [bʀusaj] *nfpl* undergrowth *sg*; **broussailleux, -euse** *adj* bushy

brousse [bʀus] *nf*: **la ~** the bush

brouter [bʀute] *vi* to graze

brugnon [bʀyɲɔ̃] *nm* (*Bot*) nectarine

bruiner [bʀɥine] *vb impers*: **il bruine** it's drizzling, there's a drizzle

bruit [bʀɥi] *nm*: **un ~** a noise, a sound; (*fig: rumeur*) a rumour; **le ~** noise; **sans ~** without a sound, noiselessly; **bruit de fond** background noise

brûlant, e [bʀylɑ̃, ɑ̃t] *adj* burning; (*liquide*) boiling (hot)

brûlé, e [bʀyle] *adj* (*fig: démasqué*) blown ▷ *nm*: **odeur de ~** smell of burning

brûler [bʀyle] *vt* to burn; (*suj: eau bouillante*) to scald; (*consommer: électricité, essence*) to use; (*feu rouge, signal*) to go through ▷ *vi* to burn; (*jeu*): **tu brûles!** you're getting hot!; **se brûler** to burn o.s.; (*s'ébouillanter*) to scald o.s.

brûlure [bʀylyʀ] *nf* (*lésion*) burn; **brûlures d'estomac** heartburn *sg*

brume [bʀym] nf mist

brun, e [bʀœ̃, bʀyn] adj (gén: bière) brown; (cheveux, tabac) dark; **elle est ~e** she's got dark hair

brunch [bʀœntʃ] nm brunch

brushing [bʀœʃiŋ] nm blow-dry

brusque [bʀysk] adj abrupt

brut, e [bʀyt] adj (minerai, soie) raw; (diamant) rough; (Comm) gross; **(pétrole) ~** crude (oil)

brutal, e, -aux [bʀytal, o] adj brutal

Bruxelles [bʀysɛl] n Brussels

bruyamment [bʀɥijamɑ̃] adv noisily

bruyant, e [bʀɥijɑ̃, ɑ̃t] adj noisy

bruyère [bʀyjɛʀ] nf heather

BTS sigle m (= brevet de technicien supérieur) vocational training certificate taken at the end of a higher education course

bu, e [by] pp de **boire**

buccal, e, -aux [bykal, o] adj: **par voie ~e** orally

bûche [byʃ] nf log; **prendre une ~** (fig) to come a cropper; **bûche de Noël** Yule log

bûcher [byʃe] nm (funéraire) pyre; (supplice) stake ▷ vi (fam) to swot (BRIT), slave (away) ▷ vt (fam) to swot up (BRIT), slave away at

budget [bydʒɛ] nm budget

buée [bɥe] nf (sur une vitre) mist

buffet [byfɛ] nm (meuble) sideboard; (de réception) buffet; **buffet (de gare)** (station) buffet, snack bar

buis [bɥi] nm box tree; (bois) box(wood)

buisson [bɥisɔ̃] nm bush

bulbe [bylb] nm (Bot, Anat) bulb

Bulgarie [bylgaʀi] nf Bulgaria

bulle [byl] nf bubble

bulletin [byltɛ̃] nm (communiqué, journal) bulletin; (Scol) report; **bulletin d'informations** news bulletin; **bulletin (de vote)** ballot paper; **bulletin météorologique** weather report

bureau, x [byʀo] nm (meuble) desk; (pièce, service) office; **bureau de change** (foreign) exchange office ou bureau; **bureau de poste** post office; **bureau de tabac** tobacconist's (shop); **bureaucratie** [byʀokʀasi] nf bureaucracy

bus¹ [by] vb voir **boire**

bus² [bys] nm bus; **à quelle heure part le ~?** what time does the bus leave?

buste [byst] nm (torse) chest; (seins) bust

but¹ [by] vb voir **boire**

but² [by(t)] nm (cible) target; (fig) goal, aim; (Football etc) goal; **de ~ en blanc** point-blank; **avoir pour ~ de faire** to aim to do; **dans le ~ de** with the intention of

butane [bytan] nm (camping) butane; (usage domestique) Calor gas®

butiner [bytine] vi (abeilles) to gather nectar

buvais etc [byvɛ] vb voir **boire**

buvard [byvaʀ] nm blotter

buvette [byvɛt] nf bar

C

c' [s] dét voir **ce**

ça [sa] pron (pour désigner) this; (: plus loin) that; (comme sujet indéfini) it; **ça m'étonne que ...** it surprises me that ...; **comment ça va?** how are you?; **ça va?** (d'accord?) O.K.?, all right?; **où ça?** where's that?; **pourquoi ça?** why's that?; **qui ça?** who's that?; **ça alors!** well really!; **ça fait 10 ans (que)** it's 10 years (since); **c'est ça** that's right; **ça y est** that's it

cabane [kaban] nf hut, cabin

cabaret [kabaʀɛ] nm night club

cabillaud [kabijo] nm cod inv

cabine [kabin] nf (de bateau) cabin; (de piscine etc) cubicle; (de camion, train) cab; (d'avion) cockpit; **cabine d'essayage** fitting room; **cabine (téléphonique)** call ou (tele)phone box

cabinet [kabinɛ] nm (petite pièce) closet; (de médecin) surgery (BRIT), office (US); (de notaire etc) office; (: clientèle) practice; (Pol) Cabinet; **cabinets** nmpl (w.-c.) toilet sg; **cabinet de toilette** toilet

câble [kɑbl] nm cable; **le ~** (TV) cable television, cablevision (US)

cacahuète [kakaɥɛt] nf peanut

cacao [kakao] nm cocoa

cache [kaʃ] nm mask, card (for masking)

cache-cache [kaʃkaʃ] nm: **jouer à ~** to play hide-and-seek

cachemire [kaʃmiʀ] nm cashmere

cacher [kaʃe] vt to hide, conceal; **se cacher** vi (volontairement) to hide; (être caché) to be hidden ou concealed; **~ qch à qn** to hide ou conceal sth from sb

cachet [kaʃɛ] nm (comprimé) tablet; (de la poste) postmark; (rétribution) fee; (fig) style, character

cachette [kaʃɛt] nf hiding place; **en ~** on the sly, secretly

cactus [kaktys] nm cactus

cadavre [kadɑvʀ] nm corpse, (dead) body

caddie® [kadi] nm (supermarket) trolley (BRIT), (grocery) cart (US)

cadeau, x [kado] nm present, gift; **faire un ~ à qn** to give sb a present ou gift; **faire ~ de qch à qn** to make a present of sth to sb, give sb sth as a present

cadenas [kadnɑ] nm padlock

cadet, te [kadɛ, ɛt] adj younger; (le plus jeune) youngest ▷ nm/f youngest child ou one

cadran [kadʀɑ̃] nm dial; **cadran solaire** sundial

cadre [kɑdʀ] nm frame; (environnement) surroundings pl ▷ nm/f (Admin) managerial employee, executive; **dans le ~ de** (fig) within the framework ou context of

cafard [kafaʀ] nm cockroach; **avoir le ~** (fam) to be down in the dumps

café [kafe] nm coffee; (bistro) café ▷ adj inv coffee(-coloured); **café au lait** white coffee; **café noir** black coffee; **café tabac** tobacconist's or newsagent's serving coffee and spirits; **cafetière** nf (pot) coffee-pot

cage [kaʒ] *nf* cage; **cage (d'escalier)** stairwell; **cage thoracique** rib cage

cageot [kaʒo] *nm* crate

cagoule [kagul] *nf* (*passe-montagne*) balaclava

cahier [kaje] *nm* notebook; **cahier de brouillon** jotter (*BRIT*), rough notebook; **cahier d'exercices** exercise book

caille [kaj] *nf* quail

caillou, x [kaju] *nm* (little) stone; **caillouteux, -euse** *adj* (*route*) stony

Caire [kɛʀ] *nm*: **le ~** Cairo

caisse [kɛs] *nf* box; (*tiroir où l'on met la recette*) till; (*où l'on paye*) cash desk (*BRIT*), check-out; (*de banque*) cashier's desk; **caisse d'épargne** savings bank; **caisse de retraite** pension fund; **caisse enregistreuse** cash register; **caissier, -ière** *nm/f* cashier

cake [kɛk] *nm* fruit cake

calandre [kalɑ̃dʀ] *nf* radiator grill

calcaire [kalkɛʀ] *nm* limestone ▷ *adj* (*eau*) hard; (*Géo*) limestone *cpd*

calcul [kalkyl] *nm* calculation; **le ~** (*Scol*) arithmetic; **calcul (biliaire)** (*gall*)stone; **calculatrice** *nf* calculator; **calculer** *vt* to calculate, work out; **calculette** *nf* pocket calculator

cale [kal] *nf* (*de bateau*) hold; (*en bois*) wedge

calé, e [kale] (*fam*) *adj* clever, bright

caleçon [kalsɔ̃] *nm* (*d'homme*) boxer shorts; (*de femme*) leggings

calendrier [kalɑ̃dʀije] *nm* calendar; (*fig*) timetable

calepin [kalpɛ̃] *nm* notebook

caler [kale] *vt* to wedge ▷ *vi* (*moteur, véhicule*) to stall

calibre [kalibʀ] *nm* calibre

câlin, e [kɑlɛ̃, in] *adj* cuddly, cuddlesome; (*regard, voix*) tender

calmant [kalmɑ̃] *nm* tranquillizer, sedative; (*pour la douleur*) painkiller

calme [kalm] *adj* calm, quiet ▷ *nm* calm(ness), quietness; **sans perdre son ~** without losing one's cool (*inf*) ou composure; **calmer** *vt* to calm (down);

(*douleur, inquiétude*) to ease, soothe; **se calmer** *vi* to calm down

calorie [kalɔʀi] *nf* calorie

camarade [kamaʀad] *nm/f* friend, pal; (*Pol*) comrade

Cambodge [kɑ̃bɔdʒ] *nm*: **le ~** Cambodia

cambriolage [kɑ̃bʀijɔlaʒ] *nm* burglary; **cambrioler** *vt* to burgle (*BRIT*), burglarize (*US*); **cambrioleur, -euse** *nm/f* burglar

camelote [kamlɔt] (*fam*) *nf* rubbish, trash, junk

caméra [kameʀa] *nf* (*Cinéma, TV*) camera; (*d'amateur*) cine-camera

Cameroun [kamʀun] *nm*: **le ~** Cameroon

caméscope® [kameskɔp] *nm* camcorder®

camion [kamjɔ̃] *nm* lorry (*BRIT*), truck; **camion de dépannage** breakdown (*BRIT*) ou tow (*US*) truck; **camionnette** *nf* (small) van; **camionneur** *nm* (*chauffeur*) lorry (*BRIT*) ou truck driver; (*entrepreneur*) haulage contractor (*BRIT*), trucker (*US*)

camomille [kamɔmij] *nf* camomile; (*boisson*) camomile tea

camp [kɑ̃] *nm* camp; (*fig*) side

campagnard, e [kɑ̃paɲaʀ, aʀd] *adj* country *cpd*

campagne [kɑ̃paɲ] *nf* country, countryside; (*Mil, Pol, Comm*) campaign; **à la ~** in the country

camper [kɑ̃pe] *vi* to camp ▷ *vt* to sketch; **se ~ devant** to plant o.s. in front of; **campeur, -euse** *nm/f* camper

camping [kɑ̃piŋ] *nm* camping; **faire du ~** to go camping; **(terrain de) camping** campsite, camping site; **camping-car** *nm* camper, motorhome (*US*); **camping-gaz®** *nm inv* camp(ing) stove

Canada [kanada] *nm*: **le ~** Canada; **canadien, ne** *adj* Canadian ▷ *nm/f*: **Canadien, ne** Canadian; **canadienne** *nf* (*veste*) fur-lined jacket

canal, -aux [kanal, o] *nm* canal;

(*naturel*, *TV*) channel; **canalisation** *nf* (*tuyau*) pipe

canapé [kanape] *nm* settee, sofa

canard [kanar] *nm* duck; (*fam*: *journal*) rag

cancer [kɑ̃sɛr] *nm* cancer; (*signe*): **le C~** Cancer

cancre [kɑ̃kr] *nm* dunce

candidat, e [kɑ̃dida, at] *nm/f* candidate; (*à un poste*) applicant, candidate; **candidature** *nf* (*Pol*) candidature; (*à poste*) application; **poser sa candidature à un poste** to apply for a job

cane [kan] *nf* (female) duck

canette [kanɛt] *nf* (*de bière*) (flip-top) bottle

canevas [kanva] *nm* (*Couture*) canvas

caniche [kaniʃ] *nm* poodle

canicule [kanikyl] *nf* scorching heat

canif [kanif] *nm* penknife, pocket knife

canne [kan] *nf* (walking) stick; **canne à pêche** fishing rod; **canne à sucre** sugar cane

cannelle [kanɛl] *nf* cinnamon

canoë [kanɔe] *nm* canoe; (*sport*) canoeing; **canoë (kayak)** kayak

canot [kano] *nm* ding(h)y; **canot de sauvetage** lifeboat; **canot pneumatique** inflatable ding(h)y

cantatrice [kɑ̃tatris] *nf* (opera) singer

cantine [kɑ̃tin] *nf* canteen

canton [kɑ̃tɔ̃] *nm* district consisting of *several communes*; (*en Suisse*) canton

caoutchouc [kautʃu] *nm* rubber; **caoutchouc mousse** foam rubber

cap [kap] *nm* (*Géo*) cape; (*promontoire*) headland; (*fig*: *tournant*) watershed; (*Navig*): **changer de ~** to change course; **mettre le ~ sur** to head *ou* steer for

CAP *sigle m* (= *Certificat d'aptitude professionnelle*) vocational training certificate taken at secondary school

capable [kapabl] *adj* able, capable; **~ de qch/faire** capable of sth/doing

capacité [kapasite] *nf* (*compétence*) ability; (*Jur*, *contenance*) capacity

cape [kap] *nf* cape, cloak; **rire sous ~** to laugh up one's sleeve

CAPES [kapɛs] *sigle m* (= *Certificat d'aptitude pédagogique à l'enseignement secondaire*) teaching diploma

capitaine [kapitɛn] *nm* captain

capital, e, -aux [kapital, o] *adj* (*œuvre*) major; (*question*, *rôle*) fundamental ▷ *nm* capital; (*fig*) stock; **d'une importance ~e** of capital importance; **capitaux** *nmpl* (*fonds*) capital *sg*; **capital (social)** authorized capital; **capitale** *nf* (*ville*) capital; (*lettre*) capital (letter); **capitalisme** *nm* capitalism; **capitaliste** *adj*, *nm/f* capitalist

caporal, -aux [kapɔral, o] *nm* lance corporal

capot [kapo] *nm* (*Auto*) bonnet (*BRIT*), hood (*US*)

câpre [kɑpr] *nf* caper

caprice [kapris] *nm* whim, caprice; **faire des ~s** to make a fuss; **capricieux, -euse** *adj* (*fantasque*) capricious, whimsical; (*enfant*) awkward

Capricorne [kaprikɔrn] *nm*: **le ~** Capricorn

capsule [kapsyl] *nf* (*de bouteille*) cap; (*Bot etc*, *spatiale*) capsule

capter [kapte] *vt* (*ondes radio*) to pick up; (*fig*) to win, capture

captivant, e [kaptivɑ̃, ɑ̃t] *adj* captivating

capturer [kaptyre] *vt* to capture

capuche [kapyʃ] *nf* hood

capuchon [kapyʃɔ̃] *nm* hood; (*de stylo*) cap, top

car [kar] *nm* coach ▷ *conj* because, for

carabine [karabin] *nf* rifle

caractère [karaktɛr] *nm* (*gén*) character; **avoir bon/mauvais ~** to be good-/ill-natured; **en ~s gras** in bold type; **en petits ~s** in small print; **~s d'imprimerie** (block) capitals

caractériser [karakterize] *vt* to be characteristic of; **se ~ par** to be characterized *ou* distinguished by

caractéristique [karakteristik] *adj*,

nf characteristic

carafe [kaʀaf] *nf* (*pour eau, vin ordinaire*) carafe

caraïbe [kaʀaib] *adj* Caribbean ▷ *n*: **les C-s** the Caribbean (Islands)

carambolage [kaʀɑ̃bɔlaʒ] *nm* multiple crash, pileup

caramel [kaʀamɛl] *nm* (*bonbon*) caramel, toffee; (*substance*) caramel

caravane [kaʀavan] *nf* caravan; **caravaning** *nm* caravanning

carbone [kaʀbɔn] *nm* carbon; (*double*) carbon (copy)

carbonique [kaʀbɔnik] *adj*: **gaz -** carbon dioxide; **neige -** dry ice

carbonisé, e [kaʀbɔnize] *adj* charred

carburant [kaʀbyʀɑ̃] *nm* (motor) fuel

carburateur [kaʀbyʀatœʀ] *nm* carburettor

cardiaque [kaʀdjak] *adj* cardiac, heart *cpd* ▷ *nm/f* heart patient; **être -** to have heart trouble

cardigan [kaʀdigɑ̃] *nm* cardigan

cardiologue [kaʀdjɔlɔg] *nm/f* cardiologist, heart specialist

carême [kaʀɛm] *nm*: **le C-** Lent

carence [kaʀɑ̃s] *nf* (*manque*) deficiency

caresse [kaʀɛs] *nf* caress

caresser [kaʀese] *vt* to caress; (*animal*) to stroke

cargaison [kaʀgɛzɔ̃] *nf* cargo, freight

cargo [kaʀgo] *nm* cargo boat, freighter

caricature [kaʀikatyʀ] *nf* caricature

carie [kaʀi] *nf*: **la - (dentaire)** tooth decay; **une -** a bad tooth

carnaval [kaʀnaval] *nm* carnival

carnet [kaʀnɛ] *nm* (*calepin*) notebook; (*de tickets, timbres etc*) book; **carnet de chèques** cheque book

carotte [kaʀɔt] *nf* carrot

carré, e [kaʀe] *adj* square; (*fig: franc*) straightforward ▷ *nm* (*Math*) square; **mètre/kilomètre -** square metre/ kilometre

carreau, x [kaʀo] *nm* (*par terre*) (floor) tile; (*au mur*) (wall) tile; (*de fenêtre*) (window) pane; (*motif*) check, square; (*Cartes: couleur*) diamonds *pl*; **tissu à -x**

checked fabric

carrefour [kaʀfuʀ] *nm* crossroads *sg*

carrelage [kaʀlaʒ] *nm* (*sol*) (tiled) floor

carrelet [kaʀlɛ] *nm* (*poisson*) plaice

carrément [kaʀemɑ̃] *adv* (*franchement*) straight out, bluntly; (*sans hésiter*) straight; (*intensif*) completely; **c'est - impossible** it's completely impossible

carrière [kaʀjɛʀ] *nf* (*métier*) career; (*de roches*) quarry; **militaire de -** professional soldier

carrosserie [kaʀɔsʀi] *nf* body, coachwork *no pl*

carrure [kaʀyʀ] *nf* build; (*fig*) stature, calibre

cartable [kaʀtabl] *nm* satchel, (school)bag

carte [kaʀt] *nf* (*de géographie*) map; (*marine, du ciel*) chart; (*d'abonnement, à jouer*) card; (*au restaurant*) menu; (*aussi*: **- de visite**) (visiting) card; **pouvez-vous me l'indiquer sur la -?** can you show me (it) on the map?; **à la -** (*au restaurant*) à la carte; **est-ce qu'on peut voir la -?** can we see the menu?; **donner - blanche à qn** to give sb a free rein; **carte bancaire** cash card; **Carte Bleue®** debit card; **carte à puce** smart card; **carte de crédit** credit card; **carte de fidélité** loyalty card; **carte d'identité** identity card; **carte de séjour** residence permit; **carte grise** (*Auto*) ≈ (car) registration book, logbook; **carte memoire** (*d'appareil-photo numérique*) memory card; **carte postale** postcard; **carte routière** road map

carter [kaʀtɛʀ] *nm* sump

carton [kaʀtɔ̃] *nm* (*matériau*) cardboard; (*boîte*) (cardboard) box; **faire un - (*fam*)** to score a hit; **carton (à dessin)** portfolio

cartouche [kaʀtuʃ] *nf* cartridge; (*de cigarettes*) carton

cas [kɑ] *nm* case; **ne faire aucun - de** to take no notice of; **en aucun -** on no account; **au - où** in case; **en - de** in case of, in the event of; **en - de besoin**

if need be; **en tout ~** in any case, at any rate

cascade [kaskad] nf waterfall, cascade

case [kɑz] nf (hutte) hut; (compartiment) compartment; (sur un formulaire, de mots croisés etc) box

caser [kɑze] (fam) vt (placer) to put (away); (loger) to put up; **se caser** vi (se marier) to settle down; (trouver un emploi) to find a (steady) job

caserne [kazɛʀn] nf barracks pl

casier [kazje] nm (pour courrier) pigeonhole; (compartiment) compartment; (à clef) locker; **casier judiciaire** police record

casino [kazino] nm casino

casque [kask] nm helmet; (chez le coiffeur) (hair-)drier; (pour audition) (head-)phones pl, headset

casquette [kaskɛt] nf cap

casse...: **casse-croûte** nm inv snack; **casse-noix** nm inv nutcrackers pl; **casse-pieds** (fam) adj inv: **il est casse-pieds** he's a pain in the neck

casser [kɑse] vt to break; (Jur) to quash; **se casser** vi to break; **~ les pieds à qn** (fam: irriter) to get on sb's nerves; **se ~ la tête** (fam) to go to a lot of trouble

casserole [kasʀɔl] nf saucepan

casse-tête [kɑstɛt] nm inv (difficultés) headache (fig)

cassette [kasɛt] nf (bande magnétique) cassette; (coffret) casket

cassis [kasis] nm blackcurrant

cassoulet [kasulɛ] nm bean and sausage hot-pot

catalogue [katalɔg] nm catalogue

catalytique [katalitik] adj: **pot ~** catalytic convertor

catastrophe [katastʀɔf] nf catastrophe, disaster

catéchisme [kateʃism] nm catechism

catégorie [kategɔʀi] nf category; **catégorique** adj categorical

cathédrale [katedʀal] nf cathedral

catholique [katɔlik] adj, nm/f (Roman) Catholic; **pas très ~** a bit shady ou fishy

cauchemar [koʃmaʀ] nm nightmare

cause [koz] nf cause; (Jur) lawsuit, case; **à ~ de** because of, owing to; **pour ~ de** on account of; **(et) pour ~** and for (a very) good reason; **être en ~** (intérêts) to be at stake; **remettre en ~** to challenge; **causer** vt to cause ▷ vi to chat, talk

caution [kosjɔ̃] nf guarantee, security; (Jur) bail (bond); (fig) backing, support; **libéré sous ~** released on bail

cavalier, -ière [kavalje, jɛʀ] adj (désinvolte) offhand ▷ nm/f rider; (au bal) partner ▷ nm (Échecs) knight

cave [kav] nf cellar

CD sigle m (= compact disc) CD

CD-ROM [sederɔm] sigle m CD-ROM

⭕ **MOT-CLÉ**

ce, cette [sə, sɛt] (devant nm **cet** + voyelle ou h aspiré; pl **ces**) dét (proximité) this; these pl; (non-proximité) that; those pl; **cette maison(-ci/là)** this/that house; **cette nuit** (qui vient) tonight; (passée) last night
▷ pron **1**: **c'est** it's ou it is; **c'est un peintre** it's ou he is a painter; **ce sont des peintres** they're ou they are painters; **c'est le facteur** etc (à la porte) it's the postman; **c'est toi qui lui a parlé** it was you who spoke to him; **qui est-ce?** who is it?; (en désignant) who is he/she?; **qu'est-ce?** what is it?
2: **ce qui, ce que**: **ce qui me plaît, c'est sa franchise** what I like about him ou her is his ou her frankness; **il est bête, ce qui me chagrine** he's stupid, which saddens me; **tout ce qui bouge** everything that ou which moves; **tout ce que je sais** all I know; **ce dont j'ai parlé** what I talked about; **ce que c'est grand!** it's so big!; voir aussi **-ci**; **est-ce que**; **n'est-ce pas**; **c'est-à-dire**

ceci [səsi] pron this

céder [sede] vt (donner) to give up ▷ vi (chaise, barrage) to give way; (personne)

to give in; **~ à** to yield to, give in to
CEDEX [sedɛks] *sigle m* (= *courrier d'entreprise à distribution exceptionnelle*) postal service for bulk users
cédille [sedij] *nf* cedilla
ceinture [sɛ̃tyʀ] *nf* belt; (*taille*) waist; **ceinture de sécurité** safety *ou* seat belt
cela [s(ə)la] *pron* indéfini) it; **~ m'étonne que …** it surprises me that …; **quand/où ~?** when/where (was that)?
célèbre [selɛbʀ] *adj* famous; **célébrer** *vt* to celebrate
céleri [selʀi] *nm*: **~(-rave)** celeriac; **céleri en branche** celery
célibataire [selibatɛʀ] *adj* single, unmarried ▷ *nm* bachelor ▷ *nf* unmarried woman
celle, celles [sɛl] *pron voir* **celui**
cellule [selyl] *nf* (*gén*) cell; **~ souche** stem cell
cellulite [selylit] *nf* cellulite

 MOT-CLÉ

celui, celle [səlɥi, sɛl] (*mpl* **ceux**, *fpl* **celles**) *pron* **1**: **celui-ci/là, celle-ci/là** this one/that one; **ceux-ci, celles-ci** these (ones); **ceux-là, celles-là** those (ones)
2: **celui qui bouge** the one which *ou* that moves; (*personne*) the one who moves; **celui que je vois** the one (which *ou* that) I see; (*personne*) the one (whom) I see; **celui dont je parle** the one I'm talking about; **celui de mon frère** my brother's; **celui du salon/du dessous** the one in (*ou* from) the lounge/below
3 (*valeur indéfinie*): **celui qui veut** whoever wants

cendre [sɑ̃dʀ] *nf* ash; **cendres** *nfpl* (*d'un défunt*) ashes; **sous la ~** (*Culin*) in (the) embers; **cendrier** *nm* ashtray
censé, e [sɑ̃se] *adj*: **être ~ faire** to be supposed to do
censeur [sɑ̃sœʀ] *nm* (*Scol*) deputy-head

(BRIT), vice-principal (US)
censure [sɑ̃syʀ] *nf* censorship; **censurer** *vt* (*Cinéma, Presse*) to censor; (*Pol*) to censure
cent [sɑ̃] *num* a hundred, one hundred ▷ *nm* (US, Canada etc) cent; (*partie de l'euro*) cent; **centaine** *nf*: **une centaine (de)** about a hundred, a hundred or so; **des centaines (de)** hundreds (of); **centenaire** *adj* hundred-year-old ▷ *nm* (*anniversaire*) centenary; (*monnaie*) cent; **centième** *num* hundredth; **centigrade** *nm* centigrade; **centilitre** *nm* centilitre; **centime** *nm* centime; **centime d'euro** *nm* euro cent; **centimètre** *nm* centimetre; (*ruban*) tape measure, measuring tape
central, e, -aux [sɑ̃tʀal, o] *adj* central ▷ *nm*: **~ (téléphonique)** (telephone) exchange; **centrale** *nf* power station; **centrale électrique/nucléaire** power/nuclear power station
centre [sɑ̃tʀ] *nm* centre; **centre commercial/sportif/culturel** shopping/sports/arts centre; **centre d'appels** call centre; **centre-ville** *nm* town centre, downtown (area) (US)
cèpe [sɛp] *nm* (*edible*) boletus
cependant [s(ə)pɑ̃dɑ̃] *adv* however
céramique [seʀamik] *nf* ceramics *sg*
cercle [sɛʀkl] *nm* circle; **cercle vicieux** vicious circle
cercueil [sɛʀkœj] *nm* coffin
céréale [seʀeal] *nf* cereal
cérémonie [seʀemɔni] *nf* ceremony; **sans ~** (*inviter, manger*) informally
cerf [sɛʀ] *nm* stag
cerf-volant [sɛʀvɔlɑ̃] *nm* kite
cerise [s(ə)ʀiz] *nf* cherry; **cerisier** *nm* cherry (tree)
cerner [sɛʀne] *vt* (*Mil etc*) to surround; (*fig: problème*) to delimit, define
certain, e [sɛʀtɛ̃, ɛn] *adj* certain ▷ *dét* certain; **d'un ~ âge** past one's prime, not so young; **un ~ temps** (quite) some time; **un ~ Georges** someone called Georges; **~s** *pron* some; **certainement** *adv* (*probablement*) most probably *ou*

likely; (*bien sûr*) certainly, of course
certes [sɛʁt] *adv* (*sans doute*)
admittedly; (*bien sûr*) of course
certificat [sɛʁtifika] *nm* certificate
certifier [sɛʁtifje] *vt*: **~ qch à qn**
to assure sb of sth; **copie certifiée conforme** certified copy of the original
certitude [sɛʁtityd] *nf* certainty
cerveau, x [sɛʁvo] *nm* brain
cervelas [sɛʁvəla] *nm* saveloy
cervelle [sɛʁvɛl] *nf* (*Anat*) brain; (*Culin*)
brains
ces [se] *dét voir* **ce**
CES *sigle m* (= *collège d'enseignement
secondaire*) ≈ (junior) secondary school
(BRIT)
cesse [sɛs]: **sans ~** *adv* (*tout le temps*)
continually, constantly; (*sans
interruption*) **il n'a eu de
~ que** he did not rest until; **cesser** *vt*
to stop ▷ *vi* to stop, cease; **cesser de
faire** to stop doing; **cessez-le-feu** *nm
inv* ceasefire
c'est-à-dire [sɛtadiʁ] *adv* that is (to say)
cet, cette [sɛt] *dét voir* **ce**
ceux [sø] *pron voir* **celui**
chacun, e [ʃakœ̃, yn] *pron* each;
(*indéfini*) everyone, everybody
chagrin [ʃagʁɛ̃] *nm* grief, sorrow; **avoir
du ~** to be grieved
chahut [ʃay] *nm* uproar; **chahuter** *vt*
to rag, bait ▷ *vi* to make an uproar
chaîne [ʃɛn] *nf* chain; (*Radio, TV:
stations*) channel; **travail à la ~**
production line work; **réactions
en ~** chain reaction *sg*; **chaîne de
montagnes** mountain range; **chaîne
(hi-fi)** hi-fi system
chair [ʃɛʁ] *nf* flesh; **avoir la ~ de poule**
to have goosepimples *ou* gooseflesh;
bien en ~ plump, well-padded; **en
~ et en os** in the flesh; **~ à saucisse**
sausage meat
chaise [ʃɛz] *nf* chair; **chaise longue**
deckchair
châle [ʃal] *nm* shawl
chaleur [ʃalœʁ] *nf* heat; (*fig: accueil*)
warmth; **chaleureux, -euse** *adj* warm

chamailler [ʃamaje]: **se chamailler** *vi*
to squabble, bicker
chambre [ʃɑ̃bʁ] *nf* bedroom; (*Pol,
Comm*) chamber; **faire ~ à part** to sleep
in separate rooms; **je voudrais une ~
pour deux personnes** I'd like a double
room; **chambre à air** (*de pneu*) (inner)
tube; **chambre à coucher** bedroom;
chambre à un lit/à deux lits (*à
l'hôtel*) single-/twin-bedded room;
chambre d'amis spare *ou* guest room;
chambre d'hôte ≈ bed and breakfast;
chambre meublée bedsit(ter) (BRIT),
furnished room; **chambre noire** (*Photo*)
darkroom
chameau, x [ʃamo] *nm* camel
chamois [ʃamwa] *nm* chamois
champ [ʃɑ̃] *nm* field; **champ de bataille**
battlefield; **champ de courses**
racecourse
champagne [ʃɑ̃paɲ] *nm* champagne
champignon [ʃɑ̃piɲɔ̃] *nm* mushroom;
(*terme générique*) fungus; **champignon
de Paris** *ou* **de couche** button
mushroom
champion, ne [ʃɑ̃pjɔ̃, jɔn] *adj,
nm/f* champion; **championnat** *nm*
championship
chance [ʃɑ̃s] *nf*: **la ~** luck; **chances** *nfpl*
(*probabilités*) chances; **avoir de la ~** to
be lucky; **il a des ~s de réussir** he's got
a good chance of passing; **bonne ~!**
good luck!
change [ʃɑ̃ʒ] *nm* (*devises*) exchange
changement [ʃɑ̃ʒmɑ̃] *nm* change;
changement de vitesses gears *pl*
changer [ʃɑ̃ʒe] *vt* (*modifier*) to change,
alter; (*remplacer, Comm*) to change ▷ *vi*
to change, alter; **se changer** *vi* to
change (o.s.); **~ de** (*remplacer: adresse,
nom, voiture etc*) to change one's;
(*échanger: place, train etc*) to change;
~ d'avis to change one's mind; **~ de
vitesse** to change gear; **il faut ~ à Lyon**
you *ou* we *etc* have to change in Lyons;
où est-ce que je peux ~ de l'argent?
where can I change some money?
chanson [ʃɑ̃sɔ̃] *nf* song

chant [ʃɑ̃] nm song; (art vocal) singing; (d'église) hymn

chantage [ʃɑ̃taʒ] nm blackmail; **faire du ~** to use blackmail

chanter [ʃɑ̃te] vt, vi to sing; **si cela lui chante** (fam) if he feels like it; **chanteur, -euse** nm/f singer

chantier [ʃɑ̃tje] nm (building) site; (sur une route) roadworks pl; **mettre en ~** to put in hand; **chantier naval** shipyard

chantilly [ʃɑ̃tiji] nf voir **crème**

chantonner [ʃɑ̃tɔne] vi, vt to sing to oneself, hum

chapeau, x [ʃapo] nm hat; **~!** well done!

chapelle [ʃapɛl] nf chapel

chapitre [ʃapitʀ] nm chapter

chaque [ʃak] dét each, every; (indéfini) every

char [ʃaʀ] nm (Mil): **~ (d'assaut)** tank; **~ à voile** sand yacht

charbon [ʃaʀbɔ̃] nm coal; **charbon de bois** charcoal

charcuterie [ʃaʀkytʀi] nf (magasin) pork butcher's shop and delicatessen; (produits) cooked pork meats pl; **charcutier, -ière** nm/f pork butcher

chardon [ʃaʀdɔ̃] nm thistle

charge [ʃaʀʒ] nf (fardeau) load, burden; (Élec, Mil, Jur) charge; (rôle, mission) responsibility; **charges** nfpl (du loyer) service charges; **à la ~ de** (dépendant de) dependent upon; (aux frais de) chargeable to; **prendre en ~** to take charge of; (suj: véhicule) to take on; (dépenses) to take care of; **charges sociales** social security contributions

chargement [ʃaʀʒəmɑ̃] nm (objets) load

charger [ʃaʀʒe] vt (voiture, fusil, caméra) to load; (batterie) to charge ▷ vi (Mil etc) to charge; **se ~ de** to see to, take care of

chariot [ʃaʀjo] nm trolley; (charrette) waggon

charité [ʃaʀite] nf charity; **faire la ~ à** to give (something) to

charmant, e [ʃaʀmɑ̃, ɑ̃t] adj charming

charme [ʃaʀm] nm charm; **charmer** vt to charm

charpente [ʃaʀpɑ̃t] nf frame(work); **charpentier** nm carpenter

charrette [ʃaʀɛt] nf cart

charter [ʃaʀtɛʀ] nm (vol) charter flight

chasse [ʃas] nf hunting; (au fusil) shooting; (poursuite) chase; (aussi: **~ d'eau**) flush; **prendre en ~** to give chase to; **tirer la ~ (d'eau)** to flush the toilet, pull the chain; **~ à courre** hunting; **chasse-neige** nm inv snowplough (BRIT), snowplow (US); **chasser** vt to hunt; (expulser) to chase away ou out, drive away ou out; **chasseur, -euse** nm/f hunter ▷ nm (avion) fighter

chat¹ [ʃa] nm cat

chat² [tʃat] nm (Internet) chat room

châtaigne [ʃatɛɲ] nf chestnut

châtain [ʃatɛ̃] adj inv (cheveux) chestnut (brown); (personne) chestnut-haired

château, x [ʃato] nm (forteresse) castle; (résidence royale) palace; (manoir) mansion; **château d'eau** water tower; **château fort** stronghold, fortified castle

châtiment [ʃatimɑ̃] nm punishment

chaton [ʃatɔ̃] nm (Zool) kitten

chatouiller [ʃatuje] vt to tickle; **chatouilleux, -euse** adj ticklish

chatte [ʃat] nf (she-)cat

chatter [tʃate] vi (Internet) to chat

chaud, e [ʃo, ʃod] adj (gén) warm; (très chaud) hot; **il fait ~** it's warm; it's hot; **avoir ~** to be warm; to be hot; **ça me tient ~** it keeps me warm; **rester au ~** to stay in the warm

chaudière [ʃodjɛʀ] nf boiler

chauffage [ʃofaʒ] nm heating; **chauffage central** central heating

chauffe-eau [ʃofo] nm inv water-heater

chauffer [ʃofe] vt to heat ▷ vi to heat up, warm up; (trop chauffer: moteur) to overheat; **se chauffer** vi (au soleil) to warm o.s.

chauffeur [ʃofœʀ] nm driver; (privé) chauffeur

chaumière [ʃomjɛʀ] nf (thatched) cottage

chaussée [ʃose] nf road(way)

chausser [ʃose] vt (bottes, skis) to put on; (enfant) to put shoes on; **~ du 38/42** to take size 38/42

chaussette [ʃosɛt] nf sock

chausson [ʃosɔ̃] nm slipper; (de bébé) bootee; **chausson (aux pommes)** (apple) turnover

chaussure [ʃosyʀ] nf shoe; **chaussures basses** flat shoes; **chaussures montantes** ankle boots; **chaussures de ski** ski boots

chauve [ʃov] adj bald; **chauve-souris** nf bat

chauvin, e [ʃovɛ̃, in] adj chauvinistic

chaux [ʃo] nf lime; **blanchi à la ~** whitewashed

chef [ʃɛf] nm head, leader; (de cuisine) chef; **commandant en ~** commander-in-chief; **chef d'accusation** charge; **chef d'entreprise** company head; **chef d'État** head of state; **chef de famille** head of the family; **chef de file** (de parti etc) leader; **chef de gare** station master; **chef d'orchestre** conductor; **chef-d'œuvre** nm masterpiece; **chef-lieu** nm county town

chemin [ʃ(ə)mɛ̃] nm path; (itinéraire, direction, trajet) way; **en ~** on the way; **chemin de fer** railway (BRIT), railroad (US)

cheminée [ʃ(ə)mine] nf chimney; (à l'intérieur) chimney piece, fireplace; (de bateau) funnel

chemise [ʃ(ə)miz] nf shirt; (dossier) folder; **chemise de nuit** nightdress

chemisier [ʃ(ə)mizje] nm blouse

chêne [ʃɛn] nm oak (tree); (bois) oak

chenil [ʃ(ə)nil] nm kennels pl

chenille [ʃ(ə)nij] nf (Zool) caterpillar

chèque [ʃɛk] nm cheque (BRIT), check (US); **est-ce que je peux payer par ~?** can I pay by cheque?; **chèque sans provision** bad cheque; **chèque de voyage** traveller's cheque; **chéquier** [ʃekje] nm cheque book

cher, -ère [ʃɛʀ] adj (aimé) dear; (coûteux) expensive, dear ▷ adv: **ça coûte ~** it's expensive

chercher [ʃɛʀʃe] vt to look for; (gloire etc) to seek; **aller ~** to go for, go and fetch; **~ à faire** to try to do; **chercheur, -euse** nm/f researcher, research worker

chéri, e [ʃeri] adj beloved, dear; **(mon) ~** darling

cheval, -aux [ʃ(ə)val, o] nm horse; (Auto): **~ (vapeur)** horsepower no pl; **faire du ~** to ride; **à ~** on horseback; **à ~ sur** astride; (fig) overlapping; **cheval de course** racehorse

chevalier [ʃ(ə)valje] nm knight

chevalière [ʃ(ə)valjɛʀ] nf signet ring

chevaux [ʃəvo] nmpl de **cheval**

chevet [ʃ(ə)vɛ] nm: **au ~ de qn** at sb's bedside; **lampe de chevet** bedside lamp

cheveu, x [ʃ(ə)vø] nm hair; **cheveux** nmpl (chevelure) hair sg; **avoir les ~x courts** to have short hair

cheville [ʃ(ə)vij] nf (Anat) ankle; (de bois) peg; (pour une vis) plug

chèvre [ʃɛvʀ] nf (she-)goat

chèvrefeuille [ʃɛvʀəfœj] nm honeysuckle

chevreuil [ʃəvʀœj] nm roe deer inv; (Culin) venison

 MOT-CLÉ

chez [ʃe] prép **1** (à la demeure de) at; (: direction) to; **chez qn** at/to sb's house ou place; **je suis chez moi** I'm at home; **je rentre chez moi** I'm going home; **allons chez Nathalie** let's go to Nathalie's

2 (+profession) at; (: direction) to; **chez le boulanger/dentiste** at ou to the baker's/dentist's

3 (dans le caractère, l'œuvre de) in; **chez ce poète** in this poet's work; **c'est ce que je préfère chez lui** that's what I like best about him

chic [ʃik] adj inv chic, smart; (fam:

généreux) nice, decent ▷ *nm* stylishness;
~ (alors)! (*fam*) great!; **avoir le ~ de** to
have the knack of
chicorée [ʃikɔʀe] *nf* (*café*) chicory;
(*salade*) endive
chien [ʃjɛ̃] *nm* dog; **chien d'aveugle**
guide dog; **chien de garde** guard dog
chienne [ʃjɛn] *nf* dog, bitch
chiffon [ʃifɔ̃] *nm* (piece of) rag;
chiffonner *vt* to crumple; (*fam:
tracasser*) to concern
chiffre [ʃifʀ] *nm* (*représentant un nombre*)
figure, numeral; (*montant, total*) total,
sum; **en ~s ronds** in round figures;
chiffre d'affaires turnover; **chiffrer**
vt (*dépense*) to put a figure to, assess;
(*message*) to (en)code, cipher; **se
chiffrer à** to add up to, amount to
chignon [ʃiɲɔ̃] *nm* chignon, bun
Chili [ʃili] *nm*: **le ~** Chile; **chilien, ne** *adj*
Chilean ▷ *nm/f*: **Chilien, ne** Chilean
chimie [ʃimi] *nf* chemistry;
chimiothérapie [ʃimjoteʀapi]
nf chemotherapy; **chimique** *adj*
chemical; **produits chimiques**
chemicals
chimpanzé [ʃɛ̃pɑ̃ze] *nm* chimpanzee
Chine [ʃin] *nf*: **la ~** China; **chinois, e** *adj*
Chinese ▷ *nm/f*: **Chinois, e** Chinese
▷ *nm* (*Ling*) Chinese
chiot [ʃjo] *nm* pup(py)
chips [ʃips] *nfpl* crisps (*BRIT*), (potato)
chips (*US*)
chirurgie [ʃiʀyʀʒi] *nf* surgery;
chirurgie esthétique plastic surgery;
chirurgien, ne *nm/f* surgeon
chlore [klɔʀ] *nm* chlorine
choc [ʃɔk] *nm* (*heurt*) impact, shock;
(*collision*) crash; (*moral*) shock;
(*affrontement*) clash
chocolat [ʃɔkɔla] *nm* chocolate;
chocolat au lait milk chocolate
chœur [kœʀ] *nm* (*chorale*) choir; (*Opéra,
Théâtre*) chorus; **en ~** in chorus
choisir [ʃwaziʀ] *vt* to choose, select
choix [ʃwa] *nm* choice, selection; **avoir
le ~** to have the choice; **premier ~**
(*Comm*) class one; **de ~** choice, selected;

au ~ as you wish
chômage [ʃomaʒ] *nm* unemployment;
mettre au ~ to make redundant,
put out of work; **être au ~** to be
unemployed *ou* out of work; **chômeur,
-euse** *nm/f* unemployed person
choquer [ʃɔke] *vt* (*offenser*) to shock;
(*deuil*) to shake
chorale [kɔʀal] *nf* choir
chose [ʃoz] *nf* thing; **c'est peu de ~** it's
nothing (really)
chou, x [ʃu] *nm* cabbage; **mon petit
~** (my) sweetheart; **chou à la crème**
choux bun; **chou de Bruxelles** Brussels
sprout; **choucroute** *nf* sauerkraut
chouette [ʃwɛt] *nf* owl ▷ *adj* (*fam*)
great, smashing
chou-fleur [ʃuflœʀ] *nm* cauliflower
chrétien, ne [kʀetjɛ̃, jɛn] *adj, nm/f*
Christian
Christ [kʀist] *nm*: **le ~** Christ;
christianisme *nm* Christianity
chronique [kʀɔnik] *adj* chronic ▷ *nf*
(*de journal*) column, page; (*historique*)
chronicle; (*Radio, TV*): **la ~ sportive** the
sports review
chronologique [kʀɔnɔlɔʒik] *adj*
chronological
chronomètre [kʀɔnɔmɛtʀ] *nm*
stopwatch; **chronométrer** *vt* to time
chrysanthème [kʀizɑ̃tɛm] *nm*
chrysanthemum

- **CHRYSANTHÈME**
-
- Chrysanthemums are strongly
- associated with funerals in France,
- and therefore should not be given
- as gifts.

chuchotement [ʃyʃɔtmɑ̃] *nm* whisper
chuchoter [ʃyʃɔte] *vt, vi* to whisper
chut [ʃyt] *excl* sh!
chute [ʃyt] *nf* fall; (*déchet*) scrap; **faire
une ~ (de 10 m)** to fall (10 m); **chute
(d'eau)** waterfall; **chute libre** free
fall; **chutes de pluie/neige** rainfall/
snowfall

Chypre [ʃipʀ] *nm/f* Cyprus

-ci [si] *adv voir* **par** ▷ *dét*: **ce garçon~** this boy; **ces femmes~** these women

cible [sibl] *nf* target

ciboulette [sibulɛt] *nf* (small) chive

cicatrice [sikatʀis] *nf* scar; **cicatriser** *vt* to heal

ci-contre [sikɔ̃tʀ] *adv* opposite

ci-dessous [sidəsu] *adv* below

ci-dessus [sidəsy] *adv* above

cidre [sidʀ] *nm* cider

Cie *abr* (= *compagnie*) Co.

ciel [sjɛl] *nm* sky; (*Rel*) heaven

cieux [sjø] *nmpl de* **ciel**

cigale [sigal] *nf* cicada

cigare [sigaʀ] *nm* cigar

cigarette [sigaʀɛt] *nf* cigarette

ci-inclus, e [siɛ̃kly, yz] *adj, adv* enclosed

ci-joint, e [siʒwɛ̃, ɛ̃t] *adj, adv* enclosed

cil [sil] *nm* (eye)lash

cime [sim] *nf* top; (*montagne*) peak

ciment [simɑ̃] *nm* cement

cimetière [simtjɛʀ] *nm* cemetery; (*d'église*) churchyard

cinéaste [sineast] *nm/f* film-maker

cinéma [sinema] *nm* cinema

cinq [sɛ̃k] *num* five; **cinquantaine** *nf*: **une cinquantaine (de)** about fifty; **avoir la cinquantaine** (*âge*) to be around fifty; **cinquante** *num* fifty; **cinquantenaire** *adj, nm/f* fifty-year-old; **cinquième** *num* fifth ▷ *nf* (*Scol*) year 8 (*BRIT*), seventh grade (*US*)

cintre [sɛ̃tʀ] *nm* coat-hanger

cintré, e [sɛ̃tʀe] *adj* (*chemise*) fitted

cirage [siʀaʒ] *nm* (shoe) polish

circonflexe [siʀkɔ̃flɛks] *adj*: **accent ~** circumflex accent

circonstance [siʀkɔ̃stɑ̃s] *nf* circumstance; (*occasion*) occasion; **circonstances atténuantes** mitigating circumstances

circuit [siʀkɥi] *nm* (*Élec, Tech*) circuit; (*trajet*) tour, (round) trip

circulaire [siʀkylɛʀ] *adj, nf* circular

circulation [siʀkylasjɔ̃] *nf* circulation; (*Auto*): **la ~** (the) traffic

circuler [siʀkyle] *vi* (*sang, devises*) to circulate; (*véhicules*) to drive (along); (*passants*) to walk along; (*train, bus*) to run; **faire ~** (*nouvelle*) to spread (about), circulate; (*badauds*) to move on

cire [siʀ] *nf* wax; **ciré** *nm* oilskin; **cirer** *vt* to wax, polish

cirque [siʀk] *nm* circus; (*fig*) chaos, bedlam; **quel ~!** what a carry-on!

ciseau, x [sizo] *nm*: **~ (à bois)** chisel; **ciseaux** *nmpl* (*paire de ciseaux*) (pair of) scissors

citadin, e [sitadɛ̃, in] *nm/f* city dweller

citation [sitasjɔ̃] *nf* (*d'auteur*) quotation; (*Jur*) summons *sg*

cité [site] *nf* town; (*plus grande*) city; **cité universitaire** students' residences *pl*

citer [site] *vt* (*un auteur*) to quote (from); (*nommer*) to name; (*Jur*) to summon

citoyen, ne [sitwajɛ̃, jɛn] *nm/f* citizen

citron [sitʀɔ̃] *nm* lemon; **citron pressé** (fresh) lemon juice; **citron vert** lime; **citronnade** *nf* still lemonade

citrouille [sitʀuj] *nf* pumpkin

civet [sivɛ] *nm*: **~ de lapin** rabbit stew

civière [sivjɛʀ] *nf* stretcher

civil, e [sivil] *adj* (*mariage, poli*) civil; (*non militaire*) civilian; **en ~** in civilian clothes; **dans le ~** in civilian life

civilisation [sivilizasjɔ̃] *nf* civilization

clair, e [klɛʀ] *adj* light; (*pièce*) light, bright; (*eau, son, fig*) clear ▷ *adv*: **voir ~** to see clearly; **tirer qch au ~** to clear sth up, clarify sth; **mettre au ~** (*notes etc*) to tidy up ▷ *nm*: **~ de lune** moonlight; **clairement** *adv* clearly

clairière [klɛʀjɛʀ] *nf* clearing

clandestin, e [klɑ̃dɛstɛ̃, in] *adj* clandestine, secret; (*mouvement*) underground; (*travailleur, immigration*) illegal; **passager ~** stowaway

claque [klak] *nf* (*gifle*) slap; **claquer** *vi* (*porte*) to bang, slam; (*fam: mourir*) to snuff it ▷ *vt* (*porte*) to slam, bang; (*doigts*) to snap; (*fam: dépenser*) to blow; **il claquait des dents** his teeth were chattering; **être claqué** (*fam*) to be dead tired; **se claquer un muscle** to pull *ou* strain a muscle; **claquettes** *nfpl* tap-dancing *sg*; (*chaussures*) flip-flops

clarinette [klaRinɛt] *nf* clarinet

classe [klɑs] *nf* class; (*Scol: local*) class(room); (: *leçon, élèves*) class; **aller en ~** to go to school; **classement** *nm* (*rang: Scol*) place; (: *Sport*) placing; (*liste: Scol*) class list (in order of merit); (: *Sport*) placings *pl*

classer [klɑse] *vt* (*idées, livres*) to classify; (*papiers*) to file; (*candidat, concurrent*) to grade; (*Jur: affaire*) to close; **se ~ premier/dernier** to come first/last; (*Sport*) to finish first/last; **classeur** *nm* file

classique [klasik] *adj* classical; (*sobre: coupe etc*) classic(al); (*habituel*) standard, classic

clavecin [klav(ə)sɛ̃] *nm* harpsichord

clavicule [klavikyl] *nf* collarbone

clavier [klavje] *nm* keyboard

clé [kle] *nf* key; (*Mus*) clef; (*de mécanicien*) spanner (*BRIT*), wrench (*US*); **prix ~s en main** (*d'une voiture*) on-the-road price; **clé de contact** ignition key; **clé USB** USB key

clef [kle] *nf* = **clé**

clergé [klɛRʒe] *nm* clergy

cliché [kliʃe] *nm* (*fig*) cliché; (*négatif*) negative; (*photo*) print

client, e [klijɑ̃, klijɑ̃t] *nm/f* (*acheteur*) customer, client; (*d'hôtel*) guest, patron; (*du docteur*) patient; (*de l'avocat*) client; **clientèle** *nf* (*du magasin*) customers *pl*, clientèle; (*du docteur, de l'avocat*) practice

cligner [kliɲe] *vi*: **~ des yeux** to blink (one's eyes); **~ de l'œil** to wink; **clignotant** *nm* (*Auto*) indicator; **clignoter** *vi* (*étoiles etc*) to twinkle; (*lumière*) to flicker

climat [klima] *nm* climate

climatisation [klimatizasjɔ̃] *nf* air conditioning; **climatisé, e** *adj* airconditioned

clin d'œil [klɛ̃dœj] *nm* wink; **en un clin d'œil** in a flash

clinique [klinik] *nf* private hospital

clip [klip] *nm* (*boucle d'oreille*) clip-on; **(vidéo) ~** (pop) video

cliquer [klike] *vt* to click; **~ sur** to click on

clochard, e [klɔʃaR, aRd] *nm/f* tramp

cloche [klɔʃ] *nf* (*d'église*) bell; (*fam*) clot; **clocher** *nm* church tower; (*en pointe*) steeple ▷ *vi* (*fam*) to be *ou* go wrong; **de clocher** (*péj*) parochial

cloison [klwazɔ̃] *nf* partition (wall)

clonage [klɔnaʒ] *nm* cloning

cloner [klone] *vt* to clone

cloque [klɔk] *nf* blister

clore [klɔR] *vt* to close

clôture [klotyR] *nf* closure; (*barrière*) enclosure

clou [klu] *nm* nail; **clous** *nmpl* (*passage clouté*) pedestrian crossing; **pneus à ~s** studded tyres; **le ~ du spectacle** the highlight of the show; **clou de girofle** clove

clown [klun] *nm* clown

club [klœb] *nm* club

CNRS *sigle m* (= *Centre nationale de la recherche scientifique*) ≈ SERC (*BRIT*), ≈ NSF (*US*)

coaguler [kɔagyle] *vt, vi* (*aussi*: **se ~**: *sang*) to coagulate

cobaye [kɔbaj] *nm* guinea-pig

coca [kɔka] *nm* Coke®

cocaïne [kɔkain] *nf* cocaine

coccinelle [kɔksinɛl] *nf* ladybird (*BRIT*), ladybug (*US*)

cocher [kɔʃe] *vt* to tick off

cochon, ne [kɔʃɔ̃, ɔn] *nm* pig ▷ *adj* (*fam*) dirty, smutty; **cochon d'Inde** guinea pig; **cochonnerie** (*fam*) *nf* (*saleté*) filth; (*marchandise*) rubbish, trash

cocktail [kɔktɛl] *nm* cocktail; (*réception*) cocktail party

cocorico [kɔkɔriko] *excl, nm* cock-a-doodle-do

cocotte [kɔkɔt] *nf* (*en fonte*) casserole; **ma ~** (*fam*) sweetie (pie); **cocotte (minute)**® pressure cooker

code [kɔd] *nm* code ▷ *adj*: **phares ~s** dipped lights; **se mettre en ~(s)** to dip one's (head)lights; **code à barres** bar code; **code civil** Common Law; **code de la route** highway code; **code pénal** penal code; **code postal** (numéro) post (BRIT) ou zip (US) code

cœur [kœʀ] nm heart; (Cartes: couleur) hearts pl; (: carte) heart; **avoir bon ~** to be kind-hearted; **avoir mal au ~** to feel sick; **par ~** by heart; **de bon ~** willingly; **cela lui tient à ~** that's (very) close to his heart

coffre [kɔfʀ] nm (meuble) chest; (d'auto) boot (BRIT), trunk (US); **coffre-fort** nm safe; **coffret** nm casket

cognac [kɔɲak] nm brandy, cognac

cogner [kɔɲe] vi to knock; **se ~ contre** to knock ou bump into; **se ~ la tête** to bang one's head

cohérent, e [kɔeʀɑ̃, ɑ̃t] adj coherent, consistent

coiffé, e [kwafe] adj: **bien/mal ~** with tidy/untidy hair; **~ d'un chapeau** wearing a hat

coiffer [kwafe] vt (fig: surmonter) to cover, top; **se coiffer** vi to do one's hair; **~ qn** to do sb's hair; **coiffeur, -euse** nm/f hairdresser; **coiffeuse** nf (table) dressing table; **coiffure** nf (cheveux) hairstyle, hairdo; (art): **la coiffure** hairdressing

coin [kwɛ̃] nm corner; (pour coincer) wedge; **l'épicerie du ~** the local grocer; **dans le ~** (aux alentours) in the area, around about; (habiter) locally; **je ne suis pas du ~** I'm not from here; **au ~ du feu** by the fireside; **regard en ~** sideways glance

coincé, e [kwɛ̃se] adj stuck, jammed; (fig: inhibé) inhibited, hung up (fam)

coïncidence [kɔɛ̃sidɑ̃s] nf coincidence

coing [kwɛ̃] nm quince

col [kɔl] nm (de chemise) collar; (encolure, cou) neck; (de montagne) pass; **col de l'utérus** cervix; **col roulé** polo-neck

colère [kɔlɛʀ] nf anger; **une ~** a fit of anger; **(se mettre) en ~ (contre qn)** (to get) angry (with sb); **coléreux, -euse, colérique** adj quick-tempered, irascible

colin [kɔlɛ̃] nm hake

colique [kɔlik] nf diarrhoea

colis [kɔli] nm parcel

collaborer [kɔ(l)labɔʀe] vi to collaborate; **~ à** to collaborate on; (revue) to contribute to

collant, e [kɔlɑ̃, ɑ̃t] adj sticky; (robe etc) clinging, skintight; (péj) clinging ▷ nm (bas) tights pl; (de danseur) leotard

colle [kɔl] nf glue; (à papiers peints) (wallpaper) paste; (fam: devinette) teaser, riddle; (Scol: fam) detention

collecte [kɔlɛkt] nf collection; **collectif, -ive** adj collective; (visite, billet) group cpd

collection [kɔlɛksjɔ̃] nf collection; (Édition) series; **collectionner** vt to collect; **collectionneur, -euse** nm/f collector

collectivité [kɔlɛktivite] nf group; **collectivités locales** (Admin) local authorities

collège [kɔlɛʒ] nm (école) (secondary) school; (assemblée) body; **collégien** nm schoolboy

collègue [kɔ(l)lɛg] nm/f colleague

coller [kɔle] vt (papier, timbre) to stick (on); (affiche) to stick up; (enveloppe) to stick down; (morceaux) to stick ou glue together; (Comput) to paste; (fam: mettre, fourrer) to stick, shove; (Scol: fam) to keep in ▷ vi (être collant) to be sticky; (adhérer) to stick; **~ à** to stick to; **être collé à un examen** (fam) to fail an exam

collier [kɔlje] nm (bijou) necklace; (de chien, Tech) collar

colline [kɔlin] nf hill

collision [kɔlizjɔ̃] nf collision, crash; **entrer en ~ (avec)** to collide (with)

collyre [kɔliʀ] nm eye drops

colombe [kɔlɔ̃b] nf dove

Colombie [kɔlɔ̃bi] nf: **la ~** Colombia

colonie [kɔlɔni] nf colony; **colonie (de vacances)** holiday camp (for children)

colonne [kɔlɔn] nf column; **se mettre en ~ par deux** to get into twos;

colonne (vertébrale) spine, spinal column

colorant [kɔlɔʀɑ̃] *nm* colouring

colorer [kɔlɔʀe] *vt* to colour

colorier [kɔlɔʀje] *vt* to colour (in)

coloris [kɔlɔʀi] *nm* colour, shade

colza [kɔlza] *nm* rape(seed)

coma [kɔma] *nm* coma; **être dans le ~** to be in a coma

combat [kɔ̃ba] *nm* fight, fighting *no pl*; **combat de boxe** boxing match; **combattant** *nm*: **ancien combattant** war veteran; **combattre** *vt* to fight; (*épidémie, ignorance*) to combat, fight against

combien [kɔ̃bjɛ̃] *adv* (*quantité*) how much; (*nombre*) how many; **~ de** (*quantité*) how much; (*nombre*) how many; **~ de temps** how long; **~ ça coûte/pèse?** how much does it cost/weigh?; **on est le ~ aujourd'hui?** (*fam*) what's the date today?

combinaison [kɔ̃binɛzɔ̃] *nf* combination; (*astuce*) scheme; (*de femme*) slip; (*de plongée*) wetsuit; (*bleu de travail*) boiler suit (BRIT), coveralls *pl* (US)

combiné [kɔ̃bine] *nm* (*aussi*: **~ téléphonique**) receiver

comble [kɔ̃bl] *adj* (*salle*) packed (full) ▷ *nm* (*du bonheur, plaisir*) height; **combles** *nmpl* (*Constr*) attic *sg*, loft *sg*; **c'est le ~!** that beats everything!

combler [kɔ̃ble] *vt* (*trou*) to fill in; (*besoin, lacune*) to fill; (*déficit*) to make good; (*satisfaire*) to fulfil

comédie [kɔmedi] *nf* comedy; (*fig*) playacting *no pl*; **faire la ~** (*fam*) to make a fuss; **comédie musicale** musical; **comédien, ne** *nm/f* actor(-tress)

comestible [kɔmɛstibl] *adj* edible

comique [kɔmik] *adj* (*drôle*) comical; (*Théâtre*) comic ▷ *nm* (*artiste*) comic, comedian

commandant [kɔmɑ̃dɑ̃] *nm* (*gén*) commander, commandant; (*Navig, Aviat*) captain

commande [kɔmɑ̃d] *nf* (*Comm*)

order; **commandes** *nfpl* (*Aviat etc*) controls; **sur ~** to order; **commander** *vt* (*Comm*) to order; (*diriger, ordonner*) to command; **commander à qn de faire** to command *ou* order sb to do; **je peux commander, s'il vous plaît?** can I order, please?

 MOT-CLÉ

comme [kɔm] *prép* **1** (*comparaison*) like; **tout comme son père** just like his father; **fort comme un bœuf** as strong as an ox; **joli comme tout** ever so pretty
2 (*manière*) like; **faites-le comme ça** do it like this, do it this way; **comme ci, comme ça** so-so, middling; **comme il faut** (*correctement*) properly
3 (*en tant que*) as a; **donner comme prix** to give as a prize; **travailler comme secrétaire** to work as a secretary
▷ *conj* **1** (*ainsi que*) as; **elle écrit comme elle parle** she writes as she talks; **comme si** as if
2 (*au moment où, alors que*) as; **il est parti comme j'arrivais** he left as I arrived
3 (*parce que, puisque*) as; **comme il était en retard, il ...** as he was late, he ...
▷ *adv*: **comme il est fort/c'est bon!** he's so strong/it's so good!

commencement [kɔmɑ̃smɑ̃] *nm* beginning, start

commencer [kɔmɑ̃se] *vt, vi* to begin, start; **~ à** *ou* **de faire** to begin *ou* start doing

comment [kɔmɑ̃] *adv* how; **~?** (*que dites-vous*) pardon?; **et ~!** and how!

commentaire [kɔmɑ̃tɛʀ] *nm* (*remarque*) comment, remark; (*exposé*) commentary

commerçant, e [kɔmɛʀsɑ̃, ɑ̃t] *nm/f* shopkeeper, trader

commerce [kɔmɛʀs] *nm* (*activité*) trade, commerce; (*boutique*) business; **~ électronique** e-commerce; **~**

équitable fair trade; **commercial, e, -aux** adj commercial, trading; (*péj*) commercial; **les commerciaux** the sales people; **commercialiser** vt to market

commissaire [kɔmisɛʀ] nm (*de police*) ≈ (police) superintendent; **commissaire aux comptes** (*Admin*) auditor; **commissariat** nm police station

commission [kɔmisjɔ̃] nf (*comité, pourcentage*) commission; (*message*) message; (*course*) errand; **commissions** nfpl (*achats*) shopping sg

commode [kɔmɔd] adj (*pratique*) convenient, handy; (*facile*) easy; (*personne*): **pas ~** awkward (to deal with) ▷ nf chest of drawers

commun, e [kɔmœ̃ yn] adj common; (*pièce*) communal, shared; (*effort*) joint; **ça sort du ~** it's out of the ordinary; **le ~ des mortels** the common run of people; **en ~** (*faire*) jointly; **mettre en ~** to pool, share; **communs** nmpl (*bâtiments*) outbuildings; **d'un ~ accord** by mutual agreement

communauté [kɔmynote] nf community

commune [kɔmyn] nf (*Admin*) commune, ≈ district; (: *urbaine*) ≈ borough

communication [kɔmynikasjɔ̃] nf communication

communier [kɔmynje] vi (*Rel*) to receive communion

communion [kɔmynjɔ̃] nf communion

communiquer [kɔmynike] vt (*nouvelle, dossier*) to pass on, convey; (*peur etc*) to communicate ▷ vi to communicate; **se communiquer à** (*se propager*) to spread to

communisme [kɔmynism] nm communism; **communiste** adj, nm/f communist

commutateur [kɔmytatœʀ] nm (*Élec*) (change-over) switch, commutator

compact, e [kɔ̃pakt] adj (*dense*) dense; (*appareil*) compact

compagne [kɔ̃paɲ] nf companion

compagnie [kɔ̃paɲi] nf (*firme, Mil*) company; **tenir ~ à qn** to keep sb company; **fausser ~ à qn** to give sb the slip, slip *ou* sneak away from sb; **compagnie aérienne** airline (company)

compagnon [kɔ̃paɲɔ̃] nm companion

comparable [kɔ̃paʀabl] adj: **~ (à)** comparable (to)

comparaison [kɔ̃paʀɛzɔ̃] nf comparison

comparer [kɔ̃paʀe] vt to compare; **~ qch/qn à** *ou* **et** (*pour choisir*) to compare sth/sb with *ou* and; (*pour établir une similitude*) to compare sth/sb to

compartiment [kɔ̃paʀtimɑ̃] nm compartment; **un ~ non-fumeurs** a non-smoking compartment (*BRIT*) *ou* car (*US*)

compas [kɔ̃pa] nm (*Géom*) (pair of) compasses pl; (*Navig*) compass

compatible [kɔ̃patibl] adj compatible

compatriote [kɔ̃patʀijɔt] nm/f compatriot

compensation [kɔ̃pɑ̃sasjɔ̃] nf compensation

compenser [kɔ̃pɑ̃se] vt to compensate for, make up for

compétence [kɔ̃petɑ̃s] nf competence

compétent, e [kɔ̃petɑ̃, ɑ̃t] adj (*apte*) competent, capable

compétition [kɔ̃petisjɔ̃] nf (*gén*) competition; (*Sport: épreuve*) event; **la ~ automobile** motor racing

complément [kɔ̃plemɑ̃] nm complement; (*reste*) remainder; **complément d'information** (*Admin*) supplementary *ou* further information; **complémentaire** adj complementary; (*additionnel*) supplementary

complet, -ète [kɔ̃plɛ, ɛt] adj complete; (*plein: hôtel etc*) full ▷ nm (*aussi:* **~-veston**) suit; **pain complet** wholemeal bread; **complètement** adv completely; **compléter** vt (*porter à la quantité voulue*) to complete;

(*augmenter: connaissances, études*) to complement, supplement; (: *garde-robe*) to add to

complexe [kɔ̃plɛks] *adj, nm* complex; **complexe hospitalier/industriel** hospital/industrial complex; **complexé, e** *adj* mixed-up, hung-up

complication [kɔ̃plikasjɔ̃] *nf* complexity, intricacy; (*difficulté, ennui*) complication; **complications** *nfpl* (*Méd*) complications

complice [kɔ̃plis] *nm* accomplice

compliment [kɔ̃plimɑ̃] *nm* (*louange*) compliment; **compliments** *nmpl* (*félicitations*) congratulations

compliqué, e [kɔ̃plike] *adj* complicated, complex; (*personne*) complicated

comportement [kɔ̃pɔʀtəmɑ̃] *nm* behaviour

comporter [kɔ̃pɔʀte] *vt* (*consister en*) to consist of, comprise; (*inclure*) to have; **se comporter** *vi* to behave

composer [kɔ̃poze] *vt* (*musique, texte*) to compose; (*mélange, équipe*) to make up; (*numéro*) to dial; (*constituer*) to make up, form ▷ *vi* (*transiger*) to come to terms; **se composer de** to be composed of, be made up of; **compositeur, -trice** *nm/f* (*Mus*) composer; **composition** *nf* composition; (*Scol*) test

composter [kɔ̃pɔste] *vt* (*billet*) to punch

- **COMPOSTER**
-
- In France you have to punch your
- ticket on the platform to validate it
- before getting onto the train.

compote [kɔ̃pɔt] *nf* stewed fruit *no pl*; **compote de pommes** stewed apples

compréhensible [kɔ̃pʀeɑ̃sibl] *adj* comprehensible; (*attitude*) understandable

compréhensif, -ive [kɔ̃pʀeɑ̃sif, iv] *adj* understanding

| Attention à ne pas traduire *compréhensif* par *comprehensive*.

comprendre [kɔ̃pʀɑ̃dʀ] *vt* to understand; (*se composer de*) to comprise, consist of

compresse [kɔ̃pʀɛs] *nf* compress

comprimé [kɔ̃pʀime] *nm* tablet

compris, e [kɔ̃pʀi, iz] *pp de* **comprendre** ▷ *adj* (*inclus*) included; **~ entre** (*situé*) contained between; **l'électricité ~e/non ~e, y/non ~ l'électricité** including/excluding electricity; **100 euros tout ~** 100 euros all inclusive *ou* all-in

comptabilité [kɔ̃tabilite] *nf* (*activité*) accounting, accountancy; (*comptes*) accounts *pl*, books *pl*; (*service*) accounts office

comptable [kɔ̃tabl] *nm/f* accountant

comptant [kɔ̃tɑ̃] *adv*: **payer ~** to pay cash; **acheter ~** to buy for cash

compte [kɔ̃t] *nm* count; (*total, montant*) count, (*right*) number; (*bancaire, facture*) account; **comptes** *nmpl* (*Finance*) accounts, books; (*fig*) explanation *sg*; **en fin de ~** all things considered; **s'en tirer à bon ~** to get off lightly; **pour le ~ de** on behalf of; **pour son propre ~** for one's own benefit; **régler un ~** (*s'acquitter de qch*) to settle an account; (*se venger*) to get one's own back; **rendre des ~s à qn** (*fig*) to be answerable to sb; **tenir ~ de** to take account of; **travailler à son ~** to work for oneself; **rendre ~ (à qn) de qch** to give (sb) an account of sth; *voir aussi* **rendre**; **compte à rebours** countdown; **compte courant** current account; **compte rendu** account, report; (*de film, livre*) review; **compte-gouttes** *nm inv* dropper

compter [kɔ̃te] *vt* to count; (*facturer*) to charge for; (*avoir à son actif, comporter*) to have; (*prévoir*) to allow, reckon; (*penser, espérer*): **~ réussir** to expect to succeed ▷ *vi* to count; (*être économe*) to economize; (*figurer*): **~ parmi** to be *ou* rank among; **~ sur** to count (up)on;

~ avec qch/qn to reckon with *ou* take account of sth/sb; **sans ~ que** besides which
compteur [kɔ̃tœʀ] *nm* meter; **compteur de vitesse** speedometer
comptine [kɔ̃tin] *nf* nursery rhyme
comptoir [kɔ̃twaʀ] *nm* (*de magasin*) counter; (*bar*) bar
con, ne [kɔ̃, kɔn] (*fam!*) *adj* damned *ou* bloody (*BRIT*) stupid (*!*)
concentrer [kɔ̃sɑ̃tʀe] *vt* to concentrate; **se concentrer** *vi* to concentrate
concerner [kɔ̃sɛʀne] *vt* to concern; **en ce qui me concerne** as far as I am concerned
concert [kɔ̃sɛʀ] *nm* concert; **de ~** (*décider*) unanimously
concessionnaire [kɔ̃sesjɔnɛʀ] *nm/f* agent, dealer
concevoir [kɔ̃s(ə)vwaʀ] *vt* (*idée, projet*) to conceive (of); (*comprendre*) to understand; (*enfant*) to conceive; **bien/mal conçu** well-/badly-designed
concierge [kɔ̃sjɛʀʒ] *nm/f* caretaker
concis, e [kɔ̃si, iz] *adj* concise
conclure [kɔ̃klyʀ] *vt* to conclude; **conclusion** *nf* conclusion
conçois *etc* [kɔ̃swa] *vb voir* **concevoir**
concombre [kɔ̃kɔ̃bʀ] *nm* cucumber
concours [kɔ̃kuʀ] *nm* competition; (*Scol*) competitive examination; (*assistance*) aid, help; **concours de circonstances** combination of circumstances; **concours hippique** horse show
concret, -ète [kɔ̃kʀɛ, ɛt] *adj* concrete
conçu, e [kɔ̃sy] *pp de* **concevoir**
concubinage [kɔ̃kybinaʒ] *nm* (*Jur*) cohabitation
concurrence [kɔ̃kyʀɑ̃s] *nf* competition; **faire ~ à** to be in competition with; **jusqu'à ~ de** up to
concurrent, e [kɔ̃kyʀɑ̃, ɑ̃t] *nm/f* (*Sport, Écon etc*) competitor; (*Scol*) candidate
condamner [kɔ̃dane] *vt* (*blâmer*) to condemn; (*Jur*) to sentence; (*porte,

ouverture*) to fill in, block up; **~ qn à 2 ans de prison** to sentence sb to 2 years' imprisonment
condensation [kɔ̃dɑ̃sasjɔ̃] *nf* condensation
condition [kɔ̃disjɔ̃] *nf* condition; **conditions** *nfpl* (*tarif, prix*) terms; (*circonstances*) conditions; **sans ~s** unconditionally; **à ~ de ou que** provided that; **conditionnel, le** *nm* conditional (tense)
conditionnement [kɔ̃disjɔnmɑ̃] *nm* (*emballage*) packaging
condoléances [kɔ̃dɔleɑ̃s] *nfpl* condolences
conducteur, -trice [kɔ̃dyktœʀ, tʀis] *nm/f* driver ▷ *nm* (*Élec etc*) conductor
conduire [kɔ̃dɥiʀ] *vt* to drive; (*délégation, troupeau*) to lead; **se conduire** *vi* to behave; **~ à** to lead to; **~ qn quelque part** to take sb somewhere; to drive sb somewhere
conduite [kɔ̃dɥit] *nf* (*comportement*) behaviour; (*d'eau, de gaz*) pipe; **sous la ~ de** led by
confection [kɔ̃fɛksjɔ̃] *nf* (*fabrication*) making; (*Couture*): **la ~** the clothing industry
conférence [kɔ̃feʀɑ̃s] *nf* conference; (*exposé*) lecture; **conférence de presse** press conference
confesser [kɔ̃fese] *vt* to confess; **confession** *nf* confession; (*culte: catholique etc*) denomination
confetti [kɔ̃feti] *nm* confetti *no pl*
confiance [kɔ̃fjɑ̃s] *nf* (*en l'honnêteté de qn*) confidence, trust; (*en la valeur de qch*) faith; **avoir ~ en** to have confidence *ou* faith in, trust; **faire ~ à qn** to trust sb; **mettre qn en ~** to win sb's trust; **confiance en soi** self-confidence
confiant, e [kɔ̃fjɑ̃, jɑ̃t] *adj* confident; trusting
confidence [kɔ̃fidɑ̃s] *nf* confidence; **confidentiel, le** *adj* confidential
confier [kɔ̃fje] *vt*: **~ à qn** (*objet, travail*) to entrust to sb; (*secret, pensée*) to

confide to sb; **se ~ à qn** to confide in sb
confirmation [kɔ̃fiʀmasjɔ̃] *nf*
confirmation
confirmer [kɔ̃fiʀme] *vt* to confirm
confiserie [kɔ̃fizʀi] *nf (magasin)*
confectioner's *ou* sweet shop;
confiseries *nfpl (bonbons)*
confectionery *sg*
confisquer [kɔ̃fiske] *vt* to confiscate
confit, e [kɔ̃fi, it] *adj*: **fruits ~s**
crystallized fruits; **confit d'oie** *nm*
conserve of goose
confiture [kɔ̃fityʀ] *nf* jam
conflit [kɔ̃fli] *nm* conflict
confondre [kɔ̃fɔ̃dʀ] *vt (jumeaux, faits)*
to confuse, mix up; *(témoin, menteur)* to
confound; **se confondre** *vi* to merge;
se ~ en excuses to apologize profusely
conforme [kɔ̃fɔʀm] *adj*: **~ à** *(loi, règle)*
in accordance with; **conformément**
adv: **conformément à** in accordance
with; **conformer** *vt*: **se conformer à**
to conform to
confort [kɔ̃fɔʀ] *nm* comfort; **tout ~**
(Comm) with all modern conveniences;
confortable *adj* comfortable
confronter [kɔ̃fʀɔ̃te] *vt* to confront
confus, e [kɔ̃fy, yz] *adj (vague)*
confused; *(embarrassé)* embarrassed;
confusion *nf (voir confus)* confusion;
embarrassment; *(voir confondre)*
confusion, mixing up
congé [kɔ̃ʒe] *nm (vacances)* holiday; **en
~** on holiday; **semaine/jour de ~** week/
day off; **prendre ~ de qn** to take one's
leave of sb; **donner son ~ à** to give in
one's notice to; **congé de maladie** sick
leave; **congé de maternité** maternity
leave; **congés payés** paid holiday
congédier [kɔ̃ʒedje] *vt* to dismiss
congélateur [kɔ̃ʒelatœʀ] *nm* freezer
congeler [kɔ̃ʒ(ə)le] *vt* to freeze; **les
produits congelés** frozen foods
congestion [kɔ̃ʒɛstjɔ̃] *nf* congestion
Congo [kɔ̃o] *nm*: **le ~** Congo, the
Democratic Republic of the Congo
congrès [kɔ̃gʀɛ] *nm* congress
conifère [kɔnifɛʀ] *nm* conifer

conjoint, e [kɔ̃ʒwɛ̃, wɛ̃t] *adj* joint
▷ *nm/f* spouse
conjonctivite [kɔ̃ʒɔ̃ktivit] *nf*
conjunctivitis
conjoncture [kɔ̃ʒɔ̃ktyʀ] *nf*
circumstances *pl*; **la ~ actuelle** the
present (economic) situation
conjugaison [kɔ̃ʒygɛzɔ̃] *nf (Ling)*
conjugation
connaissance [kɔnɛsɑ̃s] *nf (savoir)*
knowledge *no pl*; *(personne connue)*
acquaintance; **être sans ~** to be
unconscious; **perdre/reprendre ~** to
lose/regain consciousness; **à ma/sa
~** to (the best of) my/his knowledge;
faire la ~ de qn to meet sb
connaisseur, -euse [kɔnɛsœʀ, øz]
nm/f connoisseur
connaître [kɔnɛtʀ] *vt* to know;
(éprouver) to experience; *(avoir: succès)*
to have, enjoy; **~ de nom/vue** to know
by name/sight; **ils se sont connus à
Genève** they (first) met in Geneva; **s'y
~ en qch** to know a lot about sth
connecter [kɔnɛkte] *vt* to connect; **se
~ à Internet** to log onto the Internet
connerie [kɔnʀi] *(fam!) nf* stupid thing
(to do/say)
connexion [kɔnɛksjɔ̃] *nf* connection
connu, e [kɔny] *adj (célèbre)* well-
known
conquérir [kɔ̃keʀiʀ] *vt* to conquer;
conquête *nf* conquest
consacrer [kɔ̃sakʀe] *vt (employer)* to
devote, dedicate; *(Rel)* to consecrate; **se
~ à qch** to dedicate *ou* devote o.s. to sth
conscience [kɔ̃sjɑ̃s] *nf* conscience;
avoir/prendre ~ de to be/become
aware of; **perdre ~** to lose
consciousness; **avoir bonne/
mauvaise ~** to have a clear/guilty
conscience; **consciencieux, -euse**
adj conscientious; **conscient, e** *adj*
conscious
consécutif, -ive [kɔ̃sekytif, iv] *adj*
consecutive; **~ à** following upon
conseil [kɔ̃sɛj] *nm (avis)* piece of
advice; *(assemblée)* council; **des ~s**

advice; **prendre ~ (auprès de qn)** to take advice (from sb); **conseil d'administration** board (of directors); **conseil des ministres** ≈ the Cabinet; **conseil municipal** town council

conseiller, -ère [kɔ̃seje, ɛʀ] nm/f adviser ▷ vt (personne) to advise; (méthode, action) to recommend, advise; **~ à qn de** to advise sb to; **pouvez-vous me ~ un bon restaurant?** can you suggest a good restaurant?

consentement [kɔ̃sɑ̃tmɑ̃] nm consent

consentir [kɔ̃sɑ̃tiʀ] vt to agree, consent

conséquence [kɔ̃sekɑ̃s] nf consequence; **en ~** (donc) consequently; (de façon appropriée) accordingly; **conséquent, e** adj logical, rational; (fam: important) substantial; **par conséquent** consequently

conservateur, -trice [kɔ̃sɛʀvatœʀ, tʀis] nm/f (Pol) conservative; (de musée) curator ▷ nm (pour aliments) preservative

conservatoire [kɔ̃sɛʀvatwaʀ] nm academy

conserve [kɔ̃sɛʀv] nf (gén pl) canned ou tinned (BRIT) food; **en ~** canned, tinned (BRIT)

conserver [kɔ̃sɛʀve] vt (faculté) to retain, keep; (amis, livres) to keep; (préserver, Culin) to preserve

considérable [kɔ̃sideʀabl] adj considerable, significant, extensive

considération [kɔ̃sideʀasjɔ̃] nf consideration; (estime) esteem

considérer [kɔ̃sideʀe] vt to consider; **~ qch comme** to regard sth as

consigne [kɔ̃siɲ] nf (de gare) left luggage (office) (BRIT), checkroom (US); (ordre, instruction) instructions pl; **consigne automatique** left-luggage locker

consister [kɔ̃siste] vi: **~ en/à faire** to consist of/in doing

consoler [kɔ̃sɔle] vt to console

consommateur, -trice [kɔ̃sɔmatœʀ, tʀis] nm/f (Écon) consumer; (dans un café) customer

consommation [kɔ̃sɔmasjɔ̃] nf (boisson) drink; (Écon) consumption; **de ~** (biens, sociétés) consumer cpd

consommer [kɔ̃sɔme] vt (suj: personne) to eat ou drink, consume; (: voiture, machine) to use, consume; (mariage) to consummate ▷ vi (dans un café) to (have a) drink

consonne [kɔ̃sɔn] nf consonant

constamment [kɔ̃stamɑ̃] adv constantly

constant, e [kɔ̃stɑ̃, ɑ̃t] adj constant; (personne) steadfast

constat [kɔ̃sta] nm (de police, d'accident) report; **~ (à l')amiable** jointly-agreed statement for insurance purposes; **~ d'échec** acknowledgement of failure

constatation [kɔ̃statasjɔ̃] nf (observation) (observed) fact, observation

constater [kɔ̃state] vt (remarquer) to note; (Admin, Jur: attester) to certify

consterner [kɔ̃stɛʀne] vt to dismay

constipé, e [kɔ̃stipe] adj constipated

constitué, e [kɔ̃stitɥe] adj: **~ de** made up ou composed of

constituer [kɔ̃stitɥe] vt (équipe) to set up; (dossier, collection) to put together; (suj: éléments: composer) to make up, constitute; (représenter, être) to constitute; **se ~ prisonnier** to give o.s. up

constructeur, -trice [kɔ̃stʀyktœʀ, tʀis] nm/f manufacturer, builder

constructif, -ive [kɔ̃stʀyktif, iv] adj constructive

construction [kɔ̃stʀyksjɔ̃] nf construction, building

construire [kɔ̃stʀɥiʀ] vt to build, construct

consul [kɔ̃syl] nm consul; **consulat** nm consulate

consultant [kɔ̃syltɑ̃] adj, nm consultant

consultation [kɔ̃syltasjɔ̃] nf consultation; **heures de ~** (Méd) surgery (BRIT) ou office (US) hours

consulter [kɔsylte] *vt* to consult ▷ *vi* (*médecin*) to hold surgery (BRIT), be in (the office) (US)

contact [kɔtakt] *nm* contact; **au ~ de** (*air, peau*) on contact with; (*gens*) through contact with; **mettre/ couper le ~** (*Auto*) to switch on/off the ignition; **entrer en** ou **prendre ~ avec** to get in touch ou contact with; **contacter** *vt* to contact, get in touch with

contagieux, -euse [kɔtaʒjø, jøz] *adj* infectious; (*par le contact*) contagious

contaminer [kɔtamine] *vt* to contaminate

conte [kɔt] *nm* tale; **conte de fées** fairy tale

contempler [kɔtɑple] *vt* to contemplate, gaze at

contemporain, e [kɔtɑpɔrɛ̃, ɛn] *adj, nm/f* contemporary

contenir [kɔt(ə)nir] *vt* to contain; (*avoir une capacité de*) to hold

content, e [kɔtɑ, ɑt] *adj* pleased, glad; **~ de** pleased with; **contenter** *vt* to satisfy, please; **se contenter de** to content o.s. with

contenu [kɔt(ə)ny] *nm* (*d'un récipient*) contents *pl*; (*d'un texte*) content

conter [kɔte] *vt* to recount, relate

conteste [kɔtɛst]: **sans ~** *adv* unquestionably, indisputably; **contester** *vt* to question ▷ *vi* (*Pol, gén*) rebel (against established authority)

contexte [kɔtɛkst] *nm* context

continent [kɔtinɑ] *nm* continent

continu, e [kɔtiny] *adj* continuous; **faire la journée ~e** to work without taking a full lunch break; **(courant) continu** direct current, DC

continuel, le [kɔtinɥɛl] *adj* (*qui se répète*) constant, continual; (*continu*) continuous

continuer [kɔtinɥe] *vt* (*travail, voyage etc*) to continue (with), carry on (with), go on (with); (*prolonger: alignement, rue*) to continue ▷ *vi* (*vie, bruit*) to continue,

go on; **~ à** ou **de faire** to go on ou continue doing

contourner [kɔturne] *vt* to go round; (*difficulté*) to get round

contraceptif, -ive [kɔtraseptif, iv] *adj, nm* contraceptive; **contraception** *nf* contraception

contracté, e [kɔtrakte] *adj* tense

contracter [kɔtrakte] *vt* (*muscle etc*) to tense, contract; (*maladie, dette*) to contract; (*assurance*) to take out; **se contracter** *vi* (*muscles*) to contract

contractuel, le [kɔtraktɥɛl] *nm/f* (*agent*) traffic warden

contradiction [kɔtradiksjɔ] *nf* contradiction; **contradictoire** *adj* contradictory, conflicting

contraignant, e [kɔtrɛɲɑ, ɑt] *adj* restricting

contraindre [kɔtrɛdr] *vt*: **~ qn à faire** to compel sb to do; **contrainte** *nf* constraint

contraire [kɔtrɛr] *adj, nm* opposite; **~ à** contrary to; **au ~** on the contrary

contrarier [kɔtrarje] *vt* (*personne: irriter*) to annoy; (*fig: projets*) to thwart, frustrate; **contrariété** *nf* annoyance

contraste [kɔtrast] *nm* contrast

contrat [kɔtra] *nm* contract

contravention [kɔtravɑsjɔ] *nf* parking ticket

contre [kɔtr] *prép* against; (*en échange*) (in exchange) for; **par ~** on the other hand

contrebande [kɔtrəbɑd] *nf* (*trafic*) contraband, smuggling; (*marchandise*) contraband, smuggled goods *pl*; **faire la ~ de** to smuggle

contrebas [kɔtrəba]: **en ~** *adv* (down) below

contrebasse [kɔtrəbas] *nf* (double) bass

contre...: **contrecoup** *nm* repercussions *pl*; **contredire** *vt* (*personne*) to contradict; (*faits*) to refute

contrefaçon [kɔtrəfasɔ] *nf* forgery

contre...: **contre-indication** (*pl* **contre-indications**) *nf* (*Méd*) contraindication; **"contre-indication en cas d'eczéma"** "should not be used by people with eczema"; **contre-indiqué, e** adj (Méd) contraindicated; (déconseillé) unadvisable, ill-advised

contremaître [kɔ̃trəmɛtr] nm foreman

contre-plaqué [kɔ̃trəplake] nm plywood

contresens [kɔ̃trəsɑ̃s] nm (erreur) misinterpretation; (de traduction) mistranslation; **à ~** the wrong way

contretemps [kɔ̃trətɑ̃] nm hitch; **à ~** (fig) at an inopportune moment

contribuer [kɔ̃tribɥe] : **~ à** vt to contribute towards; **contribution** nf contribution; **mettre à contribution** to call upon; **contributions directes/indirectes** direct/indirect taxation

contrôle [kɔ̃trol] nm checking no pl, check; (des prix) monitoring, control; (test) test, examination; **perdre le ~ de** (véhicule) to lose control of; **contrôle continu** (Scol) continuous assessment; **contrôle d'identité** identity check

contrôler [kɔ̃trole] vt (vérifier) to check; (surveiller: opérations) to supervise; (: prix) to monitor, control; (maîtriser, Comm: firme) to control; **contrôleur, -euse** nm/f (de train) (ticket) inspector; (de bus) (bus) conductor(-tress)

controversé, e [kɔ̃trɔvɛrse] adj (personnage, question) controversial

contusion [kɔ̃tyzjɔ̃] nf bruise, contusion

convaincre [kɔ̃vɛ̃kr] vt: **~ qn (de qch)** to convince sb (of sth); **~ qn (de faire)** to persuade sb (to do)

convalescence [kɔ̃valesɑ̃s] nf convalescence

convenable [kɔ̃vnabl] adj suitable; (assez bon, respectable) decent

convenir [kɔ̃vnir] vi to be suitable; **~ à** to suit; **~ de** (bien-fondé de qch) to admit (to), acknowledge; (date, somme etc) to agree upon; **~ que** (admettre) to admit that; **~ de faire** to agree to do

convention [kɔ̃vɑ̃sjɔ̃] nf convention; **conventions** nfpl (convenances) convention sg; **convention collective** (Écon) collective agreement; **conventionné, e** adj (Admin) applying charges laid down by the state

convenu, e [kɔ̃vny] pp de **convenir** ▷ adj agreed

conversation [kɔ̃vɛrsasjɔ̃] nf conversation

convertir [kɔ̃vɛrtir] vt: **~ qn (à)** to convert sb (to); **se convertir (à)** to be converted (to); **~ qch en** to convert sth into

conviction [kɔ̃viksjɔ̃] nf conviction

convienne etc [kɔ̃vjɛn] vb voir **convenir**

convivial, e, -aux [kɔ̃vivjal, jo] adj (Inform) user-friendly

convocation [kɔ̃vɔkasjɔ̃] nf (document) notification to attend; (: Jur) summons sg

convoquer [kɔ̃vɔke] vt (assemblée) to convene; (subordonné) to summon; (candidat) to ask to attend

coopération [kɔɔperasjɔ̃] nf co-operation; (Admin): **la C~** ≈ Voluntary Service Overseas (BRIT), ≈ Peace Corps (US)

coopérer [kɔɔpere] vi: **~ (à)** to co-operate (in)

coordonné, e [kɔɔrdɔne] adj coordinated; **coordonnées** nfpl (adresse etc) address and telephone number

coordonner [kɔɔrdɔne] vt to coordinate

copain [kɔpɛ̃] (fam) nm mate, pal; (petit ami) boyfriend

copie [kɔpi] nf copy; (Scol) script, paper; **copier** vt, vi to copy; **copier coller** (Comput) copy and paste; **copier sur** to copy from; **copieur** nm (photo)copier

copieux, -euse [kɔpjø, jøz] adj copious

copine [kɔpin] (fam) nf mate, pal; (petite amie) girlfriend

coq [kɔk] nm cock, rooster

coque [kɔk] nf (de noix, mollusque) shell; (de bateau) hull; **à la ~** (Culin) (soft-)boiled

coquelicot [kɔkliko] nm poppy

coqueluche [kɔklyʃ] nf whooping-cough

coquet, te [kɔkɛ, ɛt] adj appearance-conscious; (logement) smart, charming

coquetier [kɔk(ə)tje] nm egg-cup

coquillage [kɔkijaʒ] nm (mollusque) shellfish inv; (coquille) shell

coquille [kɔkij] nf shell; (Typo) misprint; **coquille St Jacques** scallop

coquin, e [kɔkɛ̃, in] adj mischievous, roguish; (polisson) naughty

cor [kɔr] nm (Mus) horn; (Méd): **~ (au pied)** corn

corail, -aux [kɔraj, o] nm coral no pl

Coran [kɔrɑ̃] nm: **le ~** the Koran

corbeau, x [kɔrbo] nm crow

corbeille [kɔrbɛj] nf basket; **corbeille à papier** waste paper basket ou bin

corde [kɔrd] nf rope; (de violon, raquette) string; **usé jusqu'à la ~** threadbare; **corde à linge** washing ou clothes line; **corde à sauter** skipping rope; **cordes vocales** vocal cords; **cordée** nf (d'alpinistes) rope, roped party

cordialement [kɔrdjalmɑ̃] adv (formule épistolaire) (kind) regards

cordon [kɔrdɔ̃] nm cord, string; **cordon de police** police cordon; **cordon ombilical** umbilical cord

cordonnerie [kɔrdɔnri] nf shoe repairer's (shop); **cordonnier** nm shoe repairer

Corée [kɔre] nf: **la ~ du Sud/du Nord** South/North Korea

coriace [kɔrjas] adj tough

corne [kɔrn] nf horn; (de cerf) antler

cornée [kɔrne] nf cornea

corneille [kɔrnɛj] nf crow

cornemuse [kɔrnəmyz] nf bagpipes pl

cornet [kɔrnɛ] nm (paper) cone; (de glace) cornet, cone

corniche [kɔrniʃ] nf (route) coast road

cornichon [kɔrniʃɔ̃] nm gherkin

Cornouailles [kɔrnwaj] nf Cornwall

corporel, le [kɔrpɔrɛl] adj bodily; (punition) corporal

corps [kɔr] nm body; **à ~ perdu** headlong; **prendre ~** to take shape; **corps électoral** the electorate; **corps enseignant** the teaching profession

correct, e [kɔrɛkt] adj correct; (fam: acceptable: salaire, hôtel) reasonable, decent; **correcteur, -trice** nm/f (Scol) examiner; **correction** nf (voir corriger) correction; (voir correct) correctness; (coups) thrashing

correspondance [kɔrɛspɔ̃dɑ̃s] nf correspondence; (de train, d'avion) connection; **cours par ~** correspondence course; **vente par ~** mail-order business

correspondant, e [kɔrɛspɔ̃dɑ̃, ɑ̃t] nm/f correspondent; (Tél) person phoning (ou being phoned)

correspondre [kɔrɛspɔ̃dr] vi to correspond, tally; **~ à** to correspond to; **~ avec qn** to correspond with sb

corrida [kɔrida] nf bullfight

corridor [kɔridɔr] nm corridor

corrigé [kɔriʒe] nm (Scol: d'exercice) correct version

corriger [kɔriʒe] vt (devoir) to correct; (punir) to thrash; **~ qn de** (défaut) to cure sb of

corrompre [kɔrɔ̃pr] vt to corrupt; (acheter: témoin etc) to bribe

corruption [kɔrypsjɔ̃] nf corruption; (de témoins) bribery

corse [kɔrs] adj, nm/f Corsican ▷ nf: **la C~** Corsica

corsé, e [kɔrse] adj (café) full-flavoured; (sauce) spicy; (problème) tough

cortège [kɔrtɛʒ] nm procession

cortisone [kɔrtizɔn] nf cortisone

corvée [kɔrve] nf chore, drudgery no pl

cosmétique [kɔsmetik] nm beauty care product

cosmopolite [kɔsmɔpɔlit] adj cosmopolitan

costaud, e [kɔsto, od] (fam) adj strong, sturdy

costume [kɔstym] *nm* (*d'homme*) suit; (*de théâtre*) costume; **costumé, e** *adj* dressed up; **bal costumé** fancy dress ball

cote [kɔt] *nf* (*en Bourse*) quotation; **cote d'alerte** danger *ou* flood level; **cote de popularité** (popularity) rating

côte [kot] *nf* (*rivage*) coast(line); (*pente*) hill; (*Anat*) rib; (*d'un tricot, tissu*) rib, ribbing *no pl*; **~ à ~** side by side; **la Côte (d'Azur)** the (French) Riviera

côté [kote] *nm* (*gén*) side; (*direction*) way, direction; **de chaque ~ (de)** on each side (of); **de tous les ~s** from all directions; **de quel ~ est-il parti?** which way did he go?; **de ce/de l'autre ~** this/the other way; **du ~ de** (*provenance*) from; (*direction*) towards; (*proximité*) near; **de ~** (*regarder*) sideways; **mettre qch de ~** to put sth aside; **mettre de l'argent de ~** to save some money; **à ~** (*right*) nearby; (*voisins*) next door; **à ~ de** beside, next to; (*en comparaison*) compared to; **être aux ~s de** to be by the side of

Côte d'Ivoire [kotdivwaʀ] *nf*: **la Côte d'Ivoire** Côte d'Ivoire, the Ivory Coast

côtelette [kotlɛt] *nf* chop

côtier, -ière [kotje, jɛʀ] *adj* coastal

cotisation [kɔtizasjɔ̃] *nf* subscription, dues *pl*; (*pour une pension*) contributions *pl*

cotiser [kɔtize] *vi*: **~ (à)** to pay contributions (to); **se cotiser** *vi* to club together

coton [kɔtɔ̃] *nm* cotton; **coton hydrophile** cotton wool (BRIT), absorbent cotton (US); **Coton-tige®** *nm* cotton bud

cou [ku] *nm* neck

couchant [kuʃɑ̃] *adj*: **soleil ~** setting sun

couche [kuʃ] *nf* layer; (*de peinture, vernis*) coat; (*de bébé*) nappy (BRIT), diaper (US); **couches sociales** social levels *ou* strata

couché, e [kuʃe] *adj* lying down; (*au lit*) in bed

coucher [kuʃe] *vt* (*personne*) to put to bed; (: *loger*) to put up; (*objet*) to lay on its side ▷ *vi* to sleep; **~ avec qn** to sleep with sb; **se coucher** *vi* (*pour dormir*) to go to bed; (*pour se reposer*) to lie down; (*soleil*) to set; **coucher de soleil** sunset

couchette [kuʃɛt] *nf* couchette; (*pour voyageur, sur bateau*) berth

coucou [kuku] *nm* cuckoo

coude [kud] *nm* (*Anat*) elbow; (*de tuyau, de la route*) bend; **~ à ~** shoulder to shoulder, side by side

coudre [kudʀ] *vt* (*bouton*) to sew on ▷ *vi* to sew

couette [kwɛt] *nf* duvet, quilt; **couettes** *nfpl* (*cheveux*) bunches

couffin [kufɛ̃] *nm* Moses basket

couler [kule] *vi* to flow, run; (*fuir: stylo, récipient*) to leak; (*nez: sombrer: bateau*) to sink ▷ *vt* (*cloche, sculpture*) to cast; (*bateau*) to sink; (*faire échouer: personne*) to bring down

couleur [kulœʀ] *nf* colour (BRIT), color (US); (*Cartes*) suit; **film/télévision en ~s** colo(u)r film/television; **de ~** (*homme, femme: vieilli*) colo(u)red

couleuvre [kulœvʀ] *nf* grass snake

coulisses [kulis] *nfpl* (*Théâtre*) wings; (*fig*): **dans les ~** behind the scenes

couloir [kulwaʀ] *nm* corridor, passage; (*d'avion*) aisle; (*de bus*) gangway; **~ aérien/de navigation** air/shipping lane

coup [ku] *nm* (*heurt, choc*) knock; (*affectif*) blow, shock; (*agressif*) blow; (*avec arme à feu*) shot; (*de l'horloge*) stroke; (*tennis, golf*) stroke; (*boxe*) blow; (*fam: fois*) time; **donner un ~ de balai** to give the floor a sweep; **boire un ~** (*fam*) to have a drink; **être dans le ~** (*impliqué*) to be in on it; (*à la page*) to be hip *ou* trendy; **du ~ ...** as a result; **d'un seul ~** (*subitement*) suddenly; (*à la fois*) at one go; **du premier ~** first time; **du même ~** at the same time; **à tous les ~s** (*fam*) every time; **tenir le ~** to hold out; **après ~** afterwards; **à ~ sûr** definitely, without fail; **~ sur** in quick succession; **sur le ~** outright; **sous le ~ de** (surprise etc) under the influence of; **coup de chance** stroke of luck; **coup de coude** nudge (with the elbow); **coup de couteau** stab (of a knife); **coup d'envoi** kick-off; **coup d'essai** first attempt; **coup d'État** coup; **coup de feu** shot; **coup de filet** (Police) haul; **coup de foudre** (fig) love at first sight; **coup de frein** (sharp) braking no pl; **coup de grâce** coup de grâce, death blow; **coup de main:** **donner un coup de main à qn** to give sb a (helping) hand; **coup d'œil** glance; **coup de pied** kick; **coup de poing** punch; **coup de soleil** sunburn no pl; **coup de sonnette** ring of the bell; **coup de téléphone** phone call; **coup de tête** (fig) (sudden) impulse; **coup de théâtre** (fig) dramatic turn of events; **coup de tonnerre** clap of thunder; **coup de vent** gust of wind; **en coup de vent** (rapidement) in a tearing hurry; **coup franc** free kick

coupable [kupabl] adj guilty ▷ nm/f (gén) culprit; (Jur) guilty party

coupe [kup] nf (verre) goblet; (à fruits) dish; (Sport) cup; (de cheveux, de vêtement) cut; (graphique, plan) (cross) section

couper [kupe] vt to cut; (retrancher) to cut (out); (route, courant) to cut off; (appétit) to take away; (vin à table) to dilute ▷ vi to cut; (prendre un raccourci) to take a short-cut; **se couper** vi (se blesser) to cut o.s.; **~ la parole à qn** to cut sb short; **nous avons été coupés** we've been cut off

couple [kupl] nm couple

couplet [kuplɛ] nm verse

coupole [kupɔl] nf dome

coupon [kupɔ̃] nm (ticket) coupon; (reste de tissu) remnant

coupure [kupyʀ] nf cut; (billet de banque) note; (de journal) cutting; **coupure de courant** power cut

cour [kuʀ] nf (de ferme, jardin) (court)yard; (d'immeuble) back yard; (Jur,

royale) court; **faire la ~ à qn** to court sb; **cour d'assises** court of assizes; **cour de récréation** playground

courage [kuʀaʒ] nm courage, bravery; **courageux, -euse** adj brave, courageous

couramment [kuʀamɑ̃] adv commonly; (parler) fluently

courant, e [kuʀɑ̃, ɑ̃t] adj (fréquent) common; (Comm, gén: normal) standard; (en cours) current ▷ nm current; (fig) movement; (: d'opinion) trend; **être au ~ (de)** (fait, nouvelle) to know (about); **mettre qn au ~ (de)** (nouveau travail etc) to teach sb the basics (of); **se tenir au ~ (de)** (techniques etc) to keep o.s. up-to-date (on); **dans le ~ de** (pendant) in the course of; **le 10 ~** (Comm) the 10th inst.; **courant d'air** draught; **courant électrique** (electric) current, power

courbature [kuʀbatyʀ] nf ache

courbe [kuʀb] adj curved ▷ nf curve

coureur, -euse [kuʀœʀ, øz] nm/f (Sport) runner (ou driver); (péj) womanizer; manhunter

courge [kuʀʒ] nf (Culin) marrow; **courgette** nf courgette (BRIT), zucchini (US)

courir [kuʀiʀ] vi to run ▷ vt (Sport: épreuve) to compete in; (risque) to run; (danger) to face; **~ les magasins** to go round the shops; **le bruit court que** the rumour is going round that

couronne [kuʀɔn] nf crown; (de fleurs) wreath, circlet

courons etc [kuʀɔ̃] vb voir **courir**

courriel [kuʀjɛl] nm e-mail

courrier [kuʀje] nm mail, post; (lettres à écrire) letters pl; **est-ce que j'ai du ~?** are there any letters for me?; **courrier électronique** e-mail

⬛ Attention à ne pas traduire courrier par le mot anglais courier.

courroie [kuʀwa] nf strap; (Tech) belt

courrons etc [kuʀɔ̃] vb voir **courir**

cours [kuʀ] nm (leçon) class; (: particulier) lesson; (série de leçons, *cheminement*) course; (*écoulement*) flow; (*Comm: de devises*) rate; (: *de denrées*) price; **donner libre ~ à** to give free expression to; **avoir ~** (*Scol*) to have a class *ou* lecture; **en ~** (*année*) current; (*travaux*) in progress; **en ~ de route** on the way; **au ~ de** in the course of, during; **le ~ de change** the exchange rate; **cours d'eau** waterway; **cours du soir** night school

course [kuʀs] *nf* running; (*Sport: épreuve*) race; (*d'un taxi*) journey, trip; (*commission*) errand; **courses** *nfpl* (*achats*) shopping *sg*; **faire des ~s** to do some shopping

court, e [kuʀ, kuʀt(ə)] *adj* short ▷ *adv* short ▷ *nm:* **~ (de tennis)** (tennis) court; **à ~ de** short of; **prendre qn de ~** to catch sb unawares; **court-circuit** *nm* short-circuit

courtoisie [kuʀtwazi] *nf* courtesy

couru, e [kuʀy] *pp de* **courir**

cousais *etc* [kuze] *vb voir* **coudre**

couscous [kuskus] *nm* couscous

cousin, e [kuzɛ̃, in] *nm/f* cousin

coussin [kusɛ̃] *nm* cushion

cousu, e [kuzy] *pp de* **coudre**

coût [ku] *nm* cost; **le ~ de la vie** the cost of living

couteau, x [kuto] *nm* knife

coûter [kute] *vt, vi* to cost; **combien ça coûte?** how much is it?, what does it cost?; **ça coûte trop cher** it's too expensive; **coûte que coûte** at all costs; **coûteux, -euse** *adj* costly, expensive

coutume [kutym] *nf* custom

couture [kutyʀ] *nf* sewing; (*profession*) dressmaking; (*points*) seam; **couturier** *nm* fashion designer; **couturière** *nf* dressmaker

couvent [kuvɑ̃] *nm* (*de sœurs*) convent; (*de frères*) monastery

couver [kuve] *vt* to hatch; (*maladie*) to be coming down with ▷ *vi* (*feu*) to smoulder; (*révolte*) to be brewing

couvercle [kuvɛʀkl] *nm* lid; (*de bombe aérosol etc, qui se visse*) cap, top

couvert, e [kuvɛʀ, ɛʀt] *pp de* **couvrir** ▷ *adj* (*ciel*) overcast ▷ *nm* place setting; (*place à table*) place; **couverts** *nmpl* (*ustensiles*) cutlery *sg*; **~ de** covered with *ou* in; **mettre le ~** to lay the table

couverture [kuvɛʀtyʀ] *nf* blanket; (*de livre, assurance, fig*) cover; (*presse*) coverage

couvre-lit [kuvʀəli] *nm* bedspread

couvrir [kuvʀiʀ] *vt* to cover; **se couvrir** *vi* (*s'habiller*) to cover up; (*se coiffer*) to put on one's hat; (*ciel*) to cloud over

cow-boy [kɔbɔj] *nm* cowboy

crabe [kʀab] *nm* crab

cracher [kʀaʃe] *vi, vt* to spit

crachin [kʀaʃɛ̃] *nm* drizzle

craie [kʀɛ] *nf* chalk

craindre [kʀɛ̃dʀ] *vt* to fear, be afraid of; (*être sensible à: chaleur, froid*) to be easily damaged by

crainte [kʀɛ̃t] *nf* fear; **de ~ de/que** for fear of/that; **craintif, -ive** *adj* timid

crampe [kʀɑ̃p] *nf* cramp; **j'ai une ~ à la jambe** I've got cramp in my leg

cramponner [kʀɑ̃pɔne] *vb:* **se ~ (à)** to hang *ou* cling on (to)

cran [kʀɑ̃] *nm* (*entaille*) notch; (*de courroie*) hole; (*fam: courage*) guts *pl*

crâne [kʀɑn] *nm* skull

crapaud [kʀapo] *nm* toad

craquement [kʀakmɑ̃] *nm* crack, snap; (*du plancher*) creak, creaking *no pl*

craquer [kʀake] *vi* (*bois, plancher*) to creak; (*fil, branche*) to snap; (*couture*) to come apart; (*fig: accusé*) to break down; (: *fam*) to crack up ▷ *vt* (*allumette*) to strike; **j'ai craqué** (*fam*) I couldn't resist it

crasse [kʀas] *nf* grime, filth; **crasseux, -euse** *adj* grimy, filthy

cravache [kʀavaʃ] *nf* (riding) crop

cravate [kʀavat] *nf* tie

crawl [kʀol] *nm* crawl; **dos ~é** backstroke

crayon [kʀɛjɔ̃] *nm* pencil; **crayon à bille** ball-point pen; **crayon de couleur** crayon, colouring pencil; **crayon-feutre** (*pl* **crayons-feutres**) *nm* felt(-tip) pen

création [kʀeasjɔ̃] *nf* creation

crèche [kʀɛʃ] *nf* (*de Noël*) crib; (*garderie*) crèche, day nursery

crédit [kʀedi] *nm* (*gén*) credit; **crédits** *nmpl* (*fonds*) funds; **payer/acheter à ~** to pay/buy on credit *ou* on easy terms; **faire ~ à qn** to give sb credit; **créditer** *vt*: **créditer un compte (de)** to credit an account (with)

créer [kʀee] *vt* to create

crémaillère [kʀemajɛʀ] *nf*: **pendre la ~** to have a house-warming party

crème [kʀɛm] *nf* cream; (*entremets*) cream dessert ▷ *adj inv* cream(-coloured); **un (café) ~** ≈ a white coffee; **crème anglaise** (egg) custard; **crème Chantilly** whipped cream; **crème à raser** shaving cream; **crème solaire** suntan lotion

créneau, x [kʀeno] *nm* (*de fortification*) crenel(le); (*dans marché*) gap, niche; (*Auto*): **faire un ~** to reverse into a parking space (*between two cars alongside the kerb*)

crêpe [kʀɛp] *nf* (*galette*) pancake ▷ *nm* (*tissu*) crêpe; **crêperie** *nf* pancake shop *ou* restaurant

crépuscule [kʀepyskyl] *nm* twilight, dusk

cresson [kʀesɔ̃] *nm* watercress

creuser [kʀøze] *vt* (*trou, tunnel*) to dig; (*sol*) to dig a hole in; (*fig*) to go (deeply) into; **ça creuse** that gives you a real appetite; **se ~ la cervelle** (*fam*) to rack one's brains

creux, -euse [kʀø, kʀøz] *adj* hollow ▷ *nm* hollow; **heures creuses** slack periods; (*électricité, téléphone*) off-peak periods; **avoir un ~** (*fam*) to be hungry

crevaison [kʀəvɛzɔ̃] *nf* puncture

crevé, e [kʀəve] (*fam*) *adj* (*fatigué*) shattered (*BRIT*), exhausted

crever [kʀəve] *vt* (*ballon*) to burst ▷ *vi* (*pneu*) to burst; (*automobiliste*) to have a puncture (*BRIT*) *ou* a flat (tire) (*US*); (*fam*) to die

crevette [kʀəvɛt] *nf*: **~ (rose)** prawn;

crevette grise shrimp

cri [kʀi] *nm* cry, shout; (*d'animal: spécifique*) cry, call; **c'est le dernier ~** (*fig*) it's the latest fashion

criard, e [kʀijaʀ, kʀijaʀd] *adj* (*couleur*) garish, loud; (*voix*) yelling

cric [kʀik] *nm* (*Auto*) jack

crier [kʀije] *vi* (*pour appeler*) to shout, cry (out); (*de douleur etc*) to scream, yell ▷ *vt* (*injure*) to shout (out), yell (out)

crime [kʀim] *nm* crime; (*meurtre*) murder; **criminel, le** *nm/f* criminal; (*assassin*) murderer

crin [kʀɛ̃] *nm* (*de cheval*) hair *no pl*

crinière [kʀinjɛʀ] *nf* mane

crique [kʀik] *nf* creek, inlet

criquet [kʀikɛ] *nm* grasshopper

crise [kʀiz] *nf* crisis; (*Méd*) attack; (*: d'épilepsie*) fit; **piquer une ~ de nerfs** to go hysterical; **crise cardiaque** heart attack; **crise de foie**: **avoir une crise de foie** to have really bad indigestion

cristal, -aux [kʀistal, o] *nm* crystal

critère [kʀitɛʀ] *nm* criterion

critiquable [kʀitikabl] *adj* open to criticism

critique [kʀitik] *adj* critical ▷ *nm/f* (*de théâtre, musique*) critic ▷ *nf* criticism; (*Théâtre etc: article*) review

critiquer [kʀitike] *vt* (*dénigrer*) to criticize; (*évaluer*) to assess, examine (critically)

croate [kʀɔat] *adj* Croatian ▷ *nm/f*: **C~** Croat, Croatian

Croatie [kʀɔasi] *nf*: **la ~** Croatia

crochet [kʀɔʃɛ] *nm* hook; (*détour*) detour; (*Tricot: aiguille*) crochet hook; (*: technique*) crochet; **vivre aux ~s de qn** to live *ou* sponge off sb

crocodile [kʀɔkɔdil] *nm* crocodile

croire [kʀwaʀ] *vt* to believe; **se ~ fort** to think one is strong; **~ que** to believe *ou* think that; **~ à, ~ en** to believe in

croisade [kʀwazad] *nf* crusade

croisement [kʀwazmɑ̃] *nm* (*carrefour*) crossroads *sg*; (*Bio*) crossing; (*: résultat*) crossbreed

croiser [kʀwaze] *vt* (*personne, voiture*)

to pass; (*route*) to cross, cut across; (*Bio*) to cross; **se croiser** *vi* (*personnes, véhicules*) to pass each other; (*routes, lettres*) to cross; (*regards*) to meet; **~ les jambes/bras** to cross one's legs/fold one's arms

croisière [kʀwazjɛʀ] *nf* cruise

croissance [kʀwasɑ̃s] *nf* growth

croissant [kʀwasɑ̃] *nm* (*à manger*) croissant; (*motif*) crescent

croître [kʀwatʀ] *vi* to grow

croix [kʀwa] *nf* cross; **la Croix Rouge** the Red Cross

croque-monsieur [kʀɔkməsjø] *nm inv* toasted ham and cheese sandwich

croquer [kʀɔke] *vt* (*manger*) to crunch; (: *fruit*) to munch; (*dessiner*) to sketch; **chocolat à croquer** plain dessert chocolate

croquis [kʀɔki] *nm* sketch

crotte [kʀɔt] *nf* droppings *pl*; **crottin** *nm* dung, manure; (*fromage*) (small round) cheese (*of goat's milk*)

croustillant, e [kʀustijɑ̃, ɑ̃t] *adj* crisp

croûte [kʀut] *nf* crust; (*du fromage*) rind; (*Méd*) scab; **en ~** (*Culin*) in pastry

croûton [kʀutɔ̃] *nm* (*Culin*) crouton; (*bout du pain*) crust, heel

croyant, e [kʀwajɑ̃, ɑ̃t] *nm/f* believer

CRS *sigle fpl* (= *Compagnies républicaines de sécurité*) state security police force ▷ *sigle m* member of the CRS

cru, e [kʀy] *pp de* **croire** ▷ *adj* (*non cuit*) raw; (*lumière, couleur*) harsh; (*paroles*) crude ▷ *nm* (*vignoble*) vineyard; (*vin*) wine; **un grand ~** a great vintage; **jambon ~** Parma ham

crû [kʀy] *pp de* **croître**

cruauté [kʀyote] *nf* cruelty

cruche [kʀyʃ] *nf* pitcher, jug

crucifix [kʀysifi] *nm* crucifix

crudités [kʀydite] *nfpl* (*Culin*) selection of raw vegetables

crue [kʀy] *nf* (*inondation*) flood

cruel, le [kʀyɛl] *adj* cruel

crus *etc* [kʀy] *vb voir* **croire; croître**

crûs *etc* [kʀy] *vb voir* **croître**

crustacés [kʀystase] *nmpl* shellfish

Cuba [kyba] *nf* Cuba; **cubain, e** *adj* Cuban ▷ *nm/f*: **Cubain, e** Cuban

cube [kyb] *nm* cube; (*jouet*) brick; **mètre ~** cubic metre; **2 au ~** 2 cubed

cueillette [kœjɛt] *nf* picking; (*quantité*) crop, harvest

cueillir [kœjiʀ] *vt* (*fruits, fleurs*) to pick, gather; (*fig*) to catch

cuiller [kɥijɛʀ], **cuillère** [kɥijɛʀ] *nf* spoon; **cuiller à café** coffee spoon; (*Culin*) ≈ teaspoonful; **cuiller à soupe** soup-spoon; (*Culin*) ≈ tablespoonful; **cuillerée** *nf* spoonful

cuir [kɥiʀ] *nm* leather; **cuir chevelu** scalp

cuire [kɥiʀ] *vt* (*aliments*) to cook; (*au four*) to bake ▷ *vi* to cook; **bien cuit** (*viande*) well done; **trop cuit** overdone

cuisine [kɥizin] *nf* (*pièce*) kitchen; (*art culinaire*) cookery, cooking; (*nourriture*) cooking, food; **faire la ~** to cook; **cuisiné, e** *adj*: **plat cuisiné** ready-made meal *ou* dish; **cuisiner** *vt* to cook; (*fam*) to grill ▷ *vi* to cook; **cuisinier, -ière** *nm/f* cook; **cuisinière** *nf* (*poêle*) cooker

cuisse [kɥis] *nf* thigh; (*Culin*) leg

cuisson [kɥisɔ̃] *nf* cooking

cuit, e [kɥi, kɥit] *pp de* **cuire**

cuivre [kɥivʀ] *nm* copper; **les cuivres** (*Mus*) the brass

cul [ky] (*fam!*) *nm* arse (!)

culminant, e [kylminɑ̃, ɑ̃t] *adj*: **point ~** highest point

culot [kylo] (*fam*) *nm* (*effronterie*) cheek

culotte [kylɔt] *nf* (*de femme*) knickers *pl* (*BRIT*), panties *pl*

culte [kylt] *nm* (*religion*) religion; (*hommage, vénération*) worship; (*protestant*) service

cultivateur, -trice [kyltivatœʀ, tʀis] *nm/f* farmer

cultivé, e [kyltive] *adj* (*personne*) cultured, cultivated

cultiver [kyltive] *vt* to cultivate; (*légumes*) to grow, cultivate

culture [kyltyʀ] *nf* cultivation; (*connaissances etc*) culture; **les ~s**

intensives intensive farming; **culture physique** physical training; **culturel, le** *adj* cultural

cumin [kymɛ̃] *nm* cumin

cure [kyʀ] *nf* (*Méd*) course of treatment; **cure d'amaigrissement** slimming (*BRIT*) *ou* weight-loss (*US*) course; **cure de repos** rest cure

curé [kyʀe] *nm* parish priest

cure-dent [kyʀdɑ̃] *nm* toothpick

curieux, -euse [kyʀjø, jøz] *adj* (*indiscret*) curious, inquisitive; (*étrange*) strange, curious ▷ *nmpl* (*badauds*) onlookers; **curiosité** *nf* curiosity; (*site*) unusual feature

curriculum vitae [kyʀikylɔmvite] *nm inv* curriculum vitae

cutané, e [kytane] *adj* skin

cuve [kyv] *nf* vat; (*à mazout etc*) tank

cuvée [kyve] *nf* vintage

cuvette [kyvɛt] *nf* (*récipient*) bowl, basin; (*Géo*) basin

CV *sigle m* (*Auto*) = **cheval vapeur**; (*Comm*) = **curriculum vitae**

cybercafé [sibɛʀkafe] *nm* Internet café

cyberespace [sibɛʀɛspas] *nm* cyberspace

cybernaute [sibɛʀnot] *nm/f* Internet user

cyclable [siklabl] *adj*: **piste ~** cycle track

cycle [sikl] *nm* cycle; **cyclisme** *nm* cycling; **cycliste** *nm/f* cyclist ▷ *adj* cycle *cpd*; **coureur cycliste** racing cyclist

cyclomoteur [siklɔmɔtœʀ] *nm* moped

cyclone [siklon] *nm* hurricane

cygne [siɲ] *nm* swan

cylindre [silɛ̃dʀ] *nm* cylinder; **cylindrée** *nf* (*Auto*) (cubic) capacity; **une (voiture de) grosse cylindrée** a big-engined car

cymbale [sɛ̃bal] *nf* cymbal

cynique [sinik] *adj* cynical

cystite [sistit] *nf* cystitis

d' [d] *prép voir* **de**

dactylo [daktilo] *nf* (*aussi*: **~graphe**) typist; (*aussi*: **~graphie**) typing

dada [dada] *nm* hobby-horse

daim [dɛ̃] *nm* (fallow) deer *inv*; (*cuir suédé*) suede

daltonien, ne [daltɔnjɛ̃, jɛn] *adj* colour-blind

dame [dam] *nf* lady; (*Cartes, Échecs*) queen; **dames** *nfpl* (*jeu*) draughts *sg* (*BRIT*), checkers *sg* (*US*)

Danemark [danmaʀk] *nm* Denmark

danger [dɑ̃ʒe] *nm* danger; **être en ~** (*personne*) to be in danger; **mettre en ~** (*personne*) to put in danger; (*projet, carrière*) to jeopardize; **dangereux, -euse** *adj* dangerous

danois, e [danwa, waz] *adj* Danish ▷ *nm/f*: **D~, e** Dane ▷ *nm* (*Ling*) Danish

◯ MOT-CLÉ

dans [dɑ̃] *prép* **1** (*position*) in; (*à l'intérieur de*) inside; **c'est dans le tiroir/le salon**

it's in the drawer/lounge; **dans la boîte** in ou inside the box; **je l'ai lu dans le journal** I read it in the newspaper; **marcher dans la ville** to walk about the town

2 (direction) into; **elle a couru dans le salon** she ran into the lounge; **monter dans une voiture/le bus** to get into a car/on to the bus

3 (provenance) out of, from; **je l'ai pris dans le tiroir/salon** I took it out of ou from the drawer/lounge; **boire dans un verre** to drink out of ou from a glass

4 (temps) in; **dans 2 mois** in 2 months, in 2 months' time

5 (approximation) about; **dans les 20 euros** about 20 euros

danse [dɑ̃s] nf: **la ~** dancing; **une ~** dance; **la ~ classique** ballet; **danser** vi, vt to dance; **danseur, -euse** nm/f ballet dancer; (au bal etc) dancer; (: cavalier) partner

date [dat] nf date; **de longue ~** longstanding; **date de naissance** date of birth; **date limite** deadline; **dater** vt, vi to date; **dater de** to date from; **à dater de** (as) from

datte [dat] nf date

dauphin [dofɛ̃] nm (Zool) dolphin

davantage [davɑ̃taʒ] adv more; (plus longtemps) longer; **~ de** more

MOT-CLÉ

de, d' [də] (de +le = **du**, de +les = **des**) prép

1 (appartenance) of; **le toit de la maison** the roof of the house; **la voiture d'Ann/de mes parents** Ann's/my parents' car

2 (provenance) from; **il vient de Londres** he comes from London; **elle est sortie du cinéma** she came out of the cinema

3 (caractérisation, mesure): **un mur de brique/bureau d'acajou** a brick wall/mahogany desk; **un billet de 50 euros** a 50 euro note; **une pièce de 2 m de large** ou **large de 2 m** a room 2m wide,

a 2m-wide room; **un bébé de 10 mois** a 10-month-old baby; **12 mois de crédit/travail** 12 months' credit/work; **être payé 20 euros de l'heure** to be paid 20 euros an ou per hour; **augmenter de 10 euros** to increase by 10 euros; **de 14 à 18** from 14 to 18

4 (moyen) with; **je l'ai fait de mes propres mains** I did it with my own two hands

5 (cause): **mourir de faim** to die of hunger; **rouge de colère** red with fury

6 (devant infinitif) to; **il m'a dit de rester** he told me to stay

▷ dét **1** (phrases affirmatives) some (souvent omis); **du vin, de l'eau, des pommes** (some) wine, (some) water, (some) apples; **des enfants sont venus** some children came; **pendant des mois** for months

2 (phrases interrogatives et négatives) any; **a-t-il du vin?** has he got any wine?; **il n'a pas de pommes/d'enfants** he hasn't (got) any apples/children, he has no apples/children

dé [de] nm (à jouer) die ou dice; (aussi: **dé à coudre**) thimble

déballer [debale] vt to unpack

débarcadère [debarkadɛʀ] nm wharf

débardeur [debardœʀ] nm (maillot) tank top

débarquer [debarke] vt to unload, land ▷ vi to disembark; (fig: fam) to turn up

débarras [debaʀa] nm (pièce) lumber room; (placard) junk cupboard; **bon ~!** good riddance!; **débarrasser** vt to clear; **se débarrasser de** vt to get rid of; **débarrasser qn de** (vêtements, paquets) to relieve sb of; **débarrasser (la table)** to clear the table

débat [deba] nm discussion, debate; **débattre** vt to discuss, debate; **se débattre** vi to struggle

débit [debi] nm (d'un liquide, fleuve) flow; (d'un magasin) turnover (of goods); (élocution) delivery; (bancaire) debit; **débit de boissons** drinking establishment; **débit de tabac** tobacconist's

déblayer [debleje] vt to clear

débloquer [debloke] vt (prix, crédits) to free

déboîter [debwate] vt (Auto) to pull out; **se ~ le genou** etc to dislocate one's knee etc

débordé, e [deborde] adj: **être ~ (de)** (travail, demandes) to be snowed under (with)

déborder [deborde] vi to overflow; (lait etc) to boil over; **~ (de) qch** (dépasser) to extend beyond sth; **~ de** (joie, zèle) to be brimming over with ou bursting with

débouché [debuʃe] nm (pour vendre) outlet; (perspective d'emploi) opening

déboucher [debuʃe] vt (évier, tuyau etc) to unblock; (bouteille) to uncork ▷ vi: **~ de** to emerge from; **~ sur** (études) to lead on to

debout [d(ə)bu] adv: **être ~** (personne) to be standing, stand; (: levé, éveillé) to be up; **se mettre ~** to stand up; **se tenir ~** to stand; **~!** stand up!; (du lit) get up!; **cette histoire ne tient pas ~** this story doesn't hold water

déboutonner [debutɔne] vt to undo, unbutton

débraillé, e [debraje] adj slovenly, untidy

débrancher [debraʃe] vt to disconnect; (appareil électrique) to unplug

débrayage [debrejaʒ] nm (Auto) clutch; **débrayer** vi (Auto) to declutch; (cesser le travail) to stop work

débris [debri] nmpl fragments; **des ~ de verre** bits of glass

débrouillard, e [debrujar, ard] (fam) adj smart, resourceful

débrouiller [debruje] vt to disentangle, untangle; **se débrouiller** vi to manage; **débrouillez-vous** you'll have to sort things out yourself

début [deby] nm beginning, start; **débuts** nmpl (de carrière) début sg; **~**

juin in early June; **débutant, e** nm/f beginner, novice; **débuter** vi to begin, start; (faire ses débuts) to start out

décaféiné, e [dekafeine] adj decaffeinated

décalage [dekalaʒ] nm gap; **décalage horaire** time difference

décaler [dekale] vt to shift

décapotable [dekapɔtabl] adj convertible

décapsuleur [dekapsylœr] nm bottle-opener

décédé, e [desede] adj deceased

décéder [desede] vi to die

décembre [desãbr] nm December

décennie [deseni] nf decade

décent, e [desã, ãt] adj decent

déception [desɛpsjɔ̃] nf disappointment

décès [desɛ] nm death

décevoir [des(ə)vwar] vt to disappoint

décharge [deʃarʒ] nf (dépôt d'ordures) rubbish tip ou dump; (électrique) electrical discharge; **décharger** vt (marchandise, véhicule) to unload; (tirer) to discharge; **décharger qn de** (responsabilité) to relieve sb of, release sb from

déchausser [deʃose] vt (skis) to take off; **se déchausser** vi to take off one's shoes; (dent) to come ou work loose

déchet [deʃɛ] nm (reste) scrap; **déchets** nmpl (ordures) refuse sg, rubbish sg; **~s nucléaires** nuclear waste

déchiffrer [deʃifre] vt to decipher

déchirant, e [deʃirã, ãt] adj heart-rending

déchirement [deʃirmã] nm (chagrin) wrench, heartbreak; (gén pl: conflit) rift, split

déchirer [deʃire] vt to tear; (en morceaux) to tear up; (arracher) to tear out; (fig: conflit) to tear (apart); **se déchirer** vi to tear, rip; **se ~ un muscle** to tear a muscle

déchirure [deʃiryr] nf (accroc) tear, rip; **déchirure musculaire** torn muscle

décidé, e [deside] adj (personne, air) determined; **c'est ~** it's decided; **décidément** adv really

décider [deside] vt: **~ qch** to decide on sth; **~ de faire/que** to decide to do/that; **~ qn (à faire qch)** to persuade sb (to do sth); **se décider (à faire)** to decide (to do), make up one's mind (to do); **se ~ pour** to decide on ou in favour of

décimal, e, -aux [desimal, o] adj decimal

décimètre [desimetr] nm decimetre

décisif, -ive [desizif, iv] adj decisive

décision [desizjɔ̃] nf decision

déclaration [deklarasjɔ̃] nf declaration; (discours: Pol etc) statement; **déclaration d'impôts** ou **de revenus** ≈ tax return; **déclaration de vol**: **faire une déclaration de vol** to report a theft

déclarer [deklare] vt to declare; (décès, naissance) to register; **se déclarer** vi (feu) to break out

déclencher [deklɑ̃ʃe] vt (mécanisme etc) to release; (sonnerie) to set off; (attaque, grève) to launch; (provoquer) to trigger off; **se déclencher** vi (sonnerie) to go off

décliner [dekline] vi to decline ▷ vt (invitation) to decline; (nom, adresse) to state

décoiffer [dekwafe] vt: **~ qn** to mess up sb's hair; **je suis toute décoiffée** my hair is in a real mess

déçois etc [deswa] vb voir **décevoir**

décollage [dekɔlaʒ] nm (Aviat) takeoff

décoller [dekɔle] vt to unstick ▷ vi (avion) to take off; **se décoller** vi to come unstuck

décolleté, e [dekɔlte] adj low-cut ▷ nm low neck(line); (plongeant) cleavage

décolorer [dekɔlɔre]: **se décolorer** vi to fade; **se faire ~ les cheveux** to have one's hair bleached

décommander [dekɔmɑ̃de] vt to cancel; **se décommander** vi to cry off

déconcerter [dekɔ̃sɛrte] vt to disconcert, confound

décongeler [dekɔ̃ʒ(ə)le] vt to thaw

déconner [dekɔne] (fam) vi to talk rubbish

déconseiller [dekɔ̃seje] vt: **~ qch (à qn)** to advise (sb) against sth; **c'est déconseillé** it's not recommended

décontracté, e [dekɔ̃trakte] adj relaxed, laid-back (fam)

décontracter [dekɔ̃trakte]: **se décontracter** vi to relax

décor [dekɔr] nm décor; (paysage) scenery; **décorateur** nm (interior) decorator; **décoration** nf decoration; **décorer** vt to decorate

décortiquer [dekɔrtike] vt to shell; (fig: texte) to dissect

découdre [dekudr]: **se découdre** vi to come unstitched

découper [dekupe] vt (papier, tissu etc) to cut up; (viande) to carve; (article) to cut out

décourager [dekuraʒe] vt to discourage; **se décourager** vi to lose heart, become discouraged

décousu, e [dekuzy] adj unstitched; (fig) disjointed, disconnected

découvert, e [dekuver, ɛrt] adj (tête) bare, uncovered; (lieu) open, exposed ▷ nm (bancaire) overdraft; **découverte** nf discovery; **faire la découverte de** to discover

découvrir [dekuvrir] vt to discover; (enlever ce qui couvre) to uncover; (dévoiler) to reveal; **se découvrir** vi (chapeau) to take off one's hat; (vêtement) to take something off; (ciel) to clear

décrire [dekrir] vt to describe

décrocher [dekrɔʃe] vt (détacher) to take down; (téléphone) to take off the hook; (: pour répondre) to lift the receiver; (fam: contrat etc) to get, land ▷ vi (fam: abandonner) to drop out; (: cesser d'écouter) to switch off

déçu, e [desy] pp de **décevoir**

dédaigner [dedeɲe] vt to despise, scorn; (négliger) to disregard, spurn;

dédaigneux, -euse adj scornful, disdainful; **dédain** nm scorn, disdain

dedans [dədɑ̃] adv inside; (pas en plein air) indoors, inside ▷ nm inside; **au ~** inside

dédicacer [dedikase] vt: **~ (à qn)** to sign (for sb), autograph (for sb)

dédier [dedje] vt: **~ à** to dedicate to

dédommagement [dedɔmaʒmɑ̃] nm compensation

dédommager [dedɔmaʒe] vt: **~ qn (de)** to compensate sb (for)

dédouaner [dedwane] vt to clear through customs

déduire [deduir] vt: **~ qch (de)** (ôter) to deduct sth (from); (conclure) to deduce ou infer sth (from)

défaillance [defajɑ̃s] nf (syncope) blackout; (fatigue) (sudden) weakness no pl; (technique) fault, failure; **défaillance cardiaque** heart failure

défaire [defɛʀ] vt to undo; (installation) to take down, dismantle; **se défaire** vi to come undone; **se ~ de** to get rid of

défait, e [defɛ, ɛt] adj (visage) haggard, ravaged; **défaite** nf defeat

défaut [defo] nm (moral) fault, failing, defect; (tissus) fault, flaw; (manque, carence): **~ de** shortage of; **prendre qn en ~** to catch sb out; **faire ~** (manquer) to be lacking; **à ~ de** for lack ou want of

défavorable [defavɔrabl] adj unfavourable (BRIT), unfavorable (US)

défavoriser [defavɔrize] vt to put at a disadvantage

défectueux, -euse [defɛktyø, øz] adj faulty, defective

défendre [defɑ̃dr] vt to defend; (interdire) to forbid; **se défendre** vi to defend o.s.; **~ à qn qch/de faire** to forbid sb sth/to do; **il se défend** (fam: se débrouiller) he can hold his own; **se ~ de/contre** (se protéger) to protect o.s. from/against; **se ~ de** (se garder de) to refrain from

défense [defɑ̃s] nf defence; (d'éléphant etc) tusk; **ministre de la ~** Minister of Defence (BRIT), Defence Secretary (US);

"~ de fumer" "no smoking"

défi [defi] nm challenge; **lancer un ~ à qn** to challenge sb; **sur un ton de ~** defiantly

déficit [defisit] nm (Comm) deficit

défier [defje] vt (provoquer) to challenge; (mort, autorité) to defy; **~ qn de faire qch** to challenge ou defy sb to do sth

défigurer [defigyre] vt to disfigure

défilé [defile] nm (Géo) (narrow) gorge ou pass; (soldats) parade; (manifestants) procession, march

défiler [defile] vi (troupes) to march past; (sportifs) to parade; (manifestants) to march; (visiteurs) to pour, stream; **faire ~ un document** (Comput) to scroll a document; **se défiler** vi: **il s'est défilé** (fam) he wriggled out of it

définir [definir] vt to define

définitif, -ive [definitif, iv] adj (final) final, definitive; (pour longtemps) permanent, definitive; (refus) definite; **définitive** nf: **en définitive** eventually; (somme toute) in fact; **définitivement** adv (partir, s'installer) for good

déformer [defɔrme] vt to put out of shape; (pensée, fait) to distort; **se déformer** vi to lose its shape

défouler [defule]: **se défouler** vi to unwind, let off steam

défunt, e [defœ̃, œ̃t] adj (mort) late before n ▷ nm/f deceased

dégagé, e [degaʒe] adj (route, ciel) clear; **sur un ton ~** casually

dégager [degaʒe] vt (exhaler) to give off; (délivrer) to free, extricate; (désencombrer) to clear; (isoler: idée, aspect) to bring out; **~ qn de** (engagement, parole etc) to release ou free sb from; **se dégager** vi (passage, ciel) to clear

dégâts [dega] nmpl damage sg; **faire des ~** to cause damage

dégel [deʒɛl] nm thaw; **dégeler** vt to thaw (out)

dégivrer [deʒivre] vt (frigo) to defrost; (vitres) to de-ice

dégonflé, e [degɔ̃fle] *adj* (*pneu*) flat
dégonfler [degɔ̃fle] *vt* (*pneu, ballon*) to let down, deflate; **se dégonfler** *vi* (*fam*) to chicken out
dégouliner [deguline] *vi* to trickle, drip
dégourdi, e [degurdi] *adj* smart, resourceful
dégourdir [degurdir] *vt*: **se ~ les jambes** to stretch one's legs (*fig*)
dégoût [degu] *nm* disgust, distaste; **dégoûtant, e** *adj* disgusting; **dégoûté, e** *adj* disgusted; **dégoûté de** sick of; **dégoûter** *vt* to disgust; **dégoûter qn de qch** to put sb off sth
dégrader [degrade] *vt* (*Mil: officier*) to degrade; (*abîmer*) to damage, deface; **se dégrader** *vi* (*relations, situation*) to deteriorate
degré [dəgre] *nm* degree
dégressif, -ive [degresif, iv] *adj* on a decreasing scale
dégringoler [degrɛ̃gɔle] *vi* to tumble (down)
déguisement [degizmɑ̃] *nm* (*pour s'amuser*) fancy dress
déguiser [degize] *vt*: **se déguiser (en)** *vi* (*se costumer*) to dress up (as); (*pour tromper*) to disguise o.s. (as)
dégustation [degystasjɔ̃] *nf* (*de fromages etc*) sampling; **~ de vins** wine-tasting session
déguster [degyste] *vt* (*vins*) to taste; (*fromages etc*) to sample; (*savourer*) to enjoy, savour
dehors [dəɔr] *adv* outside; (*en plein air*) outdoors ▷ *nm* outside ▷ *nmpl* (*apparences*) appearances; **mettre ou jeter ~** (*expulser*) to throw out; **au ~** outside; **au ~ de** outside; **en ~ de** (*hormis*) apart from
déjà [deʒa] *adv* already; (*auparavant*) before, already
déjeuner [deʒœne] *vi* to (have) lunch; (*le matin*) to have breakfast ▷ *nm* lunch
delà [dəla] *adv*: **en ~ (de), au ~ (de)** beyond
délacer [delase] *vt* (*chaussures*) to undo

délai [delɛ] *nm* (*attente*) waiting period; (*sursis*) extension (of time); (*temps accordé*) time limit; **sans ~** without delay; **dans les ~s** within the time limit
délaisser [delese] *vt* to abandon, desert
délasser [delase] *vt* to relax; **se délasser** *vi* to relax
délavé, e [delave] *adj* faded
délayer [deleje] *vt* (*Culin*) to mix (with water *etc*); (*peinture*) to thin down
delco(r) [dɛlko] *nm* (*Auto*) distributor
délégué, e [delege] *nm/f* representative
déléguer [delege] *vt* to delegate
délibéré, e [delibere] *adj* (*conscient*) deliberate
délicat, e [delika, at] *adj* delicate; (*plein de tact*) tactful; (*attention*) thoughtful; **délicatement** *adv* delicately; (*avec douceur*) gently
délice [delis] *nm* delight
délicieux, -euse [delisjø, jøz] *adj* (*au goût*) delicious; (*sensation*) delightful
délimiter [delimite] *vt* (*terrain*) to delimit, demarcate
délinquant, e [delɛ̃kɑ̃, -ɑ̃t] *adj, nm/f* delinquent
délirer [delire] *vi* to be delirious; **tu délires!** (*fam*) you're crazy!
délit [deli] *nm* (*criminal*) offence
délivrer [delivre] *vt* (*prisonnier*) to (set) free, release; (*passeport*) to issue
deltaplane(r) [dɛltaplan] *nm* hang-glider
déluge [delyʒ] *nm* (*pluie*) downpour; (*biblique*) Flood
demain [d(ə)mɛ̃] *adv* tomorrow; **~ matin/soir** tomorrow morning/evening
demande [d(ə)mɑ̃d] *nf* (*requête*) request; (*revendication*) demand; (*d'emploi*) application; (*Écon*): **la ~** demand; **"~s d'emploi"** (*annonces*) "situations wanted"
demandé, e [d(ə)mɑ̃de] *adj* (*article etc*): **très ~** (very) much in demand
demander [d(ə)mɑ̃de] *vt* to ask for;

(*chemin, heure etc*) to ask; (*nécessiter*) to require, demand; **~ qch à qn** to ask sb for sth; **~ un service à qn** to ask sb a favour; **~ à qn de faire qch** to ask sb to do sth; **je ne demande pas mieux que de ...** I'll be only too pleased to ...; **se ~ si/pourquoi** *etc* to wonder whether/why *etc*; **demandeur, -euse** *nm/f*: **demandeur d'emploi** job-seeker; **demandeur d'asile** asylum-seeker

démangeaison [demɑ̃ʒɛzɔ̃] *nf* itching; **avoir des ~s** to be itching

démanger [demɑ̃ʒe] *vi* to itch

démaquillant [demakijɑ̃] *nm* make-up remover

démaquiller [demakije] *vt*: **se démaquiller** to remove one's make-up

démarche [demaʀʃ] *nf* (*allure*) gait, walk; (*intervention*) step; (*fig: intellectuelle*) thought processes *pl*; **faire les ~s nécessaires (pour obtenir qch)** to take the necessary steps (to obtain sth)

démarrage [demaʀaʒ] *nm* start

démarrer [demaʀe] *vi* (*conducteur*) to start (up); (*véhicule*) to move off; (*travaux*) to get moving; **démarreur** *nm* (*Auto*) starter

démêlant [demɛlɑ̃] *nm* conditioner

démêler [demele] *vt* to untangle; **démêlés** *nmpl* problems

déménagement [demenaʒmɑ̃] *nm* move; **camion de déménagement** removal van

déménager [demenaʒe] *vt* (*meubles*) to (re)move ▷ *vi* to move (house); **déménageur** *nm* removal man

démerder [demɛʀde] (*fam*): **se démerder** *vi* to sort things out for o.s.

démettre [demɛtʀ] *vt*: **~ qn de** (*fonction, poste*) to dismiss sb from; **se ~ l'épaule** *etc* to dislocate one's shoulder *etc*

demeurer [d(ə)mœʀe] *vi* (*habiter*) to live; (*rester*) to remain

demi, e [dəmi] *adj* half ▷ *nm* (*bière*) ≈ half-pint (0,25 litres) ▷ *préfixe*: **~...** half-, semi..., demi-; **trois heures/bouteilles**

et ~es three and a half hours/bottles, three hours/bottles and a half; **il est 2 heures et ~e/midi et ~** it's half past 2/half past 12; **à ~-** half-; **à la ~e** (*heure*) on the half-hour; **demi-douzaine** *nf* half-dozen, half a dozen; **demi-finale** *nf* semifinal; **demi-frère** *nm* half-brother; **demi-heure** *nf* half-hour, half an hour; **demi-journée** *nf* half-day, half a day; **demi-litre** *nm* half-litre, half a litre; **demi-livre** *nf* half-pound, half a pound; **demi-pension** *nf* (*à l'hôtel*) half-board; **demi-pensionnaire** *nm/f*: **être demi-pensionnaire** to take school lunches

démis, e [demi, iz] *adj* (*épaule etc*) dislocated

demi-sœur [dəmisœr] *nf* half-sister

démission [demisjɔ̃] *nf* resignation; **donner sa ~** to give *ou* hand in one's notice; **démissionner** *vi* to resign

demi-tarif [dəmitaʀif] *nm* half-price; **voyager à ~** to travel half-fare

demi-tour [dəmituʀ] *nm* about-turn; **faire ~** to turn (and go) back

démocratie [demɔkʀasi] *nf* democracy; **démocratique** *adj* democratic

démodé, e [demɔde] *adj* old-fashioned

demoiselle [d(ə)mwazɛl] *nf* (*jeune fille*) young lady; (*célibataire*) single lady, maiden lady; **demoiselle d'honneur** bridesmaid

démolir [demɔliʀ] *vt* to demolish

démon [demɔ̃] *nm* (*enfant turbulent*) devil, demon; **le D~** the Devil

démonstration [demɔ̃stʀasjɔ̃] *nf* demonstration

démonter [demɔ̃te] *vt* (*machine etc*) to take down, dismantle; **se démonter** (*meuble*) to be dismantled, be taken to pieces; (*personne*) to lose countenance

démontrer [demɔ̃tʀe] *vt* to demonstrate

démouler [demule] *vt* to turn out

démuni, e [demyni] *adj* (*sans argent*) impoverished; **~ de** without

dénicher [deniʃe] (*fam*) *vt* (*objet*) to

unearth; (*restaurant etc*) to discover

dénier [denje] vt to deny

dénivellation [denivelasjɔ̃] nf (*pente*) slope

dénombrer [denɔ̃bʀe] vt to count

dénomination [denɔminasjɔ̃] nf designation, appellation

dénoncer [denɔ̃se] vt to denounce; **se dénoncer** to give o.s. up, come forward

dénouement [denumɑ̃] nm outcome

dénouer [denwe] vt to unknot, undo

denrée [dɑ̃ʀe] nf: **denrées alimentaires** foodstuffs

dense [dɑ̃s] adj dense; **densité** nf density

dent [dɑ̃] nf tooth; **dent de lait/de sagesse** milk/wisdom tooth; **dentaire** adj dental; **cabinet dentaire** dental surgery (BRIT), dentist's office (US)

dentelle [dɑ̃tɛl] nf lace no pl

dentier [dɑ̃tje] nm denture

dentifrice [dɑ̃tifʀis] nm toothpaste

dentiste [dɑ̃tist] nm/f dentist

dentition [dɑ̃tisjɔ̃] nf teeth

dénué, e [denɥe] adj: **~ de** devoid of

déodorant [deɔdɔʀɑ̃] nm deodorant

déontologie [deɔ̃tɔlɔʒi] nf code of practice

dépannage [depanaʒ] nm: **service de ~** (*Auto*) breakdown service

dépanner [depane] vt (*voiture, télévision*) to fix, repair; (*fig*) to bail out, help out; **dépanneuse** nf breakdown lorry (BRIT), tow truck (US)

dépareillé, e [depaʀeje] adj (*collection, service*) incomplete; (*objet*) odd

départ [depaʀ] nm departure; (*Sport*) start; **au ~** at the start; **la veille de son ~** the day before he leaves/left

département [depaʀtəmɑ̃] nm department

● **DÉPARTEMENT**
●
● France is divided into 96
● administrative units called
● **départements**. These local
● government divisions are headed
● by a state-appointed 'préfet',
● and administered by an elected
● 'Conseil général'. **Départements**
● are usually named after prominent
● geographical features such as rivers
● or mountain ranges.

dépassé, e [depase] adj superseded, outmoded; **il est complètement ~** he's completely out of his depth, he can't cope

dépasser [depase] vt (*véhicule, concurrent*) to overtake; (*endroit*) to pass, go past; (*somme, limite*) to exceed; (*fig: en beauté etc*) to surpass, outshine ▷ vi (*jupon etc*) to show; **se dépasser** to excel o.s.

dépaysé, e [depeize] adj disoriented

dépaysement [depeizmɑ̃] nm (*changement*) change of scenery

dépêcher [depeʃe]: **se dépêcher** vi to hurry

dépendance [depɑ̃dɑ̃s] nf dependence; (*bâtiment*) outbuilding

dépendre [depɑ̃dʀ]: **~ de** vt to depend on; (*financièrement etc*) to be dependent on; **ça dépend** it depends

dépens [depɑ̃] nmpl: **aux ~ de** at the expense of

dépense [depɑ̃s] nf spending no pl, expense, expenditure no pl; **dépenser** vt to spend; (*énergie*) to expend, use up; **se dépenser** vi to exert o.s.

dépeupler [depœple]: **se dépeupler** vi to become depopulated

dépilatoire [depilatwaʀ] adj: **crème ~** hair-removing ou depilatory cream

dépister [depiste] vt to detect; (*voleur*) to track down

dépit [depi] nm vexation, frustration; **en ~ de** in spite of; **en ~ du bon sens** contrary to all good sense; **dépité, e** adj vexed, frustrated

déplacé, e [deplase] adj (*propos*) out of place, uncalled-for

déplacement [deplasmɑ̃] nm (*voyage*) trip, travelling no pl; **en ~** away

déplacer [deplase] vt (*table, voiture*) to

move, shift; **se déplacer** vi to move; (voyager) to travel; **se ~ une vertèbre** to slip a disc

déplaire [deplɛʀ] vt: **ça me déplaît** I don't like this, I dislike this; **se déplaire** vi to be unhappy; **déplaisant, e** adj disagreeable

dépliant [deplijɑ̃] nm leaflet

déplier [deplije] vt to unfold

déposer [depoze] vt (gén: mettre, poser) to lay ou put down; (à la banque, à la consigne) to deposit; (passager) to drop (off), set down; (roi) to depose; (plainte) to lodge; (marque) to register; **se déposer** vi to settle; **dépositaire** nm/f (Comm) agent; **déposition** nf statement

dépôt [depo] nm (à la banque, sédiment) deposit; (entrepôt) warehouse, store

dépourvu, e [depuʀvy] adj: **~ de** lacking in, without; **prendre qn au ~** to catch sb unprepared

dépression [depʀesjɔ̃] nf depression; **dépression (nerveuse)** (nervous) breakdown

déprimant, e [depʀimɑ̃, ɑ̃t] adj depressing

déprimer [depʀime] vi to be/get depressed

 MOT-CLÉ

depuis [dəpɥi] prép 1 (point de départ dans le temps) since; **il habite Paris depuis 1983/l'an dernier** he has been living in Paris since 1983/last year; **depuis quand?** since when?; **depuis quand le connaissez-vous?** how long have you known him?
2 (temps écoulé) for; **il habite Paris depuis 5 ans** he has been living in Paris for 5 years; **je le connais depuis 3 ans** I've known him for 3 years
3 (lieu): **il a plu depuis Metz** it's been raining since Metz; **elle a téléphoné depuis Valence** she rang from Valence
4 (quantité, rang) from; **depuis les plus petits jusqu'aux plus grands** from the youngest to the oldest
▷ adv (temps) since (then); **je ne lui ai pas parlé depuis** I haven't spoken to him since (then); **depuis que** conj (ever) since; **depuis qu'il m'a dit ça** (ever) since he said that to me

député, e [depyte] nm/f (Pol) ≈ Member of Parliament (BRIT), ≈ Member of Congress (US)

dérangement [deʀɑ̃ʒmɑ̃] nm (gêne) trouble; (gastrique etc) disorder; **en ~** (téléphone, machine) out of order

déranger [deʀɑ̃ʒe] vt (personne) to trouble, bother; (projets) to disrupt, upset; (objets, vêtements) to disarrange; **se déranger** vi: **surtout ne vous dérangez pas pour moi** please don't put yourself out on my account; **est-ce que cela vous dérange si …?** do you mind if …?

déraper [deʀape] vi (voiture) to skid; (personne, semelles) to slip

dérégler [deʀegle] vt (mécanisme) to put out of order; (estomac) to upset

dérisoire [deʀizwaʀ] adj derisory

dérive [deʀiv] nf: **aller à la ~** (Navig, fig) to drift

dérivé, e [deʀive] nm (Tech) by-product

dermatologue [dɛʀmatɔlɔg] nm/f dermatologist

dernier, -ière [dɛʀnje, jɛʀ] adj last; (le plus récent) latest, last; **lundi/le mois ~** last Monday/month; **c'est le ~ cri** it's the very latest thing; **en ~** last; **ce ~** the latter; **dernièrement** adv recently

dérogation [deʀɔgasjɔ̃] nf (special) dispensation

dérouiller [deʀuje] vt: **se ~ les jambes** to stretch one's legs (fig)

déroulement [deʀulmɑ̃] nm (d'une opération etc) progress

dérouler [deʀule] vt (ficelle) to unwind; **se dérouler** vi (avoir lieu) to take place; (se passer) to go (off); **tout s'est déroulé comme prévu** everything went as planned

dérouter [deʀute] vt (avion, train) to

reroute, divert; (*étonner*) to disconcert, throw (out)

derrière [dɛRjɛR] *adv, prép* behind ▷ *nm* (*d'une maison*) back; (*postérieur*) behind, bottom; **les pattes de ~** the back *ou* hind legs; **par ~** from behind; (*fig*) behind one's back

des [de] *dét voir* **de** ▷ *prép* +*dét* = **de +les**

dès [dɛ] *prép* from; **~ que** as soon as; **~ son retour** as soon as he was (*ou* is) back

désaccord [dezakɔR] *nm* disagreement

désagréable [dezagReabl] *adj* unpleasant

désagrément [dezagRemã] *nm* annoyance, trouble *no pl*

désaltérer [dezalteRe] *vt*: **se désaltérer** to quench one's thirst

désapprobateur, -trice [dezapRɔbatœR, tRis] *adj* disapproving

désapprouver [dezapRuve] *vt* to disapprove of

désarmant, e [dezaRmã, ãt] *adj* disarming

désastre [dezastR] *nm* disaster; **désastreux, -euse** *adj* disastrous

désavantage [dezavãtaʒ] *nm* disadvantage; **désavantager** *vt* to put at a disadvantage

descendre [desãdR] *vt* (*escalier, montagne*) to go (*ou* come) down; (*valise, paquet*) to take *ou* get down; (*étagère etc*) to lower; (*fam: abattre*) to shoot down ▷ *vi* to go (*ou* come) down; (*passager: s'arrêter*) to get out, alight; **~ à pied/en voiture** to walk/drive down; **~ de** (*famille*) to be descended from; **~ du train** to get out of *ou* get off the train; **~ de cheval** to dismount; **~ d'un arbre** to climb down from a tree; **~ à l'hôtel** to stay at a hotel

descente [desãt] *nf* descent, going down; (*chemin*) way down; (*Ski*) downhill (race); **au milieu de la ~** halfway down; **descente de lit** bedside rug; **descente (de police)** (police) raid

description [dɛskRipsjõ] *nf* description

déséquilibre [dezekilibR] *nm* (*position*): **en ~** unsteady; (*fig: des forces, du budget*) imbalance

désert, e [dezɛR, ɛRt] *adj* deserted ▷ *nm* desert; **désertique** *adj* desert *cpd*

désespéré, e [dezɛspeRe] *adj* desperate

désespérer [dezɛspeRe] *vi*: **~ (de)** to despair (of); **désespoir** *nm* despair; **en désespoir de cause** in desperation

déshabiller [dezabije] *vt* to undress; **se déshabiller** *vi* to undress (o.s.)

déshydraté, e [dezidRate] *adj* dehydrated

désigner [dezine] *vt* (*montrer*) to point out, indicate; (*dénommer*) to denote; (*candidat etc*) to name

désinfectant, e [dezɛ̃fɛktã, ãt] *adj, nm* disinfectant

désinfecter [dezɛ̃fɛkte] *vt* to disinfect

désintéressé, e [dezɛ̃teRese] *adj* disinterested, unselfish

désintéresser [dezɛ̃teRese] *vt*: **se ~ (de)** to lose interest (in)

désintoxication [dezɛ̃tɔksikasjõ] *nf*: **faire une cure de ~** to undergo treatment for alcoholism (*ou* drug addiction)

désinvolte [dezɛ̃vɔlt] *adj* casual, off-hand

désir [deziR] *nm* wish; (*sensuel*) desire; **désirer** *vt* to want, wish for; (*sexuellement*) to desire; **je désire ...** (*formule de politesse*) I would like ...

désister [deziste]: **se désister** *vi* to stand down, withdraw

désobéir [dezɔbeiR] *vi*: **~ (à qn/qch)** to disobey (sb/sth); **désobéissant, e** *adj* disobedient

désodorisant [dezɔdɔRizã] *nm* air freshener, deodorizer

désolé, e [dezɔle] *adj* (*paysage*) desolate; **je suis ~** I'm sorry

désordonné, e [dezɔRdɔne] *adj* untidy

désordre [dezɔRdR] *nm* disorder(liness), untidiness; (*anarchie*)

disorder; **en ~** in a mess, untidy
désormais [dezɔʀmɛ] *adv* from
now on
desquelles [dekɛl] *prép +pron* = **de
+lesquelles**
desquels [dekɛl] *prép +pron* = **de
+lesquels**
dessécher [deseʃe]: **se dessécher** *vi*
to dry out
desserrer [deseʀe] *vt* to loosen; (*frein*)
to release
dessert [desɛʀ] *nm* dessert, pudding
desservir [desɛʀviʀ] *vt* (*ville, quartier*)
to serve; (*débarrasser*): **~ (la table)** to
clear the table
dessin [desɛ̃] *nm* (*œuvre, art*) drawing;
(*motif*) pattern, design; **dessin animé**
cartoon (film); **dessin humoristique**
cartoon; **dessinateur, -trice** *nm/f*
drawer; (*de bandes dessinées*) cartoonist;
(*industriel*) draughtsman(-woman)
(BRIT), draftsman(-woman) (US);
dessiner *vt* to draw; (*concevoir*) to
design; **se dessiner** *vi* (*forme*) to be
outlined; (*fig: solution*) to emerge
dessous [d(ə)su] *adv* underneath,
beneath ▷ *nm* below ▷ *nmpl*
(*sous-vêtements*) underwear *sg*; **en ~,
par ~** underneath; **au-~ (de)** below;
(*peu digne de*) beneath; **avoir le ~** to get
the worst of it; **les voisins du ~** the
downstairs neighbours; **dessous-de-
plat** *nm inv* tablemat
dessus [d(ə)sy] *adv* on top; (*collé, écrit*)
on it ▷ *nm* top; **en ~** above; **par ~** *adv*
over it ▷ *prép* over; **au-~ (de)** above; **les
voisins de ~** the upstairs neighbours;
avoir le ~ to get the upper hand; **sens
~ dessous** upside down; **dessus-de-lit**
nm inv bedspread
destin [dɛstɛ̃] *nm* fate; (*avenir*) destiny
destinataire [dɛstinatɛʀ]
nm/f (*Postes*) addressee; (*d'un colis*)
consignee
destination [dɛstinasjɔ̃] *nf* (*lieu*)
destination; (*usage*) purpose; **à ~ de**
bound for, travelling to
destiner [dɛstine] *vt*: **~ qch à qn**

(*envisager de donner*) to intend sb to have
sth; (*adresser*) to intend sth for sb; **être
destiné à** (*usage*) to be meant for; **se ~
à l'enseignement** to intend to become
a teacher
détachant [detaʃɑ̃] *nm* stain remover
détacher [detaʃe] *vt* (*enlever*) to detach,
remove; (*délier*) to untie; (*Admin*): **~
qn (auprès de** *ou* **à)** to post sb (to); **se
détacher** *vi* (*se séparer*) to come off;
(: *page*) to come out; (*se défaire*) to come
undone; **se ~ sur** to stand out against;
se ~ de (*se désintéresser*) to grow away
from
détail [detaj] *nm* detail; (*Comm*): **le ~**
retail; **en ~** in detail; **au ~** (*Comm*) retail;
détaillant *nm* retailer; **détaillé, e** *adj*
(*plan, explications*) detailed; (*facture*)
itemized; **détailler** *vt* (*expliquer*) to
explain in detail
détecter [detɛkte] *vt* to detect
détective [detɛktiv] *nm*: **détective
(privé)** private detective
déteindre [detɛ̃dʀ] *vi* (*au lavage*) to
run, lose its colour; **~ sur** (*vêtement*) to
run into; (*fig*) to rub off on
détendre [detɑ̃dʀ] *vt* (*corps, esprit*) to
relax; **se détendre** *vi* (*ressort*) to lose its
tension; (*personne*) to relax
détenir [det(ə)niʀ] *vt* (*record, pouvoir,
secret*) to hold; (*prisonnier*) to detain,
hold
détente [detɑ̃t] *nf* relaxation
détention [detɑ̃sjɔ̃] *nf* (*d'armes*)
possession; (*captivité*) detention;
détention préventive custody
détenu, e [det(ə)ny] *nm/f* prisoner
détergent [detɛʀʒɑ̃] *nm* detergent
détériorer [deteʀjɔʀe] *vt* to damage;
se détériorer *vi* to deteriorate
déterminé, e [detɛʀmine] *adj* (*résolu*)
determined; (*précis*) specific, definite
déterminer [detɛʀmine] *vt* (*fixer*) to
determine; **~ qn à faire qch** to decide
sb to do sth; **se ~ à faire qch** to make
up one's mind to do sth
détester [detɛste] *vt* to hate, detest
détour [detuʀ] *nm* detour; (*tournant*)

bend, curve; **ça vaut le ~** it's worth the trip; **sans ~** (fig) plainly

détourné, e [deturne] adj (moyen) roundabout

détourner [deturne] vt to divert; (par la force) to hijack; (yeux, tête) to turn away; (de l'argent) to embezzle; **se détourner** vi to turn away

détraquer [detrake] vt to put out of order; (estomac) to upset; **se détraquer** vi (machine) to go wrong

détriment [detrimã] nm: **au ~ de** to the detriment of

détroit [detrwa] nm strait

détruire [detrɥir] vt to destroy

dette [dɛt] nf debt

DEUG sigle m (= diplôme d'études universitaires générales) diploma taken after 2 years at university

deuil [dœj] nm (perte) bereavement; (période) mourning; **être en ~** to be in mourning

deux [dø] num two; **tous les ~** both; **ses ~ mains** both his hands, his two hands; **~ fois** twice; **deuxième** num second; **deuxièmement** adv secondly; **deux-pièces** nm inv (tailleur) two-piece suit; (de bain) two-piece (swimsuit); (appartement) two-roomed flat (BRIT) ou apartment (US); **deux-points** nm inv colon sg; **deux-roues** nm inv two-wheeled vehicle

devais [dəvɛ] vb voir **devoir**

dévaluation [devalɥasjõ] nf devaluation

devancer [d(ə)vãse] vt (coureur, rival) to get ahead of; (arriver) to arrive before; (prévenir: questions, désirs) to anticipate

devant [d(ə)vã] adv in front; (à distance: en avant) ahead ▷ prép in front of; (en avant) ahead of; (avec mouvement: passer) past; (en présence de) before, in front of; (étant donné) in view of ▷ nm front; **prendre les ~s** to make the first move; **les pattes de ~** the front legs, the forelegs; **par ~** (boutonner) at the front; (entrer) the front way; **aller au-~ de**

qn to go out to meet sb; **aller au-~ de** (désirs de qn) to anticipate

devanture [d(ə)vãtyr] nf (étalage) display; (vitrine) (shop) window

développement [dev(ə)lɔpmã] nm development; **pays en voie de ~** developing countries

développer [dev(ə)lɔpe] vt to develop; **se développer** vi to develop

devenir [dəv(ə)nir] vb +attrib to become; **que sont-ils devenus?** what has become of them?

devez [dəve] vb voir **devoir**

déviation [devjasjõ] nf (Auto) diversion (BRIT), detour (US)

devienne etc [dəvjɛn] vb voir **devenir**

deviner [d(ə)vine] vt to guess; (apercevoir) to distinguish; **devinette** nf riddle

devis [d(ə)vi] nm estimate, quotation

devise [dəviz] nf (formule) motto, watchword; **devises** nfpl (argent) currency sg

dévisser [devise] vt to unscrew, undo; **se dévisser** vi to come unscrewed

devoir [d(ə)vwar] nm duty; (Scol) homework no pl; (: en classe) exercise ▷ vt (argent, respect): **~ qch (à qn)** to owe (sb) sth; (+infin: obligation): **il doit le faire** he has to do it, he must do it; (: intention): **le nouveau centre commercial doit ouvrir en mai** the new shopping centre is due to open in May; (: probabilité): **il doit être tard** it must be late; (: fatalité): **cela devait arriver** it was bound to happen; **combien est-ce que je vous dois?** how much do I owe you?

dévorer [devɔre] vt to devour

dévoué, e [devwe] adj devoted

dévouer [devwe]: **se dévouer** vi (se sacrifier) **se ~ (pour)** to sacrifice o.s. (for); (se consacrer) **se ~ à** to devote ou dedicate o.s. to

devrai [dəvre] vb voir **devoir**

dézipper [dezipe] vt to unzip

diabète [djabɛt] nm diabetes sg; **diabétique** nm/f diabetic

diable [djɑbl] nm devil
diabolo [djabɔlo] nm (boisson) lemonade with fruit cordial
diagnostic [djagnɔstik] nm diagnosis sg; **diagnostiquer** vt to diagnose
diagonal, e, -aux [djagɔnal, o] adj diagonal; **diagonale** nf diagonal; **en diagonale** diagonally
diagramme [djagʀam] nm chart, graph
dialecte [djalɛkt] nm dialect
dialogue [djalɔg] nm dialogue
diamant [djamɑ̃] nm diamond
diamètre [djamɛtʀ] nm diameter
diapositive [djapozitiv] nf transparency, slide
diarrhée [djaʀe] nf diarrhoea
dictateur [diktatœʀ] nm dictator; **dictature** nf dictatorship
dictée [dikte] nf dictation
dicter [dikte] vt to dictate
dictionnaire [diksjɔnɛʀ] nm dictionary
dièse [djɛz] nm sharp
diesel [djezɛl] nm diesel ▷ adj inv diesel
diète [djɛt] nf (jeûne) starvation diet; (régime) diet; **diététique** adj: **magasin diététique** health food shop (BRIT) ou store (US)
dieu, x [djø] nm god; **D~** God; **mon D~!** good heavens!
différemment [difeʀamɑ̃] adv differently
différence [difeʀɑ̃s] nf difference; **à la ~ de** unlike; **différencier** vt to differentiate
différent, e [difeʀɑ̃, ɑ̃t] adj (dissemblable) different; **~ de** different from; (divers) different, various
différer [difeʀe] vt to postpone, put off ▷ vi: **~ (de)** to differ (from)
difficile [difisil] adj difficult; (exigeant) hard to please; **difficilement** adv with difficulty
difficulté [difikylte] nf difficulty; **en ~** (bateau, alpiniste) in difficulties
diffuser [difyze] vt (chaleur) to diffuse;

(émission, musique) to broadcast; (nouvelle) to circulate; (Comm) to distribute
digérer [diʒeʀe] vt to digest; (fam: accepter) to stomach, put up with; **digestif** nm (after-dinner) liqueur; **digestion** nf digestion
digne [diɲ] adj dignified; **~ de** worthy of; **~ de foi** trustworthy; **dignité** nf dignity
digue [dig] nf dike, dyke
dilemme [dilɛm] nm dilemma
diligence [diliʒɑ̃s] nf stagecoach
diluer [dilɥe] vt to dilute
dimanche [dimɑ̃ʃ] nm Sunday
dimension [dimɑ̃sjɔ̃] nf (grandeur) size; (dimensions) dimensions
diminuer [diminɥe] vt to reduce, decrease; (ardeur etc) to lessen; (dénigrer) to belittle ▷ vi to decrease, diminish; **diminutif** nm (surnom) pet name
dinde [dɛ̃d] nf turkey
dindon [dɛ̃dɔ̃] nm turkey
dîner [dine] nm dinner ▷ vi to have dinner
dingue [dɛ̃g] (fam) adj crazy
dinosaure [dinozɔʀ] nm dinosaur
diplomate [diplɔmat] adj diplomatic ▷ nm diplomat; (fig) diplomatist; **diplomatie** nf diplomacy
diplôme [diplom] nm diploma; **avoir des ~s** to have qualifications; **diplômé, e** adj qualified
dire [diʀ] nm: **au ~ de** according to ▷ vt to say; (secret, mensonge, heure) to tell; **~ qch à qn** to tell sb sth; **~ à qn qu'il fasse** ou **de faire** to tell sb to do; **on dit que** they say that; **ceci** ou **cela dit** that being said; **si cela lui dit** (plaire) if he fancies it; **que dites-vous de** (penser) what do you think of; **on dirait que** it looks (ou sounds etc) as if; **dis/dites (donc)!** I say!; **se ~ (à soi-même)** to say to o.s.; **se ~ malade** (se prétendre) to claim one is ill; **ça ne se dit pas** (impoli) you shouldn't say that; (pas en usage) you don't say that
direct, e [diʀɛkt] adj direct ▷ nm (TV):

en ~ live; **directement** adv directly

irecteur, -trice [dirɛktœr, tris] nm/f (d'entreprise) director; (de service) manager(-eress); (d'école) head(teacher) (BRIT), principal (US)

irection [dirɛksjɔ̃] nf (sens) direction; (d'entreprise) management; (Auto) steering; **"toutes ~s"** "all routes"

irent [dir] vb voir **dire**

irigeant, e [diriʒɑ̃, ɑ̃t] adj (classe) ruling ▷ nm/f (d'un parti etc) leader

iriger [diriʒe] vt (entreprise) to manage, run; (véhicule) to steer; (orchestre) to conduct; (recherches, travaux) to supervise; **~ sur** (arme) to point ou level ou aim at; **~ son regard sur** to look in the direction of; **se diriger** vi (s'orienter) to find one's way; **se ~ vers** ou **sur** to make ou head for

is [di] vb voir **dire**

iscerner [disɛrne] vt to discern, make out

iscipline [disiplin] nf discipline; **discipliner** vt to discipline

iscontinu, e [diskɔ̃tiny] adj intermittent

iscontinuer [diskɔ̃tinɥe] vi: **sans ~** without stopping, without a break

iscothèque [diskɔtɛk] nf (boîte de nuit) disco(thèque)

iscours [diskur] nm speech

iscret, -ète [diskrɛ, ɛt] adj discreet; (parfum, maquillage) unobtrusive; **discrétion** nf discretion; **à discrétion** as much as one wants

iscrimination [diskriminasjɔ̃] nf discrimination; **sans ~** indiscriminately

iscussion [diskysjɔ̃] nf discussion

iscutable [diskytabl] adj debatable

iscuter [diskyte] vt (débattre) to discuss; (contester) to question, dispute ▷ vi to talk; (protester) to argue; **~ de** to discuss

ise [diz] vb voir **dire**

isjoncteur [disʒɔ̃ktœr] nm (Élec) circuit breaker

isloquer [disloke]: **se disloquer** vi

(parti, empire) to break up; (meuble) to come apart; (épaule) to be dislocated

disons [dizɔ̃] vb voir **dire**

disparaître [disparɛtr] vi to disappear; (se perdre: traditions etc) to die out; **faire ~** (tache) to remove; (douleur) to get rid of

disparition [disparisjɔ̃] nf disappearance; **espèce en voie de ~** endangered species

disparu, e [dispary] nm/f missing person ▷ adj: **être porté ~** to be reported missing

dispensaire [dispɑ̃sɛr] nm community clinic

dispenser [dispɑ̃se] vt: **~ qn de** to exempt sb from

disperser [dispɛrse] vt to scatter; **se disperser** vi to break up

disponible [dispɔnibl(ə)] adj available

disposé, e [dispoze] adj: **bien/mal ~** (humeur) in a good/bad mood; **~ à** (prêt à) willing ou prepared to

disposer [dispoze] vt to arrange ▷ vi: **vous pouvez ~** you may leave; **~ de** to have (at one's disposal); **se ~ à faire** to prepare to do, be about to do

dispositif [dispozitif] nm device; (fig) system, plan of action

disposition [dispozisjɔ̃] nf (arrangement) arrangement, layout; (humeur) mood; **prendre ses ~s** to make arrangements; **avoir des ~s pour la musique** etc to have a special aptitude for music etc; **à la ~ de qn** at sb's disposal; **je suis à votre ~** I am at your service

disproportionné, e [disproporsjone] adj disproportionate, out of all proportion

dispute [dispyt] nf quarrel, argument; **disputer** vt (match) to play; (combat) to fight; **se disputer** vi to quarrel

disqualifier [diskalifje] vt to disqualify

disque [disk] nm (Mus) record; (forme, pièce) disc; (Sport) discus; **disque compact** compact disc; **disque dur**

hard disk; **disquette** *nf* floppy disk,
diskette
dissertation [disɛrtasjɔ̃] *nf* (*Scol*)
essay
dissimuler [disimyle] *vt* to conceal
dissipé, e [disipe] *adj* (*élève*)
undisciplined, unruly
dissolvant [disɔlvɑ̃] *nm* nail polish
remover
dissuader [disɥade] *vt*: ~ **qn de faire**
to dissuade sb from doing
distance [distɑ̃s] *nf* distance; (*fig:
écart*) gap; **à ~** at *ou* from a distance;
distancer *vt* to outdistance
distant, e [distɑ̃, ɑ̃t] *adj* (*réservé*)
distant; ~ **de** (*lieu*) far away from
distillerie [distilʀi] *nf* distillery
distinct, e [distɛ̃(kt), ɛ̃kt] *adj* distinct;
distinctement *adv* distinctly, clearly;
distinctif, -ive *adj* distinctive
distingué, e [distɛ̃ge] *adj*
distinguished
distinguer [distɛ̃ge] *vt* to distinguish;
se ~ de to be distinguished by
distraction [distʀaksjɔ̃] *nf*
(*inattention*) absent-mindedness;
(*passe-temps*) distraction,
entertainment
distraire [distʀɛʀ] *vt* (*divertir*) to
entertain, divert; (*déranger*) to distract;
se distraire *vi* to amuse *ou* enjoy o.s.;
distrait, e *adj* absent-minded
distrayant, e [distʀɛjɑ̃, ɑ̃t] *adj*
entertaining
distribuer [distʀibɥe] *vt* to distribute,
hand out; (*Cartes*) to deal (out);
(*courrier*) to deliver; **distributeur** *nm*
(*Comm*) distributor; **distributeur
(automatique)** (vending) machine;
distributeur de billets (cash)
dispenser
dit, e [di, dit] *pp de* **dire** ▷ *adj* (*fixé*): **le
jour ~** the arranged day; (*surnommé*): **X,
~ Pierrot** X, known as Pierrot
dites [dit] *vb voir* **dire**
divan [divɑ̃] *nm* divan
divers, e [divɛʀ, ɛʀs] *adj* (*varié*) diverse,
varied; (*différent*) different, various; **~es

personnes** various *ou* several people
diversité [divɛʀsite] *nf* (*variété*)
diversity
divertir [divɛʀtiʀ]: **se divertir** *vi* to
amuse *ou* enjoy o.s.; **divertissement**
nm distraction, entertainment
diviser [divize] *vt* to divide; **division**
nf division
divorce [divɔʀs] *nm* divorce; **divorcé,
nm/f** divorcee; **divorcer** *vi* to get a
divorce, get divorced; **divorcer de** *ou*
d'avec qn to divorce sb
divulguer [divylge] *vt* to disclose
dix [dis] *num* ten; **dix-huit** *num*
eighteen; **dix-huitième** *num*
eighteenth; **dixième** *num* tenth; **dix-
neuf** *num* nineteen; **dix-neuvième**
num nineteenth; **dix-sept** *num*
seventeen; **dix-septième** *num*
seventeenth
dizaine [dizɛn] *nf*: **une ~ (de)** about
ten, ten or so
do [do] *nm* (*note*) C; (*en chantant la
gamme*) do(h)
docile [dɔsil] *adj* docile
dock [dɔk] *nm* dock; **docker** *nm* docker
docteur [dɔktœʀ] *nm* doctor; **doctorat**
nm doctorate
doctrine [dɔktʀin] *nf* doctrine
document [dɔkymɑ̃] *nm* document;
documentaire *adj, nm* documentary;
documentation *nf* documentation,
literature; **documenter** *vt*: **se
documenter (sur)** to gather
information (on)
dodo [dodo] *nm* (*langage enfantin*): **aller
faire ~** to go to beddy-byes
dogue [dɔg] *nm* mastiff
doigt [dwa] *nm* finger; **à deux ~s
de** within an inch of; **un ~ de lait/
whiskey** a drop of milk/whisky; **doigt
de pied** toe
doit *etc* [dwa] *vb voir* **devoir**
dollar [dɔlaʀ] *nm* dollar
domaine [dɔmɛn] *nm* estate,
property; (*fig*) domain, field
domestique [dɔmɛstik] *adj* domestic
▷ *nm/f* servant, domestic

omicile [dɔmisil] *nm* home, place of residence; **à ~** at home; **livrer à ~** to deliver; **domicilié, e** *adj*: **"domicilié à …"** "address …"

ominant, e [dɔminã, ãt] *adj* (*opinion*) predominant

ominer [dɔmine] *vt* to dominate; (*sujet*) to master; (*surpasser*) to outclass, surpass; (*surplomber*) to tower above, dominate ▷ *vi* to be in the dominant position; **se dominer** *vi* to control o.s.

omino [dɔmino] *nm* domino; **dominos** *nmpl* (*jeu*) dominoes *sg*

ommage [dɔmaʒ] *nm*: **~s** (*dégâts*) damage *no pl*; **c'est ~!** what a shame!; **c'est ~ que** it's a shame *ou* pity that

ompter [dɔ̃(p)te] *vt* to tame; **dompteur, -euse** *nm/f* trainer

OM-ROM [dɔmrɔm] *sigle m* (= *départements et régions d'outre-mer*) French overseas departments and regions

on [dɔ̃] *nm* gift; (*charité*) donation; **avoir des ~s pour** to have a gift *ou* talent for; **elle a le ~ de m'énerver** she's got a knack of getting on my nerves

onc [dɔ̃k] *conj* therefore, so; (*après une digression*) so, then

onné, e [dɔne] *adj* (*convenu: lieu, heure*) given; (*pas cher: fam*): **c'est ~** it's a gift; **étant ~ que …** given that …; **données** *nfpl* data

onner [dɔne] *vt* to give; (*vieux habits etc*) to give away; (*spectacle*) to put on; **~ qch à qn** to give sb sth, give sth to sb; **~ sur** (*suj: fenêtre, chambre*) to look (out) onto; **ça donne soif/faim** it makes you (feel) thirsty/hungry; **se ~ à fond** to give one's all; **se ~ du mal** to take (great) trouble; **s'en ~ à cœur joie** (*fam*) to have a great time

○ **MOT-CLÉ**

ont [dɔ̃] *pron relatif* **1** (*appartenance: objets*) whose, of which; (*appartenance: êtres animés*) whose; **la maison dont le toit est rouge** the house the roof of which is red, the house whose roof is red; **l'homme dont je connais la sœur** the man whose sister I know

2 (*parmi lesquel(le)s*): **2 livres, dont l'un est …** 2 books, one of which is …; **il y avait plusieurs personnes, dont Gabrielle** there were several people, among them Gabrielle; **10 blessés, dont 2 grièvement** 10 injured, 2 of them seriously

3 (*complément d'adjectif, de verbe*): **le fils dont il est si fier** the son he's so proud of; **le pays dont il est originaire** the country he's from; **la façon dont il l'a fait** the way he did it; **ce dont je parle** what I'm talking about

dopage [dɔpaʒ] *nm* (*Sport*) drug use; (*de cheval*) doping

doré, e [dɔre] *adj* golden; (*avec dorure*) gilt, gilded

dorénavant [dɔrenavã] *adv* henceforth

dorer [dɔre] *vt* to gild; **(faire) ~** (*Culin*) to brown

dorloter [dɔrlɔte] *vt* to pamper

dormir [dɔrmir] *vi* to sleep; (*être endormi*) to be asleep

dortoir [dɔrtwar] *nm* dormitory

dos [do] *nm* back; (*de livre*) spine; **"voir au ~"** "see over"; **de ~** from the back

dosage [dozaʒ] *nm* mixture

dose [doz] *nf* dose; **doser** *vt* to measure out; **il faut savoir doser ses efforts** you have to be able to pace yourself

dossier [dosje] *nm* (*documents*) file; (*de chaise*) back; (*Presse*) feature; (*Comput*) folder; **un ~ scolaire** a school report

douane [dwan] *nf* customs *pl*; **douanier, -ière** *adj* customs *cpd* ▷ *nm* customs officer

double [dubl] *adj, adv* double ▷ *nm* (2 *fois plus*): **le ~ (de)** twice as much (*ou* many) (as); (*autre exemplaire*) duplicate, copy; (*sosie*) double; (*Tennis*) doubles *sg*; **en ~ (exemplaire)** in duplicate; **faire ~ emploi** to be redundant; **double-cliquer** *vi* (*Inform*) to double-click

doubler [duble] vt (multiplier par 2) to double; (vêtement) to line; (dépasser) to overtake, pass; (film) to dub; (acteur) to stand in for ▷ vi to double

doublure [dublyʀ] nf lining; (Cinéma) stand-in

douce [dus] adj voir **doux**; **douceâtre** adj sickly sweet; **doucement** adv gently; (lentement) slowly; **douceur** nf softness; (de quelqu'un) gentleness; (de climat) mildness

douche [duʃ] nf shower; **prendre une ~** to have ou take a shower; **doucher: se doucher** vi to have ou take a shower

doué, e [dwe] adj gifted, talented; **être ~ pour** to have a gift for

douille [duj] nf (Élec) socket

douillet, te [dujɛ, ɛt] adj cosy; (péj: à la douleur) soft

douleur [dulœʀ] nf pain; (chagrin) grief, distress; **douloureux, -euse** adj painful

doute [dut] nm doubt; **sans ~** no doubt; (probablement) probably; **sans aucun ~** without a doubt; **douter** vt to doubt; **douter de** (sincérité de qn) to have (one's) doubts about; (réussite) to be doubtful of; **douter que** to doubt if ou whether; **se douter de qch/que** to suspect sth/that; **je m'en doutais** I suspected as much; **douteux, -euse** adj (incertain) doubtful; (péj) dubious-looking

Douvres [duvʀ] n Dover

doux, douce [du, dus] adj soft; (sucré) sweet; (peu fort: moutarde, clément: climat) mild; (pas brusque) gentle

douzaine [duzɛn] nf (12) dozen; (environ 12): **une ~ (de)** a dozen or so

douze [duz] num twelve; **douzième** num twelfth

dragée [dʀaʒe] nf sugared almond

draguer [dʀage] vt (rivière) to dredge; (fam) to try to pick up

dramatique [dʀamatik] adj dramatic; (tragique) tragic ▷ nf (TV) (television) drama

drame [dʀam] nm drama

drap [dʀa] nm (de lit) sheet; (tissu) woollen fabric

drapeau, x [dʀapo] nm flag

drap-housse [dʀaus] nm fitted sheet

dresser [dʀese] vt (mettre vertical, monter) to put up, erect; (liste) to draw up; (animal) to train; **se dresser** vi (obstacle) to stand; (personne) to draw o.s. up; **~ qn contre qn** to set sb against sb; **~ l'oreille** to prick up one's ears

drogue [dʀɔg] nf drug; **la ~** drugs pl; **drogué, e** nm/f drug addict; **droguer** vt (victime) to drug; **se droguer** vi (aux stupéfiants) to take drugs; (péj: de médicaments) to dose o.s. up; **droguerie** nf hardware shop; **droguiste** nm keeper/owner of a hardware shop

droit, e [dʀwa, dʀwat] adj (non courbe) straight; (vertical) upright, straight; (fig: loyal) upright, straight(forward); (opposé à gauche) right, right-hand ▷ adv straight ▷ nm (prérogative) right; (taxe) duty, tax; (: d'inscription) fee; (Jur): **le ~** law; **avoir le ~ de** to be allowed to; **avoir ~ à** to be entitled to; **être dans son ~** to be within one's rights; **à ~e** on the right; (direction) (to the) right; **droits d'auteur** royalties; **droits d'inscription** enrolment fee; **droite** nf (Pol): **la droite** the right (wing); **droitier, -ière** adj right-handed

drôle [dʀol] adj funny; **une ~ d'idée** a funny idea

dromadaire [dʀɔmadɛʀ] nm dromedary

du [dy] dét voir **de** ▷ prép +dét = **de + le**

dû, due [dy] vb voir **devoir** ▷ adj (somme) owing, owed; (causé par): **dû à** due to ▷ nm due

dune [dyn] nf dune

duplex [dyplɛks] nm (appartement) split-level apartment, duplex

duquel [dykɛl] prép +pron = **de +lequel**

dur, e [dyʀ] adj (pierre, siège, travail, problème) hard; (voix, climat) harsh; (sévère) hard, harsh; (cruel) hard(-hearted); (porte, col) stiff; (viande) tough ▷ adv hard ▷ nm (fam:

meneur) tough nut; **~ d'oreille** hard of hearing

durant [dyrɑ̃] *prép (au cours de)* during; *(pendant)* for; **des mois ~** for months

durcir [dyrsir] *vt, vi* to harden; **se durcir** *vi* to harden

durée [dyre] *nf* length; *(d'une pile etc)* life; **de courte ~** *(séjour)* short

durement [dyrmɑ̃] *adv* harshly

durer [dyre] *vi* to last

dureté [dyrte] *nf* hardness; harshness; stiffness; toughness

durit(r) [dyrit] *nf* (car radiator) hose

duvet [dyvɛ] *nm* down; *(sac de couchage)* down-filled sleeping bag

DVD *sigle m* (= *digital versatile disc*) DVD

dynamique [dinamik] *adj* dynamic; **dynamisme** *nm* dynamism

dynamo [dinamo] *nf* dynamo

dyslexie [disleksi] *nf* dyslexia, word-blindness

e

eau, x [o] *nf* water; **eaux** *nfpl (Méd)* waters; **prendre l'~** to leak, let in water; **tomber à l'~** *(fig)* to fall through; **eau de Cologne** eau de Cologne; **eau courante** running water; **eau de javel** bleach; **eau de toilette** toilet water; **eau douce** fresh water; **eau gazeuse** sparkling (mineral) water; **eau minérale** mineral water; **eau plate** still water; **eau salée** salt water; **eau-de-vie** *nf* brandy

ébène [ebɛn] *nf* ebony; **ébéniste** *nm* cabinetmaker

éblouir [ebluir] *vt* to dazzle

éboueur [ebwœr] *nm* dustman *(BRIT)*, garbageman *(US)*

ébouillanter [ebujɑ̃te] *vt* to scald; *(Culin)* to blanch

éboulement [ebulmɑ̃] *nm* rock fall

ébranler [ebrɑ̃le] *vt* to shake; *(affaiblir)* to weaken; **s'ébranler** *vi (partir)* to move off

ébullition [ebylisjɔ̃] *nf* boiling point; **en ~** boiling

écaille [ekaj] nf (de poisson) scale; (matière) tortoiseshell; **écailler** vt (poisson) to scale; **s'écailler** vi to flake ou peel (off)

écart [ekaʀ] nm gap; **à l'~** out of the way; **à l'~ de** away from; **faire un ~** (voiture) to swerve

écarté, e [ekaʀte] adj (lieu) out-of-the-way, remote; (ouvert): **les jambes ~es** legs apart; **les bras ~s** arms outstretched

écarter [ekaʀte] vt (séparer) to move apart, separate; (éloigner) to push back, move away; (ouvrir: bras, jambes) to spread, open; (: rideau) to draw (back); (éliminer: candidat, possibilité) to dismiss; **s'écarter** vi to part; (s'éloigner) to move away; **s'~ de** to wander from

échafaudage [eʃafodaʒ] nm scaffolding

échalote [eʃalɔt] nf shallot

échange [eʃɑ̃ʒ] nm exchange; **en ~ de** in exchange ou return for; **échanger** vt: **échanger qch (contre)** to exchange sth (for)

échantillon [eʃɑ̃tijɔ̃] nm sample

échapper [eʃape]: **~ à** vt (gardien) to escape (from); (punition, péril) to escape; **s'échapper** vi to escape; **~ à qn** (détail, sens) to escape sb; (objet qu'on tient) to slip out of sb's hands; **laisser ~** (cri etc) to let out; **l'~ belle** to have a narrow escape

écharde [eʃaʀd] nf splinter (of wood)

écharpe [eʃaʀp] nf scarf; **avoir le bras en ~** to have one's arm in a sling

échauffer [eʃofe] vt (moteur) to overheat; **s'échauffer** vi (Sport) to warm up; (dans la discussion) to become heated

échéance [eʃeɑ̃s] nf (d'un paiement: date) settlement date; (fig) deadline; **à brève ~** in the short term; **à longue ~** in the long run

échéant [eʃeɑ̃]: **le cas ~** adv if the case arises

échec [eʃɛk] nm failure; (Échecs): **~ et mat/au roi** checkmate/check; **échecs** nmpl (jeu) chess sg; **tenir en ~** to hold in check

échelle [eʃɛl] nf ladder; (fig, d'une carte) scale

échelon [eʃ(ə)lɔ̃] nm (d'échelle) rung; (Admin) grade; **échelonner** vt to space out

échiquier [eʃikje] nm chessboard

écho [eko] nm echo; **échographie** nf: **passer une échographie** to have a scan

échouer [eʃwe] vi to fail; **s'échouer** vi to run aground

éclabousser [eklabuse] vt to splash

éclair [eklɛʀ] nm (d'orage) flash of lightning, lightning no pl; (gâteau) éclair

éclairage [eklɛʀaʒ] nm lighting

éclaircie [eklɛʀsi] nf bright interval

éclaircir [eklɛʀsiʀ] vt to lighten; (fig: mystère) to clear up; (: point) to clarify; **s'éclaircir** vi (ciel) to clear; **s'~ la voix** to clear one's throat; **éclaircissement** nm (sur un point) clarification

éclairer [eklere] vt (lieu) to light (up); (personne: avec une lampe etc) to light the way for; (fig: problème) to shed light on ▷ vi: **~ mal/bien** to give a poor/good light; **s'~ à la bougie** to use candlelight

éclat [ekla] nm (de bombe, de verre) fragment; (du soleil, d'une couleur etc) brightness, brilliance; (d'une cérémonie) splendour; (scandale): **faire un ~** to cause a commotion; **éclats de voix** shouts; **éclat de rire** roar of laughter

éclatant, e [eklatɑ̃, ɑ̃t] adj brilliant

éclater [eklate] vi (pneu) to burst; (bombe) to explode; (guerre) to break out; (groupe, parti) to break up; **~ en sanglots/de rire** to burst out sobbing/laughing

écluse [eklyz] nf lock

écœurant, e [ekœʀɑ̃, ɑ̃t] adj (gâteau etc) sickly; (fig) sickening

écœurer [ekœʀe] vt: **~ qn** (nourriture) to make sb feel sick; (conduite, personne) to disgust sb

école [ekɔl] nf school; **aller à l'~** to go

to school; **école maternelle** nursery school; **école primaire** primary (BRIT) ou grade (US) school; **école secondaire** secondary (BRIT) ou high (US) school; **écolier, -ière** nm/f schoolboy(-girl)

écologie [ekɔlɔʒi] nf ecology; **écologique** adj environment-friendly; **écologiste** nm/f ecologist

économe [ekɔnɔm] adj thrifty ▷ nm/f (de lycée etc) bursar (BRIT), treasurer (US)

économie [ekɔnɔmi] nf economy; (gain: d'argent, de temps etc) saving; (science) economics sg; **économies** nfpl (pécule) savings; **économique** adj (avantageux) economical; (Écon) economic; **économiser** vt, vi to save

écorce [ekɔʀs] nf bark; (de fruit) peel

écorcher [ekɔʀʃe] vt: **s'~ le genou/la main** to graze one's knee/one's hand; **écorchure** nf graze

écossais, e [ekɔsɛ, ɛz] adj Scottish ▷ nm/f: **É~, e** Scot

Écosse [ekɔs] nf: **l'~** Scotland

écouter [ekute] vt to listen to; **s'écouter** (malade) to be a bit of a hypochondriac; **si je m'écoutais** if I followed my instincts; **écouteur** nm (Tél) receiver; **écouteurs** nmpl (casque) headphones pl, headset

écran [ekʀɑ̃] nm screen; **petit ~** television; **~ total** sunblock

écrasant, e [ekʀɑzɑ̃, ɑ̃t] adj overwhelming

écraser [ekʀaze] vt to crush; (piéton) to run over; **s'écraser** vi to crash; **s'~ contre** to crash into

écrémé, e [ekʀeme] adj (lait) skimmed

écrevisse [ekʀəvis] nf crayfish inv

écrire [ekʀiʀ] vt to write; **s'écrire** to write to each other; **ça s'écrit comment?** how is it spelt?; **écrit** nm (examen) written paper; **par écrit** in writing

écriteau, x [ekʀito] nm notice, sign

écriture [ekʀityʀ] nf writing; **écritures** nfpl (Comm) accounts, books; **l'É~ (sainte), les É~s** the Scriptures

écrivain [ekʀivɛ̃] nm writer

écrou [ekʀu] nm nut

écrouler [ekʀule]: **s'écrouler** vi to collapse

écru, e [ekʀy] adj (couleur) off-white, écru

écume [ekym] nf foam

écureuil [ekyʀœj] nm squirrel

écurie [ekyʀi] nf stable

eczéma [ɛgzema] nm eczema

EDF sigle f (= Électricité de France) national electricity company

Édimbourg [edɛ̃buʀ] n Edinburgh

éditer [edite] vt (publier) to publish; (annoter) to edit; **éditeur, -trice** nm/f publisher; **édition** nf edition; (industrie du livre) publishing

édredon [edʀədɔ̃] nm eiderdown

éducateur, -trice [edykatœʀ, tʀis] nm/f teacher; (en école spécialisée) instructor

éducatif, -ive [edykatif, iv] adj educational

éducation [edykasjɔ̃] nf education; (familiale) upbringing; (manières) (good) manners pl; **éducation physique** physical education

éduquer [edyke] vt to educate; (élever) to bring up

effacer [efase] vt to erase, rub out; **s'effacer** vi (inscription etc) to wear off; (pour laisser passer) to step aside

effarant, e [efaʀɑ̃, ɑ̃t] adj alarming

effectif, -ive [efɛktif, iv] adj real ▷ nm (Scol) (pupil) numbers pl; (entreprise) staff, workforce; **effectivement** adv (réellement) actually, really; (en effet) indeed

effectuer [efɛktɥe] vt (opération) to carry out; (trajet) to make

effervescent, e [efɛʀvesɑ̃, ɑ̃t] adj effervescent

effet [efɛ] nm effect; (impression) impression; **effets** nmpl (vêtements etc) things; **faire ~** (médicament) to take effect; **faire de l'~** (impressionner) to make an impression; **faire bon/ mauvais ~ sur qn** to make a good/bad impression on sb; **en ~** indeed; **effet de**

serre greenhouse effect

efficace [efikas] *adj* (*personne*) efficient; (*action, médicament*) effective; **efficacité** *nf* efficiency; effectiveness

effondrer [efɔ̃dʀe]: **s'effondrer** *vi* to collapse

efforcer [efɔʀse]: **s'efforcer de** *vt*: **s'~ de faire** to try hard to do

effort [efɔʀ] *nm* effort

effrayant, e [efʀejɑ̃, ɑ̃t] *adj* frightening

effrayer [efʀeje] *vt* to frighten, scare; **s'~ (de)** to be frightened *ou* scared (by)

effréné, e [efʀene] *adj* wild

effronté, e [efʀɔ̃te] *adj* cheeky

effroyable [efʀwajabl] *adj* horrifying, appalling

égal, e, -aux [egal, o] *adj* equal; (*constant: vitesse*) steady ▷ *nm/f* equal; **être ~ à** (*prix, nombre*) to be equal to; **ça lui est ~** it's all the same to him, he doesn't mind; **sans ~** matchless, unequalled; **d'~ à ~** as equals; **également** *adv* equally; (*aussi*) too, as well; **égaler** *vt* to equal; **égaliser** *vt* (*sol, salaires*) to level (out); (*chances*) to equalize ▷ *vi* (*Sport*) to equalize; **égalité** *nf* equality; **être à égalité** to be level

égard [egaʀ] *nm*: **~s** *mpl* consideration *sg*; **à cet ~** in this respect; **par ~ pour** out of consideration for; **à l'~ de** towards

égarer [egaʀe] *vt* to mislay; **s'égarer** *vi* to get lost, lose one's way; (*objet*) to go astray

églefin [egləfɛ̃] *nm* haddock

église [egliz] *nf* church; **aller à l'~** to go to church

égoïsme [egɔism] *nm* selfishness; **égoïste** *adj* selfish

égout [egu] *nm* sewer

égoutter [egute] *vt* to drip; **s'égoutter** *vi* to drip; **égouttoir** *nm* draining board; (*mobile*) draining rack

égratignure [egʀatiɲyʀ] *nf* scratch

Égypte [eʒipt] *nf*: **l'~** Egypt; **égyptien, ne** *adj* Egyptian ▷ *nm/f*:

Égyptien, ne Egyptian

eh [e] *excl* hey!; **eh bien!** well!

élaborer [elabɔʀe] *vt* to elaborate; (*projet, stratégie*) to work out; (*rapport*) to draft

élan [elɑ̃] *nm* (*Zool*) elk, moose; (*Sport*) run up; (*fig: de tendresse etc*) surge; **prendre de l'~** to gather speed

élancer [elɑ̃se]: **s'élancer** *vi* to dash, hurl o.s.

élargir [elaʀʒiʀ] *vt* to widen; **s'élargir** *vi* to widen; (*vêtement*) to stretch

élastique [elastik] *adj* elastic ▷ *nm* (*de bureau*) rubber band; (*pour la couture*) elastic *no pl*

élection [elɛksjɔ̃] *nf* election

électricien, ne [elɛktʀisjɛ̃, jɛn] *nm/f* electrician

électricité [elɛktʀisite] *nf* electricity; **allumer/éteindre l'~** to put on/off the light

électrique [elɛktʀik] *adj* electric(al)

électrocuter [elɛktʀɔkyte] *vt* to electrocute

électroménager [elɛktʀomenaʒe] *adj, nm*: **appareils ~s, l'~** domestic (electrical) appliances

électronique [elɛktʀɔnik] *adj* electronic ▷ *nf* electronics *sg*

élégance [elegɑ̃s] *nf* elegance

élégant, e [elegɑ̃, ɑ̃t] *adj* elegant

élément [elemɑ̃] *nm* element; (*pièce*) component, part; **élémentaire** *adj* elementary

éléphant [elefɑ̃] *nm* elephant

élevage [el(ə)vaʒ] *nm* breeding; (*de bovins*) cattle rearing; **truite d'~** farmed trout

élevé, e [el(ə)ve] *adj* high; **bien/mal ~** well-/ill-mannered

élève [elɛv] *nm/f* pupil

élever [el(ə)ve] *vt* (*enfant*) to bring up, raise; (*animaux*) to breed; (*hausser: taux, niveau*) to raise; (*édifier: monument*) to put up, erect; **s'élever** *vi* (*avion*) to go up; (*niveau, température*) to rise; **s'~ à** (*suj: frais, dégâts*) to amount to, add up to; **s'~ contre qch** to rise up against

sth; **~ la voix** to raise one's voice;
éleveur, -euse nm/f breeder
éliminatoire [eliminatwaʀ] nf
(Sport) heat
éliminer [elimine] vt to eliminate
élire [eliʀ] vt to elect
elle [ɛl] pron (sujet) she; (: chose) it;
(complément) her; it; **~s** (sujet) they;
(complément) them; **~-même** herself;
itself; **~s-mêmes** themselves; voir
aussi **il**
éloigné, e [elwaɲe] adj distant, far-off;
(parent) distant
éloigner [elwaɲe] vt (échéance) to put
off, postpone; (soupçons, danger) to
ward off; (objet): **~ qch (de)** to move
ou take sth away (from); (personne):
~ qn (de) to take sb away ou remove
sb (from); **s'éloigner (de)** (personne)
to go away (from); (véhicule) to move
away (from); (affectivement) to grow
away (from)
élu, e [ely] pp de **élire** ▷ nm/f (Pol)
elected representative
Élysée [elize] nm: **(le palais de) l'~**
the Élysee Palace (the French president's
residence)
émail, -aux [emaj, o] nm enamel
e-mail [imɛl] nm e-mail; **envoyer qch
par ~** to e-mail sth
émanciper [emãsipe]: **s'émanciper**
vi (fig) to become emancipated ou
liberated
emballage [ãbalaʒ] nm (papier)
wrapping; (boîte) packaging
emballer [ãbale] vt to wrap (up); (dans
un carton) to pack (up); (fig: fam) to thrill
(to bits); **s'emballer** vi (moteur) to race;
(cheval) to bolt; (fig: personne) to get
carried away
embarcadère [ãbaʀkadɛʀ] nm
wharf, pier
embarquement [ãbaʀkəmã] nm (de
passagers) boarding; (de marchandises)
loading
embarquer [ãbaʀke] vt (personne) to
embark; (marchandise) to load; (fam)
to cart off ▷ vi (passager) to board;

s'embarquer vi to board; **s'~ dans**
(affaire, aventure) to embark upon
embarras [ãbaʀa] nm (gêne)
embarrassment; **mettre qn dans
l'~** to put sb in an awkward position;
vous n'avez que l'~ du choix the only
problem is choosing
embarrassant, e [ãbaʀasã, ãt] adj
embarrassing
embarrasser [ãbaʀase] vt (encombrer)
to clutter (up); (gêner) to hinder,
hamper; **~** to put sb in an awkward
position; **s'~ de** to burden o.s. with
embaucher [ãboʃe] vt to take on, hire
embêter [ãbete] vt to bother;
s'embêter vi (s'ennuyer) to be bored
emblée [ãble]: **d'~** adv straightaway
embouchure [ãbuʃyʀ] nf (Géo) mouth
embourber [ãbuʀbe]: **s'embourber** vi
to get stuck in the mud
embouteillage [ãbutɛjaʒ] nm
traffic jam
embranchement [ãbʀãʃmã] nm
(routier) junction
embrasser [ãbʀase] vt to kiss; (sujet,
période) to embrace, encompass
embrayage [ãbʀɛjaʒ] nm clutch
embrouiller [ãbʀuje] vt to muddle up;
(fils) to tangle (up); **s'embrouiller** vi
(personne) to get in a muddle
embruns [ãbʀœ̃] nmpl sea spray sg
embué, e [ãbɥe] adj misted up
émeraude [em(ə)ʀod] nf emerald
émerger [emɛʀʒe] vi to emerge; (faire
saillie, aussi fig) to stand out
émeri [em(ə)ʀi] nm: **toile** ou **papier ~**
emery paper
émerveiller [emɛʀveje] vt to fill with
wonder; **s'émerveiller de** to marvel at
émettre [emɛtʀ] vt (son, lumière) to
give out, emit; (message etc: Radio) to
transmit; (billet, timbre, emprunt) to
issue; (hypothèse, avis) to voice, put
forward ▷ vi to broadcast
émeus etc [emø] vb voir **émouvoir**
émeute [emøt] nf riot
émigrer [emigʀe] vi to emigrate
émincer [emɛ̃se] vt to cut into thin

slices

émission [emisjɔ̃] nf (Radio, TV) programme, broadcast; (d'un message) transmission; (de timbre) issue

emmêler [ɑ̃mele] vt to tangle (up); (fig) to muddle up; **s'emmêler** vi to get in a tangle

emménager [ɑ̃menaʒe] vi to move in; **~ dans** to move into

emmener [ɑ̃m(ə)ne] vt to take (with one); (comme otage, capture) to take away; **~ qn au cinéma** to take sb to the cinema

emmerder [ɑ̃mɛʀde] (fam!) vt to bug, bother; **s'emmerder** vi to be bored stiff

émoticone [emɔticɔn] nm smiley

émotif, -ive [emɔtif, iv] adj emotional

émotion [emɔsjɔ̃] nf emotion

émouvoir [emuvwaʀ] vt to move; **s'émouvoir** vi to be moved; (s'indigner) to be roused

empaqueter [ɑ̃pakte] vt to parcel up

emparer [ɑ̃paʀe]: **s'emparer de** vt (objet) to seize, grab; (comme otage, MIL) to seize; (suj: peur etc) to take hold of

empêchement [ɑ̃pɛʃmɑ̃] nm (unexpected) obstacle, hitch

empêcher [ɑ̃peʃe] vt to prevent; **~ qn de faire** to prevent ou stop sb (from) doing; **il n'empêche que** nevertheless; **il n'a pas pu s'~ de rire** he couldn't help laughing

empereur [ɑ̃pʀœʀ] nm emperor

empiffrer [ɑ̃pifʀe]: **s'~** (fam) vi to stuff o.s.

empiler [ɑ̃pile] vt to pile (up)

empire [ɑ̃piʀ] nm empire; (fig) influence

empirer [ɑ̃piʀe] vi to worsen, deteriorate

emplacement [ɑ̃plasmɑ̃] nm site

emploi [ɑ̃plwa] nm (utilisation) use; (Comm, Écon) employment; (poste) job, situation; **mode d'~** directions for use; **emploi du temps** timetable, schedule

employé, e [ɑ̃plwaje] nm/f employee; **employé de bureau** office employee ou clerk

employer [ɑ̃plwaje] vt to use; (ouvrier, main-d'œuvre) to employ; **s'~ à faire** to apply ou devote o.s. to doing; **employeur, -euse** nm/f employer

empoigner [ɑ̃pwaɲe] vt to grab

empoisonner [ɑ̃pwazɔne] vt to poison; (empester: air, pièce) to stink out; (fam): **~ qn** to drive sb mad

emporter [ɑ̃pɔʀte] vt to take (with one); (en dérobant ou enlevant, emmener: blessés, voyageurs) to take away; (entraîner) to carry away; **s'emporter** vi (de colère) to lose one's temper; **l'~ (sur)** to get the upper hand (of); **plats à ~** take-away meals

empreinte [ɑ̃pʀɛ̃t] nf: **~ (de pas)** footprint; **empreintes (digitales)** fingerprints

empressé, e [ɑ̃pʀese] adj attentive

empresser [ɑ̃pʀese]: **s'empresser** vi: **s'~ auprès de qn** to surround sb with attentions; **s'~ de faire** (se hâter) to hasten to do

emprisonner [ɑ̃pʀizɔne] vt to imprison

emprunt [ɑ̃pʀœ̃] nm loan

emprunter [ɑ̃pʀœ̃te] vt to borrow; (itinéraire) to take, follow

ému, e [emy] pp de **émouvoir** ▷ adj (gratitude) touched; (compassion) moved

 MOT-CLÉ

en [ɑ̃] prép **1** (endroit, pays) in; (direction) to; **habiter en France/ville** to live in France/town; **aller en France/ville** to go to France/town

2 (moment, temps) in; **en été/juin** in summer/June; **en 3 jours** in 3 days

3 (moyen) by; **en avion/taxi** by plane/taxi

4 (composition) made of; **c'est en verre** it's (made of) glass; **un collier en argent** a silver necklace

5 (description, état): **une femme (habillée) en rouge** a woman (dressed) in red; **peindre qch en rouge** to paint sth red; **en T/étoile** T/star-shaped; **en**

chemise/chaussettes in one's shirt-sleeves/socks; **en soldat** as a soldier; **cassé en plusieurs morceaux** broken into several pieces; **en réparation** being repaired, under repair; **en vacances** on holiday; **en deuil** in mourning; **le même en plus grand** the same but *ou* only bigger

6 (*avec gérondif*) while, on, by; **en dormant** while sleeping, as one sleeps; **en sortant** on going out, as he *etc* went out; **sortir en courant** to run out

7 (*comme*) as; **je te parle en ami** I'm talking to you as a friend

▷ *pron* **1** (*indéfini*): **j'en ai/veux** I have/want some; **en as-tu?** have you got any?; **je n'en veux pas** I don't want any; **j'en ai 2** I've got 2; **combien y en a-t-il?** how many (of them) are there?; **j'en ai assez** I've got enough (of it *ou* them); (*j'en ai marre*) I've had enough

2 (*provenance*) from there; **j'en viens** I've come from there

3 (*cause*): **il en est malade/perd le sommeil** he is ill/can't sleep because of it

4 (*complément de nom, d'adjectif, de verbe*): **j'en connais les dangers** I know its *ou* the dangers; **j'en suis fier** I am proud of it *ou* him *ou* her *ou* them; **j'en ai besoin** I need it *ou* them

encadrer [ãkadʀe] *vt* (*tableau, image*) to frame; (*fig: entourer*) to surround; (*personnel, soldats etc*) to train

encaisser [ãkese] *vt* (*chèque*) to cash; (*argent*) to collect; (*fam: coup, défaite*) to take

en-cas [ãka] *nm* snack

enceinte [ãsɛ̃t] *adj f*: **~ (de 6 mois)** (6 months) pregnant ▷ *nf* (*mur*) wall; (*espace*) enclosure; **enceinte (acoustique)** (loud)speaker

encens [ãsã] *nm* incense

enchaîner [ãʃene] *vt* to chain up; (*mouvements, séquences*) to link (together) ▷ *vi* to carry on

enchanté, e [ãʃãte] *adj* (*ravi*)

delighted; (*magique*) enchanted; **~ (de faire votre connaissance)** pleased to meet you

enchère [ãʃɛʀ] *nf* bid; **mettre/vendre aux ~s** to put up for (sale by)/sell by auction

enclencher [ãklãʃe] *vt* (*mécanisme*) to engage; **s'enclencher** *vi* to engage

encombrant, e [ãkɔ̃bʀã, ãt] *adj* cumbersome, bulky

encombrement [ãkɔ̃bʀəmã] *nm*: **être pris dans un ~** to be stuck in a traffic jam

encombrer [ãkɔ̃bʀe] *vt* to clutter (up); (*gêner*) to hamper; **s'~ de** (*bagages etc*) to load *ou* burden o.s. with

 MOT-CLÉ

encore [ãkɔʀ] *adv* **1** (*continuation*) still; **il y travaille encore** he's still working on it; **pas encore** not yet

2 (*de nouveau*) again; **j'irai encore demain** I'll go again tomorrow; **encore une fois** (once) again; **(et puis) quoi encore?** what next?

3 (*en plus*) more; **encore un peu de viande?** a little more meat?; **encore deux jours** two more days

4 (*intensif*) even, still; **encore plus fort/mieux** even louder/better, louder/better still

5 (*restriction*) even so *ou* then, only; **encore pourrais-je le faire si ...** even so, I might be able to do it if ...; **si encore** if only

encourager [ãkuʀaʒe] *vt* to encourage; **~ qn à faire qch** to encourage sb to do sth

encourir [ãkuʀiʀ] *vt* to incur

encre [ãkʀ] *nf* ink; **encre de Chine** Indian ink

encyclopédie [ãsiklɔpedi] *nf* encyclopaedia

endetter [ãdete]: **s'endetter** *vi* to get into debt

endive [ãdiv] *nf* chicory *no pl*

endormi, e [ɑ̃dɔʀmi] *adj* asleep
endormir [ɑ̃dɔʀmiʀ] *vt* to put to
sleep; (*suj: chaleur etc*) to send to sleep;
(*Méd: dent, nerf*) to anaesthetize; (*fig:
soupçons*) to allay; **s'endormir** *vi* to fall
asleep, go to sleep
endroit [ɑ̃dʀwa] *nm* place; (*opposé à
l'envers*) right side; **à l'~** (*vêtement*) the
right way out; (*objet posé*) the right
way round
endurance [ɑ̃dyʀɑ̃s] *nf* endurance
endurant, e [ɑ̃dyʀɑ̃, ɑ̃t] *adj* tough,
hardy
endurcir [ɑ̃dyʀsiʀ] **s'endurcir** *vi*
(*physiquement*) to become tougher;
(*moralement*) to become hardened
endurer [ɑ̃dyʀe] *vt* to endure, bear
énergétique [enɛʀʒetik] *adj* (*aliment*)
energy-giving
énergie [enɛʀʒi] *nf* (*Physique*) energy;
(*Tech*) power; (*morale*) vigour, spirit;
énergique *adj* energetic, vigorous;
(*mesures*) drastic, stringent
énervant, e [enɛʀvɑ̃, ɑ̃t] *adj* irritating,
annoying
énerver [enɛʀve] *vt* to irritate, annoy;
s'énerver *vi* to get excited, get
worked up
enfance [ɑ̃fɑ̃s] *nf* childhood
enfant [ɑ̃fɑ̃] *nm/f* child; **enfantin, e**
adj (*puéril*) childlike; (*langage, jeu etc*)
children's *cpd*
enfer [ɑ̃fɛʀ] *nm* hell
enfermer [ɑ̃fɛʀme] *vt* to shut up; (*à
clef, interner*) to lock up; **s'enfermer** to
shut o.s. away
enfiler [ɑ̃file] *vt* (*vêtement*) to slip on,
slip into; (*perles*) to string; (*aiguille*)
to thread
enfin [ɑ̃fɛ̃] *adv* at last; (*en énumérant*)
lastly; (*toutefois*) still; (*pour conclure*) in a
word; (*somme toute*) after all
enflammer [ɑ̃flame] **s'enflammer** *vi*
to catch fire; (*Méd*) to become inflamed
enflé, e [ɑ̃fle] *adj* swollen
enfler [ɑ̃fle] *vt* to swell (up)
enfoncer [ɑ̃fɔ̃se] *vt* (*clou*) to drive in;
(*faire pénétrer*): **~ qch dans** to push (*ou*

drive) sth into; (*forcer: porte*) to break
open; **s'enfoncer** to sink; **s'~ dans** to
sink into; (*forêt, ville*) to disappear into
enfouir [ɑ̃fwiʀ] *vt* (*dans le sol*) to bury;
(*dans un tiroir etc*) to tuck away
enfuir [ɑ̃fɥiʀ]: **s'enfuir** *vi* to run away
ou off
engagement [ɑ̃gaʒmɑ̃] *nm*
commitment; **sans ~** without
obligation
engager [ɑ̃gaʒe] *vt* (*embaucher*) to take
on; (: *artiste*) to engage; (*commencer*) to
start; (*lier*) to bind, commit; (*impliquer*)
to involve; (*investir*) to invest, lay out;
(*inciter*) to urge; (*introduire: clé*) to insert;
s'engager *vi* (*promettre*) to commit
o.s.; (*Mil*) to enlist; (*débuter: conversation
etc*) to start (up); **s'~ à faire** to
undertake to do; **s'~ dans** (*rue, passage*)
to turn into; (*fig: affaire, discussion*) to
enter into, embark on
engelures [ɑ̃ʒlyʀ] *nfpl* chilblains
engin [ɑ̃ʒɛ̃] *nm* machine; (*outil*)
instrument; (*Auto*) vehicle; (*Aviat*)
aircraft *inv*

⸠ Attention à ne pas traduire *engin*
par le mot anglais *engine*.

engloutir [ɑ̃glutiʀ] *vt* to swallow up
engouement [ɑ̃gumɑ̃] *nm* (sudden)
passion
engouffrer [ɑ̃gufʀe] *vt* to swallow up,
devour; **s'engouffrer dans** to rush into
engourdir [ɑ̃guʀdiʀ] *vt* to numb;
(*fig*) to dull, blunt; **s'engourdir** *vi* to
go numb
engrais [ɑ̃gʀɛ] *nm* manure; **engrais
chimique** chemical fertilizer
engraisser [ɑ̃gʀese] *vt* to fatten (up)
engrenage [ɑ̃gʀənaʒ] *nm* gears *pl*,
gearing; (*fig*) chain
engueuler [ɑ̃gœle] (*fam*) *vt* to bawl at
enhardir [ɑ̃aʀdiʀ]: **s'enhardir** *vi* to
grow bolder
énigme [enigm] *nf* riddle
enivrer [ɑ̃nivʀe] *vt*: **s'~** to get drunk
enjamber [ɑ̃ʒɑ̃be] *vt* to stride over
enjeu, x [ɑ̃ʒø] *nm* stakes *pl*
enjoué, e [ɑ̃ʒwe] *adj* playful

enlaidir [ɑ̃lediʀ] vt to make ugly ▷ vi to become ugly

enlèvement [ɑ̃lɛvmɑ̃] nm (rapt) abduction, kidnapping

enlever [ɑ̃l(ə)ve] vt (ôter: gén) to remove; (: vêtement, lunettes etc) to take off; (emporter: ordures etc) to take away; (kidnapper) to abduct, kidnap; (obtenir: prix, contrat) to win; (prendre): **~ qch à qn** to take sth (away) from sb

enliser [ɑ̃lize]: **s'enliser** vi to sink, get stuck

enneigé, e [ɑ̃neʒe] adj (route, maison) snowed-up; (paysage) snowy

ennemi, e [ɛnmi] adj hostile; (Mil) enemy cpd ▷ nm/f enemy

ennui [ɑ̃nɥi] nm (lassitude) boredom; (difficulté) trouble no pl; **avoir des ~s** to have problems; **ennuyer** vt to bother; (lasser) to bore; **s'ennuyer** vi to be bored; **si cela ne vous ennuie pas** if it's no trouble (to you); **ennuyeux, -euse** adj boring, tedious; (embêtant) annoying

énorme [enɔʀm] adj enormous, huge; **énormément** adv enormously; **énormément de neige/gens** an enormous amount of snow/number of people

enquête [ɑ̃kɛt] nf (de journaliste, de police) investigation; (judiciaire, administrative) inquiry; (sondage d'opinion) survey; **enquêter** vi: **enquêter (sur)** to investigate

enragé, e [ɑ̃ʀaʒe] adj (Méd) rabid, with rabies; (fig) fanatical

enrageant, e [ɑ̃ʀaʒɑ̃, ɑ̃t] adj infuriating

enrager [ɑ̃ʀaʒe] vi to be in a rage

enregistrement [ɑ̃ʀ(ə)ʒistʀəmɑ̃] nm recording; **enregistrement des bagages** baggage check-in

enregistrer [ɑ̃ʀ(ə)ʒistʀe] vt (Mus etc) to record; (fig: mémoriser) to make a mental note of; (bagages: à l'aéroport) to check in

enrhumer [ɑ̃ʀyme] vt: **s'~, être enrhumé** to catch a cold

enrichir [ɑ̃ʀiʃiʀ] vt to make rich(er); (fig) to enrich; **s'enrichir** vi to get rich(er)

enrouer [ɑ̃ʀwe]: **s'enrouer** vi to go hoarse

enrouler [ɑ̃ʀule] vt (fil, corde) to wind (up); **s'~ (autour de qch)** to wind (around) sth

enseignant, e [ɑ̃sɛɲɑ̃, ɑ̃t] nm/f teacher

enseignement [ɑ̃sɛɲ(ə)mɑ̃] nm teaching; (Admin) education

enseigner [ɑ̃sɛɲe] vt, vi to teach; **~ qch à qn** to teach sb sth

ensemble [ɑ̃sɑ̃bl] adv together ▷ nm (groupement) set; (vêtements) outfit; (totalité): **l'~ du/de la** the whole ou entire; (unité, harmonie) unity; **impression/idée d'~** overall ou general impression/idea; **dans l'~** (en gros) on the whole

ensoleillé, e [ɑ̃sɔleje] adj sunny

ensuite [ɑ̃sɥit] adv then, next; (plus tard) afterwards, later

entamer [ɑ̃tame] vt (pain, bouteille) to start; (hostilités, pourparlers) to open

entasser [ɑ̃tase] vt (empiler) to pile up, heap up; **s'entasser** vi (s'amonceler) to pile up; **s'~ dans** (personnes) to cram into

entendre [ɑ̃tɑ̃dʀ] vt to hear; (comprendre) to understand; (vouloir dire) to mean; **s'entendre** vi (sympathiser) to get on; (se mettre d'accord) to agree; **j'ai entendu dire que** I've heard (it said) that; **~ parler de** to hear of

entendu, e [ɑ̃tɑ̃dy] adj (réglé) agreed; (au courant: air) knowing; **(c'est) ~** all right, agreed; **bien ~** of course

entente [ɑ̃tɑ̃t] nf understanding; (accord, traité) agreement; **à double ~** (sens) with a double meaning

enterrement [ɑ̃tɛʀmɑ̃] nm (cérémonie) funeral, burial

enterrer [ɑ̃teʀe] vt to bury

entêtant, e [ɑ̃tɛtɑ̃, ɑ̃t] adj heady

en-tête [ɑ̃tɛt] nm heading; **papier à ~** headed notepaper

entêté, e [ɑ̃tete] *adj* stubborn
entêter [ɑ̃tete]: **s'entêter** *vi*: **s'~ (à faire)** to persist (in doing)
enthousiasme [ɑ̃tuzjasm] *nm* enthusiasm; **enthousiasmer** *vt* to fill with enthusiasm; **s'enthousiasmer (pour qch)** to get enthusiastic (about sth); **enthousiaste** *adj* enthusiastic
entier, -ère [ɑ̃tje, jɛʀ] *adj* whole; (*total: satisfaction etc*) complete; (*fig: caractère*) unbending ▷ *nm* (Math) whole; **en ~** totally; **lait ~** full-cream milk; **entièrement** *adv* entirely, wholly
entonnoir [ɑ̃tɔnwaʀ] *nm* funnel
entorse [ɑ̃tɔʀs] *nf* (Méd) sprain; (fig): **~ au règlement** infringement of the rule
entourage [ɑ̃tuʀaʒ] *nm* circle; (*famille*) circle of family/friends; (*ce qui enclôt*) surround
entourer [ɑ̃tuʀe] *vt* to surround; (*apporter son soutien à*) to rally round; **~ de** to surround with; **s'~ de** to surround o.s. with
entracte [ɑ̃tʀakt] *nm* interval
entraide [ɑ̃tʀɛd] *nf* mutual aid
entrain [ɑ̃tʀɛ̃] *nm* spirit; **avec/sans ~** spiritedly/half-heartedly
entraînement [ɑ̃tʀɛnmɑ̃] *nm* training
entraîner [ɑ̃tʀene] *vt* (*charrier*) to carry *ou* drag along; (*Tech*) to drive; (*emmener: personne*) to take (off); (*influencer*) to lead; (*Sport*) to train; (*impliquer*) to entail; **s'entraîner** *vi* (Sport) to train; **s'~ à qch/à faire** to train o.s. for sth/to do; **~ qn à faire** (*inciter*) to lead sb to do; **entraîneur, -euse** *nm/f* (Sport) coach, trainer ▷ *nm* (Hippisme) trainer
entre [ɑ̃tʀ] *prép* between; (*parmi*) among(st); **l'un d'~ eux/nous** one of them/us; **ils se battent ~ eux** they are fighting among(st) themselves; **~ autres (choses)** among other things; **entrecôte** *nf* entrecôte *ou* rib steak
entrée [ɑ̃tʀe] *nf* entrance; (*accès: au cinéma etc*) admission; (*billet*) (admission) ticket; (Culin) first course
entre...: **entrefilet** *nm* paragraph (*short*

article); **entremets** *nm* (cream) dessert
entrepôt [ɑ̃tʀəpo] *nm* warehouse
entreprendre [ɑ̃tʀəpʀɑ̃dʀ] *vt* (*se lancer dans*) to undertake; (*commencer*) to begin *ou* start (upon)
entrepreneur, -euse [ɑ̃tʀəpʀənœʀ, øz] *nm/f*: **entrepreneur (en bâtiment)** (building) contractor
entreprise [ɑ̃tʀəpʀiz] *nf* (*société*) firm, concern; (*action*) undertaking, venture
entrer [ɑ̃tʀe] *vi* to go (*ou* come) in, enter ▷ *vt* (Inform) to enter, input; **(faire) ~ qch dans** to get sth into; **~ dans** (*gén*) to enter; (*pièce*) to go (*ou* come) into, enter; (*club*) to join; (*heurter*) to run into; **~ à l'hôpital** to go into hospital; **faire ~** (*visiteur*) to show in
entre-temps [ɑ̃tʀətɑ̃] *adv* meanwhile
entretenir [ɑ̃tʀət(ə)niʀ] *vt* to maintain; (*famille, maîtresse*) to support, keep; **~ qn (de)** to speak to sb (about)
entretien [ɑ̃tʀətjɛ̃] *nm* maintenance; (*discussion*) discussion, talk; (*pour un emploi*) interview
entrevoir [ɑ̃tʀəvwaʀ] *vt* (*à peine*) to make out; (*brièvement*) to catch a glimpse of
entrevue [ɑ̃tʀəvy] *nf* (*audience*) interview
entrouvert, e [ɑ̃tʀuvɛʀ, ɛʀt] *adj* half-open
énumérer [enymeʀe] *vt* to list
envahir [ɑ̃vaiʀ] *vt* to invade; (*suj: inquiétude, peur*) to come over; **envahissant, e** (*péj*) *adj* (*personne*) intrusive
enveloppe [ɑ̃v(ə)lɔp] *nf* (*de lettre*) envelope; (*crédits*) budget; **envelopper** *vt* to wrap; (*fig*) to envelop, shroud
enverrai *etc* [ɑ̃veʀe] *vb voir* **envoyer**
envers [ɑ̃vɛʀ] *prép* towards, to ▷ *nm* other side; (*d'une étoffe*) wrong side; **à l'~** (*verticalement*) upside down; (*pull*) back to front; (*chaussettes*) inside out
envie [ɑ̃vi] *nf* (*sentiment*) envy; (*souhait*) desire, wish; **avoir ~ de (faire)** to feel like (doing); (*plus fort*) to want (to

do); **avoir ~ que** to wish that; **cette glace me fait ~** I fancy some of that ice cream; **envier** vt to envy; **envieux, -euse** adj envious

environ [ãviʀɔ̃] adv: **~ 3 h/2 km** (around) about 3 o'clock/2 km; voir aussi **environs**

environnant, e [ãviʀɔnã, ãt] adj surrounding

environnement [ãviʀɔnmã] nm environment

environs [ãviʀɔ̃] nmpl surroundings; **aux ~ de** (round) about

envisager [ãvizaʒe] vt to contemplate, envisage; **~ de faire** to consider doing

envoler [ãvɔle]: **s'envoler** vi (oiseau) to fly away ou off; (avion) to take off; (papier, feuille) to blow away; (fig) to vanish (into thin air)

envoyé, e [ãvwaje] nm/f (Pol) envoy; (Presse) correspondent; **envoyé spécial** special correspondent

envoyer [ãvwaje] vt to send; (lancer) to hurl, throw; **~ chercher** to send for; **~ promener qn** (fam) to send sb packing

épagneul, e [epaɲœl] nm/f spaniel

épais, se [epɛ, ɛs] adj thick; **épaisseur** nf thickness

épanouir [epanwiʀ]: **s'épanouir** vi (fleur) to bloom, open out; (visage) to light up; (personne) to blossom

épargne [epaʀɲ] nf saving

épargner [epaʀɲe] vt to save; (ne pas tuer ou endommager) to spare ▷ vi to save; **~ qch à qn** to spare sb sth

éparpiller [epaʀpije] vt to scatter; **s'éparpiller** vi to scatter; (fig) to dissipate one's efforts

épatant, e [epatã, ãt] (fam) adj super

épater [epate] (fam) vt (étonner) to amaze; (impressionner) to impress

épaule [epol] nf shoulder

épave [epav] nf wreck

épée [epe] nf sword

épeler [ep(ə)le] vt to spell

éperon [epʀɔ̃] nm spur

épervier [epɛʀvje] nm sparrowhawk

épi [epi] nm (de blé, d'orge) ear; (de maïs) cob

épice [epis] nf spice

épicé, e [epise] adj spicy

épicer [epise] vt to spice

épicerie [episʀi] nf grocer's shop; (denrées) groceries pl; **épicerie fine** delicatessen; **épicier, -ière** nm/f grocer

épidémie [epidemi] nf epidemic

épiderme [epidɛʀm] nm skin

épier [epje] vt to spy on, watch closely

épilepsie [epilɛpsi] nf epilepsy

épiler [epile] vt (jambes) to remove the hair from; (sourcils) to pluck

épinards [epinaʀ] nmpl spinach sg

épine [epin] nf thorn, prickle; (d'oursin etc) spine

épingle [epɛ̃gl] nf pin; **épingle de nourrice** ou **de sûreté** safety pin

épisode [epizɔd] nm episode; **film/roman à ~s** serial; **épisodique** adj occasional

épluche-légumes [eplyʃlegym] nm inv (potato) peeler

éplucher [eplyʃe] vt (fruit, légumes) to peel; (fig) to go over with a fine-tooth comb; **épluchures** nfpl peelings

éponge [epɔ̃ʒ] nf sponge; **éponger** vt (liquide) to mop up; (surface) to sponge; (fig: déficit) to soak up

époque [epɔk] nf (de l'histoire) age, era; (de l'année, la vie) time; **d'~** (meuble) period cpd

épouse [epuz] nf wife; **épouser** vt to marry

épousseter [epuste] vt to dust

épouvantable [epuvãtabl] adj appalling, dreadful

épouvantail [epuvãtaj] nm scarecrow

épouvante [epuvãt] nf terror; **film d'~** horror film; **épouvanter** vt to terrify

époux [epu] nm husband ▷ nmpl (married) couple

épreuve [epʀœv] nf (d'examen) test; (malheur, difficulté) trial, ordeal; (Photo) print; (Typo) proof; (Sport) event; **à toute ~** unfailing; **mettre à l'~** to put to the test

éprouver [epʀuve] vt (tester) to

test; (*marquer, faire souffrir*) to afflict, distress; (*ressentir*) to experience

épuisé, e [epɥize] *adj* exhausted; (*livre*) out of print; **épuisement** *nm* exhaustion

épuiser [epɥize] *vt* (*fatiguer*) to exhaust, wear *ou* tire out; (*stock, sujet*) to exhaust; **s'épuiser** *vi* to wear *ou* tire o.s. out, exhaust o.s.

épuisette [epɥizɛt] *nf* shrimping net

équateur [ekwatœʀ] *nm* equator; **(la république de) l'É~** Ecuador

équation [ekwasjɔ̃] *nf* equation

équerre [ekɛʀ] *nf* (*à dessin*) (set) square

équilibre [ekilibʀ] *nm* balance; **garder/perdre l'~** to keep/lose one's balance; **être en ~** to be balanced; **équilibré, e** *adj* well-balanced; **équilibrer** *vt* to balance

équipage [ekipaʒ] *nm* crew

équipe [ekip] *nf* team; **travailler en ~** to work as a team

équipé, e [ekipe] *adj*: **bien/mal ~** well-/poorly-equipped

équipement [ekipmɑ̃] *nm* equipment

équiper [ekipe] *vt* to equip; **~ qn/qch de** to equip sb/sth with

équipier, -ière [ekipje, jɛʀ] *nm/f* team member

équitation [ekitasjɔ̃] *nf* (horse-)riding; **faire de l'~** to go riding

équivalent, e [ekivalɑ̃, ɑ̃t] *adj, nm* equivalent

équivaloir [ekivalwaʀ]: **~ à** *vt* to be equivalent to

érable [eʀabl] *nm* maple

érafler [eʀafle] *vt* to scratch; **éraflure** *nf* scratch

ère [ɛʀ] *nf* era; **en l'an 1050 de notre ~** in the year 1050 A.D.

érection [eʀɛksjɔ̃] *nf* erection

éroder [eʀɔde] *vt* to erode

érotique [eʀɔtik] *adj* erotic

errer [eʀe] *vi* to wander

erreur [eʀœʀ] *nf* mistake, error; **faire ~** to be mistaken; **par ~** by mistake

éruption [eʀypsjɔ̃] *nf* eruption; (*Méd*) rash

es [ɛ] *vb voir* **être**

ès [ɛs] *prép*: **licencié ès lettres/sciences** ≈ Bachelor of Arts/Science

ESB *sigle f* (= *encéphalopathie spongiforme bovine*) BSE

escabeau, x [ɛskabo] *nm* (*tabouret*) stool; (*échelle*) stepladder

escalade [ɛskalad] *nf* climbing *no pl*; (*Pol etc*) escalation; **escalader** *vt* to climb

escale [ɛskal] *nf* (*Navig: durée*) call; (*endroit*) port of call; (*Aviat*) stop(over); **faire ~ à** (*Navig*) to put in at; (*Aviat*) to stop over at; **vol sans ~** nonstop flight

escalier [ɛskalje] *nm* stairs *pl*; **dans l'~** *ou* **les ~s** on the stairs; **escalier mécanique** *ou* **roulant** escalator

escapade [ɛskapad] *nf*: **faire une ~** to go on a jaunt; (*s'enfuir*) to run away *ou* off

escargot [ɛskaʀgo] *nm* snail

escarpé, e [ɛskaʀpe] *adj* steep

esclavage [ɛsklavaʒ] *nm* slavery

esclave [ɛsklav] *nm/f* slave

escompte [ɛskɔ̃t] *nm* discount

escrime [ɛskʀim] *nf* fencing

escroc [ɛskʀo] *nm* swindler, conman; **escroquer** *vt*: **escroquer qch (à qn)** to swindle sth (out of sb); **escroquerie** *nf* swindle

espace [ɛspas] *nm* space; **espacer** *vt* to space out; **s'espacer** *vi* (*visites etc*) to become less frequent

espadon [ɛspadɔ̃] *nm* swordfish *inv*

espadrille [ɛspadʀij] *nf* rope-soled sandal

Espagne [ɛspaɲ] *nf*: **l'~** Spain; **espagnol, e** *adj* Spanish ▷ *nm/f*: **Espagnol, e** Spaniard ▷ *nm* (*Ling*) Spanish

espèce [ɛspɛs] *nf* (*Bio, Bot, Zool*) species *inv*; (*gén: sorte*) sort, kind, type; (*péj*): **~ de maladroit/de brute!** you clumsy oaf/you brute!; **espèces** *nfpl* (*Comm*) cash *sg*; **payer en ~** to pay (in) cash

espérance [ɛspeʀɑ̃s] *nf* hope; **espérance de vie** life expectancy

espérer [ɛspeʀe] *vt* to hope for;

j'espère (bien) I hope so; **~ que/faire** to hope that/to do

spiègle [ɛspjɛgl] *adj* mischievous

spion, ne [ɛspjɔ̃, jɔn] *nm/f* spy; **espionnage** *nm* espionage, spying; **espionner** *vt* to spy (up)on

spoir [ɛspwaʀ] *nm* hope; **dans l'~ de/que** in the hope of/that; **reprendre ~** not to lose hope

sprit [ɛspʀi] *nm* (*intellect*) mind; (*humour*) wit; (*mentalité, d'une loi etc, fantôme etc*) spirit; **faire de l'~** to try to be witty; **reprendre ses ~s** to come to; **perdre l'~** to lose one's mind

squimau, de, -x [ɛskimo, od] *adj* Eskimo ▷ *nm/f*: **E~, de** Eskimo ▷ *nm*: **E~®** ice lolly (BRIT), popsicle (US)

ssai [esɛ] *nm* (*tentative*) attempt, try; (*de produit*) testing; (*Rugby*) try; (*Littérature*) essay; **à l'~** on a trial basis; **mettre à l'~** to put to the test

ssaim [esɛ̃] *nm* swarm

ssayer [eseje] *vt* to try; (*vêtement, chaussures*) to try (on); (*méthode, voiture*) to try (out) ▷ *vi* to try; **~ de faire** to try *ou* attempt to do

ssence [esɑ̃s] *nf* (*de voiture*) petrol (BRIT), gas(oline) (US); (*extrait de plante*) essence; (*espèce: d'arbre*) species *inv*

ssentiel, le [esɑ̃sjɛl] *adj* essential; **c'est l'~** (*ce qui importe*) that's the main thing; **l'~ de** the main part of

ssieu, x [esjø] *nm* axle

ssor [esɔʀ] *nm* (*de l'économie etc*) rapid expansion

ssorer [esɔʀe] *vt* (*en tordant*) to wring (out); (*par la force centrifuge*) to spin-dry; **essoreuse** *nf* spin-dryer

ssouffler [esufle]: **s'essouffler** *vi* to get out of breath

ssuie-glace [esɥiglas] *nm inv* windscreen (BRIT) *ou* windshield (US) wiper

ssuyer [esɥije] *vt* to wipe; (*fig: échec*) to suffer; **s'essuyer** *vi* (*après le bain*) to dry o.s.; **~ la vaisselle** to dry up

st¹ [ɛ] *vb voir* **être**

st² [ɛst] *nm* east ▷ *adj inv* east; (*région*) east(ern); **à l'~** in the east; (*direction*) to the east, east(wards); **à l'~ de** (to the) east of

est-ce que [ɛskə] *adv*: **~ c'est cher/ c'était bon?** is it expensive/was it good?; **quand est-ce qu'il part?** when does he leave?, when is he leaving?; *voir aussi* **que**

esthéticienne [ɛstetisjɛn] *nf* beautician

esthétique [ɛstetik] *adj* attractive

estimation [ɛstimasjɔ̃] *nf* valuation; (*chiffre*) estimate

estime [ɛstim] *nf* esteem, regard; **estimer** *vt* (*respecter*) to esteem; (*expertiser: bijou etc*) to value; (*évaluer: coût etc*) to assess, estimate; (*penser*): **estimer que/être** to consider that/o.s. to be

estival, e, -aux [ɛstival, o] *adj* summer *cpd*

estivant, e [ɛstivɑ̃, ɑ̃t] *nm/f* (summer) holiday-maker

estomac [ɛstɔma] *nm* stomach

estragon [ɛstʀagɔ̃] *nm* tarragon

estuaire [ɛstɥɛʀ] *nm* estuary

et [e] *conj* and; **et lui?** what about him?; **et alors!** so what!

étable [etabl] *nf* cowshed

établi [etabli] *nm* (work)bench

établir [etabliʀ] *vt* (*papiers d'identité, facture*) to make out; (*liste, programme*) to draw up; (*entreprise*) to set up; (*réputation, usage, fait, culpabilité*) to establish; **s'établir** *vi* to be established; **s'~ (à son compte)** to set up in business; **s'~ à/près de** to settle in/near

établissement [etablismɑ̃] *nm* (*entreprise, institution*) establishment; **établissement scolaire** school, educational establishment

étage [eta:ʒ] *nm* (*d'immeuble*) storey, floor; **à l'~** upstairs; **au 2ème ~** on the 2nd (BRIT) *ou* 3rd (US) floor; **c'est à quel ~?** what floor is it on?

étagère [etaʒɛʀ] *nf* (*rayon*) shelf; (*meuble*) shelves *pl*

étai [etɛ] nm stay, prop

étain [etɛ̃] nm pewter no pl

étais etc [etɛ] vb voir **être**

étaler [etale] vt (carte, nappe) to spread (out); (peinture) to spread; (échelonner: paiements, vacances) to spread, stagger; (marchandises) to display; (connaissances) to parade; **s'étaler** vi (liquide) to spread out; (fam) to fall flat on one's face; **s'~ sur** (suj: paiements etc) to be spread out over

étalon [etalɔ̃] nm (cheval) stallion

étanche [etɑ̃ʃ] adj (récipient) watertight; (montre, vêtement) waterproof

étang [etɑ̃] nm pond

étant [etɑ̃] vb voir **être**; **donné**

étape [etap] nf stage; (lieu d'arrivée) stopping place; (: Cyclisme) staging point

état [eta] nm (Pol, condition) state; **en mauvais ~** in poor condition; **en ~ (de marche)** in (working) order; **remettre en ~** to repair; **hors d'~** out of order; **être en ~/hors d'~ de faire** to be in a/in no fit state to do; **être dans tous ses ~s** to be in a state; **faire ~ de** (alléguer) to put forward; **l'É~** the State; **état civil** civil status; **état des lieux** inventory of fixtures; **États-Unis** nmpl: **les États-Unis** the United States

etc. [ɛtseteʀa] adv etc

et c(a)etera [ɛtseteʀa] adv et cetera, and so on

été [ete] pp de **être** ▷ nm summer

éteindre [etɛ̃dʀ] vt (lampe, lumière, radio) to turn ou switch off; (cigarette, feu) to put out, extinguish; **s'éteindre** vi (feu, lumière) to go out; (mourir) to pass away; **éteint, e** adj (fig) lacklustre, dull; (volcan) extinct

étendre [etɑ̃dʀ] vt (pâte, liquide) to spread; (carte etc) to spread out; (linge) to hang up; (bras, jambes) to stretch out; (fig: agrandir) to extend; **s'étendre** vi (augmenter, se propager) to spread; (terrain, forêt etc) to stretch; (s'allonger) to stretch out; (se coucher) to lie down;

(fig: expliquer) to elaborate

étendu, e [etɑ̃dy] adj extensive

éternel, le [etɛʀnɛl] adj eternal

éternité [etɛʀnite] nf eternity; **ça a duré une ~** it lasted for ages

éternuement [etɛʀnymɑ̃] nm sneeze

éternuer [etɛʀnɥe] vi to sneeze

êtes [ɛt(z)] vb voir **être**

Éthiopie [etjɔpi] nf: **l'~** Ethiopia

étiez [etje] vb voir **être**

étinceler [etɛ̃s(ə)le] vi to sparkle

étincelle [etɛ̃sɛl] nf spark

étiquette [etikɛt] nf label; (protocole): **l'~** etiquette

étirer [etiʀe] **s'étirer** vi (personne) to stretch; (convoi, route): **s'~ sur** to stretch out over

étoile [etwal] nf star; **à la belle ~** in the open; **étoile de mer** starfish; **étoile filante** shooting star; **étoilé, e** adj starry

étonnant, e [etɔnɑ̃, ɑ̃t] adj amazing

étonnement [etɔnmɑ̃] nm surprise, amazement

étonner [etɔne] vt to surprise, amaze; **s'étonner que/de** to be amazed that/at; **cela m'~ait (que)** (j'en doute) I'd be very surprised (if)

étouffer [etufe] vt to suffocate; (bruit) to muffle; (scandale) to hush up ▷ vi to suffocate; **s'étouffer** vi (en mangeant etc) to choke; **on étouffe** it's stifling

étourderie [etuʀdəʀi] nf (caractère) absent-mindedness no pl; (faute) thoughtless blunder

étourdi, e [etuʀdi] adj (distrait) scatterbrained, heedless

étourdir [etuʀdiʀ] vt (assommer) to stun, daze; (griser) to make dizzy ou giddy; **étourdissement** nm dizzy spell

étrange [etʀɑ̃ʒ] adj strange

étranger, -ère [etʀɑ̃ʒe, ɛʀ] adj foreign (pas de la famille, non familier) strange ▷ nm/f foreigner; stranger ▷ nm: **à l'~** abroad

étrangler [etʀɑ̃gle] vt to strangle; **s'étrangler** vi (en mangeant etc) to choke

○ MOT-CLÉ

tre [ɛtʀ] nm being; **être humain** human being
▷ vb +attrib **1** (état, description) to be; **il est instituteur** he is ou he's a teacher; **vous êtes grand/intelligent/fatigué** you are ou you're tall/clever/tired
2 (+à: appartenir) to be; **le livre est à Paul** the book is Paul's ou belongs to Paul; **c'est à moi/eux** it is ou it's mine/theirs
3 (+de: provenance): **il est de Paris** he is from Paris; (: appartenance): **il est des nôtres** he is one of us
4 (date): **nous sommes le 10 janvier** it's the 10th of January (today)
▷ vi to be; **je ne serai pas ici demain** I won't be here tomorrow
▷ vb aux **1** to have; to be; **être arrivé/allé** to have arrived/gone; **il est parti** he has left, he has gone
2 (forme passive) to be; **être fait par** to be made by; **il a été promu** he has been promoted
3 (+à: obligation): **c'est à réparer** it needs repairing; **il est à essayer** it should be tried; **il est à espérer que ...** it is ou it's to be hoped that ...
▷ vb impers **1**: **il est** +adjectif it is +adjective; **il est impossible de le faire** it's impossible to do it
2 (heure, date): **il est 10 heures** it is ou it's 10 o'clock
3 (emphatique): **c'est moi** it's me; **c'est à lui de le faire** it's up to him to do it

trennes [etʀɛn] nfpl Christmas box sg
trier [etʀije] nm stirrup
troit, e [etʀwa, wat] adj narrow; (vêtement) tight; (fig: liens, collaboration) close; **à l'~** cramped; **~ d'esprit** narrow-minded
tude [etyd] nf studying; (ouvrage, rapport) study; (Scol: salle de travail) study room; **études** nfpl (Scol) studies; **être à l'~** (projet etc) to be under consideration; **faire des ~s (de droit/**

médecine) to study (law/medicine)
étudiant, e [etydjɑ̃, jɑ̃t] nm/f student
étudier [etydje] vt, vi to study
étui [etɥi] nm case
eu, eue [y] pp de **avoir**
euh [ø] excl er
euro [øʀo] nm euro
Europe [øʀɔp] nf: **l'~** Europe; **européen, ne** adj European ▷ nm/f: **Européen, ne** European
eus etc [y] vb voir **avoir**
eux [ø] pron (sujet) they; (objet) them
évacuer [evakɥe] vt to evacuate
évader [evade]: **s'évader** vi to escape
évaluer [evalɥe] vt (expertiser) to appraise, evaluate; (juger approximativement) to estimate
évangile [evɑ̃ʒil] nm gospel; **É~** Gospel
évanouir [evanwiʀ]: **s'évanouir** vi to faint; (disparaître) to vanish, disappear; **évanouissement** nm (syncope) fainting fit
évaporer [evapɔʀe]: **s'évaporer** vi to evaporate
évasion [evazjɔ̃] nf escape
éveillé, e [eveje] adj awake; (vif) alert, sharp; **éveiller** vt to (a)waken; (soupçons etc) to arouse; **s'éveiller** vi to (a)waken; (fig) to be aroused
événement [evɛnmɑ̃] nm event
éventail [evɑ̃taj] nm fan; (choix) range
éventualité [evɑ̃tɥalite] nf eventuality; possibility; **dans l'~ de** in the event of
éventuel, le [evɑ̃tɥɛl] adj possible

▌ Attention à ne pas traduire **éventuel** par eventual.

éventuellement adv possibly

▌ Attention à ne pas traduire **éventuellement** par eventually.

évêque [evɛk] nm bishop
évidemment [evidamɑ̃] adv (bien sûr) of course; (certainement) obviously
évidence [evidɑ̃s] nf obviousness; (fait) obvious fact; **de toute ~** quite obviously ou evidently; **être en ~** to be clearly visible; **mettre en ~** (fait) to highlight; **évident, e** adj obvious,

evident; **ce n'est pas évident!** (fam) it's not that easy!

évier [evje] nm (kitchen) sink

éviter [evite] vt to avoid; **~ de faire** to avoid doing; **~ qch à qn** to spare sb sth

évoluer [evɔlɥe] vi (enfant, maladie) to develop; (situation, moralement) to evolve, develop; (aller et venir) to move about; **évolution** nf development, evolution

évoquer [evɔke] vt to call to mind, evoke; (mentionner) to mention

ex- [eks] préfixe ex-; **son ~mari** her ex-husband; **son ~femme** his ex-wife

exact, e [egza(kt), egzakt] adj exact; (correct) correct; (ponctuel) punctual; **l'heure ~e** the right ou exact time; **exactement** adv exactly

ex aequo [egzeko] adj equally placed; **arriver ~** to finish neck and neck

exagéré, e [egzaʒeʀe] adj (prix etc) excessive

exagérer [egzaʒeʀe] vt to exaggerate ▷ vi to exaggerate; (abuser) to go too far

examen [egzamɛ̃] nm examination; (Scol) exam, examination; **à l'~** under consideration; **examen médical** (medical) examination; (analyse) test

examinateur, -trice [egzaminatœʀ, tʀis] nm/f examiner

examiner [egzamine] vt to examine

exaspérant, e [egzaspeʀɑ̃, ɑ̃t] adj exasperating

exaspérer [egzaspeʀe] vt to exasperate

exaucer [egzose] vt (vœu) to grant

excéder [eksede] vt (dépasser) to exceed; (agacer) to exasperate

excellent, e [ekselɑ̃, ɑ̃t] adj excellent

excentrique [eksɑ̃tʀik] adj eccentric

excepté, e [eksepte] adj, prép: **les élèves ~s, ~ les élèves** except for the pupils

exception [eksepsjɔ̃] nf exception; **à l'~ de** except for, with the exception of; **d'~** (mesure, loi) special, exceptional; **exceptionnel, le** adj exceptional; **exceptionnellement** adv

exceptionally

excès [eksɛ] nm surplus ▷ nmpl excesses; **faire des ~** to overindulge; **excès de vitesse** speeding no pl; **excessif, -ive** adj excessive

excitant, e [eksitɑ̃, ɑ̃t] adj exciting ▷ nm stimulant; **excitation** nf (état) excitement

exciter [eksite] vt to excite; (suj: café etc) to stimulate; **s'exciter** vi to get excited

exclamer [eksklame]: **s'exclamer** vi to exclaim

exclure [eksklyʀ] vt (faire sortir) to expel; (ne pas compter) to exclude, leave out; (rendre impossible) to exclude, rule out; **il est exclu que** it's out of the question that ...; **il n'est pas exclu que ...** it's not impossible that ...; **exclusif, -ive** adj exclusive; **exclusion** nf exclusion; **à l'exclusion de** with the exclusion ou exception of; **exclusivité** nf (Comm) exclusive rights pl; **film passant en exclusivité à** film showing only at

excursion [ekskyʀsjɔ̃] nf (en autocar) excursion, trip; (à pied) walk, hike

excuse [ekskyz] nf excuse; **excuses** nfpl (regret) apology sg, apologies; **excuser** vt to excuse; **s'excuser (de)** to apologize (for); **excusez-moi** I'm sorry; (pour attirer l'attention) excuse me

exécuter [egzekyte] vt (tuer) to execute; (tâche etc) to execute, carry out; (Mus: jouer) to perform, execute; **s'exécuter** vi to comply

exemplaire [egzɑ̃plɛʀ] nm copy

exemple [egzɑ̃pl] nm example; **par ~** for instance, for example; **donner l'~** to set an example

exercer [egzɛʀse] vt (pratiquer) to exercise, practise; (influence, contrôle) to exert; (former) to exercise, train; **s'exercer** vi (sportif, musicien) to practise

exercice [egzɛʀsis] nm exercise

exhiber [egzibe] vt (montrer: papiers, certificat) to present, produce; (péj) to

display, flaunt; **s'exhiber** vi to parade; (suj: exhibitionniste) to expose o.s;
exhibitionniste nm/f flasher
exigeant, e [ɛgziʒã, ãt] adj demanding; (péj) hard to please
exiger [ɛgziʒe] vt to demand, require
exil [ɛgzil] nm exile; **exiler** vt to exile; **s'exiler** vi to go into exile
existence [ɛgzistãs] nf existence
exister [ɛgziste] vi to exist; **il existe un/des** there is a/are (some)
exorbitant, e [ɛgzɔrbitã, ãt] adj exorbitant
exotique [ɛgzɔtik] adj exotic; **yaourt aux fruits ~s** tropical fruit yoghurt
expédier [ɛkspedje] vt (lettre, paquet) to send; (troupes) to dispatch; (fam: travail etc) to dispose of, dispatch; **expéditeur, -trice** nm/f sender; **expédition** nf sending; (scientifique, sportive, Mil) expedition
expérience [ɛksperjãs] nf (de la vie) experience; (scientifique) experiment
expérimenté, e [ɛksperimãte] adj experienced
expérimenter [ɛksperimãte] vt to test out, experiment with
expert, e [ɛksper, ɛrt] adj, nm expert; **~ en objets d'art** art appraiser; **expert-comptable** nm ≈ chartered accountant (BRIT), ≈ certified public accountant (US)
expirer [ɛkspire] vi (prendre fin, mourir) to expire; (respirer) to breathe out
explication [ɛksplikasjõ] nf explanation; (discussion) discussion; (dispute) argument
explicite [ɛksplisit] adj explicit
expliquer [ɛksplike] vt to explain; **s'expliquer** to explain (o.s.); **s'~ avec qn** (discuter) to explain o.s. to sb; **son erreur s'explique** one can understand his mistake
exploit [ɛksplwa] nm exploit, feat; **exploitant, e** nm/f: **exploitant (agricole)** farmer; **exploitation** nf exploitation; (d'une entreprise) running; **exploitation agricole** farming

concern; **exploiter** vt (personne, don) to exploit; (entreprise, ferme) to run, operate; (mine) to exploit, work
explorer [ɛksplɔre] vt to explore
exploser [ɛksploze] vi to explode, blow up; (engin explosif) to go off; (personne: de colère) to flare up; **explosif, -ive** adj, nm explosive; **explosion** nf explosion; (de joie, colère) outburst
exportateur, -trice [ɛkspɔrtatœr, tris] adj export cpd, exporting ▷ nm exporter
exportation [ɛkspɔrtasjõ] nf (action) exportation; (produit) export
exporter [ɛkspɔrte] vt to export
exposant [ɛkspozã] nm exhibitor
exposé, e [ɛkspoze] nm talk ▷ adj: **~ au sud** facing south
exposer [ɛkspoze] vt (marchandise) to display; (peinture) to exhibit, show; (parler de) to explain, set out; (mettre en danger, orienter, Photo) to expose; **s'~ à** (soleil, danger) to expose o.s. to; **exposition** nf (manifestation) exhibition; (Photo) exposure
exprès¹ [ɛksprɛ] adv (délibérément) on purpose; (spécialement) specially; **faire ~ de faire qch** to do sth on purpose
exprès², -esse [ɛksprɛs] adj inv (lettre, colis) express
express [ɛksprɛs] adj, nm: **(café) ~** espresso (coffee); **(train) ~** fast train
expressif, -ive [ɛkspresif, iv] adj expressive
expression [ɛkspresjõ] nf expression
exprimer [ɛksprime] vt (sentiment, idée) to express; (jus, liquide) to press out; **s'exprimer** vi (personne) to express o.s
expulser [ɛkspylse] vt to expel; (locataire) to evict; (Sport) to send off
exquis, e [ɛkski, iz] adj exquisite
extasier [ɛkstazje]: **s'extasier sur** vt to go into raptures over
exténuer [ɛkstenɥe] vt to exhaust
extérieur, e [ɛksterjœr] adj (porte, mur etc) outer, outside; (au dehors: escalier, w.-c.) outside; (commerce)

foreign; (*influences*) external; (*apparent: calme, gaieté etc*) surface *cpd* ▷ *nm* (*d'une maison, d'un récipient etc*) outside, exterior; (*apparence*) exterior; **à l'~** outside; (*à l'étranger*) abroad

externat [ɛkstɛʀna] *nm* day school

externe [ɛkstɛʀn] *adj* external, outer ▷ *nm/f* (*Méd*) non-resident medical student (BRIT), extern (US); (*Scol*) day pupil

extincteur [ɛkstɛ̃ktœʀ] *nm* (fire) extinguisher

extinction [ɛkstɛ̃ksjɔ̃] *nf*: **extinction de voix** loss of voice

extra [ɛkstʀa] *adj inv* first-rate; (*fam*) fantastic ▷ *nm inv* extra help

extraire [ɛkstʀɛʀ] *vt* to extract; **~ qch de** to extract sth from; **extrait** *nm* extract; **extrait de naissance** birth certificate

extraordinaire [ɛkstʀaɔʀdinɛʀ] *adj* extraordinary; (*Pol: mesures etc*) special

extravagant, e [ɛkstʀavagɑ̃, ɑ̃t] *adj* extravagant

extraverti, e [ɛkstʀavɛʀti] *adj* extrovert

extrême [ɛkstʀɛm] *adj, nm* extreme; **d'un ~ à l'autre** from one extreme to another; **extrêmement** *adv* extremely; **Extrême-Orient** *nm* Far East

extrémité [ɛkstʀemite] *nf* end; (*situation*) straits *pl*, plight; (*geste désespéré*) extreme action; **extrémités** *nfpl* (*pieds et mains*) extremities

exubérant, e [ɛgzybeʀɑ̃, ɑ̃t] *adj* exuberant

F *abr* = **franc**; (*appartement*): **un F2/F3** a one-/two-bedroom flat (BRIT) *ou* apartment (US)

fa [fa] *nm inv* (*Mus*) F; (*en chantant la gamme*) fa

fabricant, e [fabʀikɑ̃, ɑ̃t] *nm/f* manufacturer

fabrication [fabʀikasjɔ̃] *nf* manufacture

fabrique [fabʀik] *nf* factory; **fabriquer** *vt* to make; (*industriellement*) to manufacture; (*fig*): **qu'est-ce qu'il fabrique?** (*fam*) what is he doing?

fac [fak] (*fam*) *abr f* (*Scol*) = **faculté**

façade [fasad] *nf* front, façade

face [fas] *nf* face; (*fig: aspect*) side ▷ *adj*: **le côté ~** heads; **en ~ de** opposite; (*fig*) in front of; **de ~** (*voir*) face on; **~ à** facing; (*fig*) faced with, in the face of; **faire ~ à** to face; **~ à ~** *adv* facing each other ▷ *nm inv* encounter

fâché, e [fɑʃe] *adj* angry; (*désolé*) sorry

fâcher [fɑʃe] *vt* to anger; **se fâcher (contre qn)** *vi* to get angry (with sb);

se **~** avec (se brouiller) to fall out with

acile [fasil] adj easy; (caractère) easy-going; **facilement** adv easily; **facilité** nf easiness; (disposition, don) aptitude; **facilités** (possibilités) facilities; (Comm) terms; **faciliter** vt to make easier

açon [fasɔ̃] nf (manière) way; (d'une robe etc) making-up, cut; **façons** nfpl (péj) fuss sg; **de ~ à/à ce que** so as to/that; **de toute ~** anyway, in any case; **sans ~** (accepter) without fuss; **non merci, sans ~** no thanks, honestly

acteur, -trice [faktœʀ] nm/f postman(-woman) (BRIT), mailman(-woman) (US) ▷ nm (Math, fig: élément) factor

acture [faktyʀ] nf (à payer: gén) bill; (Comm) invoice

acultatif, -ive [fakyltatif, iv] adj optional

aculté [fakylte] nf (intellectuelle, d'université) faculty; (pouvoir, possibilité) power

fade [fad] adj insipid

aible [fɛbl] adj weak; (voix, lumière, vent) faint; (rendement, revenu) low ▷ nm (pour quelqu'un) weakness, soft spot; **faiblesse** nf weakness; **faiblir** vi to weaken; (lumière) to dim; (vent) to drop

aïence [fajɑ̃s] nf earthenware no pl

aillir [fajiʀ] vi: **j'ai failli tomber** I almost ou very nearly fell

aillite [fajit] nf bankruptcy; **faire ~** to go bankrupt

aim [fɛ̃] nf hunger; **avoir ~** to be hungry; **rester sur sa ~** (aussi fig) to be left wanting more

ainéant, e [fɛneɑ̃, ɑ̃t] nm/f idler, loafer

○ **MOT-CLÉ**

aire [fɛʀ] vt 1 (fabriquer, être l'auteur de) to make; **faire du vin/une offre/un film** to make wine/an offer/a film; **faire du bruit** to make a noise

2 (effectuer: travail, opération) to do; **que faites-vous?** (quel métier etc) what do

you do?; (quelle activité: au moment de la question) what are you doing?; **faire la lessive** to do the washing

3 (études) to do; (sport, musique) to play; **faire du droit/du français** to do law/French; **faire du rugby/piano** to play rugby/the piano

4 (simuler): **faire le malade/l'innocent** to act the invalid/the innocent

5 (transformer, avoir un effet sur): **faire de qn un frustré/avocat** to make sb frustrated/a lawyer; **ça ne me fait rien** (m'est égal) I don't care ou mind; (me laisse froid) it has no effect on me; **ça ne fait rien** it doesn't matter; **faire que** (impliquer) to mean that

6 (calculs, prix, mesures): **2 et 2 font 4** 2 and 2 are ou make 4; **ça fait 10 m/15 euros** it's 10 m/15 euros; **je vous le fais 10 euros** I'll let you have it for 10 euros; **je fais du 40** I take a size 40

7 (distance): **faire du 50 (à l'heure)** to do 50 (km an hour); **nous avons fait 1000 km en 2 jours** we did ou covered 1000 km in 2 days; **faire l'Europe** to tour ou do Europe; **faire les magasins** to go shopping

8: **qu'a-t-il fait de sa valise?** what has he done with his case?

9: **ne faire que**: **il ne fait que critiquer** (sans cesse) all he (ever) does is criticize; (seulement) he's only criticizing

10 (dire) to say; **"vraiment?" fit-il** "really?" he said

11 (maladie) to have; **faire du diabète** to have diabetes sg

▷ vi 1 (agir, s'y prendre) to act, do; **il faut faire vite** we (ou you etc) must act quickly; **comment a-t-il fait pour?** how did he manage to?; **faites comme chez vous** make yourself at home

2 (paraître) to look; **faire vieux/démodé** to look old/old-fashioned; **ça fait bien** it looks good

▷ vb substitut to do; **ne le casse pas comme je l'ai fait** don't break it as I did; **je peux le voir? — faites!** can I see it? — please do!

▷ *vb impers* **1** (*temps*): **il fait beau** *etc* the weather's fine *etc*; *voir aussi* **jour**; **froid** *etc*

2 (*temps écoulé, durée*): **ça fait 2 ans qu'il est parti** it's 2 years since he left; **ça fait 2 ans qu'il y est** he's been there for 2 years

▷ *vb semi-aux* **1**: **faire** (+*infinitif: action directe*) to make; **faire tomber/bouger qch** to make sth fall/move; **faire démarrer un moteur/chauffer de l'eau** to start up an engine/heat some water; **cela fait dormir** it makes you sleep; **faire travailler les enfants** to make the children work *ou* get the children to work; **il m'a fait traverser la rue** he helped me to cross the street

2 (*indirectement, par un intermédiaire*): **faire réparer qch** to get *ou* have sth repaired; **faire punir les enfants** to have the children punished

se faire *vi* **1** (*être convenable*): **cela se fait beaucoup/ne se fait pas** it's done a lot/not done

2: **se faire** +*nom ou pron*: **se faire une jupe** to make o.s. a skirt; **se faire des amis** to make friends; **se faire du souci** to worry; **il ne s'en fait pas** he doesn't worry

3: **se faire** +*adj* (*devenir*): **se faire vieux** to be getting old; **se faire beau** to do o.s. up

4: **se faire à** (*s'habituer*) to get used to; **je n'arrive pas à me faire à la nourriture/au climat** I can't get used to the food/climate

5: **se faire** +*infinitif*: **se faire examiner la vue/opérer** to have one's eyes tested/have an operation; **se faire couper les cheveux** to get one's hair cut; **il va se faire tuer/punir** he's going to get himself killed/get punished; **il s'est fait aider** he got somebody to help him; **il s'est fait aider par Simon** he got Simon to help him; **se faire faire un vêtement** to get a garment made for o.s.

6 (*impersonnel*): **comment se fait-il/faisait-il que?** how is it/was it that?

faire-part [fɛʀpaʀ] *nm inv* announcement (*of birth, marriage etc*)

faisan, e [fəzɑ̃, an] *nm/f* pheasant

faisons [fəzɔ̃] *vb voir* **faire**

fait, e [fɛ, fɛt] *adj* (*mûr: fromage, melon*) ripe ▷ *nm* (*événement*) event, occurrence; (*réalité, donnée*) fact; **être au ~ (de)** to be informed (of); **au ~** (*à propos*) by the way; **en venir au ~** to get to the point; **du ~ de ceci/qu'il a ment** because of *ou* on account of this/his having lied; **de ce ~** for this reason; **en ~** in fact; **prendre qn sur le ~** to catch sb in the act; **c'est bien ~ pour lui** (*ou eux etc*) it serves him (*ou* them *etc*) right; **fait divers** news item

faites [fɛt] *vb voir* **faire**

falaise [falɛz] *nf* cliff

falloir [falwaʀ] *vb impers*: **il faut qu'il parte/a fallu qu'il parte** (*obligation*) he has to *ou* must leave/had to leave; **il a fallu le faire** it had to be done; **il faudrait qu'elle rentre** she should come *ou* go back, she ought to come *ou* go back; **il faut faire attention** you have to be careful; **il me faudrait 100 euros** I would need 100 euros; **il vous faut tourner à gauche après l'église** you have to turn left past the church; **nous avons ce qu'il (nous) faut** we have what we need; **il ne fallait pas** you shouldn't have (done); **comme il faut** (*personne*) proper; (*agir*) properly; **s'en falloir** *vr*: **il s'en est fallu de 100 euros/5 minutes** we/they *etc* were 100 euros short/5 minutes late (*ou* early); **il s'en faut de beaucoup qu'il soit** he is far from being; **il s'en est fallu de peu que cela n'arrive** it very nearly happened

famé, e [fame] *adj*: **mal ~** disreputable, of ill repute

fameux, -euse [famø, øz] *adj* (*illustre*) famous; (*bon: repas, plat etc*) first-rate, first-class; (*valeur intensive*) real, downright

familial, e, -aux [familjal, jo] *adj* family *cpd*

familiarité [familjaRite] *nf* familiarity

familier, -ère [familje, jɛR] *adj* (*connu*) familiar; (*atmosphère*) informal, friendly; (*Ling*) informal, colloquial ▷ *nm* regular (visitor)

famille [famij] *nf* family; **il a de la ~ à Paris** he has relatives in Paris

famine [famin] *nf* famine

fanatique [fanatik] *adj* fanatical ▷ *nm/f* fanatic

faner [fane]: **se faner** *vi* to fade

fanfare [fɑ̃faR] *nf* (*orchestre*) brass band; (*musique*) fanfare

fantaisie [fɑ̃tezi] *nf* (*spontanéité*) fancy, imagination; (*caprice*) whim ▷ *adj*: **bijou ~** costume jewellery

fantasme [fɑ̃tasm] *nm* fantasy

fantastique [fɑ̃tastik] *adj* fantastic

fantôme [fɑ̃tom] *nm* ghost, phantom

faon [fɑ̃] *nm* fawn

FAQ *sigle f* (= foire aux questions) FAQ

farce [faRs] *nf* (*viande*) stuffing; (*blague*) (practical) joke; (*Théâtre*) farce; **farcir** *vt* (*viande*) to stuff

farder [faRde]: **se farder** *vi* to make (o.s.) up

farine [farin] *nf* flour

farouche [faRuʃ] *adj* (*timide*) shy, timid

fart [faRt] *nm* (ski) wax

fascination [fasinasjɔ̃] *nf* fascination

fasciner [fasine] *vt* to fascinate

fascisme [faʃism] *nm* fascism

fasse *etc* [fas] *vb voir* **faire**

fastidieux, -euse [fastidjø, jøz] *adj* tedious, tiresome

fatal, e [fatal] *adj* fatal; (*inévitable*) inevitable; **fatalité** *nf* (*destin*) fate; (*coïncidence*) fateful coincidence

fatidique [fatidik] *adj* fateful

fatigant, e [fatigɑ̃, ɑ̃t] *adj* tiring; (*agaçant*) tiresome

fatigue [fatig] *nf* tiredness, fatigue; **fatigué, e** *adj* tired; **fatiguer** *vt* to tire, make tired; (*fig: agacer*) to annoy ▷ *vi* (*moteur*) to labour, strain; **se fatiguer**

to get tired

fauché, e [foʃe] (*fam*) *adj* broke

faucher [foʃe] *vt* (*herbe*) to cut; (*champs, blés*) to reap; (*fig: véhicule*) to mow down; (*fam: voler*) to pinch

faucon [fokɔ̃] *nm* falcon, hawk

faudra [fodRa] *vb voir* **falloir**

faufiler [fofile]: **se faufiler** *vi*: **se ~ dans** to edge one's way into; **se ~ parmi/entre** to thread one's way among/between

faune [fon] *nf* (*Zool*) wildlife, fauna

fausse [fos] *adj voir* **faux**; **faussement** *adv* (*accuser*) wrongly, wrongfully; (*croire*) falsely

fausser [fose] *vt* (*objet*) to bend, buckle; (*fig*) to distort; **~ compagnie à qn** to give sb the slip

faut [fo] *vb voir* **falloir**

faute [fot] *nf* (*erreur*) mistake, error; (*mauvaise action*) misdemeanour; (*Football etc*) offence; (*Tennis*) fault; **c'est de sa/ma ~** it's his *ou* her/my fault; **être en ~** to be in the wrong; **~ de** (*temps, argent*) for *ou* through lack of; **sans ~** without fail; **faute de frappe** typing error; **faute professionnelle** professional misconduct *no pl*

fauteuil [fotœj] *nm* armchair; (*au théâtre*) seat; **fauteuil roulant** wheelchair

fautif, -ive [fotif, iv] *adj* (*responsable*) at fault, in the wrong; (*incorrect*) incorrect, inaccurate; **il se sentait ~** he felt guilty

fauve [fov] *nm* wildcat ▷ *adj* (*couleur*) fawn

faux¹ [fo] *nf* scythe

faux², fausse [fo, fos] *adj* (*inexact*) wrong; (*voix*) out of tune; (*billet*) fake, forged; (*sournois, postiche*) false ▷ *adv* (*Mus*) out of tune ▷ *nm* (*copie*) fake, forgery; **faire ~ bond à qn** to let sb down; **faire un ~ pas** to trip; (*fig*) to make a faux pas; **fausse alerte** false alarm; **fausse couche** miscarriage; **faux frais** *nmpl* extras, incidental expenses; **faux mouvement** awkward movement; **fausse note** wrong note; **faux témoignage** (*délit*) perjury; **faux-filet** nm sirloin

faveur [favœʀ] nf favour; **traitement de ~** preferential treatment; **en ~ de** in favour of

favorable [favɔʀabl] adj favourable

favori, te [favɔʀi, it] adj, nm/f favourite

favoriser [favɔʀize] vt to favour

fax [faks] nm fax

fécond, e [fekɔ̃, ɔ̃d] adj fertile; **féconder** vt to fertilize

féculent [fekylɑ̃] nm starchy food

fédéral, e, -aux [federal, o] adj federal

fée [fe] nf fairy

feignant, e [fɛɲɑ̃, ɑ̃t] nm/f = **fainéant, e**

feindre [fɛ̃dʀ] vt to feign; **~ de faire** to pretend to do

fêler [fele] vt to crack; **se fêler** to crack

félicitations [felisitasjɔ̃] nfpl congratulations

féliciter [felisite] vt: **~ qn (de)** to congratulate sb (on)

félin, e [felɛ̃, in] nm (big) cat

femelle [fəmɛl] adj, nf female

féminin, e [feminɛ̃, in] adj feminine; (*sexe*) female; (*équipe, vêtements etc*) women's ▷ nm (Ling) feminine; **féministe** adj feminist

femme [fam] nf woman; (*épouse*) wife; **femme au foyer** housewife; **femme de chambre** chambermaid; **femme de ménage** cleaning lady

fémur [femyʀ] nm femur, thighbone

fendre [fɑ̃dʀ] vt (*couper en deux*) to split; (*fissurer*) to crack; (*traverser: foule, air*) to cleave through; **se fendre** vi to crack

fenêtre [f(ə)nɛtʀ] nf window

fenouil [fənuj] nm fennel

fente [fɑ̃t] nf (*fissure*) crack; (*de boîte à lettres etc*) slit

fer [fɛʀ] nm iron; **fer à cheval** horseshoe; **fer à friser** curling tongs pl; **fer (à repasser)** iron; **fer forgé** wrought iron

ferai etc [fəʀe] vb voir **faire**

fer-blanc [fɛʀblɑ̃] nm tin(plate)

férié, e [feʀje] adj: **jour ~** public holiday

ferions etc [fəʀjɔ̃] vb voir **faire**

ferme [fɛʀm] adj firm ▷ adv (travailler etc) hard ▷ nf (exploitation) farm; (maison) farmhouse

fermé, e [fɛʀme] adj closed, shut; (gaz, eau etc) off; (fig: milieu) exclusive

fermenter [fɛʀmɑ̃te] vi to ferment

fermer [fɛʀme] vt to close, shut; (cesser l'exploitation de) to close down, shut down; (eau, électricité, robinet) to turn off; (aéroport, route) to close ▷ vi to close, shut; (magasin: definitivement) to close down, shut down; **~ à clef** to lock; **se fermer** vi to close, shut

fermeté [fɛʀməte] nf firmness

fermeture [fɛʀmətyʀ] nf closing; (dispositif) catch; **heures de ~** closing times; **fermeture éclair®** ou **à glissière** zip (fastener) (BRIT), zipper (US)

fermier [fɛʀmje] nm farmer

féroce [feʀɔs] adj ferocious, fierce

ferons [fəʀɔ̃] vb voir **faire**

ferrer [feʀe] vt (cheval) to shoe

ferroviaire [feʀɔvjɛʀ] adj rail(way) cpd (BRIT), rail(road) cpd (US)

ferry(-boat) [feʀe(-bot)] nm ferry

fertile [fɛʀtil] adj fertile; **~ en incidents** eventful, packed with incidents

fervent, e [fɛʀvɑ̃, ɑ̃t] adj fervent

fesse [fɛs] nf buttock; **fessée** nf spanking

festin [fɛstɛ̃] nm feast

festival [fɛstival] nm festival

festivités [fɛstivite] nfpl festivities

fêtard, e [fɛtaʀ, aʀd] (fam) nm/f high liver, merry-maker

fête [fɛt] nf (religieuse) feast; (publique) holiday; (réception) party; (kermesse) fête, fair; (du nom) feast day, name day; **faire la ~** to live it up; **faire ~ à qn** to give sb a warm welcome; **les ~s (de fin d'année)** the festive season; **la salle des ~s** the village hall; **la ~ des Mères/**

Pères Mother's/Father's Day; **fête foraine** (fun) fair; **fêter** vt to celebrate; (*personne*) to have a celebration for

feu, x [fø] nm (*gén*) fire; (*signal lumineux*) light; (*de cuisinière*) ring; **feux** nmpl (*Auto*) (traffic) lights; **au ~!** (*incendie*) fire!; **à ~ doux/vif** over a slow/brisk heat; **à petit ~** (*Culin*) over a gentle heat; (*fig*) slowly; **faire ~** to fire; **ne pas faire long ~** not to last long; **prendre ~** to catch fire; **mettre le ~ à** to set fire to; **faire du ~** to make a fire; **avez-vous du ~?** (*pour cigarette*) have you (got) a light?; **feu arrière** rear light; **feu d'artifice** (*spectacle*) fireworks pl; **feu de joie** bonfire; **feu orange/rouge/vert** amber (BRIT) ou yellow (US)/red/green light; **feux de brouillard** fog lights ou lamps; **feux de croisement** dipped (BRIT) ou dimmed (US) headlights; **feux de position** sidelights; **feux de route** headlights

feuillage [fœjaʒ] nm foliage, leaves pl

feuille [fœj] nf (*d'arbre*) leaf; (*de papier*) sheet; **feuille de calcul** spreadsheet; **feuille d'impôts** tax form; **feuille de maladie** medical expenses claim form; **feuille de paie** pay slip

feuillet [fœjɛ] nm leaf

feuilleté, e [fœjte] adj: **pâte ~** flaky pastry

feuilleter [fœjte] vt (*livre*) to leaf through

feuilleton [fœjtɔ̃] nm serial

feutre [føtʀ] nm felt; (*chapeau*) felt hat; (*aussi: stylo-~*) felt-tip pen; **feutré, e** adj (*atmosphère*) muffled

fève [fɛv] nf broad bean

février [fevʀije] nm February

fiable [fjabl] adj reliable

fiançailles [fjɑ̃saj] nfpl engagement sg

fiancé, e [fjɑ̃se] nm/f fiancé(e) ▷ adj: **être ~ (à)** to be engaged (to)

fiancer [fjɑ̃se]: **se fiancer (avec)** vi to become engaged (to)

fibre [fibʀ] nf fibre; **fibre de verre** fibreglass, glass fibre

ficeler [fis(ə)le] vt to tie up

ficelle [fisɛl] nf string no pl; (*morceau*) piece ou length of string

fiche [fiʃ] nf (*pour fichier*) (index) card; (*formulaire*) form; (*Élec*) plug; **fiche de paye** pay slip

ficher [fiʃe] vt (*dans un fichier*) to file; (*Police*) to put on file; (*fam: faire*) to do; (: *donner*) to give; (: *mettre*) to stick ou shove; **fiche-(moi) le camp!** (*fam*) clear off!; **fiche-moi la paix!** (*fam*) leave me alone!; **se ficher de** (*fam: rire de*) to make fun of; (*être indifférent à*) not to care about

fichier [fiʃje] nm file; **~ joint** (*Comput*) attachment

fichu, e [fiʃy] pp de **ficher** (*fam*) ▷ adj (*fam: fini, inutilisable*) bust, done for; (: *intensif*) wretched, darned ▷ nm (*foulard*) (head)scarf; **mal ~** (*fam*) feeling lousy

fictif, -ive [fiktif, iv] adj fictitious

fiction [fiksjɔ̃] nf fiction; (*fait imaginé*) invention

fidèle [fidɛl] adj faithful ▷ nm/f (*Rel*): **les ~s** (*à l'église*) the congregation sg; **fidélité** nf (*d'un conjoint*) fidelity, faithfulness; (*d'un ami, client*) loyalty

fier[1] [fje]: **se fier à** vt to trust

fier[2], **fière** [fjɛʀ] adj proud; **~ de** proud of; **fierté** nf pride

fièvre [fjɛvʀ] nf fever; **avoir de la ~/39 de ~** to have a high temperature/a temperature of 39°C; **fiévreux, -euse** adj feverish

figer [fiʒe]: **se figer** vi (*huile*) to congeal; (*personne*) to freeze

fignoler [fiɲɔle] (*fam*) vt to polish up

figue [fig] nf fig; **figuier** nm fig tree

figurant, e [figyʀɑ̃, ɑ̃t] nm/f (*Théâtre*) walk-on; (*Cinéma*) extra

figure [figyʀ] nf (*visage*) face; (*forme, personnage*) figure; (*illustration*) picture, diagram

figuré, e [figyʀe] adj (*sens*) figurative

figurer [figyʀe] vi to appear ▷ vt to represent; **se figurer que** to imagine that

fil [fil] nm (*brin, fig: d'une histoire*) thread;

(*électrique*) wire; (*d'un couteau*) edge; **au ~ des années** with the passing of the years; **au ~ de l'eau** with the stream *ou* current; **coup de ~** (*fam*) phone call; **donner/recevoir un coup de ~** to make/get *ou* receive a phone call; **fil de fer** wire; **fil de fer barbelé** barbed wire

file [fil] *nf* line; (*Auto*) lane; **en ~ indienne** in single file; **à la ~** (*d'affilée*) in succession; **file (d'attente)** queue (*BRIT*), line (*US*)

filer [file] *vt* (*tissu, toile*) to spin; (*prendre en filature*) to shadow, tail; (*fam: donner*): **~ qch à qn** to slip sb sth ▷ *vi* (*bas*) to run; (*aller vite*) to fly past; (*fam: partir*) to make *ou* be off; **~ doux** to toe the line

filet [filɛ] *nm* net; (*Culin*) fillet; (*d'eau, de sang*) trickle; **filet (à provisions)** string bag

filiale [filjal] *nf* (*Comm*) subsidiary

filière [filjɛʀ] *nf* (*carrière*) path; **suivre la ~** (*dans sa carrière*) to work one's way up (through the hierarchy)

fille [fij] *nf* girl; (*opposé à fils*) daughter; **vieille ~** old maid; **fillette** *nf* (little) girl

filleul, e [fijœl] *nm/f* godchild, godson/daughter

film [film] *nm* (*pour photo*) (roll of) film; (*œuvre*) film, picture, movie

fils [fis] *nm* son; **fils à papa** daddy's boy

filtre [filtʀ] *nm* filter; **filtrer** *vt* to filter; (*fig: candidats, visiteurs*) to screen

fin¹ [fɛ̃] *nf* end; **fins** *nfpl* (*but*) ends; **prendre ~** to come to an end; **mettre ~ à** to put an end to; **à la ~** in the end, eventually; **en ~ de compte** in the end; **sans ~** endless; **~ juin** at the end of June; **fin prêt** quite ready

fin², e [fɛ̃, fin] *adj* (*papier, couche, fil*) thin; (*cheveux, visage*) fine; (*taille*) neat, slim; (*esprit, remarque*) subtle ▷ *adv* (*couper*) finely; **fines herbes** mixed herbs; **avoir la vue/l'ouïe fine** to have keen eyesight/hearing; **repas/vin fin** gourmet meal/fine wine

final, e [final, o] *adj* final ▷ *nm* (*Mus*) finale; **finale** *nf* final; **quarts de finale** quarter finals; **finalement** *adv* finally,

in the end; (*après tout*) after all

finance [finɑ̃s]: **finances** *nfpl* (*situation*) finances; (*activités*) finance *sg*; **moyennant ~** for a fee; **financer** *vt* to finance; **financier, -ière** *adj* financial

finesse [finɛs] *nf* thinness; (*raffinement*) fineness; (*subtilité*) subtlety

fini, e [fini] *adj* finished; (*Math*) finite ▷ *nm* (*d'un objet manufacturé*) finish

finir [finiʀ] *vt* to finish ▷ *vi* to finish, end; **~ par faire** to end up *ou* finish up doing; **~ de faire** to finish doing; (*cesser*) to stop doing; **il finit par m'agacer** he's beginning to get on my nerves; **en ~ avec** to be *ou* have done with; **il va mal ~** he will come to a bad end

finition [finisjɔ̃] *nf* (*résultat*) finish

finlandais, e [fɛ̃lɑ̃dɛ, ɛz] *adj* Finnish ▷ *nm/f*: **F~, e** Finn

Finlande [fɛ̃lɑ̃d] *nf*: **la ~** Finland

finnois, e [finwa, waz] *adj* Finnish ▷ *nm* (*Ling*) Finnish

fioul [fjul] *nm* fuel oil

firme [fiʀm] *nf* firm

fis [fi] *vb voir* **faire**

fisc [fisk] *nm* tax authorities *pl*; **fiscal, e, -aux** *adj* tax *cpd*, fiscal; **fiscalité** *nf* tax system

fissure [fisyʀ] *nf* crack; **fissurer** *vt* to crack; **se fissurer** *vi* to crack

fit [fi] *vb voir* **faire**

fixation [fiksasjɔ̃] *nf* (*attache*) fastening; (*Psych*) fixation

fixe [fiks] *adj* fixed; (*emploi*) steady, regular ▷ *nm* (*salaire*) basic salary; (*téléphone*) landline; **à heure ~** at a set time; **menu à prix ~** set menu

fixé, e [fikse] *adj*: **être ~ (sur)** (*savoir à quoi s'en tenir*) to have made up one's mind (about)

fixer [fikse] *vt* (*attacher*): **~ qch (à/sur)** to fix *ou* fasten sth (to/onto); (*déterminer*) to fix, set; (*regarder*) to stare at; **se fixer** *vi* (*s'établir*) to settle down; **se ~ sur** (*suj: attention*) to focus on

flacon [flakɔ̃] *nm* bottle

lageolet [flaʒɔlɛ] *nm* (*Culin*) dwarf kidney bean

lagrant, e [flagʀɑ̃, ɑ̃t] *adj* flagrant, blatant; **en ~ délit** in the act

lair [flɛʀ] *nm* sense of smell; (*fig*) intuition; **flairer** *vt* (*humer*) to sniff (at); (*détecter*) to scent

lamand, e [flamɑ̃, ɑ̃d] *adj* Flemish ▷ *nm* (*Ling*) Flemish ▷ *nm/f*: **F~, e** Fleming

lamant [flamɑ̃] *nm* flamingo

lambant, e [flɑ̃bɑ̃, ɑ̃t] *adv*: **~ neuf** brand new

lambé, e [flɑ̃be] *adj* (*Culin*) flambéed

lambée [flɑ̃be] *nf* blaze; (*fig: des prix*) explosion

lamber [flɑ̃be] *vi* to blaze (up)

lamboyer [flɑ̃bwaje] *vi* to blaze (up)

lamme [flam] *nf* flame; (*fig*) fire, fervour; **en ~s** on fire, ablaze

lan [flɑ̃] *nm* (*Culin*) custard tart *ou* pie

lanc [flɑ̃] *nm* side; (*Mil*) flank

lancher [flɑ̃ʃe] (*fam*) *vi* to fail, pack up

lanelle [flanɛl] *nf* flannel

lâner [flɑne] *vi* to stroll

lanquer [flɑ̃ke] *vt* to flank; (*fam: mettre*) to chuck, shove; (: *jeter*): **~ par terre/à la porte** to fling to the ground/chuck out

laque [flak] *nf* (*d'eau*) puddle; (*d'huile, de sang etc*) pool

lash [flaʃ] (*pl* **~es**) *nm* (*Photo*) flash; **flash d'information** newsflash

latter [flate] *vt* to flatter; **se ~ de qch** to pride o.s. on sth; **flatteur, -euse** *adj* flattering

lèche [flɛʃ] *nf* arrow; (*de clocher*) spire; **monter en ~** (*fig*) to soar, rocket; **partir en ~** to be off like a shot; **fléchette** *nf* dart

létrir [fletʀiʀ]: **se flétrir** *vi* to wither

leur [flœʀ] *nf* flower; (*d'un arbre*) blossom; **en ~** (*arbre*) in blossom; **à ~s** flowery

leuri, e [flœʀi] *adj* (*jardin*) in flower *ou* bloom; (*tissu, papier*) flowery

leurir [flœʀiʀ] *vi* (*rose*) to flower; (*arbre*) to blossom; (*fig*) to flourish ▷ *vt*

(*tombe*) to put flowers on; (*chambre*) to decorate with flowers

fleuriste [flœʀist] *nm/f* florist

fleuve [flœv] *nm* river

flexible [flɛksibl] *adj* flexible

flic [flik] (*fam: péj*) *nm* cop

flipper [flipœʀ] *nm* pinball (machine)

flirter [flœʀte] *vi* to flirt

flocon [flɔkɔ̃] *nm* flake

flore [flɔʀ] *nf* flora

florissant, e [flɔʀisɑ̃, ɑ̃t] *adj* (*économie*) flourishing

flot [flo] *nm* flood, stream; **flots** *nmpl* (*de la mer*) waves; **être à ~** (*Navig*) to be afloat; **entrer à ~s** to stream *ou* pour in

flottant, e [flɔtɑ̃, ɑ̃t] *adj* (*vêtement*) loose

flotte [flɔt] *nf* (*Navig*) fleet; (*fam: eau*) water; (: *pluie*) rain

flotter [flɔte] *vi* to float; (*nuage, odeur*) to drift; (*drapeau*) to fly; (*vêtements*) to hang loose; (*fam: pleuvoir*) to rain; **faire ~** to float; **flotteur** *nm* float

flou, e [flu] *adj* fuzzy, blurred; (*fig*) woolly, vague

fluide [flɥid] *adj* fluid; (*circulation etc*) flowing freely ▷ *nm* fluid

fluor [flyɔʀ] *nm*: **dentifrice au ~** fluoride toothpaste

fluorescent, e [flyɔʀesɑ̃, ɑ̃t] *adj* fluorescent

flûte [flyt] *nf* flute; (*verre*) flute (glass); (*pain*) (thin) French stick; **~!** drat it!; **flûte traversière/à bec** flute/recorder

flux [fly] *nm* incoming tide; (*écoulement*) flow; **le ~ et le reflux** the ebb and flow

foc [fɔk] *nm* jib

foi [fwa] *nf* faith; **digne de ~** reliable; **être de bonne/mauvaise ~** to be sincere/insincere; **ma ~ ...** well ...

foie [fwa] *nm* liver; **crise de ~** stomach upset

foin [fwɛ̃] *nm* hay; **faire du ~** (*fig: fam*) to kick up a row

foire [fwaʀ] *nf* fair; (*fête foraine*) (fun) fair; **faire la ~** (*fig: fam*) to whoop it up; **~ aux questions** (*Internet*) FAQs; **foire (exposition)** trade fair

fois [fwa] *nf* time; **une/deux ~** once/twice; **2 ~ 2** times 2; **une ~** *(passé)* once; *(futur)* sometime; **une ~ pour toutes** once and for all; **une ~ que** once; **des ~** *(parfois)* sometimes; **à la ~** *(ensemble)* at once

fol [fɔl] *adj voir* **fou**

folie [fɔli] *nf* *(d'une décision, d'un acte)* madness, folly; *(état)* madness, insanity; **la ~ des grandeurs** delusions of grandeur; **faire des ~s** *(en dépenses)* to be extravagant

folklorique [fɔlklɔrik] *adj* folk *cpd*; *(fam)* weird

folle [fɔl] *adj, nf voir* **fou**; **follement** *adv* *(très)* madly, wildly

foncé, e [fɔ̃se] *adj* dark

foncer [fɔ̃se] *vi* to go darker; *(fam: aller vite)* to tear *ou* belt along; **~ sur** to charge at

fonction [fɔ̃ksjɔ̃] *nf* function; *(emploi, poste)* post, position; **fonctions** *nfpl* *(professionnelles)* duties; **voiture de ~** company car; **en ~ de** *(par rapport à)* according to; **faire ~ de** to serve as; **la ~ publique** the state *ou* civil service *(BRIT)*; **fonctionnaire** *nm/f* state employee, local authority employee; *(dans l'administration)* ≈ civil servant; **fonctionner** *vi* to work, function

fond [fɔ̃] *nm* *(d'un récipient, trou)* bottom; *(d'une salle, scène)* back; *(d'un tableau, décor)* background; *(opposé à la forme)* content; *(Sport)* **le ~** long distance (running); **au ~ de** at the bottom of; at the back of; **à ~** *(connaître, soutenir)* thoroughly; *(appuyer, visser)* right down *ou* home; **à ~ (de train)** *(fam)* full tilt; **dans le ~, au ~** *(en somme)* basically, really; **de ~ en comble** from top to bottom; **fond de teint** foundation (cream); *voir aussi* **fonds**

fondamental, e, -aux [fɔ̃damɑ̃tal, o] *adj* fundamental

fondant, e [fɔ̃dɑ̃, ɑ̃t] *adj* *(neige)* melting; *(poire)* that melts in the mouth

fondation [fɔ̃dasjɔ̃] *nf* founding; *(établissement)* foundation; **fondations** *nfpl* *(d'une maison)* foundations

fondé, e [fɔ̃de] *adj* *(accusation etc)* well-founded; **être ~ à** to have grounds for *ou* good reason to

fondement [fɔ̃dmɑ̃] *nm:* **sans ~** *(rumeur etc)* groundless, unfounded

fonder [fɔ̃de] *vt* to found; *(fig)* to base; **se fonder sur** *(suj: personne)* to base o.s. on

fonderie [fɔ̃dri] *nf* smelting works *sg*

fondre [fɔ̃dr] *vt* *(aussi:* **faire ~**) to melt; *(dans l'eau)* to dissolve; *(fig: mélanger)* to merge, blend ▷ *vi* *(à la chaleur)* to melt; *(dans l'eau)* to dissolve; *(fig)* to melt away; *(se précipiter):* **~ sur** to swoop down on; **~ en larmes** to burst into tears

fonds [fɔ̃] *nm* *(Comm):* **~ (de commerce)** business ▷ *nmpl* *(argent)* funds

fondu, e [fɔ̃dy] *adj* *(beurre, neige)* melted; *(métal)* molten; **fondue** *nf* *(Culin)* fondue

font [fɔ̃] *vb voir* **faire**

fontaine [fɔ̃tɛn] *nf* fountain; *(source)* spring

fonte [fɔ̃t] *nf* melting; *(métal)* cast iron; **la ~ des neiges** the (spring) thaw

foot [fut] *(fam)* *nm* football

football [futbol] *nm* football, soccer; **footballeur** *nm* footballer

footing [futiŋ] *nm* jogging; **faire du ~** to go jogging

forain, e [fɔrɛ̃, ɛn] *adj* fairground *cpd* ▷ *nm* *(marchand)* stallholder; *(acteur)* fairground entertainer

forçat [fɔrsa] *nm* convict

force [fɔrs] *nf* strength; *(Physique, Mécanique)* force; **forces** *nfpl* *(physiques)* strength *sg*; *(Mil)* forces; **à ~ d'insister** by dint of insisting; as he *(ou* I *etc)* kept on insisting; **de ~** forcibly, by force; **dans la ~ de l'âge** in the prime of life; **les forces de l'ordre** the police *no pl*

forcé, e [fɔrse] *adj* forced; **c'est ~** *(fam)* it's inevitable; **forcément** *adv* inevitably; **pas forcément** not necessarily

orcer [fɔʀse] vt to force; (voix) to strain ▷ vi (Sport) to overtax o.s.; **~ la dose** (fam) to overdo it; **se ~ (à faire)** to force o.s. (to do)

orestier, -ère [fɔʀɛstje, jɛʀ] adj forest cpd

orêt [fɔʀɛ] nf forest

orfait [fɔʀfɛ] nm (Comm) all-in deal ou price; **déclarer ~** to withdraw; **forfaitaire** adj inclusive

orge [fɔʀʒ] nf forge, smithy; **forgeron** nm (black)smith

ormaliser [fɔʀmalize]: **se formaliser** vi: **se ~ (de)** to take offence (at)

ormalité [fɔʀmalite] nf formality; **simple ~** mere formality

ormat [fɔʀma] nm size; **formater** vt (disque) to format

ormation [fɔʀmasjɔ̃] nf (développement) forming; (apprentissage) training; **formation permanente** ou **continue** continuing education

orme [fɔʀm] nf (gén) form; (d'un objet) shape, form; **formes** nfpl (bonnes manières) proprieties; (d'une femme) figure sg; **en ~ de poire** pear-shaped, in the shape of a pear; **être en ~** (Sport etc) to be on form; **en bonne et due ~** in due form

ormel, le [fɔʀmɛl] adj (catégorique) definite, positive; **formellement** adv (absolument) positively; **formellement interdit** strictly forbidden

ormer [fɔʀme] vt to form; (éduquer) to train; **se former** vi to form

ormidable [fɔʀmidabl] adj tremendous

ormulaire [fɔʀmylɛʀ] nm form

ormule [fɔʀmyl] nf (gén) formula; (expression) phrase; **formule de politesse** polite phrase; (en fin de lettre) letter ending

ort, e [fɔʀ, fɔʀt] adj strong; (intensité, rendement) high, great; (corpulent) stout; (doué) good, able ▷ adv (serrer, frapper) hard; (parler) loud(ly); (beaucoup) greatly, very much; (très) very ▷ nm (édifice) fort; (point fort) strong point,

forte; **forte tête** rebel; **forteresse** nf stronghold

fortifiant [fɔʀtifjɑ̃] nm tonic

fortune [fɔʀtyn] nf fortune; **faire ~** to make one's fortune; **de ~** makeshift; **fortuné, e** adj wealthy

forum [fɔʀɔm] nm forum; **~ de discussion** (Internet) message board

fosse [fos] nf (grand trou) pit; (tombe) grave

fossé [fose] nm ditch; (fig) gulf, gap

fossette [fosɛt] nf dimple

fossile [fosil] nm fossil

fou (fol), folle [fu, fɔl] adj mad; (déréglé etc) wild, erratic; (fam: extrême, très grand) terrific, tremendous ▷ nm/f madman(-woman) ▷ nm (du roi) jester; **être fou de** to be mad ou crazy about; **avoir le fou rire** to have the giggles

foudre [fudʀ] nf: **la ~** lightning

foudroyant, e [fudʀwajɑ̃, ɑ̃t] adj (progrès) lightning cpd; (succès) stunning; (maladie, poison) violent

fouet [fwɛ] nm whip; (Culin) whisk; **de plein ~** (se heurter) head on; **fouetter** vt to whip; (crème) to whisk

fougère [fuʒɛʀ] nf fern

fougue [fug] nf ardour, spirit; **fougueux, -euse** adj fiery

fouille [fuj] nf search; **fouilles** nfpl (archéologiques) excavations; **fouiller** vt to search; (creuser) to dig ▷ vi to rummage; **fouillis** nm jumble, muddle

foulard [fulaʀ] nm scarf

foule [ful] nf crowd; **la ~** crowds pl; **une ~ de** masses of

foulée [fule] nf stride

fouler [fule] vt to press; (sol) to tread upon; **se ~ la cheville** to sprain one's ankle; **ne pas se ~** not to overexert o.s.; **il ne se foule pas** he doesn't put himself out; **foulure** nf sprain

four [fuʀ] nm oven; (de potier) kiln; (Théâtre: échec) flop

fourche [fuʀʃ] nf pitchfork

fourchette [fuʀʃɛt] nf fork; (Statistique) bracket, margin

fourgon [fuʀgɔ̃] nm van; (Rail)

wag(g)on; **fourgonnette** nf (small) van

fourmi [fuʀmi] nf ant; **avoir des ~s dans les jambes/mains** to have pins and needles in one's legs/hands; **fourmilière** nf ant-hill; **fourmiller** vi to swarm

fourneau, x [fuʀno] nm stove

fourni, e [fuʀni] adj (barbe, cheveux) thick; (magasin): **bien ~ (en)** well stocked (with)

fournir [fuʀniʀ] vt to supply; (preuve, exemple) to provide, supply; (effort) to put in; ~ **qch à qn** to supply sth to sb, supply ou provide sb with sth; **fournisseur, -euse** nm/f supplier; **fournisseur d'accès à Internet** (Internet) service provider, ISP; **fourniture** nf supply(ing); **fournitures scolaires** school stationery

fourrage [fuʀaʒ] nm fodder

fourré, e [fuʀe] adj (bonbon etc) filled; (manteau etc) fur-lined ▷ nm thicket

fourrer [fuʀe] (fam) vt to stick, shove; **se fourrer dans/sous** to get into/under

fourrière [fuʀjɛʀ] nf pound

fourrure [fuʀyʀ] nf fur; (sur l'animal) coat

foutre [futʀ] (fam!) vt = **ficher**; **foutu, e** (fam!) adj = **fichu, e**

foyer [fwaje] nm (maison) home; (famille) family; (de cheminée) hearth; (de jeunes etc) (social) club; (résidence) hostel; (salon) foyer; **lunettes à double ~** bi-focals

fracassant, e [fʀakasɑ̃, ɑ̃t] adj (succès) thundering

fraction [fʀaksjɔ̃] nf fraction

fracture [fʀaktyʀ] nf fracture; **fracture du crâne** fractured skull; **fracturer** vt (coffre, serrure) to break open; (os, membre) to fracture; **se fracturer le crâne** to fracture one's skull

fragile [fʀaʒil] adj fragile, delicate; (fig) frail; **fragilité** nf fragility

fragment [fʀagmɑ̃] nm (d'un objet)

fragment, piece

fraîche [fʀɛʃ] adj voir **frais**; **fraîcheur** nf coolness; (d'un aliment) freshness; **fraîchir** vi to get cooler; (vent) to freshen

frais, fraîche [fʀɛ, fʀɛʃ] adj fresh; (froid) cool ▷ adv (récemment) newly, fresh(ly) ▷ nm: **mettre au ~** to put in a cool place ▷ nmpl (gén) expenses; (Comm) costs; **il fait ~** it's cool; **servir ~** serve chilled; **prendre le ~** to take a breath of cool air; **faire des ~** to go to a lot of expense; **frais de scolarité** school fees (BRIT), tuition (US); **frais généraux** overheads

fraise [fʀɛz] nf strawberry; **fraise des bois** wild strawberry

framboise [fʀɑ̃bwaz] nf raspberry

franc, franche [fʀɑ̃, fʀɑ̃ʃ] adj (personne) frank, straightforward; (visage) open; (net: refus) clear; (: coupure) clean; (intensif) downright ▷ nm franc

français, e [fʀɑ̃sɛ, ɛz] adj French ▷ nm/f: **F~, e** Frenchman(-woman) ▷ nm (Ling) French

France [fʀɑ̃s] nf: **la ~** France; **~ 2, ~ 3** public-sector television channels

⊜ **FRANCE TÉLÉVISION**

France 2 and **France 3** are public-sector television channels. France 2 is a national general interest and entertainment channel; France 3 provides regional news and information as well as programmes for the national network.

franche [fʀɑ̃ʃ] adj voir **franc**; **franchement** adv frankly; (nettement) definitely; (tout à fait: mauvais etc) downright

franchir [fʀɑ̃ʃiʀ] vt (obstacle) to clear, get over; (seuil, ligne, rivière) to cross; (distance) to cover

franchise [fʀɑ̃ʃiz] nf frankness; (douanière) exemption; (Assurances) excess

anc-maçon [fʀɑ̃masɔ̃] *nm* freemason

anco [fʀɑ̃ko] *adv* (*Comm*): **~ (de port)** postage paid

ancophone [fʀɑ̃kɔfɔn] *adj* French-speaking

anc-parler [fʀɑ̃paʀle] *nm inv* outspokenness; **avoir son ~** to speak one's mind

ange [fʀɑ̃ʒ] *nf* fringe

angipane [fʀɑ̃ʒipan] *nf* almond paste

appant, e [fʀapɑ̃, ɑ̃t] *adj* striking

appé, e [fʀape] *adj* iced

apper [fʀape] *vt* to hit, strike; (*étonner*) to strike; **~ dans ses mains** to clap one's hands; **frappé de stupeur** dumbfounded

aternel, le [fʀatɛʀnɛl] *adj* brotherly, fraternal; **fraternité** *nf* brotherhood

aude [fʀod] *nf* fraud; (*Scol*) cheating; **passer qch en ~** to smuggle sth in (*ou* out); **fraude fiscale** tax evasion

ayeur [fʀejœʀ] *nf* fright

edonner [fʀədɔne] *vt* to hum

eezer [fʀizœʀ] *nm* freezing compartment

ein [fʀɛ̃] *nm* brake; **mettre un ~ à** (*fig*) to curb, check; **frein à main** handbrake; **freiner** *vi* to brake ▷ *vt* (*progrès etc*) to check

êle [fʀɛl] *adj* frail, fragile

elon [fʀəlɔ̃] *nm* hornet

émir [fʀemiʀ] *vi* (*de peur, d'horreur*) to shudder; (*de colère*) to shake; (*feuillage*) to quiver

êne [fʀɛn] *nm* ash

équemment [fʀekamɑ̃] *adv* frequently

équent, e [fʀekɑ̃, ɑ̃t] *adj* frequent

équentation [fʀekɑ̃tasjɔ̃] *nf* frequenting; **fréquentations** *nfpl* (*relations*) company *sg*; **avoir de mauvaises ~s** to be in with the wrong crowd, keep bad company

équenté, e [fʀekɑ̃te] *adj*: **très ~** (very) busy; **mal ~** patronized by disreputable elements

fréquenter [fʀekɑ̃te] *vt* (*lieu*) to frequent; (*personne*) to see; **se fréquenter** to see each other

frère [fʀɛʀ] *nm* brother

fresque [fʀɛsk] *nf* (*Art*) fresco

fret [fʀɛ(t)] *nm* freight

friand, e [fʀijɑ̃, fʀijɑ̃d] *adj*: **~ de** very fond of ▷ *nm*: **~ au fromage** cheese puff

friandise [fʀijɑ̃diz] *nf* sweet

fric [fʀik] (*fam*) *nm* cash, bread

friche [fʀiʃ]: **en ~** *adj, adv* (lying) fallow

friction [fʀiksjɔ̃] *nf* (*massage*) rub, rub-down; (*Tech, fig*) friction

frigidaire® [fʀiʒidɛʀ] *nm* refrigerator

frigo [fʀigo] (*fam*) *nm* fridge

frigorifique [fʀigɔʀifik] *adj* refrigerating

frileux, -euse [fʀilø, øz] *adj* sensitive to (the) cold

frimer [fʀime] (*fam*) *vi* to show off

fringale [fʀɛ̃gal] (*fam*) *nf*: **avoir la ~** to be ravenous

fringues [fʀɛ̃g] (*fam*) *nfpl* clothes

fripé, e [fʀipe] *adj* crumpled

frire [fʀiʀ] *vt, vi*: **faire ~** to fry

frisé, e [fʀize] *adj* (*cheveux*) curly; (*personne*) curly-haired

frisson [fʀisɔ̃] *nm* (*de froid*) shiver; (*de peur*) shudder; **frissonner** *vi* (*de fièvre, froid*) to shiver; (*d'horreur*) to shudder

frit, e [fʀi, fʀit] *pp de* **frire**; **frite** *nf*: **(pommes) frites** chips (*BRIT*), French fries; **friteuse** *nf* chip pan; **friteuse électrique** deep fat fryer; **friture** *nf* (*huile*) (deep) fat; (*plat*) **friture (de poissons)** fried fish

froid, e [fʀwa, fʀwad] *adj, nm* cold; **il fait ~** it's cold; **avoir/prendre ~** to be/catch cold; **être en ~ avec** to be on bad terms with; **froidement** *adv* (*accueillir*) coldly; (*décider*) coolly

froisser [fʀwase] *vt* to crumple (up), crease; (*fig*) to hurt, offend; **se froisser** *vi* to crumple, crease; (*personne*) to take offence; **se ~ un muscle** to strain a muscle

frôler [fʀole] *vt* to brush against; (*suj: projectile*) to skim past; (*fig*) to come very close to

fromage [fʀɔmaʒ] *nm* cheese; **fromage blanc** soft white cheese

froment [fʀɔmɑ̃] *nm* wheat

froncer [fʀɔ̃se] *vt* to gather; **~ les sourcils** to frown

front [fʀɔ̃] *nm* forehead, brow; (*Mil*) front; **de ~** (*se heurter*) head-on; (*rouler*) together (*i.e. 2 or 3 abreast*); (*simultanément*) at once; **faire ~ à** to face up to

frontalier, -ère [fʀɔ̃talje, jɛʀ] *adj* border *cpd*, frontier *cpd*; **(travailleurs) ~s** people who commute across the border

frontière [fʀɔ̃tjɛʀ] *nf* frontier, border

frotter [fʀɔte] *vi* to rub, scrape ▷ *vt* to rub; (*pommes de terre, plancher*) to scrub; **~ une allumette** to strike a match

fruit [fʀɥi] *nm* fruit *gen no pl*; **fruits de mer** seafood(s); **fruits secs** dried fruit *sg*; **fruité, e** *adj* fruity; **fruitier, -ère** *adj*: **arbre fruitier** fruit tree

frustrer [fʀystʀe] *vt* to frustrate

fuel(-oil) [fjul(ɔjl)] *nm* fuel oil; (*domestique*) heating oil

fugace [fygas] *adj* fleeting

fugitif, -ive [fyʒitif, iv] *adj* (*fugace*) fleeting ▷ *nm/f* fugitive

fugue [fyg] *nf*: **faire une ~** to run away, abscond

fuir [fɥiʀ] *vt* to flee from; (*éviter*) to shun ▷ *vi* to run away; (*gaz, robinet*) to leak

fuite [fɥit] *nf* flight; (*écoulement, divulgation*) leak; **être en ~** to be on the run; **mettre en ~** to put to flight

fulgurant, e [fylgyʀɑ̃, ɑ̃t] *adj* lightning *cpd*, dazzling

fumé, e [fyme] *adj* (*Culin*) smoked; (*verre*) tinted; **fumée** *nf* smoke

fumer [fyme] *vi* to smoke; (*soupe*) to steam ▷ *vt* to smoke

fûmes [fym] *vb voir* **être**

fumeur, -euse [fymœʀ, øz] *nm/f* smoker

fumier [fymje] *nm* manure

funérailles [fyneʀaj] *nfpl* funeral *sg*

fur [fyʀ]: **au ~ et à mesure** *adv* as one goes along; **au ~ et à mesure que** as

furet [fyʀɛ] *nm* ferret

fureter [fyʀ(ə)te] *(péj) vi* to nose about

fureur [fyʀœʀ] *nf* fury; **être en ~** to be infuriated; **faire ~** to be all the rage

furie [fyʀi] *nf* fury; (*femme*) shrew, vixen; **en ~** (*mer*) raging; **furieux, -euse** *adj* furious

furoncle [fyʀɔ̃kl] *nm* boil

furtif, -ive [fyʀtif, iv] *adj* furtive

fus [fy] *vb voir* **être**

fusain [fyzɛ̃] *nm* (*Art*) charcoal

fuseau, x [fyzo] *nm* (*pour filer*) spindle; (*pantalon*) (ski) pants; **fuseau horaire** time zone

fusée [fyze] *nf* rocket

fusible [fyzibl] *nm* (*Élec: fil*) fuse wire; (*: fiche*) fuse

fusil [fyzi] *nm* (*de guerre, à canon rayé*) rifle, gun; (*de chasse, à canon lisse*) shotgun, gun; **fusillade** *nf* gunfire *no pl*, shooting *no pl*; **fusiller** *vt* to shoot; **fusiller qn du regard** to look daggers at sb

fusionner [fyzjɔne] *vi* to merge

fût [fy] *vb voir* **être** ▷ *nm* (*tonneau*) barrel, cask

futé, e [fyte] *adj* crafty; **Bison ~®** *TV and radio traffic monitoring service*

futile [fytil] *adj* futile; frivolous

futur, e [fytyʀ] *adj, nm* future

fuyard, e [fɥijaʀ, aʀd] *nm/f* runaway

Gabon [gabɔ̃] nm: **le ~** Gabon

gâcher [gaʃe] vt (gâter) to spoil; (gaspiller) to waste; **gâchis** nm waste no pl

gaffe [gaf] nf blunder; **faire ~** (fam) to be careful

gage [gaʒ] nm (dans un jeu) forfeit; (fig: de fidélité, d'amour) token; **gages** nmpl (salaire) wages; **mettre en ~** to pawn

gagnant, e [gaɲɑ̃, ɑ̃t] adj: **billet/ numéro ~** winning ticket/number ▷ nm/f winner

gagne-pain [gaɲpɛ̃] nm inv job

gagner [gaɲe] vt to win; (somme d'argent, revenu) to earn; (aller vers, atteindre) to reach; (envahir: sommeil, peur) to overcome; (: mal) to spread to ▷ vi to win; (fig) to gain; **~ du temps/de la place** to gain time/save space; **~ sa vie** to earn one's living

gai, e [ge] adj cheerful; (un peu ivre) merry; **gaiement** adv cheerfully; **gaieté** nf cheerfulness; **de gaieté de cœur** with a light heart

gain [gɛ̃] nm (revenu) earnings pl; (bénéfice: gén pl) profits pl

gala [gala] nm official reception; **de ~** (soirée etc) gala

galant, e [galɑ̃, ɑ̃t] adj (courtois) courteous, gentlemanly; (entreprenant) flirtatious, gallant; (scène, rendez-vous) romantic

galerie [galʀi] nf gallery; (Théâtre) circle; (de voiture) roof rack; (fig: spectateurs) audience; **galerie de peinture** (private) art gallery; **galerie marchande** shopping arcade

galet [galɛ] nm pebble

galette [galɛt] nf flat cake; **galette des Rois** cake eaten on Twelfth Night

- **GALETTE DES ROIS**
-
- A **galette des Rois** is a cake eaten on
- Twelfth Night containing a figurine.
- The person who finds it is the king
- (or queen) and gets a paper crown.
- They then choose someone else to be
- their queen (or king).

galipette [galipɛt] nf somersault

Galles [gal] nfpl: **le pays de ~** Wales; **gallois, e** adj Welsh ▷ nm/f: **Gallois, e** Welshman(-woman) ▷ nm (Ling) Welsh

galon [galɔ̃] nm (Mil) stripe; (décoratif) piece of braid

galop [galo] nm gallop; **galoper** vi to gallop

gambader [gɑ̃bade] vi (animal, enfant) to leap about

gamin, e [gamɛ̃, in] nm/f kid ▷ adj childish

gamme [gam] nf (Mus) scale; (fig) range

gang [gɑ̃g] nm (de criminels) gang

gant [gɑ̃] nm glove; **gant de toilette** face flannel (BRIT), face cloth

garage [gaʀaʒ] nm garage; **garagiste** nm/f garage owner; (employé) garage mechanic

garantie [gaʀɑ̃ti] nf guarantee; **(bon de) ~** guarantee ou warranty slip

garantir [gaʀɑ̃tiʀ] vt to guarantee; **~ à**

qn que to assure sb that

garçon [gaʀsɔ̃] nm boy; (célibataire): **vieux ~** bachelor; **garçon (de café)** (serveur) waiter; **garçon de courses** messenger

garde [gaʀd(ə)] nm (de prisonnier) guard; (de domaine etc) warden; (soldat, sentinelle) guardsman ▷ nf (soldats) guard; **de ~** on duty; **monter la ~** to stand guard; **mettre en ~** to warn; **prendre ~ (à)** to be careful (of); **garde champêtre** nm rural policeman; **garde du corps** nm bodyguard; **garde à vue** nf (Jur) ≈ police custody; **garde-boue** nm inv mudguard; **garde-chasse** nm gamekeeper

garder [gaʀde] vt (conserver) to keep; (surveiller: enfants) to look after; (: immeuble, lieu, prisonnier) to guard; **se garder** vi (aliment: se conserver) to keep; **se ~ de faire** to be careful not to do; **~ le lit/la chambre** to stay in bed/indoors; **pêche/chasse gardée** private fishing/hunting (ground)

garderie [gaʀdəʀi] nf day nursery, crèche

garde-robe [gaʀdəʀɔb] nf wardrobe

gardien, ne [gaʀdjɛ̃, jɛn] nm/f (garde) guard; (de prison) warder; (de domaine, réserve) warden; (de musée etc) attendant; (de phare, cimetière) keeper; (d'immeuble) caretaker; (fig) guardian; **gardien de but** goalkeeper; **gardien de la paix** policeman; **gardien de nuit** night watchman

gare¹ [gaʀ] nf station; **gare routière** bus station

gare² [gaʀ] excl: **~ à ...!** mind ...!; **~ à toi!** watch out!

garer [gaʀe] vt to park; **se garer** vi to park

garni, e [gaʀni] adj (plat) served with vegetables (and chips or rice etc)

garniture [gaʀnityʀ] nf (Culin) vegetables pl; **garniture de frein** brake lining

gars [gɑ] (fam) nm guy

Gascogne [gaskɔɲ] nf Gascony; **le**

golfe de ~ the Bay of Biscay

gas-oil [gazɔjl] nm diesel (oil)

gaspiller [gaspije] vt to waste

gastronome [gastʀɔnɔm] nm/f gourmet; **gastronomique** adj gastronomic

gâteau, x [gɑto] nm cake; **gâteau sec** biscuit

gâter [gɑte] vt to spoil; **se gâter** vi (dent, fruit) to go bad; (temps, situation) to change for the worse

gâteux, -euse [gɑtø, øz] adj senile

gauche [goʃ] adj left, left-hand; (maladroit) awkward, clumsy ▷ nf (Pol) left (wing); **le bras ~** the left arm; **le côté ~** the left-hand side; **à ~** on the left; (direction) (to the) left; **gaucher, -ère** adj left-handed; **gauchiste** nm/f leftist

gaufre [gofʀ] nf waffle

gaufrette [gofʀɛt] nf wafer

gaulois, e [golwa, waz] adj Gallic ▷ nm/f: **G~, e** Gaul

gaz [gaz] nm inv gas; **ça sent le ~** I can smell gas, there's a smell of gas

gaze [gaz] nf gauze

gazette [gazɛt] nf news sheet

gazeux, -euse [gazø, øz] adj (boisson) fizzy; (eau) sparkling

gazoduc [gazodyk] nm gas pipeline

gazon [gazɔ̃] nm (herbe) grass; (pelouse) lawn

geai [ʒɛ] nm jay

géant, e [ʒeɑ̃, ɑ̃t] adj gigantic; (Comm) giant-size ▷ nm/f giant

geindre [ʒɛ̃dʀ] vi to groan, moan

gel [ʒɛl] nm frost

gélatine [ʒelatin] nf gelatine

gelée [ʒ(ə)le] nf jelly; (gel) frost

geler [ʒ(ə)le] vt, vi to freeze; **il gèle** it's freezing

gélule [ʒelyl] nf (Méd) capsule

Gémeaux [ʒemo] nmpl: **les ~** Gemini

gémir [ʒemiʀ] vi to groan, moan

gênant, e [ʒɛnɑ̃, ɑ̃t] adj (irritant) annoying; (embarrassant) embarrassing

gencive [ʒɑ̃siv] nf gum

gendarme [ʒɑ̃daʀm] nm gendarme;

gendarmerie *nf* military police force in countryside and small towns; their police station or barracks

gendre [ʒɑ̃dʀ] *nm* son-in-law

gêné, e [ʒene] *adj* embarrassed

gêner [ʒene] *vt* (*incommoder*) to bother; (*encombrer*) to be in the way; (*embarrasser*): **~ qn** to make sb feel ill-at-ease; **se gêner** to put o.s. out; **ne vous gênez pas!** don't mind me!

général, e, -aux [ʒeneʀal, o] *adj*, *nm* general; **en ~** usually, in general; **généralement** *adv* generally; **généraliser** *vt*, *vi* to generalize; **se généraliser** *vi* to become widespread; **généraliste** *nm/f* general practitioner, G.P.

génération [ʒeneʀasjɔ̃] *nf* generation

généreux, -euse [ʒeneʀø, øz] *adj* generous

générique [ʒeneʀik] *nm* (*Cinéma*) credits *pl*

générosité [ʒeneʀozite] *nf* generosity

genêt [ʒ(ə)nɛ] *nm* broom *no pl* (*shrub*)

génétique [ʒenetik] *adj* genetic

Genève [ʒ(ə)nɛv] *n* Geneva

génial, e, -aux [ʒenjal, jo] *adj* of genius; (*fam: formidable*) fantastic, brilliant

génie [ʒeni] *nm* genius; (*Mil*): **le ~** the Engineers *pl*; **génie civil** civil engineering

genièvre [ʒənjɛvʀ] *nm* juniper

génisse [ʒenis] *nf* heifer

génital, e, -aux [ʒenital, o] *adj* genital; **les parties ~es** the genitals

génoise [ʒenwaz] *nf* sponge cake

genou, x [ʒ(ə)nu] *nm* knee; **à ~x** on one's knees; **se mettre à ~x** to kneel down

genre [ʒɑ̃ʀ] *nm* kind, type, sort; (*Ling*) gender; **avoir bon ~** to look a nice sort; **avoir mauvais ~** to be coarse-looking; **ce n'est pas son ~** it's not like him

gens [ʒɑ̃] *nmpl* (*f in some phrases*) people *pl*

gentil, le [ʒɑ̃ti, ij] *adj* kind; (*enfant: sage*) good; (*endroit etc*) nice;

gentillesse *nf* kindness; **gentiment** *adv* kindly

géographie [ʒeɔgʀafi] *nf* geography

géologie [ʒeɔlɔʒi] *nf* geology

géomètre [ʒeɔmɛtʀ] *nm/f* (*arpenteur*) (land) surveyor

géométrie [ʒeɔmetʀi] *nf* geometry; **géométrique** *adj* geometric

géranium [ʒeʀanjɔm] *nm* geranium

gérant, e [ʒeʀɑ̃, ɑ̃t] *nm/f* manager(-eress); **gérant d'immeuble** (managing) agent

gerbe [ʒɛʀb] *nf* (*de fleurs*) spray; (*de blé*) sheaf

gercé, e [ʒɛʀse] *adj* chapped

gerçure [ʒɛʀsyʀ] *nf* crack

gérer [ʒeʀe] *vt* to manage

germain, e [ʒɛʀmɛ̃, ɛn] *adj*: **cousin ~** first cousin

germe [ʒɛʀm] *nm* germ; **germer** *vi* to sprout; (*semence*) to germinate

geste [ʒɛst] *nm* gesture

gestion [ʒɛstjɔ̃] *nf* management

Ghana [gana] *nm*: **le ~** Ghana

gibier [ʒibje] *nm* (*animaux*) game

gicler [ʒikle] *vi* to spurt, squirt

gifle [ʒifl] *nf* slap (in the face); **gifler** *vt* to slap (in the face)

gigantesque [ʒigɑ̃tɛsk] *adj* gigantic

gigot [ʒigo] *nm* leg (of mutton *ou* lamb)

gigoter [ʒigɔte] *vi* to wriggle (about)

gilet [ʒilɛ] *nm* waistcoat; (*pull*) cardigan; **gilet de sauvetage** life jacket

gin [dʒin] *nm* gin; **~-tonic** gin and tonic

gingembre [ʒɛ̃ʒɑ̃bʀ] *nm* ginger

girafe [ʒiʀaf] *nf* giraffe

giratoire [ʒiʀatwaʀ] *adj*: **sens ~** roundabout

girofle [ʒiʀɔfl] *nf*: **clou de ~** clove

girouette [ʒiʀwɛt] *nf* weather vane *ou* cock

gitan, e [ʒitɑ̃, an] *nm/f* gipsy

gîte [ʒit] *nm* (*maison*) home; (*abri*) shelter; **gîte (rural)** (country) holiday cottage (BRIT), gîte (*self-catering accommodation in the country*)

givre [ʒivʀ] *nm* (hoar) frost; **givré, e** *adj*

covered in frost; (*fam: fou*) nuts; **orange givrée** orange sorbet (*served in peel*)

glace [glas] *nf* ice; (*crème glacée*) ice cream; (*miroir*) mirror; (*de voiture*) window

glacé, e [glase] *adj* (*mains, vent, pluie*) freezing; (*lac*) frozen; (*boisson*) iced

glacer [glase] *vt* to freeze; (*gâteau*) to ice; (*fig*): **~ qn** (*intimider*) to chill sb; (*paralyser*) to make sb's blood run cold

glacial, e [glasjal, jo] *adj* icy

glacier [glasje] *nm* (*Géo*) glacier; (*marchand*) ice-cream maker

glacière [glasjɛr] *nf* icebox

glaçon [glasɔ̃] *nm* icicle; (*pour boisson*) ice cube

glaïeul [glajœl] *nm* gladiolus

glaise [glɛz] *nf* clay

gland [glɑ̃] *nm* acorn; (*décoration*) tassel

glande [glɑ̃d] *nf* gland

glissade [glisad] *nf* (*par jeu*) slide; (*chute*) slip; **faire des ~s sur la glace** to slide on the ice

glissant, e [glisɑ̃, ɑ̃t] *adj* slippery

glissement [glismɑ̃] *nm*: **glissement de terrain** landslide

glisser [glise] *vi* (*avancer*) to glide *ou* slide along; (*coulisser, tomber*) to slide; (*déraper*) to slip; (*être glissant*) to be slippery ▷ *vt* to slip; **se glisser dans/ entre** to slip into/between

global, e, -aux [glɔbal, o] *adj* overall

globe [glɔb] *nm* globe

globule [glɔbyl] *nm* (*du sang*): **~ blanc/ rouge** white/red corpuscle

gloire [glwar] *nf* glory

glousser [gluse] *vi* to cluck; (*rire*) to chuckle

glouton, ne [glutɔ̃, ɔn] *adj* gluttonous

gluant, e [glyɑ̃, ɑ̃t] *adj* sticky, gummy

glucose [glykoz] *nm* glucose

glycine [glisin] *nf* wisteria

GO *sigle* (= *grandes ondes*) LW

goal [gol] *nm* goalkeeper

gobelet [gɔblɛ] *nm* (*en étain, verre, argent*) tumbler; (*d'enfant, de pique-nique*) beaker; (*à dés*) cup

goéland [gɔelɑ̃] *nm* (sea)gull

goélette [gɔelɛt] *nf* schooner

goinfre [gwɛ̃fr] *nm* glutton

golf [gɔlf] *nm* golf; (*terrain*) golf course; **golf miniature** crazy (*BRIT*) *ou* miniature golf

golfe [gɔlf] *nm* gulf; (*petit*) bay

gomme [gɔm] *nf* (*à effacer*) rubber (*BRIT*), eraser; **gommer** *vt* to rub out (*BRIT*), erase

gonflé, e [gɔ̃fle] *adj* swollen; **il est ~** (*fam: courageux*) he's got some nerve; (*impertinent*) he's got a nerve

gonfler [gɔ̃fle] *vt* (*pneu, ballon: en soufflant*) to blow up; (: *avec une pompe*) to pump up; (*nombre, importance*) to inflate ▷ *vi* to swell (up); (*Culin: pâte*) to rise

gonzesse [gɔ̃zɛs] (*fam*) *nf* chick, bird (*BRIT*)

gorge [gɔrʒ] *nf* (*Anat*) throat; (*vallée*) gorge; **gorgée** *nf* (*petite*) sip; (*grande*) gulp

gorille [gɔrij] *nm* gorilla; (*fam*) bodyguard

gosse [gɔs] (*fam*) *nm/f* kid

goudron [gudrɔ̃] *nm* tar; **goudronner** *vt* to tar(mac) (*BRIT*), asphalt (*US*)

gouffre [gufr] *nm* abyss, gulf

goulot [gulo] *nm* neck; **boire au ~** to drink from the bottle

goulu, e [guly] *adj* greedy

gourde [gurd] *nf* (*récipient*) flask; (*fam*) (clumsy) clot *ou* oaf ▷ *adj* oafish

gourdin [gurdɛ̃] *nm* club, bludgeon

gourmand, e [gurmɑ̃, ɑ̃d] *adj* greedy; **gourmandise** *nf* greed; (*bonbon*) sweet

gousse [gus] *nf*: **gousse d'ail** clove of garlic

goût [gu] *nm* taste; **avoir bon ~** to taste good; **de bon ~** tasteful; **de mauvais ~** tasteless; **prendre ~ à** to develop a taste *ou* a liking for

goûter [gute] *vt* (*essayer*) to taste; (*apprécier*) to enjoy ▷ *vi* to have (afternoon) tea ▷ *nm* (afternoon) tea; **je peux ~?** can I have a taste?

goutte [gut] *nf* drop; (*Méd*) gout; (*alcool*) brandy; **tomber ~ à ~** to drip;

une **~ de whisky** a drop of whisky; **goutte-à-goutte** nm (Méd) drip

gouttière [gutjɛʀ] nf gutter

gouvernail [guvɛʀnaj] nm rudder; (barre) helm, tiller

gouvernement [guvɛʀnəmɑ̃] nm government

gouverner [guvɛʀne] vt to govern

grâce [gʀɑs] nf (charme, Rel) grace; (faveur) favour; (Jur) pardon; **faire ~ à qn de qch** to spare sb sth; **demander ~** to beg for mercy; **~ à** thanks to; **gracieux, -euse** adj graceful

grade [gʀad] nm rank; **monter en ~** to be promoted

gradin [gʀadɛ̃] nm tier; step; **gradins** nmpl (de stade) terracing sg

gradué, e [gʀadɥe] adj: **verre ~** measuring jug

graduel, le [gʀadɥel] adj gradual

graduer [gʀadɥe] vt (effort etc) to increase gradually; (règle, verre) to graduate

graffiti [gʀafiti] nmpl graffiti

grain [gʀɛ̃] nm (gén) grain; (Navig) squall; **grain de beauté** beauty spot; **grain de café** coffee bean; **grain de poivre** peppercorn

graine [gʀɛn] nf seed

graissage [gʀesaʒ] nm lubrication, greasing

graisse [gʀes] nf fat; (lubrifiant) grease; **graisser** vt to lubricate, grease; (tacher) to make greasy; **graisseux, -euse** adj greasy

grammaire [gʀa(m)mɛʀ] nf grammar

gramme [gʀam] nm gramme

grand, e [gʀɑ̃, gʀɑ̃d] adj (haut) tall; (gros, vaste, long) big, large; (long) long; (plus âgé) big; (adulte) grown-up; (important, brillant) great ▷ adv: **~ ouvert** wide open; **au ~ air** in the open (air); **les blessés** the severely injured; **grand ensemble** housing scheme; **grand magasin** department store; **grande personne** grown-up; **grande surface** hypermarket; **grandes écoles** prestigious schools at university

level; **grandes lignes** (Rail) main lines; **grandes vacances** summer holidays (BRIT) ou vacation (US); **grand-chose** nm/f inv: **pas grand-chose** not much; **Grande-Bretagne** nf (Great) Britain; **grandeur** nf (dimension) size; **grandeur nature** life-size; **grandiose** adj imposing; **grandir** vi to grow ▷ vt: **grandir qn** (suj: vêtement, chaussure) to make sb look taller; **grand-mère** nf grandmother; **grand-peine: à grand-peine** adv with difficulty; **grand-père** nm grandfather; **grands-parents** nmpl grandparents

grange [gʀɑ̃ʒ] nf barn

granit [gʀanit] nm granite

graphique [gʀafik] adj graphic ▷ nm graph

grappe [gʀap] nf cluster; **grappe de raisin** bunch of grapes

gras, se [gʀɑ, gʀɑs] adj (viande, soupe) fatty; (personne) fat; (surface, main) greasy; (plaisanterie) coarse; (Typo) bold ▷ nm (Culin) fat; **faire la ~se matinée** to have a lie-in (BRIT), sleep late (US); **grassement** adv: **grassement payé** handsomely paid

gratifiant, e [gʀatifjɑ̃, jɑ̃t] adj gratifying, rewarding

gratin [gʀatɛ̃] nm (plat) cheese-topped dish; (croûte) cheese topping; (fam: élite) upper crust; **gratiné, e** adj (Culin) au gratin

gratis [gʀatis] adv free

gratitude [gʀatityd] nf gratitude

gratte-ciel [gʀatsjɛl] nm inv skyscraper

gratter [gʀate] vt (avec un outil) to scrape; (enlever: avec un outil) to scrape off; (: avec un ongle) to scratch; (enlever avec un ongle) to scratch off ▷ vi (irriter) to be scratchy; (démanger) to itch; **se gratter** to scratch (o.s.)

gratuit, e [gʀatɥi, ɥit] adj (entrée, billet) free; (fig) gratuitous

grave [gʀav] adj (maladie, accident) serious, bad; (sujet, problème) serious, grave; (air) grave, solemn; (voix, son) deep, low-pitched; **gravement** *adv* seriously; *(parler, regarder)* gravely

graver [gʀave] *vt (plaque, nom)* to engrave; *(CD, DVD)* to burn

graveur [gʀavœʀ] *nm* engraver; **graveur de CD/DVD** CD/DVD writer

gravier [gʀavje] *nm* gravel *no pl*; **gravillons** *nmpl* loose chippings *ou* gravel *sg*

gravir [gʀaviʀ] *vt* to climb (up)

gravité [gʀavite] *nf (de maladie, d'accident)* seriousness; *(de sujet, problème)* gravity

graviter [gʀavite] *vi* to revolve

gravure [gʀavyʀ] *nf* engraving; *(reproduction)* print

gré [gʀe] *nm*: **à son ~** to one's liking; **de bon ~** willingly; **contre le ~ de qn** against sb's will; **de son (plein) ~** of one's own free will; **bon ~ mal ~** like it or not; **de ~ ou de force** whether one likes it or not; **savoir ~ à qn de qch** to be grateful to sb for sth

grec, grecque [gʀɛk] *adj* Greek; *(classique: vase etc)* Grecian ▷ *nm/f*: **G~, Grecque** Greek ▷ *nm (Ling)* Greek

Grèce [gʀɛs] *nf*: **la ~** Greece

greffe [gʀɛf] *nf (Bot, Méd: de tissu)* graft; *(Méd: d'organe)* transplant; **greffer** *vt (Bot, Méd: tissu)* to graft; *(Méd: organe)* to transplant

grêle [gʀɛl] *adj* (very) thin ▷ *nf* hail; **grêler** *vb impers*: **il grêle** it's hailing; **grêlon** *nm* hailstone

grelot [gʀəlo] *nm* little bell

grelotter [gʀələte] *vi* to shiver

grenade [gʀənad] *nf (explosive)* grenade; *(Bot)* pomegranate; **grenadine** *nf* grenadine

grenier [gʀənje] *nm* attic; *(de ferme)* loft

grenouille [gʀənuj] *nf* frog

grès [gʀɛ] *nm* sandstone; *(poterie)* stoneware

grève [gʀɛv] *nf (d'ouvriers)* strike; *(plage)* shore; **se mettre en/faire ~** to go on/ be on strike; **grève de la faim** hunger strike; **grève sauvage** wildcat strike

gréviste [gʀevist] *nm/f* striker

grièvement [gʀijɛvmɑ̃] *adv* seriously

griffe [gʀif] *nf* claw; *(de couturier)* label; **griffer** *vt* to scratch

grignoter [gʀiɲɔte] *vt (personne)* to nibble at; *(souris)* to gnaw at ▷ *vi* to nibble

gril [gʀil] *nm* steak *ou* grill pan; **faire cuire au ~** to grill; **grillade** *nf (viande etc)* grill

grillage [gʀijaʒ] *nm (treillis)* wire netting; *(clôture)* wire fencing

grille [gʀij] *nf (clôture)* wire fence; *(portail)* (metal) gate; *(d'égout)* (metal) grate; *(fig)* grid

grille-pain [gʀijpɛ̃] *nm inv* toaster

griller [gʀije] *vt (pain)* to toast; *(viande)* to grill; *(fig: ampoule etc)* to blow; **faire ~** to toast; to grill; *(châtaignes)* to roast; **~ un feu rouge** to jump the lights

grillon [gʀijɔ̃] *nm* cricket

grimace [gʀimas] *nf* grimace; *(pour faire rire)*: **faire des ~s** to pull *ou* make faces

grimper [gʀɛ̃pe] *vi, vt* to climb

grincer [gʀɛ̃se] *vi (objet métallique)* to grate; *(plancher, porte)* to creak; **~ des dents** to grind one's teeth

grincheux, -euse [gʀɛ̃ʃø, øz] *adj* grumpy

grippe [gʀip] *nf* flu, influenza; **grippe aviaire** bird flu; **grippé, e** *adj*: **être grippé** to have flu

gris, e [gʀi, gʀiz] *adj* grey; *(ivre)* tipsy

grisaille [gʀizaj] *nf* greyness, dullness

griser [gʀize] *vt* to intoxicate

grive [gʀiv] *nf* thrush

Groenland [gʀɔɛnlɑ̃d] *nm* Greenland

grogner [gʀɔɲe] *vi* to growl; *(fig)* to grumble; **grognon, ne** *adj* grumpy

grommeler [gʀɔm(ə)le] *vi* to mutter to o.s.

gronder [gʀɔ̃de] *vi* to rumble; *(fig: révolte)* to be brewing ▷ *vt* to scold; **se faire ~** to get a telling-off

gros, se [gʀo, gʀos] *adj* big, large; *(obèse)* fat; *(travaux, dégâts)* extensive; *(épais)* thick; *(rhume, averse)* heavy ▷ *adv*: **risquer/gagner ~** to risk/win

a lot ▷ *nm/f* fat man/woman ▷ *nm*
(*Comm*): **le ~** the wholesale business;
le ~ de the bulk of; **prix de gros**
wholesale price; **par ~ temps/grosse
mer** in rough weather/heavy seas; **en
~** roughly; (*Comm*) wholesale; **gros lot**
jackpot; **gros mot** swearword; **gros
plan** (*Photo*) close-up; **gros sel** cooking
salt; **gros titre** headline; **grosse caisse**
big drum

groseille [grozɛj] *nf*: **~ (rouge/
blanche)** red/white currant; **groseille
à maquereau** gooseberry

grosse [gros] *adj voir* **gros**; **grossesse**
nf pregnancy; **grosseur** *nf* size;
(*tumeur*) lump

grossier, -ière [grosje, jɛr] *adj*
coarse; (*insolent*) rude; (*dessin*) rough;
(*travail*) roughly done; (*imitation,
instrument*) crude; (*évident: erreur*) gross;
grossièrement *adv* (*sommairement*)
roughly; (*vulgairement*) coarsely;
grossièreté *nf* rudeness; (*mot*):
dire des grossièretés to use coarse
language

grossir [grosir] *vi* (*personne*) to put on
weight ▷ *vt* (*exagérer*) to exaggerate;
(*au microscope*) to magnify; (*suj:
vêtement*): **~ qn** to make sb look fatter

grossiste [grosist] *nm/f* wholesaler

grotesque [grotɛsk] *adj* (*extravagant*)
grotesque; (*ridicule*) ludicrous

grotte [grot] *nf* cave

groupe [grup] *nm* group; **groupe
de parole** support group; **groupe
sanguin** blood group; **groupe scolaire**
school complex; **grouper** *vt* to group;
se grouper *vi* to gather

grue [gry] *nf* crane

GSM [ʒeesɛm] *nm, adj* GSM

guenon [gənɔ̃] *nf* female monkey

guépard [gepar] *nm* cheetah

guêpe [gɛp] *nf* wasp

guère [gɛr] *adv* (*avec adjectif, adverbe*):
ne ... ~ hardly; (*avec verbe: pas beaucoup*):
ne ... ~ tournure négative +*much*; (*pas
souvent*) hardly ever; (*pas longtemps*)
tournure négative +(*very*) *long*; **il n'y a**

~ que/de there's hardly anybody (*ou*
anything) but/hardly any; **ce n'est
~ difficile** it's hardly difficult; **nous
n'avons ~ de temps** we have hardly
any time

guérilla [gerija] *nf* guerrilla warfare

guérillero [gerijero] *nm* guerrilla

guérir [gerir] *vt* (*personne, maladie*)
to cure; (*membre, plaie*) to heal ▷ *vi*
(*malade, maladie*) to be cured; (*blessure*)
to heal; **guérison** *nf* (*de maladie*)
curing; (*de membre, plaie*) healing; (*de
malade*) recovery; **guérisseur, -euse**
nm/f healer

guerre [gɛr] *nf* war; **en ~** at war; **faire
la ~ à** to wage war against; **guerre
civile/mondiale** civil/world war;
guerrier, -ière *adj* warlike ▷ *nm/f*
warrior

guet [gɛ] *nm*: **faire le ~** to be on the
watch *ou* look-out; **guet-apens**
[gɛtapɑ̃] *nm* ambush; **guetter** *vt*
(*épier*) to watch (intently); (*attendre*) to
watch (out) for; (*hostilement*) to be lying
in wait for

gueule [gœl] *nf* (*d'animal*) mouth; (*fam:
figure*) face; (: *bouche*) mouth; **ta ~!** (*fam*)
shut up!; **avoir la ~ de bois** (*fam*) to
have a hangover, be hung over; **gueuler**
(*fam*) *vi* to bawl

gui [gi] *nm* mistletoe

guichet [giʃɛ] *nm* (*de bureau, banque*)
counter; **les ~s** (*à la gare, au théâtre*) the
ticket office *sg*

guide [gid] *nm* (*personne*) guide; (*livre*)
guide (book) ▷ *nf* (*éclaireuse*) girl guide;
guider *vt* to guide

guidon [gidɔ̃] *nm* handlebars *pl*

guignol [giɲɔl] *nm* ≈ Punch and Judy
show; (*fig*) clown

guillemets [gijmɛ] *nmpl*: **entre ~** in
inverted commas

guindé, e [gɛ̃de] *adj* (*personne, air*) stiff,
starchy; (*style*) stilted

Guinée [gine] *nf* Guinea

guirlande [girlɑ̃d] *nf* (*fleurs*) garland;
guirlande de Noël tinsel garland

guise [giz] *nf*: **à votre ~** as you wish *ou*

please; **en ~ de** by way of
guitare [gitaʀ] *nf* guitar
Guyane [gɥijan] *nf*: **la ~ (française)**
French Guiana
gym [ʒim] *nf* (*exercices*) gym; **gymnase**
nm gym(nasium); **gymnaste** *nm/f*
gymnast; **gymnastique** *nf* gymnastics
sg; (*au réveil etc*) keep-fit exercises *pl*
gynécologie [ʒinekɔlɔʒi] *nf*
gynaecology; **gynécologique** *adj*
gynaecological; **gynécologue** *nm/f*
gynaecologist

habile [abil] *adj* skilful; (*malin*) clever;
habileté [abilte] *nf* skill, skilfulness;
cleverness
habillé, e [abije] *adj* dressed; (*chic*)
dressy
habiller [abije] *vt* to dress; (*fournir en
vêtements*) to clothe; (*couvrir*) to cover;
s'habiller *vi* to dress (o.s.); (*se déguiser,
mettre des vêtements chic*) to dress up
habit [abi] *nm* outfit; **habits** *nmpl*
(*vêtements*) clothes; **habit (de soirée)**
evening dress; (*pour homme*) tails *pl*
habitant, e [abitã, ãt] *nm/f*
inhabitant; (*d'une maison*) occupant;
loger chez l'~ to stay with the locals
habitation [abitasjɔ̃] *nf* house;
habitations à loyer modéré (block of)
council flats
habiter [abite] *vt* to live in ▷ *vi*: **~
à/dans** to live in; **où habitez-vous?**
where do you live?
habitude [abityd] *nf* habit; **avoir l'~ de
qch** to be used to sth; **avoir l'~ de faire**
to be in the habit of doing; (*expérience*)

to be used to doing; **d'~** usually; **comme d'~** as usual

habitué, e [abitɥe] *nm/f (de maison)* regular visitor; *(de café)* regular (customer)

habituel, le [abitɥɛl] *adj* usual

habituer [abitɥe] *vt:* **~ qn à** to get sb used to; **s'habituer à** to get used to

'hache [ʃ] *nf* axe

'hacher [aʃe] *vt (viande)* to mince; *(persil)* to chop; **'hachis** *nm* mince *no pl;* **hachis Parmentier** ≈ shepherd's pie

'haie [ɛ] *nf* hedge; *(Sport)* hurdle

'haillons [ajɔ̃] *nmpl* rags

'haine [ɛn] *nf* hatred

'haïr [aiʀ] *vt* to detest, hate

'hâlé, e [ale] *adj* (sun)tanned, sunburnt

haleine [alɛn] *nf* breath; **hors d'~** out of breath; **tenir en ~** *(attention)* to hold spellbound; *(incertitude)* to keep in suspense; **de longue ~** long-term

'haleter [alte] *vt* to pant

'hall [ol] *nm* hall

'halle [al] *nf* (covered) market; **halles** *nfpl (d'une grande ville)* central food market *sg*

hallucination [alysinasjɔ̃] *nf* hallucination

'halte [alt] *nf* stop, break; *(endroit)* stopping place ▷ *excl* stop!; **faire halte** to stop

haltère [altɛʀ] *nm* dumbbell, barbell; **haltères** *nmpl:* **(poids de) ~s** *(activité)* weightlifting *sg;* **haltérophilie** *nf* weightlifting

'hamac [amak] *nm* hammock

'hameau, x [amo] *nm* hamlet

hameçon [amsɔ̃] *nm* (fish) hook

'hanche [ɑ̃ʃ] *nf* hip

'handball [ɑ̃dbal] *nm* handball

'handicapé, e [ɑ̃dikape] *adj* disabled, handicapped ▷ *nm/f* handicapped person; **handicapé mental/physique** mentally/physically handicapped person; **'handicapé moteur** person with a movement disorder

'hangar [ɑ̃gaʀ] *nm* shed; *(Aviat)* hangar

'hanneton [antɔ̃] *nm* cockchafer

'hanter [ɑ̃te] *vt* to haunt

'hantise [ɑ̃tiz] *nf* obsessive fear

'harceler [aʀsəle] *vt* to harass; **harceler qn de questions** to plague sb with questions

'hardi, e [aʀdi] *adj* bold, daring

'hareng [aʀɑ̃] *nm* herring; **hareng saur** kipper, smoked herring

'hargne [aʀɲ] *nf* aggressiveness; **'hargneux, -euse** *adj* aggressive

'haricot [aʀiko] *nm* bean; **'haricot blanc** haricot bean; **'haricot vert** green bean; **'haricot rouge** kidney bean

harmonica [aʀmɔnika] *nm* mouth organ

harmonie [aʀmɔni] *nf* harmony; **harmonieux, -euse** *adj* harmonious; *(couleurs, couple)* well-matched

'harpe [aʀp] *nf* harp

'hasard [azaʀ] *nm:* **le hasard** chance, fate; **un hasard** a coincidence; **au hasard** *(aller)* aimlessly; *(choisir)* at random; **par hasard** by chance; **à tout hasard** *(en cas de besoin)* just in case; *(en espérant trouver ce qu'on cherche)* on the off chance *(BRIT)*

'hâte [ɑt] *nf* haste; **à la hâte** hurriedly, hastily; **en hâte** posthaste, with all possible speed; **avoir hâte de** to be eager *ou* anxious to; **'hâter** *vt* to hasten; **se hâter** *vi* to hurry; **'hâtif, -ive** *adj (travail)* hurried; *(décision, jugement)* hasty

'hausse [os] *nf* rise, increase; **être en hausse** to be going up; **'hausser** *vt* to raise; **hausser les épaules** to shrug (one's shoulders)

'haut, e [o, ot] *adj* high; *(grand)* tall ▷ *adv* high ▷ *nm* top (part); **de 3 m de haut** 3 m high, 3 m in height; **des hauts et des bas** ups and downs; **en haut lieu** in high places; **à haute voix, (tout) haut** aloud, out loud; **du haut de** from the top of; **de haut en bas** from top to bottom; **plus haut** higher up, further up; *(dans un texte)* above;

(*parler*) louder; **en haut** (*être/aller*) at/to the top; (*dans une maison*) upstairs; **en haut de** at the top of; **'haut débit** broadband

'hautain, e ['otɛ̃, ɛn] *adj* haughty

'hautbois ['obwɑ] *nm* oboe

'hauteur ['otœR] *nf* height; **à la hauteur de** (*accident*) near; (*fig: tâche, situation*) equal to; **à la hauteur** (*fig*) up to it

'haut-parleur *nm* (loud)speaker

Hawaï [awai] *n*: **les îles ~** Hawaii

'Haye ['ɛ] *n*: **la Haye** the Hague

hebdomadaire [ɛbdɔmadɛR] *adj, nm* weekly

hébergement [ebɛRʒəmɑ̃] *nm* accommodation

héberger [ebɛRʒe] *vt* (*touristes*) to accommodate, lodge; (*amis*) to put up; (*réfugiés*) to take in

hébergeur [ebɛRʒœR] *nm* (*Internet*) host

hébreu, x [ebRø] *adj m, nm* Hebrew

Hébrides [ebRid] *nf*: **les ~** the Hebrides

hectare [ɛktaR] *nm* hectare

'hein ['ɛ̃] *excl* eh?

'hélas ['elɑs] *excl* alas! ▷ *adv* unfortunately

'héler ['ele] *vt* to hail

hélice [elis] *nf* propeller

hélicoptère [elikɔptɛR] *nm* helicopter

helvétique [ɛlvetik] *adj* Swiss

hématome [ematom] *nm* nasty bruise

hémisphère [emisfɛR] *nm*: **l'~ nord/sud** the northern/southern hemisphere

hémorragie [emɔRaʒi] *nf* bleeding *no pl*, haemorrhage

hémorroïdes [em`id] *nfpl* piles, haemorrhoids

'hennir ['eniR] *vi* to neigh, whinny

hépatite [epatit] *nf* hepatitis

herbe [ɛRb] *nf* grass; (*Culin, Méd*) herb; **~s de Provence** mixed herbs; **en ~** unripe; (*fig*) budding; **herbicide** *nm* weed-killer; **herboriste** *nm/f* herbalist

héréditaire [eReditɛR] *adj* hereditary

'hérisson ['eRisɔ̃] *nm* hedgehog

héritage [eRitaʒ] *nm* inheritance; (*coutumes, système*) heritage, legacy

hériter [eRite] *vi*: **~ qch (de qn)** to inherit sth (from sb); **héritier, -ière** *nm/f* heir(-ess)

hermétique [ɛRmetik] *adj* airtight; watertight; (*fig: obscur*) abstruse; (: *impénétrable*) impenetrable

hermine [ɛRmin] *nf* ermine

'hernie ['ɛRni] *nf* hernia

héroïne [eRɔin] *nf* heroine; (*drogue*) heroin

héroïque [eRɔik] *adj* heroic

'héron ['eRɔ̃] *nm* heron

'héros ['eRo] *nm* hero

hésitant, e [ezitɑ̃, ɑ̃t] *adj* hesitant

hésitation [ezitasjɔ̃] *nf* hesitation

hésiter [ezite] *vi*: **~ (à faire)** to hesitate (to do)

hétérosexuel, le [eteRɔsɛkɥɛl] *adj* heterosexual

'hêtre ['ɛtR] *nm* beech

heure [œR] *nf* hour; (*Scol*) period; (*moment*) time; **c'est l'~** it's time; **quelle ~ est-il?** what time is it?; **2 ~s (du matin)** 2 o'clock (in the morning); **être à l'~** to be on time; (*montre*) to be right; **mettre à l'~** to set right; **à une ~ avancée (de la nuit)** at a late hour (of the night); **de bonne ~** early; **à toute ~** at any time; **24 ~s sur 24** round the clock, 24 hours a day; **à l'~ qu'il est** at this time (of day); by now; **sur l'~** at once; **à quelle ~ ouvre le musée/magasin?** what time does the museum/shop open?; **heures de bureau** office hours; **heure de pointe** rush hour; (*téléphone*) peak period; **heures supplémentaires** overtime *sg*

heureusement [œRøzmɑ̃] *adv* (*par bonheur*) fortunately, luckily

heureux, -euse [œRø, øz] *adj* happy; (*chanceux*) lucky, fortunate

'heurt ['œR] *nm* (*choc*) collision; (*conflit*) clash

'heurter ['œRte] *vt* (*mur*) to strike, hit; (*personne*) to collide with

hexagone [ɛgzagɔn] *nm* hexagon; **l'H~** (*la France*) France (*because of its shape*)

hiberner [ibɛʀne] *vi* to hibernate

'hibou, x ['ibu] *nm* owl

'hideux, -euse ['idø, øz] *adj* hideous

hier [jɛʀ] *adv* yesterday; **~ matin/midi** yesterday morning/lunchtime; **~ soir** last night, yesterday evening; **toute la journée d'~** all day yesterday; **toute la matinée d'~** all yesterday morning

'hiérarchie ['jeʀaʀʃi] *nf* hierarchy

hindou, e [ɛ̃du] *adj* Hindu ▷ *nm/f*: **H~, e** Hindu

hippique [ipik] *adj* equestrian, horse *cpd*; **un club ~** a riding centre; **un concours ~** a horse show; **hippisme** *nm* (horse)riding

hippodrome [ipɔdʀom] *nm* racecourse

hippopotame [ipɔpɔtam] *nm* hippopotamus

hirondelle [iʀɔ̃dɛl] *nf* swallow

'hisser ['ise] *vt* to hoist, haul up

histoire [istwaʀ] *nf* (*science, événements*) history; (*anecdote, récit, mensonge*) story; (*affaire*) business *no pl*; **histoires** *nfpl* (*chichis*) fuss *no pl*; (*ennuis*) trouble *sg*; **historique** *adj* historical; (*important*) historic ▷ *nm*: **faire l'historique de** to give the background to

'hit-parade ['itpaʀad] *nm*: **le hit-parade** the charts

hiver [ivɛʀ] *nm* winter; **hivernal, e, -aux** *adj* winter *cpd*; (*glacial*) wintry; **hiverner** *vi* to winter

HLM *nm ou f* (= *habitation à loyer modéré*) council flat; **des ~** council housing

'hobby ['ɔbi] *nm* hobby

'hocher ['ɔʃe] *vt*: **hocher la tête** to nod; (*signe négatif ou dubitatif*) to shake one's head

'hockey ['ɔkɛ] *nm*: **hockey (sur glace/gazon)** (ice/field) hockey

'hold-up ['ɔldœp] *nm inv* hold-up

'hollandais, e ['ɔlɑ̃dɛ, ɛz] *adj* Dutch ▷ *nm* (*Ling*) Dutch ▷ *nm/f*: **Hollandais, e** Dutchman(-woman)

'Hollande ['ɔlɑ̃d] *nf*: **la Hollande** Holland

'homard ['ɔmaʀ] *nm* lobster

homéopathique [ɔmeɔpatik] *adj* homoeopathic

homicide [ɔmisid] *nm* murder; **homicide involontaire** manslaughter

hommage [ɔmaʒ] *nm* tribute; **rendre ~ à** to pay tribute to

homme [ɔm] *nm* man; **homme d'affaires** businessman; **homme d'État** statesman; **homme de main** hired man; **homme de paille** stooge; **l'homme de la rue** the man on the street

homo…: **homogène** *adj* homogeneous; **homologue** *nm/f* counterpart; **homologué, e** *adj* (*Sport*) ratified; (*tarif*) authorized; **homonyme** *nm* (*Ling*) homonym; (*d'une personne*) namesake; **homosexuel, le** *adj* homosexual

'Hong Kong ['ɔ̃gkɔ̃g] *n* Hong Kong

'Hongrie ['ɔ̃gʀi] *nf*: **la Hongrie** Hungary; **'hongrois, e** *adj* Hungarian ▷ *nm/f*: **Hongrois, e** Hungarian ▷ *nm* (*Ling*) Hungarian

honnête [ɔnɛt] *adj* (*intègre*) honest; (*juste, satisfaisant*) fair; **honnêtement** *adv* honestly; **honnêteté** *nf* honesty

honneur [ɔnœʀ] *nm* honour; (*mérite*) credit; **en l'~ de** in honour of; (*événement*) on the occasion of; **faire ~ à** (*engagements*) to honour; (*famille*) to be a credit to; (*fig: repas etc*) to do justice to

honorable [ɔnɔʀabl] *adj* worthy, honourable; (*suffisant*) decent

honoraire [ɔnɔʀɛʀ] *adj* honorary; **professeur ~** professor emeritus; **honoraires** *nmpl* fees

honorer [ɔnɔʀe] *vt* to honour; (*estimer*) to hold in high regard; (*faire honneur à*) to do credit to

'honte ['ɔ̃t] *nf* shame; **avoir honte de** to be ashamed of; **faire honte à qn** to make sb (feel) ashamed; **'honteux, -euse** *adj* ashamed; (*conduite, acte*) shameful, disgraceful

hôpital, -aux [ɔpital, o] *nm* hospital; **où est l'~ le plus proche?** where is the nearest hospital?

'hoquet [ˈɔkɛ] *nm*: **avoir le hoquet** to have (the) hiccoughs

horaire [ɔʀɛʀ] *adj* hourly ▷ *nm* timetable, schedule; **horaires** *nmpl* (*d'employé*) hours; **horaire souple** flexitime

horizon [ɔʀizɔ̃] *nm* horizon

horizontal, e, -aux [ɔʀizɔ̃tal, o] *adj* horizontal

horloge [ɔʀlɔʒ] *nf* clock; **l'~ parlante** the speaking clock; **horloger, -ère** *nm/f* watchmaker; clockmaker

'hormis [ˈɔʀmi] *prép* save

horoscope [ˈskɔp] *nm* horoscope

horreur [ɔʀœʀ] *nf* horror; **quelle ~!** how awful!; **avoir ~ de** to loathe *ou* detest; **horrible** *adj* horrible; **horrifier** *vt* to horrify

'hors [ˈɔʀ] *prép*: **hors de** out of; **hors pair** outstanding; **hors de propos** inopportune; **être hors de soi** to be beside o.s.; **'hors d'usage** out of service; **'hors-bord** *nm inv* speedboat (*with outboard motor*); **'hors-d'œuvre** *nm inv* hors d'œuvre; **'hors-la-loi** *nm inv* outlaw; **'hors-service** *adj inv* out of order; **'hors-taxe** *adj* (*boutique, articles*) duty-free

hortensia [ɔʀtɑ̃sja] *nm* hydrangea

hospice [ɔspis] *nm* (*de vieillards*) home

hospitalier, -ière [ɔspitalje, jɛʀ] *adj* (*accueillant*) hospitable; (*Méd: service, centre*) hospital *cpd*

hospitaliser [ɔspitalize] *vt* to take/send to hospital, hospitalize

hospitalité [ɔspitalite] *nf* hospitality

hostie [ɔsti] *nf* host (*Rel*)

hostile [ɔstil] *adj* hostile; **hostilité** *nf* hostility

hôte [ot] *nm* (*maître de maison*) host; (*invité*) guest

hôtel [otɛl] *nm* hotel; **aller à l'~** to stay in a hotel; **hôtel de ville** town hall; **hôtel (particulier)** (private) mansion; **hôtellerie** *nf* hotel business

● **HÔTELS**
●
● There are six categories of hotel
● in France, from zero ('non classé')
● to four stars and luxury four stars
● ('quatre étoiles luxe'). Prices include
● VAT but not breakfast. In some
● towns, guests pay a small additional
● tourist tax, the 'taxe de séjour'.

hôtesse [otɛs] *nf* hostess; **hôtesse (de l'air)** stewardess, air hostess (*BRIT*)

'houblon [ˈublɔ̃] *nm* (*Bot*) hop; (*pour la bière*) hops *pl*

'houille [ˈuj] *nf* coal; **'houille blanche** hydroelectric power

'houle [ˈul] *nf* swell; **'houleux, -euse** *adj* stormy

'hourra [ˈuʀa] *excl* hurrah!

'housse [ˈus] *nf* cover

'houx [ˈu] *nm* holly

'hublot [ˈyblo] *nm* porthole

'huche [ˈyʃ] *nf*: **huche à pain** bread bin

'huer [ˈɥe] *vt* to boo

huile [ɥil] *nf* oil

huissier [ɥisje] *nm* usher; (*Jur*) ≈ bailiff

'huit [ˈɥi(t)] *num* eight; **samedi en huit** a week on Saturday; **dans huit jours** in a week; **'huitaine** *nf*: **une huitaine (de jours)** a week or so; **'huitième** *num* eighth

huître [ɥitʀ] *nf* oyster

humain, e [ymɛ̃, ɛn] *adj* human; (*compatissant*) humane ▷ *nm* human (being); **humanitaire** *adj* humanitarian; **humanité** *nf* humanity

humble [œ̃bl] *adj* humble

'humer [ˈyme] *vt* (*plat*) to smell; (*parfum*) to inhale

humeur [ymœʀ] *nf* mood; **de bonne/mauvaise ~** in a good/bad mood

humide [ymid] *adj* damp; (*main, yeux*) moist; (*climat, chaleur*) humid; (*saison, route*) wet

humilier [ymilje] *vt* to humiliate

humilité [ymilite] *nf* humility, humbleness

humoristique [ymɔʀistik] *adj*

humorous

humour [ymuʀ] nm humour; **avoir de l'~** to have a sense of humour; **humour noir** black humour

'huppé, e ['ype] (fam) adj posh

'hurlement ['yʀləmɑ̃] nm howling no pl, howl, yelling no pl, yell

'hurler ['yʀle] vi to howl, yell

'hutte ['yt] nf hut

hydratant, e [idʀatɑ̃, ɑ̃t] adj (crème) moisturizing

hydraulique [idʀolik] adj hydraulic

hydravion [idʀavjɔ̃] nm seaplane

hydrogène [idʀɔʒɛn] nm hydrogen

hydroglisseur [idʀɔglisœʀ] nm hydroplane

hyène [jɛn] nf hyena

hygiène [iʒjɛn] nf hygiene

hygiénique [iʒenik] adj hygienic

hymne [imn] nm hymn

hyperlien [ipɛʀljɛ̃] nm hyperlink

hypermarché [ipɛʀmaʀʃe] nm hypermarket

hypermétrope [ipɛʀmetʀɔp] adj long-sighted

hypertension [ipɛʀtɑ̃sjɔ̃] nf high blood pressure

hypnose [ipnoz] nf hypnosis; **hypnotiser** vt to hypnotize

hypocrisie [ipɔkʀizi] nf hypocrisy; **hypocrite** adj hypocritical

hypothèque [ipɔtɛk] nf mortgage

hypothèse [ipɔtɛz] nf hypothesis

hystérique [isteʀik] adj hysterical

iceberg [ajsbɛʀg] nm iceberg

ici [isi] adv here; **jusqu'~** as far as this; (temps) so far; **d'~ demain** by tomorrow; **d'~ là** by then, in the meantime; **d'~ peu** before long

icône [ikon] nf icon

idéal, e, -aux [ideal, o] adj ideal ▷ nm ideal; **idéaliste** adj idealistic ▷ nm/f idealist

idée [ide] nf idea; **avoir dans l'~ que** to have an idea that; **se faire des ~s** to imagine things, get ideas into one's head; **avoir des ~s noires** to have black ou dark thoughts; **idées reçues** received wisdom sg

identifier [idɑ̃tifje] vt to identify; **s'identifier** vi: **s'~ avec** ou **à qn/qch** (héros etc) to identify with sb/sth

identique [idɑ̃tik] adj: **~ (à)** identical (to)

identité [idɑ̃tite] nf identity

idiot, e [idjo, idjɔt] adj idiotic ▷ nm/f idiot

idole [idɔl] nf idol

if [if] *nm* yew
ignoble [iɲɔbl] *adj* vile
ignorant, e [iɲɔrɑ̃, ɑ̃t] *adj* ignorant; **~ de** ignorant of, not aware of
ignorer [iɲɔre] *vt* not to know; (*personne*) to ignore
il [il] *pron* he; (*animal, chose, en tournure impersonnelle*) it; **il fait froid** it's cold; **Pierre est-il arrivé?** has Pierre arrived?; **il a gagné** he won; *voir* **avoir**
île [il] *nf* island; **l'île Maurice** Mauritius; **les îles anglo-normandes** the Channel Islands; **les îles britanniques** the British Isles
illégal, e, -aux [i(l)legal, o] *adj* illegal
illimité, e [i(l)limite] *adj* unlimited
illisible [i(l)lizibl] *adj* illegible; (*roman*) unreadable
illogique [i(l)lɔʒik] *adj* illogical
illuminer [i(l)lymine] *vt* to light up; (*monument, rue: pour une fête*) to illuminate; (: *au moyen de projecteurs*) to floodlight
illusion [i(l)lyzjɔ̃] *nf* illusion; **se faire des ~s** to delude o.s.; **faire ~** to delude *ou* fool people
illustration [i(l)lystrasjɔ̃] *nf* illustration
illustré, e [i(l)lystre] *adj* illustrated ▷ *nm* comic
illustrer [i(l)lystre] *vt* to illustrate; **s'illustrer** to become famous, win fame
ils [il] *pron* they
image [imaʒ] *nf* (*gén*) picture; (*métaphore*) image; **image de marque** brand image; (*fig*) public image; **imagé, e** *adj* (*texte*) full of imagery; (*langage*) colourful
imaginaire [imaʒinɛr] *adj* imaginary
imagination [imaʒinasjɔ̃] *nf* imagination; **avoir de l'~** to be imaginative
imaginer [imaʒine] *vt* to imagine; (*inventer: expédient*) to devise, think up; **s'imaginer** *vt* (*se figurer: scène etc*) to imagine, picture; **s'~ que** to imagine that

imbécile [ɛ̃besil] *adj* idiotic ▷ *nm/f* idiot
imbu, e [ɛ̃by] *adj*: **~ de** full of
imitateur, -trice [imitatœr, tris] *nm/f* (*gén*) imitator; (*Music-Hall*) impersonator
imitation [imitasjɔ̃] *nf* imitation; (*de personnalité*) impersonation
imiter [imite] *vt* to imitate; (*contrefaire*) to forge; (*ressembler à*) to look like
immangeable [ɛ̃mɑ̃ʒabl] *adj* inedible
immatriculation [imatrikylasjɔ̃] *nf* registration

○ **IMMATRICULATION**
○
○ The last two numbers on vehicle
○ licence plates show which
○ 'département' of France the vehicle
○ is registered in. For example, a car
○ registered in Paris has the number 75
○ on its licence plates.

immatriculer [imatrikyle] *vt* to register; **faire/se faire ~** to register
immédiat, e [imedja, jat] *adj* immediate ▷ *nm*: **dans l'~** for the time being; **immédiatement** *adv* immediately
immense [i(m)mɑ̃s] *adj* immense
immerger [imɛrʒe] *vt* to immerse, submerge
immeuble [imœbl] *nm* building; (*à usage d'habitation*) block of flats
immigration [imigrasjɔ̃] *nf* immigration
immigré, e [imigre] *nm/f* immigrant
imminent, e [iminɑ̃, ɑ̃t] *adj* imminent
immobile [i(m)mɔbil] *adj* still, motionless
immobilier, -ière [imɔbilje, jɛr] *adj* property *cpd* ▷ *nm*: **l'~** the property business
immobiliser [imɔbilize] *vt* (*gén*) to immobilize; (*circulation, véhicule, affaires*) to bring to a standstill; **s'immobiliser** (*personne*) to stand still; (*machine, véhicule*) to come to a halt

mmoral, e, -aux [i(m)mɔʀal, o] adj
immoral

mmortel, le [imɔʀtɛl] adj immortal

mmunisé, e [im(m)ynize] adj: **~
contre** immune to

mmunité [imynite] nf immunity

mpact [ɛ̃pakt] nm impact

mpair, e [ɛ̃pɛʀ] adj odd ▷ nm faux
pas, blunder

mpardonnable [ɛ̃paʀdɔnabl] adj
unpardonable, unforgivable

mparfait, e [ɛ̃paʀfɛ, ɛt] adj imperfect

mpartial, e, -aux [ɛ̃paʀsjal, jo] adj
impartial, unbiased

mpasse [ɛ̃pɑs] nf dead end, cul-de-
sac; (fig) deadlock

mpassible [ɛ̃pasibl] adj impassive

mpatience [ɛ̃pasjɑ̃s] nf impatience

mpatient, e [ɛ̃pasjɑ̃, jɑ̃t]
adj impatient; **impatienter**:
s'impatienter vi to get impatient

mpeccable [ɛ̃pekabl] adj (parfait)
perfect; (propre) impeccable; (fam)
smashing

mpensable [ɛ̃pɑ̃sabl] adj (événement
hypothétique) unthinkable; (événement
qui a eu lieu) unbelievable

mpératif, -ive [ɛ̃peʀatif, iv] adj
imperative ▷ nm (Ling) imperative;
impératifs nmpl (exigences: d'une
fonction, d'une charge) requirements;
(: de la mode) demands

mpératrice [ɛ̃peʀatʀis] nf empress

mperceptible [ɛ̃pɛʀsɛptibl] adj
imperceptible

mpérial, e, -aux [ɛ̃peʀjal, jo] adj
imperial

mpérieux, -euse [ɛ̃peʀjø, jøz] adj
(caractère, ton) imperious; (obligation,
besoin) pressing, urgent

mpérissable [ɛ̃peʀisabl] adj undying

mperméable [ɛ̃pɛʀmeabl] adj
waterproof; (fig): **~ à** impervious to
▷ nm raincoat

mpertinent, e [ɛ̃pɛʀtinɑ̃, ɑ̃t] adj
impertinent

mpitoyable [ɛ̃pitwajabl] adj pitiless,
merciless

implanter [ɛ̃plɑ̃te]: **s'implanter** vi
to be set up

impliquer [ɛ̃plike] vt to imply; **~ qn
(dans)** to implicate sb (in)

impoli, e [ɛ̃pɔli] adj impolite, rude

impopulaire [ɛ̃pɔpylɛʀ] adj unpopular

importance [ɛ̃pɔʀtɑ̃s] nf importance;
(de somme) size; (de retard, dégâts)
extent; **sans ~** unimportant

important, e [ɛ̃pɔʀtɑ̃, ɑ̃t] adj
important; (en quantité: somme, retard)
considerable, sizeable; (: dégâts)
extensive; (péj: airs, ton) self-important
▷ nm: **l'~** the important thing

importateur, -trice [ɛ̃pɔʀtatœʀ,
tʀis] nm/f importer

importation [ɛ̃pɔʀtasjɔ̃] nf
importation; (produit) import

importer [ɛ̃pɔʀte] vt (Comm) to
import; (maladies, plantes) to introduce
▷ vi (être important) to matter; **il
importe qu'il fasse** it is important
that he should do; **peu m'importe** (je
n'ai pas de préférence) I don't mind; (je
m'en moque) I don't care; **peu importe
(que)** it doesn't matter (if); voir aussi
n'importe

importun, e [ɛ̃pɔʀtœ̃, yn] adj
irksome, importunate; (arrivée, visite)
inopportune, ill-timed ▷ nm intruder;
importuner vt to bother

imposant, e [ɛ̃pozɑ̃, ɑ̃t] adj imposing

imposer [ɛ̃poze] vt (taxer) to tax;
s'imposer (être nécessaire) to be
imperative; **~ qch à qn** to impose sth
on sb; **en ~ à** to impress; **s'~ comme** to
emerge as; **s'~ par** to win recognition
through

impossible [ɛ̃pɔsibl] adj impossible; **il
m'est ~ de le faire** it is impossible for
me to do it, I can't possibly do it; **faire
l'~** to do one's utmost

imposteur [ɛ̃pɔstœʀ] nm impostor

impôt [ɛ̃po] nm tax; **impôt foncier** land
tax; **impôt sur le chiffre d'affaires**
corporation (BRIT) ou corporate (US)
tax; **impôt sur le revenu** income tax;
impôts locaux rates, local taxes (US),

≈ council tax (*BRIT*)

impotent, e [ɛ̃pɔtɑ̃, ɑ̃t] *adj* disabled

impraticable [ɛ̃pratikabl] *adj* (*projet*) impracticable, unworkable; (*piste*) impassable

imprécis, e [ɛ̃presi, iz] *adj* imprecise

imprégner [ɛ̃preɲe] *vt* (*tissu*) to impregnate; (*lieu, air*) to fill; **s'imprégner de** (*fig*) to absorb

imprenable [ɛ̃prənabl] *adj* (*forteresse*) impregnable; **vue ~** unimpeded outlook

impression [ɛ̃presjɔ̃] *nf* impression; (*d'un ouvrage, tissu*) printing; **faire bonne/mauvaise ~** to make a good/ bad impression; **impressionnant, e** *adj* (*imposant*) impressive; (*bouleversant*) upsetting; **impressionner** *vt* (*frapper*) to impress; (*bouleverser*) to upset

imprévisible [ɛ̃previzibl] *adj* unforeseeable

imprévu, e [ɛ̃prevy] *adj* unforeseen, unexpected ▷ *nm* (*incident*) unexpected incident; **des vacances pleines d'~** holidays full of surprises; **en cas d'~** if anything unexpected happens; **sauf ~** unless anything unexpected crops up

imprimante [ɛ̃primɑ̃t] *nf* printer; **imprimante (à) laser** laser printer

imprimé [ɛ̃prime] *nm* (*formulaire*) printed form; (*Postes*) printed matter *no pl*; (*tissu*) printed fabric; **~ à fleur** floral print

imprimer [ɛ̃prime] *vt* to print; (*publier*) to publish; **imprimerie** *nf* printing; (*établissement*) printing works *sg*; **imprimeur** *nm* printer

impropre [ɛ̃prɔpr] *adj* inappropriate; **~ à** unfit for

improviser [ɛ̃prɔvize] *vt, vi* to improvise

improviste [ɛ̃prɔvist]: **à l'~** *adv* unexpectedly, without warning

imprudence [ɛ̃prydɑ̃s] *nf* (*d'une personne, d'une action*) carelessness *no pl*; (*d'une remarque*) imprudence *no pl*; **commettre une ~** to do something foolish

imprudent, e [ɛ̃prydɑ̃, ɑ̃t] *adj* (*conducteur, geste, action*) careless; (*remarque*) unwise, imprudent; (*projet*) foolhardy

impuissant, e [ɛ̃pɥisɑ̃, ɑ̃t] *adj* helpless; (*sans effet*) ineffectual; (*sexuellement*) impotent

impulsif, -ive [ɛ̃pylsif, iv] *adj* impulsive

impulsion [ɛ̃pylsjɔ̃] *nf* (*Élec, instinct*) impulse; (*élan, influence*) impetus

inabordable [inabɔrdabl] *adj* (*cher*) prohibitive

inacceptable [inakseptabl] *adj* unacceptable

inaccessible [inaksesibl] *adj* inaccessible; **~ à** impervious to

inachevé, e [inaʃ(ə)ve] *adj* unfinished

inactif, -ive [inaktif, iv] *adj* inactive; (*remède*) ineffective; (*Bourse: marché*) slack

inadapté, e [inadapte] *adj* (*gén*): **~ à** not adapted to, unsuited to; (*Psych*) maladjusted

inadéquat, e [inadekwa(t), kwat] *adj* inadequate

inadmissible [inadmisibl] *adj* inadmissible

inadvertance [inadvɛrtɑ̃s]: **par ~** *adv* inadvertently

inanimé, e [inanime] *adj* (*matière*) inanimate; (*évanoui*) unconscious; (*sans vie*) lifeless

inanition [inanisjɔ̃] *nf*: **tomber d'~** to faint with hunger (and exhaustion)

inaperçu, e [inapɛrsy] *adj*: **passer ~** to go unnoticed

inapte [inapt] *adj*: **~ à** incapable of; (*Mil*) unfit for

inattendu, e [inatɑ̃dy] *adj* unexpected

inattentif, -ive [inatɑ̃tif, iv] *adj* inattentive; **~ à** (*dangers, détails*) heedless of; **inattention** *nf* lack of attention; **une faute** *ou* **une erreur d'inattention** a careless mistake

inaugurer [inogyre] *vt* (*monument*) to unveil; (*exposition, usine*) to open; (*fig*) to inaugurate

inavouable[inavwabl] *adj* shameful; *(bénéfices)* undisclosable

incalculable[ɛ̃kalkylabl] *adj* incalculable

incapable[ɛ̃kapabl] *adj* incapable; **~ de faire** incapable of doing; *(empêché)* unable to do

incapacité[ɛ̃kapasite] *nf* *(incompétence)* incapability; *(impossibilité)* incapacity; **dans l'~ de faire** unable to do

incarcérer[ɛ̃kaʀseʀe] *vt* to incarcerate, imprison

incassable[ɛ̃kasabl] *adj* unbreakable

incendie[ɛ̃sɑ̃di] *nm* fire; **incendie criminel** arson *no pl*; **incendie de forêt** forest fire; **incendier** *vt* *(mettre le feu à)* to set fire to, set alight; *(brûler complètement)* to burn down

incertain, e[ɛ̃sɛʀtɛ̃, ɛn] *adj* uncertain; *(temps)* unsettled; *(imprécis: contours)* indistinct, blurred; **incertitude** *nf* uncertainty

incessamment[ɛ̃sesamɑ̃] *adv* very shortly

incident[ɛ̃sidɑ̃] *nm* incident; **incident de parcours** minor hitch *ou* setback; **incident technique** technical difficulties *pl*

incinérer[ɛ̃sineʀe] *vt* *(ordures)* to incinerate; *(mort)* to cremate

incisive[ɛ̃siziv] *nf* incisor

inciter[ɛ̃site] *vt*: **~ qn à (faire) qch** to encourage sb to do sth; *(à la révolte etc)* to incite sb to do sth

incivilité[ɛ̃sivilite] *nf* *(grossièreté)* incivility; **incivilités** *nfpl* antisocial behaviour *sg*

inclinable[ɛ̃klinabl] *adj*: **siège à dossier ~** reclining seat

inclination[ɛ̃klinasjɔ̃] *nf* *(penchant)* inclination

incliner[ɛ̃kline] *vt* *(pencher)* to tilt ▷ *vi*: **~ à qch/à faire** to incline towards sth/doing; **s'incliner** *vr* *(se pencher)* to bow; **s'~ devant** *(par respect)* to pay one's respects

inclure[ɛ̃klyʀ] *vt* to include; *(joindre à un envoi)* to enclose

inclus, e[ɛ̃kly, -yz] *pp de* **inclure** ▷ *adj* included; *(joint à un envoi)* enclosed ▷ *adv*: **est-ce que le service est ~?** is service included?; **jusqu'au 10 mars ~** until 10th March inclusive

incognito[ɛ̃kɔɲito] *adv* incognito ▷ *nm*: **garder l'~** to remain incognito

incohérent, e[ɛ̃kɔeʀɑ̃, ɑ̃t] *adj* *(comportement)* inconsistent; *(geste, langage, texte)* incoherent

incollable[ɛ̃kɔlabl] *adj* *(riz)* non-stick; **il est ~** *(fam)* he's got all the answers

incolore[ɛ̃kɔlɔʀ] *adj* colourless

incommoder[ɛ̃kɔmɔde] *vt* *(chaleur, odeur)*: **~ qn** to bother sb

incomparable[ɛ̃kɔ̃paʀabl] *adj* incomparable

incompatible[ɛ̃kɔ̃patibl] *adj* incompatible

incompétent, e[ɛ̃kɔ̃petɑ̃, ɑ̃t] *adj* incompetent

incomplet, -ète[ɛ̃kɔ̃plɛ, ɛt] *adj* incomplete

incompréhensible[ɛ̃kɔ̃pʀeɑ̃sibl] *adj* incomprehensible

incompris, e[ɛ̃kɔ̃pʀi, iz] *adj* misunderstood

inconcevable[ɛ̃kɔ̃s(ə)vabl] *adj* inconceivable

inconfortable[ɛ̃kɔ̃fɔʀtabl(ə)] *adj* uncomfortable

incongru, e[ɛ̃kɔ̃gʀy] *adj* unseemly

inconnu, e[ɛ̃kɔny] *adj* unknown ▷ *nm/f* stranger ▷ *nm*: **l'~** the unknown; **inconnue** *nf* unknown factor

inconsciemment[ɛ̃kɔ̃sjamɑ̃] *adv* unconsciously

inconscient, e[ɛ̃kɔ̃sjɑ̃, jɑ̃t] *adj* unconscious; *(irréfléchi)* thoughtless, reckless; *(sentiment)* subconscious ▷ *nm* *(Psych)*: **l'~** the unconscious; **~ de** unaware of

inconsidéré, e[ɛ̃kɔ̃sideʀe] *adj* ill-considered

inconsistant, e[ɛ̃kɔ̃sistɑ̃, ɑ̃t] *adj* *(fig)* flimsy, weak

inconsolable[ɛ̃kɔ̃sɔlabl] *adj*
inconsolable

incontestable[ɛ̃kɔ̃tɛstabl] *adj*
indisputable

incontinent, e[ɛ̃kɔ̃tinɑ̃, ɑ̃t] *adj*
incontinent

incontournable[ɛ̃kɔ̃tuʀnabl] *adj*
unavoidable

incontrôlable[ɛ̃kɔ̃tʀolabl]
adj unverifiable; (*irrépressible*)
uncontrollable

inconvénient[ɛ̃kɔ̃venjɑ̃] *nm*
disadvantage, drawback; **si vous n'y
voyez pas d'~** if you have no objections

incorporer[ɛ̃kɔʀpɔʀe] *vt*: **~ (à)** to
mix in (with); **~ (dans)** (*paragraphe
etc*) to incorporate (in); (*Mil: appeler*)
to recruit (into); **il a très bien su s'~
à notre groupe** he was very easily
incorporated into our group

incorrect, e[ɛ̃kɔʀɛkt] *adj* (*impropre,
inconvenant*) improper; (*défectueux*)
faulty; (*inexact*) incorrect; (*impoli*)
impolite; (*déloyal*) underhand

incorrigible[ɛ̃kɔʀiʒibl] *adj*
incorrigible

incrédule[ɛ̃kʀedyl] *adj* incredulous;
(*Rel*) unbelieving

incroyable[ɛ̃kʀwajabl] *adj* incredible

incruster[ɛ̃kʀyste] *vt* (*Art*) to inlay;
s'incruster *vi* (*invité*) to take root

inculpé, e[ɛ̃kylpe] *nm/f* accused

inculper[ɛ̃kylpe] *vt*: **~ (de)** to charge
(with)

inculquer[ɛ̃kylke] *vt*: **~ qch à** to
inculcate sth in *ou* instil sth into

Inde[ɛ̃d] *nf*: **l'~** India

indécent, e[ɛ̃desɑ̃, ɑ̃t] *adj* indecent

indécis, e[ɛ̃desi, iz] *adj* (*par nature*)
indecisive; (*temporairement*) undecided

indéfendable[ɛ̃defɑ̃dabl] *adj*
indefensible

indéfini, e[ɛ̃defini] *adj* (*imprécis,
incertain*) undefined; (*illimité, Ling*)
indefinite; **indéfiniment** *adv*
indefinitely; **indéfinissable** *adj*
indefinable

indélébile[ɛ̃delebil] *adj* indelible

indélicat, e[ɛ̃delika, at] *adj* tactless

indemne[ɛ̃dɛmn] *adj* unharmed;
indemniser *vt*: **indemniser qn (de)** to
compensate sb (for)

indemnité[ɛ̃dɛmnite] *nf*
(*dédommagement*) compensation *no pl*;
(*allocation*) allowance; **indemnité de
licenciement** redundancy payment

indépendamment[ɛ̃depɑ̃damɑ̃]
adv independently; **~ de** (*abstraction
faite de*) irrespective of; (*en plus de*) over
and above

indépendance[ɛ̃depɑ̃dɑ̃s] *nf*
independence

indépendant, e[ɛ̃depɑ̃dɑ̃, ɑ̃t] *adj*
independent; **~ de** independent of;
travailleur ~ self-employed worker

indescriptible[ɛ̃dɛskʀiptibl] *adj*
indescribable

indésirable[ɛ̃deziʀabl] *adj*
undesirable

indestructible[ɛ̃dɛstʀyktibl] *adj*
indestructible

indéterminé, e[ɛ̃detɛʀmine] *adj*
(*date, cause, nature*) unspecified; (*forme,
longueur, quantité*) indeterminate

index[ɛ̃dɛks] *nm* (*doigt*) index finger;
(*d'un livre etc*) index; **mettre à l'~** to
blacklist

indicateur[ɛ̃dikatœʀ] *nm* (*Police*)
informer; (*Tech*) gauge, indicator ▷ *adj*:
panneau ~ signpost; **indicateur des
chemins de fer** railway timetable;
indicateur de rues street directory

indicatif, -ive[ɛ̃dikatif, iv] *adj*: **à titre
~** for (your) information ▷ *nm* (*Ling*)
indicative; (*Radio*) theme *ou* signature
tune; (*Tél*) dialling code (BRIT), area
code (US); **quel est l'~ de ...** what's the
code for ...?

indication[ɛ̃dikasjɔ̃] *nf* indication;
(*renseignement*) information *no
pl*; **indications** *nfpl* (*directives*)
instructions

indice[ɛ̃dis] *nm* (*marque, signe*)
indication, sign; (*Police: lors d'une
enquête*) clue; (*Jur: présomption*) piece
of evidence; (*Science, Écon, Tech*) index;

~ **de protection** (sun protection) factor
indicible [ɛ̃disibl] *adj* inexpressible
indien, ne [ɛ̃djɛ̃, jɛn] *adj* Indian
▷ *nm/f*: **I~, ne** Indian
indifféremment [ɛ̃diferamɑ̃] *adv*
(*sans distinction*) equally (well)
indifférence [ɛ̃diferɑ̃s] *nf* indifference
indifférent, e [ɛ̃diferɑ̃, ɑ̃t] *adj* (*peu
intéressé*) indifferent; **ça m'est ~** it
doesn't matter to me; **elle m'est ~e**
I am indifferent to her
indigène [ɛ̃diʒɛn] *adj* native,
indigenous; (*des gens du pays*) local
▷ *nm/f* native
indigeste [ɛ̃diʒɛst] *adj* indigestible
indigestion [ɛ̃diʒɛstjɔ̃] *nf* indigestion
no pl; **avoir une ~** to have indigestion
indigne [ɛ̃diɲ] *adj* unworthy
indigner [ɛ̃diɲe] *vt*: **s'~ de qch** to get
annoyed about sth; **s'~ contre qn** to
get annoyed with sb
indiqué, e [ɛ̃dike] *adj* (*date, lieu*)
agreed; (*traitement*) appropriate;
(*conseillé*) advisable
indiquer [ɛ̃dike] *vt* (*suj: pendule, aiguille*)
to show; (: *étiquette, panneau*) to show,
indicate; (*renseigner sur*) to point out,
tell; (*déterminer: date, lieu*) to give, state;
(*signaler, dénoter*) to indicate, point
to; **~ qch/qn à qn** (*montrer du doigt*) to
point sth/sb out to sb; (*faire connaître:
médecin, restaurant*) to tell sb of sth/sb;
**pourriez-vous m'~ les toilettes/
l'heure?** could you direct me to the
toilets/tell me the time?
indiscipliné, e [ɛ̃disipline] *adj*
undisciplined
indiscret, -ète [ɛ̃diskrɛ, ɛt] *adj*
indiscreet
indiscutable [ɛ̃diskytabl] *adj*
indisputable
indispensable [ɛ̃dispɑ̃sabl] *adj*
indispensable, essential
indisposé, e [ɛ̃dispoze] *adj* indisposed
indistinct, e [ɛ̃distɛ̃(kt), ɛ̃kt] *adj*
indistinct; **indistinctement** *adv* (*voir,
prononcer*) indistinctly; (*sans distinction*)
indiscriminately

individu [ɛ̃dividy] *nm* individual;
individuel, le *adj* (*gén*) individual;
(*responsabilité, propriété, liberté*)
personal; **chambre individuelle** single
room; **maison individuelle** detached
house
indolore [ɛ̃dɔlɔr] *adj* painless
Indonésie [ɛ̃dɔnezi] *nf* Indonesia
indu, e [ɛ̃dy] *adj*: **à une heure ~e** at
some ungodly hour
indulgent, e [ɛ̃dylʒɑ̃, ɑ̃t] *adj* (*parent,
regard*) indulgent; (*juge, examinateur*)
lenient
industrialisé, e [ɛ̃dystrijalize] *adj*
industrialized
industrie [ɛ̃dystri] *nf* industry;
industriel, le *adj* industrial ▷ *nm*
industrialist
inébranlable [inebrɑ̃labl] *adj* (*masse,
colonne*) solid; (*personne, certitude, foi*)
unshakeable
inédit, e [inedi, it] *adj* (*correspondance,
livre*) hitherto unpublished; (*spectacle,
moyen*) novel, original; (*film*) unreleased
inefficace [inefikas] *adj* (*remède,
moyen*) ineffective; (*machine, employé*)
inefficient
inégal, e, -aux [inegal, o] *adj*
unequal; (*irrégulier*) uneven; **inégalable**
adj matchless; **inégalé, e** *adj* (*record*)
unequalled; (*beauté*) unrivalled;
inégalité *nf* inequality
inépuisable [inepɥizabl] *adj*
inexhaustible
inerte [inɛrt] *adj* (*immobile*) lifeless;
(*sans réaction*) passive
inespéré, e [inɛspere] *adj*
unexpected, unhoped-for
inestimable [inɛstimabl] *adj*
priceless; (*fig: bienfait*) invaluable
inévitable [inevitabl] *adj*
unavoidable; (*fatal, habituel*) inevitable
inexact, e [inɛgza(kt), akt] *adj*
inaccurate
inexcusable [inɛkskyzabl] *adj*
unforgivable
inexplicable [inɛksplikabl] *adj*
inexplicable

in extremis [inɛkstremis] adv at the last minute ▷ adj last-minute

infaillible [ɛ̃fajibl] adj infallible

infarctus [ɛ̃faʀktys] nm: ~ **(du myocarde)** coronary (thrombosis)

infatigable [ɛ̃fatigabl] adj tireless

infect, e [ɛ̃fɛkt] adj revolting; (personne) obnoxious; (temps) foul

infecter [ɛ̃fɛkte] vt (atmosphère, eau) to contaminate; (Méd) to infect; **s'infecter** to become infected ou septic; **infection** nf infection; (puanteur) stench

inférieur, e [ɛ̃feʀjœʀ] adj lower; (en qualité, intelligence) inferior; ~ **à** (somme, quantité) less ou smaller than; (moins bon que) inferior to

infernal, e, -aux [ɛ̃fɛʀnal, o] adj (insupportable: chaleur, rythme) infernal; (: enfant) horrid; (satanique, effrayant) diabolical

infidèle [ɛ̃fidɛl] adj unfaithful

infiltrer [ɛ̃filtʀe]: **s'infiltrer** vr: **s'~ dans** to get into; (liquide) to seep through; (fig: groupe, ennemi) to infiltrate

infime [ɛ̃fim] adj minute, tiny

infini, e [ɛ̃fini] adj infinite ▷ nm infinity; **à l'~** endlessly; **infiniment** adv infinitely; **infinité** nf: **une infinité de** an infinite number of

infinitif [ɛ̃finitif] nm infinitive

infirme [ɛ̃fiʀm] adj disabled ▷ nm/f disabled person

infirmerie [ɛ̃fiʀməʀi] nf medical room

infirmier, -ière [ɛ̃fiʀmje] nm/f nurse; **infirmière chef** sister

infirmité [ɛ̃fiʀmite] nf disability

inflammable [ɛ̃flamabl] adj (in)flammable

inflation [ɛ̃flasjɔ̃] nf inflation

influençable [ɛ̃flyɑ̃sabl] adj easily influenced

influence [ɛ̃flyɑ̃s] nf influence; **influencer** vt to influence; **influent, e** adj influential

informaticien, ne [ɛ̃fɔʀmatisjɛ̃, jɛn] nm/f computer scientist

information [ɛ̃fɔʀmasjɔ̃] nf (renseignement) piece of information; (Presse, TV: nouvelle) item of news; (diffusion de renseignements, Inform) information; (Jur) inquiry, investigation; **informations** nfpl (TV) news sg

informatique [ɛ̃fɔʀmatik] nf (technique) data processing; (science) computer science ▷ adj computer cpd; **informatiser** vt to computerize

informer [ɛ̃fɔʀme] vt: ~ **qn (de)** to inform sb (of); **s'informer** vr: **s'~ (de/si)** to inquire ou find out (about/ whether); **s'~ sur** to inform o.s. about

infos [ɛ̃fo] nfpl: **les ~** the news sg

infraction [ɛ̃fʀaksjɔ̃] nf offence; ~ **à** violation ou breach of; **être en ~** to be in breach of the law

infranchissable [ɛ̃fʀɑ̃ʃisabl] adj impassable; (fig) insuperable

infrarouge [ɛ̃fʀaʀuʒ] adj infrared

infrastructure [ɛ̃fʀastʀyktyʀ] nf (Aviat, Mil) ground installations pl; (Écon: touristique etc) infrastructure

infuser [ɛ̃fyze] vt, vi (thé) to brew; (tisane) to infuse; **infusion** nf (tisane) herb tea

ingénier [ɛ̃ʒenje]: **s'ingénier** vi: **s'~ à faire** to strive to do

ingénierie [ɛ̃ʒeniʀi] nf engineering

ingénieur [ɛ̃ʒenjœʀ] nm engineer; **ingénieur du son** sound engineer

ingénieux, -euse [ɛ̃ʒenjø, jøz] adj ingenious, clever

ingrat, e [ɛ̃gʀa, at] adj (personne) ungrateful; (travail, sujet) thankless; (visage) unprepossessing

ingrédient [ɛ̃gʀedjɑ̃] nm ingredient

inhabité, e [inabite] adj uninhabited

inhabituel, le [inabitɥɛl] adj unusual

inhibition [inibisjɔ̃] nf inhibition

inhumain, e [inymɛ̃, ɛn] adj inhuman

inimaginable [inimaʒinabl] adj unimaginable

ininterrompu, e [inɛ̃teʀɔ̃py] adj (file, série) unbroken; (flot, vacarme) uninterrupted, non-stop; (effort) unremitting, continuous; (*suite, ligne*) unbroken

initial, e, -aux [inisjal, jo] *adj* initial; **initiales** *nfpl* (*d'un nom, sigle etc*) initials

initiation [inisjasjɔ̃] *nf*: **~ à** introduction to

initiative [inisjativ] *nf* initiative

initier [inisje] *vt*: **~ qn à** to initiate sb into; (*faire découvrir: art, jeu*) to introduce sb to

injecter [ɛ̃ʒɛkte] *vt* to inject; **injection** *nf* injection; **à injection** (*Auto*) fuel injection *cpd*

injure [ɛ̃ʒyR] *nf* insult, abuse *no pl*; **injurier** *vt* to insult, abuse; **injurieux, -euse** *adj* abusive, insulting

injuste [ɛ̃ʒyst] *adj* unjust, unfair; **injustice** *nf* injustice

inlassable [ɛ̃lasabl] *adj* tireless

inné, e [i(n)ne] *adj* innate, inborn

innocent, e [inɔsɑ̃, ɑ̃t] *adj* innocent; **innocenter** *vt* to clear, prove innocent

innombrable [i(n)nɔ̃bRabl] *adj* innumerable

innover [inɔve] *vi* to break new ground

inoccupé, e [inɔkype] *adj* unoccupied

inodore [inɔdɔR] *adj* (*gaz*) odourless; (*fleur*) scentless

inoffensif, -ive [inɔfɑ̃sif, iv] *adj* harmless, innocuous

inondation [inɔ̃dasjɔ̃] *nf* flood

inonder [inɔ̃de] *vt* to flood; **~ de** to flood with

inopportun, e [inɔpɔRtœ̃, yn] *adj* ill-timed, untimely

inoubliable [inublijabl] *adj* unforgettable

inouï, e [inwi] *adj* unheard-of, extraordinary

inox [inɔks] *nm* stainless steel

inquiet, -ète [ɛ̃kjɛ, ɛ̃kjɛt] *adj* anxious; **inquiétant, e** *adj* worrying, disturbing; **inquiéter** *vt* to worry; **s'inquiéter** to worry; **s'inquiéter de** to worry about; (*s'enquérir de*) to inquire about; **inquiétude** *nf* anxiety

insaisissable [ɛ̃sezisabl] *adj* (*fugitif, ennemi*) elusive; (*différence, nuance*)

imperceptible

insalubre [ɛ̃salybR] *adj* insalubrious

insatisfait, e [ɛ̃satisfɛ, ɛt] *adj* (*non comblé*) unsatisfied; (*mécontent*) dissatisfied

inscription [ɛ̃skRipsjɔ̃] *nf* inscription; (*immatriculation*) enrolment

inscrire [ɛ̃skRiR] *vt* (*marquer: sur son calepin etc*) to note *ou* write down; (: *sur un mur, une affiche etc*) to write; (: *dans la pierre, le métal*) to inscribe; (*mettre: sur une liste, un budget etc*) to put down; **s'inscrire** (*pour une excursion etc*) to put one's name down; **s'~ (à)** (*club, parti*) to join; (*université*) to register *ou* enrol (at); (*examen, concours*) to register (for); **~ qn à** (*club, parti*) to enrol sb at

insecte [ɛ̃sɛkt] *nm* insect; **insecticide** *nm* insecticide

insensé, e [ɛ̃sɑ̃se] *adj* mad

insensible [ɛ̃sɑ̃sibl] *adj* (*nerf, membre*) numb; (*dur, indifférent*) insensitive

inséparable [ɛ̃sepaRabl] *adj* inseparable ▷ *nm*: **~s** (*oiseaux*) lovebirds

insigne [ɛ̃siɲ] *nm* (*d'un parti, club*) badge; (*d'une fonction*) insignia ▷ *adj* distinguished

insignifiant, e [ɛ̃siɲifjɑ̃, jɑ̃t] *adj* insignificant; trivial

insinuer [ɛ̃sinɥe] *vt* to insinuate; **s'insinuer dans** (*fig*) to worm one's way into

insipide [ɛ̃sipid] *adj* insipid

insister [ɛ̃siste] *vi* to insist; (*continuer à sonner*) to keep on trying; **~ sur** (*détail, sujet*) to lay stress on

insolation [ɛ̃sɔlasjɔ̃] *nf* (*Méd*) sunstroke *no pl*

insolent, e [ɛ̃sɔlɑ̃, ɑ̃t] *adj* insolent

insolite [ɛ̃sɔlit] *adj* strange, unusual

insomnie [ɛ̃sɔmni] *nf* insomnia *no pl*; **avoir des ~s** to sleep badly, not be able to sleep

insouciant, e [ɛ̃susjɑ̃, jɑ̃t] *adj* carefree; **~ du danger** heedless of (the) danger

insoupçonnable [ɛ̃supsɔnabl] *adj* unsuspected; (*personne*) above suspicion

insoupçonné, e [ɛ̃supsɔne] *adj*
unsuspected

insoutenable [ɛ̃sut(ə)nabl] *adj*
(*argument*) untenable; (*chaleur*)
unbearable

inspecter [ɛ̃spɛkte] *vt* to inspect;
inspecteur, -trice *nm/f* inspector;
inspecteur d'Académie (regional)
director of education; **inspecteur
des finances** ≈ tax inspector (BRIT),
≈ Internal Revenue Service agent
(US); **inspecteur (de police)** (police)
inspector; **inspection** *nf* inspection

inspirer [ɛ̃spiʀe] *vt* (*gén*) to inspire ▷ *vi*
(*aspirer*) to breathe in; **s'inspirer** *vr*: **s'~
de** to be inspired by

instable [ɛ̃stabl] *adj* unstable; (*meuble,
équilibre*) unsteady; (*temps*) unsettled

installation [ɛ̃stalasjɔ̃] *nf* (*mise en
place*) installation; **installations** *nfpl*
(*de sport, dans un camping*) facilities;
l'installation électrique wiring

installer [ɛ̃stale] *vt* (*loger, placer*) to put;
(*meuble, gaz, électricité*) to put in; (*rideau,
étagère, tente*) to put up; (*appartement*)
to fit out; **s'installer** (*s'établir: artisan,
dentiste etc*) to set o.s. up; (*se loger*) to
settle; (*emménager*) to settle in; (*sur
un siège, à un emplacement*) to settle
(down); (*fig: maladie, grève*) to take a
firm hold

instance [ɛ̃stɑ̃s] *nf* (*Admin: autorité*)
authority; **affaire en ~** matter pending;
être en ~ de divorce to be awaiting
a divorce

instant [ɛ̃stɑ̃] *nm* moment, instant;
dans un ~ in a moment; **à l'~** this
instant; **je l'ai vu à l'~** I've just this
minute seen him, I saw him a moment
ago; **pour l'~** for the moment, for the
time being

instantané, e [ɛ̃stɑ̃tane] *adj* (*lait, café*)
instant; (*explosion, mort*) instantaneous
▷ *nm* snapshot

instar [ɛ̃staʀ]: **à l'~ de** *prép* following
the example of, like

instaurer [ɛ̃stɔʀe] *vt* to institute;

(*couvre-feu*) to impose; **s'instaurer** *vr*
(*paix*) to be established; (*doute*) to set in

instinct [ɛ̃stɛ̃] *nm* instinct;
instinctivement *adv* instinctively

instituer [ɛ̃stitɥe] *vt* to establish

institut [ɛ̃stity] *nm* institute; **institut
de beauté** beauty salon; **Institut
universitaire de technologie**
≈ polytechnic

instituteur, -trice [ɛ̃stitytœʀ, tʀis]
nm/f (primary school) teacher

institution [ɛ̃stitysjɔ̃] *nf* institution;
(*collège*) private school; **institutions**
nfpl (*structures politiques et sociales*)
institutions

instructif, -ive [ɛ̃stʀyktif, iv] *adj*
instructive

instruction [ɛ̃stʀyksjɔ̃] *nf*
(*enseignement, savoir*) education;
(*Jur*) (preliminary) investigation and
hearing; **instructions** *nfpl* (*ordres, mode
d'emploi*) instructions; **instruction
civique** civics *sg*

instruire [ɛ̃stʀɥiʀ] *vt* (*élèves*) to teach;
(*recrues*) to train; (*Jur: affaire*) to conduct
the investigation for; **s'instruire** to
educate o.s.; **instruit, e** *adj* educated

instrument [ɛ̃stʀymɑ̃] *nm*
instrument; **instrument à cordes/à
vent** stringed/wind instrument;
instrument de mesure measuring
instrument; **instrument de musique**
musical instrument; **instrument de
travail** (working) tool

insu [ɛ̃sy] *nm*: **à l'~ de qn** without sb
knowing (it)

insuffisant, e [ɛ̃syfizɑ̃, ɑ̃t] *adj* (*en
quantité*) insufficient; (*en qualité*)
inadequate; (*sur une copie*) poor

insulaire [ɛ̃sylɛʀ] *adj* island *cpd*;
(*attitude*) insular

insuline [ɛ̃sylin] *nf* insulin

insulte [ɛ̃sylt] *nf* insult; **insulter** *vt*
to insult

insupportable [ɛ̃sypɔʀtabl] *adj*
unbearable

insurmontable [ɛ̃syʀmɔ̃tabl] *adj*
(*difficulté*) insuperable; (*aversion*)

unconquerable

intact, e [ɛ̃takt] *adj* intact

intarissable [ɛ̃taʀisabl] *adj* inexhaustible

intégral, e, -aux [ɛ̃tegʀal, o] *adj* complete; **texte ~** unabridged version; **bronzage ~** all-over suntan; **intégralement** *adv* in full; **intégralité** *nf* whole; **dans son intégralité** in full; **intégrant, e** *adj*: **faire partie intégrante de** to be an integral part of

intègre [ɛ̃tegʀ] *adj* upright

intégrer [ɛ̃tegʀe]: **s'intégrer** *vr*: **s'~ à ou dans qch** to become integrated into sth; **bien s'~** to fit in

intégrisme [ɛ̃tegʀism] *nm* fundamentalism

intellectuel, le [ɛ̃telɛktɥel] *adj* intellectual ▷ *nm/f* intellectual; (*péj*) highbrow

intelligence [ɛ̃teliʒɑ̃s] *nf* intelligence; (*compréhension*): **l'~ de** the understanding of; (*complicité*): **regard d'~** glance of complicity; (*accord*): **vivre en bonne ~ avec qn** to be on good terms with sb

intelligent, e [ɛ̃teliʒɑ̃, ɑ̃t] *adj* intelligent

intelligible [ɛ̃teliʒibl] *adj* intelligible

intempéries [ɛ̃tɑ̃peʀi] *nfpl* bad weather *sg*

intenable [ɛ̃t(ə)nabl] *adj* (*chaleur*) unbearable

intendant, e [ɛ̃tɑ̃dɑ̃] *nm/f* (*Mil*) quartermaster; (*Scol*) bursar

intense [ɛ̃tɑ̃s] *adj* intense; **intensif, -ive** *adj* intensive; **un cours intensif** a crash course

intenter [ɛ̃tɑ̃te] *vt*: **~ un procès contre ou à** to start proceedings against

intention [ɛ̃tɑ̃sjɔ̃] *nf* intention; (*Jur*) intent; **avoir l'~ de faire** to intend to do; **à l'~ de** for; (*renseignement*) for the benefit of; (*film, ouvrage*) aimed at; **à cette ~** with this aim in view; **intentionné, e** *adj*: **bien intentionné** well-meaning *ou* -intentioned; **mal intentionné** ill-intentioned

interactif, -ive [ɛ̃teʀaktif, iv] *adj* (*Comput*) interactive

intercepter [ɛ̃teʀsepte] *vt* to intercept; (*lumière, chaleur*) to cut off

interchangeable [ɛ̃teʀʃɑ̃ʒabl] *adj* interchangeable

interdiction [ɛ̃teʀdiksjɔ̃] *nf* ban; **interdiction de fumer** no smoking

interdire [ɛ̃teʀdiʀ] *vt* to forbid; (*Admin*) to ban, prohibit; (: *journal, livre*) to ban; **~ à qn de faire** to forbid sb to do; (*suj: empêchement*) to prevent sb from doing

interdit, e [ɛ̃teʀdi, it] *pp de* **interdire** ▷ *adj* (*stupéfait*) taken aback; **film ~ aux moins de 18/12 ans** ≈ 18-/12A-rated film; **"stationnement ~"** "no parking"

intéressant, e [ɛ̃teʀesɑ̃, ɑ̃t] *adj* interesting; (*avantageux*) attractive

intéressé, e [ɛ̃teʀese] *adj* (*parties*) involved, concerned; (*amitié, motifs*) self-interested

intéresser [ɛ̃teʀese] *vt* (*captiver*) to interest; (*toucher*) to be of interest to; (*Admin: concerner*) to affect, concern; **s'intéresser** *vr*: **s'~ à** to be interested in

intérêt [ɛ̃teʀe] *nm* interest; (*égoïsme*) self-interest; **tu as ~ à accepter** it's in your interest to accept; **tu as ~ à te dépêcher** you'd better hurry

intérieur, e [ɛ̃teʀjœʀ] *adj* (*mur, escalier, poche*) inside; (*commerce, politique*) domestic; (*cour, calme, vie*) inner; (*navigation*) inland ▷ *nm*: **l'~** (*d'une maison, d'un récipient etc*) the inside; (*d'un pays, aussi: décor, mobilier*) the interior; **à l'~ (de)** inside; **ministère de l'l~e** ≈ Home Office (*BRIT*), ≈ Department of the Interior (*US*); **intérieurement** *adv* inwardly

intérim [ɛ̃teʀim] *nm* interim period; **faire de l'~** to temp; **assurer l'~ (de)** to deputize (for); **par ~** interim

intérimaire [ɛ̃teʀimeʀ] *adj* (*directeur, ministre*) acting; (*secrétaire, personnel*) temporary ▷ *nm/f* (*secrétaire*) temporary secretary, temp (*BRIT*)

interlocuteur, -trice [ɛ̃teʀlɔkytœʀ, tʀis] *nm/f* speaker; **son ~** the person he was speaking to

intermédiaire [ɛ̃tɛʀmedjɛʀ] *adj* intermediate; (*solution*) temporary ▷ *nm/f* intermediary; (*Comm*) middleman; **sans ~** directly; **par l'~ de** through

interminable [ɛ̃tɛʀminabl] *adj* endless

intermittence [ɛ̃tɛʀmitɑ̃s] *nf*: **par ~** sporadically, intermittently

internat [ɛ̃tɛʀna] *nm* boarding school

international, e, -aux [ɛ̃tɛʀnasjɔnal, o] *adj, nm/f* international

internaute [ɛ̃tɛʀnot] *nm/f* Internet user

interne [ɛ̃tɛʀn] *adj* internal ▷ *nm/f* (*Scol*) boarder; (*Méd*) houseman

Internet [ɛ̃tɛʀnɛt] *nm*: **l'~** the Internet

interpeller [ɛ̃tɛʀpəle] *vt* (*appeler*) to call out to; (*apostropher*) to shout at; (*Police, Pol*) to question; (*concerner*) to concern

interphone [ɛ̃tɛʀfɔn] *nm* intercom; (*d'immeuble*) entry phone

interposer [ɛ̃tɛʀpoze] *vt*: **s'interposer** to intervene; **par personnes interposées** through a third party

interprète [ɛ̃tɛʀpʀɛt] *nm/f* interpreter; (*porte-parole*) spokesperson; **pourriez-vous nous servir d' ~?** could you act as our interpreter?

interpréter [ɛ̃tɛʀpʀete] *vt* to interpret; (*jouer*) to play; (*chanter*) to sing

interrogatif, -ive [ɛ̃tɛʀɔgatif, iv] *adj* (*Ling*) interrogative

interrogation [ɛ̃tɛʀɔgasjɔ̃] *nf* question; (*action*) questioning; **~ écrite/orale** (*Scol*) written/oral test

interrogatoire [ɛ̃tɛʀɔgatwaʀ] *nm* (*Police*) questioning *no pl*; (*Jur, aussi fig*) cross-examination

interroger [ɛ̃tɛʀɔʒe] *vt* to question; (*Inform*) to consult; (*Scol*) to test

interrompre [ɛ̃tɛʀɔ̃pʀ] *vt* (*gén*) to interrupt; (*négociations*) to break off;

(*match*) to stop; **s'interrompre** to break off; **interrupteur** *nm* switch; **interruption** *nf* interruption; (*pause*) break; **sans interruption** without stopping; **interruption (volontaire) de grossesse** termination (of pregnancy)

intersection [ɛ̃tɛʀsɛksjɔ̃] *nf* intersection

intervalle [ɛ̃tɛʀval] *nm* (*espace*) space; (*de temps*) interval; **dans l'~** in the meantime; **à deux jours d'~** two days apart

intervenir [ɛ̃tɛʀvəniʀ] *vi* (*gén*) to intervene; **~ auprès de qn** to intervene with sb; **intervention** *nf* intervention; (*discours*) speech; **intervention chirurgicale** (*Méd*) surgical operation

interview [ɛ̃tɛʀvju] *nf* interview

intestin [ɛ̃tɛstɛ̃] *nm* intestine

intime [ɛ̃tim] *adj* intimate; (*vie*) private; (*conviction*) inmost; (*dîner, cérémonie*) quiet ▷ *nm/f* close friend; **un journal ~** a diary

intimider [ɛ̃timide] *vt* to intimidate

intimité [ɛ̃timite] *nf*: **dans l'~** in private; (*sans formalités*) with only a few friends, quietly

intolérable [ɛ̃tɔleʀabl] *adj* intolerable

intox [ɛ̃tɔks] (*fam*) *nf* brainwashing

intoxication [ɛ̃tɔksikasjɔ̃] *nf*: **intoxication alimentaire** food poisoning

intoxiquer [ɛ̃tɔksike] *vt* to poison; (*fig*) to brainwash

intraitable [ɛ̃tʀɛtabl] *adj* inflexible, uncompromising

intransigeant, e [ɛ̃tʀɑ̃ziʒɑ̃, ɑ̃t] *adj* intransigent

intrépide [ɛ̃tʀepid] *adj* dauntless

intrigue [ɛ̃tʀig] *nf* (*scénario*) plot; **intriguer** *vt* to puzzle, intrigue

introduction [ɛ̃tʀɔdyksjɔ̃] *nf* introduction

introduire [ɛ̃tʀɔdɥiʀ] *vt* to introduce; (*visiteur*) to show in; (*aiguille, clef*): **~ qch dans** to insert *ou* introduce sth into; **s'introduire** *vr* (*techniques, usages*) to be introduced; **s'~ (dans)** to get in(to); (*dans un groupe*) to get o.s. accepted (into)

introuvable [ɛ̃tʀuvabl] *adj* which cannot be found; (*Comm*) unobtainable

intrus, e [ɛ̃tʀy, yz] *nm/f* intruder

intuition [ɛ̃tɥisjɔ̃] *nf* intuition

inusable [inyzabl] *adj* hard-wearing

inutile [inytil] *adj* useless; (*superflu*) unnecessary; **inutilement** *adv* unnecessarily; **inutilisable** *adj* unusable

invalide [ɛ̃valid] *adj* disabled ▷ *nm*: ~ **de guerre** disabled ex-serviceman

invariable [ɛ̃vaʀjabl] *adj* invariable

invasion [ɛ̃vazjɔ̃] *nf* invasion

inventaire [ɛ̃vɑ̃tɛʀ] *nm* inventory; (*Comm: liste*) stocklist; (: *opération*) stocktaking *no pl*

inventer [ɛ̃vɑ̃te] *vt* to invent; (*subterfuge*) to devise, invent; (*histoire, excuse*) to make up, invent; **inventeur** *nm* inventor; **inventif, -ive** *adj* inventive; **invention** *nf* invention

inverse [ɛ̃vɛʀs] *adj* opposite ▷ *nm*: **l'~** the opposite; **dans l'ordre ~** in the reverse order; **en sens ~** in (*ou* from) the opposite direction; **dans le sens ~ des aiguilles d'une montre** anticlockwise; **tu t'es trompé, c'est l'~** you've got it wrong, it's the other way round; **inversement** *adv* conversely; **inverser** *vt* to invert, reverse; (*Élec*) to reverse

investir [ɛ̃vɛstiʀ] *vt* to invest; ~ **qn de** (*d'une fonction, d'un pouvoir*) to vest *ou* invest sb with; **s'investir** *vr*: **s'~ dans** (*Psych*) to put a lot into; **investissement** *nm* investment

invisible [ɛ̃vizibl] *adj* invisible

invitation [ɛ̃vitasjɔ̃] *nf* invitation

invité, e [ɛ̃vite] *nm/f* guest

inviter [ɛ̃vite] *vt* to invite; ~ **qn à faire qch** to invite sb to do sth

invivable [ɛ̃vivabl] *adj* unbearable

involontaire [ɛ̃vɔlɔ̃tɛʀ] *adj* (*mouvement*) involuntary; (*insulte*) unintentional; (*complice*) unwitting

invoquer [ɛ̃vɔke] *vt* (*Dieu, muse*) to call upon, invoke; (*prétexte*) to put forward (as an excuse); (*loi, texte*) to refer to

invraisemblable [ɛ̃vʀɛsɑ̃blabl] *adj* (*fait, nouvelle*) unlikely, improbable; (*insolence, habit*) incredible

iode [jɔd] *nm* iodine

irai *etc* [iʀe] *vb voir* **aller**

Irak [iʀak] *nm* Iraq; **irakien, ne** *adj* Iraqi ▷ *nm/f*: **Irakien, ne** Iraqi

Iran [iʀɑ̃] *nm* Iran; **iranien, ne** *adj* Iranian ▷ *nm/f*: **Iranien, ne** Iranian

irions *etc* [iʀjɔ̃] *vb voir* **aller**

iris [iʀis] *nm* iris

irlandais, e [iʀlɑ̃dɛ, ez] *adj* Irish ▷ *nm/f*: **I~, e** Irishman(-woman)

Irlande [iʀlɑ̃d] *nf* Ireland; **la République d'~** the Irish Republic; **la mer d'~** the Irish Sea; **Irlande du Nord** Northern Ireland

ironie [iʀɔni] *nf* irony; **ironique** *adj* ironical; **ironiser** *vi* to be ironical

irons *etc* [iʀɔ̃] *vb voir* **aller**

irradier [iʀadje] *vt* to irradiate

irraisonné, e [iʀɛzɔne] *adj* irrational

irrationnel, le [iʀasjɔnɛl] *adj* irrational

irréalisable [iʀealizabl] *adj* unrealizable; (*projet*) impracticable

irrécupérable [iʀekypeʀabl] *adj* beyond repair; (*personne*) beyond redemption

irréel, le [iʀeɛl] *adj* unreal

irréfléchi, e [iʀeflefi] *adj* thoughtless

irrégularité [iʀegylaʀite] *nf* irregularity; (*de travail, d'effort, de qualité*) unevenness *no pl*

irrégulier, -ière [iʀegylje, jɛʀ] *adj* irregular; (*travail, effort, qualité*) uneven; (*élève, athlète*) erratic

irrémédiable [iʀemedjabl] *adj* irreparable

irremplaçable [iʀɑ̃plasabl] *adj* irreplaceable

irréparable [iʀepaʀabl] *adj* (*objet*) beyond repair; (*dommage etc*) irreparable

irréprochable [iʀepʀɔʃabl] *adj* irreproachable, beyond reproach;

(tenue) impeccable
irrésistible [iʀezistibl] *adj* irresistible; *(besoin, désir, preuve, logique)* compelling; *(amusant)* hilarious
irrésolu, e [iʀezɔly] *adj (personne)* irresolute; *(problème)* unresolved
irrespectueux, -euse [iʀɛspɛktɥø, øz] *adj* disrespectful
irresponsable [iʀɛspɔ̃sabl] *adj* irresponsible
irriguer [iʀige] *vt* to irrigate
irritable [iʀitabl] *adj* irritable
irriter [iʀite] *vt* to irritate
irruption [iʀypsjɔ̃] *nf*: **faire ~ (chez qn)** to burst in (on sb)
Islam [islam] *nm*: **l'~** Islam; **islamique** *adj* Islamic; **islamophobie** *nf* Islamophobia
Islande [islɑ̃d] *nf* Iceland
isolant, e [izɔlɑ̃, ɑ̃t] *adj* insulating; *(insonorisant)* soundproofing
isolation [izɔlasjɔ̃] *nf* insulation; **~ acoustique** soundproofing
isolé, e [izɔle] *adj* isolated; *(contre le froid)* insulated
isoler [izɔle] *vt* to isolate; *(prisonnier)* to put in solitary confinement; *(ville)* to cut off, isolate; *(contre le froid)* to insulate; **s'isoler** *vi* to isolate o.s.
Israël [isʀaɛl] *nm* Israel; **israélien, ne** *adj* Israeli ▷ *nm/f*: **Israélien, ne** Israeli; **israélite** *adj* Jewish ▷ *nm/f*: **Israélite** Jew (Jewess)
issu, e [isy] *adj*: **~ de** *(né de)* descended from; *(résultant de)* stemming from; **issue** *nf (ouverture, sortie)* exit; *(solution)* way out, solution; *(dénouement)* outcome; **à l'issue de** at the conclusion *ou* close of; **voie sans issue** dead end; **issue de secours** emergency exit
Italie [itali] *nf* Italy; **italien, ne** *adj* Italian ▷ *nm/f*: **Italien, ne** Italian ▷ *nm (Ling)* Italian
italique [italik] *nm*: **en ~** in italics
itinéraire [itineʀɛʀ] *nm* itinerary, route; **itinéraire bis** alternative route
IUT *sigle m* = **Institut universitaire de technologie**

IVG *sigle f* (= *interruption volontaire de grossesse*) abortion
ivoire [ivwaʀ] *nm* ivory
ivre [ivʀ] *adj* drunk; **~ de** *(colère, bonheur)* wild with; **ivrogne** *nm/f* drunkard

[ʒ] *pron voir* **je**

jacinthe [ʒasɛ̃t] *nf* hyacinth

jadis [ʒɑdis] *adv* long ago

jaillir [ʒajiʀ] *vi* (*liquide*) to spurt out; (*cris, réponses*) to burst forth

jais [ʒɛ] *nm* jet; **(d'un noir) de ~** jet-black

jalousie [ʒaluzi] *nf* jealousy; (*store*) slatted blind

jaloux, -ouse [ʒalu, uz] *adj* jealous; **être ~ de** to be jealous of

jamaïquain, e [ʒamaikɛ̃, -ɛn] *adj* Jamaican ▷ *nm/f*: **J~, e** Jamaican

jamaïque [ʒamaik] *nf*: **la ~** Jamaica

jamais [ʒamɛ] *adv* never; (*sans négation*) ever; **ne ... ~** never; **je ne suis ~ allé en Espagne** I've never been to Spain; **si ~ vous passez dans la région, venez nous voir** if you happen to be/if you're ever in this area, come and see us; **à ~** for ever

jambe [ʒɑ̃b] *nf* leg

jambon [ʒɑ̃bɔ̃] *nm* ham

jante [ʒɑ̃t] *nf* (*wheel*) rim

janvier [ʒɑ̃vje] *nm* January

Japon [ʒapɔ̃] *nm* Japan; **japonais, e** *adj* Japanese ▷ *nm/f*: **Japonais, e** Japanese ▷ *nm* (*Ling*) Japanese

jardin [ʒaʀdɛ̃] *nm* garden; **jardin d'enfants** nursery school; **jardinage** *nm* gardening; **jardiner** *vi* to do some gardening; **jardinier, -ière** *nm/f* gardener; **jardinière** *nf* planter; (*de fenêtre*) window box; **jardinière de légumes** (*Culin*) mixed vegetables

jargon [ʒaʀgɔ̃] *nm* (*baragouin*) gibberish; (*langue professionnelle*) jargon

jarret [ʒaʀɛ] *nm* back of knee; (*Culin*) knuckle, shin

jauge [ʒoʒ] *nf* (*instrument*) gauge; **jauge (de niveau) d'huile** (*Auto*) dipstick

jaune [ʒon] *adj, nm* yellow ▷ *adv* (*fam*): **rire ~** to laugh on the other side of one's face; **jaune d'œuf** (egg) yolk; **jaunir** *vi*, *vt* to turn yellow; **jaunisse** *nf* jaundice

Javel [ʒavɛl] *nf voir* **eau**

javelot [ʒavlo] *nm* javelin

je, j' [ʒə] *pron* I

jean [dʒin] *nm* jeans *pl*

Jésus-Christ [ʒezykʀi(st)] *n* Jesus Christ; **600 avant/après ~** *ou* **J.-C.** 600 B.C./A.D.

jet [ʒɛ] *nm* (*lancer: action*) throwing *no pl*; (*: résultat*) throw; (*jaillissement: d'eaux*) jet; (*: de sang*) spurt; **jet d'eau** spray

jetable [ʒ(ə)tabl] *adj* disposable

jetée [ʒəte] *nf* jetty; (*grande*) pier

jeter [ʒ(ə)te] *vt* (*gén*) to throw; (*se défaire de*) to throw away *ou* out; **~ qch à qn** to throw sth to sb; (*de façon agressive*) to throw sth at sb; **~ un coup d'œil (à)** to take a look (at); **~ un sort à qn** to cast a spell on sb; **se ~ sur qn** to rush at sb; **se ~ dans** (*suj: fleuve*) to flow into

jeton [ʒ(ə)tɔ̃] *nm* (*au jeu*) counter

jette *etc* [ʒɛt] *vb voir* **jeter**

jeu, x [ʒø] *nm* (*divertissement, Tech: d'une pièce*) play; (*Tennis: partie, Football etc: façon de jouer*) game; (*Théâtre etc*) acting; (*série d'objets, jouet*) set; (*Cartes*) hand; (*au casino*): **le ~** gambling; **remettre en ~** (*Football*) to throw in; **être en ~** (*fig*) to be at stake; **entrer/mettre en ~** (fig) to come/bring into play; **jeu de cartes** pack of cards; **jeu d'échecs** chess set; **jeu de hasard** game of chance; **jeu de mots** pun; **jeu de société** board game; **jeu télévisé** television quiz; **jeu vidéo** video game

jeudi [ʒødi] nm Thursday

jeun [ʒœ̃]: **à ~** adv on an empty stomach; **être à ~** to have eaten nothing; **rester à ~** not to eat anything

jeune [ʒœn] adj young; **jeunes** nmpl: **les ~s** young people; **jeune fille** girl; **jeune homme** young man; **jeunes gens** young people

jeûne [ʒøn] nm fast

jeunesse [ʒœnɛs] nf youth; (aspect) youthfulness

joaillier, -ière [ʒɔaje, -jɛʀ] nm/f jeweller

jogging [dʒɔgiŋ] nm jogging; (survêtement) tracksuit; **faire du ~** to go jogging

joie [ʒwa] nf joy

joindre [ʒwɛ̃dʀ] vt to join; (à une lettre): **~ qch à** to enclose sth with; (contacter) to contact, get in touch with; **se ~ à qn** to join sb; **se ~ à qch** to join in sth

joint, e [ʒwɛ̃, ɛ̃t] adj: **pièce ~e** (de lettre) enclosure; (de mail) attachment ▷ nm joint; (ligne) join; **joint de culasse** cylinder head gasket

joli, e [ʒɔli] adj pretty, attractive; **une ~e somme/situation** a tidy sum/a nice little job; **c'est du ~!** (ironique) that's very nice!; **c'est bien ~, mais ...** that's all very well but ...

jonc [ʒɔ̃] nm (bul)rush

jonction [ʒɔ̃ksjɔ̃] nf junction

jongleur, -euse [ʒɔ̃glœʀ, øz] nm/f juggler

jonquille [ʒɔ̃kij] nf daffodil

Jordanie [ʒɔʀdani] nf: **la ~** Jordan

joue [ʒu] nf cheek

jouer [ʒwe] vt to play; (somme d'argent, réputation) to stake, wager; (simuler: sentiment) to affect, feign ▷ vi to play; (Théâtre, Cinéma) to act; (au casino) to gamble; (bois, porte: se voiler) to warp; (clef, pièce: avoir du jeu) to be loose; **~ sur** (miser) to gamble on; **~ de** (Mus) to play; **~ à** (jeu, sport, roulette) to play; **~ un tour à qn** to play a trick on sb; **~ serré** to play a close game; **~ la comédie** to put on an act; **à toi/nous de ~** it's your/our go ou turn; **bien joué!** well done!; **on joue Hamlet au théâtre X** Hamlet is on at the X theatre

jouet [ʒwɛ] nm toy; **être le ~ de** (illusion etc) to be the victim of

joueur, -euse [ʒwœʀ, øz] nm/f player; **être beau/mauvais ~** to be a good/bad loser

jouir [ʒwiʀ] vi (sexe: fam) to come ▷ vt: **~ de** to enjoy

jour [ʒuʀ] nm day; (opposé à la nuit) day, daytime; (clarté) daylight; (fig: aspect) light; (ouverture) gap; **de ~** (crème, service) day cpd; **travailler de ~** to work during the day; **voyager de ~** to travel by day; **au ~ le ~** from day to day; **de nos ~s** these days; **du ~ au lendemain** overnight; **il fait ~** it's daylight; **au grand ~** (fig) in the open; **mettre au ~** to disclose; **mettre à ~** to update; **donner le ~ à** to give birth to; **voir le ~** to be born; **le ~ J** D-day; **jour férié** publ holiday; **jour ouvrable** working day

journal, -aux [ʒuʀnal, o] nm (news)paper; (spécialisé) journal; (intime) diary; **journal de bord** log; **journal parlé/télévisé** radio/television news sg

journalier, -ière [ʒuʀnalje, jɛʀ] adj daily; (banal) everyday

journalisme [ʒuʀnalism] nm journalism; **journaliste** nm/f journalist

journée [ʒuʀne] nf day; **faire la ~ continue** to work over lunch

joyau, x [ʒwajo] nm gem, jewel

joyeux, -euse [ʒwajø, øz] adj joyful, merry; **~ Noël!** merry Christmas!; **~ anniversaire!** happy birthday!

jubiler [ʒybile] vi to be jubilant, exult

judas [ʒyda] nm (trou) spy-hole

ıdiciaire [ʒydisjɛʀ] *adj* judicial
ıdicieux, -euse [ʒydisjø, jøz] *adj* judicious
ıdo [ʒydo] *nm* judo
ıge [ʒyʒ] *nm* judge; **juge d'instruction** examining (*BRIT*) *ou* committing (*US*) magistrate; **juge de paix** justice of the peace
ıgé [ʒyʒe]: **au ~** *adv* by guesswork
ıgement [ʒyʒmɑ̃] *nm* judgment; (*Jur: au pénal*) sentence; (: *au civil*) decision
ıger [ʒyʒe] *vt* to judge; (*estimer*) to consider; **~ qn/qch satisfaisant** to consider sb/sth (to be) satisfactory; **~ bon de faire** to see fit to do
ıif, -ive [ʒɥif, ʒɥiv] *adj* Jewish ▷ *nm/f*: **J~, ive** Jew (Jewess)
ıillet [ʒɥijɛ] *nm* July

- ○ **14 JUILLET**
- ○
- ● **Le 14 juillet** is a national holiday
- ● in France and commemorates the
- ● storming of the Bastille during the
- ● French Revolution. Throughout
- ● the country there are celebrations,
- ● which feature parades, music,
- ● dancing and firework displays. In
- ● Paris a military parade along the
- ● Champs-Élysées is attended by the
- ● President.

ıin [ʒɥɛ̃] *nm* June
ımeau, -elle, x [ʒymo, ɛl] *adj, nm/f* twin
ımeler [ʒym(ə)le] *vt* to twin
ımelle [ʒymɛl] *adj, nf voir* **jumeau**; **jumelles** *nfpl* (*appareil*) binoculars
ıment [ʒymɑ̃] *nf* mare
ıngle [ʒɑ̃gl] *nf* jungle
ıpe [ʒyp] *nf* skirt
ıpon [ʒypɔ̃] *nm* waist slip
ıré, e [ʒyʀe] *nm/f* juror ▷ *adj*: **ennemi ~** sworn enemy
ırer [ʒyʀe] *vt* (*obéissance etc*) to swear, vow ▷ *vi* (*dire des jurons*) to swear, curse; (*dissoner*): **~ (avec)** to clash (with); **~ de faire/que** to swear to do/that; **~ de**

qch (*s'en porter garant*) to swear to sth
juridique [ʒyʀidik] *adj* legal
juron [ʒyʀɔ̃] *nm* curse, swearword
jury [ʒyʀi] *nm* jury; (*Art, Sport*) panel of judges; (*Scol*) board of examiners
jus [ʒy] *nm* juice; (*de viande*) gravy, (meat) juice; **jus de fruit** fruit juice
jusque [ʒysk]: **jusqu'à** *prép* (*endroit*) as far as, (up) to; (*moment*) until, till; (*limite*) up to; **~ sur/dans** up to; (*y compris*) even on/in; **jusqu'à ce que** until; **jusqu'à présent** *ou* **maintenant** so far; **jusqu'où?** how far?
justaucorps [ʒystokɔʀ] *nm* leotard
juste [ʒyst] *adj* (*équitable*) just, fair; (*légitime*) just; (*exact*) right; (*pertinent*) apt; (*étroit*) tight; (*insuffisant*) on the short side ▷ *adv* rightly, correctly; (*chanter*) in tune; (*exactement, seulement*) just; **~ assez/au-dessus** just enough/above; **au ~** exactly; **le ~ milieu** the happy medium; **c'était ~** it was a close thing; **pouvoir tout ~ faire** to be only just able to do; **justement** *adv* justly; (*précisément*) just, precisely; **justesse** *nf* (*précision*) accuracy; (*d'une remarque*) aptness; (*d'une opinion*) soundness; **de justesse** only just
justice [ʒystis] *nf* (*équité*) fairness, justice; (*Admin*) justice; **rendre ~ à qn** to do sb justice
justificatif, -ive [ʒystifikatif, iv] *adj* (*document*) supporting; **pièce justificative** written proof
justifier [ʒystifje] *vt* to justify; **~ de** to prove
juteux, -euse [ʒytø, øz] *adj* juicy
juvénile [ʒyvenil] *adj* youthful

K

kiwi [kiwi] *nm* kiwi
klaxon [klaksɔn] *nm* horn; **klaxonner**
  vi, vt to hoot (*BRIT*), honk (*US*)
km *abr* = **kilomètre**
km/h *abr* (= kilomètres/heure) ≈ mph
K.-O. (*fam*) *adj inv* shattered, knackered
Kosovo [kɔsɔvo] *nm* Kosovo
Koweit, Kuweit [kɔwɛt] *nm*: **le ~**
  Kuwait
k-way® [kawɛ] *nm* (lightweight nylon)
  cagoule
kyste [kist] *nm* cyst

K [kɑ] *nm* (*Inform*) K
kaki [kaki] *adj inv* khaki
kangourou [kãguʀu] *nm* kangaroo
karaté [kaʀate] *nm* karate
kascher [kaʃɛʀ] *adj* kosher
kayak [kajak] *nm* canoe, kayak; **faire**
  du ~ to go canoeing
képi [kepi] *nm* kepi
kermesse [kɛʀmɛs] *nf* fair; (*fête de*
  charité) bazaar, (charity) fête
kidnapper [kidnape] *vt* to kidnap
kilo [kilo] *nm* = **kilogramme**
kilo...: **kilogramme** *nm* kilogramme;
  kilométrage *nm* number of kilometres
  travelled, ≈ mileage; **kilomètre** *nm*
  kilometre; **kilométrique** *adj* (*distance*)
  in kilometres
kinésithérapeute [kineziteʀapøt]
  nm/f physiotherapist
kiosque [kjɔsk] *nm* kiosk, stall
kir [kiʀ] *nm* kir (*white wine with*
  blackcurrant liqueur)
kit [kit] *nm* kit; **~ piéton** *ou* **mains libres**
  hands-free kit; **en ~** in kit form

] art déf voir **le**

`la] art déf voir **le** ▷ nm (Mus) A; (en`
`hantant la gamme) la`

`la] adv there; (ici) here; (dans le temps)`
`hen; **elle n'est pas là** she isn't here;`
`'est là que this is where; **là où** where;`
`e là (fig) hence; **par là** (fig) by that; voir`
`ussi -ci; **ce; celui**; **là-bas** adv there`
oratoire [labɔratwaʀ] nm
aboratory; **laboratoire de langues**
anguage laboratory
orieux, -euse [labɔʀjø, jøz] adj
`âche) laborious`
ourer vt to plough
yrinthe [labiʀɛt] nm labyrinth,
haze
`:[lak] nm lake`
:et [lasɛ] nm (de chaussure) lace; (de
`ute) sharp bend; (piège) snare`
he [laʃ] adj (poltron) cowardly;
`desserré) loose, slack ▷ nm/f coward`
her [laʃe] vt to let go of; (ce qui tombe,
`bandonner) to drop; (oiseau, animal:`
`bérer) to release, set free; (fig: mot,`
remarque) to let slip, come out with ▷ vi
(freins) to fail; **~ les amarres** (Navig) to
cast off (the moorings); **~ prise** to let go
lacrymogène [lakʀimɔʒɛn] adj: **gaz
~** teargas
lacune [lakyn] nf gap
là-dedans [ladədɑ̃] adv inside (there),
in it; (fig) in that
là-dessous [ladsu] adv underneath,
under there; (fig) behind that
là-dessus [ladsy] adv on there; (fig:
sur ces mots) at that point; (: à ce sujet)
about that
lagune [lagyn] nf lagoon
là-haut [lao] adv up there
laid, e [lɛ, lɛd] adj ugly; **laideur** nf
ugliness no pl
lainage [lɛnaʒ] nm (vêtement) woollen
garment; (étoffe) woollen material
laine [lɛn] nf wool
laïque [laik] adj lay, civil; (Scol) state cpd
▷ nm/f layman(-woman)
laisse [lɛs] nf (de chien) lead, leash; **tenir
en ~** to keep on a lead ou leash
laisser [lese] vt to leave ▷ vb aux: **~ qn
faire** to let sb do; **se ~ aller** to let o.s.
go; **laisse-toi faire** let me (ou him etc)
do it; **laisser-aller** nm carelessness,
slovenliness; **laissez-passer** nm
inv pass
lait [lɛ] nm milk; **frère/sœur de ~** foster
brother/sister; **lait concentré/
condensé** condensed/evaporated
milk; **lait écrémé/entier** skimmed/
full-cream (BRIT) ou whole milk; **laitage**
nm dairy product; **laiterie** nf dairy;
laitier, -ière adj dairy cpd ▷ nm/f
milkman (dairywoman)
laiton [lɛtɔ̃] nm brass
laitue [lety] nf lettuce
lambeau, x [lɑ̃bo] nm scrap; **en ~x** in
tatters, tattered
lame [lam] nf blade; (vague) wave;
(lamelle) strip; **lame de fond** ground
swell no pl; **lame de rasoir** razor blade;
lamelle nf thin strip ou blade
lamentable [lamɑ̃tabl] adj appalling
lamenter [lamɑ̃te] vb: **se ~ (sur)** to

moan (over)

lampadaire [lɑ̃padɛʀ] *nm* (*de salon*) standard lamp; (*dans la rue*) street lamp

lampe [lɑ̃p] *nf* lamp; (*Tech*) valve; **lampe à bronzer** sun lamp; **lampe à pétrole** oil lamp; **lampe de poche** torch (*BRIT*), flashlight (*US*); **lampe halogène** halogen lamp

lance [lɑ̃s] *nf* spear; **lance d'incendie** fire hose

lancée [lɑ̃se] *nf*: **être/continuer sur sa ~** to be under way/keep going

lancement [lɑ̃smɑ̃] *nm* launching

lance-pierres [lɑ̃spjɛʀ] *nm inv* catapult

lancer [lɑ̃se] *nm* (*Sport*) throwing *no pl*, throw ▷ *vt* to throw; (*émettre, projeter*) to throw out, send out; (*produit, fusée, bateau, artiste*) to launch; (*injure*) to hurl, fling; **se lancer** *vi* (*prendre de l'élan*) to build up speed; (*se précipiter*): **se ~ sur** *ou* **contre** to rush at; **se ~ dans** (*discussion*) to launch into; (*aventure*) to embark on; **~ qch à qn** to throw sth to sb; (*de façon agressive*) to throw sth at sb; **~ un cri** *ou* **un appel** to shout *ou* call out; **lancer du poids** putting the shot

landau [lɑ̃do] *nm* pram (*BRIT*), baby carriage (*US*)

lande [lɑ̃d] *nf* moor

langage [lɑ̃gaʒ] *nm* language

langouste [lɑ̃gust] *nf* crayfish *inv*; **langoustine** *nf* Dublin Bay prawn

langue [lɑ̃g] *nf* (*Anat, Culin*) tongue; (*Ling*) language; **tirer la ~ (à)** to stick out one's tongue (at); **de ~ française** French-speaking; **quelles ~s parlez-vous?** what languages do you speak?; **langue maternelle** native language, mother tongue; **langues vivantes** modern languages

langueur [lɑ̃gœʀ] *nf* languidness

languir [lɑ̃giʀ] *vi* to languish; (*conversation*) to flag; **faire ~ qn** to keep sb waiting

lanière [lanjɛʀ] *nf* (*de fouet*) lash; (*de sac, bretelle*) strap

lanterne [lɑ̃tɛʀn] *nf* (*portable*) lantern; (*électrique*) light, lamp; (*de voiture*) (side)light

laper [lape] *vt* to lap up

lapidaire [lapidɛʀ] *adj* (*fig*) terse

lapin [lapɛ̃] *nm* rabbit; (*peau*) rabbitskin; (*fourrure*) cony; **poser un ~ qn** (*fam*) to stand sb up

Laponie [laponi] *nf* Lapland

laps [laps] *nm*: **~ de temps** space of time, time *no pl*

laque [lak] *nf* (*vernis*) lacquer; (*pour cheveux*) hair spray

laquelle [lakɛl] *pron voir* **lequel**

larcin [laʀsɛ̃] *nm* theft

lard [laʀ] *nm* (*bacon*) (streaky) bacon; (*graisse*) fat

lardon [laʀdɔ̃] *nm*: **~s** chopped bacon

large [laʀʒ] *adj* wide, broad; (*fig*) generous ▷ *adv*: **calculer/voir ~** to allow extra/think big ▷ *nm* (*largeur*): **m de ~** 5 m wide *ou* in width; (*mer*): **le** the open sea; **au ~ de** off; **large d'esp** broad-minded; **largement** *adv* wide (*de loin*) greatly; (*au moins*) easily; (*généreusement*) generously; **c'est largement suffisant** that's ample; **largesse** *nf* generosity; **largesses** *nf*, (*dons*) liberalities; **largeur** *nf* (*qu'on mesure*) width; (*impression visuelle*) wideness, width; (*d'esprit*) broadness

larguer [laʀge] *vt* to drop; **~ les amarres** to cast off (the moorings)

larme [laʀm] *nf* tear; (*fam: goutte*) dro **en ~s** in tears; **larmoyer** *vi* (*yeux*) to water; (*se plaindre*) to whimper

larvé, e [laʀve] *adj* (*fig*) latent

laryngite [laʀɛ̃ʒit] *nf* laryngitis

las, lasse [lɑ, lɑs] *adj* weary

laser [lazɛʀ] *nm*: **(rayon) ~** laser (bear **chaîne** *ou* **platine ~** laser disc (player **disque ~** laser disc

lasse [lɑs] *adj voir* **las**

lasser [lɑse] *vt* to weary, tire; **se lasse de** *vt* to grow weary *ou* tired of

latéral, e, -aux [lateʀal, o] *adj* side *cpd*, lateral

latin, e [latɛ̃, in] *adj* Latin ▷ *nm/f*: **L~,** Latin ▷ *nm* (*Ling*) Latin

titude [latityd] nf latitude
uréat, e [lɔʀea, at] nm/f winner
urier [lɔʀje] nm (Bot) laurel; **feuille de** (Culin) bay leaf
vable [lavabl] adj washable
vabo [lavabo] nm washbasin;
avabos nmpl (toilettes) toilet sg
vage [lavaʒ] nm washing no pl, wash; **avage de cerveau** brainwashing no pl
vande [lavɑ̃d] nf lavender
ve [lav] nf lava no pl
ve-linge [lavlɛ̃ʒ] nm inv washing machine
ver [lave] vt to wash; (tache) to wash off; **se laver** vi to have a wash, wash; **se ~ les mains/dents** to wash one's hands/clean one's teeth; **~ la aisselle/le linge** to wash the dishes/clothes; **~ qn de** (accusation) to clear sb of; **laverie** nf: **laverie (automatique)** launderette; **lavette** nf dish cloth; (fam) drip; **laveur, -euse** nm/f cleaner; **ave-vaisselle** nm inv dishwasher; **avoir** nm wash house; (évier) sink
xatif, -ive [laksatif, iv] adj, nm laxative
yette [lɛjɛt] nf baby clothes

O **MOT-CLÉ**

[lə], **la, l'** (pl **les**) art déf **1** the; **le ivre/la pomme/l'arbre** the book/the pple/the tree; **les étudiants** the tudents
 (noms abstraits): **le courage/ 'amour/la jeunesse** courage/love/ outh
 (indiquant la possession): **se casser la ambe** etc to break one's leg etc; **levez a main** put your hand up; **avoir les eux gris/le nez rouge** to have grey yes/a red nose
 (temps): **le matin/soir** in the norning/evening; mornings/ venings; **le jeudi** etc (d'habitude) on hursdays etc; (ce jeudi-là etc) on (the) hursday
 (distribution, évaluation) a, an; **10**

euros le mètre/kilo 10 euros a ou per metre/kilo; **le tiers/quart de** a third/quarter of
▷ pron **1** (personne: mâle) him; (: femelle) her; (: pluriel) them; **je le/la/les vois** I can see him/her/them
2 (animal, chose: singulier) it; (: pluriel) them; **je le (ou la) vois** I can see it; **je les vois** I can see them
3 (remplaçant une phrase): **je ne le savais pas** I didn't know (about it); **il était riche et ne l'est plus** he was once rich but no longer is

lécher [leʃe] vt to lick; (laper: lait, eau) to lick ou lap up; **se ~ les doigts/lèvres** to lick one's fingers/lips; **lèche-vitrines** nm: **faire du lèche-vitrines** to go window-shopping
leçon [l(ə)sɔ̃] nf lesson; **faire la ~ à** (fig) to give a lecture to; **leçons de conduite** driving lessons; **leçons particulières** private lessons ou tuition sg (BRIT)
lecteur, -trice [lɛktœʀ, tʀis] nm/f reader; (d'université) foreign language assistant ▷ nm (Tech): **~ de cassettes/ CD/DVD** cassette/CD/DVD player; **lecteur de disquette(s)** disk drive; **lecteur MP3** MP3 player
lecture [lɛktyʀ] nf reading
Attention à ne pas traduire lecture par le mot anglais lecture.
ledit [lədi], **ladite** (mpl **lesdits**, fpl **lesdites**) dét the aforesaid
légal, e, -aux [legal, o] adj legal; **légaliser** vt to legalize; **légalité** nf law
légendaire [leʒɑ̃dɛʀ] adj legendary
légende [leʒɑ̃d] nf (mythe) legend; (de carte, plan) key; (de dessin) caption
léger, -ère [leʒe, ɛʀ] adj light; (bruit, retard) slight; (personne: superficiel) thoughtless; (: volage) free and easy; **à la légère** (parler, agir) rashly, thoughtlessly; **légèrement** adv (s'habiller, bouger) lightly; (un peu) slightly; **manger légèrement** to eat a light meal; **légèreté** nf lightness; (d'une remarque) flippancy

législatif, -ive [leʒislatif, iv] *adj*
legislative; **législatives** *nfpl* general
election *sg*

légitime [leʒitim] *adj* (*Jur*) lawful,
legitimate; (*fig*) rightful, legitimate; **en
état de ~ défense** in self-defence

legs [lɛg] *nm* legacy

léguer [lege] *vt*: **~ qch à qn** (*Jur*) to
bequeath sth to sb

légume [legym] *nm* vegetable;
légumes secs pulses; **légumes verts**
green vegetables, greens

lendemain [lɑ̃dmɛ̃] *nm*: **le ~** the next
ou following day; **le ~ matin/soir** the
next *ou* following morning/evening; **le
~ de** the day after

lent, e [lɑ̃, lɑ̃t] *adj* slow; **lentement** *adv*
slowly; **lenteur** *nf* slowness *no pl*

lentille [lɑ̃tij] *nf* (*Optique*) lens *sg*;
(*Culin*) lentil; **lentilles de contact**
contact lenses

léopard [leɔpaʀ] *nm* leopard

lèpre [lɛpʀ] *nf* leprosy

 MOT-CLÉ

lequel, laquelle [ləkɛl, lakɛl] (*mpl*
lesquels, *fpl* **lesquelles**) (*à + lequel =*
auquel, *de + lequel =* **duquel** *etc*) *pron*
1 (*interrogatif*) which, which one; **lequel
des deux?** which one?
2 (*relatif: personne: sujet*) who; (*: objet,
après préposition*) whom; (*: chose*) which
▷ *adj*: **auquel cas** in which case

les [le] *dét voir* **le**

lesbienne [lɛsbjɛn] *nf* lesbian

léser [leze] *vt* to wrong

lésiner [lezine] *vi*: **ne pas ~ sur les
moyens** (*pour mariage etc*) to push the
boat out

lésion [lezjɔ̃] *nf* lesion, damage *no pl*

lessive [lesiv] *nf* (*poudre*) washing
powder; (*linge*) washing *no pl*, wash;
lessiver *vt* to wash; (*fam: fatiguer*) to
tire out, exhaust

lest [lɛst] *nm* ballast

leste [lɛst] *adj* sprightly, nimble

lettre [lɛtʀ] *nf* letter; **lettres** *nfpl*
(*littérature*) literature *sg*; (*Scol*) arts
(subjects); **à la ~** literally; **en toutes ~**
in full; **lettre piégée** letter bomb

leucémie [løsemi] *nf* leukaemia

 MOT-CLÉ

leur [lœʀ] *adj possessif* their; **leur
maison** their house; **leurs amis** their
friends
▷ *pron* **1** (*objet indirect*) (to) them; **je le
ai dit la vérité** I told them the truth;
je le leur ai donné I gave it to them, I
gave them it
2 (*possessif*): **le(la) leur, les leurs** the

levain [ləvɛ̃] *nm* leaven

levé, e [ləve] *adj*: **être ~** to be up; **levé**
nf (*Postes*) collection

lever [l(ə)ve] *vt* (*vitre, bras etc*) to raise
(*soulever de terre, supprimer: interdiction
siège*) to lift; (*impôts, armée*) to levy ▷ *v*
to rise ▷ *nm*: **au ~** on getting up; **se
lever** *vi* to get up; (*soleil*) to rise; (*jour*)
to break; (*brouillard*) to lift; **ça va se ~**
(*temps*) it's going to clear up; **lever de
soleil** sunrise; **lever du jour** daybreak

levier [ləvje] *nm* lever

lèvre [lɛvʀ] *nf* lip

lévrier [levʀije] *nm* greyhound

levure [l(ə)vyʀ] *nf* yeast; **levure
chimique** baking powder

lexique [lɛksik] *nm* vocabulary;
(*glossaire*) lexicon

lézard [lezaʀ] *nm* lizard

lézarde [lezaʀd] *nf* crack

liaison [ljɛzɔ̃] *nf* (*rapport*) connection
(*transport*) link; (*amoureuse*) affair;
(*Phonétique*) liaison; **entrer/être en ~
avec** to get/be in contact with

liane [ljan] *nf* creeper

liasse [ljas] *nf* wad, bundle

Liban [libɑ̃] *nm*: **le ~** (the) Lebanon

libeller [libele] *vt* (*chèque, mandat*): **~
(au nom de)** to make out (to); (*lettre*)
to word

libellule [libelyl] *nf* dragonfly

béral, e, -aux [libeʀal, o] *adj,
nm/f* liberal; **profession ~e** (liberal)
profession

bérer [libeʀe] *vt* (*délivrer*) to free,
liberate; (*relâcher: prisonnier*) to
discharge, release; (: *d'inhibitions*) to
liberate; (*gaz*) to release; **se libérer** *vi*
(*de rendez-vous*) to get out of previous
engagements

berté [libɛʀte] *nf* freedom; (*loisir*) free
time; **libertés** *nfpl* (*privautés*) liberties;
mettre/être en ~ to set/be free; **en ~
provisoire/surveillée/conditionnelle**
on bail/probation/parole

braire [libʀɛʀ] *nm/f* bookseller

brairie [libʀeʀi] *nf* bookshop

> Attention à ne pas traduire *librairie*
> par *library*.

bre [libʀ] *adj* free; (*route, voie*) clear;
(*place, salle*) free; (*ligne*) not engaged;
(*Scol*) non-state; **~ de qch/de faire** free
from sth/to do; **la place est ~?** is this
seat free?; **libre arbitre** free will; **libre-
échange** *nm* free trade; **libre-service**
nm self-service store

ibye [libi] *nf*: **la ~** Libya

cence [lisɑ̃s] *nf* (*permis*) permit;
(*diplôme*) degree; (*liberté*) liberty;

licencié, e *nm/f* (*Scol*): **licencié
ès lettres/en droit** ≈ Bachelor of
Arts/Law

cenciement [lisɑ̃simɑ̃] *nm*
redundancy

cencier [lisɑ̃sje] *vt* (*débaucher*) to
make redundant, lay off; (*renvoyer*)
to dismiss

cite [lisit] *adj* lawful

e [li] *nf* dregs *pl*, sediment

é, e [lje] *adj*: **très ~ avec** very friendly
with *ou* close to

echtenstein [liʃtɛnʃtain] *nm*: **le ~**
Liechtenstein

ège [ljɛʒ] *nm* cork

en [ljɛ̃] *nm* (*corde, fig: affectif*) bond;
(*rapport*) link, connection; **lien de
parenté** family tie; **lien hypertexte**
hyperlink

er [lje] *vt* (*attacher*) to tie up; (*joindre*)

to link up; (*fig: unir, engager*) to bind;
~ conversation (avec) to strike up a
conversation (with); **~ connaissance
avec** to get to know

lierre [ljɛʀ] *nm* ivy

lieu, x [ljø] *nm* place; **lieux** *nmpl*
(*locaux*) premises; (*endroit: d'un accident
etc*) scene *sg*; **en ~ sûr** in a safe place; **en
premier ~** in the first place; **en dernier
~** lastly; **avoir ~** to take place; **tenir ~
de** to serve as; **donner ~ à** to give rise
to; **au ~ de** instead of; **arriver/être sur
les ~x** to arrive at/be on the scene; **lieu
commun** cliché; **lieu-dit** (*pl* **lieux-dits**)
nm locality

lieutenant [ljøt(ə)nɑ̃] *nm* lieutenant

lièvre [ljɛvʀ] *nm* hare

ligament [ligamɑ̃] *nm* ligament

ligne [liɲ] *nf* (*gén*) line; (*Transports:
liaison*) service; (: *trajet*) route;
(*silhouette*) figure; **garder la ~** to keep
one's figure; **entrer en ~ de compte** to
come into it; **en ~** (*Inform*) online; **~ fixe**
(*Tél*) land line (phone)

lignée [liɲe] *nf* line, lineage

ligoter [ligote] *vt* to tie up

ligue [lig] *nf* league

lilas [lila] *nm* lilac

limace [limas] *nf* slug

limande [limɑ̃d] *nf* dab

lime [lim] *nf* file; **lime à ongles** nail file;
limer *vt* to file

limitation [limitasjɔ̃] *nf*: **limitation
de vitesse** speed limit

limite [limit] *nf* (*de terrain*) boundary;
(*partie ou point extrême*) limit; **à la ~** (*au
pire*) if the worst comes (*ou* came) to the
worst; **vitesse/charge ~** maximum
speed/load; **cas ~** borderline
case; **date ~** deadline; **date ~ de
vente/consommation** sell-by/best-
before date; **limiter** *vt* (*restreindre*) to
limit, restrict; (*délimiter*) to border;
limitrophe *adj* border *cpd*

limoger [limɔʒe] *vt* to dismiss

limon [limɔ̃] *nm* silt

limonade [limɔnad] *nf* lemonade

lin [lɛ̃] *nm* (*tissu*) linen

linceul [lɛ̃sœl] nm shroud

linge [lɛ̃ʒ] nm (serviettes etc) linen; (lessive) washing; (aussi: **~ de corps**) underwear; **lingerie** nf lingerie, underwear

lingot [lɛ̃go] nm ingot

linguistique [lɛ̃gɥistik] adj linguistic ▷ nf linguistics sg

lion, ne [ljɔ̃, ljɔn] nm/f lion (lioness); (signe): **le L~** Leo; **lionceau, x** nm lion cub

liqueur [likœr] nf liqueur

liquidation [likidasjɔ̃] nf (vente) sale

liquide [likid] adj liquid ▷ nm liquid; (Comm): **en ~** in ready money ou cash; **je n'ai pas de ~** I haven't got any cash; **liquider** vt to liquidate; (Comm: articles) to clear, sell off

lire [lir] nf (monnaie) lira ▷ vt, vi to read

lis [lis] nm = **lys**

Lisbonne [lizbɔn] n Lisbon

lisible [lizibl] adj legible

lisière [lizjɛr] nf (de forêt) edge

lisons [lizɔ̃] vb voir **lire**

lisse [lis] adj smooth

liste [list] nf list; **faire la ~ de** to list; **liste de mariage** wedding (present) list; **liste électorale** electoral roll; **listing** nm (Inform) printout

lit [li] nm bed; **petit ~, ~ à une place** single bed; **grand ~, ~ à deux places** double bed; **faire son ~** to make one's bed; **aller/se mettre au ~** to go to/get into bed; **lit de camp** campbed; **lit d'enfant** cot (BRIT), crib (US)

literie [litri] nf bedding, bedclothes pl

litige [litiʒ] nm dispute

litre [litr] nm litre

littéraire [literɛr] adj literary ▷ nm/f arts student; **elle est très ~** she's very literary

littéral, e, -aux [literal, o] adj literal

littérature [literatyr] nf literature

littoral, -aux [litɔral, o] nm coast

livide [livid] adj livid, pallid

livraison [livrɛzɔ̃] nf delivery

livre [livr] nm book ▷ nf (monnaie) pound; (poids) half a kilo, ≈ pound; **livre**

de poche paperback

livré, e [livre] adj: **~ à soi-même** left t o.s. one's own devices

livrer [livre] vt (Comm) to deliver; (otage, coupable) to hand over; (secret, information) to give away; **se livrer à** (se confier) to confide in; (se rendre, s'abandonner) to give o.s. up to; (faire: pratiques, actes) to indulge in; (enquête) to carry out

livret [livre] nm booklet; (d'opéra) libretto; **livret de caisse d'épargne** (savings) bank-book; **livret de famille** (official) family record book; **livret scolaire** (school) report book

livreur, -euse [livrœr, øz] nm/f delivery boy ou man/girl ou woman

local, e, -aux [lɔkal] adj local ▷ nm (salle) premises pl; voir aussi **locaux**; **localité** nf locality

locataire [lɔkatɛr] nm/f tenant; (de chambre) lodger

location [lɔkasjɔ̃] nf (par le locataire, le loueur) renting; (par le propriétaire) renting out, letting; (Théâtre) booking office; **"~ de voitures"** "car rental"; **habiter en ~** to live in rented accommodation; **prendre une ~ (pou les vacances)** to rent a house etc (for the holidays)

⏐ Attention à ne pas traduire **locatic** par le mot anglais **location**.

locomotive [lɔkɔmɔtiv] nf locomotive, engine

locution [lɔkysjɔ̃] nf phrase

loge [lɔʒ] nf (Théâtre: d'artiste) dressing room; (: de spectateurs) box; (de concierg franc-maçon) lodge

logement [lɔʒmɑ̃] nm accommodation no pl (BRIT), accommodations pl (US); (appartement flat (BRIT), apartment (US); (Pol, Admin **le ~** housing no pl

loger [lɔʒe] vt to accommodate ▷ vi to live; **être logé, nourri** to have board and lodging; **se loger** vr: **trouver à se ~** to find somewhere to live; **se ~ dans** (suj: balle, flèche) to lodge itself in

logeur, -euse *nm/f* landlord(-lady)

logiciel [lɔʒisjɛl] *nm* software

logique [lɔʒik] *adj* logical ▷ *nf* logic

logo [lɔgo] *nm* logo

loi [lwa] *nf* law; **faire la ~** to lay down the law

loin [lwɛ̃] *adv* far; (*dans le temps: futur*) a long way off; (*: passé*) a long time ago; **plus ~** further; **~ de** far from; **c'est ~ d'ici?** is it far from here?; **au ~** far off; **de ~** from a distance; (*fig: de beaucoup*) by far

lointain, e [lwɛ̃tɛ̃, ɛn] *adj* faraway, distant; (*dans le futur, passé*) distant; (*cause, parent*) remote, distant ▷ *nm*: **dans le ~** in the distance

loir [lwaʀ] *nm* dormouse

Loire [lwaʀ] *nf*: **la ~** the (River) Loire

loisir [lwaziʀ] *nm*: **heures de ~** spare time; **loisirs** *nmpl* (*temps libre*) leisure *sg*; (*activités*) leisure activities; **avoir le ~ de faire** to have the time *ou* opportunity to do; **à ~** at leisure

londonien, ne [lɔ̃dɔnjɛ̃, jɛn] *adj* London *cpd*, of London ▷ *nm/f*: **L~, ne** Londoner

Londres [lɔ̃dʀ] *n* London

long, longue [lɔ̃, lɔ̃g] *adj* long ▷ *adv*: **en savoir ~** to know a great deal ▷ *nm*: **de 3 m de ~** 3 m long, 3 m in length; **ne pas faire ~ feu** not to last long; **(tout) le ~ de** (all) along; **tout au ~ de** (*année, vie*) throughout; **de ~ en large** (*marcher*) to and fro, up and down; *voir aussi* **longue**

longer [lɔ̃ʒe] *vt* to go (*ou* walk *ou* drive) along(side); (*suj: mur, route*) to border

longiligne [lɔ̃ʒiliɲ] *adj* long-limbed

longitude [lɔ̃ʒityd] *nf* longitude

longtemps [lɔ̃tɑ̃] *adv* (for) a long time, (for) long; **avant ~** before long; **pour** *ou* **pendant ~** for a long time; **mettre ~ à faire** to take a long time to do; **il en a pour ~?** will he be long?

longue [lɔ̃g] *adj voir* **long** ▷ *nf*: **à la ~** in the end; **longuement** *adv* (*longtemps*) for a long time; (*en détail*) at length

longueur [lɔ̃gœʀ] *nf* length;

longueurs *nfpl* (*fig: d'un film etc*) tedious parts; **en ~** lengthwise; **tirer en ~** to drag on; **à ~ de journée** all day long

loquet [lɔkɛ] *nm* latch

lorgner [lɔʀɲe] *vt* to eye; (*fig*) to have one's eye on

lors [lɔʀ]: **~ de** *prép* at the time of; during

lorsque [lɔʀsk] *conj* when, as

losange [lɔzɑ̃ʒ] *nm* diamond

lot [lo] *nm* (*part*) share; (*de loterie*) prize; (*fig: destin*) fate, lot; (*Comm, Inform*) batch; **le gros ~** the jackpot

loterie [lɔtʀi] *nf* lottery

lotion [losjɔ̃] *nf* lotion; **lotion après rasage** aftershave (lotion)

lotissement [lɔtismɑ̃] *nm* housing development; (*parcelle*) plot, lot

loto [lɔto] *nm* lotto

lotte [lɔt] *nf* monkfish

louanges [lwɑ̃ʒ] *nfpl* praise *sg*

loubard [lubaʀ] (*fam*) *nm* lout

louche [luʃ] *adj* shady, fishy, dubious ▷ *nf* ladle; **loucher** *vi* to squint

louer [lwe] *vt* (*maison: suj: propriétaire*) to let, rent (out); (*: locataire*) to rent; (*voiture etc: entreprise*) to hire out (*BRIT*), rent (out); (*: locataire*) to hire, rent; (*réserver*) to book; (*faire l'éloge de*) to praise; **"à ~"** "to let" (*BRIT*), "for rent" (*US*); **je voudrais ~ une voiture** I'd like to hire (*BRIT*) *ou* rent (*US*) a car

loup [lu] *nm* wolf; **jeune ~** young go-getter

loupe [lup] *nf* magnifying glass; **à la ~** in minute detail

louper [lupe] (*fam*) *vt* (*manquer*) to miss; (*examen*) to flunk

lourd, e [luʀ, luʀd] *adj, adv* heavy; **c'est trop ~** it's too heavy; **~ de** (*conséquences, menaces*) charged with; **il fait ~** the weather is close, it's sultry; **lourdaud, e** (*péj*) *adj* clumsy; **lourdement** *adv* heavily

loutre [lutʀ] *nf* otter

louveteau, x [luv(ə)to] *nm* wolf-cub; (*scout*) cub (scout)

louvoyer [luvwaje] *vi* (*fig*) to hedge,

evade the issue

loyal, e, -aux [lwajal, o] *adj* (*fidèle*) loyal, faithful; (*fair-play*) fair; **loyauté** *nf* loyalty, faithfulness; fairness

loyer [lwaje] *nm* rent

lu, e [ly] *pp de* **lire**

lubie [lybi] *nf* whim, craze

lubrifiant [lybʁifjɑ̃] *nm* lubricant

lubrifier [lybʁifje] *vt* to lubricate

lubrique [lybʁik] *adj* lecherous

lucarne [lykaʁn] *nf* skylight

lucide [lysid] *adj* lucid; (*accidenté*) conscious

lucratif, -ive [lykʁatif, iv] *adj* lucrative, profitable; **à but non ~** non profit-making

lueur [lɥœʁ] *nf* (*pâle*) (faint) light; (*chatoyante*) glimmer *no pl*; (*fig*) glimmer; gleam

luge [lyʒ] *nf* sledge (BRIT), sled (US)

lugubre [lygybʁ] *adj* gloomy, dismal

○ MOT-CLÉ

lui [lɥi] *pron* **1** (*objet indirect: mâle*) (to) him; (: *femelle*) (to) her; (: *chose, animal*) (to) it; **je lui ai parlé** I have spoken to him (*ou* to her); **il lui a offert un cadeau** he gave him (*ou* her) a present **2** (*après préposition, comparatif: personne*) him; (: *chose, animal*) it; **elle est contente de lui** she is pleased with him; **je la connais mieux que lui** I know her better than he does; I know her better than him; **ce livre est à lui** this book is his, this is his book; **c'est à lui de jouer** it's his turn *ou* go **3** (*sujet, forme emphatique*) he; **lui, il est à Paris** HE is in Paris; **c'est lui qui l'a fait** HE did it **4** (*objet, forme emphatique*) him; **c'est lui que j'attends** I'm waiting for HIM **5**: **lui-même** himself; itself

luire [lɥiʁ] *vi* to shine; (*en rougeoyant*) to glow

lumière [lymjɛʁ] *nf* light; **mettre en ~** (*fig*) to highlight; **lumière du jour** daylight

luminaire [lyminɛʁ] *nm* lamp, light

lumineux, -euse [lyminø, øz] *adj* luminous; (*éclairé*) illuminated; (*ciel, couleur*) bright; (*rayon*) of light, light *cpd*; (*fig: regard*) radiant

lunatique [lynatik] *adj* whimsical, temperamental

lundi [lœ̃di] *nm* Monday; **on est ~** it's Monday; **le(s) ~(s)** on Mondays; **"à ~"** "see you on Monday"; **lundi de Pâques** Easter Monday

lune [lyn] *nf* moon; **lune de miel** honeymoon

lunette [lynɛt] *nf*: **~s** *nfpl* glasses, spectacles; (*protectrices*) goggles; **lunette arrière** (*Auto*) rear window; **lunettes de soleil** sunglasses; **lunettes noires** dark glasses

lustre [lystʁ] *nm* (*de plafond*) chandelier; (*fig: éclat*) lustre; **lustrer** *vt* to shine

luth [lyt] *nm* lute

lutin [lytɛ̃] *nm* imp, goblin

lutte [lyt] *nf* (*conflit*) struggle; (*sport*) wrestling; **lutter** *vi* to fight, struggle

luxe [lyks] *nm* luxury; **de ~** luxury *cpd*

Luxembourg [lyksɑ̃buʁ] *nm*: **le ~** Luxembourg

luxer [lykse] *vt*: **se ~ l'épaule** to dislocate one's shoulder

luxueux, -euse [lyksɥø, øz] *adj* luxurious

lycée [lise] *nm* ≈ secondary school; **lycéen, ne** *nm/f* secondary school pupil

Lyon [ljɔ̃] *n* Lyons

lyophilisé, e [ljɔfilize] *adj* (*café*) freeze-dried

lyrique [liʁik] *adj* lyrical; (*Opéra*) lyric; **artiste ~** opera singer

lys [lis] *nm* lily

M *abr* = **Monsieur**

m' [m] *pron voir* **me**

ma [ma] *adj voir* **mon**

macaron [makaʀɔ̃] *nm* (*gâteau*) macaroon; (*insigne*) (round) badge

macaronis [makaʀɔni] *nmpl* macaroni *sg*; **~ au fromage** *ou* **en gratin** macaroni cheese (*BRIT*), macaroni and cheese (*US*)

macédoine [masedwan] *nf*: **~ de fruits** fruit salad; **~ de légumes** mixed vegetables; **la M~** Macedonia

macérer [maseʀe] *vi, vt* to macerate; (*dans du vinaigre*) to pickle

mâcher [mɑʃe] *vt* to chew; **ne pas ~ ses mots** not to mince one's words

machin [maʃɛ̃] (*fam*) *nm* thing(umajig); (*personne*): **M~(e)** *nm(f)* what's-his(*ou* her)-name

machinal, e, -aux [maʃinal, o] *adj* mechanical, automatic

machination [maʃinasjɔ̃] *nf* frame-up

machine [maʃin] *nf* machine; (*locomotive*) engine; **machine à laver/ coudre** washing/sewing machine; **machine à sous** fruit machine

mâchoire [mɑʃwaʀ] *nf* jaw

mâchonner [maʃɔne] *vt* to chew (at)

maçon [masɔ̃] *nm* builder; (*poseur de briques*) bricklayer; **maçonnerie** *nf* (*murs*) brickwork; (*pierres*) masonry, stonework

Madagascar [madagaskaʀ] *nf* Madagascar

Madame [madam] (*pl* **Mesdames**) *nf*: **~ Dupont** Mrs Dupont; **occupez-vous de ~/Monsieur/Mademoiselle** please serve this lady/gentleman/(young) lady; **bonjour ~/Monsieur/Mademoiselle** good morning; (*ton déférent*) good morning Madam/Sir/Madam; (*le nom est connu*) good morning Mrs/Mr/Miss X; **~/Monsieur/Mademoiselle!** (*pour appeler*) Madam/Sir/Miss!; **~/Monsieur/Mademoiselle** (*sur lettre*) Dear Madam/Sir/Madam; **chère ~/ cher Monsieur/chère Mademoiselle** Dear Mrs/Mr/Miss X; **Mesdames** Ladies; **mesdames, mesdemoiselles, messieurs** ladies and gentlemen

madeleine [madlɛn] *nf* madeleine, *small sponge cake*

Mademoiselle [madmwazɛl] (*pl* **Mesdemoiselles**) *nf* Miss; *voir aussi* **Madame**

madère [madɛʀ] *nm* Madeira (wine)

Madrid [madʀid] *n* Madrid

magasin [magazɛ̃] *nm* (*boutique*) shop; (*entrepôt*) warehouse; **en ~** (*Comm*) in stock

magazine [magazin] *nm* magazine

Maghreb [magʀɛb] *nm*: **le ~** North Africa; *maghrébin*; **maghrébin, e** *adj* North African ▷ *nm/f*: **Maghrébin, e** North African

magicien, ne [maʒisjɛ̃, jɛn] *nm/f* magician

magie [maʒi] *nf* magic; **magique** *adj* magic; *(enchanteur)* magical

magistral, e, -aux [maʒistral, o] *adj (œuvre, adresse)* masterly; *(ton)* authoritative; **cours ~** lecture

magistrat [maʒistʀa] *nm* magistrate

magnétique [maɲetik] *adj* magnetic

magnétophone [maɲetɔfɔn] *nm* tape recorder; **magnétophone à cassettes** cassette recorder

magnétoscope [maɲetɔskɔp] *nm* video-tape recorder

magnifique [maɲifik] *adj* magnificent

magret [magʀɛ] *nm*: **~ de canard** duck steaklet

mai [mɛ] *nm* May

maigre [mɛgʀ] *adj* (very) thin, skinny; *(viande)* lean; *(fromage)* low-fat; *(végétation)* thin, sparse; *(fig)* poor, meagre, skimpy; **jours ~s** days of abstinence, fish days; **maigreur** *nf* thinness; **maigrir** *vi* to get thinner, lose weight; **maigrir de 2 kilos** to lose 2 kilos

mail [mɛl] *nm* e-mail

maille [maj] *nf* stitch; **maille à l'endroit/l'envers** plain/purl stitch

maillet [majɛ] *nm* mallet

maillon [majɔ̃] *nm* link

maillot [majo] *nm (aussi: ~ de corps)* vest; *(de sportif)* jersey; **maillot de bain** swimming *ou* bathing (BRIT) costume, swimsuit; *(d'homme)* (swimming *ou* bathing (BRIT)) trunks *pl*

main [mɛ̃] *nf* hand; **à la ~** *(tenir, avoir)* in one's hand; *(faire, tricoter etc)* by hand; **se donner la ~** to hold hands; **donner** *ou* **tendre la ~ à qn** to hold out one's hand to sb; **se serrer la ~** to shake hands; **serrer la ~ à qn** to shake hands with sb; **sous la ~** to *ou* at hand; **haut les ~s!** hands up!; **attaque à ~ armée** armed attack; **à remettre en ~s propres** to be delivered personally; **mettre la dernière ~ à** to put the finishing touches to; **se faire/perdre la ~** to get one's hand in/lose one's touch; **avoir qch bien en ~** to have (got) the hang of sth; **main-d'œuvre** *nf* manpower, labour; **mainmise** *nf (fig)*: **mainmise sur** complete hold on; **mains libres** *adj inv (téléphone, kit)* hands-free

maint, e [mɛ̃, mɛ̃t] *adj* many a; **~s** many; **à ~es reprises** time and (time) again

maintenant [mɛ̃t(ə)nɑ̃] *adv* now; *(actuellement)* nowadays

maintenir [mɛ̃t(ə)niʀ] *vt (retenir, soutenir)* to support; *(contenir: foule etc)* to hold back; *(conserver, affirmer)* to maintain; **se maintenir** *vi (prix)* to keep steady; *(amélioration)* to persist

maintien [mɛ̃tjɛ̃] *nm (sauvegarde)* maintenance; *(attitude)* bearing

maire [mɛʀ] *nm* mayor; **mairie** *nf (bâtiment)* town hall; *(administration)* town council

mais [mɛ] *conj* but; **~ non!** of course not!; **~ enfin** but after all; *(indignation)* look here!

maïs [mais] *nm* maize (BRIT), corn (US)

maison [mɛzɔ̃] *nf* house; *(chez-soi)*

home; (*Comm*) firm ▷ *adj inv* (*Culin*) home-made; (*fig*) in-house, own; **à la ~** at home; (*direction*) home; **maison de repos** convalescent home; **maison de retraite** old people's home; **maison close** *ou* **de passe** brothel; **maison de santé** mental home; **maison des jeunes** ≈ youth club; **maison mère** parent company

maître, -esse [mɛtʀ, mɛtʀɛs] *nm/f* master (mistress); (*Scol*) teacher, schoolmaster(-mistress) ▷ *nm* (*peintre etc*) master; (*titre*): **M~** Maître, *term of address gen for a barrister* ▷ *adj* (*principal, essentiel*) main; **être ~ de** (*soi, situation*) to be in control of; **une ~sse femme** a managing woman; **maître chanteur** blackmailer; **maître d'école** schoolmaster; **maître d'hôtel** (*domestique*) butler; (*d'hôtel*) head waiter; **maître nageur** lifeguard; **maîtresse** *nf* (*amante*) mistress; **maîtresse (d'école)** teacher, (school)mistress; **maîtresse de maison** hostess; (*ménagère*) housewife

maîtrise [mɛtʀiz] *nf* (*aussi*: **~ de soi**) self-control, self-possession; (*habileté*) skill, mastery; (*suprématie*) mastery, command; (*diplôme*) ≈ master's degree; **maîtriser** *vt* (*cheval, incendie*) to (bring under) control; (*sujet*) to master; (*émotion*) to control, master; **se maîtriser** to control o.s.

majestueux, -euse [maʒɛstɥø, øz] *adj* majestic

majeur, e [maʒœʀ] *adj* (*important*) major; (*Jur*) of age ▷ *nm* (*doigt*) middle finger; **en ~e partie** for the most part; **la ~e partie de** most of

majorer [maʒɔʀe] *vt* to increase

majoritaire [maʒɔʀitɛʀ] *adj* majority *cpd*

majorité [maʒɔʀite] *nf* (*gén*) majority; (*parti*) party in power; **en ~** mainly; **avoir la ~** to have the majority

majuscule [maʒyskyl] *adj, nf*: (**lettre**) **~** capital (letter)

mal [mal, mo] (*pl* **maux**) *nm* (*opposé au bien*) evil; (*tort, dommage*) harm; (*douleur physique*) pain, ache; (*maladie*) illness, sickness *no pl* ▷ *adj bad*, wrong; **être ~ à l'aise** to be uncomfortable; **être ~ avec qn** to be on bad terms with sb; **il a ~ compris** he misunderstood; **se sentir** *ou* **se trouver ~** to feel ill *ou* unwell; **dire/penser du ~ de** to speak/think ill of; **ne voir aucun ~ à** to see no harm in, see nothing wrong in; **faire ~ à qn** to hurt sb; **se faire ~** to hurt o.s.; **avoir du ~ à faire qch** to have trouble doing sth; **se donner du ~ pour faire qch** to go to a lot of trouble to do sth; **ça fait ~** it hurts; **j'ai ~ au dos** my back hurts; **avoir ~ à la tête/à la gorge/aux dents** to have a headache/a sore throat/toothache; **avoir le ~ du pays** to be homesick; *voir aussi* **cœur**; **maux**; **mal de mer** seasickness; **mal en point** in a bad state

malade [malad] *adj* ill, sick; (*poitrine, jambe*) bad; (*plante*) diseased ▷ *nm/f* invalid, sick person; (*à l'hôpital etc*) patient; **tomber ~** to fall ill; **être ~ du cœur** to have heart trouble *ou* a bad heart; **malade mental** mentally ill person; **maladie** *nf* (*spécifique*) disease, illness; (*mauvaise santé*) illness, sickness; **maladif, -ive** *adj* sickly; (*curiosité, besoin*) pathological

maladresse [maladʀɛs] *nf* clumsiness *no pl*; (*gaffe*) blunder

maladroit, e [maladʀwa, wat] *adj* clumsy

malaise [malɛz] *nm* (*Méd*) feeling of faintness; (*fig*) uneasiness, malaise; **avoir un ~** to feel faint

Malaisie [malɛzi] *nf*: **la ~** Malaysia

malaria [malaʀja] *nf* malaria

malaxer [malakse] *vt* (*pétrir*) to knead; (*mélanger*) to mix

malbouffe [malbuf] (*fam*) *nf*: **la ~** junk food

malchance [malʃɑ̃s] *nf* misfortune, ill luck *no pl*; **par ~** unfortunately; **malchanceux, -euse** *adj* unlucky

mâle [mɑl] *adj* (*aussi* Élec, Tech) male;
(*viril: voix, traits*) manly ▷ *nm* male
malédiction [malediksjɔ̃] *nf* curse
mal...: **malentendant, e** *nm/f*: **les
malentendants** the hard of hearing;
malentendu *nm* misunderstanding;
il y a eu un malentendu there's been
a misunderstanding; **malfaçon** *nf*
fault; **malfaisant, e** *adj* evil, harmful;
malfaiteur *nm* lawbreaker, criminal;
(*voleur*) burglar, thief; **malfamé, e** *adj*
disreputable
malgache [malgaʃ] *adj* Madagascan,
Malagasy ▷ *nm/f*: **M~** Madagascan,
Malagasy ▷ *nm* (Ling) Malagasy
malgré [malgʀe] *prép* in spite of,
despite; **~ tout** all the same
malheur [malœʀ] *nm* (*situation*)
adversity, misfortune; (*événement*)
misfortune; (*: très grave*) disaster,
tragedy; **faire un ~** to be a smash
hit; **malheureusement** *adv*
unfortunately; **malheureux, -euse** *adj*
(*triste*) unhappy, miserable; (*infortuné,
regrettable*) unfortunate; (*malchanceux*)
unlucky; (*insignifiant*) wretched ▷ *nm/f*
poor soul
malhonnête [malɔnɛt] *adj* dishonest;
malhonnêteté *nf* dishonesty
malice [malis] *nf* mischievousness;
(*méchanceté*): **par ~** out of malice *ou*
spite; **sans ~** guileless; **malicieux,
-euse** *adj* mischievous
> Attention à ne pas traduire
> *malicieux* par *malicious*.
malin, -igne [malɛ̃, maliɲ] *adj* (*futé:
f gén: aussi:* **maline**) smart, shrewd;
(Méd) malignant
malingre [malɛ̃gʀ] *adj* puny
malle [mal] *nf* trunk; **mallette** *nf*
(*small*) suitcase; (*porte-documents*)
attaché case
malmener [malməne] *vt* to
manhandle; (*fig*) to give a rough
handling to
malodorant, e [malɔdɔʀɑ̃, ɑ̃t] *adj*
foul-*ou* ill-smelling
malpoli, e [malpɔli] *adj* impolite

malsain, e [malsɛ̃, ɛn] *adj* unhealthy
malt [malt] *nm* malt
Malte [malt] *nf* Malta
maltraiter [maltʀete] *vt* to
manhandle, ill-treat
malveillance [malvejɑ̃s] *nf* (*animosité*)
ill will; (*intention de nuire*) malevolence
malversation [malvɛʀsasjɔ̃] *nf*
embezzlement
maman [mamɑ̃] *nf* mum(my), mother
mamelle [mamɛl] *nf* teat
mamelon [mam(ə)lɔ̃] *nm* (Anat) nipple
mamie [mami] (*fam*) *nf* granny
mammifère [mamifɛʀ] *nm* mammal
mammouth [mamut] *nm* mammoth
manche [mɑ̃ʃ] *nf* (*de vêtement*) sleeve;
(*d'un jeu, tournoi*) round; (Géo): **la M~**
the Channel ▷ *nm* (*d'outil, casserole*)
handle; (*de pelle, pioche etc*) shaft; **à ~s
courtes/longues** short-/long-sleeved;
manche à balai broomstick; (Inform,
Aviat) joystick *m inv*
manchette [mɑ̃ʃɛt] *nf* (*de chemise*) cuff;
(*coup*) forearm blow; (*titre*) headline
manchot [mɑ̃ʃo] *nm* one-armed man;
armless man; (Zool) penguin
mandarine [mɑ̃daʀin] *nf* mandarin
(orange), tangerine
mandat [mɑ̃da] *nm* (*postal*) postal *ou*
money order; (*d'un député etc*) mandate;
(*procuration*) power of attorney,
proxy; (Police) warrant; **mandat
d'arrêt** warrant for arrest; **mandat
de perquisition** search warrant;
mandataire *nm/f* (*représentant*)
representative; (Jur) proxy
manège [manɛʒ] *nm* riding school; (*à
la foire*) roundabout, merry-go-round;
(*fig*) game, ploy
manette [manɛt] *nf* lever, tap;
manette de jeu joystick
mangeable [mɑ̃ʒabl] *adj* edible,
eatable
mangeoire [mɑ̃ʒwaʀ] *nf* trough,
manger
manger [mɑ̃ʒe] *vt* to eat; (*ronger: suj:
rouille etc*) to eat into *ou* away ▷ *vi* to
eat; **donner à ~ (à)** (*enfant*) to feed; **est-**

ce qu'on peut ~ quelque chose? can we have something to eat?

mangue [māg] *nf* mango

maniable [manjabl] *adj* (*outil*) handy; (*voiture, voilier*) easy to handle

maniaque [manjak] *adj* finicky, fussy ▷ *nm/f* (*méticuleux*) fusspot; (*fou*) maniac

manie [mani] *nf* (*tic*) odd habit; (*obsession*) mania; **avoir la ~ de** to be obsessive about

manier [manje] *vt* to handle

manière [manjɛʀ] *nf* (*façon*) way, manner; **manières** *nfpl* (*attitude*) manners; (*chichis*) fuss *sg*; **de ~ à** so as to; **de cette ~** in this way *ou* manner; **d'une certaine ~** in a way; **de toute ~** in any case; **d'une ~ générale** generally speaking, as a general rule

maniéré, e [manjeʀe] *adj* affected

manifestant, e [manifɛstā, āt] *nm/f* demonstrator

manifestation [manifɛstasjɔ̃] *nf* (*de joie, mécontentement*) expression, demonstration; (*symptôme*) outward sign; (*culturelle etc*) event; (*Pol*) demonstration

manifeste [manifɛst] *adj* obvious, evident ▷ *nm* manifesto; **manifester** *vt* (*volonté, intentions*) to show, indicate; (*joie, peur*) to express, show ▷ *vi* to demonstrate; **se manifester** *vi* (*émotion*) to show *ou* express itself; (*difficultés*) to arise; (*symptômes*) to appear

manigancer [manigāse] *vt* to plot

manipulation [manipylasjɔ̃] *nf* handling; (*Pol, génétique*) manipulation

manipuler [manipyle] *vt* to handle; (*fig*) to manipulate

manivelle [manivɛl] *nf* crank

mannequin [mankɛ̃] *nm* (*Couture*) dummy; (*Mode*) model

manœuvre [manœvʀ] *nf* (*gén*) manoeuvre (*BRIT*), maneuver (*US*) ▷ *nm* labourer; **manœuvrer** *vt* to manoeuvre (*BRIT*), maneuver (*US*); (*levier, machine*) to operate ▷ *vi* to manoeuvre

manoir [manwaʀ] *nm* manor *ou* country house

manque [māk] *nm* (*insuffisance*): **~ de** lack of; (*vide*) emptiness, gap; (*Méd*) withdrawal; **être en état de ~** to suffer withdrawal symptoms

manqué, e [māke] *adj* failed; **garçon ~** tomboy

manquer [māke] *vi* (*faire défaut*) to be lacking; (*être absent*) to be missing; (*échouer*) to fail ▷ *vt* to miss ▷ *vb impers*: **il (nous) manque encore 10 euros** we are still 10 euros short; **il manque des pages (au livre)** there are some pages missing (from the book); **il/cela me manque** I miss him/this; **~ à** (*règles etc*) to be in breach of, fail to observe; **~ de** to lack; **je ne ~ai pas de lui dire** I'll be sure to tell him; **il a manqué (de) tuer** he very nearly got killed

mansarde [māsaʀd] *nf* attic; **mansardé, e** *adj*: **chambre mansardée** attic room

manteau, x [māto] *nm* coat

manucure [manykyʀ] *nf* manicurist

manuel, le [manɥɛl] *adj* manual ▷ *nm* (*ouvrage*) manual, handbook

manufacture [manyfaktyʀ] *nf* factory; **manufacturé, e** *adj* manufactured

manuscrit, e [manyskʀi, it] *adj* handwritten ▷ *nm* manuscript

manutention [manytāsjɔ̃] *nf* (*Comm*) handling

mappemonde [mapmɔ̃d] *nf* (*plane*) map of the world; (*sphère*) globe

maquereau, x [makʀo] *nm* (*Zool*) mackerel *inv*; (*fam*) pimp

maquette [makɛt] *nf* (*à échelle réduite*) (scale) model; (*d'une page illustrée*) paste-up

maquillage [makijaʒ] *nm* making up; (*crème etc*) make-up

maquiller [makije] *vt* (*personne, visage*) to make up; (*truquer: passeport, statistique*) to fake; (: *voiture volée*) to do over (*respray etc*); **se maquiller** *vi* to make up (one's face)

maquis [maki] *nm* (*Géo*) scrub; (*Mil*) maquis, underground fighting *no pl*

maraîcher, -ère [maʀeʃe, ɛʀ] *adj*: **cultures maraîchères** market gardening *sg* ▷ *nm/f* market gardener

marais [maʀɛ] *nm* marsh, swamp

marasme [maʀasm] *nm* stagnation, slump

marathon [maʀatɔ̃] *nm* marathon

marbre [maʀbʀ] *nm* marble

marc [maʀ] *nm* (*de raisin, pommes*) marc

marchand, e [maʀʃɑ̃, ɑ̃d] *nm/f* shopkeeper, tradesman(-woman); (*au marché*) merchant ▷ *adj*: **prix/valeur ~(e)** market price/value; **marchand de fruits** fruiterer (*BRIT*), fruit seller (*US*); **marchand de journaux** newsagent; **marchand de légumes** greengrocer (*BRIT*), produce dealer (*US*); **marchand de poissons** fishmonger (*BRIT*), fish seller (*US*); **marchander** *vi* to bargain, haggle; **marchandise** *nf* goods *pl*, merchandise *no pl*

marche [maʀʃ] *nf* (*d'escalier*) step; (*activité*) walking; (*promenade, trajet, allure*) walk; (*démarche*) walk, gait; (*Mil etc, Mus*) march; (*fonctionnement*) running; (*des événements*) course; **dans le sens de la ~** (*Rail*) facing the engine; **en ~** (*monter etc*) while the vehicle is moving *ou* in motion; **mettre en ~** to start; **se mettre en ~** (*personne*) to get moving; (*machine*) to start; **être en état de ~** to be in working order; **marche à suivre** (correct) procedure; **marche arrière** reverse (gear); **faire marche arrière** to reverse; (*fig*) to backtrack, back-pedal

marché [maʀʃe] *nm* market; (*transaction*) bargain, deal; **faire du ~ noir** to buy and sell on the black market; **marché aux puces** flea market

marcher [maʀʃe] *vi* to walk; (*Mil*) to march; (*aller: voiture, train, affaires*) to go; (*prospérer*) to go well; (*fonctionner*) to

work, run; (*fam: consentir*) to go along, agree; (: *croire naïvement*) to be taken in; **faire ~ qn** (*taquiner*) to pull sb's leg; (*tromper*) to lead sb up the garden path; **comment est-ce que ça marche?** how does this work?; **marcheur, -euse** *nm/f* walker

mardi [maʀdi] *nm* Tuesday; **Mardi gras** Shrove Tuesday

mare [maʀ] *nf* pond; (*flaque*) pool

marécage [maʀekaʒ] *nm* marsh, swamp; **marécageux, -euse** *adj* marshy

maréchal, -aux [maʀeʃal, o] *nm* marshal

marée [maʀe] *nf* tide; (*poissons*) fresh (sea) fish; **marée haute/basse** high/low tide; **marée noire** oil slick

marelle [maʀɛl] *nf*: **(jouer à) la ~** (to play) hopscotch

margarine [maʀgaʀin] *nf* margarine

marge [maʀʒ] *nf* margin; **en ~ de** (*fig*) on the fringe of; **marge bénéficiaire** profit margin

marginal, e, -aux [maʀʒinal, o] *nm/f* (*original*) eccentric; (*déshérité*) dropout

marguerite [maʀgəʀit] *nf* marguerite, (oxeye) daisy; (*d'imprimante*) daisy-wheel

mari [maʀi] *nm* husband

mariage [maʀjaʒ] *nm* marriage; (*noce*) wedding; **mariage civil/religieux** registry office (*BRIT*) *ou* civil wedding/church wedding

marié, e [maʀje] *adj* married ▷ *nm* (bride)groom; **les ~s** the bride and groom; **les (jeunes) ~s** the newly-weds

marier [maʀje] *vt* to marry; (*fig*) to blend; **se ~ (avec)** to marry, get married to

marin, e [maʀɛ̃, in] *adj* sea *cpd*, marine ▷ *nm* sailor

marine [maʀin] *adj voir* **marin** ▷ *adj inv* navy (blue) ▷ *nm* (*Mil*) marine ▷ *nf* navy; **marine marchande** merchant navy

mariner [maʀine] *vt*: **faire ~** to marinade

marionnette [maʀjɔnɛt] *nf* puppet
maritalement [maʀitalmã] *adv*:
vivre ~ to live as husband and wife
maritime [maʀitim] *adj* sea *cpd*,
maritime
mark [maʀk] *nm* mark
marmelade [maʀmǝlad] *nf* stewed
fruit, compote; **marmelade d'oranges**
marmalade
marmite [maʀmit] *nf* (cooking-)pot
marmonner [maʀmɔne] *vt, vi* to
mumble, mutter
marmotter [maʀmɔte] *vt* to mumble
Maroc [maʀɔk] *nm*: **le ~** Morocco;
marocain, e [maʀɔkɛ̃, ɛn] *adj*
Moroccan ▷ *nm/f*: **Marocain, e**
Moroccan
maroquinerie [maʀɔkinʀi] *nf*
(*articles*) fine leather goods *pl*; (*boutique*)
shop selling fine leather goods
marquant, e [maʀkã, ãt] *adj*
outstanding
marque [maʀk] *nf* mark; (*Comm: de
nourriture*) brand; (: *de voiture, produits
manufacturés*) make; (*de disques*) label;
de ~ (*produits*) high-class; (*visiteur
etc*) distinguished, well-known; **une
grande ~ de vin** a well-known brand of
wine; **marque de fabrique** trademark;
marque déposée registered
trademark
marquer [maʀke] *vt* to mark; (*inscrire*)
to write down; (*bétail*) to brand; (*Sport:
but etc*) to score; (: *joueur*) to mark;
(*accentuer: taille etc*) to emphasize;
(*manifester: refus, intérêt*) to show
▷ *vi* (*événement*) to stand out, be
outstanding; (*Sport*) to score; **~ les
points** to keep the score
marqueterie [maʀkɛtʀi] *nf* inlaid
work, marquetry
marquis [maʀki] *nm* marquis,
marquess
marraine [maʀɛn] *nf* godmother
marrant, e [maʀã, ãt] (*fam*) *adj* funny
marre [maʀ] (*fam*) *adv*: **en avoir ~ de** to
be fed up with
marrer [maʀe]: **se ~** (*fam*) *vi* to have a

(good) laugh
marron [maʀɔ̃] *nm* (*fruit*) chestnut
▷ *adj inv* brown; **marrons glacés**
candied chestnuts; **marronnier** *nm*
chestnut (tree)
mars [maʀs] *nm* March
Marseille [maʀsɛj] *n* Marseilles
marteau, x [maʀto] *nm* hammer; **être
~** (*fam*) to be nuts; **marteau-piqueur**
nm pneumatic drill
marteler [maʀtǝle] *vt* to hammer
martien, ne [maʀsjɛ̃, jɛn] *adj*
Martian, of *ou* from Mars
martyr, e [maʀtiʀ] *nm/f* martyr ▷ *adj*:
enfants ~s battered children; **martyre**
nm martyrdom; (*fig: sens affaibli*) agony,
torture; **martyriser** *vt* (*Rel*) to martyr;
(*fig*) to bully; (*enfant*) to batter, beat
marxiste [maʀksist] *adj*, *nm/f* Marxist
mascara [maskaʀa] *nm* mascara
masculin, e [maskylɛ̃, in] *adj*
masculine; (*sexe, population*) male;
(*équipe, vêtements*) men's; (*viril*) manly
▷ *nm* masculine
masochiste [mazɔʃist] *adj*
masochistic
masque [mask] *nm* mask; **masque de
beauté** face pack *ou* mask; **masque
de plongée** diving mask; **masquer** *vt*
(*cacher: paysage, porte*) to hide, conceal;
(*dissimuler: vérité, projet*) to mask,
obscure
massacre [masakʀ] *nm* massacre,
slaughter; **massacrer** *vt* to massacre,
slaughter; (*fam: texte etc*) to murder
massage [masaʒ] *nm* massage
masse [mas] *nf* mass; (*Élec*) earth;
(*maillet*) sledgehammer; (*péj*): **la ~** the
masses *pl*; **une ~ de** (*fam*) masses *ou*
loads of; **en ~** *adv* (*acheter*) in bulk;
(*en foule*) en masse ▷ *adj* (*exécutions,
production*) mass *cpd*
masser [mase] *vt* (*assembler: gens*) to
gather; (*pétrir*) to massage; **se masser**
vi (*foule*) to gather; **masseur, -euse**
nm/f masseur(-euse)
massif, -ive [masif, iv] *adj* (*porte*)
solid, massive; (*visage*) heavy, large;

(*bois, or*) solid; (*dose*) massive; (*déportations etc*) mass *cpd* ▷ *nm* (*montagneux*) massif; (*de fleurs*) clump, bank; **le M~ Central** the Massif Central

massue [masy] *nf* club, bludgeon

mastic [mastik] *nm* (*pour vitres*) putty; (*pour fentes*) filler

mastiquer [mastike] *vt* (*aliment*) to chew, masticate

mat, e [mat] *adj* (*couleur, métal*) mat(t); (*bruit, son*) dull ▷ *adj inv* (*Échecs*): **être ~** to be checkmate

mât [mɑ] *nm* (*Navig*) mast; (*poteau*) pole, post

match [matʃ] *nm* match; **faire ~ nul** to draw; **match aller** first leg; **match retour** second leg, return match

matelas [mat(ə)lɑ] *nm* mattress; **matelas pneumatique** air bed *ou* mattress

matelot [mat(ə)lo] *nm* sailor, seaman

mater [mate] *vt* (*personne*) to bring to heel, subdue; (*révolte*) to put down

matérialiser [materjalize]: **se matérialiser** *vi* to materialize

matérialiste [materjalist] *adj* materialistic

matériau [materjo] *nm* material; **matériaux** *nmpl* material(s)

matériel, le [materjɛl] *adj* material ▷ *nm* equipment *no pl*; (*de camping etc*) gear *no pl*; (*Inform*) hardware

maternel, le [matɛrnɛl] *adj* (*amour, geste*) motherly, maternal; (*grand-père, oncle*) maternal; **maternelle** *nf* (*aussi*: **école maternelle**) (state) nursery school

maternité [matɛrnite] *nf* (*établissement*) maternity hospital; (*état de mère*) motherhood, maternity; (*grossesse*) pregnancy; **congé de ~** maternity leave

mathématique [matematik] *adj* mathematical; **mathématiques** *nfpl* (*science*) mathematics *sg*

maths [mat] (*fam*) *nfpl* maths

matière [matjɛr] *nf* matter; (*Comm, Tech*) material, matter *no pl*; (*fig: d'un*

livre etc) subject matter, material; (*Scol*) subject; **en ~ de** as regards; **matières grasses** fat content *sg*; **matières premières** raw materials

Matignon [matiɲɔ̃] *nm*: **(l'hôtel) ~** *the French Prime Minister's residence*

matin [matɛ̃] *nm, adv* morning; **le ~** (*pendant le matin*) in the morning; **demain/hier/dimanche ~** tomorrow/yesterday/Sunday morning; **tous les ~s** every morning; **une heure du ~** one o'clock in the morning; **du ~ au soir** from morning till night; **de bon** *ou* **grand ~** early in the morning; **matinal, e, -aux** *adj* (*toilette, gymnastique*) morning *cpd*; **être matinal** (*personne*) to be up early; to be an early riser; **matinée** *nf* morning; (*spectacle*) matinée

matou [matu] *nm* tom(cat)

matraque [matrak] *nf* (*de policier*) truncheon (*BRIT*), billy (*US*)

matricule [matrikyl] *nm* (*Mil*) regimental number; (*Admin*) reference number

matrimonial, e, -aux [matrimɔnjal, jo] *adj* marital, marriage *cpd*

maudit, e [modi, -it] (*fam*) *adj* (*satané*) blasted, confounded

maugréer [mogree] *vi* to grumble

maussade [mosad] *adj* sullen; (*temps*) gloomy

mauvais, e [mɔvɛ, ɛz] *adj* bad; (*faux*): **le ~ numéro/moment** the wrong number/moment; (*méchant, malveillant*) malicious, spiteful ▷ *adv*: **il fait ~** the weather is bad; **sentir ~** to have a nasty smell, smell nasty; **la mer est ~e** the sea is rough; **mauvais joueur** bad loser; **mauvaise herbe** weed; **mauvaise langue** gossip, scandalmonger (*BRIT*); **mauvaise plaisanterie** nasty trick

mauve [mov] *adj* mauve

maux [mo] *nmpl de* **mal**

maximum [maksimɔm] *adj, nm* maximum; **au ~** (*le plus possible*) as much as one can; (*tout au plus*) at the (very) most *ou* maximum; **faire le ~** to do one's level best

mayonnaise [majɔnɛz] *nf* mayonnaise

mazout [mazut] *nm* (fuel) oil

me, m' [m(ə)] *pron* (*direct: téléphoner, attendre etc*) me; (*indirect: parler, donner etc*) (to) me; (*réfléchi*) myself

mec [mɛk] (*fam*) *nm* bloke, guy

mécanicien, ne [mekanisjɛ̃, jɛn] *nm/f* mechanic; (*Rail*) (train *ou* engine) driver; **pouvez-vous nous envoyer un ~?** can you send us a mechanic?

mécanique [mekanik] *adj* mechanical ▷ *nf* (*science*) mechanics *sg*; (*mécanisme*) mechanism; **ennui ~** engine trouble *no pl*

mécanisme [mekanism] *nm* mechanism

méchamment [meʃamɑ̃] *adv* nastily, maliciously, spitefully

méchanceté [meʃɑ̃ste] *nf* nastiness, maliciousness; **dire des ~s à qn** to say spiteful things to sb

méchant, e [meʃɑ̃, ɑ̃t] *adj* nasty, malicious, spiteful; (*enfant: pas sage*) naughty; (*animal*) vicious

mèche [mɛʃ] *nf* (*de cheveux*) lock; (*de lampe, bougie*) wick; (*d'un explosif*) fuse; **se faire faire des ~s** to have highlights put in one's hair; **de ~ avec** in league with

méchoui [meʃwi] *nm* barbecue of a whole roast sheep

méconnaissable [mekɔnɛsabl] *adj* unrecognizable

méconnaître [mekɔnɛtR] *vt* (*ignorer*) to be unaware of; (*mésestimer*) to misjudge

mécontent, e [mekɔ̃tɑ̃, ɑ̃t] *adj*: **~ (de)** discontented *ou* dissatisfied *ou* displeased (with); (*contrarié*) annoyed (at); **mécontentement** *nm* dissatisfaction, discontent, displeasure; (*irritation*) annoyance

Mecque [mɛk] *nf*: **la ~** Mecca

médaille [medaj] *nf* medal

médaillon [medajɔ̃] *nm* (*bijou*) locket

médecin [med(ə)sɛ̃] *nm* doctor

médecine [med(ə)sin] *nf* medicine

média [medja] *nmpl*: **les ~** the media; **médiatique** *adj* media *cpd*

médical, e, -aux [medikal, o] *adj* medical; **passer une visite ~e** to have a medical

médicament [medikamɑ̃] *nm* medicine, drug

médiéval, e, -aux [medjeval, o] *adj* medieval

médiocre [medjɔkR] *adj* mediocre, poor

méditer [medite] *vi* to meditate

Méditerranée [mediteRane] *nf*: **la (mer) ~** the Mediterranean (Sea); **méditerranéen, ne** *adj* Mediterranean ▷ *nm/f*: **Méditerranéen, ne** native *ou* inhabitant of a Mediterranean country

méduse [medyz] *nf* jellyfish

méfait [mefɛ] *nm* (*faute*) misdemeanour, wrongdoing; **méfaits** *nmpl* (*ravages*) ravages, damage *sg*

méfiance [mefjɑ̃s] *nf* mistrust, distrust

méfiant, e [mefjɑ̃, jɑ̃t] *adj* mistrustful, distrustful

méfier [mefje]: **se méfier** *vi* to be wary; to be careful; **se ~ de** to mistrust, distrust, be wary of

mégaoctet [megaɔktɛ] *nm* megabyte

mégarde [megaRd] *nf*: **par ~** (*accidentellement*) accidentally; (*par erreur*) by mistake

mégère [meʒɛR] *nf* shrew

mégot [mego] (*fam*) *nm* cigarette end

meilleur, e [mɛjœR] *adj, adv* better ▷ *nm*: **le ~** the best; **le ~ des deux** the better of the two; **il fait ~ qu'hier** it's better weather than yesterday; **meilleur marché** (*inv*) cheaper

mél [mɛl] *nm* e-mail

mélancolie [melɑ̃kɔli] *nf* melancholy, gloom; **mélancolique** *adj* melancholic, melancholy

mélange [melɑ̃ʒ] *nm* mixture;

mélanger vt to mix; (vins, couleurs) to blend; (mettre en désordre) to mix up, muddle (up)

mêlée [mele] nf mêlée, scramble; (Rugby) scrum(mage)

mêler [mele] vt (unir) to mix; (embrouiller) to muddle (up), mix up; **se mêler** vi to mix, mingle; **se ~ à** (personne: se joindre) to join; (: s'associer à) to mix with; **se ~ de** (suj: personne) to meddle with, interfere in; **mêle-toi de ce qui te regarde** ou **de tes affaires!** mind your own business!

mélodie [melɔdi] nf melody; **mélodieux, -euse** adj melodious

melon [m(ə)lɔ̃] nm (Bot) (honeydew) melon; (aussi: **chapeau ~**) bowler (hat)

membre [mɑ̃bʀ] nm (Anat) limb; (personne, pays, élément) member ▷ adj member cpd

mémé [meme] (fam) nf granny

 MOT-CLÉ

même [mɛm] adj 1 (avant le nom) same; **en même temps** at the same time; **ils ont les mêmes goûts** they have the same ou similar tastes
2 (après le nom: renforcement): **il est la loyauté même** he is loyalty itself; **ce sont ses paroles mêmes** they are his very words
▷ pron: **le(la) même** the same one
▷ adv 1 (renforcement): **il n'a même pas pleuré** he didn't even cry; **même lui l'a dit** even HE said it; **ici même** at this very place; **même si** even if
2: **à même**: **à même la bouteille** straight from the bottle; **à même la peau** next to the skin; **être à même de faire** to be in a position to do, be able to do
3: **de même**: **faire de même** to do likewise; **lui de même** so does (ou did ou is) he; **de même que** just as; **il va de même pour** the same goes for

mémoire [memwaʀ] nf memory ▷ nm (Scol) dissertation, paper; **mémoires** nmpl (souvenirs) memoirs; **à la ~ de** to the ou in memory of; **de ~** from memory; **mémoire morte** read-only memory, ROM; **mémoire vive** random access memory, RAM

mémorable [memɔʀabl] adj memorable, unforgettable

menace [mənas] nf threat; **menacer** vt to threaten

ménage [menaʒ] nm (travail) housework; (couple) (married) couple; (famille, Admin) household; **faire le ~** to do the housework; **ménagement** nm care and attention; **ménager, -ère** adj household cpd, domestic ▷ vt (traiter: personne) to handle with tact; (utiliser) to use sparingly; (prendre soin de) to take (great) care of, look after; (organiser) to arrange; **ménagère** nf housewife

mendiant, e [mɑ̃djɑ̃, jɑ̃t] nm/f beggar

mendier [mɑ̃dje] vi to beg ▷ vt to beg (for)

mener [m(ə)ne] vt to lead; (enquête) to conduct; (affaires) to manage ▷ vi: **~ à/dans** (emmener) to take to/into; **~ qch à bien** to see sth through (to a successful conclusion), complete sth successfully

meneur, -euse [mənœʀ, øz] nm/f leader; (péj) agitator

méningite [menɛ̃ʒit] nf meningitis no pl

ménopause [menopoz] nf menopause

menottes [mənɔt] nfpl handcuffs

mensonge [mɑ̃sɔ̃ʒ] nm lie; (action) lying no pl; **mensonger, -ère** adj false

mensualité [mɑ̃sɥalite] nf (traite) monthly payment

mensuel, le [mɑ̃sɥɛl] adj monthly

mensurations [mɑ̃syʀasjɔ̃] nfpl measurements

mental, e, -aux [mɑ̃tal, o] adj mental; **mentalité** nf mentality

menteur, -euse [mɑ̃tœʀ, øz] nm/f liar

menthe [mɑ̃t] nf mint

mention [mɑ̃sjɔ̃] nf (annotation) note,

comment; (Scol) grade; **~ bien** ≈ grade
B, ≈ good pass; (Université) ≈ upper 2nd
class pass (BRIT), ≈ pass with (high)
honors (US); (Admin): **"rayer les ~s
inutiles"** "delete as appropriate";
mentionner vt to mention

mentir [mɑ̃tir] vi to lie

menton [mɑ̃tɔ̃] nm chin

menu, e [məny] adj (personne) slim,
slight; (frais, difficulté) minor ▷ adv
(couper, hacher) very fine ▷ nm menu;
~ touristique/gastronomique
economy/gourmet's menu

menuiserie [mənɥizri] nf (métier)
joinery, carpentry; (passe-temps)
woodwork; **menuisier** nm joiner,
carpenter

méprendre [meprɑ̃dr]: **se méprendre**
vi: **se ~ sur** to be mistaken (about)

mépris [mepri] nm (dédain) contempt,
scorn; **au ~ de** regardless of, in defiance
of; **méprisable** adj contemptible,
despicable; **méprisant, e** adj scornful;
méprise nf mistake, error; **mépriser**
vt to scorn, despise; (gloire, danger) to
scorn, spurn

mer [mɛr] nf sea; (marée) tide; **en ~** at
sea; **en haute** ou **pleine ~** off shore, on
the open sea; **la ~ du Nord/Rouge/
Noire/Morte** the North/Red/Black/
Dead Sea

mercenaire [mɛrsənɛr] nm
mercenary, hired soldier

mercerie [mɛrsəri] nf (boutique)
haberdasher's shop (BRIT), notions
store (US)

merci [mɛrsi] excl thank you ▷ nf: **à la
~ de qn/qch** at sb's mercy/the mercy of
sth; **~ beaucoup** thank you very much;
~ de thank you for; **sans ~** merciless(ly)

mercredi [mɛrkrədi] nm Wednesday;
~ des Cendres Ash Wednesday; voir
aussi **lundi**

mercure [mɛrkyr] nm mercury

merde [mɛrd] (fam!) nf shit (!) ▷ excl
(bloody) hell (!)

mère [mɛr] nf mother; **mère
célibataire** single parent, unmarried

mother; **mère de famille** housewife,
mother

merguez [mɛrgɛz] nf merguez
sausage (type of spicy sausage from N
Africa)

méridional, e, -aux [meridjɔnal, o]
adj southern ▷ nm/f Southerner

meringue [mərɛ̃g] nf meringue

mérite [merit] nm merit; **avoir du ~ (à
faire qch)** to deserve credit (for doing
sth); **mériter** vt to deserve

merle [mɛrl] nm blackbird

merveille [mɛrvɛj] nf marvel, wonder;
faire ~ to work wonders; **à ~** perfectly,
wonderfully; **merveilleux, -euse** adj
marvellous, wonderful

mes [me] adj voir **mon**

mésange [mezɑ̃ʒ] nf tit(mouse)

mésaventure [mezavɑ̃tyr] nf
misadventure, misfortune

Mesdames [medam] nfpl de **Madame**

Mesdemoiselles [medmwazɛl] nfpl
de **Mademoiselle**

mesquin, e [mɛskɛ̃, in] adj mean,
petty; **mesquinerie** nf meanness;
(procédé) mean trick

message [mesaʒ] nm message; **est-ce
que je peux laisser un ~?** can I leave
a message?; **~ SMS** text message;
messager, -ère nm/f messenger;
messagerie nf (Internet): **messagerie
électronique** e-mail; **messagerie
vocale** (service) voice mail; **messagerie
instantanée** instant messenger

messe [mɛs] nf mass; **aller à la ~** to
go to mass

Messieurs [mesjø] nmpl de **Monsieur**

mesure [m(ə)zyr] nf (évaluation,
dimension) measurement; (récipient)
measure; (Mus: cadence) time, tempo;
(: division) bar; (retenue) moderation;
(disposition) measure, step; **sur ~**
(costume) made-to-measure; **dans la ~
où** insofar as, inasmuch as; **à ~ que** as;
être en ~ de to be in a position to; **dans
une certaine ~** to a certain extent

mesurer [məzyre] vt to measure;
(juger) to weigh up, assess; (modérer: ses

paroles etc) to moderate

métal, -aux [metal, o] *nm* metal; **métallique** *adj* metallic

météo [meteo] *nf* (*bulletin*) weather report

météorologie [meteɔʀɔlɔʒi] *nf* meteorology

méthode [metɔd] *nf* method; (*livre, ouvrage*) manual, tutor

méticuleux, -euse [metikylø, øz] *adj* meticulous

métier [metje] *nm* (*profession: gén*) job; (*: manuel*) trade; (*artisanal*) craft; (*technique, expérience*) (acquired) skill *ou* technique; (*aussi*: **~ à tisser**) (weaving) loom

métis, se [metis] *adj, nm/f* half-caste, half-breed

métrage [metʀaʒ] *nm*: **long/moyen/court ~** full-length/medium-length/short film

mètre [mɛtʀ] *nm* metre; (*règle*) (metre) rule; (*ruban*) tape measure; **métrique** *adj* metric

métro [metʀo] *nm* underground (BRIT), subway

métropole [metʀɔpɔl] *nf* (*capitale*) metropolis; (*pays*) home country

mets [mɛ] *nm* dish

metteur [metœʀ] *nm*: **~ en scène** (*Théâtre*) producer; (*Cinéma*) director

 MOT-CLÉ

mettre [mɛtʀ] *vt* **1** (*placer*) to put; **mettre en bouteille/en sac** to bottle/put in bags *ou* sacks

2 (*vêtements: revêtir*) to put on; (*: porter*) to wear; **mets ton gilet** put your cardigan on; **je ne mets plus mon manteau** I no longer wear my coat

3 (*faire fonctionner: chauffage, électricité*) to put on; (*: réveil, minuteur*) to set; (*installer: gaz, eau*) to put in, lay on; **mettre en marche** to start up

4 (*consacrer*): **mettre du temps à faire qch** to take time to do sth *ou* over sth

5 (*noter, écrire*) to say, put (down);

qu'est-ce qu'il a mis sur la carte? what did he say *ou* write on the card?; **mettez au pluriel ...** put ... into the plural

6 (*supposer*): **mettons que ...** let's suppose *ou* say that ...

7: **y mettre du sien** to pull your weight

se mettre *vi* **1** (*se placer*): **vous pouvez vous mettre là** you can sit (*ou* stand) there; **où ça se met?** where does it go?; **se mettre au lit** to get into bed; **se mettre au piano** to sit down at the piano; **se mettre de l'encre sur les doigts** to get ink on one's fingers

2 (*s'habiller*): **se mettre en maillot de bain** to get into *ou* put on a swimsuit; **n'avoir rien à se mettre** to have nothing to wear

3: **se mettre à** to begin, start; **se mettre à faire** to begin *ou* start doing *ou* to do; **se mettre au piano** to start learning the piano; **se mettre au régime** to go on a diet; **se mettre au travail/à l'étude** to get down to work/one's studies

meuble [mœbl] *nm* piece of furniture; **des ~s** furniture; **meublé** *nm* furnished flatlet (BRIT) *ou* room; **meubler** *vt* to furnish

meuf [mœf] *nf* (*fam*) woman

meugler [møgle] *vi* to low, moo

meule [møl] *nf* (*de foin, blé*) stack; (*de fromage*) round; (*à broyer*) millstone

meunier [mønje] *nm* miller

meurs *etc* [mœʀ] *vb voir* **mourir**

meurtre [mœʀtʀ] *nm* murder; **meurtrier, -ière** *adj* (*arme etc*) deadly; (*fureur, instincts*) murderous ▷ *nm/f* murderer(-eress)

meurtrir [mœʀtʀiʀ] *vt* to bruise; (*fig*) to wound

meus *etc* [mœ] *vb voir* **mouvoir**

meute [møt] *nf* pack

mexicain, e [mɛksikɛ̃, ɛn] *adj* Mexican ▷ *nm/f*: **M~, e** Mexican

Mexico [mɛksiko] *n* Mexico City

Mexique [mɛksik] *nm*: **le ~** Mexico

mi [mi] nm (Mus) E; (en chantant la gamme) **mi**; préfixe: **mi...** half(-); mid-; **à la mi-janvier** in mid-January; **à mi-jambes/corps** (up ou down) to the knees/waist; **à mi-hauteur** halfway up

miauler [mjole] vi to mew

miche [miʃ] nf round ou cob loaf

mi-chemin [miʃmɛ̃]: **à ~** adv halfway, midway

mi-clos, e [miklo, kloz] adj half-closed

micro [mikʀo] nm mike, microphone; (Inform) micro

microbe [mikʀɔb] nm germ, microbe

micro...: **micro-onde** nf: **four à micro-ondes** microwave oven; **micro-ordinateur** nm microcomputer; **microscope** nm microscope; **microscopique** adj microscopic

midi [midi] nm midday, noon; (moment du déjeuner) lunchtime; (sud) south; **à ~** at 12 (o'clock) ou midday ou noon; **le M~** the South (of France), the Midi

mie [mi] nf crumb (of the loaf)

miel [mjɛl] nm honey; **mielleux, -euse** adj (personne) unctuous, syrupy

mien, ne [mjɛ̃, mjɛn] pron: **le(la) ~(ne), les ~(ne)s** mine; **les ~s** my family

miette [mjɛt] nf (de pain, gâteau) crumb; (fig: de la conversation etc) scrap; **en ~s** in pieces ou bits

O MOT-CLÉ

mieux [mjø] adv 1 (d'une meilleure façon): **mieux (que)** better (than); **elle travaille/mange mieux** she works/eats better; **aimer mieux** to prefer; **elle va mieux** she is better; **de mieux en mieux** better and better

2 (de la meilleure façon) best; **ce que je connais le mieux** what I know best; **les livres les mieux faits** the best-made books

▷ adj 1 (plus à l'aise, en meilleure forme): **se sentir mieux** to feel better

2 (plus satisfaisant) better; **c'est mieux ainsi** it's better like this; **c'est le mieux des deux** it's the better of the two; **le(la) mieux, les mieux** the best; **demandez-lui, c'est le mieux** ask him, it's the best thing

3 (plus joli) better-looking; **il est mieux que son frère** (plus beau) he's better-looking than his brother; (plus gentil) he's nicer than his brother; **il est mieux sans moustache** he looks better without a moustache

4: **au mieux** at best; **au mieux avec** on the best of terms with; **pour le mieux** for the best

▷ nm 1 (progrès) improvement

2: **de mon/ton mieux** as best I/you can (ou could); **faire de son mieux** to do one's best

mignon, ne [miɲɔ̃, ɔn] adj sweet, cute

migraine [migʀɛn] nf headache; (Méd) migraine

mijoter [miʒɔte] vt to simmer; (préparer avec soin) to cook lovingly; (fam: tramer) to plot, cook up ▷ vi to simmer

milieu, x [miljø] nm (centre) middle; (Bio, Géo) environment; (entourage social) milieu; (provenance) background; (pègre): **le ~** the underworld; **au ~ de** in the middle of; **au beau** ou **en plein ~ (de)** right in the middle (of); **un juste ~** a happy medium

militaire [militɛʀ] adj military, army cpd ▷ nm serviceman

militant, e [militɑ̃, ɑ̃t] adj, nm/f militant

militer [milite] vi to be a militant

mille [mil] num a ou one thousand ▷ nm (mesure): **~ (marin)** nautical mile; **mettre dans le ~** (fig) to be bang on target; **millefeuille** nm cream ou vanilla slice; **millénaire** nm millennium ▷ adj thousand-year-old; (fig) ancient; **mille-pattes** nm inv centipede

millet [mijɛ] nm millet

milliard [miljaʀ] nm milliard, thousand million (BRIT), billion (US); **milliardaire** nm/f multimillionaire

(_BRIT_), billionaire (_US_)

millier [milje] _nm_ thousand; **un ~ (de)** a thousand or so, about a thousand; **par ~s** in (their) thousands, by the thousand

milligramme [miligʀam] _nm_ milligramme

millimètre [milimɛtʀ] _nm_ millimetre

million [miljɔ̃] _nm_ million; **deux ~s de** two million; **millionnaire** _nm/f_ millionaire

mime [mim] _nm/f_ (_acteur_) mime(r) ▷ _nm_ (_art_) mime, miming; **mimer** _vt_ to mime; (_singer_) to mimic, take off

minable [minabl] _adj_ (_décrépit_) shabby(-looking); (_médiocre_) pathetic

mince [mɛ̃s] _adj_ thin; (_personne, taille_) slim, slender; (_fig: profit, connaissances_) slight, small, weak ▷ _excl_ **~ alors!** drat it!, darn it! (_US_); **minceur** _nf_ thinness; (_d'une personne_) slimness, slenderness; **mincir** _vi_ to get slimmer

mine [min] _nf_ (_physionomie_) expression, look; (_allure_) exterior, appearance; (_de crayon_) lead; (_gisement, explosif, fig: source_) mine; **avoir bonne ~** (_personne_) to look well; (_ironique_) to look an utter idiot; **avoir mauvaise ~** to look unwell _ou_ poorly; **faire ~ de faire** to make a pretence of doing; **~ de rien** although you wouldn't think so

miner [mine] _vt_ (_saper_) to undermine, erode; (_Mil_) to mine

minerai [minʀɛ] _nm_ ore

minéral, e, -aux [mineʀal, o] _adj, nm_ mineral

minéralogique [mineʀalɔʒik] _adj_: **plaque ~** number (_BRIT_) _ou_ license (_US_) plate; **numéro ~** registration (_BRIT_) _ou_ license (_US_) number

minet, te [minɛ, ɛt] _nm/f_ (_chat_) pussy-cat; (_péj_) young trendy

mineur, e [minœʀ] _adj_ minor ▷ _nm/f_ (_Jur_) minor, person under age ▷ _nm_ (_travailleur_) miner

miniature [minjatyʀ] _adj, nf_ miniature

minibus [minibys] _nm_ minibus

minier, -ière [minje, jɛʀ] _adj_ mining

mini-jupe [miniʒyp] _nf_ mini-skirt

minime [minim] _adj_ minor, minimal

minimessage [minimesaʒ] _nm_ text message

minimiser [minimize] _vt_ to minimize; (_fig_) to play down

minimum [minimɔm] _adj, nm_ minimum; **au ~** (_au moins_) at the very least

ministère [ministɛʀ] _nm_ (_aussi Rel_) ministry; (_cabinet_) government

ministre [ministʀ] _nm_ (_aussi Rel_) minister; **ministre d'État** senior minister _ou_ secretary

Minitel® [minitɛl] _nm_ videotext terminal and service

- **MINITEL®**
-
- **Minitel®** is a public information
- system provided by France-Télécom
- to telephone subscribers since
- the early 80s. Among the services
- available are a computerized
- telephone directory and information
- on travel timetables, stock-market
- news and situations vacant.
- Subscribers pay for their time on
- screen as part of their phone bill.
- Although this information is now
- also available on the Internet, the
- special Minitel® screens, terminals
- and keyboards are still very much a
- part of French daily life.

minoritaire [minɔʀitɛʀ] _adj_ minority

minorité [minɔʀite] _nf_ minority; **être en ~** to be in the _ou_ a minority

minuit [minɥi] _nm_ midnight

minuscule [minyskyl] _adj_ minute, tiny ▷ _nf_: **(lettre) ~** small letter

minute [minyt] _nf_ minute; **à la ~** (_just this instant_); (_faire_) there and then; **minuter** _vt_ to time; **minuterie** _nf_ time switch

minutieux, -euse [minysjø, jøz] _adj_ (_personne_) meticulous; (_travail_) minutely detailed

mirabelle [miʀabɛl] nf (cherry) plum

miracle [miʀakl] nm miracle

mirage [miʀaʒ] nm mirage

mire [miʀ] nf: **point de ~** (fig) focal point

miroir [miʀwaʀ] nm mirror

miroiter [miʀwate] vi to sparkle, shimmer; **faire ~ qch à qn** to paint sth in glowing colours for sb, dangle sth in front of sb's eyes

mis, e [mi, miz] pp de **mettre** ▷ adj: **bien ~** well-dressed

mise [miz] nf (argent: au jeu) stake; (tenue) clothing, attire; **être de ~** to be acceptable ou in season; **mise à jour** updating; **mise au point** (fig) clarification; **mise de fonds** capital outlay; **mise en plis** set; **mise en scène** production

miser [mize] vt (enjeu) to stake, bet; **~ sur** (cheval, numéro) to bet on; (fig) to bank ou count on

misérable [mizeʀabl] adj (lamentable, malheureux) pitiful, wretched; (pauvre) poverty-stricken; (insignifiant, mesquin) miserable ▷ nm/f wretch

misère [mizeʀ] nf (extreme) poverty, destitution; **misères** nfpl (malheurs) woes, miseries; (ennuis) little troubles; **salaire de ~** starvation wage

missile [misil] nm missile

mission [misjɔ̃] nf mission; **partir en ~** (Admin, Pol) to go on an assignment; **missionnaire** nm/f missionary

mité, e [mite] adj moth-eaten

mi-temps [mitɑ̃] nf inv (Sport: période) half; (: pause) half-time; **à ~** part-time

miteux, -euse [mitø, øz] adj (lieu) seedy

mitigé, e [mitiʒe] adj: **sentiments ~s** mixed feelings

mitoyen, ne [mitwajɛ̃, jɛn] adj (mur) common, party cpd; **maisons ~nes** semi-detached houses; (plus de deux) terraced (BRIT) ou row (US) houses

mitrailler [mitʀaje] vt to machine-gun; (fig) to pelt, bombard;

(: photographier) to take shot after shot of; **mitraillette** nf submachine gun; **mitrailleuse** nf machine gun

mi-voix [mivwa]: **à ~** adv in a low ou hushed voice

mixage [miksaʒ] nm (Cinéma) (sound) mixing

mixer [miksœʀ] nm (food) mixer

mixte [mikst] adj (gén) mixed; (Scol) mixed, coeducational; **cuisinière ~** combined gas and electric cooker (BRIT) ou stove (US)

mixture [mikstyʀ] nf mixture; (fig) concoction

Mlle (pl **~s**) abr = **Mademoiselle**

MM abr = **Messieurs**

Mme (pl **~s**) abr = **Madame**

mobile [mɔbil] adj mobile; (pièce de machine) moving ▷ nm (motif) motive; (œuvre d'art) mobile; **(téléphone) ~** mobile (phone)

mobilier, -ière [mɔbilje, jɛʀ] nm furniture

mobiliser [mɔbilize] vt to mobilize

mocassin [mɔkasɛ̃] nm moccasin

moche [mɔʃ] (fam) adj (laid) ugly; (mauvais) rotten

modalité [mɔdalite] nf form, mode

mode [mɔd] nf fashion ▷ nm (manière) form, mode; (Ling) mood; (Mus, Inform) mode; **à la ~** fashionable, in fashion; **mode d'emploi** directions pl (for use); **mode de paiement** method of payment; **mode de vie** lifestyle

modèle [mɔdɛl] adj, nm model; (qui pose: de peintre) sitter; **modèle déposé** registered design; **modèle réduit** small-scale model; **modeler** vt to model

modem [mɔdɛm] nm modem

modéré, e [mɔdeʀe] adj, nm/f moderate

modérer [mɔdeʀe] vt to moderate; **se modérer** vi to restrain o.s.

moderne [mɔdɛʀn] adj modern ▷ nm (style) modern style; (meubles) modern furniture; **moderniser** vt to modernize

modeste [mɔdɛst] adj modest;

modestie nf modesty

modifier [mɔdifje] vt to modify, alter; **se modifier** vi to alter

modique [mɔdik] adj modest

module [mɔdyl] nm module

moelle [mwal] nf marrow

moelleux, -euse [mwalø, øz] adj soft; (gâteau) light and moist

mœurs [mœʀ] nfpl (conduite) morals; (manières) manners; (pratiques sociales, mode de vie) habits

moi [mwa] pron me; (emphatique): ~, **je ...** for my part, I ..., I myself ...; **c'est ~ qui l'ai fait** I did it, it was me who did it; **apporte-le-~** bring it to me; **à ~** mine; (dans un jeu) my turn; **moi-même** pron myself; (emphatique) I myself

moindre [mwɛ̃dʀ] adj lesser; lower; **le(la) ~, les ~s** the least, the slightest; **merci — c'est la ~ des choses!** thank you — it's a pleasure!

moine [mwan] nm monk, friar

moineau, x [mwano] nm sparrow

● **MOT-CLÉ**

moins [mwɛ̃] adv **1** (comparatif): **moins (que)** less (than); **moins grand que** less tall than, not as tall as; **il a 3 ans de moins que moi** he's 3 years younger than me; **moins je travaille, mieux je me porte** the less I work, the better I feel

2 (superlatif): **le moins** (the) least; **c'est ce que j'aime le moins** it's what I like (the) least; **le(la) moins doué(e)** the least gifted; **au moins, du moins** at least; **pour le moins** at the very least

3: **moins de** (quantité) less (than); (nombre) fewer (than); **moins de sable/d'eau** less sand/water; **moins de livres/gens** fewer books/people; **moins de 2 ans** less than 2 years; **moins de midi** not yet midday

4: **de moins, en moins: 100 euros/3 jours de moins** 100 euros/3 days less; **3 livres en moins** 3 books fewer; 3 books too few; **de l'argent en moins** less money; **le soleil en moins** but for the sun, minus the sun; **de moins en moins** less and less

5: **à moins de, à moins que** unless; **à moins de faire** unless we do (ou he does etc); **à moins que tu ne fasses** unless you do; **à moins d'un accident** barring any accident

▷ prép: **4 moins 2** 4 minus 2; **il est moins 5** it's 5 to; **il fait moins 5** it's 5 (degrees) below (freezing), it's minus 5

mois [mwa] nm month

moisi [mwazi] nm mould, mildew; **odeur de ~** musty smell; **moisir** vi to go mouldy; **moisissure** nf mould no pl

moisson [mwasɔ̃] nf harvest; **moissonner** vt to harvest, reap; **moissonneuse** nf (machine) harvester

moite [mwat] adj sweaty, sticky

moitié [mwatje] nf half; **la ~** half; **la ~ de** half (of); **la ~ du temps** half the time; **à la ~ de** halfway through; **à ~** (avant le verbe) half; (avant l'adjectif) half-; **à ~ prix** (at) half-price

molaire [mɔlɛʀ] nf molar

molester [mɔlɛste] vt to manhandle, maul (about)

molle [mɔl] adj voir **mou**; **mollement** adv (péj: travailler) sluggishly; (protester) feebly

mollet [mɔlɛ] nm calf ▷ adj m: **œuf ~** soft-boiled egg

molletonné, e [mɔltɔne] adj fleece-lined

mollir [mɔliʀ] vi (fléchir) to relent; (substance) to go soft

mollusque [mɔlysk] nm mollusc

môme [mom] (fam) nm/f (enfant) brat

moment [mɔmɑ̃] nm moment; **ce n'est pas le ~** this is not the (right) time; **au même ~** at the same time; (instant) at the same moment; **pour un bon ~** for a good while; **pour le ~** for the moment, for the time being; **au ~ de** at the time of; **au ~ où** just as; **à tout ~** (peut arriver etc) at any time ou moment; (constamment) constantly, continually;

en ce ~ at the moment; at present; **sur le ~** at the time; **par ~s** now and then, at times; **d'un ~ à l'autre** any time (now); **du ~ où** ou **que** seeing that, since; **momentané, e** adj temporary, momentary; **momentanément** adv (court instant) for a short while

momie [mɔmi] nf mummy

mon, ma [mɔ̃, ma] (pl **mes**) adj my

Monaco [mɔnako] nm Monaco

monarchie [mɔnaʀʃi] nf monarchy

monastère [mɔnastɛʀ] nm monastery

mondain, e [mɔ̃dɛ̃, ɛn] adj (vie) society cpd

monde [mɔ̃d] nm world; (haute société) **le ~** (high) society; **il y a du ~** (beaucoup de gens) there are a lot of people; (quelques personnes) there are some people; **beaucoup/peu de ~** many/few people; **mettre au ~** to bring into the world; **pas le moins du ~** not in the least; **mondial, e, -aux** adj (population) world cpd; (influence) world-wide; **mondialement** adv throughout the world; **mondialisation** nf globalization

monégasque [mɔnegask] adj Monegasque, of ou from Monaco ▷ nm/f: **M~** Monegasque, person from ou inhabitant of Monaco

monétaire [mɔnetɛʀ] adj monetary

moniteur, -trice [mɔnitœʀ, tʀis] nm/f (Sport) instructor(-tress); (de colonie de vacances) supervisor ▷ nm (écran) monitor

monnaie [mɔnɛ] nf (Écon, gén: moyen d'échange) currency; (petites pièces): **avoir de la ~** to have (some) change; **une pièce de ~** a coin; **faire de la ~** to get (some) change; **avoir/faire la ~ de 20 euros** to have change of/get change for 20 euros; **rendre à qn la ~ (sur 20 euros)** to give sb the change (out of ou from 20 euros); **gardez la ~** keep the change; **désolé, je n'ai pas de ~** sorry, I don't have any change; **avez-vous de la ~?** do you have any change?

monologue [mɔnɔlɔg] nm monologue, soliloquy; **monologuer** vi to soliloquize

monopole [mɔnɔpɔl] nm monopoly

monotone [mɔnɔtɔn] adj monotonous

Monsieur [məsjø] (pl **Messieurs**) titre Mr ▷ nm (homme quelconque): **un/le monsieur** a/the gentleman; **~, ...** (en tête de lettre) Dear Sir, ...; voir aussi **Madame**

monstre [mɔ̃stʀ] nm monster ▷ adj (fam: colossal) monstrous; **un travail ~** a fantastic amount of work; **monstrueux, -euse** adj monstrous

mont [mɔ̃] nm: **par ~s et par vaux** up hill and down dale; **le Mont Blanc** Mont Blanc

montage [mɔ̃taʒ] nm (assemblage: d'appareil) assembly; (Photo) photomontage; (Cinéma) editing

montagnard, e [mɔ̃taɲaʀ, aʀd] adj mountain cpd ▷ nm/f mountain-dweller

montagne [mɔ̃taɲ] nf (cime) mountain; (région): **la ~** the mountains pl; **montagnes russes** big dipper sg, switchback sg; **montagneux, -euse** adj mountainous; (basse montagne) hilly

montant, e [mɔ̃tɑ̃, ɑ̃t] adj rising; **pull à col ~** high-necked jumper ▷ nm (somme, total) (sum) total, (total) amount; (de fenêtre) upright; (de lit) post

monte-charge [mɔ̃tʃaʀʒ] nm inv goods lift, hoist

montée [mɔ̃te] nf (des prix, hostilités) rise; (escalade) climb; (côte) hill; **au milieu de la ~** halfway up

monter [mɔ̃te] vt (escalier, côte) to go (ou come) up; (valise, paquet) to take (ou bring) up; (étagère) to raise; (tente, échafaudage) to put up; (machine) to assemble; (Cinéma) to edit; (Théâtre) to put on, stage; (société etc) to set up ▷ vi to go (ou come) up; (prix, niveau, température) to rise; **~ à cheval** (faire du cheval) to ride (a horse); **~ sur** to climb up onto; **~**

sur ou **à un arbre/une échelle** to climb (up) a tree/ladder; **se monter à** (*frais etc*) to add up to, come to

montgolfière [mɔ̃gɔlfjɛʀ] *nf* hot-air balloon

montre [mɔ̃tʀ] *nf* watch; **contre la ~** (*Sport*) against the clock

Montréal [mɔ̃ʀeal] *n* Montreal

montrer [mɔ̃tʀe] *vt* to show; **~ qch à qn** to show sb sth; **pouvez-vous me ~ où c'est?** can you show me where it is?

monture [mɔ̃tyʀ] *nf* (*cheval*) mount; (*de lunettes*) frame; (*d'une bague*) setting

monument [mɔnymɑ̃] *nm* monument; **monument aux morts** war memorial

moquer [mɔke]: **se moquer de** *vt* to make fun of, laugh at; (*fam: se désintéresser de*) not to care about; (*tromper*): **se ~ de qn** to take sb for a ride

moquette [mɔkɛt] *nf* fitted carpet

moqueur, -euse [mɔkœʀ, øz] *adj* mocking

moral, e, -aux [mɔʀal, o] *adj* moral ▷ *nm* morale; **avoir le ~** (*fam*) to be in good spirits; **avoir le ~ à zéro** (*fam*) to be really down; **morale** *nf* (*mœurs*) morals *pl*; (*valeurs*) moral standards *pl*, morality; (*d'une fable etc*) moral; **faire la morale à** to lecture, preach at; **moralité** *nf* morality; (*de fable*) moral

morceau, x [mɔʀso] *nm* piece, bit; (*d'une œuvre*) passage, extract; (*Mus*) piece; (*Culin: de viande*) cut; (*de sucre*) lump; **mettre en ~x** to pull to pieces ou bits; **manger un ~** to have a bite (to eat)

morceler [mɔʀsəle] *vt* to break up, divide up

mordant, e [mɔʀdɑ̃, ɑ̃t] *adj* (*ton, remarque*) scathing, cutting; (*ironie, froid*) biting ▷ *nm* (*style*) bite, punch

mordiller [mɔʀdije] *vt* to nibble at, chew at

mordre [mɔʀdʀ] *vt* to bite ▷ *vi* (*poisson*) to bite; **~ sur** (*fig*) to go over into, overlap into; **~ à l'hameçon** to bite, rise to the bait

mordu, e [mɔʀdy] (*fam*) *nm/f* enthusiast; **un ~ de jazz** a jazz fanatic

morfondre [mɔʀfɔ̃dʀ]: **se morfondre** *vi* to mope

morgue [mɔʀg] *nf* (*arrogance*) haughtiness; (*lieu: de la police*) morgue; (: *à l'hôpital*) mortuary

morne [mɔʀn] *adj* dismal, dreary

morose [mɔʀoz] *adj* sullen, morose

mors [mɔʀ] *nm* bit

morse [mɔʀs] *nm* (*Zool*) walrus; (*Tél*) Morse (code)

morsure [mɔʀsyʀ] *nf* bite

mort¹ [mɔʀ] *nf* death

mort², e [mɔʀ, mɔʀt] *pp de* **mourir** ▷ *adj* dead ▷ *nm/f* (*défunt*) dead man ou woman; (*victime*): **il y a eu plusieurs ~s** several people were killed, there were several killed; **~ de peur/fatigue** frightened to death/dead tired

mortalité [mɔʀtalite] *nf* mortality, death rate

mortel, le [mɔʀtɛl] *adj* (*poison etc*) deadly, lethal; (*accident, blessure*) fatal; (*silence, ennemi*) deadly; (*péché*) mortal; (*fam: ennuyeux*) deadly boring

mort-né, e [mɔʀne] *adj* (*enfant*) stillborn

mortuaire [mɔʀtɥeʀ] *adj*: **avis ~** death announcement

morue [mɔʀy] *nf* (*Zool*) cod *inv*

mosaïque [mɔzaik] *nf* mosaic

Moscou [mɔsku] *n* Moscow

mosquée [mɔske] *nf* mosque

mot [mo] *nm* word; (*message*) line, note; **~ à ~** word for word; **mot de passe** password; **mots croisés** crossword (puzzle) *sg*

motard [mɔtaʀ] *nm* biker; (*policier*) motorcycle cop

motel [mɔtɛl] *nm* motel

moteur, -trice [mɔtœʀ, tʀis] *adj* (*Anat, Physiol*) motor; (*Tech*) driving; (*Auto*): **à 4 roues motrices** 4-wheel drive ▷ *nm* engine, motor; **à ~** power-driven, motor *cpd*; **moteur de recherche** search engine

motif [mɔtif] *nm* (*cause*) motive;

(*décoratif*) design, pattern, motif; **sans ~** groundless

motivation [mɔtivasjɔ̃] *nf* motivation

motiver [mɔtive] *vt* to motivate; (*justifier*) to justify, account for

moto [mɔto] *nf* (motor)bike; **motocycliste** *nm/f* motorcyclist

motorisé, e [mɔtɔrize] *adj* (*personne*) having transport *ou* a car

motrice [mɔtris] *adj voir* **moteur**

motte [mɔt] *nf*: **~ de terre** lump of earth, clod (of earth); **motte de beurre** lump of butter

mou (mol), molle [mu, mɔl] *adj* soft; (*personne*) lethargic; (*protestations*) weak ▷ *nm*: **avoir du mou** to be slack

mouche [muʃ] *nf* fly

moucher [muʃe]: **se moucher** *vi* to blow one's nose

moucheron [muʃRɔ̃] *nm* midge

mouchoir [muʃwaR] *nm* handkerchief, hanky; **mouchoir en papier** tissue, paper hanky

moudre [mudR] *vt* to grind

moue [mu] *nf* pout; **faire la ~** to pout; (*fig*) to pull a face

mouette [mwɛt] *nf* (sea)gull

moufle [mufl] *nf* (*gant*) mitt(en)

mouillé, e [muje] *adj* wet

mouiller [muje] *vt* (*humecter*) to wet, moisten; (*tremper*): **~ qn/qch** to make sb/sth wet ▷ *vi* (*Navig*) to lie *ou* be at anchor; **se mouiller** to get wet; (*fam: prendre des risques*) to commit o.s.

moulant, e [mulɑ̃, ɑ̃t] *adj* figure-hugging

moule [mul] *nf* mussel ▷ *nm* (*Culin*) mould; **moule à gâteaux** *nm* cake tin (BRIT) *ou* pan (US)

mouler [mule] *vt* (*suj: vêtement*) to hug, fit closely round

moulin [mulɛ̃] *nm* mill; **moulin à café** coffee mill; **moulin à eau** watermill; **moulin à légumes** (vegetable) shredder; **moulin à paroles** (*fig*) chatterbox; **moulin à poivre** pepper mill; **moulin à vent** windmill

moulinet [mulinɛ] *nm* (*de canne à pêche*) reel; (*mouvement*): **faire des ~s avec qch** to whirl sth around

moulinette® [mulinɛt] *nf* (vegetable) shredder

moulu, e [muly] *pp de* **moudre**

mourant, e [murɑ̃, ɑ̃t] *adj* dying

mourir [murir] *vi* to die; (*civilisation*) to die out; **~ de froid/faim** to die of exposure/hunger; **~ de faim/d'ennui** (*fig*) to be starving/be bored to death; **~ d'envie de faire** to be dying to do

mousse [mus] *nf* (*Bot*) moss; (*de savon*) lather; (*écume: sur eau, bière*) froth, foam; (*Culin*) mousse ▷ *nm* (*Navig*) ship's boy; **mousse à raser** shaving foam

mousseline [muslin] *nf* muslin; **pommes ~** mashed potatoes

mousser [muse] *vi* (*bière, détergent*) to foam; (*savon*) to lather; **mousseux, -euse** *adj* frothy ▷ *nm*: **(vin) mousseux** sparkling wine

mousson [musɔ̃] *nf* monsoon

moustache [mustaʃ] *nf* moustache; **moustaches** *nfpl* (*du chat*) whiskers *pl*; **moustachu, e** *adj* with a moustache

moustiquaire [mustikɛr] *nf* mosquito net

moustique [mustik] *nm* mosquito

moutarde [mutard] *nf* mustard

mouton [mutɔ̃] *nm* sheep *inv*; (*peau*) sheepskin; (*Culin*) mutton

mouvement [muvmɑ̃] *nm* movement; (*fig: impulsion*) gesture; **avoir un bon ~** to make a nice gesture; **en ~** in motion; on the move; **mouvementé, e** *adj* (*vie, poursuite*) eventful; (*réunion*) turbulent

mouvoir [muvwaR]: **se mouvoir** *vi* to move

moyen, ne [mwajɛ̃, jɛn] *adj* average; (*tailles, prix*) medium; (*de grandeur moyenne*) medium-sized ▷ *nm* (*façon*) means *sg*, way; **moyens** *nmpl* (*capacités*) means; **très ~** (*résultats*) pretty poor; **je n'en ai pas les ~s** I can't afford it; **au ~ de** by means of; **par tous les ~s** by every possible means, every possible way; **par ses propres ~s** all by oneself; **moyen âge** Middle Ages pl; **moyen de transport** means of transport

moyennant [mwajɛnɑ̃] prép (somme) for; (service, conditions) in return for; (travail, effort) with

moyenne [mwajɛn] nf average; (Math) mean; (Scol) pass mark; **en ~** (an) average; **moyenne d'âge** average age

Moyen-Orient [mwajɛnɔʀjɑ̃] nm: **le ~** the Middle East

moyeu, x [mwajø] nm hub

MST sigle f (= maladie sexuellement transmissible) STD

mû, mue [my] pp de **mouvoir**

muer [mɥe] vi (oiseau, mammifère) to moult; (serpent) to slough; (jeune garçon): **il mue** his voice is breaking

muet, te [mɥɛ, mɥɛt] adj dumb; (fig): **~ d'admiration** etc speechless with admiration etc; (Cinéma) silent ▷ nm/f mute

mufle [myfl] nm muzzle; (fam: goujat) boor

mugir [myʒiʀ] vi (taureau) to bellow; (vache) to low; (fig) to howl

muguet [mygɛ] nm lily of the valley

mule [myl] nf (Zool) (she-)mule

mulet [mylɛ] nm (Zool) (he-)mule

multinationale [myltinasjɔnal] nf multinational

multiple [myltipl] adj multiple, numerous; (varié) many, manifold; **multiplication** nf multiplication; **multiplier** vt to multiply; **se multiplier** vi to multiply

municipal, e, -aux [mynisipal, o] adj (élections, stade) municipal; (conseil) town cpd; **piscine/bibliothèque ~e** public swimming pool/library; **municipalité** nf (ville) municipality; (conseil) town council

munir [myniʀ] vt: **~ qch de** to equip sth with; **se ~ de** to arm o.s. with

munitions [mynisjɔ̃] nfpl ammunition sg

mur [myʀ] nm wall; **mur du son** sound barrier

mûr, e [myʀ] adj ripe; (personne) mature

muraille [myʀaj] nf (high) wall

mural, e, -aux [myʀal, o] adj wall cpd; (art) mural

mûre [myʀ] nf blackberry

muret [myʀɛ] nm low wall

mûrir [myʀiʀ] vi (fruit, blé) to ripen; (abcès) to come to a head; (fig: idée, personne) to mature ▷ vt (projet) to nurture; (personne) to (make) mature

murmure [myʀmyʀ] nm murmur; **murmurer** vi to murmur

muscade [myskad] nf (aussi: **noix (de) ~**) nutmeg

muscat [myska] nm (raisins) muscat grape; (vin) muscatel (wine)

muscle [myskl] nm muscle; **musclé, e** adj muscular; (fig) strong-arm

museau, x [myzo] nm muzzle; (Culin) brawn

musée [myze] nm museum; (de peinture) art gallery

museler [myz(ə)le] vt to muzzle; **muselière** nf muzzle

musette [myzɛt] nf (sac) lunchbag

musical, e, -aux [myzikal, o] adj musical

music-hall [myzikol] nm (salle) variety theatre; (genre) variety

musicien, ne [myzisjɛ̃, jɛn] adj musical ▷ nm/f musician

musique [myzik] nf music

● **FÊTE DE LA MUSIQUE**
●
● The **Fête de la Musique** is a music
● festival which takes place every year
● on 21 June. Throughout France, local
● musicians perform free of charge in
● parks, streets and squares.

musulman, e [myzylmɑ̃, an] adj, nm/f Moslem, Muslim

mutation [mytasjɔ̃] nf (Admin) transfer

muter [myte] vt to transfer, move

mutilé, e [mytile] nm/f disabled

person (through loss of limbs)

nutiler [mytile] *vt* to mutilate, maim

nutin, e [mytɛ̃, in] *adj* (*air, ton*) mischievous, impish ▷ *nm/f* (*Mil, Navig*) mutineer; **mutinerie** *nf* mutiny

nutisme [mytism] *nm* silence

nutuel, le [mytyɛl] *adj* mutual; **mutuelle** *nf* voluntary insurance premiums for back-up health cover

nyope [mjɔp] *adj* short-sighted

nyosotis [mjɔzɔtis] *nm* forget-me-not

nyrtille [miʀtij] *nf* bilberry

nystère [mistɛʀ] *nm* mystery; **mystérieux, -euse** *adj* mysterious

nystifier [mistifje] *vt* to fool

nythe [mit] *nm* myth

nythologie [mitɔlɔʒi] *nf* mythology

n' [n] *adv voir* **ne**

nacre [nakʀ] *nf* mother of pearl

nage [naʒ] *nf* swimming; (*manière*) style of swimming, stroke; **traverser/s'éloigner à la ~** to swim across/away; **en ~** bathed in sweat; **nageoire** *nf* fin; **nager** *vi* to swim; **nageur, -euse** *nm/f* swimmer

naïf, -ïve [naif, naiv] *adj* naïve

nain, e [nɛ̃, nɛn] *nm/f* dwarf

naissance [nɛsɑ̃s] *nf* birth; **donner ~ à** to give birth to; (*fig*) to give rise to; **lieu de ~** place of birth

naître [nɛtʀ] *vi* to be born; (*fig*): **~ de** to arise from, be born out of; **il est né en 1960** he was born in 1960; **faire ~** (*fig*) to give rise to, arouse

naïveté [naivte] *nf* naïvety

nana [nana] (*fam*) *nf* (*fille*) chick, bird (*BRIT*)

nappe [nap] *nf* tablecloth; (*de pétrole, gaz*) layer; **napperon** *nm* table-mat

naquit *etc* [naki] *vb voir* **naître**

narguer [naʀge] *vt* to taunt

narine [naʀin] nf nostril

natal, e [natal] adj native; **natalité** nf birth rate

natation [natasjɔ̃] nf swimming

natif, -ive [natif, iv] adj native

nation [nasjɔ̃] nf nation; **national, e, -aux** adj national; **nationale** nf: **(route) nationale** ≈ A road (BRIT), ≈ state highway (US); **nationaliser** vt to nationalize; **nationalisme** nm nationalism; **nationalité** nf nationality

natte [nat] nf (cheveux) plait; (tapis) mat

naturaliser [natyʀalize] vt to naturalize

nature [natyʀ] nf nature ▷ adj, adv (Culin) plain, without seasoning or sweetening; (café, thé) black, without sugar; (yaourt) natural; **payer en ~** to pay in kind; **nature morte** still life; **naturel, le** adj (gén, aussi enfant) natural ▷ nm (absence d'affectation) naturalness; (caractère) disposition, nature; **naturellement** adv naturally; (bien sûr) of course

naufrage [nofʀaʒ] nm (ship)wreck; **faire ~** to be shipwrecked

nausée [noze] nf nausea; **avoir la ~** to feel sick

nautique [notik] adj nautical, water cpd; **sports ~s** water sports

naval, e [naval] adj naval; (industrie) shipbuilding

navet [navε] nm turnip; (péj: film) rubbishy film

navette [navεt] nf shuttle; **faire la ~ (entre)** to go to and fro ou shuttle (between)

navigateur [navigatœʀ] nm (Navig) seafarer; (Inform) browser

navigation [navigasjɔ̃] nf navigation, sailing

naviguer [navige] vi to navigate, sail; **~ sur Internet** to browse the Internet

navire [naviʀ] nm ship

navrer [navʀe] vt to upset, distress; **je suis navré** I'm so sorry

ne, n' [n(ə)] adv voir **pas**; **plus**; **jamais** etc; (sans valeur négative: non traduit): **c'est plus loin que je ne le croyais** it's further than I thought

né, e [ne] pp (voir naître): **né en 1960** born in 1960; **née Scott** née Scott

néanmoins [neɑ̃mwɛ̃] adv nevertheless

néant [neɑ̃] nm nothingness; **réduire à ~** to bring to nought; (espoir) to dash

nécessaire [neseseʀ] adj necessary ▷ nm necessary; (sac) kit; **je vais faire le ~** I'll see to it; **nécessaire de couture** sewing kit; **nécessaire de toilette** toilet bag; **nécessité** nf necessity; **nécessiter** vt to require

nectar [nɛktaʀ] nm nectar

néerlandais, e [neɛʀlɑ̃dɛ, ɛz] adj Dutch

nef [nɛf] nf (d'église) nave

néfaste [nefast] adj (nuisible) harmful; (funeste) ill-fated

négatif, -ive [negatif, iv] adj negative ▷ nm (Photo) negative

négligé, e [negliʒe] adj (en désordre) slovenly ▷ nm (tenue) negligee

négligeable [negliʒabl] adj negligible

négligent, e [negliʒɑ̃, ɑ̃t] adj careless, negligent

négliger [negliʒe] vt (tenue) to be careless about; (avis, précautions) to disregard; (épouse, jardin) to neglect; **~ de faire** to fail to do, not bother to do

négociant, e [negosjɑ̃, jɑ̃t] nm/f merchant

négociation [negosjasjɔ̃] nf negotiation

négocier [negosje] vi, vt to negotiate

nègre [nɛgʀ] (péj) nm (écrivain) ghost (writer)

neige [nɛʒ] nf snow; **neiger** vi to snow

nénuphar [nenyfaʀ] nm water-lily

néon [neɔ̃] nm neon

néo-zélandais, e [neozelɑ̃dɛ, ɛz] adj New Zealand cpd ▷ nm/f: **Néo-Zélandais, e** New Zealander

Népal [nepal] nm: **le ~** Nepal

nerf [nɛʀ] nm nerve; **être sur les ~s**

to be all keyed up; **nerveux, -euse**
adj nervous; (irritable) touchy, nervy;
(voiture) nippy, responsive; **nervosité**
nf excitability, tenseness; (irritabilité
passagère) irritability, nerviness

n'est-ce pas? [nɛspɑ] adv isn't it?,
won't you? etc, selon le verbe qui précède
Net [nɛt] nm (Internet): **le ~** the Net
net, nette [nɛt] adj (sans équivoque,
distinct) clear; (évident: amélioration,
différence) marked, distinct; (propre)
neat, clean; (Comm: prix, salaire) net
▷ adv (refuser) flatly ▷ nm: **mettre au ~**
to copy out; **s'arrêter ~** to stop dead;
nettement adv clearly, distinctly;
(incontestablement) decidedly; **netteté**
nf clearness
nettoyage [netwajaʒ] nm cleaning;
nettoyage à sec dry cleaning
nettoyer [netwaje] vt to clean
neuf¹ [nœf] num nine
neuf², neuve [nœf, nœv] adj new;
remettre à ~ to do up (as good as new),
refurbish; **quoi de ~?** what's new?
neutre [nøtʀ] adj neutral; (Ling) neuter
neuve [nœv] adj voir **neuf²**
neuvième [nœvjɛm] num ninth
neveu, x [n(ə)vø] nm nephew
New York [njujɔʀk] n New York
nez [ne] nm nose; **~ à ~ avec** face to face
with; **avoir du ~** to have flair
ni [ni] conj: **ni ... ni** neither ... nor; **je
n'aime ni les lentilles ni les épinards**
I like neither lentils nor spinach; **il n'a
dit ni oui ni non** he didn't say either yes
or no; **elles ne sont venues ni l'une
ni l'autre** neither of them came; **il n'a
rien vu ni entendu** he didn't see or
hear anything
niche [niʃ] nf (du chien) kennel; (de mur)
recess, niche; **nicher** vi to nest
nid [ni] nm nest; **nid de poule** pothole
nièce [njɛs] nf niece
nier [nje] vt to deny
Nil [nil] nm: **le ~** the Nile
n'importe [nɛ̃pɔʀt] adv: **n'importe
qui/quoi/où** anybody/anything/
anywhere; **n'importe quand** any time;

n'importe quel/quelle any; **n'importe
lequel/laquelle** any (one); **n'importe
comment** (sans soin) carelessly
niveau, x [nivo] nm level; (des élèves,
études) standard; **niveau de vie**
standard of living
niveler [niv(ə)le] vt to level
noble [nɔbl] adj noble; **noblesse** nf
nobility; (d'une action etc) nobleness
noce [nɔs] nf wedding; (gens) wedding
party (ou guests pl); **faire la ~** (fam) to
go on a binge; **noces d'argent/d'or/de
diamant** silver/golden/diamond
wedding (anniversary)
nocif, -ive [nɔsif, iv] adj harmful
nocturne [nɔktyʀn] adj nocturnal ▷ nf
late-night opening
Noël [nɔɛl] nm Christmas
nœud [nø] nm knot; (ruban) bow; **nœud
papillon** bow tie
noir, e [nwaʀ] adj black; (obscur, sombre)
dark ▷ nm/f black man/woman ▷ nm:
dans le ~ in the dark; **travail au ~**
moonlighting; **travailler au ~** to work
on the side; **noircir** vt, vi to blacken;
noire nf (Mus) crotchet (BRIT), quarter
note (US)
noisette [nwazɛt] nf hazelnut
noix [nwa] nf walnut; (Culin): **une ~ de
beurre** a knob of butter; **à la ~** (fam)
worthless; **noix de cajou** cashew nut;
noix de coco coconut; **noix muscade**
nutmeg
nom [nɔ̃] nm name; (Ling) noun; **nom
de famille** surname; **nom de jeune
fille** maiden name
nomade [nɔmad] nm/f nomad
nombre [nɔ̃bʀ] nm number; **venir en
~** to come in large numbers; **depuis ~
d'années** for many years; **au ~ de
mes amis** among my friends;
nombreux, -euse adj many,
numerous; (avec nom sg: foule etc)
large; **peu nombreux** few; **de
nombreux cas** many cases
nombril [nɔ̃bʀi(l)] nm navel
nommer [nɔme] vt to name; (élire) to
appoint, nominate; **se nommer**; **il se**

nomme Pascal his name's Pascal, he's called Pascal

non [nɔ̃] adv (réponse) no; (avec loin, sans, seulement) not; **~ (pas) que** not that; **moi ~ plus** neither do I, I don't either; **c'est bon ~?** (exprimant le doute) it's good, isn't it?; **je pense que ~** I don't think so

non alcoolisé, e [nɔ̃alkɔlize] adj non alcoholic

nonchalant, e [nɔ̃ʃalɑ̃, ɑ̃t] adj nonchalant

non-fumeur, -euse [nɔ̃fymœr, øz] nm/f non-smoker

non-sens [nɔ̃sɑ̃s] nm absurdity

nord [nɔr] nm North ▷ adj northern; north; **au ~** (situation) in the north; (direction) to the north; **au ~ de** (to the) north of; **nord-africain, e** adj North-African ▷ nm/f: **Nord-Africain, e** North African; **nord-est** nm North-East; **nord-ouest** nm North-West

normal, e, -aux [nɔrmal, o] adj normal; **c'est tout à fait ~** it's perfectly natural; **vous trouvez ça ~?** does it seem right to you?; **normale** nf: **la normale** the norm, the average; **normalement** adv (en général) normally

normand, e [nɔrmɑ̃, ɑ̃d] adj of Normandy ▷ nm/f: **N~, e** (de Normandie) Norman

Normandie [nɔrmɑ̃di] nf Normandy

norme [nɔrm] nf norm; (Tech) standard

Norvège [nɔrvɛʒ] nf Norway; **norvégien, ne** adj Norwegian ▷ nm/f: **Norvégien, ne** Norwegian ▷ nm (Ling) Norwegian

nos [no] adj voir **notre**

nostalgie [nɔstalʒi] nf nostalgia; **nostalgique** adj nostalgic

notable [nɔtabl] adj (fait) notable, noteworthy; (marqué) noticeable, marked ▷ nm prominent citizen

notaire [nɔtɛr] nm solicitor

notamment [nɔtamɑ̃] adv in particular, among others

note [nɔt] nf (écrite, Mus) note; (Scol) mark (BRIT), grade; (facture) bill; **note de service** memorandum

noter [nɔte] vt (écrire) to write down; (remarquer) to note, notice; (devoir) to mark, grade

notice [nɔtis] nf summary, short article; (brochure) leaflet, instruction book

notifier [nɔtifje] vt: **~ qch à qn** to notify sb of sth, notify sth to sb

notion [nosjɔ̃] nf notion, idea

notoire [nɔtwar] adj widely known; (en mal) notorious

notre [nɔtr] (pl nos) adj our

nôtre [notr] pron: **le ~, la ~, les ~s** ours ▷ adj ours; **les ~s** ours; (alliés etc) our own people; **soyez des ~s** join us

nouer [nwe] vt to tie, knot; (fig: alliance etc) to strike up

noueux, -euse [nwø, øz] adj gnarled

nourrice [nuris] nf (gardienne) child-minder

nourrir [nurir] vt to feed; (fig: espoir) to harbour, nurse; **nourrissant, e** adj nourishing, nutritious; **nourrisson** nm (unweaned) infant; **nourriture** nf food

nous [nu] pron (sujet) we; (objet) us; **nous-mêmes** pron ourselves

nouveau (nouvel), -elle, x [nuvo, nuvɛl] adj new ▷ nm: **y a-t-il du nouveau?** is there anything new on this? ▷ nm/f new pupil (ou employee); **de nouveau, à nouveau** again; **nouveau venu, nouvelle venue** newcomer; **nouveaux mariés** newly-weds; **nouveau-né, e** nm/f newborn baby; **nouveauté** nf novelty; (objet) new thing ou article

nouvel [nuvɛl] adj voir **nouveau**; **Nouvel An** New Year

nouvelle [nuvɛl] adj voir **nouveau** ▷ n (piece of) news sg; (Littérature) short story; **les ~s** (Presse, TV) the news; **je suis sans ~s de lui** I haven't heard from him; **Nouvelle-Calédonie** nf New Caledonia; **Nouvelle-Zélande** nf New Zealand

novembre [nɔvɑ̃bʀ] *nm* November

- **NOVEMBRE**
-
-
- **Le 11 novembre** is a public holiday in
- France commemorating the signing
- of the armistice, near Compiègne, at
- the end of World War I.

noyade [nwajad] *nf* drowning *no pl*
noyau, x [nwajo] *nm* (*de fruit*) stone;
(*Bio, Physique*) nucleus; (*fig: centre*) core
noyer [nwaje] *nm* walnut (tree); (*bois*)
walnut ▷ *vt* to drown; (*moteur*) to flood;
se noyer *vi* to be drowned, drown;
(*suicide*) to drown o.s.
nu, e [ny] *adj* naked; (*membres*) naked,
bare; (*pieds, mains, chambre, fil électrique*)
bare ▷ *nm* (*Art*) nude; **tout nu** stark
naked; **se mettre nu** to strip
nuage [nɥaʒ] *nm* cloud; **nuageux,**
-euse *adj* cloudy
nuance [nɥɑ̃s] *nf* (*de couleur, sens*)
shade; **il y a une ~ (entre)** there's a
slight difference (between); **nuancer**
vt (*opinion*) to bring some reservations
ou qualifications to
nucléaire [nykleeʀ] *adj* nuclear ▷ *nm*:
le ~ nuclear energy
nudiste [nydist] *nm/f* nudist
nuée [nɥe] *nf*: **une ~ de** a cloud *ou* host
ou swarm of
nuire [nɥiʀ] *vi* to be harmful; **~ à** to
harm, do damage to; **nuisible** *adj*
harmful; **animal nuisible** pest
nuit [nɥi] *nf* night; **il fait ~** it's dark;
cette ~ (*hier*) last night; (*aujourd'hui*)
tonight; **de ~** (*vol, service*) night *cpd*;
nuit blanche sleepless night
nul, nulle [nyl] *adj* (*aucun*) no; (*minime*)
nil, non-existent; (*non valable*) null; (*péj*):
être ~ (en) to be useless *ou* hopeless
(at) ▷ *pron* none, no one; **match** *ou*
résultat ~ draw; **~le part** nowhere;
nullement *adv* by no means
numérique [nymeʀik] *adj* numerical;
(*affichage, son, télévision*) digital
numéro [nymeʀo] *nm* number;
(*spectacle*) act, turn; (*Presse*) issue,
number; **numéro de téléphone**
(tele)phone number; **numéro vert**
≈ freefone® number (*BRIT*), ≈ toll-free
number (*US*); **numéroter** *vt* to number
nuque [nyk] *nf* nape of the neck
nu-tête [nytɛt] *adj inv, adv* bareheaded
nutritif, -ive [nytʀitif, iv] *adj* (*besoins,*
valeur) nutritional; (*nourrissant*)
nutritious
nylon [nilɔ̃] *nm* nylon

oasis[ɔazis] *nf* oasis
obéir[ɔbeiʀ] *vi* to obey; **~ à** to obey;
obéissance *nf* obedience;
obéissant, e *adj* obedient
obèse[ɔbɛz] *adj* obese; **obésité** *nf*
obesity
objecter[ɔbʒɛkte] *vt*: **~ que** to object
that; **objecteur** *nm*: **objecteur de
conscience** conscientious objector
objectif, -ive[ɔbʒɛktif, iv] *adj*
objective ▷ *nm* objective; (*Photo*) lens
sg, objective
objection[ɔbʒɛksjɔ̃] *nf* objection
objectivité[ɔbʒɛktivite] *nf* objectivity
objet[ɔbʒɛ] *nm* object; (*d'une discussion,
recherche*) subject; **être** ou **faire l'~
de** (*discussion*) to be the subject of;
(*soins*) to be given ou shown; **sans ~**
purposeless; (*craintes*) groundless;
(bureau des) ~s trouvés lost property
sg (BRIT), lost-and-found *sg* (US); **objet
d'art** objet d'art; **objets de valeur**
valuables; **objets personnels** personal
items

obligation[ɔbligasjɔ̃] *nf* obligation;
(*Comm*) bond, debenture; **obligatoire**
adj compulsory, obligatory;
obligatoirement *adv* necessarily;
(*fam: sans aucun doute*) inevitably
obliger[ɔbliʒe] *vt* (*contraindre*): **~ qn à
faire** to force ou oblige sb to do; **je suis
bien obligé (de le faire)** I have to (do it
oblique[ɔblik] *adj* oblique; **en ~**
diagonally
oblitérer[ɔblitere] *vt* (*timbre-poste*)
to cancel
obnubiler[ɔbnybile] *vt* to obsess
obscène[ɔpsɛn] *adj* obscene
obscur, e[ɔpskyʀ] *adj* dark; (*méconnu*)
obscure; **obscurcir** *vt* to darken; (*fig*)
to obscure; **s'obscurcir** *vi* to grow
dark; **obscurité** *nf* darkness; **dans
l'obscurité** in the dark, in darkness
obsédé, e[ɔpsede] *nm/f*: **un ~ de jazz** a
jazz fanatic; **obsédé sexuel** sex maniac
obséder[ɔpsede] *vt* to obsess, haunt
obsèques[ɔpsɛk] *nfpl* funeral *sg*
observateur, -trice[ɔpsɛʀvatœʀ,
tʀis] *adj* observant, perceptive ▷ *nm/f*
observer
observation[ɔpsɛʀvasjɔ̃] *nf*
observation; (*d'un règlement etc*)
observance; (*reproche*) reproof; **être en
~** (*Méd*) to be under observation
observatoire[ɔpsɛʀvatwaʀ] *nm*
observatory
observer[ɔpsɛʀve] *vt* (*regarder*) to
observe, watch; (*scientifiquement; aussi
règlement etc*) to observe; (*surveiller*) to
watch; (*remarquer*) to observe, notice;
faire ~ qch à qn (*dire*) to point out
sth to sb
obsession[ɔpsesjɔ̃] *nf* obsession
obstacle[ɔpstakl] *nm* obstacle;
(*Équitation*) jump, hurdle; **faire ~ à**
(*projet*) to hinder, put obstacles in
the path of
obstiné, e[ɔpstine] *adj* obstinate
obstiner[ɔpstine]: **s'obstiner** *vi* to
insist, dig one's heels in; **s'~ à faire** to
persist (obstinately) in doing
obstruer[ɔpstʀye] *vt* to block,

obstruct

btenir [ɔptənir] vt to obtain, get; (résultat) to achieve, obtain; **~ de pouvoir faire** to obtain permission to do

bturateur [ɔptyratœr] nm (Photo) shutter

bus [ɔby] nm shell

ccasion [ɔkazjɔ̃] nf (aubaine, possibilité) opportunity; (circonstance) occasion; (Comm: article non neuf) secondhand buy; (: acquisition avantageuse) bargain; **à plusieurs ~s** on several occasions; **à l'~** sometimes, on occasions; **d'~** secondhand; **occasionnel, le** adj (non régulier) occasional

ccasionner [ɔkazjɔne] vt to cause

ccident [ɔksidɑ̃] nm: **l'O~** the West; **occidental, e, -aux** adj western; (Pol) Western ▷ nm/f Westerner

ccupation [ɔkypasjɔ̃] nf occupation

ccupé, e [ɔkype] adj (personne) busy; (place, sièges) taken; (toilettes) engaged; (Mil, Pol) occupied; **la ligne est ~e** the line's engaged (BRIT) ou busy (US)

ccuper [ɔkype] vt to occupy; (poste) to hold; **s'occuper de** (être responsable de) to be in charge of; (se charger de: affaire) to take charge of, deal with; (: clients etc) to attend to; **s'~ (à qch)** to occupy o.s. ou keep o.s. busy (with sth)

ccurrence [ɔkyrɑ̃s] nf: **en l'~** in this case

céan [ɔseɑ̃] nm ocean

ctet [ɔktɛ] nm byte

ctobre [ɔktɔbr] nm October

culiste [ɔkylist] nm/f eye specialist

deur [ɔdœr] nf smell

dieux, -euse [ɔdjø, jøz] adj hateful

dorant, e [ɔdɔrɑ̃, ɑ̃t] adj sweet-smelling, fragrant

dorat [ɔdɔra] nm (sense of) smell

eil [œj] (pl **yeux**) nm eye; **avoir un ~ au beurre noir** ou **poché** to have a black eye; **à l'~** (fam) for free; **à l'~ nu** with the naked eye; **ouvrir l'~** (fig) to keep one's eyes open ou an eye out; **fermer**

les yeux (sur) (fig) to turn a blind eye (to); **les yeux fermés** (aussi fig) with one's eyes shut

œillères [œjɛr] nfpl blinkers (BRIT), blinders (US)

œillet [œjɛ] nm (Bot) carnation

œuf [œf, pl ø] nm egg; **œuf à la coque** boiled egg; **œuf au plat** fried egg; **œuf dur** hard-boiled egg; **œuf de Pâques** Easter egg; **œufs brouillés** scrambled eggs

œuvre [œvr] nf (tâche) task, undertaking; (livre, tableau etc) work; (ensemble de la production artistique) works pl ▷ nm (Constr): **le gros ~** the shell; **mettre en ~** (moyens) to make use of; **œuvre de bienfaisance** charity; **œuvre d'art** work of art

offense [ɔfɑ̃s] nf insult; **offenser** vt to offend, hurt; **s'offenser de qch** to take offence (BRIT) ou offense (US) at sth

offert, e [ɔfɛr, ɛrt] pp de **offrir**

office [ɔfis] nm (agence) bureau, agency; (Rel) service ▷ nm ou nf (pièce) pantry; **faire ~ de** to act as; **d'~** automatically; **office du tourisme** tourist bureau

officiel, le [ɔfisjɛl] adj, nm/f official

officier [ɔfisje] nm officer

officieux, -euse [ɔfisjø, jøz] adj unofficial

offrande [ɔfrɑ̃d] nf offering

offre [ɔfr] nf offer; (aux enchères) bid; (Admin: soumission) tender; (Écon): **l'~ et la demande** supply and demand; **"~s d'emploi"** "situations vacant"; **offre d'emploi** job advertised; **offre publique d'achat** takeover bid

offrir [ɔfrir] vt: **~ (à qn)** to offer (to sb); (faire cadeau de) to give (to sb); **s'offrir** vt (vacances, voiture) to treat o.s. to; **~ (à qn) de faire qch** to offer to do sth (for sb); **~ à boire à qn** (chez soi) to offer sb a drink; **je vous offre un verre** I'll buy you a drink

OGM sigle m (= organisme génétiquement modifié) GMO

oie [wa] nf (Zool) goose

oignon [ɔɲɔ̃] nm onion; (de tulipe

etc) bulb

oiseau, x [wazo] *nm* bird; **oiseau de proie** bird of prey

oisif, -ive [wazif, iv] *adj* idle

oléoduc [ɔleɔdyk] *nm* (oil) pipeline

olive [ɔliv] *nf* (*Bot*) olive; **olivier** *nm* olive (tree)

OLP *sigle f* (= *Organisation de libération de la Palestine*) PLO

olympique [ɔlɛ̃pik] *adj* Olympic

ombragé, e [ɔ̃braʒe] *adj* shaded, shady

ombre [ɔ̃br] *nf* (*espace non ensoleillé*) shade; (*ombre portée, tache*) shadow; **à l'~** in the shade; **dans l'~** (*fig*) in the dark; **ombre à paupières** eyeshadow

omelette [ɔmlɛt] *nf* omelette; **omelette norvégienne** baked Alaska

omettre [ɔmɛtr] *vt* to omit, leave out

omoplate [ɔmɔplat] *nf* shoulder blade

⭘ **MOT-CLÉ**

on [ɔ̃] *pron* **1** (*indéterminé*) you, one; **on peut le faire ainsi** you *ou* one can do it like this, it can be done like this

2 (*quelqu'un*): **on les a attaqués** they were attacked; **on vous demande au téléphone** there's a phone call for you, you're wanted on the phone

3 (*nous*) we; **on va y aller demain** we're going tomorrow

4 (*les gens*) they; **autrefois, on croyait ...** they used to believe ...

5: **on ne peut plus** *adv*: **on ne peut plus stupide** as stupid as can be

oncle [ɔ̃kl] *nm* uncle

onctueux, -euse [ɔ̃ktɥø, øz] *adj* creamy, smooth

onde [ɔ̃d] *nf* wave; **~s courtes/ moyennes** short/medium wave *sg*; **grandes ~s** long wave *sg*

ondée [ɔ̃de] *nf* shower

on-dit [ɔ̃di] *nm inv* rumour

onduler [ɔ̃dyle] *vi* to undulate; (*cheveux*) to wave

onéreux, -euse [ɔnerø, øz] *adj* costly

ongle [ɔ̃gl] *nm* nail

ont [ɔ̃] *vb voir* **avoir**

ONU *sigle f* (= *Organisation des Nations Unies*) UN

onze [ɔ̃z] *num* eleven; **onzième** *num* eleventh

OPA *sigle f* = **offre publique d'achat**

opaque [ɔpak] *adj* opaque

opéra [ɔpera] *nm* opera; (*édifice*) opera house

opérateur, -trice [ɔperatœr, tris] *nm/f* operator; **opérateur (de prise de vues)** cameraman

opération [ɔperasjɔ̃] *nf* operation; (*Comm*) dealing

opératoire [ɔperatwar] *adj* (*choc etc*) post-operative

opérer [ɔpere] *vt* (*personne*) to operate on; (*faire, exécuter*) to carry out, make ▷ *vi* (*remède: faire effet*) to act, work; (*Méd*) to operate; **s'opérer** *vi* (*avoir lieu* to occur, take place; **se faire ~** to have an operation

opérette [ɔperɛt] *nf* operetta, light opera

opinion [ɔpinjɔ̃] *nf* opinion; **l'opinion (publique)** public opinion

opportun, e [ɔpɔrtœ̃, yn] *adj* timely, opportune; **opportuniste** *nm/f* opportunist

opposant, e [ɔpozɑ̃, ɑ̃t] *nm/f* opponent

opposé, e [ɔpoze] *adj* (*direction*) opposite; (*faction*) opposing; (*opinions, intérêts*) conflicting; (*contre*): **~ à** opposed to, against ▷ *nm*: **l'~** the other *ou* opposite side (*ou* direction); (*contraire*) the opposite; **à l'~** (*fig*) on the other hand; **à l'~ de** (*fig*) contrary to, unlike

opposer [ɔpoze] *vt* (*personnes, équipes*) to oppose; (*couleurs*) to contrast; **s'opposer** *vi* (*équipes*) to confront each other; (*opinions*) to conflict; (*couleurs, styles*) to contrast; **s'~ à** (*interdire*) to oppose; **~ qch à** (*comme obstacle, défense*) to set sth against; (*comme objection*) to put sth forward against

pposition [ɔpozisjɔ̃] nf opposition; **par ~ à** as opposed to; **entrer en ~ avec** to come into conflict with; **faire ~ à un chèque** to stop a cheque

ppressant, e [ɔpresɑ̃, ɑ̃t] adj oppressive

ppresser [ɔprese] vt to oppress; **oppression** nf oppression

pprimer [ɔprime] vt to oppress

pter [ɔpte] vi: **~ pour** to opt for

pticien, ne [ɔptisjɛ̃, jɛn] nm/f optician

ptimisme [ɔptimism] nm optimism; **optimiste** nm/f optimist ▷ adj optimistic

ption [ɔpsjɔ̃] nf option; **matière à ~** (Scol) optional subject

ptique [ɔptik] adj (nerf) optic; (verres) optical ▷ nf (fig: manière de voir) perspective

r [ɔʀ] nm gold ▷ conj now, but; **en or** (objet) gold cpd; **une affaire en or** a real bargain; **il croyait gagner or il a perdu** he was sure he would win and yet he lost

rage [ɔʀaʒ] nm (thunder)storm; **orageux, -euse** adj stormy

ral, e, -aux [ɔʀal, o] adj, nm oral; **par voie ~e** (Méd) orally

range [ɔʀɑ̃ʒ] nf orange ▷ adj inv orange; **orangé, e** adj orangey, orange-coloured; **orangeade** nf orangeade; **oranger** nm orange tree

rateur [ɔʀatœʀ] nm speaker

rbite [ɔʀbit] nf (Anat) (eye-)socket; (Physique) orbit

rcades [ɔʀkad] nfpl: **les ~** the Orkneys, the Orkney Islands

rchestre [ɔʀkɛstʀ] nm orchestra; (de jazz) band; (places) stalls pl (BRIT), orchestra (US)

rchidée [ɔʀkide] nf orchid

rdinaire [ɔʀdinɛʀ] adj ordinary; (qualité) standard; (péj: commun) common ▷ nm ordinary; (menus) everyday fare ▷ nf (essence) ≈ two-star (petrol) (BRIT), ≈ regular gas (US); **d'~** usually, normally; **comme à l'~** as usual

ordinateur [ɔʀdinatœʀ] nm computer; **ordinateur individuel** ou **personnel** personal computer; **ordinateur portable** laptop (computer)

ordonnance [ɔʀdɔnɑ̃s] nf (Méd) prescription; (Mil) orderly, batman (BRIT); **pouvez-vous me faire une ~?** can you write me a prescription?

ordonné, e [ɔʀdɔne] adj tidy, orderly

ordonner [ɔʀdɔne] vt (agencer) to organize, arrange; (donner un ordre): **~ à qn de faire** to order sb to do; (Rel) to ordain; (Méd) to prescribe

ordre [ɔʀdʀ] nm order; (propreté et soin) orderliness, tidiness; (nature): **d'~ pratique** of a practical nature; **ordres** nmpl (Rel) holy orders; **mettre en ~** to tidy (up), put in order; **par ~ alphabétique/d'importance** in alphabetical order/in order of importance; **à l'~ de qn** payable to sb; **être aux ~s de qn/sous les ~s de qn** to be at sb's disposal/under sb's command; **jusqu'à nouvel ~** until further notice; **de premier ~** first-rate; **ordre du jour** (d'une réunion) agenda; **à l'ordre du jour** (fig) topical; **ordre publique** law and order

ordure [ɔʀdyʀ] nf filth no pl; **ordures** nfpl (balayures, déchets) rubbish sg, refuse sg; **ordures ménagères** household refuse

oreille [ɔʀɛj] nf ear; **avoir de l'~** to have a good ear (for music)

oreiller [ɔʀeje] nm pillow

oreillons [ɔʀɛjɔ̃] nmpl mumps sg

ores [ɔʀ]: **d'~ et déjà** adv already

orfèvrerie [ɔʀfɛvʀəʀi] nf goldsmith's (ou silversmith's) trade; (ouvrage) gold (ou silver) plate

organe [ɔʀgan] nm organ; (porte-parole) representative, mouthpiece

organigramme [ɔʀganigʀam] nm (tableau hiérarchique) organization chart; (schéma) flow chart

organique [ɔʀganik] adj organic

organisateur, -trice [ɔʀganizatœʀ,

tris] nm/f organizer
organisation [ɔʀganizasjɔ̃] nf
organization; **Organisation des
Nations Unies** United Nations
(Organization)
organiser [ɔʀganize] vt to organize;
(mettre sur pied: service etc) to set up;
s'organiser to get organized
organisme [ɔʀganism] nm (Bio)
organism; (corps, Admin) body
organiste [ɔʀganist] nm/f organist
orgasme [ɔʀgasm] nm orgasm, climax
orge [ɔʀʒ] nf barley
orgue [ɔʀg] nm organ
orgueil [ɔʀgœj] nm pride; **orgueilleux,
-euse** adj proud
oriental, e, -aux [ɔʀjɑ̃tal, -o] adj
(langue, produit) oriental; (frontière)
eastern
orientation [ɔʀjɑ̃tasjɔ̃] nf (de
recherches) orientation; (d'une maison
etc) aspect; (d'un journal) leanings pl;
avoir le sens de l'~ to have a (good)
sense of direction; **orientation
professionnelle** careers advisory
service
orienté, e [ɔʀjɑ̃te] adj (fig: article,
journal) slanted; **bien/mal ~**
(appartement) well/badly positioned; **~
au sud** facing south, with a southern
aspect
orienter [ɔʀjɑ̃te] vt (tourner: antenne)
to direct, turn; (personne, recherches)
to direct; (fig: élève) to orientate;
s'orienter (se repérer) to find one's
bearings; **s'~ vers** (fig) to turn towards
origan [ɔʀigɑ̃] nm oregano
originaire [ɔʀiʒinɛʀ] adj: **être ~ de** to
be a native of
original, e, -aux [ɔʀiʒinal, o] adj
original; (bizarre) eccentric ▷ nm/f
eccentric ▷ nm (document etc, Art)
original
origine [ɔʀiʒin] nf origin; **origines** nfpl
(d'une personne) origins; **d'~** (pays) of
origin; **d'~ suédoise** of Swedish origin;
(pneus etc) original; **à l'~** originally;
originel, le adj original

orme [ɔʀm] nm elm
ornement [ɔʀnəmɑ̃] nm ornament
orner [ɔʀne] vt to decorate, adorn
ornière [ɔʀnjɛʀ] nf rut
orphelin, e [ɔʀfəlɛ̃, in] adj orphan(ed)
▷ nm/f orphan; **orphelin de
mère/de père** motherless/fatherless;
orphelinat nm orphanage
orteil [ɔʀtɛj] nm toe; **gros ~** big toe
orthographe [ɔʀtɔgʀaf] nf spelling
ortie [ɔʀti] nf (stinging) nettle
os [ɔs] nm bone; **os à moelle**
marrowbone
osciller [ɔsile] vi (au vent etc) to rock;
(fig): **~ entre** to waver ou fluctuate
between
osé, e [oze] adj daring, bold
oseille [ozɛj] nf sorrel
oser [oze] vi, vt to dare; **~ faire** to dare
(to) do
osier [ozje] nm willow; **d'~, en ~**
wicker(work)
osseux, -euse [ɔsø, øz] adj bony;
(tissu, maladie, greffe) bone cpd
otage [ɔtaʒ] nm hostage; **prendre qn
comme ~** to take sb hostage
OTAN sigle f (= Organisation du traité de
l'Atlantique Nord) NATO
otarie [ɔtaʀi] nf sea-lion
ôter [ote] vt to remove; (soustraire)
to take away; **~ qch à qn** to take sth
(away) from sb; **~ qch de** to remove
sth from
otite [ɔtit] nf ear infection
ou [u] conj or; **ou ... ou** either ... or; **ou
bien** or (else)

MOT-CLÉ

où [u] pron relatif **1** (position, situation)
where, that (souvent omis); **la chambre
où il était** the room (that) he was in,
the room where he was; **la ville où
je l'ai rencontré** the town where I
met him; **la pièce d'où il est sorti** the
room he came out of; **le village d'où
je viens** the village I come from; **les
villes par où il est passé** the towns he

went through
2 (*temps, état*) that (*souvent omis*); **le jour où il est parti** the day (that) he left; **au prix où c'est** at the price it is ▷ *adv* : **où est-il/va-t-il?** where is he/is he going?; **par où?** which way?; **d'où vient que ...?** how come ...?
2 (*position*) where; **je sais où il est** I know where he is; **où que l'on aille** wherever you go

ouate ['wat] *nf* cotton wool (BRIT), cotton (US)

oubli [ubli] *nm* (*acte*): **l'~ de** forgetting; (*trou de mémoire*) lapse of memory; (*négligence*) omission, oversight; **tomber dans l'~** to sink into oblivion

oublier [ublije] *vt* to forget; (*laisser quelque part: chapeau etc*) to leave behind; (*ne pas voir: erreurs etc*) to miss; **j'ai oublié ma clé/mon passeport** I've forgotten my key/passport

ouest [wɛst] *nm* west ▷ *adj inv* west; (*région*) western; **à l'~** in the west; (*direction*) (to the) west, westwards; **à l'~ de** (to the) west of

ouf ['uf] *excl* phew!

oui ['wi] *adv* yes

ouï-dire ['widiʀ]: **par ~** *adv* by hearsay

ouïe [wi] *nf* hearing; **ouïes** *nfpl* (*de poisson*) gills

ouragan [uʀagɑ̃] *nm* hurricane

ourlet [uʀlɛ] *nm* hem

ours [uʀs] *nm* bear; **ours blanc/brun** polar/brown bear; **ours (en peluche)** teddy (bear)

oursin [uʀsɛ̃] *nm* sea urchin

ourson [uʀsɔ̃] *nm* (bear-)cub

ouste [ust] *excl* hop it!

outil [uti] *nm* tool; **outiller** *vt* to equip

outrage [utʀaʒ] *nm* insult; **outrage à la pudeur** indecent conduct *no pl*

outrance [utʀɑ̃s]: **à ~** *adv* excessively, to excess

outre [utʀ] *prép* besides ▷ *adv*: **passer ~ à** to disregard, take no notice of; **en ~** besides, moreover; **~ mesure** to excess; (*manger, boire*) immoderately; **outre-Atlantique** *adv* across the Atlantic; **outre-mer** *adv* overseas

ouvert, e [uvɛʀ, ɛʀt] *pp de* ouvrir ▷ *adj* open; (*robinet, gaz etc*) on; **ouvertement** *adv* openly; **ouverture** *nf* opening; (*Mus*) overture; **heures d'ouverture** (*Comm*) opening hours; **ouverture d'esprit** open-mindedness

ouvrable [uvʀabl] *adj*: **jour ~** working day, weekday

ouvrage [uvʀaʒ] *nm* (*tâche, de tricot etc*) work *no pl*; (*texte, livre*) work

ouvre-boîte(s) [uvʀəbwat] *nm inv* tin (BRIT) *ou* can opener

ouvre-bouteille(s) [uvʀəbutɛj] *nm inv* bottle-opener

ouvreuse [uvʀøz] *nf* usherette

ouvrier, -ière [uvʀije, ijɛʀ] *nm/f* worker ▷ *adj* working-class; (*conflit*) industrial; (*mouvement*) labour *cpd*; **classe ouvrière** working class

ouvrir [uvʀiʀ] *vt* (*gén*) to open; (*brèche, passage, Méd: abcès*) to open up; (*commencer l'exploitation de, créer*) to open (up); (*eau, électricité, chauffage, robinet*) to turn on ▷ *vi* to open; to open up; **s'ouvrir** *vi* to open; **s'~ à qn** to open one's heart to sb; **est-ce ouvert au public?** is it open to the public?; **quand est-ce que le musée est ouvert?** when is the museum open?; **à quelle heure ouvrez-vous?** what time do you open?; **~ l'appétit à qn** to whet sb's appetite

ovaire [ɔvɛʀ] *nm* ovary

ovale [ɔval] *adj* oval

OVNI [ɔvni] *sigle m* (= *objet volant non identifié*) UFO

oxyder [ɔkside]: **s'oxyder** *vi* to become oxidized

oxygène [ɔksiʒɛn] *nm* oxygen

oxygéné, e [ɔksiʒene] *adj*: **eau ~e** hydrogen peroxide

ozone [ozon] *nf* ozone; **la couche d'~** the ozone layer

P

pacifique [pasifik] adj peaceful ▷ nm: **le P~, l'océan P~** the Pacific (Ocean)

pack [pak] nm pack

pacotille [pakɔtij] nf cheap junk

PACS sigle m (= pacte civil de solidarité) contract of civil partnership; **pacser**: **se pacser** vi to sign a contract of civil partnership

pacte [pakt] nm pact, treaty

pagaille [pagaj] nf mess, shambles sg

page [paʒ] nf page ▷ nm page (boy); **à la ~** (fig) up-to-date; **page d'accueil** (Inform) home page; **page Web** (Inform) web page

paiement [pɛmɑ̃] nm payment

païen, ne [pajɛ̃, pajɛn] adj, nm/f pagan, heathen

paillasson [pajasɔ̃] nm doormat

paille [paj] nf straw

pain [pɛ̃] nm (substance) bread; (unité) loaf (of bread); (morceau): **~ de savon** etc bar of soap etc; **pain au chocolat** chocolate-filled pastry; **pain aux raisins** currant bun; **pain bis/complet** brown/wholemeal (BRIT) ou wholewheat (US) bread; **pain d'épice** ≈ gingerbread; **pain de mie** sandwich loaf; **pain grillé** toast

pair, e [pɛR] adj (nombre) even ▷ nm peer; **aller de ~** to go hand in hand ou together; **jeune fille au ~** au pair; **paire** nf pair

paisible [pezibl] adj peaceful, quiet

paix [pɛ] nf peace; **faire/avoir la ~** to make/have peace; **fiche-lui la ~!** (fam) leave him alone!

Pakistan [pakistɑ̃] nm: **le ~** Pakistan

palais [palɛ] nm palace; (Anat) palate

pâle [pɑl] adj pale; **bleu ~** pale blue

Palestine [palɛstin] nf: **la ~** Palestine

palette [palɛt] nf (de peintre) palette; (produits) range

pâleur [pɑlœR] nf paleness

palier [palje] nm (d'escalier) landing; (fig) level, plateau; **par ~s** in stages

pâlir [paliR] vi to turn ou go pale; (couleur) to fade

pallier [palje] vt to offset, make up for

palme [palm] nf (de plongeur) flipper; **palmé, e** adj (pattes) webbed

palmier [palmje] nm palm tree; (gâteau) heart-shaped biscuit made of flaky pastry

pâlot, te [palo, ɔt] adj pale, peaky

palourde [paluRd] nf clam

palper [palpe] vt to feel, finger

palpitant, e [palpitɑ̃, ɑ̃t] adj thrilling

palpiter [palpite] vi (cœur, pouls) to beat; (: plus fort) to pound, throb

paludisme [palydism] nm malaria

pamphlet [pɑ̃flɛ] nm lampoon, satirical tract

pamplemousse [pɑ̃pləmus] nm grapefruit

pan [pɑ̃] nm section, piece ▷ excl bang!

panache [panaʃ] nm plume; (fig) spirit, panache

panaché, e [panaʃe] adj: **glace ~e** mixed-flavour ice cream ▷ nm (bière) shandy

pancarte [pɑ̃kaRt] nf sign, notice

pancréas [pɑ̃kReas] nm pancreas

pané, e [pane] *adj* fried in breadcrumbs
panier [panje] *nm* basket; **mettre au
~** to chuck away; **panier à provisions**
shopping basket; **panier-repas** *nm*
packed lunch
panique [panik] *nf, adj* panic;
paniquer *vi* to panic
panne [pan] *nf* breakdown; **être/
tomber en ~** to have broken down/
break down; **être en ~ d'essence** *ou*
sèche to have run out of petrol (BRIT)
ou gas (US); **ma voiture est en ~** my car
has broken down; **panne d'électricité**
ou **de courant** power cut *ou* failure
panneau, x [pano] *nm* (*écriteau*) sign,
notice; **panneau d'affichage** notice
board; **panneau de signalisation**
roadsign; **panneau indicateur**
signpost
panoplie [panɔpli] *nf* (*jouet*) outfit;
(*fig*) array
panorama [panɔrama] *nm* panorama
panse [pãs] *nf* paunch
pansement [pãsmã] *nm* dressing,
bandage; **pansement adhésif** sticking
plaster
pantacourt [pãtakur] *nm* three-
quarter length trousers *pl*
pantalon [pãtalɔ̃] *nm* trousers *pl*,
pair of trousers; **pantalon de ski** ski
pants *pl*
panthère [pãter] *nf* panther
pantin [pãtɛ̃] *nm* puppet
pantoufle [pãtufl] *nf* slipper
paon [pã] *nm* peacock
papa [papa] *nm* dad(dy)
pape [pap] *nm* pope
paperasse [papras] (*péj*) *nf* bumf
no pl, papers *pl*; **paperasserie** (*péj*)
nf paperwork *no pl*; (*tracasserie*) red
tape *no pl*
papeterie [papetri] *nf* (*magasin*)
stationer's (shop)
papi *nm* (*fam*) granddad
papier [papje] *nm* paper; (*article*)
article; **papiers** *nmpl* (*aussi*: **~s
d'identité**) (identity) papers; **papier
à lettres** writing paper, notepaper;

papier (d')aluminium aluminium
(BRIT) *ou* aluminum (US) foil, tinfoil;
papier calque tracing paper; **papier de
verre** sandpaper; **papier hygiénique**
ou **(de) toilette** toilet paper; **papier
journal** newspaper; **papier peint**
wallpaper
papillon [papijɔ̃] *nm* butterfly; (*fam*:
contravention) (parking) ticket; **papillon
de nuit** moth
papillote [papijɔt] *nf*: **en ~** cooked
in tinfoil
papoter [papɔte] *vi* to chatter
paquebot [pak(ə)bo] *nm* liner
pâquerette [pakrɛt] *nf* daisy
Pâques [pak] *nm, nfpl* Easter

paquet [pakɛ] *nm* packet; (*colis*) parcel;
(*fig*: *tas*): **~ de** pile *ou* heap of; **un ~ de
cigarettes, s'il vous plaît** a packet of
cigarettes, please; **paquet-cadeau** *nm*:
**pouvez-vous me faire un paquet-
cadeau, s'il vous plaît?** can you
gift-wrap it for me, please?
par [par] *prép* by; **finir** *etc* **~** to end *etc*
with; **~ amour** out of love; **passer ~
Lyon/la côte** to go via *ou* through
Lyons/along the coast; **~ la fenêtre**
(*jeter, regarder*) out of the window; **3 ~
jour/personne** 3 a *ou* per day/person; **2
~ 2** in twos; **~ ici** this way; (*dans le coin*)
round here; **~-ci, ~-là** here and there; **~
temps de pluie** in wet weather
parabolique [parabɔlik] *adj*: **antenne
~** parabolic *ou* dish aerial
parachute [paraʃyt] *nm* parachute;
parachutiste *nm/f* parachutist; (*Mil*)
paratrooper
parade [parad] *nf* (*spectacle, défilé*)
parade; (*Escrime, Boxe*) parry

paradis [paʀadi] nm heaven, paradise

paradoxe [paʀadɔks] nm paradox

paraffine [paʀafin] nf paraffin

parages [paʀaʒ] nmpl: **dans les ~ (de)** in the area ou vicinity (of)

paragraphe [paʀagʀaf] nm paragraph

paraître [paʀɛtʀ] vb +attrib to seem, look, appear ▷ vi to appear; (être visible) to show; (Presse, Édition) to be published, come out, appear ▷ vb impers: **il paraît que** it seems ou appears that, they say that

parallèle [paʀalɛl] adj parallel; (non officiel) unofficial ▷ nm (comparaison): **faire un ~ entre** to draw a parallel between ▷ nf parallel (line)

paralyser [paʀalize] vt to paralyse

paramédical, e, -aux [paʀamedikal, o] adj: **personnel ~** paramedics pl, paramedical workers pl

paraphrase [paʀafʀaz] nf paraphrase

parapluie [paʀaplɥi] nm umbrella

parasite [paʀazit] nm parasite; **parasites** nmpl (Tél) interference sg

parasol [paʀasɔl] nm parasol, sunshade

paratonnerre [paʀatɔnɛʀ] nm lightning conductor

parc [paʀk] nm (public) park, gardens pl; (de château etc) grounds pl; (d'enfant) playpen; **parc à thème** theme park; **parc d'attractions** amusement park; **parc de stationnement** car park

parcelle [paʀsɛl] nf fragment, scrap; (de terrain) plot, parcel

parce que [paʀsk(ə)] conj because

parchemin [paʀʃəmɛ̃] nm parchment

parc(o)mètre [paʀkmɛtʀ] nm parking meter

parcourir [paʀkuʀiʀ] vt (trajet, distance) to cover; (article, livre) to skim ou glance through; (lieu) to go all over, travel up and down; (suj: frisson) to run through

parcours [paʀkuʀ] nm (trajet) journey; (itinéraire) route

par-dessous [paʀd(ə)su] prép, adv under(neath)

pardessus [paʀdəsy] nm overcoat

par-dessus [paʀd(ə)sy] prép over (the top of) ▷ adv over (the top); **~ le marché** on top of all that; **~ tout** above all; **en avoir ~ la tête** to have had enough

par-devant [paʀd(ə)vɑ̃] adv (passer) round the front

pardon [paʀdɔ̃] nm forgiveness no pl ▷ excl sorry!; (pour interpeller etc) excuse me!; **demander ~ à qn (de)** to apologize to sb (for); **je vous demande ~** I'm sorry; (pour interpeller) excuse me; **pardonner** vt to forgive; **pardonner qch à qn** to forgive sb for sth

pare... : **pare-brise** nm inv windscreen (BRIT), windshield (US); **pare-chocs** nm inv bumper; **pare-feu** nm inv (de foyer) fireguard; (Inform) firewall

pareil, le [paʀɛj] adj (identique) the same, alike; (similaire) similar; (tel): **un courage/livre ~** such courage/a book, courage/a book like this; **de ~s livres** such books; **faire ~** to do the same (thing); **~ à** the same as; (similaire) similar to; **sans ~** unparalleled, unequalled

parent, e [paʀɑ̃, ɑ̃t] nm/f: **un(e) ~(e)** a relative ou relation; **parents** nmpl (père et mère) parents; **parenté** nf (lien) relationship

parenthèse [paʀɑ̃tɛz] nf (ponctuation) bracket, parenthesis; (digression) parenthesis, digression; **entre ~s** in brackets; (fig) incidentally

paresse [paʀɛs] nf laziness; **paresseux, -euse** adj lazy

parfait, e [paʀfɛ, ɛt] adj perfect ▷ nm (Ling) perfect (tense); **parfaitement** adv perfectly ▷ excl (most) certainly

parfois [paʀfwa] adv sometimes

parfum [paʀfœ̃] nm (produit) perfume, scent; (odeur: de fleur) scent, fragrance; (goût) flavour; **quels ~s avez-vous?** what flavours do you have?; **parfumé, e** adj (fleur, fruit) fragrant; (femme) perfumed; **parfumé au café** coffee-flavoured; **parfumer** vt (suj: odeur, bouquet) to perfume; (crème, gâteau) to flavour; **parfumerie** nf (produits) perfumes pl; (boutique) perfume shop

pari[paʀi] nm bet; **parier** vt to bet

Paris[paʀi] n Paris; **parisien, ne** adj Parisian; (Géo, Admin) Paris cpd ▷ nm/f: **Parisien, ne** Parisian

parité[paʀite] nf (Pol): ~ **hommes-femmes** balanced representation of men and women

parjure [paʀʒyʀ] nm perjury

parking [paʀkiŋ] nm (lieu) car park

Attention à ne pas traduire **parking** par le mot anglais **parking**.

parlant, e [paʀlɑ̃, ɑ̃t] adj (regard) eloquent; (Cinéma) talking

parlement [paʀləmɑ̃] nm parliament; **parlementaire** adj parliamentary ▷ nm/f member of parliament

parler [paʀle] vi to speak, talk; (avouer) to talk; ~ **(à qn) de** to talk ou speak (to sb) about; **le/en français** to speak French/in French; ~ **affaires** to talk business; **sans ~ de** (fig) not to mention, to say nothing of; **tu parles!** (fam: bien sûr) you bet!; **parlez-vous français?** do you speak French?; **je ne parle pas anglais** I don't speak English; **est-ce que je peux ~ à ...?** can I speak to ...?

parloir [paʀlwaʀ] nm (de prison, d'hôpital) visiting room

parmi [paʀmi] prép among(st)

paroi [paʀwa] nf wall; (cloison) partition

paroisse [paʀwas] nf parish

parole [paʀɔl] nf (faculté): **la ~** speech; (mot, promesse) word; **paroles** nfpl (Mus) words, lyrics; **tenir ~** to keep one's word; **prendre la ~** to speak; **demander la ~** to ask for permission to speak; **je te crois sur ~** I'll take your word for it

parquet [paʀkɛ] nm (parquet) floor; (Jur): **le ~** the Public Prosecutor's department

parrain [paʀɛ̃] nm godfather;

parrainer vt (suj: entreprise) to sponsor

pars [paʀ] vb voir **partir**

parsemer [paʀsəme] vt (suj: feuilles, papiers) to be scattered over; ~ **qch de** to scatter sth with

part [paʀ] nf (qui revient à qn) share; (fraction, partie) part; **à ~** adv (séparément) separately; (de côté) aside ▷ prép apart from, except for; **prendre ~ à** (débat etc) to take part in; (soucis, douleur de qn) to share in; **faire ~ de qch à qn** to announce sth to sb, inform sb of sth; **pour ma ~** as for me, as far as I'm concerned; **à ~ entière** full; **de la ~ de** (au nom de) on behalf of; (donné par) from; **de toute(s) ~(s)** from all sides ou quarters; **de ~ et d'autre** on both sides, on either side; **d'une ~ ... d'autre ~** on the one hand ... on the other hand; **d'autre ~** (de plus) moreover; **faire la ~ des choses** to make allowances

partage [paʀtaʒ] nm (fractionnement) dividing up; (répartition) sharing (out) no pl, share-out

partager [paʀtaʒe] vt to share; (distribuer, répartir) to share (out); (morceler, diviser) to divide (up); **se partager** vt (héritage etc) to share between themselves (ou ourselves)

partenaire [paʀtənɛʀ] nm/f partner

parterre [paʀtɛʀ] nm (de fleurs) (flower) bed; (Théâtre) stalls pl

parti [paʀti] nm (Pol) party; (décision) course of action; (personne à marier) match; **tirer ~ de** to take advantage of, turn to good account; **prendre ~ (pour/contre)** to take sides ou a stand (for/against); **parti pris** bias

partial, e, -aux [paʀsjal, jo] adj biased, partial

participant, e [paʀtisipɑ̃, ɑ̃t] nm/f participant; (à un concours) entrant

participation [paʀtisipasjɔ̃] nf participation; (financière) contribution

participer [paʀtisipe]: ~ **à** vt (course, réunion) to take part in; (frais etc) to contribute to; (chagrin, succès de qn) to share (in)

particularité [partikylarite] *nf*
(distinctive) characteristic
particulier, -ière [partikylje, jɛʀ]
adj (*spécifique*) particular; (*spécial*)
special, particular; (*personnel, privé*)
private; (*étrange*) peculiar, odd ▷ *nm*
(*individu: Admin*) private individual; **~ à**
peculiar to; **en ~** (*surtout*) in particular,
particularly; (*en privé*) in private;
particulièrement *adv* particularly
partie [parti] *nf* (*gén*) part; (*Jur etc:
protagonistes*) party; (*de cartes, tennis etc*)
game; **une ~ de pêche** a fishing party
ou trip; **en ~** partly, in part; **faire ~ de**
(*suj: chose*) to be part of; **prendre qn à ~**
to take sb to task; **en grande ~** largely,
in the main; **partie civile** (*Jur*) party
claiming damages in a criminal case
partiel, le [parsjɛl] *adj* partial ▷ *nm*
(*Scol*) class exam
partir [partir] *vi* (*gén*) to go; (*quitter*)
to go, leave; (*tache*) to go, come out; **~
de** (*lieu: quitter*) to leave; (*: commencer
à*) to start from; **~ pour/à** (*lieu, pays
etc*) to leave for/go off to; **à ~ de** from;
le train/le bus part à quelle heure?
what time does the train/bus leave?
partisan, e [partizã, an] *nm/f*
partisan ▷ *adj*: **être ~ de qch/de faire**
to be in favour of sth/doing
partition [partisjɔ̃] *nf* (*Mus*) score
partout [partu] *adv* everywhere; **~
où il allait** everywhere *ou* wherever
he went
paru [pary] *pp de* **paraître**
parution [parysjɔ̃] *nf* publication
parvenir [parvənir]: **~ à** *vt* (*atteindre*)
to reach; (*réussir*): **~ à faire** to manage
to do, succeed in doing; **faire ~ qch à
qn** to have sth sent to sb
pas¹ [pa] *nm* (*enjambée, Danse*) step;
(*allure, mesure*) pace; (*bruit*) (foot)step;
(*trace*) footprint; **~ à ~** step by step;
au ~ at walking pace; **marcher à
grands ~** to stride along; **à ~ de loup**
stealthily; **faire les cent ~** to pace up
and down; **faire le premier ~** to make
the first move; **sur le ~ de la porte** on

the doorstep

 MOT-CLÉ

pas² [pa] *adv* **1** (*en corrélation avec
ne, non etc*) not; **il ne pleure pas**
(*habituellement*) he does not *ou* doesn't
cry; (*maintenant*) he's not *ou* isn't crying;
il n'a pas pleuré/ne pleurera pas he
did not *ou* didn't/will not *ou* won't cry;
ils n'ont pas de voiture/d'enfants
they don't have *ou* haven't got a car/any
children; **il m'a dit de ne pas le faire** he
told me not to do it; **non pas que ...**
not that ...
2 (*employé sans ne etc*): **pas moi** not
me, I don't (*ou* can't *etc*); **elle travaille,
(mais) lui pas** *ou* **pas lui** she works but
he doesn't *ou* does not; **une pomme
pas mûre** an unripe apple; **pas du
tout** not at all; **pas de sucre, merci**
no sugar, thanks; **ceci est à vous ou
pas?** is this yours or not?, is this yours
or isn't it?
3: **pas mal** (*joli: personne, maison*) not
bad; **pas mal fait** not badly done *ou*
made; **comment ça va? — pas mal**
how are things? — not bad; **pas mal de**
quite a lot of

passage [pasaʒ] *nm* (*fait de passer*)
voir **passer**; (*lieu, prix de la traversée,
extrait*) passage; (*chemin*) way; **de ~**
(*touristes*) passing through; **passage à
niveau** level crossing; **passage clouté**
pedestrian crossing; **passage interdit**
no entry; **passage souterrain** subway
(*BRIT*), underpass
passager, -ère [pasaʒe, ɛʀ] *adj*
passing ▷ *nm/f* passenger
passant, e [pasã, ãt] *adj* (*rue, endroit*)
busy ▷ *nm/f* passer-by; **en ~** in passing
passe [pas] *nf* (*Sport, Navig*) pass; **être
en ~ de faire** to be on the way to doing;
être dans une mauvaise ~ to be going
through a rough patch
passé, e [pase] *adj* (*révolu*) past; (*dernier:
semaine etc*) last; (*couleur*) faded ▷ *prép*

after ▷ *nm* past; (*Ling*) past (tense); **~ de mode** out of fashion; **passé composé** perfect (tense); **passé simple** past historic (tense)

passe-partout [pɑspaʀtu] *nm inv* master *ou* skeleton key ▷ *adj inv* all-purpose

passeport [pɑspɔʀ] *nm* passport

passer [pɑse] *vi* (*aller*) to go; (*voiture, piétons: défiler*) to pass (by), go by; (*facteur, laitier etc*) to come, call; (*pour rendre visite*) to call ou drop in; (*film, émission*) to be on; (*temps, jours*) to pass, go by; (*couleur*) to fade; (*mode*) to die out; (*douleur*) to pass, go away; (*Scol*) **~ dans la classe supérieure** to go up to the next class ▷ *vt* (*frontière, rivière etc*) to cross; (*douane*) to go through; (*examen*) to sit, take; (*visite médicale etc*) to have; (*journée, temps*) to spend; (*enfiler: vêtement*) to slip on; (*film, pièce*) to show, put on; (*disque*) to play, put on; (*commande*) to place; (*marché, accord*) to agree on; **se passer** *vi* (*avoir lieu: scène, action*) to take place; (*se dérouler: entretien etc*) to go; (*s'écouler: semaine etc*) to pass, go by; (*arriver*) **que s'est-il passé?** what happened?; **~ qch à qn** (*sel etc*) to pass sth to sb; (*prêter*) to lend sb sth; (*lettre, message*) to pass sth on to sb; (*tolérer*) to let sb get away with sth; **~ par** to go through; **~ avant qch/qn** (*fig*) to come before sth/sb; **~ un coup de fil à qn** (*fam*) to give sb a ring; **laisser ~** (*air, lumière, personne*) to let through; (*occasion*) to let slip, miss; (*erreur*) to overlook; **~ à la radio/télévision** to be on the radio/on television; **~ à table** to sit down to eat; **~ au salon** to go into the sitting-room; **~ son tour** to miss one's turn; **~ la seconde** (*Auto*) to change into second; **~ le balai/l'aspirateur** to sweep up/hoover; **je vous passe M. Dupont** (*je vous mets en communication avec lui*) I'm putting you through to Mr Dupont; (*je lui passe l'appareil*) here is Mr Dupont, I'll hand you over to Mr Dupont; **se ~ de** to go ou

do without

passerelle [pɑsʀɛl] *nf* footbridge; (*de navire, avion*) gangway

passe-temps [pɑstɑ̃] *nm inv* pastime

passif, -ive [pasif, iv] *adj* passive

passion [pɑsjɔ̃] *nf* passion; **passionnant, e** *adj* fascinating; **passionné, e** *adj* (*personne*) passionate; (*récit*) impassioned; **être passionné de** to have a passion for; **passionner** *vt* (*personne*) to fascinate, grip

passoire [pɑswaʀ] *nf* sieve; (*à légumes*) colander; (*à thé*) strainer

pastèque [pastɛk] *nf* watermelon

pasteur [pastœʀ] *nm* (*protestant*) minister, pastor

pastille [pastij] *nf* (*à sucer*) lozenge, pastille

patate [patat] *nf* (*fam: pomme de terre*) spud; **patate douce** sweet potato

patauger [patoʒe] *vi* to splash about

pâte [pɑt] *nf* (*à tarte*) pastry; (*à pain*) dough; (*à frire*) batter; **pâtes** *nfpl* (*macaroni etc*) pasta *sg*; **pâte à modeler** modelling clay, Plasticine® (BRIT); **pâte brisée** shortcrust pastry; **pâte d'amandes** almond paste, marzipan; **pâte de fruits** crystallized fruit *no pl*; **pâte feuilletée** puff *ou* flaky pastry

pâté [pɑte] *nm* (*charcuterie*) pâté; (*tache*) ink blot; **pâté de maisons** block (of houses); **pâté (de sable)** sandpie; **pâté en croûte** ≈ pork pie

pâtée [pɑte] *nf* mash, feed

patente [patɑ̃t] *nf* (*Comm*) trading licence

paternel, le [patɛʀnɛl] *adj* (*amour, soins*) fatherly; (*ligne, autorité*) paternal

pâteux, -euse [pɑtø, øz] *adj* pasty; (*langue*) coated

pathétique [patetik] *adj* moving

patience [pasjɑ̃s] *nf* patience

patient, e [pasjɑ̃, jɑ̃t] *adj, nm/f* patient; **patienter** *vi* to wait

patin [patɛ̃] *nm* skate; (*sport*) skating; **patins (à glace)** (ice) skates; **patins à roulettes** roller skates

patinage [patinaʒ] *nm* skating

patiner [patine] *vi* to skate; (*roue, voiture*) to spin; **se patiner** *vi* (*meuble, cuir*) to acquire a sheen; **patineur, -euse** *nm/f* skater; **patinoire** *nf* skating rink, (ice) rink

pâtir [pɑtiʀ]: **~ de** *vt* to suffer because of

pâtisserie [pɑtisʀi] *nf* (*boutique*) cake shop; (*gâteau*) cake, pastry; (*à la maison*) pastry- *ou* cake-making, baking; **pâtissier, -ière** *nm/f* pastrycook

patois [patwa] *nm* dialect, patois

patrie [patʀi] *nf* homeland

patrimoine [patʀimwan] *nm* (*culture*) heritage

● **JOURNÉES DU PATRIMOINE**
●
● Once a year, important public
● buildings are open to the public for
● a weekend. During these **Journées**
● **du Patrimoine**, there are guided
● visits and talks based on a particular
● theme.

patriotique [patʀijɔtik] *adj* patriotic

patron, ne [patʀɔ̃, ɔn] *nm/f* boss; (*Rel*) patron saint ▷ *nm* (*Couture*) pattern; **patronat** *nm* employers *pl*; **patronner** *vt* to sponsor, support

patrouille [patʀuj] *nf* patrol

patte [pat] *nf* (*jambe*) leg; (*pied: de chien, chat*) paw; (: *d'oiseau*) foot

pâturage [pɑtyʀaʒ] *nm* pasture

paume [pom] *nf* palm

paumé, e [pome] (*fam*) *nm/f* drop-out

paupière [popjɛʀ] *nf* eyelid

pause [poz] *nf* (*arrêt*) break; (*en parlant, Mus*) pause

pauvre [povʀ] *adj* poor; **les pauvres** *nmpl* the poor; **pauvreté** *nf* (*état*) poverty

pavé, e [pave] *adj* (*cour*) paved; (*chaussée*) cobbled ▷ *nm* (*bloc*) paving stone; cobblestone

pavillon [pavijɔ̃] *nm* (*de banlieue*) small (detached) house; pavilion; (*drapeau*) flag

payant, e [pɛjɑ̃, ɑ̃t] *adj* (*spectateurs etc*) paying; (*fig: entreprise*) profitable; (*effort*) which pays off; **c'est ~** you have to pay, there is a charge

paye [pɛj] *nf* pay, wages *pl*

payer [peje] *vt* (*créancier, employé, loyer*) to pay; (*achat, réparations, fig: faute*) to pay for ▷ *vi* to pay; (*métier*) to be well-paid; (*tactique etc*) to pay off; **il me l'a fait ~ 10 euros** he charged me 10 euros for it; **~ qch à qn** to buy sth for sb, buy sb sth; **se ~ la tête de qn** (*fam*) to take the mickey out of sb; **est-ce que je peux ~ par carte de crédit?** can I pay by credit card?

pays [pei] *nm* country; (*région*) region; **du ~** local

paysage [peizaʒ] *nm* landscape

paysan, ne [peizɑ̃, an] *nm/f* farmer; (*péj*) peasant ▷ *adj* (*agricole*) farming; (*rural*) country

Pays-Bas [peiba] *nmpl*: **les ~** the Netherlands

PC *nm* (*Inform*) PC

PDA *sigle m* (= *personal digital assistant*) PDA

PDG *sigle m* = **président directeur général**

péage [peaʒ] *nm* toll; (*endroit*) tollgate

peau, x [po] *nf* skin; **gants de ~** fine leather gloves; **être bien/mal dans sa ~** to be quite at ease/ill-at-ease; **peau de chamois** (*chiffon*) chamois leather, shammy

pêche [pɛʃ] *nf* (*fruit*) peach; (*sport, activité*) fishing; (*poissons pêchés*) catch; **pêche à la ligne** (*en rivière*) angling

péché [peʃe] *nm* sin

pécher [peʃe] *vi* (*Rel*) to sin

pêcher [peʃe] *nm* peach tree ▷ *vi* to go fishing ▷ *vt* (*attraper*) to catch; (*être pêcheur de*) to fish for

pécheur, -eresse [peʃœʀ, peʃʀɛs] *nm/f* sinner

pêcheur [peʃœʀ] *nm* fisherman; (*à la ligne*) angler

pédagogie [pedagoʒi] *nf* educational methods *pl*, pedagogy; **pédagogique**

adj educational

pédaie [pedal] *nf* pedal

pédalo [pedalo] *nm* pedal-boat

pédant, e [pedã, ãt] (*péj*) *adj* pedantic

pédestre [pedɛstʀ] *adj*: **randonnée ~**
ramble; **sentier ~** pedestrian footpath

pédiatre [pedjatʀ] *nm/f* paediatrician,
child specialist

pédicure [pedikyʀ] *nm/f* chiropodist

pègre [pɛgʀ] *nf* underworld

peigne [pɛɲ] *nm* comb; **peigner** *vt* to
comb (the hair of); **se peigner** *vi* to
comb one's hair; **peignoir** *nm* dressing
gown; **peignoir de bain** bathrobe

peindre [pɛ̃dʀ] *vt* to paint; (*fig*) to
portray, depict

peine [pɛn] *nf* (*affliction*) sorrow,
sadness *no pl*; (*mal, effort*) trouble *no
pl*, (*difficulté*) difficulty; (*Jur*)
sentence; **avoir de la ~** to be sad;
faire de la ~ à qn to distress *ou* upset
sb; **prendre la ~ de faire** to go to the
trouble of doing; **se donner de la ~** to
make an effort; **ce n'est pas la ~ de
faire** there's no point in doing, it's not
worth doing; **à ~** scarcely, barely; **à ~ …
que** hardly … than, no sooner … than;
peine capitale capital punishment;
peine de mort death sentence *ou*
penalty; **peiner** *vi* (*personne*) to work
hard; (*moteur, voiture*) to labour ▷ *vt* to
grieve, sadden

peintre [pɛ̃tʀ] *nm* painter; **peintre en
bâtiment** painter (and decorator)

peinture [pɛ̃tyʀ] *nf* painting; (*matière*)
paint; (*surfaces peintes: aussi:* **~s**)
paintwork; **"~ fraîche"** "wet paint"

péjoratif, -ive [peʒɔʀatif, iv] *adj*
pejorative, derogatory

Pékin [pekɛ̃] *n* Beijing

pêle-mêle [pɛlmɛl] *adv* higgledy-
piggledy

peler [pəle] *vt, vi* to peel

pèlerin [pɛlʀɛ̃] *nm* pilgrim

pèlerinage [pɛlʀinaʒ] *nm* pilgrimage

pelle [pɛl] *nf* shovel; (*d'enfant, de
terrassier*) spade

pellicule [pelikyl] *nf* film; **pellicules**
nfpl (*Méd*) dandruff *sg*; **je voudrais une
~ de 36 poses** I'd like a 36-exposure film

pelote [p(ə)lɔt] *nf* (*de fil, laine*) ball;
pelote basque pelota

peloton [p(ə)lɔtɔ̃] *nm* group, squad;
(*Cyclisme*) pack

pelotonner [p(ə)lɔtɔne]: **se
pelotonner** *vi* to curl (o.s.) up

pelouse [p(ə)luz] *nf* lawn

peluche [p(ə)lyʃ] *nf*: (**animal en**) **~**
fluffy animal, soft toy; **chien/lapin en
~** fluffy dog/rabbit

pelure [p(ə)lyʀ] *nf* peeling, peel *no pl*

pénal, e, -aux [penal, o] *adj* penal;
pénalité *nf* penalty

penchant [pãʃã] *nm* (*tendance*)
tendency, propensity; (*faible*) liking,
fondness

pencher [pãʃe] *vi* to tilt, lean over ▷ *vt*
to tilt; **se pencher** *vi* to lean over; (*se
baisser*) to bend down; **se ~ sur** (*fig:
problème*) to look into; **~ pour** to be
inclined to favour

pendant [pãdã] *prép* (*au cours de*)
during; (*indique la durée*) for; **~ que** while

pendentif [pãdãtif] *nm* pendant

penderie [pãdʀi] *nf* wardrobe

pendre [pãdʀ] *vt, vi* to hang; **se ~** (*se
suicider*) to hang o.s.; **~ qch à** (*mur*) to
hang sth (up) on; (*plafond*) to hang sth
(up) from

pendule [pãdyl] *nf* clock ▷ *nm*
pendulum

pénétrer [penetʀe] *vi, vt* to penetrate;
~ dans to enter

pénible [penibl] *adj* (*travail*) hard;
(*sujet*) painful; (*personne*) tiresome;
péniblement *adv* with difficulty

péniche [peniʃ] *nf* barge

pénicilline [penisilin] *nf* penicillin

péninsule [penɛ̃syl] *nf* peninsula

pénis [penis] *nm* penis

pénitence [penitãs] *nf* (*peine*)
penance; (*repentir*) penitence;
pénitencier *nm* penitentiary

pénombre [penɔ̃bʀ] *nf* (*faible clarté*)
half-light; (*obscurité*) darkness

pensée [pãse] *nf* thought; (*démarche,*

doctrine) thinking *no pl*; (*fleur*) pansy; **en ~** in one's mind

penser [pɑ̃se] *vi, vt* to think; **~ à** (*ami, vacances*) to think of *ou* about; (*réfléchir à: problème, offre*) to think about *ou* over; (*prévoir*) to think of; **faire ~ à** to remind one of; **~ faire qch** to be thinking of doing sth, intend to do sth; **pensif, -ive** *adj* pensive, thoughtful

pension [pɑ̃sjɔ̃] *nf* (*allocation*) pension; (*prix du logement*) board and lodgings, bed and board; (*école*) boarding school; **pension alimentaire** (*de divorcée*) maintenance allowance, alimony; **pension complète** full board; **pension de famille** boarding house, guesthouse; **pensionnaire** *nm/f* (*Scol*) boarder; **pensionnat** *nm* boarding school

pente [pɑ̃t] *nf* slope; **en ~** sloping

Pentecôte [pɑ̃tkot] *nf*: **la ~** Whitsun (*BRIT*), Pentecost

pénurie [penyri] *nf* shortage

pépé [pepe] (*fam*) *nm* grandad

pépin [pepɛ̃] *nm* (*Bot: graine*) pip; (*ennui*) snag, hitch

pépinière [pepinjɛr] *nf* nursery

perçant, e [pɛrsɑ̃, ɑ̃t] *adj* (*cri*) piercing, shrill; (*regard*) piercing

percepteur, -trice [pɛrsɛptœr, tris] *nm/f* tax collector

perception [pɛrsɛpsjɔ̃] *nf* perception; (*bureau*) tax office

percer [pɛrse] *vt* to pierce; (*ouverture etc*) to make; (*mystère, énigme*) to penetrate ▷ *vi* to break through; **perceuse** *nf* drill

percevoir [pɛrsəvwar] *vt* (*distinguer*) to perceive, detect; (*taxe, impôt*) to collect; (*revenu, indemnité*) to receive

perche [pɛrʃ] *nf* (*bâton*) pole

percher [pɛrʃe] *vt, vi* to perch; **se percher** *vi* to perch; **perchoir** *nm* perch

perçois *etc* [pɛrswa] *vb voir* **percevoir**

perçu, e [pɛrsy] *pp de* **percevoir**

percussion [pɛrkysjɔ̃] *nf* percussion

percuter [pɛrkyte] *vt* to strike; (*suj:*

véhicule) to crash into

perdant, e [pɛrdɑ̃, ɑ̃t] *nm/f* loser

perdre [pɛrdr] *vt* to lose; (*gaspiller: temps, argent*) to waste; (*personne: moralement etc*) to ruin ▷ *vi* to lose; (*sur une vente etc*) to lose out; **se perdre** *vi* (*s'égarer*) to get lost, lose one's way; (*denrées*) to go to waste; **j'ai perdu mon portefeuille/passeport** I've lost my wallet/passport; **je me suis perdu** (*et je le suis encore*) I'm lost; (*et je ne le suis plus*) I got lost

perdrix [pɛrdri] *nf* partridge

perdu, e [pɛrdy] *pp de* **perdre** ▷ *adj* (*isolé*) out-of-the-way; (*Comm: emballage*) non-returnable; (*malade*): **il est ~** there's no hope left for him; **à vos moments ~s** in your spare time

père [pɛr] *nm* father; **père de famille** father; **le père Noël** Father Christmas

perfection [pɛrfɛksjɔ̃] *nf* perfection; **à la ~** to perfection; **perfectionné, e** *adj* sophisticated; **perfectionner** *vt* to improve, perfect; **se perfectionner en anglais** to improve one's English

perforer [pɛrfɔre] *vt* (*poinçonner*) to punch

performant, e [pɛrfɔrmɑ̃, ɑ̃t] *adj*: **très ~** high-performance *cpd*

perfusion [pɛrfyzjɔ̃] *nf*: **faire une ~ à qn** to put sb on a drip

péril [peril] *nm* peril

périmé, e [perime] *adj* (*Admin*) out-of-date, expired

périmètre [perimetr] *nm* perimeter

période [perjɔd] *nf* period; **périodique** *adj* periodic ▷ *nm* periodical; **garniture** *ou* **serviette périodique** sanitary towel (*BRIT*) *ou* napkin (*US*)

périphérique [periferik] *adj* (*quartiers*) outlying ▷ *nm* (*Auto*): **boulevard ~** ring road (*BRIT*), beltway (*US*)

périr [perir] *vi* to die, perish

périssable [perisabl] *adj* perishable

perle [pɛrl] *nf* pearl; (*de plastique, métal, sueur*) bead

permanence [pɛrmanɑ̃s] *nf*

permanence; (*local*) (duty) office;
assurer une ~ (*service public, bureaux*)
to operate *ou* maintain a basic service;
être de ~ to be on call *ou* duty; **en ~**
continuously

permanent, e [pɛrmanɑ̃, ɑ̃t] *adj*
permanent; (*spectacle*) continuous;
permanente *nf* perm

perméable [pɛrmeabl] *adj* (*terrain*)
permeable; **~ à** (*fig*) receptive *ou* open to

permettre [pɛrmɛtr] *vt* to allow,
permit; **~ à qn de faire/qch** to allow
sb to do/sth; **se ~ de faire** to take the
liberty of doing

permis [pɛrmi] *nm* permit, licence;
permis de conduire driving licence
(*brit*), driver's license (*us*); **permis de
construire** planning permission (*brit*),
building permit (*us*); **permis de séjour**
residence permit; **permis de travail**
work permit

permission [pɛrmisjɔ̃] *nf* permission;
(*Mil*) leave; **avoir la ~ de faire** to have
permission to do; **en ~** on leave

Pérou [peru] *nm* Peru

perpétuel, le [pɛrpetɥɛl] *adj*
perpetual; **perpétuité** *nf*: **à perpétuité**
for life; **être condamné à perpétuité**
to receive a life sentence

perplexe [pɛrplɛks] *adj* perplexed,
puzzled

perquisitionner [pɛrkizisjɔne] *vi* to
carry out a search

perron [pɛrɔ̃] *nm* steps *pl* (*leading to
entrance*)

perroquet [pɛrɔkɛ] *nm* parrot

perruche [peryʃ] *nf* budgerigar (*brit*),
budgie (*brit*), parakeet (*us*)

perruque [peryk] *nf* wig

persécuter [pɛrsekyte] *vt* to
persecute

persévérer [pɛrsevere] *vi* to
persevere

persil [pɛrsi] *nm* parsley

persique [pɛrsik] *adj*: **le golfe ~** the
(Persian) Gulf

persistant, e [pɛrsistɑ̃, ɑ̃t] *adj*
persistent

persister [pɛrsiste] *vi* to persist; **~ à
faire qch** to persist in doing sth

personnage [pɛrsɔnaʒ] *nm* (*individu*)
character, individual; (*célébrité*)
important person; (*de roman, film*)
character; (*Peinture*) figure

personnalité [pɛrsɔnalite] *nf*
personality; (*personnage*) prominent
figure

personne [pɛrsɔn] *nf* person ▷ *pron*
nobody, no one; (*avec négation en
anglais*) anybody, anyone; **personne
âgée** elderly person; **personnel, le** *adj*
personal; (*égoïste*) selfish ▷ *nm* staff,
personnel; **personnellement** *adv*
personally

perspective [pɛrspɛktiv] *nf* (*Art*)
perspective; (*vue*) view; (*point de vue*)
viewpoint, angle; (*chose envisagée*)
prospect; **en ~** in prospect

perspicace [pɛrspikas] *adj* clear-
sighted, gifted with (*ou* showing)
insight; **perspicacité** *nf* clear-
sightedness

persuader [pɛrsɥade] *vt*: **~ qn (de
faire)** to persuade sb (to do); **persuasif,
-ive** *adj* persuasive

perte [pɛrt] *nf* loss; (*de temps*) waste;
(*fig: morale*) ruin; **à ~ de vue** as far as the
eye can (*ou* could) see; **pertes blanches**
(vaginal) discharge *sg*

pertinent, e [pɛrtinɑ̃, ɑ̃t] *adj* apt,
relevant

perturbation [pɛrtyrbasjɔ̃] *nf*:
perturbation (atmosphérique)
atmospheric disturbance

perturber [pɛrtyrbe] *vt* to disrupt;
(*Psych*) to perturb, disturb

pervers, e [pɛrvɛr, ɛrs] *adj* perverted

pervertir [pɛrvɛrtir] *vt* to pervert

pesant, e [pəzɑ̃, ɑ̃t] *adj* heavy; (*fig:
présence*) burdensome

pèse-personne [pɛzpɛrsɔn] *nm*
(bathroom) scales *pl*

peser [pəze] *vt* to weigh ▷ *vi* to weigh;
(*fig: avoir de l'importance*) to carry
weight; **~ lourd** to be heavy

pessimiste [pesimist] *adj* pessimistic

▷ *nm/f* pessimist
peste [pɛst] *nf* plague
pétale [petal] *nm* petal
pétanque [petɑ̃k] *nf* type of bowls

● **PÉTANQUE**
●
● **Pétanque** is a version of the game
● of 'boules', played on a variety of
● hard surfaces. Standing with their
● feet together, players throw steel
● bowls at a wooden jack. **Pétanque**
● originated in the South of France
● and is still very much associated
● with that area.

pétard [petaʀ] *nm* banger (*BRIT*),
firecracker
péter [pete] *vi* (*fam: casser*) to bust;
(*fam!*) to fart (!)
pétillant, e [petijɑ̃, ɑ̃t] *adj* (*eau etc*)
sparkling
pétiller [petije] *vi* (*feu*) to crackle;
(*champagne*) to bubble; (*yeux*) to sparkle
petit, e [p(ə)ti, it] *adj* small; (*avec
nuance affective*) little; (*voyage*) short,
little; (*bruit etc*) faint, slight ▷ *nm/f*
(*petit enfant*) little boy/girl, child; **petits**
nmpl (*d'un animal*) young *no pl*; **faire des
~s** to have kittens (*ou* puppies *etc*); **la
classe des ~s** the infant class; **les tout-
~s** the tiny tots (*fam*); **~ à
~** bit by bit, gradually; **petit(e) ami(e)**
boyfriend/girlfriend; **petit déjeuner**
breakfast; **le petit déjeuner est à
quelle heure?** what time is breakfast?;
petit four petit four; **petit pain** (bread)
roll; **les petites annonces** the small
ads; **petits pois** (garden) peas; **petite-
fille** *nf* granddaughter; **petit-fils** *nm*
grandson
pétition [petisjɔ̃] *nf* petition
petits-enfants [pətizɑ̃fɑ̃] *nmpl*
grandchildren
pétrin [petʀɛ̃] *nm* (*fig*): **dans le ~** (*fam*)
in a jam *ou* fix
pétrir [petʀiʀ] *vt* to knead
pétrole [petʀɔl] *nm* oil; (*pour lampe,*

réchaud etc) paraffin (oil); **pétrolier,
-ière** *nm* oil tanker

 Attention à ne pas traduire *pétrole*
par le mot anglais *petrol*.

○ **MOT-CLÉ**

peu [pø] *adv* **1** (*modifiant verbe, adjectif,
adverbe*): **il boit peu** he doesn't drink
(very much); **il est peu bavard** he's
not very talkative; **peu avant/après**
shortly before/afterwards
2 (*modifiant nom*): **peu de**: **peu de
gens/d'arbres** few *ou* not (very) many
people/trees; **il a peu d'espoir** he
hasn't (got) much hope, he has little
hope; **pour peu de temps** for (only) a
short while
3: **peu à peu** little by little; **à peu près**
just about, more *ou* less; **à peu près
10 kg/10 euros** approximately 10
kg/10 euros
▷ *nm* **1**: **le peu de gens qui** the few
people who; **le peu de sable qui** what
little sand, the little sand which
2: **un peu** a little; **un petit peu** a little
bit; **un peu d'espoir** a little hope;
elle est un peu bavarde she's quite
ou rather talkative; **un peu plus de**
slightly more than; **un peu moins de**
slightly less than; (*avec pluriel*) slightly
fewer than
▷ *pron*: **peu le savent** few know (it); **de
peu** (only) just

peuple [pœpl] *nm* people; **peupler** *vt*
(*pays, région*) to populate; (*étang*) to
stock; (*suj: hommes, poissons*) to inhabit
peuplier [pøplije] *nm* poplar (tree)
peur [pœʀ] *nf* fear; **avoir ~ (de/de
faire/que)** to be frightened *ou* afraid
(of/of doing/that); **faire ~ à** to
frighten; **de ~ de/que** for fear of/that;
peureux, -euse *adj* fearful, timorous
peut [pø] *vb voir* **pouvoir**
peut-être [pøtɛtʀ] *adv* perhaps,
maybe; **~ que** perhaps, maybe; **~ bien
qu'il fera/est** he may well do/be

phare [faʀ] nm (en mer) lighthouse; (de véhicule) headlight

pharmacie [faʀmasi] nf (magasin) chemist's (BRIT), pharmacy; (de salle de bain) medicine cabinet; **pharmacien, ne** nm/f pharmacist, chemist (BRIT)

phénomène [fenɔmɛn] nm phenomenon

philosophe [filɔzɔf] nm/f philosopher ▷ adj philosophical

philosophie [filɔzɔfi] nf philosophy

phobie [fɔbi] nf phobia

phoque [fɔk] nm seal

phosphorescent, e [fɔsfɔʀesɑ̃, ɑ̃t] adj luminous

photo [fɔto] nf photo(graph); **prendre en ~** to take a photo of; **pourriez-vous nous prendre en ~, s'il vous plaît?** would you take a picture of us, please?; **faire de la ~** to take photos; **photo d'identité** passport photograph; **photocopie** nf photocopy; **photocopier** vt to photocopy; **photocopieuse** nf photocopier; **photographe** nm/f photographer; **photographie** nf (technique) photography; (cliché) photograph; **photographier** vt to photograph

phrase [fʀɑz] nf sentence

physicien, ne [fizisjɛ̃, jɛn] nm/f physicist

physique [fizik] adj physical ▷ nm physique ▷ nf physics sg; **au ~** physically; **physiquement** adv physically

pianiste [pjanist] nm/f pianist

piano [pjano] nm piano; **pianoter** vi to tinkle away (at the piano)

pic [pik] nm (instrument) pick(axe); (montagne) peak; (Zool) woodpecker; **à ~** vertically; (fig: tomber, arriver) just at the right time

pichet [piʃɛ] nm jug

picorer [pikɔʀe] vt to peck

pie [pi] nf magpie

pièce [pjɛs] nf (d'un logement) room; (Théâtre) play; (de machine) part; (de monnaie) coin; (document) document; (fragment, de collection) piece; **dix euros ~** ten euros each; **vendre à la ~** to sell separately; **travailler à la ~** to do piecework; **un maillot une ~** a one-piece swimsuit; **un deux-~s cuisine** a two-room(ed) flat (BRIT) ou apartment (US) with kitchen; **pièce à conviction** exhibit; **pièce d'eau** ornamental lake ou pond; **pièce de rechange** spare (part); **pièce d'identité** : **avez-vous une pièce d'identité?** have you got any (means of) identification?; **pièce jointe** (Comput) attachment; **pièce montée** tiered cake; **pièces détachées** spares, (spare) parts; **pièces justificatives** supporting documents

pied [pje] nm foot; (de table) leg; (de lampe) base; **~s nus** ou **nus-~s** barefoot; **à ~** on foot; **au ~ de la lettre** literally; **avoir ~** to be able to touch the bottom, not to be out of one's depth; **avoir le ~ marin** to be a good sailor; **sur ~** (debout, rétabli) up and about; **mettre sur ~** (entreprise) to set up; **c'est le ~** (fam) it's brilliant; **mettre les ~s dans le plat** (fam) to put one's foot in it; **il se débrouille comme un ~** (fam) he's completely useless; **pied-noir** nm Algerian-born Frenchman

piège [pjɛʒ] nm trap; **prendre au ~** to trap; **piéger** vt (avec une bombe) to booby-trap; **lettre/voiture piégée** letter-/car-bomb

piercing [pjɛʀsiŋ] nm body piercing

pierre [pjɛʀ] nf stone; **pierre tombale** tombstone; **pierreries** nfpl gems, precious stones

piétiner [pjetine] vi (trépigner) to stamp (one's foot); (fig) to be at a standstill ▷ vt to trample on

piéton, ne [pjetɔ̃, ɔn] nm/f pedestrian; **piétonnier, -ière** adj: **rue** ou **zone piétonnière** pedestrian precinct

pieu, x [pjø] nm post; (pointu) stake

pieuvre [pjœvʀ] nf octopus

pieux, -euse [pjø, pjøz] adj pious

pigeon [piʒɔ̃] nm pigeon

piger [piʒe] (fam) vi, vt to understand

pigiste [piʒist] nm/f freelance(r)

pignon [piɲɔ̃] nm (de mur) gable

pile [pil] nf (tas) pile; (Élec) battery ▷ adv (fam: s'arrêter etc) dead; **à deux heures ~** at two on the dot; **jouer à ~ ou face** to toss up (for it); **~ ou face?** heads or tails?

piler [pile] vt to crush, pound

pilier [pilje] nm pillar

piller [pije] vt to pillage, plunder, loot

pilote [pilɔt] nm pilot; (de voiture) driver ▷ adj pilot cpd; **pilote de course** racing driver; **pilote de ligne** airline pilot; **piloter** vt (avion) to pilot, fly; (voiture) to drive

pilule [pilyl] nf pill; **prendre la ~** to be on the pill

piment [pimã] nm (aussi: **~ rouge**) chilli; (fig) spice, piquancy; **~ doux** pepper, capsicum; **pimenté, e** adj (plat) hot, spicy

pin [pɛ̃] nm pine

pinard [pinaʀ] (fam) nm (cheap) wine, plonk (BRIT)

pince [pɛ̃s] nf (outil) pliers pl; (de homard, crabe) pincer, claw; (Couture: pli) dart; **pince à épiler** tweezers pl; **pince à linge** clothes peg (BRIT) ou pin (US)

pincé, e [pɛ̃se] adj (air) stiff

pinceau, x [pɛ̃so] nm (paint)brush

pincer [pɛ̃se] vt to pinch; (fam) to nab

pinède [pinɛd] nf pinewood, pine forest

pingouin [pɛ̃gwɛ̃] nm penguin

ping-pong® [piŋpɔ̃g] nm table tennis

pinson [pɛ̃sɔ̃] nm chaffinch

pintade [pɛ̃tad] nf guinea-fowl

pion [pjɔ̃] nm (Échecs) pawn; (Dames) piece; (Scol) supervisor

pionnier [pjɔnje] nm pioneer

pipe [pip] nf pipe; **fumer la ~** to smoke a pipe

piquant, e [pikã, ãt] adj (barbe, rosier etc) prickly; (saveur, sauce) hot, pungent; (détail) titillating; (froid) biting ▷ nm (épine) thorn, prickle; (fig) spiciness, spice

pique [pik] nf pike; (fig) cutting remark

▷ nm (Cartes) spades pl

pique-nique [piknik] nm picnic; **pique-niquer** vi to have a picnic

piquer [pike] vt (suj: guêpe, fumée, orties) to sting; (: moustique) to bite; (: barbe) to prick; (: froid) to bite; (Méd) to give a jab to; (: chien, chat) to put to sleep; (intérêt) to arouse; (fam: voler) to pinch ▷ vi (avion) to go into a dive

piquet [pikɛ] nm (pieu) post, stake; (de tente) peg

piqûre [pikyʀ] nf (d'épingle) prick; (d'ortie) sting; (de moustique) bite; (Méd) injection, shot (US); **faire une ~ à qn** to give sb an injection

pirate [piʀat] nm, adj pirate; **pirate de l'air** hijacker

pire [piʀ] adj worse; (superlatif): **le(la) ~ ...** the worst ... ▷ nm: **le ~ (de)** the worst (of); **au ~** at (the very) worst

pis [pi] nm (de vache) udder ▷ adj, adv worse; **de mal en ~** from bad to worse

piscine [pisin] nf (swimming) pool; **piscine couverte** indoor (swimming) pool

pissenlit [pisãli] nm dandelion

pistache [pistaʃ] nf pistachio (nut)

piste [pist] nf (d'un animal, sentier) track, trail; (indice) lead; (de stade) track; (de cirque) ring; (de danse) floor; (de patinage) rink; (de ski) run; (Aviat) runway; **piste cyclable** cycle track

pistolet [pistɔlɛ] nm (arme) pistol, gun; (à peinture) spray gun; **pistolet-mitrailleur** nm submachine gun

piston [pistɔ̃] nm (Tech) piston; **avoir du ~** (fam) to have friends in the right places; **pistonner** vt (candidat) to pull strings for

piteux, -euse [pitø, øz] adj pitiful, sorry (avant le nom); **en ~ état** in a sorry state

pitié [pitje] nf pity; **il me fait ~** I feel sorry for him; **avoir ~ de** (compassion) to pity, feel sorry for; (merci) to have pity ou mercy on

pitoyable [pitwajabl] adj pitiful

pittoresque [pitɔʀɛsk] adj

picturesque

PJ sigle f (= police judiciaire) ≈ CID (BRIT), ≈ FBI (US)

placard [plakar] nm (armoire) cupboard; (affiche) poster, notice

place [plas] nf (emplacement, classement) place; (de ville, village) square; (espace libre) room, space; (de parking) space; (siège: de train, cinéma, voiture) seat; (emploi) job; **en ~** (mettre) in its place; **sur ~** on the spot; **faire ~ à** to give way to; **ça prend de la ~** it takes up a lot of room ou space; **à la ~ de** in place of, instead of; **à votre ~ ...** if I were you ...; **je voudrais réserver deux ~s** I'd like to book two seats; **la ~ est prise?** is this seat taken?; **se mettre à la ~ de qn** to put o.s. in sb's place ou in sb's shoes

placé, e [plase] adj: **haut ~** (fig) high-ranking; **être bien/mal ~** (spectateur) to have a good/a poor seat; (concurrent) to be in a good/bad position; **il est bien ~ pour le savoir** he is in a position to know

placement [plasmã] nm (Finance) investment; **agence** ou **bureau de ~** employment agency

placer [plase] vt to place; (convive, spectateur) to seat; (argent) to place, invest; **se ~ au premier rang** to go and stand (ou sit) in the first row

plafond [plafɔ̃] nm ceiling

plage [plaʒ] nf beach; **plage arrière** (Auto) parcel ou back shelf

plaider [plede] vi (avocat) to plead ▷ vt to plead; **~ pour** (fig) to speak for; **plaidoyer** nm (Jur) speech for the defence; (fig) plea

plaie [plε] nf wound

plaignant, e [plεɲã, ãt] nm/f plaintiff

plaindre [plɛ̃dʀ] vt to pity, feel sorry for; **se plaindre** vi (gémir) to moan; (protester): **se ~ (à qn) (de)** to complain (to sb) (about); (souffrir): **se ~ de** to complain of

plaine [plεn] nf plain

plain-pied [plɛ̃pje] adv: **de ~ (avec)** on the same level (as)

plainte [plɛ̃t] nf (gémissement) moan, groan; (doléance) complaint; **porter ~** to lodge a complaint

plaire [plεʀ] vi to be a success, be successful; **ça plaît beaucoup aux jeunes** it's very popular with young people; **~ à**: **cela me plaît** I like it; **se ~ quelque part** to like being somewhere ou like it somewhere; **s'il vous plaît** please

plaisance [plεzãs] nf (aussi: **navigation de ~**) (pleasure) sailing, yachting

plaisant, e [plεzã, ãt] adj pleasant; (histoire, anecdote) amusing

plaisanter [plεzãte] vi to joke; **plaisanterie** nf joke

plaisir [pleziʀ] nm pleasure; **faire ~ à qn** (délibérément) to be nice to sb, please sb; **ça me fait ~** I like (doing) it; **j'espère que ça te fera ~** I hope you'll like it; **pour le ~** for pleasure

plaît [plε] vb voir **plaire**

plan, e [plã, an] adj flat ▷ nm plan; (fig) level, plane; (Cinéma) shot; **au premier/second ~** in the foreground/middle distance; **à l'arrière ~** in the background; **plan d'eau** lake

planche [plãʃ] nf (pièce de bois) plank, (wooden) board; (illustration) plate; **planche à repasser** ironing board; **planche (à roulettes)** skateboard; **planche (à voile)** (sport) windsurfing

plancher [plãʃe] nm floor; floorboards pl ▷ vi (fam) to work hard

planer [plane] vi to glide; (fam: rêveur) to have one's head in the clouds; **~ sur** (fig: danger) to hang over

planète [planεt] nf planet

planeur [planœʀ] nm glider

planifier [planifje] vt to plan

planning [planiŋ] nm programme, schedule; **planning familial** family planning

plant [plã] nm seedling, young plant

plante [plãt] nf plant; **la plante du pied** the sole (of the foot); **plante verte** ou **d'appartement** house plant

planter [plɑ̃te] *vt* (*plante*) to plant; (*enfoncer*) to hammer *ou* drive in; (*tente*) to put up, pitch; (*fam: personne*) to dump; **se planter** (*fam: se tromper*) to get it wrong

plaque [plak] *nf* plate; (*de verglas, d'eczéma*) patch; (*avec inscription*) plaque; **plaque chauffante** hotplate; **plaque de chocolat** bar of chocolate; **plaque tournante** (*fig*) centre

plaqué, e [plake] *adj*: **~ or/argent** gold-/silver-plated

plaquer [plake] *vt* (*Rugby*) to bring down; (*fam: laisser tomber*) to drop

plaquette [plakɛt] *nf* (*de chocolat*) bar; (*beurre*) pack(et); **plaquette de frein** brake pad

plastique [plastik] *adj, nm* plastic; **plastiquer** *vt* to blow up (*with a plastic bomb*)

plat, e [pla, -at] *adj* flat; (*cheveux*) straight; (*style*) flat, dull ▷ *nm* (*récipient, Culin*) dish; (*d'un repas*) course; **à ~ ventre** face down; **à ~** (*pneu, batterie*) flat; (*fam: personne*) dead beat; **plat cuisiné** pre-cooked meal; **plat de résistance** main course; **plat du jour** dish of the day

platane [platan] *nm* plane tree

plateau, x [plato] *nm* (*support*) tray; (*Géo*) plateau; (*Cinéma*) set; **plateau à fromages** cheese board

plate-bande [platbɑ̃d] *nf* flower bed

plate-forme [platfɔrm] *nf* platform; **plate-forme de forage/pétrolière** drilling/oil rig

platine [platin] *nm* platinum ▷ *nf* (*d'un tourne-disque*) turntable; **platine laser** compact disc *ou* CD player

plâtre [plɑtr] *nm* (*matériau*) plaster; (*statue*) plaster statue; (*Méd*) (plaster) cast; **avoir un bras dans le ~** to have an arm in plaster

plein, e [plɛ̃, plɛn] *adj* full ▷ *nm*: **faire le ~ (d'essence)** to fill up (with petrol); **à ~es mains** (*ramasser*) in handfuls; **à ~ temps** full-time; **en ~ air** in the open air; **en ~ soleil** in direct sunlight; **en ~e**

nuit/rue in the middle of the night/street; **en ~ jour** in broad daylight; **le ~, s'il vous plaît** fill it up, please

pleurer [plœre] *vi* to cry; (*yeux*) to water ▷ *vt* to mourn (for); **~ sur** to lament (over), to bemoan

pleurnicher [plœrniʃe] *vi* to snivel, whine

pleurs [plœr] *nmpl*: **en ~** in tears

pleut [plø] *vb voir* **pleuvoir**

pleuvoir [pløvwar] *vb impers* to rain ▷ *vi* (*coups*) to rain down; (*critiques, invitations*) to shower down; **il pleut** it's raining; **il pleut des cordes** it's pouring (down), it's raining cats and dogs

pli [pli] *nm* fold; (*de jupe*) pleat; (*de pantalon*) crease

pliant, e [plijɑ̃, plijɑ̃t] *adj* folding

plier [plije] *vt* to fold; (*pour ranger*) to fold up; (*genou, bras*) to bend ▷ *vi* to bend; (*fig*) to yield; **se ~ à** to submit to

plisser [plise] *vt* (*jupe*) to put pleats in; (*yeux*) to screw up; (*front*) to crease

plomb [plɔ̃] *nm* (*métal*) lead; (*d'une cartouche*) (lead) shot; (*Pêche*) sinker; (*Élec*) fuse; **sans ~** (*essence etc*) unleaded

plomberie [plɔ̃bri] *nf* plumbing

plombier [plɔ̃bje] *nm* plumber

plonge [plɔ̃ʒ] *nf* washing-up

plongeant, e [plɔ̃ʒɑ̃, ɑ̃t] *adj* (*vue*) from above; (*décolleté*) plunging

plongée [plɔ̃ʒe] *nf* (*Sport*) diving *no pl*; (*sans scaphandre*) skin diving; **~ sous-marine** diving

plongeoir [plɔ̃ʒwar] *nm* diving board

plongeon [plɔ̃ʒɔ̃] *nm* dive

plonger [plɔ̃ʒe] *vi* to dive ▷ *vt*: **~ qch dans** to plunge sth into; **se ~ dans** (*études, lecture*) to bury *ou* immerse o.s. in; **plongeur** *nm* diver

plu [ply] *pp de* **plaire**; *de* **pleuvoir**

pluie [plɥi] *nf* rain

plume [plym] *nf* feather; (*pour écrire*) (pen) nib; (*fig*) pen

plupart [plypar]: **la ~** *pron* the majority, most (of them); **la ~ des** most, the majority of; **la ~ du temps/d'entre nous** most of the time/of us;

pour la ~ for the most part, mostly

pluriel [plyʀjɛl] *nm* plural

plus¹ [ply] *vb voir* **plaire**

○ **MOT-CLÉ**

plus² [ply] *adv* **1** (*forme négative*): **ne ... plus** no more, no longer; **je n'ai plus d'argent** I've got no more money *ou* no money left; **il ne travaille plus** he's no longer working, he doesn't work any more

2 [ply, plyz + *voyelle*] (*comparatif*) more, ...+er; (*superlatif*): **le plus** the most, the ...+est; **plus grand/intelligent (que)** bigger/more intelligent (than); **le plus grand/intelligent** the biggest/ most intelligent; **tout au plus** at the very most

3 [plys, plyz + *voyelle*] (*davantage*) more; **il travaille plus (que)** he works more (than); **plus il travaille, plus il est heureux** the more he works, the happier he is; **plus de 10 personnes/3 heures** more than *ou* over 10 people/3 hours; **3 heures de plus que** 3 hours more than; **de plus** what's more, moreover; **il a 3 ans de plus que moi** he's 3 years older than me; **3 kilos en plus** 3 kilos more; **en plus de** in addition to; **de plus en plus** more and more; **plus ou moins** more or less; **ni plus ni moins** no more, no less ▷ *prép* [plys]: **4 plus 2** 4 plus 2

plusieurs [plyzjœʀ] *dét, pron* several; **ils sont ~** there are several of them

plus-value [plyvaly] *nf* (*bénéfice*) surplus

plutôt [plyto] *adv* rather; **je préfère ~ celui-ci** I'd rather have this one; **~ que (de) faire** rather than *ou* instead of doing

pluvieux, -euse [plyvjø, jøz] *adj* rainy, wet

PME *sigle f* (= *petite(s) et moyenne(s) entreprise(s)*) small business(es)

PMU *sigle m* (= *Pari mutuel urbain*) system

of betting on horses; (*café*) betting agency

PNB *sigle m* (= *produit national brut*) GNP

pneu [pnø] *nm* tyre (BRIT), tire (US); **j'ai un ~ crevé** I've got a flat tyre

pneumonie [pnømɔni] *nf* pneumonia

poche [pɔʃ] *nf* pocket; (*sous les yeux*) bag, pouch; **argent de ~** pocket money

pochette [pɔʃɛt] *nf* (*d'aiguilles etc*) case; (*mouchoir*) breast pocket handkerchief; (*sac à main*) clutch bag; **pochette de disque** record sleeve

poêle [pwal] *nm* stove ▷ *nf*: **~ (à frire)** frying pan

poème [pɔɛm] *nm* poem

poésie [pɔezi] *nf* (*poème*) poem; (*art*): **la ~** poetry

poète [pɔɛt] *nm* poet

poids [pwa] *nm* weight; (*Sport*) shot; **vendre au ~** to sell by weight; **perdre/prendre du ~** to lose/put on weight; **poids lourd** (*camion*) lorry (BRIT), truck (US)

poignant, e [pwaɲɑ̃, ɑ̃t] *adj* poignant

poignard [pwaɲaʀ] *nm* dagger; **poignarder** *vt* to stab, knife

poigne [pwaɲ] *nf* grip; **avoir de la ~** (*fig*) to rule with a firm hand

poignée [pwaɲe] *nf* (*de sel etc, fig*) handful; (*de couvercle, porte*) handle; **poignée de main** handshake

poignet [pwaɲɛ] *nm* (*Anat*) wrist; (*de chemise*) cuff

poil [pwal] *nm* (*Anat*) hair; (*de pinceau, brosse*) bristle; (*de tapis*) strand; (*pelage*) coat; **à ~** (*fam*) starkers; **au ~** (*fam*) hunky-dory; **poilu, e** *adj* hairy

poinçonner [pwɛ̃sɔne] *vt* (*bijou*) to hallmark; (*billet*) to punch

poing [pwɛ̃] *nm* fist; **coup de ~** punch

point [pwɛ̃] *nm* point; (*endroit*) spot; (*marque, signe*) dot; (: *de ponctuation*) full stop, period (US); (*Couture, Tricot*) stitch ▷ *adv* = **pas²**; **faire le ~** (*fig*) to take stock (of the situation); **sur le ~ de faire** (just) about to do; **à tel ~ que** so much so that; **mettre au ~** (*procédé*) to develop; (*affaire*) to settle; **à ~** (*Culin: viande*) medium; **à ~ (nommé)**

just at the right time; **deux ~s** colon;
point de côté stitch (pain); **point
d'exclamation/d'interrogation**
exclamation/question mark; **point
de repère** landmark; (dans le temps)
point of reference; **point de vente**
retail outlet; **point de vue** viewpoint;
(fig: opinion) point of view; **point faible**
weak spot; **point final** full stop, period
(us); **point mort: au point mort** (Auto)
in neutral; **points de suspension**
suspension points

pointe [pwɛ̃t] nf point; (clou) tack; (fig):
une ~ de a hint of; **être à la ~ de** (fig)
to be in the forefront of; **sur la ~ des
pieds** on tiptoe; **en ~** pointed, tapered;
de ~ (technique etc) leading; **heures de
~** peak hours

pointer [pwɛ̃te] vt (diriger: canon, doigt):
~ sur qch to point at sth ▷ vi (employé)
to clock in

pointillé [pwɛ̃tije] nm (trait) dotted line

pointilleux, -euse [pwɛ̃tijø, øz] adj
particular, pernickety

pointu, e [pwɛ̃ty] adj pointed; (voix)
shrill; (analyse) precise

pointure [pwɛ̃tyʀ] nf size

point-virgule [pwɛ̃viʀgyl] nm
semi-colon

poire [pwaʀ] nf pear; (fam: péj) mug

poireau, x [pwaʀo] nm leek

poirier [pwaʀje] nm pear tree

pois [pwɑ] nm (Bot) pea; (sur une étoffe)
dot, spot; **~ chiche** chickpea; **à ~**
(cravate etc) spotted, polka-dot cpd

poison [pwazɔ̃] nm poison

poisseux, -euse [pwasø, øz] adj sticky

poisson [pwasɔ̃] nm fish gén inv;
(Astrol): **P~s** Pisces; **~ d'avril** April fool;
(blague) April Fool's Day trick; see note;
poisson rouge goldfish; **poissonnerie**
nf fish-shop; **poissonnier, -ière** nm/f
fishmonger (brit), fish merchant (us)

- **POISSON D'AVRIL**
-
- The traditional April Fools' Day prank
- in France involves attaching a cut-

- out paper fish, known as a 'poisson
- d'avril', to the back of one's victim,
- without being caught.

poitrine [pwatʀin] nf chest; (seins)
bust, bosom; (Culin) breast

poivre [pwavʀ] nm pepper

poivron [pwavʀɔ̃] nm pepper,
capsicum

polaire [pɔlɛʀ] adj polar

pôle [pol] nm (Géo, Élec) pole; **le ~ Nord/
Sud** the North/South Pole

poli, e [pɔli] adj polite; (lisse) smooth

police [pɔlis] nf police; **police
judiciaire** ≈ Criminal Investigation
Department (brit), ≈ Federal Bureau
of Investigation (us); **police secours**
≈ emergency services pl (brit),
≈ paramedics pl (us); **policier, -ière**
adj police cpd ▷ nm policeman; (aussi:
roman policier) detective novel

polir [pɔliʀ] vt to polish

politesse [pɔlitɛs] nf politeness

politicien, ne [pɔlitisjɛ̃, jɛn] (péj) nm/f
politician

politique [pɔlitik] adj political ▷ nf
politics sg; (mesures, méthode) policies p

politiquement [pɔlitikmɑ̃] adv
politically; **~ correct** politically correct

pollen [pɔlɛn] nm pollen

polluant, e [pɔlɥɑ̃, ɑ̃t] adj polluting
▷ nm (produit): **~** pollutant; **non ~**
non-polluting

polluer [pɔlɥe] vt to pollute; **pollution**
nf pollution

polo [pɔlo] nm (chemise) polo shirt

Pologne [pɔlɔɲ] nf: **la ~** Poland;
polonais, e adj Polish ▷ nm/f:
Polonais, e Pole ▷ nm (Ling) Polish

poltron, ne [pɔltʀɔ̃, ɔn] adj cowardly

polycopier [pɔlikɔpje] vt to duplicate

Polynésie [pɔlinezi] nf: **la ~** Polynesia;
la ~ française French Polynesia

polyvalent, e [pɔlivalɑ̃, ɑ̃t] adj (rôle)
varied; (salle) multi-purpose

pommade [pɔmad] nf ointment,
cream

pomme [pɔm] nf apple; **tomber**

dans les ~s (fam) to pass out; **pomme d'Adam** Adam's apple; **pomme de pin** pine ou fir cone; **pomme de terre** potato

ommette [pɔmɛt] nf cheekbone

ommier [pɔmje] nm apple tree

ompe [pɔ̃p] nf pump; (faste) pomp (and ceremony); **pompe (à essence)** petrol pump; **pompes funèbres** funeral parlour sg, undertaker's sg; **pomper** vt to pump; (aspirer) to pump up; (absorber) to soak up

ompeux, -euse [pɔ̃pø, øz] adj pompous

ompier [pɔ̃pje] nm fireman

ompiste [pɔ̃pist] nm/f petrol (BRIT) ou gas (US) pump attendant

oncer [pɔ̃se] vt to sand (down)

onctuation [pɔ̃ktɥasjɔ̃] nf punctuation

onctuel, le [pɔ̃ktɥɛl] adj punctual

ondéré, e [pɔ̃deʀe] adj level-headed, composed

ondre [pɔ̃dʀ] vt to lay

oney [pɔnɛ] nm pony

ont [pɔ̃] nm bridge; (Navig) deck; **faire le ~** to take the extra day off; see note; **pont suspendu** suspension bridge; **pont-levis** nm drawbridge

○ **PONT**

The expression 'faire le pont' refers to the practice of taking a Monday or Friday off to make a long weekend if a public holiday falls on a Tuesday or Thursday. The French commonly take an extra day off work to give four consecutive days' holiday at 'l'Ascension', 'le 14 juillet' and 'le 15 août'.

op [pɔp] adj inv pop

opulaire [pɔpylɛʀ] adj popular; (manifestation) mass cpd; (milieux, quartier) working-class; (expression) vernacular

opularité [pɔpylaʀite] nf popularity

population [pɔpylasjɔ̃] nf population

populeux, -euse [pɔpylø, øz] adj densely populated

porc [pɔʀ] nm pig; (Culin) pork

porcelaine [pɔʀsəlɛn] nf porcelain, china; piece of china(ware)

porc-épic [pɔʀkepik] nm porcupine

porche [pɔʀʃ] nm porch

porcherie [pɔʀʃəʀi] nf pigsty

pore [pɔʀ] nm pore

porno [pɔʀno] adj porno ▷ nm porn

port [pɔʀ] nm harbour, port; (ville) port; (de l'uniforme etc) wearing; (pour lettre) postage; (pour colis, aussi: posture) carriage; **port d'arme** (Jur) carrying of a firearm; **port payé** postage paid

portable [pɔʀtabl] adj (portatif) portable; (téléphone) mobile ▷ nm (Comput) laptop (computer); (téléphone) mobile (phone)

portail [pɔʀtaj] nm gate

portant, e [pɔʀtɑ̃, ɑ̃t] adj: **bien/mal ~** in good/poor health

portatif, -ive [pɔʀtatif, iv] adj portable

porte [pɔʀt] nf door; (de ville, jardin) gate; **mettre à la ~** to throw out; **porte-avions** nm inv aircraft carrier; **porte-bagages** nm inv luggage rack; **porte-bonheur** nm inv lucky charm; **porte-clefs** nm inv key ring; **porte-documents** nm inv attaché ou document case

porté, e [pɔʀte] adj: **être ~ à faire** to be inclined to do; **être ~ sur qch** to be keen on sth; **portée** nf (d'une arme) range; (fig: effet) impact, import; (: capacité) scope, capability; (de chatte etc) litter; (Mus) stave, staff; **à/hors de portée (de)** within/out of reach (of); **à portée de (la) main** within (arm's) reach; **à la portée de qn** (fig) at sb's level, within sb's capabilities

porte...: portefeuille nm wallet; **portemanteau, x** nm (cintre) coat hanger; (au mur) coat rack; **porte-monnaie** nm inv purse; **porte-parole** nm inv spokesman

porter [pɔʀte] vt to carry; (sur soi: vêtement, barbe, bague) to wear; (fig: responsabilité etc) to bear, carry; (inscription, nom, fruits) to bear; (coup) to deal; (attention) to turn; (apporter): **~ qch à qn** to take sth to sb ▷ vi (voix) to carry; (coup, argument) to hit home; **se porter** vi (se sentir): **se ~ bien/mal** to be well/unwell; **~ sur** (recherches) to be concerned with; **se faire ~ malade** to report sick

porteur, -euse [pɔʀtœʀ, øz] nm/f (de bagages) porter; (de chèque) bearer

porte-voix [pɔʀtəvwa] nm inv megaphone

portier [pɔʀtje] nm doorman

portière [pɔʀtjɛʀ] nf door

portion [pɔʀsjɔ̃] nf (part) portion, share; (partie) portion, section

porto [pɔʀto] nm port (wine)

portrait [pɔʀtʀɛ] nm (peinture) portrait; (photo) photograph; **portrait-robot** nm Identikit® ou photo-fit® picture

portuaire [pɔʀtɥɛʀ] adj port cpd, harbour cpd

portugais, e [pɔʀtygɛ, ɛz] adj Portuguese ▷ nm/f: **P~, e** Portuguese ▷ nm (Ling) Portuguese

Portugal [pɔʀtygal] nm: **le ~** Portugal

pose [poz] nf (de moquette) laying; (attitude, d'un modèle) pose; (Photo) exposure

posé, e [poze] adj serious

poser [poze] vt to put; (installer: moquette, carrelage) to lay; (rideaux, papier peint) to hang; (question) to ask; (principe, conditions) to lay ou set down; (difficulté) to pose; (formuler: problème) to formulate ▷ vi (modèle) to pose; **se poser** vi (oiseau, avion) to land; (question) to arise; **~ qch (sur)** (déposer) to put sth down (on); **~ qch sur/quelque part** (placer) to put sth on/somewhere; **~ sa candidature à un poste** to apply for a post

positif, -ive [pozitif, iv] adj positive

position [pozisjɔ̃] nf position; **prendre ~** (fig) to take a stand

posologie [pozɔlɔʒi] nf dosage

posséder [pɔsede] vt to own, possess; (qualité, talent) to have, possess; (sexuellement) to possess; **possession** nf ownership no pl, possession; **prendre possession de qch** to take possession of sth

possibilité [pɔsibilite] nf possibility; **possibilités** nfpl (potentiel) potential s₉

possible [pɔsibl] adj possible; (projet, entreprise) feasible ▷ nm: **faire son ~** to do all one can, do one's utmost; **le plus/moins de livres ~** as many/few books as possible; **le plus vite ~** as quickly as possible; **aussitôt/dès que ~** as soon as possible

postal, e, -aux [pɔstal, o] adj postal

poste¹ [pɔst] nf (service) post, postal service; (administration, bureau) post office; **mettre à la ~** to post; **poste restante** poste restante (BRIT), general delivery (US)

poste² [pɔst] nm (fonction, Mil) post; (Tél) extension; (de radio etc) set; **poste (de police)** police station; **poste de secours** first-aid post; **poste d'essence** filling station; **poste d'incendie** fire point; **poste de pilotage** cockpit, flight deck

poster [pɔste] vt to post; **où est-ce que je peux ~ ces cartes postales?** where can I post these cards?

postérieur, e [pɔsteʀjœʀ] adj (date) later; (partie) back ▷ nm (fam) behind

postuler [pɔstyle] vi: **~ à** ou **pour un emploi** to apply for a job

pot [po] nm (en verre) jar; (en terre) pot; (en plastique, carton) carton; (en métal) tin; (fam: chance) luck; **avoir du ~** (fam) to be lucky; **boire** ou **prendre un ~** (fam) to have a drink; **petit ~ (pour bébé)** (jar of) baby food; **~ catalytique** catalytic converter; **pot d'échappement** exhaust pipe

potable [pɔtabl] adj: **eau (non) ~** (non-)drinking water

potage [pɔtaʒ] nm soup; **potager,**

-ère adj: **(jardin) potager** kitchen ou vegetable garden

ot-au-feu [pɔtofø] nm inv (beef) stew

ot-de-vin [podvɛ̃] nm bribe

ote [pɔt] (fam) nm pal

oteau, x [pɔto] nm post; **poteau indicateur** signpost

otelé, e [pɔt(ə)le] adj plump, chubby

otentiel, le [pɔtɑ̃sjɛl] adj, nm potential

oterie [pɔtri] nf pottery; (objet) piece of pottery

otier, -ière [pɔtje, jɛr] nm/f potter

otiron [pɔtirɔ̃] nm pumpkin

ou, x [pu] nm louse

oubelle [pubɛl] nf (dust)bin

ouce [pus] nm thumb

oudre [pudr] nf powder; (fard) (face) powder; (explosif) gunpowder; **en ~**: **café en ~** instant coffee; **lait en ~** dried ou powdered milk; **poudreuse** nf powder snow; **poudrier** nm (powder) compact

ouffer [pufe] vi: **~ (de rire)** to burst out laughing

oulailler [pulaje] nm henhouse

oulain [pulɛ̃] nm foal; (fig) protégé

oule [pul] nf hen; (Culin) (boiling) fowl; **poule mouillée** coward

oulet [pulɛ] nm chicken; (fam) cop

oulie [puli] nf pulley

ouls [pu] nm pulse; **prendre le ~ de qn** to feel sb's pulse

oumon [pumɔ̃] nm lung

oupée [pupe] nf doll

our [pur] prép for ▷ nm: **le ~ et le contre** the pros and cons; **~ faire** (so as) to do, in order to do; **~ avoir fait** for having done; **~ que** so that, in order that; **fermé ~ (cause de) travaux** closed for refurbishment ou alterations; **c'est ~ ça que ...** that's why ...; **~ quoi faire?** what for?; **~ 20 euros d'essence** 20 euros' worth of petrol; **~ cent** per cent; **~ ce qui est de** as for

ourboire [purbwar] nm tip; **combien de ~ est-ce qu'il faut laisser?** how much should I tip?

pourcentage [pursɑ̃taʒ] nm percentage

pourchasser [purʃase] vt to pursue

pourparlers [purparle] nmpl talks, negotiations

pourpre [purpr] adj crimson

pourquoi [purkwa] adv, conj why ▷ nm inv: **le ~ (de)** the reason (for)

pourrai etc [pure] vb voir **pouvoir**

pourri, e [puri] adj rotten

pourrir [purir] vi to rot; (fruit) to go rotten ou bad ▷ vt to rot; (fig) to spoil thoroughly; **pourriture** nf rot

poursuite [pursɥit] nf pursuit, chase; **poursuites** nfpl (Jur) legal proceedings

poursuivre [pursɥivr] vt to pursue, chase (after); (obséder) to haunt; (Jur) to bring proceedings against, prosecute; (: au civil) to sue; (but) to strive towards; (continuer: études etc) to carry on with, continue; **se poursuivre** vi to go on, continue

pourtant [purtɑ̃] adv yet; **c'est ~ facile** (and) yet it's easy

pourtour [purtur] nm perimeter

pourvoir [purvwar] vt: **~ qch/qn de** to equip sth/sb with ▷ vi: **~ à** to provide for; **pourvu, e** adj: **pourvu de** equipped with; **pourvu que** (si) provided that, so long as; (espérons que) let's hope (that)

pousse [pus] nf growth; (bourgeon) shoot

poussée [puse] nf thrust; (d'acné) eruption; (fig: prix) upsurge

pousser [puse] vt to push; (émettre: cri, soupir) to give; (stimuler: élève) to urge on; (poursuivre: études, discussion) to carry on (further) ▷ vi to push; (croître) to grow; **se pousser** vi to move over; **~ qn à** (inciter) to urge ou press sb to; (acculer) to drive sb to; **faire ~** (plante) to grow

poussette [pusɛt] nf push chair (BRIT), stroller (US)

poussière [pusjɛr] nf dust; **poussiéreux, -euse** adj dusty

poussin [pusɛ̃] nm chick
poutre [putʀ] nf beam

 MOT-CLÉ

pouvoir [puvwaʀ] nm power; (Pol:
dirigeants): **le pouvoir** those in power;
les pouvoirs publics the authorities;
pouvoir d'achat purchasing power
▷ vb semi-aux **1** (être en état de) can,
be able to; **je ne peux pas le réparer**
I can't ou I am not able to repair it;
déçu de ne pas pouvoir le faire
disappointed not to be able to do it
2 (avoir la permission) can, may, be
allowed to; **vous pouvez aller au
cinéma** you can ou may go to the
pictures
3 (probabilité, hypothèse) may, might,
could; **il a pu avoir un accident** he
may ou might ou could have had an
accident; **il aurait pu le dire!** he might
ou could have said (so)!
▷ vb impers may, might, could; **il peut
arriver que** it may ou might ou could
happen that; **il pourrait pleuvoir** it
might rain
▷ vt can, be able to; **j'ai fait tout ce que
j'ai pu** I did all I could; **je n'en peux plus**
(épuisé) I'm exhausted; (à bout) I can't
take any more
▷ vi: **se pouvoir: il se peut que** it may
ou might be that; **cela se pourrait**
that's quite possible

prairie [pʀeʀi] nf meadow
praline [pʀalin] nf sugared almond
praticable [pʀatikabl] adj passable,
practicable
pratiquant, e [pʀatikɑ̃, ɑ̃t] nm/f
(regular) churchgoer
pratique [pʀatik] nf practice ▷ adj
practical; **pratiquement** adv (pour ainsi
dire) practically, virtually; **pratiquer**
vt to practise; (l'équitation, la pêche)
to go in for; (le golf, football) to play;
(intervention, opération) to carry out
pré [pʀe] nm meadow

préalable [pʀealabl] adj preliminary;
au ~ beforehand
préambule [pʀeɑ̃byl] nm preamble;
(fig) prelude; **sans ~** straight away
préau [pʀeo] nm (Scol) covered
playground
préavis [pʀeavi] nm notice
précaution [pʀekosjɔ̃] nf precaution;
avec ~ cautiously; **par ~** as a
precaution
précédemment [pʀesedamɑ̃] adv
before, previously
précédent, e [pʀesedɑ̃, ɑ̃t] adj
previous ▷ nm precedent; **sans ~**
unprecedented; **le jour ~** the day
before, the previous day
précéder [pʀesede] vt to precede
prêcher [pʀeʃe] vt to preach
précieux, -euse [pʀesjø, jøz] adj
precious; (aide, conseil) invaluable
précipice [pʀesipis] nm drop, chasm
précipitamment [pʀesipitamɑ̃] adv
hurriedly, hastily
précipitation [pʀesipitasjɔ̃] nf (hâte)
haste
précipité, e [pʀesipite] adj hurried,
hasty
précipiter [pʀesipite] vt (hâter: départ)
to hasten; (faire tomber): **~ qn/qch du
haut de** to throw ou hurl sb/sth off ou
from; **se précipiter** (ou to speed up; **se ~
sur/vers** to rush at/towards
précis, e [pʀesi, iz] adj precise;
(mesures) accurate, precise; **à 4 heures
~es** at 4 o'clock sharp; **précisément**
adv precisely; **préciser** vt (expliquer)
to be more specific about, clarify;
(spécifier) to state, specify; **se préciser**
vi to become clear(er); **précision**
nf precision; (détail) point ou detail;
demander des précisions to ask for
further explanation
précoce [pʀekɔs] adj early; (enfant)
precocious
préconçu, e [pʀekɔ̃sy] adj
preconceived
préconiser [pʀekɔnize] vt to advocat
prédécesseur [pʀedesesœʀ] nm

predecessor

rédilection [pʀedilɛksjɔ̃] nf: **avoir une ~ pour** to be partial to

rédire [pʀedir] vt to predict

rédominer [pʀedɔmine] vi to predominate

réface [pʀefas] nf preface

réfecture [pʀefɛktyʀ] nf prefecture; **préfecture de police** police headquarters pl

référable [pʀefeʀabl] adj preferable

référé, e [pʀefeʀe] adj, nm/f favourite

référence [pʀefeʀɑ̃s] nf preference; **de ~** preferably

référer [pʀefeʀe] vt: **~ qn/qch (à)** to prefer sb/sth (to), like sb/sth better (than); **~ faire** to prefer to do; **je préférerais du thé** I would rather have tea, I'd prefer tea

réfet [pʀefɛ] nm prefect

réhistorique [pʀeistɔʀik] adj prehistoric

réjudice [pʀeʒydis] nm (matériel) loss; (moral) harm no pl; **porter ~ à** to harm, be detrimental to; **au ~ de** at the expense of

réjugé [pʀeʒyʒe] nm prejudice; **avoir un ~ contre** to be prejudiced ou biased against

rélasser [pʀelɑse]: **se prélasser** vi to lounge

rélèvement [pʀelɛvmɑ̃] nm (montant) deduction; **faire un ~ de sang** to take a blood sample

rélever [pʀel(ə)ve] vt (échantillon) to take; **~ (sur)** (montant) to deduct (from); (argent: sur son compte) to withdraw (from)

rématuré, e [pʀematyʀe] adj premature ▷ nm premature baby

remier, -ière [pʀəmje, jɛʀ] adj first; (rang) front; (fig: objectif) basic; **le ~ venu** the first person to come along; **de ~ ordre** first-rate; **Premier ministre** Prime Minister; **première** nf (Scol) year 2 (BRIT), eleventh grade (US); (Aviat, Rail etc) first class; **premièrement** adv firstly

prémonition [pʀemɔnisjɔ̃] nf premonition

prenant, e [pʀənɑ̃, ɑ̃t] adj absorbing, engrossing

prénatal, e [pʀenatal] adj (Méd) antenatal

prendre [pʀɑ̃dʀ] vt to take; (repas) to have; (se procurer) to get; (malfaiteur, poisson) to catch; (passager) to pick up; (personnel) to take on; (traiter: personne) to handle; (voix, ton) to put on; (ôter): **~ qch à** to take sth from; (coincer): **se ~ les doigts dans** to get one's fingers caught in ▷ vi (liquide, ciment) to set; (greffe, vaccin) to take; (feu: foyer) to go; (se diriger): **~ à gauche** to turn (to the) left; **~ froid** to catch cold; **se ~ pour** to think one is; **s'en ~ à** to attack; **se ~ d'amitié pour** to befriend; **s'y ~** (procéder) to set about it

preneur [pʀənœʀ] nm: **être/trouver ~** to be willing to buy/find a buyer

prénom [pʀenɔ̃] nm first ou Christian name

préoccupation [pʀeɔkypasjɔ̃] nf (souci) concern; (idée fixe) preoccupation

préoccuper [pʀeɔkype] vt (inquiéter) to worry; (absorber) to preoccupy; **se ~ de** to be concerned with

préparatifs [pʀepaʀatif] nmpl preparations

préparation [pʀepaʀasjɔ̃] nf preparation

préparer [pʀepaʀe] vt to prepare; (café, thé) to make; (examen) to prepare for; (voyage, entreprise) to plan; **se préparer** vi (orage, tragédie) to brew, be in the air; **~ qch à qn** (surprise etc) to have sth in store for sb; **se ~ (à qch/faire)** to prepare (o.s.) ou get ready (for sth/to do)

prépondérant, e [pʀepɔ̃deʀɑ̃, ɑ̃t] adj major, dominating

préposé, e [pʀepoze] nm/f employee; (facteur) postman

préposition [pʀepozisjɔ̃] nf preposition

près [pʀɛ] *adv* near, close; **~ de** near (to), close to; (*environ*) nearly, almost; **de ~** closely; **à 5 kg ~** to within about 5 kg; **il n'est pas à 10 minutes ~** he can spare 10 minutes; **est-ce qu'il y a une banque ~ d'ici?** is there a bank nearby?

présage [pʀezaʒ] *nm* omen

presbyte [pʀɛsbit] *adj* long-sighted

presbytère [pʀɛsbitɛʀ] *nm* presbytery

prescription [pʀɛskʀipsjɔ̃] *nf* prescription

prescrire [pʀɛskʀiʀ] *vt* to prescribe

présence [pʀezɑ̃s] *nf* presence; (*au bureau, à l'école*) attendance

présent, e [pʀezɑ̃, ɑ̃t] *adj, nm* present; **à ~ (que)** now (that)

présentation [pʀezɑ̃tasjɔ̃] *nf* presentation; (*de nouveau venu*) introduction; (*allure*) appearance; **faire les ~s** to do the introductions

présenter [pʀezɑ̃te] *vt* to present; (*excuses, condoléances*) to offer; (*invité, conférencier*): **~ qn (à)** to introduce sb (to) ▷ *vi*: **~ bien** to have a pleasing appearance; **se présenter** *vi* (*occasion*) to arise; **se ~ à** (*examen*) to sit; (*élection*) to stand at, run for; **je vous présente Nadine** this is Nadine, could I introduce you to Nadine?

préservatif [pʀezɛʀvatif] *nm* condom, sheath

préserver [pʀezɛʀve] *vt*: **~ de** (*protéger*) to protect from

président [pʀezidɑ̃] *nm* (*Pol*) president; (*d'une assemblée, Comm*) chairman; **président directeur général** chairman and managing director; **présidentielles** *nfpl* presidential elections

présider [pʀezide] *vt* to preside over; (*dîner*) to be the guest of honour at

presque [pʀɛsk] *adv* almost, nearly; **~ personne** hardly anyone; **~ rien** hardly anything; **~ pas** hardly (at all); **~ pas (de)** hardly any

presqu'île [pʀɛskil] *nf* peninsula

pressant, e [pʀesɑ̃, ɑ̃t] *adj* urgent

presse [pʀɛs] *nf* press; (*affluence*): **heures de ~** busy times

pressé, e [pʀese] *adj* in a hurry; (*travail*) urgent; **orange ~e** freshly-squeezed orange juice

pressentiment [pʀesɑ̃timɑ̃] *nm* foreboding, premonition

pressentir [pʀesɑ̃tiʀ] *vt* to sense

presse-papiers [pʀɛspapje] *nm inv* paperweight

presser [pʀese] *vt* (*fruit, éponge*) to squeeze; (*bouton*) to press; (*allure*) to speed up; (*inciter*): **~ qn de faire** to urge *ou* press sb to do ▷ *vi* to be urgent; **se presser** *vi* (*se hâter*) to hurry (up); **se ~ contre qn** to squeeze up against sb; **le temps presse** there's not much time; **rien ne presse** there's no hurry

pressing [pʀesiŋ] *nm* (*magasin*) dry-cleaner's

pression [pʀesjɔ̃] *nf* pressure; (*bouton*) press stud; (*fam: bière*) draught beer; **faire ~ sur** to put pressure on; **sous ~** pressurized, under pressure; (*fig*) under pressure; **pression artérielle** blood pressure

prestataire [pʀɛstatɛʀ] *nm/f* supplier

prestation [pʀɛstasjɔ̃] *nf* (*allocation*) benefit; (*d'une entreprise*) service provided; (*d'un artiste*) performance

prestidigitateur, -trice [pʀɛstidiʒitatœʀ, tʀis] *nm/f* conjurer

prestige [pʀɛstiʒ] *nm* prestige; **prestigieux, -euse** *adj* prestigious

présumer [pʀezyme] *vt*: **~ que** to presume *ou* assume that

prêt, e [pʀɛ, pʀɛt] *adj* ready ▷ *nm* (*somme*) loan; **quand est-ce que mes photos seront ~es?** when will my photos be ready?; **prêt-à-porter** *nm* ready-to-wear *ou* off-the-peg (*BRIT*) clothes *pl*

prétendre [pʀetɑ̃dʀ] *vt* (*affirmer*): **~ que** to claim that; (*avoir l'intention de*): **faire qch** to mean *ou* intend to do sth; **prétendu, e** *adj* (*supposé*) so-called

⯀ Attention à ne pas traduire *prétendre* par *to pretend*.

prétentieux, -euse [pʀetɑ̃sjø, jøz]

adj pretentious

prétention [pretɑ̃sjɔ̃] *nf* claim; (*vanité*) pretentiousness

prêter [prete] *vt* (*livres, argent*): **~ qch (à)** to lend sth (to); (*supposer*): **~ à qn** (*caractère, propos*) to attribute to sb; **pouvez-vous me ~ de l'argent?** can you lend me some money?

prétexte [pretɛkst] *nm* pretext, excuse; **sous aucun ~** on no account; **prétexter** *vt* to give as a pretext *ou* an excuse

prêtre [pretr] *nm* priest

preuve [prœv] *nf* proof; (*indice*) proof, evidence *no pl*; **faire ~ de** to show; **faire ses ~s** to prove o.s. (*ou* itself)

prévaloir [prevalwar] *vi* to prevail

prévenant, e [prev(ə)nɑ̃, ɑ̃t] *adj* thoughtful, kind

prévenir [prev(ə)nir] *vt* (*éviter: catastrophe etc*) to avoid, prevent; (*anticiper: désirs, besoins*) to anticipate; **~ qn (de)** (*avertir*) to warn sb (about); (*informer*) to tell *ou* inform sb (about)

préventif, -ive [prevɑ̃tif, iv] *adj* preventive

prévention [prevɑ̃sjɔ̃] *nf* prevention; **prévention routière** road safety

prévenu, e [prev(ə)ny] *nm/f* (*Jur*) defendant, accused

prévision [previzjɔ̃] *nf*: **~s** predictions; (*Écon*) forecast *sg*; **en ~ de** in anticipation of; **prévisions météorologiques** weather forecast *sg*

prévoir [prevwar] *vt* (*anticiper*) to foresee; (*s'attendre à*) to expect, reckon on; (*organiser: voyage etc*) to plan; (*envisager*) to allow; **comme prévu** as planned; **prévoyant, e** *adj* gifted with (*ou* showing) foresight; **prévu, e** *pp de* **prévoir**

prier [prije] *vi* to pray ▷ *vt* (*Dieu*) to pray to; (*implorer*) to beg; (*demander*): **~ qn de faire** to ask sb to do; **se faire ~** to need coaxing *ou* persuading; **je vous en prie** (*allez-y*) please do; (*de rien*) don't mention it; **prière** *nf* prayer; **"prière de ..."** "please ..."

primaire [primer] *adj* primary ▷ *nm* (*Scol*) primary education

prime [prim] *nf* (*bonus*) bonus; (*subvention*) premium; (*Comm: cadeau*) free gift; (*Assurances, Bourse*) premium ▷ *adj*: **de ~ abord** at first glance; **primer** *vt* (*récompenser*) to award a prize to ▷ *vi* to dominate; to be most important

primevère [primver] *nf* primrose

primitif, -ive [primitif, iv] *adj* primitive; (*originel*) original

prince [prɛ̃s] *nm* prince; **princesse** *nf* princess

principal, e, -aux [prɛ̃sipal, o] *adj* principal, main ▷ *nm* (*Scol*) principal, head(master); (*essentiel*) main thing

principe [prɛ̃sip] *nm* principle; **par ~** on principle; **en ~** (*habituellement*) as a rule; (*théoriquement*) in principle

printemps [prɛ̃tɑ̃] *nm* spring

priorité [prijorite] *nf* priority; (*Auto*) right of way; **priorité à droite** right of way to vehicles coming from the right

pris, e [pri, priz] *pp de* **prendre** ▷ *adj* (*place*) taken; (*mains*) full; (*personne*) busy; **avoir le nez/la gorge ~(e)** to have a stuffy nose/a hoarse throat; **être ~ de panique** to be panic-stricken

prise [priz] *nf* (*d'une ville*) capture; (*Pêche, Chasse*) catch; (*point d'appui ou pour empoigner*) hold; (*Élec: fiche*) plug; (*: femelle*) socket; **être aux ~s avec** to be grappling with; **prise de courant** power point; **prise de sang** blood test; **prise multiple** adaptor

priser [prize] *vt* (*estimer*) to prize, value

prison [prizɔ̃] *nf* prison; **aller/être en ~** to go to/be in prison *ou* jail; **prisonnier, -ière** *nm/f* prisoner ▷ *adj* captive

privé, e [prive] *adj* private; (*en punition*): **tu es ~ de télé!** no TV for you! ▷ *nm* (*Comm*) private sector; **en ~** in private

priver [prive] *vt*: **~ qn de** to deprive sb of; **se priver de** to go *ou* do without

privilège [privilɛʒ] *nm* privilege

prix [pri] *nm* price; (*récompense, Scol*) prize; **hors de ~** exorbitantly priced;

à aucun ~ not at any price; **à tout ~** at all costs

probable [pʀɔbabl] *adj* likely, probable; **probablement** *adv* probably

problème [pʀɔblɛm] *nm* problem

procédé [pʀɔsede] *nm* (*méthode*) process; (*comportement*) behaviour *no pl*

procéder [pʀɔsede] *vi* to proceed; (*moralement*) to behave; **~ à** to carry out

procès [pʀɔsɛ] *nm* trial; (*poursuites*) proceedings *pl*; **être en ~ avec** to be involved in a lawsuit with

processus [pʀɔsesys] *nm* process

procès-verbal, -aux [pʀɔsɛvɛʀbal, o] *nm* (*de réunion*) minutes *pl*; (*aussi*: **P.-V.**) parking ticket

prochain, e [pʀɔʃɛ̃, ɛn] *adj* next; (*proche: départ, arrivée*) impending ▷ *nm* fellow man; **la ~e fois/semaine ~e** next time/week; **prochainement** *adv* soon, shortly

proche [pʀɔʃ] *adj* nearby; (*dans le temps*) imminent; (*parent, ami*) close; **proches** *nmpl* (*parents*) close relatives; **être ~ (de)** to be near, be close (to)

proclamer [pʀɔklame] *vt* to proclaim

procuration [pʀɔkyʀasjɔ̃] *nf* proxy

procurer [pʀɔkyʀe] *vt*: **~ qch à qn** (*fournir*) to obtain sth for sb; (*causer: plaisir etc*) to bring sb sth; **se procurer** *vt* to get; **procureur** *nm* public prosecutor

prodige [pʀɔdiʒ] *nm* marvel, wonder; (*personne*) prodigy; **prodiguer** *vt* (*soins, attentions*): **prodiguer qch à qn** to give sb sth

producteur, -trice [pʀɔdyktœʀ, tʀis] *nm/f* producer

productif, -ive [pʀɔdyktif, iv] *adj* productive

production [pʀɔdyksjɔ̃] *nf* production; (*rendement*) output

productivité [pʀɔdyktivite] *nf* productivity

produire [pʀɔdɥiʀ] *vt* to produce; **se produire** *vi* (*événement*) to happen, occur; (*acteur*) to perform, appear

produit [pʀɔdɥi] *nm* product;

produit chimique chemical; **produits agricoles** farm produce *sg*; **produits de beauté** beauty products, cosmetics; **produits d'entretien** cleaning products

prof [pʀɔf] (*fam*) *nm* teacher

proférer [pʀɔfeʀe] *vt* to utter

professeur, e [pʀɔfesœʀ] *nm/f* teacher; (*de faculté*) (university) lecturer; (: *titulaire d'une chaire*) professor

profession [pʀɔfesjɔ̃] *nf* occupation; **~ libérale** (liberal) profession; **sans ~** unemployed; **professionnel, le** *adj*, *nm/f* professional

profil [pʀɔfil] *nm* profile; **de ~** in profile

profit [pʀɔfi] *nm* (*avantage*) benefit, advantage; (*Comm, Finance*) profit; **au ~ de** in aid of; **tirer ~ de** to profit from; **profitable** *adj* (*utile*) beneficial; (*lucratif*) profitable; **profiter** *vi*: **profiter de** (*situation, occasion*) to take advantage of; (*vacances, jeunesse etc*) to make the most of

profond, e [pʀɔfɔ̃, ɔ̃d] *adj* deep; (*sentiment, intérêt*) profound; **profondément** *adv* deeply; **il dort profondément** he is sound asleep; **profondeur** *nf* depth; **l'eau à quelle profondeur?** how deep is the water?

programme [pʀɔgʀam] *nm* programme; (*Scol*) syllabus, curriculum; (*Inform*) program; **programmer** *vt* (*émission*) to schedule; (*Inform*) to program; **programmeur, -euse** *nm/f* programmer

progrès [pʀɔgʀɛ] *nm* progress *no pl*; **faire des ~** to make progress; **progresser** *vi* to progress; **progressif, -ive** *adj* progressive

proie [pʀwa] *nf* prey *no pl*

projecteur [pʀɔʒɛktœʀ] *nm* (*pour film*) projector; (*de théâtre, cirque*) spotlight

projectile [pʀɔʒɛktil] *nm* missile

projection [pʀɔʒɛksjɔ̃] *nf* projection; (*séance*) showing

projet [pʀɔʒɛ] *nm* plan; (*ébauche*) draft; **projet de loi** bill; **projeter** *vt* (*envisager* to plan; (*film, photos*) to project; (*ombre, lueur*) to throw, cast; (*jeter*) to throw up (*ou off ou out*)

prolétaire[pʀɔletɛʀ] *adj, nmf* proletarian

prolongement[pʀɔlɔ̃ʒmɑ̃] *nm* extension; **dans le ~ de** running on from

prolonger[pʀɔlɔ̃ʒe] *vt* (*débat, séjour*) to prolong; (*délai, billet, rue*) to extend; **se prolonger** *vi* to go on

promenade[pʀɔm(ə)nad] *nf* walk (*ou drive ou ride*); **faire une ~** to go for a walk; **une ~ en voiture/à vélo** a drive/(bicycle) ride

promener[pʀɔm(ə)ne] *vt* (*chien*) to take out for a walk; (*doigts, regard*): **~ qch sur** to run sth over; **se promener** *vi* to go for (*ou be out for*) a walk

promesse[pʀɔmɛs] *nf* promise

promettre[pʀɔmɛtʀ] *vt* to promise ▷ *vi* to be *ou* look promising; **~ à qn de faire** to promise sb that one will do

promiscuité[pʀɔmiskɥite] *nf* (*chambre*) lack of privacy

promontoire[pʀɔmɔ̃twaʀ] *nm* headland

promoteur, -trice[pʀɔmɔtœʀ, tʀis] *nm/f*: **promoteur (immobilier)** property developer (*BRIT*), real estate promoter (*US*)

promotion[pʀɔmosjɔ̃] *nf* promotion; **en ~** on special offer

promouvoir[pʀɔmuvwaʀ] *vt* to promote

prompt, e[pʀɔ̃(pt), pʀɔ̃(p)t] *adj* swift, rapid

prôner[pʀone] *vt* (*préconiser*) to advocate

pronom[pʀɔnɔ̃] *nm* pronoun

prononcer[pʀɔnɔ̃se] *vt* to pronounce; (*dire*) to utter; (*discours*) to deliver; **se prononcer** *vi* to be pronounced; **comment est-ce que ça se prononce?** how do you pronounce *ou* say it?; **se ~ (sur)** (*se décider*) to reach a decision (on *ou* about), give a verdict (on); **prononciation** *nf* pronunciation

pronostic[pʀɔnɔstik] *nm* (*Méd*) prognosis; (*fig: aussi*: **~s**) forecast

propagande[pʀɔpagɑ̃d] *nf* propaganda

propager[pʀɔpaʒe] *vt* to spread; **se propager** *vi* to spread

prophète[pʀɔfɛt] *nm* prophet

prophétie[pʀɔfesi] *nf* prophecy

propice[pʀɔpis] *adj* favourable

proportion[pʀɔpɔʀsjɔ̃] *nf* proportion; **toute(s) ~(s) gardée(s)** making due allowance(s)

propos[pʀɔpo] *nm* (*intention*) intention, aim; (*sujet*): **à quel ~?** what about? ▷ *nmpl* (*paroles*) talk *no pl*, remarks; **à ~ de** about, regarding; **à tout ~** for the slightest thing *ou* reason; **à ~** by the way; (*opportunément*) at the right moment

proposer[pʀɔpoze] *vt* to propose; **~ qch (à qn)** (*suggérer*) to suggest sth (to sb), propose sth (to sb); (*offrir*) to offer (sb) sth; **se ~ (pour faire)** to offer one's services (to do); **proposition** (*suggestion*) *nf* proposal, suggestion; (*Ling*) clause

propre[pʀɔpʀ] *adj* clean; (*net*) neat, tidy; (*possessif*) own; (*sens*) literal; (*particulier*): **~ à** peculiar to; (*approprié*): **~ à** suitable for ▷ *nm*: **recopier au ~** to make a fair copy of; **proprement** *adv* (*avec propreté*) cleanly; **le village proprement dit** the village itself; **à proprement parler** strictly speaking; **propreté** *nf* cleanliness

propriétaire[pʀɔpʀijetɛʀ] *nm/f* owner; (*pour le locataire*) landlord(-lady)

propriété[pʀɔpʀijete] *nf* property; (*droit*) ownership

propulser[pʀɔpylse] *vt* to propel

prose[pʀoz] *nf* (*style*) prose

prospecter[pʀɔspɛkte] *vt* to prospect; (*Comm*) to canvass

prospectus[pʀɔspɛktys] *nm* leaflet

prospère[pʀɔspɛʀ] *adj* prosperous; **prospérer** *vi* to prosper

prosterner[pʀɔstɛʀne]: **se prosterner** *vi* to bow low, prostrate o.s.

prostituée [pʀɔstitɥe] nf prostitute

prostitution [pʀɔstitysjɔ̃] nf
prostitution

protecteur, -trice [pʀɔtɛktœʀ, tʀis]
adj protective; (air, ton: péj) patronizing
▷ nm/f protector

protection [pʀɔtɛksjɔ̃] nf protection;
(d'un personnage influent: aide) patronage

protéger [pʀɔteʒe] vt to protect; **se ~
de/contre** to protect o.s. from

protège-slip [pʀɔtɛʒslip] nm panty
liner

protéine [pʀɔtein] nf protein

protestant, e [pʀɔtɛstɑ̃, ɑ̃t] adj, nm/f
Protestant

protestation [pʀɔtɛstasjɔ̃] nf (plainte)
protest

protester [pʀɔtɛste] vi: ~ **(contre)** to
protest (against ou about); ~ **de** (son
innocence) to protest

prothèse [pʀɔtɛz] nf: **prothèse
dentaire** denture

protocole [pʀɔtɔkɔl] nm (fig) etiquette

proue [pʀu] nf bow(s pl), prow

prouesse [pʀuɛs] nf feat

prouver [pʀuve] vt to prove

provenance [pʀɔv(ə)nɑ̃s] nf origin;
avion en ~ de plane (arriving) from

provenir [pʀɔv(ə)niʀ]: ~ **de** vt to
come from

proverbe [pʀɔvɛʀb] nm proverb

province [pʀɔvɛ̃s] nf province

proviseur [pʀɔvizœʀ] nm
≈ head(teacher) (BRIT), ≈ principal (US)

provision [pʀɔvizjɔ̃] nf (réserve)
stock, supply; **provisions** nfpl (vivres)
provisions, food no pl

provisoire [pʀɔvizwaʀ] adj
temporary; **provisoirement** adv
temporarily

provocant, e [pʀɔvɔkɑ̃, ɑ̃t] adj
provocative

provoquer [pʀɔvɔke] vt (défier) to
provoke; (causer) to cause, bring about;
(inciter): ~ **qn à** to incite sb to

proxénète [pʀɔksenɛt] nm procurer

proximité [pʀɔksimite] nf nearness,

closeness; (dans le temps) imminence,
closeness; **à ~** near ou close by; **à ~ de**
near (to), close to

prudemment [pʀydamɑ̃] adv
carefully; wisely, sensibly

prudence [pʀydɑ̃s] nf carefulness;
avec ~ carefully; **par ~** as a precaution

prudent, e [pʀydɑ̃, ɑ̃t] adj (pas
téméraire) careful; (: en général) safety-
conscious; (sage, conseillé) wise,
sensible; **c'est plus ~** it's wiser

prune [pʀyn] nf plum

pruneau, x [pʀyno] nm prune

prunier [pʀynje] nm plum tree

PS sigle m = **parti socialiste**

pseudonyme [psødɔnim] nm (gén)
fictitious name; (d'écrivain) pseudonym
pen name

psychanalyse [psikanaliz] nf
psychoanalysis

psychiatre [psikjatʀ] nm/f
psychiatrist; **psychiatrique** adj
psychiatric

psychique [psiʃik] adj psychological

psychologie [psikɔlɔʒi] nf
psychology; **psychologique** adj
psychological; **psychologue** nm/f
psychologist

pu [py] pp de **pouvoir**

puanteur [pɥɑ̃tœʀ] nf stink, stench

pub [pyb] nf (fam: annonce) ad, advert;
(pratique) advertising

public, -ique [pyblik] adj public;
(école, instruction) state cpd ▷ nm public
(assistance) audience; **en ~** in public

publicitaire [pyblisitɛʀ] adj
advertising cpd; (film) publicity cpd

publicité [pyblisite] nf (méthode,
profession) advertising; (annonce)
advertisement; (révélations) publicity

publier [pyblije] vt to publish

publipostage [pyblipɔstaʒ] nm
mailing m

publique [pyblik] adj voir **public**

puce [pys] nf flea; (Inform) chip; **carte
à ~** smart card; **(marché aux) ~s** flea
market sg

pudeur [pydœʀ] nf modesty; **pudique**

adj (chaste) modest; (discret) discreet
■uer [pɥe] (péj) vi to stink
■uéricultrice [pɥerikyltris] nf
p(a)ediatric nurse
■uéril, e [pɥeril] adj childish
■uis [pɥi] vb voir **pouvoir** ▷ adv then
■uiser [pɥize] vt: **~ (dans)** to draw
(from)
■uisque [pɥisk] conj since
■uissance [pɥisɑ̃s] nf power; **en ~** adj
potential
■uissant, e [pɥisɑ̃, ɑ̃t] adj powerful
■uits [pɥi] nm well
■ull(-over) [pyl(ɔvɛr)] nm sweater
■ulluler [pylyle] vi to swarm
■ulpe [pylp] nf pulp
■ulvériser [pylverize] vt to pulverize;
(liquide) to spray
■unaise [pynɛz] nf (Zool) bug; (clou)
drawing pin (BRIT), thumbtack (US)
■unch [pɔ̃ʃ] nm (boisson) punch
■unir [pynir] vt to punish; **punition** nf
punishment
■upille [pypij] nf (Anat) pupil ▷ nm/f
(enfant) ward
■upitre [pypitr] nm (Scol) desk
■ur, e [pyr] adj pure; (vin) undiluted;
(whisky) neat; **en ~e perte** to no avail;
c'est de la folie ~e it's sheer madness
■urée [pyre] nf: **~ (de pommes de
terre)** mashed potatoes pl; **purée de
marrons** chestnut purée
■urement [pyrmɑ̃] adv purely
■urgatoire [pyrgatwar] nm
purgatory
■urger [pyrʒe] vt (Méd, Pol) to purge;
(Jur: peine) to serve
■ur-sang [pyrsɑ̃] nm inv thoroughbred
■us [py] nm pus
■utain [pytɛ̃] (fam!) nf whore (!)
■uzzle [pœzl] nm jigsaw (puzzle)
■.-V. [peve] sigle m = **procès-verbal**
■yjama [piʒama] nm pyjamas pl (BRIT),
pajamas pl (US)
■yramide [piramid] nf pyramid
■yrénées [pirene] nfpl: **les ~** the
Pyrenees

QI sigle m (= quotient intellectuel) IQ
quadragénaire [k(w)adraʒenɛr]
nm/f man/woman in his/her forties
quadruple [k(w)adrypl] nm: **le ~ de**
four times as much as
quai [ke] nm (de port) quay; (de gare)
platform; **être à ~** (navire) to be
alongside; **de quel ~ part le train pour
Paris?** which platform does the Paris
train go from?
qualification [kalifikasjɔ̃] nf
(aptitude) qualification
qualifier [kalifje] vt to qualify; **se
qualifier** vi to qualify; **~ qch/qn de** to
describe sth/sb as
qualité [kalite] nf quality
quand [kɑ̃] conj, adv when; **~ je serai
riche** when I'm rich; **~ même** all the
same; **~ même, il exagère!** really, he
overdoes it!; **~ bien même** even though
quant [kɑ̃]: **~ à** prép (pour ce qui est de) as
for, as to; (au sujet de) regarding
quantité [kɑ̃tite] nf quantity, amount;
(grand nombre): **une** ou **des ~(s) de** a

great deal of

quarantaine [karɑ̃tɛn] *nf* (*Méd*) quarantine; **avoir la ~** (*âge*) to be around forty; **une ~ (de)** forty or so, about forty

quarante [karɑ̃t] *num* forty

quart [kar] *nm* (*fraction*) quarter; (*surveillance*) watch; **un ~ de vin** a quarter litre of wine; **le ~ de** a quarter of; **quart d'heure** quarter of an hour; **quarts de finale** quarter finals

quartier [kartje] *nm* (*de ville*) district, area; (*de bœuf*) quarter; (*de fruit*) piece; **cinéma de ~** local cinema; **avoir ~ libre** (*fig*) to be free; **quartier général** headquarters *pl*

quartz [kwarts] *nm* quartz

quasi [kazi] *adv* almost, nearly; **quasiment** *adv* almost, nearly; **quasiment jamais** hardly ever

quatorze [katɔrz] *num* fourteen

quatorzième [katɔrzjɛm] *num* fourteenth

quatre [katr] *num* four; **à ~ pattes** on all fours; **se mettre en ~ pour qn** to go out of one's way for sb; **~ à ~** (*monter, descendre*) four at a time; **quatre-vingt-dix** *num* ninety; **quatre-vingts** *num* eighty; **quatrième** *num* fourth ▷ *nf* (*Scol*) year 9 (*BRIT*), eighth grade (*US*)

quatuor [kwatɥɔr] *nm* quartet(te)

O **MOT-CLÉ**

que [kə] *conj* **1** (*introduisant complétive*) that; **il sait que tu es là** he knows (that) you're here; **je veux que tu acceptes** I want you to accept; **il a dit que oui** he said he would (*ou* it was *etc*)
2 (*reprise d'autres conjonctions*): **quand il rentrera et qu'il aura mangé** when he gets back and (when) he has eaten; **si vous y allez et que vous ...** if you go there and if you ...
3 (*en tête de phrase: hypothèse, souhait etc*): **qu'il le veuille ou non** whether he likes it or not; **qu'il fasse ce qu'il voudra!** let him do as he pleases!

4 (*après comparatif*) than, as; *voir aussi* **plus**; **aussi**; **autant** *etc*
5 (*seulement*): **ne ... que** only; **il ne boit que de l'eau** he only drinks water
6 (*temps*): **il y a 4 ans qu'il est parti** it is 4 years since he left, he left 4 years ago
▷ *adv* (*exclamation*): **qu'il ou qu'est-ce qu'il est bête/court vite!** he's so silly!/he runs so fast!; **que de livres!** what a lot of books!
▷ *pron* **1** (*relatif: personne*) whom; (: *chose*) that, which; **l'homme que je vois** the man (whom) I see; **le livre que tu vois** the book (that *ou* which) you see; **un jour que j'étais ...** a day when I was ...
2 (*interrogatif*) what; **que fais-tu?, qu'est-ce que tu fais?** what are you doing?; **qu'est-ce que c'est?** what is it?, what's that?; **que faire?** what can one do?

Québec [kebɛk] *n*: **le ~** Quebec; **québecois, e** *adj* Quebec ▷ *nm/f*: **Québecois, e** Quebecker ▷ *nm* (*Ling*) Quebec French

O **MOT-CLÉ**

quel, quelle [kɛl] *adj* **1** (*interrogatif: personne*) who; (: *chose*) what; **quel est cet homme?** who is this man?; **quel est ce livre?** what is this book?; **quel livre/homme?** what book/man?; (*parmi un certain choix*) which book/man?; **quels acteurs préférez-vous?** which actors do you prefer?; **dans quels pays êtes-vous allé?** which *ou* what countries did you go to?
2 (*exclamatif*): **quelle surprise!** what a surprise!
3: **quel que soit le coupable** whoever is guilty; **quel que soit votre avis** whatever your opinion

quelconque [kɛlkɔ̃k] *adj* (*indéfini*): **un ami/prétexte ~** some friend/pretext or other; (*médiocre: repas*) indifferent, poor; (*laid: personne*) plain-looking

🔵 **MOT-CLÉ**

quelque [kɛlk] *adj* **1** (*au singulier*) some; (*au pluriel*) a few, some; (*tournure interrogative*) any; **quelque espoir** some hope; **il a quelques amis** he has a few *ou* some friends; **a-t-il quelques amis?** does he have any friends?; **les quelques livres qui** the few books which; **20 kg et quelque(s)** a bit over 20 kg
2: quelque ... que: **quelque livre qu'il choisisse** whatever (*ou* whichever) book he chooses
3: quelque chose something; (*tournure interrogative*) anything; **quelque chose d'autre** something else; anything else; **quelque part** somewhere; anywhere; **en quelque sorte** as it were
▷ *adv* **1** (*environ*): **quelque 100 mètres** some 100 metres
2: quelque peu rather, somewhat

quelquefois [kɛlkəfwa] *adv* sometimes
quelques-uns, -unes [kɛlkəzœ̃, yn] *pron* a few, some
quelqu'un [kɛlkœ̃] *pron* someone, somebody; (*+ tournure interrogative*) anyone, anybody; **quelqu'un d'autre** someone *ou* somebody else; (*+ tournure interrogative*) anybody else
qu'en dira-t-on [kɑ̃diratɔ̃] *nm inv*: **le qu'en dira-t-on** gossip, what people say
querelle [kərɛl] *nf* quarrel; **quereller: se quereller** *vi* to quarrel
qu'est-ce que [kɛskə] *vb + conj voir* **que**
qu'est-ce qui [kɛski] *vb + conj voir* **qui**
question [kɛstjɔ̃] *nf* question; (*fig*) matter, issue; **il a été ~ de** we (*ou* they) spoke about; **de quoi est-il ~?** what is it about?; **il n'en est pas ~** there's no question of it; **en ~** in question; **hors de ~** out of the question; **remettre**

en ~ to question; **questionnaire** *nm* questionnaire; **questionner** *vt* to question
quête [kɛt] *nf* collection; (*recherche*) quest, search; **faire la ~** (*à l'église*) to take the collection; (*artiste*) to pass the hat round
quetsche [kwɛtʃ] *nf* kind of dark-red plum
queue [kø] *nf* tail; (*fig: du classement*) bottom; (: *de poêle*) handle; (: *de fruit, feuille*) stalk; (: *de train, colonne, file*) rear; **faire la ~** to queue (up) (BRIT), line up (US); **queue de cheval** ponytail; **queue de poisson** (*Auto*): **faire une queue de poisson à qn** to cut in front of sb

🔵 **MOT-CLÉ**

qui [ki] *pron* **1** (*interrogatif: personne*) who; (: *chose*): **qu'est-ce qui est sur la table?** what is on the table?; **qui est-ce qui?** who?; **qui est-ce que?** who?; **à qui est ce sac?** whose bag is this?; **à qui parlais-tu?** who were you talking to?, to whom were you talking?; **chez qui allez-vous?** whose house are you going to?
2 (*relatif: personne*) who; (*+prép*) whom; **l'ami de qui je vous ai parlé** the friend I told you about; **la dame chez qui je suis allé** the lady whose house I went to
3 (*sans antécédent*): **amenez qui vous voulez** bring who you like; **qui que ce soit** whoever it may be

quiconque [kikɔ̃k] *pron* (*celui qui*) whoever, anyone who; (*n'importe qui*) anyone, anybody
quille [kij] *nf*: **(jeu de) ~s** skittles *sg* (BRIT), bowling (US)
quincaillerie [kɛ̃kajʀi] *nf* (*ustensiles*) hardware; (*magasin*) hardware shop
quinquagénaire [kɛ̃kaʒenɛʀ] *nm/f* man/woman in his/her fifties
quinquennat [kɛ̃kena] *nm five year term of office (of French President)*

quinte [kɛ̃t] *nf*: **~ (de toux)** coughing fit
quintuple [kɛ̃typl] *nm*: **le ~ de** five times as much as
quinzaine [kɛ̃zɛn] *nf*: **une ~ (de)** about fifteen, fifteen or so; **une ~ (de jours)** a fortnight (BRIT), two weeks
quinze [kɛ̃z] *num* fifteen; **dans ~ jours** in a fortnight('s time), in two weeks(' time)
quinzième [kɛ̃zjɛm] *num* fifteenth
quiproquo [kipʀɔko] *nm* misunderstanding
quittance [kitɑ̃s] *nf* (*reçu*) receipt
quitte [kit] *adj*: **être ~ envers qn** to be no longer in sb's debt; (*fig*) to be quits with sb; **~ à faire** even if it means doing
quitter [kite] *vt* to leave; (*vêtement*) to take off; **se quitter** *vi* (*couples, interlocuteurs*) to part; **ne quittez pas** (*au téléphone*) hold the line
qui-vive [kiviv] *nm*: **être sur le ~** to be on the alert

⭕ **MOT-CLÉ**

quoi [kwa] *pron interrog* **1** what; **quoi de neuf?** what's new?; **quoi?** (*qu'est-ce que tu dis?*) what?
2 (*avec prép*): **à quoi tu penses?** what are you thinking about?; **de quoi parlez-vous?** what are you talking about?; **à quoi bon?** what's the use?
▷ *pron rel*: **as-tu de quoi écrire?** do you have something to write with?; **il n'y a pas de quoi** (please) don't mention it; **il n'y a pas de quoi rire** there's nothing to laugh about
▷ *pron* (*locutions*): **quoi qu'il arrive** whatever happens; **quoi qu'il en soit** be that as it may; **quoi que ce soit** anything at all
▷ *excl* what!

quoique [kwak] *conj* (al)though
quotidien, ne [kɔtidjɛ̃, jɛn] *adj* daily; (*banal*) everyday ▷ *nm* (*journal*) daily (paper); **quotidiennement** *adv* daily

r

r. *abr* = **route**; **rue**
rab [ʀab] (*fam*) *nm* (*nourriture*) extra; **est-ce qu'il y a du ~?** are there any seconds?
rabâcher [ʀabaʃe] *vt* to keep on repeating
rabais [ʀabɛ] *nm* reduction, discount; **rabaisser** *vt* (*dénigrer*) to belittle; (*rabattre: prix*) to reduce
Rabat [ʀaba(t)] *n* Rabat
rabattre [ʀabatʀ] *vt* (*couvercle, siège*) to pull down; (*déduire*) to reduce; **se rabattre** *vi* (*se refermer: couvercle*) to fall shut; (*véhicule, coureur*) to cut in; **se ~ sur** to fall back on
rabbin [ʀabɛ̃] *nm* rabbi
rabougri, e [ʀabugʀi] *adj* stunted
raccommoder [ʀakɔmɔde] *vt* to mend, repair
raccompagner [ʀakɔ̃paɲe] *vt* to take *ou* see back
raccord [ʀakɔʀ] *nm* link; (*retouche*) touch up; **raccorder** *vt* to join (up), link up; (*suj: pont etc*) to connect, link

accourci [Rakursi] *nm* short cut
accourcir [Rakursir] *vt* to shorten
▷ *vi (jours)* to grow shorter, draw in
accrocher [Rakrɔʃe] *vt (tableau)* to
hang back up; *(récepteur)* to put down
▷ *vi (Tél)* to hang up, ring off
ace [Ras] *nf* race; *(d'animaux, fig)* breed;
de ~ purebred, pedigree
achat [Raʃa] *nm* buying; *(du même
objet)* buying back
acheter [Raʃ(ə)te] *vt (article perdu)* to
buy another; *(après avoir vendu)* to buy
back; *(d'occasion)* to buy; *(Comm: part,
firme)* to buy up; *(davantage)* **~ du lait/3
œufs** to buy more milk/another 3 eggs
ou 3 more eggs; **se racheter** *vi (fig)* to
make amends
acial, e, -aux [Rasjal, jo] *adj* racial
acine [Rasin] *nf* root; **racine carrée/
cubique** square/cube root
acisme [Rasism] *nm* racism
aciste [Rasist] *adj, nm/f* racist
acket [Raket] *nm* racketeering *no pl*
aclée [Rakle] *(fam) nf* hiding,
thrashing
acler [Rakle] *vt (surface)* to scrape; **se ~
la gorge** to clear one's throat
acontars [Rakɔ̃tar] *nmpl* story, lie
aconter [Rakɔ̃te] *vt:* **~ (à qn)** *(décrire)*
to relate to sb, tell (sb) about; *(dire de
mauvaise foi)* to tell (sb); **~ une histoire**
to tell a story
adar [Radar] *nm* radar
ade [Rad] *nf (natural)* harbour; **rester
en ~** *(fig)* to be left stranded
adeau, x [Rado] *nm* raft
adiateur [Radjatœr] *nm* radiator,
heater; *(Auto)* radiator; **radiateur
électrique** electric heater *ou* fire
adiation [Radjasjɔ̃] *nf (Physique)*
radiation
adical, e, -aux [Radikal, o] *adj*
radical
adieux, -euse [Radjø, jøz] *adj* radiant
adin, e [Radɛ̃, in] *(fam) adj* stingy
adio [Radjo] *nf* radio; *(Méd)* X-ray
▷ *nm* radio operator; **à la ~** on the
radio; **radioactif, -ive** *adj* radioactive;

radiocassette *nm* cassette radio,
radio cassette player; **radiographie** *nf*
radiography; *(photo)* X-ray photograph;
radiophonique *adj* radio *cpd*; **radio-
réveil** *(pl* **radios-réveils)** *nm* radio
alarm clock
radis [Radi] *nm* radish
radoter [Radɔte] *vi* to ramble on
radoucir [Radusir]: **se radoucir** *vi
(temps)* to become milder; *(se calmer)*
to calm down
rafale [Rafal] *nf (vent)* gust (of wind);
(tir) burst of gunfire
raffermir [Rafɛrmir] *vt* to firm up
raffiner [Rafine] *vt* to refine; **raffinerie**
nf refinery
raffoler [Rafɔle]: **~ de** *vt* to be very
keen on
rafle [Rafl] *nf (de police)* raid; **rafler** *(fam)*
vt to swipe, nick
rafraîchir [Rafreʃir] *vt (atmosphère,
température)* to cool (down); *(aussi:*
mettre à ~) to chill; *(fig: rénover)* to
brighten up; **se rafraîchir** *vi (temps)*
to grow cooler; *(en se lavant)* to
freshen up; *(en buvant)* to refresh o.s.;
rafraîchissant, e *adj* refreshing;
rafraîchissement *nm (boisson)* cool
drink; **rafraîchissements** *nmpl
(boissons, fruits etc)* refreshments
rage [Raʒ] *nf (Méd):* **la ~** rabies; *(fureur)*
rage, fury; **faire ~** to rage; **rage de
dents** (raging) toothache
ragot [Rago] *(fam) nm* malicious
gossip *no pl*
ragoût [Ragu] *nm* stew
raide [Rɛd] *adj (câble)* taut, tight; *(escarpé)*
steep; *(droit: cheveux)* straight;
(fam: sans argent) flat broke; *(osé)*
daring, bold ▷ *adv (en pente)* steeply; **~
mort** stone dead; **raideur** *nf (rigidité)*
stiffness; **avec raideur** *(répondre)* stiffly,
abruptly; **raidir** *vt (muscles)* to stiffen;
se raidir *vi (tissu)* to stiffen; *(personne)*
to tense up; *(: se préparer moralement)* to
brace o.s.; *(fig: position)* to harden
raie [Rɛ] *nf (Zool)* skate, ray; *(rayure)*
stripe; *(des cheveux)* parting

raifort [RɛfɔR] nm horseradish

rail [Raj] nm rail; (chemins de fer) railways pl; **par ~** by rail

railler [Raje] vt to scoff at, jeer at

rainure [RenyR] nf groove

raisin [Rezɛ̃] nm (aussi: **~s**) grapes pl; **raisins secs** raisins

raison [Rezɔ̃] nf reason; **avoir ~** to be right; **donner ~ à qn** to agree with sb; (événement) to prove sb right; **perdre la ~** to become insane; **se faire une ~** to learn to live with it; **~ de plus** all the more reason; **à plus forte ~** all the more so; **en ~ de** because of; **à ~ de** at the rate of; **sans ~** for no reason; **raison sociale** corporate name; **raisonnable** adj reasonable, sensible

raisonnement [Rezɔnmɑ̃] nm (façon de réfléchir) reasoning; (argumentation) argument

raisonner [Rezɔne] vi (penser) to reason; (argumenter, discuter) to argue ▷ vt (personne) to reason with

rajeunir [RaʒœniR] vt (suj: coiffure, robe): **~ qn** to make sb look younger; (fig: personnel) to inject new blood into ▷ vi to become (ou look) younger

rajouter [Raʒute] vt to add

rajuster [RaʒystE] vt (vêtement) to straighten, tidy; (salaires) to adjust

ralenti [Ralɑ̃ti] nm: **au ~** (fig) at a slower pace; **tourner au ~** (Auto) to tick over, idle

ralentir [Ralɑ̃tiR] vt to slow down

râler [Rale] vi to groan; (fam) to grouse, moan (and groan)

rallier [Ralje] vt (rejoindre) to rejoin; (gagner à sa cause) to win over

rallonge [Ralɔ̃ʒ] nf (de table) (extra) leaf

rallonger [Ralɔ̃ʒe] vt to lengthen

rallye [Rali] nm rally; (Pol) march

ramassage [Ramasaʒ] nm: **ramassage scolaire** school bus service

ramasser [Ramase] vt (objet tombé ou par terre, fam) to pick up; (recueillir: copies, ordures) to collect; (récolter) to gather; **ramassis** (péj) nm (de voyous) bunch; (d'objets) jumble

rambarde [Rɑ̃baRd] nf guardrail

rame [Ram] nf (aviron) oar; (de métro) train; (de papier) ream

rameau, x [Ramo] nm (small) branch; **les Rameaux** (Rel) Palm Sunday sg

ramener [Ram(ə)ne] vt to bring back; (reconduire) to take back; **~ qch à** (réduire à) to reduce sth to

ramer [Rame] vi to row

ramollir [RamɔliR] vt to soften; **se ramollir** vi to go soft

rampe [Rɑ̃p] nf (d'escalier) banister(s pl); (dans un garage) ramp; (Théâtre): **la ~** the footlights pl; **rampe de lancement** launching pad

ramper [Rɑ̃pe] vi to crawl

rancard [Rɑ̃kaR] (fam) nm (rendez-vous) date

rancart [Rɑ̃kaR] nm: **mettre au ~** (fam) to scrap

rance [Rɑ̃s] adj rancid

rancœur [Rɑ̃kœR] nf rancour

rançon [Rɑ̃sɔ̃] nf ransom

rancune [Rɑ̃kyn] nf grudge, rancour; **garder ~ à qn (de qch)** to bear sb a grudge (for sth); **sans ~!** no hard feelings!; **rancunier, -ière** adj vindictive, spiteful

randonnée [Rɑ̃dɔne] nf (pédestre) walk, ramble; (: en montagne) hike, hiking no pl; **la ~** (activité) hiking, walking; **une ~ à cheval** a pony trek

rang [Rɑ̃] nm (rangée) row; (grade, classement) rank; **rangs** nmpl (Mil) ranks; **se mettre en ~s** to get into ou form rows; **au premier ~** in the first row; (fig) ranking first

rangé, e [Rɑ̃ʒe] adj (vie) well-ordered; (personne) steady

rangée [Rɑ̃ʒe] nf row

ranger [Rɑ̃ʒe] vt (mettre de l'ordre dans) to tidy up; (classer, grouper) to order, arrange; (mettre à sa place) to put away; (fig: classer): **~ qn/qch parmi** to rank sb/sth among; **se ranger** vi (véhicule, conducteur) to pull over ou in; (piéton) to step aside; (s'assagir) to settle down; **se ~ à** (avis) to come round to

animer [ʀanime] vt (personne) to bring round; (douleur, souvenir) to revive; (feu) to rekindle

apace [ʀapas] nm bird of prey

âpe [ʀɑp] nf (Culin) grater; **râper** vt (Culin) to grate

apide [ʀapid] adj fast; (prompt: coup d'œil, mouvement) quick ▷ nm express (train); (de cours d'eau) rapid; **rapidement** adv fast; quickly

apiécer [ʀapjese] vt to patch

appel [ʀapɛl] nm (Théâtre) curtain call; (Méd: vaccination) booster; (deuxième avis) reminder; **rappeler** vt to call back; (ambassadeur, Mil) to recall; (faire se souvenir): **rappeler qch à qn** to remind sb of sth; **se rappeler** vt (se souvenir de) to remember, recall; **pouvez-vous rappeler plus tard?** can you call back later?

apport [ʀapɔʀ] nm (lien, analogie) connection; (compte rendu) report; (profit) yield, return; **rapports** nmpl (entre personnes, pays) relations; **avoir ~ à** to have something to do with; **être/se mettre en ~ avec qn** to be/get in touch with sb; **par ~ à** in relation to; **rapports (sexuels)** (sexual) intercourse sg; **rapport qualité-prix** value (for money)

apporter [ʀapɔʀte] vt (rendre, ramener) to bring back; (bénéfice) to yield, bring in; (mentionner, répéter) to report ▷ vi (investissement) to give a good return ou yield; (activité) to be very profitable; **se ~ à** to relate to

approchement [ʀapʀɔʃmã] nm (de nations) reconciliation; (rapport) parallel

approcher [ʀapʀɔʃe] vt (deux objets) to bring closer together; (fig: ennemis, partis etc) to bring together; (comparer) to establish a parallel between; (chaise d'une table): **~ qch (de)** to bring sth closer (to); **se rapprocher** vi to draw closer ou nearer; **se ~ de** to come closer to; (présenter une analogie avec) to be close to

aquette [ʀakɛt] nf (de tennis) racket; (de ping-pong) bat

rare [ʀaʀ] adj rare; **se faire ~** to become scarce; **rarement** adv rarely, seldom

ras, e [ʀɑ, ʀɑz] adj (poil, herbe) short; (tête) close-cropped ▷ adv short; **en ~e campagne** in open country; **à ~ bords** to the brim; **en avoir ~ le bol** (fam) to be fed up

raser [ʀɑze] vt (barbe, cheveux) to shave off; (menton, personne) to shave; (fam: ennuyer) to bore; (démolir) to raze (to the ground); (frôler) to graze, skim; **se raser** vi to shave; (fam) to be bored (to tears); **rasoir** nm razor

rassasier [ʀasazje] vt: **être rassasié** to have eaten one's fill

rassemblement [ʀasɑ̃bləmɑ̃] nm (groupe) gathering; (Pol) union

rassembler [ʀasɑ̃ble] vt (réunir) to assemble, gather; (documents, notes) to gather together, collect; **se rassembler** vi to gather

rassurer [ʀasyʀe] vt to reassure; **se rassurer** vi to reassure o.s.; **rassure-toi** don't worry

rat [ʀa] nm rat

rate [ʀat] nf spleen

raté, e [ʀate] adj (tentative) unsuccessful, failed ▷ nm/f (fam: personne) failure

râteau, x [ʀɑto] nm rake

rater [ʀate] vi (affaire, projet etc) to go wrong, fail ▷ vt (fam: cible, train, occasion) to miss; (plat) to spoil; (fam: examen) to fail; **nous avons raté notre train** we missed our train

ration [ʀasjɔ̃] nf ration

RATP sigle f (= Régie autonome des transports parisiens) Paris transport authority

rattacher [ʀataʃe] vt (animal, cheveux) to tie up again; (fig: relier): **~ qch à** to link sth with

rattraper [ʀatʀape] vt (fugitif) to recapture; (empêcher de tomber) to catch (hold of); (atteindre, rejoindre) to catch up with; (réparer: erreur) to make up for; **se rattraper** vi to make up for it; **se ~**

(à) (se raccrocher) to stop o.s. falling (by catching hold of)

rature [RatyR] nf deletion, erasure

rauque [Rok] adj (voix) hoarse

ravages [Rava3] nmpl: **faire des ~** to wreak havoc

ravi, e [Ravi] adj: **être ~ de/que** to be delighted with/that

ravin [Ravɛ̃] nm gully, ravine

ravir [RaviR] vt (enchanter) to delight; **à ~** adv beautifully

raviser [Ravize]: **se raviser** vi to change one's mind

ravissant, e [Ravisɑ̃, ɑ̃t] adj delightful

ravisseur, -euse [RavisœR, øz] nm/f abductor, kidnapper

ravitailler [Ravitaje] vt (en vivres, munitions) to provide with fresh supplies; (avion) to refuel; **se ~ (en)** to get fresh supplies (of)

raviver [Ravive] vt (feu, douleur) to revive; (couleurs) to brighten up

rayé, e [Reje] adj (à rayures) striped

rayer [Reje] vt (érafler) to scratch; (barrer) to cross out; (d'une liste) to cross off

rayon [Rejɔ̃] nm (de soleil etc) ray; (Géom) radius; (de roue) spoke; (étagère) shelf; (de grand magasin) department; **dans un ~ de** within a radius of; **rayon de soleil** sunbeam; **rayons X** X-rays

rayonnement [Rejɔnmɑ̃] nm (fig: d'une culture) influence

rayonner [Rejɔne] vi (fig) to shine forth; (personne: de joie, de beauté) to be radiant; (touriste) to go touring (from one base)

rayure [RejyR] nf (motif) stripe; (éraflure) scratch; **à ~s** striped

raz-de-marée [RɑdmaRe] nm inv tidal wave

ré [Re] nm (Mus) D; (en chantant la gamme) re

reaction [Reaksjɔ̃] nf reaction

réadapter [Readapte]: **se réadapter (à)** vi to readjust (to)

réagir [ReajiR] vi to react

réalisateur, -trice [RealizatœR, tRis]

nm/f (TV, Cinéma) director

réalisation [Realizasjɔ̃] nf realization; (cinéma) production; **en cours de ~** under way

réaliser [Realize] vt (projet, opération) to carry out, realize; (rêve, souhait) to realize, fulfil; (exploit) to achieve; (film) to produce; (se rendre compte de) to realize; **se réaliser** vi to be realized

réaliste [Realist] adj realistic

réalité [Realite] nf reality; **en ~** in (actual) fact; **dans la ~** in reality

réanimation [Reanimasjɔ̃] nf resuscitation; **service de ~** intensive care unit

rébarbatif, -ive [RebaRbatif, iv] adj forbidding

rebattu, e [R(ə)baty] adj hackneyed

rebelle [Rəbɛl] nm/f rebel ▷ adj (troupes) rebel; (enfant) rebellious; (mèche etc) unruly

rebeller [R(ə)bele]: **se rebeller** vi to rebel

rebondir [R(ə)bɔ̃diR] vi (ballon: au sol) to bounce; (: contre un mur) to rebound; (fig) to get moving again

rebord [R(ə)bɔR] nm edge; **le ~ de la fenêtre** the windowsill

rebours [R(ə)buR]: **à ~** adv the wrong way

rebrousser [R(ə)bRuse] vt: **~ chemin** to turn back

rebuter [Rəbyte] vt to put off

récalcitrant, e [Rekalsitrɑ̃, ɑ̃t] adj refractory

récapituler [Rekapityle] vt to recapitulate, sum up

receler [R(ə)səle] vt (produit d'un vol) to receive; (fig) to conceal; **receleur, -euse** nm/f receiver

récemment [Resamɑ̃] adv recently

recensement [R(ə)sɑ̃smɑ̃] nm (population) census

recenser [R(ə)sɑ̃se] vt (population) to take a census of; (inventorier) to list

récent, e [Resɑ̃, ɑ̃t] adj recent

récépissé [Resepise] nm receipt

récepteur [ReseptœR] nm receiver

réception [Resɛpsjɔ̃] nf receiving no pl; (accueil) reception, welcome; (bureau) reception desk; (réunion mondaine) reception, party; **réceptionniste** nm/f receptionist

recette [R(ə)sɛt] nf recipe; (Comm) takings pl; **recettes** nfpl (Comm: rentrées) receipts; **faire ~** (spectacle, exposition) to be a winner

recevoir [R(ə)səvwaR] vt to receive; (client, patient) to see; **être reçu** (à un examen) to pass

rechange [R(ə)ʃɑ̃ʒ]: **de ~** adj (pièces, roue) spare; (fig: solution) alternative; **des vêtements de ~** a change of clothes

recharge [R(ə)ʃaRʒ] nf refill; **rechargeable** adj (stylo etc) refillable; **recharger** vt (stylo) to refill; (batterie) to recharge

réchaud [Reʃo] nm (portable) stove

réchauffer [Reʃofe] vt (plat) to reheat; (mains, personne) to warm; **se réchauffer** vi (température) to get warmer; (personne) to warm o.s. (up)

rêche [Rɛʃ] adj rough

recherche [R(ə)ʃɛRʃ] nf (action) search; (raffinement) studied elegance; (scientifique etc): **la ~** research; **recherches** nfpl (de la police) investigations; (scientifiques) research sg; **la ~ de** the search for; **être à la ~ de qch** to be looking for sth

recherché, e [R(ə)ʃɛRʃe] adj (rare, demandé) much sought-after; (raffiné: style) mannered; (: tenue) elegant

rechercher [R(ə)ʃɛRʃe] vt (objet égaré, personne) to look for; (causes, nouveau procédé) to try to find; (bonheur, compliments) to seek

rechute [R(ə)ʃyt] nf (Méd) relapse

récidiver [Residive] vi to commit a subsequent offence; (fig) to do it again

récif [Resif] nm reef

récipient [Resipjɑ̃] nm container

réciproque [ResipRɔk] adj reciprocal

récit [Resi] nm story; **récital** nm recital; **réciter** vt to recite

réclamation [Reklamasjɔ̃] nf complaint; **(service des) ~s** complaints department

réclame [Reklam] nf ad, advert(isement); **en ~** on special offer; **réclamer** vt to ask for; (revendiquer) to claim, demand ▷ vi to complain

réclusion [Reklyzjɔ̃] nf imprisonment

recoin [Rəkwɛ̃] nm nook, corner

reçois etc [Rəswa] vb voir **recevoir**

récolte [Rekɔlt] nf harvesting, gathering; (produits) harvest, crop; **récolter** vt to harvest, gather (in); (fig) to collect

recommandé [R(ə)kɔmɑ̃de] nm (Postes): **en ~** by registered mail

recommander [R(ə)kɔmɑ̃de] vt to recommend; (Postes) to register

recommencer [R(ə)kɔmɑ̃se] vt (reprendre: lutte, séance) to resume, start again; (refaire: travail, explications) to start afresh, start (over) again ▷ vi to start again; (récidiver) to do it again

récompense [Rekɔ̃pɑ̃s] nf reward; (prix) award; **récompenser** vt: **récompenser qn (de** ou **pour)** to reward sb (for)

réconcilier [Rekɔ̃silje] vt to reconcile; **se réconcilier (avec)** to make up (with)

reconduire [R(ə)kɔ̃dɥiR] vt (raccompagner) to take ou see back; (renouveler) to renew

réconfort [Rekɔ̃fɔR] nm comfort; **réconforter** vt (consoler) to comfort

reconnaissance [R(ə)kɔnɛsɑ̃s] nf (gratitude) gratitude, gratefulness; (action de reconnaître) recognition; (Mil) reconnaissance, recce; **reconnaissant, e** adj grateful; **je vous serais reconnaissant de bien vouloir ...** I would be most grateful if you would (kindly) ...

reconnaître [R(ə)kɔnɛtR] vt to recognize; (Mil: lieu) to reconnoitre; (Jur: enfant, torts) to acknowledge; **~ que** to admit ou acknowledge that; **~ qn/qch à** (l'identifier grâce à) to recognize sb/sth

by; **reconnu, e** adj (indiscuté, connu)
recognized
reconstituer [R(ə)kɔ̃stitɥe] vt
(événement, accident) to reconstruct;
(fresque, vase brisé) to piece together,
reconstitute
reconstruire [R(ə)kɔ̃strɥir] vt to
rebuild
reconvertir [R(ə)kɔ̃vɛrtir]: **se
reconvertir dans** vr (un métier, une
branche) to go into
record [R(ə)kɔr] nm, adj record
recoupement [R(ə)kupmɑ̃] nm: **par ~**
by cross-checking
recouper [R(ə)kupe]: **se recouper** vi
(témoignages) to tie ou match up
recourber [R(ə)kurbe]: **se recourber**
vi to curve (up), bend (up)
recourir [R(ə)kurir]: **~ à** vt (ami,
agence) to turn ou appeal to; (force, ruse,
emprunt) to resort to
recours [R(ə)kur] nm: **avoir ~ à
= recourir à; en dernier ~** as a last
resort
recouvrer [R(ə)kuvre] vt (vue, santé
etc) to recover, regain
recouvrir [R(ə)kuvrir] vt (couvrir
à nouveau) to re-cover; (couvrir
entièrement, aussi fig) to cover
récréation [Rekreasjɔ̃] nf (Scol) break
recroqueviller [R(ə)krɔk(ə)vije]:
se recroqueviller vi (personne) to
huddle up
recrudescence [R(ə)krydesɑ̃s] nf
fresh outbreak
recruter [R(ə)kryte] vt to recruit
rectangle [Rɛktɑ̃gl] nm rectangle;
rectangulaire adj rectangular
rectificatif [Rɛktifikatif] nm
correction
rectifier [Rɛktifje] vt (calcul, adresse,
paroles) to correct; (erreur) to rectify
rectiligne [Rɛktiliɲ] adj straight
recto [Rɛkto] nm front (of a page); **~
verso** on both sides (of the page)
reçu, e [R(ə)sy] pp de **recevoir** ▷ adj
(candidat) successful; (admis, consacré)
accepted ▷ nm (Comm) receipt; **je peux

avoir un ~, s'il vous plaît? can I have a
receipt, please?
recueil [Rəkœj] nm collection;
recueillir vt to collect; (voix, suffrages)
to win; (accueillir: réfugiés, chat) to take
in; **se recueillir** vi to gather one's
thoughts, meditate
recul [R(ə)kyl] nm (éloignement)
distance; (déclin) decline; **être en ~**
to be on the decline; **avec du ~** with
hindsight; **avoir un mouvement
de ~** to recoil; **prendre du ~** to stand
back; **reculé, e** adj remote; **reculer**
vi to move back, back away; (Auto) to
reverse, back (up); (fig) to be on the
decline ▷ vt to move back; (véhicule)
to reverse, back (up); (date, décision) to
postpone; **reculer devant** (danger,
difficulté) to shrink from; **reculons; à
reculons** adv backwards
récupérer [Rekypere] vt to recover,
get back; (heures de travail) to make up;
(déchets) to salvage ▷ vi to recover
récurer [Rekyre] vt to scour; **poudre à
~** scouring powder
reçut [Rəsy] vb voir **recevoir**
recycler [R(ə)sikle] vt (Tech) to recycle;
se recycler vi to retrain
rédacteur, -trice [Redaktœr, tris]
nm/f (journaliste) writer; subeditor;
(d'ouvrage de référence) editor, compiler
rédaction [Redaksjɔ̃] nf writing;
(rédacteurs) editorial staff; (Scol: devoir)
essay, composition
redescendre [R(ə)desɑ̃dr] vi to go
back down ▷ vt (pente etc) to go down
rédiger [Redize] vt to write; (contrat)
to draw up
redire [R(ə)dir] vt to repeat; **trouver à
~ à** to find fault with
redoubler [R(ə)duble] vi (tempête,
violence) to intensify; (Scol) to repeat a
year; **~ de patience/prudence** to be
doubly patient/careful
redoutable [R(ə)dutabl] adj
formidable, fearsome
redouter [R(ə)dute] vt to dread
redressement [R(ə)drɛsmɑ̃] nm

(économique) recovery

redresser [R(ə)dRese] vt *(relever)* to set upright; *(pièce tordue)* to straighten out; *(situation, économie)* to put right; **se redresser** vi *(personne)* to sit *(ou* stand) up (straight); *(économie)* to recover

réduction [Redyksjɔ̃] nf reduction; **y a-t-il une ~ pour les étudiants?** is there a reduction for students?

réduire [RedɥiR] vt to reduce; *(prix, dépenses)* to cut, reduce; **réduit** nm *(pièce)* tiny room

rééducation [Reedykasjɔ̃] nf *(d'un membre)* re-education; *(de délinquants, d'un blessé)* rehabilitation

réel, le [Reɛl] adj real; **réellement** adv really

réexpédier [Reɛkspedje] vt *(à l'envoyeur)* to return, send back; *(au destinataire)* to send on, forward

refaire [R(ə)fɛR] vt to do again; *(faire de nouveau: sport)* to take up again; *(réparer, restaurer)* to do up

réfectoire [RefɛktwaR] nm refectory

référence [RefeRɑ̃s] nf reference; **références** nfpl *(recommandations)* reference sg

référer [RefeRe]: **se référer à** vt to refer to

refermer [R(ə)fɛRme] vt to close *ou* shut again; **se refermer** vi *(porte)* to close *ou* shut (again)

refiler [R(ə)file] vi *(fam)* to palm off

réfléchi, e [Refleʃi] adj *(caractère)* thoughtful; *(action)* well-thought-out; *(Ling)* reflexive; **c'est tout ~** my mind's made up

réfléchir [RefleʃiR] vt to reflect ▷ vi to think; **~ à** to think about

reflet [R(ə)flɛ] nm reflection; *(sur l'eau etc)* sheen no pl, glint; **refléter** vt to reflect; **se refléter** vi to be reflected

réflexe [Reflɛks] nm, adj reflex

réflexion [Reflɛksjɔ̃] nf *(de la lumière etc)* reflection; *(fait de penser)* thought; *(remarque)* remark; **~ faite, à la ~** on reflection

réflexologie [Reflɛksɔlɔʒi] nf reflexology

réforme [RefɔRm] nf reform; *(Rel)*: **la R~** the Reformation; **réformer** vt to reform; *(Mil)* to declare unfit for service

refouler [R(ə)fule] vt *(envahisseurs)* to drive back; *(larmes)* to force back; *(désir, colère)* to repress

refrain [R(ə)fRɛ̃] nm refrain, chorus

refréner [RəfRene], **réfréner** [RefRene] vt to curb, check

réfrigérateur [RefRiʒeRatœR] nm refrigerator, fridge

refroidir [R(ə)fRwadiR] vt to cool; *(fig: personne)* to put off ▷ vi to cool (down); **se refroidir** vi *(temps)* to get cooler *ou* colder; *(fig: ardeur)* to cool (off); **refroidissement** nm *(grippe etc)* chill

refuge [R(ə)fyʒ] nm refuge; **réfugié, e** adj, nm/f refugee; **réfugier: se réfugier** vi to take refuge

refus [R(ə)fy] nm refusal; **ce n'est pas de ~** I won't say no, it's welcome; **refuser** vt to refuse; *(Scol: candidat)* to fail; **refuser qch à qn** to refuse sb sth; **refuser du monde** to have to turn people away; **se refuser à faire** to refuse to do

regagner [R(ə)gaɲe] vt *(faveur)* to win back; *(lieu)* to get back to

régal [Regal] nm treat; **régaler: se régaler** vi to have a delicious meal; *(fig)* to enjoy o.s.

regard [R(ə)gaR] nm *(coup d'œil)* look, glance; *(expression)* look (in one's eye); **au ~ de** *(loi, morale)* from the point of view of; **en ~ de** in comparison with

regardant, e [R(ə)gaRdɑ̃, ɑ̃t] adj *(économe)* tight-fisted; **peu ~ (sur)** very free (about)

regarder [R(ə)gaRde] vt to look at; *(film, télévision, match)* to watch; *(concerner)* to concern ▷ vi to look; **ne pas ~ à la dépense** to spare no expense; **~ qn/qch comme** to regard sb/sth as

régie [Reʒi] nf *(Comm, Industrie)* state-owned company; *(Théâtre, Cinéma)* production; *(Radio, TV)* control room

régime [ʀeʒim] *nm* (*Pol*) régime; (*Méd*) diet; (*Admin: carcéral, fiscal etc*) system; (*de bananes, dattes*) bunch; **se mettre au/suivre un ~** to go on/be on a diet

régiment [ʀeʒimɑ̃] *nm* regiment

région [ʀeʒjɔ̃] *nf* region; **régional, e, -aux** *adj* regional

régir [ʀeʒiʀ] *vt* to govern

régisseur [ʀeʒisœʀ] *nm* (*d'un domaine*) steward; (*Cinéma, TV*) assistant director; (*Théâtre*) stage manager

registre [ʀeʒistʀ] *nm* register

réglage [ʀeglaʒ] *nm* adjustment

règle [ʀegl] *nf* (*instrument*) ruler; (*loi*) rule; **règles** *nfpl* (*menstruation*) period *sg*; **en ~** (*papiers d'identité*) in order; **en ~ générale** as a (general) rule

réglé, e [ʀegle] *adj* (*vie*) well-ordered; (*arrangé*) settled

règlement [ʀegləmɑ̃] *nm* (*paiement*) settlement; (*arrêté*) regulation; (*règles, statuts*) regulations *pl*, rules *pl*; **réglementaire** *adj* conforming to the regulations; (*tenue*) regulation *cpd*; **réglementation** *nf* (*règles*) regulations; **réglementer** *vt* to regulate

régler [ʀegle] *vt* (*conflit, facture*) to settle; (*personne*) to settle up with; (*mécanisme, machine*) to regulate, adjust; (*thermostat etc*) to set, adjust

réglisse [ʀeglis] *nf* liquorice

règne [ʀeɲ] *nm* (*d'un roi etc, fig*) reign; **le ~ végétal/animal** the vegetable/animal kingdom; **régner** *vi* to rule, reign; (*fig*) to reign

regorger [ʀ(ə)gɔʀʒe] *vi*: **~ de** to overflow with, be bursting with

regret [ʀ(ə)gʀɛ] *nm* regret; **à ~** with regret; **sans ~** with no regrets; **regrettable** *adj* regrettable; **regretter** *vt* to regret; (*personne*) to miss; **je regrette mais ...** I'm sorry but ...

regrouper [ʀ(ə)gʀupe] *vt* (*grouper*) to group together; (*contenir*) to include, comprise; **se regrouper** *vi* to gather (together)

régulier, -ière [ʀegylje, jɛʀ] *adj* (*gén*) regular; (*vitesse, qualité*) steady; (*égal: couche, ligne*) even; (*Transports: ligne, service*) scheduled, regular; (*légal*) lawful, in order; (*honnête*) straight, on the level; **régulièrement** *adv* regularly; (*uniformément*) evenly

rehausser [ʀəose] *vt* (*relever*) to heighten, raise; (*fig: souligner*) to set off, enhance

rein [ʀɛ̃] *nm* kidney; **reins** *nmpl* (*dos*) back *sg*

reine [ʀɛn] *nf* queen

reine-claude [ʀɛnklod] *nf* greengage

réinscriptible [ʀeɛ̃skʀiptibl] *adj* (*CD, DVD*) rewritable

réinsertion [ʀeɛ̃sɛʀsjɔ̃] *nf* (*de délinquant*) reintegration, rehabilitation

réintégrer [ʀeɛ̃tegʀe] *vt* (*lieu*) to return to; (*fonctionnaire*) to reinstate

rejaillir [ʀ(ə)ʒajiʀ] *vi* to splash up; **~ sur** (*fig: scandale*) to rebound on; (*: gloire*) to be reflected on

rejet [ʀaʒɛ] *nm* rejection; **rejeter** *vt* (*relancer*) to throw back; (*écarter*) to reject; (*déverser*) to throw out, discharge; (*vomir*) to bring *ou* throw up; **rejeter la responsabilité de qch sur qn** to lay the responsibility for sth at sb's door

rejoindre [ʀ(ə)ʒwɛ̃dʀ] *vt* (*famille, régiment*) to rejoin, return to; (*lieu*) to get (back) to; (*suj: route etc*) to meet, join; (*rattraper*) to catch up (with); **se rejoindre** *vi* to meet; **je te rejoins à la gare** I'll see *ou* meet you at the station

réjouir [ʀeʒwiʀ] *vt* to delight; **se ~ (de qch/de faire)** to be delighted (about sth/to do); **réjouissances** *nfpl* (*fête*) festivities

relâche [ʀəlɑʃ] *nm ou nf*: **sans ~** without respite *ou* a break; **relâché, e** *adj* loose, lax; **relâcher** *vt* (*libérer*) to release; (*desserrer*) to loosen; **se relâcher** *vi* (*discipline*) to become slack *ou* lax; (*élève etc*) to slacken off

relais [ʀ(ə)lɛ] *nm* (*Sport*): **(course de) ~** relay (race); **prendre le ~ (de)** to take over (from); **relais routier** ≈ transport café (BRIT), ≈ truck stop (US)

relancer [R(ə)lãse] vt (balle) to throw back; (moteur) to restart; (fig) to boost, revive; (harceler): **~ qn** to pester sb

relatif, -ive [R(ə)latif, iv] adj relative

relation [R(ə)lasjõ] nf (rapport) relation(ship); (connaissance) acquaintance; **relations** nfpl (rapports) relations; (connaissances) connections; **être/entrer en ~(s) avec** to be/get in contact with

relaxer [Rəlakse]: **se relaxer** vi to relax

relayer [R(ə)leje] vt (collaborateur, coureur etc) to relieve; **se relayer** vi (dans une activité) to take it in turns

reléguer [R(ə)lege] vt to relegate

relevé, e [Rəl(ə)ve] adj (manches) rolled-up; (sauce) highly-seasoned ▷ nm (de compteur) reading; **relevé bancaire** ou **de compte** bank statement

relève [Rəlɛv] nf (personne) relief; **prendre la ~** to take over

relever [Rəl(ə)ve] vt (meuble) to stand up again; (personne tombée) to help up; (vitre, niveau de vie) to raise; (inf) to turn up; (style) to elevate; (plat, sauce) to season; (sentinelle, équipe) to relieve; (fautes) to pick out; (défi) to accept, take up; (noter: adresse etc) to take down, note; (: plan) to sketch; (compteur) to read; (ramasser: cahiers) to collect, take in; **se relever** vi (se remettre debout) to get up; **~ de** (maladie) to be recovering from; (être du ressort de) to be a matter for; (fig) to pertain to; **~ qn de** (fonctions) to relieve sb of; **~ la tête** to look up

relief [Rəljɛf] nm relief; **mettre en ~** (fig) to bring out, highlight

relier [Rəlje] vt to link up; (livre) to bind; **~ qch à** to link sth to

religieux, -euse [R(ə)liʒjø, jøz] adj religious ▷ nm monk

religion [R(ə)liʒjõ] nf religion

relire [R(ə)liR] vt (à nouveau) to reread, read again; (vérifier) to read over

reluire [R(ə)lɥiR] vi to gleam

remanier [R(ə)manje] vt to reshape, recast; (Pol) to reshuffle

remarquable [R(ə)maRkabl] adj remarkable

remarque [R(ə)maRk] nf remark; (écrite) note

remarquer [R(ə)maRke] vt (voir) to notice; **se remarquer** vi to be noticeable; **faire ~ (à qn) que** to point out (to sb) that; **faire ~ qch (à qn)** to point sth out (to sb); **remarquez, ...** mind you ...; **se faire ~** to draw attention to o.s.

rembourrer [Rãbure] vt to stuff

remboursement [Rãbursəmã] nm (de dette, d'emprunt) repayment; (de frais) refund; **rembourser** vt to pay back, repay; (frais, billet etc) to refund; **se faire rembourser** to get a refund

remède [R(ə)mɛd] nm (médicament) medicine; (traitement, fig) remedy, cure

remémorer [R(ə)memɔRe]: **se remémorer** vt to recall, recollect

remerciements [RəmɛRsimã] nmpl thanks; **(avec) tous mes ~** (with) grateful ou many thanks

remercier [R(ə)mɛRsje] vt to thank; (congédier) to dismiss; **~ qn de/d'avoir fait** to thank sb for/for having done

remettre [R(ə)mɛtR] vt (replacer) to put back; (vêtement) to put back on; (ajouter) to add; (ajourner): **~ qch (à)** to postpone sth (until); **se remettre** vi: **se ~ (de)** to recover (from); **~ qch à qn** (donner: lettre, clé etc) to hand over sth to sb; (: prix, décoration) to present sb with sth; **se ~ à faire qch** to start doing sth again; **s'en ~ à** to leave it (up) to

remise [R(ə)miz] nf (rabais) discount; (local) shed; **remise de peine** reduction of sentence; **remise des prix** prize-giving; **remise en cause** ou **question** calling into question, challenging; **remise en jeu** (Football) throw-in

remontant [R(ə)mõtã] nm tonic, pick-me-up

remonte-pente [R(ə)mõtpãt] nm ski-lift

remonter [R(ə)mõte] vi to go back

up; (*prix, température*) to go up again
▷ *vt* (*pente*) to go up; (*fleuve*) to sail (*ou*
swim *etc*) up; (*manches, pantalon*) to
roll up; (*col*) to turn up; (*niveau, limite*)
to raise; (*fig: personne*) to buck up;
(*qch de démonté*) to put back together,
reassemble; (*montre*) to wind up; **~ le
moral à qn** to raise sb's spirits; **~ à**
(*dater de*) to date *ou* go back to
remords [R(ə)mɔR] *nm* remorse *no pl*;
avoir des ~ to feel remorse
remorque [R(ə)mɔRk] *nf* trailer;
remorquer *vt* to tow; **remorqueur**
nm tug(boat)
remous [Rəmu] *nm* (*d'un navire*)
(back)wash *no pl*; (*de rivière*) swirl, eddy
▷ *nmpl* (*fig*) stir *sg*
remparts [RɑpaR] *nmpl* walls,
ramparts
remplaçant, e [Rɑ̃plasɑ̃, ɑ̃t] *nm/f*
replacement, stand-in; (*Scol*) supply
teacher
remplacement [Rɑ̃plasmɑ̃] *nm*
replacement; **faire des ~s** (*professeur*) to
do supply teaching; (*secrétaire*) to temp
remplacer [Rɑ̃plase] *vt* to replace; **~
qch/qn par** to replace sth/sb with
rempli, e [Rɑ̃pli] *adj* (*emploi du temps*)
full, busy; **~ de** full of, filled with
remplir [Rɑ̃pliR] *vt* to fill (up);
(*questionnaire*) to fill out *ou* up;
(*obligations, fonction, condition*) to fulfil;
se remplir *vi* to fill up
remporter [Rɑ̃pɔRte] *vt* (*marchandise*)
to take away; (*fig*) to win, achieve
remuant, e [Rəmɥɑ̃, ɑ̃t] *adj* restless
remue-ménage [R(ə)mymenaʒ] *nm
inv* commotion
remuer [Rəmɥe] *vt* to move; (*café,
sauce*) to stir ▷ *vi* to move; **se remuer** *vi*
to move; (*fam: s'activer*) to get a move on
rémunérer [Remynere] *vt* to
remunerate
renard [R(ə)naR] *nm* fox
renchérir [Rɑ̃ʃeRiR] *vi* (*fig*): **~ (sur)** (*en
paroles*) to add something (to)
rencontre [Rɑ̃kɔtR] *nf* meeting;
(*imprévue*) encounter; **aller à la ~ de qn**

to go and meet sb; **rencontrer** *vt* to
meet; (*mot, expression*) to come across;
(*difficultés*) to meet with; **se rencontrer**
vi to meet
rendement [Rɑ̃dmɑ̃] *nm* (*d'un
travailleur, d'une machine*) output; (*d'un
champ*) yield
rendez-vous [Rɑ̃devu] *nm*
appointment; (*d'amoureux*) date;
(*lieu*) meeting place; **donner ~ à qn**
to arrange to meet sb; **avoir/
prendre ~ (avec)** to have/make an
appointment (with); **j'ai ~ avec ...**
I have an appointment with ...; **je
voudrais prendre ~** I'd like to make an
appointment
rendre [Rɑ̃dR] *vt* (*restituer*) to give back,
return; (*invitation*) to return, repay;
(*vomir*) to bring up; (*exprimer, traduire*) to
render; (*faire devenir*): **~ qn célèbre/qch
possible** to make sb famous/sth
possible; **se rendre** *vi* (*capituler*) to
surrender, give o.s. up; (*aller*): **se ~
quelque part** to go somewhere; **~ la
monnaie à qn** to give sb his change; **se
~ compte de qch** to realize sth
rênes [REn] *nfpl* reins
renfermé, e [RɑfɛRme] *adj* (*fig*)
withdrawn ▷ *nm*: **sentir le ~** to smell
stuffy
renfermer [RɑfɛRme] *vt* to contain
renforcer [RɑfɔRse] *vt* to
reinforce; **renfort: renforts** *nmpl*
reinforcements; **à grand renfort de**
with a great deal of
renfrogné, e [RɑfRɔɲe] *adj* sullen
renier [Rənje] *vt* (*personne*) to disown,
repudiate; (*foi*) to renounce
renifler [R(ə)nifle] *vi, vt* to sniff
renne [REn] *nm* reindeer *inv*
renom [Rənɔ̃] *nm* reputation; (*célébrité*)
renown; **renommé, e** *adj* celebrated,
renowned; **renommée** *nf* fame
renoncer [R(ə)nɔse]: **~ à** *vt* to give up;
~ à faire to give up the idea of doing
renouer [Rənwe] *vt*: **~ avec** (*habitude*)
to take up again
renouveler [R(ə)nuv(ə)le] *vt* to

renew; (exploit, méfait) to repeat; **se
renouveler** vi (incident) to recur,
happen again; **renouvellement** nm
(remplacement) renewal

énover [Renɔve] vt (immeuble) to
renovate, do up; (quartier) to redevelop

enseignement [Rãsɛɲmã] nm
information no pl, piece of information;
(guichet des) ~s information office;
(service des) ~s (Tél) directory
enquiries (BRIT), information (US)

enseigner [Rãseɲe] vt: **~ qn (sur)**
to give information to sb (about); **se
renseigner** vi to ask for information,
make inquiries

entabilité [Rãtabilite] nf profitability

entable [Rãtabl] adj profitable

ente [Rãt] nf private income; (pension)
pension

entrée [Rãtre] nf: **~ (d'argent)** cash
no pl coming in; **la ~ (des classes)** the
start of the new school year

entrer [Rãtre] vi (revenir chez soi) to
go (ou come) back home; (entrer de
nouveau) to go (ou come) back in; (entrer)
to go (ou come) in; (air, clou: pénétrer) to
go in; (revenu) to come in ▷ vt to bring
in; (véhicule) to put away; (chemise dans
pantalon etc) to tuck in; (griffes) to draw
in; **~ le ventre** to pull in one's stomach;
~ dans (heurter) to crash into; **~ dans
l'ordre** to be back to normal; **~ dans
ses frais** to recover one's expenses;
je rentre mardi I'm going ou coming
home on Tuesday

enverse [Rãvɛrs] **à la ~** adv
backwards

enverser [Rãvɛrse] vt (faire tomber:
chaise, verre) to knock over, overturn;
(liquide, contenu) to spill, upset; (piéton)
to knock down; (retourner) to turn
upside down; (: ordre des mots etc)
to reverse; (fig: gouvernement etc) to
overthrow; (fam: stupéfier) to bowl over;
se renverser vi (verre, vase) to fall over;
(contenu) to spill

envoi [Rãvwa] nm (d'employé)
dismissal; (d'élève) expulsion; (référence)

cross-reference; (éructation) belch;
renvoyer vt to send back; (congédier) to
dismiss; (élève: définitivement) to expel;
(lumière) to reflect; (ajourner): **renvoyer
qch (à)** to put sth off ou postpone
sth (until)

repaire [RəpɛR] nm den

répandre [RepãdR] vt (renverser) to
spill; (étaler, diffuser) to spread; (odeur)
to give off; **se répandre** vi to spill; (se
propager) to spread; **répandu, e** adj
(opinion, usage) widespread

réparation [Reparasjõ] nf repair

réparer [Repare] vt to repair; (fig:
offense) to make up for, atone for;
(: oubli, erreur) to put right; **où est-ce
que je peux le faire ~?** where can I
get it fixed?

repartie [Reparti] nf retort; **avoir de
la ~** to be quick at repartee

repartir [R(ə)partiR] vi to leave again;
(voyageur) to set off again; (fig) to get
going again; **~ à zéro** to start from
scratch (again)

répartir [RepartiR] vt (pour attribuer)
to share out; (pour disperser, disposer)
to divide up; (poids) to distribute; **se
répartir** vt (travail, rôles) to share out
between themselves; **répartition** nf
(des richesses etc) distribution

repas [R(ə)pa] nm meal

repassage [R(ə)pasaʒ] nm ironing

repasser [R(ə)pase] vi to come (ou
go) back ▷ vt (vêtement, tissu) to iron;
(examen) to retake, resit; (film) to show
again; (leçon: revoir) to go over (again)

repentir [Rəpãtiʀ] nm repentance; **se
repentir** vi to repent; **se ~ d'avoir fait
qch** (regretter) to regret having done sth

répercussions [Repɛrkysjõ] nfpl (fig)
repercussions

répercuter [Repɛrkyte]: **se répercuter**
vi (bruit) to reverberate; (fig): **se ~ sur** to
have repercussions on

repère [R(ə)pɛR] nm mark; (monument,
événement) landmark

repérer [R(ə)pere] vt (fam: erreur,
personne) to spot; (: endroit) to locate; **se**

repérer vi to find one's way about

répertoire [ʀɛpɛʀtwaʀ] nm (liste) (alphabetical) list; (carnet) index notebook; (Inform) folder, directory; (d'un artiste) repertoire

répéter [ʀepete] vt to repeat; (préparer: leçon) to learn, go over; (Théâtre) to rehearse; **se répéter** vi (redire) to repeat o.s.; (se reproduire) to be repeated, recur; **pouvez-vous ~, s'il vous plaît?** can you repeat that, please?

répétition [ʀepetisjɔ̃] nf repetition; (Théâtre) rehearsal; ~ **générale** (final) dress rehearsal

répit [ʀepi] nm respite; **sans ~** without letting up

replier [ʀ(ə)plije] vt (rabattre) to fold down ou over; **se replier** vi (troupes, armée) to withdraw, fall back; (sur soi-même) to withdraw into o.s.

réplique [ʀeplik] nf (repartie, fig) reply; (Théâtre) line; (copie) replica; **répliquer** vi to reply; (riposter) to retaliate

répondeur [ʀepɔ̃dœʀ] nm: ~ **(automatique)** (Tél) answering machine

répondre [ʀepɔ̃dʀ] vi to answer, reply; (freins) to respond; ~ **à** to reply to, answer; (affection, salut) to return; (provocation) to respond to; (correspondre à: besoin) to answer; (: conditions) to meet; (: description) to match; (avec impertinence): ~ **à qn** to answer sb back; ~ **de** to answer for

réponse [ʀepɔ̃s] nf answer, reply; **en ~ à** in reply to

reportage [ʀ(ə)pɔʀtaʒ] nm report

reporter¹ [ʀapɔʀtɛʀ] nm reporter

reporter² [ʀapɔʀte] vt (ajourner): ~ **qch (à)** to postpone sth (until); (transférer): ~ **qch sur** to transfer sth to; **se reporter à** (époque) to think back to; (document) to refer to

repos [ʀ(ə)po] nm rest; (tranquillité) peace (and quiet); (Mil): ~! stand at ease!; **ce n'est pas de tout ~!** it's no picnic!

reposant, e [ʀ(ə)pozɑ̃, ɑ̃t] adj restful

reposer [ʀ(ə)poze] vt (verre, livre) to put down; (délasser) to rest ▷ vi: **laisser ~** (pâte) to leave to stand; **se reposer** vi to rest; **se ~ sur qn** to rely on sb; ~ **sur** (fig) to rest on

repoussant, e [ʀ(ə)pusɑ̃, ɑ̃t] adj repulsive

repousser [ʀ(ə)puse] vi to grow again ▷ vt to repel, repulse; (offre) to turn down, reject; (personne) to push back; (différer) to put back

reprendre [ʀ(ə)pʀɑ̃dʀ] vt (objet prêté, donné) to take back; (prisonnier, ville) to recapture; (firme, entreprise) to take over; (le travail) to resume; (emprunter: argument, idée) to take up, use; (refaire: article etc) to go over again; (vêtement) to alter; (réprimander) to tell off; (corriger) to correct; (chercher): **je viendrai te ~ à 4** I'll come and fetch you at 4; (se resservir de): ~ **du pain/un œuf** to take (ou eat) more bread/another egg ▷ vi (classes, pluie) to start (up) again; (activités, travaux, combats) to resume, start (up) again; (affaires) to pick up; (dire): **reprit il** he went on; ~ **des forces** to recover one's strength; ~ **courage** to take new heart; ~ **la route** to resume one's journey, set off again; ~ **haleine** ou **son souffle** to get one's breath back

représentant, e [ʀ(ə)pʀezɑ̃tɑ̃, ɑ̃t] nm/f representative

représentation [ʀ(ə)pʀezɑ̃tasjɔ̃] nf (symbole, image) representation; (spectacle) performance

représenter [ʀ(ə)pʀezɑ̃te] vt to represent; (donner: pièce, opéra) to perform; **se représenter** vt (se figurer) to imagine

répression [ʀepʀesjɔ̃] nf repression

réprimer [ʀepʀime] vt (émotions) to suppress; (peuple etc) to repress

repris [ʀ(ə)pʀi] nm: ~ **de justice** ex-prisoner, ex-convict

reprise [ʀ(ə)pʀiz] nf (recommencement) resumption; (économique) recovery; (TV) repeat; (Comm) trade-in, part exchange; (*raccommodage*) mend; **à plusieurs ~s** on several occasions

priser [ʀ(ə)pʀize] vt (*chaussette, ainage*) to darn; (*tissu*) to mend

proche [ʀ(ə)pʀɔʃ] nm (*remontrance*) reproach; **faire des ~s à qn** to reproach sb; **sans ~(s)** beyond reproach;

reprocher vt: **reprocher qch à qn** to reproach ou blame sb for sth; **reprocher qch à** (*critiquer*) to have sth against

production [ʀ(ə)pʀɔdyksjɔ̃] nf reproduction

produire [ʀ(ə)pʀɔdɥiʀ] vt to reproduce; **se reproduire** vi (*Bio*) to reproduce; (*recommencer*) to recur, re-occur

ptile [ʀɛptil] nm reptile

publique [ʀepyblik] nf republic

pugnant, e [ʀepyɲɑ̃, ɑ̃t] adj disgusting

pugner [ʀepyɲe]: **~ à** vt : **~ à qn** to repel ou disgust sb; **~ à faire** to be loath ou reluctant to do

putation [ʀepytasjɔ̃] nf reputation;

réputé, e adj renowned

quérir [ʀəkeʀiʀ] vt (*nécessiter*) to require, call for

quête [ʀəkɛt] nf request

quin [ʀəkɛ̃] nm shark

quis, e [ʀəki, iz] adj required

ER sigle m (= *réseau express régional*) Greater Paris high-speed train service

scapé, e [ʀɛskape] nm/f survivor

scousse [ʀɛskus] nf: **aller à la ~ de qn** to go to sb's aid ou rescue

seau, x [ʀezo] nm network

servation [ʀezɛʀvasjɔ̃] nf booking, reservation; **j'ai confirmé ma ~ par fax/e-mail** I confirmed my booking by fax/e-mail

serve [ʀezɛʀv] nf (*retenue*) reserve; (*entrepôt*) storeroom; (*restriction, d'Indiens*) reservation; (*de pêche, chasse*) preserve; **de ~** (*provisions etc*) in reserve

servé, e [ʀezɛʀve] adj reserved; **chasse/pêche ~e** private hunting/fishing

server [ʀezɛʀve] vt to reserve;

(*chambre, billet etc*) to book, reserve; (*fig: destiner*) to have in store; (*garder*): **~ qch pour/à** to keep ou save sth for; **je voudrais ~ une chambre pour deux personnes** I'd like to book a double room; **j'ai réservé une table au nom de ...** I booked a table in the name of ...

réservoir [ʀezɛʀvwaʀ] nm tank

résidence [ʀezidɑ̃s] nf residence; **résidence secondaire** second home; **résidence universitaire** hall of residence (BRIT), dormitory (US); **résidentiel, le** adj residential; **résider** vi: **résider à/dans/en** to reside in; **résider dans** (*fig*) to lie in

résidu [ʀezidy] nm residue *no pl*

résigner [ʀeziɲe]: **se résigner** vi: **se ~ (à qch/à faire)** to resign o.s. (to sth/to doing)

résilier [ʀezilje] vt to terminate

résistance [ʀezistɑ̃s] nf resistance; (*de réchaud, bouilloire: fil*) element

résistant, e [ʀezistɑ̃, ɑ̃t] adj (*personne*) robust, tough; (*matériau*) strong, hard-wearing

résister [ʀeziste] vi to resist; **~ à** (*assaut, tentation*) to resist; (*supporter: gel etc*) to withstand; (*désobéir à*) to stand up to, oppose

résolu, e [ʀezɔly] pp de **résoudre** ▷ adj: **être ~ à qch/faire** to be set upon sth/doing

résolution [ʀezɔlysjɔ̃] nf (*fermeté, décision*) resolution; (*d'un problème*) solution

résolve etc [ʀezɔlv] vb voir **résoudre**

résonner [ʀezɔne] vi (*cloche, pas*) to reverberate, resound; (*salle*) to be resonant

résorber [ʀezɔʀbe]: **se résorber** vi (*fig: chômage*) to be reduced; (: *déficit*) to be absorbed

résoudre [ʀezudʀ] vt to solve; **se ~ à faire** to bring o.s. to do

respect [ʀɛspɛ] nm respect; **tenir en ~** to keep at bay; **présenter ses ~s à qn** to pay one's respects to sb; **respecter** vt to respect; **respectueux, -euse** adj respectful

respiration [ʀɛspiʀasjɔ̃] nf
breathing no pl

respirer [ʀɛspiʀe] vi to breathe; (fig: se
détendre) to get one's breath;
(: se rassurer) to breathe again ▷ vt to
breathe (in), inhale; (manifester: santé,
calme etc) to exude

resplendir [ʀɛsplɑ̃diʀ] vi to shine;
(fig): ~ **(de)** to be radiant (with)

responsabilité [ʀɛspɔ̃sabilite] nf
responsibility; (légale) liability

responsable [ʀɛspɔ̃sabl] adj
responsible ▷ nm/f (coupable) person
responsible; (personne compétente)
person in charge; (de parti, syndicat)
official; ~ **de** responsible for

ressaisir [ʀ(ə)seziʀ]: **se ressaisir** vi to
regain one's self-control

ressasser [ʀ(ə)sase] vt to keep going
over

ressemblance [ʀ(ə)sɑ̃blɑ̃s] nf
resemblance, similarity, likeness

ressemblant, e [ʀ(ə)sɑ̃blɑ̃, ɑ̃t] adj
(portrait) lifelike, true to life

ressembler [ʀ(ə)sɑ̃ble]: ~ **à** vt to
be like, resemble; (visuellement) to
look like; **se ressembler** vi to be (ou
look) alike

ressentiment [ʀ(ə)sɑ̃timɑ̃] nm
resentment

ressentir [ʀ(ə)sɑ̃tiʀ] vt to feel; **se ~ de**
to feel (ou show) the effects of

resserrer [ʀ(ə)seʀe] vt (nœud, boulon)
to tighten (up); (fig: liens) to strengthen

resservir [ʀ(ə)seʀviʀ] vi to do ou serve
again; ~ **qn (d'un plat)** to give sb a
second helping (of a dish); **se ~ de** (plat)
to take a second helping of; (outil etc)
to use again

ressort [ʀəsɔʀ] nm (pièce) spring;
(énergie) spirit; (recours): **en dernier ~** as
a last resort; (compétence): **être du ~ de**
to fall within the competence of

ressortir [ʀəsɔʀtiʀ] vi to go (ou come)
out (again); (contraster) to stand out;
~ **de** to emerge from; **faire ~** (fig:
souligner) to bring out

ressortissant, e [ʀ(ə)sɔʀtisɑ̃, ɑ̃t]
nm/f national

ressources [ʀ(ə)suʀs] nfpl (moyens)
resources

ressusciter [ʀesysite] vt (fig) to revive,
bring back ▷ vi to rise (from the dead)

restant, e [ʀɛstɑ̃, ɑ̃t] adj remaining
▷ nm: **le ~ (de)** the remainder (of); **un ~
de** (de trop) some left-over

restaurant [ʀɛstɔʀɑ̃] nm restaurant;
**pouvez-vous m'indiquer un bon
~?** can you recommend a good
restaurant?

restauration [ʀɛstɔʀasjɔ̃] nf
restoration; (hôtellerie) catering;
restauration rapide fast food

restaurer [ʀɛstɔʀe] vt to restore; **se
restaurer** vi to have something to eat

reste [ʀɛst] nm (restant): **le ~ (de)** the
rest (of); (de trop): **un ~ (de)** some
left-over; **restes** nmpl (nourriture) left-
overs; (d'une cité etc, dépouille mortelle)
remains; **du ~, au ~** besides, moreover

rester [ʀɛste] vi to stay, remain;
(subsister) to remain, be left; (durer)
to last, live on ▷ vb impers: **il reste du
pain/2 œufs** there's some bread/there
are 2 eggs left (over); **restons-en là** let's
leave it at that; **il me reste assez de
temps** I have enough time left; **il ne me
reste plus qu'à ...** I've just got to ...

restituer [ʀɛstitɥe] vt (objet, somme):
qch (à qn) to return sth (to sb)

restreindre [ʀɛstʀɛ̃dʀ] vt to restrict,
limit

restriction [ʀɛstʀiksjɔ̃] nf restriction

résultat [ʀezylta] nm result; **résultats**
nmpl (d'examen, d'élection) results pl

résulter [ʀezylte]: ~ **de** vt to result
from, be the result of

résumé [ʀezyme] nm summary,
résumé; **en ~** in brief; (pour conclure)
to sum up

résumer [ʀezyme] vt (texte) to
summarize; (récapituler) to sum up
⬛ Attention à ne pas traduire *résumé*
par *to resume*.

résurrection [ʀezyʀɛksjɔ̃] nf

resurrection

établir [Retabliʀ] vt to restore, re-establish; **se rétablir** vi (guérir) to recover; (silence, calme) to return, be restored; **rétablissement** nm restoring; (guérison) recovery

étaper [R(ə)tape] (fam) vt (maison, voiture etc) to do up; (revigorer) to buck up

étard [R(ə)taʀ] nm (d'une personne attendue) lateness no pl; (sur l'horaire, un programme) delay; (fig: scolaire, mental etc) backwardness; **en ~ (de 2 heures)** (2 hours) late; **avoir du ~** to be late; (sur un programme) to be behind (schedule); **prendre du ~** (train, avion) to be delayed; **sans ~** without delay; **désolé d'être en ~** sorry I'm late; **le vol a deux heures de ~** the flight is two hours late

étardataire [R(ə)taʀdatɛʀ] nm/f latecomer

étardement [R(ə)taʀdəmã]: **à ~** adj delayed action cpd; **bombe à ~** time bomb

étarder [R(ə)taʀde] vt to delay; (montre) to put back ▷ vi (montre) to be slow; **~ qn (d'une heure)** (sur un horaire) to delay sb (an hour); **~ qch (de 2 jours)** (départ, date) to put back (2 days)

étenir [Rət(ə)niʀ] vt (garder, retarder) to keep, detain; (maintenir: objet qui glisse, fig: colère, larmes) to hold back; (se rappeler) to retain; (réserver) to reserve; (accepter: proposition etc) to accept; (fig: empêcher d'agir): **~ qn (de faire)** to hold sb back (from doing); (prélever): **~ qch (sur)** to deduct sth from; **se retenir** vi (se raccrocher): **se ~ à** to hold onto; (se contenir): **se ~ de faire** to restrain o.s. from doing; **~ son souffle** to hold one's breath

étentir [R(ə)tãtiʀ] vi to ring out; **retentissant, e** adj resounding

étenue [Rət(ə)ny] nf (prélèvement) deduction; (Scol) detention; (modération) (self-)restraint

ticence [Retisãs] nf hesitation, reluctance no pl; **réticent, e** adj

hesitant, reluctant

rétine [Retin] nf retina

retiré, e [R(ə)tiRe] adj (vie) secluded; (lieu) remote

retirer [R(ə)tiRe] vt (vêtement, lunettes) to take off, remove; (argent, plainte) to withdraw; (reprendre: bagages, billets) to collect, pick up; (extraire): **~ qch de** to take sth out of, remove sth from

retomber [R(ə)tɔ̃be] vi (à nouveau) to fall again; (atterrir: après un saut etc) to land; (échoir): **~ sur qn** to fall on sb

rétorquer [Retɔʀke] vt: **~ (à qn) que** to retort (to sb) that

retouche [R(ə)tuʃ] nf (sur vêtement) alteration; **retoucher** vt (photographie) to touch up; (texte, vêtement) to alter

retour [R(ə)tuʀ] nm return; **au ~** (en route) on the way back; **à mon ~** when I get/got back; **être de ~ (de)** to be back (from); **par ~ du courrier** by return of post; **quand serons-nous de ~?** when do we get back?

retourner [R(ə)tuRne] vt (dans l'autre sens: matelas, crêpe etc) to turn (over); (: sac, vêtement) to turn inside out; (fam: bouleverser) to shake; (renvoyer, restituer): **~ qch à qn** to return sth to sb ▷ vi (aller, revenir): **~ quelque part/à** to go back ou return somewhere/to; **se retourner** vi (tourner la tête) to turn round; **~ à** (état, activité) to return to, go back to; **se ~ contre** (fig) to turn against

retrait [R(ə)tʀɛ] nm (d'argent) withdrawal; **en ~** set back; **retrait du permis (de conduire)** disqualification from driving (BRIT), revocation of driver's license (US)

retraite [R(ə)tʀɛt] nf (d'un employé) retirement; (revenu) pension; (d'une armée, Rel) retreat; **prendre sa ~** to retire; **retraite anticipée** early retirement; **retraité, e** adj retired ▷ nm/f pensioner

retrancher [R(ə)tʀãʃe] vt (nombre, somme): **~ qch de** to take ou deduct sth from; **se ~ derrière/dans** to take refuge behind/in

rétrécir [ʀetʀesiʀ] vt (vêtement) to take in ▷ vi to shrink; **se rétrécir** (route, vallée) to narrow

rétro [ʀetʀo] adj inv: **la mode ~** the nostalgia vogue

rétroprojecteur [ʀetʀopʀɔʒɛktœʀ] nm overhead projector

rétrospective [ʀetʀɔspɛktiv] nf (Art) retrospective; (Cinéma) season, retrospective; **rétrospectivement** adv in retrospect

retrousser [ʀ(ə)tʀuse] vt to roll up

retrouvailles [ʀ(ə)tʀuvaj] nfpl reunion sg

retrouver [ʀ(ə)tʀuve] vt (fugitif, objet perdu) to find; (calme, santé) to regain; (revoir) to see again; (rejoindre) to meet (again), join; **se retrouver** vi to meet; (s'orienter) to find one's way; **se ~ quelque part** to find o.s. somewhere; **s'y ~** (y voir clair) to make sense of it; (rentrer dans ses frais) to break even; **je ne retrouve plus mon portefeuille** I can't find my wallet (BRIT) ou billfold (US)

rétroviseur [ʀetʀɔvizœʀ] nm (rearview) mirror

réunion [ʀeynjɔ̃] nf (séance) meeting

réunir [ʀeyniʀ] vt (rassembler) to gather together; (inviter: amis, famille) to have round; (cumuler: qualités etc) to combine; (rapprocher: ennemis) to bring together (again), reunite; (rattacher: parties) to join (together); **se réunir** vi (se rencontrer) to meet

réussi, e [ʀeysi] adj successful

réussir [ʀeysiʀ] vi to succeed, be successful; (à un examen) to pass ▷ vt to make a success of; **~ à faire** to succeed in doing; **~ à qn** (être bénéfique à) to agree with sb; **réussite** nf success; (Cartes) patience

revaloir [ʀ(ə)valwaʀ] vt: **je vous revaudrai cela** I'll repay you some day; (en mal) I'll pay you back for this

revanche [ʀ(ə)vɑ̃ʃ] nf revenge; (sport) revenge match; **en ~** on the other hand

rêve [ʀɛv] nm dream; **de ~** dream cpd;

faire un ~ to have a dream

réveil [ʀevɛj] nm waking up no pl; (fig) awakening; (pendule) alarm (clock); **au ~** on waking (up); **réveiller** vt (personne) to wake up; (fig) to awaken, revive; **se réveiller** vi to wake up; **pouvez-vous me réveiller à 7 heures, s'il vous plaît?** could I have an alarm call at 7am, please?

réveillon [ʀevɛjɔ̃] nm Christmas Eve; (de la Saint-Sylvestre) New Year's Eve; **réveillonner** vi to celebrate Christmas Eve (ou New Year's Eve)

révélateur, -trice [ʀevelatœʀ, tʀis] adj: **~ (de qch)** revealing (sth)

révéler [ʀevele] vt to reveal; **se révéler** vi to be revealed, reveal itself ▷ vb +attrib: **se ~ difficile/aisé** to prove difficult/easy

revenant, e [ʀ(ə)vənɑ̃, ɑ̃t] nm/f ghost

revendeur, -euse [ʀ(ə)vɑ̃dœʀ, øz] nm/f (détaillant) retailer; (de drogue) (drug-)dealer

revendication [ʀ(ə)vɑ̃dikasjɔ̃] nf claim, demand

revendiquer [ʀ(ə)vɑ̃dike] vt to claim, demand; (responsabilité) to claim

revendre [ʀ(ə)vɑ̃dʀ] vt (d'occasion) to resell; (détailler) to sell; **à ~** (en abondance) to spare

revenir [ʀəv(ə)niʀ] vi to come back; (coûter): **~ cher/à 100 euros (à qn)** to cost (sb) a lot/100 euros; **~ à** (reprendre: études, projet) to return to, go back to; (équivaloir à) to amount to; **~ à qn** (part, honneur) to go to sb, be sb's; (souvenir, nom) to come back to sb; **~ sur** (question, sujet) to go back over; (engagement) to go back on; **~ à soi** to come round; **n'en pas ~: je n'en reviens pas** I can't get over it; **~ sur ses pas** to retrace one's steps; **cela revient à dire que/au même** it amounts to saying that/the same thing; **faire ~** (Culin) to brown

revenu [ʀəv(ə)ny] nm income; **revenus** nmpl income sg

rêver [ʀeve] vi, vt to dream; **~ de/à** to dream of

éverbère [ʀeveʀbɛʀ] *nm* street lamp *ou* light; **réverbérer** *vt* to reflect

évers [ʀ(ə)vɛʀ] *nm* (*de feuille, main*) back; (*d'étoffe*) wrong side; (*de pièce, médaille*) back, reverse; (*Tennis, Ping-Pong*) backhand; (*de veste*) lapel; (*fig: échec*) setback

évêtement [ʀ(ə)vɛtmɑ̃] *nm* (*des sols*) flooring; (*de chaussée*) surface

évêtir [ʀ(ə)vetiʀ] *vt* (*habit*) to don, put on; (*prendre: importance, apparence*) to take on; **~ qch de** to cover sth with

éveur, -euse [ʀɛvœʀ, øz] *adj* dreamy ▷ *nm/f* dreamer

évient [ʀəvjɛ̃] *vb voir* **revenir**

évigorer [ʀ(ə)vigɔʀe] *vt* (*air frais*) to invigorate, brace up; (*repas, boisson*) to revive, buck up

évirement [ʀ(ə)viʀmɑ̃] *nm* change of mind; (*d'une situation*) reversal

éviser [ʀevize] *vt* to revise; (*machine*) to overhaul, service

évision [ʀevizjɔ̃] *nf* revision; (*de voiture*) servicing *no pl*

évivre [ʀ(ə)vivʀ] *vi* (*reprendre des forces*) to come alive again ▷ *vt* (*épreuve, moment*) to relive

évoir [ʀəvwaʀ] *vt* to see again; (*réviser*) to revise ▷ *nm*: **au ~** goodbye

évoltant, e [ʀevɔltɑ̃, ɑ̃t] *adj* revolting, appalling

évolte [ʀevɔlt] *nf* rebellion, revolt

évolter [ʀevɔlte] *vt* to revolt; **se révolter (contre)** to rebel (against)

évolu, e [ʀevɔly] *adj* past; (*Admin*): **âgé de 18 ans ~s** over 18 years of age

évolution [ʀevɔlysjɔ̃] *nf* revolution; **révolutionnaire** *adj, nm/f* evolutionary

évolver [ʀevɔlvɛʀ] *nm* gun; (*à barillet*) evolver

évoquer [ʀevɔke] *vt* (*fonctionnaire*) to dismiss; (*arrêt, contrat*) to revoke

évue [ʀ(ə)vy] *nf* review; (*périodique*) review, magazine; (*de music-hall*) variety show; **passer en ~** (*mentalement*) to go through

z-de-chaussée [ʀed(ə)ʃose] *nm inv*
ground floor

RF *sigle f* = **République française**

Rhin [ʀɛ̃] *nm* Rhine

rhinocéros [ʀinɔseʀɔs] *nm* rhinoceros

Rhône [ʀon] *nm* Rhone

rhubarbe [ʀybaʀb] *nf* rhubarb

rhum [ʀɔm] *nm* rum

rhumatisme [ʀymatism] *nm* rheumatism *no pl*

rhume [ʀym] *nm* cold; **rhume de cerveau** head cold; **le rhume des foins** hay fever

ricaner [ʀikane] *vi* (*avec méchanceté*) to snigger; (*bêtement*) to giggle

riche [ʀiʃ] *adj* rich; (*personne, pays*) rich, wealthy; **~ en** rich in; **richesse** *nf* wealth; (*fig: de sol, musée etc*) richness; **richesses** *nfpl* (*ressources, argent*) wealth *sg*; (*fig: trésors*) treasures

ricochet [ʀikɔʃɛ] *nm*: **faire des ~s** to skip stones

ride [ʀid] *nf* wrinkle

rideau, x [ʀido] *nm* curtain; **rideau de fer** (*boutique*) metal shutter(s)

rider [ʀide] *vt* to wrinkle; **se rider** *vi* to become wrinkled

ridicule [ʀidikyl] *adj* ridiculous ▷ *nm*: **le ~** ridicule; **ridiculiser** *vt* to ridicule; **se ridiculiser** *vi* to make a fool of o.s.

rien [ʀjɛ̃] *pron* **1**: **(ne) ... rien** nothing, *tournure négative + anything*; **qu'est-ce que vous avez? — rien** what have you got? — nothing; **il n'a rien dit/fait** he said/did nothing; he hasn't said/done anything; **n'avoir peur de rien** to be afraid *ou* frightened of nothing, not to be afraid *ou* frightened of anything; **il n'a rien** (*n'est pas blessé*) he's all right; **ça ne fait rien** it doesn't matter; **de rien!** not at all!

2: **rien de**: **rien d'intéressant** nothing interesting; **rien d'autre** nothing else; **rien du tout** nothing at all

3: **rien que** just, only; nothing but; **rien que pour lui faire plaisir** only *ou* just to please him; **rien que la vérité** nothing but the truth; **rien que cela** that alone ▷ *nm*: **un petit rien** (*cadeau*) a little something; **des riens** trivia *pl*; **un rien de** a hint of; **en un rien de temps** in no time at all

rieur, -euse [ʀ(i)jœʀ, ʀ(i)jøz] *adj* cheerful

rigide [ʀiʒid] *adj* stiff; (*fig*) rigid; strict

rigoler [ʀigɔle] *vi* (*fam: rire*) to laugh; (*s'amuser*) to have (some) fun; (*plaisanter*) to be joking *ou* kidding; **rigolo, -ote** (*fam*) *adj* funny ▷ *nm/f* comic; (*péj*) fraud, phoney

rigoureusement [ʀiguʀøzmɑ̃] *adv* (*vrai*) absolutely; (*interdit*) strictly

rigoureux, -euse [ʀiguʀø, øz] *adj* rigorous; (*hiver*) hard, harsh

rigueur [ʀigœʀ] *nf* rigour; **"tenue de soirée de ~"** "formal dress only"; **à la ~** at a pinch; **tenir ~ à qn de qch** to hold sth against sb

rillettes [ʀijɛt] *nfpl* potted meat (*made from pork or goose*)

rime [ʀim] *nf* rhyme

rinçage [ʀɛ̃saʒ] *nm* rinsing (out); (*opération*) rinse

rincer [ʀɛ̃se] *vt* to rinse; (*récipient*) to rinse out

ringard, e [ʀɛ̃gaʀ, aʀd] (*fam*) *adj* old-fashioned

riposter [ʀipɔste] *vi* to retaliate ▷ *vt*: **~ que** to retort that

rire [ʀiʀ] *vi* to laugh; (*se divertir*) to have fun ▷ *nm* laugh; **le ~** laughter; **~ de** to laugh at; **pour ~** (*pas sérieusement*) for a joke *ou* a laugh

risible [ʀizibl] *adj* laughable

risque [ʀisk] *nm* risk; **le ~** danger; **à ses ~s et périls** at his own risk; **risqué, e** *adj* risky; (*plaisanterie*) risqué, daring; **risquer** *vt* to venture, hazard; (*allusion, question*) to venture, hazard; **ça ne risque rien** it's quite safe; **risquer de**: **il risque de se tuer** he could get himself killed; **ce qui risque de se produire** what might *ou* could well happen; **il ne risque pas de recommencer** there's no chance of him doing that again; **se risquer à faire** (*tenter*) to venture *ou* dare to do

rissoler [ʀisɔle] *vi, vt*: **(faire) ~** to brown

ristourne [ʀistuʀn] *nf* discount

rite [ʀit] *nm* rite; (*fig*) ritual

rivage [ʀivaʒ] *nm* shore

rival, e, -aux [ʀival, o] *adj, nm/f* rival; **rivaliser** *vi*: **rivaliser avec** (*personne*) to rival, vie with; **rivalité** *nf* rivalry

rive [ʀiv] *nf* shore; (*de fleuve*) bank; **riverain, e** *nm/f* riverside (*ou* lakeside) resident; (*d'une route*) local resident

rivière [ʀivjɛʀ] *nf* river

riz [ʀi] *nm* rice; **rizière** *nf* paddy-field, ricefield

RMI *sigle m* (= *revenu minimum d'insertion*) ≈ income support (BRIT), ≈ welfare (US)

RN *sigle f* = **route nationale**

robe [ʀɔb] *nf* dress; (*de juge*) robe; (*pelage*) coat; **robe de chambre** dressing gown; **robe de mariée** wedding dress; **robe de soirée** evening dress

robinet [ʀɔbinɛ] *nm* tap (BRIT), faucet (US)

robot [ʀɔbo] *nm* robot; **robot de cuisine** food processor

robuste [ʀɔbyst] *adj* robust, sturdy; **robustesse** *nf* robustness, sturdiness

roc [ʀɔk] *nm* rock

rocade [ʀɔkad] *nf* bypass

rocaille [ʀɔkaj] *nf* loose stones *pl*; (*jardin*) rockery, rock garden

roche [ʀɔʃ] *nf* rock

rocher [ʀɔʃe] *nm* rock

rocheux, -euse [ʀɔʃø, øz] *adj* rocky

rodage [ʀɔdaʒ] *nm*: **en ~** running in

rôder [ʀode] *vi* to roam about; (*de façon suspecte*) to lurk (about *ou* around); **rôdeur, -euse** *nm/f* prowler

rogne [ʀɔɲ] (*fam*) *nf*: **être en ~** to be in a temper

rogner [ʀɔɲe] *vt* to clip; **~ sur** (*fig*) to cut down *ou* back on

rognons [ʀɔɲɔ̃] *nmpl* (*Culin*) kidneys

roi [ʀwa] *nm* king; **la fête des Rois, le**

Rois Twelfth Night

ôle [Rol] nm role, part

ôllers [RɔlœR] nmpl Rollerblades®

omain, e [Rɔmɛ̃, ɛn] adj Roman
▷ nm/f: **R~, e** Roman

oman, e [Rɔmɑ̃, an] adj (Archit)
Romanesque ▷ nm novel; **roman
policier** detective story

omancer [Rɔmɑ̃se] vt (agrémenter) to
romanticize; **romancier, -ière** nm/f
novelist; **romanesque** adj (amours,
aventures) storybook cpd; (sentimental:
personne) romantic

oman-feuilleton [Rɔmɑ̃fœjtɔ̃] nm
serialized novel

omanichel, le [Rɔmaniʃɛl] (péj)
nm/f gipsy

omantique [Rɔmɑ̃tik] adj romantic

omarin [RɔmaRɛ̃] nm rosemary

ome [Rɔm] n Rome

ompre [Rɔ̃pR] vt to break; (entretien,
fiançailles) to break off ▷ vi (fiancés) to
break it off; **se rompre** vi to break;
rompu, e adj (fourbu) exhausted

onces [Rɔ̃s] nfpl brambles

onchonner [Rɔ̃ʃɔne] (fam) vi to
grouse, grouch

ond, e [Rɔ̃, Rɔ̃d] adj round; (joues,
mollets) well-rounded; (fam: ivre) tight
▷ nm (cercle) ring; (fam: sou): **je n'ai
plus un ~** I haven't a penny left; **en ~**
(s'asseoir, danser) in a ring; **ronde** nf
(gén: de surveillance) rounds pl, patrol;
(danse) round (dance); (Mus) semibreve
(BRIT), whole note (US); **à la ronde**
(alentour): **à 10 km à la ronde** for 10 km
round; **rondelet, te** adj plump

ondelle [Rɔ̃dɛl] nf (tranche) slice,
round; (Tech) washer

ond-point [Rɔ̃pwɛ̃] nm roundabout

onflement [Rɔ̃fləmɑ̃] nm snore,
snoring

onfler [Rɔ̃fle] vi to snore; (moteur,
poêle) to hum

onger [Rɔ̃ʒe] vt to gnaw (at); (suj: vers,
rouille) to eat into; **se ~ les ongles** to
bite one's nails; **se ~ les sangs** to worry
o.s. sick; **rongeur** nm rodent

ronronner [Rɔ̃Rɔne] vi to purr

rosbif [Rɔsbif] nm: **du ~** roasting beef;
(cuit) roast beef

rose [Roz] nf rose ▷ adj pink; **rose
bonbon** adj inv candy pink

rosé, e [Roze] adj pinkish; **(vin) ~** rosé

roseau, x [Rozo] nm reed

rosée [Roze] nf dew

rosier [Rozje] nm rosebush, rose tree

rossignol [Rɔsiɲɔl] nm (Zool)
nightingale

rotation [Rɔtasjɔ̃] nf rotation

roter [Rɔte] (fam) vi to burp, belch

rôti [Roti] nm: **du ~** roasting meat; (cuit)
roast meat; **un ~ de bœuf/porc** a joint
of beef/pork

rotin [Rɔtɛ̃] nm rattan (cane); **fauteuil
en ~** cane (arm)chair

rôtir [RotiR] vi, vt (aussi: **faire ~**)
to roast; **rôtisserie** nf (restaurant)
steakhouse; (traiteur) roast meat shop;
rôtissoire nf (roasting) spit

rotule [Rɔtyl] nf kneecap

rouage [Rwaʒ] nm cog(wheel),
gearwheel; **les ~s de l'État** the wheels
of State

roue [Ru] nf wheel; **roue de secours**
spare wheel

rouer [Rwe] vt: **~ qn de coups** to give
sb a thrashing

rouge [Ruʒ] adj, nm/f red ▷ nm red;
(vin) ~ red wine; **sur la liste ~** ex-
directory (BRIT), unlisted (US); **passer
au ~** (signal) to go red; (automobiliste)
to go through a red light; **rouge à joue**
blusher; **rouge (à lèvres)** lipstick;
rouge-gorge nm robin (redbreast)

rougeole [Ruʒɔl] nf measles sg

rougeoyer [Ruʒwaje] vi to glow red

rouget [Ruʒe] nm mullet

rougeur [RuʒœR] nf redness; (Méd:
tache) red blotch

rougir [RuʒiR] vi to turn red; (de honte,
timidité) to blush, flush; (de plaisir, colère)
to flush

rouille [Ruj] nf rust; **rouillé, e** adj rusty;
rouiller vt to rust ▷ vi to rust, go rusty

roulant, e [Rulɑ̃, ɑ̃t] adj (meuble) on

wheels; (*tapis etc*) moving; **escalier ~** escalator

rouleau, x [ʀulo] *nm* roll; (*à mise en plis, à peinture, vague*) roller; **rouleau à pâtisserie** rolling pin

roulement [ʀulmɑ̃] *nm* (*rotation*) rotation; (*bruit*) rumbling *no pl*, rumble; **travailler par ~** to work on a rota (BRIT) *ou* rotation (US) basis; **roulement (à billes)** ball bearings *pl*; **roulement de tambour** drum roll

rouler [ʀule] *vt* to roll; (*papier, tapis*) to roll up; (*Culin: pâte*) to roll out; (*fam: duper*) to do, con ▷ *vi* (*bille, boule*) to roll; (*voiture, train*) to go, run; (*automobiliste*) to drive; (*bateau*) to roll; **se ~ dans** (*boue*) to roll in; (*couverture*) to roll o.s. (up) in

roulette [ʀulɛt] *nf* (*de table, fauteuil*) castor; (*de dentiste*) drill; (*jeu*) roulette; **à ~s** on castors; **ça a marché comme sur des ~s** (*fam*) it went off very smoothly

roulis [ʀuli] *nm* roll(ing)

roulotte [ʀulɔt] *nf* caravan

roumain, e [ʀumɛ̃, ɛn] *adj* Rumanian ▷ *nm/f*: **R~, e** Rumanian

Roumanie [ʀumani] *nf* Rumania

rouquin, e [ʀukɛ̃, in] (*péj*) *nm/f* redhead

rouspéter [ʀuspete] (*fam*) *vi* to moan

rousse [ʀus] *adj voir* **roux**

roussir [ʀusiʀ] *vt* to scorch ▷ *vi* (*Culin*): **faire ~** to brown

route [ʀut] *nf* road; (*fig: chemin*) way; (*itinéraire, parcours*) route; (*fig: voie*) road, path; **il y a 3h de ~** it's a 3-hour ride *ou* journey; **en ~** on the way; **en ~!** let's go!; **mettre en ~** to start up; **se mettre en ~** to set off; **quelle ~ dois-je prendre pour aller à …?** which road do I take for …?; **route nationale** ≈ A road (BRIT), ≈ state highway (US); **routier, -ière** *adj* road *cpd* ▷ *nm* (*camionneur*) (long-distance) lorry (BRIT) *ou* truck (US) driver; (*restaurant*) ≈ transport café (BRIT), ≈ truck stop (US)

routine [ʀutin] *nf* routine; **routinier, -ière** (*péj*) *adj* (*activité*) humdrum;

(*personne*) addicted to routine

rouvrir [ʀuvʀiʀ] *vt, vi* to reopen, open again; **se rouvrir** *vi* to reopen, open again

roux, rousse [ʀu, ʀus] *adj* red; (*personne*) red-haired ▷ *nm/f* redhead

royal, e, -aux [ʀwajal, o] *adj* royal; (*cadeau etc*) fit for a king

royaume [ʀwajom] *nm* kingdom; (*fig*) realm; **le Royaume-Uni** the United Kingdom

royauté [ʀwajote] *nf* (*régime*) monarchy

ruban [ʀybɑ̃] *nm* ribbon; **ruban adhésif** adhesive tape

rubéole [ʀybeɔl] *nf* German measles *sg*, rubella

rubis [ʀybi] *nm* ruby

rubrique [ʀybʀik] *nf* (*titre, catégorie*) heading; (*Presse: article*) column

ruche [ʀyʃ] *nf* hive

rude [ʀyd] *adj* (*au toucher*) rough; (*métier, tâche*) hard, tough; (*climat*) severe, harsh; (*bourru*) harsh, rough; (*fruste: manières*) rugged, tough; (*fam: fameux*) jolly good; **rudement** (*fam*) *ad* (*très*) terribly

rudimentaire [ʀydimɑ̃tɛʀ] *adj* rudimentary, basic

rudiments [ʀydimɑ̃] *nmpl*: **avoir des ~ d'anglais** to have a smattering of English

rue [ʀy] *nf* street

ruée [ʀɥe] *nf* rush

ruelle [ʀɥɛl] *nf* alley(-way)

ruer [ʀɥe] *vi* (*cheval*) to kick out; **se ruer** *vi*: **se ~ sur** to pounce on; **se ~ vers/dans/hors de** to rush *ou* dash towards/into/out of

rugby [ʀygbi] *nm* rugby (football)

rugir [ʀyʒiʀ] *vi* to roar

rugueux, -euse [ʀygø, øz] *adj* rough

ruine [ʀɥin] *nf* ruin; **ruiner** *vt* to ruin; **ruineux, -euse** *adj* ruinous

ruisseau, x [ʀɥiso] *nm* stream, brook

ruisseler [ʀɥis(ə)le] *vi* to stream

rumeur [ʀymœʀ] *nf* (*nouvelle*) rumour; (*bruit confus*) rumbling

miner [Rymine] vt (herbe) to
uminate; (fig) to ruminate on ou over,
hew over

pture [RyptyR] nf (séparation,
ésunion) break-up, split; (de
égociations etc) breakdown; (de contrat)
reach; (dans continuité) break

ral, e, -aux [RyRal, o] adj rural,
ountry cpd

se [Ryz] nf: **la ~** cunning, craftiness;
pour tromper) trickery; **une ~** a trick, a
use; **rusé, e** adj cunning, crafty

sse [Rys] adj Russian ▷ nm/f: **R~**
ussian ▷ nm (Ling) Russian

ssie [Rysi] nf: **la ~** Russia

stine® [Rystin] nf rubber repair
atch (for bicycle tyre)

stique [Rystik] adj rustic

thme [Ritm] nm rhythm; (vitesse)
ate; (: de la vie) pace, tempo; **rythmé, e**
dj rhythmic(al)

S

s' [s] pron voir **se**
sa [sa] adj voir **son'**
sable [sabl] nm sand
sablé [sable] nm shortbread biscuit
sabler [sable] vt (contre le verglas)
to grit; **~ le champagne** to drink
champagne
sabot [sabo] nm clog; (de cheval) hoof;
sabot de frein brake shoe
saboter [sabɔte] vt to sabotage;
(bâcler) to make a mess of, botch
sac [sak] nm bag; (à charbon etc) sack;
mettre à ~ to sack; **sac à dos** rucksack;
sac à main handbag; **sac de couchage**
sleeping bag; **sac de voyage** travelling
bag
saccadé, e [sakade] adj jerky;
(respiration) spasmodic
saccager [sakaʒe] vt (piller) to sack;
(dévaster) to create havoc in
saccharine [sakaRin] nf saccharin
sachet [saʃɛ] nm (small) bag; (de sucre,
café) sachet; **du potage en ~** packet
soup; **sachet de thé** tea bag

sacoche[sakɔʃ] nf (gén) bag; (de bicyclette) saddlebag

sacré, e[sakre] adj sacred; (fam: satané) blasted; (: fameux): **un ~ toupet** a heck of a cheek

sacrement[sakrəmɑ̃] nm sacrament

sacrifice[sakrifis] nm sacrifice; **sacrifier** vt to sacrifice

sacristie[sakristi] nf (catholique) sacristy; (protestante) vestry

sadique[sadik] adj sadistic

safran[safrɑ̃] nm saffron

sage[saʒ] adj wise; (enfant) good

sage-femme[saʒfam] nf midwife

sagesse[saʒɛs] nf wisdom

Sagittaire[saʒitɛʀ] nm: **le ~** Sagittarius

Sahara[saaʀa] nm: **le ~** the Sahara (desert)

saignant, e[sɛɲɑ̃, ɑ̃t] adj (viande) rare

saigner[seɲe] vi to bleed ▷ vt to bleed; (animal) to kill (by bleeding); **~ du nez** to have a nosebleed

saillir[sajiʀ] vi to project, stick out; (veine, muscle) to bulge

sain, e[sɛ̃, sɛn] adj healthy; **~ et sauf** safe and sound, unharmed; **~ d'esprit** sound in mind, sane

saindoux[sɛ̃du] nm lard

saint, e[sɛ̃, sɛ̃t] adj holy ▷ nm/f saint; **le Saint Esprit** the Holy Spirit ou Ghost; **la Sainte Vierge** the Blessed Virgin; **la Saint-Sylvestre** New Year's Eve; **sainteté** nf holiness

sais etc [se] vb voir **savoir**

saisie[sezi] nf seizure; **saisie (de données)**(data) capture

saisir[seziʀ] vt to take hold of, grab; (fig: occasion) to seize; (comprendre) to grasp; (entendre) to get, catch; (données) to capture; (Culin) to fry quickly; (Jur: biens, publication) to seize; **saisissant, e** adj startling, striking

saison[sezɔ̃] nf season; **haute/basse/morte ~** high/low/slack season; **saisonnier, -ière** adj seasonal

salade[salad] nf (Bot) lettuce etc; (Culin: green) salad; (fam: confusion) tangle, muddle; **salade composée** mixed salad; **salade de fruits** fruit salad; **saladier** nm (salad) bowl

salaire[salɛʀ] nm (annuel, mensuel) salary; (hebdomadaire, journalier) pay, wages pl; **salaire minimum interprofessionnel de croissance** index-linked guaranteed minimum wage

salarié, e[salaʀje] nm/f salaried employee; wage-earner

salaud[salo] (fam!) nm sod (!), bastard (!)

sale[sal] adj dirty, filthy; (fam: mauvai) nasty

salé, e[sale] adj (mer, goût) salty; (Culin: amandes, beurre etc) salted; (: gâteaux) savoury; (fam: grivois) spicy; (facture) steep

saler[sale] vt to salt

saleté[salte] nf (état) dirtiness; (cras) dirt, filth; (tache etc) dirt no pl; (fam: méchanceté) dirty trick; (: camelote) rubbish no pl; (: obscénité) filthy thing (to say)

salière[saljɛʀ] nf saltcellar

salir[saliʀ] vt to (make) dirty; (fig: quelqu'un) to soil the reputation of; **s**e **salir** vi to get dirty; **salissant, e** adj (tissu) which shows the dirt; (travail) dirty, messy

salle[sal] nf room; (d'hôpital) ward; (d restaurant) dining room; (d'un cinéma` auditorium; (: public) audience; **salle à manger** dining room; **salle d'attente** waiting room; **salle de bain(s)** bathroom; **salle de classe** classroom; **salle de concert** concert hall; **salle de eau** shower-room; **salle d'embarquement** (à l'aéroport) departure lounge; **salle de jeux** (pou enfants) playroom; **salle de séjour** living room; **salle des ventes** salero

salon[salɔ̃] nm lounge, sitting room (mobilier) lounge suite; (exposition) exhibition, show; **salon de coiffure** hairdressing salon; **salon de thé** tearoom

salope[salɔp] (fam!) nf bitch (!);

saloperie (fam!) nf (action) dirty trick; (chose sans valeur) rubbish no pl

salopette [salɔpɛt] nf dungarees pl; (d'ouvrier) overall(s)

salsifis [salsifi] nm salsify

salubre [salybʀ] adj healthy, salubrious

saluer [salɥe] vt (pour dire bonjour, fig) to greet; (pour dire au revoir) to take one's leave of; (Mil) to salute

salut [saly] nm (geste) wave; (parole) greeting; (Mil) salute; (sauvegarde) safety; (Rel) salvation ▷ excl (fam: bonjour) hi (there); (: au revoir) see you, bye

salutations [salytasjɔ̃] nfpl greetings; **veuillez agréer, Monsieur, mes ~ distinguées** yours faithfully

samedi [samdi] nm Saturday

SAMU [samy] sigle m (= service d'assistance médicale d'urgence) ≈ ambulance (service) (BRIT), paramedics pl (US)

sanction [sɑ̃ksjɔ̃] nf sanction; **sanctionner** vt (loi, usage) to sanction; (punir) to punish

sandale [sɑ̃dal] nf sandal

sandwich [sɑ̃dwi(t)ʃ] nm sandwich; **je voudrais un ~ au jambon/fromage** I'd like a ham/cheese sandwich

sang [sɑ̃] nm blood; **en ~** covered in blood; **se faire du mauvais ~** to fret, get in a state; **sang-froid** nm calm, sangfroid; **de sang-froid** in cold blood; **sanglant, e** adj bloody

sangle [sɑ̃gl] nf strap

sanglier [sɑ̃glije] nm (wild) boar

sanglot [sɑ̃glo] nm sob; **sangloter** to sob

sangsue [sɑ̃sy] nf leech

sanguin, e [sɑ̃gɛ̃, in] adj blood cpd

sanitaire [sanitɛʀ] adj health cpd; **sanitaires** nmpl (lieu) bathroom sg

sans [sɑ̃] prép without; **un pull ~ manches** a sleeveless jumper; **~ faute** without fail; **~ arrêt** without break; **~ ça** (fam) otherwise; **~ qu'il s'en aperçoive** without him

ou his noticing; **sans-abri** nmpl homeless; **sans-emploi** nm/f inv unemployed person; **les sans-emploi** the unemployed; **sans-gêne** adj inv inconsiderate

santé [sɑ̃te] nf health; **en bonne ~** in good health; **boire à la ~ de qn** to drink (to) sb's health; **à ta/votre ~!** cheers!

saoudien, ne [saudjɛ̃, jɛn] adj Saudi Arabian ▷ nm/f: **S~, ne** Saudi Arabian

saoul, e [su, sul] adj = **soûl**

saper [sape] vt to undermine, sap

sapeur-pompier [sapœʀpɔ̃pje] nm fireman

saphir [safiʀ] nm sapphire

sapin [sapɛ̃] nm fir (tree); (bois) fir; **sapin de Noël** Christmas tree

sarcastique [saʀkastik] adj sarcastic

Sardaigne [saʀdɛɲ] nf: **la ~** Sardinia

sardine [saʀdin] nf sardine

SARL sigle f (= société à responsabilité limitée) ≈ plc (BRIT), ≈ Inc. (US)

sarrasin [saʀazɛ̃] nm buckwheat

satané, e [satane] (fam) adj confounded

satellite [satelit] nm satellite

satin [satɛ̃] nm satin

satire [satiʀ] nf satire; **satirique** adj satirical

satisfaction [satisfaksjɔ̃] nf satisfaction

satisfaire [satisfɛʀ] vt to satisfy; **~ à** (conditions) to meet; **satisfaisant, e** adj (acceptable) satisfactory; **satisfait, e** adj satisfied; **satisfait de** happy ou satisfied with

saturer [satyʀe] vt to saturate

sauce [sos] nf sauce; (avec un rôti) gravy; **sauce tomate** tomato sauce; **saucière** nf sauceboat

saucisse [sosis] nf sausage

saucisson [sosisɔ̃] nm (slicing) sausage

sauf, sauve [sof, sov] adj unharmed, unhurt; (fig: honneur) intact, saved ▷ prép except; **laisser la vie sauve à qn** to spare sb's life; **~ si** (à moins que) unless; **~ erreur** if I'm not mistaken;

~ avis contraire unless you hear to the contrary

sauge [soʒ] nf sage

saugrenu, e [sogrəny] adj preposterous

saule [sol] nm willow (tree)

saumon [somɔ̃] nm salmon inv

saupoudrer [supudʀe] vt: **~ qch de** to sprinkle sth with

saur [sɔʀ] adj m: **hareng ~** smoked herring, kipper

saut [so] nm jump; (discipline sportive) jumping; **faire un ~ chez qn** to pop over to sb's (place); **saut à l'élastique** bungee jumping; **saut à la perche** pole vaulting; **saut en hauteur/longueur** high/long jump; **saut périlleux** somersault

sauter [sote] vi to jump, leap, (exploser) to blow up, explode; (: fusibles) to blow; (se détacher) to pop out (ou off) ▷ vt to jump (over), leap (over); (fig: omettre) to skip, miss (out); **faire ~** to blow up; (Culin) to sauté; **~ à la corde** to skip; **~ au cou de qn** to fly into sb's arms; **~ sur une occasion** to jump at an opportunity; **~ aux yeux** to be (quite) obvious

sauterelle [sotʀɛl] nf grasshopper

sautiller [sotije] vi (oiseau) to hop; (enfant) to skip

sauvage [sovaʒ] adj (gén) wild; (peuplade) savage; (farouche: personne) unsociable; (barbare) wild, savage; (non officiel) unauthorized, unofficial; **faire du camping ~** to camp in the wild ▷ nm/f savage; (timide) unsociable type

sauve [sov] adj f voir **sauf**

sauvegarde [sovgaʀd] nf safeguard; (Inform) backup; **sauvegarder** vt to safeguard; (Inform: enregistrer) to save; (: copier) to back up

sauve-qui-peut [sovkipø] excl run for your life!

sauver [sove] vt to save; (porter secours à) to rescue; (récupérer) to salvage, rescue; **se sauver** vi (s'enfuir) to run away; (fam: partir) to be off; **sauvetage**

nm rescue; **sauveteur** nm rescuer; **sauvette: à la sauvette** adv (se mari etc) hastily, hurriedly; **sauveur** nm saviour (BRIT), savior (US)

savant, e [savɑ̃, ɑ̃t] adj scholarly, learned ▷ nm scientist

saveur [savœʀ] nf flavour; (fig) savou

savoir [savwaʀ] vt to know; (être capable de): **il sait nager** he can swim ▷ nm knowledge; **se savoir** vi (être connu) to be known; **je ne sais pas** I don't know; **je ne sais pas parler français** I don't speak French; **savez-vous où je peux ...?** do you know where I can ...?; **je n'en sais rien** I (really) don't know; **à ~** that is, name **faire ~ qch à qn** to let sb know sth; **p que je sache** not as far as I know

savon [savɔ̃] nm (produit) soap; (morceau) bar of soap; (fam): **passer u ~ à qn** to give sb a good dressing-dov **savonner** vt to soap; **savonnette** n bar of soap

savourer [savuʀe] vt to savour; **savoureux, -euse** adj tasty; (fig: anecdote) spicy, juicy

saxo(phone) [saksɔ(fɔn)] nm sax(ophone)

scabreux, -euse [skabʀø, øz] adj risky; (indécent) improper, shocking

scandale [skɑ̃dal] nm scandal; **faire ~** (scène) to make a scene; (Jur) to crea a disturbance; **faire ~** to scandalize people; **scandaleux, -euse** adj scandalous, outrageous

scandinave [skɑ̃dinav] adj Scandinavian ▷ nm/f: **S~** Scandinavi

Scandinavie [skɑ̃dinavi] nf Scandinavia

scarabée [skaʀabe] nm beetle

scarlatine [skaʀlatin] nf scarlet fev

scarole [skaʀɔl] nf endive

sceau, x [so] nm seal

sceller [sele] vt to seal

scénario [senaʀjo] nm scenario

scène [sɛn] nf (gén) scene; (estrade, fig théâtre) stage; **entrer en ~** to come o stage; **mettre en ~** (Théâtre) to stage

(Cinéma) to direct; **faire une ~ (à qn)** to make a scene (with sb); **scène de ménage** domestic scene

ceptique [sɛptik] adj sceptical

chéma [ʃema] nm (diagramme) diagram, sketch; **schématique** adj diagrammatic(al), schematic; (fig) oversimplified

ciatique [sjatik] nf sciatica

cie [si] nf saw

ciemment [sjamɑ̃] adv knowingly

cience [sjɑ̃s] nf science; (savoir) knowledge; **sciences humaines/ sociales** social sciences; **sciences naturelles** (Scol) natural science sg, biology sg; **sciences po** political science ou studies pl; **science-fiction** nf science fiction; **scientifique** adj scientific ▷ nm/f scientist; (étudiant) science student

cier [sje] vt to saw; (retrancher) to saw off; **scierie** nf sawmill

cintiller [sɛ̃tije] vi to sparkle; (étoile) to twinkle

ciure [sjyʀ] nf: **~ (de bois)** sawdust

clérose [skleʀoz] nf: **sclérose en plaques** multiple sclerosis

colaire [skɔlɛʀ] adj school cpd; **scolariser** vt to provide with schooling/schools; **scolarité** nf schooling

cooter [skutœʀ] nm (motor) scooter

core [skɔʀ] nm score

corpion [skɔʀpjɔ̃] nm (signe): **le S~** Scorpio

cotch [skɔtʃ] nm (whisky) scotch, whisky; **S~®** (adhésif) Sellotape® (BRIT), Scotch® tape (US)

cout, e [skut] adj, nm scout

cript [skʀipt] nm (écriture) printing; (Cinéma) (shooting) script

crupule [skʀypyl] nm scruple

cruter [skʀyte] vt to scrutinize; (l'obscurité) to peer into

crutin [skʀytɛ̃] nm (vote) ballot; (ensemble des opérations) poll

culpter [skylte] vt to sculpt; (bois) to carve; **sculpteur** nm sculptor;

sculpture nf sculpture

SDF sigle m: **sans domicile fixe** homeless person; **les ~** the homeless

 MOT-CLÉ

se [sə], **s'** pron **1** (emploi réfléchi) oneself; (: masc) himself; (: fém) herself; (: sujet non humain) itself; (: pl) themselves; **se savonner** to soap o.s.
2 (réciproque) one another, each other; **ils s'aiment** they love one another ou each other
3 (passif): **cela se répare facilement** it is easily repaired
4 (possessif): **se casser la jambe/se laver les mains** to break one's leg/ wash one's hands

séance [seɑ̃s] nf (d'assemblée) meeting, session; (de tribunal) sitting, session; (musicale, Cinéma, Théâtre) performance

seau, x [so] nm bucket, pail

sec, sèche [sɛk, sɛʃ] adj dry; (raisins, figues) dried; (cœur: insensible) hard, cold ▷ nm: **tenir au ~** to keep in a dry place ▷ adv hard; **je le bois ~** I drink it straight ou neat; **à ~** (puits) dried up

sécateur [sekatœʀ] nm secateurs pl (BRIT), shears pl

sèche [sɛʃ] adj f voir **sec**; **sèche-cheveux** nm inv hair-drier; **sèche-linge** nm inv tumble dryer; **sèchement** adv (répondre) drily

sécher [seʃe] vt to dry; (dessécher: peau, blé) to dry (out); (: étang) to dry up; (fam: cours) to skip ▷ vi to dry; to dry out; to dry up; (fam: candidat) to be stumped; **se sécher** (après le bain) to dry o.s.; **sécheresse** nf dryness; (absence de pluie) drought; **séchoir** nm drier

second, e [s(ə)gɔ̃, ɔ̃d] adj second ▷ nm (assistant) second in command; (Navig) first mate ▷ nf (Scol) year 11 (BRIT), tenth grade (US); (Aviat, Rail etc) second class; **voyager en ~e** to travel second-class; **secondaire** adj secondary; **seconde²** nf second; **seconder** vt to assist

secouer [s(ə)kwe] vt to shake; (passagers) to rock; (traumatiser) to shake (up)

secourir [s(ə)kuriR] vt (venir en aide à) to assist, aid; **secourisme** nm first aid; **secouriste** nm/f first-aid worker

secours [s(ə)kuR] nm help, aid, assistance ▷ nmpl aid sg; **au ~!** help!; **appeler au ~** to shout ou call for help; **porter ~ à qn** to give sb assistance, help sb; **les premiers ~** first aid sg

● **ÉQUIPES DE SECOURS**
●
● Emergency phone numbers can
● be dialled free from public phones.
● For the police ('la police') dial 17; for
● medical services ('le SAMU') dial
● 15; for the fire brigade ('les sapeurs
● pompiers'), dial 18.

secousse [s(ə)kus] nf jolt, bump; (électrique) shock; (fig: psychologique) jolt, shock

secret, -ète [səkRɛ, ɛt] adj secret; (fig: renfermé) reticent, reserved ▷ nm secret; (discrétion absolue): **le ~** secrecy; **en ~** in secret, secretly; **secret professionnel** professional secrecy

secrétaire [s(ə)kRetɛR] nm/f secretary ▷ nm (meuble) writing desk; **secrétaire de direction** private ou personal secretary; **secrétaire d'État** junior minister; **secrétariat** nm (profession) secretarial work; (bureau) office; (: d'organisation internationale) secretariat

secteur [sɛktœR] nm sector; (zone) area; (Élec): **branché sur ~** plugged into the mains (supply)

section [sɛksjɔ̃] nf section; (de parcours d'autobus) fare stage; (Mil: unité) platoon; **sectionner** vt to sever

sécu [seky] abr f = **sécurité sociale**

sécurité [sekyRite] nf (absence de danger) safety; (absence de troubles) security; **système de ~** security system; **être en ~** to be safe; **la sécurité routière** road safety; **la sécurité sociale** ≈ (the) Social Security (BRIT), ≈ Welfare (US)

sédentaire [sedãtɛR] adj sedentary

séduction [sedyksjɔ̃] nf seduction; (charme, attrait) appeal, charm

séduire [seduiR] vt to charm; (femme: abuser de) to seduce; **séduisant, e** adj (femme) seductive; (homme, offre) very attractive

ségrégation [segRegasjɔ̃] nf segregation

seigle [sɛgl] nm rye

seigneur [sɛɲœR] nm lord

sein [sɛ̃] nm breast; (entrailles) womb; **au ~ de** (équipe, institution) within

séisme [seism] nm earthquake

seize [sɛz] num sixteen; **seizième** num sixteenth

séjour [seʒuR] nm stay; (pièce) living room; **séjourner** vi to stay

sel [sɛl] nm salt; (fig: piquant) spice

sélection [selɛksjɔ̃] nf selection; **sélectionner** vt to select

self-service [sɛlfsɛRvis] adj, nm self-service

selle [sɛl] nf saddle; **selles** nfpl (Méd) stools; **seller** vt to saddle

selon [s(ə)lɔ̃] prép according to; (en se conformant à) in accordance with; **~ que** according to whether; **~ moi** as I see it

semaine [s(ə)mɛn] nf week; **en ~** during the week, on weekdays

semblable [sãblabl] adj similar; (de ce genre): **de ~s mésaventures** such mishaps ▷ nm fellow creature ou man; **~ à** similar to, like

semblant [sãblã] nm: **un ~ de ...** a semblance of ...; **faire ~ (de faire)** to pretend (to do)

sembler [sãble] vb +attrib to seem ▷ vb impers: **il semble (bien) que/inutile de** it (really) seems ou appears that/ useless to; **il me semble que** it seems to me that; **comme bon lui semble** as he sees fit

semelle [s(ə)mɛl] nf sole; (intérieure) insole, inner sole

semer [s(ə)me] vt to sow; (fig: éparpiller) to scatter; (: confusion) to spread; (fam: poursuivants) to lose, shake off; **semé de** (difficultés) riddled with

semestre [s(ə)mɛstʀ] nm half-year; (Scol) semester

séminaire [seminɛʀ] nm seminar

semi-remorque [səmiʀəmɔʀk] nm articulated lorry (BRIT), semi(trailer) (US)

semoule [s(ə)mul] nf semolina

sénat [sena] nm senate; **sénateur** nm senator

Sénégal [senegal] nm: **le ~** Senegal

sens [sɑ̃s] nm (Physiol,) sense; (signification) meaning, sense; (direction) direction; **à mon ~** to my mind; **dans le ~ des aiguilles d'une montre** clockwise; **dans le ~ contraire des aiguilles d'une montre** anticlockwise; **dans le mauvais ~** (aller) the wrong way, in the wrong direction; **le bon ~** common sense; **sens dessus dessous** upside down; **sens interdit/unique** one-way street

sensation [sɑ̃sasjɔ̃] nf sensation; **à ~** (péj) sensational; **faire ~** to cause ou create a sensation; **sensationnel, le** adj (fam) fantastic, terrific

sensé, e [sɑ̃se] adj sensible

sensibiliser [sɑ̃sibilize] vt: **~ qn à** to make sb sensitive to

sensibilité [sɑ̃sibilite] nf sensitivity

sensible [sɑ̃sibl] adj sensitive; (aux sens) perceptible; (appréciable: différence, progrès) appreciable, noticeable; **~ à** sensitive to; **sensiblement** adv (à peu près): **ils sont sensiblement du même âge** they are approximately the same age; **sensiblerie** nf sentimentality

▮ Attention à ne pas traduire sensible par le mot anglais sensible.

sensuel, le [sɑ̃suɛl] adj (personne) sensual; (musique) sensuous

sentence [sɑ̃tɑ̃s] nf (jugement) sentence

sentier [sɑ̃tje] nm path

sentiment [sɑ̃timɑ̃] nm feeling; **recevez mes ~s respectueux** (personne nommée) yours sincerely; (personne non nommée) yours faithfully; **sentimental, e, -aux** adj sentimental; (vie, aventure) love cpd

sentinelle [sɑ̃tinɛl] nf sentry

sentir [sɑ̃tiʀ] vt (par l'odorat) to smell; (par le goût) to taste; (au toucher, fig) to feel; (répandre une odeur de) to smell of; (: ressemblance) to smell like ▷ vi to smell; **~ mauvais** to smell bad; **se ~ bien** to feel good; **se ~ mal** (être indisposé) to feel unwell ou ill; **se ~ le courage/la force de faire** to feel brave/strong enough to do; **il ne peut pas le ~** (fam) he can't stand him; **je ne me sens pas bien** I don't feel well

séparation [separasjɔ̃] nf separation; (cloison) division, partition

séparé, e [separe] adj (distinct) separate; (époux) separated; **séparément** adv separately

séparer [separe] vt to separate; (désunir) to drive apart; (détacher): **~ qch de** to pull sth (off) from; **se séparer** vi (époux, amis) to separate, part; (se diviser: route etc) to divide; **se ~ de** (époux) to separate ou part from; (employé, objet personnel) to part with

sept [sɛt] num seven; **septante** (BELGIQUE, SUISSE) adj inv seventy

septembre [sɛptɑ̃bʀ] nm September

septicémie [sɛptisemi] nf blood poisoning, septicaemia

septième [sɛtjɛm] num seventh

séquelles [sekɛl] nfpl after-effects; (fig) aftermath sg

serbe [sɛʀb(ə)] adj Serbian

Serbie [sɛʀbi] nf: **la ~** Serbia

serein, e [səʀɛ̃, ɛn] adj serene

sergent [sɛʀʒɑ̃] nm sergeant

série [seʀi] nf series inv; (de clés, casseroles, outils) set; (catégorie: Sport) rank; **en ~** in quick succession; (Comm) mass cpd; **de ~** (voiture) standard; **hors ~** (Comm) custom-built; **série noire** (crime) thriller

sérieusement [seʀjøzmɑ̃] adv seriously

sérieux, -euse [seʀjø, jøz] *adj* serious; (*élève, employé*) reliable, responsible; (*client, maison*) reliable, dependable ▷ *nm* seriousness; (*d'une entreprise etc*) reliability; **garder son ~** to keep a straight face; **prendre qch/qn au ~** to take sth/sb seriously

serin [s(ə)ʀɛ̃] *nm* canary

seringue [s(ə)ʀɛ̃g] *nf* syringe

serment [sɛʀmɑ̃] *nm* (*juré*) oath; (*promesse*) pledge, vow

sermon [sɛʀmɔ̃] *nm* sermon

séropositif, -ive [seʀopozitif, iv] *adj* (*Méd*) HIV positive

serpent [sɛʀpɑ̃] *nm* snake; **serpenter** *vi* to wind

serpillière [sɛʀpijɛʀ] *nf* floorcloth

serre [sɛʀ] *nf* (*Agr*) greenhouse; **serres** *nfpl* (*griffes*) claws, talons

serré, e [seʀe] *adj* (*habits*) tight; (*fig: lutte, match*) tight, close-fought; (*passagers etc*) (tightly) packed; (*réseau*) dense; **avoir le cœur ~** to have a heavy heart

serrer [seʀe] *vt* (*tenir*) to grip *ou* hold tight; (*comprimer, coincer*) to squeeze; (*poings, mâchoires*) to clench; (*suj: vêtement*) to be too tight for; (*ceinture, nœud, vis*) to tighten ▷ *vi*: **~ à droite** to keep *ou* get over to the right

serrure [seʀyʀ] *nf* lock; **serrurier** *nm* locksmith

sert *etc* [sɛʀ] *vb voir* **servir**

servante [sɛʀvɑ̃t] *nf* (maid)servant

serveur, -euse [sɛʀvœʀ, øz] *nm/f* waiter (waitress)

serviable [sɛʀvjabl] *adj* obliging, willing to help

service [sɛʀvis] *nm* service; (*assortiment de vaisselle*) set, service; (*bureau: de la vente etc*) department, section; (*travail*) duty; **premier ~** (*série de repas*) first sitting; **être de ~** to be on duty; **faire le ~** to serve; **rendre un ~ à qn** to do sb a favour; (*objet: s'avérer utile*) to come in useful *ou* handy for sb; **mettre en ~** to put into service *ou* operation; **~ compris/non compris** service included/not included; **hors ~** out of order; **service après vente** after sales service; **service d'ordre** police (*ou* stewards) in charge of maintaining order; **service militaire** military service; *see note*; **services secrets** secret service *sg*

● **SERVICE MILITAIRE**
●
● Until 1997, French men over the age
● of 18 who were passed as fit, and
● who were not in full-time higher
● education, were required to do
● ten months' "service militaire".
● Conscientious objectors were
● required to do two years' community
● service.
● Since 1997, military service has been
● suspended in France. However, all
● sixteen-year-olds, both male and
● female, are required to register for
● a compulsory one-day training
● course, the "JAPD" ("journée d'appel
● de préparation à la défense"), which
● covers basic information on the
● principles and organization of
● defence in France, and also advises
● on career opportunities in the
● military and in the voluntary sector.
● Young people must attend the
● training day before their eighteenth
● birthday.

serviette [sɛʀvjɛt] *nf* (*de table*) (table) napkin, serviette; (*de toilette*) towel; (*porte-documents*) briefcase; **serviette hygiénique** sanitary towel

servir [sɛʀviʀ] *vt* to serve; (*au restaurant*) to wait on; (*au magasin*) to serve, attend to ▷ *vi* (*Tennis*) to serve; (*Cartes*) to deal; **se servir** *vi* (*prendre d'un plat*) to help o.s.; **vous êtes servi?** are you being served?; **~ à qn** (*diplôme, livre*) to be of use to sb; **~ à qch/faire** (*outil etc*) to be used for sth/doing; **ne sert à rien** it's no use; **~ (à qn) de** to serve as (for sb); **se ~ de** (*plat*) to help o.s. to;

(*voiture, outil, relations*) to use; **sers-toi!** help yourself!

serviteur [sɛʀvitœʀ] *nm* servant

ses [se] *adj voir* **son¹**

seuil [sœj] *nm* doorstep; (*fig*) threshold

seul, e [sœl] *adj* (*sans compagnie*) alone; (*unique*): **un ~ livre** only one book, a single book ▷ *adv* (*vivre*) alone, on one's own ▷ *nm, nf*: **il en reste un(e) ~(e)** there's only one left; **le ~ livre** the only book; **parler tout ~** to talk to oneself; **faire qch (tout) ~** to do sth (all) on one's own *ou* (all) by oneself; **à lui (tout) ~** single-handed, on his own; **se sentir ~** to feel lonely; **seulement** *adv* only; **non seulement ... mais aussi** *ou* **encore** not only ... but also

sève [sɛv] *nf* sap

sévère [sevɛʀ] *adj* severe

sexe [sɛks] *nm* sex; (*organes génitaux*) genitals, sex organs; **sexuel, le** *adj* sexual

shampooing [ʃɑ̃pwɛ̃] *nm* shampoo

Shetland [ʃɛtlɑ̃d] *n*: **les îles ~** the Shetland Islands, Shetland

short [ʃɔʀt] *nm* (pair of) shorts *pl*

○ **MOT-CLÉ**

si [si] *adv* **1** (*oui*) yes; **"Paul n'est pas venu" — "si!"** "Paul hasn't come" — "yes, he has!"; **je vous assure que si** I assure you he did *ou* she is *etc*
2 (*tellement*) so; **si gentil/rapidement** so kind/fast; **(tant et) si bien que** so much so that; **si rapide qu'il soit** however fast he may be
▷ *conj* if; **si tu veux** if you want; **je me demande si** I wonder if *ou* whether; **si seulement** if only
▷ *nm* (*Mus*) B; (*en chantant la gamme*) ti

Sicile [sisil] *nf*: **la ~** Sicily

SIDA [sida] *sigle m* (= *syndrome immuno-déficitaire acquis*) AIDS *sg*

sidéré, e [sideʀe] *adj* staggered

sidérurgie [sideʀyʀʒi] *nf* steel industry

siècle [sjɛkl] *nm* century

siège [sjɛʒ] *nm* seat; (*d'entreprise*) head office; (*d'organisation*) headquarters *pl*; (*Mil*) siege; **siège social** registered office; **siéger** *vi* to sit

sien, ne [sjɛ̃, sjɛn] *pron*: **le(la) ~(ne), les ~(ne)s** (*homme*) his; (*femme*) hers; (*chose, animal*) its

sieste [sjɛst] *nf* (afternoon) snooze *ou* nap; **faire la ~** to have a snooze *ou* nap

sifflement [siflømɑ̃] *nm*: **un ~** a whistle

siffler [sifle] *vi* (*gén*) to whistle; (*en respirant*) to wheeze; (*serpent, vapeur*) to hiss ▷ *vt* (*chanson*) to whistle; (*chien etc*) to whistle for; (*fille*) to whistle at; (*pièce, orateur*) to hiss, boo; (*fin du match, départ*) to blow one's whistle for; (*fam: verre*) to guzzle

sifflet [siflɛ] *nm* whistle; **coup de ~** whistle

siffloter [siflɔte] *vi, vt* to whistle

sigle [sigl] *nm* acronym

signal, -aux [siɲal, o] *nm* signal; (*indice, écriteau*) sign; **donner le ~ de** to give the signal for; **signal d'alarme** alarm signal; **signalement** *nm* description, particulars *pl*

signaler [siɲale] *vt* to indicate; (*personne: faire un signe*) to signal; (*vol, perte*) to report; (*fig: contacter*) **~ qch à qn/(à qn) que** to point out sth to sb/(to sb) that; **je voudrais ~ un vol** I'd like to report a theft

signature [siɲatyʀ] *nf* signature; (*action*) signing

signe [siɲ] *nm* sign; (*Typo*) mark; **faire un ~ de la main** to give a sign with one's hand; **faire ~ à qn** (*fig: contacter*) to get in touch with sb; **faire ~ à qn d'entrer** to motion (to) sb to come in; **signer** *vt* to sign; **se signer** *vi* to cross o.s.; **où dois-je signer?** where do I sign?

significatif, -ive [siɲifikatif, iv] *adj* significant

signification [siɲifikasjɔ̃] *nf* meaning

signifier [siɲifje] *vt* (*vouloir dire*) to mean; (*faire connaître*): **~ qch (à qn)** to make sth known (to sb)

silence [silɑ̃s] nm silence; (Mus) rest;
garder le ~ to keep silent, say nothing;
silencieux, -euse adj quiet, silent
▷ nm silencer

silhouette [silwɛt] nf outline,
silhouette; (allure) figure

sillage [sijaʒ] nm wake

sillon [sijɔ̃] nm furrow; (de disque)
groove; **sillonner** vt to criss-cross

simagrées [simagʀe] nfpl fuss sg

similaire [similɛʀ] adj similar;
similicuir nm imitation leather;
similitude nf similarity

simple [sɛ̃pl] adj simple; (non multiple)
single ▷ nm: **~ messieurs/dames**
men's/ladies' singles sg ▷ nm/f: **~
d'esprit** simpleton

simplicité [sɛ̃plisite] nf simplicity; **en
toute ~** quite simply

simplifier [sɛ̃plifje] vt to simplify

simuler [simyle] vt to sham, simulate

simultané, e [simyltane] adj
simultaneous

sincère [sɛ̃sɛʀ] adj sincere;
sincèrement adv sincerely; (pour parler
franchement) honestly, really; **sincérité**
nf sincerity

Singapour [sɛ̃gapuʀ] nm Singapore

singe [sɛ̃ʒ] nm monkey; (de grande taille)
ape; **singer** vt to ape, mimic; **singeries**
nfpl antics

singulariser [sɛ̃gylaʀize]: **se
singulariser** vi to call attention to o.s.

singularité [sɛ̃gylaʀite] nf peculiarity

singulier, -ière [sɛ̃gylje, jɛʀ] adj
remarkable, singular ▷ nm singular

sinistre [sinistʀ] adj sinister ▷ nm
(incendie) blaze; (catastrophe) disaster;
(Assurances) damage (giving rise to a
claim); **sinistré, e** adj disaster-stricken
▷ nm/f disaster victim

sinon [sinɔ̃] conj (autrement, sans quoi)
otherwise, or else; (sauf) except, other
than; (si ce n'est) if not

sinueux, -euse [sinɥø, øz] adj
winding

sinus [sinys] nm (Anat) sinus; (Géom)

sine; **sinusite** nf sinusitis

sirène [siʀɛn] nf siren; **sirène d'alarme**
fire alarm; (en temps de guerre) air-raid
siren

sirop [siʀo] nm (à diluer: de fruit etc)
syrup; (pharmaceutique) syrup, mixture;
~ pour la toux cough mixture

siroter [siʀɔte] vt to sip

sismique [sismik] adj seismic

site [sit] nm (paysage, environnement)
setting; (d'une ville etc: emplacement)
site; **site (pittoresque)** beauty spot;
sites touristiques places of interest;
site Web (Inform) website

sitôt [sito] adv: **~ parti** as soon as he etc
had left; **~ que** as soon as; **pas de ~** not
for a long time

situation [sitɥasjɔ̃] nf situation; (d'un
édifice, d'une ville) position, location;
situation de famille marital status

situé, e [sitɥe] adj situated

situer [sitɥe] vt to site, situate; (en
pensée) to set, place; **se situer** vi to
be situated

six [sis] num six; **sixième** num sixth ▷ nf
(Scol) year 7 (BRIT), sixth grade (US)

skaï® [skaj] nm Leatherette®

ski [ski] nm (objet) ski; (sport) skiing;
faire du ~ to ski; **ski de fond** cross-
country skiing; **ski nautique** water-
skiing; **ski de piste** downhill skiing; **ski
de randonnée** cross-country skiing;
skier vi to ski; **skieur, -euse** nm/f skier

slip [slip] nm (sous-vêtement) pants pl,
briefs pl; (de bain: d'homme) trunks pl; (:
du bikini) (bikini) briefs pl

slogan [slɔgɑ̃] nm slogan

Slovaquie [slɔvaki] nf: **la ~** Slovakia

SMIC [smik] sigle m = **salaire minimum
interprofessionnel de croissance**

smoking [smɔkiŋ] nm dinner ou
evening suit

SMS sigle m (= short message service)
(service) SMS; (message) text message

SNCF sigle f (= Société nationale des
chemins de fer français) French railways

snob [snɔb] adj snobbish ▷ nm/f snob;
snobisme nm snobbery, snobbishness

sobre [sɔbʀ] adj (personne) temperate, abstemious; (élégance, style) sober

sobriquet [sɔbʀikɛ] nm nickname

social, e, -aux [sɔsjal, jo] adj social

socialisme [sɔsjalism] nm socialism; **socialiste** nm/f socialist

société [sɔsjete] nf society; (sportive) club; (Comm) company; **la ~ de consommation** the consumer society; **société anonyme** ≈ limited (BRIT) ou incorporated (US) company

sociologie [sɔsjɔlɔʒi] nf sociology

socle [sɔkl] nm (de colonne, statue) plinth, pedestal; (de lampe) base

socquette [sɔkɛt] nf ankle sock

sœur [sœʀ] nf sister; (religieuse) nun, sister

soi [swa] pron oneself; **en ~** (intrinsèquement) in itself; **cela va de ~** that ou it goes without saying; **soi-disant** adj inv so-called ▷ adv supposedly

soie [swa] nf silk; **soierie** nf (tissu) silk

soif [swaf] nf thirst; **avoir ~** to be thirsty; **donner ~ à qn** to make sb thirsty

soigné, e [swaɲe] adj (tenue) well-groomed, neat; (travail) careful, meticulous

soigner [swaɲe] vt (malade, maladie: suj: docteur) to treat; (suj: infirmière, mère) to nurse, look after; (travail, détails) to take care over; (jardin, invités) to look after; **soigneux, -euse** adj (propre) tidy, neat; (appliqué) painstaking, careful

soi-même [swamɛm] pron oneself

soin [swɛ̃] nm (application) care; (propreté, ordre) tidiness, neatness; **soins** nmpl (à un malade, blessé) treatment sg, medical attention sg; (hygiène) care sg; **prendre ~ de** to take care of, look after; **prendre ~ de faire** to take care to do; **les premiers ~s** first aid sg

soir [swaʀ] nm evening; **ce ~** this evening, tonight; **à ce ~!** see you this evening (ou tonight)!; **sept/dix heures du ~** seven in the evening/ten at

night; **demain ~** tomorrow evening, tomorrow night; **soirée** nf evening; (réception) party

soit[1] [swa] vb voir **être** ▷ conj (à savoir) namely; (ou): **~ ... ~** either ... or; **~ que ... ~ que** ou **ou que** whether ... or whether

soit[2] [swat] adv so be it, very well

soixantaine [swasɑ̃tɛn] nf: **une ~ (de)** sixty or so, about sixty; **avoir la ~** (âge) to be around sixty

soixante [swasɑ̃t] num sixty; **soixante-dix** num seventy

soja [sɔʒa] nm soya; (graines) soya beans pl; **germes de ~** beansprouts

sol [sɔl] nm ground; (de logement) floor; (Agr) soil; (Mus) G; (: en chantant la gamme) so(h)

solaire [sɔlɛʀ] adj (énergie etc) solar; (crème etc) sun cpd

soldat [sɔlda] nm soldier

solde [sɔld] nf pay ▷ nm (Comm) balance; **soldes** nm ou f pl (articles) sale goods; (vente) sales; **en ~** at sale price; **solder** vt (marchandise) to sell at sale price, sell off

sole [sɔl] nf sole inv (fish)

soleil [sɔlɛj] nm sun; (lumière) sun(light); (temps ensoleillé) sun(shine); **il fait du ~** it's sunny; **au ~** in the sun

solennel, le [sɔlanɛl] adj solemn

solfège [sɔlfɛʒ] nm musical theory

solidaire [sɔlidɛʀ] adj: **être ~s** to show solidarity, stand ou stick together; **être ~ de** (collègues) to stand by; **solidarité** nf solidarity; **par solidarité (avec)** in sympathy (with)

solide [sɔlid] adj solid; (mur, maison, meuble) solid, sturdy; (connaissances, argument) sound; (personne, estomac) robust, sturdy ▷ nm solid

soliste [sɔlist] nm/f soloist

solitaire [sɔlitɛʀ] adj (sans compagnie) solitary, lonely; (lieu) lonely ▷ nm/f (ermite) recluse; (fig: ours) loner

solitude [sɔlityd] nf loneliness; (tranquillité) solitude

solliciter [sɔlisite] vt (personne) to appeal to; (emploi, faveur) to seek

sollicitude [sɔlisityd] nf concern

soluble [sɔlybl] adj soluble

solution [sɔlysjɔ̃] nf solution; **solution de facilité** easy way out

solvable [sɔlvabl] adj solvent

sombre [sɔ̃bʀ] adj dark; (fig) gloomy; **sombrer** vi (bateau) to sink; **sombrer dans** (misère, désespoir) to sink into

sommaire [sɔmɛʀ] adj (simple) basic; (expéditif) summary ▷ nm summary

somme [sɔm] nf (Math) sum; (quantité) amount; (argent) sum, amount ▷ nm: **faire un ~** to have a (short) nap; **en ~** all in all; **~ toute** all in all

sommeil [sɔmɛj] nm sleep; **avoir ~** to be sleepy; **sommeiller** vi to doze

sommet [sɔmɛ] nm top; (d'une montagne) summit, top; (fig: de la perfection, gloire) height

sommier [sɔmje] nm (bed) base

somnambule [sɔmnɑ̃byl] nm/f sleepwalker

somnifère [sɔmnifɛʀ] nm sleeping drug no pl (ou pill)

somnoler [sɔmnɔle] vi to doze

somptueux, -euse [sɔ̃ptɥø, øz] adj sumptuous

son¹, sa [sɔ̃, sa] (pl **ses**) adj (antécédent humain: mâle) his; (: femelle) her; (: valeur indéfinie) one's, his/her; (antécédent non humain) its

son² [sɔ̃] nm sound; (de blé) bran

sondage [sɔ̃daʒ] nm: **sondage (d'opinion)** (opinion) poll

sonde [sɔ̃d] nf (Navig) lead ou sounding line; (Méd) probe; (Tech: de forage) borer, driller

sonder [sɔ̃de] vt (Navig) to sound; (Tech) to bore, drill; (fig: personne) to sound out; **~ le terrain** (fig) to test the ground

songe [sɔ̃ʒ] nm dream; **songer** vi: **songer à** (penser à) to think over; (envisager) to consider, think of; **songer que** to think that; **songeur, -euse** adj pensive

sonnant, e [sɔnɑ̃, ɑ̃t] adj: **à 8 heures ~es** on the stroke of 8

sonné, e [sɔne] adj (fam) cracked; **il est**

midi ~ it's gone twelve

sonner [sɔne] vi to ring ▷ vt (cloche) to ring; (glas, tocsin) to sound; (portier, infirmière) to ring for; **~ faux** (instrument) to sound out of tune; (rire) to ring false

sonnerie [sɔnʀi] nf (son) ringing; (sonnette) bell; (de portable) ringtone; **sonnerie d'alarme** alarm bell

sonnette [sɔnɛt] nf bell; **sonnette d'alarme** alarm bell

sonore [sɔnɔʀ] adj (voix) sonorous, ringing; (salle) resonant; (film, signal) sound cpd; **sonorisation** nf (équipement: de salle de conférences) public address system, P.A. system; (: de discothèque) sound system; **sonorité** nf (de piano, violon) tone; (d'une salle) acoustics pl

sophistiqué, e [sɔfistike] adj sophisticated

sorbet [sɔrbɛ] nm water ice, sorbet

sorcier [sɔrsje] nm sorcerer

sordide [sɔrdid] adj (lieu) squalid; (action) sordid

sort [sɔr] nm (destinée) fate; (condition) lot; (magique) curse, spell; **tirer au ~** to draw lots

sorte [sɔrt] nf sort, kind; **de la ~** in that way; **de (telle) ~ que** so that; **en quelque ~** in a way; **faire en ~ que** to see to it that; **quelle ~ de ...?** what kind of ...?

sortie [sɔrti] nf (issue) way out, exit; (remarque drôle) sally; (promenade) outing; (le soir: au restaurant etc) night out; (Comm: d'un disque) release; (: d'un livre) publication; (: d'un modèle) launching; **où est la ~?** where's the exit?; **sortie de bain** (vêtement) bathrobe

sortilège [sɔrtilɛʒ] nm (magic) spell

sortir [sɔrtiʀ] vi (gén) to come out; (partir, se promener, aller au spectacle) to go out; (numéro gagnant) to come up ▷ vt (gén) to take out; (produit, modèle) to bring out; (fam: dire) to come out with; **~ avec qn** to be going out with sb; **s'en ~** (malade) to pull through;

(d'une difficulté etc) to get through; **~ de** *(endroit)* to go *(ou* come) out of, leave; *(provenir de)* to come from; *(compétence)* to be outside

sosie [sɔzi] *nm* double

sot, sotte [so, sɔt] *adj* silly, foolish ▷ *nm/f* fool; **sottise** *nf (caractère)* silliness, foolishness; *(action)* silly *ou* foolish thing

sou [su] *nm:* **près de ses ~s** tight-fisted; **sans le ~** penniless

soubresaut [subRəso] *nm* start; *(cahot)* jolt

souche [suʃ] *nf (d'arbre)* stump; *(de carnet)* counterfoil *(BRIT)*

souci [susi] *nm (inquiétude)* worry; *(préoccupation)* concern; *(Bot)* marigold; **se faire du ~** to worry; **soucier: se soucier de** *vt* to care about; **soucieux, -euse** *adj* concerned, worried

soucoupe [sukup] *nf* saucer; **soucoupe volante** flying saucer

soudain, e [sudɛ̃, ɛn] *adj (douleur, mort)* sudden ▷ *adv* suddenly, all of a sudden

Soudan [sudã] *nm:* **le ~** Sudan

soude [sud] *nf* soda

souder [sude] *vt (avec fil à souder)* to solder; *(par soudure autogène)* to weld; *(fig)* to bind together

soudure [sudyR] *nf* soldering; welding; *(joint)* soldered joint; weld

souffle [sufl] *nm (en expirant)* breath; *(en soufflant)* puff, blow; *(respiration)* breathing; *(d'explosion, de ventilateur)* blast; *(du vent)* blowing; **être à bout de ~** to be out of breath; **un ~ d'air** a breath of air

soufflé, e [sufle] *adj (fam: stupéfié)* staggered ▷ *nm (Culin)* soufflé

souffler [sufle] *vi (gén)* to blow; *(haleter)* to puff (and blow) ▷ *vt (feu, bougie)* to blow out; *(chasser: poussière etc)* to blow away; *(Tech: verre)* to blow; *(dire):* **~ qch à qn** to whisper sth to sb

souffrance [sufRɑ̃s] *nf* suffering; **en ~** *(affaire)* pending

souffrant, e [sufRɑ̃, ɑ̃t] *adj* unwell

souffre-douleur [sufRədulœR] *nm inv* butt, underdog

souffrir [sufRiR] *vi* to suffer, be in pain ▷ *vt* to suffer, endure; *(supporter)* to bear, stand; **~ de** *(maladie, froid)* to suffer from; **elle ne peut pas le ~** she can't stand *ou* bear him

soufre [sufR] *nm* sulphur

souhait [swɛ] *nm* wish; **tous nos ~s pour la nouvelle année** (our) best wishes for the New Year; **à vos ~s!** bless you!; **souhaitable** *adj* desirable

souhaiter [swete] *vt* to wish for; **~ la bonne année à qn** to wish sb a happy New Year; **~ que** to hope that

soûl, e [su, sul] *adj* drunk ▷ *nm:* **tout son ~** to one's heart's content

soulagement [sulaʒmɑ̃] *nm* relief

soulager [sulaʒe] *vt* to relieve

soûler [sule] *vt:* **~ qn** to get sb drunk; *(suj: boisson)* to make sb drunk; *(fig)* to make sb's head spin *ou* reel; **se soûler** *vi* to get drunk

soulever [sul(ə)ve] *vt* to lift; *(poussière)* to send up; *(enthousiasme)* to arouse; *(question, débat)* to raise; **se soulever** *vi (peuple)* to rise up; *(personne couchée)* to lift o.s. up

soulier [sulje] *nm* shoe

souligner [suliɲe] *vt* to underline; *(fig)* to emphasize, stress

soumettre [sumɛtR] *vt (pays)* to subject, subjugate; *(rebelle)* to put down, subdue; **~ qch à qn** *(projet etc)* to submit sth to sb; **se soumettre (à)** to submit (to)

soumis, e [sumi, iz] *adj* submissive; **soumission** *nf* submission

soupçon [supsɔ̃] *nm* suspicion; *(petite quantité):* **un ~ de** a hint *ou* touch of; **soupçonner** *vt* to suspect; **soupçonneux, -euse** *adj* suspicious

soupe [sup] *nf* soup

souper [supe] *vi* to have supper ▷ *nm* supper

soupeser [supəze] *vt* to weigh in one's hand(s); *(fig)* to weigh up

soupière [supjeR] *nf* (soup) tureen

soupir [supiR] *nm* sigh; **pousser un**

~ de soulagement to heave a sigh of relief

soupirer [supire] *vi* to sigh

souple [supl] *adj* supple; (*fig: règlement, caractère*) flexible; (: *démarche, taille*) lithe, supple; **souplesse** *nf* suppleness; (*de caractère*) flexibility

source [surs] *nf* (*point d'eau*) spring; (*d'un cours d'eau, fig*) source; **de bonne ~** on good authority

sourcil [sursi] *nm* (eye)brow; **sourciller** *vi*: **sans sourciller** without turning a hair *ou* batting an eyelid

sourd, e [sur, surd] *adj* deaf; (*bruit*) muffled; (*douleur*) dull ▷ *nm/f* deaf person; **faire la ~e oreille** to turn a deaf ear; **sourdine** *nf* (*Mus*) mute; **en sourdine** softly, quietly; **sourd-muet, sourde-muette** *adj* deaf-and-dumb ▷ *nm/f* deaf-mute

souriant, e [surjā, jāt] *adj* cheerful

sourire [surir] *nm* smile ▷ *vi* to smile; **~ à qn** to smile at sb; (*fig: plaire à*) to appeal to sb; (*suj: chance*) to smile on sb; **garder le ~** to keep smiling

souris [suri] *nf* mouse

sournois, e [surnwa, waz] *adj* deceitful, underhand

sous [su] *prép* under; **~ la pluie** in the rain; **~ terre** underground; **~ peu** shortly, before long; **sous-bois** *nm inv* undergrowth

souscrire [suskrir]: **~ à** *vt* to subscribe to

sous...: sous-directeur, -trice *nm/f* assistant manager(-manageress); **sous-entendre** *vt* to imply, infer; **sous-entendu, e** *adj* implied ▷ *nm* innuendo, insinuation; **sous-estimer** *vt* to underestimate; **sous-jacent, e** *adj* underlying; **sous-louer** *vt* to sublet; **sous-marin, e** *adj* (*flore, faune*) submarine; (*pêche*) underwater ▷ *nm* submarine; **sous-pull** *nm* thin poloneck jersey; **soussigné, e** *adj*: **je soussigné** I the undersigned; **sous-sol** *nm* basement; **sous-titre** *nm* subtitle

soustraction [sustraksjɔ̃] *nf* subtraction

soustraire [sustrɛr] *vt* to subtract, take away; (*dérober*): **~ qch à qn** to remove sth from sb; **se soustraire à** (*autorité etc*) to elude, escape from

sous...: sous-traitant *nm* sub-contractor; **sous-traiter** *vt* to sub-contract; **sous-vêtements** *nmpl* underwear *sg*

soutane [sutan] *nf* cassock, soutane

soute [sut] *nf* hold

soutenir [sut(ə)nir] *vt* to support; (*assaut, choc*) to stand up to, withstand; (*intérêt, effort*) to keep up; (*assurer*): **~ que** to maintain that; **soutenu, e** *adj* (*efforts*) sustained, unflagging; (*style*) elevated

souterrain, e [sutɛrɛ̃, ɛn] *adj* underground ▷ *nm* underground passage

soutien [sutjɛ̃] *nm* support; **soutien-gorge** *nm* bra

soutirer [sutire] *vt*: **~ qch à qn** to squeeze *ou* get sth out of sb

souvenir [suv(ə)nir] *nm* (*réminiscence*) memory; (*objet*) souvenir ▷ *vb*: **se ~ de** to remember; **se ~ que** to remember that; **en ~ de** in memory *ou* remembrance of; **avec mes affectueux/meilleurs ~s, ...** with love from, .../regards, ...

souvent [suvā] *adv* often; **peu ~** seldom, infrequently

souverain, e [suv(ə)rɛ̃, ɛn] *nm/f* sovereign, monarch

soyeux, -euse [swajø, øz] *adj* silky

spacieux, -euse [spasjø, jøz] *adj* spacious, roomy

spaghettis [spageti] *nmpl* spaghetti *sg*

sparadrap [sparadra] *nm* sticking plaster (*BRIT*), Bandaid® (*US*)

spatial, e, -aux [spasjal, jo] *adj* (*Aviat*) space *cpd*

speaker, ine [spikœr, krin] *nm/f* announcer

spécial, e, -aux [spesjal, jo] *adj* special; (*bizarre*) peculiar; **spécialement** *adv* especially,

particularly; (*tout exprès*) specially;
spécialiser: **se spécialiser** *vi* to
specialize; **spécialiste** *nm/f* specialist;
spécialité *nf* speciality; (*branche*)
special field
spécifier [spesifje] *vt* to specify, state
spécimen [spesimɛn] *nm* specimen
spectacle [spɛktakl] *nm* (*scène*)
sight; (*représentation*) show; (*industrie*)
show business; **spectaculaire** *adj*
spectacular
spectateur, -trice [spɛktatœr,
tris] *nm/f* (*Cinéma etc*) member of
the audience; (*Sport*) spectator; (*d'un
événement*) onlooker, witness
spéculer [spekyle] *vi* to speculate
spéléologie [speleɔlɔʒi] *nf* potholing
sperme [spɛrm] *nm* semen, sperm
sphère [sfɛr] *nf* sphere
spirale [spiral] *nf* spiral
spirituel, le [spirityɛl] *adj* spiritual;
(*fin, piquant*) witty
splendide [splɑ̃did] *adj* splendid
spontané, e [spɔ̃tane] *adj*
spontaneous; **spontanéité** *nf*
spontaneity
sport [spɔr] *nm* sport ▷ *adj inv*
(*vêtement*) casual; **faire du ~** to do sport;
sports d'hiver winter sports; **sportif,
-ive** *adj* (*journal, association, épreuve*)
sports *cpd*; (*allure, démarche*) athletic;
(*attitude, esprit*) sporting
spot [spɔt] *nm* (*lampe*) spot(light);
(*annonce*); **spot (publicitaire)**
commercial (break)
square [skwar] *nm* public garden(s)
squelette [skəlɛt] *nm* skeleton;
squelettique *adj* scrawny
SRAS [sras] *sigle m* (= *syndrome
respiratoire aigu sévère*) SARS
Sri Lanka [srilɑ̃ka] *nm*: **le ~** Sri Lanka
stabiliser [stabilize] *vt* to stabilize
stable [stabl] *adj* stable, steady
stade [stad] *nm* (*Sport*) stadium; (*phase,
niveau*) stage
stage [staʒ] *nm* (*cours*) training course;
~ de formation (professionnelle)
vocational (training) course; **~ de**

perfectionnement advanced training
course; **stagiaire** *nm/f, adj* trainee
▎ Attention à ne pas traduire *stage*
par le mot anglais *stage*.
stagner [stagne] *vi* to stagnate
stand [stɑ̃d] *nm* (*d'exposition*) stand; (*de
foire*) stall; **stand de tir** (*à la foire, Sport*)
shooting range
standard [stɑ̃dar] *adj inv* standard
▷ *nm* switchboard; **standardiste** *nm/f*
switchboard operator
standing [stɑ̃diŋ] *nm* standing; **de
grand ~** luxury
starter [starter] *nm* (*Auto*) choke
station [stasjɔ̃] *nf* station; (*de
bus*) stop; (*de villégiature*) resort;
station de ski ski resort; **station
de taxis** taxi rank (BRIT) *ou* stand
(US); **stationnement** *nm* parking;
stationner *vi* to park; **station-service**
nf service station
statistique [statistik] *nf* (*science*)
statistics *sg*; (*rapport, étude*) statistic
▷ *adj* statistical
statue [staty] *nf* statue
statu quo [statykwo] *nm* status quo
statut [staty] *nm* status; **statuts** *nmpl*
(*Jur, Admin*) statutes; **statutaire** *adj*
statutory
Sté *abr* = **société**
steak [stɛk] *nm* steak; **~ haché**
hamburger
sténo(graphie) [stenɔ(grafi)] *nf*
shorthand
stérile [steril] *adj* sterile
stérilet [sterilɛ] *nm* coil, loop
stériliser [sterilize] *vt* to sterilize
stimulant [stimylɑ̃] *nm* (*fig*) stimulus,
incentive; (*physique*) stimulant
stimuler [stimyle] *vt* to stimulate
stipuler [stipyle] *vt* to stipulate
stock [stɔk] *nm* stock; **stocker** *vt* to
stock
stop [stɔp] *nm* (*Auto: écriteau*) stop sign;
(: *feu arrière*) brake-light; **faire du ~**
(*fam*) to hitch(hike); **stopper** *vt, vi* to
stop, halt
store [stɔr] *nm* blind; (*de magasin*)

shade, awning

strabisme [stʀabism] nm squinting

strapontin [stʀapɔ̃tɛ̃] nm jump ou foldaway seat

stratégie [stʀateʒi] nf strategy; **stratégique** adj strategic

stress [stʀɛs] nm stress; **stressant, e** adj stressful; **stresser** vt: **stresser qn** to make sb (feel) tense

strict, e [stʀikt] adj strict; (tenue, décor) severe, plain; **le ~ nécessaire/ minimum** the bare essentials/ minimum

strident, e [stʀidɑ̃, ɑ̃t] adj shrill, strident

strophe [stʀɔf] nf verse, stanza

structure [stʀyktyʀ] nf structure; **~s d'accueil** reception facilities

studieux, -euse [stydjø, jøz] adj studious

studio [stydjo] nm (logement) (one-roomed) flatlet (BRIT) ou apartment (US); (d'artiste, TV etc) studio

stupéfait, e [stypefɛ, ɛt] adj astonished

stupéfiant, e [stypefjɑ̃, jɑ̃t] adj (étonnant) stunning, astounding ▷ nm (Méd) drug, narcotic

stupéfier [stypefje] vt (étonner) to stun, astonish

stupeur [stypœʀ] nf astonishment

stupide [stypid] adj stupid; **stupidité** nf stupidity; (parole, acte) stupid thing (to do ou say)

style [stil] nm style

stylé, e [stile] adj well-trained

styliste [stilist] nm/f designer

stylo [stilo] nm: **~ (à encre)** (fountain) pen; **stylo (à) bille** ball-point pen

su, e [sy] pp de **savoir** ▷ nm: **au su de** with the knowledge of

suave [sɥav] adj sweet

subalterne [sybaltɛʀn] adj (employé, officier) junior; (rôle) subordinate, subsidiary ▷ nm/f subordinate

subconscient [sypkɔ̃sjɑ̃] nm subconscious

subir [sybiʀ] vt (affront, dégâts) to suffer;

(opération, châtiment) to undergo

subit, e [sybi, it] adj sudden; **subitement** adv suddenly, all of a sudden

subjectif, -ive [sybʒɛktif, iv] adj subjective

subjonctif [sybʒɔ̃ktif] nm subjunctive

subjuguer [sybʒyge] vt to captivate

submerger [sybmɛʀʒe] vt to submerge; (fig) to overwhelm

subordonné, e [sybɔʀdɔne] adj, nm/f subordinate

subrepticement [sybʀɛptismɑ̃] adv surreptitiously

subside [sybzid] nm grant

subsidiaire [sybzidjɛʀ] adj: **question ~** deciding question

subsister [sybziste] vi (rester) to remain, subsist; (survivre) to live on

substance [sypstɑ̃s] nf substance

substituer [sypstitɥe] vt: **~ qn/qch à** to substitute sb/sth for; **se ~ à qn** (évincer) to substitute o.s. for sb

substitut [sypstity] nm (succédané) substitute

subterfuge [syptɛʀfyʒ] nm subterfuge

subtil, e [syptil] adj subtle

subvenir [sybvəniʀ]: **~ à** vt to meet

subvention [sybvɑ̃sjɔ̃] nf subsidy, grant; **subventionner** vt to subsidize

suc [syk] nm (Bot) sap; (de viande, fruit) juice

succéder [syksede]: **~ à** vt to succeed; **se succéder** vi (accidents, années) to follow one another

succès [syksɛ] nm success; **avoir du ~** to be a success, be successful; **à ~** successful; **succès de librairie** bestseller

successeur [syksesœʀ] nm successor

successif, -ive [syksesif, iv] adj successive

succession [syksesjɔ̃] nf (série, Pol) succession; (Jur: patrimoine) estate, inheritance

succomber [sykɔ̃be] vi to die, succumb; (fig): **~ à** to succumb to

succulent, e [sykylɑ̃, ɑ̃t] adj (repas,

mets) delicious

succursale [sykyʀsal] *nf* branch

sucer [syse] *vt* to suck; **sucette** *nf* (*bonbon*) lollipop; (*de bébé*) dummy (BRIT), pacifier (US)

sucre [sykʀ] *nm*: **le ~** (*substance*) sugar; (*morceau*) lump of sugar, sugar lump *ou* cube; **sucre d'orge** barley sugar; **sucre en morceaux/cristallisé/en poudre** lump/granulated/caster sugar; **sucre glace** icing sugar (BRIT), confectioner's sugar (US); **sucré, e** *adj* (*produit alimentaire*) sweetened; (*au goût*) sweet; **sucrer** *vt* (*thé, café*) to sweeten, put sugar in; **sucreries** *nfpl* (*bonbons*) sweets, sweet things; **sucrier** *nm* (*récipient*) sugar bowl

sud [syd] *nm*: **le ~** the south ▷ *adj inv* south; (*côte*) south, southern; **au ~** (*situation*) in the south; (*direction*) to the south; **au ~ de** (to the) south of; **sud-africain, e** *adj* South African ▷ *nm/f*: **Sud-Africain, e** South African; **sud-américain, e** *adj* South American ▷ *nm/f*: **Sud-Américain, e** South American; **sud-est** *nm, adj inv* south-east; **sud-ouest** *nm, adj inv* south-west

Suède [sɥɛd] *nf*: **la ~** Sweden; **suédois, e** *adj* Swedish ▷ *nm/f*: **Suédois, e** Swede ▷ *nm* (*Ling*) Swedish

suer [sɥe] *vi* to sweat; (*suinter*) to ooze; **sueur** *nf* sweat; **en sueur** sweating, in a sweat; **donner des sueurs froides à qn** to put sb in(to) a cold sweat

suffire [syfiʀ] *vi* (*être assez*): **~ (à qn/pour qch/pour faire)** to be enough *ou* sufficient (for sb/for sth/to do); **il suffit d'une négligence ...** it only takes one act of carelessness ...; **il suffit qu'on oublie pour que ...** one only needs to forget for ...; **ça suffit!** that's enough!

suffisamment [syfizamɑ̃] *adv* sufficiently, enough; **~ de** sufficient, enough

suffisant, e [syfizɑ̃, ɑ̃t] *adj* sufficient; (*résultats*) satisfactory; (*vaniteux*) self-important, bumptious

suffixe [syfiks] *nm* suffix

suffoquer [syfɔke] *vt* to choke, suffocate; (*stupéfier*) to stagger, astound ▷ *vi* to choke, suffocate

suffrage [syfʀaʒ] *nm* (*Pol: voix*) vote

suggérer [sygʒeʀe] *vt* to suggest; **suggestion** *nf* suggestion

suicide [sɥisid] *nm* suicide; **suicider**: **se suicider** *vi* to commit suicide

suie [sɥi] *nf* soot

suisse [sɥis] *adj* Swiss ▷ *nm*: **S~** Swiss *pl inv* ▷ *nf*: **la S~** Switzerland; **la S~ romande/allemande** French-speaking/German-speaking Switzerland

suite [sɥit] *nf* (*continuation: d'énumération etc*) rest, remainder; (: *de feuilleton*) continuation; (: *film etc sur le même thème*) sequel; (*série*) series, succession; (*conséquence*) result; (*ordre, liaison logique*) coherence; (*appartement, Mus*) suite; (*escorte*) retinue, suite; **suites** *nfpl* (*d'une maladie etc*) effects; **prendre la ~ de** (*directeur etc*) to succeed, take over from; **donner ~ à** (*requête, projet*) to follow up; **faire ~ à** to follow; **(faisant) ~ à votre lettre du ...** further to your letter of the ...; **de ~** (*d'affilée*) in succession; (*immédiatement*) at once; **par la ~** afterwards, subsequently; **à la ~** one after the other; **à la ~ de** (*derrière*) behind; (*en conséquence de*) following

suivant, e [sɥivɑ̃, ɑ̃t] *adj* next, following ▷ *prép* (*selon*) according to; **au ~!** next!

suivi, e [sɥivi] *adj* (*effort, qualité*) consistent; (*cohérent*) coherent; **très/peu ~** (*cours*) well-/poorly-attended

suivre [sɥivʀ] *vt* (*gén*) to follow; (*Scol: cours*) to attend; (*comprendre*) to keep up with; (*Comm: article*) to continue to stock ▷ *vi* to follow; (*élève: assimiler*) to keep up; **se suivre** *vi* (*accidents etc*) to follow one after the other; **faire ~** (*lettre*) to forward; **"à ~"** "to be continued"

sujet, te [syʒɛ, ɛt] *adj*: **être ~ à** (*vertige etc*) to be liable *ou* subject to ▷ *nm/f*

(*d'un souverain*) subject ▷ *nm* subject;
au ~ de about; **sujet de conversation**
topic *ou* subject of conversation;
sujet d'examen (*Scol*) examination
question

super [sypɛʀ] (*fam*) *adj inv* terrific,
great, fantastic, super

superbe [sypɛʀb] *adj* magnificent,
superb

superficie [sypɛʀfisi] *nf* (surface) area

superficiel, le [sypɛʀfisjɛl] *adj*
superficial

superflu, e [sypɛʀfly] *adj* superfluous

supérieur, e [sypeʀjœʀ] *adj* (*lèvre,
étages, classes*) upper; (*plus élevé:
température, niveau, enseignement*): **~ (à)**
higher (than); (*meilleur: qualité, produit*):
~ (à) superior (to); (*excellent, hautain*)
superior ▷ *nm, nf* superior; **supériorité**
nf superiority

supermarché [sypɛʀmaʀʃe] *nm*
supermarket

superposer [sypɛʀpoze] *vt* (*faire
chevaucher*) to superimpose; **lits
superposés** bunk beds

superpuissance [sypɛʀpɥisɑ̃s] *nf*
super-power

superstitieux, -euse [sypɛʀstisjø,
jøz] *adj* superstitious

superviser [sypɛʀvize] *vt* to
supervise

supplanter [syplɑ̃te] *vt* to supplant

suppléant, e [sypleɑ̃, -ɑ̃t] *adj*
(*professeur*) supply *cpd*; (*juge,
fonctionnaire*) deputy *cpd* ▷ *nm/f*
(*professeur*) supply teacher

suppléer [syplee] *vt* (*ajouter: mot
manquant etc*) to supply, provide;
(*compenser: lacune*) to fill in; **~ à** to
make up for

supplément [syplemɑ̃] *nm*
supplement; (*de frites etc*) extra portion;
un ~ de travail extra *ou* additional
work; **payer un ~** to pay an additional
charge; **le vin est en ~** wine is extra;
supplémentaire *adj* additional,
further; (*train, bus*) relief *cpd*, extra

supplications [syplikasjɔ̃] *nfpl* pleas,
entreaties

supplice [syplis] *nm* torture *no pl*

supplier [syplije] *vt* to implore,
beseech

support [sypɔʀ] *nm* support;
(*publicitaire*) medium; (*audio-visuel*) aid

supportable [sypɔʀtabl] *adj* (*douleur*)
bearable

supporter¹ [sypɔʀtɛʀ] *nm* supporter,
fan

supporter² [sypɔʀte] *vt* (*conséquences,
épreuve*) to bear, endure; (*défauts,
personne*) to put up with; (*suj: chose:
chaleur etc*) to withstand; (: *personne:
chaleur, vin*) to be able to take

> Attention à ne pas traduire
> *supporter* par *to support*.

supposer [sypoze] *vt* to suppose;
(*impliquer*) to presuppose; **à ~ que**
supposing (that)

suppositoire [sypozitwaʀ] *nm*
suppository

suppression [sypʀesjɔ̃] *nf* (*voir
supprimer*) cancellation; removal;
deletion

supprimer [sypʀime] *vt* (*congés,
service d'autobus etc*) to cancel; (*emplois,
privilèges, témoin gênant*) to do away
with; (*cloison, cause, anxiété*) to remove;
(*clause, mot*) to delete

suprême [sypʀɛm] *adj* supreme

 MOT-CLÉ

sur [syʀ] *prép* **1** (*position*) on; (*par-dessus*)
over; (*au-dessus*) above; **pose-le sur
la table** put it on the table; **je n'ai
pas d'argent sur moi** I haven't any
money on me
2 (*direction*) towards; **en allant sur
Paris** going towards Paris; **sur votre
droite** on *ou* to your right
3 (*à propos de*) on, about; **un livre/une
conférence sur Balzac** a book/lecture
on *ou* about Balzac
4 (*proportion*) out of; **un sur 10** one in
10; (*Scol*) one out of 10
5 (*mesures*) by; **4 m sur 2** 4 m by 2

6 (*succession*): **avoir accident sur accident** to have one accident after the other

sûr, e [syʀ] *adj* sure, certain; (*digne de confiance*) reliable; (*sans danger*) safe; (*diagnostic, goût*) reliable; **le plus ~ est de** the safest thing is to; **sûr de soi** self-assured, self-confident

surcharge [syʀʃaʀʒ] *nf* (*de passagers, marchandises*) excess load; **surcharger** *vt* to overload

surcroît [syʀkʀwa] *nm*: **un ~ de** additional +*nom*; **par** *ou* **de ~** moreover; **en ~** in addition

surdité [syʀdite] *nf* deafness

sûrement [syʀmã] *adv* (*certainement*) certainly; (*sans risques*) safely

surenchère [syʀãʃeʀ] *nf* (*aux enchères*) higher bid; **surenchérir** *vi* to bid higher; (*fig*) to try and outbid each other

surestimer [syʀɛstime] *vt* to overestimate

sûreté [syʀte] *nf* (*sécurité*) safety; (*exactitude: de renseignements etc*) reliability; (*d'un geste*) steadiness; **mettre en ~** to put in a safe place; **pour plus de ~** as an extra precaution, to be on the safe side

surf [sœʀf] *nm* surfing

surface [syʀfas] *nf* surface; (*superficie*) surface area; **une grande ~** a supermarket; **faire ~** to surface; **en ~** near the surface; (*fig*) superficially

surfait, e [syʀfɛ, ɛt] *adj* overrated

surfer [syʀfe] *vi*: **~ sur Internet** to surf *ou* browse the Internet

surgelé, e [syʀʒəle] *adj* (deep-)frozen ▷ *nm*: **les ~s** (deep-)frozen food

surgir [syʀʒiʀ] *vi* to appear suddenly; (*fig: problème, conflit*) to arise

sur...: **surhumain, e** *adj* superhuman; **sur-le-champ** *adv* immediately; **surlendemain** *nm*: **le surlendemain (soir)** two days later (in the evening); **le surlendemain de** two days after; **surmenage** *nm* overwork(ing);

surmener: **se surmener** *vi* to overwork

surmonter [syʀmõte] *vt* (*vaincre*) to overcome; (*être au-dessus de*) to top

surnaturel, le [syʀnatyʀɛl] *adj, nm* supernatural

surnom [syʀnõ] *nm* nickname

surnombre [syʀnõbʀ] *nm*: **être en ~** to be too many (*ou* one too many)

surpeuplé, e [syʀpœple] *adj* overpopulated

surplace [syʀplas] *nm*: **faire du ~** to mark time

surplomber [syʀplõbe] *vt, vi* to overhang

surplus [syʀply] *nm* (*Comm*) surplus; (*reste*): **~ de bois** wood left over

surprenant, e [syʀpʀənã, ãt] *adj* amazing

surprendre [syʀpʀãdʀ] *vt* (*étonner*) to surprise; (*tomber sur: intrus etc*) to catch; (*entendre*) to overhear

surpris, e [syʀpʀi, iz] *adj*: **~ (de/que)** surprised (at/that); **surprise** *nf* surprise; **faire une surprise à qn** to give sb a surprise; **surprise-partie** *nf* party

sursaut [syʀso] *nm* start, jump; **~ de** (*énergie, indignation*) sudden fit *ou* burst of; **en ~** with a start; **sursauter** *vi* to (give a) start, jump

sursis [syʀsi] *nm* (*Jur: gén*) suspended sentence; (*fig*) reprieve

surtout [syʀtu] *adv* (*avant tout, d'abord*) above all; (*spécialement, particulièrement*) especially; **~, ne dites rien!** whatever you do don't say anything!; **~ pas!** certainly *ou* definitely not!; **~ que ...** especially as ...

surveillance [syʀvejãs] *nf* watch; (*Police, Mil*) surveillance; **sous ~ médicale** under medical supervision

surveillant, e [syʀvejã, ãt] *nm/f* (*de prison*) warder; (*Scol*) monitor

surveiller [syʀveje] *vt* (*enfant, élèves, bagages*) to watch, keep an eye on; (*prisonnier, suspect*) to keep (a) watch on; (*territoire, bâtiment*) to (keep) watch

over; (*travaux, cuisson*) to supervise;
(*Scol: examen*) to invigilate; **~ son
langage/sa ligne** to watch one's
language/figure
survenir [syʀvəniʀ] *vi* (*incident, retards*)
to occur, arise; (*événement*) to take place
survêtement [syʀvɛtmɑ̃] *nm*
tracksuit
survie [syʀvi] *nf* survival; **survivant, e**
nm/f survivor; **survivre** *vi* to survive;
survivre à (*accident etc*) to survive
survoler [syʀvɔle] *vt* to fly over; (*fig:
livre*) to skim through
survolté, e [syʀvɔlte] *adj* (*fig*)
worked up
sus [sy(s)]: **en ~ de** *prép* in addition to,
over and above; **en ~** in addition
susceptible [syseptibl] *adj* touchy,
sensitive; **~ de faire** (*hypothèse*) liable
to do
susciter [sysite] *vt* (*admiration*) to
arouse; (*ennuis*): **~ (à qn)** to create
(for sb)
suspect, e [syspɛ(kt), ɛkt] *adj*
suspicious; (*témoignage, opinions*)
suspect ▷ *nm/f* suspect; **suspecter**
vt to suspect; (*honnêteté de qn*) to
question, have one's suspicions about
suspendre [syspɑ̃dʀ] *vt* (*accrocher:
vêtement*): **~ qch (à)** to hang sth up (on);
(*interrompre, démettre*) to suspend
suspendu, e [syspɑ̃dy] *adj* (*accroché*):
~ à hanging on (*ou* from); (*perché*): **~
au-dessus de** suspended over
suspens [syspɑ̃]: **en ~** *adv* (*affaire*)
in abeyance; **tenir en ~** to keep in
suspense
suspense [syspɛns, syspɑ̃s] *nm*
suspense
suspension [syspɑ̃sjɔ̃] *nf* suspension;
(*lustre*) light fitting *ou* fitment
suture [sytyʀ] *nf* (*Méd*): **point de ~**
stitch
svelte [svɛlt] *adj* slender, svelte
SVP *abr* (= *s'il vous plaît*) please
sweat [swit] *nm* (*fam*) sweatshirt
sweat-shirt [switʃœʀt] (*pl* **~s**) *nm*
sweatshirt

syllabe [si(l)lab] *nf* syllable
symbole [sɛ̃bɔl] *nm* symbol;
symbolique *adj* symbolic(al); (*geste,
offrande*) token *cpd*; **symboliser** *vt* to
symbolize
symétrique [simetʀik] *adj*
symmetrical
sympa [sɛ̃pa] (*fam*) *adj inv* nice; **sois ~,
prête-le moi** be a pal and lend it to me
sympathie [sɛ̃pati] *nf* (*inclination*)
liking; (*affinité*) friendship;
(*condoléances*) sympathy; **j'ai
beaucoup de ~ pour lui** I like him a lot;
sympathique *adj* nice, friendly
Attention à ne pas traduire
sympathique par *sympathetic*.
sympathisant, e [sɛ̃patizɑ̃, ɑ̃t] *nm/f*
sympathizer
sympathiser [sɛ̃patize] *vi* (*voisins
etc: s'entendre*) to get on (*BRIT*) *ou* along
(*US*) (well)
symphonie [sɛ̃fɔni] *nf* symphony
symptôme [sɛ̃ptom] *nm* symptom
synagogue [sinagɔg] *nf* synagogue
syncope [sɛ̃kɔp] *nf* (*Méd*) blackout;
tomber en ~ to faint, pass out
syndic [sɛ̃dik] *nm* (*d'immeuble*)
managing agent
syndical, e, -aux [sɛ̃dikal, o] *adj*
(trade) union *cpd*; **syndicaliste** *nm/f*
trade unionist
syndicat [sɛ̃dika] *nm* (*d'ouvriers,
employés*) (trade) union; **syndicat
d'initiative** tourist office; **syndiqué, e**
adj belonging to a (trade) union;
syndiquer: **se syndiquer** *vi* to form
a trade union; (*adhérer*) to join a trade
union
synonyme [sinɔnim] *adj* synonymous
▷ *nm* synonym; **~ de** synonymous with
syntaxe [sɛ̃taks] *nf* syntax
synthèse [sɛ̃tɛz] *nf* synthesis
synthétique [sɛ̃tetik] *adj* synthetic
Syrie [siʀi] *nf*: **la ~** Syria
systématique [sistematik] *adj*
systematic
système [sistɛm] *nm* system; **le ~ D**
resourcefulness

t' [t] *pron voir* **te**
ta [ta] *adj voir* **ton¹**
tabac [taba] *nm* tobacco; (*magasin*)
tobacconist's (shop)
tabagisme [tabaʒism] *nm*: **tabagisme
passif** passive smoking
table [tabl] *nf* table; **à ~!** dinner *etc* is
ready!; **se mettre à ~** to sit down to
eat; **mettre la ~** to lay the table; **une
~ pour 4, s'il vous plaît** a table for 4,
please; **table à repasser** ironing board;
table de cuisson hob; **table de nuit**
ou **de chevet** bedside table; **table des
matières** (table of) contents *pl*; **table
d'orientation** viewpoint indicator;
table roulante trolley (BRIT), tea
wagon (US)
tableau, x [tablo] *nm* (*peinture*)
painting; (*reproduction, fig*) picture;
(*panneau*) board; (*schéma*) table, chart;
tableau d'affichage notice board;
tableau de bord dashboard; (*Aviat*)
instrument panel; **tableau noir**
blackboard

tablette [tablɛt] *nf* (*planche*) shelf;
tablette de chocolat bar of chocolate
tablier [tablije] *nm* apron
tabou [tabu] *nm* taboo
tabouret [taburɛ] *nm* stool
tac [tak] *nm*: **il m'a répondu du ~ au ~**
he answered me right back
tache [taʃ] *nf* (*saleté*) stain, mark; (*Art,
de couleur, lumière*) spot; **tache de
rousseur** freckle
tâche [taʃ] *nf* task
tacher [taʃe] *vt* to stain, mark
tâcher [taʃe] *vi*: **~ de faire** to try *ou*
endeavour to do
tacheté, e [taʃte] *adj* spotted
tact [takt] *nm* tact; **avoir du ~** to be
tactful
tactique [taktik] *adj* tactical ▷ *nf*
(*technique*) tactics *sg*; (*plan*) tactic
taie [tɛ] *nf*: **~ (d'oreiller)** pillowslip,
pillowcase
taille [taj] *nf* cutting; (*d'arbre etc*)
pruning; (*milieu du corps*) waist;
(*hauteur*) height; (*grandeur*) size; **de ~ à
faire** capable of doing; **de ~** sizeable;
taille-crayon(s) *nm* pencil sharpener
tailler [taje] *vt* (*pierre, diamant*) to cut;
(*arbre, plante*) to prune; (*vêtement*) to cut
out; (*crayon*) to sharpen
tailleur [tajœʀ] *nm* (*couturier*) tailor;
(*vêtement*) suit; **en ~** (*assis*) cross-legged
taillis [taji] *nm* copse
taire [tɛʀ] *vi*: **faire ~ qn** to make sb be
quiet; **se taire** *vi* to be silent *ou* quiet;
taisez-vous! be quiet!
Taiwan [tajwan] *nf* Taiwan
talc [talk] *nm* talc, talcum powder
talent [talɑ̃] *nm* talent
talkie-walkie [tokiwoki] *nm* walkie-
talkie
talon [talɔ̃] *nm* heel; (*de chèque, billet*)
stub, counterfoil (BRIT); **talons plats/
aiguilles** flat/stiletto heels
talus [taly] *nm* embankment
tambour [tɑ̃buʀ] *nm* (*Mus, aussi Tech*)
drum; (*musicien*) drummer; (*porte*)
revolving door(s *pl*); **tambourin** *nm*
tambourine

Tamise [tamiz] nf: **la ~** theThames
tamisé, e [tamize] adj (fig) subdued, soft
tampon [tɑ̃pɔ̃] nm (de coton, d'ouate) wad, pad; (amortisseur) buffer; (bouchon) plug, stopper; (cachet, timbre) stamp; **(mémoire) ~** (Inform) buffer; **tampon (hygiénique)** tampon; **tamponner** vt (timbres) to stamp; (heurter) to crash ou ram into; **tamponneuse** adj f: **autos tamponneuses** dodgems
tandem [tɑ̃dɛm] nm tandem
tandis [tɑ̃di]: **~ que** conj while
tanguer [tɑ̃ge] vi to pitch (and toss)
tant [tɑ̃] adv so much; **~ de** (sable, eau) so much; (gens, livres) so many; **~ que** as long as; (autant que) as much as; **~ mieux** that's great; (avec une certaine réserve) so much the better; **~ pis** too bad; (conciliant) never mind; **~ bien que mal** as well as can be expected
tante [tɑ̃t] nf aunt
tantôt [tɑ̃to] adv (parfois): **~ ... ~** now ... now; (cet après-midi) this afternoon
taon [tɑ̃] nm horsefly
tapage [tapaʒ] nm uproar, din
tapageur, -euse [tapaʒœʀ, øz] adj noisy; (voyant) loud, flashy
tape [tap] nf slap
tape-à-l'œil [tapalœj] adj inv flashy, showy
taper [tape] vt (porte) to bang, slam; (enfant) to slap; (dactylographier) to type (out); (fam: emprunter): **~ qn de 10 euros** to touch sb for 10 euros ▷ vi (soleil) to beat down; **se taper** vt (repas) to put away; (fam: corvée) to get landed with; **~ sur qn** to thump sb; (fig) to run sb down; **~ sur un clou** to hit a nail; **~ sur la table** to bang on the table; **~ à** (porte etc) to knock on; **~ dans** (se servir) to dig into; **~ des mains/pieds** to clap one's hands/stamp one's feet; **~ (à la machine)** to type
tapi, e [tapi] adj (blotti) crouching; (caché) hidden away
tapis [tapi] nm carpet; (petit) rug; **tapis de sol** (de tente) groundsheet;

tapis de souris (Inform) mouse mat;
tapis roulant (pour piétons) moving walkway; (pour bagages) carousel
tapisser [tapise] vt (avec du papier peint) to paper; (recouvrir): **~ qch (de)** to cover sth (with); **tapisserie** nf (tenture, broderie) tapestry; (papier peint) wallpaper; **tapissier-décorateur** nm interior decorator
tapoter [tapɔte] vt (joue, main) to pat; (objet) to tap
taquiner [takine] vt to tease
tard [taʀ] adv late; **plus ~** later (on); **au plus ~** at the latest; **sur le ~** late in life; **il est trop ~** it's too late
tarder [taʀde] vi (chose) to be a long time coming; (personne): **à faire** to delay doing; **il me tarde d'être** I am longing to be; **sans (plus) ~** without (further) delay
tardif, -ive [taʀdif, iv] adj late
tarif [taʀif] nm: **~ des consommations** price list; **~s postaux/douaniers** postal/customs rates; **~ des taxis** taxi fares; **~ plein/réduit** (train) full/reduced fare; (téléphone) peak/off-peak rate
tarir [taʀiʀ] vi to dry up, run dry
tarte [taʀt] nf tart; **~ aux fraises** strawberry tart; **~ Tatin** ≈ apple upside-down tart
tartine [taʀtin] nf slice of bread; **tartine de miel** slice of bread and honey; **tartiner** vt to spread; **fromage à tartiner** cheese spread
tartre [taʀtʀ] nm (des dents) tartar; (de bouilloire) fur, scale
tas [tɑ] nm heap, pile; (fig): **un ~ de** heaps of, lots of; **en ~** in a heap ou pile; **formé sur le ~** trained on the job
tasse [tɑs] nf cup; **tasse à café** coffee cup
tassé, e [tɑse] adj: **bien ~** (café etc) strong
tasser [tɑse] vt (terre, neige) to pack down; (entasser): **~ qch dans** to cram sth into; **se tasser** vi (se serrer) to squeeze up; (s'affaisser) to settle; (fig) to

settle down

tâter [tate] vt to feel; (fig) to try out; **se tâter** (hésiter) to be in two minds; **~ de** (prison etc) to have a taste of

tatillon, ne [tatijɔ̃, ɔn] adj pernickety

tâtonnement [tatɔnmã] nm: **par ~s** (fig) by trial and error

tâtonner [tatɔne] vi to grope one's way along

tâtons [tatɔ̃]: **à ~** adv: **chercher/ avancer à ~** to grope around for/grope one's way forward

tatouage [tatwaʒ] nm tattoo

tatouer [tatwe] vt to tattoo

taudis [todi] nm hovel, slum

taule [tol] (fam) nf nick (fam), prison

taupe [top] nf mole

taureau, x [tɔro] nm bull; (signe): **le T~** Taurus

taux [to] nm rate; (d'alcool) level; **taux d'intérêt** interest rate

taxe [taks] nf tax; (douanière) duty; **toutes ~s comprises** inclusive of tax; **la boutique hors ~s** the duty-free shop; **taxe à la valeur ajoutée** value-added tax; **taxe de séjour** tourist tax

taxer [takse] vt (personne) to tax; (produit) to put a tax on, tax

taxi [taksi] nm taxi; (chauffeur: fam) taxi driver; **pouvez-vous m'appeler un ~, s'il vous plaît?** can you call me a taxi, please?

Tchécoslovaquie [tʃekɔslɔvaki] nf Czechoslovakia; **tchèque** adj Czech ▷ nm/f: **Tchèque** Czech ▷ nm (Ling) Czech; **la République tchèque** the Czech Republic

Tchétchénie [tʃetʃeni] nf: **la ~** Chechnya

te, t' [tə] pron you; (réfléchi) yourself

technicien, ne [tɛknisjɛ̃, jɛn] nm/f technician

technico-commercial, e, -aux [tɛknikɔkɔmɛrsjal, jo] adj: **agent ~** sales technician

technique [tɛknik] adj technical ▷ nf technique; **techniquement** adv technically

techno [tɛkno] nf (Mus) techno (music)

technologie [tɛknɔlɔʒi] nf technology; **technologique** adj technological

teck [tɛk] nm teak

tee-shirt [tiʃœrt] nm T-shirt, tee-shirt

teindre [tɛ̃dr] vt to dye; **se ~ les cheveux** to dye one's hair; **teint, e** adj dyed ▷ nm (du visage) complexion; (momentané) colour ▷ nf shade; **grand teint** colourfast

teinté, e [tɛ̃te] adj: **~ de** (fig) tinged with

teinter [tɛ̃te] vt (verre, papier) to tint; (bois) to stain

teinture [tɛ̃tyr] nf dye; **teinture d'iode** tincture of iodine; **teinturerie** nf dry cleaner's; **teinturier** nm dry cleaner

tel, telle [tɛl] adj (pareil) such; (comme): **~ un/des ...** like a/like ...; (indéfini) such-and-such a; (intensif): **un ~/de ~s ...** such (a)/such ...; **rien de ~** nothing like it; **~ que** like, such as; **~ quel** as it is ou stands (ou was etc); **venez ~ jour** come on such-and-such a day

télé [tele] (fam) nf TV; **à la ~** on TV ou telly

télé...: télécabine nf (benne) cable car; **télécarte** nf phonecard; **téléchargeable** adj downloadable; **téléchargement** nm (action) downloading; (fichier) download; **télécharger** vt to download; **télécommande** nf remote control; **télécopieur** nm fax machine; **télédistribution** nf cable TV; **télégramme** nm telegram; **télégraphier** vt to telegraph, cable; **téléguider** vt to radio-control; **télématique** nf telematics sg; **téléobjectif** nm telephoto lens sg; **télépathie** nf telepathy; **téléphérique** nm cable car

téléphone [telefɔn] nm telephone; **avoir le ~** to be on the (tele)phone; **au ~** on the phone; **téléphoner** vi to make a phone call; **téléphoner à** to phone,

call up; **est-ce que je peux téléphoner d'ici?** can I make a call from here?; **téléphonique** adj (tele)phone cpd
télé…: téléréalité nf reality TV
télescope [telɛskɔp] nm telescope
télescoper [telɛskɔpe] vt to smash up; **se télescoper** (véhicules) to concertina
télé…: téléscripteur nm teleprinter; **télésiège** nm chairlift; **téléski** nm ski-tow; **téléspectateur, -trice** nm/f (television) viewer; **télétravail** nm telecommuting; **télévente** nf telesales; **téléviseur** nm television set; **télévision** nf television; **à la télévision** on television; **télévision numérique** digital TV; **télévision par câble/satellite** cable/satellite television
télex [telɛks] nm telex
telle [tel] adj voir **tel**; **tellement** adv (tant) so much; (si) so; **tellement de** (sable, eau) so much; (gens, livres) so many; **il s'est endormi tellement il était fatigué** he was so tired (that) he fell asleep; **pas tellement** not (all) that much; not (all) that +adjectif
téméraire [temerɛr] adj reckless, rash
témoignage [temwaɲaʒ] nm (Jur: déclaration) testimony no pl, evidence no pl; (rapport, récit) account; (fig: d'affection etc: cadeau) token, mark; (: geste) expression
témoigner [temwaɲe] vt (intérêt, gratitude) to show ▷ vi (Jur) to testify, give evidence; **~ de** to bear witness to, testify to
témoin [temwɛ̃] nm witness ▷ adj: **appartement ~** show flat (BRIT); **être ~ de** to witness; **témoin oculaire** eyewitness
tempe [tɑ̃p] nf temple
tempérament [tɑ̃peramɑ̃] nm temperament, disposition; **à ~** (vente) on deferred (payment) terms; (achat) by instalments, hire purchase cpd
température [tɑ̃peratyr] nf temperature; **avoir** ou **faire de la ~** to be running ou have a temperature

tempête [tɑ̃pɛt] nf storm; **tempête de sable/neige** sand/snowstorm
temple [tɑ̃pl] nm temple; (protestant) church
temporaire [tɑ̃pɔrɛr] adj temporary
temps [tɑ̃] nm (atmosphérique) weather; (durée) time; (époque) time, times pl; (Ling) tense; (Mus) beat; (Tech) stroke; **un ~ de chien** (fam) rotten weather; **quel ~ fait-il?** what's the weather like?; **il fait beau/mauvais ~** the weather is fine/bad; **avoir le ~/tout son ~** to have time/plenty of time; **en ~ de paix/guerre** in peacetime/wartime; **en ~ utile** ou **voulu** in due time ou course; **ces derniers ~** lately; **dans quelque ~** in a (little) while; **de ~ en ~, de ~ à autre** from time to time; **à ~** (partir, arriver) in time; **à ~ complet, à plein ~** full-time; **à ~ partiel, à mi-~** part-time; **dans le ~** at one time; **temps d'arrêt** pause, halt; **temps libre** free ou spare time; **temps mort** (Comm) slack period
tenable [t(ə)nabl] adj bearable
tenace [tənas] adj persistent
tenant, e [tənɑ̃, ɑ̃t] nm/f (Sport): **~ du titre** title-holder
tendance [tɑ̃dɑ̃s] nf tendency; (opinions) leanings pl, sympathies pl; (évolution) trend; **avoir ~ à** to have a tendency to, tend to
tendeur [tɑ̃dœr] nm (attache) elastic strap
tendre [tɑ̃dr] adj tender; (bois, roche, couleur) soft ▷ vt (élastique, peau) to stretch; (corde) to tighten; (muscle) to tense; (fig: piège) to set, lay; (donner): **~ qch à qn** to hold sth out to sb; (offrir) to offer sb sth; **se tendre** vi (corde) to tighten; (relations) to become strained; **~ à qch/à faire** to tend towards sth/to do; **~ l'oreille** to prick up one's ears; **~ la main/le bras** to hold out one's hand/ stretch out one's arm; **tendrement** adv tenderly; **tendresse** nf tenderness
tendu, e [tɑ̃dy] pp de **tendre** ▷ adj (corde) tight; (muscles) tensed; (relations) strained

ténèbres [tenɛbʀ] *nfpl* darkness *sg*

teneur [tənœʀ] *nf* content; (*d'une lettre*) terms *pl*, content

tenir [t(ə)niʀ] *vt* to hold; (*magasin, hôtel*) to run; (*promesse*) to keep ▷ *vi* to hold; (*neige, gel*) to last; **se tenir** *vi* (*avoir lieu*) to be held, take place; (*être: personne*) to stand; **~ à** (*personne, objet*) to be attached to; (*réputation*) to care about; **~ à faire** to be determined to do; **~ de** (*ressembler à*) to take after; **ça ne tient qu'à lui** it is entirely up to him; **~ qn pour** to regard sb as; **~ qch de qn** (*histoire*) to have heard *ou* learnt sth from sb; (*qualité, défaut*) to have inherited *ou* got sth from sb; **~ dans** to fit into; **~ compte de qch** to take sth into account; **~ les comptes** to keep the books; **~ bon** to stand fast; **~ le coup** to hold out; **~ au chaud** (*café, plat*) to keep hot; **un manteau qui tient chaud** a warm coat; **tiens/tenez, voilà le stylo** there's the pen!; **tiens, voilà Alain!** look, here's Alain!; **tiens?** (*surprise*) really?; **se ~ droit** to stand (*ou* sit) up straight; **bien se ~** to behave well; **se ~ à qch** to hold on to sth; **s'en ~ à qch** to confine o.s. to sth

tennis [tenis] *nm* tennis; (*court*) tennis court ▷ *nm ou f pl* (*aussi:* **chaussures de ~**) tennis *ou* gym shoes; **tennis de table** table tennis; **tennisman** *nm* tennis player

tension [tɑ̃sjɔ̃] *nf* tension; (*Méd*) blood pressure; **avoir de la ~** to have high blood pressure

tentation [tɑ̃tasjɔ̃] *nf* temptation

tentative [tɑ̃tativ] *nf* attempt

tente [tɑ̃t] *nf* tent

tenter [tɑ̃te] *vt* (*éprouver, attirer*) to tempt; (*essayer*): **~ qch/de faire** to attempt *ou* try sth/to do; **~ sa chance** to try one's luck

tenture [tɑ̃tyʀ] *nf* hanging

tenu, e [t(ə)ny] *pp de* **tenir** ▷ *adj* (*maison, comptes*): **bien ~** well-kept; (*obligé*): **~ de faire** obliged to do ▷ *nf* (*vêtements*) clothes *pl*; (*comportement*) (good) manners *pl*, good behaviour; (*d'une maison*) upkeep; **en petite ~e** scantily dressed *ou* clad

ter [tɛʀ] *adj*: **16 ~** 16b *ou* B

terme [tɛʀm] *nm* term; (*fin*) end; **à court/long ~** *adj* short-/long-term ▷ *adv* in the short/long term; **avant ~** (*Méd*) prematurely; **mettre un ~ à** to put an end *ou* a stop to; **en bons ~s** on good terms

terminaison [tɛʀminɛzɔ̃] *nf* (*Ling*) ending

terminal, -aux [tɛʀminal, o] *nm* terminal; **terminale** *nf* (*Scol*) ≈ year 13 (*BRIT*), ≈ twelfth grade (*US*)

terminer [tɛʀmine] *vt* to finish; **se terminer** *vi* to end; **quand est-ce que le spectacle se termine?** when does the show finish?

terne [tɛʀn] *adj* dull

ternir [tɛʀniʀ] *vt* to dull; (*fig*) to sully, tarnish; **se ternir** *vi* to become dull

terrain [tɛʀɛ̃] *nm* (*sol, fig*) ground; (*Comm: étendue de terre*) land *no pl*; (*parcelle*) plot (of land); (*à bâtir*) site; **sur le ~** (*fig*) on the field; **terrain d'aviation** airfield; **terrain de camping** campsite; **terrain de football/rugby** football/rugby pitch (*BRIT*) *ou* field (*US*); **terrain de golf** golf course; **terrain de jeu** games field; (*pour les petits*) playground; **terrain de sport** sports ground; **terrain vague** waste ground *no pl*

terrasse [tɛʀas] *nf* terrace; **à la ~** (*café*) outside; **terrasser** *vt* (*adversaire*) to floor; (*suj: maladie etc*) to strike down

terre [tɛʀ] *nf* (*gén, aussi Élec*) earth; (*substance*) soil, earth; (*opposé à mer*) land *no pl*; (*contrée*) earth; **terres** *nfpl* (*terrains*) lands, land *sg*; **en ~** (*pipe, poterie*) clay *cpd*; **à ~** *ou* **par ~** (*mettre, être, s'asseoir*) on the ground (*ou* floor); (*jeter, tomber*) to the ground, down; **terre à terre** *adj inv* (*considération, personne*) down-to-earth; **terre cuite** terracotta; **la terre ferme** dry land; **terre glaise** clay

terreau [tɛʀo] *nm* compost

terre-plein [tɛʀplɛ̃] *nm* platform; (*sur chaussée*) central reservation

terrestre [teʀɛstʀ] *adj* (*surface*) earth's, of the earth; (*Bot, Zool, Mil*) land *cpd*; (*Rel*) earthly

terreur [teʀœʀ] *nf* terror *no pl*

terrible [teʀibl] *adj* terrible, dreadful; (*fam*) terrific; **pas ~** nothing special

terrien, ne [teʀjɛ̃, jɛn] *adj*: **propriétaire ~** landowner ▷ *nm/f* (*non martien etc*) earthling

terrier [teʀje] *nm* burrow, hole; (*chien*) terrier

terrifier [teʀifje] *vt* to terrify

terrine [teʀin] *nf* (*récipient*) terrine; (*Culin*) pâté

territoire [teʀitwaʀ] *nm* territory

terroriser [teʀɔʀize] *vt* to terrorize

terrorisme [teʀɔʀism] *nm* terrorism; **terroriste** *nm/f* terrorist

tertiaire [tɛʀsjɛʀ] *adj* tertiary ▷ *nm* (*Écon*) service industries *pl*

tes [te] *adj voir* **ton¹**

test [tɛst] *nm* test

testament [tɛstamɑ̃] *nm* (*Jur*) will; (*Rel*) Testament; (*fig*) legacy

tester [tɛste] *vt* to test

testicule [tɛstikyl] *nm* testicle

tétanos [tetanos] *nm* tetanus

têtard [tɛtaʀ] *nm* tadpole

tête [tɛt] *nf* head; (*cheveux*) hair *no pl*; (*visage*) face; **de ~** (*comme adj: wagon etc*) front *cpd*; (*comme adv: calculer*) in one's head, mentally; **perdre la ~** (*fig: s'affoler*) to lose one's head; (: *devenir fou*) to go off one's head; **tenir ~ à qn** to stand up to sb; **la ~ en bas** with one's head down; **la ~ la première** (*tomber*) headfirst; **faire une ~** (*Football*) to head the ball; **faire la ~** (*fig*) to sulk; **en ~** at the front; (*Sport*) in the lead; **à la ~ de** at the head of; **à ~ reposée** in a more leisurely moment; **n'en faire qu'à sa ~** to do as one pleases; **en avoir par-dessus la ~** to be fed up; **en ~ à ~** in private, alone together; **de la ~ aux pieds** from head to toe; **tête de lecture** (playback) head; **tête de liste** (*Pol*) chief candidate; **tête**

de mort skull and crossbones; **tête de série** (*Tennis*) seeded player, seed; **tête de Turc** (*fig*) whipping boy (*BRIT*), butt; **tête-à-queue** *nm inv*: **faire un tête-à-queue** to spin round

téter [tete] *vt*: **~ (sa mère)** to suck at one's mother's breast, feed

tétine [tetin] *nf* teat; (*sucette*) dummy (*BRIT*), pacifier (*US*)

têtu, e [tety] *adj* stubborn, pigheaded

texte [tɛkst] *nm* text; (*morceau choisi*) passage

textile [tɛkstil] *adj* textile *cpd* ▷ *nm* textile; **le ~** the textile industry

Texto® [tɛksto] *nm* text message

texture [tɛkstyʀ] *nf* texture

TGV *sigle m* (= *train à grande vitesse*) high-speed train

thaïlandais, e [tajlɑ̃dɛ, ɛz] *adj* Thai ▷ *nm/f*: **T~, e** Thai

Thaïlande [tailɑ̃d] *nf* Thailand

thé [te] *nm* tea; **~ au citron** lemon tea; **~ au lait** tea with milk; **prendre le ~** to have tea; **faire le ~** to make the tea

théâtral, e, -aux [teɑtʀal, o] *adj* theatrical

théâtre [teɑtʀ] *nm* theatre; (*péj: simulation*) playacting; (*fig: lieu*): **le ~ de** the scene of; **faire du ~** to act

théière [tejɛʀ] *nf* teapot

thème [tɛm] *nm* theme; (*Scol: traduction*) prose (composition)

théologie [teɔlɔʒi] *nf* theology

théorie [teɔʀi] *nf* theory; **théorique** *adj* theoretical

thérapie [teʀapi] *nf* therapy

thermal, e, -aux [tɛʀmal, o] *adj*: **station ~e** spa; **cure ~e** water cure

thermomètre [tɛʀmɔmɛtʀ] *nm* thermometer

thermos® [tɛʀmos] *nm ou nf*: **(bouteille) thermos** vacuum *ou* Thermos® flask

thermostat [tɛʀmɔsta] *nm* thermostat

thèse [tɛz] *nf* thesis

thon [tɔ̃] *nm* tuna (fish)

thym [tɛ̃] *nm* thyme

Tibet [tibɛ] *nm*: **le ~** Tibet

tibia [tibja] *nm* shinbone, tibia; *(partie antérieure de la jambe)* shin

TIC *sigle fpl* (= *technologies de l'information et de la communication*) ICT *sg*

tic [tik] *nm* tic, (nervous) twitch; *(de langage etc)* mannerism

ticket [tikɛ] *nm* ticket; **ticket de caisse** receipt; **je peux avoir un ticket de caisse, s'il vous plaît?** can I have a receipt, please?

tiède [tjɛd] *adj* lukewarm; *(vent, air)* mild, warm; **tiédir** *vi* to cool; *(se réchauffer)* to grow warmer

tien, ne [tjɛ̃, tjɛn] *pron*: **le(la) ~(ne), les ~(ne)s** yours; **à la ~ne!** cheers!

tiens [tjɛ̃] *vb, excl voir* **tenir**

tiercé [tjɛrse] *nm system of forecast betting giving first 3 horses*

tiers, tierce [tjɛr, tjɛrs] *adj* third ▷ *nm* (*Jur*) third party; *(fraction)* third; **le tiers monde** the Third World

tige [tiʒ] *nf* stem; *(baguette)* rod

tignasse [tiɲas] *(péj) nf* mop of hair

tigre [tigr] *nm* tiger; **tigré, e** *adj (rayé)* striped; *(tacheté)* spotted; *(chat)* tabby; **tigresse** *nf* tigress

tilleul [tijœl] *nm* lime (tree), linden (tree); *(boisson)* lime(-blossom) tea

timbre [tɛ̃br] *nm (tampon)* stamp; *(aussi:* **~-poste**) (postage) stamp; *(Mus: de voix, instrument)* timbre, tone

timbré, e [tɛ̃bre] *(fam) adj* cracked

timide [timid] *adj* shy; *(timoré)* timid; **timidement** *adv* shyly; timidly; **timidité** *nf* shyness; timidity

tintamarre [tɛ̃tamar] *nm* din, uproar

tinter [tɛ̃te] *vi* to ring, chime; *(argent, clefs)* to jingle

tique [tik] *nf (parasite)* tick

tir [tir] *nm (sport)* shooting; *(fait ou manière de tirer)* firing *no pl*; *(rafale)* fire; *(stand)* shooting gallery; **tir à l'arc** archery

tirage [tiraʒ] *nm (action)* printing; *(Photo)* print; *(de journal)* circulation; *(de livre: nombre d'exemplaires)* (print) run; *(: édition)* edition; *(de loterie)* draw; **par ~**

au sort by drawing lots

tire [tir] *nf*: **vol à la ~** pickpocketing

tiré, e [tire] *adj (traits)* drawn; **~ par les cheveux** far-fetched

tire-bouchon [tirbuʃɔ̃] *nm* corkscrew

tirelire [tirlir] *nf* moneybox

tirer [tire] *vt (gén)* to pull; *(trait, rideau, carte, conclusion, chèque)* to draw; *(langue)* to stick out; *(en faisant feu: balle, coup)* to fire; *(: animal)* to shoot; *(journal, livre, photo)* to print; *(Football: corner etc)* to take ▷ *vi (faire feu)* to fire; *(faire du tir, Football)* to shoot; **se tirer** *vi (fam)* to push off; **s'en ~** *(éviter le pire)* to get off; *(survivre)* to pull through; *(se débrouiller)* to manage; **~ qch de** *(extraire)* to take *ou* pull sth out of; **~ qn de** *(embarras etc)* to help *ou* get sb out of; **~ sur** *(corde)* to pull on *ou* at; *(faire feu sur)* to shoot *ou* fire at; *(pipe)* to draw on; *(approcher de: couleur)* to verge *ou* border on; **~ à l'arc/la carabine** to shoot with a bow and arrow/with a rifle; **~ à sa fin** to be drawing to a close; **~ qch au clair** to clear sth up; **~ au sort** to draw lots; **~ parti de** to take advantage of; **~ profit de** to profit from; **~ les cartes** to read *ou* tell the cards

tiret [tirɛ] *nm* dash

tireur [tirœr] *nm* gunman; **tireur d'élite** marksman

tiroir [tirwar] *nm* drawer; **tiroir-caisse** *nm* till

tisane [tizan] *nf* herb tea

tisser [tise] *vt* to weave

tissu [tisy] *nm* fabric, material, cloth *no pl*; *(Anat, Bio)* tissue; **tissu-éponge** *nm* (terry) towelling *no pl*

titre [titr] *nm (gén)* title; *(de journal)* headline; *(diplôme)* qualification; *(Comm)* security; **en ~** *(champion)* official; **à juste ~** rightly; **à quel ~?** on what grounds?; **à aucun ~** on no account; **au même ~ (que)** in the same way (as); **à ~ d'information** for (your) information; **à ~ gracieux** free of charge; **à ~ d'essai** on a trial basis; **à ~ privé** in a private capacity;

titre de propriété title deed; **titre de transport** ticket

tituber [titybe] *vi* to stagger (along)

titulaire [titylɛR] *adj* (*Admin*) with tenure ▷ *nm/f* (*de permis*) holder; **être ~ de** (*diplôme, permis*) to hold

toast [tost] *nm* slice *ou* piece of toast; (*de bienvenue*) (welcoming) toast; **porter un ~ à qn** to propose *ou* drink a toast to sb

toboggan [tɔbɔgɑ̃] *nm* slide; (*Auto*) flyover

toc [tɔk] *excl*: **~, ~** knock knock ▷ *nm*: **en ~** fake

tocsin [tɔksɛ̃] *nm* alarm (bell)

tohu-bohu [tɔybɔy] *nm* hubbub

toi [twa] *pron* you

toile [twal] *nf* (*tableau*) canvas; **de** *ou* **en ~** (*pantalon*) cotton; (*sac*) canvas; **la T~** (*Internet*) the Web; **toile cirée** oilcloth; **toile d'araignée** cobweb; **toile de fond** (*fig*) backdrop

toilette [twalɛt] *nf* (*habits*) outfit; **toilettes** *nfpl* (*w.-c.*) toilet *sg*; **faire sa ~** to have a wash, get washed; **articles de ~** toiletries; **où sont les ~s?** where's the toilet?

toi-même [twamɛm] *pron* yourself

toit [twa] *nm* roof; **toit ouvrant** sunroof

toiture [twatyR] *nf* roof

Tokyo [tɔkjo] *n* Tokyo

tôle [tol] *nf* (*plaque*) steel *ou* iron sheet; **tôle ondulée** corrugated iron

tolérable [tɔleRabl] *adj* tolerable

tolérant, e [tɔleRɑ̃, ɑ̃t] *adj* tolerant

tolérer [tɔleRe] *vt* to tolerate; (*Admin: hors taxe etc*) to allow

tollé [tɔ(l)le] *nm* outcry

tomate [tɔmat] *nf* tomato; **~s farcies** stuffed tomatoes

tombe [tɔ̃b] *nf* (*sépulture*) grave; (*avec monument*) tomb

tombeau, x [tɔ̃bo] *nm* tomb

tombée [tɔ̃be] *nf*: **à la ~ de la nuit** at nightfall

tomber [tɔ̃be] *vi* to fall; (*fièvre, vent*) to drop; **laisser ~** (*objet*) to drop; (*personne*) to let down; (*activité*) to give up; **laisse ~!** forget it!; **faire ~** to knock over; (*sur* (*rencontrer*) to bump into; **~ de fatigue/sommeil** to drop from exhaustion/be falling asleep on one's feet; **ça tombe bien** that's come at the right time; **il est bien tombé** he's been lucky; **~ à l'eau** (*projet*) to fall through; **~ en panne** to break down

tombola [tɔ̃bɔla] *nf* raffle

tome [tɔm] *nm* volume

ton¹, ta [tɔ̃, ta] (*pl* **tes**) *adj* your

ton² [tɔ̃] *nm* (*gén*) tone; (*couleur*) shade, tone; **de bon ~** in good taste

tonalité [tɔnalite] *nf* (*au téléphone*) dialling tone

tondeuse [tɔ̃døz] *nf* (*à gazon*) (lawn)mower; (*du coiffeur*) clippers *pl*; (*pour les moutons*) shears *pl*

tondre [tɔ̃dR] *vt* (*pelouse, herbe*) to mow; (*haie*) to cut, clip; (*mouton, toison*) to shear; (*cheveux*) to crop

tongs [tɔ̃g] *nfpl* flip-flops

tonifier [tɔnifje] *vt* (*peau, organisme*) to tone up

tonique [tɔnik] *adj* fortifying ▷ *nm* tonic

tonne [tɔn] *nf* metric ton, tonne

tonneau, x [tɔno] *nm* (*à vin, cidre*) barrel; **faire des ~x** (*voiture, avion*) to roll over

tonnelle [tɔnɛl] *nf* bower, arbour

tonner [tɔne] *vi* to thunder; **il tonne** it is thundering, there's some thunder

tonnerre [tɔnɛR] *nm* thunder

tonus [tɔnys] *nm* energy

top [tɔp] *nm*: **au 3ème ~** at the 3rd stroke ▷ *adj*: **~ secret** top secret

topinambour [tɔpinɑ̃buR] *nm* Jerusalem artichoke

torche [tɔRʃ] *nf* torch

torchon [tɔRʃɔ̃] *nm* cloth; (*à vaisselle*) tea towel *ou* cloth

tordre [tɔRdR] *vt* (*chiffon*) to wring; (*barre, fig: visage*) to twist; **se tordre** *vi*: **se ~ le poignet/la cheville** to twist one's wrist/ankle; **se ~ de douleur/rire** to be doubled up with pain/laughter;

tordu, e adj bent; (fig) crazy

tornade [tɔʀnad] nf tornado

torrent [tɔʀɑ̃] nm mountain stream

torsade [tɔʀsad] nf: **un pull à ~s** a cable sweater

torse [tɔʀs] nm chest; (Anat, Sculpture) torso; **~ nu** stripped to the waist

tort [tɔʀ] nm (défaut) fault; **torts** nmpl (Jur) fault sg; **avoir ~** to be wrong; **être dans son ~** to be in the wrong; **donner ~ à qn** to lay the blame on sb; **causer du ~ à qn** to harm sb; **à ~** wrongly; **à ~ et à travers** wildly

torticolis [tɔʀtikɔli] nm stiff neck

tortiller [tɔʀtije] vt to twist; (moustache) to twirl; **se tortiller** vi to wriggle; (en dansant) to wiggle

tortionnaire [tɔʀsjɔnɛʀ] nm torturer

tortue [tɔʀty] nf tortoise; (d'eau douce) terrapin; (d'eau de mer) turtle

tortueux, -euse [tɔʀtɥø, øz] adj (rue) twisting; (fig) tortuous

torture [tɔʀtyʀ] nf torture; **torturer** vt to torture; (fig) to torment

tôt [to] adv early; **~ ou tard** sooner or later; **si ~** so early; (déjà) so soon; **plus ~** earlier; **au plus ~** at the earliest

total, e, -aux [tɔtal, o] adj, nm total; **au ~** in total; (fig) on the whole; **faire le ~** to work out the total; **totalement** adv totally; **totaliser** vt to total; **totalitaire** adj totalitarian; **totalité** nf: **la totalité de** all (of); the whole +sg; **en totalité** entirely

toubib [tubib] (fam) nm doctor

touchant, e [tuʃɑ̃, ɑ̃t] adj touching

touche [tuʃ] nf (de piano, de machine à écrire) key; (de téléphone) button; (Peinture etc) stroke, touch; (fig: de nostalgie) touch; (Football: aussi: **remise en ~**) throw-in; (aussi: **ligne de ~**) touch-line; **touche dièse** (de téléphone, clavier) hash key

toucher [tuʃe] nm touch ▷ vt to touch; (palper) to feel; (atteindre: d'un coup de feu etc) to hit; (concerner) to concern, affect; (contacter) to reach, contact; (recevoir: récompense) to receive, get; (: salaire) to draw, get; (: chèque) to cash; **se toucher** (être en contact) to touch; **au ~** to the touch; **~ à** to touch; (concerner) to have to do with, concern; **je vais lui en ~ un mot** I'll have a word with him about it; **~ au but** (fig) to near one's goal; **~ à sa fin** to be drawing to a close

touffe [tuf] nf tuft

touffu, e [tufy] adj thick, dense

toujours [tuʒuʀ] adv always; (encore) still; (constamment) forever; **~ plus** more and more; **pour ~** forever; **~ est-il que** the fact remains that; **essaie ~** (you can) try anyway

toupie [tupi] nf (spinning) top

tour¹ [tuʀ] nf tower; (immeuble) high-rise block (BRIT) ou building (US); (Échecs) castle, rook; **tour de contrôle** nf control tower; **la tour Eiffel** the Eiffel Tower

tour² [tuʀ] nm (excursion) trip; (à pied) stroll, walk; (en voiture) run, ride; (Sport: aussi: **~ de piste**) lap; (d'être servi ou de jouer etc) turn; (de roue etc) revolution; (Pol: aussi: **~ de scrutin**) ballot; (ruse, de prestidigitation) trick; (de potier) wheel; (à bois, métaux) lathe; (circonférence): **de 3 m de ~** 3 m round, with a circumference ou girth of 3 m; **faire le ~ de** to go round; (à pied) to walk round; **c'est au ~ de Renée** it's Renée's turn; **à ~ de rôle, ~ à ~** in turn; **tour de chant** nm song recital; **tour de force** tour de force; **tour de garde** nm spell of duty; **tour d'horizon** nm (fig) general survey; **tour de taille/tête** nm waist/head measurement; **un 33 tours** an LP; **un 45 tours** a single

tourbe [tuʀb] nf peat

tourbillon [tuʀbijɔ̃] nm whirlwind; (d'eau) whirlpool; (fig) whirl, swirl; **tourbillonner** vi to whirl (round)

tourelle [tuʀɛl] nf turret

tourisme [tuʀism] nm tourism; **agence de ~** tourist agency; **faire du ~** to go touring; (en ville) to go sightseeing; **touriste** nm/f tourist; **touristique** adj tourist cpd; (région) touristic

tourment [tuʀmɑ̃] *nm* torment; **tourmenter** *vt* to torment; **se tourmenter** to fret, worry o.s.

tournage [tuʀnaʒ] *nm* (*Cinéma*) shooting

tournant [tuʀnɑ̃] *nm* (*de route*) bend; (*fig*) turning point

tournée [tuʀne] *nf* (*du facteur etc*) round; (*d'artiste, politicien*) tour; (*au café*) round (of drinks)

tourner [tuʀne] *vt* to turn; (*sauce, mélange*) to stir; (*Cinéma: faire les prises de vues*) to shoot; (: *produire*) to make ▷ *vi* to turn; (*moteur*) to run; (*taximètre*) to tick away; (*lait etc*) to turn (sour); **se tourner** *vi* to turn round; **tournez à gauche/droite au prochain carrefour** turn left/right at the next junction; **mal ~** to go wrong; **~ autour de** to go round; (*péj*) to hang round; **~ à/en** to turn into; **~ qn en ridicule** to ridicule sb; **~ le dos à** (*mouvement*) to turn one's back on; (*position*) to have one's back to; **~ de l'œil** to pass out; **se ~ vers** to turn towards; (*fig*) to turn to; **se ~ les pouces** to twiddle one's thumbs

tournesol [tuʀnəsɔl] *nm* sunflower

tournevis [tuʀnəvis] *nm* screwdriver

tournoi [tuʀnwa] *nm* tournament

tournure [tuʀnyʀ] *nf* (*Ling*) turn of phrase; (*évolution*): **la ~ de qch** the way sth is developing; **tournure d'esprit** turn *ou* cast of mind

tourte [tuʀt] *nf* pie

tourterelle [tuʀtəʀɛl] *nf* turtledove

tous [tu] *adj, pron voir* **tout**

Toussaint [tusɛ̃] *nf*: **la ~** All Saints' Day

tousser [tuse] *vi* to cough

○ **MOT-CLÉ**

tout, e [tu, tut] (*mpl* **tous**, *fpl* **toutes**) *adj* **1** (*avec article singulier*) all; **tout le lait** all the milk; **toute la nuit** all night, the whole night; **tout le livre** the whole book; **tout un pain** a whole loaf; **tout le temps** all the time; the whole time; **tout le monde** everybody; **c'est tout le contraire** it's quite the opposite

2 (*avec article pluriel*) all; **tous les livres** all the books; **toutes les nuits** every night; **toutes les fois** every time; **toutes les trois/deux semaines** every third/other *ou* second week, every three/two weeks; **tous les deux** both *ou* each of us (*ou* them *ou* you); **toutes les trois** all three of us (*ou* them *ou* you)

3 (*sans article*): **à tout âge** at any age; **pour toute nourriture, il avait ...** his only food was ...

▷ *pron* everything, all; **il a tout fait** he's done everything; **je les vois tous** I can see them all *ou* all of them; **nous y sommes tous allés** all of us went, we all went; **c'est tout** that's all; **en tout** in all; **tout ce qu'il sait** all he knows

▷ *nm* whole; **le tout** all of it (*ou* them); **le tout est de ...** the main thing is to ...; **pas du tout** not at all

▷ *adv* **1** (*très, complètement*) very; **tout près** very near; **le tout premier** the very first; **tout seul** all alone; **le livre tout entier** the whole book; **tout en haut** right at the top; **tout droit** straight ahead

2: **tout en** while; **tout en travaillant** while working, as he *etc* works *ou* worked

3: **tout d'abord** first of all; **tout à coup** suddenly; **tout à fait** absolutely; **tout à l'heure** a short while ago; (*futur*) in a short while, shortly; **à tout à l'heure!** see you later!; **tout de même** all the same; **tout de suite** immediately, straight away; **tout simplement** quite simply

toutefois [tutfwa] *adv* however

outes [tut] adj, pron voir **tout**

out-terrain [tutɛʀɛ̃] adj: **vélo ~** mountain bike; **véhicule ~** four-wheel drive

oux [tu] nf cough

oxicomane [tɔksikɔman] nm/f drug addict

oxique [tɔksik] adj toxic

rac [tʀak] nm (au théâtre, en public) stage fright; (aux examens) nerves pl; **avoir le ~** (au théâtre, en public) to have stage fright; (aux examens) to be feeling nervous

racasser [tʀakase] vt to worry, bother; **se tracasser** vi to worry

race [tʀas] nf (empreintes) tracks pl; (marques, aussi fig) mark; (quantité infime, indice, vestige) trace; **traces de pas** footprints

racer [tʀase] vt to draw; (piste) to open up

ract [tʀakt] nm tract, pamphlet

racteur [tʀaktœʀ] nm tractor

raction [tʀaksjɔ̃] nf: **~ avant/arrière** front-wheel/rear-wheel drive

radition [tʀadisjɔ̃] nf tradition; **traditionnel, le** adj traditional

raducteur, -trice [tʀadyktœʀ, tʀis] nm/f translator

raduction [tʀadyksjɔ̃] nf translation

raduire [tʀaduiʀ] vt to translate; (exprimer) to convey; **~ qn en justice** to bring sb before the courts; **pouvez-vous me ~ ceci?** can you translate this for me?

rafic [tʀafik] nm traffic; **trafic d'armes** arms dealing; **trafiquant, e** nm/f trafficker; (d'armes) dealer; **trafiquer** (péj) vt (vin) to doctor; (moteur, document) to tamper with

ragédie [tʀaʒedi] nf tragedy; **tragique** adj tragic

rahir [tʀaiʀ] vt to betray; **trahison** nf betrayal; (Jur) treason

rain [tʀɛ̃] nm (Rail) train; (allure) pace; **être en ~ de faire qch** to be doing sth; **c'est bien le ~ pour ...?** is this the train for ...?; **train d'atterrissage**

undercarriage; **train de vie** lifestyle; **train électrique** (jouet) (electric) train set

traîne [tʀɛn] nf (de robe) train; **être à la ~** to lag behind

traîneau, x [tʀɛno] nm sleigh, sledge

traîner [tʀene] vt (remorque) to pull; (enfant, chien) to drag ou trail along ▷ vi (robe, manteau) to trail; (être en désordre) to lie around; (aller lentement) to dawdle (along); (vagabonder, agir lentement) to hang about; (durer) to drag on; **se traîner** vi: **se ~ par terre** to crawl (on the ground); **~ les pieds** to drag one's feet

train-train [tʀɛ̃tʀɛ̃] nm humdrum routine

traire [tʀɛʀ] vt to milk

trait [tʀɛ] nm (ligne) line; (de dessin) stroke; (caractéristique) feature, trait; **traits** nmpl (du visage) features; **d'un ~** (boire) in one gulp; **de ~** (animal) draught; **avoir ~ à** to concern; **trait d'union** hyphen

traitant, e [tʀɛtɑ̃, ɑ̃t] adj (shampooing) medicated; **votre médecin ~** your usual ou family doctor

traite [tʀɛt] nf (Comm) draft; (Agr) milking; **d'une ~** without stopping

traité [tʀete] nm treaty

traitement [tʀɛtmɑ̃] nm treatment; (salaire) salary; **traitement de données** data processing; **traitement de texte** word processing; (logiciel) word processing package

traiter [tʀete] vt to treat; (qualifier): **~ qn d'idiot** to call sb a fool ▷ vi to deal; **~ de** to deal with

traiteur [tʀɛtœʀ] nm caterer

traître, -esse [tʀɛtʀ, tʀɛtʀɛs] adj (dangereux) treacherous ▷ nm traitor

trajectoire [tʀaʒɛktwaʀ] nf path

trajet [tʀaʒɛ] nm (parcours, voyage) journey; (itinéraire) route; (distance à parcourir) distance; **il y a une heure de ~** the journey takes one hour

trampoline [tʀɑ̃pɔlin] nm trampoline

tramway [tʀamwɛ] nm tram(way);

(voiture) tram(car) (BRIT), streetcar (US)

tranchant, e [tʀɑ̃ʃɑ̃, ɑ̃t] adj sharp; (fig) peremptory ▷ nm (d'un couteau) cutting edge; (de la main) edge; **à double ~** double-edged

tranche [tʀɑ̃ʃ] nf (morceau) slice; (arête) edge; **~ d'âge/de salaires** age/wage bracket

tranché, e [tʀɑ̃ʃe] adj (couleurs) distinct; (opinions) clear-cut

trancher [tʀɑ̃ʃe] vt to cut, sever ▷ vi to take a decision; **~ avec** to contrast sharply with

tranquille [tʀɑ̃kil] adj quiet; (rassuré) easy in one's mind, with one's mind at rest; **se tenir ~** (enfant) to be quiet; **laisse-moi/laisse-ça ~** leave me/it alone; **avoir la conscience ~** to have a clear conscience; **tranquillisant** nm tranquillizer; **tranquillité** nf peace (and quiet); (d'esprit) peace of mind

transférer [tʀɑ̃sfeʀe] vt to transfer; **transfert** nm transfer

transformation [tʀɑ̃sfɔʀmasjɔ̃] nf change, alteration; (radicale) transformation; (Rugby) conversion; **transformations** nfpl (travaux) alterations

transformer [tʀɑ̃sfɔʀme] vt to change; (radicalement) to transform; (vêtement) to alter; (matière première, appartement, Rugby) to convert; **(se) ~ en** to turn into

transfusion [tʀɑ̃sfyzjɔ̃] nf: **~ sanguine** blood transfusion

transgénique [tʀɑ̃sʒenik] adj transgenic

transgresser [tʀɑ̃sgʀese] vt to contravene

transi, e [tʀɑ̃zi] adj numb (with cold), chilled to the bone

transiger [tʀɑ̃ziʒe] vi to compromise

transit [tʀɑ̃zit] nm transit; **transiter** vi to pass in transit

transition [tʀɑ̃zisjɔ̃] nf transition; **transitoire** adj transitional

transmettre [tʀɑ̃smɛtʀ] vt (passer): **~ qch à qn** to pass sth on to sb;

(Tech, Tél, Méd) to transmit; (TV, Radio: retransmettre) to broadcast; **transmission** nf transmission

transparent, e [tʀɑ̃spaʀɑ̃, ɑ̃t] adj transparent

transpercer [tʀɑ̃spɛʀse] vt (froid, pluie) to go through, pierce; (balle) to go through

transpiration [tʀɑ̃spiʀasjɔ̃] nf perspiration

transpirer [tʀɑ̃spiʀe] vi to perspire

transplanter [tʀɑ̃splɑ̃te] vt (Méd, Bot) to transplant

transport [tʀɑ̃spɔʀ] nm transport; **transports en commun** public transport sg; **transporter** vt to carry, move; (Comm) to transport, convey; **transporteur** nm haulage contractor (BRIT), trucker (US)

transvaser [tʀɑ̃svaze] vt to decant

transversal, e, -aux [tʀɑ̃svɛʀsal, o] adj (rue) which runs across; **coupe ~e** cross section

trapèze [tʀapɛz] nm (au cirque) trapeze

trappe [tʀap] nf trap door

trapu, e [tʀapy] adj squat, stocky

traquenard [tʀaknaʀ] nm trap

traquer [tʀake] vt to track down; (harceler) to hound

traumatiser [tʀomatize] vt to traumatize

travail, -aux [tʀavaj] nm (gén) work; (tâche, métier) work no pl, job; (Écon, Méd) labour; **être sans ~** (employé) to be unemployed; voir aussi **travaux**; **travail (au) noir** moonlighting

travailler [tʀavaje] vi to work; (bois) to warp ▷ vt (bois, métal) to work; (objet d'art, discipline) to work on; **cela le travaille** it is on his mind; **travailleur, -euse** adj hard-working ▷ nm/f worker; **travailleur social** social worker; **travailliste** adj ≈ Labour cpd

travaux [tʀavo] nmpl (de réparation, agricoles etc) work sg; (sur route) roadworks pl; (de construction) building (work); **travaux des champs** farmwork sg; **travaux dirigés** (Scol) tutorial *sg*; **travaux forcés** hard labour *no pl*; **travaux manuels** (*Scol*) handicrafts; **travaux ménagers** housework *no pl*; **travaux pratiques** (*Scol*) practical work; (*en laboratoire*) lab work

travers [tʀavɛʀ] *nm* fault, failing; **en ~ (de)** across; **au ~ (de)/à ~** through; **de ~** (*nez, bouche*) crooked; (*chapeau*) askew; **comprendre de ~** to misunderstand; **regarder de ~** (*fig*) to look askance at

traverse [tʀavɛʀs] *nf* (*de voie ferrée*) sleeper; **chemin de ~** shortcut

traversée [tʀavɛʀse] *nf* crossing; **combien de temps dure la ~?** how long does the crossing take?

traverser [tʀavɛʀse] *vt* (*gén*) to cross; (*ville, tunnel, aussi: percer, fig*) to go through; (*suj: ligne, trait*) to run across

traversin [tʀavɛʀsɛ̃] *nm* bolster

travesti [tʀavɛsti] *nm* transvestite

trébucher [tʀebyʃe] *vi*: **~ (sur)** to stumble (over), trip (against)

trèfle [tʀɛfl] *nm* (*Bot*) clover; (*Cartes: couleur*) clubs *pl*; (: *carte*) club; **~ à quatre feuilles** four-leaf clover

treize [tʀɛz] *num* thirteen; **treizième** *num* thirteenth

tréma [tʀema] *nm* diaeresis

tremblement [tʀɑ̃bləmɑ̃] *nm*: **tremblement de terre** earthquake

trembler [tʀɑ̃ble] *vi* to tremble, shake; **~ de** (*froid, fièvre*) to shiver ou tremble with; (*peur*) to shake ou tremble with; **~ pour qn** to fear for sb

trémousser [tʀemuse]: **se trémousser** *vi* to jig about, wriggle about

trempé, e [tʀɑ̃pe] *adj* soaking (wet), drenched; (*Tech*) tempered

tremper [tʀɑ̃pe] *vt* to soak, drench; (*aussi*: **faire ~, mettre à ~**) to soak; (*plonger*): **~ qch dans** to dip sth in(to) ♦ *vi* to soak; (*fig*): **~ dans** to be involved ou have a hand in; **se tremper** *vi* to have a quick dip

tremplin [tʀɑ̃plɛ̃] *nm* springboard; (*Ski*) ski-jump

trentaine [tʀɑ̃tɛn] *nf*: **une ~ (de)** thirty or so, about thirty; **avoir la ~** (*âge*) to be around thirty

trente [tʀɑ̃t] *num* thirty; **être sur son ~ et un** to be wearing one's Sunday best; **trentième** *num* thirtieth

trépidant, e [tʀepidɑ̃, ɑ̃t] *adj* (*fig: rythme*) pulsating; (: *vie*) hectic

trépigner [tʀepiɲe] *vi* to stamp (one's feet)

très [tʀɛ] *adv* very; much +*pp*, highly +*pp*

trésor [tʀezɔʀ] *nm* treasure; **Trésor (public)** public revenue; **trésorerie** *nf* (*gestion*) accounts *pl*; (*bureaux*) accounts department; **difficultés de trésorerie** cash problems, shortage of cash *ou* funds; **trésorier, -ière** *nm/f* treasurer

tressaillir [tʀesajiʀ] *vi* to shiver, shudder

tressauter [tʀesote] *vi* to start, jump

tresse [tʀɛs] *nf* braid, plait; **tresser** *vt* (*cheveux*) to braid, plait; (*fil, jonc*) to plait; (*corbeille*) to weave; (*corde*) to twist

tréteau, x [tʀeto] *nm* trestle

treuil [tʀœj] *nm* winch

trêve [tʀɛv] *nf* (*Mil, Pol*) truce; (*fig*) respite; **~ de ...** enough of this ...

tri [tʀi] *nm*: **faire le ~ (de)** to sort out; **le (bureau de) ~** (*Postes*) the sorting office

triangle [tʀijɑ̃gl] *nm* triangle; **triangulaire** *adj* triangular

tribord [tʀibɔʀ] *nm*: **à ~** to starboard, on the starboard side

tribu [tʀiby] *nf* tribe

tribunal, -aux [tʀibynal, o] *nm* (*Jur*) court; (*Mil*) tribunal

tribune [tʀibyn] *nf* (*estrade*) platform, rostrum; (*débat*) forum; (*d'église, de tribunal*) gallery; (*de stade*) stand

tribut [tʀiby] *nm* tribute

tributaire [tʀibytɛʀ] *adj*: **être ~ de** to be dependent on

tricher [tʀiʃe] *vi* to cheat; **tricheur, -euse** *nm/f* cheat(er)

tricolore [tʀikɔlɔʀ] *adj* three-coloured; (*français*) red, white and blue

tricot [tʀiko] nm (technique, ouvrage) knitting no pl; (vêtement) jersey, sweater; **~ de peau** vest; **tricoter** vt to knit

tricycle [tʀisikl] nm tricycle

trier [tʀije] vt to sort out; (Postes, fruits) to sort

trimestre [tʀimɛstʀ] nm (Scol) term; (Comm) quarter; **trimestriel, le** adj quarterly; (Scol) end-of-term

trinquer [tʀɛ̃ke] vi to clink glasses

triomphe [tʀijɔ̃f] nm triumph; **triompher** vi to triumph, win; **triompher de** to triumph over, overcome

tripes [tʀip] nfpl (Culin) tripe sg

triple [tʀipl] adj triple ▷ nm: **le ~ (de)** (comparaison) three times as much (as); **en ~ exemplaire** in triplicate; **tripler** vi, vt to triple, treble

triplés, -ées [tʀiple] nm/fpl triplets

tripoter [tʀipɔte] vt to fiddle with

triste [tʀist] adj sad; (couleur, temps, journée) dreary; (péj): **~ personnage/ affaire** sorry individual/affair; **tristesse** nf sadness

trivial, e, -aux [tʀivjal, jo] adj coarse, crude; (commun) mundane

troc [tʀɔk] nm barter

trognon [tʀɔɲɔ̃] nm (de fruit) core; (de légume) stalk

trois [tʀwa] num three; **troisième** num third ▷ nf (Scol) year 10 (BRIT), ninth grade (US); **le troisième âge** (période de vie) one's retirement years; (personnes âgées) senior citizens pl

trombe [tʀɔ̃b] nf: **des ~s d'eau** a downpour; **en ~** like a whirlwind

trombone [tʀɔ̃bɔn] nm (Mus) trombone; (de bureau) paper clip

trompe [tʀɔ̃p] nf (d'éléphant) trunk; (Mus) trumpet, horn

tromper [tʀɔ̃pe] vt to deceive; (vigilance, poursuivants) to elude; **se tromper** vi to make a mistake, be mistaken; **se ~ de voiture/jour** to take the wrong car/get the day wrong; **se ~ de 3 cm/20 euros** to be out by 3 cm/20

euros; **je me suis trompé de route** I took the wrong road

trompette [tʀɔ̃pɛt] nf trumpet; **en ~** (nez) turned-up

trompeur, -euse [tʀɔ̃pœʀ, øz] adj deceptive

tronc [tʀɔ̃] nm (Bot, Anat) trunk; (d'église) collection box

tronçon [tʀɔ̃sɔ̃] nm section; **tronçonner** vt to saw up; **tronçonneuse** nf chainsaw

trône [tʀon] nm throne

trop [tʀo] adv (+vb) too much; (+adjectif, adverbe) too; **~ (nombreux)** too many; **peu (nombreux)** too few; **~ (souvent)** too often; **~ (longtemps)** (for) too long; **~ de** (nombre) too many; (quantité) too much; **de ~, en ~: des livres en ~** a few books too many; **du lait en ~** too much milk; **3 livres/3 euros de ~** 3 books too many/3 euros too much; **ça coûte ~ cher** it's too expensive

tropical, e, -aux [tʀɔpikal, o] adj tropical

tropique [tʀɔpik] nm tropic

trop-plein [tʀɔplɛ̃] nm (tuyau) overflow ou outlet (pipe); (liquide) overflow

troquer [tʀɔke] vt: **~ qch contre** to barter ou trade sth for; (fig) to swap sth for

trot [tʀo] nm trot; **trotter** vi to trot

trottinette [tʀɔtinɛt] nf (child's) scooter

trottoir [tʀɔtwaʀ] nm pavement (BRIT), sidewalk (US); **faire le ~** (péj) to walk the streets; **trottoir roulant** moving walkway, travellator

trou [tʀu] nm hole; (fig) gap; (Comm) deficit; **trou d'air** air pocket; **trou de mémoire** blank, lapse of memory

troublant, e [tʀublɑ̃, ɑ̃t] adj disturbing

trouble [tʀubl] adj (liquide) cloudy; (image, photo) blurred; (affaire) shady, murky ▷ adv: **voir ~** to have blurred vision ▷ nm agitation; **troubles** nmpl (Pol) disturbances, troubles, unrest sg

(*Méd*) trouble sg, disorders; **trouble-fête** nm spoilsport

oubler [tʀuble] vt to disturb; (*liquide*) to make cloudy; (*intriguer*) to bother; **se troubler** vi (*personne*) to become flustered *ou* confused

ouer [tʀue] vt to make a hole (*ou* holes) in

ouille [tʀuj] (*fam*) nf: **avoir la ~** to be scared to death

oupe [tʀup] nf troop; **troupe (de théâtre)** (theatrical) company

oupeau, x [tʀupo] nm (*de moutons*) flock; (*de vaches*) herd

ousse [tʀus] nf case, kit; (*d'écolier*) pencil case; **aux ~s de** (*fig*) on the heels *ou* tail of; **trousse à outils** toolkit; **trousse de toilette** toilet bag

ousseau, x [tʀuso] nm (*de mariée*) trousseau; **trousseau de clefs** bunch of keys

ouvaille [tʀuvaj] nf find

ouver [tʀuve] vt to find; (*rendre visite*): **aller/venir ~ qn** to go/come and see sb; **se trouver** vi (*être*) to be; **je trouve que** I find *ou* think that; **~ à boire/critiquer** to find something to drink/criticize; **se ~ mal** to pass out

uand [tʀɥɑ̃] nf gangster; **truander** vt: **se faire truander** to be swindled

uc [tʀyk] nm (*astuce*) way, trick; (*de cinéma, prestidigitateur*) trick, effect; (*chose*) thing, thingumajig; **avoir le ~** to have the knack; **c'est pas mon ~** (*fam*) it's not really my thing

uffe [tʀyf] nf truffle; (*nez*) nose

uffé, e [tʀyfe] adj (*Culin*) garnished with truffles; **~ de** (*fig: citations*) peppered with; (: *fautes*) riddled with; (: *pièges*) bristling with

uie [tʀɥi] nf sow

uite [tʀɥit] nf trout inv

uquage [tʀyka3] nm special effects pl

uquer [tʀyke] vt (*élections, serrure, dés*) to fix

SVP sigle (= tournez svp) PTO

TC sigle (= toutes taxes comprises) inclusive of tax

tu¹ [ty] pron you; **dire tu à qn** to use the "tu" form to sb

tu², e [ty] pp de **taire**

tuba [tyba] nm (*Mus*) tuba; (*Sport*) snorkel

tube [tyb] nm tube; (*chanson*) hit

tuberculose [tybɛʀkyloz] nf tuberculosis

tuer [tɥe] vt to kill; **se tuer** vi to be killed; (*suicide*) to kill o.s.; **se ~ au travail** (*fig*) to work o.s. to death; **tuerie** nf slaughter no pl

tue-tête [tytɛt]: **à ~** adv at the top of one's voice

tueur [tɥœʀ] nm killer; **tueur à gages** hired killer

tuile [tɥil] nf tile; (*fam*) spot of bad luck, blow

tulipe [tylip] nf tulip

tuméfié, e [tymefje] adj puffed-up, swollen

tumeur [tymœʀ] nf growth, tumour

tumulte [tymylt] nm commotion; **tumultueux, -euse** adj stormy, turbulent

tunique [tynik] nf tunic

Tunis [tynis] n Tunis

Tunisie [tynizi] nf: **la ~** Tunisia; **tunisien, ne** adj Tunisian ▷ nm/f: **Tunisien, ne** Tunisian

tunnel [tynɛl] nm tunnel; **le ~ sous la Manche** the Channel Tunnel

turbulent, e [tyʀbylɑ̃, ɑ̃t] adj boisterous, unruly

turc, turque [tyʀk] adj Turkish ▷ nm/f: **T~, Turque** Turk/Turkish woman ▷ nm (*Ling*) Turkish

turf [tyʀf] nm racing; **turfiste** nm/f racegoer

Turquie [tyʀki] nf: **la ~** Turkey

turquoise [tyʀkwaz] nf turquoise ▷ adj inv turquoise

tutelle [tytɛl] nf (*Jur*) guardianship; (*Pol*) trusteeship; **sous la ~ de** (*fig*) under the supervision of

tuteur [tytœʀ] nm (*Jur*) guardian; (*de plante*) stake, support

tutoyer [tytwaje] vt: **~ qn** to address

sb as "tu"

tuyau, x [tɥijo] *nm* pipe; *(flexible)* tube; *(fam)* tip; **tuyau d'arrosage** hosepipe; **tuyau d'échappement** exhaust pipe; **tuyauterie** *nf* piping *no pl*

TVA *sigle f* (= *taxe à la valeur ajoutée*) VAT

tympan [tɛ̃pɑ̃] *nm* (*Anat*) eardrum

type [tip] *nm* type; *(fam)* chap, guy ▷ *adj* typical, classic

typé, e [tipe] *adj* ethnic

typique [tipik] *adj* typical

tyran [tiʀɑ̃] *nm* tyrant; **tyrannique** *adj* tyrannical

tzigane [dzigan] *adj* gipsy, tzigane

ulcère [ylsɛʀ] *nm* ulcer

ultérieur, e [ylteʀjœʀ] *adj* later, subsequent; **remis à une date ~e** postponed to a later date; **ultérieurement** *adv* later, subsequently

ultime [yltim] *adj* final

 MOT-CLÉ

un, une [œ̃, yn] *art indéf* a; *(devant voyelle)* an; **un garçon/vieillard** a boy/an old man; **une fille** a girl ▷ *pron* one; **l'un des meilleurs** one of the best; **l'un ..., l'autre** (the) one ..., the other; **les uns ..., les autres** some ..., others; **l'un et l'autre** both (of them); **l'un ou l'autre** either (of them); **l'un l'autre** each other; **les uns les autres** one another; **pas un seul** not a single one; **un par un** one by one ▷ *num* one; **un pamplemousse seulement** one grapefruit only, just

one grapefruit
▷ nf: **la une** (Presse) the front page

nanime [ynanim] adj unanimous;
unanimité nf: **à l'unanimité**
unanimously
ni, e [yni] adj (ton, tissu) plain; (surface)
smooth, even; (famille) close(-knit);
(pays) united
nifier [ynifje] vt to unite, unify
niforme [ynifɔʀm] adj uniform;
(surface, ton) even ▷ nm uniform;
uniformiser vt (systèmes) to
standardize
nion [ynjɔ̃] nf union; **union de
consommateurs** consumers'
association; **union libre: vivre en
union libre** (en concubinage) to cohabit;
Union européenne European Union;
Union soviétique Soviet Union
nique [ynik] adj (seul) only;
(exceptionnel) unique; (le même): **un
prix/système** ~ a single price/system;
fils/fille ~ only son/daughter,
only child; **sens** ~ one-way street;
uniquement adv only, solely; (juste)
only, merely
nir [yniʀ] vt (nations) to unite; (en
mariage) to unite, join together; **s'unir**
vi to unite; (en mariage) to be joined
together
nitaire [yniteʀ] adj: **prix** ~ unit price
nité [ynite] nf unit; (harmonie,
cohésion) unity
nivers [yniveʀ] nm universe;
universel, le adj universal
niversitaire [yniveʀsiteʀ] adj
university cpd; (diplôme, études)
academic, university cpd ▷ nm/f
academic
niversité [yniveʀsite] nf university
rbain, e [yʀbɛ̃, ɛn] adj urban, city
cpd, town cpd; **urbanisme** nm town
planning
rgence [yʀʒɑ̃s] nf urgency; (Méd etc)
emergency; **d'**~ adj emergency cpd
▷ adv as a matter of urgency; **(service
des)** ~s casualty

urgent, e [yʀʒɑ̃, ɑ̃t] adj urgent
urine [yʀin] nf urine; **urinoir** nm
(public) urinal
urne [yʀn] nf (électorale) ballot box;
(vase) urn
urticaire [yʀtikeʀ] nf nettle rash
us [ys] nmpl: **us et coutumes** (habits
and) customs
usage [yzaʒ] nm (emploi, utilisation) use;
(coutume) custom; **à l'**~ with use; **à l'**~
de (pour) for (use of); **en** ~ in use; **hors
d'**~ out of service; **à** ~ **interne** (Méd) to
be taken (internally); **à** ~ **externe** (Méd)
for external use only; **usagé, e** adj (usé)
worn; **usager, -ère** nm/f user
usé, e [yze] adj worn; (banal: argument
etc) hackneyed
user [yze] vt (outil) to wear down;
(vêtement) to wear out; (matière) to wear
away; (consommer: charbon etc) to use;
s'user vi (tissu, vêtement) to wear out;
~ **de** (moyen, procédé) to use, employ;
(droit) to use
usine [yzin] nf factory
usité, e [yzite] adj common
ustensile [ystɑ̃sil] nm implement;
ustensile de cuisine kitchen utensil
usuel, le [yzɥɛl] adj everyday, common
usure [yzyʀ] nf wear
utérus [yteʀys] nm uterus, womb
utile [ytil] adj useful
utilisation [ytilizasjɔ̃] nf use
utiliser [ytilize] vt to use
utilitaire [ytiliteʀ] adj utilitarian
utilité [ytilite] nf usefulness no pl; **de
peu d'**~ of little use ou help
utopie [ytɔpi] nf utopia

V

va [va] *vb voir* **aller**

vacance [vakɑ̃s] *nf* (*Admin*) vacancy; **vacances** *nfpl* holiday(s *pl* (BRIT)), vacation *sg* (US)): **les grandes ~s** the summer holidays; **prendre des/ses ~s** to take a holiday/one's holiday(s); **aller en ~s** to go on holiday; **je suis ici en ~s** I'm here on holiday; **vacancier, -ière** *nm/f* holiday-maker

vacant, e [vakɑ̃, ɑ̃t] *adj* vacant

vacarme [vakarm] *nm* (*bruit*) racket

vaccin [vaksɛ̃] *nm* vaccine; (*opération*) vaccination; **vaccination** *nf* vaccination; **vacciner** *vt* to vaccinate; **être vacciné contre qch** (*fam*) to be cured of sth

vache [vaʃ] *nf* (*Zool*) cow; (*cuir*) cowhide ▷ *adj* (*fam*) rotten, mean; **vachement** (*fam*) *adv* (*très*) really; (*pleuvoir, travailler*) a hell of a lot; **vacherie** *nf* (*action*) dirty trick; (*remarque*) nasty remark

vaciller [vasije] *vi* to sway, wobble; (*bougie, lumière*) to flicker; (*fig*) to be failing, falter

va-et-vient [vaevjɛ̃] *nm inv* (*de personnes, véhicules*) comings and goings *pl*, to-ings and fro-ings *pl*

vagabond [vagabɔ̃] *nm* (*rôdeur*) tramp, vagrant; (*voyageur*) wanderer; **vagabonder** *vi* to roam, wander

vagin [vaʒɛ̃] *nm* vagina

vague [vag] *nf* wave ▷ *adj* vague; (*regard*) faraway; (*manteau, robe*) loose(-fitting); (*quelconque*): **un ~ bureau/cousin** some office/cousin or other; **vague de fond** ground swell **vague de froid** cold spell

vaillant, e [vajɑ̃, ɑ̃t] *adj* (*courageux*) gallant; (*robuste*) hale and hearty

vain, e [vɛ̃, vɛn] *adj* vain; **en ~** in vain

vaincre [vɛ̃kʀ] *vt* to defeat; (*fig*) to conquer, overcome; **vaincu, e** *nm/f* defeated party; **vainqueur** *nm* victor; (*Sport*) winner

vaisseau, x [vɛso] *nm* (*Anat*) vessel; (*Navig*) ship, vessel; **vaisseau spatial** spaceship

vaisselier [vɛsəlje] *nm* dresser

vaisselle [vɛsɛl] *nf* (*service*) crockery; (*plats etc à laver*) (dirty) dishes *pl*; **faire la ~** to do the washing-up (BRIT) *ou* the dishes

valable [valabl] *adj* valid; (*acceptable*) decent, worthwhile

valet [valɛ] *nm* manservant; (*Cartes*) jack

valeur [valœʀ] *nf* (*gén*) value; (*mérite*) worth, merit; (*Comm: titre*) security; **valeurs** *nfpl* (*morales*) values; **mettre en ~** (*détail*) to highlight; (*objet décoratif*) to show off to advantage; **avoir de la ~** to be valuable; **sans ~** worthless; **prendre de la ~** to go up *ou* gain in value

valide [valid] *adj* (*en bonne santé*) fit; (*valable*) valid; **valider** *vt* to validate

valise [valiz] *nf* (suit)case; **faire ses ~s** to pack one's bags

vallée [vale] *nf* valley

vallon [valɔ̃] *nm* small valley

valoir [valwaʀ] *vi* (*être valable*) to hold, apply ▷ *vt* (*prix, valeur, effort*) to be worth; (*causer*): **~ qch à qn** to earn sb sth; **se valoir** *vi* to be of equal merit; (*péj*) to be two of a kind; **faire ~** (*droits, prérogatives*) to assert; **se faire ~** to make the most of o.s.; **à ~ sur** to be deducted from; **vaille que vaille** somehow or other; **cela ne me dit rien qui vaille** I don't like the look of it at all; **ce climat ne me vaut rien** this climate doesn't suit me; **~ le coup** *ou* **la peine** to be worth the trouble *ou* worth it; **~ mieux: il vaut mieux se taire** it's better to say nothing; **ça ne vaut rien** it's worthless; **que vaut ce candidat?** how good is this applicant?

valse [vals] *nf* waltz

vandalisme [vɑ̃dalism] *nm* vandalism

vanille [vanij] *nf* vanilla

vanité [vanite] *nf* vanity; **vaniteux, -euse** *adj* vain, conceited

vanne [van] *nf* gate; (*fig*) joke

vannerie [vanri] *nf* basketwork

vantard, e [vɑ̃tar, ard] *adj* boastful

vanter [vɑ̃te] *vt* to speak highly of, praise; **se vanter** *vi* to boast, brag; **se ~ de** to pride o.s. on; (*péj*) to boast of

vapeur [vapœr] *nf* steam; (*émanation*) vapour, fumes *pl*; **vapeurs** *nfpl* (*bouffées*) vapours; **à ~** steam-powered, steam *cpd*; **cuit à la ~** steamed;

vaporeux, -euse *adj* (*flou*) hazy, misty; (*léger*) filmy; **vaporisateur** *nm* spray;

vaporiser *vt* (*parfum etc*) to spray

varappe [varap] *nf* rock climbing

vareuse [varøz] *nf* (*blouson*) pea jacket; (*d'uniforme*) tunic

variable [varjabl] *adj* variable; (*temps, humeur*) changeable; (*divers: résultats*) varied, various

varice [varis] *nf* varicose vein

varicelle [varisεl] *nf* chickenpox

varié, e [varje] *adj* varied; (*divers*) various; **hors d'œuvre ~s** selection of hors d'œuvres

varier [varje] *vi* to vary; (*temps, humeur*) to change ▷ *vt* to vary; **variété** *nf* variety; **variétés** *nfpl*: **spectacle/ émission de variétés** variety show

variole [varjɔl] *nf* smallpox

Varsovie [varsɔvi] *n* Warsaw

vas [va] *vb voir* **aller**; **~-y!** [vazi] go on!

vase [vaz] *nm* vase ▷ *nf* silt, mud; **vaseux, -euse** *adj* silty, muddy; (*fig: confus*) woolly, hazy; (: *fatigué*) woozy

vasistas [vazistas] *nm* fanlight

vaste [vast] *adj* vast, immense

vautour [votur] *nm* vulture

vautrer [votre] *vb*: **se ~ dans/sur** to wallow in/sprawl on

va-vite [vavit]: **à la ~** *adv* in a rush *ou* hurry

VDQS *sigle* (= *vin délimité de qualité supérieure*) *label guaranteeing the quality of wine*

veau, x [vo] *nm* (*Zool*) calf; (*Culin*) veal; (*peau*) calfskin

vécu, e [veky] *pp de* **vivre**

vedette [vədεt] *nf* (*artiste etc*) star; (*canot*) motor boat; (*police*) launch

végétal, e, -aux [veʒetal, o] *adj* vegetable ▷ *nm* vegetable, plant; **végétalien, ne** *adj, nm/f* vegan

végétarien, ne [veʒetarjɛ̃, jεn] *adj, nm/f* vegetarian; **avez-vous des plats ~s?** do you have any vegetarian dishes?

végétation [veʒetasjɔ̃] *nf* vegetation; **végétations** *nfpl* (*Méd*) adenoids

véhicule [veikyl] *nm* vehicle; **véhicule utilitaire** commercial vehicle

veille [vεj] *nf* (*état*) wakefulness; (*jour*): **la ~ (de)** the day before; **la ~ au soir** the previous evening; **à la ~ de** on the eve of; **la ~ de Noël** Christmas Eve; **la ~ du jour de l'An** New Year's Eve

veillée [veje] *nf* (*soirée*) evening; (*réunion*) evening gathering; **veillée (funèbre)** wake

veiller [veje] *vi* to stay up ▷ *vt* (*malade, mort*) to watch over, sit up with; **~ à** to attend to, see to; **~ à ce que** to make sure that; **~ sur** to watch over; **veilleur** *nm*: **veilleur de nuit** night watchman; **veilleuse** *nf* (*lampe*) night light; (*Auto*) sidelight; (*flamme*) pilot light

veinard, e [venar, ard] *nm/f* lucky devil

veine [vɛn] nf (Anat, du bois etc) vein; (filon) vein, seam; (fam: chance): **avoir de la ~** to be lucky

véliplanchiste [veliplɑ̃ʃist] nm/f windsurfer

vélo [velo] nm bike, cycle; **faire du ~** to go cycling; **vélomoteur** nm moped

velours [v(ə)luR] nm velvet; **velours côtelé** corduroy; **velouté, e** adj velvety ▷ nm: **velouté de tomates** cream of tomato soup

velu, e [vəly] adj hairy

vendange [vɑ̃dɑ̃ʒ] nf (aussi: **~s**) grape harvest; **vendanger** vi to harvest the grapes

vendeur, -euse [vɑ̃dœR, øz] nm/f shop assistant ▷ nm (Jur) vendor, seller

vendre [vɑ̃dR] vt to sell; **~ qch à qn** to sell sb sth; **"à ~"** "for sale"

vendredi [vɑ̃dRədi] nm Friday; **vendredi saint** Good Friday

vénéneux, -euse [venenø, øz] adj poisonous

vénérien, ne [veneRjɛ̃, jɛn] adj venereal

vengeance [vɑ̃ʒɑ̃s] nf vengeance no pl, revenge no pl

venger [vɑ̃ʒe] vt to avenge; **se venger** vi to avenge o.s.; **se ~ de qch** to avenge o.s. for sth, take one's revenge for sth; **se ~ de qn** to take revenge on sb; **se ~ sur** to take revenge on

venimeux, -euse [vənimø, øz] adj poisonous, venomous; (fig: haineux) venomous, vicious

venin [vənɛ̃] nm venom, poison

venir [v(ə)niR] vi to come; **~ de** to come from; **~ de faire: je viens d'y aller/de le voir** I've just been there/seen him; **s'il vient à pleuvoir** if it should rain; **j'en viens à croire que** I have come to believe that; **où veux-tu en ~?** what are you getting at?; **faire ~** (docteur, plombier) to call (out)

vent [vɑ̃] nm wind; **il y a du ~** it's windy; **c'est du ~** it's all hot air; **dans le ~** (fam) trendy

vente [vɑ̃t] nf sale; **la ~** (activité) selling; (secteur) sales pl; **mettre en ~** (produit) to put on sale; (maison, objet personnel) to put up for sale; **vente aux enchères** auction sale; **vente de charité** jumble sale

venteux, -euse [vɑ̃tø, øz] adj windy

ventilateur [vɑ̃tilatœR] nm fan

ventiler [vɑ̃tile] vt to ventilate

ventouse [vɑ̃tuz] nf (de caoutchouc) suction pad

ventre [vɑ̃tR] nm (Anat) stomach; (légèrement péj) belly; (utérus) womb; **avoir mal au ~** to have stomach ache (BRIT) ou a stomach ache (US)

venu, e [v(ə)ny] pp de **venir** ▷ adj: **bien ~** timely; **mal ~** out of place; **être mal ~ à** ou **de faire** to have no grounds for doing, be in no position to do

ver [vɛR] nm worm; (des fruits etc) maggot; (du bois) woodworm no pl; voir aussi **vers**; **ver à soie** silkworm; **ver de terre** earthworm; **ver luisant** glow-worm; **ver solitaire** tapeworm

verbe [vɛRb] nm verb

verdâtre [vɛRdɑtR] adj greenish

verdict [vɛRdik(t)] nm verdict

verdir [vɛRdiR] vi, vt to turn green; **verdure** nf greenery

véreux, -euse [verø, øz] adj worm-eaten; (malhonnête) shady, corrupt

verge [vɛRʒ] nf (Anat) penis

verger [vɛRʒe] nm orchard

verglacé, e [vɛRglase] adj icy, iced-over

verglas [vɛRglɑ] nm (black) ice

véridique [veRidik] adj truthful

vérification [veRifikasjɔ̃] nf (action) checking no pl; (contrôle) check

vérifier [veRifje] vt to check; (corroborer) to confirm, bear out

véritable [veRitabl] adj real; (ami, amour) true; **un ~ désastre** an absolut disaster

vérité [veRite] nf truth; **en ~** really, actually

verlan [vɛRlɑ̃] nm (fam) (back) slang

vermeil, le [vɛRmɛj] adj ruby red

vermine [vɛRmin] nf vermin pl

vermoulu, e [vɛʀmuly] *adj* worm-eaten

verni, e [vɛʀni] *adj* (*fam*) lucky; **cuir ~** patent leather

vernir [vɛʀniʀ] *vt* (*bois, tableau, ongles*) to varnish; (*poterie*) to glaze; **vernis** *nm* (*enduit*) varnish; glaze; (*fig*) veneer; **vernis à ongles** nail polish *ou* varnish; **vernissage** *nm* (*d'une exposition*) preview

vérole [veʀɔl] *nf* (*variole*) smallpox

verre [vɛʀ] *nm* glass; (*de lunettes*) lens *sg*; **boire** *ou* **prendre un ~** to have a drink; **verres de contact** contact lenses; **verrière** *nf* (*paroi vitrée*) glass wall; (*toit vitré*) glass roof

verrou [veʀu] *nm* (*targette*) bolt; **mettre qn sous les ~s** to put sb behind bars; **verrouillage** *nm* locking; **verrouillage centralisé** central locking; **verrouiller** *vt* (*porte*) to bolt; (*ordinateur*) to lock

verrue [veʀy] *nf* wart

vers [vɛʀ] *nm* line ▷ *nmpl* (*poésie*) verse *sg* ▷ *prép* (*en direction de*) toward(s); (*près de*) around (about); (*temporel*) about, around

versant [vɛʀsɑ̃] *nm* slopes *pl*, side

versatile [vɛʀsatil] *adj* fickle, changeable

verse [vɛʀs]: **à ~** *adv*: **il pleut à ~** it's pouring (with rain)

Verseau [vɛʀso] *nm*: **le ~** Aquarius

versement [vɛʀsəmɑ̃] *nm* payment; **en 3 ~s** in 3 instalments

verser [vɛʀse] *vt* (*liquide, grains*) to pour; (*larmes, sang*) to shed; (*argent*) to pay; **~ qch sur un compte** to pay sth into an account

version [vɛʀsjɔ̃] *nf* version; (*Scol*) translation (*into the mother tongue*); **film en ~ originale** film in the original language

verso [vɛʀso] *nm* back; **voir au ~** see over(leaf)

vert, e [vɛʀ, vɛʀt] *adj* green; (*vin*) young; (*vigoureux*) sprightly ▷ *nm* green; **les V~s** (*Pol*) the Greens

vertèbre [vɛʀtɛbʀ] *nf* vertebra

vertement [vɛʀtəmɑ̃] *adv* (*réprimander*) sharply

vertical, e, -aux [vɛʀtikal, o] *adj* vertical; **verticale** *nf* vertical; **à la verticale** vertically; **verticalement** *adv* vertically

vertige [vɛʀtiʒ] *nm* (*peur du vide*) vertigo; (*étourdissement*) dizzy spell; (*fig*) fever; **vertigineux, -euse** *adj* breathtaking

vertu [vɛʀty] *nf* virtue; **en ~ de** in accordance with; **vertueux, -euse** *adj* virtuous

verve [vɛʀv] *nf* witty eloquence; **être en ~** to be in brilliant form

verveine [vɛʀvɛn] *nf* (*Bot*) verbena, vervain; (*infusion*) verbena tea

vésicule [vezikyl] *nf* vesicle; **vésicule biliaire** gall-bladder

vessie [vesi] *nf* bladder

veste [vɛst] *nf* jacket; **veste droite/ croisée** single-/double-breasted jacket

vestiaire [vɛstjɛʀ] *nm* (*au théâtre etc*) cloakroom; (*de stade etc*) changing-room (BRIT), locker-room (US)

vestibule [vɛstibyl] *nm* hall

vestige [vɛstiʒ] *nm* relic; (*fig*) vestige; **vestiges** *nmpl* (*de ville*) remains

vestimentaire [vɛstimɑ̃tɛʀ] *adj* (*détail*) of dress; (*élégance*) sartorial; **dépenses ~s** clothing expenditure

veston [vɛstɔ̃] *nm* jacket

vêtement [vɛtmɑ̃] *nm* garment, item of clothing; **vêtements** *nmpl* clothes

vétérinaire [veteʀinɛʀ] *nm/f* vet, veterinary surgeon

vêtir [vetiʀ] *vt* to clothe, dress

vêtu, e [vety] *pp de* **vêtir** ▷ *adj*: **~ de** dressed in, wearing

vétuste [vetyst] *adj* ancient, timeworn

veuf, veuve [vœf, vœv] *adj* widowed ▷ *nm* widower

veuve [vœv] *nf* widow

vexant, e [vɛksɑ̃, ɑ̃t] *adj* (*contrariant*) annoying; (*blessant*) hurtful

vexation [vɛksasjɔ̃] *nf* humiliation

vexer [vɛkse] *vt*: **~ qn** to hurt sb's feelings; **se vexer** *vi* to be offended

viable [vjabl] *adj* viable; (*économie, industrie etc*) sustainable

viande [vjɑ̃d] *nf* meat; **je ne mange pas de ~** I don't eat meat

vibrer [vibʀe] *vi* to vibrate; (*son, voix*) to be vibrant; (*fig*) to be stirred; **faire ~** to (cause to) vibrate; (*fig*) to stir, thrill

vice [vis] *nm* vice; (*défaut*) fault ▷ *préfixe*: **~...** vice-; **vice de forme** legal flaw *ou* irregularity

vicié, e [visje] *adj* (*air*) polluted, tainted; (*Jur*) invalidated

vicieux, -euse [visjø, jøz] *adj* (*pervers*) lecherous; (*rétif*) unruly ▷ *nm/f* lecher

vicinal, e, -aux [visinal, o] *adj*: **chemin ~** by-road, byway

victime [viktim] *nf* victim; (*d'accident*) casualty

victoire [viktwaʀ] *nf* victory

victuailles [viktɥaj] *nfpl* provisions

vidange [vidɑ̃ʒ] *nf* (*d'un fossé, réservoir*) emptying; (*Auto*) oil change; (*de lavabo: bonde*) waste outlet; **vidanges** *nfpl* (*matières*) sewage *sg*; **vidanger** *vt* to empty

vide [vid] *adj* empty ▷ *nm* (*Physique*) vacuum; (*espace*) (empty) space, gap; (*futilité, néant*) void; **avoir peur du ~** to be afraid of heights; **emballé sous ~** vacuum packed; **à ~** (*sans occupants*) empty; (*sans charge*) unladen

vidéo [video] *nf* video ▷ *adj*: **cassette ~** video cassette; **jeu ~** video game; **vidéoclip** *nm* music video; **vidéoconférence** *nf* videoconference

vide-ordures [vidɔʀdyʀ] *nm inv* (rubbish) chute

vider [vide] *vt* to empty; (*Culin: volaille, poisson*) to gut, clean out; **se vider** *vi* to empty; **~ les lieux** to quit *ou* vacate the premises; **videur** *nm* (*de boîte de nuit*) bouncer, doorman

vie [vi] *nf* life; **être en ~** to be alive; **sans ~** lifeless; **à ~** for life; **que faites-vous dans la ~?** what do you do?

vieil [vjɛj] *adj m voir* **vieux**; **vieillard**

nm old man; **vieille** *adj*, *nf voir* **vieux**; **vieilleries** *nfpl* old things; **vieillesse** *nf* old age; **vieillir** *vi* (*prendre de l'âge*) to grow old; (*population, vin*) to age; (*doctrine, auteur*) to become dated ▷ *vt* to age; **vieillissement** *nm* growing old; ageing

Vienne [vjɛn] *nf* Vienna

viens [vjɛ̃] *vb voir* **venir**

vierge [vjɛʀʒ] *adj* virgin; (*page*) clean, blank ▷ *nf* virgin; (*signe*): **la V~** Virgo

Vietnam, Viet-Nam [vjɛtnam] *nm* Vietnam; **vietnamien, ne** *adj* Vietnamese ▷ *nm/f*: **Vietnamien, ne** Vietnamese

vieux, vieil, vieille [vjø, vjɛj] *adj* old ▷ *nm/f* old man (woman); **les vieux** *nmpl* old people; **un petit ~** a little old man; **mon ~/ma vieille** (*fam*) old man/girl; **prendre un coup de ~** to put years on; **vieux garçon** bachelor; **vieux jeu** *adj inv* old-fashioned

vif, vive [vif, viv] *adj* (*animé*) lively; (*alerte, brusque, aigu*) sharp; (*lumière, couleur*) bright; (*air*) crisp; (*vent, émotion*) keen; (*fort: regret, déception*) great, deep; (*vivant*): **brûlé ~** burnt alive; **de vive voix** personally; **avoir l'esprit ~** to be quick-witted; **piquer qn au ~** to cut sb to the quick; **à ~** (*plaie*) open; **avoir les nerfs à ~** to be on edge

vigne [viɲ] *nf* (*plante*) vine; (*plantation*) vineyard; **vigneron** *nm* wine grower

vignette [viɲɛt] *nf* (*Admin*) ≈ (road) tax disc (*BRIT*), ≈ license plate sticker (*US*); (*de médicament*) price label (*used for reimbursement*)

vignoble [viɲɔbl] *nm* (*plantation*) vineyard; (*vignes d'une région*) vineyards *pl*

vigoureux, -euse [viguʀø, øz] *adj* vigorous, robust

vigueur [vigœʀ] *nf* vigour; **entrer en ~** to come into force; **en ~** current

vilain, e [vilɛ̃, ɛn] *adj* (*laid*) ugly; (*affaire, blessure*) nasty; (*pas sage: enfant*) naughty; **vilain mot** naughty *ou* bad word

villa [vila] *nf* (detached) house; **~ en multipropriété** time-share villa

village [vilaʒ] *nm* village; **villageois, e** *adj* village *cpd* ▷ *nm/f* villager

ville [vil] *nf* town; (*importante*) city; (*administration*): **la ~** the (town) council, the local authority; **ville d'eaux** spa; **ville nouvelle** new town

vin [vɛ̃] *nm* wine; **avoir le ~ gai** to get happy after a few drinks; **vin d'honneur** reception (*with wine and snacks*); **vin de pays** local wine; **vin ordinaire** *ou* **de table** table wine

vinaigre [vinɛgʀ] *nm* vinegar; **vinaigrette** *nf* vinaigrette, French dressing

vindicatif, -ive [vɛ̃dikatif, iv] *adj* vindictive

vingt [vɛ̃] *num* twenty; **~-quatre heures sur ~-quatre** twenty-four hours a day, round the clock; **vingtaine** *nf*: **une vingtaine (de)** about twenty, twenty or so; **vingtième** *num* twentieth

vinicole [vinikɔl] *adj* wine *cpd*, wine-growing

vinyle [vinil] *nm* vinyl

viol [vjɔl] *nm* (*d'une femme*) rape; (*d'un lieu sacré*) violation

violacé, e [vjɔlase] *adj* purplish, mauvish

violemment [vjɔlamɑ̃] *adv* violently

violence [vjɔlɑ̃s] *nf* violence

violent, e [vjɔlɑ̃, ɑ̃t] *adj* violent; (*remède*) drastic

violer [vjɔle] *vt* (*femme*) to rape; (*sépulture, loi, traité*) to violate

violet, te [vjɔlɛ, ɛt] *adj, nm* purple, mauve; **violette** *nf* (*fleur*) violet

violon [vjɔlɔ̃] *nm* violin; (*fam: prison*) lock-up; **violon d'Ingres** hobby; **violoncelle** *nm* cello; **violoniste** *nm/f* violinist

vipère [vipɛʀ] *nf* viper, adder

virage [viʀaʒ] *nm* (*d'un véhicule*) turn; (*d'une route, piste*) bend

virée [viʀe] *nf* trip; (*à pied*) walk; (*longue*) walking tour; (*dans les cafés*) tour

virement [viʀmɑ̃] *nm* (*Comm*) transfer

virer [viʀe] *vt* (*Comm*): **~ qch (sur)** to transfer sth (into); (*fam: expulser*): **~ qn** to kick sb out ▷ *vi* to turn; (*Chimie*) to change colour; **~ au bleu/rouge** to turn blue/red; **~ de bord** to tack

virevolter [viʀvɔlte] *vi* to twirl around

virgule [viʀgyl] *nf* comma; (*Math*) point

viril, e [viʀil] *adj* (*propre à l'homme*) masculine; (*énergique, courageux*) manly, virile

virtuel, le [viʀtɥɛl] *adj* potential; (*théorique*) virtual

virtuose [viʀtɥoz] *nm/f* (*Mus*) virtuoso; (*gén*) master

virus [viʀys] *nm* virus

vis¹ [vi] *vb voir* **voir**; **vivre**

vis² [vis] *nf* screw

visa [viza] *nm* (*sceau*) stamp; (*validation de passeport*) visa

visage [vizaʒ] *nm* face

vis-à-vis [vizavi] *prép*: **~ de qn** to(wards) sb; **en ~** facing each other

visées [vize] *nfpl* (*intentions*) designs

viser [vize] *vi* to aim ▷ *vt* to aim at; (*concerner*) to be aimed *ou* directed at; (*apposer un visa sur*) to stamp, visa; **~ à qch/faire** to aim at sth/at doing *ou* to do

visibilité [vizibilite] *nf* visibility

visible [vizibl] *adj* visible; (*disponible*): **est-il ~?** can he see me?, will he see visitors?

visière [vizjɛʀ] *nf* (*de casquette*) peak; (*qui s'attache*) eyeshade

vision [vizjɔ̃] *nf* vision; (*sens*) (eye)sight, vision; (*fait de voir*): **la ~ de** the sight of; **visionneuse** *nf* viewer

visiophone [vizjɔfɔn] *nm* videophone

visite [vizit] *nf* visit; **~ médicale** medical examination; **~ accompagnée** *ou* **guidée** guided tour; **la ~ guidée commence à quelle heure?** what time does the guided tour start?; **faire une ~ à qn** to call on sb, pay sb a visit; **rendre ~ à qn** to visit sb, pay sb a visit; **être en ~ (chez qn)** to be visiting (sb); **avoir**

de la ~ to have visitors; **heures de ~**
(*hôpital*, *prison*) visiting hours
visiter [vizite] *vt* to visit; **visiteur,**
-euse *nm/f* visitor
vison [vizɔ̃] *nm* mink
visser [vise] *vt*: **~ qch** (*fixer*, *serrer*) to
screw sth on
visuel, le [vizɥɛl] *adj* visual
vital, e, -aux [vital, o] *adj* vital
vitamine [vitamin] *nf* vitamin
vite [vit] *adv* (*rapidement*) quickly, fast;
(*sans délai*) quickly; (*sous peu*) soon; **~!**
quick!; **faire ~** to be quick; **le temps**
passe ~ time flies
vitesse [vites] *nf* speed; (*Auto: dispositif*)
gear; **prendre de la ~** to pick up *ou*
gather speed; **à toute ~** at full *ou* top
speed; **en ~** (*rapidement*) quickly; (*en*
hâte) in a hurry

● **LIMITE DE VITESSE**
●
● The speed limit in France is 50 km/h
● in built-up areas, 90 km/h on main
● roads, and 130 km/h on motorways
● (110 km/h when it is raining).

viticulteur [vitikyltœr] *nm* wine
grower
vitrage [vitraʒ] *nm*: **double ~** double
glazing
vitrail, -aux [vitraj, o] *nm* stained-
glass window
vitre [vitr] *nf* (*window*) pane; (*de*
portière, voiture) window; **vitré, e** *adj*
glass *cpd*
vitrine [vitrin] *nf* (*shop*) window;
(*petite armoire*) display cabinet; **en ~** in
the window
vivable [vivabl] *adj* (*personne*) livable-
with; (*maison*) fit to live in
vivace [vivas] *adj* (*arbre, plante*) hardy;
(*fig*) indestructible, inveterate
vivacité [vivasite] *nf* liveliness,
vivacity
vivant, e [vivɑ̃, ɑ̃t] *adj* (*qui vit*) living,
alive; (*animé*) lively; (*preuve, exemple*)
living ▷ *nm*: **du ~ de qn** in sb's lifetime;

les ~s the living
vive [viv] *adj voir* **vif** ▷ *vb voir* **vivre**
▷ *excl*: **~ le roi!** long live the king!;
vivement *adv* deeply ▷ *excl*: **vivement**
les vacances! roll on the holidays!
vivier [vivje] *nm* (*étang*) fish tank;
(*réservoir*) fishpond
vivifiant, e [vivifjɑ̃, jɑ̃t] *adj*
invigorating
vivoter [vivɔte] *vi* (*personne*) to scrape
a living, get by; (*fig: affaire etc*) to
struggle along
vivre [vivr] *vi, vt* to live; (*période*) to live
through; **vivres** *nmpl* provisions, food
supplies; **~ de** to live on; **il vit encore**
he is still alive; **se laisser ~** to take life
as it comes; **ne plus ~** (*être anxieux*) to
live on one's nerves; **il a vécu** (*eu une vie*
aventureuse) he has seen life; **être facile**
à ~ to be easy to get on with; **faire ~ qn**
(*pourvoir à sa subsistance*) to provide (a
living) for sb
vlan [vlɑ̃] *excl* wham!, bang!
VO [veo] *nf*: **film en VO** film in the
original version; **en VO sous-titrée** in
the original version with subtitles
vocabulaire [vɔkabylɛr] *nm*
vocabulary
vocation [vɔkasjɔ̃] *nf* vocation, calling
vœu, x [vø] *nm* wish; (*promesse*) vow;
faire ~ de to take a vow of; **tous nos ~x**
de bonne année, meilleurs ~x best
wishes for the New Year
vogue [vɔg] *nf* fashion, vogue; **en ~** in
fashion, in vogue
voici [vwasi] *prép* (*pour introduire*,
désigner) here is +*sg*, here are +*pl*; **et**
~ que ... and now it (*ou* he) ...; *voir*
aussi **voilà**
voie [vwa] *nf* way; (*Rail*) track, line;
(*Auto*) lane; **être en bonne ~** to be
going well; **mettre qn sur la ~** to
put sb on the right track; **pays en**
~ de développement developing
country; **être en ~ d'achèvement/de**
rénovation to be nearing completion
in the process of renovation; **par ~**
buccale *ou* **orale** orally; **route à ~**

unique single-track road; **route à 2/3 ~s** 2-/3-lane road; **voie de garage** (*Rail*) siding; **voie express** expressway; **voie ferrée** track; railway line (BRIT), railroad (US); **la voie lactée** the Milky Way; **la voie publique** the public highway

voilà [vwala] *prép* (*en désignant*) there is +*sg*, there are +*pl*; **les ~ qui voici** here *ou* there they are; **en ~ ou voici un** here's one, there's one; **voici mon frère et ~ ma sœur** this is my brother and that's my sister; **~ ou voici deux ans** two years ago; **~ ou voici dix ans que** it's two years since; **et ~!** there we are!; **~ tout** that's all; **~ ou voici** (*en offrant etc*) there *ou* here you are; **tiens! ~ Paul** look! there's Paul

voile [vwal] *nm* veil; (*tissu léger*) net ⊳ *nf* sail; (*sport*) sailing; **voiler** *vt* to veil; (*fausser: roue*) to buckle; (*: bois*) to warp; **se voiler** *vi* (*lune, regard*) to mist over; (*voix*) to become husky; (*roue, disque*) to buckle; (*planche*) to warp; **voilier** *nm* sailing ship; (*de plaisance*) sailing boat; **voilure** *nf* (*de voilier*) sails *pl*

voir [vwaʀ] *vi, vt* to see; **se voir** *vi* (*être visible*) to show; (*se fréquenter*) to see each other; (*se produire*) to happen; **cela se voit** (*c'est visible*) that's obvious, it shows; **faire ~ qch à qn** to show sb sth; **en faire ~ à qn** (*fig*) to give sb a hard time; **ne pas pouvoir ~ qn** not to be able to stand sb; **voyons!** let's see now; (*indignation etc*) come on!; **ça n'a rien à ~ avec lui** that has nothing to do with him

voire [vwaʀ] *adv* even

voisin, e [vwazɛ̃, in] *adj* (*proche*) neighbouring; (*contigu*) next; (*ressemblant*) connected ⊳ *nm/f* neighbour; **voisinage** *nm* (*proximité*) proximity; (*environs*) vicinity; (*quartier, voisins*) neighbourhood

voiture [vwatyʀ] *nf* car; (*wagon*) coach, carriage; **voiture de course** racing car; **voiture de sport** sports car

voix [vwa] *nf* voice; (*Pol*) vote; **à haute ~** aloud; **à ~ basse** in a low voice; **à 2/4 ~** (*Mus*) in 2/4 parts; **avoir ~ au chapitre** to have a say in the matter

vol [vɔl] *nm* (*d'oiseau, d'avion*) flight; (*larcin*) theft; **~ régulier** scheduled flight; **à d'oiseau** as the crow flies; **au ~: attraper qch au ~** to catch sth as it flies past; **en ~** in flight; **je voudrais signaler un ~** I'd like to report a theft; **vol à main armée** armed robbery; **vol à voile** gliding; **vol libre** hang-gliding

volage [vɔlaʒ] *adj* fickle

volaille [vɔlaj] *nf* (*oiseaux*) poultry *pl*; (*viande*) poultry *no pl*; (*oiseau*) fowl

volant, e [vɔlɑ̃, ɑ̃t] *adj voir* **feuille** *etc* ⊳ *nm* (*d'automobile*) (steering) wheel; (*de commande*) wheel; (*objet lancé*) shuttlecock; (*bande de tissu*) flounce

volcan [vɔlkɑ̃] *nm* volcano

volée [vɔle] *nf* (*Tennis*) volley; **à la ~: rattraper à la ~** to catch in mid-air; **à toute ~** (*sonner les cloches*) vigorously; (*lancer un projectile*) with full force

voler [vɔle] *vi* (*avion, oiseau, fig*) to fly; (*voleur*) to steal ⊳ *vt* (*objet*) to steal; (*personne*) to rob; **~ qch à qn** to steal sth from sb; **on m'a volé mon portefeuille** my wallet (BRIT) *ou* billfold (US) has been stolen; **il ne l'a pas volé!** he asked for it!

volet [vɔlɛ] *nm* (*de fenêtre*) shutter; (*de feuillet, document*) section

voleur, -euse [vɔlœʀ, øz] *nm/f* thief ⊳ *adj* thieving; **"au ~!"** "stop thief!"

volontaire [vɔlɔ̃tɛʀ] *adj* (*acte, enrôlement, prisonnier*) voluntary; (*oubli*) intentional; (*caractère, personne: décidé*) self-willed ⊳ *nm/f* volunteer

volonté [vɔlɔ̃te] *nf* (*faculté de vouloir*) will; (*énergie, fermeté*) will(power); (*souhait, désir*) wish; **à ~** as much as one likes; **bonne ~** goodwill, willingness; **mauvaise ~** lack of goodwill, unwillingness

volontiers [vɔlɔ̃tje] *adv* (*avec plaisir*) willingly, gladly; (*habituellement, souvent*) readily, willingly; **voulez-vous boire quelque chose? — ~!** would you like something to drink? — yes, please!

volt [vɔlt] nm volt

volte-face [vɔltəfas] nf inv: **faire ~** to turn round

voltige [vɔltiʒ] nf (Équitation) trick riding; (au cirque) acrobatics sg; **voltiger** vi to flutter (about)

volubile [vɔlybil] adj voluble

volume [vɔlym] nm volume; (Géom: solide) solid; **volumineux, -euse** adj voluminous, bulky

volupté [vɔlypte] nf sensual delight ou pleasure

vomi [vɔmi] nm vomit; **vomir** vi to vomit, be sick ▷ vt to vomit, bring up; (fig) to belch out, spew out; (exécrer) to loathe, abhor

vorace [vɔʀas] adj voracious

vos [vo] adj voir **votre**

vote [vɔt] nm vote; **vote par correspondance/procuration** postal/proxy vote; **voter** vi to vote ▷ vt (projet de loi) to vote for; (loi, réforme) to pass

votre [vɔtʀ] (pl **vos**) adj your

vôtre [votʀ] pron: **le ~, la ~, les ~s** yours; **les ~s** (fig) your family ou folks; **à la ~** (toast) your (good) health!

vouer [vwe] vt: **~ sa vie à** (étude, cause etc) to devote one's life to; **~ une amitié éternelle à qn** to vow undying friendship to sb

⊙ **MOT-CLÉ**

vouloir [vulwaʀ] nm: **le bon vouloir de qn** sb's goodwill; sb's pleasure ▷ vt **1** (exiger, désirer) to want; **vouloir faire/que qn fasse** to want to do/sb to do; **voulez-vous du thé?** would you like ou do you want some tea?; **que me veut-il?** what does he want with me?; **sans le vouloir** (involontairement) without meaning to, unintentionally; **je voudrais ceci/faire** I would ou I'd like this/to do; **le hasard a voulu que ...** as fate would have it ...; **la tradition veut que ...** it is a tradition that ...

2 (consentir): **je veux bien** (bonne volonté) I'll be happy to; (concession) fair enough, that's fine; **je peux le faire, si vous voulez** I can do it if you like; **oui, si on veut** (en quelque sorte) yes, if you like; **veuillez attendre** please wait; **veuillez agréer ...** (formule épistolaire: personne nommée) yours sincerely; (personne non nommée) yours faithfully

3: **en vouloir à qn** to bear sb a grudge; **s'en vouloir (de)** to be annoyed with o.s. (for); **il en veut à mon argent** he's after my money

4: **vouloir de**: **l'entreprise ne veut plus de lui** the firm doesn't want him any more; **elle ne veut pas de son aide** she doesn't want his help

5: **vouloir dire** to mean

voulu, e [vuly] adj (requis) required, requisite; (délibéré) deliberate, intentional; voir aussi **vouloir**

vous [vu] pron you; (objet indirect) (to) you; (réfléchi: sg) yourself; (: pl) yourselves; (réciproque) each other ▷ nm: **employer le ~** (vouvoyer) to use the "vous" form; **~-même** yourself; **~-mêmes** yourselves

vouvoyer [vuvwaje] vt: **~ qn** to address sb as "vous"

voyage [vwajaʒ] nm journey, trip; (fait de voyager): **le ~** travel(ling); **partir/être en ~** to go off/be away on a journey ou trip; **faire bon ~** to have a good journey; **votre ~ s'est bien passé?** how was your journey?; **voyage d'affaires/d'agrément** business/pleasure trip; **voyage de noces** honeymoon; **nous sommes en voyage de noces** we're on honeymoon; **voyage organisé** package tour

voyager [vwajaʒe] vi to travel; **voyageur, -euse** nm/f traveller; (passager) passenger; **voyageur de commerce** sales representative, commercial traveller

voyant, e [vwajɑ̃, ɑ̃t] adj (couleur) loud, gaudy ▷ nm (signal) (warning) light

voyelle [vwajɛl] *nf* vowel
voyou [vwaju] *nm* hooligan
vrac [vʀak]: **en ~** *adv* (*au détail*) loose;
(*en gros*) in bulk; (*en désordre*) in a jumble
vrai, e [vʀɛ] *adj* (*véridique: récit,
faits*) true; (*non factice, authentique*)
real; **à ~ dire** to tell the truth;
vraiment *adv* really; **vraisemblable**
adj likely; (*excuse*) convincing;
vraisemblablement *adj* probably;
vraisemblance *nf* likelihood;
(*romanesque*) verisimilitude
vrombir [vʀɔ̃biʀ] *vi* to hum
VRP *sigle m* (= *voyageur, représentant,
placier*) sales rep (*fam*)
VTT *sigle m* (= *vélo tout-terrain*) mountain
bike
vu, e [vy] *pp de* **voir** ▷ *adj*: **bien/mal vu**
(*fig: personne*) popular/unpopular;
(: *chose*) approved/disapproved of
▷ *prép* (*en raison de*) in view of; **vu que**
in view of the fact that
vue [vy] *nf* (*fait de voir*): **la ~ de** the sight
of; (*sens, faculté*) (eye)sight; (*panorama,
image, photo*) view; **vues** *nfpl* (*idées*)
views; (*dessein*) designs; **hors de ~** out
of sight; **avoir en ~** to have in mind;
tirer à ~ to shoot on sight; **à ~ d'œil**
visibly; **à première ~** at first sight; **de ~**
by sight; **perdre de ~** to lose sight of; **en
~** (*visible*) in sight; (*célèbre*) in the public
eye; **en ~ de faire** with a view to doing;
perdre la ~ to lose one's (eye)sight;
avoir ~ sur (*suj: fenêtre*) to have a view
of; **vue d'ensemble** overall view
vulgaire [vylgɛʀ] *adj* (*grossier*) vulgar,
coarse; (*ordinaire*) commonplace,
mundane; (*péj: quelconque*): **de ~s
touristes** common tourists; (*Bot, Zool:
non latin*) common; **vulgariser** *vt* to
popularize
vulnérable [vylneʀabl] *adj* vulnerable

wagon [vagɔ̃] *nm* (*de voyageurs*)
carriage; (*de marchandises*) truck,
wagon; **wagon-lit** *nm* sleeper,
sleeping car; **wagon-restaurant** *nm*
restaurant *ou* dining car
wallon, ne [walɔ̃, ɔn] *adj* Walloon
▷ *nm* (*Ling*) Walloon ▷ *nm/f*: **W~, ne**
Walloon
watt [wat] *nm* watt
w-c *sigle mpl* (= *water-closet(s)*) toilet
Web [wɛb] *nm inv*: **le ~** the (World
Wide) Web; **webmaster** [-mastœʀ],
webmestre [-mɛstʀ] *nm/f* webmaster
week-end [wikɛnd] *nm* weekend
western [wɛstɛʀn] *nm* western
whisky [wiski] (*pl* **whiskies**) *nm*
whisky

X y

xénophobe [gzenɔfɔb] *adj*
  xenophobic ▷ *nm/f* xenophobe
xérès [gzeʀɛs] *nm* sherry
xylophone [gzilɔfɔn] *nm* xylophone

y [i] *adv* (*à cet endroit*) there; (*dessus*) on
  it (*ou* them); (*dedans*) in it (*ou* them)
  ▷ *pron* (*about ou on ou of*) it (*d'après le
  verbe employé*); **j'y pense** I'm thinking
  about it; **ça y est!** that's it!; *voir aussi*
  aller; avoir
yacht [jɔt] *nm* yacht
yaourt [jauʀt] *nm* yoghourt; **~ nature/
  aux fruits** plain/fruit yogurt
yeux [jø] *nmpl de* **œil**
yoga [jɔga] *nm* yoga
yoghourt [jɔguʀt] *nm* = **yaourt**
yougoslave [jugɔslav] (*Histoire*) *adj*
  Yugoslav(ian) ▷ *nm/f*: **Y~** Yugoslav
Yougoslavie [jugɔslavi] *nf* (*Histoire*)
  Yugoslavia; **l'ex-~** the former
  Yugoslavia

Z

≈ restricted parking area; **zone industrielle** industrial estate

zoo [zo(o)] *nm* zoo

zoologie [zɔɔlɔʒi] *nf* zoology; **zoologique** *adj* zoological

zut [zyt] *excl* dash (it)! (*BRIT*), nuts! (*US*)

zapper [zape] *vi* to zap

zapping [zapiŋ] *nm*: **faire du ~** to flick through the channels

zèbre [zɛbʀ(ə)] *nm* (*Zool*) zebra; **zébré, e** *adj* striped, streaked

zèle [zɛl] *nm* zeal; **faire du ~** (*péj*) to be over-zealous; **zélé, e** *adj* zealous

zéro [zeʀo] *nm* zero, nought (*BRIT*); **au-dessous de ~** below zero (Centigrade) *ou* freezing; **partir de ~** to start from scratch; **trois (buts) à ~** 3 (goals to) nil

zeste [zɛst] *nm* peel, zest

zézayer [zezeje] *vi* to have a lisp

zigzag [zigzag] *nm* zigzag; **zigzaguer** *vi* to zigzag

Zimbabwe [zimbabwe] *nm*: **le ~** Zimbabwe

zinc [zɛ̃g] *nm* (*Chimie*) zinc

zipper [zipe] *vt* (*Inform*) to zip

zizi [zizi] *nm* (*langage enfantin*) willy

zodiaque [zɔdjak] *nm* zodiac

zona [zona] *nm* shingles *sg*

zone [zon] *nf* zone, area; (*fam: quartiers pauvres*): **la ~** the slums; **zone bleue**

French in focus

Introduction

French in focus gives you a fascinating introduction to the French-speaking world. The following pages look at where French is spoken throughout the world, helping you to get to know the language and the people that speak it. Practical language tips and notes on common translation difficulties will allow you to become more confident in French and a useful correspondence section gives you all the information you need to be able to communicate effectively.

We've also included a number of links to useful websites, which will give you the opportunity to read and learn more about French-speaking countries and the French language.

We hope that you will enjoy using your *French in focus* supplement. We are sure that it will help you to find out more about French-speaking countries and become more confident in writing and speaking French.

Allez-y!

France and its regions

©Collins Bartholomew Ltd 2005

3

France and its regions

The six biggest French cities

City	Name of inhabitants	Population
Paris	les Parisiens	9,645,000 (Paris area)
		2,125,000 (the city proper
Marseille–Aix-en-Provence	les Marseillais	1,350,000
	les Aixois	
Lyon	les Lyonnais	1,349,000
Lille	les Lillois	1,001,000
Nice	les Niçois	889,000
Toulouse	les Toulousains	761,000

Note that the names of the city inhabitants start with a capital letter, but when they are used as adjectives, they begin with a small letter: *les musées parisiens* (Paris museums), *la cuisine lyonnaise* (cooking from Lyons).

French speakers often refer to mainland France as *l'Hexagone* because of its shape. The head of state is the President (*le Président de la République*), who is elected for five years. The President appoints a Prime Minister (*le Premier Ministre*), who heads the government.

France is organized into twenty-two areas called *régions*. Each *région* is made up of several smaller *départements*, four of which lie far beyond Europe's borders.

Useful links:
www.premier-ministre.gouv.fr
  Office of the Prime Minister.
www.service-public.fr
  Links to most government departments.

The overseas *Départements* (*Départements d'outre-mer – DOM* and *Régions d'outre-mer – ROM*) consist of:
• the Caribbean islands of *Martinique* and *Guadeloupe*
• *Réunion* in the Indian Ocean
• *Guyane française* in South America
They have the same legal system as mainland France.

France's overseas territories (*Collectivités d'outre-mer – COM*) include:
• *Polynésie française, Wallis-et-Futuna* and *Nouvelle-Calédonie* in the South Pacific
• *Mayotte* in the Indian Ocean
• *Saint-Pierre et Miquelon*
• polar territories in the Antarctic

A useful link:
www.outre-mer.gouv.fr
  Information on the DOM-ROM.

A snapshot of France

- France is the biggest country by area in Western Europe, covering 549 000 km² (well over twice the size of the UK).

- The Loire is the longest river in France, and is around 1010 km long. It rises in the Cévennes mountains and flows into the Atlantic Ocean at Saint-Nazaire.

- The highest mountain in the Alps, Mont Blanc (4807 m), lies just within France's border with Italy.

- 59.3 million people live in metropolitan France, and there are another 1.7 million in the overseas départements.

- France is the world's fifth largest economy after the US, Japan, Germany and the UK.

- The main religion in France is Roman Catholicism; Islam is the second largest religion.

- After Italy, France is the world's biggest wine-producing country.

- The Tour de France is the world's most famous cycle race. Competitors cover approximately 3500 km nationwide.

A useful link:
www.insee.fr
  The French statistical office.

The French-speaking world

r c t i q u e

que
—Luxembourg
uisse
— Val d'Aoste
MONACO

unisie

Liban   Egypte

Tchad
in

Djibouti
Cameroun
République
centrafricaine
Guinée équatoriale
République du Congo
Rwanda
Burundi

publique
ocratique
du Congo

Seychelles
Comores
MAYOTTE

Madagascar
Île Maurice
LA RÉUNION

Laos   Vietnam
Cambodge

*océan
Pacifique*

*océan
Indien*

Vanuatu

NOUVELLE-
CALÉDONIE

©Collins Bartholomew Ltd 2005

COUNTRIES OR REGIONS WHERE FRENCH IS THE MOTHER TONGUE

Countries where French is one of the official languages

Countries or regions where French is used

Varieties of French

French is the first language for nearly 80 million people, which makes it the eighth most widely spoken language in the world. Around 57 million students all over the globe are currently learning French.

Outside France, French is mostly spoken in:

- Belgium and Switzerland

- Algeria, Morocco, Tunisia, Cameroon, Côte d'Ivoire and the Democratic Republic of the Congo

- Canada

A useful link :
www.academie-francaise.fr
  The Académie française web site.

Le Québec
Québec is the largest Canadian province, with an area of around 1 540 680 km². Over 80% of the province's inhabitants speak French as their first language, although it is rather different from the language of mainland France. The French spoken in Québec is called *Québécois*.

French regional languages

Other languages spoken within France:

Language	French name	Brief description	Where spoken
Alsatian	l'alsacien	Close to German	Near the border with Germany
Breton	le breton	A Celtic language	Brittany in north-west France
Basque	le basque	Not related to any other known language	Near the border with Spain
Catalan	le catalan	Close to Spanish	Near the border with Spain
Corsican	le corse	Close to Italian	The island of Corsica
Flemish	le flamand	Close to Dutch	Near the border with Belgium
Occitan	l'occitan	Close to Spanish and French	The southern part of France

Words that have crossed the Channel

When the Normans invaded England in 1066, French became the language of the ruling classes. Since then, it has played a central part in the development of English.

English has absorbed thousands of French words over time, for example, 'beef' comes from *bœuf*, 'marriage' comes from *mariage* and so on.

However, English also uses words that come directly from French and don't change at all: for example, 'au pair', 'eau de toilette' and 'rendez-vous'.

With the spread of English as a global means of communication, English terms have become more widespread in the French language.

Some of these terms mean the same in both languages:

le brunch	*un cocktail*
le hit-parade	*une interview*
un self-service	*le stress*
un tee-shirt	*les WC*
le Web	*le week-end*
un western	*un yacht*

Others have different meanings in French and English:

un agenda	diary
les baskets	trainers (BRIT), sneakers (US)
les chips	crisps (BRIT), chips (US)
la lecture	reading
un parking	a car park
un smoking	a dinner jacket
un stop	a stop sign, a brake-light

Be careful!
Some words are singular in French but plural in English and vice versa:

un jean (a pair of) jeans
un short (a pair of) shorts
les WC the WC

A useful link:
www.academie-francaise.fr
   The Académie française web site.

Some informal French

We all use different language styles – more relaxed, more formal – depending on the situation we find ourselves in.

When you visit a French-speaking country, you're sure to hear some informal expressions in everyday situations.

Here are some examples of French informal words:

la bagnole	car
le boulot	work
dingue	crazy
génial	fantastic
le mec	guy
moche	ugly, rotten
le prof	teacher

Informal language is marked very clearly in the dictionary to help you choose the appropriate word or phrase.

Be careful when using items marked 'informal' (*fam*) in your dictionary, and avoid ones marked 'offensive' (*fam!*) altogether.

Le verlan
Verlan is a kind of slang in which words are invented by swapping round syllables and often chopping off the end of the new word: for example, *femme* becomes *meuf*, and *Arabe* becomes *beur*.

Improving your pronunciation

There are a number of different methods you can use to improve your pronunciation and increase your confidence in speaking French:

- read out loud to yourself to improve your confidence
- listen to French radio
- watch French-language films
- chat with French-speakers

Useful links:

www.radiofrance.fr
France Info, France Inter and France Culture.

www.rfi.fr
Radio France Internationale, the equivalent of the BBC World Service.

Some points to help you with your pronunciation

- **U and ou.** For *ou*, round your lips as for English 'oo!' For *u*, round your lips but say 'ee'.

- **Silent consonant endings and *liaison*.** Consonants at the end of words are not normally pronounced but you do pronounce them when the following word starts with a vowel (*mes amis* sounds like 'mayzamee', *c'est ici* sounds like 'seteesee'). This is called *liaison*.

- **Elision.** When the words *je, le, la, me, te, se* and *ne* are immediately followed by a word starting with any vowel, the *e* is dropped (and replaced by an apostrophe in writing): *j'adore l'été, elle s'habille, je t'aime.*

- **Letter *h*.** The letter *h* is never pronounced at the beginning of French words. So, *haricot* is pronounced 'areeko' and *hôtel* as 'otel'.

Words beginning with *h* can behave in one of two ways as regards pronunciation.

In some cases, the word behaves as if it began with a vowel, and preceding words like *le* and *la* are shortened: *à l'hôtel, l'huile, ils l'hébergent*. For such words liaison also takes place: *les hôtels* is pronounced as 'layzotel'.

In other cases, *le, la* and similar words are not shortened: *la Hollande, le haricot*, and liaison does not happen: *les haricots* is pronounced as 'lay ariko' and not 'layzariko'. Words which behave like this are preceded by an apostrophe in the dictionary: *'hasard*.

Improving your fluency

Conversational words and phrases

In English we insert lots of words and phrases, such as *so, then, by the way,* into our conversation, to give our thoughts a structure and often to show our attitude. The French words shown below do the same thing. If you use them they will make you sound more fluent and natural.

- **alors**
  Tu as fini? **Alors** je m'en vais. (= then)
  Alors tu viens (oui ou non)? (= well, then)
- **bon**
  Bon! J'y vais. (= right!)
  Bon! Ça suffit maintenant. (= OK!)
- **ah bon**
  Je pars aux États-Unis demain. – **Ah bon**? (= really?)
- **c'est ça**
  Vous avez vingt-cinq ans, alors? – Oui, **c'est ça**. (= that's right)
- **donc**
  Voilà **donc** la solution. (= so, then)
  C'était **donc** un espion? (= then, so)
- **enfin**
  Enfin, vous voyez, c'est la catastrophe! (= in a word)
  Enfin, tu aurais pu le faire! (= even so)

- **de toute façon**
  De toute façon, je ne veux pas y aller. (= anyway)
  Tu peux m'appeler, je serai à la maison **de toute façon**. (= in any case)
- **au fait**
  Au fait, est-ce que tu as aimé le film? (= by the way)
  C'est quand, **au fait**, ton anniversaire? (= in fact)
- **en fait**
  En fait, je n'ai pas beaucoup de temps. (= actually)
  En fait, on devrait partir maintenant. (= in fact)
- **quand même**
  C'est **quand même** ennuyeux. (= after all)
  Merci **quand même**. (= all the same)

Improving your fluency

Varying the words you use to get your message across will make you sound more fluent in French. For example, you already know *J'aime* *bien les gâteaux*, but for a change you could say *J'adore les gâteaux* to mean the same thing. Here are some other suggestions:

Saying what you like or dislike

J'ai bien aimé le film.	I liked ...
La visite des vignobles m'a beaucoup plu.	I really enjoyed ...
Je n'aime pas (du tout) le poisson.	I don't like ... (at all).
J'ai horreur du sport.	I loathe ...

Expressing your opinion

Je pense que c'est trop cher.	I think ...
Je trouve que c'est normal.	I think ...
Je crois que c'est un peu tard.	I think ...
Je suis certain/sûr que Marc va gagner.	I'm sure ...
À mon avis, il n'a pas changé.	In my opinion ...

Agreeing or disagreeing

Je trouve que vous avez raison.	I think you're right.
Je suis d'accord avec vous.	I agree with you.
Il a tort.	He's wrong.
Je ne suis pas d'accord.	I disagree.

Correspondence

The following section on correspondence has been designed to help you communicate confidently in written as well as spoken French. Sample letters, e-mails and sections on text messaging and making telephone calls will ensure that you have all the vocabulary you need to correspond successfully in French.

Text messaging

Texto	French	English
@+	*à plus tard*	see you later
@2m1	*à demain*	see you tomorrow
biito	*bientôt*	soon
cpg	*c'est pas grave*	it's no big deal
dsl	*désolé*	I'm sorry
entouk	*en tout cas*	in any case
G la N	*J'ai la haine*	I'm gutted
je t'M	*je t'aime*	I love you
mdr	*mort de rire*	rolling on the floor laughing
mr6	*merci*	thanks
MSG	*message*	message
p2k	*pas de quoi*	you're welcome
parske	*parce que*	because
qqn	*quelqu'un*	someone
ri1	*rien*	nothing
svp	*s'il vous plaît*	please
TOK	*t'es OK?*	are you OK?
TOQP	*t'es occupé?*	are you busy?
we	*week-end*	weekend
Xlnt	*excellent*	excellent

Writing an e-mail

Fichier	Edition	Affichage	Outils	**Composer**	Aide	Envoyer

		Nouveau message
A:	michel@europost.fr	Répondre
Cc:		Répondre à tous
Copie cachée:		Faire suivre
Object:	Demain soir	Fichier joint

Tu veux sortir demain soir? Le nouveau James Bond passe à l'Odéon, si ça t'intéresse.

Si tu ne peux pas demain, je suis libre samedi midi. On pourrait déjeuner ensemble.

Grosses bises

Nadia

> **Saying your e-mail address**
> In French, when you tell someone your e-mail address, you say:
> *michel arobase europost point ef-ayr*

fichier (m)	file	*répondre à tous*	reply to all
édition (f)	edit	*faire suivre*	forward
affichage (m)	view	*fichier (m) joint*	attachment
outils (mpl)	tools	*à*	to
composer	compose	*cc*	cc (carbon copy)
aide (f)	help	*copie (f) cachée*	bcc (blind carbon copy)
envoyer	send	*objet (m)*	subject
nouveau message (m)	new	*de*	from
répondre	reply to sender	*date (f)*	sent

ere is some additional useful Internet vocabulary:

arre (f) de éfilement	scroll bar		icône (f)	icon
ase (f) de données	database		imprimer	to print
avier (m)	keyboard		l'Internet (m)	the Internet
ic (m) droit	right click		liens (mpl)	links
iquer	to click		menu (m)	menu
ore une session	to log off		moniteur (m)	monitor
oller	to paste		moteur (m) de recherche	search engine
opier	to copy		navigateur (m)	browser
orbeille (f)	recycle bin		ouvrir une session	to log on
ouper	to cut		page (f) d'accueil	home page
ossier (m)	folder		page (f) Web	web page
ouble-cliquer	to double click		précédente	back
nvoyé	sent		rechercher	to search
AQ	FAQs		sauvegarder	to save
voris	favourites		site (m) Web	website
nêtre (f)	window		suivante	forward
uille (f) de calcul	spreadsheet		surfer sur Internet	to surf the Net
ournisseur (m) accès à Internet	Internet Service Provider		télécharger	to download
storique	history		transmission (f) à haut débit	broadband

Writing a personal letter

→ *Guy Leduc*
18, rue des Tulipes
65004 Gervais

→ *Gervais, le 14 février 2006*

Salut Frédéric !

Merci beaucoup pour les CD que tu m'as envoyés. Tu as vraiment bien choisi puisqu'il s'agit de mes deux chanteurs préférés: je n'arrête pas de les écouter!

Sinon, rien de nouveau ici. Je passe presque tout mon temps à préparer mes examens qui commencent dans quinze jours. J'espère que je les réussirai tous, mais j'ai le trac pour mon examen de maths: c'est la matière que j'aime le moins.

Maman m'a dit que tu pars en Crète avec ta famille la semaine prochaine. Je te souhaite de très bonnes vacances, et je suis sûr que tu reviendras tout bronzé.

À bientôt!

Maxime

Writing a personal letter

Other ways of starting a personal letter	Other ways of ending a personal letter
Chers Jean et Sylvie	*Affectueusement*
Chère tante Laure	*Je t'embrasse*
Mon cher Laurent	*Grosses bises* (informal)

Some useful phrases

Je te remercie de ta lettre.	Thank you for your letter.
J'ai été très content d'avoir de tes nouvelles.	It was great to hear from you.
Je suis désolé de ne pas vous avoir répondu plus vite.	I'm sorry I didn't reply sooner.
Transmettez mes amitiés à Sophie.	Give my regards to Sophie.
Dis bonjour à Martin de ma part.	Say hello to Martin for me.
Maman t'embrasse.	Mum sends her love.

Writing a formal letter

Jeanne Judon ← *Your own name and address*
89, bd des Tertres
75008 Paris

                                Hôtel Renoir

Name and address of the person/company you are writing to → 15, av. Jean Médecin
                                06000 Nice

Paris, le 2 juin 2006 ← *Town/city you are writing from, and the date*

Madame ou Monsieur,

Suite à notre conversation téléphonique de ce matin, je vous écris afin de confirmer ma réservation pour une chambre avec salle de bains pour deux nuits du mercredi 1er au jeudi 2 juillet 2007 inclus.

Comme convenu, veuillez trouver ci-joint un chèque de 30€ correspondant au montant des arrhes.

Je vous prie de croire, Madame, Monsieur, à l'assurance de mes sentiments distingués.

Jeanne Judon

20

Writing a formal letter

Other ways of starting a formal letter	Other ways of ending a formal letter
Monsieur le Directeur (or le Maire etc) *Madame le Directeur* *Messieurs* *Madame* *Cher Monsieur* *Chère Madame*	*Veuillez accepter, [...]*, l'expression de mes sentiments distingués.* *Fill in the brackets with the words you used to start your letter: *Messieurs, chère Madame* etc.

Some useful phrases

Je vous serais reconnaissant(e) de ...	I would be grateful if you would ...
Je vous prie de ...	Please ...
Nous vous remercions de votre lettre.	Thank you for your letter.
Dans l'attente de votre réponse ...	I look forward to hearing from you ...
Je vous remercie dès à présent de ...	Thank you in advance for ...

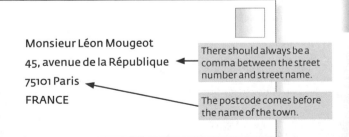

Monsieur Léon Mougeot
45, avenue de la République
75101 Paris
FRANCE

There should always be a comma between the street number and street name.

The postcode comes before the name of the town.

21

Making a call

Asking for information

Quel est l'indicatif de Bordeaux?

Comment fait-on pour avoir une ligne
  extérieure?

Pouvez-vous me donner le numéro du poste
  de M Durand?

What's the code for Bordeaux?

How do I get an outside line?

Could you give me the extension
  number for Mr Durand?

When your number answers

Bonjour! J'aimerais parler à Valérie.

Pourriez-vous me passer le docteur
  Leduc, s'il vous plaît?

Pourriez-vous lui demander de me rappeler,
  s'il vous plaît?

Je rappellerai dans une demi-heure.

Je peux laisser un message, s'il vous plaît?

Hello! Could I speak to Valérie,
  please?

Could you put me through to
  Dr Leduc, please?

Would you ask him/her to call me
  back, please?

I'll call back in half an hour.

Could I leave a message, please?

When you answer the telephone

Allô! C'est Marc à l'appareil.

C'est moi.

Qui est à l'appareil?

Hello! It's Marc speaking.

Speaking.

Who's speaking?

What you may hear

C'est de la part de qui?

Je vous le/la passe.

Ne quittez pas.

Ça ne répond pas.

Voulez-vous laisser un message?

Who shall I say is calling?

I'm putting you through.

Please hold.

There's no reply.

Would you like to leave a message?

Making a call

you have a problem

suis désolé, j'ai dû faire un faux numéro.	I'm sorry, I must have dialled the wrong number.
a ligne est très mauvaise.	This is a very bad line.
a coupe.	You're breaking up.
a batterie est presque à plat.	My battery's low.
ne t'entends plus.	I can't hear you.

Saying your phone number

To tell someone your phone number in French, you divide the number up into pairs instead of saying each digit separately. For example:

01 40 32 37 12

zéro-un / quarante / trente-deux / trente-sept / douze

If there's one extra number, you say that first:

0 26 23 84 47 46

zéro / vingt-six / vingt-trois / quatre-vingt-quatre / quarante-sept / quarante-six

French phrases and sayings

In French, as in many languages, people use vivid expressions based on images from their experience of real life. We've grouped the common expressions below according to the type of image they use. For fun, we have given you the word-for-word translation as well as the true English equivalent.

Fruit and vegetables

Ce ne sont pas mes oignons! → This is none of my business!
word for word: *these aren't my onions*

C'est la fin des haricots. → It's the last straw.
word for word: *it's the end of beans*

être haut comme trois pommes → to be knee-high to a grasshopper
word for word: *to be high as three apples*

tomber dans les pommes → to faint
word for word: *to fall into the apples*

Animals and Insects

donner sa langue au chat → to give in or up (*when guessing*)
word for word: *to give one's tongue to the cat*

appeler un chat un chat → to call a spade a spade
word for word: *to call a cat a cat*

quand les poules auront des dents → pigs might fly
word for word: *when hens have teeth*

passer du coq à l'âne → to jump from one subject to another
word for word: *to go from the cockerel to the donkey*

avoir un chat dans la gorge → to have a frog in one's throat
word for word: *to have a cat in one's throat*

French phrases and sayings

The weather

Ce n'est pas la mer à boire. → It's not the end of the world.

    word for word: *it's not like having to drink the sea*

Je ne suis pas tombé de la dernière pluie. → I wasn't born yesterday.

    word for word: *I didn't come down with the last shower of rain*

passer entre les gouttes → to come through without a scratch

    word for word: *to run between the raindrops*

pleuvoir des cordes → to be bucketing down

    word for word: *to be raining ropes*

Ça ne me fait ni chaud ni froid. → It doesn't make any difference to me.

    word for word: *it makes me neither hot nor cold*

Parts of the body

avoir une dent contre quelqu'un → to have a grudge against somebody

    word for word: *to have a tooth against somebody*

Il n'a pas la langue dans sa poche. → He's never at a loss for words.

    word for word: *he doesn't keep his tongue in his pocket*

avoir un poil dans la main → to be bone idle

    word for word: *to have a hair growing on one's palm*

gagner les doigts dans le nez → to win hands down

    word for word: *to win with one's fingers up one's nose*

French phrases and sayings

Clothes

changer d'avis comme de chemise → to be always changing one's mind

word for word: *to change one's mind as often as one's shirt*

trouver chaussure à son pied → to find a suitable match

word for word: *to find a shoe for one's foot*

Lâche-moi la chemise! or **Lâche-moi les baskets!** → Get off my back!

word for word: *let go of my shirt, let go of my trainers*

C'est bonnet blanc et blanc bonnet. → It's six of one and half a dozen of the other.

word for word: *it's white hat and hat white*

Colours

voir tout en rose → to see life through rose-tinted spectacles

word for word: *to see everything in pink*

avoir une peur bleue de quelque chose → to be scared stiff of something

word for word: *to have a blue fear of something*

regarder qn dans le blanc des yeux → to look somebody straight in the eye

word for word: *to look into the whites of somebody's eyes*

Some common translation difficulties

On the following pages we have shown some of the translation difficulties that you are most likely to come across. We hope that the tips we have given will help you to avoid these common pitfalls when writing and speaking French.

Tu or *vous*?

In French the word for 'you' depends on who you are talking to:

- To a person you know well, use **tu**:

    Will **you** lend me this CD?   →   *Tu me prêtes ce CD?*

- To a person you do not know so well, use **vous**:

    Have **you** met my wife?   →   *Vous connaissez ma femme?*

To more than one person, whether you know them well or not, use **vous**:

    Do **you** understand, children?   →   *Vous comprenez, les enfants?*

Getting friendly

When you get to know someone, they may ask you:

On se tutoie?   →   Shall we use 'tu' to each other?

On is the usual way of saying 'we' in conversation.

On est allé voir la Tour Eiffel.   →   We went to see the Eiffel Tower.

Some common translation difficulties

Showing possession

In English -**'s** is a common way of showing who or what something belongs to. In French you have to use *de*:

my brother**'s** car	➔	*la voiture **de** mon frère*
the children**'s** bedroom	➔	*la chambre **des** enfants*

Singular versus plural

A word that is singular in English may be plural in French, and vice versa. Check in the dictionary if you are not sure:

Singular:		*Plural:*
luggage	➔	***les** bagage**s***
Plural:		*Singular:*
my trouser**s**	➔	***mon** pantalon*

'There is' and 'there are'

In French these are both translated by *il y a*:

There is someone at the door.	➔	*il y a quelqu'un à la porte.*
There are five books on the table.	➔	*il y a cinq livres sur la table.*

Some common translation difficulties

Using *en*

When the word *en* is used with numbers, it is often not translated in English but it can <u>never</u> be missed out in French:

I want **two (of them)**.	→	*J'**en** veux **deux**.*
Have you got a dictionary? – Yes, I've got **one**.	→	*Tu as un dictionnaire? – Oui, j'**en** ai **un**.*

Translating 'to'

'To' is generally translated by *à*, but remember:

• When you are talking about the time, use *moins*:

five **to** ten	→	*dix heures **moins** cinq*

• In front of verbs, it is shown by the verb ending:

to eat	→	*mang**er***
to leave	→	*part**ir***
to wait	→	*attend**re***

• When you mean 'in order to', use *pour*:

He's going into town **(in order) to** buy a present.	→	*Il va en ville **pour** acheter un cadeau.*

Using *ne … pas* and other negatives

You often find the verb 'do' in English negatives, but *faire* is never used like this. You use set word pairs instead:

English negative with 'do':	French negative word pair:
I do**n't** smoke.	→ *Je **ne** fume **pas**.*
Do**n't** change **anything**.	→ ***Ne** changez **rien**.*

Some common translation difficulties

Translating 'to be'

'To be' usually corresponds to être, but remember:

• In phrases describing how you feel, use **avoir**:

to be warm/cold	→	**avoir** chaud/froid
to be hungry/thirsty	→	**avoir** faim/soif
to be afraid	→	**avoir** peur

• To describe the weather, use **faire**:

It**'s** lovely weather today.	→	Il **fait** beau aujourd'hui.

• To say your age, use **avoir**:

I**'m** fifteen.	→	J'**ai** quinze ans.

• To talk about your health, use **aller**:

I**'m** very well, thank you.	→	Je **vais** très bien, merci.

Translating verbs

Many English verbs can be followed by a preposition or adverb such as 'on' or 'back' – 'to go on', 'to give back'. These additions often give the verb a new meaning. There is no similar way of doing this in French – you just use a different word, for example:

Verb (+ preposition/adverb):		Translation:
to go	→	aller
to go on	→	continuer
to give	→	donner
to give back	→	rendre

Some common translation difficulties

Sentences that contain a verb and preposition in English might not contain a preposition in French, and vice versa. The dictionary can help you with these. For example:

- Verb + preposition:

    to pay **for** something   →   *payer quelque chose*

    Verb without preposition:

- Verb without preposition:

    to change something   →   *changer **de** quelque chose*

    Verb + preposition:

A [eɪ] *n* (*Mus*) la *m*

 KEYWORD

a [eɪ, ə] (*before vowel or silent h* **an**) *indef art* **1** un(e); **a book** un livre; **an apple** une pomme; **she's a doctor** elle est médecin
2 (*instead of the number "one"*) un(e); **a year ago** il y a un an; **a hundred/thousand** *etc* **pounds** cent/mille *etc* livres
3 (*in expressing ratios, prices etc*): **3 a day/week** 3 par jour/semaine; **10 km an hour** 10 km à l'heure; **£5 a person** 5£ par personne; **30p a kilo** 30p le kilo

A2 *n* (*BRIT: Scol*) deuxième partie de l'examen équivalent au baccalauréat
A.A. *n abbr* (*BRIT: = Automobile Association*) ≈ ACF *m*; (= *Alcoholics Anonymous*) AA
A.A.A. *n abbr* (= *American Automobile Association*) ≈ ACF *m*

aback [ə'bæk] *adv*: **to be taken ~** être décontenancé(e)
abandon [ə'bændən] *vt* abandonner
abattoir ['æbətwɑːʳ] *n* (*BRIT*) abattoir *m*
abbey ['æbɪ] *n* abbaye *f*
abbreviation [əbriːvɪ'eɪʃən] *n* abréviation *f*
abdomen ['æbdəmən] *n* abdomen *m*
abduct [æb'dʌkt] *vt* enlever
abide [ə'baɪd] *vt* souffrir, supporter; **I can't ~ it/him** je ne le supporte pas; **abide by** *vt fus* observer, respecter
ability [ə'bɪlɪtɪ] *n* compétence *f*; capacité *f*; (*skill*) talent *m*
able ['eɪbl] *adj* compétent(e); **to be ~ to do sth** pouvoir faire qch, être capable de faire qch
abnormal [æb'nɔːməl] *adj* anormal(e)
aboard [ə'bɔːd] *adv* à bord ▷ *prep* à bord de; (*train*) dans
abolish [ə'bɔlɪʃ] *vt* abolir
abolition [æbə'lɪʃən] *n* abolition *f*
abort [ə'bɔːt] *vt* (*Med*) faire avorter; (*Comput, fig*) abandonner; **abortion** [ə'bɔːʃən] *n* avortement *m*; **to have an abortion** se faire avorter

 KEYWORD

about [ə'baut] *adv* **1** (*approximately*) environ, à peu près; **about a hundred/thousand** *etc* environ cent/mille *etc*, une centaine (de)/un millier (de) *etc*; **it takes about 10 hours** ça prend environ *or* à peu près 10 heures; **at about 2 o'clock** vers 2 heures; **I've just about finished** j'ai presque fini
2 (*referring to place*) çà et là, de-ci de-là; **to run about** courir çà et là; **to walk about** se promener, aller et venir; **they left all their things lying about** ils ont laissé traîner toutes leurs affaires
3: **to be about to do sth** être sur le point de faire qch
▷ *prep* **1** (*relating to*) au sujet de, à propos de; **a book about London** un livre sur Londres; **what is it about?** de

quoi s'agit-il?; **we talked about it** nous en avons parlé; **what** or **how about doing this?** et si nous faisions ceci? **2** (*referring to place*) dans; **to walk about the town** se promener dans la ville

above [ə'bʌv] *adv* au-dessus ▷ *prep* au-dessus de; (*more than*) plus de; **mentioned ~** mentionné ci-dessus; **~ all** par-dessus tout, surtout

abroad [ə'brɔːd] *adv* à l'étranger

abrupt [ə'brʌpt] *adj* (*steep, blunt*) abrupt(e); (*sudden, gruff*) brusque

abscess ['æbsɛs] *n* abcès *m*

absence ['æbsəns] *n* absence *f*

absent ['æbsənt] *adj* absent(e); **absent-minded** *adj* distrait(e)

absolute ['æbsəluːt] *adj* absolu(e); **absolutely** [æbsə'luːtlɪ] *adv* absolument

absorb [əb'zɔːb] *vt* absorber; **to be ~ed in a book** être plongé(e) dans un livre; **absorbent cotton** *n* (*US*) coton *m* hydrophile; **absorbing** *adj* absorbant(e); (*book, film etc*) captivant(e)

abstain [əb'steɪn] *vi*: **to ~ (from)** s'abstenir (de)

abstract ['æbstrækt] *adj* abstrait(e)

absurd [əb'səːd] *adj* absurde

abundance [ə'bʌndəns] *n* abondance *f*

abundant [ə'bʌndənt] *adj* abondant(e)

abuse *n* [ə'bjuːs] (*insults*) insultes *fpl*, injures *fpl*; (*ill-treatment*) mauvais traitements *mpl*; (*of power etc*) abus *m* ▷ *vt* [ə'bjuːz] (*insult*) insulter; (*ill-treat*) malmener; (*power etc*) abuser de; **abusive** *adj* grossier(-ière), injurieux(-euse)

abysmal [ə'bɪzməl] *adj* exécrable; (*ignorance etc*) sans bornes

academic [ækə'dɛmɪk] *adj* universitaire; (*person: scholarly*) intellectuel(-le); (*pej: issue*) oiseux(-euse), purement théorique ▷ *n* universitaire *m/f*; **academic year** *n*

(*University*) année *f* universitaire; (*Scol*) année scolaire

academy [ə'kædəmɪ] *n* (*learned body*) académie *f*; (*school*) collège *m*; **~ of music** conservatoire *m*

accelerate [æk'sɛləreɪt] *vt, vi* accélérer; **acceleration** [æksɛlə'reɪʃən] *n* accélération *f*; **accelerator** *n* (*BRIT*) accélérateur *m*

accent ['æksɛnt] *n* accent *m*

accept [ək'sɛpt] *vt* accepter; **acceptable** *adj* acceptable; **acceptance** *n* acceptation *f*

access ['æksɛs] *n* accès *m*; **to have ~ to** (*information, library etc*) avoir accès à, pouvoir utiliser or consulter; (*person*) avoir accès auprès de; **accessible** [æk'sɛsəbl] *adj* accessible

accessory [æk'sɛsərɪ] *n* accessoire *m*; **~ to** (*Law*) accessoire à

accident ['æksɪdənt] *n* accident *m*; (*chance*) hasard *m*; **I've had an ~** j'ai eu un accident; **by ~** (*by chance*) par hasard; (*not deliberately*) accidentellement; **accidental** [æksɪ'dɛntl] *adj* accidentel(le); **accidentally** [æksɪ'dɛntəlɪ] *adv* accidentellement; **Accident and Emergency Department** *n* (*BRIT*) service *m* des urgences; **accident insurance** *n* assurance *f* accident

acclaim [ə'kleɪm] *vt* acclamer ▷ *n* acclamations *fpl*

accommodate [ə'kɔmədeɪt] *vt* loger, recevoir; (*oblige, help*) obliger; (*car etc*) contenir

accommodation (*US* **accommodations**) [əkɔmə'deɪʃən(z)] *n(pl)* logement *m*

accompaniment [ə'kʌmpənɪmənt] *n* accompagnement *m*

accompany [ə'kʌmpənɪ] *vt* accompagner

accomplice [ə'kʌmplɪs] *n* complice *m/f*

accomplish [ə'kʌmplɪʃ] *vt* accomplir; **accomplishment** *n* (*skill: gen pl*) talent *m*; (*completion*) accomplissement *m*;

(*achievement*) réussite *f*

accord [ə'kɔːd] *n* accord *m* ▷ *vt* accorder; **of his own ~** de son plein gré; **accordance** *n*: **in accordance with** conformément à; **according**: **according to** *prep* selon; **accordingly** *adv* (*appropriately*) en conséquence; (*as a result*) par conséquent

account [ə'kaunt] *n* (*Comm*) compte *m*; (*report*) compte rendu, récit *m*; **accounts** *npl* (*Comm: records*) comptabilité *f*, comptes; **of no ~** sans importance; **on ~** en acompte; **to buy sth on ~** acheter qch à crédit; **on no ~** en aucun cas; **on ~ of** à cause de; **to take into ~**, **take ~ of** tenir compte de; **account for** *vt fus* (*explain*) expliquer, rendre compte de; (*represent*) représenter; **accountable** *adj*: **accountable (to)** responsable (devant); **accountant** *n* comptable *m/f*; **account number** *n* numéro *m* de compte

accumulate [ə'kjuːmjuleɪt] *vt* accumuler, amasser ▷ *vi* s'accumuler, s'amasser

accuracy ['ækjurəsɪ] *n* exactitude *f*, précision *f*

accurate ['ækjurɪt] *adj* exact(e), précis(e); (*device*) précis; **accurately** *adv* avec précision

accusation [ækju'zeɪʃən] *n* accusation *f*

accuse [ə'kjuːz] *vt*: **to ~ sb (of sth)** accuser qn (de qch); **accused** *n* (*Law*) accusé(e)

accustomed [ə'kʌstəmd] *adj*: **~ to** habitué(e) *or* accoutumé(e) à

ace [eɪs] *n* as *m*

ache [eɪk] *n* mal *m*, douleur *f* ▷ *vi* (*be sore*) faire mal, être douloureux(-euse); **my head ~s** j'ai mal à la tête

achieve [ə'tʃiːv] *vt* (*aim*) atteindre; (*victory, success*) remporter, obtenir; **achievement** *n* exploit *m*, réussite *f*; (*of aims*) réalisation *f*

acid ['æsɪd] *adj, n* acide (*m*)

acknowledge [ək'nɔlɪdʒ] *vt* (*also: ~*

receipt of) accuser réception de; (*fact*) reconnaître; **acknowledgement** *n* (*of letter*) accusé *m* de réception

acne ['æknɪ] *n* acné *m*

acorn ['eɪkɔːn] *n* gland *m*

acoustic [ə'kuːstɪk] *adj* acoustique

acquaintance [ə'kweɪntəns] *n* connaissance *f*

acquire [ə'kwaɪə'] *vt* acquérir; **acquisition** [ækwɪ'zɪʃən] *n* acquisition *f*

acquit [ə'kwɪt] *vt* acquitter; **to ~ o.s. well** s'en tirer très honorablement

acre ['eɪkə'] *n* acre *f* (= 4047 m²)

acronym ['ækrənɪm] *n* acronyme *m*

across [ə'krɔs] *prep* (*on the other side*) de l'autre côté de; (*crosswise*) en travers de ▷ *adv* de l'autre côté; en travers; **to run/swim ~** traverser en courant/à la nage; **~ from** en face de

acrylic [ə'krɪlɪk] *adj, n* acrylique (*m*)

act [ækt] *n* acte *m*, action *f*; (*Theat: part of play*) acte; (: *of performer*) numéro *m*; (*Law*) loi *f* ▷ *vi* aller; (*Theat*) jouer; (*pretend*) jouer la comédie ▷ *vt* (*role*) jouer, tenir; **to catch sb in the ~** prendre qn sur le fait *or* en flagrant délit; **to ~ as** servir de; **act up** (*inf*) ▷ *vi* (*person*) se conduire mal; (*knee, back, injury*) jouer des tours; (*machine*) être capricieux(-ieuse); **acting** *adj* suppléant(e), par intérim ▷ *n* (*activity*): **to do some acting** faire du théâtre (*or* du cinéma)

action ['ækʃən] *n* action *f*; (*Mil*) combat(s) *m(pl)*; (*Law*) procès *m*, action en justice; **out of ~** hors de combat; (*machine etc*) hors d'usage; **to take ~** agir, prendre des mesures; **action replay** *n* (*BRIT TV*) ralenti *m*

activate ['æktɪveɪt] *vt* (*mechanism*) actionner, faire fonctionner

active ['æktɪv] *adj* actif(-ive); (*volcano*) en activité; **actively** *adv* activement; (*discourage*) vivement

activist ['æktɪvɪst] *n* activiste *m/f*

activity [æk'tɪvɪtɪ] *n* activité *f*; **activity holiday** *n* vacances actives

actor ['æktər] n acteur m

actress ['æktrɪs] n actrice f

actual ['æktjuəl] adj réel(le), véritable; (emphatic use) lui-même (elle-même).

▌Be careful not to translate **actual** by the French word **actuel**.

actually ['æktjuəlɪ] adv réellement, véritablement; (in fact) en fait

▌Be careful not to translate **actually** by the French word **actuellement**.

acupuncture ['ækjupʌŋktʃər] n acuponcture f

acute [ə'kjuːt] adj aigu(ë); (mind, observer) pénétrant(e)

A.D. adv abbr (= Anno Domini) ap. J.-C.

ad [æd] n abbr = **advertisement**

adamant ['ædəmənt] adj inflexible

adapt [ə'dæpt] vt adapter ▷ vi: **to ~ (to)** s'adapter (à); **adapter, adaptor** n (Elec) adaptateur m; (for several plugs) prise f multiple

add [æd] vt ajouter; (figures: also: **to ~ up**) additionner ▷ vi (fig): **it doesn't ~ up** cela ne rime à rien; **add up to** vt fus (Math) s'élever à; (fig: mean) signifier

addict ['ædɪkt] n toxicomane m/f; (fig) fanatique m/f; **addicted** [ə'dɪktɪd] adj: **to be addicted to** (drink, drugs) être adonné(e) à; (fig: football etc) être un(e) fanatique de; **addiction** [ə'dɪkʃən] n (Med) dépendance f; **addictive** [ə'dɪktɪv] adj qui crée une dépendance

addition [ə'dɪʃən] n (adding up) addition f; (thing added) ajout m; **in ~** de plus, de surcroît; **in ~ to** en plus de; **additional** adj supplémentaire

additive ['ædɪtɪv] n additif m

address [ə'drɛs] n adresse f; (talk) discours m, allocution f ▷ vt adresser; (speak to) s'adresser à; **my ~ is ...** mon adresse, c'est ...; **address book** n carnet m d'adresses

adequate ['ædɪkwɪt] adj (enough) suffisant(e); (satisfactory) satisfaisant(e)

adhere [əd'hɪər] vi: **to ~ to** adhérer à; (fig: rule, decision) se tenir à

adhesive [əd'hiːzɪv] n adhésif m;

adhesive tape n (BRIT) ruban m adhésif; (US Med) sparadrap m

adjacent [ə'dʒeɪsənt] adj adjacent(e), contigu(ë); **~ to** adjacent à

adjective ['ædʒɛktɪv] n adjectif m

adjoining [ə'dʒɔɪnɪŋ] adj voisin(e), adjacent(e), attenant(e)

adjourn [ə'dʒəːn] vt ajourner ▷ vi suspendre la séance; lever séance; clore la session

adjust [ə'dʒʌst] vt (machine) ajuster, régler; (prices, wages) rajuster ▷ vi: **to ~ (to)** s'adapter (à); **adjustable** adj réglable; **adjustment** n (of machine) ajustage m, réglage m; (of prices, wages) rajustement m; (of person) adaptation f

administer [əd'mɪnɪstər] vt administrer; **administration** [ədmɪnɪs'treɪʃən] n (management) administration f; (government) gouvernement m; **administrative** [əd'mɪnɪstrətɪv] adj administratif(-ive)

administrator [əd'mɪnɪstreɪtər] n administrateur(-trice)

admiral ['ædmərəl] n amiral m

admiration [ædmə'reɪʃən] n admiration f

admire [əd'maɪər] vt admirer; **admirer** n (fan) admirateur(-trice)

admission [əd'mɪʃən] n admission f; (to exhibition, night club etc) entrée f; (confession) aveu m

admit [əd'mɪt] vt laisser entrer; admettre; (agree) reconnaître, admettre; (crime) reconnaître avoir commis; **"children not ~ted"** "entrée interdite aux enfants"; **admit to** vt fus reconnaître, avouer; **admittance** n admission f, (droit m d')entrée f; **admittedly** adv il faut en convenir

adolescent [ædəu'lɛsnt] adj, n adolescent(e)

adopt [ə'dɔpt] vt adopter; **adopted** adj adoptif(-ive), adopté(e); **adoption** [ə'dɔpʃən] n adoption f

adore [ə'dɔːr] vt adorer

adorn [ə'dɔːn] vt orner

Adriatic (Sea) [eɪdrɪ'ætɪk-] n, adj:
the Adriatic (Sea) la mer Adriatique,
l'Adriatique f

drift [ə'drɪft] adv à la dérive

adult ['ædʌlt] n adulte m/f ▷ adj
(grown-up) adulte; (for adults) pour
adultes; **adult education** n éducation
f des adultes

adultery [ə'dʌltərɪ] n adultère m

advance [əd'vɑːns] n avance f ▷ vt
avancer ▷ vi s'avancer; **in ~** en avance,
d'avance; **to make ~s to sb** (gen) faire
des propositions à qn; (amorously) faire
des avances à qn; **~ booking** location f;
~ notice, ~ warning préavis m; (verbal)
avertissement m; **do I need to book in
~?** est-ce qu'il faut réserver à l'avance?;
advanced adj avancé(e); (Scol: studies)
supérieur(e)

advantage [əd'vɑːntɪdʒ] n (also Tennis)
avantage m; **to take ~ of** (person)
exploiter; (opportunity) profiter de

advent ['ædvənt] n avènement m,
venue f; **A~** (Rel) avent m

adventure [əd'vɛntʃəʳ] n aventure f;
adventurous [əd'vɛntʃərəs] adj
aventureux(-euse)

adverb ['ædvəːb] n adverbe m

adversary ['ædvəsərɪ] n adversaire
m/f

adverse ['ædvəːs] adj adverse; (effect)
négatif(-ive); (weather, publicity)
mauvais(e); (wind) contraire

advert ['ædvəːt] n abbr (BRIT)
= **advertisement**

advertise ['ædvətaɪz] vi faire de la
publicité or de la réclame; (in classified
ads etc) mettre une annonce ▷ vt faire
de la publicité or de la réclame pour; (in
classified ads etc) mettre une annonce
pour vendre; **to ~ for** (staff) recruter
par (voie d')annonce; **advertisement**
[əd'vəːtɪsmənt] n (Comm) publicité
f, réclame f; (in classified ads etc)
annonce f; **advertiser** n annonceur m;
advertising n publicité f

advice [əd'vaɪs] n conseils mpl;
(notification) avis m; **a piece of ~** un

conseil; **to take legal ~** consulter
un avocat

advisable [əd'vaɪzəbl] adj
recommandable, indiqué(e)

advise [əd'vaɪz] vt conseiller; **to ~ sb
of sth** aviser or informer qn de qch; **to
~ against sth/doing sth** déconseiller
qch/conseiller de ne pas faire qch;
adviser, advisor n conseiller(-ère);
advisory adj consultatif(-ive)

advocate n ['ædvəkɪt] (lawyer)
avocat (plaidant); (upholder) défenseur
m, avocat(e) ▷ vt ['ædvəkeɪt]
recommander, prôner; **to be an ~ of**
être partisan(e) de

Aegean [iː'dʒiːən] n, adj: **the ~ (Sea)** la
mer Égée, l'Égée f

aerial ['ɛərɪəl] n antenne f ▷ adj
aérien(ne)

aerobics [ɛə'rəubɪks] n aérobic m

aeroplane ['ɛərəpleɪn] n (BRIT) avion m

aerosol ['ɛərəsɔl] n aérosol m

affair [ə'fɛəʳ] n affaire f; (also: **love ~**)
liaison f; aventure f

affect [ə'fɛkt] vt affecter; (subj: disease)
atteindre; **affected** adj affecté(e);
affection n affection f; **affectionate**
adj affectueux(-euse)

afflict [ə'flɪkt] vt affliger

affluent ['æfluənt] adj (person, family,
surroundings) aisé(e), riche; **the ~
society** la société d'abondance

afford [ə'fɔːd] vt (behaviour) se
permettre; (provide) fournir, procurer;
can we ~ a car? avons-nous de quoi
acheter or les moyens d'acheter une
voiture?; **affordable** adj abordable

Afghanistan [æf'gænɪstæn] n
Afghanistan m

afraid [ə'freɪd] adj effrayé(e); **to be ~
of or to** avoir peur de; **I am ~ that** je
crains que + sub; **I'm ~ so/not** oui/non,
malheureusement

Africa ['æfrɪkə] n Afrique f; **African** adj
africain(e) ▷ n Africain(e); **African-
American** adj afro-américain(e) ▷ n
Afro-Américain(e)

after ['ɑːftəʳ] prep, adv après ▷ conj

après que; **it's quarter ~ two** (US) il est deux heures et quart; **~ having done/~ he left** après avoir fait/ après son départ; **to name sb ~ sb** donner à qn le nom de qn; **to ask ~ sb** demander des nouvelles de qn; **what/who are you ~?** que/qui cherchez-vous?; **~ you!** après vous!; **~ all** après tout; **after-effects** npl (of disaster, radiation, drink etc) répercussions fpl; (of illness) séquelles fpl, suites fpl; **aftermath** n conséquences fpl; **afternoon** n après-midi m or f; **after-shave (lotion)** n lotion f après-rasage; **aftersun (lotion/cream)** n après-soleil m inv; **afterwards** (US **afterward**) adv après

again [əˈgɛn] adv de nouveau, encore (une fois); **to do sth ~** refaire qch; **~ and ~** à plusieurs reprises

against [əˈgɛnst] prep contre; (compared to) par rapport à

age [eɪdʒ] n âge m ▷ vt, vi vieillir; **he is 20 years of ~** il a 20 ans; **to come of ~** atteindre sa majorité; **it's been ~s since I saw you** ça fait une éternité que je ne t'ai pas vu; **~d 10** âgé(e) de 10 ans; **age group** n tranche f d'âge; **age limit** n limite f d'âge

agency [ˈeɪdʒənsɪ] n agence f

agenda [əˈdʒɛndə] n ordre m du jour

> Be careful not to translate agenda by the French word agenda.

agent [ˈeɪdʒənt] n agent m; (firm) concessionnaire m

aggravate [ˈægrəveɪt] vt (situation) aggraver; (annoy) exaspérer, agacer

aggression [əˈgrɛʃən] n agression f

aggressive [əˈgrɛsɪv] adj agressif(-ive)

agile [ˈædʒaɪl] adj agile

agitated [ˈædʒɪteɪtɪd] adj inquiet(-ète)

AGM n abbr (= annual general meeting) AG f

ago [əˈgəu] adv: **2 days ~** il y a 2 jours; **not long ~** il n'y a pas longtemps; **how long ~?** il y a combien de temps (de cela)?

agony [ˈægənɪ] n (pain) douleur f atroce; (distress) angoisse f; **to be in ~**

souffrir le martyre

agree [əˈgriː] vt (price) convenir de ▷ vi: **to ~ with** (person) être d'accord avec; (statements etc) concorder avec; (Ling) s'accorder avec; **to ~ to do** accepter de or consentir à faire; **to ~ to sth** consentir à qch; **to ~ that** (admit) convenir or reconnaître que; **garlic doesn't ~ with me** je ne supporte pas l'ail; **agreeable** adj (pleasant) agréable; (willing) consentant(e), d'accord; **agreed** adj (time, place) convenu(e); **agreement** n accord m; **in agreement** d'accord

agricultural [ægrɪˈkʌltʃərəl] adj agricole

agriculture [ˈægrɪkʌltʃər] n agriculture f

ahead [əˈhɛd] adv en avant; devant; **go right** or **straight ~** (direction) allez tout droit; **go ~!** (permission) allez-y!; **~ of** devant; (fig: schedule etc) en avance sur; **~ of time** en avance

aid [eɪd] n aide f; (device) appareil m ▷ vt aider; **in ~ of** en faveur de

aide [eɪd] n (person) assistant(e)

AIDS [eɪdz] n abbr (= acquired immune (or immuno-)deficiency syndrome) SIDA m

ailing [ˈeɪlɪŋ] adj (person) souffreteux(euse); (economy) malade

ailment [ˈeɪlmənt] n affection f

aim [eɪm] vt: **to ~ sth (at)** (gun, camera) braquer or pointer qch (sur); (missile) lancer qch (à or contre or en direction de); (remark, blow) destiner or adresser qch (à) ▷ vi (also: **to take ~**) viser ▷ n (objective) but m; (skill): **his ~ is bad** il vise mal; **to ~ at** viser; (fig) viser (à); **to ~ to do** avoir l'intention de faire

ain't [eɪnt] (inf) = **am not**; **aren't**; **isn't**

air [ɛər] n air m ▷ vt aérer; (idea, grievance, views) mettre sur le tapis ▷ cpd (currents, attack etc) aérien(ne); **to throw sth into the ~** (ball etc) jeter qch en l'air; **by ~** par avion; **to be on the ~** (Radio, TV: programme) être diffusé(e); (: station) émettre; **airbag** n airbag m; **airbed** n (BRIT) matelas *m* pneumatique; **airborne** *adj* (*plane*) en vol; **as soon as the plane was airborne** dès que l'avion eut décollé; **air-conditioned** *adj* climatisé(e), à air conditionné; **air conditioning** *n* climatisation *f*; **aircraft** *n inv* avion *m*; **airfield** *n* terrain *m* d'aviation; **Air Force** *n* Armée *f* de l'air; **air hostess** *n* (*BRIT*) hôtesse *f* de l'air; **airing cupboard** *n* (*BRIT*) placard qui contient la chaudière et dans lequel on met le linge à sécher; **airlift** *n* pont aérien; **airline** *n* ligne aérienne, compagnie aérienne; **airliner** *n* avion *m* de ligne; **airmail** *n*: **by airmail** par avion; **airplane** *n* (*US*) avion *m*; **airport** *n* aéroport *m*; **air raid** *n* attaque aérienne; **airsick** *adj*: **to be airsick** avoir le mal de l'air; **airspace** *n* espace *m* aérien; **airstrip** *n* terrain *m* d'atterrissage; **air terminal** *n* aérogare *f*; **airtight** *adj* hermétique; **air-traffic controller** *n* aiguilleur *m* du ciel; **airy** *adj* bien aéré(e); (*manners*) dégagé(e)

isle [aɪl] *n* (*of church: central*) allée *f* centrale; (: *side*) nef latérale, bas-côté *m*; (*in theatre, supermarket*) allée; (*on plane*) couloir *m*; **aisle seat** *n* place *f* côté couloir

jar [əˈdʒɑːʳ] *adj* entrouvert(e)

la carte [ælæˈkɑːt] *adv* à la carte

larm [əˈlɑːm] *n* alarme *f* ▷ *vt* alarmer; **alarm call** *n* coup *m* de fil pour réveiller; **could I have an alarm call at 7 am, please?** pouvez-vous me réveiller à 7 heures, s'il vous plaît?; **alarm clock** *n* réveille-matin *m inv*, réveil *m*; **alarmed** *adj* (*frightened*) alarmé(e); (*protected by an alarm*) protégé(e) par un système d'alarme; **alarming** *adj* alarmant(e)

lbania [ælˈbeɪnɪə] *n* Albanie *f*

lbeit [ɔːlˈbiːɪt] *conj* bien que + *sub*, encore que + *sub*

lbum [ˈælbəm] *n* album *m*

cohol [ˈælkəhɒl] *n* alcool *m*; **alcohol-free** *adj* sans alcool; **alcoholic** [ælkəˈhɒlɪk] *adj, n* alcoolique (*m/f*)

alcove [ˈælkəʊv] *n* alcôve *f*

ale [eɪl] *n* bière *f*

alert [əˈlɜːt] *adj* alerte, vif (vive); (*watchful*) vigilant(e) ▷ *n* alerte *f* ▷ *vt* alerter; **on the ~** sur le qui-vive; (*Mil*) en état d'alerte

algebra [ˈældʒɪbrə] *n* algèbre *m*

Algeria [ælˈdʒɪərɪə] *n* Algérie *f*

Algerian [ælˈdʒɪərɪən] *adj* algérien(ne) ▷ *n* Algérien(ne)

Algiers [ælˈdʒɪəz] *n* Alger

alias [ˈeɪlɪəs] *adv* alias ▷ *n* faux nom, nom d'emprunt

alibi [ˈælɪbaɪ] *n* alibi *m*

alien [ˈeɪlɪən] *n* (*from abroad*) étranger(-ère); (*from outer space*) extraterrestre ▷ *adj*: **~ (to)** étranger(-ère) (à); **alienate** *vt* aliéner; (*subj: person*) s'aliéner

alight [əˈlaɪt] *adj* en feu ▷ *vi* mettre pied à terre; (*passenger*) descendre; (*bird*) se poser

align [əˈlaɪn] *vt* aligner

alike [əˈlaɪk] *adj* semblable, pareil(le) ▷ *adv* de même; **to look ~** se ressembler

alive [əˈlaɪv] *adj* vivant(e); (*active*) plein(e) de vie

O **KEYWORD**

all [ɔːl] *adj* (*singular*) tout(e); (*plural*) tous (toutes); **all day** toute la journée; **all night** toute la nuit; **all men** tous les hommes; **all five** tous les cinq; **all the books** tous les livres; **all his life** toute sa vie
▷ *pron* **1** tout; **I ate it all**, **I ate all of it** j'ai tout mangé; **all of us went** nous y sommes tous allés; **all of the boys went** tous les garçons y sont allés; **is that all?** c'est tout?; (*in shop*) ce sera tout?
2 (*in phrases*): **above all** surtout, par-dessus tout; **after all** après tout; **at all**: **not at all** (*in answer to question*) pas du tout; (*in answer to thanks*) je vous en prie!; **I'm not at all tired** je ne suis pas du tout fatigué(e); **anything at all will**

do n'importe quoi fera l'affaire; **all in all** tout bien considéré, en fin de compte ▷ adv: **all alone** tout(e) seul(e); **it's not as hard as all that** ce n'est pas si difficile que ça; **all the more/the better** d'autant plus/mieux; **the score is 2 all** le score est de 2 partout

Allah ['ælə] n Allah m

allegation [ælɪ'geɪʃən] n allégation f

alleged [ə'ledʒd] adj prétendu(e); **allegedly** adv à ce que l'on prétend, paraît-il

allegiance [ə'li:dʒəns] n fidélité f, obéissance f

allergic [ə'lə:dʒɪk] adj: **~ to** allergique à; **I'm ~ to penicillin** je suis allergique à la pénicilline

allergy ['ælədʒɪ] n allergie f

alleviate [ə'li:vɪeɪt] vt soulager, adoucir

alley ['ælɪ] n ruelle f

alliance [ə'laɪəns] n alliance f

allied ['ælaɪd] adj allié(e)

alligator ['ælɪgeɪtər] n alligator m

all-in ['ɔ:lɪn] adj, adv (BRIT: charge) tout compris

allocate ['æləkeɪt] vt (share out) répartir, distribuer; **to ~ sth to** (duties) assigner or attribuer qch à; (sum, time) allouer qch à

allot [ə'lɔt] vt (share out) répartir, distribuer; **to ~ sth to** (time) allouer qch à; (duties) assigner qch à

all-out ['ɔ:laut] adj (effort etc) total(e)

allow [ə'lau] vt (practice, behaviour) permettre, autoriser; (sum to spend etc) accorder, allouer; (sum, time estimated) compter, prévoir; (claim, goal) admettre; (concede): **to ~ that** convenir que; **to ~ sb to do** permettre à qn de faire, autoriser qn à faire; **he is ~ed to ...** on lui permet de ...; **allow for** vt fus tenir compte de; **allowance** n (money received) allocation f; (: from parent etc) subside m; (: for expenses) indemnité f; (US: pocket money) argent m

de poche; (Tax) somme f déductible du revenu imposable, abattement m; **to make allowances for** (person) essayer de comprendre; (thing) tenir compte de

all right adv (feel, work) bien; (as answer) d'accord

ally n ['ælaɪ] allié m ▷ vt [ə'laɪ]: **to ~ o.s. with** s'allier avec

almighty [ɔ:l'maɪtɪ] adj tout(e)-puissant(e); (tremendous) énorme

almond ['ɑ:mənd] n amande f

almost ['ɔ:lməust] adv presque

alone [ə'ləun] adj, adv seul(e); **to leave sb ~** laisser qn tranquille; **to leave sth ~** ne pas toucher à qch; **let ~ ...** sans parler de ...; encore moins ...

along [ə'lɔŋ] prep le long de ▷ adv: **is he coming ~ with us?** vient-il avec nous? **he was hopping/limping ~** il venait en avançait en sautillant/boitant; **~ with** avec, en plus de; (person) en compagnie de; **all ~** (all the time) depuis le début; **alongside** prep (along) le long de; (beside) à côté de ▷ adv bord à bord; côte à côte

aloof [ə'lu:f] adj distant(e) ▷ adv: **to stand ~** se tenir à l'écart or à distance

aloud [ə'laud] adv à haute voix

alphabet ['ælfəbɛt] n alphabet m

Alps [ælps] npl: **the ~** les Alpes fpl

already [ɔ:l'rɛdɪ] adv déjà

alright ['ɔ:l'raɪt] adv (BRIT) = **all right**

also ['ɔ:lsəu] adv aussi

altar ['ɔltər] n autel m

alter ['ɔltər] vt, vi changer; **alteration** [ɔltə'reɪʃən] n changement m, modification f; **alterations** npl (Sewing) retouches fpl; (Archit) modifications fpl

alternate adj [ɔl'tə:nɪt] alterné(e), alternant(e), alternatif(-ive); (US) = **alternative** ▷ vi ['ɔltə:neɪt] alterner; **to ~ with** alterner avec; **on ~ days** un jour sur deux, tous les deux jours

alternative [ɔl'tə:nətɪv] adj (solution, plan) autre, de remplacement; (lifestyle) parallèle ▷ n (choice) alternative f; (other possibility) autre possibilité f;

~ medicine médecine alternative, médecine douce; **alternatively** adv: **alternatively one could ...** une autre or l'autre solution serait de ...

although [ɔːlˈðəu] conj bien que + sub

altitude [ˈæltɪtjuːd] n altitude f

altogether [ɔːltəˈgɛðəˀ] adv entièrement, tout à fait; (on the whole) tout compte fait; (in all) en tout

aluminium [æljuˈmɪnɪəm] (BRIT **aluminum**) [əˈluːmɪnəm] (US) n aluminium m

always [ˈɔːlweɪz] adv toujours

Alzheimer's (disease) [ˈæltshaɪməz-] n maladie f d'Alzheimer

am [æm] vb see **be**

a.m. adv abbr (= ante meridiem) du matin

amalgamate [əˈmælgəmeɪt] vt, vi fusionner

amass [əˈmæs] vt amasser

amateur [ˈæmətəˀ] n amateur m

amaze [əˈmeɪz] vt stupéfier; **to be ~d (at)** être stupéfait(e) (de); **amazed** adj stupéfait(e); **amazement** n surprise f, étonnement m; **amazing** adj étonnant(e), incroyable; (bargain, offer) exceptionnel(le)

Amazon [ˈæməzən] n (Geo) Amazone f

ambassador [æmˈbæsədəˀ] n ambassadeur m

amber [ˈæmbəˀ] n ambre m; **at ~** (BRIT Aut) à l'orange

ambiguous [æmˈbɪgjuəs] adj ambigu(ë)

ambition [æmˈbɪʃən] n ambition f; **ambitious** [æmˈbɪʃəs] adj ambitieux(-euse)

ambulance [ˈæmbjuləns] n ambulance f; **call an ~!** appelez une ambulance!

ambush [ˈæmbuʃ] n embuscade f ▷ vt tendre une embuscade à

amen [ˈɑːmɛn] excl amen

amend [əˈmɛnd] vt (law) amender; (text) corriger; **to make ~s** réparer ses torts, faire amende honorable; **amendment** n (to law) amendement m; (to text) correction f

amenities [əˈmiːnɪtɪz] npl aménagements mpl, équipements mpl

America [əˈmɛrɪkə] n Amérique f; **American** adj américain(e) ▷ n Américain(e); **American football** n (BRIT) football m américain

amicable [ˈæmɪkəbl] adj amical(e); (Law) à l'amiable

amid(st) [əˈmɪd(st)] prep parmi, au milieu de

ammunition [æmjuˈnɪʃən] n munitions fpl

amnesty [ˈæmnɪstɪ] n amnistie f

among(st) [əˈmʌŋ(st)] prep parmi, entre

amount [əˈmaunt] n (sum of money) somme f; (total) montant m; (quantity) quantité f; nombre m ▷ vi: **to ~ to** (total) s'élever à; (be same as) équivaloir à, revenir à

amp(ère) [ˈæmp(ɛəˀ)] n ampère m

ample [ˈæmpl] adj ample, spacieux(-euse); (enough): **this is ~** c'est largement suffisant; **to have ~ time/room** avoir bien assez de temps/place

amplifier [ˈæmplɪfaɪəˀ] n amplificateur m

amputate [ˈæmpjuteɪt] vt amputer

Amtrak [ˈæmtræk] (US) n société mixte de transports ferroviaires interurbains pour voyageurs

amuse [əˈmjuːz] vt amuser; **amusement** n amusement m; (pastime) distraction f; **amusement arcade** n salle f de jeu; **amusement park** n parc m d'attractions

amusing [əˈmjuːzɪŋ] adj amusant(e), divertissant(e)

an [æn, ən, n] indef art see **a**

anaemia [əˈniːmɪə] (US **anemia**) n anémie f

anaemic [əˈniːmɪk] (US **anemic**) adj anémique

anaesthetic [ænɪsˈθɛtɪk] (US **anesthetic**) n anesthésique m

analog(ue) [ˈænəlɔg] adj (watch, computer) analogique

analogy [əˈnælədʒɪ] n analogie f

analyse ['ænəlaɪz] (US **analyze**) vt analyser; **analysis** (pl **analyses**) [ə'næləsɪs, -siːz] n analyse f; **analyst** ['ænəlɪst] n (political analyst etc) analyste m/f; (US) psychanalyste m/f

analyze ['ænəlaɪz] vt (US) = **analyse**

anarchy ['ænəkɪ] n anarchie f

anatomy [ə'nætəmɪ] n anatomie f

ancestor ['ænsɪstər] n ancêtre m, aïeul m

anchor ['æŋkər] n ancre f ▷ vi (also: **to drop ~**) jeter l'ancre, mouiller ▷ vt mettre à l'ancre; (fig): **to ~ sth to** fixer qch à

anchovy ['æntʃəvɪ] n anchois m

ancient ['eɪnʃənt] adj ancien(ne), antique; (person) d'un âge vénérable; (car) antédiluvien(ne)

and [ænd] conj et; **~ so on** et ainsi de suite; **try ~ come** tâchez de venir; **come ~ sit here** venez vous asseoir ici; **he talked ~ talked** il a parlé pendant des heures; **better ~ better** de mieux en mieux; **more ~ more** de plus en plus

Andorra [æn'dɔːrə] n (principauté f d')Andorre f

anemia etc [ə'niːmɪə] (US) = **anaemia** etc

anesthetic [ænɪs'θɛtɪk] (US) = **anaesthetic**

angel ['eɪndʒəl] n ange m

anger ['æŋɡər] n colère f

angina [æn'dʒaɪnə] n angine f de poitrine

angle ['æŋɡl] n angle m; **from their ~** de leur point de vue

angler ['æŋɡlər] n pêcheur(-euse) à la ligne

Anglican ['æŋɡlɪkən] adj, n anglican(e)

angling ['æŋɡlɪŋ] n pêche f à la ligne

angrily ['æŋɡrɪlɪ] adv avec colère

angry ['æŋɡrɪ] adj en colère, furieux(-euse); (wound) enflammé(e); **to be ~ with sb/at sth** être furieux contre qn/de qch; **to get ~** se fâcher, se mettre en colère

anguish ['æŋɡwɪʃ] n angoisse f

animal ['ænɪməl] n animal m ▷ adj animal(e)

animated ['ænɪmeɪtɪd] adj animé(e)

animation [ænɪ'meɪʃən] n (of person) entrain m; (of street, Cine) animation f

aniseed ['ænɪsiːd] n anis m

ankle ['æŋkl] n cheville f

annex ['ænɛks] n (BRIT: also: **~e**) annexe f ▷ vt [ə'nɛks] annexer

anniversary [ænɪ'vɜːsərɪ] n anniversaire m

announce [ə'naʊns] vt annoncer; (birth, death) faire part de; **announcement** n annonce f; (for births etc: in newspaper) avis m de faire-part; (: letter, card) faire-part m; **announcer** n (Radio, TV: between programmes) speaker(ine); (: in a programme) présentateur(-trice)

annoy [ə'nɔɪ] vt agacer, ennuyer, contrarier; **don't get ~ed!** ne vous fâchez pas!; **annoying** adj agaçant(e), contrariant(e)

annual ['ænjuəl] adj annuel(le) ▷ n (Bot) plante annuelle; (book) album m; **annually** adv annuellement

annum ['ænəm] n see **per**

anonymous [ə'nɔnɪməs] adj anonyme

anorak ['ænəræk] n anorak m

anorexia [ænə'rɛksɪə] n (also: **~ nervosa**) anorexie f

anorexic [ænə'rɛksɪk] adj, n anorexique (m/f)

another [ə'nʌðər] adj: **~ book** (one more) un autre livre, encore un livre, un livre de plus; (a different one) un autre livre ▷ pron un(e) autre, encore un(e), un(e) de plus; see also **one**

answer ['ɑːnsər] n réponse f; (to problem) solution f ▷ vi répondre ▷ vt (reply to) répondre à; (problem) résoudre; (prayer) exaucer; **in ~ to your letter** suite à ou en réponse à votre lettre; **to ~ the phone** répondre (au téléphone); **to ~ the bell** or **the door** aller ou venir ouvrir (la porte); **answer back** vi répondre, répliquer; **answerphone** n (esp BRIT) répondeur m (téléphonique)

nt [ænt] n fourmi f

ntarctic [ænt'ɑːktɪk] n: **the ~** l'Antarctique m

ntelope ['æntɪləup] n antilope f

ntenatal ['æntɪ'neɪtl] adj prénatal(e)

ntenna (pl **~e**) [æn'tɛnə, -niː] n antenne f

nthem ['ænθəm] n: **national ~** hymne national

nthology [æn'θɔlədʒɪ] n anthologie f

nthrax ['ænθræks] n anthrax m

nthropology [ænθrə'pɔlədʒɪ] n anthropologie f

nti ['æntɪ] prefix anti-; **antibiotic** ['æntɪbaɪ'ɔtɪk] n antibiotique m; **antibody** ['æntɪbɔdɪ] n anticorps m

nticipate [æn'tɪsɪpeɪt] vt s'attendre à, prévoir; (wishes, request) aller au devant de, devancer; **anticipation** [æntɪsɪ'peɪʃən] n attente f

nticlimax ['æntɪ'klaɪmæks] n déception f

nticlockwise ['æntɪ'klɔkwaɪz] (BRIT) adv dans le sens inverse des aiguilles d'une montre

ntics ['æntɪks] npl singeries fpl

nti: **antidote**: **antidote** ['æntɪdəut] n antidote m, contrepoison m; **antifreeze** ['æntɪfriːz] n antigel m; **anti-globalization** n antimondialisation f; **antihistamine** [æntɪ'hɪstəmɪn] n antihistaminique m; **antiperspirant** [æntɪ'pəːspɪrənt] n déodorant m

ntique [æn'tiːk] n (ornament) objet m d'art ancien; (furniture) meuble ancien ▷ adj ancien(ne); **antique shop** n magasin m d'antiquités

ntiseptic [æntɪ'sɛptɪk] adj, n antiseptique (m)

ntisocial ['æntɪ'səuʃəl] adj (unfriendly) peu liant(e), insociable; (against society) antisocial(e)

ntlers ['æntləz] npl bois mpl, ramure f

nxiety [æŋ'zaɪətɪ] n anxiété f; (keenness): **~ to do** grand désir or impatience f de faire

nxious ['æŋkʃəs] adj (très) inquiet(-ète); (always worried)

anxieux(-euse); (worrying) angoissant(e); (keen): **~ to do/that** qui tient beaucoup à faire/à ce que + sub; impatient(e) de faire/que + sub

 KEYWORD

any ['ɛnɪ] adj **1** (in questions etc: singular) du, de l', de la, ; (: plural) des; **do you have any butter/children/ink?** avez-vous du beurre/des enfants/de l'encre?
2 (with negative) de, d'; **I don't have any money/books** je n'ai pas d'argent/de livres
3 (no matter which) n'importe quel(le); (each and every) tout(e), chaque; **choose any book you like** vous pouvez choisir n'importe quel livre; **any teacher you ask will tell you** n'importe quel professeur vous le dira
4 (in phrases): **in any case** de toute façon; **any day now** d'un jour à l'autre; **at any moment** à tout moment, d'un instant à l'autre; **at any rate** en tout cas; **any time** n'importe quand; **he might come (at) any time** il pourrait venir n'importe quand; **come (at) any time** venez quand vous voulez
▷ pron **1** (in questions etc) en; **have you got any?** est-ce que vous en avez?; **can any of you sing?** est-ce que parmi vous il y en a qui savent chanter?
2 (with negative) en; **I don't have any (of them)** je n'en ai pas, je n'en ai aucun
3 (no matter which one(s)) n'importe lequel (or laquelle); (anybody) n'importe qui; **take any of those books (you like)** vous pouvez prendre n'importe lequel de ces livres
▷ adv **1** (in questions etc): **do you want any more soup/sandwiches?** voulez-vous encore de la soupe/des sandwichs?; **are you feeling any better?** est-ce que vous vous sentez mieux?
2 (with negative): **I can't hear him any more** je ne l'entends plus; **don't wait any longer** n'attendez pas plus

longtemps; **anybody** pron n'importe qui; (in interrogative sentences) quelqu'un; (in negative sentences): **I don't see anybody** je ne vois personne; **if anybody should phone ...** si quelqu'un téléphone ...; **anyhow** adv quoi qu'il en soit; (haphazardly) n'importe comment; **do it anyhow you like** faites-le comme vous voulez; **she leaves things just anyhow** elle laisse tout traîner; **I shall go anyhow** j'irai de toute façon; **anyone** pron = **anybody**; **anything** pron (no matter what) n'importe quoi; (in questions) quelque chose; (with negative) ne ... rien; **can you see anything?** tu vois quelque chose?; **if anything happens to me ...** s'il m'arrive quoi que ce soit ...; **you can say anything you like** vous pouvez dire ce que vous voulez; **anything will do** n'importe quoi fera l'affaire; **he'll eat anything** il mange de tout; **anytime** adv (at any moment) d'un moment à l'autre; (whenever) n'importe quand; **anyway** adv de toute façon; **anyway, I couldn't come even if I wanted to** de toute façon, je ne pouvais pas venir même si je le voulais; **I shall go anyway** j'irai quand même; **why are you phoning, anyway?** au fait, pourquoi tu me téléphones?; **anywhere** adv n'importe où; (in interrogative sentences) quelque part; (in negative sentences): **I can't see him anywhere** je ne le vois nulle part; **can you see him anywhere?** tu le vois quelque part?; **put the books down anywhere** pose les livres n'importe où; **anywhere in the world** (no matter where) n'importe où dans le monde

apart [ə'pɑːt] adv (to one side) à part; de côté; à l'écart; (separately) séparément; **to take/pull ~** démonter; **10 miles/a long way ~** à 10 miles/très éloignés l'un de l'autre; **~ from** prep à part, excepté

apartment [ə'pɑːtmənt] n (us) appartement m, logement m; (room) chambre f; **apartment building** n (us) immeuble m; maison divisée en appartements

apathy ['æpəθɪ] n apathie f, indifférence f

ape [eɪp] n (grand) singe ▷ vt singer

aperitif [ə'pɛrɪtɪf] n apéritif m

aperture ['æpətʃjuəʳ] n orifice m, ouverture f; (Phot) ouverture (du diaphragme)

APEX ['eɪpɛks] n abbr (Aviat: = advance purchase excursion) APEX m

apologize [ə'pɔlədʒaɪz] vi: **to ~ (for sth to sb)** s'excuser (de qch auprès de qn), présenter des excuses (à qn pour qch)

apology [ə'pɔlədʒɪ] n excuses fpl

apostrophe [ə'pɔstrəfɪ] n apostrophe

appal [ə'pɔːl] (us **appall**) vt consterner atterrer; horrifier; **appalling** adj épouvantable; (stupidity) consternant(e)

apparatus [æpə'reɪtəs] n appareil m, dispositif m; (in gymnasium) agrès m

apparent [ə'pærənt] adj apparent(e); **apparently** adv apparemment

appeal [ə'piːl] vi (Law) faire or interjeter appel ▷ n (Law) appel m; (request) appel prière f; (charm) attrait m, charme m; **to ~ for** demander (instamment); implorer; **to ~ to** (beg) faire appel à; (be attractive) plaire à; **it doesn't ~ to me** cela ne m'attire pas; **appealing** ad (attractive) attrayant(e)

appear [ə'pɪəʳ] vi apparaître, se montrer; (Law) comparaître; (publication) paraître, sortir, être publié(e); (seem) paraître, sembler; **it would ~ that** il semble que; **to ~ in Hamlet** jouer dans Hamlet; **to ~ on TV** passer à la télé; **appearance** n apparition f; parution f; (look, aspect) apparence f, aspect m

appendices [ə'pɛndɪsiːz] npl of **appendix**

appendicitis [əpɛndɪ'saɪtɪs] n appendicite f

appendix (pl **appendices**) [ə'pɛndɪks]

-siːz] n appendice m

ppetite ['æpɪtaɪt] n appétit m

ppetizer ['æpɪtaɪzər] n (food) amuse-gueule m; (drink) apéritif m

pplaud [ə'plɔːd] vt, vi applaudir

pplause [ə'plɔːz] n applaudissements mpl

pple ['æpl] n pomme f; **apple pie** n tarte f aux pommes

ppliance [ə'plaɪəns] n appareil m

pplicable [ə'plɪkəbl] adj applicable; **to be ~ to** (relevant) valoir pour

pplicant ['æplɪkənt] n: **~ (for)** candidat(e) (à)

pplication [æplɪ'keɪʃən] n application f; (for a job, a grant etc) demande f; candidature f; **application form** n formulaire m de demande

pply [ə'plaɪ] vt: **to ~ (to)** (paint, ointment) appliquer (sur); (law, etc) appliquer (à) ▷ vi: **to ~ to** (ask) s'adresser à; (be suitable for, relevant to) s'appliquer à; **to ~ (for)** (permit, grant) faire une demande (en vue d'obtenir); (job) poser sa candidature (pour), faire une demande d'emploi (concernant); **to ~ o.s. to** s'appliquer à

ppoint [ə'pɔɪnt] vt (to post) nommer, engager; (date, place) fixer, désigner; **appointment** n (to post) nomination f; (job) poste m; (arrangement to meet) rendez-vous m; **to have an appointment** avoir un rendez-vous; **to make an appointment (with)** prendre rendez-vous (avec); **I'd like to make an appointment** je voudrais prendre rendez-vous

ppraisal [ə'preɪzl] n évaluation f

ppreciate [ə'priːʃɪeɪt] vt (like) apprécier, faire cas de; (be grateful for) être reconnaissant(e) de; (be aware of) comprendre, se rendre compte de ▷ vi (Finance) prendre de la valeur; **appreciation** [əpriːʃɪ'eɪʃən] n appréciation f; (gratitude) reconnaissance f; (Finance) hausse f, valorisation f

pprehension [æprɪ'hɛnʃən] n

appréhension f, inquiétude f

apprehensive [æprɪ'hɛnsɪv] adj inquiet(-ète), appréhensif(-ive)

apprentice [ə'prɛntɪs] n apprenti m

approach [ə'prəʊtʃ] vi approcher ▷ vt (come near) approcher de; (ask, apply to) s'adresser à; (subject, problem) aborder ▷ n approche f; accès m, abord m; démarche f (intellectuelle)

appropriate adj [ə'prəʊprɪɪt] (tool etc) qui convient, approprié(e); (moment, remark) opportun(e) ▷ vt [ə'prəʊprɪeɪt] (take) s'approprier

approval [ə'pruːvəl] n approbation f; **on ~** (Comm) à l'examen

approve [ə'pruːv] vt approuver; **approve of** vt fus (thing) approuver; (person): **they don't ~ of her** ils n'ont pas bonne opinion d'elle

approximate [ə'prɔksɪmɪt] adj approximatif(-ive); **approximately** adv approximativement

Apr. abbr = **April**

apricot ['eɪprɪkɔt] n abricot m

April ['eɪprəl] n avril m; **April Fools' Day** n le premier avril

- **APRIL FOOLS' DAY**
-
- **April Fools' Day** est le 1er avril, à
- l'occasion duquel on fait des farces
- de toutes sortes. Les victimes de
- ces farces sont les "April fools".
- Traditionnellement, on n'est censé
- faire des farces que jusqu'à midi.

apron ['eɪprən] n tablier m

apt [æpt] adj (suitable) approprié(e); (likely): **~ to do** susceptible de faire; ayant tendance à faire

aquarium [ə'kwɛərɪəm] n aquarium m

Aquarius [ə'kwɛərɪəs] n le Verseau

Arab ['ærəb] n Arabe m/f ▷ adj arabe

Arabia [ə'reɪbɪə] n Arabie f; **Arabian** adj arabe; **Arabic** ['ærəbɪk] adj, n arabe (m)

arbitrary ['ɑːbɪtrərɪ] adj arbitraire

arbitration [ɑːbɪ'treɪʃən] n

arbitrage m

arc [ɑːk] n arc m

arcade [ɑːˈkeɪd] n arcade f; (passage with shops) passage m, galerie f; (with games) salle f de jeu

arch [ɑːtʃ] n arche f; (of foot) cambrure f, voûte f plantaire ▷ vt arquer, cambrer

archaeology [ɑːkɪˈɒlədʒɪ] (US **archeology**) n archéologie f

archbishop [ɑːtʃˈbɪʃəp] n archevêque m

archeology [ɑːkɪˈɒlədʒɪ] (US) = **archaeology**

architect ['ɑːkɪtɛkt] n architecte m; **architectural** [ɑːkɪˈtɛktʃərəl] adj architectural(e); **architecture** n architecture f

archive ['ɑːkaɪv] n (often pl) archives fpl

Arctic ['ɑːktɪk] adj arctique ▷ n: **the ~** l'Arctique m

are [ɑːʳ] vb see **be**

area ['ɛərɪə] n (Geom) superficie f; (zone) région f; (: smaller) secteur m; (in room) coin m; (knowledge, research) domaine m; **area code** (US) n (Tel) indicatif m de zone

arena [əˈriːnə] n arène f

aren't [ɑːnt] = **are not**

Argentina [ɑːdʒənˈtiːnə] n Argentine f; **Argentinian** [ɑːdʒənˈtɪnɪən] adj argentin(e) ▷ n Argentin(e)

arguably ['ɑːgjuəblɪ] adv: **it is ~ ...** on peut soutenir que c'est ...

argue ['ɑːgjuː] vi (quarrel) se disputer; (reason) argumenter; **to ~ that** objecter or alléguer que, donner comme argument que

argument ['ɑːgjumənt] n (quarrel) dispute f, discussion f; (reasons) argument m

Aries ['ɛərɪz] n le Bélier

arise (pt **arose**, pp **~n**) [əˈraɪz, əˈrəuz, əˈrɪzn] vi survenir, se présenter

arithmetic [əˈrɪθmətɪk] n arithmétique f

arm [ɑːm] n bras m ▷ vt armer; **arms** npl (weapons, Heraldry) armes fpl; **~ in ~** bras dessus bras dessous; **armchair**

['ɑːtʃɛəʳ] n fauteuil m

armed [ɑːmd] adj armé(e); **armed forces** npl: **the armed forces** les forces armées; **armed robbery** n vol m à main armée

armour (US **armor**) ['ɑːməʳ] n armure f; (Mil: tanks) blindés mpl

armpit ['ɑːmpɪt] n aisselle f

armrest ['ɑːmrɛst] n accoudoir m

army ['ɑːmɪ] n armée f

A road n (BRIT) ≈ route nationale

aroma [əˈrəumə] n arôme m; **aromatherapy** n aromathérapie f

arose [əˈrəuz] pt of **arise**

around [əˈraund] adv (tout) autour; (nearby) dans les parages ▷ prep autour de; (near) près de; (fig: about) environ; (: date, time) vers; **is he ~?** est-il dans les parages or là?

arouse [əˈrauz] vt (sleeper) éveiller; (curiosity, passions) éveiller, susciter; (anger) exciter

arrange [əˈreɪndʒ] vt arranger; **to ~ to do sth** prévoir de faire qch; **arrangement** n arrangement m; **arrangements** npl (plans etc) arrangements mpl, dispositions fpl

array [əˈreɪ] n (of objects) déploiement m, étalage m

arrears [əˈrɪəz] npl arriéré m; **to be in ~ with one's rent** devoir un arriéré de loyer

arrest [əˈrɛst] vt arrêter; (sb's attention) retenir, attirer ▷ n arrestation f; **under ~** en état d'arrestation

arrival [əˈraɪvl] n arrivée f; **new ~** nouveau venu/nouvelle venue; (baby) nouveau-né(e)

arrive [əˈraɪv] vi arriver; **arrive at** vt fus (decision, solution) parvenir à

arrogance ['ærəgəns] n arrogance f

arrogant ['ærəgənt] adj arrogant(e)

arrow ['ærəu] n flèche f

arse [ɑːs] n (BRIT inf!) cul m (!)

arson ['ɑːsn] n incendie criminel

art [ɑːt] n art m; **Arts** npl (Scol) les lettres fpl; **art college** n école f des beaux-arts

rtery ['ɑ:tərɪ] n artère f
rt gallery n musée m d'art; (saleroom) galerie f de peinture
rthritis [ɑ:'θraɪtɪs] n arthrite f
rtichoke ['ɑ:tɪtʃəuk] n artichaut m; **Jerusalem ~** topinambour m
rticle ['ɑ:tɪkl] n article m
rticulate adj [ɑ:'tɪkjulɪt] (person) qui s'exprime clairement et aisément; (speech) bien articulé(e), prononcé(e) clairement ▷ vb [ɑ:'tɪkjuleɪt] ▷ vi articuler, parler distinctement ▷ vt articuler
rtificial [ɑ:tɪ'fɪʃəl] adj artificiel(le)
rtist ['ɑ:tɪst] n artiste m/f; **artistic** [ɑ:'tɪstɪk] adj artistique
rt school n ≈ école f des beaux-arts

○ **KEYWORD**

s [æz] conj **1** (time: moment) comme, alors que; à mesure que; **he came in as I was leaving** il est arrivé comme je partais; **as the years went by** à mesure que les années passaient; **as from tomorrow** à partir de demain **2** (since, because) comme, puisque; **he left early as he had to be home by 10** comme il or puisqu'il devait être de retour avant 10h, il est parti de bonne heure
3 (referring to manner, way) comme; **do as you wish** faites comme vous voudrez; **as she said** comme elle disait ▷ adv **1** (in comparisons): **as big as** aussi grand que; **twice as big as** deux fois plus grand que; **as much** or **many as** autant que; **as much money/many books as** autant d'argent/de livres que; **as soon as** dès que
2 (concerning): **as for** or **to that** quant à cela, pour ce qui est de cela
3: **as if** or **though** comme si; **he looked as if he was ill** il avait l'air d'être malade; see also **long**; **such**; **well** ▷ prep (in the capacity of) en tant que, en qualité de; **he works as a driver** il travaille comme chauffeur; **as**

chairman of the company, he ... en tant que président de la société, il ...; **he gave me it as a present** il me l'a offert, il m'en a fait cadeau

a.s.a.p. abbr = **as soon as possible**
asbestos [æz'bɛstəs] n asbeste m, amiante m
ascent [ə'sɛnt] n (climb) ascension f
ash [æʃ] n (dust) cendre f; (also: **~ tree**) frêne m
ashamed [ə'ʃeɪmd] adj honteux(-euse), confus(e); **to be ~ of** avoir honte de
ashore [ə'ʃɔːʳ] adv à terre
ashtray ['æʃtreɪ] n cendrier m
Ash Wednesday n mercredi m des Cendres
Asia ['eɪʃə] n Asie f; **Asian** n (from Asia) Asiatique m/f; (BRIT: from Indian subcontinent) Indo-Pakistanais(-e) ▷ adj asiatique; indo-pakistanais(-e)
aside [ə'saɪd] adv de côté; à l'écart ▷ n aparté m
ask [ɑ:sk] vt demander; (invite) inviter; **to ~ sb sth/to do sth** demander à qn qch/de faire qch; **to ~ sb about sth** questionner qn au sujet de qch; se renseigner auprès de qn au sujet de qch; **to ~ (sb) a question** poser une question (à qn); **to ~ sb out to dinner** inviter qn au restaurant; **ask for** vt fus demander; **it's just ~ing for trouble** or **for it** ce serait chercher des ennuis
asleep [ə'sli:p] adj endormi(e); **to fall ~** s'endormir
AS level n abbr (= Advanced Subsidiary level) première partie de l'examen équivalent au baccalauréat
asparagus [əs'pærəgəs] n asperges fpl
aspect ['æspɛkt] n aspect m; (direction in which a building etc faces) orientation f, exposition f
aspirations [æspə'reɪʃənz] npl (hopes, ambition) aspirations fpl
aspire [əs'paɪəʳ] vi: **to ~ to** aspirer à
aspirin ['æsprɪn] n aspirine f
ass [æs] n âne m; (inf) imbécile m/f; (us

infl) cul m (!)

assassin [əˈsæsɪn] n assassin m;
assassinate vt assassiner

assault [əˈsɔːlt] n (Mil) assaut m; (gen:
attack) agression f ▷ vt attaquer;
(*sexually*) violenter

assemble [əˈsɛmbl] vt assembler ▷ vi
s'assembler, se rassembler

assembly [əˈsɛmblɪ] n (*meeting*)
rassemblement m; (*parliament*)
assemblée f; (*construction*)
assemblage m

assert [əˈsəːt] vt affirmer, déclarer;
(*authority*) faire valoir; (*innocence*)
protester de; **assertion** [əˈsəːʃən] n
assertion f, affirmation f

assess [əˈsɛs] vt évaluer, estimer; (*tax,
damages*) établir or fixer le montant de;
(*person*) juger la valeur de; **assessment**
n évaluation f, estimation f; (*of tax*)
fixation f

asset [ˈæsɛt] n avantage m, atout m;
(*person*) atout; **assets** npl (Comm)
capital m; avoir(s) m(pl); actif m

assign [əˈsaɪn] vt (*date*) fixer, arrêter; **to
~ sth to** (*task*) assigner qch à; (*resources*)
affecter qch à; **assignment** n (*task*)
mission f; (*homework*) devoir m

assist [əˈsɪst] vt aider, assister;
assistance n aide f, assistance f;
assistant n assistant(e), adjoint(e);
(BRIT: *also*: **shop assistant**)
vendeur(-euse)

associate adj, n [əˈsəʊʃɪɪt] associé(e)
▷ vb [əˈsəʊʃɪeɪt] ▷ vt associer ▷ vi: **to ~
with sb** fréquenter qn

association [əsəʊsɪˈeɪʃən] n
association f

assorted [əˈsɔːtɪd] adj assorti(e)

assortment [əˈsɔːtmənt] n
assortiment m; (*of people*) mélange m

assume [əˈsjuːm] vt supposer;
(*responsibilities etc*) assumer; (*attitude,
name*) prendre, adopter

assumption [əˈsʌmpʃən] n
supposition f, hypothèse f; (*of power*)
assomption f, prise f

assurance [əˈʃuərəns] n assurance f

assure [əˈʃuəʳ] vt assurer

asterisk [ˈæstərɪsk] n astérisque m

asthma [ˈæsmə] n asthme m

astonish [əˈstɒnɪʃ] vt étonner,
stupéfier; **astonished** adj étonné(e);
to be astonished at être étonné(e)
de; **astonishing** adj étonnant(e),
stupéfiant(e); **I find it astonishing
that ...** je trouve incroyable que ... + su
astonishment n (grand) étonnemen
stupéfaction f

astound [əˈstaund] vt stupéfier,
sidérer

astray [əˈstreɪ] adv: **to go ~** s'égarer;
(*fig*) quitter le droit chemin; **to lead ~**
(*morally*) détourner du droit chemin

astrology [əsˈtrɒlədʒɪ] n astrologie f

astronaut [ˈæstrənɔːt] n
astronaute m/f

astronomer [əsˈtrɒnəməʳ] n
astronome m

astronomical [æstrəˈnɒmɪkl] adj
astronomique

astronomy [əsˈtrɒnəmɪ] n
astronomie f

astute [əsˈtjuːt] adj astucieux(-euse),
malin(-igne)

asylum [əˈsaɪləm] n asile m; **asylum
seeker** [-siːkəʳ] n demandeur(-euse)
d'asile

 KEYWORD

at [æt] prep **1** (*referring to position,
direction*) à; **at the top** au sommet; **at
home/school** à la maison or chez soi
l'école; **at the baker's** à la boulangeri
chez le boulanger; **to look at sth**
regarder qch

2 (*referring to time*): **at 4 o'clock** à 4
heures; **at Christmas** à Noël; **at night**
la nuit; **at times** par moments, parfoi

3 (*referring to rates, speed etc*): **at £1
a kilo** une livre le kilo; **two at a time**
deux à la fois; **at 50 km/h** à 50 km/h

4 (*referring to manner*): **at a stroke** d'un
seul coup; **at peace** en paix

5 (*referring to activity*): **to be at work** (i

the office etc) être au travail; (working) travailler; **to play at cowboys** jouer aux cowboys; **to be good at sth** être bon en qch

6 (referring to cause): **shocked/ surprised/annoyed at sth** choqué par/étonné de/agacé par qch; **I went at his suggestion** j'y suis allé sur son conseil

7 (symbol) arobase f

ate [eɪt] pt of **eat**

atheist ['eɪθɪɪst] n athée m/f

Athens ['æθɪnz] n Athènes

athlete ['æθliːt] n athlète m/f

athletic [æθ'lɛtɪk] adj athlétique; **athletics** n athlétisme m

Atlantic [ət'læntɪk] adj atlantique ▷ n: **the ~ (Ocean)** l'(océan m) Atlantique m

atlas ['ætləs] n atlas m

A.T.M. n abbr (= Automated Telling Machine) guichet m automatique

atmosphere ['ætməsfɪər] n (air) atmosphère f; (fig: of place etc) atmosphère, ambiance f

atom ['ætəm] n atome m; **atomic** [ə'tɔmɪk] adj atomique; **atom(ic) bomb** n bombe f atomique

A to Z® n (map) plan m des rues

atrocity [ə'trɔsɪtɪ] n atrocité f

attach [ə'tætʃ] vt (gen) attacher; (document, letter) joindre; **to be ~ed to sb/sth** (to like) être attaché à qn/qch; **attachment** n (tool) accessoire m; (Comput) fichier m joint; (love): **attachment (to)** affection f (pour), attachement m (à)

attack [ə'tæk] vt attaquer; (task etc) s'attaquer à ▷ n attaque f; **heart ~** crise f cardiaque; **attacker** n attaquant m; agresseur m

attain [ə'teɪn] vt (also: **to ~ to**) parvenir à, atteindre; (knowledge) acquérir

attempt [ə'tɛmpt] n tentative f ▷ vt essayer, tenter

attend [ə'tɛnd] vt (course) suivre; (meeting, talk) assister à; (school, church) aller à, fréquenter; (patient) soigner,

s'occuper de; **attend to** vt fus (needs, affairs etc) s'occuper de; (customer) s'occuper de, servir; **attendance** n (being present) présence f; (people present) assistance f; **attendant** n employé(e); gardien(ne) ▷ adj concomitant(e), qui accompagne or s'ensuit

Be careful not to translate **to attend** by the French word **attendre**.

attention [ə'tɛnʃən] n attention f ▷ excl (Mil) garde-à-vous!; **for the ~ of** (Admin) à l'attention de

attic ['ætɪk] n grenier m, combles mpl

attitude ['ætɪtjuːd] n attitude f

attorney [ə'tɜːnɪ] n (US: lawyer) avocat m; **Attorney General** n (BRIT) ≈ procureur général; (US) ≈ garde m des Sceaux, ministre m de la Justice

attract [ə'trækt] vt attirer; **attraction** [ə'trækʃən] n (gen pl: pleasant things) attraction f, attrait m; (Physics) attraction; (fig: towards sb, sth) attirance f; **attractive** adj séduisant(e), attrayant(e)

attribute n ['ætrɪbjuːt] attribut m ▷ vt [ə'trɪbjuːt]: **to ~ sth to** attribuer qch à

aubergine ['əubəʒiːn] n aubergine f

auburn ['ɔːbən] adj auburn inv, châtain roux inv

auction ['ɔːkʃən] n (also: **sale by ~**) vente f aux enchères ▷ vt (also: **to sell by ~**) vendre aux enchères

audible ['ɔːdɪbl] adj audible

audience ['ɔːdɪəns] n (people) assistance f, public m; (on radio) auditeurs mpl; (at theatre) spectateurs mpl; (interview) audience f

audit ['ɔːdɪt] vt vérifier

audition [ɔː'dɪʃən] n audition f

auditor ['ɔːdɪtər] n vérificateur m des comptes

auditorium [ɔːdɪ'tɔːrɪəm] n auditorium m, salle f de concert or de spectacle

Aug. abbr = **August**

August ['ɔːgəst] n août m

aunt [ɑːnt] n tante f; **auntie, aunty** n diminutive of **aunt**

au pair [ˈəʊˈpɛəʳ] n (also: ~ **girl**) jeune fille f au pair

aura [ˈɔːrə] n atmosphère f; (of person) aura f

austerity [ɔsˈtɛrɪtɪ] n austérité f

Australia [ɔsˈtreɪlɪə] n Australie f; **Australian** adj australien(ne) ▷ n Australien(ne)

Austria [ˈɔstrɪə] n Autriche f; **Austrian** adj autrichien(ne) ▷ n Autrichien(ne)

authentic [ɔːˈθɛntɪk] adj authentique

author [ˈɔːθəʳ] n auteur m

authority [ɔːˈθɔrɪtɪ] n autorité f; (permission) autorisation (formelle); **the authorities** les autorités fpl, l'administration f

authorize [ˈɔːθəraɪz] vt autoriser

auto [ˈɔːtəu] n (US) auto f, voiture f; **autobiography** [ɔːtəbaɪˈɔgrəfɪ] n autobiographie f; **autograph** [ˈɔːtəgrɑːf] n autographe m ▷ vt signer, dédicacer; **automatic** [ɔːtəˈmætɪk] adj automatique ▷ n (gun) automatique m; (car) voiture f à transmission automatique; **automatically** adv automatiquement; **automobile** [ˈɔːtəməbiːl] n (US) automobile f; **autonomous** [ɔːˈtɔnəməs] adj autonome; **autonomy** [ɔːˈtɔnəmɪ] n autonomie f

autumn [ˈɔːtəm] n automne m

auxiliary [ɔːgˈzɪlɪərɪ] adj, n auxiliaire (m/f)

avail [əˈveɪl] vt: **to ~ o.s. of** user de; profiter de ▷ n: **to no ~** sans résultat, en vain, en pure perte

availability [əveɪləˈbɪlɪtɪ] n disponibilité f

available [əˈveɪləbl] adj disponible

avalanche [ˈævəlɑːnʃ] n avalanche f

Ave. abbr = **avenue**

avenue [ˈævənjuː] n avenue f; (fig) moyen m

average [ˈævərɪdʒ] n moyenne f ▷ adj moyen(ne) ▷ vt (a certain figure) atteindre or faire etc en moyenne; **on ~** en moyenne

avert [əˈvəːt] vt (danger) prévenir, écarter; (one's eyes) détourner

avid [ˈævɪd] adj avide

avocado [ævəˈkɑːdəu] n (BRIT: also: ~ **pear**) avocat m

avoid [əˈvɔɪd] vt éviter

await [əˈweɪt] vt attendre

awake [əˈweɪk] adj éveillé(e) ▷ vb (pt **awoke**, pp **awoken**) ▷ vt éveiller ▷ vi s'éveiller; **to be ~** être réveillé(e)

award [əˈwɔːd] n (for bravery) récompense f; (prize) prix m; (Law: damages) dommages-intérêts mpl ▷ vt (prize) décerner; (Law: damages) accorder

aware [əˈwɛəʳ] adj: **~ of** (conscious) conscient(e) de; (informed) au courant de; **to become ~ of/that** prendre conscience de/que; se rendre compte de/que; **awareness** n conscience f, connaissance f

away [əˈweɪ] adv (au) loin; (movement): **she went ~** elle est partie ▷ adj (not in, not here) absent(e); **far ~** (au) loin; **two kilometres ~** à (une distance de) deux kilomètres, à deux kilomètres de distance; **two hours ~ by car** à deux heures de voiture or de route; **the holiday was two weeks ~** il restait deux semaines jusqu'aux vacances; **he's ~ for a week** il est parti (pour) une semaine; **to take sth ~ from sb** prendre qch à qn; **to take sth ~ from sth** (subtract) ôter qch de qch; **to work/pedal ~** travailler/pédaler à cœur joie; **to fade ~** (colour) s'estompe(r) (sound) s'affaiblir

awe [ɔː] n respect mêlé de crainte, effro mêlé d'admiration; **awesome** [ˈɔːsəm] (US) adj (inf: excellent) génial(e)

awful [ˈɔːfəl] adj affreux(-euse); **an ~ lo of** énormément de; **awfully** adv (very) terriblement, vraiment

awkward [ˈɔːkwəd] adj (clumsy) gauche, maladroit(e); (inconvenient) pe pratique; (embarrassing) gênant

awoke [əˈwəuk] pt of **awake**

awoken [əˈwəukən] pp of **awake**

xe [æks] (US **ax**) n hache f ▷ vt (project etc) abandonner; (jobs) supprimer
:le ['æksl] n essieu m
y(e) [aɪ] excl (yes) oui
:alea [ə'zeɪlɪə] n azalée f

B [biː] n (Mus): **B** si m
B.A. abbr (Scol) = **Bachelor of Arts**
baby ['beɪbɪ] n bébé m; **baby carriage**
n (US) voiture f d'enfant; **baby-sit**
vi garder les enfants; **baby-sitter** n
baby-sitter m/f; **baby wipe** n lingette
f (pour bébé)
bachelor ['bætʃələʳ] n célibataire m; **B~**
of Arts/Science (BA/BSc) ≈ licencié(e)
ès or en lettres/sciences
back [bæk] n (of person, horse) dos m; (of
hand) dos, revers m; (of house) derrière
m; (of car, train) arrière m; (of chair)
dossier m; (of page) verso m; (of crowd):
can the people at the ~ hear me
properly? est-ce que les gens du fond
peuvent m'entendre?; (Football) arrière
m; **~ to front** à l'envers ▷ vt (financially)
soutenir (financièrement); (candidate:
also: **~ up**) soutenir, appuyer; (horse: at
races) parier or miser sur; (car) (faire)
reculer ▷ vi reculer; (car etc) faire
marche arrière ▷ adj (in compounds) de
derrière, à l'arrière; **~ seat/wheel** (Aut)

siège *m*/roue *f* arrière *inv*; **~ payments/ rent** arriéré *m* de paiements/loyer; **~ garden/room** jardin/pièce sur l'arrière ▷ *adv* (*not forward*) en arrière; (*returned*): **he's ~** il est rentré, il est de retour; **he ran ~** il est revenu en courant; (*restitution*): **throw the ball ~** renvoie la balle; **can I have it ~?** puis-je le ravoir?, peux-tu me le rendre?; (*again*): **he called ~** il a rappelé; **back down** *vi* rabattre de ses prétentions; **back out** *vi* (*of promise*) se dédire; **back up** *vt* (*person*) soutenir; (*Comput*) faire une copie de sauvegarde de; **backache** *n* mal *m* au dos; **backbencher** (*BRIT*) *n* membre du parlement sans portefeuille; **backbone** *n* colonne vertébrale, épine dorsale; **back door** *n* porte *f* de derrière; **backfire** *vi* (*Aut*) pétarader; (*plans*) mal tourner; **backgammon** *n* trictrac *m*; **background** *n* arrière-plan *m*; (*of events*) situation *f*, conjoncture *f*; (*basic knowledge*) éléments *mpl* de base; (*experience*) formation *f*; **family background** milieu familial; **backing** *n* (*fig*) soutien *m*, appui *m*; **backlog** *n*: **backlog of work** travail *m* en retard; **backpack** *n* sac *m* à dos; **backpacker** *n* randonneur(-euse); **backslash** *n* barre oblique inversée; **backstage** *adv* dans les coulisses; **backstroke** *n* dos crawlé; **backup** *adj* (*train, plane*) supplémentaire, de réserve; (*Comput*) de sauvegarde ▷ *n* (*support*) appui *m*, soutien *m*; (*Comput: also*: **backup file**) sauvegarde *f*; **backward** *adj* (*movement*) en arrière; (*person, country*) arriéré(e), attardé(e); **backwards** *adv* (*move, go*) en arrière; (*read a list*) à l'envers, à rebours; (*fall*) à la renverse; (*walk*) à reculons; **backyard** *n* arrière-cour *f*
bacon [ˈbeɪkən] *n* bacon *m*, lard *m*
bacteria [bækˈtɪərɪə] *npl* bactéries *fpl*
bad [bæd] *adj* mauvais(e); (*child*) vilain(e); (*mistake, accident*) grave; (*meat, food*) gâté(e), avarié(e); **his ~ leg** sa jambe malade; **to go ~** (*meat, food*) se gâter; (*milk*) tourner

bade [bæd] *pt of* **bid**
badge [bædʒ] *n* insigne *m*; (*of policeman*) plaque *f*; (*stick-on, sew-on*) badge *m*
badger [ˈbædʒər] *n* blaireau *m*
badly [ˈbædlɪ] *adv* (*work, dress etc*) mal; **to reflect ~ on sb** donner une mauvaise image de qn; **~ wounded** grièvement blessé; **he needs it ~** il en a absolument besoin; **~ off** *adj, adv* dans la gêne
bad-mannered [ˈbædˈmænəd] *adj* mal élevé(e)
badminton [ˈbædmɪntən] *n* badminton *m*
bad-tempered [ˈbædˈtɛmpəd] *adj* (*by nature*) ayant mauvais caractère; (*on one occasion*) de mauvaise humeur
bag [bæg] *n* sac *m*; **~s of** (*inf: lots of*) des tas de; **baggage** *n* bagages *mpl*; **baggage allowance** *n* franchise *f* de bagages; **baggage reclaim** *n* (*at airport*) livraison *f* des bagages; **baggy** *adj* avachi(e), qui fait des poches; **bagpipes** *npl* cornemuse *f*
bail [beɪl] *n* caution *f* ▷ *vt* (*prisoner: also*: **grant ~ to**) mettre en liberté sous caution; (*boat: also*: **~ out**) écoper; **to be released on ~** être libéré(e) sous caution; **bail out** *vt* (*prisoner*) payer la caution de
bait [beɪt] *n* appât *m* ▷ *vt* appâter; (*fig: tease*) tourmenter
bake [beɪk] *vt* (*faire*) cuire au four ▷ *vi* (*bread etc*) cuire (au four); (*make cakes etc*) faire de la pâtisserie; **baked beans** *npl* haricots blancs à la sauce tomate; **baked potato** *n* pomme *f* de terre en robe des champs; **baker** *n* boulanger *m*; **bakery** *n* boulangerie *f*; **baking** *n* (*process*) cuisson *f*; **baking powder** *n* levure *f* (chimique)
balance [ˈbæləns] *n* équilibre *m*; (*Comm: sum*) solde *m*; (*remainder*) reste *m*; (*scales*) balance *f* ▷ *vt* mettre or faire tenir en équilibre; (*pros and cons*) peser; (*budget*) équilibrer; (*account*) balancer; (*compensate*) compenser,

contrebalancer; **~ of trade/payments** balance commerciale/des comptes et paiements; **balanced** adj (personality, diet) équilibré(e); (report) objectif(-ive);
balance sheet n bilan m

balcony ['bælkənɪ] n balcon m; **do you have a room with a ~?** avez-vous une chambre avec balcon?

bald [bɔːld] adj chauve; (tyre) lisse

ball [bɔːl] n boule f; (football) ballon m; (for tennis, golf) balle f; (dance) bal m; **to play ~** jouer au ballon (or à la balle); (fig) coopérer

ballerina [bælə'riːnə] n ballerine f

ballet ['bæleɪ] n ballet m; (art) danse f (classique); **ballet dancer** n danseur(-euse) de ballet

balloon [bə'luːn] n ballon m

ballot ['bælət] n scrutin m

ballpoint (pen) ['bɔːlpɔɪnt-] n stylo m à bille

ballroom ['bɔːlrum] n salle f de bal

Baltic [bɔːltɪk] n: **the ~ (Sea)** la (mer) Baltique

bamboo [bæm'buː] n bambou m

ban [bæn] n interdiction f ▷ vt interdire

banana [bə'nɑːnə] n banane f

band [bænd] n bande f; (at a dance) orchestre m; (Mil) musique f, fanfare f

bandage ['bændɪdʒ] n bandage m, pansement m ▷ vt (wound, leg) mettre un pansement or un bandage sur

Band-Aid® ['bændeɪd] n (us) pansement adhésif

B. & B. n abbr = **bed and breakfast**

bandit ['bændɪt] n bandit m

bang [bæŋ] n détonation f; (of door) claquement m; (blow) coup (violent) ▷ vt frapper (violemment); (door) claquer ▷ vi détoner; claquer

Bangladesh [bæŋglə'dɛʃ] n Bangladesh m

Bangladeshi [bæŋglə'dɛʃɪ] adj du Bangladesh ▷ n habitant(e) du Bangladesh

bangle ['bæŋgl] n bracelet m

bangs [bæŋz] npl (us: fringe) frange f

banish ['bænɪʃ] vt bannir

banister(s) ['bænɪstə(z)] n(pl) rampe f (d'escalier)

banjo (pl **~es** or **~s**) ['bændʒəu] n banjo m

bank [bæŋk] n banque f; (of river, lake) bord m, rive f; (of earth) talus m, remblai m ▷ vi (Aviat) virer sur l'aile; **bank on** vt fus miser or tabler sur; **bank account** n compte m en banque; **bank balance** n solde m bancaire; **bank card** (BRIT) n carte f d'identité bancaire; **bank charges** npl (BRIT) frais mpl de banque; **banker** n banquier m; **bank holiday** n (BRIT) jour férié (où les banques sont fermées); voir encadré; **banking** n opérations fpl bancaires; profession f de banquier; **bank manager** n directeur m d'agence (bancaire); **banknote** n billet m de banque

- **BANK HOLIDAY**
-
- Le terme **bank holiday** s'applique
- au Royaume-Uni aux jours fériés
- pendant lesquels banques et
- commerces sont fermés. Les
- principaux **bank holidays** à part
- Noël et Pâques se situent au mois
- de mai et fin août, et contrairement
- aux pays de tradition catholique, ne
- coïncident pas nécessairement avec
- une fête religieuse.

bankrupt ['bæŋkrʌpt] adj en faillite; **to go ~** faire faillite; **bankruptcy** n faillite f

bank statement n relevé m de compte

banner ['bænər] n bannière f

bannister(s) ['bænɪstə(z)] n(pl) = **banister(s)**

banquet ['bæŋkwɪt] n banquet m, festin m

baptism ['bæptɪzəm] n baptême m

baptize [bæp'taɪz] vt baptiser

bar [bɑːr] n (pub) bar m; (counter) comptoir m, bar; (rod: of metal etc) barre f; (of window etc) barreau m; (of chocolate)

tablette f, plaque f; (fig: obstacle)
obstacle m; (prohibition) mesure f
d'exclusion; (Mus) mesure f ▷ vt (road)
barrer; (person) exclure; (activity)
interdire; **~ of soap** savonnette
f; **behind ~s** (prisoner) derrière les
barreaux; **the B~** (Law) le barreau; **~
none** sans exception
barbaric [bɑːˈbærɪk] adj barbare
barbecue [ˈbɑːbɪkjuː] n barbecue m
barbed wire [ˈbɑːbd-] n fil m de fer
barbelé
barber [ˈbɑːbəʳ] n coiffeur m (pour
hommes); **barber's (shop)** (US **barber
(shop))** n salon m de coiffure (pour
hommes)
bar code n code m à barres, code-
barre m
bare [bɛəʳ] adj nu(e) ▷ vt mettre à nu,
dénuder; (teeth) montrer; **barefoot** adj,
adv nu-pieds, (les) pieds nus; **barely**
adv à peine
bargain [ˈbɑːgɪn] n (transaction)
marché m; (good buy) affaire f, occasion
f ▷ vi (haggle) marchander; (negotiate)
négocier, traiter; **into the ~** par-dessus
le marché; **bargain for** vt fus (inf): **he
got more than he ~ed for!** il en a eu
pour son argent!
barge [bɑːdʒ] n péniche f; **barge in** vi
(walk in) faire irruption; (interrupt talk)
intervenir mal à propos
bark [bɑːk] n (of tree) écorce f; (of dog)
aboiement m ▷ vi aboyer
barley [ˈbɑːlɪ] n orge f
barmaid [ˈbɑːmeɪd] n serveuse f (de
bar), barmaid f
barman [ˈbɑːmən] n serveur m (de bar),
barman m
barn [bɑːn] n grange f
barometer [bəˈrɒmɪtəʳ] n baromètre m
baron [ˈbærən] n baron m; **baroness**
n baronne f
barracks [ˈbærəks] npl caserne f
barrage [ˈbærɑːʒ] n (Mil) tir m de
barrage; (dam) barrage m; (of criticism)
feu m
barrel [ˈbærəl] n tonneau m; (of gun)

canon m
barren [ˈbærən] adj stérile
barrette [bəˈrɛt] (US) n barrette f
barricade [bærɪˈkeɪd] n barricade f
barrier [ˈbærɪəʳ] n barrière f
barring [ˈbɑːrɪŋ] prep sauf
barrister [ˈbærɪstəʳ] n (BRIT) avocat
(plaidant)
barrow [ˈbærəu] n (cart) charrette
f à bras
bartender [ˈbɑːtɛndəʳ] n (US) serveur
m (de bar), barman m
base [beɪs] n base f ▷ vt (opinion, belief)
to ~ sth on baser or fonder qch sur ▷ a⊘
vil(e), bas(se)
baseball [ˈbeɪsbɔːl] n base-ball m;
baseball cap n casquette f de base-ba
Basel [bɑːl] n = **Basle**
basement [ˈbeɪsmənt] n sous-sol m
bases [ˈbeɪsiːz] npl of **basis**
bash [bæʃ] vt (inf) frapper, cogner
basic [ˈbeɪsɪk] adj (precautions, rules)
élémentaire; (principles, research)
fondamental(e); (vocabulary, salary) de
base; (minimal) réduit(e) au minimum
rudimentaire; **basically** adv (in fact) e⊘
fait; (essentially) fondamentalement;
basics npl: **the basics** l'essentiel m
basil [ˈbæzl] n basilic m
basin [ˈbeɪsn] n (vessel, also Geo) cuvett
f, bassin m; (BRIT: for food) bol m; (also:
wash~) lavabo m
basis (pl **bases**) [ˈbeɪsɪs, -siːz] n base
f; **on a part-time/trial ~** à temps
partiel/à l'essai
basket [ˈbɑːskɪt] n corbeille f; (with
handle) panier m; **basketball** n
basket-ball m
Basle [bɑːl] n **Bâle**
Basque [bæsk] adj basque ▷ n Basque
m/f; **the ~ Country** le Pays basque
bass [beɪs] n (Mus) basse f
bastard [ˈbɑːstəd] n enfant naturel(le⊘
bâtard(e); (inf!) salaud m (!)
bat [bæt] n chauve-souris f; (for baseba
etc) batte f; (BRIT: for table tennis)
raquette f ▷ vt: **he didn't ~ an eyelid**
n'a pas sourcillé or bronché

atch [bætʃ] n (of bread) fournée f; (of papers) liasse f; (of applicants, letters) paquet m

ath (pl **~s**) [bɑːθ, bɑːðz] n bain m; (bathtub) baignoire f ▷ vt baigner, donner un bain à; **to have a ~** prendre un bain; see also **baths**

athe [beɪð] vi se baigner ▷ vt baigner; (wound etc) laver

athing ['beɪðɪŋ] n baignade f; **bathing costume** (us **bathing suit**) n maillot m (de bain)

ath: bathrobe n peignoir m de bain; **bathroom** n salle f de bains; **baths** [bɑːðz] npl (BRIT: also: **swimming baths**) piscine f; **bath towel** n serviette f de bain; **bathtub** n baignoire f

aton ['bætən] n bâton m; (Mus) baguette f; (club) matraque f

atter ['bætə'] vt battre ▷ n pâte f à frire; **battered** adj (hat, pan) cabossé(e); **battered wife/child** épouse/enfant maltraité(e) or martyr(e)

attery ['bætərɪ] n (for torch, radio) pile f; (Aut, Mil) batterie f; **battery farming** n élevage m en batterie

attle ['bætl] n bataille f, combat m ▷ vi se battre, lutter; **battlefield** n champ m de bataille

ay [beɪ] n (of sea) baie f; (BRIT: for parking) place f de stationnement; (: for loading) aire f de chargement; **B~ of Biscay** golfe m de Gascogne; **to hold sb at ~** tenir qn à distance or en échec

ay leaf n laurier m

azaar [bə'zɑː'] n (shop, market) bazar m; (sale) vente f de charité

BC n abbr (= British Broadcasting Corporation) office de la radiodiffusion et télévision britannique

.C. adv abbr (= before Christ) av. J.-C.

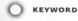 **KEYWORD**

e [biː] (pt **was, were**, pp **been**) aux vb **1** (with present participle: forming continuous tenses): **what are you doing?** que faites-vous?; **they're coming tomorrow** ils viennent demain; **I've been waiting for you for 2 hours** je t'attends depuis 2 heures **2** (with pp: forming passives) être; **to be killed** être tué(e); **the box had been opened** la boîte avait été ouverte; **he was nowhere to be seen** on ne le voyait nulle part

3 (in tag questions): **it was fun, wasn't it?** c'était drôle, n'est-ce pas?; **he's good-looking, isn't he?** il est beau, n'est-ce pas?; **she's back, is she?** elle est rentrée, n'est-ce pas or alors?

4 (+to +infinitive): **the house is to be sold** (necessity) la maison doit être vendue; (future) la maison va être vendue; **he's not to open it** il ne doit pas l'ouvrir

▷ vb + complement **1** (gen) être; **I'm English** je suis anglais(e); **I'm tired** je suis fatigué(e); **I'm hot/cold** j'ai chaud/froid; **he's a doctor** il est médecin; **be careful/good/quiet!** faites attention/soyez sages/taisez-vous!; **2 and 2 are 4** 2 et 2 font 4

2 (of health) aller; **how are you?** comment allez-vous?; **I'm better now** je vais mieux maintenant; **he's very ill** il est très malade

3 (of age) avoir; **how old are you?** quel âge avez-vous?; **I'm sixteen (years old)** j'ai seize ans

4 (cost) coûter; **how much was the meal?** combien a coûté le repas?; **that'll be £5, please** ça fera 5 livres, s'il vous plaît; **this shirt is £17** cette chemise coûte 17 livres

▷ vi **1** (exist, occur etc) être, exister; **the prettiest girl that ever was** la fille la plus jolie qui ait jamais existé; **is there a God?** y a-t-il un dieu?; **be that as it may** quoi qu'il en soit; **so be it** soit

2 (referring to place) être, se trouver; **I won't be here tomorrow** je ne serai pas là demain

3 (referring to movement) aller; **where have you been?** où êtes-vous allé(s)?

▷ *impers vb* **1** (*referring to time*) être; **it's 5 o'clock** il est 5 heures; **it's the 28th of April** c'est le 28 avril
2 (*referring to distance*): **it's 10 km to the village** le village est à 10 km
3 (*referring to the weather*) faire; **it's too hot/cold** il fait trop chaud/froid; **it's windy today** il y a du vent aujourd'hui
4 (*emphatic*): **it's me/the postman** c'est moi/le facteur; **it was Maria who paid the bill** c'est Maria qui a payé la note

beach [biːtʃ] *n* plage *f* ▷ *vt* échouer
beacon ['biːkən] *n* (*lighthouse*) fanal *m*; (*marker*) balise *f*
bead [biːd] *n* perle *f*; (*of dew, sweat*) goutte *f*; **beads** *npl* (*necklace*) collier *m*
beak [biːk] *n* bec *m*
beam [biːm] *n* (*Archit*) poutre *f*; (*of light*) rayon *m* ▷ *vi* rayonner
bean [biːn] *n* haricot *m*; (*of coffee*) grain *m*; **beansprouts** *npl* pousses *fpl* or germes *mpl* de soja
bear [bɛəʳ] *n* ours *m* ▷ *vb* (*pt* **bore**, *pp* **borne**) ▷ *vt* porter; (*endure*) supporter, rapporter ▷ *vi*: **to ~ right/left** obliquer à droite/gauche, se diriger vers la droite/gauche
beard [bɪəd] *n* barbe *f*
bearer ['bɛərəʳ] *n* porteur *m*; (*of passport etc*) titulaire *mf*
bearing ['bɛərɪŋ] *n* maintien *m*, allure *f*; (*connection*) rapport *m*; (*Tech*): **(ball) bearings** *npl* roulement *m* (à billes)
beast [biːst] *n* bête *f*; (*inf: person*) brute *f*
beat [biːt] *n* battement *m*; (*Mus*) temps *m*, mesure *f*; (*of policeman*) ronde *f* ▷ *vt, vi* (*pt ~*, *pp ~en*) battre; **off the ~en track** hors des chemins or sentiers battus; **to ~ it** (*inf*) ficher le camp; **beat up** *vt* (*inf: person*) tabasser; **beating** *n* raclée *f*
beautiful ['bjuːtɪful] *adj* beau (belle); **beautifully** *adv* admirablement
beauty ['bjuːtɪ] *n* beauté *f*; **beauty parlour** (*US* **beauty parlor**) [-'pɑːləʳ] *n* institut *m* de beauté; **beauty salon** *n* institut *m* de beauté; **beauty spot**

n (*on skin*) grain *m* de beauté; (*BRIT Tourism*) site naturel (d'une grande beauté)
beaver ['biːvəʳ] *n* castor *m*
became [bɪ'keɪm] *pt of* **become**
because [bɪ'kɔz] *conj* parce que; **~ of** *prep* à cause de
beckon ['bɛkən] *vt* (*also*: **~ to**) faire signe (de venir) à
become [bɪ'kʌm] *vi* devenir; **to ~ fat/thin** grossir/maigrir; **to ~ angry** s mettre en colère
bed [bɛd] *n* lit *m*; (*of flowers*) parterre *m*; (*of coal, clay*) couche *f*; (*of sea, lake*) fond *m*; **to go to ~** aller se coucher; **bed and breakfast** *n* (*terms*) chambre et petit déjeuner; (*place*) ≈ chambre *f* d'hôte; *voi* encadré; **bedclothes** *npl* couvertures *fpl* et draps *mpl*; **bedding** *n* literie *f*; **bed linen** *n* draps *mpl* de lit (et taies *fpl* d'oreillers), literie *f*; **bedroom** *n* chambre *f* (à coucher); **bedside** *n*: **at sb's bedside** au chevet de qn; **bedside lamp** *n* lampe *f* de chevet; **bedside table** *n* table *f* de chevet; **bedsit(ter)** *n* (*BRIT*) chambre meublée, studio *m*; **bedspread** *n* couvre-lit *m*, dessus-de-lit *m*; **bedtime** *n*: **it's bedtime** c'est l'heure de se coucher

- **BED AND BREAKFAST**
-
- Un **bed and breakfast** est une
- petite pension dans une maison
- particulière ou une ferme où l'on
- peut louer une chambre avec
- petit déjeuner compris pour un
- prix modique par rapport à ce que
- l'on paierait dans un hôtel. Ces
- établissements sont communémen
- appelés "B & B", et sont signalés par
- une pancarte dans le jardin ou au-
- dessus de la porte.

bee [biː] *n* abeille *f*
beech [biːtʃ] *n* hêtre *m*
beef [biːf] *n* bœuf *m*; **roast ~** rosbif *m*; **beefburger** *n* hamburger *m*;

Beefeater n hallebardier m (de la tour de Londres)

een [bi:n] pp of **be**

eer [bɪər] n bière f; **beer garden** n (BRIT) jardin m d'un pub (où l'on peut emmener ses consommations)

eet [bi:t] n (vegetable) betterave f; (US: also: **red ~**) betterave f (potagère)

eetle ['bi:tl] n scarabée m, coléoptère m

eetroot ['bi:tru:t] n (BRIT) betterave f

efore [bɪ'fɔːr] prep (of time) avant; (of space) devant ▷ conj avant que + sub; avant de ▷ adv avant; **~ going** avant de partir; **~ she goes** avant qu'elle (ne) parte; **the week ~** la semaine précédente or d'avant; **I've never seen it ~** c'est la première fois que je le vois; **beforehand** adv au préalable, à l'avance

eg [bɛg] vi mendier ▷ vt mendier; (forgiveness, mercy etc) demander; (entreat) supplier; **to ~ sb to do sth** supplier qn de faire qch; see also **pardon**

egan [bɪ'gæn] pt of **begin**

eggar ['bɛgər] n mendiant(e)

egin [bɪ'gɪn] (pt **began**, pp **begun**) vt, vi commencer; **to ~ doing** or **to do sth** commencer à faire qch; **beginner** n débutant(e); **beginning** n commencement m, début m

egun [bɪ'gʌn] pp of **begin**

ehalf [bɪ'hɑːf] n: **on ~ of**, (US) **in ~ of** (representing) de la part de; (for benefit of) pour le compte de; **on my/his ~** de ma/sa part

ehave [bɪ'heɪv] vi se conduire, se comporter; (well: also: **~ o.s.**) se conduire bien or comme il faut; **behaviour** (US **behavior**) n comportement m, conduite f

ehind [bɪ'haɪnd] prep derrière; (time) en retard sur; (supporting): **to be ~ sb** soutenir qn ▷ adv derrière; en retard ▷ n derrière m; **~ the scenes** dans les coulisses; **to be ~ (schedule) with sth** être en retard dans qch

eige [beɪʒ] adj beige

Beijing ['beɪ'dʒɪŋ] n Pékin

being ['bi:ɪŋ] n être m; **to come into ~** prendre naissance

belated [bɪ'leɪtɪd] adj tardif(-ive)

belch [bɛltʃ] vi avoir un renvoi, roter ▷ vt (also: **~ out**: smoke etc) vomir, cracher

Belgian ['bɛldʒən] adj belge, de Belgique ▷ n Belge m/f

Belgium ['bɛldʒəm] n Belgique f

belief [bɪ'li:f] n (opinion) conviction f; (trust, faith) foi f

believe [bɪ'li:v] vt, vi croire, estimer; **to ~ in** (God) croire en; (ghosts, method) croire à; **believer** n (in idea, activity) partisan(e); (Rel) croyant(e)

bell [bɛl] n cloche f; (small) clochette f, grelot m; (on door) sonnette f; (electric) sonnerie f

bellboy ['bɛlbɔɪ] (US **bellhop** ['bɛlhɔp]) n groom m, chasseur m

bellow ['bɛləu] vi (bull) meugler; (person) brailler

bell pepper n (esp US) poivron m

belly ['bɛlɪ] n ventre m; **belly button** (inf) n nombril m

belong [bɪ'lɔŋ] vi: **to ~ to** appartenir à; (club etc) faire partie de; **this book ~s here** ce livre va ici, la place de ce livre est ici; **belongings** npl affaires fpl, possessions fpl

beloved [bɪ'lʌvɪd] adj (bien-)aimé(e), chéri(e)

below [bɪ'ləu] prep sous, au-dessous de ▷ adv en dessous; en contre-bas; **see ~** voir plus bas or plus loin or ci-dessous

belt [bɛlt] n ceinture f; (Tech) courroie f ▷ vt (thrash) donner une raclée à; **beltway** n (US Aut) route f de ceinture; (: motorway) périphérique m

bemused [bɪ'mju:zd] adj médusé(e)

bench [bɛntʃ] n banc m; (in workshop) établi m; **the B~** (Law: judges) la magistrature, la Cour

bend [bɛnd] vb (pt, pp **bent**) ▷ vt courber; (leg, arm) plier ▷ vi se courber ▷ n (BRIT: in road) virage m, tournant m; (in pipe, river) coude m; **bend down** vi se baisser; **bend over** vi se pencher

beneath [bɪˈniːθ] prep sous, au-dessous de; (unworthy of) indigne de ▷ adv dessous, au-dessous, en bas

beneficial [bɛnɪˈfɪʃəl] adj: **~ (to)** salutaire (pour), bénéfique (à)

benefit [ˈbɛnɪfɪt] n avantage m, profit m; (allowance of money) allocation f ▷ vt faire du bien à, profiter à ▷ vi: **he'll ~ from it** cela lui fera du bien, il y gagnera or s'en trouvera bien

Benelux [ˈbɛnɪlʌks] n Bénélux m

benign [bɪˈnaɪn] adj (person, smile) bienveillant(e), affable; (Med) bénin(-igne)

bent [bɛnt] pt, pp of **bend** ▷ n inclination f, penchant m ▷ adj: **to be ~ on** être résolu(e) à

bereaved [bɪˈriːvd] n: **the ~** la famille du disparu

beret [ˈbɛreɪ] n béret m

Berlin [bəːˈlɪn] n Berlin

Bermuda [bəːˈmjuːdə] n Bermudes fpl

Bern [bəːn] n Berne

berry [ˈbɛrɪ] n baie f

berth [bəːθ] n (bed) couchette f; (for ship) poste m d'amarrage, mouillage m ▷ vi (in harbour) venir à quai; (at anchor) mouiller

beside [bɪˈsaɪd] prep à côté de; (compared with) par rapport à; **that's ~ the point** ça n'a rien à voir; **to be ~ o.s. (with anger)** être hors de soi; **besides** adv en outre, de plus ▷ prep en plus de; (except) excepté

best [bɛst] adj meilleur(e) ▷ adv le mieux; **the ~ part of** (quantity) le plus clair de, la plus grande partie de; **at ~** au mieux; **to make the ~ of sth** s'accommoder de qch (du mieux que l'on peut); **to do one's ~** faire de son mieux; **to the ~ of my knowledge** pour autant que je sache; **to the ~ of my ability** du mieux que je pourrai; **best-before date** n date f de limite d'utilisation or de consommation; **best man** (irreg) n garçon m d'honneur; **bestseller** n best-seller m, succès m

de librairie

bet [bɛt] n pari m ▷ vt, vi (pt, pp ~ or **~ted**) parier; **to ~ sb sth** parier qch à q

betray [bɪˈtreɪ] vt trahir

better [ˈbɛtər] adj meilleur(e) ▷ adv mieux ▷ vt améliorer ▷ n: **to get the ~ of** triompher de, l'emporter sur; **you had ~ do it** vous feriez mieux de le faire; **he thought ~ of it** il s'est ravisé; **to get ~** (Med) aller mieux; (improve) s'améliorer

betting [ˈbɛtɪŋ] n paris mpl; **betting shop** n (BRIT) bureau m de paris

between [bɪˈtwiːn] prep entre ▷ adv a milieu, dans l'intervalle

beverage [ˈbɛvərɪdʒ] n boisson f (gén sans alcool)

beware [bɪˈwɛər] vi: **to ~ (of)** prendre garde (à); **"~ of the dog"** "(attention) chien méchant"

bewildered [bɪˈwɪldəd] adj dérouté(e ahuri(e)

beyond [bɪˈjɒnd] prep (in space, time) au-delà de; (exceeding) au-dessus de ▷ adv au-delà; **~ doubt** hors de doute; **repair** irréparable

bias [ˈbaɪəs] n (prejudice) préjugé m, parti pris; (preference) prévention f; **bias(s)ed** adj partial(e), montrant un parti pris

bib [bɪb] n bavoir m

Bible [ˈbaɪbl] n Bible f

bicarbonate of soda [baɪˈkɑːbənɪt-] n bicarbonate m de soude

biceps [ˈbaɪsɛps] n biceps m

bicycle [ˈbaɪsɪkl] n bicyclette f; **bicycle pump** n pompe f à vélo

bid [bɪd] n offre f; (at auction) enchère f; (attempt) tentative f ▷ vb (pt ~ or **bade**, pp ~ or **~den**) ▷ vi faire une enchère or offre ▷ vt faire une enchère or offre de; **to ~ sb good day** souhaiter le bonjour à qn; **bidder** n: **the highest bidder** le plus offrant

bidet [ˈbiːdeɪ] n bidet m

big [bɪg] adj (in height: person, building, tree) grand(e); (in bulk, amount: person, parcel, book) gros(se); **bigheaded** adj prétentieux(-euse); **big toe** n gros orteil

● **BIG APPLE**
●
● Si l'on sait que "The Big Apple"
● désigne la ville de New York ("apple"
● est en réalité un terme d'argot
● signifiant "grande ville"), on connaît
● moins les surnoms donnés aux
● autres grandes villes américaines.
● Chicago est surnommée "Windy
● City" à cause des rafales soufflant du
● lac Michigan, La Nouvelle-Orléans
● doit son sobriquet de "Big Easy"
● à son style de vie décontracté, et
● l'industrie automobile a donné à
● Detroit son surnom de "Motown".

ike [baɪk] n vélo m; **bike lane** n piste f cyclable
ikini [bɪˈkiːnɪ] n bikini m
ilateral [baɪˈlætərl] adj bilatéral(e)
ilingual [baɪˈlɪŋgwəl] adj bilingue
ill [bɪl] n note f, facture f; (in restaurant) addition f, note f; (Pol) projet m de loi; (US: banknote) billet m (de banque); (notice) affiche f; (of bird) bec m; **put it on my ~** mettez-le sur mon compte; **"post no ~s"** "défense d'afficher"; **to fit** or **fill the ~** (fig) faire l'affaire; **billboard** (US) n panneau m d'affichage; **billfold** [ˈbɪlfəuld] n (US) portefeuille m
illiards [ˈbɪljədz] n (jeu m de) billard m
illion [ˈbɪljən] n (BRIT) billion m (million de millions); (US) milliard m
in [bɪn] n boîte f; (BRIT: also: **dust~**, **litter ~**) poubelle f; (for coal) coffre m
ind (pt, pp **bound**) [baɪnd, baund] vt attacher; (book) relier; (oblige) obliger, contraindre ▷ n (inf: nuisance) scie f
inge [bɪndʒ] n (inf): **to go on a ~** faire la bringue
ingo [ˈbɪngəu] n sorte de jeu de loto pratiqué dans des établissements publics
inoculars [bɪˈnɔkjuləz] npl jumelles fpl
io... [baɪə'] prefix: **biochemistry**

n biochimie f; **biodegradable** [ˈbaɪəudɪˈgreɪdəbl] adj biodégradable; **biography** [baɪˈɔgrəfɪ] n biographie f; **biological** adj biologique; **biology** [baɪˈɔlədʒɪ] n biologie f; **biometric** [baɪəˈmɛtrɪk] adj biométrique
birch [bəːtʃ] n bouleau m
bird [bəːd] n oiseau m; (BRIT inf: girl) nana f; **bird flu** n grippe f aviaire; **bird of prey** n oiseau m de proie; **birdwatching** n ornithologie f (d'amateur)
Biro® [ˈbaɪərəu] n stylo m à bille
birth [bəːθ] n naissance f; **to give ~ to** donner naissance à, mettre au monde; (subj: animal) mettre bas; **birth certificate** n acte m de naissance; **birth control** n (policy) limitation f des naissances; (methods) méthode(s) contraceptive(s); **birthday** n anniversaire m ▷ cpd (cake, card etc) d'anniversaire; **birthmark** n envie f, tache f de vin; **birthplace** n lieu m de naissance
biscuit [ˈbɪskɪt] n (BRIT) biscuit m; (US) petit pain au lait
bishop [ˈbɪʃəp] n évêque m; (Chess) fou m
bistro [ˈbiːstrəu] n petit restaurant m, bistrot m
bit [bɪt] pt of **bite** ▷ n morceau m; (Comput) bit m, élément m binaire; (of tool) mèche f; (of horse) mors m; **a ~ of** un peu de; **a ~ mad/dangerous** un peu fou/risqué; **~ by ~** petit à petit
bitch [bɪtʃ] n (dog) chienne f; (inf!) salope f(!), garce f
bite [baɪt] vt, vi (pt **bit**, pp **bitten**) mordre; (insect) piquer ▷ n morsure f; (insect bite) piqûre f; (mouthful) bouchée f; **let's have a ~ (to eat)** mangeons un morceau; **to ~ one's nails** se ronger les ongles
bitten [ˈbɪtn] pp of **bite**
bitter [ˈbɪtər] adj amer(-ère); (criticism) cinglant(e); (icy: weather, wind) glacial(e) ▷ n (BRIT: beer) bière f (à forte teneur en houblon)
bizarre [bɪˈzaːr] adj bizarre

black [blæk] *adj* noir(e) ▷ *n* (*colour*) noir *m*; (*person*): **B~** noir(e) ▷ *vt* (*BRIT Industry*) boycotter; **to give sb a ~ eye** pocher l'œil à qn, faire un œil au beurre noir à qn; **to be in the ~** (*in credit*) avoir un compte créditeur; **~ and blue** (*bruised*) couvert(e) de bleus; **black out** *vi* (*faint*) s'évanouir; **blackberry** *n* mûre *f*; **blackbird** *n* merle *m*; **blackboard** *n* tableau noir; **black coffee** *n* café noir; **blackcurrant** *n* cassis *m*; **black ice** *n* verglas *m*; **blackmail** *n* chantage *m* ▷ *vt* faire chanter, soumettre au chantage; **black market** *n* marché noir; **blackout** *n* panne *f* d'électricité; (*in wartime*) black-out *m*; (*TV*) interruption *f* d'émission; (*fainting*) syncope *f*; **black pepper** *n* poivre noir; **black pudding** *n* boudin (noir); **Black Sea** *n*: **the Black Sea** la mer Noire

bladder ['blædə'] *n* vessie *f*

blade [bleɪd] *n* lame *f*; (*of propeller*) pale *f*; **a ~ of grass** un brin d'herbe

blame [bleɪm] *n* faute *f*, blâme *m* ▷ *vt*: **to ~ sb/sth for sth** attribuer à qn/qch la responsabilité de qch; reprocher qch à qn/qch; **I'm not to ~** ce n'est pas ma faute

bland [blænd] *adj* (*taste, food*) doux (douce), fade

blank [blæŋk] *adj* blanc (blanche); (*look*) sans expression, dénué(e) d'expression ▷ *n* espace *m* vide, blanc *m*; (*cartridge*) cartouche f à blanc; **his mind was a ~** il avait la tête vide

blanket ['blæŋkɪt] *n* couverture *f*; (*of snow, cloud*) couche *f*

blast [blɑːst] *n* explosion *f*; (*shock wave*) souffle *m*; (*of air, steam*) bouffée *f* ▷ *vt* faire sauter *or* exploser

blatant ['bleɪtənt] *adj* flagrant(e), criant(e)

blaze [bleɪz] *n* (*fire*) incendie *m*; (*fig*) flamboiement *m* ▷ *vi* (*fire*) flamber; (*fig*) flamboyer, resplendir ▷ *vt*: **to ~ a trail** (*fig*) montrer la voie; **in a ~ of publicity** à grand renfort de publicité

blazer ['bleɪzə'] *n* blazer *m*

bleach [bliːtʃ] *n* (*also*: **household ~**) eau *f* de Javel ▷ *vt* (*linen*) blanchir; **bleachers** *npl* (*US Sport*) gradins *mpl* (*en plein soleil*)

bleak [bliːk] *adj* morne, désolé(e); (*weather*) triste, maussade; (*smile*) lugubre; (*prospect, future*) morose

bled [blɛd] *pt, pp of* **bleed**

bleed (*pt, pp* **bled**) [bliːd, blɛd] *vt* saigner; (*brakes, radiator*) purger ▷ *vi* saigner; **my nose is ~ing** je saigne du nez

blemish ['blɛmɪʃ] *n* défaut *m*; (*on reputation*) tache *f*

blend [blɛnd] *n* mélange *m* ▷ *vt* mélanger ▷ *vi* (*colours etc: also*: **~ in**) se mélanger, se fondre, s'allier; **blender** *n* (*Culin*) mixeur *m*

bless (*pt, pp* **~ed** *or* **blest**) [blɛs, blɛst] *vt* bénir; **~ you!** (*after sneeze*) à tes souhaits!; **blessing** *n* bénédiction *f*; (*godsend*) bienfait *m*

blew [bluː] *pt of* **blow**

blight [blaɪt] *vt* (*hopes etc*) anéantir, briser

blind [blaɪnd] *adj* aveugle ▷ *n* (*for window*) store *m* ▷ *vt* aveugler; **the blind** *npl* les aveugles *mpl*; **blind alley** *n* impasse *f*; **blindfold** *n* bandeau *m* ▷ *adj, adv* les yeux bandés ▷ *vt* bander les yeux à

blink [blɪŋk] *vi* cligner des yeux; (*light*) clignoter

bliss [blɪs] *n* félicité *f*, bonheur *m* sans mélange

blister ['blɪstə'] *n* (*on skin*) ampoule *f*, cloque *f*; (*on paintwork*) boursouflure *f* ▷ *vi* (*paint*) se boursoufler, se cloquer

blizzard ['blɪzəd] *n* blizzard *m*, tempête *f* de neige

bloated ['bləʊtɪd] *adj* (*face*) bouffi(e); (*stomach, person*) gonflé(e)

blob [blɔb] *n* (*drop*) goutte *f*; (*stain, spot*) tache *f*

block [blɔk] *n* bloc *m*; (*in pipes*) obstruction *f*; (*toy*) cube *m*; (*of buildings*) pâté *m* (de maisons) ▷ *vt* bloquer;

(fig) faire obstacle à; **the sink is ~ed** l'évier est bouché; **~ of flats** (BRIT) immeuble (locatif); **mental ~** blocage m; **block up** vt boucher; **blockade** [blɔ'keɪd] n blocus m ▷ vt faire le blocus de; **blockage** n obstruction f; **blockbuster** n (film, book) grand succès; **block capitals** npl majuscules fpl d'imprimerie; **block letters** npl majuscules fpl

log [blɔg] n blog m, blogue m

loke [bləʊk] n (BRIT inf) type m

lond(e) [blɔnd] adj, n blond(e)

lood [blʌd] n sang m; **blood donor** n donneur(-euse) de sang; **blood group** n groupe sanguin; **blood poisoning** n empoisonnement m du sang; **blood pressure** n tension (artérielle); **bloodshed** n effusion f de sang, carnage m; **bloodshot** adj: **bloodshot eyes** yeux injectés de sang; **bloodstream** n sang m, système sanguin; **blood test** n analyse f de sang; **blood transfusion** n transfusion f de sang; **blood type** n groupe sanguin; **blood vessel** n vaisseau sanguin; **bloody** adj sanglant(e); (BRIT inf!): **this bloody ...** ce foutu ..., ce putain de ... (!) ▷ adv: **bloody strong/good** (BRIT inf!) vachement or sacrément fort/bon

loom [bluːm] n fleur f ▷ vi être en fleur

lossom ['blɔsəm] n fleur(s) f(pl) ▷ vi être en fleurs; (fig) s'épanouir

lot [blɔt] n tache f ▷ vt tacher; (ink) sécher

louse [blauz] n (feminine garment) chemisier m, corsage m

low [bləʊ] n coup m ▷ vb (pt blew, pp ~n) ▷ vi souffler ▷ vt (instrument) jouer de; (fuse) faire sauter; **to ~ one's nose** se moucher; **blow away** vi s'envoler ▷ vt chasser, faire s'envoler; **blow out** vi (fire, flame) s'éteindre; (tyre) éclater; (fuse) sauter; **blow up** vi exploser, sauter ▷ vt faire sauter; (tyre) gonfler; (Phot) agrandir; **blow-dry** n (hairstyle) brushing m

blown [bləʊn] pp of **blow**

blue [bluː] adj bleu(e); (depressed) triste; **~ film/joke** film m/histoire f pornographique; **out of the ~** (fig) à l'improviste, sans qu'on s'y attende; **bluebell** n jacinthe f des bois; **blueberry** n myrtille f, airelle f; **blue cheese** n (fromage) bleu m; **blues** npl: **the blues** (Mus) le blues; **to have the blues** (inf: feeling) avoir le cafard; **bluetit** n mésange bleue

bluff [blʌf] vi bluffer ▷ n bluff m; **to call sb's ~** mettre qn au défi d'exécuter ses menaces

blunder ['blʌndəʳ] n gaffe f, bévue f ▷ vi faire une gaffe or une bévue

blunt [blʌnt] adj (knife) émoussé(e), peu tranchant(e); (pencil) mal taillé(e); (person) brusque, ne mâchant pas ses mots

blur [bləːʳ] n (shape): **to become a ~** devenir flou ▷ vt brouiller, rendre flou(e); **blurred** adj flou(e)

blush [blʌʃ] vi rougir ▷ n rougeur f; **blusher** n rouge m à joues

board [bɔːd] n (wooden) planche f; (on wall) panneau m; (for chess etc) plateau m; (cardboard) carton m; (committee) conseil m, comité m; (in firm) conseil d'administration; (Naut, Aviat): **on ~** à bord ▷ vt (ship) monter à bord de; (train) monter dans; **full ~** (BRIT) pension complète; **half ~** (BRIT) demi-pension f; **~ and lodging** n chambre f avec pension; **to go by the ~** (hopes, principles) être abandonné(e); **board game** n jeu m de société; **boarding card** n (Aviat, Naut) carte f d'embarquement; **boarding pass** n (BRIT) = **boarding card**; **boarding school** n internat m, pensionnat m; **board room** n salle f du conseil d'administration

boast [bəʊst] vi: **to ~ (about or of)** se vanter (de)

boat [bəʊt] n bateau m; (small) canot m; barque f

bob [bɔb] vi (boat, cork on water: also: ~

up and down) danser, se balancer
bobby pin ['bɔbɪ-] n (US) pince f à cheveux
body ['bɔdɪ] n corps m; (of car) carrosserie f; (fig: society) organe m, organisme m; **body-building** n body-building m, culturisme m; **bodyguard** n garde m du corps; **bodywork** n carrosserie f
bog [bɔg] n tourbière f ▷ vt: **to get ~ged down (in)** (fig) s'enliser (dans)
bogus ['bəugəs] adj bidon inv; fantôme
boil [bɔɪl] vt (faire) bouillir ▷ vi bouillir ▷ n (Med) furoncle m; **to come to the** or (US) **a ~** bouillir; **boil down** vi (fig): **to ~ down to** se réduire or ramener à; **boil over** vi déborder; **boiled egg** n œuf m à la coque; **boiled potatoes** n pommes fpl à l'anglaise or à l'eau; **boiler** n chaudière f; **boiling** ['bɔɪlɪŋ] adj: **I'm boiling (hot)** (inf) je crève de chaud; **boiling point** n point m d'ébullition
bold [bəuld] adj hardi(e), audacieux(-euse); (pej) effronté(e); (outline, colour) franc (franche), tranché(e), marqué(e)
bollard ['bɔləd] n (BRIT Aut) borne lumineuse or de signalisation
bolt [bəult] n verrou m; (with nut) boulon m ▷ adv: **~ upright** droit(e) comme un piquet ▷ vt (door) verrouiller; (food) engloutir ▷ vi se sauver, filer (comme une flèche); (horse) s'emballer
bomb [bɔm] n bombe f ▷ vt bombarder; **bombard** [bɔm'bɑːd] vt bombarder; **bomber** n (Aviat) bombardier m; (terrorist) poseur m de bombes; **bomb scare** n alerte f à la bombe
bond [bɔnd] n lien m; (binding promise) engagement m, obligation f; (Finance) obligation; **bonds** npl (chains) chaînes fpl; **in ~** (of goods) en entrepôt
bone [bəun] n os m; (of fish) arête f ▷ vt désosser; ôter les arêtes de
bonfire ['bɔnfaɪə'] n feu m (de joie); (for rubbish) feu
bonnet ['bɔnɪt] n bonnet m; (BRIT: of car) capot m
bonus ['bəunəs] n (money) prime f; (advantage) avantage m
boo [buː] excl hou!, peuh! ▷ vt huer
book [buk] n livre m; (of stamps, tickets etc) carnet m; (Comm): **books** npl comptes mpl, comptabilité f ▷ vt (ticket) prendre; (seat, room) réserver; (football player) prendre le nom de, donner un carton à; **I ~ed a table in the name of ...** j'ai réservé une table au nom de ...; **book in** vi (BRIT: at hotel) prendre sa chambre; **book up** vt réserver; **the hotel is ~ed up** l'hôtel est complet; **bookcase** n bibliothèque f (meuble); **booking** n (BRIT) réservation f; **I confirmed my booking by fax/e-mail** j'ai confirmé ma réservation par fax/e-mail; **booking office** n (BRIT) bureau m de location; **book-keeping** n comptabilité f; **booklet** n brochure f; **bookmaker** n bookmaker m; **bookmark** n (for book) marque-page m; (Comput) signet m; **bookseller** n libraire m/f; **bookshelf** n (single) étagère f (à livres); (bookcase) bibliothèque f; **bookshop, bookstore** n librairie f
boom [buːm] n (noise) grondement m; (in prices, population) forte augmentation; (busy period) boom m, vague f de prospérité ▷ vi gronder; prospérer
boost [buːst] n stimulant m, remontant m ▷ vt stimuler
boot [buːt] n botte f; (for hiking) chaussure f (de marche); (ankle boot) bottine f; (BRIT: of car) coffre m ▷ vt (Comput) lancer, mettre en route; **to ~ (in addition)** par-dessus le marché, en plus
booth [buːð] n (at fair) baraque (foraine); (of telephone etc) cabine f; (also: **voting ~**) isoloir m
booze [buːz] (inf) n boissons fpl alcooliques, alcool m
border ['bɔːdə'] n bordure f; bord m; (of a country) frontière f; **borderline** n (fig)

ligne f de démarcation

ore [bɔːʳ] *pt of* **bear** ▷ *vt* (*person*) ennuyer; raser; (*hole*) percer; (*well, tunnel*) creuser ▷ *n* (*person*) raseur(-euse); (*boring thing*) barbe f; (*of gun*) calibre m; **bored** *adj*: **to be bored** s'ennuyer; **boredom** *n* ennui m

oring ['bɔːrɪŋ] *adj* ennuyeux(-euse)

orn [bɔːn] *adj*: **to be ~** naître; **I was ~ in 1960** je suis né en 1960

orne [bɔːn] *pp of* **bear**

orough ['bʌrə] *n* municipalité f

orrow ['bɔrəu] *vt*: **to ~ sth (from sb)** emprunter qch (à qn)

osnia(-Herzegovina) ['bɔːsnɪə(hɛrzəˈgəuviːnə)] *n* Bosnie-Herzégovine f; **Bosnian** *adj* bosniaque, bosnien(ne) ▷ *n* Bosniaque m/f, Bosnien(ne)

osom ['buzəm] *n* poitrine f; (*fig*) sein m

oss [bɔs] *n* patron(ne) ▷ *vt* (*also*: **~ about, ~ around**) mener à la baguette; **bossy** *adj* autoritaire

oth [bəuθ] *adj* les deux, l'un(e) et l'autre ▷ *pron*: **~ (of them)** les deux, tous (toutes) les deux, l'un(e) et l'autre; **~ of us went, we ~ went** nous y sommes allés tous les deux ▷ *adv*: **~ A and B** A et B

other ['bɔðəʳ] *vt* (*worry*) tracasser; (*needle, bait*) importuner, ennuyer; (*disturb*) déranger ▷ *vi* (*also*: **~ o.s.**) se tracasser, se faire du souci ▷ *n* (*trouble*) ennuis mpl; **to ~ doing** prendre la peine de faire; **don't ~** ce n'est pas la peine; **it's no ~** aucun problème

ottle ['bɔtl] *n* bouteille f; (*baby's*) biberon m; (*of perfume, medicine*) flacon m ▷ *vt* mettre en bouteille(s); **bottle bank** *n* conteneur m (de bouteilles); **bottle-opener** *n* ouvre-bouteille m

ottom ['bɔtəm] *n* (*of container, sea etc*) fond m; (*buttocks*) derrière m; (*of page, list*) bas m; (*of mountain, tree, hill*) pied m ▷ *adj* (*shelf, step*) du bas

ought [bɔːt] *pt, pp of* **buy**

oulder ['bəuldəʳ] *n* gros rocher (*gén lisse, arrondi*)

bounce [bauns] *vi* (*ball*) rebondir; (*cheque*) être refusé (*étant sans provision*) ▷ *vt* faire rebondir ▷ *n* (*rebound*) rebond m; **bouncer** *n* (*inf: at dance, club*) videur m

bound [baund] *pt, pp of* **bind** ▷ *n* (*gen pl*) limite f; (*leap*) bond m ▷ *vi* (*leap*) bondir ▷ *vt* (*limit*) borner ▷ *adj*: **to be ~ to do sth** (*obliged*) être obligé(e) or avoir obligation de faire qch; **he's ~ to fail** (*likely*) il est sûr d'échouer, son échec est inévitable or assuré; **~ by** (*law, regulation*) engagé(e) par; **~ for** à destination de; **out of ~s** dont l'accès est interdit

boundary ['baundrɪ] *n* frontière f

bouquet ['bukeɪ] *n* bouquet m

bourbon ['buəbən] *n* (*us: also:* **~ whiskey**) bourbon m

bout [baut] *n* période f; (*of malaria etc*) accès m, crise f, attaque f; (*Boxing etc*) combat m, match m

boutique [buːˈtiːk] *n* boutique f

bow¹ [bəu] *n* nœud m; (*weapon*) arc m; (*Mus*) archet m

bow² [bau] *n* (*with body*) révérence f, inclination f (du buste *or* corps); (*Naut: also:* **~s**) proue f ▷ *vi* faire une révérence, s'incliner

bowels [bauəlz] *npl* intestins mpl; (*fig*) entrailles fpl

bowl [bəul] *n* (*for eating*) bol m; (*for washing*) cuvette f; (*ball*) boule f ▷ *vi* (*Cricket*) lancer (la balle); **bowler** *n* (*Cricket*) lanceur m (de la balle); (*BRIT: also:* **bowler hat**) chapeau m melon m; **bowling** *n* (*game*) jeu m de boules, jeu de quilles; **bowling alley** *n* bowling m; **bowling green** *n* terrain m de boules (*gazonné et carré*); **bowls** *n* (jeu m de) boules fpl

bow tie [bəu-] *n* nœud m papillon

box [bɔks] *n* boîte f; (*also:* **cardboard ~**) carton m; (*Theat*) loge f ▷ *vt* mettre en boîte ▷ *vi* boxer, faire de la boxe; **boxer** ['bɔksəʳ] *n* (*person*) boxeur m; **boxer shorts** *npl* caleçon m; **boxing** ['bɔksɪŋ] *n* (*sport*) boxe f; **Boxing Day**

n (BRIT) le lendemain de Noël; voir encadré; **boxing gloves** npl gants mpl de boxe; **boxing ring** n ring m; **box junction** n (BRIT Aut) zone f (de carrefour) d'accès réglementé; **box office** n bureau m de location

● **BOXING DAY**
●
● **Boxing Day** est le lendemain de
● Noël, férié en Grande-Bretagne. Ce
● nom vient d'une coutume du XIXe
● siècle qui consistait à donner des
● cadeaux de Noël (dans des boîtes) à
● ses employés etc le 26 décembre.

boy [bɔɪ] n garçon m; **boy band** n boys band m
boycott ['bɔɪkɔt] n boycottage m ▷ vt boycotter
boyfriend ['bɔɪfrɛnd] n (petit) ami
bra [brɑː] n soutien-gorge m
brace [breɪs] n (support) attache f, agrafe f; (BRIT: also: ~s: on teeth) appareil m (dentaire); (tool) vilebrequin m ▷ vt (support) consolider, soutenir; **braces** npl (BRIT: for trousers) bretelles fpl; **to ~ o.s.** (fig) se préparer mentalement
bracelet ['breɪslɪt] n bracelet m
bracket ['brækɪt] n (Tech) tasseau m, support m; (group) classe f, tranche f; (also: **brace ~**) accolade f; (also: **round ~**) parenthèse f; (also: **square ~**) crochet m ▷ vt mettre entre parenthèses; **in ~s** entre parenthèses or crochets
brag [bræg] vi se vanter
braid [breɪd] n (trimming) galon m; (of hair) tresse f, natte f
brain [breɪn] n cerveau m; **brains** npl (intellect, food) cervelle f
braise [breɪz] vt braiser
brake [breɪk] n frein m ▷ vt, vi freiner; **brake light** n feu m de stop
bran [bræn] n son m
branch [brɑːntʃ] n branche f; (Comm) succursale f; (: of bank) agence f; **branch off** vi (road) bifurquer; **branch out** vi diversifier ses activités

brand [brænd] n marque (commerciale) ▷ vt (cattle) marquer (au fer rouge); **brand name** n nom m de marque; **brand-new** adj tout(e) neuf (neuve), flambant neuf (neuve)
brandy ['brændɪ] n cognac m
brash [bræʃ] adj effronté(e)
brass [brɑːs] n cuivre m (jaune), laiton m; **the ~** (Mus) les cuivres; **brass band** n fanfare f
brat [bræt] n (pej) mioche m/f, môme m/f
brave [breɪv] adj courageux(-euse), brave ▷ vt braver, affronter; **bravery** n bravoure f, courage m
brawl [brɔːl] n rixe f, bagarre f
Brazil [brə'zɪl] n Brésil m; **Brazilian** adj brésilien(ne) ▷ n Brésilien(ne)
breach [briːtʃ] vt ouvrir une brèche dans ▷ n (gap) brèche f; (breaking): **~ of contract** rupture f de contrat; **~ of the peace** attentat m à l'ordre public
bread [brɛd] n pain m; **breadbin** n (BRIT) boîte f or huche f à pain; **breadbox** n (US) boîte f or huche f à pain; **breadcrumbs** npl miettes fpl de pain; (Culin) chapelure f, panure f
breadth [brɛtθ] n largeur f
break [breɪk] (pt broke, pp broken) vt casser, briser; (promise) rompre; (law) violer ▷ vi se casser, se briser; (weather) tourner; (storm) éclater; (day) se lever ▷ n (gap) brèche f; (fracture) cassure f; (rest) interruption f, arrêt m; (: short) pause f; (: at school) récréation f; (chance) chance f, occasion f favorable; **to ~ one's leg** etc se casser la jambe etc; **to ~ a record** battre un record; **to ~ the news to sb** annoncer la nouvelle à qn; **break down** vt (door etc) enfoncer; (figures, data) décomposer, analyser ▷ vi s'effondrer; (Med) faire une dépression (nerveuse); (Aut) tomber en panne; **my car has broken down** ma voiture est en panne; **break in** vt (horse etc) dresser ▷ vi (burglar) entrer par effraction; (interrupt) interrompre; **break into** vt fus (house) s'introduire or pénétrer par

effraction dans; **break off** vi (speaker) s'interrompre; (branch) se rompre ▷ vt (talks, engagement) rompre; **break out** vi éclater, se déclarer; (prisoner) s'évader; **to ~ out in spots** se couvrir de boutons; **break up** vi (partnership) cesser, prendre fin; (marriage) se briser; (line) couper; **the line's** or **you're ~ing up** ça coupe ▷ vt fracasser, casser; (fight etc) interrompre, faire cesser; (marriage) désunir; **breakdown** n (Aut) panne f; (in communications, marriage) rupture f; (Med: also: **nervous breakdown**) dépression (nerveuse); (of figures) ventilation f, répartition f; **breakdown truck** (us **breakdown van**) n dépanneuse f

breakfast ['brɛkfəst] n petit déjeuner m; **what time is ~?** le petit déjeuner est à quelle heure?

break: **break-in** n cambriolage m; **breakthrough** n percée f

breast [brɛst] n (of woman) sein m; (chest) poitrine f; (of chicken, turkey) blanc m; **breast-feed** vt, vi (irreg: like **feed**) allaiter; **breast-stroke** n brasse f

breath [brɛθ] n haleine f, souffle m; **to take a deep ~** respirer à fond; **out of ~** à bout de souffle, essoufflé(e)

breathalyser® ['brɛθəlaɪzər] (BRIT) n alcootest m

breathe [briːð] vt, vi respirer; **breathe in** vi inspirer ▷ vt aspirer; **breathe out** vt, vi expirer; **breathing** n respiration f

breath: **breathless** adj essoufflé(e), haletant(e); **breathtaking** adj stupéfiant(e), à vous couper le souffle; **breath test** n alcootest m

bred [brɛd] pt, pp of **breed**

breed [briːd] (pt, pp **bred**) vt élever, faire l'élevage de ▷ vi se reproduire ▷ n race f, variété f

breeze [briːz] n brise f

breezy ['briːzɪ] adj (day, weather) venteux(-euse); (manner) désinvolte; (person) jovial(e)

brew [bruː] vt (tea) faire infuser; (beer) brasser ▷ vi (fig) se préparer, couver; **brewery** n brasserie f (fabrique)

bribe [braɪb] n pot-de-vin m ▷ vt acheter; soudoyer; **bribery** n corruption f

bric-a-brac ['brɪkəbræk] n bric-à-brac m

brick [brɪk] n brique f; **bricklayer** n maçon m

bride [braɪd] n mariée f, épouse f; **bridegroom** n marié m, époux m; **bridesmaid** n demoiselle f d'honneur

bridge [brɪdʒ] n pont m; (Naut) passerelle f (de commandement); (of nose) arête f; (Cards, Dentistry) bridge m ▷ vt (gap) combler

bridle ['braɪdl] n bride f

brief [briːf] adj bref (brève) ▷ n (Law) dossier m, cause f; (gen) tâche f ▷ vt mettre au courant; **briefs** npl slip m; **briefcase** n serviette f, porte-documents m inv; **briefing** n instructions fpl; (Press) briefing m; **briefly** adv brièvement

brigadier [brɪgə'dɪər] n brigadier général

bright [braɪt] adj brillant(e); (room, weather) clair(e); (person: clever) intelligent(e), doué(e); (: cheerful) gai(e); (idea) génial(e); (colour) vif (vive)

brilliant ['brɪljənt] adj brillant(e); (light, sunshine) éclatant(e); (inf: great) super

brim [brɪm] n bord m

brine [braɪn] n (Culin) saumure f

bring (pt, pp **brought**) [brɪŋ, brɔːt] vt (thing) apporter; (person) amener; **bring about** vt provoquer, entraîner; **bring back** vt rapporter; (person) ramener; **bring down** vt (lower) abaisser; (shoot down) abattre; (government) faire s'effondrer; **bring in** vt (person) faire entrer; (object) rentrer; (Pol: legislation) introduire; (produce: income) rapporter; **bring on** vt (illness, attack) provoquer; (player, substitute) amener; **bring out** vt sortir; (meaning) faire ressortir, mettre en relief; **bring up** vt élever; (carry up) monter; (*question*) soulever; (*food: vomit*) vomir, rendre

brink [brɪŋk] n bord m

brisk [brɪsk] adj vif (vive); (*abrupt*) brusque; (*trade etc*) actif(-ive)

bristle [ˈbrɪsl] n poil m ▷ vi se hérisser

Brit [brɪt] n abbr (*inf*: = British person) Britannique m/f

Britain [ˈbrɪtən] n (*also*: **Great ~**) la Grande-Bretagne

British [ˈbrɪtɪʃ] adj britannique ▷ npl: **the ~** les Britanniques mpl; **British Isles** npl: **the British Isles** les îles fpl Britanniques

Briton [ˈbrɪtən] n Britannique m/f

Brittany [ˈbrɪtənɪ] n Bretagne f

brittle [ˈbrɪtl] adj cassant(e), fragile

B road n (*BRIT*) ≈ route départementale

broad [brɔːd] adj large; (*distinction*) général(e); (*accent*) prononcé(e); **in ~ daylight** en plein jour; **broadband** n transmission f à haut débit; **broad bean** n fève f; **broadcast** n émission f ▷ vb (*pt, pp* **broadcast**) ▷ vt (*Radio*) radiodiffuser; (*TV*) téléviser ▷ vi émettre; **broaden** vt élargir; **to broaden one's mind** élargir ses horizons ▷ vi s'élargir; **broadly** adv en gros, généralement; **broad-minded** adj large d'esprit

broccoli [ˈbrɔkəlɪ] n brocoli m

brochure [ˈbrəuʃjuər] n prospectus m, dépliant m

broil [brɔɪl] (*US*) vt rôtir

broiler [ˈbrɔɪlər] n (*fowl*) poulet m (à rôtir); (*US*: *grill*) gril m

broke [brəuk] pt of **break** ▷ adj (*inf*) fauché(e)

broken [ˈbrəukn] pp of **break** ▷ adj (*stick, leg etc*) cassé(e); (*machine*: *also*: **~ down**) fichu(e); **in ~ French/English** dans un français/anglais approximatif or hésitant

broker [ˈbrəukər] n courtier m

bronchitis [brɔŋˈkaɪtɪs] n bronchite f

bronze [brɔnz] n bronze m

brooch [brəutʃ] n broche f

brood [bruːd] n couvée f ▷ vi (*person*)

méditer (sombrement), ruminer

broom [brum] n balai m; (*Bot*) genêt m

Bros. abbr (*Comm*: = brothers) Frères

broth [brɔθ] n bouillon m de viande et de légumes

brothel [ˈbrɔθl] n maison close, bordel m

brother [ˈbrʌðər] n frère m; **brother-in-law** n beau-frère m

brought [brɔːt] pt, pp of **bring**

brow [brau] n front m; (*eyebrow*) sourcil m; (*of hill*) sommet m

brown [braun] adj brun(e), marron inv; (*hair*) châtain inv; (*tanned*) bronzé(e) ▷ n (*colour*) brun m, marron m ▷ vt brunir; (*Culin*) faire dorer, faire roussir; **brown bread** n pain m bis

Brownie [ˈbraunɪ] n jeannette f éclaireuse (cadette)

brown rice n riz m complet

brown sugar n cassonade f

browse [brauz] vi (*in shop*) regarder (*sans acheter*); **to ~ through a book** feuilleter un livre; **browser** n (*Comput*) navigateur m

bruise [bruːz] n bleu m, ecchymose f, contusion f ▷ vt contusionner, meurtrir

brunette [bruːˈnɛt] n (femme) brune

brush [brʌʃ] n brosse f; (*for painting*) pinceau m; (*for shaving*) blaireau m; (*quarrel*) accrochage m, prise f de bec ▷ vt brosser; (*also*: **~ past, ~ against**) effleurer, frôler

Brussels [ˈbrʌslz] n Bruxelles

Brussels sprout [-spraut] n chou m de Bruxelles

brutal [ˈbruːtl] adj brutal(e)

B.Sc. n abbr = **Bachelor of Science**

BSE n abbr (= bovine spongiform encephalopathy) ESB f, BSE f

bubble [ˈbʌbl] n bulle f ▷ vi bouillonner faire des bulles; (*sparkle, fig*) pétiller; **bubble bath** n bain moussant; **bubble gum** n chewing-gum m; **bubblejet printer** [ˈbʌbldʒɛt-] n imprimante f à bulle d'encre

buck [bʌk] n mâle m (*d'un lapin, lièvre,*

daim etc); (*US inf*) dollar *m* ▷ *vi* ruer, lancer une ruade; **to pass the ~ (to sb)** se décharger de la responsabilité (sur qn)

bucket ['bʌkɪt] *n* seau *m*

buckle ['bʌkl] *n* boucle *f* ▷ *vt* (*belt etc*) boucler, attacher ▷ *vi* (*warp*) tordre, gauchir; (: *wheel*) se voiler

bud [bʌd] *n* bourgeon *m*; (*of flower*) bouton *m* ▷ *vi* bourgeonner; (*flower*) éclore

Buddhism ['budɪzəm] *n* bouddhisme *m*

Buddhist ['budɪst] *adj* bouddhiste ▷ *n* Bouddhiste *m/f*

buddy ['bʌdɪ] *n* (*US*) copain *m*

budge [bʌdʒ] *vt* faire bouger ▷ *vi* bouger

budgerigar ['bʌdʒərɪgɑːʳ] *n* perruche *f*

budget ['bʌdʒɪt] *n* budget *m* ▷ *vi*: **to ~ for sth** inscrire qch au budget

budgie ['bʌdʒɪ] *n* = **budgerigar**

buff [bʌf] *adj* (*couleur f*) chamois *m* ▷ *n* (*inf: enthusiast*) mordu(e)

buffalo (*pl ~ or ~es*) ['bʌfələu] *n* (*BRIT*) buffle *m*; (*US*) bison *m*

buffer ['bʌfəʳ] *n* tampon *m*; (*Comput*) mémoire *f* tampon

buffet *n* [*'bufei*] (*food BRIT: bar*) buffet *m* ▷ *vt* ['bʌfɪt] secouer, ébranler; **buffet car** *n* (*BRIT Rail*) voiture-bar *f*

bug [bʌg] *n* (*bedbug etc*) punaise *f*; (*esp US: any insect*) insecte *m*, bestiole *f*; (*fig: germ*) virus *m*, microbe *m*; (*spy device*) dispositif *m* d'écoute (électronique), micro clandestin; (*Comput: of program*) erreur *f* ▷ *vt* (*room*) poser des micros dans; (*inf: annoy*) embêter

buggy ['bʌgɪ] *n* poussette *f*

build [bɪld] *n* (*of person*) carrure *f*, charpente *f* ▷ *vt* (*pt, pp* **built**) construire, bâtir; **build up** *vt* accumuler, amasser; (*business*) développer; (*reputation*) bâtir; **builder** *n* entrepreneur *m*; **building** *n* (*trade*) construction *f*; (*structure*) bâtiment *m*, construction *f*; (: *residential, offices*) immeuble *m*; **building site** *n* chantier

m (de construction); **building society** *n* (*BRIT*) société *f* de crédit immobilier

built [bɪlt] *pt, pp of* **build**; **built-in** *adj* (*cupboard*) encastré(e); (*device*) incorporé(e); intégré(e); **built-up** *adj*: **built-up area** zone urbanisée

bulb [bʌlb] *n* (*Bot*) bulbe *m*, oignon *m*; (*Elec*) ampoule *f*

Bulgaria [bʌl'gɛərɪə] *n* Bulgarie *f*; **Bulgarian** *adj* bulgare ▷ *n* Bulgare *m/f*

bulge [bʌldʒ] *n* renflement *m*, gonflement *m* ▷ *vi* faire saillie; présenter un renflement; (*pocket, file*) **to be bulging with** être plein(e) à craquer de

bulimia [bə'lɪmɪə] *n* boulimie *f*

bulimic [bju:'lɪmɪk] *adj, n* boulimique (*m/f*)

bulk [bʌlk] *n* masse *f*, volume *m*; **in ~** (*Comm*) en gros, en vrac; **the ~ of** la plus grande *or* grosse partie de; **bulky** *adj* volumineux(-euse), encombrant(e)

bull [bul] *n* taureau *m*; (*male elephant, whale*) mâle *m*

bulldozer ['buldəuzəʳ] *n* bulldozer *m*

bullet ['bulɪt] *n* balle *f* (*de fusil etc*)

bulletin ['bulɪtɪn] *n* bulletin *m*, communiqué *m*; (*also*: **news ~**) (bulletin d')informations *fpl*; **bulletin board** *n* (*Comput*) messagerie *f* (électronique)

bullfight ['bulfaɪt] *n* corrida *f*, course *f* de taureaux; **bullfighter** *n* torero *m*; **bullfighting** *n* tauromachie *f*

bully ['bulɪ] *n* brute *f*, tyran *m* ▷ *vt* tyranniser, rudoyer

bum [bʌm] *n* (*inf: BRIT: backside*) derrière *m*; (: *esp US: tramp*) vagabond(e), traîne-savates *m/f inv*; (: *idler*) glandeur *m*

bumblebee ['bʌmblbi:] *n* bourdon *m*

bump [bʌmp] *n* (*blow*) coup *m*, choc *m*; (*jolt*) cahot *m*; (*on road etc, on head*) bosse *f* ▷ *vt* heurter, cogner; (*car*) emboutir; **bump into** *vt fus* rentrer dans, tamponner; (*inf: meet*) tomber sur; **bumper** *n* pare-chocs *m inv* ▷ *adj*: **bumper crop/harvest** récolte/moisson exceptionnelle; **bumpy** *adj* (*road*) cahoteux(-euse); **it was a**

bumpy flight/ride on a été secoués dans l'avion/la voiture

bun [bʌn] n (cake) petit gâteau; (bread) petit pain au lait; (of hair) chignon m

bunch [bʌntʃ] n (of flowers) bouquet m; (of keys) trousseau m; (of bananas) régime m; (of people) groupe m; **bunches** npl (in hair) couettes fpl; **~ of grapes** grappe f de raisin

bundle [bʌndl] n paquet m ▷ vt (also: **~ up**) faire un paquet de; (put): **to ~ sth/sb into** fourrer or enfourner qch/qn dans

bungalow ['bʌŋgələu] n bungalow m

bungee jumping ['bʌndʒiː'dʒʌmpɪŋ] n saut m à l'élastique

bunion ['bʌnjən] n oignon m (au pied)

bunk [bʌŋk] n couchette f; **bunk beds** npl lits superposés

bunker ['bʌŋkəʳ] n (coal store) soute f à charbon; (Mil, Golf) bunker m

bunny ['bʌnɪ] n (also: **~ rabbit**) lapin m

buoy [bɔɪ] n bouée f; **buoyant** adj (ship) flottable; (carefree) gai(e), plein(e) d'entrain; (Comm: market, economy) actif(-ive)

burden ['bəːdn] n fardeau m, charge f ▷ vt charger; (oppress) accabler, surcharger

bureau (pl **~x**) ['bjuərəu, -z] n (BRIT: writing desk) bureau m, secrétaire m; (US: chest of drawers) commode f; (office) bureau, office m

bureaucracy [bjuə'rɔkrəsɪ] n bureaucratie f

bureaucrat ['bjuərəkræt] n bureaucrate m/f, rond-de-cuir m

bureau de change [-də'ʃɑ̃ʒ] (pl **bureaux de change**) n bureau m de change

bureaux ['bjuərəuz] npl of **bureau**

burger ['bəːgəʳ] n hamburger m

burglar ['bəːgləʳ] n cambrioleur m; **burglar alarm** n sonnerie f d'alarme; **burglary** n cambriolage m

Burgundy ['bəːgəndɪ] n Bourgogne f

burial ['bɛrɪəl] n enterrement m

burn [bəːn] vt, vi (pt, pp **~ed** or **~t**) brûler ▷ n brûlure f; **burn down** vt incendier, détruire par le feu; **burn out** vt (writer etc): **to ~ o.s. out** s'user (à force de travailler); **burning** adj (building, forest) en flammes; (issue, question) brûlant(e); (ambition) dévorant(e)

Burns' Night [bəː nz-] n fête écossaise à la mémoire du poète Robert Burns

○ **BURNS NIGHT**

○ **Burns Night** est une fête qui a lieu
○ le 25 janvier, à la mémoire du poète
○ écossais Robert Burns (1759 - 1796),
○ à l'occasion de laquelle les Écossais
○ partout dans le monde organisent
○ un souper, en général arrosé de
○ whisky. Le plat principal est toujours
○ le haggis, servi avec de la purée de
○ pommes de terre et de la purée de
○ rutabagas. On apporte le haggis au
○ son des cornemuses et au cours du
○ repas on lit des poèmes de Burns et
○ on chante ses chansons.

burnt [bəːnt] pt, pp of **burn**

burp [bəːp] (inf) n rot m ▷ vi roter

burrow ['bʌrəu] n terrier m ▷ vi (rabbit) creuser un terrier; (rummage) fouiller

burst [bəːst] (pt, pp **~**) vt faire éclater; (river: banks etc) rompre ▷ vi éclater; (tyre) crever ▷ n explosion f; (also: **~ pipe**) fuite f (due à une rupture); **a ~ of enthusiasm/energy** un accès d'enthousiasme/d'énergie; **to ~ into flames** s'enflammer soudainement; **to ~ out laughing** éclater de rire; **to ~ into tears** fondre en larmes; **to ~ open** vi s'ouvrir violemment or soudainement; **to be ~ing with** (container) être plein(e) (à craquer) de, regorger de; (fig) être débordant(e) de; **burst into** vt fus (room etc) faire irruption dans

bury ['bɛrɪ] vt enterrer

bus (pl **~es**) [bʌs, 'bʌsɪz] n autobus m; **bus conductor** n receveur(-euse) m/f de bus

bush [buʃ] n buisson m; (scrub land)

brousse f; **to beat about the ~** tourner autour du pot

business [ˈbɪznɪs] n (matter, firm) affaire f; (trading) affaires fpl; (job, duty) travail m; **to be away on ~** être en déplacement d'affaires; **it's none of my ~** cela ne me regarde pas, ce ne sont pas mes affaires; **he means ~** il ne plaisante pas, il est sérieux; **business class** n (on plane) classe f affaires; **businesslike** adj sérieux(-euse), efficace; **businessman** (irreg) n homme m d'affaires; **business trip** n voyage m d'affaires; **businesswoman** (irreg) n femme f d'affaires

busker [ˈbʌskəʳ] n (BRIT) artiste ambulant(e)

bus: **bus pass** n carte f de bus; **bus shelter** n abribus m; **bus station** n gare routière; **bus-stop** n arrêt m d'autobus

bust [bʌst] n buste m; (measurement) tour m de poitrine ▷ adj (inf: broken) fichu(e), fini(e); **to go ~** faire faillite

bustling [ˈbʌslɪŋ] adj (town) très animé(e)

busy [ˈbɪzɪ] adj occupé(e); (shop, street) très fréquenté(e); (us: telephone, line) occupé ▷ vt: **to ~ o.s.** s'occuper; **busy signal** n (US) tonalité f occupé inv

⭕ **KEYWORD**

but [bʌt] conj mais; **I'd love to come, but I'm busy** j'aimerais venir mais je suis occupé; **he's not English but French** il n'est pas anglais mais français; **but that's far too expensive!** mais c'est bien trop cher!
▷ prep (apart from, except) sauf, excepté; **nothing but** rien d'autre que; **we've had nothing but trouble** nous n'avons eu que des ennuis; **no-one but him can do it** lui seul peut le faire; **who but a lunatic would do such a thing?** qui sinon un fou ferait une chose pareille!; **but for you/your help** sans toi/ton aide; **anything but that** tout sauf or

excepté ça, tout mais pas ça
▷ adv (just, only) ne ... que; **she's but a child** elle n'est qu'une enfant; **had I but known** si seulement j'avais su; **I can but try** je peux toujours essayer; **all but finished** pratiquement terminé

butcher [ˈbutʃəʳ] n boucher m ▷ vt massacrer; (cattle etc for meat) tuer; **butcher's (shop)** n boucherie f

butler [ˈbʌtləʳ] n maître m d'hôtel

butt [bʌt] n (cask) gros tonneau; (of gun) crosse f; (of cigarette) mégot m; (BRIT fig: target) cible f ▷ vt donner un coup de tête à

butter [ˈbʌtəʳ] n beurre m ▷ vt beurrer; **buttercup** n bouton m d'or

butterfly [ˈbʌtəflaɪ] n papillon m; (Swimming: also: **~ stroke**) brasse f papillon

buttocks [ˈbʌtəks] npl fesses fpl

button [ˈbʌtn] n bouton m; (us: badge) pin m ▷ vt (also: **~ up**) boutonner ▷ vi se boutonner

buy [baɪ] (pt, pp bought) vt acheter ▷ n achat m; **to ~ sb sth/sth from sb** acheter qch à qn; **to ~ sb a drink** offrir un verre or à boire à qn; **can I ~ you a drink?** je vous offre un verre?; **where can I ~ some postcards?** où est-ce que je peux acheter des cartes postales?; **buy out** vt (partner) désintéresser; **buy up** vt acheter en bloc, rafler; **buyer** n acheteur(-euse) m/f

buzz [bʌz] n bourdonnement m; (inf: phone call): **to give sb a ~** passer un coup de fil à qn ▷ vi bourdonner; **buzzer** n timbre m électrique

⭕ **KEYWORD**

by [baɪ] prep **1** (referring to cause, agent) par, de; **killed by lightning** tué par la foudre; **surrounded by a fence** entouré d'une barrière; **a painting by Picasso** un tableau de Picasso
2 (referring to method, manner, means): **by bus/car** en autobus/voiture; **by train**

par le or en train; **to pay by cheque** payer par chèque; **by moonlight/candlelight** à la lueur de la lune/d'une bougie; **by saving hard, he ...** à force d'économiser, il ...

3 (*via, through*) par; **we came by Dover** nous sommes venus par Douvres

4 (*close to, past*) à côté de; **the house by the school** la maison à côté de l'école; **a holiday by the sea** des vacances au bord de la mer; **she went by me** elle est passée à côté de moi; **I go by the post office every day** je passe devant la poste tous les jours

5 (*with time: not later than*) avant; (: *during*): **by daylight** à la lumière du jour; **by night** la nuit, de nuit; **by 4 o'clock** avant 4 heures; **by this time tomorrow** d'ici demain à la même heure; **by the time I got here it was too late** lorsque je suis arrivé il était déjà trop tard

6 (*amount*) à; **by the kilo/metre** au kilo/au mètre; **paid by the hour** payé à l'heure

7 (*Math: measure*): **to divide/multiply by 3** diviser/multiplier par 3; **a room 3 metres by 4** une pièce de 3 mètres sur 4; **it's broader by a metre** c'est plus large d'un mètre

8 (*according to*) d'après, selon; **it's 3 o'clock by my watch** il est 3 heures à ma montre; **it's all right by me** je n'ai rien contre

9: **(all) by oneself** etc tout(e) seul(e)
▷ adv **1** see **go**; **pass** etc

2: **by and by** un peu plus tard, bientôt; **by and large** dans l'ensemble

bye(-bye) ['baɪ('baɪ)] *excl* au revoir!, salut!

by-election ['baɪɪlɛkʃən] *n* (BRIT) élection (législative) partielle

bypass ['baɪpɑːs] *n* rocade *f*; (*Med*) pontage *m* ▷ *vt* éviter

byte [baɪt] *n* (*Comput*) octet *m*

C [siː] *n* (*Mus*): **C** do *m*

cab [kæb] *n* taxi *m*; (*of train, truck*) cabine *f*

cabaret ['kæbəreɪ] *n* (*show*) spectacle *m* de cabaret

cabbage ['kæbɪdʒ] *n* chou *m*

cabin ['kæbɪn] *n* (*house*) cabane *f*, hutte *f*; (*on ship*) cabine *f*; (*on plane*) compartiment *m*; **cabin crew** *n* (*Aviat*) équipage *m*

cabinet ['kæbɪnɪt] *n* (*Pol*) cabinet *m*; (*furniture*) petit meuble à tiroirs et rayons; (*also*: **display ~**) vitrine *f*, petite armoire vitrée; **cabinet minister** *n* ministre *m* (*membre du cabinet*)

cable ['keɪbl] *n* câble *m* ▷ *vt* câbler, télégraphier; **cable car** *n* téléphérique *m*; **cable television** *n* télévision *f* par câble

cactus (*pl* **cacti**) ['kæktəs, -taɪ] *n* cactus *m*

café ['kæfeɪ] *n* ≈ café(-restaurant) *m* (*sans alcool*)

cafeteria [kæfɪ'tɪərɪə] *n* cafétéria *f*

caffein(e) ['kæfi:n] n caféine f
cage [keɪdʒ] n cage f
cagoule [kə'guːl] n K-way® m
Cairo ['kaɪərəʊ] n le Caire
cake [keɪk] n gâteau m; **~ of soap**
savonnette f
calcium ['kælsɪəm] n calcium m
calculate ['kælkjuleɪt] vt calculer;
(estimate: chances, effect) évaluer;
calculation [kælkju'leɪʃən] n calcul m;
calculator n calculatrice f
calendar ['kæləndəʳ] n calendrier m
calf (pl **calves**) [kɑːf, kɑːvz] n (of cow)
veau m; (of other animals) petit m;
(also: **~skin**) veau m, vachette f; (Anat)
mollet m
calibre (US **caliber**) ['kælɪbəʳ] n
calibre m
call [kɔːl] vt appeler; (meeting)
convoquer ▷ vi appeler; (visit: also: **~
in**, **~ round**) passer ▷ n (shout) appel
m, cri m; (also: **telephone ~**) coup
m de téléphone; **to be on ~** être de
permanence; **to be ~ed** s'appeler; **can
I make a ~ from here?** est-ce que je
peux téléphoner d'ici?; **call back** vi
(return) repasser ▷ vt (Tel) rappeler ▷ vt
(Tel) rappeler; **can you ~ back later?**
pouvez-vous rappeler plus tard?; **call
for** vt fus (demand) demander; (fetch)
passer prendre; **call in** vt (doctor, expert,
police) appeler, faire venir; **call off** vt
annuler; **call on** vt fus (visit) rendre
visite à, passer voir; (request): **to ~ on
sb to do** inviter qn à faire; **call out** vi
pousser un cri or des cris; **call up** vt
(Mil) appeler, mobiliser; (Tel) appeler;
callbox n (BRIT) cabine f téléphonique;
call centre (US **call center**) n centre m
d'appels; **caller** n (Tel) personne f qui
appelle; (visitor) visiteur m
callous ['kæləs] adj dur(e), insensible
calm [kɑːm] adj calme ▷ n calme m
▷ vt calmer, apaiser; **calm down** vi se
calmer, s'apaiser ▷ vt calmer, apaiser;
calmly ['kɑːmlɪ] adv calmement,
avec calme
Calor gas® ['kæləʳ-] n (BRIT) butane m,

butagaz® m
calorie ['kælərɪ] n calorie f
calves [kɑːvz] npl of **calf**
Cambodia [kæm'bəʊdɪə] n
Cambodge m
camcorder ['kæmkɔːdəʳ] n
caméscope m
came [keɪm] pt of **come**
camel ['kæməl] n chameau m
camera ['kæmərə] n appareil-photo m;
(Cine, TV) caméra f; **in ~** à huis clos, en
privé; **cameraman** n caméraman m;
camera phone n téléphone m avec
appareil photo numérique intégré
camouflage ['kæməflɑːʒ] n
camouflage m ▷ vt camoufler
camp [kæmp] n camp m ▷ vi camper
▷ adj (man) efféminé(e)
campaign [kæm'peɪn] n (Mil,
Pol etc) campagne f ▷ vi (also fig)
faire campagne; **campaigner** n:
campaigner for partisan(e) de;
campaigner against opposant(e) à
camp: campbed n (BRIT) lit m de camp;
camper n campeur(-euse); (vehicle)
camping-car m; **campground** (US) n
(terrain m de) camping m; **camping** n
camping m; **to go camping** faire du
camping; **campsite** n (terrain m de)
camping m
campus ['kæmpəs] n campus m
can¹ [kæn] n (of milk, oil, water) bidon m;
(tin) boîte f (de conserve) ▷ vt mettre
en conserve

○ **KEYWORD**

can² [kæn] (negative **cannot, can't**,
conditional and pt **could**) aux vb **1** (be able
to) pouvoir; **you can do it if you try**
vous pouvez le faire si vous essayez; **I
can't hear you** je ne t'entends pas
2 (know how to) savoir; **I can swim/
play tennis/drive** je sais nager/jouer
au tennis/conduire; **can you speak
French?** parlez-vous français?
3 (may) pouvoir; **can I use your phone?**
puis-je me servir de votre téléphone?

4 (expressing disbelief, puzzlement etc):
it can't be true! ce n'est pas possible!;
what can he want? qu'est-ce qu'il peut
bien vouloir?

5 (expressing possibility, suggestion etc):
he could be in the library il est peut-
être dans la bibliothèque; **she could
have been delayed** il se peut qu'elle ait
été retardée

Canada ['kænədə] n Canada m;
Canadian [kə'neɪdɪən] adj
canadien(ne) ▷ n Canadien(ne)
canal [kə'næl] n canal m
canary [kə'nɛərɪ] n canari m, serin m
cancel ['kænsəl] vt annuler; (train)
supprimer; (party, appointment)
décommander; (cross out) barrer, rayer;
(cheque) faire opposition à; **I would
like to ~ my booking** je voudrais
annuler ma réservation; **cancellation**
[kænsə'leɪʃən] n annulation f;
suppression f
Cancer ['kænsər] n (Astrology) le Cancer
cancer ['kænsər] n cancer m
candidate ['kændɪdeɪt] n candidat(e)
candle ['kændl] n bougie f; (in church)
cierge m; **candlestick** n (also: **candle
holder**) bougeoir m; (bigger, ornate)
chandelier m
candy ['kændɪ] n sucre candi; (us)
bonbon m; **candy bar** (us) n barre f
chocolatée; **candyfloss** n (BRIT) barbe
f à papa
cane [keɪn] n canne f; (for baskets, chairs
etc) rotin m ▷ vt (BRIT Scol) administrer
des coups de bâton à
canister ['kænɪstər] n boîte f (gén en
métal); (of gas) bombe f
cannabis ['kænəbɪs] n (drug)
cannabis m
canned ['kænd] adj (food) en boîte,
en conserve; (inf: music) enregistré(e);
(BRIT inf: drunk) bourré(e); (US inf: worker)
mis(e) à la porte
cannon (pl ~ or **~s**) ['kænən] n (gun)
canon m
cannot ['kænɔt] = **can not**

canoe [kə'nu:] n pirogue f; (Sport)
canoë m; **canoeing** n (sport) canoë m
canon ['kænən] n (clergyman) chanoine
m; (standard) canon m
can-opener [-'əupnər] n ouvre-boîte m
can't [kɑ:nt] = **can't**
canteen [kæn'ti:n] n (eating place)
cantine f; (BRIT: of cutlery) ménagère f
canter ['kæntər] vi aller au petit galop
canvas ['kænvəs] n toile f
canvass ['kænvəs] vi (Pol): **to ~ for**
faire campagne pour ▷ vt (citizens,
opinions) sonder
canyon ['kænjən] n cañon m, gorge
(profonde)
cap [kæp] n casquette f; (for swimming)
bonnet m de bain; (of pen) capuchon m;
(of bottle) capsule f; (BRIT: contraceptive:
also: **Dutch ~**) diaphragme m ▷ vt
(outdo) surpasser; (put limit on)
plafonner
capability [keɪpə'bɪlɪtɪ] n aptitude
f, capacité f
capable ['keɪpəbl] adj capable
capacity [kə'pæsɪtɪ] n (of container)
capacité f, contenance f; (ability)
aptitude f
cape [keɪp] n (garment) cape f; (Geo)
cap m
caper ['keɪpər] n (Culin: gen pl) câpre f;
(prank) farce f
capital ['kæpɪtl] n (also: **~ city**)
capitale f; (money) capital m; (also:
~ letter) majuscule f; **capitalism**
n capitalisme m; **capitalist** adj, n
capitaliste m/f; **capital punishment** n
peine capitale
Capitol ['kæpɪtl] n: **the ~** le Capitole
Capricorn ['kæprɪkɔ:n] n le Capricorne
capsize [kæp'saɪz] vt faire chavirer
▷ vi chavirer
capsule ['kæpsju:l] n capsule f
captain ['kæptɪn] n capitaine m
caption ['kæpʃən] n légende f
captivity [kæp'tɪvɪtɪ] n captivité f
capture ['kæptʃər] vt (prisoner, animal)
capturer; (town) prendre; (attention)
capter; (Comput) saisir ▷ n capture f; (of

data) saisie *f* de données

ar [kɑːʳ] *n* voiture *f*, auto *f*; *(US Rail)* wagon *m*, voiture

arafe [kəˈræf] *n* carafe *f*

aramel [ˈkærəməl] *n* caramel *m*

arat [ˈkærət] *n* carat *m*

aravan [ˈkærəvæn] *n* caravane *f*; **caravan site** *n* (BRIT) camping *m* pour caravanes

arbohydrate [kɑːbəuˈhaɪdreɪt] *n* hydrate *m* de carbone; *(food)* féculent *m*

arbon [ˈkɑːbən] *n* carbone *m*; **carbon dioxide** [-daɪˈɔksaɪd] *n* gaz *m* carbonique, dioxyde *m* de carbone; **carbon monoxide** [-mɔˈnɔksaɪd] *n* oxyde *m* de carbone

ar boot sale *n* voir encadré

- **CAR BOOT SALE**
-
- Type de brocante très populaire, où
- chacun vide sa cave ou son grenier.
- Les articles sont présentés dans
- des coffres de voitures et la vente
- a souvent lieu sur un parking ou
- dans un champ. Les brocanteurs
- d'un jour doivent s'acquitter d'une
- petite contribution pour participer
- à la vente.

arburettor (US **carburetor**) [kɑːbjuˈrɛtəʳ] *n* carburateur *m*

ard [kɑːd] *n* carte *f*; *(material)* carton *m*; **cardboard** *n* carton *m*; **card game** *n* jeu *m* de cartes

ardigan [ˈkɑːdɪgən] *n* cardigan *m*

ardinal [ˈkɑːdɪnl] *adj* cardinal(e); *(importance)* capital(e) ▷ *n* cardinal *m*

ardphone [ˈkɑːdfəun] *n* téléphone *m* à carte *(magnétique)*

are [kɛəʳ] *n* soin *m*, attention *f*; *(worry)* souci *m* ▷ *vi*: **to ~ about** *(feel interest for)* se soucier de, s'intéresser à; *(person: love)* être attaché(e) à; **in sb's ~** à la garde de qn, confié à qn; **~ of** *(on letter)* chez; **to take ~ (to do)** faire attention (à faire); **to take ~ of** *vt* s'occuper de; **I don't ~** ça m'est bien

égal, peu m'importe; **I couldn't ~ less** cela m'est complètement égal, je m'en fiche complètement; **care for** *vt fus* s'occuper de; *(like)* aimer

career [kəˈrɪəʳ] *n* carrière *f* ▷ *vi (also:* **~ along***)* aller à toute allure

care: **carefree** *adj* sans souci, insouciant(e); **careful** *adj* soigneux(-euse); *(cautious)* prudent(e); **(be) careful!** (fais) attention!; **carefully** *adv* avec soin, soigneusement; prudemment; **caregiver** (US) *n (professional)* travailleur social; *(unpaid)* personne qui s'occupe d'un proche qui est malade; **careless** *adj* négligent(e); *(heedless)* insouciant(e); **carelessness** *n* manque *m* de soin, négligence *f*; insouciance *f*; **carer** [ˈkɛərəʳ] *n (professional)* travailleur social; *(unpaid)* personne qui s'occupe d'un proche qui est malade; **caretaker** *n* gardien(ne), concierge *m/f*

car-ferry [ˈkɑːfɛrɪ] *n (on sea)* ferry(-boat) *m*; *(on river)* bac *m*

cargo (*pl* **~es**) [ˈkɑːgəu] *n* cargaison *f*, chargement *m*

car hire *n* (BRIT) location *f* de voitures

Caribbean [kærɪˈbiːən] *adj, n*: **the ~ (Sea)** la mer des Antilles *or* des Caraïbes

caring [ˈkɛərɪŋ] *adj (person)* bienveillant(e); *(society, organization)* humanitaire

carnation [kɑːˈneɪʃən] *n* œillet *m*

carnival [ˈkɑːnɪvl] *n (public celebration)* carnaval *m*; *(US: funfair)* fête foraine

carol [ˈkærəl] *n*: **(Christmas) ~** chant *m* de Noël

carousel [kærəˈsɛl] *n (for luggage)* carrousel *m*; *(US)* manège *m*

car park (BRIT) *n* parking *m*, parc *m* de stationnement

carpenter [ˈkɑːpɪntəʳ] *n* charpentier *m*; *(joiner)* menuisier *m*

carpet [ˈkɑːpɪt] *n* tapis *m* ▷ *vt* recouvrir (d'un tapis); **fitted ~** (BRIT) moquette *f*

car rental *n* (US) location *f* de voitures

carriage [ˈkærɪdʒ] *n* (BRIT Rail)

wagon m; (horse-drawn) voiture f; (of goods) transport m; (: cost) port m; **carriageway** n (BRIT: part of road) chaussée f

carrier ['kærɪəʳ] n transporteur m, camionneur m; (company) entreprise f de transport; (Med) porteur(-euse); **carrier bag** n (BRIT) sac m en papier or en plastique

carrot ['kærət] n carotte f

carry ['kærɪ] vt (subj: person) porter; (: vehicle) transporter; (involve: responsibilities etc) comporter; impliquer; (Med: disease) être porteur de ▷ vi (sound) porter; **to get carried away** (fig) s'emballer, s'enthousiasmer; **carry on** vi (continue) continuer ▷ vt (conduct: business) diriger; (: conversation) entretenir; (continue: business, conversation) continuer; **to ~ on with sth/doing** continuer qch/à faire; **carry out** vt (orders) exécuter; (investigation) effectuer

cart [kɑːt] n charrette f ▷ vt (inf) transporter

carton ['kɑːtən] n (box) carton m; (of yogurt) pot m (en carton)

cartoon [kɑːˈtuːn] n (Press) dessin m (humoristique); (satirical) caricature f; (comic strip) bande dessinée; (Cine) dessin animé

cartridge ['kɑːtrɪdʒ] n (for gun, pen) cartouche f

carve [kɑːv] vt (meat: also: ~ up) découper; (wood, stone) tailler, sculpter; **carving** n (in wood etc) sculpture f

car wash n station f de lavage (de voitures)

case [keɪs] n cas m; (Law) affaire f, procès m; (box) caisse f, boîte f; (for glasses) étui m; (BRIT: also: **suit~**) valise f; **in ~ of** en cas de; **in ~ he** au cas où il; **just in ~** à tout hasard; **in any ~** en tout cas, de toute façon

cash [kæʃ] n argent m; (Comm) (argent m) liquide m ▷ vt encaisser; **to pay (in) ~** payer (en argent) comptant or en espèces; **~ with order/on delivery**

(Comm) payable or paiement à la commande/livraison; **I haven't got any ~** je n'ai pas de liquide; **cashback** n (discount) remise f; (at supermarket etc) retrait m (à la caisse); **cash card** n carte f de retrait; **cash desk** n (BRIT) caisse f; **cash dispenser** n distributeur m automatique de billets

cashew [kæˈʃuː] n (also: ~ nut) noix f de cajou

cashier [kæˈʃɪəʳ] n caissier(-ère)

cashmere ['kæʃmɪəʳ] n cachemire m

cash point n distributeur m automatique de billets

cash register n caisse enregistreuse

casino [kəˈsiːnəu] n casino m

casket ['kɑːskɪt] n coffret m; (US: coffin) cercueil m

casserole ['kæsərəul] n (pot) cocotte f; (food) ragoût m (en cocotte)

cassette [kæˈset] n cassette f; **cassette player** n lecteur m de cassettes

cast [kɑːst] (vb: pt, pp ~) vt (throw) jeter; (shadow: lit) projeter; (: fig) jeter; (glance) jeter ▷ n (Theat) distribution f; (also: **plaster ~**) plâtre m; **to ~ sb as Hamlet** attribuer à qn le rôle d'Hamlet; **to ~ one's vote** voter, exprimer son suffrage; **to ~ doubt on** jeter un doute sur; **cast off** vi (Naut) larguer les amarres; (Knitting) arrêter les mailles

castanets [kæstəˈnɛts] npl castagnettes fpl

caster sugar ['kɑːstə-] n (BRIT) sucre m semoule

cast-iron ['kɑːstaɪən] adj (lit) de or en fonte; (fig: will) de fer; (alibi) en béton

castle ['kɑːsl] n château m; (fortress) château-fort m; (Chess) tour f

casual ['kæʒjul] adj (by chance) de hasard, fait(e) au hasard, fortuit(e); (irregular: work etc) temporaire; (unconcerned) désinvolte; **~ wear** vêtements mpl sport inv

casualty ['kæʒjultɪ] n accidenté(e), blessé(e); (dead) victime f, mort(e); (BRIT: Med: department) urgences fpl

cat [kæt] n chat m

Catalan ['kætəlæn] *adj* catalan(e)
catalogue (*US* **catalog**) ['kætəlɔg] *n*
catalogue *m* ▷ *vt* cataloguer
catalytic converter
[kætə'lɪtɪkkən'vɜ:tə^r] *n* pot *m*
catalytique
cataract ['kætərækt] *n* (*also Med*)
cataracte *f*
catarrh [kə'tɑ:^r] *n* rhume *m* chronique,
catarrhe *f*
catastrophe [kə'tæstrəfɪ] *n*
catastrophe *f*
catch [kætʃ] (*pt, pp* **caught**) *vt* attraper;
(*person: by surprise*) prendre, surprendre;
(*understand*) saisir; (*get entangled*)
accrocher ▷ *vi* (*fire*) prendre; (*get
entangled*) s'accrocher ▷ *n* (*fish etc*)
prise *f*; (*hidden problem*) attrape *f*; (*Tech*)
loquet *m*; cliquet *m*; **to ~ sb's attention**
or eye attirer l'attention de qn; **to ~ fire**
prendre feu; **to ~ sight of** apercevoir;
catch up *vi* (*with work*) se rattraper,
combler son retard ▷ *vt* (*also*: **~ up**
with) rattraper; **catching** ['kætʃɪŋ] *adj*
(*Med*) contagieux(-euse)
category ['kætɪgərɪ] *n* catégorie *f*
cater ['keɪtə^r] *vi*: **to ~ for** (*BRIT: needs*)
satisfaire, pourvoir à; (: *readers,
consumers*) s'adresser à, pourvoir aux
besoins de; (*Comm: parties etc*) préparer
des repas pour
caterpillar ['kætəpɪlə^r] *n* chenille *f*
cathedral [kə'θi:drəl] *n* cathédrale *f*
Catholic ['kæθəlɪk] (*Rel*) *adj* catholique
▷ *n* catholique *m/f*
Catseye® ['kæts'aɪ] *n* (*BRIT Aut*) (clou
m à) catadioptre *m*
cattle ['kætl] *npl* bétail *m*, bestiaux *mpl*
catwalk ['kætwɔ:k] *n* passerelle *f*; (*for
models*) podium *m* (*de défilé de mode*)
caught [kɔ:t] *pt, pp of* **catch**
cauliflower ['kɔlɪflauə^r] *n* chou-
fleur *m*
cause [kɔ:z] *n* cause *f* ▷ *vt* causer
caution ['kɔ:ʃən] *n* prudence *f*;
(*warning*) avertissement *m* ▷ *vt* avertir,
donner un avertissement à; **cautious**
adj prudent(e)

cave [keɪv] *n* caverne *f*, grotte *f*; **cave in**
vi (*roof etc*) s'effondrer
caviar(e) ['kævɪɑ:^r] *n* caviar *m*
cavity ['kævɪtɪ] *n* cavité *f*; (*Med*) carie *f*
cc *abbr* (*= cubic centimetre*) cm³; (*on letter
etc*) = **carbon copy**
CCTV *n abbr* = **closed-circuit television**
CD *n abbr* (*= compact disc*) CD *m*; **CD
burner** *n* graveur *m* de CD; **CD player**
n platine *f* laser; **CD-ROM** [si:di:'rɔm]
n abbr (*= compact disc read-only memory*)
CD-ROM *m inv*; **CD writer** *n* graveur
m de CD
cease [si:s] *vt, vi* cesser; **ceasefire** *n*
cessez-le-feu *m*
cedar ['si:də^r] *n* cèdre *m*
ceilidh ['keɪlɪ] *n* bal *m* folklorique
écossais *or* irlandais
ceiling ['si:lɪŋ] *n* (*also fig*) plafond *m*
celebrate ['sɛlɪbreɪt] *vt, vi* célébrer;
celebration [sɛlɪ'breɪʃən] *n*
célébration *f*
celebrity [sɪ'lɛbrɪtɪ] *n* célébrité *f*
celery ['sɛlərɪ] *n* céleri *m* (en branches)
cell [sɛl] *n* (*gen*) cellule *f*; (*Elec*) élément
m (*de pile*)
cellar ['sɛlə^r] *n* cave *f*
cello ['tʃɛləu] *n* violoncelle *m*
Cellophane® ['sɛləfeɪn] *n*
cellophane® *f*
cellphone ['sɛlfəun] *n* téléphone *m*
cellulaire
Celsius ['sɛlsɪəs] *adj* Celsius *inv*
Celtic ['kɛltɪk, 'sɛltɪk] *adj* celte, celtique
cement [sə'mɛnt] *n* ciment *m*
cemetery ['sɛmɪtrɪ] *n* cimetière *m*
censor ['sɛnsə^r] *n* censeur *m* ▷ *vt*
censurer; **censorship** *n* censure *f*
census ['sɛnsəs] *n* recensement *m*
cent [sɛnt] *n* (*unit of dollar, euro*) cent
m (*= un centième du dollar, de l'euro*); *see
also* **per**
centenary [sɛn'ti:nərɪ] (*US
centennial*) [sɛn'tɛnɪəl] *n*
centenaire *m*
center ['sɛntə^r] (*US*) = **centre**
centi... [sɛntɪ] *prefix*: **centigrade**
adj centigrade; **centimetre** (*US*

centimeter) n centimètre m;
centipede ['sɛntɪpiːd] n mille-
pattes m inv
central ['sɛntrəl] adj central(e);
Central America n Amérique centrale;
central heating n chauffage central;
central reservation n (BRIT Aut) terre-
plein central
centre (US **center**) ['sɛntər] n centre m
▷ vt centrer; **centre-forward** n (Sport)
avant-centre m; **centre-half** n (Sport)
demi-centre m
century ['sɛntjʊrɪ] n siècle m; **in the
twentieth ~** au vingtième siècle
CEO n abbr (US) = **chief executive
officer**
ceramic [sɪ'ræmɪk] adj céramique
cereal ['siːrɪəl] n céréale f
ceremony ['sɛrɪmənɪ] n cérémonie f;
to stand on ~ faire des façons
certain ['səːtən] adj certain(e);
to make ~ of s'assurer de; **for ~**
certainement, sûrement; **certainly**
adv certainement; **certainty** n
certitude f
certificate [sə'tɪfɪkɪt] n certificat m
certify ['səːtɪfaɪ] vt certifier; (award
diploma to) conférer un diplôme etc
à; (declare insane) déclarer malade
mental(e)
cf. abbr (= compare) cf., voir
CFC n abbr (= chlorofluorocarbon) CFC m
chain [tʃeɪn] n (gen) chaîne f ▷ vt
(also: ~ **up**) enchaîner, attacher (avec
une chaîne); **chain-smoke** vi fumer
cigarette sur cigarette
chair [tʃɛər] n chaise f; (armchair)
fauteuil m; (of university) chaire f; (of
meeting) présidence f ▷ vt (meeting)
présider; **chairlift** n télésiège m;
chairman n président m; **chairperson**
n président(e); **chairwoman** n
présidente f
chalet ['ʃæleɪ] n chalet m
chalk [tʃɔːk] n craie f; **chalkboard** (US)
n tableau noir
challenge ['tʃælɪndʒ] n défi m ▷ vt
défier; (statement, right) mettre en

question, contester; **to ~ sb to do**
mettre qn au défi de faire; **challenging**
adj (task, career) qui représente un défi
or une gageure; (tone, look) de défi,
provocateur(-trice)
chamber ['tʃeɪmbər] n chambre f; (BRIT
Law: gen pl) cabinet m; **~ of commerce**
chambre de commerce; **chambermaid**
n femme f de chambre
champagne [ʃæm'peɪn] n
champagne m
champion ['tʃæmpɪən] n (also of cause)
champion(ne); **championship** n
championnat m
chance [tʃɑːns] n (luck) hasard m;
(opportunity) occasion f, possibilité f;
(hope, likelihood) chance f; (risk) risque
m ▷ vt (risk) risquer ▷ adj fortuit(e), de
hasard; **to take a ~** prendre un risque;
by ~ par hasard; **to ~ it** risquer le coup,
essayer
chancellor ['tʃɑːnsələr] n chancelier m;
Chancellor of the Exchequer
[-ɪks'tʃɛkər] (BRIT) n chancelier m de
l'Échiquier
chandelier [ʃændə'lɪər] n lustre m
change [tʃeɪndʒ] vt (alter, replace:
Comm: money) changer; (switch,
substitute: hands, trains, clothes,
one's name etc) changer de ▷ vi (gen)
changer; (change clothes) se changer;
(be transformed): **to ~ into** se changer
or transformer en ▷ n changement
m; (money) monnaie f; **to ~ gear** (Aut)
changer de vitesse; **to ~ one's mind**
changer d'avis; **a ~ of clothes** des
vêtements de rechange; **for a ~** pour
changer; **do you have ~ for £10?** vous
avez la monnaie de 10 livres?; **where
can I ~ some money?** où est-ce que je
peux changer de l'argent?; **keep the
~!** gardez la monnaie!; **change over**
vi (swap) échanger; (change: drivers
etc) changer; (change sides: players etc)
changer de côté; **to ~ over from sth to
sth** passer de qch à qch; **changeable**
adj (weather) variable; **change
machine** n distributeur m de monnaie

changing room n (BRIT: in shop) salon m d'essayage; (: Sport) vestiaire m

hannel ['tʃænl] n (TV) chaîne f; (waveband, groove, fig: medium) canal m; (of river, sea) chenal m ▷ vt canaliser; **the (English) C~** la Manche; **Channel Islands** npl: **the Channel Islands** les îles fpl Anglo-Normandes; **Channel Tunnel** n: **the Channel Tunnel** le tunnel sous la Manche

hant [tʃɑːnt] n chant m; (Rel) psalmodie f ▷ vt chanter; scander

haos ['keɪɔs] n chaos m

haotic [keɪˈɔtɪk] adj chaotique

hap [tʃæp] n (BRIT inf: man) type m

hapel ['tʃæpl] n chapelle f

happed [tʃæpt] adj (skin, lips) gercé(e)

hapter ['tʃæptəʳ] n chapitre m

haracter ['kærɪktəʳ] n caractère m; (in novel, film) personnage m; (eccentric person) numéro m, phénomène m; **characteristic** ['kærɪktəˈrɪstɪk] adj, n caractéristique (f); **characterize** ['kærɪktəraɪz] vt caractériser

harcoal ['tʃɑːkəʊl] n charbon m de bois; (Art) charbon

harge [tʃɑːdʒ] n (accusation) accusation f; (Law) inculpation f; (cost) prix (demandé) ▷ vt (gun, battery, Mil: enemy) charger; (customer, sum) faire payer à; vi foncer; **charges** npl (costs) frais mpl; (BRIT Tel): **to reverse the ~s** téléphoner en PCV; **to take ~ of** se charger de; **to be in ~ of** être responsable de, s'occuper de; **to ~ sb (with)** (Law) inculper qn (de); **charge card** n carte f de client (émise par un grand magasin); **charger** n (also: **battery charger**) chargeur m

harismatic [kærɪzˈmætɪk] adj charismatique

harity ['tʃærɪtɪ] n charité f; (organization) institution f charitable or de bienfaisance, œuvre f (de charité); **charity shop** n (BRIT) boutique vendant des articles d'occasion au profit d'une organisation caritative

harm [tʃɑːm] n charme m; (on bracelet)

breloque f ▷ vt charmer, enchanter; **charming** adj charmant(e)

chart [tʃɑːt] n tableau m, diagramme m; graphique m; (map) carte marine ▷ vt dresser or établir la carte de; (sales, progress) établir la courbe de; **charts** npl (Mus) hit-parade m; **to be in the ~s** (record, pop group) figurer au hit-parade

charter ['tʃɑːtəʳ] vt (plane) affréter ▷ n (document) charte f; **chartered accountant** n (BRIT) expert-comptable m; **charter flight** n charter m

chase [tʃeɪs] vt poursuivre, pourchasser; (also: **~ away**) chasser ▷ n poursuite f, chasse f

chat [tʃæt] vi (also: **have a ~**) bavarder, causer; (on Internet) chatter ▷ n conversation f; **chat up** vt (BRIT inf: girl) baratiner; **chat room** n (Internet) forum m de discussion; **chat show** n (BRIT) talk-show m

chatter ['tʃætəʳ] vi (person) bavarder, papoter ▷ n bavardage m, papotage m; **my teeth are ~ing** je claque des dents

chauffeur ['ʃəʊfəʳ] n chauffeur m (de maître)

chauvinist ['ʃəʊvɪnɪst] n (also: **male ~**) phallocrate m, macho m; (nationalist) chauvin(e)

cheap [tʃiːp] adj bon marché inv, pas cher (chère); (reduced: ticket) à prix réduit; (: fare) réduit(e); (joke) facile, d'un goût douteux; (poor quality) à bon marché, de qualité médiocre ▷ adv à bon marché, pour pas cher; **can you recommend a ~ hotel/restaurant, please?** pourriez-vous m'indiquer un hôtel/restaurant bon marché?; **cheap day return** n billet m d'aller et retour réduit (valable pour la journée); **cheaply** adv à bon marché, à bon compte

cheat [tʃiːt] vi tricher; (in exam) copier ▷ vt tromper, duper; (rob): **to ~ sb out of sth** escroquer qch à qn ▷ n tricheur(-euse) m/f; escroc m; **cheat on** vt fus tromper

Chechnya [tʃɪtʃˈnjaː] n Tchétchénie f

check [tʃɛk] vt vérifier; (*passport, ticket*) contrôler; (*halt*) enrayer; (*restrain*) maîtriser ▷ vi (*official etc*) se renseigner ▷ n vérification f; contrôle m; (*curb*) frein m; (BRIT: *bill*) addition f; (US) = **cheque**; (*pattern: gen pl*) carreaux mpl; **to ~ with sb** demander à qn; **check in** vi (*in hotel*) remplir sa fiche (d'hôtel); (*at airport*) se présenter à l'enregistrement ▷ vt (*luggage*) (faire) enregistrer; **check off** vt (*tick off*) cocher; **check out** vi (*in hotel*) régler sa note ▷ vt (*investigate: story*) vérifier; **check up** vi: **to ~ up (on sth)** vérifier (qch); **to ~ up on sb** se renseigner sur le compte de qn; **checkbook** (US) = **chequebook**; **checked** adj (*pattern, cloth*) à carreaux; **checkers** n (US) jeu m de dames; **check-in** n (*also*: **check-in desk**: *at airport*) enregistrement m; **checking account** n (US) compte courant; **checklist** n liste f de contrôle; **checkmate** n échec et mat m; **checkout** n (*in supermarket*) caisse f; **checkpoint** n contrôle m; **checkroom** (US) n consigne f; **checkup** n (Med) examen médical, check-up m

cheddar ['tʃɛdə'] n (*also*: **~ cheese**) cheddar m

cheek [tʃiːk] n joue f; (*impudence*) toupet m, culot m; **what a ~!** quel toupet!; **cheekbone** n pommette f; **cheeky** adj effronté(e), culotté(e)

cheer [tʃɪə'] vt acclamer, applaudir; (*gladden*) réjouir, réconforter ▷ vi applaudir ▷ n (*gen pl*) acclamations fpl, applaudissements mpl; bravos mpl, hourras mpl; **~s!** à la vôtre!; **cheer up** vi se dérider, reprendre courage ▷ vt remonter le moral à or de, dérider, égayer; **cheerful** adj gai(e), joyeux(-euse)

cheerio [tʃɪərɪ'əu] excl (BRIT) salut!, au revoir!

cheerleader ['tʃɪəliːdə'] n membre d'un groupe de majorettes qui chantent et dansent pour soutenir leur équipe pendant les matchs de football américain

cheese [tʃiːz] n fromage m; **cheeseburger** n cheeseburger m; **cheesecake** n tarte f au fromage

chef [ʃɛf] n chef (cuisinier)

chemical ['kɛmɪkl] adj chimique ▷ n produit m chimique

chemist ['kɛmɪst] n (BRIT: *pharmacist*) pharmacien(ne); (*scientist*) chimiste m/f; **chemistry** n chimie f; **chemist's (shop)** n (BRIT) pharmacie f

cheque (US **check**) [tʃɛk] n chèque m; **chequebook** (US **checkbook**) n chéquier m, carnet m de chèques; **cheque card** n (BRIT) carte f (d'identité) bancaire

cherry ['tʃɛrɪ] n cerise f; (*also*: **~ tree**) cerisier m

chess [tʃɛs] n échecs mpl

chest [tʃɛst] n poitrine f; (*box*) coffre m, caisse f

chestnut ['tʃɛsnʌt] n châtaigne f; (*also*: **~ tree**) châtaignier m

chest of drawers n commode f

chew [tʃuː] vt mâcher; **chewing gum** n chewing-gum m

chic [ʃiːk] adj chic inv, élégant(e)

chick [tʃɪk] n poussin m; (*inf*) pépée f

chicken ['tʃɪkɪn] n poulet m; (*inf: coward*) poule mouillée; **chicken out** vi (*inf*) se dégonfler; **chickenpox** n varicelle f

chickpea ['tʃɪkpiː] n pois m chiche

chief [tʃiːf] n chef m ▷ adj principal(e); **chief executive** (US **chief executive officer**) n directeur(-trice) général(e); **chiefly** adv principalement, surtout

child (*pl* **~ren**) [tʃaɪld, 'tʃɪldrən] n enfant m/f; **child abuse** n maltraitance f d'enfants; (*sexual*) abus mpl sexuels sur des enfants; **child benefit** n (BRIT) ≈ allocations familiales; **childbirth** n accouchement m; **child-care** n (*for working parents*) garde f des enfants (*pour les parents qui travaillent*); **childhood** n enfance f; **childish** adj puéril(e), enfantin(e); **child minder** n (BRIT) garde f d'enfants; **children** ['tʃɪldrən] npl of **child**

Chile ['tʃɪlɪ] n Chili m

chill [tʃɪl] n (of water) froid m; (of air) fraîcheur f; (Med) refroidissement m, coup m de froid ▷ vt (person) faire frissonner; (Culin) mettre au frais, rafraîchir; **chill out** vi (inf: esp US) se relaxer

chil(l)i ['tʃɪlɪ] n piment m (rouge)

chilly ['tʃɪlɪ] adj froid(e), glacé(e); (sensitive to cold) frileux(-euse)

chimney ['tʃɪmnɪ] n cheminée f

chimpanzee [tʃɪmpæn'ziː] n chimpanzé m

chin [tʃɪn] n menton m

China ['tʃaɪnə] n Chine f

china ['tʃaɪnə] n (material) porcelaine f; (crockery) (vaisselle f en) porcelaine

Chinese [tʃaɪ'niːz] adj chinois(e) ▷ n (pl inv) Chinois(e); (Ling) chinois m

chip [tʃɪp] n (gen pl: Culin: BRIT) frite f; (: US: also: **potato ~**) chip m; (of wood) copeau m; (of glass, stone) éclat m; (also: **micro~**) puce f; (in gambling) fiche f ▷ vt (cup, plate) ébrécher; **chip shop** n (BRIT) friterie f

- **CHIP SHOP**
-
- Un **chip shop**, que l'on appelle
- également un "fish-and-chip shop",
- est un magasin où l'on vend des plats
- à emporter. Les **chip shops** sont
- d'ailleurs à l'origine des "takeaways".
- On y achète en particulier du
- poisson frit et des frites, mais
- on y trouve également des plats
- traditionnels britanniques ("steak
- pies", saucisses, etc). Tous les plats
- étaient à l'origine emballés dans du
- papier journal. Dans certains de ces
- magasins, on peut s'asseoir pour
- consommer sur place.

chiropodist [kɪ'rɔpədɪst] n (BRIT) pédicure m/f

chisel ['tʃɪzl] n ciseau m

chives [tʃaɪvz] npl ciboulette f, civette f

chlorine ['klɔːriːn] n chlore m

choc-ice ['tʃɔkaɪs] n (BRIT) esquimau® m

chocolate ['tʃɔklɪt] n chocolat m

choice [tʃɔɪs] n choix m ▷ adj de choix

choir ['kwaɪər] n chœur m, chorale f

choke [tʃəuk] vi étouffer ▷ vt étrangler; étouffer; (block) boucher, obstruer ▷ n (Aut) starter m

cholesterol [kə'lɛstərɔl] n cholestérol m

choose (pt **chose**, pp **chosen**) [tʃuːz, tʃəuz, 'tʃəuzn] vt choisir; **to ~ to do** décider de faire, juger bon de faire

chop [tʃɔp] vt (wood) couper (à la hache); (Culin: also: **~ up**) couper (fin), émincer, hacher (en morceaux) ▷ n (Culin) côtelette f; **chop down** vt (tree) abattre; **chop off** vt trancher; **chopsticks** ['tʃɔpstɪks] npl baguettes fpl

chord [kɔːd] n (Mus) accord m

chore [tʃɔːr] n travail m de routine; **household ~s** travaux mpl du ménage

chorus ['kɔːrəs] n chœur m; (repeated part of song, also fig) refrain m

chose [tʃəuz] pt of **choose**

chosen ['tʃəuzn] pp of **choose**

Christ [kraɪst] n Christ m

christen ['krɪsn] vt baptiser; **christening** n baptême m

Christian ['krɪstɪən] adj, n chrétien(ne); **Christianity** [krɪstɪ'ænɪtɪ] n christianisme m; **Christian name** n prénom m

Christmas ['krɪsməs] n Noël m or f; **happy** or **merry ~!** joyeux Noël!; **Christmas card** n carte f de Noël; **Christmas carol** n chant m de Noël; **Christmas Day** n le jour de Noël; **Christmas Eve** n la veille de Noël; la nuit de Noël; **Christmas pudding** n (esp BRIT) Christmas m pudding; **Christmas tree** n arbre m de Noël

chrome [krəum] n chrome m

chronic ['krɔnɪk] adj chronique

chrysanthemum [krɪ'sænθəməm] n chrysanthème m

chubby ['tʃʌbɪ] adj potelé(e),

rondelet(te)

chuck [tʃʌk] vt (inf) lancer, jeter; (BRIT: also: ~ **up**: job) lâcher; **chuck out** vt (inf: person) flanquer dehors or à la porte; (: rubbish etc) jeter

chuckle [ˈtʃʌkl] vi glousser

chum [tʃʌm] n copain (copine)

chunk [tʃʌŋk] n gros morceau

church [tʃəːtʃ] n église f; **churchyard** n cimetière m

churn [tʃəːn] n (for butter) baratte f; (also: **milk ~**) (grand) bidon à lait

chute [ʃuːt] n goulotte f; (also: **rubbish ~**) vide-ordures m inv; (BRIT: children's slide) toboggan m

chutney [ˈtʃʌtnɪ] n chutney m

CIA n abbr (= Central Intelligence Agency) CIA f

CID n abbr (= Criminal Investigation Department) ≈ P.J. f

cider [ˈsaɪdəʳ] n cidre m

cigar [sɪˈɡɑːʳ] n cigare m

cigarette [sɪɡəˈrɛt] n cigarette f; **cigarette lighter** n briquet m

cinema [ˈsɪnəmə] n cinéma m

cinnamon [ˈsɪnəmən] n cannelle f

circle [ˈsəːkl] n cercle m; (in cinema) balcon m ▷ vi faire or décrire des cercles ▷ vt (surround) entourer, encercler; (move round) faire le tour de, tourner autour de

circuit [ˈsəːkɪt] n circuit m; (lap) tour m

circular [ˈsəːkjuləʳ] adj circulaire ▷ n circulaire f; (as advertisement) prospectus m

circulate [ˈsəːkjuleɪt] vi circuler ▷ vt faire circuler; **circulation** [səːkjuˈleɪʃən] n circulation f; (of newspaper) tirage m

circumstances [ˈsəːkəmstənsɪz] npl circonstances fpl; (financial condition) moyens mpl, situation financière

circus [ˈsəːkəs] n cirque m

cite [saɪt] vt citer

citizen [ˈsɪtɪzn] n (Pol) citoyen(ne); (resident): **the ~s of this town** les habitants de cette ville; **citizenship** n citoyenneté f; (BRIT: Scol) ≈ éducation

f civique

citrus fruits [ˈsɪtrəs-] npl agrumes mpl

city [ˈsɪtɪ] n (grande) ville f; **the C~** la Cité de Londres (centre des affaires); **city centre** n centre ville m; **city technology college** n (BRIT) établissement m d'enseignement technologique (situé dans un quartier défavorisé)

civic [ˈsɪvɪk] adj civique; (authorities) municipal(e)

civil [ˈsɪvɪl] adj civil(e); (polite) poli(e), civil(e); **civilian** [sɪˈvɪlɪən] adj, n civil(e

civilization [sɪvɪlaɪˈzeɪʃən] n civilisation f

civilized [ˈsɪvɪlaɪzd] adj civilisé(e); (fig) où règnent les bonnes manières

civil: **civil law** n code civil; (study) droit civil; **civil rights** npl droits mpl civiques; **civil servant** n fonctionnair m/f; **Civil Service** n fonction publique administration f; **civil war** n guerre civile

CJD n abbr (= Creutzfeldt-Jakob disease) MCJ f

claim [kleɪm] vt (rights etc) revendique (compensation) réclamer; (assert) déclarer, prétendre ▷ vi (for insurance) faire une déclaration de sinistre ▷ n revendication f; prétention f; (right) droit m; **(insurance) ~** demande f d'indemnisation, déclaration f de sinistre; **claim form** n (gen) formulaire m de demande

clam [klæm] n palourde f

clamp [klæmp] n crampon m; (on workbench) valet m; (on car) sabot m de Denver ▷ vt attacher; (car) mettre un sabot à; **clamp down on** vt fus sévir contre, prendre des mesures draconiennes à l'égard de

clan [klæn] n clan m

clap [klæp] vi applaudir

claret [ˈklærət] n (vin m de) bordeaux m (rouge)

clarify [ˈklærɪfaɪ] vt clarifier

clarinet [klærɪˈnɛt] n clarinette f

clarity [ˈklærɪtɪ] n clarté f

lash [klæʃ] n (sound) choc m, fracas m; (with police) affrontement m; (fig) conflit m ▷ vi se heurter; être or entrer en conflit; (colours) jurer; (dates, events) tomber en même temps

lasp [klɑːsp] n (of necklace, bag) fermoir m ▷ vt serrer, étreindre

lass [klɑːs] n (gen) classe f; (group, category) catégorie f ▷ vt classer, classifier

lassic ['klæsɪk] adj classique ▷ n (author, work) classique m; **classical** adj classique

lassification [klæsɪfɪ'keɪʃən] n classification f

lassify ['klæsɪfaɪ] vt classifier, classer

lassmate ['klɑːsmeɪt] n camarade m/f de classe

lassroom ['klɑːsrʊm] n (salle f de) classe f; **classroom assistant** n assistant(-e) d'éducation

lassy ['klɑːsɪ] (inf) adj classe (inf)

latter ['klætə^r] n cliquetis m ▷ vi cliqueter

lause [klɔːz] n clause f; (Ling) proposition f

laustrophobic [klɔːstrə'fəʊbɪk] adj (person) claustrophobe; (place) où l'on se sent claustrophobe

law [klɔː] n griffe f; (of bird of prey) serre f; (of lobster) pince f

lay [kleɪ] n argile f

lean [kliːn] adj propre; (clear, smooth) net(te); (record, reputation) sans tache; (joke, story) correct(e) ▷ vt nettoyer; **clean up** vt nettoyer; (fig) remettre de l'ordre dans; **cleaner** n (person) nettoyeur(-euse), femme f de ménage; (product) détachant m; **cleaner's** n (also: **dry cleaner's**) teinturier m; **cleaning** n nettoyage m

leanser ['klɛnzə^r] n (for face) démaquillant n

lear [klɪə^r] adj clair(e); (glass, plastic) transparent(e); (road, way) libre, dégagé(e); (profit, majority) net(te); (conscience) tranquille; (skin) frais (fraîche); (sky) dégagé(e) ▷ vt (road)

dégager, déblayer; (table) débarrasser; (room etc: of people) faire évacuer; (cheque) compenser; (Law: suspect) innocenter; (obstacle) franchir or sauter sans heurter ▷ vi (weather) s'éclaircir; (fog) se dissiper ▷ adv: **~ of** à distance de, à l'écart de; **to ~ the table** débarrasser la table, desservir; **clear away** vt (things, clothes etc) enlever, retirer; **to ~ away the dishes** débarrasser la table; **clear up** vt ranger, mettre en ordre; (mystery) éclaircir, résoudre; **clearance** n (removal) déblayage m; (permission) autorisation f; **clear-cut** adj précis(e), nettement défini(e); **clearing** n (in forest) clairière f; **clearly** adv clairement; (obviously) de toute évidence; **clearway** n (BRIT) route f à stationnement interdit

clench [klɛntʃ] vt serrer

clergy ['klɜːdʒɪ] n clergé m

clerk [klɑːk, US klɜːrk] n (BRIT) employé(e) de bureau; (US: salesman/ woman) vendeur(-euse)

clever ['klɛvə^r] adj (intelligent) intelligent(e); (skilful) habile, adroit(e); (device, arrangement) ingénieux(-euse), astucieux(-euse)

cliché ['kliːʃeɪ] n cliché m

click [klɪk] vi (Comput) cliquer ▷ vt: **to ~ one's tongue** faire claquer sa langue; **to ~ one's heels** claquer des talons; **to ~ on an icon** cliquer sur une icône

client ['klaɪənt] n client(e)

cliff [klɪf] n falaise f

climate ['klaɪmɪt] n climat m; **climate change** n changement m climatique

climax ['klaɪmæks] n apogée m, point culminant; (sexual) orgasme m

climb [klaɪm] vi grimper, monter; (plane) prendre de l'altitude ▷ vt (stairs) monter; (mountain) escalader; (tree) grimper à ▷ n montée f, escalade f; **to ~ over a wall** passer par dessus un mur; **climb down** vi (re)descendre; (BRIT fig) rabattre de ses prétentions; **climber** n (also: **rock climber**) grimpeur(-euse), varappeur(-euse); (*plant*) plante grimpante; **climbing** n (*also*: **rock climbing**) escalade f, varappe f

clinch [klɪntʃ] vt (*deal*) conclure, sceller

cling (*pt, pp* **clung**) [klɪŋ, klʌŋ] vi: **to ~ (to)** se cramponner (à), s'accrocher (à); (*clothes*) coller (à)

Clingfilm® ['klɪŋfɪlm] n film m alimentaire

clinic ['klɪnɪk] n clinique f; centre médical

clip [klɪp] n (*for hair*) barrette f; (*also:* **paper ~**) trombone m; (*TV, Cinema*) clip m ▷ vt (*also:* **~ together**: *papers*) attacher; (*hair, nails*) couper; (*hedge*) tailler; **clipping** n (*from newspaper*) coupure f de journal

cloak [kləuk] n grande cape ▷ vt (*fig*) masquer, cacher; **cloakroom** n (*for coats etc*) vestiaire m; (*BRIT*: W.C.) toilettes fpl

clock [klɔk] n (*large*) horloge f; (*small*) pendule f; **clock in** or **on** (*BRIT*) vi (*with card*) pointer (en arrivant); (*start work*) commencer à travailler; **clock off** or **out** (*BRIT*) vi (*with card*) pointer (en partant); (*leave work*) quitter le travail; **clockwise** adv dans le sens des aiguilles d'une montre; **clockwork** n rouages mpl, mécanisme m; (*of clock*) mouvement m (d'horlogerie) ▷ adj (*toy, train*) mécanique

clog [klɔg] n sabot m ▷ vt boucher, encrasser ▷ vi (*also:* **~ up**) se boucher, s'encrasser

clone [kləun] n clone m ▷ vt cloner

close¹ [kləus] adj (*near*): **~ (to)** près (de), proche (de); (*contact, link, watch*) étroit(e); (*examination*) attentif(-ive), minutieux(-euse); (*contest*) très serré(e); (*weather*) lourd(e), étouffant(e) ▷ adv près, à proximité; **~ to** prep près de; **~ by, ~ at hand** adj, adv tout(e) près; **a ~ friend** un ami intime; **to have a ~ shave** (*fig*) l'échapper belle

close² [kləuz] vt fermer ▷ vi (*shop etc*) fermer; (*lid, door etc*) se fermer; (*end*) se terminer, se conclure ▷ n (*end*)

conclusion f; **what time do you ~?** à quelle heure fermez-vous?; **close down** vi fermer (*définitivement*); **closed** adj (*shop etc*) fermé(e)

closely ['kləuslɪ] adv (*examine, watch*) de près

closet ['klɔzɪt] n (*cupboard*) placard m, réduit m

close-up ['kləusʌp] n gros plan

closing time n heure f de fermeture

closure ['kləuʒər] n fermeture f

clot [klɔt] n (*of blood, milk*) caillot m; (*inf: person*) ballot m ▷ vi (: *external bleeding*) se coaguler

cloth [klɔθ] n (*material*) tissu m, étoffe f; (*BRIT: also:* **tea ~**) torchon m; lavette f; (*also:* **table~**) nappe f

clothes [kləuðz] npl vêtements mpl, habits mpl; **clothes line** n corde f (à linge); **clothes peg** (*us* **clothes pin**) n pince f à linge

clothing ['kləuðɪŋ] n = **clothes**

cloud [klaud] n nuage m; **cloud over** vi se couvrir; (*fig*) s'assombrir; **cloudy** adj nuageux(-euse), couvert(e); (*liquid*) trouble

clove [kləuv] n clou m de girofle; **a ~ of garlic** une gousse d'ail

clown [klaun] n clown m ▷ vi (*also:* **~ about, ~ around**) faire le clown

club [klʌb] n (*society*) club m; (*weapon*) massue f, matraque f; (*also:* **golf ~**) club ▷ vt matraquer ▷ vi: **to ~ together** s'associer; **clubs** npl (*Cards*) trèfle m; **club class** n (*Aviat*) classe f club

clue [klu:] n indice m; (*in crosswords*) définition f; **I haven't a ~** je n'en ai pas la moindre idée

clump [klʌmp] n: **~ of trees** bouquet m d'arbres

clumsy ['klʌmzɪ] adj (*person*) gauche, maladroit(e); (*object*) malcommode, peu maniable

clung [klʌŋ] pt, pp of **cling**

cluster ['klʌstər] n (petit) groupe; (*of flowers*) grappe f ▷ vi se rassembler

clutch [klʌtʃ] n (*Aut*) embrayage m; (*grasp*): **~es** étreinte f, prise f ▷ vt (*grasp* agripper; (*hold tightly*) serrer fort; (*hold on to*) se cramponner à

n *abbr* (= *centimetre*) cm

o. *abbr* = **company, county**

/o *abbr* (= *care of*) c/o, aux bons soins de

oach [kəutʃ] *n* (*bus*) autocar *m*; (*horse-drawn*) diligence *f*; (*of train*) voiture *f*, wagon *m*; (*Sport: trainer*) entraîneur(-euse); (*school: tutor*) répétiteur(-trice) ▷ *vt* (*Sport*) entraîner; (*student*) donner des leçons particulières à; **coach station** (*BRIT*) *n* gare routière; **coach trip** *n* excursion *f* en car

oal [kəul] *n* charbon *m*

oalition [kəuə'lɪʃən] *n* coalition *f*

oarse [kɔːs] *adj* grossier(-ère), rude; (*vulgar*) vulgaire

oast [kəust] *n* côte *f* ▷ *vi* (*car, cycle*) descendre en roue libre; **coastal** *adj* côtier(-ère); **coastguard** *n* garde-côte *m*; **coastline** *n* côte *f*, littoral *m*

oat [kəut] *n* manteau *m*; (*of animal*) pelage *m*, poil *m*; (*of paint*) couche *f* ▷ *vt* couvrir, enduire; **coat hanger** *n* cintre *m*; **coating** *n* couche *f*, enduit *m*

oax [kəuks] *vt* persuader par des cajoleries

ob [kɔb] *n see* **corn**

obbled [ˈkɔbld] *adj* pavé(e)

obweb [ˈkɔbwɛb] *n* toile *f* d'araignée

ocaine [kə'keɪn] *n* cocaïne *f*

ock [kɔk] *n* (*rooster*) coq *m*; (*male bird*) mâle *m* ▷ *vt* (*gun*) armer; **cockerel** *n* jeune coq *m*

ockney [ˈkɔknɪ] *n* cockney *m/f* (*habitant des quartiers populaires de l'East End de Londres*), ≈ faubourien(ne)

ockpit [ˈkɔkpɪt] *n* (*in aircraft*) poste *m* de pilotage, cockpit *m*

ockroach [ˈkɔkrəutʃ] *n* cafard *m*, cancrelat *m*

ocktail [ˈkɔkteɪl] *n* cocktail *m*

ocoa [ˈkəukəu] *n* cacao *m*

oconut [ˈkəukənʌt] *n* noix *f* de coco

.O.D. *abbr* = **cash on delivery**

od [kɔd] *n* morue fraîche, cabillaud *m*

ode [kəud] *n* code *m*; (*Tel: area code*)

indicatif *m*

coeducational [ˈkəuɛdju'keɪʃənl] *adj* mixte

coffee [ˈkɔfɪ] *n* café *m*; **coffee bar** *n* (*BRIT*) café *m*; **coffee bean** *n* grain *m* de café; **coffee break** *n* pause-café *f*; **coffee maker** *n* cafetière *f*; **coffeepot** *n* cafetière *f*; **coffee shop** *n* café *m*; **coffee table** *n* (petite) table basse

coffin [ˈkɔfɪn] *n* cercueil *m*

cog [kɔg] *n* (*wheel*) roue dentée; (*tooth*) dent *f* (d'engrenage)

cognac [ˈkɔnjæk] *n* cognac *m*

coherent [kəu'hɪərənt] *adj* cohérent(e)

coil [kɔɪl] *n* rouleau *m*, bobine *f*; (*contraceptive*) stérilet *m* ▷ *vt* enrouler

coin [kɔɪn] *n* pièce *f* (de monnaie) ▷ *vt* (*word*) inventer

coincide [kəuɪn'saɪd] *vi* coïncider; **coincidence** [kəu'ɪnsɪdəns] *n* coïncidence *f*

Coke® [kəuk] *n* coca *m*

coke [kəuk] *n* (*coal*) coke *m*

colander [ˈkɔləndər] *n* passoire *f* (à légumes)

cold [kəuld] *adj* froid(e) ▷ *n* froid *m*; (*Med*) rhume *m*; **it's ~** il fait froid; **to be ~** (*person*) avoir froid; **to catch a ~** s'enrhumer, attraper un rhume; **in ~ blood** de sang-froid; **cold cuts** (*US*) *npl* viandes froides; **cold sore** *n* bouton *m* de fièvre

coleslaw [ˈkəulslɔː] *n* sorte de salade de chou cru

colic [ˈkɔlɪk] *n* colique(s) *f(pl)*

collaborate [kə'læbəreɪt] *vi* collaborer

collapse [kə'læps] *vi* s'effondrer, s'écrouler; (*Med*) avoir un malaise ▷ *n* effondrement *m*, écroulement *m*; (*of government*) chute *f*

collar [ˈkɔlər] *n* (*of coat, shirt*) col *m*; (*for dog*) collier *m*; **collarbone** *n* clavicule *f*

colleague [ˈkɔliːg] *n* collègue *m/f*

collect [kə'lɛkt] *vt* rassembler; (*pick up*) ramasser; (*as a hobby*) collectionner; (*BRIT: call for*) (passer) prendre; (*mail*) faire la levée de, ramasser; (*money owed*) encaisser; (*donations, subscriptions*) recueillir ▷ *vi* (*people*) se rassembler; (*dust, dirt*) s'amasser; **to call ~** (*us Tel*) téléphoner en PCV; **collection** [kəˈlɛkʃən] *n* collection *f*; (*of mail*) levée *f*; (*for money*) collecte *f*, quête *f*; **collective** [kəˈlɛktɪv] *adj* collectif(-ive); **collector** *n* collectionneur *m*

college [ˈkɔlɪdʒ] *n* collège *m*; (*of technology, agriculture etc*) institut *m*

collide [kəˈlaɪd] *vi*: **to ~ (with)** entrer en collision (avec)

collision [kəˈlɪʒən] *n* collision *f*, heurt *m*

cologne [kəˈləun] *n* (*also:* **eau de ~**) eau *f* de cologne

colon [ˈkəulən] *n* (*sign*) deux-points *mpl*; (*Med*) côlon *m*

colonel [ˈkəːnl] *n* colonel *m*

colonial [kəˈləunɪəl] *adj* colonial(e)

colony [ˈkɔlənɪ] *n* colonie *f*

colour *etc* (*us* **color** *etc*) [ˈkʌləʳ] *n* couleur *f* ▷ *vt* colorer; (*dye*) teindre; (*paint*) peindre; (*with crayons*) colorier; (*news*) fausser, exagérer ▷ *vi* (*blush*) rougir; **I'd like a different ~** je le voudrais dans un autre coloris; **colour in** *vt* colorier; **colour-blind** *adj* daltonien(ne); **coloured** *adj* coloré(e); (*photo*) en couleur; **colour film** *n* (*for camera*) pellicule *f* (en) couleur; **colourful** *adj* coloré(e), vif (vive); (*personality*) pittoresque, haut(e) en couleurs; **colouring** *n* colorant *m*; (*complexion*) teint *m*; **colour television** *n* télévision *f* (en) couleur

column [ˈkɔləm] *n* colonne *f*; (*fashion column, sports column etc*) rubrique *f*

coma [ˈkəumə] *n* coma *m*

comb [kəum] *n* peigne *m* ▷ *vt* (*hair*) peigner; (*area*) ratisser, passer au peigne fin

combat [ˈkɔmbæt] *n* combat *m* ▷ *vt* combattre, lutter contre

combination [kɔmbɪˈneɪʃən] *n* (*gen*) combinaison *f*

combine *vb* [kəmˈbaɪn] ▷ *vt* combiner ▷ *vi* s'associer; (*Chem*) se combiner ▷ *n*

[ˈkɔmbaɪn] (*Econ*) trust *m*; **to ~ sth with sth** (*one quality with another*) joindre ou allier qch à qch

come (*pt* **came**, *pp* ~) [kʌm, keɪm] *vi* **1** (*movement towards*) venir; **to ~ running** arriver en courant; **he's ~ here to work** il est venu ici pour travailler; **~ with me** suivez-moi

2 (*arrive*) arriver; **to ~ home** rentrer (chez soi *or* à la maison); **we've just ~ from Paris** nous arrivons de Paris

3 (*reach*): **to ~ to** (*decision etc*) parvenir à, arriver à; **the bill came to £40** la note s'est élevée à 40 livres

4 (*occur*): **an idea came to me** il m'est venu une idée

5 (*be, become*): **to ~ loose/undone** se défaire/desserrer; **I've ~ to like him** j'ai fini par bien l'aimer; **come across** *vt fus* rencontrer par hasard, tomber sur; **come along** *vi* (BRIT: *pupil, work*) faire des progrès, avancer; **come back** *vi* revenir; **come down** *vi* descendre; (*prices*) baisser; (*buildings*) s'écrouler; (: *be demolished*) être démoli(e); **come from** *vt fus* (*source*) venir de; (*place*) venir de, être originaire de; **come in** *vi* entrer; (*train*) arriver; (*fashion*) entrer en vogue; (*on deal etc*) participer; **come off** *vi* (*button*) se détacher; (*attempt*) réussir; **come on** *vi* (*lights, electricity*) s'allumer; (*central heating*) se mettre en marche; (*pupil, work, project*) faire des progrès, avancer; **~ on!** viens!; allons!, allez!; **come out** *vi* sortir; (*sun*) se montrer; (*book*) paraître; (*stain*) s'enlever; (*strike*) cesser le travail, se mettre en grève; **come round** *vi* (*after faint, operation*) revenir à soi, reprendre connaissance; **come to** *vi* revenir à soi; **come up** *vi* monter; (*sun*) se lever; (*problem*) se poser; (*event*) survenir; (*in conversation*) être soulevé; **come up with** *vt fus* (*money*) fournir; **he came up with an idea** il a eu une idée, il a proposé quelque chose

comeback [ˈkʌmbæk] *n* (*Theat etc*) rentrée *f*

omedian [kə'miːdɪən] n (comic) comique m; (Theat) comédien m

omedy ['kɔmɪdɪ] n comédie f; (humour) comique m

omet ['kɔmɪt] n comète f

omfort ['kʌmfət] n confort m, bien-être m; (solace) consolation f, réconfort m ▷ vt consoler, réconforter; **comfortable** adj confortable; (person) à l'aise; (financially) aisé(e); (patient) dont l'état est stationnaire; **comfort station** n (us) toilettes fpl

omic ['kɔmɪk] adj (also: ~al) comique ▷ n (person) comique m; (BRIT: magazine: for children) magazine m de bandes dessinées or de BD; (: for adults) illustré m; **comic book** (us) n (for children) magazine m de bandes dessinées or de BD; (for adults) illustré m; **comic strip** n bande dessinée

omma ['kɔmə] n virgule f

ommand [kə'mɑːnd] n ordre m, commandement m; (Mil: authority) commandement m; (mastery) maîtrise f ▷ vt (troops) commander; **to ~ sb to do** donner l'ordre or commander à qn de faire; **commander** n (Mil) commandant m

ommemorate [kə'mɛmərent] vt commémorer

ommence [kə'mɛns] vt, vi commencer; **commencement** (us) n (University) remise f des diplômes

ommend [kə'mɛnd] vt louer; (recommend) recommander

omment ['kɔmɛnt] n commentaire m ▷ vi: **to ~ on** faire des remarques sur; **"no ~"** "je n'ai rien à déclarer"; **commentary** ['kɔməntərɪ] n commentaire m; (Sport) reportage m (en direct); **commentator** ['kɔmənteɪtə'] n commentateur m; (Sport) reporter m

ommerce ['kɔmə:s] n commerce m

ommercial [kə'məːʃəl] adj commercial(e) ▷ n (Radio, TV) annonce f publicitaire, spot m (publicitaire); **commercial break** n (Radio, TV) spot m (publicitaire)

commission [kə'mɪʃən] n (committee, fee) commission f ▷ vt commander, charger un artiste de l'exécution de; **out of ~** (machine) hors service; **commissioner** n (Police) préfet m (de police)

commit [kə'mɪt] vt (act) commettre; (resources) consacrer; (to sb's care) confier (à); **to ~ o.s. (to do)** s'engager (à faire); **to ~ suicide** se suicider; **commitment** n engagement m; (obligation) responsabilité(s) (fpl)

committee [kə'mɪtɪ] n comité m; commission f

commodity [kə'mɔdɪtɪ] n produit m, marchandise f, article m

common ['kɔmən] adj (gen) commun(e); (usual) courant(e) ▷ n terrain communal; **commonly** adv communément, généralement; couramment; **commonplace** adj banal(e), ordinaire; **Commons** npl (BRIT Pol): **the (House of) Commons** la chambre des Communes; **common sense** n bon sens; **Commonwealth** n: **the Commonwealth** le Commonwealth

communal ['kɔmjuːnl] adj (life) communautaire; (for common use) commun(e)

commune n ['kɔmjuːn] (group) communauté f ▷ vi [kə'mjuːn]: **to ~ with** (nature) communier avec

communicate [kə'mjuːnɪkeɪt] vt communiquer, transmettre ▷ vi: **to ~ (with)** communiquer (avec)

communication [kəmjuːnɪ'keɪʃən] n communication f

communion [kə'mjuːnɪən] n (also: **Holy C~**) communion f

communism ['kɔmjunɪzəm] n communisme m; **communist** adj, n communiste m/f

community [kə'mjuːnɪtɪ] n communauté f; **community centre** (us **community center**) n foyer socio-éducatif, centre m de loisirs;

community service n ≈ travail m d'intérêt général, TIG m

commute [kə'mjuːt] vi faire le trajet journalier (de son domicile à un lieu de travail assez éloigné) ▷ vt (Law) commuer; **commuter** n banlieusard(e) (qui fait un trajet journalier pour se rendre à son travail)

compact adj [kəm'pækt] compact(e) ▷ n ['kɒmpækt] (also: **powder ~**) poudrier m; **compact disc** n disque compact; **compact disc player** n lecteur m de disques compacts

companion [kəm'pænjən] n compagnon (compagne)

company ['kʌmpəni] n compagnie f; **to keep sb ~** tenir compagnie à qn; **company car** n voiture f de fonction; **company director** n administrateur(-trice)

comparable ['kɒmpərəbl] adj comparable

comparative [kəm'pærətɪv] adj (study) comparatif(-ive); (relative) relatif(-ive); **comparatively** adv (relatively) relativement

compare [kəm'pɛər] vt: **to ~ sth/sb with** or **to** comparer qch/qn avec or à ▷ vi: **to ~ (with)** se comparer (à); être comparable (à); **comparison** [kəm'pærɪsn] n comparaison f

compartment [kəm'pɑːtmənt] n (also Rail) compartiment m; **a non-smoking ~** un compartiment non-fumeurs

compass ['kʌmpəs] n boussole f; **compasses** npl (Math) compas m

compassion [kəm'pæʃən] n compassion f, humanité f

compatible [kəm'pætɪbl] adj compatible

compel [kəm'pɛl] vt contraindre, obliger; **compelling** adj (fig: argument) irrésistible

compensate ['kɒmpənseɪt] vt indemniser, dédommager ▷ vi: **to ~ for** compenser; **compensation** [kɒmpən'seɪʃən] n compensation

f; (money) dédommagement m, indemnité f

compete [kəm'piːt] vi (take part) concourir; (vie): **to ~ (with)** rivaliser (avec), faire concurrence (à)

competent ['kɒmpɪtənt] adj compétent(e), capable

competition [kɒmpɪ'tɪʃən] n (contest) compétition f, concours m; (Econ) concurrence f

competitive [kəm'pɛtɪtɪv] adj (Econ) concurrentiel(le); (sports) de compétition; (person) qui a l'esprit de compétition

competitor [kəm'pɛtɪtər] n concurrent(e)

complacent [kəm'pleɪsnt] adj (trop) content(e) de soi

complain [kəm'pleɪn] vi: **to ~ (about)** se plaindre (de); (in shop etc) réclamer (au sujet de); **complaint** n plainte f; (in shop etc) réclamation f; (Med) affection

complement ['kɒmplɪmənt] n complément m; (esp of ship's crew etc) effectif complet ▷ vt (enhance) compléter; **complementary** [kɒmplɪ'mɛntəri] adj complémentaire

complete [kəm'pliːt] adj complet(-ète); (finished) achevé(e) ▷ vt achever, parachever; (set, group) compléter; (a form) remplir; **completely** adv complètement; **completion** [kəm'pliːʃən] n achèvement m; (of contract) exécution f

complex ['kɒmplɛks] adj complexe ▷ n (Psych, buildings etc) complexe m

complexion [kəm'plɛkʃən] n (of face) teint m

compliance [kəm'plaɪəns] n (submission) docilité f; (agreement): **~ with** le fait de se conformer à; **in ~ with** en conformité avec, conformément à

complicate ['kɒmplɪkeɪt] vt compliquer; **complicated** adj compliqué(e); **complication** [kɒmplɪ'keɪʃən] n complication f

compliment n ['kɒmplɪmənt] compliment m ▷ vt ['kɒmplɪmɛnt]

complimenter; **complimentary**
[kɔmplɪˈmɛntərɪ] adj flatteur(-euse);
(free) à titre gracieux

omply [kəmˈplaɪ] vi: **to ~ with** se
soumettre à, se conformer à

omponent [kəmˈpəʊnənt] adj
composant(e), constituant(e) ▷ n
composant m, élément m

ompose [kəmˈpəʊz] vt composer;
(form): **to be ~d of** se composer de; **to ~
o.s.** se calmer, se maîtriser; **composer**
n (Mus) compositeur m; **composition**
[kɔmpəˈzɪʃən] n composition f

omposure [kəmˈpəʊʒəʳ] n calme m,
maîtrise f de soi

ompound [ˈkɔmpaʊnd] n (Chem,
Ling) composé m; (enclosure) enclos m,
enceinte f ▷ adj composé(e); (fracture)
compliqué(e)

omprehension [kɔmprɪˈhɛnʃən] n
compréhension f

omprehensive [kɔmprɪˈhɛnsɪv]
adj (très) complet(-ète); **~ policy**
(Insurance) assurance f tous risques;
comprehensive (school) n (BRIT)
école secondaire non sélective avec libre
circulation d'une section à l'autre, ≈ CES m

▌ Be careful not to translate
comprehensive by the French word
compréhensif.

ompress vt [kəmˈprɛs] comprimer;
(text, information) condenser ▷ n
[ˈkɔmprɛs] (Med) compresse f

omprise [kəmˈpraɪz] vt (also: **be ~d
of**) comprendre; (constitute) constituer,
représenter

ompromise [ˈkɔmprəmaɪz] n
compromis m ▷ vt compromettre ▷ vi
transiger, accepter un compromis

ompulsive [kəmˈpʌlsɪv] adj (Psych)
compulsif(-ive); (book, film etc)
captivant(e)

ompulsory [kəmˈpʌlsərɪ] adj
obligatoire

omputer [kəmˈpjuːtəʳ] n
ordinateur m; **computer game** n jeu
m vidéo; **computer-generated** adj
de synthèse; **computerize** vt (data)

traiter par ordinateur; (system, office)
informatiser; **computer programmer**
n programmeur(-euse); **computer
programming** n programmation f;
computer science n informatique f;
computer studies npl informatique f;
computing [kəmˈpjuːtɪŋ] n
informatique f

con [kɔn] vt duper; (cheat) escroquer ▷ n
escroquerie f

conceal [kənˈsiːl] vt cacher, dissimuler

concede [kənˈsiːd] vt concéder ▷ vi
céder

conceited [kənˈsiːtɪd] adj
vaniteux(-euse), suffisant(e)

conceive [kənˈsiːv] vt, vi concevoir

concentrate [ˈkɔnsəntreɪt] vi se
concentrer ▷ vt concentrer

concentration [kɔnsənˈtreɪʃən] n
concentration f

concept [ˈkɔnsɛpt] n concept m

concern [kənˈsəːn] n affaire f;
(Comm) entreprise f, firme f; (anxiety)
inquiétude f, souci m ▷ vt (worry)
inquiéter; (involve) concerner; (relate
to) se rapporter à; **to be ~ed (about)**
s'inquiéter (de), être inquiet(-ète) (au
sujet de); **concerning** prep en ce qui
concerne, à propos de

concert [ˈkɔnsət] n concert m; **concert
hall** n salle f de concert

concerto [kənˈtʃəːtəʊ] n concerto m

concession [kənˈsɛʃən] n (compromise)
concession f; (reduced price) réduction
f; **tax ~** dégrèvement fiscal; **"~s"** tarif
réduit

concise [kənˈsaɪs] adj concis(e)

conclude [kənˈkluːd] vt conclure;
conclusion [kənˈkluːʒən] n
conclusion f

concrete [ˈkɔŋkriːt] n béton m ▷ adj
concret(-ète); (Constr) en béton

concussion [kənˈkʌʃən] n (Med)
commotion (cérébrale)

condemn [kənˈdɛm] vt condamner

condensation [kɔndɛnˈseɪʃən] n
condensation f

condense [kənˈdɛns] vi se condenser

▷ *vt* condenser

condition [kən'dɪʃən] *n* condition *f*; (*disease*) maladie *f* ▷ *vt* déterminer, conditionner; **on ~ that** à condition que + *sub*, à condition de; **conditional** [kən'dɪʃənl] *adj* conditionnel(le); **conditioner** *n* (*for hair*) baume démêlant; (*for fabrics*) assouplissant *m*

condo ['kɔndəu] *n* (*US inf*) = **condominium**

condom ['kɔndəm] *n* préservatif *m*

condominium [kɔndə'mɪnɪəm] *n* (*US: building*) immeuble *m* (en copropriété); (*: rooms*) appartement *m* (dans un immeuble en copropriété)

condone [kən'dəun] *vt* fermer les yeux sur, approuver (tacitement)

conduct *n* ['kɔndʌkt] conduite *f* ▷ *vt* [kən'dʌkt] conduire; (*manage*) mener, diriger; (*Mus*) diriger; **to ~ o.s.** se conduire, se comporter; **conducted tour** (*BRIT*) *n* voyage organisé; (*of building*) visite guidée; **conductor** *n* (*of orchestra*) chef *m* d'orchestre; (*on bus*) receveur *m*; (*US: on train*) chef *m* de train; (*Elec*) conducteur *m*

cone [kəun] *n* cône *m*; (*for ice-cream*) cornet *m*; (*Bot*) pomme *f* de pin, cône

confectionery [kən'fɛkʃənrɪ] *n* (*sweets*) confiserie *f*

confer [kən'fəːʳ] *vt*: **to ~ sth on** conférer qch à ▷ *vi* conférer, s'entretenir

conference ['kɔnfərns] *n* conférence *f*

confess [kən'fɛs] *vt* confesser, avouer ▷ *vi* (*admit sth*) avouer; (*Rel*) se confesser; **confession** [kən'fɛʃən] *n* confession *f*

confide [kən'faɪd] *vi*: **to ~ in** s'ouvrir à, se confier à

confidence ['kɔnfɪdns] *n* confiance *f*; (*also*: **self-~**) assurance *f*, confiance en soi; (*secret*) confidence *f*; **in ~** (*speak, write*) en confidence, confidentiellement; **confident** *adj* (*self-assured*) sûr(e) de soi; (*sure*) sûr; **confidential** [kɔnfɪ'dɛnʃəl] *adj* confidentiel(le)

confine [kən'faɪn] *vt* limiter, borner; (*shut up*) confiner, enfermer; **confined** *adj* (*space*) restreint(e), réduit(e)

confirm [kən'fəːm] *vt* (*report, Rel*) confirmer; (*appointment*) ratifier; **confirmation** [kɔnfə'meɪʃən] *n* confirmation *f*; ratification *f*

confiscate ['kɔnfɪskeɪt] *vt* confisquer

conflict *n* ['kɔnflɪkt] conflit *m*, lutte *f* ▷ *vi* [kən'flɪkt] (*opinions*) s'opposer, se heurter

conform [kən'fɔːm] *vi*: **to ~ (to)** se conformer (à)

confront [kən'frʌnt] *vt* (*two people*) confronter; (*enemy, danger*) affronter, faire face à; (*problem*) faire face à; **confrontation** [kɔnfrən'teɪʃən] *n* confrontation *f*

confuse [kən'fjuːz] *vt* (*person*) troubler; (*situation*) embrouiller; (*one thing with another*) confondre; **confused** *adj* (*person*) dérouté(e), désorienté(e); (*situation*) embrouillé(e); **confusing** *adj* peu clair(e), déroutant(e); **confusion** [kən'fjuːʒən] *n* confusion *f*

congestion [kən'dʒɛstʃən] *n* (*Med*) congestion *f*; (*fig: traffic*) encombrement *m*

congratulate [kən'grætjuleɪt] *vt*: **to ~ sb (on)** féliciter qn (de); **congratulations** [kəngrætju'leɪʃənz] *npl*: **congratulations (on)** félicitations *fpl* (pour) ▷ *excl*: **congratulations!** (toutes mes) félicitations!

congregation [kɔŋgrɪ'geɪʃən] *n* assemblée *f* (des fidèles)

congress ['kɔŋgrɛs] *n* congrès *m*; (*Pol*) **C~** Congrès *m*; **congressman** *n* membre *m* du Congrès; **congresswoman** *n* membre *m* du Congrès

conifer ['kɔnɪfəʳ] *n* conifère *m*

conjugate ['kɔndʒugeɪt] *vt* conjuguer

conjugation [kɔndʒə'geɪʃən] *n* conjugaison *f*

conjunction [kən'dʒʌŋkʃən] *n* conjonction *f*; **in ~ with** (conjointement) avec

conjure ['kʌndʒəʳ] *vi* faire des tours de

passe-passe

onnect [kə'nɛkt] vt joindre, relier; (Elec) connecter; (Tel: caller) mettre en connexion; (: subscriber) brancher; (fig) établir un rapport entre, faire un rapprochement entre ▷ vi (train): **to ~ with** assurer la correspondance avec; **to be ~ed with** avoir un rapport avec; (have dealings with) avoir des rapports avec, être en relation avec; **connecting flight** n (vol m de) correspondance f; **connection** [kə'nɛkʃən] n relation f, lien m; (Elec) connexion f; (Tel) communication f; (train etc) correspondance f

onquer ['kɔŋkə⁽ʳ⁾] vt conquérir; (feelings) vaincre, surmonter

onquest ['kɔŋkwɛst] n conquête f

ons [kɔnz] npl see **convenience**; **pro**

onscience ['kɔnʃəns] n conscience f

onscientious [kɔnʃi'ɛnʃəs] adj consciencieux(-euse)

conscious ['kɔnʃəs] adj conscient(e); (deliberate: insult, error) délibéré(e); **consciousness** n conscience f; (Med) connaissance f

onsecutive [kən'sɛkjutɪv] adj consécutif(-ive); **on three ~ occasions** trois fois de suite

onsensus [kən'sɛnsəs] n consensus m

onsent [kən'sɛnt] n consentement m ▷ vi: **to ~ (to)** consentir (à)

onsequence ['kɔnsɪkwəns] n suites fpl, conséquence f; (significance) importance f

onsequently ['kɔnsɪkwəntlɪ] adv par conséquent, donc

onservation [kɔnsə'veɪʃən] n préservation f, protection f; (also: **nature ~**) défense f de l'environnement

onservative [kən'sə:vətɪv] adj conservateur(-trice); (cautious) prudent(e); **Conservative** adj, n (BRIT Pol) conservateur(-trice)

onservatory [kən'sə:vətrɪ] n (room) jardin m d'hiver; (Mus) conservatoire m

onsider [kən'sɪdə⁽ʳ⁾] vt (study)

considérer, réfléchir à; (take into account) penser à, prendre en considération; (regard, judge) considérer, estimer; **to ~ doing sth** envisager de faire qch; **considerable** adj considérable; **considerably** adv nettement; **considerate** adj prévenant(e), plein(e) d'égards; **consideration** [kənsɪdə'reɪʃən] n considération f; (reward) rétribution f, rémunération f; **considering** prep: **considering (that)** étant donné (que)

consignment [kən'saɪnmənt] n arrivage m, envoi m

consist [kən'sɪst] vi: **to ~ of** consister en, se composer de

consistency [kən'sɪstənsɪ] n (thickness) consistance f; (fig) cohérence f

consistent [kən'sɪstənt] adj logique, cohérent(e)

consolation [kɔnsə'leɪʃən] n consolation f

console¹ [kən'səul] vt consoler

console² ['kɔnsəul] n console f

consonant ['kɔnsənənt] n consonne f

conspicuous [kən'spɪkjuəs] adj voyant(e), qui attire l'attention

conspiracy [kən'spɪrəsɪ] n conspiration f, complot m

constable ['kʌnstəbl] n (BRIT) ≈ agent m de police, gendarme m; **chief ~** ≈ préfet m de police

constant ['kɔnstənt] adj constant(e); incessant(e); **constantly** adv constamment, sans cesse

constipated ['kɔnstɪpeɪtɪd] adj constipé(e); **constipation** [kɔnstɪ'peɪʃən] n constipation f

constituency [kən'stɪtjuənsɪ] n (Pol: area) circonscription électorale; (: electors) électorat m

constitute ['kɔnstɪtjuːt] vt constituer

constitution [kɔnstɪ'tjuːʃən] n constitution f

constraint [kən'streint] n contrainte f

construct [kən'strʌkt] vt construire; **construction** [kən'strʌkʃən] n

construction f; **constructive** adj
constructif(-ive)

consul ['kɒnsl] n consul m; **consulate**
['kɒnsjulɪt] n consulat m

consult [kən'sʌlt] vt consulter;
consultant n (Med) médecin
consultant; (other specialist) consultant
m, (expert-)conseil m; **consultation**
[kɒnsəl'teɪʃən] n consultation f;
consulting room n (BRIT) cabinet m de
consultation

consume [kən'sjuːm] vt consommer;
(subj: flames, hatred, desire) consumer;
consumer n consommateur(-trice)

consumption [kən'sʌmpʃən] n
consommation f

cont. abbr (= continued) suite

contact ['kɒntækt] n contact m;
(person) connaissance f, relation f ▷ vt
se mettre en contact or en rapport
avec; **contact lenses** npl verres mpl
de contact

contagious [kən'teɪdʒəs] adj
contagieux(-euse)

contain [kən'teɪn] vt contenir;
to ~ o.s. se contenir, se maîtriser;
container n récipient m; (for shipping
etc) conteneur m

contaminate [kən'tæmɪneɪt] vt
contaminer

cont'd abbr (= continued) suite

contemplate ['kɒntəmpleɪt] vt
contempler; (consider) envisager

contemporary [kən'tempərərɪ] adj
contemporain(e); (design, wallpaper)
moderne ▷ n contemporain(e)

contempt [kən'tempt] n mépris m,
dédain m; **~ of court** (Law) outrage m à
l'autorité de la justice

contend [kən'tend] vt: **to ~ that**
soutenir or prétendre que ▷ vi: **to ~
with** (compete) rivaliser avec; (struggle)
lutter avec

content [kən'tent] adj content(e),
satisfait(e) ▷ vt contenter, satisfaire
▷ n ['kɒntent] contenu m; (of fat,
moisture) teneur f; **contents** npl (of
container etc) contenu m; **(table of) ~s**
table f des matières; **contented** adj
content(e), satisfait(e)

contest n ['kɒntest] combat m, lutte f;
(competition) concours m ▷ vt [kən'test]
contester, discuter; (compete for)
disputer; (Law) attaquer; **contestant**
[kən'testənt] n concurrent(e); (in fight)
adversaire m/f

context ['kɒntekst] n contexte m

continent ['kɒntɪnənt] n continent
m; **the C~** (BRIT) l'Europe continentale;
continental [kɒntɪ'nentl] adj
continental(e); **continental breakfast**
n café (or thé) complet; **continental
quilt** n (BRIT) couette f

continual [kən'tɪnjuəl] adj
continuel(le); **continually** adv
continuellement, sans cesse

continue [kən'tɪnjuː] vi continuer ▷ vt
continuer; (start again) reprendre

continuity [kɒntɪ'njuːɪtɪ] n continuité
f; (TV etc) enchaînement m

continuous [kən'tɪnjuəs] adj
continu(e), permanent(e); (Ling)
progressif(-ive); **continuous
assessment** (BRIT) n contrôle
continu; **continuously** adv (repeatedly)
continuellement; (uninterruptedly) sans
interruption

contour ['kɒntuər] n contour m, profil
m; (also: ~ line) courbe f de niveau

contraception [kɒntrə'sepʃən] n
contraception f

contraceptive [kɒntrə'septɪv]
adj contraceptif(-ive),
anticonceptionnel(le) ▷ n
contraceptif m

contract n ['kɒntrækt] contrat m ▷ vi
[kən'trækt] (become smaller) se
contracter, se resserrer ▷ vt contracter;
(Comm): **to ~ to do sth** s'engager (par
contrat) à faire qch; **contractor** n
entrepreneur m

contradict [kɒntrə'dɪkt] vt contredire;
contradiction [kɒntrə'dɪkʃən] n
contradiction f

contrary¹ ['kɒntrərɪ] adj contraire,
opposé(e) ▷ n contraire m; **on the ~** au

contraire; **unless you hear to the ~**
sauf avis contraire

contrary² [kən'trɛərɪ] adj (perverse)
contrariant(e), entêté(e)

contrast n ['kɒntrɑːst] contraste
m ▷ vt [kən'trɑːst] mettre en
contraste, contraster; **in ~ to** or **with**
contrairement à, par opposition à

contribute [kən'trɪbjuːt] vi
contribuer ▷ vt: **to ~ £10/an article
to** donner 10 livres/un article à; **to
~ to** (gen) contribuer à; (newspaper)
collaborer à; (discussion) prendre part
à; **contribution** [kɒntrɪ'bjuːʃən]
n contribution f; (BRIT: for social
security) cotisation f; (to publication)
article m; **contributor** n (to newspaper)
collaborateur(-trice); (of money, goods)
donateur(-trice)

control [kən'trəul] vt (process,
machinery) commander; (temper)
maîtriser; (disease) enrayer ▷ n
maîtrise f; (power) autorité f; **controls**
npl (of machine etc) commandes fpl;
(on radio) boutons mpl de réglage; **to
be in ~ of** être maître de, maîtriser;
(in charge of) être responsable de;
everything is under ~ j'ai (or il a etc) la
situation en main; **the car went out
of ~** j'ai (or il a etc) perdu le contrôle du
véhicule; **control tower** n (Aviat) tour
f de contrôle

controversial [kɒntrə'vəːʃl] adj
discutable, controversé(e)

controversy ['kɒntrəvəːsɪ] n
controverse f, polémique f

convenience [kən'viːnɪəns] n
commodité f; **at your ~** quand or
comme cela vous convient; **all modern
~s, all mod cons** (BRIT) avec tout le
confort moderne, tout confort

convenient [kən'viːnɪənt] adj
commode

convent ['kɒnvənt] n couvent m

convention [kən'vɛnʃən] n
convention f; (custom) usage m;
conventional adj conventionnel(le)

conversation [kɒnvə'seɪʃən] n

conversation f

conversely [kɒn'vəːslɪ] adv
inversement, réciproquement

conversion [kən'vəːʃən] n conversion
f; (BRIT: of house) transformation
f, aménagement m; (Rugby)
transformation f

convert vt [kən'vəːt] (Rel, Comm)
convertir; (alter) transformer; (house)
aménager ▷ n ['kɒnvəːt] converti(e);
convertible adj convertible ▷ n
(voiture f) décapotable f

convey [kən'veɪ] vt transporter;
(thanks) transmettre; (idea)
communiquer; **conveyor belt** n
convoyeur m tapis roulant

convict vt [kən'vɪkt] déclarer (or
reconnaître) coupable ▷ n ['kɒnvɪkt]
forçat m, convict m; **conviction**
[kən'vɪkʃən] n (Law) condamnation f;
(belief) conviction f

convince [kən'vɪns] vt convaincre,
persuader; **convinced** adj: **convinced
of/that** convaincu(e) de/que;
convincing adj persuasif(-ive),
convaincant(e)

convoy ['kɒnvɔɪ] n convoi m

cook [kuk] vt (faire) cuire ▷ vi
cuire; (person) faire la cuisine ▷ n
cuisinier(-ière); **cookbook** n livre m de
cuisine; **cooker** n cuisinière f; **cookery**
n cuisine f; **cookery book** n (BRIT)
= **cookbook**; **cookie** n (US) biscuit m,
petit gâteau sec; **cooking** n cuisine f

cool [kuːl] adj frais (fraîche); (not afraid)
calme; (unfriendly) froid(e); (inf: trendy)
cool inv (inf); (: great) super inv (inf)
▷ vt, vi refroidir; **cool down**
vi refroidir; (fig: person, situation) se
calmer; **cool off** vi (become calmer) se
calmer; (lose enthusiasm) perdre son
enthousiasme

cop [kɒp] n (inf) flic m

cope [kəup] vi s'en sortir, tenir le coup;
to ~ with (problem) faire face à

copper ['kɒpə'] n cuivre m; (BRIT: inf:
policeman) flic m

copy ['kɒpɪ] n copie f; (book etc)

exemplaire m ▷ vt copier; (imitate) imiter; **copyright** n droit m d'auteur, copyright m

coral ['kɔrəl] n corail m

cord [kɔːd] n corde f; (fabric) velours côtelé; (Elec) cordon m (d'alimentation), fil m (électrique); **cords** npl (trousers) pantalon m de velours côtelé; **cordless** adj sans fil

corduroy ['kɔːdərɔɪ] n velours côtelé

core [kɔːʳ] n (of fruit) trognon m, cœur m; (fig: of problem etc) cœur ▷ vt enlever le trognon or le cœur de

coriander [kɔrɪ'ændəʳ] n coriandre f

cork [kɔːk] n (material) liège m; (of bottle) bouchon m; **corkscrew** n tire-bouchon m

corn [kɔːn] n (BRIT: wheat) blé m; (US: maize) maïs m; (on foot) cor m; **~ on the cob** (Culin) épi m de maïs au naturel

corned beef ['kɔːnd-] n corned-beef m

corner ['kɔːnəʳ] n coin m; (in road) tournant m, virage m; (Football) corner m ▷ vt (trap: prey) acculer; (fig) coincer; (Comm: market) accaparer ▷ vi prendre un virage; **corner shop** (BRIT) n magasin m du coin

cornflakes ['kɔːnfleɪks] npl cornflakes mpl

cornflour ['kɔːnflauəʳ] n (BRIT) farine f de maïs, maïzena® f

cornstarch ['kɔːnstɑːtʃ] n (US) farine f de maïs, maïzena® f

Cornwall ['kɔːnwəl] n Cornouailles f

coronary ['kɔrənərɪ] n: **~ (thrombosis)** infarctus m (du myocarde), thrombose f coronaire

coronation [kɔrə'neɪʃən] n couronnement m

coroner ['kɔrənəʳ] n coroner m, officier m de police judiciaire chargé de déterminer les causes d'un décès

corporal ['kɔːpərl] n caporal m, brigadier m ▷ adj: **~ punishment** châtiment corporel

corporate ['kɔːpərɪt] adj (action, ownership) en commun; (Comm) de la société

corporation [kɔːpə'reɪʃən] n (of town) municipalité f, conseil municipal; (Comm) société f

corps [kɔːʳ, pl kɔːz] n corps m; **the diplomatic ~** le corps diplomatique; **the press ~** la presse

corpse [kɔːps] n cadavre m

correct [kə'rɛkt] adj (accurate) correct(e), exact(e); (proper) correct, convenable ▷ vt corriger; **correction** [kə'rɛkʃən] n correction f

correspond [kɔrɪs'pɔnd] vi correspondre; **to ~ to sth** (be equivalent to) correspondre à qch; **correspondence** n correspondance f; **correspondent** n correspondant(e); **corresponding** adj correspondant(e)

corridor ['kɔrɪdɔːʳ] n couloir m, corridor m

corrode [kə'rəud] vt corroder, ronger ▷ vi se corroder

corrupt [kə'rʌpt] adj corrompu(e); (Comput) altéré(e) ▷ vt corrompre; (Comput) altérer; **corruption** n corruption f; (Comput) altération f (de données)

Corsica ['kɔːsɪkə] n Corse f

cosmetic [kɔz'mɛtɪk] n produit m de beauté, cosmétique m ▷ adj (fig: reforms) symbolique, superficiel(le); **cosmetic surgery** n chirurgie f esthétique

cosmopolitan [kɔzmə'pɔlɪtn] adj cosmopolite

cost [kɔst] n coût m ▷ vb (pt, pp ~) ▷ vi coûter ▷ vt établir or calculer le prix de revient de; **costs** npl (Comm) frais mpl; (Law) dépens mpl; **how much does it ~?** combien ça coûte?; **to ~ sb time/effort** demander du temps/un effort à qn; **it ~ him his life/job** ça lui a coûté la vie/son emploi; **at all ~s** coûte que coûte, à tout prix

co-star ['kəustɑːʳ] n partenaire m/f

costly ['kɔstlɪ] adj coûteux(-euse)

cost of living n coût m de la vie

costume ['kɔstjuːm] n costume m; (BRIT: also: **swimming ~**) maillot m

(de bain)

osy (US **cozy**) ['kəʊzɪ] adj (room, bed) douillet(te); **to be ~** (person) être bien (au chaud)

ot [kɒt] n (BRIT: child's) lit m d'enfant, petit lit; (US: campbed) lit de camp

ottage ['kɒtɪdʒ] n petite maison (à la campagne), cottage m; **cottage cheese** n fromage blanc (maigre)

otton ['kɒtn] n coton m; (thread) fil m (de coton); **cotton on** vi (inf): **to ~ on (to sth)** piger (qch); **cotton bud** (BRIT) n coton-tige ® m; **cotton candy** (US) n barbe f à papa; **cotton wool** n (BRIT) ouate f, coton m hydrophile

ouch [kautʃ] n canapé m; divan m

ough [kɒf] vi tousser ▷ n toux f; **I've got a ~** j'ai la toux; **cough mixture, cough syrup** n sirop m pour la toux

ould [kʊd] pt of **can²**; **couldn't = could not**

ouncil ['kaunsl] n conseil m; **city** or **town ~** conseil municipal; **council estate** n (BRIT) (quartier m or zone f de) logements loués à/par la municipalité; **council house** n (BRIT) maison f (à loyer modéré) louée par la municipalité; **councillor** (US **councilor**) n conseiller(-ère); **council tax** n (BRIT) impôts locaux

ounsel ['kaunsl] n conseil m; (lawyer) avocat(e) ▷ vt: **to ~ (sb to do sth)** conseiller (à qn de faire qch); **counselling** (US **counseling**) n (Psych) aide psychosociale; **counsellor** (US **counselor**) n conseiller(-ère); (US Law) avocat m

ount [kaunt] vt, vi compter ▷ n compte m; (nobleman) comte m; **count in** vt (inf): **to ~ sb in on sth** inclure qn dans qch; **count on** vt fus compter sur; **countdown** n compte m à rebours

ounter ['kauntər] n comptoir m; (in post office, bank) guichet m; (in game) jeton m ▷ vt aller à l'encontre de, opposer ▷ adv: **~ to** à l'encontre de; contrairement à; **counterclockwise** (US) adv en sens inverse des aiguilles

d'une montre

counterfeit ['kauntəfɪt] n faux m, contrefaçon f ▷ vt contrefaire ▷ adj faux (fausse)

counterpart ['kauntəpɑːt] n (of person) homologue m/f

countess ['kauntɪs] n comtesse f

countless ['kauntlɪs] adj innombrable

country ['kʌntrɪ] n pays m; (native land) patrie f; (as opposed to town) campagne f; (region) région f, pays; **country and western (music)** n musique f country; **country house** n manoir m, (petit) château; **countryside** n campagne f

county ['kauntɪ] n comté m

coup [kuː, pl kuːz] n (achievement) beau coup; (also: **~ d'état**) coup d'État

couple ['kʌpl] n couple m; **a ~ of** (two) deux; (a few) deux ou trois

coupon ['kuːpɒn] n (voucher) bon m de réduction; (detachable form) coupon m détachable, coupon-réponse m

courage ['kʌrɪdʒ] n courage m; **courageous** [kə'reɪdʒəs] adj courageux(-euse)

courgette [kuə'ʒɛt] n (BRIT) courgette f

courier ['kurɪər] n messager m, courrier m; (for tourists) accompagnateur(-trice)

course [kɔːs] n cours m; (of ship) route f; (for golf) terrain m; (part of meal) plat m; **of ~** adv bien sûr; **(no,) of ~ not!** bien sûr que non!, évidemment que non!; **~ of treatment** (Med) traitement m

court [kɔːt] n cour f; (Law) cour, tribunal m; (Tennis) court m ▷ vt (woman) courtiser, faire la cour à; **to take to ~** actionner or poursuivre en justice

courtesy ['kɜːtəsɪ] n courtoisie f, politesse f; **(by) ~ of** avec l'aimable autorisation de; **courtesy bus, courtesy coach** n navette gratuite

court: **court-house** ['kɔːthaus] n (US) palais m de justice; **courtroom** ['kɔːtrum] n salle f de tribunal; **courtyard** ['kɔːtjɑːd] n cour f

cousin ['kʌzn] n cousin(e); **first ~** cousin(e) germain(e)

cover ['kʌvər] vt couvrir; (Press: report

on) faire un reportage sur; (*feelings, mistake*) cacher; (*include*) englober; (*discuss*) traiter ▷ *n* (*of book, Comm*) couverture *f*; (*of pan*) couvercle *m*; (*over furniture*) housse *f*; (*shelter*) abri *m*; **covers** *npl* (*on bed*) couvertures; **to take ~** se mettre à l'abri; **under ~** à l'abri; **under ~ of darkness** à la faveur de la nuit; **under separate ~** (*Comm*) sous pli séparé; **cover up** *vi*: **to ~ up for sb** (*fig*) couvrir qn; **coverage** *n* (*in media*) reportage *m*; **cover charge** *n* couvert *m* (*supplément à payer*); **cover-up** *n* tentative *f* pour étouffer une affaire

cow [kau] *n* vache *f* ▷ *vt* effrayer, intimider

coward ['kauəd] *n* lâche *m/f*; **cowardly** *adj* lâche

cowboy ['kaubɔɪ] *n* cow-boy *m*

cozy ['kəuzɪ] *adj* (*US*) = **cosy**

crab [kræb] *n* crabe *m*

crack [kræk] *n* (*split*) fente *f*, fissure *f*; (*in cup, bone*) fêlure *f*; (*in wall*) lézarde *f*; (*noise*) craquement *m*, coup (sec); (*Drugs*) crack *m* ▷ *vt* fendre, fissurer; fêler; lézarder; (*whip*) faire claquer; (*nut*) casser; (*problem*) résoudre; (*code*) déchiffrer ▷ *cpd* (*athlete*) de première classe, d'élite; **crack down on** *vt fus* (*crime*) sévir contre, réprimer; **cracked** *adj* (*cup, bone*) fêlé(e); (*broken*) cassé(e); (*wall*) lézardé(e); (*surface*) craquelé(e); (*inf*) toqué(e), timbré(e); **cracker** *n* (*also*: **Christmas cracker**) pétard *m*; (*biscuit*) biscuit (salé), craquelin *m*

crackle ['krækl] *vi* crépiter, grésiller

cradle ['kreɪdl] *n* berceau *m*

craft [krɑːft] *n* métier (*artisanal*); (*cunning*) ruse *f*, astuce *f*; (*boat: pl inv*) embarcation *f*, barque *f*; (*plane: pl inv*) appareil *m*; **craftsman** (*irreg*) *n* artisan *m* ouvrier (qualifié); **craftsmanship** *n* métier *m*, habileté *f*

cram [kræm] *vt* (*fill*): **to ~ sth with** bourrer qch de; (*put*): **to ~ sth into** fourrer qch dans ▷ *vi* (*for exams*) bachoter

cramp [kræmp] *n* crampe *f*; **I've got ~ in my leg** j'ai une crampe à la jambe; **cramped** *adj* à l'étroit, très serré(e)

cranberry ['krænbərɪ] *n* canneberge *f*

crane [kreɪn] *n* grue *f*

crap [kræp] *n* (*inf!*: *nonsense*) conneries *fpl* (!); (: *excrement*) merde *f*(!)

crash [kræʃ] *n* (*noise*) fracas *m*; (*of car, plane*) collision *f*; (*of business*) faillite *f* ▷ *vt* (*plane*) écraser ▷ *vi* (*plane*) s'écraser; (*two cars*) se percuter, s'emboutir; (*business*) s'effondrer; **to ~ into** se jeter *or* se fracasser contre; **crash course** *n* cours intensif; **crash helmet** *n* casque (protecteur)

crate [kreɪt] *n* cageot *m*; (*for bottles*) caisse *f*

crave [kreɪv] *vt, vi*: **to ~ (for)** avoir une envie irrésistible de

crawl [krɔːl] *vi* ramper; (*vehicle*) avancer au pas ▷ *n* (*Swimming*) crawl *m*

crayfish ['kreɪfɪʃ] *n* (*pl inv*: *freshwater*) écrevisse *f*; (*saltwater*) langoustine *f*

crayon ['kreɪən] *n* crayon *m* (de couleur)

craze [kreɪz] *n* engouement *m*

crazy ['kreɪzɪ] *adj* fou (folle); **to be ~ about sb/sth** (*inf*) être fou de qn/qch

creak [kriːk] *vi* (*hinge*) grincer; (*floor, shoes*) craquer

cream [kriːm] *n* crème *f* ▷ *adj* (*colour*) crème *inv*; **cream cheese** *n* fromage *m* à la crème, fromage blanc; **creamy** *adj* crémeux(-euse)

crease [kriːs] *n* pli *m* ▷ *vt* froisser, chiffonner ▷ *vi* se froisser, se chiffonne

create [kriː'eɪt] *vt* créer; **creation** [kriː'eɪʃən] *n* création *f*; **creative** *adj* créatif(-ive); **creator** *n* créateur(-trice)

creature ['kriːtʃə*'*] *n* créature *f*

crèche [krɛʃ] *n* garderie *f*, crèche *f*

credentials [krɪ'dɛnʃlz] *npl* (*references*) références *fpl*; (*identity papers*) pièce *f* d'identité

credibility [krɛdɪ'bɪlɪtɪ] *n* crédibilité *f*

credible ['krɛdɪbl] *adj* digne de foi, crédible

credit ['krɛdɪt] *n* crédit *m*; (*recognition*)

honneur m; (Scol) unité f de valeur ▷ vt (Comm) créditer; (believe: also: **give ~ to**) ajouter foi à, croire; **credits** npl (Cine) générique m; **to be in ~** (person, bank account) être créditeur(-trice); **to ~ sb with** (fig) prêter or attribuer à qn; **credit card** n carte f de crédit; **do you take credit cards?** acceptez-vous les cartes de crédit?

creek [kri:k] n (inlet) crique f, anse f; (US: stream) ruisseau m, petit cours d'eau

creep (pt, pp **crept**) [kri:p, krɛpt] vi ramper

cremate [krɪ'meɪt] vt incinérer

crematorium (pl **crematoria**) [krɛmə'tɔ:rɪəm, -'tɔ:rɪə] n four m crématoire

crept [krɛpt] pt, pp of **creep**

crescent ['krɛsnt] n croissant m; (street) rue f (en arc de cercle)

cress [krɛs] n cresson m

crest [krɛst] n crête f; (of coat of arms) timbre m

crew [kru:] n équipage m; (Cine) équipe f (de tournage); **crew-neck** n col ras

crib [krɪb] n lit m d'enfant; (for baby) berceau m ▷ vt (inf) copier

cricket ['krɪkɪt] n (insect) grillon m, cri-cri m inv; (game) cricket m; **cricketer** n joueur m de cricket

crime [kraɪm] n crime m; **criminal** ['krɪmɪnl] adj, n criminel(le)

crimson ['krɪmzn] adj cramoisi(e)

cringe [krɪndʒ] vi avoir un mouvement de recul

cripple ['krɪpl] n boiteux(-euse), infirme m/f ▷ vt (person) estropier, paralyser; (ship, plane) immobiliser; (production, exports) paralyser

crisis (pl **crises**) ['kraɪsɪs, -si:z] n crise f

crisp [krɪsp] adj croquant(e); (weather) vif (vive); (manner etc) brusque; **crisps** (BRIT) npl (pommes fpl) chips fpl; **crispy** adj croustillant(e)

criterion (pl **criteria**) [kraɪ'tɪərɪən, -'tɪərɪə] n critère m

critic ['krɪtɪk] n critique m/f; **critical** adj critique; **criticism** ['krɪtɪsɪzəm]

n critique f; **criticize** ['krɪtɪsaɪz] vt critiquer

Croat ['krəuæt] adj, n = **Croatian**

Croatia [krəu'eɪʃə] n Croatie f; **Croatian** adj croate ▷ n Croate m/f; (Ling) croate m

crockery ['krɔkərɪ] n vaisselle f

crocodile ['krɔkədaɪl] n crocodile m

crocus ['krəukəs] n crocus m

croissant ['krwasɑ̃] n croissant m

crook [kruk] n escroc m; (of shepherd) houlette f; **crooked** ['krukɪd] adj courbé(e), tordu(e); (action) malhonnête

crop [krɔp] n (produce) culture f; (amount produced) récolte f; (riding crop) cravache f ▷ vt (hair) tondre; **crop up** vi surgir, se présenter, survenir

cross [krɔs] n croix f; (Biol) croisement m ▷ vt (street etc) traverser; (arms, legs, Biol) croiser; (cheque) barrer ▷ adj en colère, fâché(e); **cross off** vt **cross out** vt barrer, rayer; **cross over** vi traverser; **cross-Channel ferry** ['krɔs'tʃænl-] n ferry m qui fait la traversée de la Manche; **crosscountry (race)** n cross(-country) m; **crossing** n (sea passage) traversée f; (also: **pedestrian crossing**) passage clouté; **how long does the crossing take?** combien de temps dure la traversée?; **crossing guard** (US) n contractuel qui fait traverser la rue aux enfants; **crossroads** n carrefour m; **crosswalk** n (US) passage clouté; **crossword** n mots mpl croisés

crotch [krɔtʃ] n (of garment) entrejambe m; (Anat) entrecuisse m

crouch [krautʃ] vi s'accroupir; (hide) se tapir; (before springing) se ramasser

crouton ['kru:tɔn] n croûton m

crow [krəu] n (bird) corneille f; (of cock) chant m du coq, cocorico m ▷ vi (cock) chanter

crowd [kraud] n foule f ▷ vt bourrer, remplir ▷ vi affluer, s'attrouper, s'entasser; **crowded** adj bondé(e), plein(e)

crown [kraun] n couronne f; (of head)

sommet m de la tête; (of hill) sommet m ▷ vt (also tooth) couronner; **crown jewels** npl joyaux mpl de la Couronne

crucial ['kru:ʃl] adj crucial(e), décisif(-ive)

crucifix ['kru:sıfıks] n crucifix m

crude [kru:d] adj (materials) brut(e); non raffiné(e); (basic) rudimentaire, sommaire; (vulgar) cru(e), grossier(-ière); **crude (oil)** n (pétrole) brut m

cruel ['kruəl] adj cruel(le); **cruelty** n cruauté f

cruise [kru:z] n croisière f ▷ vi (ship) croiser; (car) rouler; (aircraft) voler

crumb [krʌm] n miette f

crumble ['krʌmbl] vt émietter ▷ vi (plaster etc) s'effriter; (land, earth) s'ébouler; (building) s'écrouler, crouler; (fig) s'effondrer

crumpet ['krʌmpıt] n petite crêpe (épaisse)

crumple ['krʌmpl] vt froisser, friper

crunch [krʌntʃ] vt croquer; (underfoot) faire craquer, écraser; faire crisser ▷ n (fig) instant m or moment m critique, moment m de vérité; **crunchy** adj croquant(e), croustillant(e)

crush [krʌʃ] n (crowd) foule f, cohue f; (love): **to have a ~ on sb** avoir le béguin pour qn; (drink): **lemon ~** citron pressé ▷ vt écraser; (crumple) froisser; (grind, break up: garlic, ice) piler; (: grapes) presser; (hopes) anéantir

crust [krʌst] n croûte f; **crusty** adj (bread) croustillant(e); (inf: person) revêche, bourru(e)

crutch [krʌtʃ] n béquille f; (also: **crotch**) entrejambe m

cry [kraı] vi pleurer; (shout: also: **~ out**) crier ▷ n cri m; **cry out** vi (call out, shout) pousser un cri ▷ vt crier

crystal ['krıstl] n cristal m

cub [kʌb] n petit m (d'un animal); (also: **~ scout**) louveteau m

Cuba ['kju:bə] n Cuba m

cube [kju:b] n cube m ▷ vt (Math) élever au cube

cubicle ['kju:bıkl] n (in hospital) box m; (at pool) cabine f

cuckoo ['kuku:] n coucou m

cucumber ['kju:kʌmbər] n concombre m

cuddle ['kʌdl] vt câliner, caresser ▷ vi se blottir l'un contre l'autre

cue [kju:] n queue f de billard; (Theat etc) signal m

cuff [kʌf] n (Brit: of shirt, coat etc) poignet m, manchette f; (us: on trousers) revers m; (blow) gifle f; **off the ~** adv à l'improviste; **cufflinks** n boutons m de manchette

cuisine [kwı'zi:n] n cuisine f

cul-de-sac ['kʌldəsæk] n cul-de-sac m, impasse f

cull [kʌl] vt sélectionner ▷ n (of animals) abattage sélectif

culminate ['kʌlmıneıt] vi: **to ~ in** finir or se terminer par; (lead to) mener à

culprit ['kʌlprıt] n coupable m/f

cult [kʌlt] n culte m

cultivate ['kʌltıveıt] vt cultiver

cultural ['kʌltʃərəl] adj culturel(le)

culture ['kʌltʃər] n culture f

cumin ['kʌmın] n (spice) cumin m

cunning ['kʌnıŋ] n ruse f, astuce f ▷ adj rusé(e), malin(-igne); (clever: device, idea) astucieux(-euse)

cup [kʌp] n tasse f; (prize, event) coupe f; (of bra) bonnet m

cupboard ['kʌbəd] n placard m

cup final n (Brit Football) finale f de la coupe

curator [kjuə'reıtər] n conservateur m (d'un musée etc)

curb [kə:b] vt refréner, mettre un frein à ▷ n (fig) frein m; (us) bord m du trottoir

curdle ['kə:dl] vi (se) cailler

cure [kjuər] vt guérir; (Culin: salt) saler; (: smoke) fumer; (: dry) sécher ▷ n remède m

curfew ['kə:fju:] n couvre-feu m

curiosity [kjuərı'ɔsıtı] n curiosité f

curious ['kjuərıəs] adj curieux(-euse); **I'm ~ about him** il m'intrigue

curl [kə:l] n boucle f (de cheveux) ▷ vt,

vi boucler; (*tightly*) friser; **curl up** vi s'enrouler; (*person*) se pelotonner; **curler** n bigoudi m, rouleau m; **curly** adj bouclé(e); (*tightly curled*) frisé(e)

currant ['kʌrnt] n raisin m de Corinthe, raisin sec; (*fruit*) groseille f

currency ['kʌrnsɪ] n monnaie f; **to gain ~** (*fig*) s'accréditer

current ['kʌrnt] n courant m ▷ adj (*common*) courant(e); (*tendency, price, event*) actuel(le); **current account** n (*BRIT*) compte courant; **current affairs** npl (questions fpl d')actualité f; **currently** adv actuellement

curriculum (pl **~s** or **curricula**) [kə'rɪkjuləm, -lə] n programme m d'études; **curriculum vitae** [-'viːtaɪ] n curriculum vitae (CV) m

curry ['kʌrɪ] n curry m ▷ vt: **to ~ favour with** chercher à gagner la faveur or à s'attirer les bonnes grâces de; **curry powder** n poudre f de curry

curse [kəːs] vi jurer, blasphémer ▷ vt maudire ▷ n (*spell*) malédiction f; (*problem, scourge*) fléau m; (*swearword*) juron m

cursor ['kəːsər] n (*Comput*) curseur m

curt [kəːt] adj brusque, sec(-sèche)

curtain ['kəːtn] n rideau m

curve [kəːv] n courbe f; (*in the road*) tournant m, virage m ▷ vi se courber; (*road*) faire une courbe; **curved** adj courbe

cushion ['kuʃən] n coussin m ▷ vt (*fall, shock*) amortir

custard ['kʌstəd] n (*for pouring*) crème anglaise

custody ['kʌstədɪ] n (*of child*) garde f; (*for offenders*): **to take sb into ~** placer qn en détention préventive

custom ['kʌstəm] n coutume f, usage m; (*Comm*) clientèle f

customer ['kʌstəmər] n client(e)

customized ['kʌstəmaɪzd] adj personnalisé(e); (*car etc*) construit(e) sur commande

customs ['kʌstəmz] npl douane f; **customs officer** n douanier m

cut [kʌt] vb (pt, pp **~**) ▷ vt couper; (*meat*) découper; (*reduce*) réduire ▷ vi couper ▷ n (*gen*) coupure f; (*of clothes*) coupe f; (*in salary etc*) réduction f; (*of meat*) morceau m; **to ~ a tooth** percer une dent; **to ~ one's finger** se couper le doigt; **to get one's hair ~** se faire couper les cheveux; **I've ~ myself** je me suis coupé; **cut back** vt (*plants*) tailler; (*production, expenditure*) réduire; **cut down** vt (*tree*) abattre; (*reduce*) réduire; **cut off** vt couper; (*fig*) isoler; **cut out** vt (*picture etc*) découper; (*remove*) supprimer; **cut up** vt découper; **cutback** n réduction f

cute [kjuːt] adj mignon(ne), adorable

cutlery ['kʌtlərɪ] n couverts mpl

cutlet ['kʌtlɪt] n côtelette f

cut-price ['kʌt'praɪs] (*US* **cut-rate** ['kʌt'reɪt]) adj au rabais, à prix réduit

cutting ['kʌtɪŋ] adj (*fig*) cinglant(e) ▷ n (*BRIT: from newspaper*) coupure f (de journal); (*from plant*) bouture f

CV n abbr = **curriculum vitae**

cwt abbr = **hundredweight(s)**

cyberspace ['saɪbəspeɪs] n cyberespace m

cycle ['saɪkl] n cycle m; (*bicycle*) bicyclette f, vélo m ▷ vi faire de la bicyclette; **cycle hire** n location f de vélos; **cycle lane, cycle path** n piste f cyclable; **cycling** n cyclisme m; **cyclist** n cycliste m/f

cyclone ['saɪkləun] n cyclone m

cylinder ['sɪlɪndər] n cylindre m

cymbals ['sɪmblz] npl cymbales fpl

cynical ['sɪnɪkl] adj cynique

Cypriot ['sɪprɪət] adj cypriote, chypriote ▷ n Cypriote m/f, Chypriote m/f

Cyprus ['saɪprəs] n Chypre f

cyst [sɪst] n kyste m; **cystitis** [sɪs'taɪtɪs] n cystite f

czar [zɑːr] n tsar m

Czech [tʃɛk] adj tchèque ▷ n Tchèque m/f; (*Ling*) tchèque m; **Czech Republic** n: **the Czech Republic** la République tchèque

D [di:] n (*Mus*): **D** ré m
dab [dæb] vt (*eyes, wound*) tamponner; (*paint, cream*) appliquer (par petites touches *or* rapidement)
dad, daddy ['dæd, 'dædɪ] n papa m
daffodil ['dæfədɪl] n jonquille f
daft [dɑ:ft] adj (*inf*) idiot(e), stupide
dagger ['dægəʳ] n poignard m
daily ['deɪlɪ] adj quotidien(ne), journalier(-ière) ▷ adv tous les jours
dairy ['dɛərɪ] n (*shop*) crémerie f, laiterie f; (*on farm*) laiterie f; **dairy produce** n produits laitiers
daisy ['deɪzɪ] n pâquerette f
dam [dæm] n (*wall*) barrage m; (*water*) réservoir m, lac m de retenue ▷ vt endiguer
damage ['dæmɪdʒ] n dégâts mpl, dommages mpl; (*fig*) tort m ▷ vt endommager, abîmer; (*fig*) faire du tort à; **damages** npl (*Law*) dommages-intérêts mpl
damn [dæm] vt condamner; (*curse*) maudire ▷ n (*inf*): **I don't give a ~** je m'en fous ▷ adj (*inf: also:* **~ed**): **this ~ ...** ce sacré *or* foutu ...; **~ (it)!** zut!
damp [dæmp] adj humide ▷ n humidité f ▷ vt (*also:* **~en**: *cloth, rag*) humecter; (: *enthusiasm etc*) refroidir
dance [dɑ:ns] n danse f; (*ball*) bal m ▷ vi danser; **dance floor** n piste f de danse; **dancer** n danseur(-euse); **dancing** n danse f
dandelion ['dændɪlaɪən] n pissenlit m
dandruff ['dændrəf] n pellicules fpl
D & T n abbr (BRIT: *Scol*) = **design and technology**
Dane [deɪn] n Danois(e)
danger ['deɪndʒəʳ] n danger m; **~!** (*on sign*) danger!; **in ~** en danger; **he was in ~ of falling** il risquait de tomber; **dangerous** adj dangereux(-euse)
dangle ['dæŋgl] vt balancer ▷ vi pendre, se balancer
Danish ['deɪnɪʃ] adj danois(e) ▷ n (*Ling*) danois m
dare [dɛəʳ] vt: **to ~ sb to do** défier qn *or* mettre qn au défi de faire ▷ vi: **to ~ (to) do sth** oser faire qch; **I ~ say he'll turn up** il est probable qu'il viendra; **daring** adj hardi(e), audacieux(-euse) ▷ n audace f, hardiesse f
dark [dɑ:k] adj (*night, room*) obscur(e), sombre; (*colour, complexion*) foncé(e), sombre ▷ n: **in the ~** dans le noir; **to be in the ~ about** (*fig*) ignorer tout de; **after ~** après la tombée de la nuit; **darken** vt obscurcir, assombrir ▷ vi s'obscurcir, s'assombrir; **darkness** n obscurité f; **darkroom** n chambre noire
darling ['dɑ:lɪŋ] adj, n chéri(e)
dart [dɑ:t] n fléchette f; (*in sewing*) pince f ▷ vi: **to ~ towards** se précipiter *or* s'élancer vers; **dartboard** n cible f (de jeu de fléchettes); **darts** n jeu m de fléchettes
dash [dæʃ] n (*sign*) tiret m; (*small quantity*) goutte f, larme f ▷ vt (*throw*) jeter *or* lancer violemment; (*hopes*) anéantir ▷ vi: **to ~ towards** se précipiter *or* se ruer vers

dashboard ['dæʃbɔːd] n (Aut) tableau m de bord

data ['deɪtə] npl données fpl; **database** n base f de données; **data processing** n traitement m (électronique) de l'information

date [deɪt] n date f; (with sb) rendez-vous m; (fruit) datte f ▷ vt dater; (person) sortir avec; ~ **of birth** date de naissance; **to ~** adv à ce jour; **out of ~** périmé(e); **up to ~** à la page, mis(e) à jour, moderne; **dated** adj démodé(e)

daughter ['dɔːtər] n fille f; **daughter-in-law** n belle-fille f, bru f

daunting ['dɔːntɪŋ] adj décourageant(e), intimidant(e)

dawn [dɔːn] n aube f, aurore f ▷ vi (day) se lever, poindre; **it ~ed on him that ...** il lui vint à l'esprit que ...

day [deɪ] n jour m; (as duration) journée f; (period of time, age) époque f, temps m; **the ~ before** la veille, le jour précédent; **the ~ after, the following ~** le lendemain, le jour suivant; **the ~ before yesterday** avant-hier; **the ~ after tomorrow** après-demain; **by ~** de jour; **day-care centre** ['deɪkɛə-] n (for elderly etc) centre m d'accueil de jour; (for children) garderie f; **daydream** vi rêver (tout éveillé); **daylight** n (lumière f du) jour m; **day return** n (BRIT) billet m d'aller-retour (valable pour la journée); **daytime** n jour m, journée f; **day-to-day** adj (routine, expenses) journalier(-ière); **day trip** n excursion f (d'une journée)

dazed [deɪzd] adj abruti(e)

dazzle ['dæzl] vt éblouir, aveugler; **dazzling** adj (light) aveuglant(e), éblouissant(e); (fig) éblouissant(e)

DC abbr (Elec) = **direct current**

dead [dɛd] adj mort(e); (numb) engourdi(e), insensible; (battery) à plat ▷ adv (completely) absolument, complètement; (exactly) juste; **he was shot ~** il a été tué d'un coup de revolver; **~ tired** éreinté(e), complètement fourbu(e); **to stop ~** s'arrêter pile or net;

the line is ~ (Tel) la ligne est coupée; **dead end** n impasse f; **deadline** n date for heure f limite; **deadly** adj mortel(le); (weapon) meurtrier(-ière); **Dead Sea** n: **the Dead Sea** la mer Morte

deaf [dɛf] adj sourd(e); **deafen** vt rendre sourd(e); **deafening** adj assourdissant(e)

deal [diːl] n affaire f, marché m ▷ vt (pt, pp ~t) (blow) porter; (cards) donner, distribuer; **a great ~ of** beaucoup de; **deal with** vt fus (handle) s'occuper or se charger de; (be about: book etc) traiter de; **dealer** n (Comm) marchand m; (Cards) donneur m; **dealings** npl (in goods, shares) opérations fpl, transactions fpl; (relations) relations fpl, rapports fpl

dealt [dɛlt] pt, pp of **deal**

dean [diːn] n (Rel, BRIT Scol) doyen m; (US Scol) conseiller principal (conseillère principale) d'éducation

dear [dɪər] adj cher (chère); (expensive) cher, coûteux(-euse) ▷ n: **my ~** mon cher (ma chère) ▷ excl: **~ me!** mon Dieu!; **D~ Sir/Madam** (in letter) Monsieur/Madame; **D~ Mr/Mrs X** Cher Monsieur X (Chère Madame X); **dearly** adv (love) tendrement; (pay) cher

death [dɛθ] n mort f; (Admin) décès m; **death penalty** n peine f de mort; **death sentence** n condamnation f à mort

debate [dɪˈbeɪt] n discussion f, débat m ▷ vt discuter, débattre

debit ['dɛbɪt] n débit m ▷ vt: **to ~ a sum to sb** or **to sb's account** porter une somme au débit de qn, débiter qn d'une somme; **debit card** n carte f de paiement

debris ['dɛbriː] n débris mpl, décombres mpl

debt [dɛt] n dette f; **to be in ~** avoir des dettes, être endetté(e)

debut ['deɪbjuː] n début(s) m(pl)

Dec. abbr (= December) déc

decade ['dɛkeɪd] n décennie f, décade f

decaffeinated [dɪˈkæfɪneɪtɪd] *adj*
décaféiné(e)

decay [dɪˈkeɪ] *n* (*of building*)
délabrement *m*; (*also*: **tooth ~**) carie
f (dentaire) ▷ *vi* (*rot*) se décomposer,
pourrir; (: *teeth*) se carier

deceased [dɪˈsiːst] *n*: **the ~** le (la)
défunt(e)

deceit [dɪˈsiːt] *n* tromperie *f*,
supercherie *f*; **deceive** [dɪˈsiːv] *vt*
tromper

December [dɪˈsɛmbəʳ] *n* décembre *m*

decency [ˈdiːsənsɪ] *n* décence *f*

decent [ˈdiːsənt] *adj* (*proper*) décent(e),
convenable

deception [dɪˈsɛpʃən] *n* tromperie *f*

deceptive [dɪˈsɛptɪv] *adj*
trompeur(-euse)

decide [dɪˈsaɪd] *vt* (*subj: person*) décider;
(*question, argument*) trancher, régler ▷ *vi*
se décider, décider; **to ~ to do/that**
décider de faire/que; **to ~ on** décider,
se décider pour

decimal [ˈdɛsɪməl] *adj* décimal(e) ▷ *n*
décimale *f*

decision [dɪˈsɪʒən] *n* décision *f*

decisive [dɪˈsaɪsɪv] *adj* décisif(-ive);
(*manner, person*) décidé(e), catégorique

deck [dɛk] *n* (*Naut*) pont *m*; (*of cards*) jeu
m; (*record deck*) platine *f*; (*of bus*): **top ~**
impériale *f*; **deckchair** *n* chaise longue

declaration [dɛkləˈreɪʃən] *n*
déclaration *f*

declare [dɪˈklɛəʳ] *vt* déclarer

decline [dɪˈklaɪn] *n* (*decay*) déclin *m*;
(*lessening*) baisse *f* ▷ *vt* refuser, décliner
▷ *vi* décliner; (*business*) baisser

decorate [ˈdɛkəreɪt] *vt* (*adorn, give
a medal to*) décorer; (*paint and paper*)
peindre et tapisser; **decoration**
[dɛkəˈreɪʃən] *n* (*medal etc, adornment*)
décoration *f*; **decorator** *n* peintre *m*
en bâtiment

decrease *n* [ˈdiːkriːs] diminution *f*
▷ *vt, vi* [diːˈkriːs] diminuer

decree [dɪˈkriː] *n* (*Pol, Rel*) décret *m*;
(*Law*) arrêt *m*, jugement *m*

dedicate [ˈdɛdɪkeɪt] *vt* consacrer; (*book
etc*) dédier; **dedicated** *adj* (*person*)
dévoué(e); (*Comput*) spécialisé(e),
dédié(e); **dedicated word processor**
station *f* de traitement de texte;
dedication [dɛdɪˈkeɪʃən] *n* (*devotion*)
dévouement *m*; (*in book*) dédicace *f*

deduce [dɪˈdjuːs] *vt* déduire, conclure

deduct [dɪˈdʌkt] *vt*: **to ~ sth (from)**
déduire qch (de), retrancher qch (de);
deduction [dɪˈdʌkʃən] *n* (*deducting,
deducing*) déduction *f*; (*from wage etc*)
prélèvement *m*, retenue *f*

deed [diːd] *n* action *f*, acte *m*; (*Law*) acte
notarié, contrat *m*

deem [diːm] *vt* (*formal*) juger, estimer

deep [diːp] *adj* profond(e); (*voice*) grave
▷ *adv*: **spectators stood 20 ~** il y avait
20 rangs de spectateurs; **4 metres ~**
de 4 mètres de profondeur; **how ~ is
the water?** l'eau a quelle profondeur?;
deep-fry *vt* faire frire (dans une
friteuse); **deeply** *adv* profondément;
(*regret, interested*) vivement

deer [dɪəʳ] *n* (*pl inv*) (**red**) **~** cerf *m*;
(**fallow**) **~** daim *m*; (**roe**) **~** chevreuil *m*

default [dɪˈfɔːlt] *n* (*Comput: also*: **~
value**) valeur *f* par défaut; **by ~** (*Law*)
par défaut, par contumace; (*Sport*)
par forfait

defeat [dɪˈfiːt] *n* défaite *f* ▷ *vt* (*team,
opponents*) battre

defect *n* [ˈdiːfɛkt] défaut *m* ▷ *vi*
[dɪˈfɛkt]: **to ~ to the enemy/the West**
passer à l'ennemi/l'Ouest; **defective**
[dɪˈfɛktɪv] *adj* défectueux(-euse)

defence (*us* **defense**) [dɪˈfɛns] *n*
défense *f*

defend [dɪˈfɛnd] *vt* défendre;
defendant *n* défendeur(-deresse); (*in
criminal case*) accusé(e), prévenu(e);
defender *n* défenseur *m*

defense [dɪˈfɛns] (*us*) = **defence**

defensive [dɪˈfɛnsɪv] *adj* défensif(-ive)
▷ *n*: **on the ~** sur la défensive

defer [dɪˈfəːʳ] *vt* (*postpone*) différer,
ajourner

defiance [dɪˈfaɪəns] *n* défi *m*; **in ~ of**
au mépris de; **defiant** [dɪˈfaɪənt] *adj*

provocant(e), de défi; (*person*) rebelle, intraitable

deficiency [dɪˈfɪʃənsɪ] *n* (*lack*) insuffisance *f*; (: *Med*) carence *f*; (*flaw*) faiblesse *f*; **deficient** [dɪˈfɪʃənt] *adj* (*inadequate*) insuffisant(e); **to be deficient in** manquer de

deficit [ˈdefɪsɪt] *n* déficit *m*

define [dɪˈfaɪn] *vt* définir

definite [ˈdefɪnɪt] *adj* (*fixed*) défini(e), (bien) déterminé(e); (*clear*, *obvious*) net(te), manifeste; (*certain*) sûr(e); **he was ~ about it** il a été catégorique; **definitely** *adv* sans aucun doute

definition [defɪˈnɪʃən] *n* définition *f*; (*clearness*) netteté *f*

deflate [diːˈfleɪt] *vt* dégonfler

deflect [dɪˈflekt] *vt* détourner, faire dévier

defraud [dɪˈfrɔːd] *vt*: **to ~ sb of sth** escroquer qch à qn

defrost [diːˈfrɔst] *vt* (*fridge*) dégivrer; (*frozen food*) décongeler

defuse [diːˈfjuːz] *vt* désamorcer

defy [dɪˈfaɪ] *vt* défier; (*efforts etc*) résister à; **it defies description** cela défie toute description

degree [dɪˈɡriː] *n* degré *m*; (*Scol*) diplôme *m* (universitaire); **a (first) ~ in maths** (*BRIT*) une licence en maths; **by ~s** (*gradually*) par degrés; **to some ~** jusqu'à un certain point, dans une certaine mesure

dehydrated [diːhaɪˈdreɪtɪd] *adj* déshydraté(e); (*milk*, *eggs*) en poudre

de-icer [diːˈaɪsər] *n* dégivreur *m*

delay [dɪˈleɪ] *vt* retarder; (*payment*) différer ▷ *vi* s'attarder ▷ *n* délai *m*, retard *m*; **to be ~ed** être en retard

delegate *n* [ˈdelɪɡɪt] délégué(e) ▷ *vt* [ˈdelɪɡeɪt] déléguer

delete [dɪˈliːt] *vt* rayer, supprimer; (*Comput*) effacer

deli [ˈdelɪ] *n* épicerie fine

deliberate *adj* [dɪˈlɪbərɪt] (*intentional*) délibéré(e); (*slow*) mesuré(e) ▷ *vi* [dɪˈlɪbəreɪt] délibérer, réfléchir; **deliberately** *adv* (*on purpose*) exprès,

délibérément

delicacy [ˈdelɪkəsɪ] *n* délicatesse *f*; (*choice food*) mets fin *or* délicat, friandise *f*

delicate [ˈdelɪkɪt] *adj* délicat(e)

delicatessen [delɪkəˈtesn] *n* épicerie fine

delicious [dɪˈlɪʃəs] *adj* délicieux(-euse)

delight [dɪˈlaɪt] *n* (grande) joie, grand plaisir ▷ *vt* enchanter; **she's a ~ to work with** c'est un plaisir de travailler avec elle; **to take ~ in** prendre grand plaisir à; **delighted** *adj*: **delighted (at *or* with sth)** ravi(e) (de qch); **to be delighted to do sth/that** être enchanté(e) *or* ravi(e) de faire qch/que; **delightful** *adj* (*person*) adorable; (*meal*, *evening*) merveilleux(-euse)

delinquent [dɪˈlɪŋkwənt] *adj*, *n* délinquant(e)

deliver [dɪˈlɪvər] *vt* (*mail*) distribuer; (*goods*) livrer; (*message*) remettre; (*speech*) prononcer; (*Med*: *baby*) mettre au monde; **delivery** *n* (*of mail*) distribution *f*; (*of goods*) livraison *f*; (*of speaker*) élocution *f*; (*Med*) accouchement *m*; **to take delivery of** prendre livraison de

delusion [dɪˈluːʒən] *n* illusion *f*

de luxe [dəˈlʌks] *adj* de luxe

delve [delv] *vi*: **to ~ into** fouiller dans

demand [dɪˈmɑːnd] *vt* réclamer, exiger ▷ *n* exigence *f*; (*claim*) revendication *f*; (*Econ*) demande *f*; **in ~** demandé(e), recherché(e); **on ~** sur demande; **demanding** *adj* (*person*) exigeant(e); (*work*) astreignant(e)

> Be careful not to translate **to demand** by the French word **demander**.

demise [dɪˈmaɪz] *n* décès *m*

demo [ˈdeməu] *n abbr* (*inf*) = *demonstration* (*protest*) manif *f*; (*Comput*) démonstration *f*

democracy [dɪˈmɔkrəsɪ] *n* démocratie *f*; **democrat** [ˈdeməkræt] *n* démocrate *m/f*; **democratic** [deməˈkrætɪk] *adj* démocratique

demolish [dɪ'mɔlɪʃ] vt démolir

demolition [dɛmə'lɪʃən] n démolition f

demon ['di:mən] n démon m

demonstrate ['demənstreɪt] vt démontrer, prouver; (show) faire une démonstration de ▷ vi: **to ~ (for/against)** manifester (en faveur de/contre); **demonstration** [dɛmən'streɪʃən] n démonstration f; (Pol etc) manifestation f; **demonstrator** n (Pol etc) manifestant(e)

demote [dɪ'məut] vt rétrograder

den [dɛn] n (of lion) tanière f; (room) repaire m

denial [dɪ'naɪəl] n (of accusation) démenti m; (of rights, guilt, truth) dénégation f

denim ['dɛnɪm] n jean m; **denims** npl (blue-)jeans mpl

Denmark ['dɛnmɑːk] n Danemark m

denomination [dɪnɔmɪ'neɪʃən] n (money) valeur f; (Rel) confession f

denounce [dɪ'nauns] vt dénoncer

dense [dɛns] adj dense; (inf: stupid) obtus(e)

density ['dɛnsɪtɪ] n densité f; **single-/double-~ disk** (Comput) disquette f (à) simple/double densité

dent [dɛnt] n bosse f ▷ vt (also: **make a ~ in**) cabosser

dental ['dɛntl] adj dentaire; **dental floss** [-flɔs] n fil m dentaire; **dental surgery** n cabinet m de dentiste

dentist ['dɛntɪst] n dentiste m/f

dentures ['dɛntʃəz] npl dentier msg

deny [dɪ'naɪ] vt nier; (refuse) refuser

deodorant [diː'əudərənt] n déodorant m

depart [dɪ'pɑːt] vi partir; **to ~ from** (fig: differ from) s'écarter de

department [dɪ'pɑːtmənt] n (Comm) rayon m; (Scol) section f; (Pol) ministère m, département m; **department store** n grand magasin

departure [dɪ'pɑːtʃəʳ] n départ m; (fig): **a new ~** une nouvelle voie; **departure lounge** n salle f de départ

depend [dɪ'pɛnd] vi: **to ~ (up)on** dépendre de; (rely on) compter sur; **it ~s** cela dépend; **~ing on the result ...** selon le résultat ...; **dependant** n personne f à charge; **dependent** adj: **to be dependent (on)** dépendre (de) ▷ n = **dependant**

depict [dɪ'pɪkt] vt (in picture) représenter; (in words) (dé)peindre, décrire

deport [dɪ'pɔːt] vt déporter, expulser

deposit [dɪ'pɔzɪt] n (Chem, Comm, Geo) dépôt m; (of ore, oil) gisement m; (part payment) arrhes fpl, acompte m; (on bottle etc) consigne f; (for hired goods etc) cautionnement m, garantie f ▷ vt déposer; **deposit account** n compte m sur livret

depot ['dɛpəu] n dépôt m; (us: Rail) gare f

depreciate [dɪ'priːʃɪeɪt] vi se déprécier, se dévaloriser

depress [dɪ'prɛs] vt déprimer; (press down) appuyer sur, abaisser; (wages etc) faire baisser; **depressed** adj (person) déprimé(e); (area) en déclin, touché(e) par le sous-emploi; **depressing** adj déprimant(e); **depression** [dɪ'prɛʃən] n dépression f

deprive [dɪ'praɪv] vt: **to ~ sb of** priver qn de; **deprived** adj déshérité(e)

dept. abbr (= department) dép, dépt

depth [dɛpθ] n profondeur f; **to be in the ~s of despair** être au plus profond du désespoir; **to be out of one's ~** (brit: swimmer) ne plus avoir pied; (fig) être dépassé(e), nager

deputy ['dɛpjutɪ] n (second in command) adjoint m; (Pol) député m; (us: also: **~ sheriff**) shérif adjoint ▷ adj: **~ head** (Scol) directeur(-trice) adjoint(e), sous-directeur(-trice)

derail [dɪ'reɪl] vt: **to be ~ed** dérailler

derelict ['dɛrɪlɪkt] adj abandonné(e), à l'abandon

derive [dɪ'raɪv] vt: **to ~ sth from** tirer qch de; trouver qch dans ▷ vi: **to ~ from**

provenir de, dériver de
descend [dɪˈsɛnd] vt, vi descendre;
to ~ from descendre de, être issu(e)
de; **to ~ to** s'abaisser à; **descendant** n
descendant(e); **descent** n descente f;
(origin) origine f
describe [dɪsˈkraɪb] vt décrire;
description [dɪsˈkrɪpʃən] n
description f; (sort) sorte f, espèce f
desert n [ˈdɛzət] désert m ▷ vb
[dɪˈzəːt] ▷ vt déserter, abandonner
▷ vi (Mil) déserter; **deserted** [dɪˈzəːtɪd]
adj désert(e)
deserve [dɪˈzəːv] vt mériter
design [dɪˈzaɪn] n (sketch) plan m,
dessin m; (layout, shape) conception f,
ligne f; (pattern) dessin, motif(s) m(pl);
(of dress, car) modèle m; (art) design m,
stylisme m; (intention) dessein m ▷ vt
dessiner; (plan) concevoir; **design and
technology** n (BRIT: Scol) technologie f
designate vt [ˈdɛzɪɡneɪt] désigner
▷ adj [ˈdɛzɪɡnɪt] désigné(e)
designer [dɪˈzaɪnəʳ] n (Archit,
Art) dessinateur(-trice); (Industry)
concepteur m, designer m; (Fashion)
styliste m/f
desirable [dɪˈzaɪərəbl] adj (property,
location, purchase) attrayant(e)
desire [dɪˈzaɪəʳ] n désir m ▷ vt désirer,
vouloir
desk [dɛsk] n (in office) bureau m;
(for pupil) pupitre m; (BRIT: in shop,
restaurant) caisse f; (in hotel, at airport)
réception f; **desk-top publishing**
[ˈdɛsktɔp-] n publication assistée par
ordinateur, PAO f
despair [dɪsˈpɛəʳ] n désespoir m ▷ vi: **to
~ of** désespérer de
despatch [dɪsˈpætʃ] n, vt = **dispatch**
desperate [ˈdɛspərɪt] adj désespéré(e);
(fugitive) prêt(e) à tout; **to be ~ for sth/
to do sth** avoir désespérément besoin
de qch/de faire qch; **desperately** adv
désespérément; (very) terriblement,
extrêmement; **desperation**
[dɛspəˈreɪʃən] n désespoir m; **in
(sheer) desperation** en désespoir

de cause
despise [dɪsˈpaɪz] vt mépriser
despite [dɪsˈpaɪt] prep malgré, en
dépit de
dessert [dɪˈzəːt] n dessert m;
dessertspoon n cuiller f à dessert
destination [dɛstɪˈneɪʃən] n
destination f
destined [ˈdɛstɪnd] adj: **~ for London** à
destination de Londres
destiny [ˈdɛstɪnɪ] n destinée f, destin m
destroy [dɪsˈtrɔɪ] vt détruire; (injured
horse) abattre; (dog) faire piquer
destruction [dɪsˈtrʌkʃən] n
destruction f
destructive [dɪsˈtrʌktɪv] adj
destructeur(-trice)
detach [dɪˈtætʃ] vt détacher; **detached**
adj (attitude) détaché(e); **detached
house** n pavillon m maison(nette)
(individuelle)
detail [ˈdiːteɪl] n détail m ▷ vt raconter
en détail, énumérer; **in ~** en détail;
detailed adj détaillé(e)
detain [dɪˈteɪn] vt retenir; (in captivity)
détenir
detect [dɪˈtɛkt] vt déceler, percevoir;
(Med, Police) dépister; (Mil, Radar,
Tech) détecter; **detection** [dɪˈtɛkʃən]
n découverte f; **detective** n policier
m; **private detective** détective privé;
detective story n roman policier
detention [dɪˈtɛnʃən] n détention f;
(Scol) retenue f, consigne f
deter [dɪˈtəːʳ] vt dissuader
detergent [dɪˈtəːdʒənt] n détersif m,
détergent m
deteriorate [dɪˈtɪərɪəreɪt] vi se
détériorer, se dégrader
determination [dɪtəːmɪˈneɪʃən] n
détermination f
determine [dɪˈtəːmɪn] vt déterminer;
to ~ to do résoudre de faire, se
déterminer à faire; **determined** adj
(person) déterminé(e), décidé(e);
determined to do bien décidé à faire
deterrent [dɪˈtɛrənt] n effet m de
dissuasion; force f de dissuasion

detest [dɪ'tɛst] vt détester, avoir
horreur de

detour ['diːtuəʳ] n détour m; (us Aut:
diversion) déviation f

detract [dɪ'trækt] vt: **to ~ from** (*quality,*
pleasure) diminuer; (*reputation*) porter
atteinte à

detrimental [dɛtrɪ'mɛntl] adj: **~ to**
préjudiciable or nuisible à

devastating ['dɛvəsteɪtɪŋ] adj
dévastateur(-trice); (*news*) accablant(e)

develop [dɪ'vɛləp] vt (*gen*) développer;
(*disease*) commencer à souffrir
de; (*resources*) mettre en valeur,
exploiter; (*land*) aménager ▷ vi se
développer; (*situation, disease: evolve*)
évoluer; (*facts, symptoms: appear*) se
manifester, se produire; **can you ~**
this film? pouvez-vous développer
cette pellicule?; **developing country**
n pays m en voie de développement;
development n développement m;
(*of land*) exploitation f; (*new fact, event*)
rebondissement m, fait(s) nouveau(x)

device [dɪ'vaɪs] n (*apparatus*) appareil
m, dispositif m

devil ['dɛvl] n diable m; démon m

devious ['diːvɪəs] adj (*person*)
sournois(e), dissimulé(e)

devise [dɪ'vaɪz] vt imaginer, concevoir

devote [dɪ'vəut] vt: **to ~ sth to**
consacrer qch à; **devoted** adj
dévoué(e); **to be devoted to** être
dévoué(e) or très attaché(e) à; (*book*
etc) être consacré(e) à; **devotion** n
dévouement m, attachement m; (*Rel*)
dévotion f, piété f

devour [dɪ'vauəʳ] vt dévorer

devout [dɪ'vaut] adj pieux(-euse),
dévot(e)

dew [djuː] n rosée f

diabetes [daɪə'biːtiːz] n diabète m

diabetic [daɪə'bɛtɪk] n diabétique m/f
▷ adj (*person*) diabétique

diagnose [daɪəg'nəuz] vt
diagnostiquer

diagnosis (*pl* **diagnoses**)
[daɪəg'nəusɪs, -siːz] n diagnostic m

diagonal [daɪ'ægənl] adj diagonal(e)
▷ n diagonale f

diagram ['daɪəgræm] n diagramme
m, schéma m

dial ['daɪəl] n cadran m ▷ vt (*number*)
faire, composer

dialect ['daɪəlɛkt] n dialecte m

dialling code ['daɪəlɪŋ-] (us **dial code**)
n indicatif m (téléphonique); **what's**
the ~ for Paris? quel est l'indicatif
de Paris?

dialling tone ['daɪəlɪŋ-] (us **dial tone**)
n tonalité f

dialogue (us **dialog**) ['daɪəlɔg] n
dialogue m

diameter [daɪ'æmɪtəʳ] n diamètre m

diamond ['daɪəmənd] n diamant
m; (*shape*) losange m; **diamonds** npl
(*Cards*) carreau m

diaper ['daɪəpəʳ] n (us) couche f

diarrhoea (us **diarrhea**) [daɪə'riːə] n
diarrhée f

diary ['daɪərɪ] n (*daily account*) journal
m; (*book*) agenda m

dice [daɪs] n (*pl inv*) dé m ▷ vt (*Culin*)
couper en dés or en cubes

dictate [dɪk'teɪt] vt dicter; **dictation**
[dɪk'teɪʃən] n dictée f

dictator [dɪk'teɪtəʳ] n dictateur m

dictionary ['dɪkʃənrɪ] n dictionnaire m

did [dɪd] pt of **do**

didn't [dɪdnt] = **did not**

die [daɪ] vi mourir; **to be dying for**
sth avoir une envie folle de qch; **to be**
dying to do sth mourir d'envie de faire
qch; **die down** vi se calmer, s'apaiser;
die out vi disparaître, s'éteindre

diesel ['diːzl] n (*vehicle*) diesel m; (*also:* **~**
oil) carburant m diesel, gas-oil m

diet ['daɪət] n alimentation f; (*restricted*
food) régime m ▷ vi (*also:* **be on a ~**)
suivre un régime

differ ['dɪfəʳ] vi: **to ~ from sth** (*be*
different) être différent(e) de qch,
différer de qch; **to ~ from sb over sth**
ne pas être d'accord avec qn au sujet de
qch; **difference** n différence f; (*quarrel*)
différend m, désaccord m; **different**

adj différent(e); **differentiate**
[dɪfə'rɛnʃɪeɪt] *vi*: **to differentiate**
between faire une différence entre;
differently *adv* différemment

difficult ['dɪfɪkəlt] *adj* difficile;
difficulty *n* difficulté *f*

dig [dɪg] *vt* (*pt, pp* **dug**) (*hole*) creuser;
(*garden*) bêcher ▷ *n* (*prod*) coup *m* de
coude; (*fig: remark*) coup de griffe *or* de
patte; (*Archaeology*) fouille *f*; **to ~ one's**
nails into enfoncer ses ongles dans;
dig up *vt* déterrer

digest *vt* [daɪ'dʒɛst] digérer ▷ *n*
['daɪdʒɛst] sommaire *m*, résumé *m*;
digestion [dɪ'dʒɛstʃən] *n* digestion *f*

digit ['dɪdʒɪt] *n* (*number*) chiffre *m* (*de o*
à 9); (*finger*) doigt *m*; **digital** *adj* (*system,*
recording, radio) numérique, digital(e);
(*watch*) à affichage numérique *or*
digital; **digital camera** *n* appareil
m photo numérique; **digital TV** *n*
télévision *f* numérique

dignified ['dɪgnɪfaɪd] *adj* digne

dignity ['dɪgnɪti] *n* dignité *f*

digs [dɪgz] *npl* (*BRIT inf*) piaule *f*,
chambre meublée

dilemma [daɪ'lɛmə] *n* dilemme *m*

dill [dɪl] *n* aneth *m*

dilute [daɪ'luːt] *vt* diluer

dim [dɪm] *adj* (*light, eyesight*) faible;
(*memory, outline*) vague, indécis(e);
(*room*) sombre; (*inf: stupid*) borné(e),
obtus(e) ▷ *vt* (*light*) réduire, baisser; (*US*
Aut) mettre en code, baisser

dime [daɪm] *n* (*US*) pièce *f* de 10 cents

dimension [daɪ'mɛnʃən] *n*
dimension *f*

diminish [dɪ'mɪnɪʃ] *vt, vi* diminuer

din [dɪn] *n* vacarme *m*

dine [daɪn] *vi* dîner; **diner** *n* (*person*)
dîneur(-euse); (*US: eating place*) petit
restaurant

dinghy ['dɪŋɡɪ] *n* youyou *m*; (*inflatable*)
canot *m* pneumatique; (*also*: **sailing ~**)
voilier *m*, dériveur *m*

dingy ['dɪndʒɪ] *adj* miteux(-euse),
minable

dining car ['daɪnɪŋ-] *n* (*BRIT*) voiture-

restaurant *f*, wagon-restaurant *m*

dining room ['daɪnɪŋ-] *n* salle *f* à
manger

dining table [daɪnɪŋ-] *n* table *f* de (la)
salle à manger

dinner ['dɪnər] *n* (*evening meal*) dîner *m*;
(*lunch*) déjeuner *m*; (*public*) banquet *m*;
dinner jacket *n* smoking *m*; **dinner**
party *n* dîner *m*; **dinner time** *n*
(*evening*) heure *f* du dîner; (*midday*)
heure du déjeuner

dinosaur ['daɪnəsɔːr] *n* dinosaure *m*

dip [dɪp] *n* (*slope*) déclivité *f*; (*in sea*)
baignade *f*, bain *m*; (*Culin*) ≈ sauce *f*
▷ *vt* tremper, plonger; (*BRIT Aut: lights*)
mettre en code, baisser ▷ *vi* plonger

diploma [dɪ'pləumə] *n* diplôme *m*

diplomacy [dɪ'pləuməsɪ] *n*
diplomatie *f*

diplomat ['dɪpləmæt] *n* diplomate *m*;
diplomatic [dɪplə'mætɪk] *adj*
diplomatique

dipstick ['dɪpstɪk] *n* (*BRIT Aut*) jauge *f*
de niveau d'huile

dire [daɪər] *adj* (*poverty*) extrême; (*awful*)
affreux(-euse)

direct [daɪ'rɛkt] *adj* direct(e) ▷ *vt* (*tell*
way) diriger, orienter; (*letter, remark*)
adresser; (*Cine, TV*) réaliser; (*Theat*)
mettre en scène; (*order*): **to ~ sb to do**
sth ordonner à qn de faire qch ▷ *adv*
directement; **can you ~ me to ...?**
pouvez-vous m'indiquer le chemin
de ...?; **direct debit** *n* (*BRIT Banking*)
prélèvement *m* automatique

direction [dɪ'rɛkʃən] *n* direction *f*;
directions *npl* (*to a place*) indications
fpl; **~s for use** mode *m* d'emploi; **sense**
of ~ sens *m* de l'orientation

directly [dɪ'rɛktlɪ] *adv* (*in straight line*)
directement, tout droit; (*at once*) tout
de suite, immédiatement

director [dɪ'rɛktər] *n* directeur *m*;
(*Theat*) metteur *m* en scène; (*Cine, TV*)
réalisateur(-trice)

directory [dɪ'rɛktərɪ] *n* annuaire
m; (*Comput*) répertoire *m*; **directory**
enquiries (*US* **directory assistance**) *n*

(*Tel: service*) renseignements *mpl*

dirt [dəːt] *n* saleté *f*; (*mud*) boue *f*; **dirty** *adj* sale; (*joke*) cochon(ne) ▷ *vt* salir

disability [dɪsə'bɪlɪtɪ] *n* invalidité *f*, infirmité *f*

disabled [dɪs'eɪbld] *adj* handicapé(e); (*maimed*) mutilé(e)

disadvantage [dɪsəd'vɑːntɪdʒ] *n* désavantage *m*, inconvénient *m*

disagree [dɪsə'griː] *vi* (*differ*) ne pas concorder; (*be against, think otherwise*): **to ~ (with)** ne pas être d'accord (avec); **disagreeable** *adj* désagréable; **disagreement** *n* désaccord *m*, différend *m*

disappear [dɪsə'pɪəʳ] *vi* disparaître; **disappearance** *n* disparition *f*

disappoint [dɪsə'pɔɪnt] *vt* décevoir; **disappointed** *adj* déçu(e); **disappointing** *adj* décevant(e); **disappointment** *n* déception *f*

disapproval [dɪsə'pruːvəl] *n* désapprobation *f*

disapprove [dɪsə'pruːv] *vi*: **to ~ of** désapprouver

disarm [dɪs'ɑːm] *vt* désarmer; **disarmament** [dɪs'ɑːməmənt] *n* désarmement *m*

disaster [dɪ'zɑːstəʳ] *n* catastrophe *f*, désastre *m*; **disastrous** *adj* désastreux(-euse)

disbelief ['dɪsbə'liːf] *n* incrédulité *f*

disc [dɪsk] *n* disque *m*; (*Comput*) = **disk**

discard [dɪs'kɑːd] *vt* (*old things*) se débarrasser de; (*fig*) écarter, renoncer à

discharge *vt* (*duties*) s'acquitter de; (*waste etc*) déverser; décharger; (*patient*) renvoyer (chez lui); (*employee, soldier*) congédier, licencier ▷ *n* ['dɪstʃɑːdʒ] (*Elec, Med*) émission *f*; (*dismissal*) renvoi *m*; licenciement *m*

discipline ['dɪsɪplɪn] *n* discipline *f* ▷ *vt* discipliner; (*punish*) punir

disc jockey *n* disque-jockey *m* (DJ)

disclose [dɪs'kləuz] *vt* révéler, divulguer

disco ['dɪskəu] *n abbr* discothèque *f*

discoloured [dɪs'kʌləd] (*US*

discolored) *adj* décoloré(e), jauni(e)

discomfort [dɪs'kʌmfət] *n* malaise *m*, gêne *f*; (*lack of comfort*) manque *m* de confort

disconnect [dɪskə'nɛkt] *vt* (*Elec, Radio*) débrancher; (*gas, water*) couper

discontent [dɪskən'tɛnt] *n* mécontentement *m*

discontinue [dɪskən'tɪnjuː] *vt* cesser, interrompre; **"~d"** (*Comm*) "fin de série"

discount *n* ['dɪskaunt] remise *f*, rabais *m* ▷ *vt* [dɪs'kaunt] (*report etc*) ne pas tenir compte de

discourage [dɪs'kʌrɪdʒ] *vt* décourager

discover [dɪs'kʌvəʳ] *vt* découvrir; **discovery** *n* découverte *f*

discredit [dɪs'krɛdɪt] *vt* (*idea*) mettre en doute; (*person*) discréditer

discreet [dɪ'skriːt] *adj* discret(-ète)

discrepancy [dɪ'skrɛpənsɪ] *n* divergence *f*, contradiction *f*

discretion [dɪ'skrɛʃən] *n* discrétion *f*; **at the ~ of** à la discrétion de

discriminate [dɪ'skrɪmɪneɪt] *vi*: **to ~ between** établir une distinction entre, faire la différence entre; **to ~ against** pratiquer une discrimination contre; **discrimination** [dɪskrɪmɪ'neɪʃən] *n* discrimination *f*; (*judgment*) discernement *m*

discuss [dɪ'skʌs] *vt* discuter de; (*debate*) discuter; **discussion** [dɪ'skʌʃən] *n* discussion *f*

disease [dɪ'ziːz] *n* maladie *f*

disembark [dɪsɪm'bɑːk] *vt, vi* débarquer

disgrace [dɪs'greɪs] *n* honte *f*; (*disfavour*) disgrâce *f* ▷ *vt* déshonorer, couvrir de honte; **disgraceful** *adj* scandaleux(-euse), honteux(-euse)

disgruntled [dɪs'grʌntld] *adj* mécontent(e)

disguise [dɪs'gaɪz] *n* déguisement *m* ▷ *vt* déguiser; **in ~** déguisé(e)

disgust [dɪs'gʌst] *n* dégoût *m*, aversion *f* ▷ *vt* dégoûter, écœurer

disgusted [dɪs'gʌstɪd] *adj* dégoûté(e), écœuré(e)

disgusting [dɪs'gʌstɪŋ] *adj* dégoûtant(e)

dish [dɪʃ] *n* plat *m*; **to do** *or* **wash the ~es** faire la vaisselle; **dishcloth** *n* (*for drying*) torchon *m*; (*for washing*) lavette *f*

dishonest [dɪs'ɔnɪst] *adj* malhonnête

dishtowel [ˈdɪʃtauəl] *n* (US) torchon *m* (à vaisselle)

dishwasher [ˈdɪʃwɔʃəʳ] *n* lave-vaisselle *m*

disillusion [dɪsɪ'luːʒən] *vt* désabuser, désenchanter

disinfectant [dɪsɪn'fɛktənt] *n* désinfectant *m*

disintegrate [dɪs'ɪntɪgreɪt] *vi* se désintégrer

disk [dɪsk] *n* (Comput) disquette *f*; **single-/double-sided ~** disquette une face/double face; **disk drive** *n* lecteur *m* de disquette; **diskette** *n* (Comput) disquette *f*

dislike [dɪs'laɪk] *n* aversion *f*, antipathie *f* ▷ *vt* ne pas aimer

dislocate [ˈdɪsləkeɪt] *vt* disloquer, déboîter

disloyal [dɪs'lɔɪəl] *adj* déloyal(e)

dismal [ˈdɪzml] *adj* (*gloomy*) lugubre, maussade; (*very bad*) lamentable

dismantle [dɪs'mæntl] *vt* démonter

dismay [dɪs'meɪ] *n* consternation *f* ▷ *vt* consterner

dismiss [dɪs'mɪs] *vt* congédier, renvoyer; (*idea*) écarter; (Law) rejeter; **dismissal** *n* renvoi *m*

disobedient [dɪsə'biːdɪənt] *adj* désobéissant(e), indiscipliné(e)

disobey [dɪsə'beɪ] *vt* désobéir à

disorder [dɪs'ɔːdəʳ] *n* désordre *m*; (*rioting*) désordres *mpl*; (Med) troubles *mpl*

disorganized [dɪs'ɔːgənaɪzd] *adj* désorganisé(e)

disown [dɪs'əun] *vt* renier

dispatch [dɪs'pætʃ] *vt* expédier, envoyer ▷ *n* envoi *m*, expédition *f*; (Mil, Press) dépêche *f*

dispel [dɪs'pɛl] *vt* dissiper, chasser

dispense [dɪs'pɛns] *vt* (*medicine*) préparer (et vendre); **dispense with** *vt fus* se passer de; **dispenser** *n* (*device*) distributeur *m*

disperse [dɪs'pəːs] *vt* disperser ▷ *vi* se disperser

display [dɪs'pleɪ] *n* (*of goods*) étalage *m*; affichage *m*; (Comput: *information*) visualisation *f*; (: *device*) visuel *m*; (*of feeling*) manifestation *f* ▷ *vt* montrer; (*goods*) mettre à l'étalage, exposer; (*results, departure times*) afficher; (*pej*) faire étalage de

displease [dɪs'pliːz] *vt* mécontenter, contrarier

disposable [dɪs'pəuzəbl] *adj* (*pack etc*) jetable; (*income*) disponible

disposal [dɪs'pəuzl] *n* (*of rubbish*) évacuation *f*, destruction *f*; (*of property etc: by selling*) vente *f*; (: *by giving away*) cession *f*; **at one's ~** à sa disposition

dispose [dɪs'pəuz] *vi*: **to ~ of** (*unwanted goods*) se débarrasser de, se défaire de; (*problem*) expédier; **disposition** [dɪspə'zɪʃən] *n* disposition *f*; (*temperament*) naturel *m*

disproportionate [dɪsprə'pɔːʃənət] *adj* disproportionné(e)

dispute [dɪs'pjuːt] *n* discussion *f*; (*also*: **industrial ~**) conflit *m* ▷ *vt* (*question*) contester; (*matter*) discuter

disqualify [dɪs'kwɔlɪfaɪ] *vt* (Sport) disqualifier; **to ~ sb for sth/from doing** rendre qn inapte à qch/à faire

disregard [dɪsrɪ'gɑːd] *vt* ne pas tenir compte de

disrupt [dɪs'rʌpt] *vt* (*plans, meeting, lesson*) perturber, déranger; **disruption** [dɪs'rʌpʃən] *n* perturbation *f*, dérangement *m*

dissatisfaction [dɪssætɪs'fækʃən] *n* mécontentement *m*, insatisfaction *f*

dissatisfied [dɪs'sætɪsfaɪd] *adj*: **~ (with)** insatisfait(e) (de)

dissect [dɪ'sɛkt] *vt* disséquer

dissent [dɪ'sɛnt] *n* dissentiment *m*, différence *f* d'opinion

dissertation [dɪsə'teɪʃən] *n* (Scol) mémoire *m*

dissolve [dɪˈzɔlv] vt dissoudre ▷ vi se
dissoudre, fondre; **to ~ in(to) tears**
fondre en larmes
distance [ˈdɪstns] n distance f; **in the
~** au loin
distant [ˈdɪstnt] adj lointain(e),
éloigné(e); (manner) distant(e), froid(e)
distil (us **distill**) [dɪsˈtɪl] vt distiller;
distillery n distillerie f
distinct [dɪsˈtɪŋkt] adj distinct(e);
(clear) marqué(e); **as ~ from** par
opposition à; **distinction** [dɪsˈtɪŋkʃən]
n distinction f; (in exam) mention f très
bien; **distinctive** adj distinctif(-ive)
distinguish [dɪsˈtɪŋgwɪʃ] vt
distinguer; **to ~ o.s.** se distinguer;
distinguished adj (eminent, refined)
distingué(e)
distort [dɪsˈtɔːt] vt déformer
distract [dɪsˈtrækt] vt distraire,
déranger; **distracted** adj (not
concentrating) distrait(e); (worried)
affolé(e); **distraction** [dɪsˈtrækʃən] n
distraction f
distraught [dɪsˈtrɔːt] adj éperdu(e)
distress [dɪsˈtrɛs] n détresse
f ▷ vt affliger; **distressing** adj
douloureux(-euse), pénible
distribute [dɪsˈtrɪbjuːt] vt distribuer;
distribution [dɪstrɪˈbjuːʃən] n
distribution f; **distributor** n (gen:
Tech) distributeur m; (Comm)
concessionnaire m/f
district [ˈdɪstrɪkt] n (of country) région f;
(of town) quartier m; (Admin) district m;
district attorney n (us) ≈ procureur m
de la République
distrust [dɪsˈtrʌst] n méfiance f, doute
m ▷ vt se méfier de
disturb [dɪsˈtəːb] vt troubler;
(inconvenience) déranger; **disturbance**
n dérangement m; (political etc)
troubles mpl; **disturbed** adj (worried,
upset) agité(e), troublé(e); **to be
emotionally disturbed** avoir des
problèmes affectifs; **disturbing** adj
troublant(e), inquiétant(e)
ditch [dɪtʃ] n fossé m; (for irrigation)

rigole f ▷ vt (inf) abandonner; (person)
plaquer
ditto [ˈdɪtəu] adv idem
dive [daɪv] n plongeon m; (of submarine)
plongée f ▷ vi plonger; **to ~ into** (bag
etc) plonger la main dans; (place) se
précipiter dans; **diver** n plongeur m
diverse [daɪˈvəːs] adj divers(e)
diversion [daɪˈvəːʃən] n (BRIT Aut)
déviation f; (distraction, Mil) diversion f
diversity [daɪˈvəːsɪtɪ] n diversité f,
variété f
divert [daɪˈvəːt] vt (BRIT: traffic) dévier;
(plane) dérouter; (train, river) détourner
divide [dɪˈvaɪd] vt diviser; (separate)
séparer ▷ vi se diviser; **divided
highway** (us) n route f à quatre voies
divine [dɪˈvaɪn] adj divin(e)
diving [ˈdaɪvɪŋ] n plongée (sous-
marine); **diving board** n plongeoir m
division [dɪˈvɪʒən] n division f;
(separation) séparation f; (Comm)
service m
divorce [dɪˈvɔːs] n divorce m ▷ vt
divorcer d'avec; **divorced** adj
divorcé(e); **divorcee** [dɪvɔːˈsiː] n
divorcé(e)
D.I.Y. adj, n abbr (BRIT) = **do-it-yourself**
dizzy [ˈdɪzɪ] adj: **I feel ~** la tête me
tourne, j'ai la tête qui tourne
DJ n abbr = **disc jockey**
DNA n abbr (= deoxyribonucleic acid)
ADN m

○ **KEYWORD**

do [duː] (pt **did**, pp **done**) n (inf: party etc)
soirée f, fête f
▷ vb **1** (in negative constructions) non
traduit; **I don't understand** je ne
comprends pas
2 (to form questions) non traduit; **didn't
you know?** vous ne le saviez pas?; **what
do you think?** qu'en pensez-vous?
3 (for emphasis, in polite expressions):
**people do make mistakes
sometimes** on peut toujours se
tromper; **she does seem rather late** j

trouve qu'elle est bien en retard; **do sit down/help yourself** asseyez-vous/ servez-vous je vous en prie; **do take care!** faites bien attention à vous!
4 (*used to avoid repeating vb*): **she swims better than I do** elle nage mieux que moi; **do you agree? - yes, I do/no I don't** vous êtes d'accord? - oui/non; **she lives in Glasgow - so do I** elle habite Glasgow - moi aussi; **he didn't like it and neither did we** il n'a pas aimé ça, et nous non plus; **who broke it? - I did** qui l'a cassé? - c'est moi; **he asked me to help him and I did** il m'a demandé de l'aider, et c'est ce que j'ai fait
5 (*in question tags*): **you like him, don't you?** vous l'aimez bien, n'est-ce pas?; **I don't know him, do I?** je ne crois pas le connaître
▷ *vt* **1** (*gen: carry out, perform etc*) faire; (*visit: city, museum*) faire, visiter; **what are you doing tonight?** qu'est-ce que vous faites ce soir?; **what do you do?** (*job*) que faites-vous dans la vie?; **what can I do for you?** que puis-je faire pour vous?; **to do the cooking/washing-up** faire la cuisine/la vaisselle; **to do one's teeth/hair/nails** se brosser les dents/se coiffer/se faire les ongles
2 (*Aut etc: distance*) faire; (: *speed*) faire du; **we've done 200 km already** nous avons déjà fait 200 km; **the car was doing 100** la voiture faisait du 100 (à l'heure); **he can do 100 in that car** il peut faire du 100 (à l'heure) dans cette voiture-là
▷ *vi* **1** (*act, behave*) faire; **do as I do** faites comme moi
2 (*get on, fare*) marcher; **the firm is doing well** l'entreprise marche bien; **he's doing well/badly at school** ça marche bien/mal pour lui à l'école; **how do you do?** comment allez-vous?; (*on being introduced*) enchanté(e)!
3 (*suit*) aller; **will it do?** est-ce que ça ira?
4 (*be sufficient*) suffire, aller; **will £10**

do? est-ce que 10 livres suffiront?; **that'll do** ça suffit, ça ira; **that'll do!** (*in annoyance*) ça va or suffit comme ça!; **to make do (with)** se contenter (de)
do up *vt* (*laces, dress*) attacher; (*buttons*) boutonner; (*zip*) fermer; (*renovate: room*) refaire; (: *house*) remettre à neuf
do with *vt fus* (*need*): **I could do with a drink/some help** quelque chose à boire/un peu d'aide ne serait pas de refus; **it could do with a wash** ça ne lui ferait pas de mal d'être lavé; (*be connected with*): **that has nothing to do with you** cela ne vous concerne pas; **I won't have anything to do with it** je ne veux pas m'en mêler
do without *vi* s'en passer; **if you're late for tea then you'll do without** si vous êtes en retard pour le dîner il faudra vous en passer
▷ *vt fus* se passer de; **I can do without a car** je peux me passer de voiture

dock [dɔk] *n* dock *m*; (*wharf*) quai *m*; (*Law*) banc *m* des accusés ▷ *vi* se mettre à quai; (*Space*) s'arrimer; **docks** *npl* (*Naut*) docks
doctor ['dɔktər] *n* médecin *m*, docteur *m*; (*PhD etc*) docteur ▷ *vt* (*drink*) frelater; **call a ~!** appelez un docteur *or* un médecin!; **Doctor of Philosophy (PhD)** *n* (*degree*) doctorat *m*; (*person*) titulaire *m/f* d'un doctorat
document ['dɔkjumənt] *n* document *m*; **documentary** [dɔkju'mɛntəri] *adj, n* documentaire (*m*); **documentation** [dɔkjumən'teɪʃən] *n* documentation *f*
dodge [dɔdʒ] *n* truc *m*; combine *f* ▷ *vt* esquiver, éviter
dodgy ['dɔdʒi] *adj* (*inf: uncertain*) douteux(-euse); (: *shady*) louche
does [dʌz] *vb see* **do**
doesn't ['dʌznt] = **does not**
dog [dɔg] *n* chien(ne) ▷ *vt* (*follow closely*) suivre de près; (*fig: memory etc*) poursuivre, harceler; **doggy bag** ['dɔgɪ-] *n* petit sac pour emporter les restes

do-it-yourself ['du:ɪtjɔ:'sɛlf] n
bricolage m

dole [dəul] n (BRIT: payment) allocation f
de chômage; **on the ~** au chômage

doll [dɒl] n poupée f

dollar ['dɒləʳ] n dollar m

dolphin ['dɒlfɪn] n dauphin m

dome [dəum] n dôme m

domestic [də'mɛstɪk] adj (duty,
happiness) familial(e); (policy,
affairs, flight) intérieur(e); (animal)
domestique; **domestic appliance** n
appareil ménager

dominant ['dɒmɪnənt] adj
dominant(e)

dominate ['dɒmɪneɪt] vt dominer

domino ['dɒmɪnəu] (pl **~es**) n
domino m; **dominoes** n (game)
dominos mpl

donate [də'neɪt] vt faire don de,
donner; **donation** [də'neɪʃən] n
donation f, don m

done [dʌn] pp of **do**

donkey ['dɒŋkɪ] n âne m

donor ['dəunəʳ] n (of blood etc)
donneur(-euse); (to charity)
donateur(-trice); **donor card** n carte f
de don d'organes

don't [dəunt] = **do not**

donut ['dəunʌt] (US) n = **doughnut**

doodle ['du:dl] vi griffonner, gribouiller

doom [du:m] n (fate) destin m ▷ vt: **to
be ~ed to failure** être voué(e) à l'échec

door [dɔ:ʳ] n porte f; (Rail, car) portière f;
doorbell n sonnette f; **door handle**
n poignée f de porte; (of car) poignée
de portière; **doorknob** n poignée f or
bouton m de porte; **doorstep** n pas
m de (la) porte, seuil m; **doorway** n
(embrasure f de) porte f

dope [dəup] n (inf: drug) drogue f;
(: person) andouille f ▷ vt (horse etc)
doper

dormitory ['dɔ:mɪtrɪ] n (BRIT) dortoir
m; (US: hall of residence) résidence f
universitaire

DOS [dɒs] n abbr (= disk operating system)
DOS m

dosage ['dəusɪdʒ] n dose f; dosage m;
(on label) posologie f

dose [dəus] n dose f

dot [dɒt] n point m; (on material) pois m
▷ vt: **~ted with** parsemé(e) de; **on the
~** à l'heure tapante; **dotcom** [dɒt'kɔm]
n point com m, pointcom m; **dotted
line** ['dɒtɪd-] n ligne pointillée; **to sign
on the dotted line** signer à l'endroit
indiqué or sur la ligne pointillée

double ['dʌbl] adj double ▷ adv (twice):
to cost ~ (sth) coûter le double
(de qch) or deux fois plus (que qch) ▷ n
double m; (Cine) doublure f ▷ vt
doubler; (fold) plier en deux ▷ vi
doubler; **on the ~, at the ~** au pas
de course; **double back** vi (person)
revenir sur ses pas; **double bass** n
contrebasse f; **double bed** n grand
lit; **double-check** vt, vi revérifier;
double-click vi (Comput) double-
cliquer; **double-cross** vt doubler,
trahir; **doubledecker** n autobus m à
impériale; **double glazing** n (BRIT)
double vitrage m; **double room** n
chambre f pour deux; **doubles** n
(Tennis) double m; **double yellow
lines** npl (BRIT: Aut) double bande jaune
marquant l'interdiction de stationner

doubt [daut] n doute m ▷ vt douter
de; **no ~** sans doute; **to ~ that** douter
que + sub; **doubtful** adj douteux(-euse)
(person) incertain(e); **doubtless** adv
sans doute, sûrement

dough [dəu] n pâte f; **doughnut** (US
donut) n beignet m

dove [dʌv] n colombe f

Dover ['dəuvəʳ] n Douvres

down [daun] n (fluff) duvet m ▷ adv
en bas, vers le bas; (on the ground) par
terre ▷ prep en bas de; (along) le long
de ▷ vt (inf: drink) siffler; **to walk ~ a
hill** descendre une colline; **to run ~ the
street** descendre la rue en courant;
~ with X! à bas X!; **down-and-out** n
(tramp) clochard(e); **downfall** n chute
f; ruine f; **downhill** adv: **to go downhill**
descendre; (business) péricliter

Owning Street ['daunɪŋ-] n (BRIT):
10 ~ résidence du Premier ministre

● **DOWNING STREET**
●
● **Downing Street** est une rue de
● Westminster (à Londres) où se
● trouvent la résidence officielle
● du Premier ministre et celle du
● ministre des Finances. Le nom
● **Downing Street** est souvent utilisé
● pour désigner le gouvernement
● britannique.

Town: **download** vt (Comput)
télécharger; **downright** adj (lie etc)
effronté(e); (refusal) catégorique
Down's syndrome [daunz-] n
trisomie f
Town: **downstairs** adv (on or to
ground floor) au rez-de-chaussée; (on
or to floor below) à l'étage inférieur;
down-to-earth adj terre à terre inv;
downtown adv en ville; **down under**
adv en Australie or Nouvelle Zélande;
downward ['daunwəd] adj, adv vers
le bas; **downwards** ['daunwədz] adv
vers le bas
doz. abbr = **dozen**
doze [dəuz] vi sommeiller
dozen ['dʌzn] n douzaine f; **a ~ books**
une douzaine de livres; **~s of** des
centaines de
Dr. abbr (= doctor) Dr; (in street names)
= **drive**
drab [dræb] adj terne, morne
draft [drɑːft] n (of letter, school
work) brouillon m; (of literary work)
ébauche f; (Comm) traite f; (US: call-up)
conscription f ▷ vt faire le brouillon de;
(Mil: send) détacher; see also **draught**
drag [dræg] vt traîner; (river) draguer
▷ vi traîner ▷ n (inf) casse-pieds m/f;
(women's clothing): **in ~** (en) travesti; **to
~ and drop** (Comput) glisser-poser
dragon ['drægn] n dragon m
dragonfly ['drægənflaɪ] n libellule f
drain [dreɪn] n égout m; (on resources)

saignée f ▷ vt (land, marshes) drainer,
assécher; (vegetables) égoutter;
(reservoir etc) vider ▷ vi (water) s'écouler;
drainage n (system) système m
d'égouts; (act) drainage m; **drainpipe** n
tuyau m d'écoulement
drama ['drɑːmə] n (art) théâtre m, art
m dramatique; (play) pièce f; (event)
drame m; **dramatic** [drə'mætɪk]
adj (Theat) dramatique; (impressive)
spectaculaire
drank [dræŋk] pt of **drink**
drape [dreɪp] vt draper; **drapes** npl (US)
rideaux mpl
drastic ['dræstɪk] adj (measures)
d'urgence, énergique; (change)
radical(e)
draught (US **draft**) [drɑːft] n courant m
d'air; **on ~** (beer) à la pression; **draught
beer** n bière f (à la) pression; **draughts**
n (BRIT: game) (jeu m de) dames fpl
draw [drɔː] (vb: pt **drew**, pp **~n**) vt tirer;
(picture) dessiner; (attract) attirer; (line,
circle) tracer; (money) retirer; (wages)
toucher ▷ vi (Sport) faire match nul ▷ n
match nul; (lottery) loterie f; (: picking
of ticket) tirage m au sort; **draw out**
vi (lengthen) s'allonger ▷ vt (money)
retirer; **draw up** vi (stop) s'arrêter
▷ vt (document) établir, dresser; (plan)
formuler, dessiner; (chair) approcher;
drawback n inconvénient m,
désavantage m
drawer [drɔːʳ] n tiroir m
drawing ['drɔːɪŋ] n dessin m; **drawing
pin** n (BRIT) punaise f; **drawing room**
n salon m
drawn [drɔːn] pp of **draw**
dread [drɛd] n épouvante f, effroi m ▷ vt
redouter, appréhender; **dreadful** adj
épouvantable, affreux(-euse)
dream [driːm] n rêve m ▷ vt, vi (pt,
pp **~ed** or **~t**) rêver; **dreamer** n
rêveur(-euse)
dreamt [drɛmt] pt, pp of **dream**
dreary ['drɪərɪ] adj triste; monotone
drench [drɛntʃ] vt tremper
dress [drɛs] n robe f; (clothing)

habillement *m*, tenue *f* ▷ *vt* habiller; (*wound*) panser ▷ *vi*: **to get ~ed** s'habiller; **dress up** *vi* s'habiller; (*in fancy dress*) se déguiser; **dress circle** *n* (BRIT) premier balcon; **dresser** *n* (*furniture*) vaisselier *m*; (: *US*) coiffeuse *f*, commode *f*; **dressing** *n* (*Med*) pansement *m*; (*Culin*) sauce *f*, assaisonnement *m*; **dressing gown** *n* (BRIT) robe *f* de chambre; **dressing room** *n* (*Theat*) loge *f*; (*Sport*) vestiaire *m*; **dressing table** *n* coiffeuse *f*; **dressmaker** *n* couturière *f*

drew [druː] *pt of* **draw**

dribble ['drɪbl] *vi* (*baby*) baver ▷ *vt* (*ball*) dribbler

dried [draɪd] *adj* (*fruit, beans*) sec (sèche); (*eggs, milk*) en poudre

drier ['draɪə'] *n* = **dryer**

drift [drɪft] *n* (*of current etc*) force *f*; direction *f*; (*of snow*) rafale *f*, coulée *f*; (: *on ground*) congère *f*; (*general meaning*) sens général ▷ *vi* (*boat*) aller à la dérive, dériver; (*sand, snow*) s'amonceler, s'entasser

drill [drɪl] *n* perceuse *f*; (*bit*) foret *m*; (*of dentist*) roulette *f*, fraise *f*; (*Mil*) exercice *m* ▷ *vt* percer; (*troops*) entraîner ▷ *vi* (*for oil*) faire un or des forage(s)

drink [drɪŋk] *n* boisson *f*; (*alcoholic*) verre *m* ▷ *vt, vi* (*pt* **drank**, *pp* **drunk**) boire; **to have a ~** boire quelque chose, boire un verre; **a ~ of water** un verre d'eau; **would you like a ~?** tu veux boire quelque chose?; **drink-driving** *n* conduite *f* en état d'ivresse; **drinker** *n* buveur(-euse); **drinking water** *n* eau *f* potable

drip [drɪp] *n* (*drop*) goutte *f*; (*Med: device*) goutte-à-goutte *m inv*; (: *liquid*) perfusion *f* ▷ *vi* tomber goutte à goutte; (*tap*) goutter

drive [draɪv] *n* (*drop*) promenade *f* or trajet *m* en voiture; (*also*: **~way**) allée *f*; (*energy*) dynamisme *m*, énergie *f*; (*push*) effort (concerté); campagne *f*; (*Comput: also*: **disk ~**) lecteur *m* de disquette ▷ *vb* (*pt* **drove**, *pp* **~n**) ▷ *vt* conduire; (*nail*)

enfoncer; (*push*) chasser, pousser; (*Tech: motor*) actionner; entraîner ▷ *vi* (*be at the wheel*) conduire; (*travel by car*) aller en voiture; **left-/right-hand ~** (*Aut*) conduite *f* à gauche/droite; **to ~ sb mad** rendre qn fou (folle); **drive out** *vt* (*force out*) chasser; **drive-in** *adj, n* (*esp US*) drive-in *m*

driven ['drɪvn] *pp of* **drive**

driver ['draɪvə'] *n* conducteur(-trice); (*of taxi, bus*) chauffeur *m*; **driver's license** *n* (*US*) permis *m* de conduire

driveway ['draɪvweɪ] *n* allée *f*

driving ['draɪvɪŋ] *n* conduite *f*; **driving instructor** *n* moniteur *m* d'auto-école; **driving lesson** *n* leçon *f* de conduite; **driving licence** *n* (BRIT) permis *m* de conduire; **driving test** *n* examen *m* du permis de conduire

drizzle ['drɪzl] *n* bruine *f*, crachin *m*

droop [druːp] *vi* (*flower*) commencer à se faner; (*shoulders, head*) tomber

drop [drɔp] *n* (*of liquid*) goutte *f*; (*fall*) baisse *f*; (*also*: **parachute ~**) saut *m* ▷ *vt* laisser tomber; (*voice, eyes, price*) baisser; (*passenger*) déposer ▷ *vi* tomber; **drop in** *vi* (*inf: visit*): **to ~ in (on)** faire un saut (chez), passer (chez); **drop off** *vi* (*sleep*) s'assoupir ▷ *vt* (*passenger*) déposer; **drop out** *vi* (*withdraw*) se retirer; (*student etc*) abandonner, décrocher

drought [draut] *n* sécheresse *f*

drove [drəuv] *pt of* **drive**

drown [draun] *vt* noyer ▷ *vi* se noyer

drowsy ['drauzɪ] *adj* somnolent(e)

drug [drʌg] *n* médicament *m*; (*narcotic*) drogue *f* ▷ *vt* droguer; **to be on ~s** se droguer; **drug addict** *n* toxicomane *m/f*; **drug dealer** *n* revendeur(-euse) de drogue; **druggist** *n* (*US*) pharmacien(ne)-droguiste; **drugstore** *n* (*US*) pharmacie-droguerie *f*, drugstore *m*

drum [drʌm] *n* tambour *m*; (*for oil, petrol*) bidon *m*; **drums** *npl* (*Mus*) batterie *f*; **drummer** *n* (joueur *m* de) tambour *m*

runk [drʌŋk] pp of **drink** ▷ adj ivre,
soûl(e) ▷ n (also: **~ard**) ivrogne m/f;
to get ~ se soûler; **drunken** adj ivre,
soûl(e); (rage, stupor) ivrogne, d'ivrogne

ry [draɪ] adj sec (sèche); (day) sans
pluie ▷ vt sécher; (clothes) faire sécher
▷ vi sécher; **dry off** vi, vt sécher; **dry up**
vi (river, supplies) se tarir; **dry-cleaner's**
n teinturerie f; **dry-cleaning** n (process)
nettoyage m à sec; **dryer** n (tumble-
dryer) sèche-linge m inv; (for hair) sèche-
cheveux m inv

DSS n abbr (BRIT) = **Department of
Social Security**

DTP n abbr (= desktop publishing) PAO f

ual ['djuəl] adj double; **dual
carriageway** n (BRIT) route f à quatre
voies

ubious ['dju:bɪəs] adj hésitant(e),
incertain(e); (reputation, company)
douteux(-euse)

uck [dʌk] n canard m ▷ vi se baisser
vivement, baisser subitement la tête

ue [dju:] adj (money, payment) dû
(due); (expected) attendu(e); (fitting)
qui convient ▷ adv: **~ north** droit vers
le nord; **~ to** (because of) en raison de;
(caused by) dû à; **the train is ~ at 8 a.m.**
le train est attendu à 8 h; **she is ~ back
tomorrow** elle doit rentrer demain; **he
is ~ £10** on lui doit 10 livres; **to give sb
his** or **her ~** être juste envers qn

uel ['djuəl] n duel m

uet [dju:'ɛt] n duo m

ug [dʌg] pt, pp of **dig**

uke [dju:k] n duc m

ull [dʌl] adj (boring) ennuyeux(-euse);
(not bright) morne, terne; (sound,
pain) sourd(e); (weather, day) gris(e),
maussade ▷ vt (pain, grief) atténuer;
(mind, senses) engourdir

umb [dʌm] adj muet(te); (stupid) bête

ummy ['dʌmɪ] n (tailor's model)
mannequin m; (mock-up) factice m,
maquette f; (BRIT: for baby) tétine f ▷ adj
faux (fausse), factice

ump [dʌmp] n (also: **rubbish ~**)
décharge (publique); (inf: place) trou m

▷ vt (put down) déposer; déverser; (get
rid of) se débarrasser de; (Comput) lister

dumpling ['dʌmplɪŋ] n boulette f
(de pâte)

dune [dju:n] n dune f

dungarees [dʌŋgə'ri:z] npl bleu(s)
m(pl); (for child, woman) salopette f

dungeon ['dʌndʒən] n cachot m

duplex ['dju:plɛks] n (US: also: **~
apartment**) duplex m

duplicate n ['dju:plɪkət] double m
▷ vt ['dju:plɪkeɪt] faire un double de;
(on machine) polycopier; **in ~** en deux
exemplaires, en double

durable ['djuərəbl] adj durable;
(clothes, metal) résistant(e), solide

duration [djuə'reɪʃən] n durée f

during ['djuərɪŋ] prep pendant, au
cours de

dusk [dʌsk] n crépuscule m

dust [dʌst] n poussière f ▷ vt
(furniture) essuyer, épousseter;
(cake etc): **to ~ with** saupoudrer de;
dustbin n (BRIT) poubelle f; **duster**
n chiffon m; **dustman** n (BRIT: irreg)
boueux m, éboueur m; **dustpan**
n pelle f à poussière; **dusty** adj
poussiéreux(-euse)

Dutch [dʌtʃ] adj hollandais(e),
néerlandais(e) ▷ n (Ling) hollandais m,
néerlandais m ▷ adv: **to go ~** or **dutch**
(inf) partager les frais; **the Dutch**
npl les Hollandais, les Néerlandais;
Dutchman (irreg) n Hollandais m;
Dutchwoman (irreg) n Hollandaise f

duty ['dju:tɪ] n devoir m; (tax) droit m,
taxe f; **on ~** de service; (at night etc) de
garde; **off ~** libre, pas de service or de
garde; **duty-free** adj exempté(e) de
douane, hors-taxe

duvet ['du:veɪ] n (BRIT) couette f

DVD n abbr (= digital versatile or video disc)
DVD m; **DVD burner** n graveur m de
DVD; **DVD player** n lecteur m de DVD;
DVD writer n graveur m de DVD

dwarf (pl **dwarves**) [dwɔ:f, dwɔ:vz] n
nain(e) ▷ vt écraser

dwell (pt, pp **dwelt**) [dwɛl, dwɛlt] vi

demeurer; **dwell on** vt fus s'étendre sur
dwelt [dwɛlt] pt, pp of **dwell**
dwindle ['dwɪndl] vi diminuer,
décroître
dye [daɪ] n teinture f ▷ vt teindre
dying ['daɪɪŋ] adj mourant(e),
agonisant(e)
dynamic [daɪ'næmɪk] adj dynamique
dynamite ['daɪnəmaɪt] n dynamite f
dyslexia [dɪs'lɛksɪə] n dyslexie f
dyslexic [dɪs'lɛksɪk] adj, n dyslexique
m/f

E [iː] n (Mus): **E** mi m
E111 n abbr (= form E111) formulaire m E111
each [iːtʃ] adj chaque ▷ pron chacun(e);
~ other l'un l'autre; **they hate ~ other**
ils se détestent (mutuellement); **they
have 2 books ~** ils ont 2 livres chacun;
they cost £5 ~ ils coûtent 5 livres
(la) pièce
eager ['iːgəʳ] adj (person, buyer)
empressé(e); (keen: pupil, worker)
enthousiaste; **to be ~ to do sth**
(impatient) brûler de faire qch; (keen)
désirer vivement faire qch; **to be ~ for**
(event) désirer vivement; (vengeance,
affection, information) être avide de
eagle ['iːgl] n aigle m
ear [ɪəʳ] n oreille f; (of corn) épi m;
earache n mal m aux oreilles; **eardrum**
n tympan m
earl [əːl] n comte m
earlier ['əːlɪəʳ] adj (date etc) plus
rapproché(e); (edition etc) plus
ancien(ne), antérieur(e) ▷ adv plus tôt
early ['əːlɪ] adv tôt, de bonne heure;

(*ahead of time*) en avance; (*near the beginning*) au début ▷ *adj* précoce, qui se manifeste (*or* se fait) tôt *or* de bonne heure; (*Christians, settlers*) premier(-ière); (*reply*) rapide; (*death*) prématuré(e); (*work*) de jeunesse; **to have an ~ night/start** se coucher/partir tôt *or* de bonne heure; **in the ~** *or* **~ in the spring/19th century** au début *or* commencement du printemps/19ème siècle; **early retirement** *n* retraite anticipée

earmark ['ɪəmɑːk] *vt*: **to ~ sth for** réserver *or* destiner qch à

earn [əːn] *vt* gagner; (*Comm: yield*) rapporter; **to ~ one's living** gagner sa vie

earnest ['əːnɪst] *adj* sérieux(-euse) ▷ *n*: **in ~** *adv* sérieusement, pour de bon

earnings ['əːnɪŋz] *npl* salaire *m*; gains *mpl*; (*of company etc*) profits *mpl*, bénéfices *mpl*

ear: **earphones** *npl* écouteurs *mpl*; **earplugs** *npl* boules *fpl* Quiès®; (*to keep out water*) protège-tympans *mpl*; **earring** *n* boucle *f* d'oreille

earth [əːθ] *n* (*gen, also* BRIT *Elec*) terre *f* ▷ *vt* (BRIT *Elec*) relier à la terre; **earthquake** *n* tremblement *m* de terre, séisme *m*

ease [iːz] *n* facilité *f*, aisance *f*; (*comfort*) bien-être *m* ▷ *vt* (*soothe: mind*) tranquilliser; (*reduce: pain, problem*) atténuer; (: *tension*) réduire; (*loosen*) relâcher, détendre; (*help pass*): **to ~ sth in/out** faire pénétrer/sortir qch délicatement *or* avec douceur, faciliter la pénétration/la sortie de qch; **at ~** à l'aise; (*Mil*) au repos

easily ['iːzɪlɪ] *adv* facilement; (*by far*) de loin

east [iːst] *n* est *m* ▷ *adj* (*wind*) d'est; (*side*) est *inv* ▷ *adv* à l'est, vers l'est; **the E~** l'Orient *m*; (*Pol*) les pays *mpl* de l'Est; **eastbound** *adj* en direction de l'est; (*carriageway*) est *inv*

Easter ['iːstər] *n* Pâques *fpl*; **Easter egg** *n* œuf *m* de Pâques

eastern ['iːstən] *adj* de l'est, oriental(e)

Easter Sunday *n* le dimanche de Pâques

easy ['iːzɪ] *adj* facile; (*manner*) aisé(e) ▷ *adv*: **to take it** *or* **things ~** (*rest*) ne pas se fatiguer; (*not worry*) ne pas (trop) s'en faire; **easy-going** *adj* accommodant(e), facile à vivre

eat (*pt* **ate**, *pp* **~en**) [iːt, eɪt, 'iːtn] *vt*, *vi* manger; **can we have something to ~?** est-ce qu'on peut manger quelque chose?; **eat out** *vi* manger au restaurant

eavesdrop ['iːvzdrɒp] *vi*: **to ~ (on)** écouter de façon indiscrète

e-book ['iːbuk] *n* livre *m* électronique

e-business ['iːbɪznɪs] *n* (*company*) entreprise *f* électronique; (*commerce*) commerce *m* électronique

EC *n abbr* (= *European Community*) CE *f*

eccentric [ɪk'sɛntrɪk] *adj*, *n* excentrique *m/f*

echo, echoes ['ɛkəu] *n* écho *m* ▷ *vt* répéter ▷ *vi* résonner; faire écho

eclipse [ɪ'klɪps] *n* éclipse *f*

eco-friendly [iːkəu'frɛndlɪ] *adj* non nuisible à *or* qui ne nuit pas à l'environnement

ecological [iːkə'lɔdʒɪkəl] *adj* écologique

ecology [ɪ'kɔlədʒɪ] *n* écologie *f*

e-commerce [iːkɔməːs] *n* commerce *m* électronique

economic [iːkə'nɔmɪk] *adj* économique; (*profitable*) rentable; **economical** *adj* économique; (*person*) économe; **economics** *n* (*Scol*) économie *f* politique ▷ *npl* (*of project etc*) côté *m* or aspect *m* économique

economist [ɪ'kɔnəmɪst] *n* économiste *m/f*

economize [ɪ'kɔnəmaɪz] *vi* économiser, faire des économies

economy [ɪ'kɔnəmɪ] *n* économie *f*; **economy class** *n* (*Aviat*) classe *f* touriste; **economy class syndrome** *n* syndrome *m* de la classe économique

ecstasy ['ɛkstəsɪ] *n* extase *f*; (*Drugs*)

ecstasy *m*; **ecstatic** [ɛks'tætɪk] *adj* extatique, en extase

eczema ['ɛksɪmə] *n* eczéma *m*

edge [ɛdʒ] *n* bord *m*; (*of knife etc*) tranchant *m*, fil *m* ▷ *vt* border; **on ~** (*fig*) crispé(e), tendu(e)

edgy ['ɛdʒɪ] *adj* crispé(e), tendu(e)

edible ['ɛdɪbl] *adj* comestible; (*meal*) mangeable

Edinburgh ['ɛdɪnbərə] *n* Édimbourg

edit ['ɛdɪt] *vt* (*text, book*) éditer; (*report*) préparer; (*film*) monter; (*magazine*) diriger; (*newspaper*) être le rédacteur *or* la rédactrice en chef de; **edition** [ɪ'dɪʃən] *n* édition *f*; **editor** *n* (*of newspaper*) rédacteur(-trice), rédacteur(-trice) en chef; (*of sb's work*) éditeur(-trice); (*also*: **film editor**) monteur(-euse); **political/foreign editor** rédacteur politique/au service étranger; **editorial** [ɛdɪ'tɔːrɪəl] *adj* de la rédaction, éditorial(e) ▷ *n* éditorial *m*

educate ['ɛdjukeɪt] *vt* (*teach*) instruire; (*bring up*) éduquer; **educated** ['ɛdjukeɪtɪd] *adj* (*person*) cultivé(e)

education [ɛdju'keɪʃən] *n* éducation *f*; (*studies*) études *fpl*; (*teaching*) enseignement *m*, instruction *f*; **educational** *adj* pédagogique; (*institution*) scolaire; (*game, toy*) éducatif(-ive)

eel [iːl] *n* anguille *f*

eerie ['ɪərɪ] *adj* inquiétant(e), spectral(e), surnaturel(le)

effect [ɪ'fɛkt] *n* effet *m* ▷ *vt* effectuer; **effects** *npl* (*property*) effets, affaires *fpl*; **to take ~** (*Law*) entrer en vigueur, prendre effet; (*drug*) agir, faire son effet; **in ~** en fait; **effective** *adj* efficace; (*actual*) véritable; **effectively** *adv* efficacement; (*in reality*) effectivement, en fait

efficiency [ɪ'fɪʃənsɪ] *n* efficacité *f*; (*of machine, car*) rendement *m*

efficient [ɪ'fɪʃənt] *adj* efficace; (*machine, car*) d'un bon rendement; **efficiently** *adv* efficacement

effort ['ɛfət] *n* effort *m*; **effortless** *adj* sans effort, aisé(e); (*achievement*) facile

e.g. *adv abbr* (= *exempli gratia*) par exemple, p. ex.

egg [ɛg] *n* œuf *m*; **hard-boiled/soft-boiled ~** œuf dur/à la coque; **eggcup** *n* coquetier *m*; **egg plant** (*us*) *n* aubergine *f*; **eggshell** *n* coquille *f* d'œuf; **egg white** *n* blanc *m* d'œuf; **egg yolk** *n* jaune *m* d'œuf

ego ['iːgəu] *n* (*self-esteem*) amour-propre *m*; (*Psych*) moi *m*

Egypt ['iːdʒɪpt] *n* Égypte *f*; **Egyptian** [ɪ'dʒɪpʃən] *adj* égyptien(ne) ▷ *n* Égyptien(ne)

Eiffel Tower ['aɪfəl-] *n* tour *f* Eiffel

eight [eɪt] *num* huit; **eighteen** *num* dix-huit; **eighteenth** *num* dix-huitième; **eighth** *num* huitième; **eightieth** ['eɪtɪɪθ] *num* quatre-vingtième

eighty ['eɪtɪ] *num* quatre-vingt(s)

Eire ['ɛərə] *n* République *f* d'Irlande

either ['aɪðəʳ] *adj* l'un ou l'autre; (*both, each*) chaque ▷ *pron*: **~ (of them)** l'un ou l'autre ▷ *adv* non plus ▷ *conj*: **~ good or bad** soit bon soit mauvais; **on ~ side** de chaque côté; **I don't like ~** je n'aime ni l'un ni l'autre; **no, I don't ~** moi non plus; **which bike do you want? - ~ will do** quel vélo voulez-vous? - n'importe lequel; **answer with ~ yes or no** répondez par oui ou par non

eject [ɪ'dʒɛkt] vt (tenant etc) expulser; (object) éjecter

elaborate adj [ɪ'læbərɪt] compliqué(e), recherché(e), minutieux(-euse) ▷ vb [ɪ'læbəreɪt] ▷ vt élaborer ▷ vi entrer dans les détails

elastic [ɪ'læstɪk] adj, n élastique (m); **elastic band** n (BRIT) élastique m

elbow ['ɛlbəu] n coude m

elder ['ɛldəʳ] adj aîné(e) ▷ n (tree) sureau m; **one's ~s** ses aînés; **elderly** adj âgé(e) ▷ npl: **the elderly** les personnes âgées

eldest ['ɛldɪst] adj, n: **the ~ (child)** l'aîné(e) (des enfants)

elect [ɪ'lɛkt] vt élire; (choose): **to ~ to do** choisir de faire ▷ adj: **the president ~** le président désigné; **election** [ɪ'lɛkʃən] n élection f; **electoral** adj électoral(e); **electorate** n électorat m

electric [ɪ'lɛktrɪk] adj électrique; **electrical** adj électrique; **electric blanket** n couverture chauffante; **electric fire** n (BRIT) radiateur m électrique; **electrician** [ɪlɛk'trɪʃən] n électricien m; **electricity** [ɪlɛk'trɪsɪtɪ] n électricité f; **electric shock** n choc m or décharge f électrique; **electrify** [ɪ'lɛktrɪfaɪ] vt (Rail) électrifier; (audience) électriser

electronic [ɪlɛk'trɔnɪk] adj électronique; **electronic mail** n courrier m électronique; **electronics** n électronique f

elegance ['ɛlɪgəns] n élégance f

elegant ['ɛlɪgənt] adj élégant(e)

element ['ɛlɪmənt] n (gen) élément m; (of heater, kettle etc) résistance f

elementary [ɛlɪ'mɛntərɪ] adj élémentaire; (school, education) primaire; **elementary school** n (US) école f primaire

elephant ['ɛlɪfənt] n éléphant m

elevate ['ɛlɪveɪt] vt élever

elevator ['ɛlɪveɪtəʳ] n (in warehouse etc) élévateur m, monte-charge m inv; (US: lift) ascenseur m

eleven [ɪ'lɛvn] num onze; **eleventh** num onzième

eligible ['ɛlɪdʒəbl] adj éligible; (for membership) admissible; **an ~ young man** un beau parti; **to be ~ for sth** remplir les conditions requises pour qch

eliminate [ɪ'lɪmɪneɪt] vt éliminer

elm [ɛlm] n orme m

eloquent ['ɛləkwənt] adj éloquent(e)

else [ɛls] adv: **something ~** quelque chose d'autre, autre chose; **somewhere ~** ailleurs, autre part; **everywhere ~** partout ailleurs; **everyone ~** tous les autres; **nothing ~** rien d'autre; **where ~?** à quel autre endroit?; **little ~** pas grand-chose d'autre; **elsewhere** adv ailleurs, autre part

elusive [ɪ'lu:sɪv] adj insaisissable

e-mail ['i:meɪl] n abbr (= electronic mail) e-mail m, courriel m ▷ vt: **to ~ sb** envoyer un e-mail ou un courriel à qn; **e-mail address** n adresse f e-mail

embankment [ɪm'bæŋkmənt] n (of road, railway) remblai m, talus m; (of river) berge f, quai m; (dyke) digue f

embargo, embargoes [ɪm'bɑ:gəu] n (Comm, Naut) embargo m; (prohibition) interdiction f

embark [ɪm'bɑ:k] vi embarquer ▷ vt embarquer; **to ~ on** (journey etc) commencer, entreprendre; (fig) se lancer or s'embarquer dans

embarrass [ɪm'bærəs] vt embarrasser, gêner; **embarrassed** adj gêné(e); **embarrassing** adj gênant(e), embarrassant(e); **embarrassment** n embarras m, gêne f; (embarrassing thing, person) source f d'embarras

embassy ['ɛmbəsɪ] n ambassade f

embrace [ɪm'breɪs] vt embrasser, étreindre; (include) embrasser ▷ vi s'embrasser, s'étreindre ▷ n étreinte f

embroider [ɪm'brɔɪdəʳ] vt broder; **embroidery** n broderie f

embryo ['ɛmbrɪəu] n (also fig) embryon m

emerald ['ɛmərəld] n émeraude f

emerge [ɪ'mə:dʒ] vi apparaître; (from room, car) surgir; (from sleep, imprisonment) sortir

emergency [ɪ'mə:dʒənsɪ] n (crisis) cas m d'urgence; (Med) urgence f; **in an ~** en cas d'urgence; **state of ~** état m d'urgence; **emergency brake** (us) n frein m à main; **emergency exit** n sortie f de secours; **emergency landing** n atterrissage forcé; **emergency room** n (us: Med) urgences fpl; **emergency services** npl: **the emergency services** (fire, police, ambulance) les services mpl d'urgence

emigrate ['ɛmɪgreɪt] vi émigrer; **emigration** [ɛmɪ'greɪʃən] n émigration f

eminent ['ɛmɪnənt] adj éminent(e)

emissions [ɪ'mɪʃənz] npl émissions fpl

emit [ɪ'mɪt] vt émettre

emotion [ɪ'məuʃən] n sentiment m; **emotional** adj (person) émotif(-ive), très sensible; (needs) affectif(-ive); (scene) émouvant(e); (tone, speech) qui fait appel aux sentiments

emperor ['ɛmpərər] n empereur m

emphasis (pl **-ases**) ['ɛmfəsɪs, -si:z] n accent m; **to lay** or **place ~ on sth** (fig) mettre l'accent sur, insister sur

emphasize ['ɛmfəsaɪz] vt (syllable, word, point) appuyer or insister sur; (feature) souligner, accentuer

empire ['ɛmpaɪər] n empire m

employ [ɪm'plɔɪ] vt employer; **employee** [ɪmplɔɪ'i:] n employé(e); **employer** n employeur(-euse); **employment** n emploi m; **employment agency** n agence for bureau m de placement

empower [ɪm'pauər] vt: **to ~ sb to do** autoriser or habiliter qn à faire

empress ['ɛmprɪs] n impératrice f

emptiness ['ɛmptɪnɪs] n vide m; (of area) aspect m désertique

empty ['ɛmptɪ] adj vide; (street, area) désert(e); (threat, promise) en l'air, vain(e) ▷ vt vider ▷ vi se vider; (liquid) s'écouler; **empty-handed** adj les mains vides

EMU n abbr (= European Monetary Union) UME f

emulsion [ɪ'mʌlʃən] n émulsion f; (also: ~ paint) peinture mate

enable [ɪ'neɪbl] vt: **to ~ sb to do** permettre à qn de faire

enamel [ɪ'næməl] n émail m; (also: ~ paint) (peinture f) laque f

enchanting [ɪn'tʃɑ:ntɪŋ] adj ravissant(e), enchanteur(-eresse)

encl. abbr (on letters etc: = enclosed) ci-joint(e); (= enclosure) PJ f

enclose [ɪn'kləuz] vt (land) clôturer; (space, object) entourer; (letter etc): **to ~ (with)** joindre (à); **please find ~d** veuillez trouver ci-joint

enclosure [ɪn'kləuʒər] n enceinte f

encore [ɔŋ'kɔ:r] excl, n bis (m)

encounter [ɪn'kauntər] n rencontre f ▷ vt rencontrer

encourage [ɪn'kʌrɪdʒ] vt encourager; **encouragement** n encouragement m

encouraging [ɪn'kʌrɪdʒɪŋ] adj encourageant(e)

encyclop(a)edia [ɛnsaɪkləu'pi:dɪə] n encyclopédie f

end [ɛnd] n fin f; (of table, street, rope etc) bout m, extrémité f ▷ vt terminer; (also: **bring to an ~**, **put an ~ to**) mettre fin à ▷ vi se terminer, finir; **in the ~** finalement; **on ~** (object) debout, dressé(e); **to stand on ~** (hair) se dresser sur la tête; **for hours on ~** pendant des heures (et des heures); **end up** vi: **to ~ up in** (condition) finir or se terminer par; (place) finir or aboutir à

endanger [ɪn'deɪndʒər] vt mettre en danger; **an ~ed species** une espèce en voie de disparition

endearing [ɪn'dɪərɪŋ] adj attachant(e)

endeavour (us **endeavor**) [ɪn'dɛvər] n effort m; (attempt) tentative f ▷ vt: **to ~ to do** tenter or s'efforcer de faire

ending ['ɛndɪŋ] n dénouement m, conclusion f; (Ling) terminaison f

endless ['ɛndlɪs] adj sans fin, interminable

endorse [ɪn'dɔːs] vt (cheque) endosser; (approve) appuyer, approuver, sanctionner; **endorsement** n (approval) appui m, aval m; (BRIT: on driving licence) contravention f (portée au permis de conduire)

endurance [ɪn'djuərəns] n endurance f

endure [ɪn'djuəʳ] vt (bear) supporter, endurer ▷ vi (last) durer

enemy ['ɛnəmɪ] adj, n ennemi(e)

energetic [ɛnə'dʒɛtɪk] adj énergique; (activity) très actif(-ive), qui fait se dépenser (physiquement)

energy ['ɛnədʒɪ] n énergie f

enforce [ɪn'fɔːs] vt (law) appliquer, faire respecter

engaged [ɪn'geɪdʒd] adj (BRIT: busy, in use) occupé(e); (betrothed) fiancé(e); **to get ~** se fiancer; **the line's ~** la ligne est occupée; **engaged tone** n (BRIT Tel) tonalité f occupé inv

engagement [ɪn'geɪdʒmənt] n (undertaking) obligation f, engagement m; (appointment) rendez-vous m inv; (to marry) fiançailles fpl; **engagement ring** n bague f de fiançailles

engaging [ɪn'geɪdʒɪŋ] adj engageant(e), attirant(e)

engine ['ɛndʒɪn] n (Aut) moteur m; (Rail) locomotive f

> Be careful not to translate engine by the French word engin.

engineer [ɛndʒɪ'nɪəʳ] n ingénieur m; (BRIT: repairer) dépanneur m; (Navy, us Rail) mécanicien m; **engineering** n engineering m, ingénierie f; (of bridges, ships) génie m; (of machine) mécanique f

England ['ɪŋglənd] n Angleterre f

English ['ɪŋglɪʃ] adj anglais(e) ▷ n (Ling) anglais m; **the ~** npl les Anglais; **English Channel** n: **the English Channel** la Manche; **Englishman** (irreg) n Anglais m; **Englishwoman** (irreg) n Anglaise f

engrave [ɪn'greɪv] vt graver

engraving [ɪn'greɪvɪŋ] n gravure f

enhance [ɪn'hɑːns] vt rehausser, mettre en valeur

enjoy [ɪn'dʒɔɪ] vt aimer, prendre plaisir à; (have benefit of: health, fortune) jouir de; (: success) connaître; **to ~ o.s.** s'amuser; **enjoyable** adj agréable; **enjoyment** n plaisir m

enlarge [ɪn'lɑːdʒ] vt accroître; (Phot) agrandir ▷ vi: **to ~ on** (subject) s'étendre sur; **enlargement** n (Phot) agrandissement m

enlist [ɪn'lɪst] vt recruter; (support) s'assurer ▷ vi s'engager

enormous [ɪ'nɔːməs] adj énorme

enough [ɪ'nʌf] adj: **~ time/books** assez or suffisamment de temps/livres ▷ adv: **big ~** assez or suffisamment grand ▷ pron: **have you got ~?** (en) avez-vous assez?; **~ to eat** assez à manger; **that's ~, thanks** cela suffit or c'est assez, merci; **I've had ~ of him** j'en ai assez de lui; **he has not worked ~** il n'a pas assez or suffisamment travaillé, il n'a pas travaillé assez or suffisamment; **... which, funnily** or **oddly ~ ...** qui, chose curieuse

enquire [ɪn'kwaɪəʳ] vt, vi = **inquire**

enquiry [ɪn'kwaɪərɪ] n = **inquiry**

enrage [ɪn'reɪdʒ] vt mettre en fureur or en rage, rendre furieux(-euse)

enrich [ɪn'rɪtʃ] vt enrichir

enrol (us **enroll**) [ɪn'rəul] vt inscrire ▷ vi s'inscrire; **enrolment** (us **enrollment**) n inscription f

en route [ɔn'ruːt] adv en route, en chemin

en suite ['ɔnswiːt] adj: **with ~ bathroom** avec salle de bains en attenante

ensure [ɪn'ʃuəʳ] vt assurer, garantir

entail [ɪn'teɪl] vt entraîner, nécessiter

enter ['ɛntəʳ] vt (room) entrer dans, pénétrer dans; (club, army) entrer à; (competition) s'inscrire à or pour; (sb for a competition) (faire) inscrire; (write down) inscrire, noter; (Comput) entrer, introduire ▷ vi entrer

enterprise ['ɛntəpraɪz] n (company, undertaking) entreprise f; (initiative) (esprit *m* d')initiative *f*; **free ~** libre entreprise; **private ~** entreprise privée; **enterprising** *adj* entreprenant(e), dynamique; (*scheme*) audacieux(-euse)

entertain [ɛntə'teɪn] *vt* amuser, distraire; (*invite*) recevoir (à dîner); (*idea, plan*) envisager; **entertainer** *n* artiste *m/f* de variétés; **entertaining** *adj* amusant(e), distrayant(e); **entertainment** *n* (*amusement*) distraction *f*, divertissement *m*, amusement *m*; (*show*) spectacle *m*

enthusiasm [ɪn'θu:zɪæzəm] *n* enthousiasme *m*

enthusiast [ɪn'θu:zɪæst] *n* enthousiaste *m/f*; **enthusiastic** [ɪnθu:zɪ'æstɪk] *adj* enthousiaste; **to be enthusiastic about** être enthousiasmé(e) par

entire [ɪn'taɪə*r*] *adj* (tout) entier(-ère); **entirely** *adv* entièrement, complètement

entitle [ɪn'taɪtl] *vt*: **to ~ sb to sth** donner droit à qch à qn; **entitled** *adj* (*book*) intitulé(e); **to be entitled to do** avoir le droit de faire

entrance *n* ['ɛntrns] entrée *f* ▷ *vt* [ɪn'trɑːns] enchanter, ravir; **where's the ~?** où est l'entrée?; **to gain ~ to** (*university etc*) être admis à; **entrance examination** *n* examen *m* d'entrée or d'admission; **entrance fee** *n* (*to museum etc*) prix *m* d'entrée; (*to join club etc*) droit *m* d'inscription; **entrance ramp** *n* (*US Aut*) bretelle *f* d'accès; **entrant** *n* (*in race etc*) participant(e), concurrent(e); (*BRIT: in exam*) candidat(e)

entrepreneur ['ɔntrəprə'nə:*r*] *n* entrepreneur *m*

entrust [ɪn'trʌst] *vt*: **to ~ sth to** confier qch à

entry ['ɛntrɪ] *n* entrée *f*; (*in register, diary*) inscription *f*; **"no ~"** "défense d'entrer", "entrée interdite"; (*Aut*) "sens interdit"; **entry phone** *n* (*BRIT*) interphone *m* (*à l'entrée d'un immeuble*)

envelope ['ɛnvələup] *n* enveloppe *f*

envious ['ɛnvɪəs] *adj* envieux(-euse)

environment [ɪn'vaɪrnmənt] *n* (*social, moral*) milieu *m*; (*natural world*): **the ~** l'environnement *m*; **environmental** [ɪnvaɪərn'mɛntl] *adj* (*of surroundings*) du milieu; (*issue, disaster*) écologique; **environmentally** [ɪnvaɪərn'mɛntlɪ] *adv*: **environmentally sound/friendly** qui ne nuit pas à l'environnement

envisage [ɪn'vɪzɪdʒ] *vt* (*foresee*) prévoir

envoy ['ɛnvɔɪ] *n* envoyé(e); (*diplomat*) ministre *m* plénipotentiaire

envy ['ɛnvɪ] *n* envie *f* ▷ *vt* envier; **to ~ sb sth** envier qch à qn

epic ['ɛpɪk] *n* épopée *f* ▷ *adj* épique

epidemic [ɛpɪ'dɛmɪk] *n* épidémie *f*

epilepsy ['ɛpɪlɛpsɪ] *n* épilepsie *f*; **epileptic** *adj, n* épileptique *m/f*; **epileptic fit** *n* crise *f* d'épilepsie

episode ['ɛpɪsəud] *n* épisode *m*

equal ['i:kwl] *adj* égal(e) ▷ *vt* égaler; **~ to** (*task*) à la hauteur de; **equality** [i:'kwɔlɪtɪ] *n* égalité *f*; **equalize** *vt, vi* (*Sport*) égaliser; **equally** *adv* également; (*share*) en parts égales; (*treat*) de la même façon; (*pay*) autant; (*just as*) tout aussi

equation [ɪ'kweɪʃən] *n* (*Math*) équation *f*

equator [ɪ'kweɪtə*r*] *n* équateur *m*

equip [ɪ'kwɪp] *vt* équiper; **to ~ sb/sth with** équiper or munir qn/qch de; **equipment** *n* équipement *m*; (*electrical etc*) appareillage *m*, installation *f*

equivalent [ɪ'kwɪvələnt] *adj* équivalent(e) ▷ *n* équivalent *m*; **to be ~ to** équivaloir à, être équivalent(e) à

ER *abbr* (*BRIT*: = Elizabeth Regina) la reine Élisabeth; (*US: Med*: = emergency room) urgences *fpl*

era ['ɪərə] *n* ère *f*, époque *f*

erase [ɪ'reɪz] *vt* effacer; **eraser** *n* gomme *f*

erect [ɪ'rɛkt] *adj* droit(e) ▷ *vt* construire; (*monument*) ériger, élever; (*tent etc*) dresser; **erection** [ɪ'rɛkʃən] *n* (*Physiol*) érection *f*; (*of building*) construction f

ERM n abbr (= Exchange Rate Mechanism) mécanisme m des taux de change

erode [ɪ'rəud] vt éroder; (metal) ronger

erosion [ɪ'rəuʒən] n érosion f

erotic [ɪ'rɔtɪk] adj érotique

errand ['ɛrnd] n course f, commission f

erratic [ɪ'rætɪk] adj irrégulier(-ière), inconstant(e)

error ['ɛrər] n erreur f

erupt [ɪ'rʌpt] vi entrer en éruption; (fig) éclater; **eruption** [ɪ'rʌpʃən] n éruption f; (of anger, violence) explosion f

escalate ['ɛskəleɪt] vi s'intensifier; (costs) monter en flèche

escalator ['ɛskəleɪtər] n escalier roulant

escape [ɪ'skeɪp] n évasion f, fuite f; (of gas etc) fuite ▷ vi s'échapper, fuir; (from jail) s'évader; (fig) s'en tirer; (leak) s'échapper ▷ vt échapper à; **to ~ from** (person) échapper à; (place) s'échapper de; (fig) fuir; **his name ~s me** son nom m'échappe

escort vt [ɪ'skɔːt] escorter ▷ n ['ɛskɔːt] (Mil) escorte f

especially [ɪ'spɛʃlɪ] adv (particularly) particulièrement; (above all) surtout

espionage ['ɛspɪənɑːʒ] n espionnage m

essay ['ɛseɪ] n (Scol) dissertation f; (Literature) essai m

essence ['ɛsns] n essence f; (Culin) extrait m

essential [ɪ'sɛnʃl] adj essentiel(le); (basic) fondamental(e); **essentials** npl éléments essentiels; **essentially** adv essentiellement

establish [ɪ'stæblɪʃ] vt établir; (business) fonder, créer; (one's power etc) asseoir, affermir; **establishment** n établissement m; (founding) création f; (institution) établissement; **the Establishment** les pouvoirs établis, l'ordre établi

estate [ɪ'steɪt] n (land) domaine m, propriété f; (Law) biens mpl, succession f; (BRIT: also: **housing ~**)

lotissement m; **estate agent** n (BRIT) agent immobilier; **estate car** n (BRIT) break m

estimate n ['ɛstɪmət] estimation f; (Comm) devis m ▷ vb ['ɛstɪmeɪt] ▷ vt estimer

etc abbr (= et cetera) etc

eternal [ɪ'tɜːnl] adj éternel(le)

eternity [ɪ'tɜːnɪtɪ] n éternité f

ethical ['ɛθɪkl] adj moral(e); **ethics** ['ɛθɪks] n éthique f ▷ npl moralité f

Ethiopia [iːθɪ'əupɪə] n Éthiopie f

ethnic ['ɛθnɪk] adj ethnique; (clothes, food) folklorique, exotique, propre aux minorités ethniques non-occidentales; **ethnic minority** n minorité f ethnique

e-ticket ['iːtɪkɪt] n billet m électronique

etiquette ['ɛtɪkɛt] n convenances fpl, étiquette f

EU n abbr (= European Union) UE f

euro ['juərəu] n (currency) euro m

Europe ['juərəp] n Europe f; **European** [juərə'piːən] adj européen(ne) ▷ n Européen(ne); **European Community** n Communauté européenne; **European Union** n Union européenne

Eurostar® ['juərəustɑːr] n Eurostar® m

evacuate [ɪ'vækjueɪt] vt évacuer

evade [ɪ'veɪd] vt échapper à; (question etc) éluder; (duties) se dérober à

evaluate [ɪ'væljueɪt] vt évaluer

evaporate [ɪ'væpəreɪt] vi s'évaporer; (fig: hopes, fear) s'envoler; (anger) se dissiper

eve [iːv] n: **on the ~ of** à la veille de

even ['iːvn] adj (level, smooth) régulier(-ière); (equal) égal(e); (number) pair(e) ▷ adv même; **~ if** même si + indic; **~ though** alors même que + cond; **~ more** encore plus; **~ faster** encore plus vite; **~ so** quand même; **not ~** pas même; **~ he was there** même lui était là; **~ on Sundays** même le dimanche; **to get ~ with sb** prendre sa revanche sur qn

evening ['iːvnɪŋ] n soir m; (as duration,

event) soirée f; **in the ~** le soir; **evening class** n cours m du soir; **evening dress** n (man's) tenue f de soirée, smoking m; (woman's) robe f de soirée

event [ɪ'vɛnt] n événement m; (Sport) épreuve f; **in the ~ of** en cas de; **eventful** adj mouvementé(e)

eventual [ɪ'vɛntʃuəl] adj final(e)

> Be careful not to translate *eventual* by the French word *éventuel*.

eventually [ɪ'vɛntʃuəlɪ] adv finalement

> Be careful not to translate *eventually* by the French word *éventuellement*.

ever ['ɛvə'] adv jamais; (at all times) toujours; (in questions): **why ~ not?** mais enfin, pourquoi pas?; **the best ~** le meilleur qu'on ait jamais vu; **have you ~ seen it?** l'as-tu déjà vu?, as-tu eu l'occasion or t'est-il arrivé de le voir?; **~ since** (as adv) depuis; (as conj) depuis que; **~ so pretty** si joli; **evergreen** n arbre m à feuilles persistantes

KEYWORD

every ['ɛvrɪ] adj 1 (each) chaque; **every one of them** tous (sans exception); **every shop in town was closed** tous les magasins en ville étaient fermés
2 (all possible) tous (toutes) les; **I gave you every assistance** j'ai fait tout mon possible pour vous aider; **I have every confidence in him** j'ai entièrement or pleinement confiance en lui; **we wish you every success** nous vous souhaitons beaucoup de succès
3 (showing recurrence) tous les; **every day** tous les jours, chaque jour; **every other car** une voiture sur deux; **every other/third day** tous les deux/trois jours; **every now and then** de temps en temps; **everybody = everyone**; **everyday** adj (expression) courant(e), d'usage courant; (use) courant; (clothes, life) de tous les jours; (occurrence,

problem) quotidien(ne); **everyone** pron tout le monde, tous pl; **everything** pron tout; **everywhere** adv partout; **everywhere you go you meet ...** où qu'on aille, on rencontre ...

evict [ɪ'vɪkt] vt expulser

evidence ['ɛvɪdns] n (proof) preuve(s) f(pl); (of witness) témoignage m; (sign): **to show ~ of** donner des signes de; **to give ~** témoigner, déposer

evident ['ɛvɪdnt] adj évident(e); **evidently** adv de toute évidence; (apparently) apparemment

evil ['iːvl] adj mauvais(e) ▷ n mal m

evoke [ɪ'vəʊk] vt évoquer

evolution [iːvə'luːʃən] n évolution f

evolve [ɪ'vɒlv] vt élaborer ▷ vi évoluer, se transformer

ewe [juː] n brebis f

ex [ɛks] n (inf): **my ex** mon ex

ex- [ɛks] prefix ex-

exact [ɪg'zækt] adj exact(e) ▷ vt: **to ~ sth (from)** (signature, confession) extorquer qch (à); (apology) exiger qch (de); **exactly** adv exactement

exaggerate [ɪg'zædʒəreɪt] vt, vi exagérer; **exaggeration** [ɪgzædʒə'reɪʃən] n exagération f

exam [ɪg'zæm] n abbr (Scol) = **examination**

examination [ɪgzæmɪ'neɪʃən] n (Scol, Med) examen m; **to take** or **sit an ~** (BRIT) passer un examen

examine [ɪg'zæmɪn] vt (gen) examiner; (Scol, Law: person) interroger; **examiner** n examinateur(-trice)

example [ɪg'zaːmpl] n exemple m; **for ~** par exemple

exasperated [ɪg'zaːspəreɪtɪd] adj exaspéré(e)

excavate ['ɛkskəveɪt] vt (site) fouiller, excaver; (object) mettre au jour

exceed [ɪk'siːd] vt dépasser; (one's powers) outrepasser; **exceedingly** adv extrêmement

excel [ɪk'sɛl] vi exceller ▷ vt surpasser; **to ~ o.s.** se surpasser

excellence [ˈɛksələns] n excellence f
excellent [ˈɛksələnt] adj excellent(e)
except [ɪkˈsɛpt] prep (also: **~ for, ~ing**)
sauf, excepté, à l'exception de ▷ vt
excepter; **~ if/when** sauf si/quand;
~ that excepté que, si ce n'est que;
exception [ɪkˈsɛpʃən] n exception
f; **to take exception to** s'offusquer
de; **exceptional** [ɪkˈsɛpʃənl] adj
exceptionnel(le); **exceptionally**
[ɪkˈsɛpʃənəlɪ] adv exceptionnellement
excerpt [ˈɛksəːpt] n extrait m
excess [ɪkˈsɛs] n excès m; **excess
baggage** n excédent m de bagages;
excessive adj excessif(-ive)
exchange [ɪksˈtʃeɪndʒ] n échange m;
(also: **telephone ~**) central m ▷ vt: **to ~
(for)** échanger (contre); **could I ~ this,
please?** est-ce que je peux échanger
ceci, s'il vous plaît?; **exchange rate** n
taux m de change
excite [ɪkˈsaɪt] vt exciter; **excited** adj
(tout (toute)) excité(e); **to get excited**
s'exciter; **excitement** n excitation f;
exciting adj passionnant(e)
exclaim [ɪkˈskleɪm] vi s'exclamer;
exclamation [ɛkskləˈmeɪʃən] n
exclamation f; **exclamation mark** n
(US **exclamation point**) n point m
d'exclamation
exclude [ɪkˈskluːd] vt exclure
excluding [ɪkˈskluːdɪŋ] prep: **~ VAT** la
TVA non comprise
exclusion [ɪkˈskluːʒən] n exclusion f
exclusive [ɪkˈskluːsɪv] adj
exclusif(-ive), (club, district) sélect(e);
(item of news) en exclusivité; **~ of VAT**
TVA non comprise; **exclusively** adv
exclusivement
excruciating [ɪkˈskruːʃɪeɪtɪŋ]
adj (pain) atroce, déchirant(e);
(embarrassing) pénible
excursion [ɪkˈskəːʃən] n excursion f
excuse n [ɪkˈskjuːs] excuse f ▷ vt
[ɪkˈskjuːz] (forgive) excuser; **to ~ sb
from** (activity) dispenser qn de; **~ me!**
excusez-moi!, pardon!; **now if you
will ~ me, ...** maintenant, si vous (le)

permettez …
ex-directory [ˈɛksdɪˈrɛktərɪ] adj (BRIT)
sur la liste rouge
execute [ˈɛksɪkjuːt] vt exécuter;
execution [ɛksɪˈkjuːʃən] n exécution f
executive [ɪgˈzɛkjutɪv] n (person) cadre
m; (managing group) bureau m; (Pol)
exécutif m ▷ adj exécutif(-ive); (position,
job) de cadre
exempt [ɪgˈzɛmpt] adj: **~ from**
exempté(e) or dispensé(e) de ▷ vt: **to ~
sb from** exempter or dispenser qn de
exercise [ˈɛksəsaɪz] n exercice m ▷ vt
exercer; (patience etc) faire preuve de;
(dog) promener ▷ vi (also: **to take ~**)
prendre de l'exercice; **exercise book**
n cahier m
exert [ɪgˈzəːt] vt exercer, employer; **to
~ o.s.** se dépenser; **exertion** [ɪgˈzəːʃən]
n effort m
exhale [ɛksˈheɪl] vt exhaler ▷ vi expirer
exhaust [ɪgˈzɔːst] n (also: **~ fumes**)
gaz mpl d'échappement; (also: **~ pipe**)
tuyau m d'échappement ▷ vt épuiser;
exhausted adj épuisé(e); **exhaustion**
[ɪgˈzɔːstʃən] n épuisement m; **nervous
exhaustion** fatigue nerveuse
exhibit [ɪgˈzɪbɪt] n (Art) pièce f or objet
m exposé(e); (Law) pièce à conviction
▷ vt (Art) exposer; (courage, skill) faire
preuve de; **exhibition** [ɛksɪˈbɪʃən] n
exposition f
exhilarating [ɪgˈzɪləreɪtɪŋ] adj
grisant(e), stimulant(e)
exile [ˈɛksaɪl] n exil m; (person) exilé(e)
▷ vt exiler
exist [ɪgˈzɪst] vi exister; **existence** n
existence f; **existing** adj actuel(le)
exit [ˈɛksɪt] n sortie f ▷ vi (Comput,
Theat) sortir; **where's the ~?** où est la
sortie?; **exit ramp** n (US Aut) bretelle
f d'accès
exotic [ɪgˈzɔtɪk] adj exotique
expand [ɪkˈspænd] vt (area) agrandir;
(quantity) accroître ▷ vi (trade, etc) se
développer, s'accroître; (gas, metal)
se dilater
expansion [ɪkˈspænʃən] n (territorial,

economic) expansion *f*; *(of trade, influence etc)* développement *m*; *(of production)* accroissement *m*; *(of population)* croissance *f*; *(of gas, metal)* expansion, dilatation *f*

expect [ɪk'spɛkt] *vt (anticipate)* s'attendre à, s'attendre à ce que + *sub*; *(count on)* compter sur, escompter; *(require)* demander, exiger; *(suppose)* supposer; *(await: also baby)* attendre ▷ *vi*: **to be ~ing** *(pregnant woman)* être enceinte; **expectation** [ɛkspɛk'teɪʃən] *n (hope)* attente *f*, espérance(s) *f(pl)*; *(belief)* attente

expedition [ɛkspə'dɪʃən] *n* expédition *f*

expel [ɪk'spɛl] *vt* chasser, expulser; *(Scol)* renvoyer, exclure

expenditure [ɪk'spɛndɪtʃər] *n (act of spending)* dépense *f*; *(money spent)* dépenses *fpl*

expense [ɪk'spɛns] *n (high cost)* coût *m*; *(spending)* dépense *f*, frais *mpl*; **expenses** *npl* frais *mpl*; **dépenses**; **at the ~ of** *(fig)* aux dépens de; **expense account** *n* (note *f* de) frais *mpl*

expensive [ɪk'spɛnsɪv] *adj* cher (chère), coûteux(-euse); **it's too ~** ça coûte trop cher

experience [ɪk'spɪərɪəns] *n* expérience *f* ▷ *vt* connaître; *(feeling)* éprouver; **experienced** *adj* expérimenté(e)

experiment [ɪk'spɛrɪmənt] *n* expérience *f* ▷ *vi* faire une expérience; **experimental** [ɪkspɛrɪ'mɛntl] *adj* expérimental(e)

expert ['ɛkspəːt] *adj* expert(e) ▷ *n* expert *m*; **expertise** [ɛkspəː'tiːz] *n* (grande) compétence

expire [ɪk'spaɪər] *vi* expirer; **expiry** *n* expiration *f*; **expiry date** *n* date *f* d'expiration; *(on label)* à utiliser avant …

explain [ɪk'spleɪn] *vt* expliquer; **explanation** [ɛksplə'neɪʃən] *n* explication *f*

explicit [ɪk'splɪsɪt] *adj* explicite; *(definite)* formel(le)

explode [ɪk'spləud] *vi* exploser

exploit *n* ['ɛksplɔɪt] exploit *m* ▷ *vt* [ɪk'splɔɪt] exploiter; **exploitation** [ɛksplɔɪ'teɪʃən] *n* exploitation *f*

explore [ɪk'splɔːr] *vt* explorer; *(possibilities)* étudier, examiner; **explorer** *n* explorateur(-trice)

explosion [ɪk'spləuʒən] *n* explosion *f*; **explosive** [ɪk'spləusɪv] *adj* explosif(-ive) ▷ *n* explosif *m*

export *vt* [ɛk'spɔːt] exporter ▷ *n* ['ɛkspɔːt] exportation *f* ▷ *cpd* d'exportation; **exporter** *n* exportateur *m*

expose [ɪk'spəuz] *vt* exposer; *(unmask)* démasquer, dévoiler; **exposed** *adj (land, house)* exposé(e); **exposure** [ɪk'spəuʒər] *n* exposition *f*; *(publicity)* couverture *f*; *(Phot: speed)* (temps *m* de) pose *f*; *(: shot)* pose; **to die of exposure** *(Med)* mourir de froid

express [ɪk'sprɛs] *adj (definite)* formel(le), exprès(-esse); *(BRIT: letter etc)* exprès *inv* ▷ *n (train)* rapide *m* ▷ *vt* exprimer; **expression** [ɪk'sprɛʃən] *n* expression *f*; **expressway** *n (US)* voie *f* express (à plusieurs files)

exquisite [ɛk'skwɪzɪt] *adj* exquis(e)

extend [ɪk'stɛnd] *vt (visit, street)* prolonger, remettre; *(building)* agrandir; *(offer)* présenter, offrir; *(hand, arm)* tendre ▷ *vi (land)* s'étendre; **extension** *n (of visit, street)* prolongation *f*; *(building)* annexe *f*; *(telephone: in offices)* poste *m*; *(: in private house)* téléphone *m* supplémentaire; **extension cable**, **extension lead** *n (Elec)* rallonge *f*; **extensive** *adj* étendu(e), vaste; *(damage, alterations)* considérable; *(inquiries)* approfondi(e)

extent [ɪk'stɛnt] *n* étendue *f*; **to some ~** dans une certaine mesure; **to the ~ of …** au point de …; **to what ~?** dans quelle mesure?, jusqu'à quel point?; **to such an ~ that …** à tel point que …

exterior [ɛk'stɪərɪər] *adj* extérieur(e) ▷ *n* extérieur *m*

external [ɛk'stəːnl] *adj* externe

xtinct [ɪkˈstɪŋkt] adj (volcano) éteint(e); (species) disparu(e); **extinction** n extinction f

xtinguish [ɪkˈstɪŋgwɪʃ] vt éteindre

xtra [ˈɛkstrə] adj supplémentaire, de plus ▷ adv (in addition) en plus ▷ n supplément m; (perk) à-coté m; (Cine, Theat) figurant(e)

xtract vt [ɪkˈstrækt] extraire; (tooth) arracher; (money, promise) soutirer ▷ n [ˈɛkstrækt] extrait m

xtradite [ˈɛkstrədaɪt] vt extrader

xtraordinary [ɪkˈstrɔːdnrɪ] adj extraordinaire

xtravagance [ɪkˈstrævəgəns] n (excessive spending) prodigalités fpl; (thing bought) folie f, dépense excessive; **extravagant** adj extravagant(e); (in spending: person) prodigue, dépensier(-ière); (: tastes) dispendieux(-euse)

xtreme [ɪkˈstriːm] adj, n extrême (m); **extremely** adv extrêmement

xtremist [ɪkˈstriːmɪst] adj, n extrémiste m/f

xtrovert [ˈɛkstrəvəːt] n extraverti(e)

ye [aɪ] n œil m ((yeux) pl); (of needle) trou m, chas m ▷ vt examiner; **to keep an ~ on** surveiller; **eyeball** n globe m oculaire; **eyebrow** n sourcil m; **eyedrops** npl gouttes fpl pour les yeux; **eyelash** n cil m; **eyelid** n paupière f; **eyeliner** n eye-liner m; **eyeshadow** n ombre f à paupières; **eyesight** n vue f; **eye witness** n témoin m oculaire

F [ɛf] n (Mus): **F** fa m

fabric [ˈfæbrɪk] n tissu m

fabulous [ˈfæbjuləs] adj fabuleux(-euse); (inf: super) formidable, sensationnel(le)

face [feɪs] n visage m, figure f; (expression) air m; (of clock) cadran m; (of cliff) paroi f; (of mountain) face f; (of building) façade f ▷ vt faire face à; (facts etc) accepter; **~ down** (person) à plat ventre; (card) face en dessous; **to lose/save ~** perdre/sauver la face; **to pull a ~** faire une grimace; **in the ~ of** (difficulties etc) face à, devant; **on the ~ of it** à première vue; **~ to ~** face à face; **face up to** vt fus faire face à, affronter; **face cloth** n (BRIT) gant m de toilette; **face pack** n (BRIT) masque m (de beauté)

facial [ˈfeɪʃl] adj facial(e) ▷ n soin complet du visage

facilitate [fəˈsɪlɪteɪt] vt faciliter

facilities [fəˈsɪlɪtɪz] npl installations fpl, équipement m; **credit ~** facilités

de paiement
fact [fækt] n fait m; **in ~** en fait
faction ['fækʃən] n faction f
factor ['fæktə^r] n facteur m; (of sun cream) indice m (de protection); **I'd like a ~ 15 suntan lotion** je voudrais une crème solaire d'indice 15
factory ['fæktəri] n usine f, fabrique f
factual ['fæktjuəl] adj basé(e) sur les faits
faculty ['fækəlti] n faculté f; (US: teaching staff) corps enseignant
fad [fæd] n (personal) manie f; (craze) engouement m
fade [feid] vi se décolorer, passer; (light, sound) s'affaiblir; (flower) se faner; **fade away** vi (sound) s'affaiblir
fag [fæg] n (BRIT inf: cigarette) clope f
Fahrenheit ['fɑːrənhait] n Fahrenheit m inv
fail [feil] vt (exam) échouer à; (candidate) recaler; (subj: courage, memory) faire défaut à ▷ vi échouer; (eyesight, health, light: also: **be ~ing**) baisser, s'affaiblir; (brakes) lâcher; **to ~ to do sth** (neglect) négliger de or ne pas faire qch; (be unable) ne pas arriver or parvenir à faire qch; **without ~** à coup sûr; sans faute; **failing** n défaut m ▷ prep faute de; **failing that** à défaut, sinon; **failure** ['feiljə^r] n échec m; (person) raté(e); (mechanical etc) défaillance f
faint [feint] adj faible; (recollection) vague; (mark) à peine visible ▷ n évanouissement m ▷ vi s'évanouir; **to feel ~** défaillir; **faintest** adj: **I haven't the faintest idea** je n'en ai pas la moindre idée; **faintly** adv faiblement; (vaguely) vaguement
fair [feə^r] adj équitable, juste; (hair) blond(e); (skin, complexion) pâle, blanc (blanche); (weather) beau (belle); (good enough) assez bon(ne); (sizeable) considérable ▷ adv: **to play ~** jouer franc jeu ▷ n foire f; (BRIT: funfair) fête (foraine); **fairground** n champ m de foire; **fair-haired** adj (person) aux cheveux clairs, blond(e); **fairly** adv

(justly) équitablement; (quite) assez; **fair trade** n commerce m équitable; **fairway** n (Golf) fairway m
fairy ['feəri] n fée f; **fairy tale** n conte m de fées
faith [feiθ] n foi f; (trust) confiance f; (sect) culte m, religion f; **faithful** adj fidèle; **faithfully** adv fidèlement; **yours faithfully** (BRIT: in letters) veuillez agréer l'expression de mes salutations les plus distinguées
fake [feik] n (painting etc) faux m; (person) imposteur m ▷ adj faux (fausse) ▷ vt (emotions) simuler; (painting) faire un faux de
falcon ['fɔːlkən] n faucon m
fall [fɔːl] n chute f; (decrease) baisse f; (US: autumn) automne m ▷ vi (pt **fell**, pp **~en**) tomber; (price, temperature, dollar) baisser; **falls** npl (waterfall) chute f d'eau, cascade f; **to ~ flat** vi (on one's face) tomber de tout son long, s'étaler; (joke) tomber à plat; (plan) échouer; **fall apart** vi (object) tomber en morceaux; **fall down** vi (person) tomber; (building) s'effondrer, s'écrouler; **fall for** vt fus (trick) se laisser prendre à; (person) tomber amoureux(-euse) de; **fall off** vi tomber; (diminish) baisser, diminuer; **fall out** vi (friends etc) se brouiller; (hair, teeth) tomber; **fall over** vi tomber (par terre); **fall through** vi (plan, project) tomber à l'eau
fallen ['fɔːlən] pp of **fall**
fallout ['fɔːlaut] n retombées (radioactives)
false [fɔːls] adj faux (fausse); **under ~ pretences** sous un faux prétexte; **false alarm** n fausse alerte; **false teeth** npl (BRIT) fausses dents, dentier m
fame [feim] n renommée f, renom m
familiar [fə'miliə^r] adj familier(-ière); **to be ~ with sth** connaître qch; **familiarize** [fə'miliəraiz] vt: **to familiarize o.s. with** se familiariser avec
family ['fæmili] n famille f; **family doctor** n médecin m de famille; **family**

planning n planning familial
amine ['fæmɪn] n famine f
amous ['feɪməs] adj célèbre
an [fæn] n (folding) éventail m; (Elec) ventilateur m; (person) fan m, admirateur(-trice); (Sport) supporter m/f ▷ vt éventer; (fire, quarrel) attiser
anatic [fə'nætɪk] n fanatique m/f
an belt n courroie f de ventilateur
an club n fan-club m
ancy ['fænsɪ] n (whim) fantaisie f, envie f; (imagination) imagination f ▷ adj (luxury) de luxe; (elaborate: jewellery, packaging) fantaisie inv ▷ vt (feel like, want) avoir envie de; (imagine) imaginer; **to take a ~ to** se prendre d'affection pour; s'enticher de; **he fancies her** elle lui plaît; **fancy dress** n déguisement m, travesti m
an heater n (BRIT) radiateur soufflant
antasize ['fæntəsaɪz] vi fantasmer
antastic [fæn'tæstɪk] adj fantastique
antasy ['fæntəsɪ] n imagination f, fantaisie f; (unreality) fantasme m
anzine ['fænziːn] n fanzine m
AQ n abbr (= frequently asked question) FAQ f inv, faq f inv
ar [fɑːʳ] adj (distant) lointain(e), éloigné(e) ▷ adv loin; **the ~ side/end** l'autre côté/bout; **it's not ~ (from here)** ce n'est pas loin (d'ici); **~ away, ~ off** au loin, dans le lointain; **~ better** beaucoup mieux; **~ from** loin de; **by ~** de loin, de beaucoup; **go as ~ as the bridge** allez jusqu'au pont; **as ~ as I know** pour autant que je sache; **how ~ is it to ...?** combien y a-t-il jusqu'à ...?; **how ~ have you got with your work?** où en êtes-vous dans votre travail?
arce [fɑːs] n farce f
are [fɛəʳ] n (on trains, buses) prix m du billet; (in taxi) prix de la course; (food) table f, chère f; **half ~** demi-tarif; **full ~** plein tarif
ar East n: **the ~** l'Extrême-Orient m
arewell [fɛə'wɛl] excl, n adieu m
arm [fɑːm] n ferme f ▷ vt cultiver; **farmer** n fermier(-ière); **farmhouse**

n (maison f de) ferme f; **farming** n agriculture f; (of animals) élevage m; **farmyard** n cour f de ferme
far-reaching ['fɑː'riːtʃɪŋ] adj d'une grande portée
fart [fɑːt] (inf!) vi péter
farther ['fɑːðəʳ] adv plus loin ▷ adj plus eloigné(e), plus lointain(e)
farthest ['fɑːðɪst] superlative of **far**
fascinate ['fæsɪneɪt] vt fasciner, captiver; **fascinated** adj fasciné(e)
fascinating ['fæsɪneɪtɪŋ] adj fascinant(e)
fascination [fæsɪ'neɪʃən] n fascination f
fascist ['fæʃɪst] adj, n fasciste m/f
fashion ['fæʃən] n mode f; (manner) façon f, manière f ▷ vt façonner; **in ~** à la mode; **out of ~** démodé(e); **fashionable** adj à la mode; **fashion show** n défilé m de mannequins or de mode
fast [fɑːst] adj rapide; (clock): **to be ~** avancer; (dye, colour) grand or bon teint inv ▷ adv vite, rapidement; (stuck, held) solidement ▷ n jeûne m ▷ vi jeûner; **~ asleep** profondément endormi
fasten ['fɑːsn] vt attacher, fixer; (coat) attacher, fermer ▷ vi se fermer, s'attacher
fast food n fast food m, restauration f rapide
fat [fæt] adj gros(se) ▷ n graisse f; (on meat) gras m; (for cooking) matière grasse
fatal ['feɪtl] adj (mistake) fatal(e); (injury) mortel(le); **fatality** [fə'tælɪtɪ] n (road death etc) victime f, décès m; **fatally** adv fatalement; (injured) mortellement
fate [feɪt] n destin m; (of person) sort m
father ['fɑːðəʳ] n père m; **Father Christmas** n le Père Noël; **father-in-law** n beau-père m
fatigue [fə'tiːg] n fatigue f
fattening ['fætnɪŋ] adj (food) qui fait grossir
fatty ['fætɪ] adj (food) gras(se) ▷ n (inf) gros (grosse)

faucet ['fɔːsɪt] n (US) robinet m
fault [fɔːlt] n faute f; (defect) défaut m;
(Geo) faille f ▷ vt trouver des défauts à,
prendre en défaut; **it's my ~** c'est de ma
faute; **to find ~ with** trouver à redire or
à critiquer à; **at ~** fautif(-ive), coupable;
faulty adj défectueux(-euse)
fauna ['fɔːnə] n faune f
favour etc (US **favor** etc) ['feɪvə'ʳ]
n faveur f; (help) service m ▷ vt
(proposition) être en faveur de; (pupil
etc) favoriser; (team, horse) donner
gagnant; **to do sb a ~** rendre un service
à qn; **in ~ of** en faveur de; **to find ~
with sb** trouver grâce aux yeux de qn;
favourable adj favorable; **favourite**
['feɪvrɪt] adj, n favori(te)
fawn [fɔːn] n (deer) faon m ▷ adj (also:
~-coloured) fauve ▷ vi: **to ~ (up)on**
flatter servilement
fax [fæks] n (document) télécopie f;
(machine) télécopieur m ▷ vt envoyer
par télécopie
FBI n abbr (US: = Federal Bureau of
Investigation) FBI m
fear [fɪə'ʳ] n crainte f, peur f ▷ vt
craindre; **for ~ of** de peur que + sub or
de + infinitive; **fearful** adj craintif(-ive);
(sight, noise) affreux(-euse),
épouvantable; **fearless** adj intrépide
feasible ['fiːzəbl] adj faisable,
réalisable
feast [fiːst] n festin m, banquet m; (Rel:
also: **~ day**) fête f ▷ vi festoyer
feat [fiːt] n exploit m, prouesse f
feather ['fɛðə'ʳ] n plume f
feature ['fiːtʃə'ʳ] n caractéristique f;
(article) chronique f, rubrique f ▷ vt
(film) avoir pour vedette(s) ▷ vi figurer
(en bonne place); **features** npl (of face)
traits mpl; **a (special) ~ on sth/sb** un
reportage sur qch/qn; **feature film** n
long métrage
Feb. abbr (= February) fév
February ['fɛbruərɪ] n février m
fed [fɛd] pt, pp of **feed**
federal ['fɛdərəl] adj fédéral(e)
federation [fɛdə'reɪʃən] n fédération f

fed up adj: **to be ~ (with)** en avoir marre
or plein le dos (de)
fee [fiː] n rémunération f; (of doctor,
lawyer) honoraires mpl; (of school,
college etc) frais mpl de scolarité; (for
examination) droits mpl
feeble ['fiːbl] adj faible; (attempt, excuse,
pauvre; (joke) piteux(-euse)
feed [fiːd] n (of animal) nourriture f,
pâture f; (on printer) mécanisme m
d'alimentation ▷ vt (pt, pp **fed**) (person)
nourrir; (BRIT: baby: breastfeed) allaiter;
(: with bottle) donner le biberon à;
(horse etc) donner à manger à; (machine)
alimenter; (data etc): **to ~ sth into**
enregistrer qch dans; **feedback** n
(Elec) effet m Larsen; (from person)
réactions fpl
feel [fiːl] n (sensation) sensation f;
(impression) impression f ▷ vt (pt, pp
felt) (touch) toucher; (explore) tâter,
palper; (cold, pain) sentir; (grief, anger)
ressentir, éprouver; (think, believe): **to ~
(that)** trouver que; **to ~ hungry/cold**
avoir faim/froid; **to ~ lonely/better**
se sentir seul/mieux; **I don't ~ well**
je ne me sens pas bien; **it ~s soft** c'est
doux au toucher; **to ~ like** (want) avoir
envie de; **feeling** n (physical) sensation
f; (emotion, impression) sentiment m; **to
hurt sb's feelings** froisser qn
feet [fiːt] npl of **foot**
fell [fɛl] pt of **fall** ▷ vt (tree) abattre
fellow ['fɛləʊ] n type m; (comrade)
compagnon m; (of learned
society) membre m ▷ cpd: **their ~
prisoners/students** leurs camarades
prisonniers/étudiants; **fellow citizen**
n concitoyen(ne); **fellow countryman**
n (irreg) compatriote m; **fellow men** npl
semblables mpl; **fellowship** n (society)
association f; (comradeship) amitié
f, camaraderie f; (Scol) sorte de bourse
universitaire
felony ['fɛlənɪ] n crime m, forfait m
felt [fɛlt] pt, pp of **feel** ▷ n feutre m; **felt-
tip** n (also: **felt-tip pen**) stylo-feutre m
female ['fiːmeɪl] n (Zool) femelle f;

(*pej: woman*) bonne femme ▷ *adj* (*Biol*) femelle; (*sex, character*) féminin(e); (*vote etc*) des femmes

feminine ['fɛmɪnɪn] *adj* féminin(e)

feminist ['fɛmɪnɪst] *n* féministe *m/f*

fence [fɛns] *n* barrière *f* ▷ *vi* faire de l'escrime; **fencing** *n* (*sport*) escrime *m*

fend [fɛnd] *vi*: **to ~ for o.s.** se débrouiller (tout seul); **fend off** *vt* (*attack etc*) parer; (*questions*) éluder

fender ['fɛndər] *n* garde-feu *m inv*; (*on boat*) défense *f*; (*us: of car*) aile *f*

fennel ['fɛnl] *n* fenouil *m*

ferment *vi* [fə'mɛnt] fermenter ▷ *n* ['fə:mɛnt] (*fig*) agitation *f*, effervescence *f*

fern [fə:n] *n* fougère *f*

ferocious [fə'rəuʃəs] *adj* féroce

ferret ['fɛrɪt] *n* furet *m*

ferry ['fɛrɪ] *n* (*small*) bac *m*; (*large: also: ~boat*) ferry(-boat *m*) *m* ▷ *vt* transporter

fertile ['fə:taɪl] *adj* fertile; (*Biol*) fécond(e); **fertilize** ['fə:tɪlaɪz] *vt* fertiliser; (*Biol*) féconder; **fertilizer** *n* engrais *m*

festival ['fɛstɪvəl] *n* (*Rel*) fête *f*; (*Art, Mus*) festival *m*

festive ['fɛstɪv] *adj* de fête; **the ~ season** (*BRIT: Christmas*) la période des fêtes

fetch [fɛtʃ] *vt* aller chercher; (*BRIT: sell for*) rapporter

fête [feɪt] *n* fête *f*, kermesse *f*

fetus ['fi:təs] *n* (*us*) = **foetus**

feud [fju:d] *n* querelle *f*, dispute *f*

fever ['fi:vər] *n* fièvre *f*; **feverish** *adj* fiévreux(-euse), fébrile

few [fju:] *adj* (*not many*) peu de ▷ *pron* peu; **a ~** (*as adj*) quelques; (*as pron*) quelques-uns(-unes); **quite a ~ ...** *adj* un certain nombre de ..., pas mal de ...; **in the past ~ days** ces derniers jours; **fewer** *adj* moins de; **fewest** *adj* le moins nombreux

fiancé [fɪ'ɑ̃:ŋseɪ] *n* fiancé *m*; **fiancée** *n* fiancée *f*

fiasco [fɪ'æskəu] *n* fiasco *m*

fib [fɪb] *n* bobard *m*

fibre (*us* **fiber**) ['faɪbər] *n* fibre *f*; **fibreglass** (*us* **Fiberglass®**) *n* fibre *f* de verre

fickle ['fɪkl] *adj* inconstant(e), volage, capricieux(-euse)

fiction ['fɪkʃən] *n* romans *mpl*, littérature *f* romanesque; (*invention*) fiction *f*; **fictional** *adj* fictif(-ive)

fiddle ['fɪdl] *n* (*Mus*) violon *m*; (*cheating*) combine *f*; escroquerie *f* ▷ *vt* (*BRIT: accounts*) falsifier, maquiller; **fiddle with** *vt fus* tripoter

fidelity [fɪ'dɛlɪtɪ] *n* fidélité *f*

fidget ['fɪdʒɪt] *vi* se trémousser, remuer

field [fi:ld] *n* champ *m*; (*fig*) domaine *m*, champ; (*Sport: ground*) terrain *m*; **field marshal** *n* maréchal *m*

fierce [fɪəs] *adj* (*look, animal*) féroce, sauvage; (*wind, attack, person*) (très) violent(e); (*fighting, enemy*) acharné(e)

fifteen [fɪf'ti:n] *num* quinze; **fifteenth** *num* quinzième

fifth [fɪfθ] *num* cinquième

fiftieth ['fɪftɪɪθ] *num* cinquantième

fifty ['fɪftɪ] *num* cinquante; **fifty-fifty** *adv* moitié-moitié ▷ *adj*: **to have a fifty-fifty chance (of success)** avoir une chance sur deux (de réussir)

fig [fɪg] *n* figue *f*

fight [faɪt] *n* (*between persons*) bagarre *f*; (*argument*) dispute *f*; (*Mil*) combat *m*; (*against cancer etc*) lutte *f* ▷ *vb* (*pt, pp* **fought**) ▷ *vt* se battre contre; (*cancer, alcoholism, emotion*) combattre, lutter contre; (*election*) se présenter à ▷ *vi* se battre; (*argue*) se disputer; (*fig*): **to ~ (for/against)** lutter (pour/contre); **fight back** *vi* rendre les coups; (*after illness*) reprendre le dessus ▷ *vt* (*tears*) réprimer; **fight off** *vt* repousser; (*disease, sleep, urge*) lutter contre; **fighting** *n* combats *mpl*; (*brawls*) bagarres *fpl*

figure ['fɪgər] *n* (*Drawing, Geom*) figure *f*; (*number*) chiffre *m*; (*body, outline*) silhouette *f*; (*person's shape*) ligne *f*, formes *fpl*; (*person*) personnage *m*

▷ *vt* (*US: think*) supposer ▷ *vi* (*appear*) figurer; (*US: make sense*) s'expliquer; **figure out** *vt* (*understand*) arriver à comprendre; (*plan*) calculer

file [faɪl] *n* (*tool*) lime *f*; (*dossier*) dossier *m*; (*folder*) dossier, chemise *f*; (: *binder*) classeur *m*; (*Comput*) fichier *m*; (*row*) file *f* ▷ *vt* (*nails, wood*) limer; (*papers*) classer; (*Law: claim*) faire enregistrer; déposer; **filing cabinet** *n* classeur *m* (*meuble*)

Filipino [fɪlɪˈpiːnəu] *adj* philippin(e) ▷ *n* (*person*) Philippin(e)

fill [fɪl] *vt* remplir; (*vacancy*) pourvoir à ▷ *n*: **to eat one's ~** manger à sa faim; **to ~ with** remplir de; **fill in** *vt* (*hole*) boucher; (*form*) remplir; **fill out** *vt* (*form, receipt*) remplir; **fill up** *vt* remplir ▷ *vi* (*Aut*) faire le plein

fillet [ˈfɪlɪt] *n* filet *m*; **fillet steak** *n* filet *m* de bœuf, tournedos *m*

filling [ˈfɪlɪŋ] *n* (*Culin*) garniture *f*, farce *f*; (*for tooth*) plombage *m*; **filling station** *n* station-service *f*, station *f* d'essence

film [fɪlm] *n* film *m*; (*Phot*) pellicule *f*, film *m*; (*of powder, liquid*) couche *f*, pellicule *f* ▷ *vt* (*scene*) filmer ▷ *vi* tourner; **I'd like a 36-exposure ~** je voudrais une pellicule de 36 poses; **film star** *n* vedette *f* de cinéma

filter [ˈfɪltər] *n* filtre *m* ▷ *vt* filtrer; **filter lane** *n* (*BRIT Aut: at traffic lights*) voie *f* de dégagement; (: *on motorway*) voie *f* de sortie

filth [fɪlθ] *n* saleté *f*; **filthy** *adj* sale, dégoûtant(e); (*language*) ordurier(-ière), grossier(-ière)

fin [fɪn] *n* (*of fish*) nageoire *f*; (*of shark*) aileron *m*; (*of diver*) palme *f*

final [ˈfaɪnl] *adj* final(e), dernier(-ière); (*decision, answer*) définitif(-ive) ▷ *n* (*BRIT Sport*) finale *f*; **finals** *npl* (*Scol*) examens *mpl* de dernière année; (*US Sport*) finale *f*; **finale** [fɪˈnɑːlɪ] *n* finale *m*; **finalist** *n* (*Sport*) finaliste *m/f*; **finalize** *vt* mettre au point; **finally** *adv* (*eventually*) enfin, finalement; (*lastly*) en dernier lieu

finance [faɪˈnæns] *n* finance *f* ▷ *vt* financer; **finances** *npl* finances *fpl*; **financial** [faɪˈnænʃəl] *adj* financier(-ière); **financial year** *n* année *f* budgétaire

find [faɪnd] *vt* (*pt, pp* **found**) trouver; (*lost object*) retrouver ▷ *n* trouvaille *f*, découverte *f*; **to ~ sb guilty** (*Law*) déclarer qn coupable; **find out** *vt* se renseigner sur; (*truth, secret*) découvrir; (*person*) démasquer ▷ *vi*: **to ~ out about** (*make enquiries*) se renseigner sur; (*by chance*) apprendre; **findings** *npl* (*Law*) conclusions *fpl*, verdict *m*; (*of report*) constatations *fpl*

fine [faɪn] *adj* (*weather*) beau (belle); (*excellent*) excellent(e); (*thin, subtle, not coarse*) fin(e); (*acceptable*) bien *inv* ▷ *adv* (*well*) très bien; (*small*) fin, finement ▷ *n* (*Law*) amende *f*; contravention *f* ▷ *vt* (*Law*) condamner à une amende; donner une contravention à; **he's ~** il va bien; **the weather is ~** il fait beau; **fine arts** *npl* beaux-arts *mpl*

finger [ˈfɪŋɡər] *n* doigt *m* ▷ *vt* palper, toucher; **index ~** index *m*; **fingernail** *n* ongle *m* (de la main); **fingerprint** *n* empreinte digitale; **fingertip** *n* bout *m* du doigt

finish [ˈfɪnɪʃ] *n* fin *f*; (*Sport*) arrivée *f*; (*polish etc*) finition *f* ▷ *vt* finir, terminer ▷ *vi* finir, se terminer; **to ~ doing sth** finir de faire qch; **to ~ third** arriver *or* terminer troisième; **when does the show ~?** quand est-ce que le spectacle se termine?; **finish off** *vt* finir, terminer; (*kill*) achever; **finish up** *vi, vt* finir

Finland [ˈfɪnlənd] *n* Finlande *f*; **Finn** *n* Finnois(e), Finlandais(e); **Finnish** *adj* finnois(e), finlandais(e) ▷ *n* (*Ling*) finnois *m*

fir [fəːr] *n* sapin *m*

fire [ˈfaɪər] *n* feu *m*; (*accidental*) incendie *m*; (*heater*) radiateur *m* ▷ *vt* (*discharge*): **to ~ a gun** tirer un coup de feu; (*fig: interest*) enflammer, animer; (*inf: dismiss*) mettre à la porte, renvoyer ▷ *vi* (*shoot*) tirer, faire feu; **~!** au feu!; **on ~** en feu; **to set ~ to sth, set sth on ~** mettre le feu à qch; **fire alarm** n avertisseur m d'incendie; **firearm** n arme f à feu; **fire brigade** n (US **fire department**) (régiment m de sapeurs-)pompiers mpl; **fire engine** n (BRIT) pompe f à incendie; **fire escape** n escalier m de secours; **fire exit** n issue f or sortie f de secours; **fire extinguisher** n extincteur m; **fireman** (irreg) n pompier m; **fireplace** n cheminée f; **fire station** n caserne f de pompiers; **fire truck** (US) n = **fire engine**; **firewall** n (Internet) pare-feu m; **firewood** n bois m de chauffage; **fireworks** npl (display) feu(x) m(pl) d'artifice

firm [fə:m] adj ferme ▷ n compagnie f, firme f; **firmly** adv fermement

first [fə:st] adj premier(-ière) ▷ adv (before other people) le premier, la première; (before other things) en premier, d'abord; (when listing reasons etc) en premier lieu, premièrement; (in the beginning) au début ▷ n (person: in race) premier(-ière); (BRIT Scol) mention f très bien; (Aut) première f; **the ~ of January** le premier janvier; **at ~** au commencement, au début; **~ of all** tout d'abord, pour commencer; **first aid** n premiers secours or soins; **first-aid kit** n trousse f à pharmacie; **first-class** adj (ticket etc) de première classe; (excellent) excellent(e), exceptionnel(le); (post) en tarif prioritaire; **first-hand** adj de première main; **first lady** n (US) femme f du président; **firstly** adv premièrement, en premier lieu; **first name** n prénom m; **first-rate** adj excellent(e)

iscal ['fɪskl] adj fiscal(e); **fiscal year** n exercice financier

ish [fɪʃ] n (pl inv) poisson m ▷ vt, vi pêcher; **~ and chips** poisson frit et frites; **fisherman** (irreg) n pêcheur m; **fish fingers** npl (BRIT) bâtonnets de poisson (congelés); **fishing** n pêche f; **to go fishing** aller à la pêche;

fishing boat n barque f de pêche; **fishing line** n ligne f (de pêche); **fishmonger** n (BRIT) marchand m de poisson; **fishmonger's (shop)** n (BRIT) poissonnerie f; **fish sticks** npl (US) = **fish fingers**; **fishy** adj (inf) suspect(e), louche

fist [fɪst] n poing m

fit [fɪt] adj (Med, Sport) en (bonne) forme; (proper) convenable; approprié(e) ▷ vt (subj: clothes) aller à; (put in, attach) installer, poser; (equip) équiper, garnir, munir; (suit) convenir à ▷ vi (clothes) aller; (parts) s'adapter; (in space, gap) entrer, s'adapter ▷ n (Med) accès m, crise f; (of anger) accès; (of hysterics, jealousy) crise; **~ to** (ready to) en état de; **~ for** (worthy) digne de; (capable) apte à; **to keep ~** se maintenir en forme; **this dress is a tight/good ~** cette robe est un peu juste/(me) va très bien; **a ~ of coughing** une quinte de toux; **by ~s and starts** par à-coups; **fit in** vi (add up) cadrer; (integrate) s'intégrer; (to new situation) s'adapter; **fitness** n (Med) forme f physique; **fitted** adj (jacket, shirt) ajusté(e); **fitted carpet** n moquette f; **fitted kitchen** n (BRIT) cuisine équipée; **fitted sheet** n drap-housse m; **fitting** adj approprié(e) ▷ n (of dress) essayage m; (of piece of equipment) pose f, installation f; **fitting room** n (in shop) cabine f d'essayage; **fittings** npl installations fpl

five [faɪv] num cinq; **fiver** n (inf: BRIT) billet m de cinq livres; (: US) billet de cinq dollars

fix [fɪks] vt (date, amount etc) fixer; (sort out) arranger; (mend) réparer; (make ready: meal, drink) préparer ▷ n: **to be in a ~** être dans le pétrin; **fix up** vt (meeting) arranger; **to ~ sb up with sth** faire avoir qch à qn; **fixed** adj (prices etc) fixe; **fixture** n installation f (fixe); (Sport) rencontre f (au programme)

fizzy ['fɪzɪ] adj pétillant(e), gazeux(-euse)

flag [flæg] n drapeau m; (also: **~stone**)

dalle f ▷ vi faiblir; fléchir; **flag down**
vt héler, faire signe (de s'arrêter) à;
flagpole n mât m

flair [flɛər] n flair m

flak [flæk] n (Mil) tir antiaérien; (inf:
criticism) critiques fpl

flake [fleɪk] n (of rust, paint) écaille f; (of
snow, soap powder) flocon m ▷ vi (also: ~
off) s'écailler

flamboyant [flæm'bɔɪənt] adj
flamboyant(e), éclatant(e); (person)
haut(e) en couleur

flame [fleɪm] n flamme f

flamingo [flə'mɪŋɡəu] n flamant
m (rose)

flammable ['flæməbl] adj
inflammable

flan [flæn] n (BRIT) tarte f

flank [flæŋk] n flanc m ▷ vt flanquer

flannel ['flænl] n (BRIT: also: **face ~**)
gant m de toilette; (fabric) flanelle f

flap [flæp] n (of pocket, envelope) rabat
m ▷ vt (wings) battre (de) ▷ vi (sail,
flag) claquer

flare [flɛər] n (signal) signal lumineux;
(Mil) fusée éclairante; (in skirt etc)
évasement m; **flares** npl (trousers)
pantalon m à pattes d'éléphant; **flare
up** vi s'embraser; (fig: person) se mettre
en colère, s'emporter; (: revolt) éclater

flash [flæʃ] n éclair m; (also: **news ~**)
flash m (d'information); (Phot) flash
m ▷ vt (switch on) allumer (brièvement);
(direct): **to ~ sth at** braquer qch sur;
(send: message) câbler; (smile) lancer
▷ vi briller; jeter des éclairs; (light
on ambulance etc) clignoter; **a ~ of
lightning** un éclair; **in a ~** en un clin
d'œil; **to ~ one's headlights** faire un
appel de phares; **he ~ed by or past** il
passa (devant nous) comme un éclair;
flashback n flashback m, retour m en
arrière; **flashbulb** n ampoule f de flash;
flashlight n lampe f de poche

flask [flɑ:sk] n flacon m, bouteille f;
(also: **vacuum ~**) bouteille f thermos®

flat [flæt] adj plat(e); (tyre) dégonflé(e),
à plat; (beer) éventé(e); (battery) à plat;

(denial) catégorique; (Mus) bémol inv;
(: voice) faux (fausse) ▷ n (BRIT:
apartment) appartement m; (Aut)
crevaison f, pneu crevé; (Mus) bémol m;
~ out (work) sans relâche; (race) à fond;
flatten vt (also: **flatten out**) aplatir;
(crop) coucher; (house, city) raser

flatter ['flætər] vt flatter; **flattering** adj
flatteur(-euse); (clothes etc) seyant(e)

flaunt [flɔ:nt] vt faire étalage de

flavour etc (us **flavor** etc) ['fleɪvər]
n goût m, saveur f; (of ice cream etc)
parfum m ▷ vt parfumer, aromatiser;
vanilla-~ed à l'arôme de vanille,
vanillé(e); **what ~s do you have?** quels
parfums avez-vous?; **flavouring** n
arôme m (synthétique)

flaw [flɔ:] n défaut m; **flawless** adj
sans défaut

flea [fli:] n puce f; **flea market** n
marché m aux puces

flee (pt, pp **fled**) [fli:, flɛd] vt fuir, s'enfuir
de ▷ vi fuir, s'enfuir

fleece [fli:s] n (of sheep) toison f; (top)
(laine f) polaire f ▷ vt (inf) voler, filouter

fleet [fli:t] n flotte f; (of lorries, cars etc)
parc m; convoi m

fleeting ['fli:tɪŋ] adj fugace,
fugitif(-ive); (visit) très bref (brève)

Flemish ['flɛmɪʃ] adj flamand(e)
▷ n (Ling) flamand m; **the ~** npl les
Flamands

flesh [flɛʃ] n chair f

flew [flu:] pt of **fly**

flex [flɛks] n fil m or câble m électrique
(souple) ▷ vt (knee) fléchir; (muscles)
tendre; **flexibility** n flexibilité f;
flexible adj flexible; (person, schedule)
souple; **flexitime** (us **flextime**) n
horaire m variable or à la carte

flick [flɪk] n petit coup; (with finger)
chiquenaude f ▷ vt donner un petit
coup à; (switch) appuyer sur; **flick
through** vt fus feuilleter

flicker ['flɪkər] vi (light, flame) vaciller

flies [flaɪz] npl of **fly**

flight [flaɪt] n vol m; (escape) fuite f;
(also: **~ of steps**) escalier m; **flight**

attendant n steward m, hôtesse f de l'air

flimsy ['flɪmzɪ] adj peu solide; (clothes) trop léger(-ère); (excuse) pauvre, mince

flinch [flɪntʃ] vi tressaillir; **to ~ from** se dérober à, reculer devant

fling [flɪŋ] vt (pt, pp **flung**) jeter, lancer

flint [flɪnt] n silex m; (in lighter) pierre f (à briquet)

flip [flɪp] vt (throw) donner une chiquenaude à; (switch) appuyer sur; (us: pancake) faire sauter; **to ~ sth over** retourner qch

flip-flops ['flɪpflɒps] npl (esp BRIT) tongs fpl

flipper ['flɪpə^r] n (of animal) nageoire f; (for swimmer) palme f

flirt [flɜːt] vi flirter ▷ n flirteur(-euse)

float [fləʊt] n flotteur m; (in procession) char m; (sum of money) réserve f ▷ vi flotter

flock [flɒk] n (of sheep) troupeau m; (of birds) vol m; (of people) foule f

flood [flʌd] n inondation f; (of letters, refugees etc) flot m ▷ vt inonder ▷ vi (place) être inondé; (people): **to ~ into** envahir; **flooding** n inondation f; **floodlight** n projecteur m

floor [flɔː^r] n sol m; (storey) étage m; (of sea, valley) fond m ▷ vt (knock down) terrasser; (baffle) désorienter; **ground ~**, (us) **first ~** rez-de-chaussée m; **first ~**, (us) **second ~** premier étage; **what ~ is it on?** c'est à quel étage?; **floorboard** n planche f (du plancher); **flooring** n sol m; (wooden) plancher m; (covering) revêtement m de sol; **floor show** n spectacle m de variétés

flop [flɒp] n fiasco m ▷ vi (fail) faire fiasco; (fall) s'affaler, s'effondrer; **floppy** adj lâche, flottant(e) ▷ n (Comput: also: **floppy disk**) disquette f

¹lora ['flɔːrə] n flore f

¹loral ['flɔːrl] adj floral(e); (dress) à fleurs

¹lorist ['flɒrɪst] n fleuriste m/f; **florist's (shop)** n magasin m or boutique f de fleuriste

¹lotation [fləʊ'teɪʃən] n (of shares)

émission f; (of company) lancement m (en Bourse)

flour ['flaʊə^r] n farine f

flourish ['flʌrɪʃ] vi prospérer ▷ n (gesture) moulinet m

flow [fləʊ] n (of water, traffic etc) écoulement m; (tide, influx) flux m; (of blood, Elec) circulation f; (of river) courant m ▷ vi couler; (traffic) s'écouler; (robes, hair) flotter

flower ['flaʊə^r] n fleur f ▷ vi fleurir; **flower bed** n plate-bande f; **flowerpot** n pot m (à fleurs)

flown [fləʊn] pp of **fly**

fl. oz. abbr = **fluid ounce**

flu [fluː] n grippe f

fluctuate ['flʌktjueɪt] vi varier, fluctuer

fluent ['fluːənt] adj (speech, style) coulant(e), aisé(e); **he speaks ~ French, he's ~ in French** il parle le français couramment

fluff [flʌf] n duvet m; (on jacket, carpet) peluche f; **fluffy** adj duveteux(-euse); (toy) en peluche

fluid ['fluːɪd] n fluide m; (in diet) liquide m ▷ adj fluide; **fluid ounce** n (BRIT) = 0.028 l; 0.05 pints

fluke [fluːk] n coup m de veine

flung [flʌŋ] pt, pp of **fling**

fluorescent [fluə'resnt] adj fluorescent(e)

fluoride ['fluəraɪd] n fluor m

flurry ['flʌrɪ] n (of snow) rafale f, bourrasque f; **a ~ of activity** un affairement soudain

flush [flʌʃ] n (on face) rougeur f; (fig: of youth etc) éclat m ▷ vt nettoyer à grande eau ▷ vi rougir ▷ adj (level): **~ with** au ras de, de niveau avec; **to ~ the toilet** tirer la chasse (d'eau)

flute [fluːt] n flûte f

flutter ['flʌtə^r] n (of panic, excitement) agitation f; (of wings) battement m ▷ vi (bird) battre des ailes, voleter

fly [flaɪ] n (insect) mouche f; (on trousers: also: **flies**) braguette f ▷ vb (pt **flew**, pp **flown**) ▷ vt (plane) piloter; (passengers, *cargo*) transporter (par avion); (*distance*) parcourir ▷ *vi* voler; (*passengers*) aller en avion; (*escape*) s'enfuir, fuir; (*flag*) se déployer; **fly away, fly off** *vi* s'envoler; **fly-drive** *n* formule *f* avion plus voiture; **flying** *n* (*activity*) aviation *f*; (*action*) vol *m* ▷ *adj*: **flying visit** visite *f* éclair *inv*; **with flying colours** haut la main; **flying saucer** *n* soucoupe volante; **flyover** *n* (BRIT: *overpass*) pont routier

FM *abbr* (*Radio*: = *frequency modulation*) FM

foal [fəul] *n* poulain *m*

foam [fəum] *n* écume *f*; (*on beer*) mousse *f*; (*also*: **~ rubber**) caoutchouc *m* mousse ▷ *vi* (*liquid*) écumer; (*soapy water*) mousser

focus ['fəukəs] *n* (*pl* **~es**) foyer *m*; (*of interest*) centre *m* ▷ *vt* (*field glasses etc*) mettre au point ▷ *vi*: **to ~ (on)** (*with camera*) régler la mise au point (sur); (*with eyes*) fixer son regard (sur); (*fig: concentrate*) se concentrer; **out of/in ~** (*picture*) flou(e)/net(te); (*camera*) pas au point/au point

foetus (*us* **fetus**) ['fi:təs] *n* fœtus *m*

fog [fɔg] *n* brouillard *m*; **foggy** *adj*: **it's foggy** il y a du brouillard; **fog lamp** (*us* **fog light**) *n* (*Aut*) phare *m* anti-brouillard

foil [fɔil] *vt* déjouer, contrecarrer ▷ *n* feuille *f* de métal; (*kitchen foil*) papier *m* d'alu(minium); **to act as a ~ to** (*fig*) servir de repoussoir *or* de faire-valoir à

fold [fəuld] *n* (*bend, crease*) pli *m*; (*Agr*) parc *m* à moutons; (*fig*) bercail *m* ▷ *vt* plier; **to ~ one's arms** croiser les bras; **fold up** *vi* (*map etc*) se plier, se replier; (*business*) fermer boutique ▷ *vt* (*map etc*) plier, replier; **folder** *n* (*for papers*) chemise *f*; (: *binder*) classeur *m*; (*Comput*) dossier *m*; **folding** *adj* (*chair, bed*) pliant(e)

foliage ['fəuliidʒ] *n* feuillage *m*

folk [fəuk] *npl* gens *mpl* ▷ *cpd* folklorique; **folks** *npl* (*inf: parents*) famille *f*, parents *mpl*; **folklore**

['fəuklɔːʳ] *n* folklore *m*; **folk music** *n* musique *f* folklorique; (*contemporary*) musique folk, folk *m*; **folk song** *n* chanson *f* folklorique; (*contemporary*) chanson folk *inv*

follow ['fɔləu] *vt* suivre ▷ *vi* suivre; (*result*) s'ensuivre; **to ~ suit** (*fig*) faire de même; **follow up** *vt* (*letter, offer*) donner suite à; (*case*) suivre; **follower** *n* disciple *m/f*, partisan(e); **following** *adj* suivant(e) ▷ *n* partisans *mpl*, disciples *mpl*; **follow-up** *n* suite *f*; (*on file, case*) suivi *m*

fond [fɔnd] *adj* (*memory, look*) tendre, affectueux(-euse); (*hopes, dreams*) un peu fou (folle); **to be ~ of** aimer beaucoup

food [fu:d] *n* nourriture *f*; **food mixer** *n* mixeur *m*; **food poisoning** *n* intoxication *f* alimentaire; **food processor** *n* robot *m* de cuisine; **food stamp** *n* (*us*) bon *m* de nourriture (*pour indigents*)

fool [fu:l] *n* idiot(e); (*Culin*) mousse *f* de fruits ▷ *vt* berner, duper; **fool about, fool around** *vi* (*pej: waste time*) traînailler, glandouiller; (: *behave foolishly*) faire l'idiot *or* l'imbécile; **foolish** *adj* idiot(e), stupide; (*rash*) imprudent(e); **foolproof** *adj* (*plan etc*) infaillible

foot (*pl* **feet**) [fut, fi:t] *n* pied *m*; (*of animal*) patte *f*; (*measure*) pied (= 30.48 cm; 12 inches) ▷ *vt* (*bill*) payer; **on ~** à pied; **footage** *n* (*Cine: length*) ≈ métrage *m*; (: *material*) séquences *fpl*; **foot-and-mouth (disease)** [futənd'mauθ-] *n* fièvre aphteuse; **football** *n* (*ball*) ballon *m* (de football); (*sport*: BRIT) football *m*; (: *us*) football américain; **footballer** *n* (BRIT) = **football player**; **football match** *n* (BRIT) match *m* de foot(ball); **football player** *n* footballeur(-euse), joueur(-euse) de football; (*us*) joueur(-euse) de football américain; **footbridge** *n* passerelle *f*; **foothills** *npl* contreforts *mpl*; **foothold** *n* prise *f* (de pied); **footing** *n* (*fig*) position *f*; **to lose**

one's footing perdre pied; **footnote** n note f (en bas de page); **footpath** n sentier m; **footprint** n trace f (de pied); **footstep** n pas m; **footwear** n chaussures fpl

KEYWORD

for [fɔːʳ] prep **1** (indicating destination, intention, purpose) pour; **the train for London** le train pour (or à destination de) Londres; **he left for Rome** il est parti pour Rome; **he went for the paper** il est allé chercher le journal; **is this for me?** c'est pour moi?; **it's time for lunch** c'est l'heure du déjeuner; **what's it for?** ça sert à quoi?; **what for?** (why) pourquoi?; (to what end) pour quoi faire?, à quoi bon?; **for sale** à vendre; **to pray for peace** prier pour la paix
2 (on behalf of, representing) pour; **the MP for Hove** le député de Hove; **to work for sb/sth** travailler pour qn/qch; **I'll ask him for you** je vais lui demander pour toi; **G for George** G comme Georges
3 (because of) pour; **for this reason** pour cette raison; **for fear of being criticized** de peur d'être critiqué
4 (with regard to) pour; **it's cold for July** il fait froid pour juillet; **a gift for languages** un don pour les langues
5 (in exchange for): **I sold it for £5** je l'ai vendu 5 livres; **to pay 50 pence for a ticket** payer un billet 50 pence
6 (in favour of) pour; **are you for or against us?** êtes-vous pour ou contre nous?; **I'm all for it** je suis tout à fait pour; **vote for X** votez pour X
7 (referring to distance) pendant, sur; **there are roadworks for 5 km** il y a des travaux sur or pendant 5 km; **we walked for miles** nous avons marché pendant des kilomètres
8 (referring to time) pendant; depuis; pour; **he was away for 2 years** il a été absent pendant 2 ans; **she will be away for a month** elle sera absente

(pendant) un mois; **it hasn't rained for 3 weeks** ça fait 3 semaines qu'il ne pleut pas, il ne pleut pas depuis 3 semaines; **I have known her for years** je la connais depuis des années; **can you do it for tomorrow?** est-ce que tu peux le faire pour demain?
9 (with infinitive clauses): **it is not for me to decide** ce n'est pas à moi de décider; **it would be best for you to leave** le mieux serait que vous partiez; **there is still time for you to do it** vous avez encore le temps de le faire; **for this to be possible ...** pour que cela soit possible ..
10 (in spite of): **for all that** malgré cela, néanmoins; **for all his work/efforts** malgré tout son travail/tous ses efforts; **for all his complaints, he's very fond of her** il a beau se plaindre, il l'aime beaucoup
▷ conj (since, as: rather formal) car

forbid (pt **forbad(e)**, pp **~den**) [fə'bɪd, -'bæd, -'bɪdn] vt défendre, interdire; **to ~ sb to do** défendre or interdire à qn de faire; **forbidden** adj défendu(e)
force [fɔːs] n force f ▷ vt forcer; (push) pousser (de force); **to ~ o.s. to do** se forcer à faire; **in ~** (being used: rule, law, prices) en vigueur; (in large numbers) en force; **forced** adj forcé(e); **forceful** adj énergique
ford [fɔːd] n gué m
fore [fɔːʳ] n: **to the ~** en évidence; **forearm** n avant-bras m inv; **forecast** n prévision f; (also: **weather forecast**) prévisions fpl météorologiques, météo f ▷ vt (irreg: like **cast**) prévoir; **forecourt** n (of garage) devant m; **forefinger** n index m; **forefront** n: **in the forefront of** au premier rang or plan de; **foreground** n premier plan; **forehead** ['fɔrɪd] n front m
foreign ['fɔrɪn] adj étranger(-ère); (trade) extérieur(e); (travel) à l'étranger; **foreign currency** n devises étrangères; **foreigner** n étranger(-ère);

foreign exchange n (system) change m; (money) devises fpl; **Foreign Office** n (BRIT) ministère m des Affaires étrangères; **Foreign Secretary** n (BRIT) ministre m des Affaires étrangères

fore: **foreman** (irreg) n (in construction) contremaître m; **foremost** adj le (la) plus en vue, premier(-ière) ▷ adv: **first and foremost** avant tout, tout d'abord; **forename** n prénom m

forensic [fə'rɛnsɪk] adj: ~ **medicine** médecine légale

foresee (pt **foresaw**, pp ~n) [fɔː'siː, -'sɔː, -'siːn] vt prévoir; **foreseeable** adj prévisible

forest ['fɒrɪst] n forêt f; **forestry** n sylviculture f

forever [fə'rɛvər] adv pour toujours; (fig: endlessly) continuellement

foreword ['fɔːwəːd] n avant-propos m inv

forfeit ['fɔːfɪt] vt perdre

forgave [fə'geɪv] pt of **forgive**

forge [fɔːdʒ] n forge f ▷ vt (signature) contrefaire; (wrought iron) forger; **to ~ money** (BRIT) fabriquer de la fausse monnaie; **forger** n faussaire m; **forgery** n faux m, contrefaçon f

forget (pt **forgot**, pp **forgotten**) [fə'gɛt, -'gɒt, -'gɒtn] vt, vi oublier; **I've forgotten my key/passport** j'ai oublié ma clé/mon passeport; **forgetful** adj distrait(e), étourdi(e)

forgive (pt **forgave**, pp ~n) [fə'gɪv, -'geɪv, -'gɪvn] vt pardonner; **to ~ sb for sth/for doing sth** pardonner qch à qn/à qn de faire qch

forgot [fə'gɒt] pt of **forget**

forgotten [fə'gɒtn] pp of **forget**

fork [fɔːk] n (for eating) fourchette f; (for gardening) fourche f; (of roads) bifurcation f ▷ vi (road) bifurquer

forlorn [fə'lɔːn] adj (deserted) abandonné(e); (hope, attempt) désespéré(e)

form [fɔːm] n forme f; (Scol) classe f; (questionnaire) formulaire m ▷ vt former; (habit) contracter; **to ~ part**

of sth faire partie de qch; **on top ~** en pleine forme

formal ['fɔːməl] adj (offer, receipt) en bonne et due forme; (person) cérémonieux(-euse); (occasion, dinner) officiel(le); (garden) à la française; (clothes) de soirée; **formality** [fɔː'mælɪtɪ] n formalité f

format ['fɔːmæt] n format m ▷ vt (Comput) formater

formation [fɔː'meɪʃən] n formation f

former ['fɔːmər] adj ancien(ne); (before n) précédent(e); **the ~ ... the latter** le premier ... le second, celui-là ... celui-ci; **formerly** adv autrefois

formidable ['fɔːmɪdəbl] adj redoutable

formula ['fɔːmjulə] n formule f

fort [fɔːt] n fort m

forthcoming [fɔːθ'kʌmɪŋ] adj qui va paraître or avoir lieu prochainement; (character) ouvert(e), communicatif(-ive); (available) disponible

fortieth ['fɔːtɪɪθ] num quarantième

fortify ['fɔːtɪfaɪ] vt (city) fortifier; (person) remonter

fortnight ['fɔːtnaɪt] n (BRIT) quinzaine f, quinze jours mpl; **fortnightly** adj bimensuel(le) ▷ adv tous les quinze jours

fortress ['fɔːtrɪs] n forteresse f

fortunate ['fɔːtʃənɪt] adj heureux(-euse); (person) chanceux(-euse); **it is ~ that** c'est une chance que, il est heureux que; **fortunately** adv heureusement, par bonheur

fortune ['fɔːtʃən] n chance f; (wealth) fortune f; **fortune-teller** n diseuse f de bonne aventure

forty ['fɔːtɪ] num quarante

forum ['fɔːrəm] n forum m, tribune f

forward ['fɔːwəd] adj (movement, position) en avant, vers l'avant; (not shy) effronté(e); (in time) en avance ▷ adv (also: ~s) en avant ▷ n (Sport) avant m ▷ vt (letter) faire suivre; (parcel, goods) expédier; (*fig*) promouvoir, favoriser; **to move ~** avancer; **forwarding address** n adresse f de réexpédition

orward slash n barre f oblique

ossil ['fɔsl] adj, n fossile m

oster ['fɔstə'] vt (*encourage*) encourager, favoriser; (*child*) élever (*sans adopter*); **foster child** n enfant élevé dans une famille d'accueil

oster parent n parent qui élève un enfant sans l'adopter

ought [fɔ:t] pt, pp of **fight**

oul [faul] adj (*weather, smell, food*) infect(e); (*language*) ordurier(-ière) ▷ n (*Football*) faute f ▷ vt (*dirty*) salir, encrasser; **he's got a ~ temper** il a un caractère de chien; **foul play** n (*Law*) acte criminel

ound [faund] pt, pp of **find** ▷ vt (*establish*) fonder; **foundation** [faun'deɪʃən] n (*act*) fondation f; (*base*) fondement m; (*also*: **foundation cream**) fond m de teint; **foundations** npl (*of building*) fondations fpl

ounder ['faundə'] n fondateur m ▷ vi couler, sombrer

ountain ['fauntɪn] n fontaine f; **fountain pen** n stylo m (à encre)

our [fɔ:'] num quatre; **on all ~s** à quatre pattes; **four-letter word** n obscénité f, gros mot; **four-poster** n (*also*: **four-poster bed**) lit m à baldaquin; **fourteen** num quatorze; **fourteenth** num quatorzième; **fourth** num quatrième ▷ n (*Aut*: *also*: **fourth gear**) quatrième f; **four-wheel drive** n (*Aut*: *car*) voiture f à quatre roues motrices

owl [faul] n volaille f

ox [fɔks] n renard m ▷ vt mystifier

oyer ['fɔɪeɪ] n (*in hotel*) vestibule m; (*Theat*) foyer m

raction ['frækʃən] n fraction f

racture ['fræktʃə'] n fracture f ▷ vt fracturer

ragile ['frædʒaɪl] adj fragile

ragment ['frægmənt] n fragment m

ragrance ['freɪgrəns] n parfum m

rail [freɪl] adj fragile, délicat(e);

(*person*) frêle

frame [freɪm] n (*of building*) charpente f; (*of human, animal*) charpente, ossature f; (*of picture*) cadre m; (*of door, window*) encadrement m, chambranle m; (*of spectacles*: *also*: **~s**) monture f ▷ vt (*picture*) encadrer; **~ of mind** disposition f d'esprit; **framework** n structure f

France [frɑːns] n la France

franchise ['fræntʃaɪz] n (*Pol*) droit m de vote; (*Comm*) franchise f

frank [fræŋk] adj franc (franche) ▷ vt (*letter*) affranchir; **frankly** adv franchement

frantic ['fræntɪk] adj (*hectic*) frénétique; (*distraught*) hors de soi

fraud [frɔːd] n supercherie f, fraude f, tromperie f; (*person*) imposteur m

fraught [frɔːt] adj (*tense: person*) très tendu(e); (: *situation*) pénible; **~ with** (*difficulties etc*) chargé(e) de, plein(e) de

fray [freɪ] vt effilocher ▷ vi s'effilocher

freak [friːk] n (*eccentric person*) phénomène m; (*unusual event*) hasard m extraordinaire; (*pej: fanatic*): **health food ~** fana m/f or obsédé(e) de l'alimentation saine ▷ adj (*storm*) exceptionnel(le); (*accident*) bizarre

freckle ['frɛkl] n tache f de rousseur

free [friː] adj libre; (*gratis*) gratuit(e) ▷ vt (*prisoner etc*) libérer; (*jammed object or person*) dégager; **is this seat ~?** la place est libre?; **~ (of charge)** gratuitement; **freedom** n liberté f; **Freefone®** n numéro vert; **free gift** n prime f; **free kick** n (*Sport*) coup franc; **freelance** adj (*journalist etc*) indépendant(e), free-lance inv ▷ adv en free-lance; **freely** adv librement; (*liberally*) libéralement; **Freepost®** n (*BRIT*) port payé; **free-range** adj (*egg*) de ferme; (*chicken*) fermier; **freeway** n (*US*) autoroute f; **free will** n libre arbitre m; **of one's own free will** de son plein gré

freeze [friːz] vb (pt **froze**, pp **frozen**) ▷ vi geler ▷ vt geler; (*food*) congeler; (*prices, salaries*) bloquer, geler ▷ n gel m;

(*of prices, salaries*) blocage m; **freezer** n
congélateur m; **freezing** adj: **freezing
(cold)** (*room etc*) glacial(e); (*person,
hands*) gelé(e), glacé(e) ▷ n: **3 degrees
below freezing** 3 degrés au-dessous
de zéro; **it's freezing** il fait un froid
glacial; **freezing point** n point m de
congélation
freight [freɪt] n (*goods*) fret m,
cargaison f; (*money charged*) fret, prix m
du transport; **freight train** n (*US*) train
m de marchandises
French [frɛntʃ] adj français(e)
▷ n (*Ling*) français m; **the ~** npl les
Français; **what's the ~ (word) for ...?**
comment dit-on ... en français?;
French bean n (*BRIT*) haricot vert;
French bread n pain m français;
French dressing n (*Culin*) vinaigrette f;
French fried potatoes (*US* **French
fries**) npl (pommes de terre fpl) frites
fpl; **Frenchman** (*irreg*) n Français m;
French stick n ≈ baguette f;
French window n porte-fenêtre f;
Frenchwoman (*irreg*) n Française f
frenzy ['frɛnzɪ] n frénésie f
frequency ['friːkwənsɪ] n fréquence f
frequent adj ['friːkwənt] fréquent(e)
▷ vt [frɪ'kwɛnt] fréquenter;
frequently ['friːkwəntlɪ] adv
fréquemment
fresh [frɛʃ] adj frais (fraîche);
(*new*) nouveau (nouvelle); (*cheeky*)
familier(-ière), culotté(e); **freshen** vi
(*wind, air*) fraîchir; **freshen up** vi faire
un brin de toilette; **fresher** n (*BRIT
University: inf*) bizuth m, étudiant(e)
de première année; **freshly** adv
nouvellement, récemment; **freshman**
(*US: irreg*) n = **fresher**; **freshwater** adj
(*fish*) d'eau douce
fret [frɛt] vi s'agiter, se tracasser
Fri abbr (= Friday) ve
friction ['frɪkʃən] n friction f,
frottement m
Friday ['fraɪdɪ] n vendredi m
fridge [frɪdʒ] n (*BRIT*) frigo m,
frigidaire® m

fried [fraɪd] adj frit(e); **~ egg** œuf m
sur le plat
friend [frɛnd] n ami(e); **friendly**
adj amical(e); (*kind*) sympathique,
gentil(le); (*place*) accueillant(e); (*Pol:
country*) ami(e) ▷ n (*also:* **friendly
match**) match amical; **friendship**
n amitié f
fries [fraɪz] (*esp US*) npl = **French fried
potatoes**
frigate ['frɪgɪt] n frégate f
fright [fraɪt] n peur f, effroi m; **to
give sb a ~** faire peur à qn; **to take ~**
prendre peur, s'effrayer; **frighten** vt
effrayer, faire peur à; **frightened** adj:
to be frightened (of) avoir peur (de);
frightening adj effrayant(e); **frightful**
adj affreux(-euse)
frill [frɪl] n (*of dress*) volant m; (*of shirt*)
jabot m
fringe [frɪndʒ] n (*BRIT: of hair*) frange f;
(*edge: of forest etc*) bordure f
Frisbee® ['frɪzbɪ] n Frisbee® m
fritter ['frɪtə'] n beignet m
frivolous ['frɪvələs] adj frivole
fro [frəu] *see* **to**
frock [frɔk] n robe f
frog [frɔg] n grenouille f; **frogman**
(*irreg*) n homme-grenouille m

 KEYWORD

from [frɔm] prep **1** (*indicating starting
place, origin etc*) de; **where do you
come from?, where are you from?**
d'où venez-vous?; **where has he come
from?** d'où arrive-t-il?; **from London
to Paris** de Londres à Paris; **to escape
from sb/sth** échapper à qn/qch; **a
letter/telephone call from my sister**
une lettre/un appel de ma sœur; **to
drink from the bottle** boire à (même)
la bouteille; **tell him from me that ...**
dites-lui de ma part que ...
2 (*indicating time*) (à partir) de; **from
one o'clock to** *or* **until** *or* **till two** d'une
heure à deux heures; **from January
(on)** à partir de janvier

3 (*indicating distance*) de; **the hotel is one kilometre from the beach** l'hôtel est à un kilomètre de la plage
4 (*indicating price, number etc*) de; **prices range from £10 to £50** les prix varient entre 10 livres et 50 livres; **the interest rate was increased from 9% to 10%** le taux d'intérêt est passé de 9% à 10%
5 (*indicating difference*) de; **he can't tell red from green** il ne peut pas distinguer le rouge du vert; **to be different from sb/sth** être différent de qn/qch
6 (*because of, on the basis of*): **from what he says** d'après ce qu'il dit; **weak from hunger** affaibli par la faim

front [frʌnt] n (*of house, dress*) devant m; (*of coach, train*) avant m; (*promenade: also*: **sea ~**) bord m de mer; (*Mil, Pol, Meteorology*) front m; (*fig: appearances*) contenance f, façade f ▷ adj de devant; (*seat, wheel*) avant ▷ vi: **in ~ (of)** devant; **front door** n porte f d'entrée; (*of car*) portière f avant; **frontier** ['frʌntɪəʳ] n frontière f; **front page** n première page f; **front-wheel drive** n traction f avant

frost [frɒst] n gel m, gelée f; (*also*: **hoar~**) givre m; **frostbite** n gelures fpl; **frosting** n (*esp US: on cake*) glaçage m; **frosty** adj (*window*) couvert(e) de givre; (*weather, welcome*) glacial(e)

froth [frɒθ] n mousse f; écume f

frown [fraun] n froncement m de sourcils ▷ vi froncer les sourcils

froze [frəuz] pt of **freeze**

frozen ['frəuzn] pp of **freeze** ▷ adj (*food*) congelé(e); (*very cold: person: Comm: assets*) gelé(e)

fruit [fruːt] n (*pl inv*) fruit m; **fruit juice** n jus m de fruit; **fruit machine** n (BRIT) machine f à sous; **fruit salad** n salade f de fruits

frustrate [frʌs'treɪt] vt frustrer; **frustrated** adj frustré(e)

fry (*pt, pp* **fried**) [fraɪ, -d] vt (faire) frire;

small ~ le menu fretin; **frying pan** n poêle f (à frire)

ft. abbr = **foot**; **feet**

fudge [fʌdʒ] n (*Culin*) sorte de confiserie à base de sucre, de beurre et de lait

fuel [fjuəl] n (*for heating*) combustible m; (*for engine*) carburant m; **fuel tank** n (*in vehicle*) réservoir m de or à carburant

fulfil (*US* **fulfill**) [ful'fɪl] vt (*function, condition*) remplir; (*order*) exécuter; (*wish, desire*) satisfaire, réaliser

full [ful] adj plein(e); (*details, hotel, bus*) complet(-ète); (*busy: day*) chargé(e); (*skirt*) ample, large ▷ adv: **to know ~ well that** savoir fort bien que; **I'm ~ (up)** j'ai bien mangé; **~ employment/ fare** plein emploi/tarif; **a ~ two hours** deux bonnes heures; **at ~ speed** à toute vitesse; **in ~** (*reproduce, quote, pay*) intégralement; (*write name etc*) en toutes lettres; **full-length** adj (*portrait*) en pied; (*coat*) long(ue); **full-length film** long métrage; **full moon** n pleine lune; **full-scale** adj (*model*) grandeur nature inv; (*search, retreat*) complet(-ète), total(e); **full stop** n point m; **full-time** adj, adv (*work*) à plein temps; **fully** adv entièrement, complètement; (*at least*)

fumble ['fʌmbl] vi fouiller, tâtonner; **fumble with** vt fus tripoter

fume [fjuːm] vi (*rage*) rager; **fumes** npl vapeurs fpl, émanations fpl, gaz mpl

fun [fʌn] n amusement m, divertissement m; **to have ~** s'amuser; **for ~** pour rire; **to make ~ of** se moquer de

function ['fʌŋkʃən] n fonction f; (*reception, dinner*) cérémonie f, soirée officielle f ▷ vi fonctionner

fund [fʌnd] n caisse f, fonds m; (*source, store*) source f, mine f; **funds** npl (*money*) fonds mpl

fundamental [fʌndə'mɛntl] adj fondamental(e)

funeral ['fjuːnərəl] n enterrement m, obsèques fpl (*more formal occasion*); **funeral director** n entrepreneur m des pompes funèbres; **funeral parlour** [-'pɑːlə'] n (BRIT) dépôt m mortuaire

funfair ['fʌnfɛə'] n (BRIT) fête (foraine)

fungus (pl **fungi**) ['fʌŋgəs, -gaɪ] n champignon m; (mould) moisissure f

funnel ['fʌnl] n entonnoir m; (of ship) cheminée f

funny ['fʌnɪ] adj amusant(e), drôle; (strange) curieux(-euse), bizarre

fur [fəː'] n fourrure f; (BRIT: in kettle etc) (dépôt m de) tartre m; **fur coat** n manteau m de fourrure

furious ['fjʊərɪəs] adj furieux(-euse); (effort) acharné(e)

furnish ['fəːnɪʃ] vt meubler; (supply) fournir; **furnishings** npl mobilier m, articles mpl d'ameublement

furniture ['fəːnɪtʃə'] n meubles mpl, mobilier m; **piece of ~** meuble m

furry ['fəːrɪ] adj (animal) à fourrure; (toy) en peluche

further ['fəːðə'] adj supplémentaire, autre; nouveau (nouvelle) ▷ adv plus loin; (more) davantage; (moreover) de plus ▷ vt faire avancer or progresser, promouvoir; **further education** n enseignement m postscolaire (recyclage, formation professionnelle); **furthermore** adv de plus, en outre

furthest ['fəːðɪst] superlative of **far**

fury ['fjʊərɪ] n fureur f

fuse (US **fuze**) [fjuːz] n fusible m; (for bomb etc) amorce f, détonateur m ▷ vt, vi (metal) fondre; (BRIT: Elec): **to ~ the lights** faire sauter les fusibles or les plombs; **fuse box** n boîte f à fusibles

fusion ['fjuːʒən] n fusion f

fuss [fʌs] n (anxiety, excitement) chichis mpl, façons fpl; (commotion) tapage m; (complaining, trouble) histoire(s) f(pl); **to make a ~** faire des façons (or des histoires); **to make a ~ of sb** dorloter qn; **fussy** adj (person) tatillon(ne), difficile, chichiteux(-euse); (dress, style) tarabiscoté(e)

future ['fjuːtʃə'] adj futur(e) ▷ n avenir m; (Ling) futur m; **futures** npl (Comm) opérations fpl à terme; **in (the) ~** à

l'avenir

fuze [fjuːz] n, vt, vi (US) = **fuse**

fuzzy ['fʌzɪ] adj (Phot) flou(e); (hair) crépu(e)

g

g [dʒiː] n (Mus): **G** sol m

g abbr (= gram) g

gadget ['gædʒɪt] n gadget m

Gaelic ['geɪlɪk] adj, n (Ling) gaélique (m)

gag [gæg] n (on mouth) bâillon m; (joke)
gag m ▷ vt (prisoner etc) bâillonner

gain [geɪn] n (improvement) gain m;
(profit) gain, profit m ▷ vt gagner ▷ vi
(watch) avancer; **to ~ from/by** gagner
de/à; **to ~ on sb** (catch up) rattraper qn;
to ~ 3lbs (in weight) prendre 3 livres;
to ~ ground gagner du terrain

gal. abbr = **gallon**

gala ['gɑːlə] n gala m

galaxy ['gæləksɪ] n galaxie f

gale [geɪl] n coup m de vent

gall bladder ['gɔːl-] n vésicule f biliaire

gallery ['gælərɪ] n (also: **art ~**) musée
m; (: private) galerie; (: in theatre) dernier
balcon

gallon ['gæln] n gallon m (BRIT = 4.543
l; US = 3.785 l)

gallop ['gæləp] n galop m ▷ vi galoper

gallstone ['gɔːlstəun] n calcul m

(biliaire)

gamble ['gæmbl] n pari m, risque
calculé ▷ vt, vi jouer; **to ~ on** (fig) miser
sur; **gambler** n joueur m; **gambling**
n jeu m

game [geɪm] n jeu m; (event) match m;
(of tennis, chess, cards) partie f; (Hunting)
gibier m ▷ adj (willing): **to be ~ (for)**
être prêt(e) (à or pour); **big ~** gros
gibier; **games** npl (Scol) sport m; (sport
event) jeux; **games console** ['geɪmz-]
n console f de jeux vidéo; **game show**
n jeu télévisé

gammon ['gæmən] n (bacon) quartier
m de lard fumé; (ham) jambon fumé
or salé

gang [gæŋ] n bande f; (of workmen)
équipe f

gangster ['gæŋstəʳ] n gangster m,
bandit m

gap [gæp] n trou m; (in time) intervalle
m; (difference): **~ (between)** écart m
(entre)

gape [geɪp] vi (person) être or rester
bouche bée; (hole, shirt) être ouvert(e)

gap year n année que certains étudiants
prennent pour voyager ou pour travailler
avant d'entrer à l'université

garage ['gærɑːʒ] n garage m; **garage
sale** n vide-grenier m

garbage ['gɑːbɪdʒ] n (US: rubbish)
ordures fpl, détritus mpl; (inf: nonsense)
âneries fpl; **garbage can** n (US)
poubelle f, boîte f à ordures; **garbage
collector** n (US) éboueur m

garden ['gɑːdn] n jardin m; **gardens** npl
(public) jardin public; (private) parc m;
garden centre (BRIT) n pépinière f,
jardinerie f; **gardener** n jardinier m;
gardening n jardinage m

garlic ['gɑːlɪk] n ail m

garment ['gɑːmənt] n vêtement m

garnish ['gɑːnɪʃ] (Culin) vt garnir ▷ n
décoration f

garrison ['gærɪsn] n garnison f

gas [gæs] n gaz m; (US: gasoline) essence
f ▷ vt asphyxier; **I can smell ~** ça sent le
gaz; **gas cooker** n (BRIT) cuisinière f à

gaz; **gas cylinder** n bouteille f de gaz;
gas fire n (BRIT) radiateur m à gaz

gasket ['gæskɪt] n (Aut) joint m de
culasse

gasoline ['gæsəliːn] n (US) essence f

gasp [gɑːsp] n halètement m; (of shock
etc): **she gave a small ~ of pain** la
douleur lui coupa le souffle ▷ vi haleter;
(fig) avoir le souffle coupé

gas: **gas pedal** n (US) accélérateur m;
gas station n (US) station-service f;
gas tank n (US Aut) réservoir m
d'essence

gate [geɪt] n (of garden) portail m; (of
field, at level crossing) barrière f; (of
building, town, at airport) porte f

gateau (pl **-x**) ['gætəʊ, -z] n gros
gâteau à la crème

gatecrash ['geɪtkræʃ] vt s'introduire
sans invitation dans

gateway ['geɪtweɪ] n porte f

gather ['gæðə'] vt (flowers, fruit)
cueillir; (pick up) ramasser; (assemble:
objects) rassembler; (: people) réunir;
(: information) recueillir; (understand)
comprendre; (Sewing) froncer ▷ vi
(assemble) se rassembler; **to ~ speed**
prendre de la vitesse; **gathering** n
rassemblement m

gauge [geɪdʒ] n (instrument) jauge f ▷ vt
jauger; (fig) juger de

gave [geɪv] pt of **give**

gay [geɪ] adj (homosexual)
homosexuel(le); (colour) gai, vif (vive)

gaze [geɪz] n regard m fixe ▷ vi: **to ~ at**
vt fixer du regard

GB abbr = **Great Britain**

GCSE n abbr (BRIT: = General Certificate of
Secondary Education) examen passé à l'âge
de 16 ans sanctionnant les connaissances
de l'élève

gear [gɪə'] n matériel m, équipement
m; (Tech) engrenage m; (Aut) vitesse
f ▷ vt (fig: adapt) adapter; **top** or (US)
high/low ~ quatrième (or cinquième)/
première vitesse; **in ~** en prise; **gear up**
vi: **to ~ up (to do)** se préparer (à faire);
gear box n boîte f de vitesse; **gear**

lever n levier m de vitesse; **gear shift**
(US) n = **gear lever**; **gear stick** (BRIT) n
= **gear lever**

geese [giːs] npl of **goose**

gel [dʒɛl] n gelée f

gem [dʒɛm] n pierre précieuse

Gemini ['dʒɛmɪnaɪ] n les Gémeaux mpl

gender ['dʒɛndə'] n genre m; (person's
sex) sexe m

gene [dʒiːn] n (Biol) gène m

general ['dʒɛnərl] n général m ▷ adj
général(e); **in ~** en général; **general
anaesthetic** (US **general anesthetic**)
n anesthésie générale; **general
election** n élection(s) législative(s);
generalize vi généraliser; **generally**
adv généralement; **general
practitioner** n généraliste m/f;
general store n épicerie f

generate ['dʒɛnəreɪt] vt engendrer;
(electricity) produire

generation [dʒɛnəˈreɪʃən] n
génération f; (of electricity etc)
production f

generator ['dʒɛnəreɪtə'] n
générateur m

generosity [dʒɛnəˈrɒsɪtɪ] n
générosité f

generous ['dʒɛnərəs] adj
généreux(-euse); (copious)
copieux(-euse)

genetic [dʒɪˈnɛtɪk] adj génétique; **~
engineering** ingénierie m génétique;
fingerprinting système m d'empreint
génétique; **genetically modified** adj
(food etc) génétiquement modifié(e);
genetics n génétique f

Geneva [dʒɪˈniːvə] n Genève

genitals ['dʒɛnɪtlz] npl organes
génitaux

genius ['dʒiːnɪəs] n génie m

gent [dʒɛnt] n abbr (BRIT inf)
= **gentleman**

gentle ['dʒɛntl] adj doux (douce);
(breeze, touch) léger(-ère)

gentleman (irreg) ['dʒɛntlmən]
n monsieur m; (well-bred man)
gentleman m

ently ['dʒentlɪ] *adv* doucement
ents [dʒents] *n* W.-C. *mpl* (pour
hommes)
enuine ['dʒenjuɪn] *adj* véritable,
authentique; (*person, emotion*) sincère;
genuinely *adv* sincèrement, vraiment
eographic(al) [dʒɪə'græfɪk(l)] *adj*
géographique
eography [dʒɪ'ɔgrəfɪ] *n* géographie *f*
eology [dʒɪ'ɔlədʒɪ] *n* géologie *f*
eometry [dʒɪ'ɔmətrɪ] *n* géométrie *f*
eranium [dʒɪ'reɪnɪəm] *n* géranium *m*
eriatric [dʒerɪ'ætrɪk] *adj* gériatrique
▷ *n* patient(e) gériatrique
erm [dʒə:m] *n* (*Med*) microbe *m*
erman ['dʒə:mən] *adj* allemand(e)
▷ *n* Allemand(e); (*Ling*) allemand *m*;
German measles *n* rubéole *f*
ermany ['dʒə:mənɪ] *n* Allemagne *f*
esture ['dʒestjər] *n* geste *m*

 KEYWORD

et [get] (*pt, pp* **got**, *pp* **gotten** (us)) *vi*
1 (*become, be*) devenir; **to get old/tired**
devenir vieux/fatigué, vieillir/se
fatiguer; **to get drunk** s'enivrer; **to get
dirty** se salir; **to get married** se marier;
when do I get paid? quand est-ce
que je serai payé?; **it's getting late** il
se fait tard
2 (*go*): **to get to/from** aller à/de; **to get
home** rentrer chez soi; **how did you
get here?** comment es-tu arrivé ici?
3 (*begin*) commencer *or* se mettre
à; **to get to know sb** apprendre à
connaître qn; **I'm getting to like him**
je commence à l'apprécier; **let's get
going** *or* **started** allons-y
4 (*modal aux vb*): **you've got to do it** il
faut que vous le fassiez; **I've got to tell
the police** je dois le dire à la police
▷ *vt* **1**: **to get sth done** (*do*) faire qch;
(*have done*) faire faire qch; **to get sth/sb
ready** préparer qch/qn; **to get one's
hair cut** se faire couper les cheveux;
to get the car going *or* **to go** (faire)
démarrer la voiture; **to get sb to do sth**

faire faire qch à qn
2 (*obtain: money, permission, results*)
obtenir, avoir; (*buy*) acheter; (*find:
job, flat*) trouver; (*fetch: person, doctor,
object*) aller chercher; **to get sth for sb**
procurer qch à qn; **get me Mr Jones,
please** (*on phone*) passez-moi Mr Jones,
s'il vous plaît; **can I get you a drink?**
est-ce que je peux vous servir à boire?
3 (*receive: present, letter*) recevoir,
avoir; (*acquire: reputation*) avoir; (*prize*)
obtenir; **what did you get for your
birthday?** qu'est-ce que tu as eu pour
ton anniversaire?; **how much did you
get for the painting?** combien avez-
vous vendu le tableau?
4 (*catch*) prendre, saisir, attraper;
(*hit: target etc*) atteindre; **to get sb by
the arm/throat** prendre *or* saisir *or*
attraper qn par le bras/à la gorge; **get
him!** arrête-le!; **the bullet got him in
the leg** il a pris la balle dans la jambe
5 (*take, move*): **to get sth to sb** faire
parvenir qch à qn; **do you think we'll
get it through the door?** on arrivera à
le faire passer par la porte?
6 (*catch, take: plane, bus etc*) prendre;
**where do I get the train for
Birmingham?** où prend-on le train
pour Birmingham?
7 (*understand*) comprendre, saisir; (*hear*)
entendre; **I've got it!** j'ai compris!; **I
don't get your meaning** je ne vois
or comprends pas ce que vous voulez
dire; **I didn't get your name** je n'ai pas
entendu votre nom
8 (*have, possess*): **to have got** avoir;
how many have you got? vous en avez
combien?
9 (*illness*) avoir; **I've got a cold** j'ai le
rhume; **she got pneumonia and died**
elle a fait une pneumonie et elle en
est morte
get away *vi* partir, s'en aller; (*escape*)
s'échapper
get away with *vt fus* (*punishment*)
en être quitte pour; (*crime etc*) se faire
pardonner

get back vi (return) rentrer
▷ vt récupérer, recouvrer; **when do we get back?** quand serons-nous de retour?

get in vi entrer; (arrive home) rentrer; (train) arriver

get into vt fus entrer dans; (car, train etc) monter dans; (clothes) mettre, enfiler, endosser; **to get into bed/a rage** se mettre au lit/en colère

get off vi (from train etc) descendre; (depart: person, car) s'en aller
▷ vt (remove: clothes, stain) enlever
▷ vt fus (train, bus) descendre de; **where do I get off?** où est-ce que je dois descendre?

get on vi (at exam etc) se débrouiller; (agree): **to get on (with)** s'entendre (avec); **how are you getting on?** comment ça va?
▷ vt fus monter dans; (horse) monter sur

get out vi sortir; (of vehicle) descendre
▷ vt sortir

get out of vt fus sortir de; (duty etc) échapper à, se soustraire à

get over vt fus (illness) se remettre de

get through vi (Tel) avoir la communication; **to get through to sb** atteindre qn

get up vi (rise) se lever
▷ vt fus monter

getaway ['gɛtəweɪ] n fuite f
Ghana ['gɑːnə] n Ghana m
ghastly ['gɑːstlɪ] adj atroce, horrible
ghetto ['gɛtəu] n ghetto m
ghost [gəust] n fantôme m, revenant m
giant ['dʒaɪənt] n géant(e) ▷ adj géant(e), énorme
gift [gɪft] n cadeau m; (donation, talent) don m; **gifted** adj doué(e); **gift shop** (us **gift store**) n boutique f de cadeaux; **gift token, gift voucher** n chèque-cadeau m
gig [gɪg] n (inf: concert) concert m
gigabyte ['dʒɪgəbaɪt] n gigaoctet m
gigantic [dʒaɪ'gæntɪk] adj gigantesque

giggle ['gɪgl] vi pouffer, ricaner sottement
gills [gɪlz] npl (of fish) ouïes fpl, branchies fpl
gilt [gɪlt] n dorure f ▷ adj doré(e)
gimmick ['gɪmɪk] n truc m
gin [dʒɪn] n gin m
ginger ['dʒɪndʒər] n gingembre m
gipsy ['dʒɪpsɪ] n = **gypsy**
giraffe [dʒɪ'rɑːf] n girafe f
girl [gəːl] n fille f, fillette f; (young unmarried woman) jeune fille; (daughter) fille; **an English** ~ une jeune Anglaise; **girl band** n girls band m; **girlfriend** n (of girl) amie f; (of boy) petite amie; **Girl Guide** n (BRIT) éclaireuse f; (Roman Catholic) guide f; **Girl Scout** n (US) = **Girl Guide**
gist [dʒɪst] n essentiel m
give [gɪv] vb (pt **gave**, pp ~**n**) ▷ vt donner ▷ vi (break) céder; (stretch: fabric) se prêter; **to** ~ **sb sth**, ~ **sth to sb** donner qch à qn; (gift) offrir qch à qn; (message) transmettre qch à qn; **to** ~ **sb a call/kiss** donner un coup de fil/embrasser qn; **to** ~ **a cry/sigh** pousser un cri/un soupir; **give away** vt donner; (give free) faire cadeau de; (betray) donner, trahir; (disclose) révéler; **give back** vt rendre; **give in** vi céder ▷ vt donner; **give out** vt (food etc) distribuer; **give up** vi renoncer ▷ vt renoncer à; **to** ~ **up smoking** arrêter de fumer; **to** ~ **o.s. up** se rendre
given ['gɪvn] pp of **give** ▷ adj (fixed: time, amount) donné(e), déterminé(e) ▷ conj: ~ **the circumstances …** étant donné les circonstances …, vu les circonstances …; ~ **that …** étant donné que …
glacier ['glæsɪər] n glacier m
glad [glæd] adj content(e); **gladly** ['glædlɪ] adv volontiers
glamorous ['glæmərəs] adj (person) séduisant(e); (job) prestigieux(-euse)
glamour (US **glamor**) ['glæmər] n éclat m, prestige m
glance [glɑːns] n coup m d'œil ▷ vi: **to**

at jeter un coup d'œil à

gland [glænd] n glande f

glare [glɛəʳ] n (of anger) regard furieux; (of light) lumière éblouissante; (of publicity) feux mpl ▷ vi briller d'un éclat aveuglant; **to ~ at** lancer un regard or des regards furieux à; **glaring** adj (mistake) criant(e), qui saute aux yeux

glass [glɑːs] n verre m; **glasses** npl (spectacles) lunettes fpl

glaze [gleɪz] vt (door) vitrer; (pottery) vernir ▷ n vernis m

gleam [gliːm] vi luire, briller

glen [glɛn] n vallée f

glide [glaɪd] vi glisser; (Aviat, bird) planer; **glider** n (Aviat) planeur m

glimmer [ˈglɪməʳ] n lueur f

glimpse [glɪmps] n vision passagère, aperçu m ▷ vt entrevoir, apercevoir

glint [glɪnt] vi étinceler

glisten [ˈglɪsn] vi briller, luire

glitter [ˈglɪtəʳ] vi scintiller, briller

global [ˈgləubl] adj (world-wide) mondial(e); (overall) global(e); **globalization** n mondialisation f; **global warming** n réchauffement m de la planète

globe [gləub] n globe m

gloom [gluːm] n obscurité f; (sadness) tristesse f, mélancolie f; **gloomy** adj (person) morose; (place, outlook) sombre

glorious [ˈglɔːrɪəs] adj glorieux(-euse); (beautiful) splendide

glory [ˈglɔːrɪ] n gloire f; splendeur f

gloss [glɔs] n (shine) brillant m, vernis m; (also: ~ **paint**) peinture brillante or laquée

glossary [ˈglɔsərɪ] n glossaire m, lexique m

glossy [ˈglɔsɪ] adj brillant(e), luisant(e) ▷ n (also: ~ **magazine**) revue f de luxe

glove [glʌv] n gant m; **glove compartment** n (Aut) boîte f à gants, vide-poches m inv

glow [gləu] vi rougeoyer; (face) rayonner; (eyes) briller

glucose [ˈgluːkəus] n glucose m

glue [gluː] n colle f ▷ vt coller

GM abbr (= genetically modified) génétiquement modifié(e)

gm abbr (= gram) g

GMO n abbr (= genetically modified organism) OGM m

GMT abbr (= Greenwich Mean Time) GMT

gnaw [nɔː] vt ronger

go [gəu] vb (pt **went**, pp **gone**) ▷ vi aller; (depart) partir, s'en aller; (work) marcher; (break) céder; (time) passer; (be sold): **to go for £10** se vendre 10 livres; (become): **to go pale/mouldy** pâlir/moisir ▷ n (pl **goes**): **to have a go (at)** essayer (de faire); **to be on the go** être en mouvement; **whose go is it?** à qui est-ce de jouer?; **he's going to do it** il va le faire, il est sur le point de le faire; **to go for a walk** aller se promener; **to go dancing/shopping** aller danser/faire les courses; **to go and see sb, go to see sb** aller voir qn; **how did it go?** comment est-ce que ça s'est passé?; **to go round the back/by the shop** passer par derrière/devant le magasin; **... to go** (US: food) ... à emporter; **go ahead** vi (take place) avoir lieu; (get going) y aller; **go away** vi partir, s'en aller; **go back** vi rentrer; revenir; (go again) retourner; **go by** vi (years, time) passer, s'écouler ▷ vt fus s'en tenir à; (believe) en croire; **go down** vi descendre; (number, price, amount) baisser; (ship) couler; (sun) se coucher ▷ vt fus descendre; **go for** vt fus (fetch) aller chercher; (like) aimer; (attack) s'en prendre à; attaquer; **go in** vi entrer; **go into** vt fus entrer dans; (investigate) étudier, examiner; (embark on) se lancer dans; **go off** vi partir, s'en aller; (food) se gâter; (milk) tourner; (bomb) sauter; (alarm clock) sonner; (alarm) se déclencher; (lights etc) s'éteindre; (event) se dérouler ▷ vt fus ne plus aimer; **the gun went off** le coup est parti; **go on** vi continuer; (happen) se passer; (lights) s'allumer ▷ vt fus: **to go on doing** continuer à faire; **go out** vi sortir; (fire, light) s'éteindre;

(tide) descendre; **to go out with sb** sortir avec qn; **go over** vi, vt fus (check) revoir, vérifier; **go past** vt fus: **to go past sth** passer devant qch; **go round** vi (circulate: news, rumour) circuler; (revolve) tourner; (suffice) suffire (pour tout le monde); (visit): **to go round to sb's** passer chez qn; aller chez qn; (make a detour): **to go round (by)** faire un détour (par); **go through** vt fus (town etc) traverser; (search through) fouiller; (suffer) subir; **go up** vi monter; (price) augmenter ▷ vt fus gravir; **go with** vt fus aller avec; **go without** vt fus se passer de

go-ahead ['gəuəhɛd] adj dynamique, entreprenant(e) ▷ n feu vert

goal [gəul] n but m; **goalkeeper** n gardien m de but; **goal-post** n poteau m de but

goat [gəut] n chèvre f

gobble ['gɔbl] vt (also: ~ down, ~ up) engloutir

god [gɔd] n dieu m; **G~** Dieu; **godchild** n filleul(e); **goddaughter** n filleule f; **goddess** n déesse f; **godfather** n parrain m; **godmother** n marraine f; **godson** n filleul m

goggles ['gɔglz] npl (for skiing etc) lunettes (protectrices); (for swimming) lunettes de piscine

going ['gəuɪŋ] n (conditions) état m du terrain ▷ adj: **the ~ rate** le tarif (en vigueur)

gold [gəuld] n or m ▷ adj en or; (reserves) d'or; **golden** adj (made of gold) en or; (gold in colour) doré(e); **goldfish** n poisson m rouge; **goldmine** n mine f d'or; **gold-plated** adj plaqué(e) or inv

golf [gɔlf] n golf m; **golf ball** n balle f de golf; (on typewriter) boule f; **golf club** n club m de golf; (stick) crosse f de golf; **golf course** n terrain m de golf; **golfer** n joueur(-euse) de golf

gone [gɔn] pp of **go**

gong [gɔŋ] n gong m

good [gud] adj bon(ne); (kind) gentil(le); (child) sage; (weather) beau (belle) ▷ n

bien m; **goods** npl marchandise f, articles mpl; **~!** bon!, très bien!; **to be ~ at** être bon en; **to be ~ for** être bon pour; **it's no ~ complaining** cela ne sert à rien de se plaindre; **to make ~** (deficit) combler; (losses) compenser; **for ~ (for ever)** pour de bon, une fois pour toutes; **would you be ~ enough to …?** auriez-vous la bonté or l'amabilité de …?; **is this any ~?** (will it do?) est-ce que ceci fera l'affaire?, est-ce que cela peut vous rendre service?; (what's it like?) qu'est-ce que ça vaut?; **a ~ deal (of)** beaucoup (de); **a ~ many** beaucoup (de); **~ morning/afternoon!** bonjour!; **~ evening!** bonsoir!; **~ night!** bonsoir!; (on going to bed) bonne nuit!; **goodbye** excl au revoir!; **to say goodbye to sb** dire au revoir à qn; **Good Friday** n Vendredi saint; **good-looking** adj beau (belle), bien inv; **good-natured** adj (person) qui a un bon naturel; **goodness** n (of person) bonté f; **for goodness sake!** je vous en prie!; **goodness gracious!** mon Dieu!; **goods train** n (BRIT) train m de marchandises; **goodwill** n bonne volonté

goose (pl geese) [gu:s, gi:s] n oie f

gooseberry ['guzbərɪ] n groseille f à maquereau; **to play ~** (BRIT) tenir la chandelle

goose bumps, goose pimples npl chair f de poule

gorge [gɔ:dʒ] n gorge f ▷ vt: **to ~ o.s. (on)** se gorger (de)

gorgeous ['gɔ:dʒəs] adj splendide, superbe

gorilla [gə'rɪlə] n gorille m

gosh (inf) [gɔʃ] excl mince alors!

gospel ['gɔspl] n évangile m

gossip ['gɔsɪp] n (chat) bavardages mpl; (malicious) commérage m, cancans mpl; (person) commère f ▷ vi bavarder; cancaner, faire des commérages; **gossip column** n (Press) échos mpl

got [gɔt] pt, pp of **get**

gotten ['gɔtn] (US) pp of **get**

gourmet ['guəmeɪ] n gourmet m,

astronome *m/f*

•vern ['gʌvən] *vt* gouverner; *influence*) déterminer; **government** gouvernement *m*; (BRIT: *ministers*) ministère *m*; **governor** *n* (*of colony, tate, bank*) gouverneur *m*; (*of school, ospital etc*) administrateur(-trice); BRIT: *of prison*) directeur(-trice)

•wn [gaun] *n* robe *f*; (*of teacher, BRIT: f judge*) toge *f*

P. *n abbr* (*Med*) = **general practitioner**

ab [græb] *vt* saisir, empoigner ▷ *vi*: **to • at** essayer de saisir

ace [greɪs] *n* grâce *f*; (*honour*) honorer; (*adorn*) orner; **5 days' ~** un répit de 5 jours; **graceful** *adj* gracieux(-euse), élégant(e); **gracious** ['greɪʃəs] *adj* bienveillant(e)

ade [greɪd] *n* (Comm: *quality*) qualité ; (*size*) calibre *m*; (*type*) catégorie ; (*in hierarchy*) grade *m*, échelon *m*; Scol) note *f*; (US: *school class*) classe ; (: (*gradient*) pente *f* ▷ *vt* classer; (*by ize*) calibrer; **grade crossing** *n* (US) passage *m* à niveau; **grade school** *n* US) école *f* primaire

adient ['greɪdɪənt] *n* inclinaison , pente *f*

adual ['grædjuəl] *adj* graduel(le), progressif(-ive); **gradually** *adv* peu à peu, graduellement

aduate *n* ['grædjuɪt] diplômé(e) d'université; (US: *of high school*) diplômé(e) de fin d'études ▷ *vi* ['grædjueɪt] obtenir un diplôme d'université (*or* de fin d'études); **graduation** [grædju'eɪʃən] *n* cérémonie *f* de remise des diplômes

affiti [grə'fiːtɪ] *npl* graffiti *mpl*

aft [grɑːft] *n* (Agr, Med) greffe *f*; (*bribery*) corruption *f* ▷ *vt* greffer; **hard ~** (BRIT: *inf*) boulot acharné

ain [greɪn] *n* (*single piece*) grain *m*; (*no pl: cereals*) céréales *fpl*; (US: *corn*) blé *m*

am [græm] *n* gramme *m*

ammar ['græmər] *n* grammaire *f*; **grammar school** *n* (BRIT) ≈ lycée *m*

amme [græm] *n* = **gram**

gran (*inf*) [græn] *n* (BRIT) mamie *f* (*inf*), mémé *f* (*inf*)

grand [grænd] *adj* magnifique, splendide; (*gesture etc*) noble; **grandad** (*inf*) *n* = **granddad**; **grandchild** (*pl* **~ren**) *n* petit-fils *m*, petite-fille *f*; **grandchildren** *npl* petits-enfants; **granddad** *n* (*inf*) papy *m* (*inf*), papi *m* (*inf*), pépé *m* (*inf*); **granddaughter** *n* petite-fille *f*; **grandfather** *n* grand-père *m*; **grandma** *n* (*inf*) = **gran**; **grandmother** *n* grand-mère *f*; **grandpa** *n* (*inf*) = **granddad**; **grandparents** *npl* grands-parents *mpl*; **grand piano** *n* piano *m* à queue; **Grand Prix** ['grɑ̃:'priː] *n* (Aut) grand prix automobile; **grandson** *n* petit-fils *m*

granite ['grænɪt] *n* granit *m*

granny ['grænɪ] *n* (*inf*) = **gran**

grant [grɑːnt] *vt* accorder; (*a request*) accéder à; (*admit*) concéder ▷ *n* (Scol) bourse *f*; (Admin) subside *m*, subvention *f*; **to take sth for ~ed** considérer qch comme acquis; **to take sb for ~ed** considérer qn comme faisant partie du décor

grape [greɪp] *n* raisin *m*

grapefruit ['greɪpfruːt] *n* pamplemousse *m*

graph [grɑːf] *n* graphique *m*, courbe *f*; **graphic** ['græfɪk] *adj* graphique; (*vivid*) vivant(e); **graphics** *n* (*art*) arts *mpl* graphiques; (*process*) graphisme *m* ▷ *npl* (*drawings*) illustrations *fpl*

grasp [grɑːsp] *vt* saisir ▷ *n* (*grip*) prise *f*; (*fig*) compréhension *f*, connaissance *f*

grass [grɑːs] *n* herbe *f*; (*lawn*) gazon *m*; **grasshopper** *n* sauterelle *f*

grate [greɪt] *n* grille *f* de cheminée ▷ *vi* grincer ▷ *vt* (Culin) râper

grateful ['greɪtful] *adj* reconnaissant(e)

grater ['greɪtər] *n* râpe *f*

gratitude ['grætɪtjuːd] *n* gratitude *f*

grave [greɪv] *n* tombe *f* ▷ *adj* grave, sérieux(-euse)

gravel ['grævl] *n* gravier *m*

gravestone ['greɪvstəun] *n* pierre

tombale

graveyard ['greɪvjɑːd] n cimetière m

gravity ['grævɪtɪ] n (Physics) gravité f; pesanteur f; (seriousness) gravité

gravy ['greɪvɪ] n jus m (de viande), sauce f (au jus de viande)

gray [greɪ] adj (US) = **grey**

graze [greɪz] vi paître, brouter ▷ vt (touch lightly) frôler, effleurer; (scrape) écorcher ▷ n écorchure f

grease [griːs] n (fat) graisse f; (lubricant) lubrifiant m ▷ vt graisser; lubrifier; **greasy** adj gras(se), graisseux(-euse); (hands, clothes) graisseux

great [greɪt] adj grand(e); (heat, pain etc) très fort(e), intense; (inf) formidable; **Great Britain** n Grande-Bretagne f; **great-grandfather** n arrière-grand-père m; **great-grandmother** n arrière-grand-mère f; **greatly** adv très, grandement; (with verbs) beaucoup

Greece [griːs] n Grèce f

greed [griːd] n (also: **~iness**) avidité f; (for food) gourmandise f; **greedy** adj avide; (for food) gourmand(e)

Greek [griːk] adj grec (grecque) ▷ n Grec (Grecque); (Ling) grec m

green [griːn] adj vert(e); (inexperienced) (bien) jeune, naïf(-ïve); (ecological: product etc) écologique ▷ n (colour) vert m; (on golf course) green m; (stretch of grass) pelouse f; **greens** npl (vegetables) légumes verts; **green card** n (Aut) carte verte; (US: work permit) permis m de travail; **greengage** n reine-claude f; **greengrocer** n (BRIT) marchand m de fruits et légumes; **greengrocer's (shop)** n magasin m de fruits et légumes; **greenhouse** n serre f; **greenhouse effect** n: **the greenhouse effect** l'effet m de serre

Greenland ['griːnlənd] n Groenland m

green salad n salade verte

greet [griːt] vt accueillir; **greeting** n salutation f; **Christmas/birthday greetings** souhaits mpl de Noël/de bon anniversaire; **greeting(s) card** n carte f de vœux

grew [gruː] pt of **grow**

grey (US **gray**) [greɪ] adj gris(e); (dismal) sombre; **grey-haired** adj aux cheveux gris; **greyhound** n lévrier m

grid [grɪd] n grille f; (Elec) réseau m; **gridlock** n (traffic jam) embouteillage m

grief [griːf] n chagrin m, douleur f

grievance ['griːvəns] n doléance f, grief m; (cause for complaint) grief

grieve [griːv] vi avoir du chagrin; se désoler ▷ vt faire de la peine à, affliger; **to ~ for sb** pleurer qn

grill [grɪl] n (on cooker) gril m; (also: **mixed ~**) grillade(s) f(pl) ▷ vt (BRIT) griller; (inf: question) cuisiner

grille [grɪl] n grillage m; (Aut) calandre

grim [grɪm] adj sinistre, lugubre; (serious, stern) sévère

grime [graɪm] n crasse f

grin [grɪn] n large sourire m ▷ vi sourire

grind [graɪnd] vb (pt, pp ground) ▷ vt écraser; (coffee, pepper etc) moudre; (US: meat) hacher ▷ n (work) corvée f

grip [grɪp] n (handclasp) poigne f; (control) prise f; (handle) poignée f; (holdall) sac m de voyage ▷ vt saisir, empoigner; (viewer, reader) captiver; **to come to ~s with** se colleter avec, en venir aux prises avec; **to ~ the road** (Aut) adhérer à la route; **gripping** adj prenant(e), palpitant(e)

grit [grɪt] n gravillon m; (courage) cran m ▷ vt (road) sabler; **to ~ one's teeth** serrer les dents

grits [grɪts] npl (US) gruau m de maïs

groan [grəʊn] n (of pain) gémissement m ▷ vi gémir

grocer ['grəʊsəʳ] n épicier m; **groceries** npl provisions fpl; **grocer's (shop), grocery** n épicerie f

groin [grɔɪn] n aine f

groom [gruːm] n (for horses) palefrenier m; (also: **bride~**) marié m ▷ vt (horse) panser; (fig): **to ~ sb for** former qn pour

groove [gruːv] n sillon m, rainure f

grope [grəʊp] vi tâtonner; **to ~ for** chercher à tâtons

gross [grəus] *adj* grossier(-ière); (*Comm*) brut(e); **grossly** *adv* (*greatly*) très, grandement

grotesque [grə'tɛsk] *adj* grotesque

ground [graund] *pt, pp of* **grind** ▷ *n* sol *m*, terre *f*; (*land*) terrain *m*, terres *fpl*; (*Sport*) terrain; (*reason: gen pl*) raison *f*; (*us: also*: **~ wire**) terre *f* ▷ *vt* (*plane*) empêcher de décoller, retenir au sol; (*us Elec*) équiper d'une prise de terre; **grounds** *npl* (*gardens etc*) parc *m*, domaine *m*; (*of coffee*) marc *m*; **on the ~, to the ~** par terre; **to gain/lose ~** gagner/perdre du terrain; **ground floor** *n* (*BRIT*) rez-de-chaussée *m*; **groundsheet** *n* (*BRIT*) tapis *m* de sol; **groundwork** *n* préparation *f*

group [gruːp] *n* groupe *m* ▷ *vt* (*also*: **~ together**) grouper ▷ *vi* (*also*: **~ together**) se grouper

grouse [graus] *n* (*pl inv*: *bird*) grouse *f* (*sorte de coq de bruyère*) ▷ *vi* (*complain*) rouspéter, râler

grovel ['grɒvl] *vi* (*fig*): **to ~ (before)** ramper (devant)

grow (*pt grew, pp ~n*) [grəu, gruː, grəun] *vi* (*plant*) pousser, croître; (*person*) grandir; (*increase*) augmenter, se développer; (*become*) devenir; **to ~ rich/weak** s'enrichir/s'affaiblir ▷ *vt* cultiver, faire pousser; (*hair, beard*) laisser pousser; **grow on** *vt fus*: **that painting is ~ing on me** je finirai par aimer ce tableau; **grow up** *vi* grandir

growl [graul] *vi* grogner

grown [grəun] *pp of* **grow**; **grown-up** *n* adulte *m/f*, grande personne

growth [grəuθ] *n* croissance *f*, développement *m*; (*what has grown*) pousse *f*, poussée *f*; (*Med*) grosseur *f*, tumeur *f*

grub [grʌb] *n* larve *f*; (*inf: food*) bouffe *f*

grubby ['grʌbɪ] *adj* crasseux(-euse)

grudge [grʌdʒ] *n* rancune *f* ▷ *vt*: **to ~ sb sth** (*in giving*) donner qch à qn à contre-cœur; (*resent*) reprocher qch à qn; **to bear sb a ~ (for)** garder rancune *or* en vouloir à qn (de)

gruelling (*us* **grueling**) ['gruəlɪŋ] *adj* exténuant(e)

gruesome ['gruːsəm] *adj* horrible

grumble ['grʌmbl] *vi* rouspéter, ronchonner

grumpy ['grʌmpɪ] *adj* grincheux(-euse)

grunt [grʌnt] *vi* grogner

guarantee [gærən'tiː] *n* garantie *f* ▷ *vt* garantir

guard [gɑːd] *n* garde *f*; (*one man*) garde *m*; (*BRIT Rail*) chef *m* de train; (*safety device: on machine*) dispositif *m* de sûreté; (*also*: **fire~**) garde-feu *m inv* ▷ *vt* garder, surveiller; (*protect*): **to ~ sb/sth (against *or* from)** protéger qn/qch (contre); **to be on one's ~** (*fig*) être sur ses gardes; **guardian** *n* gardien(ne); (*of minor*) tuteur(-trice)

guerrilla [gə'rɪlə] *n* guérillero *m*

guess [gɛs] *vi* deviner ▷ *vt* deviner; (*estimate*) évaluer; (*us*) croire, penser ▷ *n* supposition *f*, hypothèse *f*; **to take *or* have a ~** essayer de deviner

guest [gɛst] *n* invité(e); (*in hotel*) client(e); **guest house** *n* pension *f*; **guest room** *n* chambre *f* d'amis

guidance ['gaɪdəns] *n* (*advice*) conseils *mpl*

guide [gaɪd] *n* (*person*) guide *m/f*; (*book*) guide *m*; (*also*: **Girl G~**) éclaireuse *f*; (*Roman Catholic*) guide *f* ▷ *vt* guider; **is there an English-speaking ~?** est-ce que l'un des guides parle anglais?; **guidebook** *n* guide *m*; **guide dog** *n* chien *m* d'aveugle; **guided tour** *n* visite guidée; **what time does the guided tour start?** la visite guidée commence à quelle heure?; **guidelines** *npl* (*advice*) instructions générales, conseils *mpl*

guild [gɪld] *n* (*History*) corporation *f*; (*sharing interests*) cercle *m*, association *f*

guilt [gɪlt] *n* culpabilité *f*; **guilty** *adj* coupable

guinea pig ['gɪnɪ-] *n* cobaye *m*

guitar [gɪ'tɑːʳ] *n* guitare *f*; **guitarist** *n* guitariste *m/f*

gulf [gʌlf] *n* golfe *m*; (*abyss*) gouffre *m*

gull [gʌl] *n* mouette *f*

gulp [gʌlp] vi avaler sa salive; (from emotion) avoir la gorge serrée, s'étrangler ▷ vt (also: **~ down**) avaler
gum [gʌm] n (Anat) gencive f; (glue) colle f; (also: **chewing-~**) chewing-gum m ▷ vt coller
gun [gʌn] n (small) revolver m, pistolet m; (rifle) fusil m, carabine f; (cannon) canon m; **gunfire** n fusillade f; **gunman** (irreg) n bandit armé; **gunpoint** n: **at gunpoint** sous la menace du pistolet (or fusil); **gunpowder** n poudre f à canon; **gunshot** n coup m de feu
gush [gʌʃ] vi jaillir; (fig) se répandre en effusions
gust [gʌst] n (of wind) rafale f
gut [gʌt] n intestin m, boyau m; **guts** npl (Anat) boyaux mpl; (inf: courage) cran m
gutter ['gʌtər] n (of roof) gouttière f; (in street) caniveau m
guy [gaɪ] n (inf: man) type m; (also: **~rope**) corde f; (figure) effigie de Guy Fawkes
Guy Fawkes' Night [gaɪ'fɔːks-] n voir encadré

- GUY FAWKES' NIGHT
-
- **Guy Fawkes' Night**, que l'on
- appelle également "bonfire night",
- commémore l'échec du complot (le
- "Gunpowder Plot") contre James Ist
- et son parlement le 5 novembre 1605.
- L'un des conspirateurs, Guy Fawkes,
- avait été surpris dans les caves du
- parlement alors qu'il s'apprêtait à y
- mettre le feu. Chaque année pour le
- 5 novembre, les enfants préparent à
- l'avance une effigie de Guy Fawkes
- et ils demandent aux passants "un
- penny pour le guy" avec lequel ils
- pourront s'acheter des fusées de feu
- d'artifice. Beaucoup de gens font
- encore un feu dans leur jardin sur
- lequel ils brûlent le "guy".

gym [dʒɪm] n (also: **~nasium**) gymnase m; (also: **~nastics**) gym f; **gymnasium** n gymnase m; **gymnast** n gymnaste m/f; **gymnastics** n, npl gymnastique f; **gym shoes** npl chaussures fpl de gym(nastique)
gynaecologist (US **gynecologist**) [gaɪnɪ'kɔlədʒɪst] n gynécologue m/f
gypsy ['dʒɪpsɪ] n gitan(e), bohémien(ne)

h

haberdashery [hæbə'dæʃərɪ] n (BRIT) mercerie f

habit ['hæbɪt] n habitude f; (costume: Rel) habit m

habitat ['hæbɪtæt] n habitat m

hack [hæk] vt hacher, tailler ▷ n (pej: writer); **hacker** n (Comput) pirate m (informatique)

had [hæd] pt, pp of **have**

haddock (pl ~ or ~s) ['hædək] n églefin m; **smoked ~** haddock m

hadn't ['hædnt] = **had not**

haemorrhage (US **hemorrhage**) ['hɛmərɪdʒ] n hémorragie f

haemorrhoids (US **hemorrhoids**) ['hɛmərɔɪdz] npl hémorroïdes fpl

haggle ['hægl] vi marchander

Hague [heɪg] n: **The ~** La Haye

hail [heɪl] n grêle f ▷ vt (call) héler; (greet) acclamer ▷ vi grêler; **hailstone** n grêlon m

hair [hɛəʳ] n cheveux mpl; (on body) poils mpl; (of animal) pelage m; (single hair: on head) cheveu m; (: on body, of animal) poil m; **to do one's ~** se coiffer; **hairband** n (elasticated) bandeau m; (plastic) serre-tête m; **hairbrush** n brosse f à cheveux; **haircut** n coupe f (de cheveux); **hairdo** n coiffure f; **hairdresser** n coiffeur(-euse); **hairdresser's** n salon m de coiffure, coiffeur m; **hair dryer** n sèche-cheveux m, séchoir m; **hair gel** n gel m pour cheveux; **hair spray** n laque f (pour les cheveux); **hairstyle** n coiffure f; **hairy** adj poilu(e), chevelu(e); (inf: frightening) effrayant(e)

hake (pl ~ or ~s) [heɪk] n colin m, merlu m

half [hɑːf] n (pl halves) moitié f; (of beer: also: ~ **pint**) ≈ demi m; (Rail, bus: also: ~ **fare**) demi-tarif m; (Sport: of match) mi-temps f ▷ adj demi(e) ▷ adv (à) moitié, à demi; ~ **an hour** une demi-heure; ~ **a dozen** une demi-douzaine; ~ **a pound** une demi-livre, ≈ 250 g; **two and a ~** deux et demi; **to cut sth in ~** couper qch en deux; **half board** n (BRIT: in hotel) demi-pension f; **half-brother** n demi-frère m; **half day** n demi-journée f; **half fare** n demi-tarif m; **half-hearted** adj tiède, sans enthousiasme; **half-hour** n demi-heure f; **half-price** adj à moitié prix ▷ adv (also: **at half-price**) à moitié prix; **half term** n (BRIT Scol) vacances fpl (de demi-trimestre); **half-time** n mi-temps f; **halfway** adv à mi-chemin; **halfway through sth** au milieu de qch

hall [hɔːl] n salle f; (entrance way: big) hall m; (small) entrée f; (US: corridor) couloir m; (mansion) château m, manoir m

hallmark ['hɔːlmɑːk] n poinçon m; (fig) marque f

hallo [hə'ləu] excl = **hello**

hall of residence n (BRIT) pavillon m or résidence f universitaire

Halloween, Hallowe'en ['hæləu'iːn] n veille f de la Toussaint; voir encadré

- **HALLOWEEN**
- Selon la tradition, **Halloween** est la
- nuit des fantômes et des sorcières.
- En Écosse et aux États-Unis surtout
- (et de plus en plus en Angleterre) les
- enfants, pour fêter **Halloween**, se
- déguisent ce soir-là et ils vont ainsi
- de porte en porte en demandant de
- petits cadeaux (du chocolat, une
- pomme etc).

hallucination [həluːsɪˈneɪʃən] n
hallucination f

hallway ['hɔːlweɪ] n (entrance)
vestibule m; (corridor) couloir m

halo ['heɪləu] n (of saint etc) auréole f

halt [hɔːlt] n halte f, arrêt m ▷ vt faire
arrêter; (progress etc) interrompre ▷ vi
faire halte, s'arrêter

halve [hɑːv] vt (apple etc) partager or
diviser en deux; (reduce by half) réduire
de moitié

halves [hɑːvz] npl of **half**

ham [hæm] n jambon m

hamburger ['hæmbəːgəʳ] n
hamburger m

hamlet ['hæmlɪt] n hameau m

hammer ['hæməʳ] n marteau m ▷ vt
(nail) enfoncer; (fig) éreinter, démolir
▷ vi (at door) frapper à coups redoublés;
to ~ a point home to sb faire rentrer
qch dans la tête de qn

hammock ['hæmək] n hamac m

hamper ['hæmpəʳ] vt gêner ▷ n panier
m (d'osier)

hamster ['hæmstəʳ] n hamster m

hamstring ['hæmstrɪŋ] n (Anat)
tendon m du jarret

hand [hænd] n main f; (of clock) aiguille
f; (handwriting) écriture f; (at cards) jeu
m; (worker) ouvrier(-ière) ▷ vt passer,
donner; **to give sb a ~** donner un coup
de main à qn; **at ~** à portée de la main;
in ~ (situation) en main; (work) en cours;
to be on ~ (person) être disponible;
(emergency services) se tenir prêt(e) (à
intervenir); **to ~** (information etc) sous

la main, à portée de la main; **on the
one ~ …, on the other ~** d'une part …,
d'autre part; **hand down** vt passer;
(tradition, heirloom) transmettre; (us:
sentence, verdict) prononcer; **hand in**
vt remettre; **hand out** vt distribuer;
hand over vt remettre; (powers etc)
transmettre; **handbag** n sac m à main;
hand baggage n = **hand luggage**;
handbook n manuel m; **handbrake**
n frein m à main; **handcuffs** npl
menottes fpl; **handful** n poignée f

handicap ['hændɪkæp] n handicap m
▷ vt handicaper; **mentally/physically
~ped** handicapé(e) mentalement/
physiquement

handkerchief ['hæŋkətʃɪf] n
mouchoir m

handle ['hændl] n (of door etc) poignée
f; (of cup etc) anse f; (of knife etc) manche
m; (of saucepan) queue f; (for winding)
manivelle f ▷ vt toucher, manier;
(deal with) s'occuper de; (treat: people)
prendre; **"~ with care"** "fragile"; **to fly
off the ~** s'énerver; **handlebar(s)** n(pl)
guidon m

hand: **hand luggage** n bagages mpl
à main; **handmade** adj fait(e) à la
main; **handout** n (money) aide f, don
m; (leaflet) prospectus m; (at lecture)
polycopié m; **hands-free** adj (phone)
mains libres inv ▷ n (also: **hands-free
kit**) kit m mains libres inv

handsome ['hænsəm] adj beau (belle);
(profit) considérable

handwriting ['hændraɪtɪŋ] n
écriture f

handy ['hændɪ] adj (person) adroit(e);
(close at hand) sous la main; (convenient)
pratique

hang (pt, pp hung) [hæŋ, hʌŋ] vt
accrocher; (criminal: pt, pp **~ed**) pendre
▷ vi pendre; (hair, drapery) tomber
▷ n: **to get the ~ of (doing) sth** (inf)
attraper le coup pour faire qch; **hang
about, hang around** vi traîner; **hang
down** vi pendre; **hang on** vi (wait)
attendre; **hang out** vt (washing)

étendre (dehors) ▷ vi (inf: live) habiter, percher; (: spend time) traîner; **hang round** vi = **hang around**; **hang up** vi (Tel) raccrocher ▷ vt (coat, painting etc) accrocher, suspendre

hanger ['hæŋər] n cintre m, portemanteau m

hang-gliding ['hæŋglaɪdɪŋ] n vol m libre or sur aile delta

hangover ['hæŋəuvər] n (after drinking) gueule f de bois

hankie, hanky ['hæŋkɪ] n abbr = **handkerchief**

happen ['hæpən] vi arriver, se passer, se produire; **what's ~ing?** que se passe-t-il?; **she ~ed to be free** il s'est trouvé (or se trouvait) qu'elle était libre; **as it ~s** justement

happily ['hæpɪlɪ] adv heureusement; (cheerfully) joyeusement

happiness ['hæpɪnɪs] n bonheur m

happy ['hæpɪ] adj heureux(-euse); **~ with** (arrangements etc) satisfait(e) de; **to be ~ to do** faire volontiers; **~ birthday!** bon anniversaire!

harass ['hærəs] vt accabler, tourmenter; **harassment** n tracasseries fpl

harbour (US **harbor**) ['hɑːbər] n port m ▷ vt héberger, abriter; (hopes, suspicions) entretenir

hard [hɑːd] adj dur(e); (question, problem) difficile; (facts, evidence) concret(-ète) ▷ adv (work) dur; (think, try) sérieusement; **to look ~ at** regarder fixement; (thing) regarder de près; **no ~ feelings!** sans rancune!; **to be ~ of hearing** être dur(e) d'oreille; **to be ~ done by** être traité(e) injustement; **hardback** n livre relié; **hardboard** n Isorel® m; **hard disk** n (Comput) disque dur; **harden** vt durcir; (fig) endurcir ▷ vi (substance) durcir

ardly ['hɑːdlɪ] adv (scarcely) à peine; (harshly) durement; **~ anywhere/ever** presque nulle part/jamais

ard: hardship n (difficulties) épreuves fpl; (deprivation) privations fpl; **hard**

shoulder n (BRIT Aut) accotement stabilisé; **hard-up** adj (inf) fauché(e); **hardware** n quincaillerie f; (Comput, Mil) matériel m; **hardware shop** (US **hardware store**) n quincaillerie f; **hard-working** adj travailleur(-euse), consciencieux(-euse)

hardy ['hɑːdɪ] adj robuste; (plant) résistant(e) au gel

hare [hɛər] n lièvre m

harm [hɑːm] n mal m; (wrong) tort m ▷ vt (person) faire du mal or du tort à; (thing) endommager; **out of ~'s way** à l'abri du danger, en lieu sûr; **harmful** adj nuisible; **harmless** adj inoffensif(-ive)

harmony ['hɑːmənɪ] n harmonie f

harness ['hɑːnɪs] n harnais m ▷ vt (horse) harnacher; (resources) exploiter

harp [hɑːp] n harpe f ▷ vi: **to ~ on about** revenir toujours sur

harsh [hɑːʃ] adj (hard) dur(e); (severe) sévère; (unpleasant: sound) discordant(e); (: light) cru(e)

harvest ['hɑːvɪst] n (of corn) moisson f; (of fruit) récolte f; (of grapes) vendange f ▷ vt moissonner; récolter; vendanger

has [hæz] vb see **have**

hasn't ['hæznt] = **has not**

hassle ['hæsl] n (inf: fuss) histoire(s) f(pl)

haste [heɪst] n hâte f, précipitation f; **hasten** ['heɪsn] vt hâter, accélérer ▷ vi se hâter, s'empresser; **hastily** adv à la hâte; (leave) précipitamment; **hasty** adj (decision, action) hâtif(-ive); (departure, escape) précipité(e)

hat [hæt] n chapeau m

hatch [hætʃ] n (Naut: also: **~way**) écoutille f; (BRIT: also: **service ~**) passe-plats m inv ▷ vi éclore

hatchback ['hætʃbæk] n (Aut) modèle m avec hayon arrière

hate [heɪt] vt haïr, détester ▷ n haine f; **hatred** ['heɪtrɪd] n haine f

haul [hɔːl] vt traîner, tirer ▷ n (of fish) prise f; (of stolen goods etc) butin m

haunt [hɔːnt] vt (subj: ghost, fear)

hanter; (: *person*) fréquenter ▷ *n* repaire *m*; **haunted** *adj* (*castle etc*) hanté(e); (*look*) égaré(e), hagard(e)

 KEYWORD

have [hæv] (*pt, pp* **had**) *aux vb* **1** (*gen*) avoir; être; **to have eaten/slept** avoir mangé/dormi; **to have arrived/gone** être arrivé(e)/allé(e); **having finished** *or* **when he had finished, he left** quand il a eu fini, il est parti; **we'd already eaten** nous avions déjà mangé **2** (*in tag questions*): **you've done it, haven't you?** vous l'avez fait, n'est-ce pas?
3 (*in short answers and questions*): **no I haven't!/yes we have!** mais non!/mais si!; **so I have!** ah oui!, oui c'est vrai!; **I've been there before, have you?** j'y suis déjà allé, et vous?
▷ *modal aux vb* (*be obliged*): **to have (got) to do sth** devoir faire qch, être obligé(e) de faire qch; **she has (got) to do it** elle doit le faire, il faut qu'elle le fasse; **you haven't to tell her** vous n'êtes pas obligé de le lui dire; (*must not*) ne le lui dites surtout pas; **do you have to book?** il faut réserver?
▷ *vt* **1** (*possess*) avoir; **he has (got) blue eyes/dark hair** il a les yeux bleus/les cheveux bruns
2 (*referring to meals etc*): **to have breakfast** prendre le petit déjeuner; **to have dinner/lunch** dîner/déjeuner; **to have a drink** prendre un verre; **to have a cigarette** fumer une cigarette
3 (*receive*) avoir, recevoir; (*obtain*) avoir; **may I have your address?** puis-je avoir votre adresse?; **you can have it for £5** vous pouvez l'avoir pour 5 livres; **I must have it for tomorrow** il me le faut pour demain; **to have a baby** avoir un bébé
4 (*maintain, allow*): **I won't have it!** ça ne se passera pas comme ça!; **we can't have that** nous ne tolérerons pas ça
5 (*by sb else*): **to have sth done** faire

faire qch; **to have one's hair cut** se faire couper les cheveux; **to have sb do sth** faire faire qch à qn
6 (*experience, suffer*) avoir; **to have a cold/flu** avoir un rhume/la grippe; **to have an operation** se faire opérer; **she had her bag stolen** elle s'est fait voler son sac
7 (+*noun*): **to have a swim/walk** nager, se promener; **to have a bath/shower** prendre un bain/une douche; **let's have a look** regardons; **to have a meeting** se réunir; **to have a party** organiser une fête; **let me have a try** laissez-moi essayer

haven ['heɪvn] *n* port *m*; (*fig*) havre *m*
haven't ['hævnt] = **have not**
havoc ['hævək] *n* ravages *mpl*
Hawaii [hə'waɪː] *n* (îles *fpl*) Hawaï *m*
hawk [hɔːk] *n* faucon *m*
hawthorn ['hɔːθɔːn] *n* aubépine *f*
hay [heɪ] *n* foin *m*; **hay fever** *n* rhume *n* des foins; **haystack** *n* meule *f* de foin
hazard ['hæzəd] *n* (*risk*) danger *m*, risque *m* ▷ *vt* risquer, hasarder; **hazardous** *adj* hasardeux(-euse), risqué(e); **hazard warning lights** *npl* (*Aut*) feux *mpl* de détresse
haze [heɪz] *n* brume *f*
hazel ['heɪzl] *n* (*tree*) noisetier *m* ▷ *adj* (*eyes*) noisette *inv*; **hazelnut** *n* noisette *f*
hazy ['heɪzɪ] *adj* brumeux(-euse); (*idea*) vague
he [hiː] *pron* il; **it is he who ...** c'est lui qui ...; **here he is** le voici
head [hɛd] *n* tête *f*; (*leader*) chef *m*; (*of school*) directeur(-trice); (*of secondary school*) proviseur *m* ▷ *vt* (*list*) être en tête de; (*group, company*) être à la tête de; **~s or tails** pile ou face; **~ first** la tête la première; **~ over heels in love** follement *or* éperdument amoureux(-euse); **to ~ the ball** faire une tête; **head for** *vt fus* se diriger vers (*disaster*) aller à; **head off** *vt* (*threat, danger*) détourner; **headache** *n* mal *m*

de tête; **to have a headache** avoir mal à la tête; **heading** n titre m; (subject title) rubrique f; **headlamp** (BRIT) n = **headlight**; **headlight** n phare m; **headline** n titre m; **head office** n siège m, bureau m central; **headphones** npl casque m (à écouteurs); **headquarters** npl (of business) bureau or siège central; (Mil) quartier général; **headroom** n (in car) hauteur f de plafond; (under bridge) hauteur limite; **headscarf** n foulard m; **headset** n = **headphones**; **headteacher** n directeur(-trice) f; (of secondary school) proviseur m; **head waiter** n maître m d'hôtel

heal [hiːl] vt, vi guérir

health [hɛlθ] n santé f; **health care** n services médicaux; **health centre** n (BRIT) centre m de santé; **health food** n aliment(s) naturel(s); **Health Service** n: **the Health Service** (BRIT) ≈ la Sécurité Sociale; **healthy** adj (person) en bonne santé; (climate, food, attitude etc) sain(e)

heap [hiːp] n tas m ▷ vt (also: ~ **up**) entasser, amonceler; **she ~ed her plate with cakes** elle a chargé son assiette de gâteaux; **~s (of)** (inf: lots) des tas (de)

hear (pt, pp ~**d**) [hɪəʳ, həːd] vt entendre; (news) apprendre ▷ vi entendre; **to ~ about** entendre parler de; (have news of) avoir des nouvelles de; **to ~ from sb** recevoir des nouvelles de qn

heard [həːd] pt, pp of **hear**

hearing ['hɪərɪŋ] n (sense) ouïe f; (of witnesses) audition f; (of a case) audience f; **hearing aid** n appareil m acoustique

hearse [həːs] n corbillard m

heart [haːt] n cœur m; **hearts** npl (Cards) cœur; **at ~** au fond; **by ~** (learn, know) par cœur; **to lose/take ~** perdre/prendre courage; **heart attack** n crise f cardiaque; **heartbeat** n battement m de cœur; **heartbroken** adj: **to be heartbroken** avoir beaucoup de chagrin; **heartburn** n brûlures fpl d'estomac; **heart disease** n maladie

f cardiaque

hearth [haːθ] n foyer m, cheminée f

heartless ['haːtlɪs] adj (person) sans cœur, insensible; (treatment) cruel(le)

hearty ['haːtɪ] adj chaleureux(-euse); (appetite) solide; (dislike) cordial(e); (meal) copieux(-euse)

heat [hiːt] n chaleur f; (Sport: also: **qualifying ~**) éliminatoire f ▷ vt chauffer; **heat up** vi (liquid) chauffer; (room) se réchauffer ▷ vt réchauffer; **heated** adj chauffé(e); (fig) passionné(e), échauffé(e), excité(e); **heater** n appareil m de chauffage; radiateur m; (in car) chauffage m; (water heater) chauffe-eau m

heather ['hɛðəʳ] n bruyère f

heating ['hiːtɪŋ] n chauffage m

heatwave ['hiːtweɪv] n vague f de chaleur

heaven ['hɛvn] n ciel m, paradis m; (fig) paradis; **heavenly** adj céleste, divin(e)

heavily ['hɛvɪlɪ] adv lourdement; (drink, smoke) beaucoup; (sleep, sigh) profondément

heavy ['hɛvɪ] adj lourd(e); (work, rain, user, eater) gros(se); (drinker, smoker) grand(e); (schedule, week) chargé(e)

Hebrew ['hiːbruː] adj hébraïque ▷ n (Ling) hébreu m

Hebrides ['hɛbrɪdiːz] npl: **the ~** les Hébrides fpl

hectare ['hɛktaːʳ] n (BRIT) hectare m

hectic ['hɛktɪk] adj (schedule) très chargé(e); (day) mouvementé(e); (lifestyle) trépidant(e)

he'd [hiːd] = **he would**; **he had**

hedge [hɛdʒ] n haie f ▷ vi se dérober ▷ vt: **to ~ one's bets** (fig) se couvrir

hedgehog ['hɛdʒhɔg] n hérisson m

heed [hiːd] vt (also: **take ~ of**) tenir compte de, prendre garde à

heel [hiːl] n talon m ▷ vt retalonner

hefty ['hɛftɪ] adj (person) costaud(e); (parcel) lourd(e); (piece, price) gros(se)

height [haɪt] n (of person) taille f, grandeur f; (of object) hauteur f; (of plane, mountain) altitude f; (high ground) hauteur, éminence f; (fig: of glory, fame, power) sommet m; (: of luxury, stupidity) comble m; **at the ~ of summer** au cœur de l'été; **heighten** vt hausser, surélever; (fig) augmenter

heir [ɛərʳ] n héritier m; **heiress** n héritière f

held [hɛld] pt, pp of **hold**

helicopter ['hɛlɪkɔptəʳ] n hélicoptère m

hell [hɛl] n enfer m; **oh ~!** (inf) merde!

he'll [hiːl] = **he will**; **he shall**

hello [hə'ləu] excl bonjour!; (to attract attention) hé!; (surprise) tiens!

helmet ['hɛlmɪt] n casque m

help [hɛlp] n aide f; (cleaner etc) femme f de ménage ▷ vt, vi aider; **~!** au secours!; **~ yourself** servez-vous; **can you ~ me?** pouvez-vous m'aider?; **can I ~ you?** (in shop) vous désirez?; **he can't ~ it** il n'y peut rien; **help out** vi aider ▷ vt: **to ~ sb out** aider qn; **helper** n aide m/f, assistant(e); **helpful** adj serviable, obligeant(e); (useful) utile; **helping** n portion f; **helpless** adj impuissant(e); (baby) sans défense; **helpline** n service m d'assistance téléphonique; (free) ≈ numéro vert

hem [hɛm] n ourlet m ▷ vt ourler

hemisphere ['hɛmɪsfɪəʳ] n hémisphère m

hemorrhage ['hɛmərɪdʒ] n (US) = **haemorrhage**

hemorrhoids ['hɛmərɔɪdz] npl (US) = **haemorrhoids**

hen [hɛn] n poule f; (female bird) femelle f

hence [hɛns] adv (therefore) d'où, de là; **2 years ~** d'ici 2 ans

hen night, hen party n soirée f entre filles (avant le mariage de l'une d'elles)

hepatitis [hɛpə'taɪtɪs] n hépatite f

her [həːʳ] pron (direct) la, l' + vowel or h mute; (indirect) lui; (stressed, after prep) elle ▷ adj son (sa), ses pl; see also **me; my**

herb [həːb] n herbe f; **herbal** adj à base de plantes; **herbal tea** n tisane f

herd [həːd] n troupeau m

here [hɪəʳ] adv ici; (time) alors ▷ excl tiens!, tenez!; **~!** (present) présent!; **~ is, ~ are** voici; **~ he/she is** le (la) voici

hereditary [hɪ'rɛdɪtrɪ] adj héréditaire

heritage ['hɛrɪtɪdʒ] n héritage m, patrimoine m

hernia ['həːnɪə] n hernie f

hero (pl **~es**) ['hɪərəu] n héros m; **heroic** [hɪ'rəuɪk] adj héroïque

heroin ['hɛrəuɪn] n héroïne f (drogue)

heroine ['hɛrəuɪn] n héroïne f (femme)

heron ['hɛrən] n héron m

herring ['hɛrɪŋ] n hareng m

hers [həːz] pron le (la) sien(ne), les siens (siennes); see also **mine¹**

herself [həː'sɛlf] pron (reflexive) se; (emphatic) elle-même; (after prep) elle; see also **oneself**

he's [hiːz] = **he is; he has**

hesitant ['hɛzɪtənt] adj hésitant(e), indécis(e)

hesitate ['hɛzɪteɪt] vi: **to ~ (about/to do)** hésiter (sur/à faire); **hesitation** [hɛzɪ'teɪʃən] n hésitation f

heterosexual ['hɛtərəu'sɛksjuəl] adj, n hétérosexuel(le)

hexagon ['hɛksəgən] n hexagone m

hey [heɪ] excl hé!

heyday ['heɪdeɪ] n: **the ~ of** l'âge m d'or de, les beaux jours de

HGV n abbr = **heavy goods vehicle**

hi [haɪ] excl salut!; (to attract attention) hé!

hibernate ['haɪbəneɪt] vi hiberner

hiccough, hiccup ['hɪkʌp] vi hoqueter ▷ n: **to have (the) ~s** avoir le hoquet

hid [hɪd] pt of **hide**

hidden ['hɪdn] pp of **hide** ▷ adj: **~ agenda** intentions non déclarées

hide [haɪd] n (skin) peau f ▷ vb (pt **hid**, pp **hidden**) ▷ vt cacher ▷ vi: **to ~ (from sb)** se cacher (de qn)

hideous ['hɪdɪəs] adj hideux(-euse), atroce

hiding ['haɪdɪŋ] n (beating) correction f, volée f de coups; **to be in ~** (concealed) se tenir caché(e)

hi-fi ['haɪfaɪ] *adj, n abbr* (= high fidelity) hi-fi *f inv*

high [haɪ] *adj* haut(e); (*speed, respect, number*) grand(e); (*price*) élevé(e); (*wind*) fort(e), violent(e); (*voice*) aigu(ë) ▷ *adv* haut, en haut; **20 m** ~ haut(e) de 20 m; ~ **in the air** haut dans le ciel; **highchair** *n* (*child's*) chaise haute; **high-class** *adj* (*neighbourhood, hotel*) chic *inv*, de grand standing; **higher education** *n* études supérieures; **high heels** *npl* talons hauts, hauts talons; **high jump** *n* (*Sport*) saut *m* en hauteur; **highlands** ['haɪləndz] *npl* région montagneuse; **the Highlands** (*in Scotland*) les Highlands *mpl*; **highlight** *n* (*fig: of event*) point culminant ▷ *vt* (*emphasize*) faire ressortir, souligner; **highlights** *npl* (*in hair*) reflets *mpl*; **highlighter** *n* (*pen*) surligneur (lumineux); **highly** *adv* extrêmement, très; (*unlikely*) fort; (*recommended, skilled, qualified*) hautement; **to speak highly of** dire beaucoup de bien de; **highness** *n*: **His/Her Highness** son Altesse *f*; **high-rise** *n* (*also*: **high-rise block, high-rise building**) tour *f* (d'habitation); **high school** *n* lycée *m*; (*US*) établissement *m* d'enseignement supérieur; **high season** *n* (*BRIT*) haute saison *f*; **high street** *n* (*BRIT*) grand-rue *f*; **high-tech** (*inf*) *adj* de pointe; **highway** *n* (*BRIT*) route *f*; (*US*) route nationale; **Highway Code** *n* (*BRIT*) code *m* de la route

hijack ['haɪdʒæk] *vt* détourner (*par la force*); **hijacker** *n* auteur *m* d'un détournement d'avion, pirate *m* de l'air

hike [haɪk] *vi* faire des excursions à pied ▷ *n* excursion *f* à pied, randonnée *f*; **hiker** *n* promeneur(-euse), excursionniste *m/f*; **hiking** *n* excursions *fpl* à pied, randonnée *f*

hilarious [hɪ'lɛərɪəs] *adj* (*behaviour, event*) désopilant(e)

hill [hɪl] *n* colline *f*; (*fairly high*) montagne *f*; (*on road*) côte *f*; **hillside** *n* (flanc *m* de) coteau *m*; **hill walking** *n*

randonnée *f* de basse montagne; **hilly** *adj* vallonné(e), montagneux(-euse)

him [hɪm] *pron* (*direct*) le, l' + *vowel or h mute*; (*stressed, indirect, after prep*) lui; *see also* **me**; **himself** *pron* (*reflexive*) se; (*emphatic*) lui-même; (*after prep*) lui; *see also* **oneself**

hind [haɪnd] *adj* de derrière

hinder ['hɪndə'] *vt* gêner; (*delay*) retarder

hindsight ['haɪndsaɪt] *n*: **with (the benefit of)** ~ avec du recul, rétrospectivement

Hindu ['hɪnduː] *n* Hindou(e); **Hinduism** *n* (*Rel*) hindouisme *m*

hinge [hɪndʒ] *n* charnière *f* ▷ *vi* (*fig*): **to ~ on** dépendre de

hint [hɪnt] *n* allusion *f*; (*advice*) conseil *m*; (*clue*) indication *f* ▷ *vt*: **to ~ that** insinuer que ▷ *vi*: **to ~ at** faire une allusion à

hip [hɪp] *n* hanche *f*

hippie, hippy ['hɪpɪ] *n* hippie *m/f*

hippo ['hɪpəʊ] (*pl* **~s**) *n* hippopotame *m*

hippopotamus [hɪpə'pɔtəməs] (*pl* **~es** *or* **hippopotami**) *n* hippopotame *m*

hippy ['hɪpɪ] *n* = **hippie**

hire ['haɪə'] *vt* (*BRIT: car, equipment*) louer; (*worker*) embaucher, engager ▷ *n* location *f*; **for** ~ à louer; (*taxi*) libre; **I'd like to** ~ **a car** je voudrais louer une voiture; **hire(d) car** *n* (*BRIT*) voiture *f* de location; **hire purchase** *n* (*BRIT*) achat *m* (*or* vente *f*) à tempérament *or* crédit

his [hɪz] *pron* le (la) sien(ne), les siens (siennes) ▷ *adj* son (sa), ses *pl*; *see also* **mine**[1]; **my**

Hispanic [hɪs'pænɪk] *adj* (*in US*) hispano-américain(e) ▷ *n* Hispano-Américain(e)

hiss [hɪs] *vi* siffler

historian [hɪ'stɔːrɪən] *n* historien(ne)

historic(al) [hɪ'stɔrɪk(l)] *adj* historique

history ['hɪstərɪ] *n* histoire *f*

hit [hɪt] *vt* (*pt, pp* ~) frapper; (*reach: target*) atteindre, toucher; (*collide with: car*) entrer en collision avec, heurter;

(fig: affect) toucher ▷ n coup m; (success) succès m; (song) tube m; (to website) visite f; (on search engine) résultat m de recherche; **to ~ it off with sb** bien s'entendre avec qn; **hit back** vi: **to ~ back at sb** prendre sa revanche sur qn

hitch [hɪtʃ] vt (fasten) accrocher, attacher; (also: ~ **up**) remonter d'une saccade ▷ vi faire de l'autostop ▷ n (difficulty) anicroche f, contretemps m; **to ~ a lift** faire du stop; **hitch-hike** vi faire de l'auto-stop; **hitch-hiker** n auto-stoppeur(-euse); **hitch-hiking** n auto-stop m, stop m (inf)

hi-tech ['haɪtɛk] adj de pointe

hitman ['hɪtmæn] (irreg) n (inf) tueur m à gages

HIV n abbr (= human immunodeficiency virus) HIV m, VIH m; **~-negative/ positive** séronégatif(-ive)/positif(-ive)

hive [haɪv] n ruche f

hoard [hɔːd] n (of food) provisions fpl, réserves fpl; (of money) trésor m ▷ vt amasser

hoarse [hɔːs] adj enroué(e)

hoax [həʊks] n canular m

hob [hɒb] n plaque chauffante

hobble ['hɒbl] vi boitiller

hobby ['hɒbɪ] n passe-temps favori

hobo ['həʊbəʊ] n (us) vagabond m

hockey ['hɒkɪ] n hockey m; **hockey stick** n crosse f de hockey

hog [hɒg] n porc (châtré) ▷ vt (fig) accaparer; **to go the whole ~** aller jusqu'au bout

Hogmanay [hɒgmə'neɪ] n réveillon m du jour de l'An, Saint-Sylvestre f; voir encadré

● **HOGMANAY**
●
● La Saint-Sylvestre ou "New Year's
● Eve" se nomme **Hogmanay** en
● Écosse. En cette occasion, la famille
● et les amis se réunissent pour
● entendre sonner les douze coups de
● minuit et pour fêter le "first-footing",
● une coutume qui veut qu'on se

● rende chez ses amis et voisins en
● apportant quelque chose à boire (du
● whisky en général) et un morceau de
● charbon en gage de prospérité pour
● la nouvelle année.

hoist [hɔɪst] n palan m ▷ vt hisser

hold [həʊld] (pt, pp held) vt tenir; (contain) contenir; (meeting) tenir; (keep back) retenir; (believe) considérer; (possess) avoir ▷ vi (withstand pressure) tenir (bon); (be valid) valoir; (on telephone) attendre ▷ n prise f; (find) influence f; (Naut) cale f; **to catch or get (a) ~ of** saisir; **to get ~ of** (find) trouver; **~ the line!** (Tel) ne quittez pas!; **to ~ one's own** (fig) (bien) se défendre; **hold back** vt retenir; (secret) cacher; **hold on** vi tenir bon; (wait) attendre; **~ on!** (Tel) ne quittez pas!; **to ~ on to sth** (grasp) se cramponner à qch; (keep) conserver or garder qch; **hold out** vt offrir ▷ vi (resist): **to ~ out (against)** résister (devant), tenir bon (devant); **hold up** vt (raise) lever; (support) soutenir; (delay) retarder; (: traffic) ralentir; (rob) braquer; **holdall** n (BRIT) fourre-tout m inv; **holder** n (container) support m; (of ticket, record) détenteur(-trice); (of office, title, passport etc) titulaire m/f

hole [həʊl] n trou m

holiday ['hɒlədɪ] n (BRIT: vacation) vacances fpl; (day off) jour m de congé; (public) jour férié; **to be on ~** être en vacances; **I'm here on ~** je suis ici en vacances; **holiday camp** n (also: **holiday centre**) camp m de vacances; **holiday job** n (BRIT) boulot m (inf) de vacances; **holiday-maker** n (BRIT) vacancier(-ière); **holiday resort** n centre m de villégiature or de vacances

Holland ['hɒlənd] n Hollande f

hollow ['hɒləʊ] adj creux(-euse); (fig) faux (fausse) ▷ n creux m; (in land) dépression f (de terrain), cuvette f ▷ vt: **to ~ out** creuser, évider

holly ['hɒlɪ] n houx m

Hollywood ['hɒlɪwʊd] n Hollywood

olocaust ['hɔləkɔːst] n holocauste m

oly ['həʊlɪ] adj saint(e); (bread, water) bénit(e); (ground) sacré(e)

ome [həʊm] n foyer m, maison f; (country) pays natal, patrie f; (institution) maison ▷ adj de famille; (Econ, Pol) national(e), intérieur(e); (Sport: team) qui reçoit; (: match, win) sur leur (or notre) terrain ▷ adv chez soi, à la maison; au pays natal; (right in: nail etc) à fond; **at ~** chez soi, à la maison; **to go (or come) ~** rentrer (chez soi), rentrer à la maison (or au pays); **make yourself at ~** faites comme chez vous; **home address** n domicile permanent; **homeland** n patrie f; **homeless** adj sans foyer, sans abri; **homely** adj (plain) simple, sans prétention; (welcoming) accueillant(e); **home-made** adj fait(e) à la maison; **home match** n match m à domicile; **Home Office** n (BRIT) ministère m de l'Intérieur; **home owner** n propriétaire occupant; **home page** n (Comput) page f d'accueil; **Home Secretary** n (BRIT) ministre m de l'Intérieur; **homesick** adj: **to be homesick** avoir le mal du pays; (missing one's family) s'ennuyer de sa famille; **home town** n ville natale; **homework** n devoirs mpl

omicide ['hɔmɪsaɪd] n (US) homicide m

omoeopathic (US **homeopathic**) [həʊmɪə'pæθɪk] adj (medicine) homéopathique; (doctor) homéopathe

omoeopathy (US **homeopathy**) [həʊmɪ'ɔpəθɪ] n homéopathie f

omosexual [hɔməʊ'sɛksjʊəl] adj, n homosexuel(le)

onest ['ɔnɪst] adj honnête; (sincere) franc (franche); **honestly** adv honnêtement; franchement; **honesty** n honnêteté f

oney ['hʌnɪ] n miel m; **honeymoon** n lune f de miel, voyage m de noces; **we're on honeymoon** nous sommes en voyage de noces; **honeysuckle** n chèvrefeuille m

Hong Kong ['hɔŋ'kɔŋ] n Hong Kong

honorary ['ɔnərərɪ] adj honoraire; (duty, title) honorifique; **~ degree** diplôme m honoris causa

honour (US **honor**) ['ɔnəʳ] vt honorer ▷ n honneur m; **to graduate with ~s** obtenir sa licence avec mention; **honourable** (US **honorable**) adj honorable; **honours degree** n (Scol) ≈ licence f avec mention

hood [hud] n capuchon m; (of cooker) hotte f; (BRIT Aut) capote f; (US Aut) capot m; **hoodie** ['hudɪ] n (top) sweat m à capuche

hoof (pl **~s** or **hooves**) [huːf, huːvz] n sabot m

hook [huk] n crochet m; (on dress) agrafe f; (for fishing) hameçon m ▷ vt accrocher; **off the ~** (Tel) décroché

hooligan ['huːlɪgən] n voyou m

hoop [huːp] n cerceau m

hooray [huː'reɪ] excl = **hurray**

hoot [huːt] vi (BRIT: Aut) klaxonner; (siren) mugir; (owl) hululer

Hoover® ['huːvəʳ] n (BRIT) aspirateur m ▷ vt: **to hoover** (room) passer l'aspirateur dans; (carpet) passer l'aspirateur sur

hooves [huːvz] npl of **hoof**

hop [hɔp] vi sauter; (on one foot) sauter à cloche-pied; (bird) sautiller

hope [həʊp] vt, vi espérer ▷ n espoir m; **I ~ so** je l'espère; **I ~ not** j'espère que non; **hopeful** adj (person) plein(e) d'espoir; (situation) prometteur(-euse), encourageant(e); **hopefully** adv (expectantly) avec espoir, avec optimisme; (one hopes) avec un peu de chance; **hopeless** adj désespéré(e); (useless) nul(le)

hops [hɔps] npl houblon m

horizon [hə'raɪzn] n horizon m; **horizontal** [hɔrɪ'zɔntl] adj horizontal(e)

hormone ['hɔːməʊn] n hormone f

horn [hɔːn] n corne f; (Mus) cor m; (Aut) klaxon m

horoscope ['hɔrəskəʊp] n

horoscope m

horrendous [hə'rɛndəs] adj horrible, affreux(-euse)

horrible ['hɔrɪbl] adj horrible, affreux(-euse)

horrid ['hɔrɪd] adj (person) détestable; (weather, place, smell) épouvantable

horrific [hɔ'rɪfɪk] adj horrible

horrifying ['hɔrɪfaɪɪŋ] adj horrifiant(e)

horror ['hɔrəʳ] n horreur f; **horror film** n film m d'épouvante

hors d'œuvre [ɔː'dəːvrə] n hors d'œuvre m

horse [hɔːs] n cheval m; **horseback**: **on horseback** adj, adv à cheval; **horse chestnut** n (nut) marron m (d'Inde); (tree) marronnier m (d'Inde); **horsepower** n puissance f (en chevaux); (unit) cheval-vapeur m (CV); **horse-racing** n courses fpl de chevaux; **horseradish** n raifort m; **horse riding** n (BRIT) équitation f

hose [həuz] n (also: ~pipe) tuyau m; (also: **garden ~**) tuyau d'arrosage; **hosepipe** n tuyau m; (in garden) tuyau d'arrosage

hospital ['hɔspɪtl] n hôpital m; **in ~** à l'hôpital; **where's the nearest ~?** où est l'hôpital le plus proche?

hospitality [hɔspɪ'tælɪtɪ] n hospitalité f

host [həust] n hôte m; (TV, Radio) présentateur(-trice), animateur(-trice); (large number): **a ~ of** une foule de; (Rel) hostie f

hostage ['hɔstɪdʒ] n otage m

hostel ['hɔstl] n foyer m; (also: **youth ~**) auberge f de jeunesse

hostess ['həustɪs] n hôtesse f; (BRIT: also: **air ~**) hôtesse de l'air; (TV, Radio) animatrice f

hostile ['hɔstaɪl] adj hostile

hostility [hɔ'stɪlɪtɪ] n hostilité f

hot [hɔt] adj chaud(e); (as opposed to only warm) très chaud; (spicy) fort(e); (fig: contest) acharné(e); (topic) brûlant(e); (temper) violent(e), passionné(e); **to be ~** (person) avoir chaud; (thing) être (très)

chaud; (weather) faire chaud; **hot dog** n hot-dog m

hotel [həu'tɛl] n hôtel m

hot-water bottle [hɔt'wɔːtə-] n bouillotte f

hound [haund] vt poursuivre avec acharnement ▷ n chien courant

hour ['auəʳ] n heure f; **hourly** adj toutes les heures; (rate) horaire

house n [haus] maison f; (Pol) chambre f; (Theat) salle f; auditoire m ▷ vt [hauz] (person) loger, héberger; **on the ~** (fig) aux frais de la maison; **household** n (Admin etc) ménage m; (people) famille f, maisonnée f; **householder** n propriétaire m/f; (head of house) chef m de famille; **housekeeper** n gouvernante f; **housekeeping** n (work) ménage m; **housewife** (irreg) n ménagère f; femme f au foyer; **house wine** n cuvée f maison or du patron; **housework** n (travaux mpl du) ménage m

housing ['hauzɪŋ] n logement m; **housing development** (BRIT **housing estate**) n (blocks of flats) cité f; (houses) lotissement m

hover ['hɔvəʳ] vi planer; **hovercraft** n aéroglisseur m, hovercraft m

how [hau] adv comment; **~ are you?** comment allez-vous?; **~ do you do?** bonjour; (on being introduced) enchanté(e), **~ long have you been here?** depuis combien de temps êtes-vous là?; **~ lovely/awful!** que or comme c'est joli/affreux!; **~ much time/many people?** combien de temps/gens?; **~ much does it cost?** ça coûte combien? **~ old are you?** quel âge avez-vous?; **~ tall is he?** combien mesure-t-il?; **~ is school?** ça va à l'école?; **~ was the film?** comment était le film?

however [hau'ɛvəʳ] conj pourtant, cependant ▷ adv: **~ I do it** de quelque manière que je m'y prenne; **~ cold it is** même s'il fait très froid; **~ did you do it** comment y êtes-vous donc arrivé?

howl [haul] n hurlement m ▷ vi hurler;

(wind) mugir

H.P. *n abbr* (BRIT) = **hire purchase**

h.p. *abbr* (*Aut*) = **horsepower**

HQ *n abbr* (= *headquarters*) QG *m*

hr(s) *abbr* (= *hour(s)*) h

HTML *n abbr* (= *hypertext markup language*) HTML *m*

hubcap ['hʌbkæp] *n* (*Aut*) enjoliveur *m*

huddle ['hʌdl] *vi*: **to ~ together** se blottir les uns contre les autres

huff [hʌf] *n*: **in a ~** fâché(e)

hug [hʌg] *vt* serrer dans ses bras; (*shore, kerb*) serrer ▷ *n*: **to give sb a ~** serrer qn dans ses bras

huge [hjuːdʒ] *adj* énorme, immense

hull [hʌl] *n* (*of ship*) coque *f*

hum [hʌm] *vt* (*tune*) fredonner ▷ *vi* fredonner; (*insect*) bourdonner; (*plane, tool*) vrombir

human ['hjuːmən] *adj* humain(e) ▷ *n* (*also*: **~ being**) être humain

humane [hjuː'meɪn] *adj* humain(e), humanitaire

humanitarian [hjuːmænɪ'tɛərɪən] *adj* humanitaire

humanity [hjuː'mænɪtɪ] *n* humanité *f*

human rights *npl* droits *mpl* de l'homme

humble ['hʌmbl] *adj* humble, modeste

humid ['hjuːmɪd] *adj* humide; **humidity** [hjuː'mɪdɪtɪ] *n* humidité *f*

humiliate [hjuː'mɪlɪeɪt] *vt* humilier

humiliating [hjuː'mɪlɪeɪtɪŋ] *adj* humiliant(e)

humiliation [hjuːmɪlɪ'eɪʃən] *n* humiliation *f*

hummus ['huməs] *n* houm(m)ous *m*

humorous ['hjuːmərəs] *adj* humoristique

humour (*us* **humor**) ['hjuːmər] *n* humour *m*; (*mood*) humeur *f* ▷ *vt* (*person*) faire plaisir à; se prêter aux caprices de

hump [hʌmp] *n* bosse *f*

hunch [hʌntʃ] *n* (*premonition*) intuition *f*

hundred ['hʌndrəd] *num* cent; **~s of** des centaines de; **hundredth** [-ɪdθ]

num centième

hung [hʌŋ] *pt, pp of* **hang**

Hungarian [hʌŋ'gɛərɪən] *adj* hongrois(e) ▷ *n* Hongrois(e); (*Ling*) hongrois *m*

Hungary ['hʌŋgərɪ] *n* Hongrie *f*

hunger ['hʌŋgər] *n* faim *f* ▷ *vi*: **to ~ for** avoir faim de, désirer ardemment

hungry ['hʌŋgrɪ] *adj* affamé(e); **to be ~** avoir faim; **~ for** (*fig*) avide de

hunt [hʌnt] *vt* (*seek*) chercher; (*Sport*) chasser ▷ *vi* (*search*): **to ~ for** chercher (partout); (*Sport*) chasser ▷ *n* (*Sport*) chasse *f*; **hunter** *n* chasseur *m*; **hunting** *n* chasse *f*

hurdle ['həːdl] *n* (*Sport*) haie *f*; (*fig*) obstacle *m*

hurl [həːl] *vt* lancer (avec violence); (*abuse, insults*) lancer

hurrah, hurray [hu'rɑː, hu'reɪ] *excl* hourra!

hurricane ['hʌrɪkən] *n* ouragan *m*

hurry ['hʌrɪ] *n* hâte *f*, précipitation *f* ▷ *vi* se presser, se dépêcher ▷ *vt* (*person*) faire presser, faire se dépêcher; (*work*) presser; **to be in a ~** être pressé(e); **to do sth in a ~** faire qch en vitesse; **hurry up** *vi* se dépêcher

hurt [həːt] (*pt, pp* **~**) *vt* (*cause pain to*) faire mal à; (*injure, fig*) blesser ▷ *vi* faire mal ▷ *adj* blessé(e); **my arm ~s** j'ai mal au bras; **to ~ o.s.** se faire mal

husband ['hʌzbənd] *n* mari *m*

hush [hʌʃ] *n* calme *m*, silence *m* ▷ *vt* faire taire; **~!** chut!

husky ['hʌskɪ] *adj* (*voice*) rauque ▷ *n* chien *m* esquimau *or* de traîneau

hut [hʌt] *n* hutte *f*; (*shed*) cabane *f*

hyacinth ['haɪəsɪnθ] *n* jacinthe *f*

hydrangea [haɪ'dreɪndʒə] *n* hortensia *m*

hydrofoil ['haɪdrəfɔɪl] *n* hydrofoil *m*

hydrogen ['haɪdrədʒən] *n* hydrogène *m*

hygiene ['haɪdʒiːn] *n* hygiène *f*; **hygienic** [haɪ'dʒiːnɪk] *adj* hygiénique

hymn [hɪm] *n* hymne *m*; cantique *m*

hype [haɪp] *n* (*inf*) matraquage *m*

publicitaire *or* médiatique
hypermarket ['haɪpəmɑːkɪt] (*BRIT*) *n*
hypermarché *m*
hyphen ['haɪfn] *n* trait *m* d'union
hypnotize ['hɪpnətaɪz] *vt* hypnotiser
hypocrite ['hɪpəkrɪt] *n* hypocrite *m/f*
hypocritical [hɪpə'krɪtɪkl] *adj*
hypocrite
hypothesis (*pl* **hypotheses**)
[haɪ'pɔθɪsɪs, -siːz] *n* hypothèse *f*
hysterical [hɪ'sterɪkl] *adj* hystérique;
(*funny*) hilarant(e)
hysterics [hɪ'sterɪks] *npl*: **to be in/
have ~** (*anger, panic*) avoir une crise de
nerfs; (*laughter*) attraper un fou rire

I [aɪ] *pron* je; (*before vowel*) j'; (*stressed*)
moi
ice [aɪs] *n* glace *f*; (*on road*) verglas *m*
▷ *vt* (*cake*) glacer ▷ *vi* (*also*: **~ over**)
geler; (*also*: **~ up**) se givrer; **iceberg**
n iceberg *m*; **ice cream** *n* glace *f*; **ice
cube** *n* glaçon *m*; **ice hockey** *n* hockey
m sur glace
Iceland ['aɪslənd] *n* Islande *f*; **Icelander**
n Islandais(e); **Icelandic** [aɪs'lændɪk]
adj islandais(e) ▷ *n* (*Ling*) islandais *m*
ice: **ice lolly** *n* (*BRIT*) esquimau *m*;
ice rink *n* patinoire *f*; **ice skating** *n*
patinage *m* (sur glace)
icing ['aɪsɪŋ] *n* (*Culin*) glaçage *m*; **icing
sugar** *n* (*BRIT*) sucre *m* glace
icon ['aɪkɔn] *n* icône *f*
ICT *n abbr* (*BRIT: Scol*: = *information and
communications technology*) TIC *fpl*
icy ['aɪsɪ] *adj* glacé(e); (*road*) verglacé(e);
(*weather, temperature*) glacial(e)
I'd [aɪd] = **I would**; **I had**
ID card *n* carte *f* d'identité
idea [aɪ'dɪə] *n* idée *f*

ideal [aɪ'dɪəl] n idéal m ▷ adj idéal(e);
ideally [aɪ'dɪəlɪ] adv (preferably) dans
l'idéal; (perfectly): **he is ideally suited
to the job** il est parfait pour ce poste
identical [aɪ'dɛntɪkl] adj identique
identification [aɪdɛntɪfɪ'keɪʃən] n
identification f; **means of ~** pièce f
d'identité
identify [aɪ'dɛntɪfaɪ] vt identifier
identity [aɪ'dɛntɪtɪ] n identité f;
identity card n carte f d'identité;
identity theft n usurpation f
d'identité
ideology [aɪdɪ'ɔlədʒɪ] n idéologie f
idiom ['ɪdɪəm] n (phrase) expression f
idiomatique; (style) style m
idiot ['ɪdɪət] n idiot(e), imbécile m/f
idle ['aɪdl] adj (doing nothing) sans
occupation, désœuvré(e); (lazy)
oisif(-ive), paresseux(-euse);
(unemployed) au chômage; (machinery)
au repos; (question, pleasures) vain(e),
futile ▷ vi (engine) tourner au ralenti
idol ['aɪdl] n idole f
idyllic [ɪ'dɪlɪk] adj idyllique
i.e. abbr (= id est: that is) c. à d., c'est-
à-dire
if [ɪf] conj si; **if necessary** si nécessaire,
le cas échéant; **if so** si c'est le cas; **if not**
sinon; **if only I could!** si seulement je
pouvais!; see also **as; even**
ignite [ɪg'naɪt] vt mettre le feu à,
enflammer ▷ vi s'enflammer
ignition [ɪg'nɪʃən] n (Aut) allumage m;
to switch on/off the ~ mettre/couper
le contact
ignorance ['ɪgnərəns] n ignorance f
ignorant ['ɪgnərənt] adj ignorant(e);
to be ~ of (subject) ne rien connaître en;
(events) ne pas être au courant de
ignore [ɪg'nɔːʳ] vt ne tenir aucun
compte de; (mistake) ne pas relever;
(person: pretend to not see) faire
semblant de ne pas reconnaître; (: pay
no attention to) ignorer
ill [ɪl] adj (sick) malade; (bad) mauvais(e)
▷ n mal m ▷ adv: **to speak/think ~
of sb** dire/penser du mal de qn; **to be**

taken ~ tomber malade
I'll [aɪl] = **I will; I shall**
illegal [ɪ'liːgl] adj illégal(e)
illegible [ɪ'lɛdʒɪbl] adj illisible
illegitimate [ɪlɪ'dʒɪtɪmət] adj
illégitime
ill health n mauvaise santé
illiterate [ɪ'lɪtərət] adj illettré(e)
illness ['ɪlnɪs] n maladie f
illuminate [ɪ'luːmɪneɪt] vt (room,
street) éclairer; (for special effect)
illuminer
illusion [ɪ'luːʒən] n illusion f
illustrate ['ɪləstreɪt] vt illustrer
illustration [ɪlə'streɪʃən] n
illustration f
I'm [aɪm] = **I am**
image ['ɪmɪdʒ] n image f; (public face)
image de marque
imaginary [ɪ'mædʒɪnərɪ] adj
imaginaire
imagination [ɪmædʒɪ'neɪʃən] n
imagination f
imaginative [ɪ'mædʒɪnətɪv] adj
imaginatif(-ive); (person) plein(e)
d'imagination
imagine [ɪ'mædʒɪn] vt s'imaginer;
(suppose) imaginer, supposer
imbalance [ɪm'bæləns] n
déséquilibre m
imitate ['ɪmɪteɪt] vt imiter; **imitation**
[ɪmɪ'teɪʃən] n imitation f
immaculate [ɪ'mækjulət] adj
impeccable; (Rel) immaculé(e)
immature [ɪmə'tjuəʳ] adj (fruit) qui
n'est pas mûr(e); (person) qui manque
de maturité
immediate [ɪ'miːdɪət] adj
immédiat(e); **immediately** adv (at
once) immédiatement; **immediately
next to** juste à côté de
immense [ɪ'mɛns] adj immense,
énorme; **immensely** adv (+adj)
extrêmement; (+vb) énormément
immerse [ɪ'məːs] vt immerger,
plonger; **to be ~d in** (fig) être plongé
dans
immigrant ['ɪmɪgrənt] n

immigrant(e); (already established) immigré(e); **immigration** [ɪmɪ'greɪʃən] n immigration f

imminent ['ɪmɪnənt] adj imminent(e)

immoral [ɪ'mɔrl] adj immoral(e)

immortal [ɪ'mɔːtl] adj, n immortel(le)

immune [ɪ'mjuːn] adj: **~ (to)** immunisé(e) (contre); **immune system** n système m immunitaire

immunize ['ɪmjunaɪz] vt immuniser

impact ['ɪmpækt] n choc m, impact m; (fig) impact

impair [ɪm'pɛər] vt détériorer, diminuer

impartial [ɪm'pɑːʃl] adj impartial(e)

impatience [ɪm'peɪʃəns] n impatience f

impatient [ɪm'peɪʃənt] adj impatient(e); **to get** or **grow ~** s'impatienter

impeccable [ɪm'pɛkəbl] adj impeccable, parfait(e)

impending [ɪm'pɛndɪŋ] adj imminent(e)

imperative [ɪm'pɛrətɪv] adj (need) urgent(e), pressant(e); (tone) impérieux(-euse) ▷ n (Ling) impératif m

imperfect [ɪm'pəːfɪkt] adj imparfait(e); (goods etc) défectueux(-euse) ▷ n (Ling: also: **~ tense**) imparfait m

imperial [ɪm'pɪərɪəl] adj impérial(e); (BRIT: measure) légal(e)

impersonal [ɪm'pəːsənl] adj impersonnel(le)

impersonate [ɪm'pəːsəneɪt] vt se faire passer pour; (Theat) imiter

impetus ['ɪmpətəs] n impulsion f; (of runner) élan m

implant [ɪm'plɑːnt] vt (Med) implanter; (fig: idea, principle) inculquer

implement n ['ɪmplɪmənt] outil m, instrument m; (for cooking) ustensile m ▷ vt ['ɪmplɪment] exécuter

implicate ['ɪmplɪkeɪt] vt impliquer, compromettre

implication [ɪmplɪ'keɪʃən] n implication f; **by ~** indirectement

implicit [ɪm'plɪsɪt] adj implicite; (complete) absolu(e), sans réserve

imply [ɪm'plaɪ] vt (hint) suggérer, laisser entendre; (mean) indiquer, supposer

impolite [ɪmpə'laɪt] adj impoli(e)

import vt [ɪm'pɔːt] importer ▷ n ['ɪmpɔːt] (Comm) importation f; (meaning) portée f, signification f

importance [ɪm'pɔːtns] n importance f

important [ɪm'pɔːtnt] adj important(e); **it's not ~** c'est sans importance, ce n'est pas important

importer [ɪm'pɔːtər] n importateur(-trice)

impose [ɪm'pəuz] vt imposer ▷ vi: **to ~ on sb** abuser de la gentillesse de qn; **imposing** adj imposant(e), impressionnant(e)

impossible [ɪm'pɔsɪbl] adj impossible

impotent ['ɪmpətnt] adj impuissant(e)

impoverished [ɪm'pɔvərɪʃt] adj pauvre, appauvri(e)

impractical [ɪm'præktɪkl] adj pas pratique; (person) qui manque d'esprit pratique

impress [ɪm'prɛs] vt impressionner, faire impression sur; (mark) imprimer, marquer; **to ~ sth on sb** faire bien comprendre qch à qn

impression [ɪm'prɛʃən] n impression f; (of stamp, seal) empreinte f; (imitation) imitation f; **to be under the ~ that** avoir l'impression que

impressive [ɪm'prɛsɪv] adj impressionnant(e)

imprison [ɪm'prɪzn] vt emprisonner, mettre en prison; **imprisonment** n emprisonnement m; (period): **to sentence sb to 10 years' imprisonment** condamner qn à 10 ans de prison

improbable [ɪm'prɔbəbl] adj improbable; (excuse) peu plausible

improper [ɪm'prɔpər] adj (unsuitable) déplacé(e), de mauvais goût; (indecent)

indécent(e); (*dishonest*) malhonnête
improve [ɪmˈpruːv] *vt* améliorer ▷ *vi*
s'améliorer; (*pupil etc*) faire des progrès;
improvement *n* amélioration *f*; (*of
pupil etc*) progrès *m*
improvise [ˈɪmprəvaɪz] *vt*, *vi*
improviser
impulse [ˈɪmpʌls] *n* impulsion *f*;
on ~ impulsivement, sur un coup
de tête; **impulsive** [ɪmˈpʌlsɪv] *adj*
impulsif(-ive)

 KEYWORD

in [ɪn] *prep* **1** (*indicating place, position*)
dans; **in the house/the fridge** dans la
maison/le frigo; **in the garden** dans
le *or* au jardin; **in town** en ville; **in the
country** à la campagne; **in school** à
l'école; **in here/there** ici/là
2 (*with place names: of town, region,
country*): **in London** à Londres; **in
England** en Angleterre; **in Japan**
au Japon; **in the United States** aux
États-Unis
3 (*indicating time: during*): **in spring**
au printemps; **in summer** en été;
in May/2005 en mai/2005; **in the
afternoon** (dans) l'après-midi; **at 4
o'clock in the afternoon** à 4 heures de
l'après-midi
4 (*indicating time: in the space of*) en;
(: *future*) dans; **I did it in 3 hours/days**
je l'ai fait en 3 heures/jours; **I'll see you
in 2 weeks** *or* **in 2 weeks' time** je te
verrai dans 2 semaines
5 (*indicating manner etc*) à; **in a
loud/soft voice** à voix haute/basse;
in pencil au crayon; **in writing** par
écrit; **in French** en français; **the boy
in the blue shirt** le garçon à *or* avec la
chemise bleue
6 (*indicating circumstances*): **in the sun**
au soleil; **in the shade** à l'ombre; **in the
rain** sous la pluie; **a change in policy**
un changement de politique
7 (*indicating mood, state*): **in tears** en
larmes; **in anger** sous le coup de la

colère; **in despair** au désespoir; **in
good condition** en bon état; **to live in
luxury** vivre dans le luxe
8 (*with ratios, numbers*): **1 in 10
households, 1 household in 10** 1
ménage sur 10; **20 pence in the pound**
20 pence par livre sterling; **they lined
up in twos** ils se mirent en rangs (deux)
par deux; **in hundreds** par centaines
9 (*referring to people, works*) chez; **the
disease is common in children** c'est
une maladie courante chez les enfants;
in (the works of) Dickens chez
Dickens, dans (l'œuvre de) Dickens
10 (*indicating profession etc*) dans; **to be
in teaching** être dans l'enseignement
11 (*after superlative*) de; **the best pupil
in the class** le meilleur élève de la
classe
12 (*with present participle*): **in saying
this** en disant ceci
▷ *adv*: **to be in** (*person: at home, work*)
être là; (*train, ship, plane*) être arrivé(e);
(*in fashion*) être à la mode; **to ask sb in**
inviter qn à entrer; **to run/limp** *etc* **in**
entrer en courant/boitant *etc*
▷ *n*: **the ins and outs (of)** (*of
proposal, situation etc*) les tenants et
aboutissants (de)

inability [ɪnəˈbɪlɪtɪ] *n* incapacité *f*; **~ to
pay** incapacité de payer
inaccurate [ɪnˈækjʊrət] *adj*
inexact(e); (*person*) qui manque de
précision
inadequate [ɪnˈædɪkwət] *adj*
insuffisant(e), inadéquat(e)
inadvertently [ɪnədˈvɜːtntlɪ] *adv* par
mégarde
inappropriate [ɪnəˈprəʊprɪət] *adj*
inopportun(e), mal à propos; (*word,
expression*) impropre
inaugurate [ɪˈnɔːgjʊreɪt] *vt*
inaugurer; (*president, official*) investir de
ses fonctions
Inc. *abbr* = **incorporated**
incapable [ɪnˈkeɪpəbl] *adj*: **~ (of)**
incapable (de)

incense n ['ɪnsɛns] encens m ▷ vt [ɪn'sɛns] (*anger*) mettre en colère

incentive [ɪn'sɛntɪv] n encouragement m, raison f de se donner de la peine

inch [ɪntʃ] n pouce m (=25 mm; 12 in a foot); **within an ~ of** à deux doigts de; **he wouldn't give an ~** (*fig*) il n'a pas voulu céder d'un pouce

incidence ['ɪnsɪdns] n (*of crime, disease*) fréquence f

incident ['ɪnsɪdnt] n incident m

incidentally [ɪnsɪ'dɛntəlɪ] adv (*by the way*) à propos

inclination [ɪnklɪ'neɪʃən] n inclination f; (*desire*) envie f

incline n ['ɪnklaɪn] pente f, plan incliné ▷ vb [ɪn'klaɪn] ▷ vt incliner ▷ vi (*surface*) s'incliner; **to be ~d to do** (*have a tendency to do*) avoir tendance à faire

include [ɪn'kluːd] vt inclure, comprendre; **service is/is not ~d** le service est compris/n'est pas compris; **including** prep y compris; **inclusion** n inclusion f; **inclusive** adj inclus(e), compris(e); **inclusive of tax** taxes comprises

income ['ɪnkʌm] n revenu m; (*from property etc*) rentes fpl; **income support** n (*BRIT*) ≈ revenu m minimum d'insertion, RMI m; **income tax** n impôt m sur le revenu

incoming ['ɪnkʌmɪŋ] adj (*passengers, mail*) à l'arrivée; (*government, tenant*) nouveau (nouvelle)

incompatible [ɪnkəm'pætɪbl] adj incompatible

incompetence [ɪn'kɒmpɪtns] n incompétence f, incapacité f

incompetent [ɪn'kɒmpɪtnt] adj incompétent(e), incapable

incomplete [ɪnkəm'pliːt] adj incomplet(-ète)

inconsistent [ɪnkən'sɪstnt] adj qui manque de constance; (*work*) irrégulier(-ière); (*statement*) peu cohérent(e); **~ with** en contradiction avec

inconvenience [ɪnkən'viːnjəns] n inconvénient m; (*trouble*) dérangement m ▷ vt déranger

inconvenient [ɪnkən'viːnjənt] adj malcommode; (*time, place*) mal choisi(e), qui ne convient pas; (*visitor*) importun(e)

incorporate [ɪn'kɔːpəreɪt] vt incorporer; (*contain*) contenir

incorrect [ɪnkə'rɛkt] adj incorrect(e); (*opinion, statement*) inexact(e)

increase n ['ɪnkriːs] augmentation f ▷ vi, vt [ɪn'kriːs] augmenter; **increasingly** adv de plus en plus

incredible [ɪn'krɛdɪbl] adj incroyable; **incredibly** adv incroyablement

incur [ɪn'kəː^r] vt (*expenses*) encourir; (*anger, risk*) s'exposer à; (*debt*) contracter; (*loss*) subir

indecent [ɪn'diːsnt] adj indécent(e), inconvenant(e)

indeed [ɪn'diːd] adv (*confirming, agreeing*) en effet, effectivement; (*for emphasis*) vraiment; (*furthermore*) d'ailleurs; **yes ~!** certainement!

indefinitely [ɪn'dɛfɪnɪtlɪ] adv (*wait*) indéfiniment

independence [ɪndɪ'pɛndns] n indépendance f; **Independence Day** n (*US*) fête de l'Indépendance américaine; *voir encadré*

- **INDEPENDENCE DAY**
-
- L'**Independence Day** est la fête
- nationale aux États-Unis, le 4
- juillet. Il commémore l'adoption
- de la déclaration d'Indépendance,
- en 1776, écrite par Thomas Jefferson
- et proclamant la séparation des 13
- colonies américaines de la Grande-
- Bretagne.

independent [ɪndɪ'pɛndnt] adj indépendant(e); (*radio*) libre; **independent school** n (*BRIT*) école privée

index ['ɪndɛks] n (pl **~es**) (*in book*)

index m; (: in library etc) catalogue m (pl
indices) (ratio, sign) indice m
India['ɪndɪə] n Inde f; **Indian** adj
indien(ne) ▷ n Indien(ne); **(American)**
Indian Indien(ne) (d'Amérique)
indicate['ɪndɪkeɪt] vt indiquer ▷ vi
(BRIT Aut): **to ~ left/right** mettre
son clignotant à gauche/à droite;
indication[ɪndɪ'keɪʃən] n indication
f, signe m; **indicative**[ɪn'dɪkətɪv]
adj: **to be indicative of sth** être
symptomatique de qch ▷ n (Ling)
indicatif m; **indicator** n (sign)
indicateur m; (Aut) clignotant m
indices['ɪndɪsiːz] npl of **index**
indict[ɪn'daɪt] vt accuser; **indictment**
n accusation f
indifference[ɪn'dɪfrəns] n
indifférence f
indifferent[ɪn'dɪfrənt] adj
indifférent(e); (poor) médiocre,
quelconque
indigenous[ɪn'dɪdʒɪnəs] adj indigène
indigestion[ɪndɪ'dʒɛstʃən] n
indigestion f, mauvaise digestion
indignant[ɪn'dɪgnənt] adj: **~ (at sth/
with sb)** indigné(e) (de qch/contre qn)
indirect[ɪndɪ'rɛkt] adj indirect(e)
indispensable[ɪndɪ'spɛnsəbl] adj
indispensable
individual[ɪndɪ'vɪdjuəl] n individu
m ▷ adj individuel(le); (characteristic)
particulier(-ière), original(e);
individually adv individuellement
Indonesia[ɪndə'niːzɪə] n Indonésie f
indoor['ɪndɔːr] adj d'intérieur; (plant)
d'appartement; (swimming pool)
couvert(e); (sport, games) pratiqué(e) en
salle; **indoors**[ɪn'dɔːz] adv à l'intérieur
induce[ɪn'djuːs] vt (persuade)
persuader; (bring about) provoquer;
(labour) déclencher
indulge[ɪn'dʌldʒ] vt (whim) céder à,
satisfaire; (child) gâter ▷ vi: **to ~ in sth**
(luxury) s'offrir qch, se permettre qch;
(fantasies etc) se livrer à qch; **indulgent**
adj indulgent(e)
industrial[ɪn'dʌstrɪəl] adj

industriel(le); (injury) du travail;
(dispute) ouvrier(-ière); **industrial
estate** n (BRIT) zone industrielle;
industrialist n industriel m; **industrial
park** n (US) zone industrielle
industry['ɪndəstrɪ] n industrie f;
(diligence) zèle m, application f
inefficient[ɪnɪ'fɪʃənt] adj inefficace
inequality[ɪnɪ'kwɔlɪtɪ] n inégalité f
inevitable[ɪn'ɛvɪtəbl] adj inévitable;
inevitably adv inévitablement,
fatalement
inexpensive[ɪnɪk'spɛnsɪv] adj bon
marché inv
inexperienced[ɪnɪk'spɪərɪənst] adj
inexpérimenté(e)
inexplicable[ɪnɪk'splɪkəbl] adj
inexplicable
infamous['ɪnfəməs] adj infâme,
abominable
infant['ɪnfənt] n (baby) nourrisson m;
(young child) petit(e) enfant
infantry['ɪnfəntrɪ] n infanterie f
infant school n (BRIT) classes fpl
préparatoires (entre 5 et 7 ans)
infect[ɪn'fɛkt] vt (wound) infecter;
(person, blood) contaminer; **infection**
[ɪn'fɛkʃən] n infection f; (contagion)
contagion f; **infectious**[ɪn'fɛkʃəs]
adj infectieux(-euse); (also fig)
contagieux(-euse)
infer[ɪn'fəːr] vt: **to ~ (from)** conclure
(de), déduire (de)
inferior[ɪn'fɪərɪər] adj inférieur(e);
(goods) de qualité inférieure ▷ n
inférieur(e); (in rank) subalterne m/f
infertile[ɪn'fəːtaɪl] adj stérile
infertility[ɪnfəː'tɪlɪtɪ] n infertilité f,
stérilité f
infested[ɪn'fɛstɪd] adj: **~ (with)**
infesté(e) (de)
infinite['ɪnfɪnɪt] adj infini(e); (time,
money) illimité(e); **infinitely** adv
infiniment
infirmary[ɪn'fəːmərɪ] n hôpital m; (in
school, factory) infirmerie f
inflamed[ɪn'fleɪmd] adj enflammé(e)
inflammation[ɪnflə'meɪʃən] n

inflammation f

inflatable [ɪnˈfleɪtəbl] *adj* gonflable

inflate [ɪnˈfleɪt] *vt* (*tyre, balloon*) gonfler; (*fig: exaggerate*) grossir; (*: increase*) gonfler; **inflation** [ɪnˈfleɪʃən] *n* (*Econ*) inflation f

inflexible [ɪnˈflɛksɪbl] *adj* inflexible, rigide

inflict [ɪnˈflɪkt] *vt*: **to ~ on** infliger à

influence [ˈɪnfluəns] *n* influence f ▷ *vt* influencer; **under the ~ of alcohol** en état d'ébriété; **influential** [ɪnfluˈɛnʃl] *adj* influent(e)

influenza [ɪnfluˈɛnzə] *n* grippe f

influx [ˈɪnflʌks] *n* afflux m

info (*inf*) [ˈɪnfəu] *n* (= *information*) renseignements *mpl*

inform [ɪnˈfɔːm] *vt*: **to ~ sb (of)** informer *or* avertir qn (de) ▷ *vi*: **to ~ on sb** dénoncer qn, informer contre qn

informal [ɪnˈfɔːml] *adj* (*person, manner, party*) simple; (*visit, discussion*) dénué(e) de formalités; (*announcement, invitation*) non officiel(le); (*colloquial*) familier(-ère)

information [ɪnfəˈmeɪʃən] *n* information(s) f(pl); renseignements *mpl*; (*knowledge*) connaissances *fpl*; **a piece of ~** un renseignement; **information office** *n* bureau *m* de renseignements; **information technology** *n* informatique f

informative [ɪnˈfɔːmətɪv] *adj* instructif(-ive)

infra-red [ɪnfrəˈrɛd] *adj* infrarouge

infrastructure [ˈɪnfrəstrʌktʃəʳ] *n* infrastructure f

infrequent [ɪnˈfriːkwənt] *adj* peu fréquent(e), rare

infuriate [ɪnˈfjuərɪeɪt] *vt* mettre en fureur

infuriating [ɪnˈfjuərɪeɪtɪŋ] *adj* exaspérant(e)

ingenious [ɪnˈdʒiːnjəs] *adj* ingénieux(-euse)

ingredient [ɪnˈɡriːdɪənt] *n* ingrédient *m*; (*fig*) élément *m*

inhabit [ɪnˈhæbɪt] *vt* habiter;

inhabitant *n* habitant(e)

inhale [ɪnˈheɪl] *vt* inhaler; (*perfume*) respirer; (*smoke*) avaler ▷ *vi* (*breathe in*) aspirer; (*in smoking*) avaler la fumée; **inhaler** *n* inhalateur *m*

inherent [ɪnˈhɪərənt] *adj*: **~ (in** *or* **to)** inhérent(e) (à)

inherit [ɪnˈhɛrɪt] *vt* hériter (de); **inheritance** *n* héritage *m*

inhibit [ɪnˈhɪbɪt] *vt* (*Psych*) inhiber; (*growth*) freiner; **inhibition** [ɪnhɪˈbɪʃən] *n* inhibition f

initial [ɪˈnɪʃl] *adj* initial(e) ▷ *n* initiale f ▷ *vt* parafer; **initials** *npl* initiales *fpl*; (*as signature*) parafe *m*; **initially** *adv* initialement, au début

initiate [ɪˈnɪʃɪeɪt] *vt* (*start*) entreprendre; amorcer; (*enterprise*) lancer; (*person*) initier; **to ~ proceedings against sb** (*Law*) intenter une action à qn, engager des poursuites contre qn

initiative [ɪˈnɪʃətɪv] *n* initiative f

inject [ɪnˈdʒɛkt] *vt* injecter; (*person*): **to ~ sb with sth** faire une piqûre de qch à qn; **injection** [ɪnˈdʒɛkʃən] *n* injection f, piqûre f

injure [ˈɪndʒəʳ] *vt* blesser; (*damage: reputation etc*) compromettre; **to ~ o.s.** se blesser; **injured** *adj* (*person, leg etc*) blessé(e); **injury** *n* blessure f; (*wrong*) tort *m*

injustice [ɪnˈdʒʌstɪs] *n* injustice f

ink [ɪŋk] *n* encre f; **ink-jet printer** [ˈɪŋkdʒɛt-] *n* imprimante f à jet d'encre

inland *adj* [ˈɪnlənd] intérieur(e) ▷ *adv* [ɪnˈlænd] à l'intérieur, dans les terres; **Inland Revenue** *n* (*BRIT*) fisc *m*

in-laws [ˈɪnlɔːz] *npl* beaux-parents *mpl*; belle famille

inmate [ˈɪnmeɪt] *n* (*in prison*) détenu(e); (*in asylum*) interné(e)

inn [ɪn] *n* auberge f

inner [ˈɪnəʳ] *adj* intérieur(e); **inner-city** *adj* (*schools, problems*) de quartiers déshérités

inning [ˈɪnɪŋ] *n* (*US: Baseball*) tour *m* de batte; **innings** *npl* (*Cricket*) tour de batte

innocence ['ɪnəsns] n innocence f

innocent ['ɪnəsnt] adj innocent(e)

innovation [ɪnəʊ'veɪʃən] n innovation f

innovative ['ɪnəʊveɪtɪv] adj novateur(-trice); (product) innovant(e)

in-patient ['ɪnpeɪʃənt] n malade hospitalisé(e)

input ['ɪnpʊt] n (contribution) contribution f; (resources) ressources fpl; (Comput) entrée f (de données); (: data) données fpl ▷ vt (Comput) introduire, entrer

inquest ['ɪnkwɛst] n enquête (criminelle); (coroner's) enquête judiciaire

inquire [ɪn'kwaɪə^r] vi demander ▷ vt demander; **to ~ about** s'informer de, se renseigner sur; **to ~ when/where/whether** demander quand/où/si; **inquiry** n demande f de renseignements; (Law) enquête f, investigation f; **"inquiries"** "renseignements"

ins. abbr = **inches**

insane [ɪn'seɪn] adj fou (folle); (Med) aliéné(e)

insanity [ɪn'sænɪtɪ] n folie f; (Med) aliénation (mentale)

insect ['ɪnsɛkt] n insecte m; **insect repellent** n crème f anti-insectes

insecure [ɪnsɪ'kjʊə^r] adj (person) anxieux(-euse); (job) précaire; (building etc) peu sûr(e)

insecurity [ɪnsɪ'kjʊərɪtɪ] n insécurité f

insensitive [ɪn'sɛnsɪtɪv] adj insensible

insert vt [ɪn'səːt] insérer ▷ n ['ɪnsəːt] insertion f

inside ['ɪn'saɪd] n intérieur m ▷ adj intérieur(e) ▷ adv à l'intérieur, dedans ▷ prep à l'intérieur de; (of time): **~ 10 minutes** en moins de 10 minutes; **to go ~** rentrer; **inside lane** n (Aut: in Britain) voie f de gauche; (: in US, Europe) voie f de droite; **inside out** adv à l'envers; (know) à fond; **to turn sth inside out** retourner qch

insight ['ɪnsaɪt] n perspicacité f; (glimpse, idea) aperçu m

insignificant [ɪnsɪg'nɪfɪknt] adj insignifiant(e)

insincere [ɪnsɪn'sɪə^r] adj hypocrite

insist [ɪn'sɪst] vi insister; **to ~ on doing** insister pour faire; **to ~ on sth** exiger qch; **to ~ that** insister pour que + sub; (claim) maintenir or soutenir que; **insistent** adj insistant(e), pressant(e); (noise, action) ininterrompu(e)

insomnia [ɪn'sɔmnɪə] n insomnie f

inspect [ɪn'spɛkt] vt inspecter; (BRIT: ticket) contrôler; **inspection** [ɪn'spɛkʃən] n inspection f; (BRIT: of tickets) contrôle m; **inspector** n inspecteur(-trice); (BRIT: on buses, trains) contrôleur(-euse)

inspiration [ɪnspə'reɪʃən] n inspiration f; **inspire** [ɪn'spaɪə^r] vt inspirer; **inspiring** adj inspirant(e)

instability [ɪnstə'bɪlɪtɪ] n instabilité f

install (US **instal**) [ɪn'stɔːl] vt installer; **installation** [ɪnstə'leɪʃən] n installation f

instalment (US **installment**) [ɪn'stɔːlmənt] n (payment) acompte m, versement partiel; (of TV serial etc) épisode m; **in ~s** (pay) à tempérament; (receive) en plusieurs fois

instance ['ɪnstəns] n exemple m; **for ~** par exemple; **in the first ~** tout d'abord, en premier lieu

instant ['ɪnstənt] n instant m ▷ adj immédiat(e), urgent(e); (coffee, food) instantané(e), en poudre; **instantly** adv immédiatement, tout de suite; **instant messaging** n messagerie f instantanée

instead [ɪn'stɛd] adv au lieu de cela; **~ of** au lieu de; **~ of sb** à la place de qn

instinct ['ɪnstɪŋkt] n instinct m; **instinctive** adj instinctif(-ive)

institute ['ɪnstɪtjuːt] n institut m ▷ vt instituer, établir; (inquiry) ouvrir; (proceedings) entamer

institution [ɪnstɪ'tjuːʃən] n institution f; (school) établissement *m* (scolaire); (*for care*) établissement (psychiatrique *etc*)

instruct [ɪnˈstrʌkt] *vt*: **to ~ sb in sth** enseigner qch à qn; **to ~ sb to do** charger qn *or* ordonner à qn de faire; **instruction** [ɪnˈstrʌkʃən] *n* instruction *f*; **instructions** *npl* (*orders*) directives *fpl*; **instructions for use** mode *m* d'emploi; **instructor** *n* professeur *m*; (*for skiing, driving*) moniteur *m*

instrument [ˈɪnstrəmənt] *n* instrument *m*; **instrumental** [ɪnstruˈmɛntl] *adj* (*Mus*) instrumental(e); **to be instrumental in sth/in doing sth** contribuer à qch/à faire qch

insufficient [ɪnsəˈfɪʃənt] *adj* insuffisant(e)

insulate [ˈɪnsjuleɪt] *vt* isoler; (*against sound*) insonoriser; **insulation** [ɪnsjuˈleɪʃən] *n* isolation *f*; (*against sound*) insonorisation *f*

insulin [ˈɪnsjulɪn] *n* insuline *f*

insult *n* [ˈɪnsʌlt] insulte *f*, affront *m* ▷ *vt* [ɪnˈsʌlt] insulter, faire un affront à; **insulting** *adj* insultant(e), injurieux(-euse)

insurance [ɪnˈʃuərəns] *n* assurance *f*; **fire/life ~** assurance-incendie/-vie; **insurance company** *n* compagnie *f* *or* société *f* d'assurances; **insurance policy** *n* police *f* d'assurance

insure [ɪnˈʃuəʳ] *vt* assurer; **to ~ (o.s.) against** (*fig*) parer à

intact [ɪnˈtækt] *adj* intact(e)

intake [ˈɪnteɪk] *n* (*Tech*) admission *f*; (*consumption*) consommation *f*; (*BRIT Scol*): **an ~ of 200 a year** 200 admissions par an

integral [ˈɪntɪɡrəl] *adj* (*whole*) intégral(e); (*part*) intégrant(e)

integrate [ˈɪntɪɡreɪt] *vt* intégrer ▷ *vi* s'intégrer

integrity [ɪnˈtɛɡrɪtɪ] *n* intégrité *f*

intellect [ˈɪntəlɛkt] *n* intelligence *f*; **intellectual** [ɪntəˈlɛktjuəl] *adj, n* intellectuel(le)

intelligence [ɪnˈtɛlɪdʒəns] *n*

intelligence *f*; (*Mil etc*) informations *fpl*, renseignements *mpl*

intelligent [ɪnˈtɛlɪdʒənt] *adj* intelligent(e)

intend [ɪnˈtɛnd] *vt* (*gift etc*): **to ~ sth for** destiner qch à; **to ~ to do** avoir l'intention de faire

intense [ɪnˈtɛns] *adj* intense; (*person*) véhément(e)

intensify [ɪnˈtɛnsɪfaɪ] *vt* intensifier

intensity [ɪnˈtɛnsɪtɪ] *n* intensité *f*

intensive [ɪnˈtɛnsɪv] *adj* intensif(-ive); **intensive care** *n*: **to be in intensive care** être en réanimation; **intensive care unit** *n* service *m* de réanimation

intent [ɪnˈtɛnt] *n* intention *f* ▷ *adj* attentif(-ive), absorbé(e); **to all ~s and purposes** en fait, pratiquement; **to be ~ on doing sth** être (bien) décidé à faire qch

intention [ɪnˈtɛnʃən] *n* intention *f*; **intentional** *adj* intentionnel(le), délibéré(e)

interact [ɪntərˈækt] *vi* avoir une action réciproque; (*people*) communiquer; **interaction** [ɪntərˈækʃən] *n* interaction *f*; **interactive** *adj* (*Comput*) interactif, conversationnel(le)

intercept [ɪntəˈsɛpt] *vt* intercepter; (*person*) arrêter au passage

interchange *n* [ˈɪntətʃeɪndʒ] (*exchange*) échange *m*; (*on motorway*) échangeur *m*

intercourse [ˈɪntəkɔːs] *n*: **sexual ~** rapports sexuels

interest [ˈɪntrɪst] *n* intérêt *m*; (*Comm: stake, share*) participation *f*, intérêts *mpl* ▷ *vt* intéresser; **interested** *adj* intéressé(e); **to be interested in sth** s'intéresser à qch; **I'm interested in going** ça m'intéresse d'y aller; **interesting** *adj* intéressant(e); **interest rate** *n* taux *m* d'intérêt

interface [ˈɪntəfeɪs] *n* (*Comput*) interface *f*

interfere [ɪntəˈfɪəʳ] *vi*: **to ~ in** (*quarrel*) s'immiscer dans; (*other people's business*) se mêler de; **to ~ with** (*object*) tripoter, toucher à; (plans) contrecarrer; (duty) être en conflit avec; **interference** n (gen) ingérence f; (Radio, TV) parasites mpl

interim ['ɪntərɪm] adj provisoire; (post) intérimaire ▷ n: **in the ~** dans l'intérim

interior [ɪn'tɪərɪə[r]] n intérieur m ▷ adj intérieur(e); (minister, department) de l'intérieur; **interior design** n architecture f d'intérieur

intermediate [ɪntə'miːdɪət] adj intermédiaire; (Scol: course, level) moyen(ne)

intermission [ɪntə'mɪʃən] n pause f; (Theat, Cine) entracte m

intern vt [ɪn'təːn] interner ▷ n ['ɪntəːn] (us) interne m/f

internal [ɪn'təːnl] adj interne; (dispute, reform etc) intérieur(e); **Internal Revenue Service** n (us) fisc m

international [ɪntə'næʃənl] adj international(e) ▷ n (BRIT Sport) international m

Internet [ɪntə'nɛt] n: **the ~** l'Internet m; **Internet café** n cybercafé m; **Internet Service Provider** n fournisseur m d'accès à Internet; **Internet user** n internaute m/f

interpret [ɪn'təːprɪt] vt interpréter ▷ vi servir d'interprète; **interpretation** [ɪntəːprɪ'teɪʃən] n interprétation f; **interpreter** n interprète m/f; **could you act as an interpreter for us?** pourriez-vous nous servir d'interprète?

interrogate [ɪn'tɛrəugeɪt] vt interroger; (suspect etc) soumettre à un interrogatoire; **interrogation** [ɪntɛrəu'geɪʃən] n interrogation f; (by police) interrogatoire m

interrogative [ɪntə'rɔgətɪv] adj interrogateur(-trice) ▷ n (Ling) interrogatif m

interrupt [ɪntə'rʌpt] vt, vi interrompre; **interruption** [ɪntə'rʌpʃən] n interruption f

intersection [ɪntə'sɛkʃən] n (of roads) croisement m

interstate ['ɪntərsteɪt] (us) n

autoroute f (qui relie plusieurs États)

interval ['ɪntəvl] n intervalle m; (BRIT: Theat) entracte m; (: Sport) mi-temps f; **at ~s** par intervalles

intervene [ɪntə'viːn] vi (time) s'écouler (entre-temps); (event) survenir; (person) intervenir

interview ['ɪntəvjuː] n (Radio, TV etc) interview f; (for job) entrevue f ▷ vt interviewer; avoir une entrevue avec; **interviewer** n (Radio, TV etc) interviewer m

intimate adj ['ɪntɪmət] intime; (friendship) profond(e); (knowledge) approfondi(e) ▷ vt ['ɪntɪmeɪt] suggérer, laisser entendre; (announce) faire savoir

intimidate [ɪn'tɪmɪdeɪt] vt intimider

intimidating [ɪn'tɪmɪdeɪtɪŋ] adj intimidant(e)

into ['ɪntu] prep dans; **~ pieces/French** en morceaux/français

intolerant [ɪn'tɔlərnt] adj: **~ (of)** intolérant(e) (de)

intranet [ɪn'trənet] n intranet m

intransitive [ɪn'trænsɪtɪv] adj intransitif(-ive)

intricate ['ɪntrɪkət] adj complexe, compliqué(e)

intrigue [ɪn'triːg] n intrigue f ▷ vt intriguer; **intriguing** adj fascinant(e)

introduce [ɪntrə'djuːs] vt introduire; (TV show etc) présenter; **to ~ sb (to sb)** présenter qn (à qn); **to ~ sb to** (pastime, technique) initier qn à; **introduction** [ɪntrə'dʌkʃən] n introduction f; (of person) présentation f; (to new experience) initiation f; **introductory** [ɪntrə'dʌktərɪ] adj préliminaire, introductif(-ive)

intrude [ɪn'truːd] vi (person) être importun(e); **to ~ on** or **into** (conversation etc) s'immiscer dans; **intruder** n intrus(e)

intuition [ɪntjuː'ɪʃən] n intuition f

inundate ['ɪnʌndeɪt] vt: **to ~ with** inonder de

invade [ɪn'veɪd] vt envahir

invalid n [ˈɪnvəlɪd] malade m/f; (with disability) invalide m/f ▷ adj [ɪnˈvælɪd] (not valid) invalide, non valide

invaluable [ɪnˈvæljuəbl] adj inestimable, inappréciable

invariably [ɪnˈvɛərɪəblɪ] adv invariablement; **she is ~ late** elle est toujours en retard

invasion [ɪnˈveɪʒən] n invasion f

invent [ɪnˈvɛnt] vt inventer; **invention** [ɪnˈvɛnʃən] n invention f; **inventor** n inventeur(-trice)

inventory [ˈɪnvəntrɪ] n inventaire m

inverted commas [ɪnˈvəːtɪd-] npl (BRIT) guillemets mpl

invest [ɪnˈvɛst] vt investir ▷ vi: **to ~ in** placer de l'argent or investir dans; (fig: acquire) s'offrir, faire l'acquisition de

investigate [ɪnˈvɛstɪɡeɪt] vt étudier, examiner; (crime) faire une enquête sur; **investigation** [ɪnvɛstɪˈɡeɪʃən] n (of crime) enquête f, investigation f

investigator [ɪnˈvɛstɪɡeɪtəʳ] n investigateur(-trice); **private ~** détective privé

investment [ɪnˈvɛstmənt] n investissement m, placement m

investor [ɪnˈvɛstəʳ] n épargnant(e); (shareholder) actionnaire m/f

invisible [ɪnˈvɪzɪbl] adj invisible

invitation [ɪnvɪˈteɪʃən] n invitation f

invite [ɪnˈvaɪt] vt inviter; (opinions etc) demander; **inviting** adj engageant(e), attrayant(e)

invoice [ˈɪnvɔɪs] n facture f ▷ vt facturer

involve [ɪnˈvɔlv] vt (entail) impliquer; (concern) concerner; (require) nécessiter; **to ~ sb in** (theft etc) impliquer qn dans; (activity, meeting) faire participer qn à; **involved** adj (complicated) complexe; **to be involved in** (take part) participer à; **involvement** n (personal role) rôle m; (participation) participation f; (enthusiasm) enthousiasme m

inward [ˈɪnwəd] adj (movement) vers l'intérieur; (thought, feeling) profond(e), intime ▷ adv = **inwards**; **inwards** adv vers l'intérieur

IQ n abbr (= intelligence quotient) Q.I. m

IRA n abbr (= Irish Republican Army) IRA f

Iran [ɪˈrɑːn] n Iran m; **Iranian** [ɪˈreɪnɪən] adj iranien(ne) ▷ n Iranien(ne)

Iraq [ɪˈrɑːk] n Irak m; **Iraqi** adj irakien(ne) ▷ n Irakien(ne)

Ireland [ˈaɪələnd] n Irlande f

iris, irises [ˈaɪrɪs, -ɪz] n iris m

Irish [ˈaɪrɪʃ] adj irlandais(e) ▷ npl: **the ~** les Irlandais; **Irishman** (irreg) n Irlandais m; **Irishwoman** (irreg) n Irlandaise f

iron [ˈaɪən] n fer m; (for clothes) fer m à repasser ▷ adj de or en fer ▷ vt (clothes) repasser

ironic(al) [aɪˈrɔnɪk(l)] adj ironique; **ironically** adv ironiquement

ironing [ˈaɪənɪŋ] n (activity) repassage m; (clothes: ironed) linge repassé; (: to be ironed) linge à repasser; **ironing board** n planche f à repasser

irony [ˈaɪrənɪ] n ironie f

irrational [ɪˈræʃənl] adj irrationnel(le); (person) qui n'est pas rationnel

irregular [ɪˈrɛɡjuləʳ] adj irrégulier(-ière); (surface) inégal(e); (action, event) peu orthodoxe

irrelevant [ɪˈrɛləvənt] adj sans rapport, hors de propos

irresistible [ɪrɪˈzɪstɪbl] adj irrésistible

irresponsible [ɪrɪˈspɔnsɪbl] adj (act) irréfléchi(e); (person) qui n'a pas le sens des responsabilités

irrigation [ɪrɪˈɡeɪʃən] n irrigation f

irritable [ˈɪrɪtəbl] adj irritable

irritate [ˈɪrɪteɪt] vt irriter; **irritating** adj irritant(e); **irritation** [ɪrɪˈteɪʃən] n irritation f

IRS n abbr (US) = **Internal Revenue Service**

is [ɪz] vb see **be**

ISDN n abbr (= Integrated Services Digital Network) RNIS m

Islam [ˈɪzlɑːm] n Islam m; **Islamic** [ɪzˈlæmɪk] adj islamique

island [ˈaɪlənd] n île f; (also: **traffic ~**) refuge m (pour piétons); **islander** n

habitant(e) d'une île, insulaire *m/f*
isle [aɪl] *n* île *f*
isn't ['ɪznt] = **is not**
isolated ['aɪsəleɪtɪd] *adj* isolé(e)
isolation [aɪsə'leɪʃən] *n* isolement *m*
ISP *n abbr* = **Internet Service Provider**
Israel ['ɪzreɪl] *n* Israël *m*; **Israeli** [ɪz'reɪlɪ]
adj israélien(ne) ▷ *n* Israélien(ne)
issue ['ɪʃuː] *n* question *f*, problème *m*;
(*of banknotes*) émission *f*; (*of newspaper*)
numéro *m*; (*of book*) publication *f*,
parution *f* ▷ *vt* (*rations, equipment*)
distribuer; (*orders*) donner; (*statement*)
publier, faire; (*certificate, passport*)
délivrer; (*banknotes, cheques, stamps*)
émettre, mettre en circulation; **at ~** en
jeu, en cause; **to take ~ with sb (over
sth)** exprimer son désaccord avec qn
(sur qch)
IT *n abbr* = **information technology**

○ KEYWORD

it [ɪt] *pron* **1** (*specific: subject*) il (elle);
(: *direct object*) le (la, l'); (: *indirect object*)
lui; **it's on the table** c'est *or* il (*or*
elle) est sur la table; **I can't find it** je
n'arrive pas à le trouver; **give it to me**
donne-le-moi
2 (*after prep*): **about/from/of it** en; **I
spoke to him about it** je lui en ai parlé;
what did you learn from it? qu'est-ce
que vous en avez retiré?; **I'm proud
of it** j'en suis fier; **in/to it** y; **put the
book in it** mettez-y le livre; **he agreed
to it** il y a consenti; **did you go to it?**
(*party, concert etc*) est-ce que vous y
êtes allé(s)?
3 (*impersonal*) il; ce, cela, ça; **it's raining**
il pleut; **it's Friday tomorrow** demain,
c'est vendredi *or* nous sommes,
vendredi; **it's 6 o'clock** il est 6 heures;
how far is it? — it's 10 miles c'est loin?
— c'est à 10 miles; **who is it? — it's me**
qui est-ce? — c'est moi

Italian [ɪ'tæljən] *adj* italien(ne) ▷ *n*
Italien(ne); (*Ling*) italien *m*

italics [ɪ'tælɪks] *npl* italique *m*
Italy ['ɪtəlɪ] *n* Italie *f*
itch [ɪtʃ] *n* démangeaison *f* ▷ *vi* (*person*)
éprouver des démangeaisons; (*part
of body*) démanger; **I'm ~ing to do**
l'envie me démange de faire; **itchy**
adj: **my back is itchy** j'ai le dos qui me
démange
it'd ['ɪtd] = **it would**; **it had**
item ['aɪtəm] *n* (*gen*) article *m*; (*on
agenda*) question *f*, point *m*; (*also*: **news
~**) nouvelle *f*
itinerary [aɪ'tɪnərərɪ] *n* itinéraire *m*
it'll ['ɪtl] = **it will**; **it shall**
its [ɪts] *adj* son (sa), ses *pl*
it's [ɪts] = **it is**; **it has**
itself [ɪt'sɛlf] *pron* (*reflexive*) se;
(*emphatic*) lui-même (elle-même)
ITV *n abbr*: = *Independent Television*)
chaîne de télévision commerciale
I've [aɪv] = **I have**
ivory ['aɪvərɪ] *n* ivoire *m*
ivy ['aɪvɪ] *n* lierre *m*

j

jab [dʒæb] vt: **to ~ sth into** enfoncer or
planter qch dans ▷ n (Med: inf) piqûre f
jack [dʒæk] n (Aut) cric m; (Cards) valet m
jacket ['dʒækɪt] n veste f, veston m; (of
book) couverture f, jaquette f; **jacket
potato** n pomme f de terre en robe
des champs
jackpot ['dʒækpɔt] n gros lot
Jacuzzi® [dʒə'kuːzɪ] n jacuzzi® m
jagged ['dʒægɪd] adj dentelé(e)
jail [dʒeɪl] n prison f ▷ vt emprisonner,
mettre en prison; **jail sentence** n
peine f de prison
jam [dʒæm] n confiture f; (also: **traffic
~**) embouteillage m ▷ vt (passage etc)
encombrer, obstruer; (mechanism,
drawer etc) bloquer, coincer; (Radio)
brouiller ▷ vi (mechanism, sliding part)
se coincer, se bloquer; (gun) s'enrayer;
to be in a ~ (inf) être dans le pétrin; **to ~
sth into** (stuff) entasser or comprimer
qch dans; (thrust) enfoncer qch dans
Jamaica [dʒə'meɪkə] n Jamaïque f
jammed [dʒæmd] adj (window etc)
coincé(e)
Jan abbr (= January) janv
janitor ['dʒænɪtər] n (caretaker)
concierge m
January ['dʒænjuərɪ] n janvier m
Japan [dʒə'pæn] n Japon m; **Japanese**
[dʒæpə'niːz] adj japonais(e) ▷ n (pl inv)
Japonais(e); (Ling) japonais m
jar [dʒɑːr] n (stone, earthenware) pot m;
(glass) bocal m ▷ vi (sound) produire un
son grinçant or discordant; (colours etc)
détonner, jurer
jargon ['dʒɑːgən] n jargon m
javelin ['dʒævlɪn] n javelot m
jaw [dʒɔː] n mâchoire f
jazz [dʒæz] n jazz m
jealous ['dʒɛləs] adj jaloux(-ouse);
jealousy n jalousie f
jeans [dʒiːnz] npl jean m
Jello® ['dʒɛləu] (US) n gelée f
jelly ['dʒɛlɪ] n (dessert) gelée f; (US: jam)
confiture f; **jellyfish** n méduse f
jeopardize ['dʒɛpədaɪz] vt mettre en
danger or péril
jerk [dʒəːk] n secousse f, saccade f; (of
muscle) spasme m; (inf) pauvre type
m ▷ vt (shake) donner une secousse à;
(pull) tirer brusquement ▷ vi (vehicles)
cahoter
jersey ['dʒəːzɪ] n tricot m; (fabric)
jersey m
Jesus ['dʒiːzəs] n Jésus
jet [dʒɛt] n (of gas, liquid) jet m; (Aviat)
avion m à réaction, jet m; **jet lag** n
décalage m horaire; **jet-ski** vi faire du
jet-ski or scooter des mers
jetty ['dʒɛtɪ] n jetée f, digue f
Jew [dʒuː] n Juif m
jewel ['dʒuːəl] n bijou m, joyau m; (in
watch) rubis m; **jeweller** (US **jeweler**) n
bijoutier(-ière), joaillier m; **jeweller's
(shop)** (US **jewelry store**) n bijouterie
f, joaillerie f; **jewellery** (US **jewelry**) n
bijoux mpl
Jewish ['dʒuːɪʃ] adj juif (juive)
jigsaw ['dʒɪgsɔː] n (also: **~ puzzle**)
puzzle m
job [dʒɔb] n (chore, task) travail m, tâche

f; (*employment*) emploi *m*, poste *m*, place f; **it's a good ~ that ...** c'est heureux or c'est une chance que ... + *sub*; **just the ~!** (c'est) juste or exactement ce qu'il faut!;
job centre (BRIT) *n* ≈ ANPE *f*, ≈ Agence nationale pour l'emploi; **jobless** *adj* sans travail, au chômage

ockey ['dʒɔkɪ] *n* jockey *m* ▷ *vi*: **to ~ for position** manœuvrer pour être bien placé

og [dʒɔg] *vt* secouer ▷ *vi* (*Sport*) faire du jogging; **to ~ sb's memory** rafraîchir la mémoire de qn; **jogging** *n* jogging *m*

oin [dʒɔɪn] *vt* (*put together*) unir, assembler; (*become member of*) s'inscrire à; (*meet*) rejoindre, retrouver; (*queue*) se joindre à ▷ *vi* (*roads, rivers*) se rejoindre, se rencontrer ▷ *n* raccord *m*; **join in** *vi* se mettre de la partie ▷ *vt fus* se mêler à; **join up** *vi* (*meet*) se rejoindre; (*Mil*) s'engager

oiner ['dʒɔɪnəʳ] (BRIT) *n* menuisier *m*

oint [dʒɔɪnt] *n* (*Tech*) jointure *f*; joint *m*; (*Anat*) articulation *f*, jointure; (BRIT *Culin*) rôti *m*; (*inf*: *place*) boîte *f*; (*of cannabis*) joint ▷ *adj* commun(e); (*committee*) mixte, paritaire; (*winner*) ex aequo; **joint account** *n* compte joint; **jointly** *adv* ensemble, en commun

oke [dʒəuk] *n* plaisanterie *f*; (*also*: **practical ~**) farce *f*; ▷ *vi* plaisanter; **to play a ~ on** jouer un tour à, faire une farce à; **joker** *n* (*Cards*) joker *m*

olly ['dʒɔlɪ] *adj* gai(e), enjoué(e); (*enjoyable*) amusant(e), plaisant(e) ▷ *adv* (BRIT *inf*) rudement, drôlement

olt [dʒəult] *n* cahot *m*, secousse *f*; (*shock*) choc *m* ▷ *vt* cahoter, secouer

ordan [dʒɔːdən] *n* (*country*) Jordanie *f*

ournal ['dʒəːnl] *n* journal *m*; **journalism** *n* journalisme *m*; **journalist** *n* journaliste *m/f*

ourney ['dʒəːnɪ] *n* voyage *m*; (*distance covered*) trajet *m*; **the ~ takes two hours** le trajet dure deux heures; **how was your ~?** votre voyage s'est bien passé?

oy [dʒɔɪ] *n* joie *f*; **joyrider** *n*

voleur(-euse) de voiture (*qui fait une virée dans le véhicule volé*); **joy stick** *n* (*Aviat*) manche *m* à balai; (*Comput*) manche à balai, manette *f* (de jeu)

Jr *abbr* = **junior**

judge [dʒʌdʒ] *n* juge *m* ▷ *vt* juger; (*estimate*: *weight, size etc*) apprécier; (*consider*) estimer

judo ['dʒuːdəu] *n* judo *m*

jug [dʒʌg] *n* pot *m*, cruche *f*

juggle ['dʒʌgl] *vi* jongler; **juggler** *n* jongleur *m*

juice [dʒuːs] *n* jus *m*; **juicy** *adj* juteux(-euse)

Jul *abbr* (= *July*) juil

July [dʒuː'laɪ] *n* juillet *m*

jumble ['dʒʌmbl] *n* fouillis *m* ▷ *vt* (*also*: **~ up, ~ together**) mélanger, brouiller; **jumble sale** *n* (BRIT) vente *f* de charité

- **JUMBLE SALE**
-
- Les **jumble sales** ont lieu dans les
- églises, salles des fêtes ou halls
- d'écoles, et l'on y vend des articles
- de toutes sortes, en général bon
- marché et surtout d'occasion, pour
- collecter des fonds pour une œuvre
- de charité, une école (par exemple,
- pour acheter un ordinateur), ou
- encore une église (pour réparer un
- toit etc).

jumbo ['dʒʌmbəu] *adj* (*also*: **~ jet**) (avion) gros porteur (à réaction)

jump [dʒʌmp] *vi* sauter, bondir; (*with fear etc*) sursauter; (*increase*) monter en flèche ▷ *vt* sauter, franchir ▷ *n* saut *m*, bond *m*; (*with fear etc*) sursaut *m*; (*fence*) obstacle *m*; **to ~ the queue** (BRIT) passer avant son tour

jumper ['dʒʌmpəʳ] *n* (BRIT: *pullover*) pull-over *m*; (US: *pinafore dress*) robe-chasuble *f*

jump leads (US **jumper cables**) *npl* câbles *mpl* de démarrage

Jun. *abbr* = **June; junior**

junction ['dʒʌŋkʃən] *n* (BRIT:

of roads) carrefour m; (of rails) embranchement m

June [dʒuːn] n juin m

jungle ['dʒʌŋgl] n jungle f

junior ['dʒuːnɪəʳ] adj, n: **he's ~ to me (by 2 years)**, **he's my ~ (by 2 years)** il est mon cadet (de 2 ans), il est plus jeune que moi (de 2 ans); **he's ~ to me** (seniority) il est en dessous de moi (dans la hiérarchie), j'ai plus d'ancienneté que lui; **junior high school** n (US) ≈ collège m d'enseignement secondaire; see also **high school**; **junior school** n (BRIT) école f primaire, cours moyen

junk [dʒʌŋk] n (rubbish) camelote f; (cheap goods) bric-à-brac m inv; **junk food** n snacks vite prêts (sans valeur nutritive)

junkie ['dʒʌŋkɪ] n (inf) junkie m, drogué(e)

junk mail n prospectus mpl; (Comput) messages mpl publicitaires

Jupiter ['dʒuːpɪtəʳ] n (planet) Jupiter f

jurisdiction [dʒuərɪs'dɪkʃən] n juridiction f; **it falls** or **comes within/ outside our ~** cela est/n'est pas de notre compétence or ressort

jury ['dʒuərɪ] n jury m

just [dʒʌst] adj juste ▷ adv: **he's ~ done it/left** il vient de le faire/partir; **~ right/two o'clock** exactement or juste ce qu'il faut/deux heures; **we were ~ going** nous partions; **I was ~ about to phone** j'allais téléphoner; **~ as he was leaving** au moment or à l'instant précis où il partait; **~ before/enough/here** juste avant/assez/là; **it's ~ me/a mistake** ce n'est que moi/(rien) qu'une erreur; **~ missed/caught** manqué/ attrapé de justesse; **~ listen to this!** écoutez un peu ça!; **she's ~ as clever as you** elle est tout aussi intelligente que vous; **it's ~ as well that you ...** heureusement que vous ...; **~ a minute!**, **~ one moment!** un instant (s'il vous plaît)!

justice ['dʒʌstɪs] n justice f; (US: judge) juge m de la Cour suprême

justification [dʒʌstɪfɪ'keɪʃən] n justification f

justify ['dʒʌstɪfaɪ] vt justifier

jut [dʒʌt] vi (also: ~ out) dépasser, faire saillie

juvenile ['dʒuːvənaɪl] adj juvénile; (court, books) pour enfants ▷ n adolescent(e)

K, k [keɪ] *abbr* (= *one thousand*) K;
(= *kilobyte*) Ko

kangaroo [kæŋgə'ru:] *n* kangourou *m*

karaoke [kɑːrə'əʊkɪ] *n* karaoké *m*

karate [kə'rɑːtɪ] *n* karaté *m*

kebab [kə'bæb] *n* kébab *m*

keel [ki:l] *n* quille *f*; **on an even ~**
(*fig*) à flot

keen [ki:n] *adj* (*eager*) plein(e)
d'enthousiasme; (*interest, desire,
competition*) vif(vive); (*eye, intelligence*)
pénétrant(e); (*edge*) effilé(e); **to be ~ to
do** *or* **on doing sth** désirer vivement
faire qch, tenir beaucoup à faire qch;
to be ~ on sth/sb aimer beaucoup
qch/qn

keep [ki:p] (*pt, pp* **kept**) *vt* (*retain,
preserve*) garder; (*hold back*) retenir;
(*shop, accounts, promise, diary*) tenir;
(*support*) entretenir; (*chickens, bees,
pigs etc*) élever ▷ *vi* (*food*) se conserver;
(*remain: in a certain state or place*)
rester ▷ *n* (*of castle*) donjon *m*; (*food
etc*): **enough for his ~** assez pour

(*assure*) sa subsistance; **to ~ doing
sth** (*continue*) continuer à faire qch;
(*repeatedly*) ne pas arrêter de faire
qch; **to ~ sb from doing/sth from
happening** empêcher qn de faire *or* que
qn (ne) fasse/que qch (n')arrive; **to ~ sb
happy/a place tidy** faire que qn soit
content/qu'un endroit reste propre; **to
~ sth to o.s.** garder qch pour soi, tenir
qch secret; **to ~ sth from sb** cacher qch
à qn; **to ~ time** (*clock*) être à l'heure,
ne pas retarder; **for ~s** (*inf*) pour de
bon, pour toujours; **keep away** *vt*: **to
~ sth/sb away from sb** tenir qch/qn
éloigné de qn ▷ *vi*: **to ~ away (from)**
ne pas s'approcher (de); **keep back** *vt*
(*crowds, tears, money*) retenir; (*conceal:
information*): **to ~ sth back from sb**
cacher qch à qn ▷ *vi* rester en arrière;
keep off *vt* (*dog, person*) éloigner ▷ *vi*: **if
the rain ~s off** s'il ne pleut pas; **~ your
hands off!** pas touché! (*inf*); **"~ off the
grass"** "pelouse interdite"; **keep on** *vi*
continuer; **to ~ on doing** continuer à
faire; **don't ~ on about it!** arrête (d'en
parler)!; **keep out** *vt* empêcher d'entrer
▷ *vi* (*stay out*) rester en dehors; **"~ out"**
"défense d'entrer"; **keep up** *vi* (*fig: in
comprehension*) suivre ▷ *vt* continuer,
maintenir; **to ~ up with sb** (*in work
etc*) se maintenir au même niveau
que qn; (*in race etc*) aller aussi vite que
qn; **keeper** *n* gardien(ne); **keep-fit** *n*
gymnastique *f* (d'entretien); **keeping**
n (*care*) garde *f*; **in keeping with** en
harmonie avec

kennel ['kɛnl] *n* niche *f*; **kennels** *npl*
(*for boarding*) chenil *m*

Kenya ['kɛnjə] *n* Kenya *m*

kept [kɛpt] *pt, pp of* **keep**

kerb [kə:b] *n* (*BRIT*) bordure *f* du trottoir

kerosene ['kɛrəsi:n] *n* kérosène *m*

ketchup ['kɛtʃəp] *n* ketchup *m*

kettle ['kɛtl] *n* bouilloire *f*

key [ki:] *n* (*gen, Mus*) clé *f*; (*of piano,
typewriter*) touche *f*; (*on map*) légende
f ▷ *adj* (*factor, role, area*) clé *inv* ▷ *vt*
(*also*: **~ in**: *text*) saisir; **can I have my**

~? je peux avoir ma clé?; **a ~ issue** un problème fondamental; **keyboard** n clavier m; **keyhole** n trou m de la serrure; **keyring** n porte-clés m

kg abbr (= kilogram) K

khaki ['kɑːkɪ] adj, n kaki m

kick [kɪk] vt donner un coup de pied à ▷ vi (horse) ruer ▷ n coup m de pied; (inf: thrill): **he does it for ~s** il le fait parce que ça l'excite, il le fait pour le plaisir; **to ~ the habit** (inf) arrêter; **kick off** vi (Sport) donner le coup d'envoi; **kick-off** n (Sport) coup m d'envoi

kid [kɪd] n (inf: child) gamin(e), gosse m/f; (animal, leather) chevreau m ▷ vi (inf) plaisanter, blaguer

kidnap ['kɪdnæp] vt enlever, kidnapper; **kidnapping** n enlèvement m

kidney ['kɪdnɪ] n (Anat) rein m; (Culin) rognon m; **kidney bean** n haricot m rouge

kill [kɪl] vt tuer ▷ n mise f à mort; **to ~ time** tuer le temps; **killer** n tueur(-euse); (murderer) meurtrier(-ière); **killing** n meurtre m; (of group of people) tuerie f, massacre m; (inf): **to make a killing** se remplir les poches, réussir un beau coup

kiln [kɪln] n four m

kilo ['kiːləʊ] n kilo m; **kilobyte** (Comput) kilo-octet m; **kilogram(me)** n kilogramme m; **kilometre** (US **kilometer**) ['kɪləmiːtəʳ] n kilomètre m; **kilowatt** n kilowatt m

kilt [kɪlt] n kilt m

kin [kɪn] n see **next-of-kin**

kind [kaɪnd] adj gentil(le), aimable ▷ n sorte f, espèce f; (species) genre m; **to be two of a ~** se ressembler; **in ~** (Comm) en nature; **~ of** (inf: rather) plutôt; **a ~ of** une sorte de; **what ~ of ...?** quelle sorte de ...?

kindergarten ['kɪndəgɑːtn] n jardin m d'enfants

kindly ['kaɪndlɪ] adj bienveillant(e), plein(e) de gentillesse ▷ adv avec bonté; **will you ~ ...** auriez-vous la bonté or l'obligeance de ...

kindness ['kaɪndnɪs] n (quality) bonté f, gentillesse f

king [kɪŋ] n roi m; **kingdom** n royaume m; **kingfisher** n martin-pêcheur m; **king-size(d) bed** n grand lit (de 1,95 m de large)

kiosk ['kiːɒsk] n kiosque m; (BRIT: also: **telephone ~**) cabine f (téléphonique)

kipper ['kɪpəʳ] n hareng fumé et salé

kiss [kɪs] n baiser m ▷ vt embrasser; **to ~ (each other)** s'embrasser; **kiss of life** n (BRIT) bouche à bouche m

kit [kɪt] n équipement m, matériel m; (set of tools etc) trousse f; (for assembly) kit m

kitchen ['kɪtʃɪn] n cuisine f

kite [kaɪt] n (toy) cerf-volant m

kitten ['kɪtn] n petit chat, chaton m

kitty ['kɪtɪ] n (money) cagnotte f

kiwi ['kiːwiː] n (also: **~ fruit**) kiwi m

km abbr (= kilometre) km

km/h abbr (= kilometres per hour) km/h

knack [næk] n: **to have the ~ (of doing)** avoir le coup (pour faire)

knee [niː] n genou m; **kneecap** n rotule f

kneel (pt, pp **knelt**) [niːl, nɛlt] vi (also: **~ down**) s'agenouiller

knelt [nɛlt] pt, pp of **kneel**

knew [njuː] pt of **know**

knickers ['nɪkəz] npl (BRIT) culotte f (de femme)

knife [naɪf] n (pl **knives**) couteau m ▷ vt poignarder, frapper d'un coup de couteau

knight [naɪt] n chevalier m; (Chess) cavalier m

knit [nɪt] vt tricoter ▷ vi tricoter; (broken bones) se ressouder; **to ~ one's brows** froncer les sourcils; **knitting** n tricot m; **knitting needle** n aiguille f à tricoter; **knitwear** n tricots mpl, lainages mpl

knives [naɪvz] npl of **knife**

knob [nɔb] n bouton m; (BRIT): **a ~ of butter** une noix de beurre

knock [nɔk] vt frapper; (bump into) heurter; (fig: col) dénigrer ▷ vi (at

door etc): **to ~ at/on** frapper à/sur ▷ n
coup m; **knock down** vt renverser;
(price) réduire; **knock off** vi (inf: finish)
s'arrêter (de travailler) ▷ vt (vase,
object) faire tomber; (inf: steal) piquer;
(fig: from price etc): **to ~ off £10** faire
une remise de 10 livres; **knock out**
vt assommer; (Boxing) mettre k.-o.;
(in competition) éliminer; **knock over**
vt (object) faire tomber; (pedestrian)
renverser; **knockout** n (Boxing) knockout m, K.-O. m; **knockout competition**
(BRIT) compétition f avec épreuves
éliminatoires

knot [nɔt] n (gen) nœud m ▷ vt nouer
know [nəu] vt (pt **knew**, pp **~n**) savoir;
(person, place) connaître; **to ~ that**
savoir que; **to ~ how to do** savoir faire;
to ~ how to swim savoir nager; **to ~
about/of sth** (event) être au courant
de qch; (subject) connaître qch; **I don't
~** je ne sais pas; **do you ~ where I
can ...?** savez-vous où je peux ...?;
know-all n (BRIT pej) je-sais-tout
m/f; **know-how** n savoir-faire m,
technique f, compétence f; **knowing**
adj (look etc) entendu(e); **knowingly**
adv (on purpose) sciemment; (smile, look)
d'un air entendu; **know-it-all** n (US)
= **know-all**
knowledge ['nɔlɪdʒ] n connaissance
f; (learning) connaissances, savoir
m; **without my ~** à mon insu;
knowledgeable adj bien informé(e)
known [nəun] pp of **know** ▷ adj (thief,
facts) notoire; (expert) célèbre
knuckle ['nʌkl] n articulation f (des
phalanges), jointure f
koala [kəu'ɑːlə] n (also: **~ bear**) koala m
Koran [kɔ'rɑːn] n Coran m
Korea [kə'rɪə] n Corée f; **Korean** adj
coréen(ne) ▷ n Coréen(ne)
kosher ['kəuʃəʳ] adj kascher inv
Kosovar, Kosovan ['kɔsəvɑːʳ,
'kɔsəvən] adj kosovar(e)
Kosovo ['kɔsəvəu] n Kosovo m
Kuwait [ku'weɪt] n Koweït m

L abbr (BRIT Aut: = learner) signale un
conducteur débutant
l. abbr (= litre) l
lab [læb] n abbr (= laboratory) labo m
label ['leɪbl] n étiquette f; (brand: of
record) marque f ▷ vt étiqueter
labor etc ['leɪbəʳ] (US) = **labour** etc
laboratory [lə'bɔrətərɪ] n laboratoire m
Labor Day n (US, CANADA) fête f du
travail (le premier lundi de septembre)

● **LABOR DAY**
●
● La fête du Travail aux États-Unis et au
● Canada est fixée au premier lundi de
● septembre. Instituée par le Congrès
● en 1894 après avoir été réclamée par
● les mouvements ouvriers pendant
● douze ans, elle a perdu une grande
● partie de son caractère politique
● pour devenir un jour férié assez
● ordinaire et l'occasion de partir pour
● un long week-end avant la rentrée
● des classes.

labor union n (US) syndicat m
Labour ['leɪbər] n (BRIT Pol: also:
the ~ Party) le parti travailliste, les
travaillistes mpl
labour (US **labor**) ['leɪbər] n (work)
travail m; (workforce) main-d'œuvre f
▷ vi: **to ~ (at)** travailler dur (à), peiner
(sur) ▷ vt: **to ~ a point** insister sur un
point; **in ~** (Med) en travail; **labourer** n
manœuvre m; **farm labourer** ouvrier
m agricole
lace [leɪs] n dentelle f; (of shoe etc) lacet
m ▷ vt (shoe: also: ~ **up**) lacer
lack [læk] n manque m ▷ vt manquer
de; **through** or **for ~ of** faute de, par
manque de; **to be ~ing** manquer, faire
défaut; **to be ~ing in** manquer de
lacquer ['lækər] n laque f
lacy ['leɪsɪ] adj (of lace) en dentelle; (like
lace) comme de la dentelle
lad [læd] n garçon m, gars m
ladder ['lædər] n échelle f; (BRIT:
in tights) maille filée ▷ vt, vi (BRIT:
tights) filer
ladle ['leɪdl] n louche f
lady ['leɪdɪ] n dame f; **"ladies and
gentlemen ..."** "Mesdames (et)
Messieurs ..."; **young ~** jeune fille f;
(married) jeune femme f; **the ladies'
(room)** les toilettes fpl des dames;
ladybird (US **ladybug**) n coccinelle f
lag [læg] n retard m ▷ vi (also: ~ **behind**)
rester en arrière, traîner; (fig) rester à la
traîne ▷ vt (pipes) calorifuger
lager ['lɑːgər] n bière blonde
lagoon [lə'guːn] n lagune f
laid [leɪd] pt, pp of **lay; laid back** adj (inf)
relaxe, décontracté(e)
lain [leɪn] pp of **lie**
lake [leɪk] n lac m
lamb [læm] n agneau m
lame [leɪm] adj (also fig) boiteux(-euse)
lament [lə'mɛnt] n lamentation f ▷ vt
pleurer, se lamenter sur
lamp [læmp] n lampe f; **lamppost**
n (BRIT) réverbère m; **lampshade** n
abat-jour m inv
land [lænd] n (as opposed to sea)

terre f (ferme); (country) pays m; (soil)
terre; (piece of land) terrain m; (estate)
terre(s), domaine(s) m(pl) ▷ vi (from
ship) débarquer; (Aviat) atterrir; (fig:
fall) (re)tomber ▷ vt (passengers,
goods) débarquer; (obtain) décrocher;
to ~ sb with sth (inf) coller qch à qn;
landing n (from ship) débarquement
m; (Aviat) atterrissage m; (of staircase)
palier m; **landing card** n carte f
de débarquement; **landlady** n
propriétaire f, logeuse f; (of pub)
patronne f; **landlord** n propriétaire
m, logeur m; (of pub etc) patron m;
landmark n (point m de) repère m;
to be a landmark (fig) faire date or
époque; **landowner** n propriétaire
foncier or terrien; **landscape**
n paysage m; **landslide** n (Geo)
glissement m (de terrain); (fig: Pol) raz-
de-marée (électoral)
lane [leɪn] n (in country) chemin m; (Aut:
of road) voie f; (: line of traffic) file f; (in
race) couloir m
language ['læŋgwɪdʒ] n langue f; (way
one speaks) langage m; **what ~s do you
speak?** quelles langues parlez-vous?;
bad ~ grossièretés fpl, langage grossier
language laboratory n laboratoire m
de langues; **language school** n école
f de langue
lantern ['læntn] n lanterne f
lap [læp] n (of track) tour m (de piste); (of
body): **in** or **on one's ~** sur les genoux
▷ vt (also: ~ **up**) laper ▷ vi (waves)
clapoter
lapel [lə'pɛl] n revers m
lapse [læps] n défaillance f; (in
behaviour) écart m (de conduite) ▷ vi
(Law) cesser d'être en vigueur; (contract)
expirer; **to ~ into bad habits** prendre
de mauvaises habitudes; **~ of time** lap
m de temps, intervalle m
laptop (computer) ['læptɔp-] n
portable m
lard [lɑːd] n saindoux m
larder ['lɑːdər] n garde-manger m inv
large [lɑːdʒ] adj grand(e); (person,

animal) gros (grosse); **at ~** (*free*) en liberté; (*generally*) en général; pour la plupart; *see also* **by**; **largely** *adv* en grande partie; (*principally*) surtout; **large-scale** *adj* (*map, drawing etc*) à grande échelle; (*fig*) important(e)

ark [lɑːk] *n* (*bird*) alouette *f*; (*joke*) blague *f*, farce *f*

aryngitis [lærɪnˈdʒaɪtɪs] *n* laryngite *f*

asagne [ləˈzænjə] *n* lasagne *f*

aser [ˈleɪzəʳ] *n* laser *m*; **laser printer** *n* imprimante *f* laser

ash [læʃ] *n* coup *m* de fouet; (*also*: **eye~**) cil *m* ▷ *vt* fouetter; (*tie*) attacher; **lash out** *vi*: **to ~ out** (**at** *or* **against sb/sth**) attaquer violemment (qn/qch)

ass [læs] (*BRIT*) *n* (jeune) fille *f*

ast [lɑːst] *adj* dernier(-ière) ▷ *adv* en dernier; (*most recently*) la dernière fois; (*finally*) finalement ▷ *vi* durer; **~ week** la semaine dernière; **~ night** (*evening*) hier soir; (*night*) la nuit dernière; **at ~** enfin; **~ but one** avant-dernier(-ière); **lastly** *adv* en dernier lieu, pour finir; **last-minute** *adj* de dernière minute

atch [lætʃ] *n* loquet *m*; **latch onto** *vt fus* (*cling to: person, group*) s'accrocher à; (*idea*) se mettre en tête

ate [leɪt] *adj* (*not on time*) en retard; (*far on in day etc*) tardif(-ive); (: *edition, delivery*) dernier(-ière); (: *dead*) défunt(e) ▷ *adv* tard; (*behind time, schedule*) en retard; **to be 10 minutes ~** avoir 10 minutes de retard; **sorry I'm ~** désolé d'être en retard; **it's too ~** il est trop tard; **of ~** dernièrement; **in ~ May** vers la fin (du mois) de mai, fin mai; **the ~ Mr X** feu M. X; **latecomer** *n* retardataire *m/f*; **lately** *adv* récemment; **later** *adj* (*date etc*) ultérieur(e); (*version etc*) plus récent(e) ▷ *adv* plus tard; **latest** [ˈleɪtɪst] *adj* tout(e) dernier(-ière); **at the latest** au plus tard

ather [ˈlɑːðəʳ] *n* mousse *f* (de savon) ▷ *vt* savonner

atin [ˈlætɪn] *n* latin *m* ▷ *adj* latin(e); **Latin America** *n* Amérique latine;

Latin American *adj* latino-américain(e), d'Amérique latine ▷ *n* Latino-Américain(e)

latitude [ˈlætɪtjuːd] *n* (*also fig*) latitude *f*

latter [ˈlætəʳ] *adj* deuxième, dernier(-ière) ▷ *n*: **the ~** ce dernier, celui-ci

laugh [lɑːf] *n* rire *m* ▷ *vi* rire; **(to do sth) for a ~** (faire qch) pour rire; **laugh at** *vt fus* se moquer de; (*joke*) rire de; **laughter** *n* rire *m*; (*of several people*) rires *mpl*

launch [lɔːntʃ] *n* lancement *m*; (*also*: **motor ~**) vedette *f* ▷ *vt* (*ship, rocket, plan*) lancer; **launch into** *vt fus* se lancer dans

launder [ˈlɔːndəʳ] *vt* laver; (*fig: money*) blanchir

Launderette® [lɔːnˈdrɛt] (*BRIT*) (*US* **Laundromat®** [ˈlɔːndrəmæt]) *n* laverie *f* (automatique)

laundry [ˈlɔːndrɪ] *n* (*clothes*) linge *m*; (*business*) blanchisserie *f*; (*room*) buanderie *f*; **to do the ~** faire la lessive

lava [ˈlɑːvə] *n* lave *f*

lavatory [ˈlævətərɪ] *n* toilettes *fpl*

lavender [ˈlævəndəʳ] *n* lavande *f*

lavish [ˈlævɪʃ] *adj* (*amount*) copieux(-euse); (*person: giving freely*): **~ with** prodigue de ▷ *vt*: **to ~ sth on sb** prodiguer qch à qn; (*money*) dépenser qch sans compter pour qn

law [lɔː] *n* loi *f*; (*science*) droit *m*; **lawful** *adj* légal(e), permis(e); **lawless** *adj* (*action*) illégal(e); (*place*) sans loi

lawn [lɔːn] *n* pelouse *f*; **lawnmower** *n* tondeuse *f* à gazon

lawsuit [ˈlɔːsuːt] *n* procès *m*

lawyer [ˈlɔːjəʳ] *n* (*consultant, with company*) juriste *m*; (*for sales, wills etc*) ≈ notaire *m*; (*partner, in court*) ≈ avocat *m*

lax [læks] *adj* relâché(e)

laxative [ˈlæksətɪv] *n* laxatif *m*

lay [leɪ] *pt of* **lie** ▷ *adj* laïque; (*not expert*) profane ▷ *vt* (*pt, pp* **laid**) poser, mettre; (*eggs*) pondre; (*trap*) tendre; (*plans*) élaborer; **to ~ the table** mettre la table;

lay down vt poser; (rules etc) établir; **to ~ down the law** (fig) faire la loi; **lay off** vt (workers) licencier; (provide: meal etc) fournir; **lay out** vt (design) dessiner, concevoir; (display) disposer; (spend) dépenser; **lay-by** n (BRIT) aire f de stationnement, sur le bas-côté
layer ['leɪəʳ] n couche f
layman ['leɪmən] (irreg) n (Rel) laïque m; (non-expert) profane m
layout ['leɪaut] n disposition f, plan m, agencement m; (Press) mise f en page
lazy ['leɪzɪ] adj paresseux(-euse)
lb. abbr (weight) = **pound**
lead¹ [li:d] n (front position) tête f; (distance, time ahead) avance f; (clue) piste f; (Elec) fil m; (for dog) laisse f; (Theat) rôle principal ▷ vb (pt, pp **led**) ▷ vt (guide) mener, conduire; (be leader of) être à la tête de ▷ vi (Sport) mener, être en tête; **to ~ to** (road, pipe) mener à, conduire à; (result in) conduire à; aboutir à; **to be in the ~** (Sport: in race) mener, être en tête; (: in match) mener (à la marque); **to ~ sb to do sth** amener qn à faire qch; **to ~ the way** montrer le chemin; **lead up to** vt conduire à; (in conversation) en venir à
lead² [lɛd] n (metal) plomb m; (in pencil) mine f
leader ['li:dəʳ] n (of team) chef m; (of party etc) dirigeant(e), leader m; (Sport: in league) leader; (: in race) coureur m de tête; **leadership** n (position) direction f; **under the leadership of ...** sous la direction de ...; **qualities of leadership** qualités fpl de chef or de meneur
lead-free ['lɛdfri:] adj sans plomb
leading ['li:dɪŋ] adj de premier plan; (main) principal(e); (in race) de tête
lead singer [li:d-] n (in pop group) (chanteur m) vedette f
leaf (pl **leaves**) [li:f, li:vz] n feuille f; (of table) rallonge f; **to turn over a new ~** (fig) changer de conduite or d'existence; **leaf through** vt (book) feuilleter
leaflet ['li:flɪt] n prospectus m, brochure f; (Pol, Rel) tract m

league [li:g] n ligue f; (Football) championnat m; **to be in ~ with** avoir partie liée avec, être de mèche avec
leak [li:k] n (out: also fig) fuite f ▷ vi (pipe, liquid etc) fuir; (shoes) prendre l'eau; (ship) faire eau ▷ vt (liquid) répandre; (information) divulguer
lean [li:n] adj maigre ▷ vb (pt, pp **~ed** or **~t**) ▷ vt: **to ~ sth on** appuyer qch sur ▷ vi (slope) pencher; (rest): **to ~ against** s'appuyer contre; être appuyé(e) contre; **to ~ on** s'appuyer sur; **lean forward** vi se pencher en avant; **lean over** vi se pencher; **leaning** n: **leaning (towards)** penchant m (pour)
leant [lɛnt] pt, pp of **lean**
leap [li:p] n bond m, saut m ▷ vi (pt, pp **~ed** or **~t**) bondir, sauter
leapt [lɛpt] pt, pp of **leap**
leap year n année f bissextile
learn (pt, pp **~ed** or **~t**) [lə:n, -t] vt, vi apprendre; **to ~ (how) to do sth** apprendre à faire qch; **to ~ about sth** (Scol) étudier qch; (hear, read) apprendre qch; **learner** n débutant(e); (BRIT: also: **learner driver**) (conducteur(-trice)) débutant(e); **learning** n savoir m
learnt [lə:nt] pp of **learn**
lease [li:s] n bail m ▷ vt louer à bail
leash [li:ʃ] n laisse f
least [li:st] adj: **the ~** (+ noun) le (la) plus petit(e), le (la) moindre; (smallest amount of) le moins de ▷ pron: **(the) ~** le moins ▷ adv (+ verb) le moins; (+ adj): **the ~** la (la) moins; **the ~ money** le moins d'argent; **the ~ expensive** le (la) moins cher (chère); **the ~ possible effort** le moins d'effort possible; **at ~** au moins; (or rather) du moins; **you could at ~ have written** tu aurais au moins pu écrire; **not in the ~** pas le moins du monde
leather ['lɛðəʳ] n cuir m
leave [li:v] (vb: pt, pp **left**) vt laisser; (go away from) quitter; (forget) oublier ▷ vi partir, s'en aller ▷ n (time off) congé m; (Mil, also: consent) permission f; **what time does the train/bus ~?** le train/le

bus part à quelle heure?; **to ~ sth to sb** (money etc) laisser qch à qn; **to be left** rester; **there's some milk left over** il reste du lait; **~ it to me!** laissez-moi faire!, je m'en occupe!; **on ~** en permission; **leave behind** vt (also fig) laisser; (forget) laisser, oublier; **leave out** vt oublier, omettre

leaves [li:vz] npl of **leaf**

Lebanon ['lɛbənən] n Liban m

lecture ['lɛktʃəʳ] n conférence f; (Scol) cours (magistral) ▷ vi donner des cours; enseigner ▷ vt (scold) sermonner, réprimander; **to give a ~ (on)** faire une conférence (sur), faire un cours (sur); **lecture hall** n amphithéâtre m; **lecturer** n (speaker) conférencier(-ière); (BRIT: at university) professeur m (d'université), prof m/f de fac (inf); **lecture theatre** n = **lecture hall**

> Be careful not to translate **lecture** by the French word **lecture**.

led [lɛd] pt, pp of **lead¹**

ledge [lɛdʒ] n (of window, on wall) rebord m; (of mountain) saillie f, corniche f

leek [li:k] n poireau m

left [lɛft] pt, pp of **leave** ▷ adj gauche ▷ adv à gauche ▷ n gauche f; **there are two ~** il en reste deux; **on the ~, to the ~** à gauche; **the L~** (Pol) la gauche; **left-hand** adj: **the left-hand side** la gauche; **left-hand drive** n (BRIT: vehicle) véhicule m avec la conduite à gauche; **left-handed** adj gaucher(-ère); (scissors etc) pour gauchers; **left-luggage locker** n (BRIT) casier m à consigne f automatique; **left-luggage (office)** n (BRIT) consigne f; **left-overs** npl restes mpl; **left-wing** adj (Pol) de gauche

leg [lɛg] n jambe f; (of animal) patte f; (of furniture) pied m; (Culin: of chicken) cuisse f; (of journey) étape f; **1st/2nd ~** (Sport) match m aller/retour; **~ of lamb** (Culin) gigot m d'agneau

legacy ['lɛgəsɪ] n (also fig) héritage m, legs m

legal ['li:gl] adj (permitted by law) légal(e); (relating to law) juridique; **legal holiday** (US) n jour férié; **legalize** vt légaliser; **legally** adv légalement

legend ['lɛdʒənd] n légende f; **legendary** ['lɛdʒəndərɪ] adj légendaire

leggings ['lɛgɪŋz] npl caleçon m

legible ['lɛdʒəbl] adj lisible

legislation [lɛdʒɪs'leɪʃən] n législation f

legislative ['lɛdʒɪslətɪv] adj législatif(-ive)

legitimate [lɪ'dʒɪtɪmət] adj légitime

leisure ['lɛʒəʳ] n (free time) temps libre, loisirs mpl; **at ~** (tout) à loisir; **at your ~** (later) à tête reposée; **leisure centre** n (BRIT) centre m de loisirs; **leisurely** adj tranquille, fait(e) sans se presser

lemon ['lɛmən] n citron m; **lemonade** n (fizzy) limonade f; **lemon tea** n thé m au citron

lend (pt, pp **lent**) [lɛnd, lɛnt] vt: **to ~ sth (to sb)** prêter qch (à qn); **could you ~ me some money?** pourriez-vous me prêter de l'argent?

length [lɛŋθ] n longueur f; (section: of road, pipe etc) morceau m, bout m; **~ of time** durée f; **it is 2 metres in ~** cela fait 2 mètres de long; **at ~** (at last) enfin, à la fin; (lengthily) longuement; **lengthen** vt allonger, prolonger ▷ vi s'allonger; **lengthways** adv dans le sens de la longueur, en long; **lengthy** adj (très) long (longue)

lens [lɛnz] n lentille f; (of spectacles) verre m; (of camera) objectif m

Lent [lɛnt] n carême m

lent [lɛnt] pt, pp of **lend**

lentil ['lɛntl] n lentille f

Leo ['li:əu] n le Lion

leopard ['lɛpəd] n léopard m

leotard ['li:əta:d] n justaucorps m

leprosy ['lɛprəsɪ] n lèpre f

lesbian ['lɛzbɪən] n lesbienne f ▷ adj lesbien(ne)

less [lɛs] adj moins de ▷ pron, adv moins ▷ prep: **~ tax/10% discount** avant impôt/moins 10% de remise; **~ than**

that/you moins que cela/vous; **~ than half** moins de la moitié; **~ than ever** moins que jamais; **~ and ~** de moins en moins; **the ~ he works ...** moins il travaille ...; **lessen** vi diminuer, s'amoindrir, s'atténuer ▷ vt diminuer, réduire, atténuer; **lesser** ['lɛsər] adj moindre; **to a lesser extent** or **degree** à un degré moindre

lesson ['lɛsn] n leçon f; **to teach sb a ~** (fig) donner une bonne leçon à qn

let (pt, pp ~) [lɛt] vt laisser; (BRIT: lease) louer; **to ~ sb do sth** laisser qn faire qch; **to ~ sb know sth** faire savoir qch à qn, prévenir qn de qch; **to ~ go** lâcher prise; **to ~ go of sth, to ~ sth go** lâcher qch; **~'s go** allons-y; **~ him come** qu'il vienne; **"to ~"** (BRIT) "à louer"; **let down** vt (lower) baisser; (BRIT: tyre) dégonfler; (disappoint) décevoir; **let in** vt laisser entrer; (visitor etc) faire entrer; **let off** vt (allow to leave) laisser partir; (not punish) ne pas punir; (firework etc) faire partir; (bomb) faire exploser; **let out** vt laisser sortir; (scream) laisser échapper; (BRIT: rent out) louer

lethal ['li:θl] adj mortel(le), fatal(e); (weapon) meurtrier(-ère)

letter ['lɛtər] n lettre f; **letterbox** n (BRIT) boîte f aux or à lettres

lettuce ['lɛtɪs] n laitue f, salade f

leukaemia (US **leukemia**) [lu:'ki:mɪə] n leucémie f

level ['lɛvl] adj (flat) plat(e), plan(e), uni(e); (horizontal) horizontal(e) ▷ n niveau m ▷ vt niveler, aplanir; **"A" ~s** npl (BRIT) ≈ baccalauréat m; **to be ~ with** être au même niveau que; **to draw ~ with** (runner, car) arriver à la hauteur de, rattraper; **on the ~** (fig: honest) régulier(-ière); **level crossing** n (BRIT) passage m à niveau

lever ['li:vər] n levier m; **leverage** n (influence): **leverage (on** or **with)** prise f(sur)

levy ['lɛvɪ] n taxe f, impôt m ▷ vt (tax) lever; (fine) infliger

liability [laɪə'bɪlətɪ] n responsabilité f;

(handicap) handicap m

liable ['laɪəbl] adj (subject): **~ to** sujet(te) à, passible de; (responsible): **~ (for)** responsable (de); (likely): **~ to do** susceptible de faire

liaise [lɪ:'eɪz] vi: **to ~ with** assurer la liaison avec

liar ['laɪər] n menteur(-euse)

libel ['laɪbl] n diffamation f; (document) écrit m diffamatoire ▷ vt diffamer

liberal ['lɪbərl] adj libéral(e); (generous): **~ with** prodigue de, généreux(-euse) avec ▷ n: **L~** (Pol) libéral(e); **Liberal Democrat** n (BRIT) libéral(e)-démocrate m/f

liberate ['lɪbəreɪt] vt libérer

liberation [lɪbə'reɪʃən] n libération f

liberty ['lɪbətɪ] n liberté f; **to be at ~** (criminal) être en liberté; **at ~ to do** être libre de faire; **to take the ~ of** prendre la liberté de, se permettre de

Libra ['li:brə] n la Balance

librarian [laɪ'brɛərɪən] n bibliothécaire m/f

library ['laɪbrərɪ] n bibliothèque f.

> Be careful not to translate *library* by the French word *librairie*.

Libya ['lɪbɪə] n Libye f

lice [laɪs] npl of **louse**

licence (US **license**) ['laɪsns] n autorisation f, permis m; (Comm) licence f; (Radio, TV) redevance f; (also: **driving ~,** US: also: **driver's license**) permis m (de conduire)

license ['laɪsns] n (US) = **licence**; **licensed** adj (for alcohol) patenté(e) pour la vente des spiritueux, qui a une patente de débit de boissons; (car) muni(e) de la vignette; **license plate** n (US Aut) plaque f minéralogique; **licensing hours** (BRIT) npl heures fpl d'ouvertures (des pubs)

lick [lɪk] vt lécher; (inf: defeat) écraser, flanquer une piquette or raclée à; **to ~ one's lips** (fig) se frotter les mains

lid [lɪd] n couvercle m; (eyelid) paupière f

lie [laɪ] n mensonge m ▷ vi (pt, pp ~d) (tell lies) mentir; (pt **lay**, pp **lain**)

(rest) être étendu(e) or allongé(e)
or couché(e); (object: be situated) se
trouver, être; **to ~ low** (fig) se cacher,
rester caché(e); **to tell ~s** mentir; **lie
about, lie around** vi (things) traîner;
(BRIT: person) traînasser, flemmarder;
lie down vi se coucher, s'étendre

Liechtenstein ['lɪktənstaɪn] n
Liechtenstein m

lie-in ['laɪɪn] n (BRIT): **to have a ~** faire
la grasse matinée

lieutenant [lɛf'tɛnənt, US luː'tɛnənt]
n lieutenant m

life (pl **lives**) [laɪf, laɪvz] n vie f; **to come
to ~** (fig) s'animer; **life assurance**
n (BRIT) = **life insurance**; **lifeboat** n
canot m or chaloupe f de sauvetage;
lifeguard n surveillant m de baignade;
life insurance n assurance-vie f;
life jacket n gilet m or ceinture f de
sauvetage; **lifelike** adj qui semble
vrai(e) or vivant(e), ressemblant(e);
(painting) réaliste; **life preserver** n (US)
gilet m or ceinture f de sauvetage; **life
sentence** n condamnation f à vie or à
perpétuité; **lifestyle** n style m de vie;
lifetime n: **in his lifetime** de son vivant

lift [lɪft] vt soulever, lever; (end)
supprimer, lever ▷ vi (fog) se lever ▷ n
(BRIT: elevator) ascenseur m; **to give sb
a ~** (BRIT) emmener or prendre qn en
voiture; **can you give me a ~ to the
station?** pouvez-vous m'emmener à
la gare?; **lift up** vt soulever; **lift-off** n
décollage m

light [laɪt] n lumière f; (lamp) lampe f;
(Aut: rear light) feu m; (: headlamp) phare
m; (for cigarette etc): **have you got a ~?**
avez-vous du feu? ▷ vt (pt, pp **~ed** or **lit**)
(candle, cigarette, fire) allumer; (room)
éclairer ▷ adj (room, colour) clair(e); (not
heavy, also fig) léger(-ère); (not strenuous)
peu fatigant(e); **lights** npl (traffic lights)
feux mpl; **to come to ~** être dévoilé(e)
or découvert(e); **in the ~ of** à la lumière
de; étant donné; **light up** vi s'allumer;
(face) s'éclairer; (smoke) allumer une
cigarette or une pipe etc ▷ vt (illuminate)

éclairer, illuminer; **light bulb** n
ampoule f; **lighten** vt (light up) éclairer;
(make lighter) éclaircir; (make less heavy)
alléger; **lighter** n (also: **cigarette
lighter**) briquet m; **light-hearted**
adj gai(e), joyeux(-euse), enjoué(e);
lighthouse n phare m; **lighting** n
éclairage m; (in theatre) éclairages m;
lightly adv légèrement; **to get off
lightly** s'en tirer à bon compte

lightning ['laɪtnɪŋ] n foudre f; (flash)
éclair m

lightweight ['laɪtweɪt] adj (suit)
léger(-ère) ▷ n (Boxing) poids léger

like [laɪk] vt aimer (bien) ▷ prep comme
▷ adj semblable, pareil(le) ▷ n: **the
~** (pej) (d')autres du même genre or
acabit; **his ~s and dislikes** ses goûts
mpl or préférences fpl; **I would ~**, **I'd
~** je voudrais, j'aimerais; **would you
~ a coffee?** voulez-vous du café?; **to
be/look ~ sb/sth** ressembler à qn/qch;
what's he ~? comment est-il?; **what
does it look ~?** de quoi est-ce que ça a
l'air?; **what does it taste ~?** quel goût
est-ce que ça a?; **that's just ~ him** c'est
bien de lui, ça lui ressemble; **do it ~ this**
fais-le comme ceci; **it's nothing ~ ...**
ce n'est pas du tout comme ...; **likeable**
adj sympathique, agréable

likelihood ['laɪklɪhud] n probabilité f

likely ['laɪklɪ] adj (result, outcome)
probable; (excuse) plausible; **he's ~ to
leave** il va sûrement partir, il risque
fort de partir; **not ~!** (inf) pas de danger!

likewise ['laɪkwaɪz] adv de même,
pareillement

liking ['laɪkɪŋ] n (for person) affection f;
(for thing) penchant m, goût m; **to be to
sb's ~** être au goût de qn, plaire à qn

lilac ['laɪlək] n lilas m

Lilo® ['laɪləu] n matelas m
pneumatique

lily ['lɪlɪ] n lis m; **~ of the valley**
muguet m

limb [lɪm] n membre m

limbo ['lɪmbəu] n: **to be in ~** (fig) être
tombé(e) dans l'oubli

lime [laɪm] n (tree) tilleul m; (fruit) citron vert, lime f; (Geo) calcaire m
limelight ['laɪmlaɪt] n: **in the ~** (fig) en vedette, au premier plan
limestone ['laɪmstəun] n pierre f à chaux; (Geo) calcaire m
limit ['lɪmɪt] n limite f ▷ vt limiter; **limited** adj limité(e), restreint(e); **to be limited to** se limiter à, ne concerner que
limousine ['lɪməzi:n] n limousine f
limp [lɪmp] n: **to have a ~** boiter ▷ vi boiter ▷ adj mou (molle)
line [laɪn] n (gen) ligne f; (stroke) trait m; (wrinkle) ride f; (rope) corde f; (wire) fil m; (of poem) vers m; (row, series) rangée f; (of people) file f, queue f; (railway track) voie f; (Comm: series of goods) article(s) m(pl), ligne de produits; (work) métier m ▷ vt: **to ~ (with)** (clothes) doubler (de); (box) garnir or tapisser (de); (subj: trees, crowd) border; **to stand in ~** (us) faire la queue; **in his ~ of business** dans sa partie, dans son rayon; **to be in ~ for sth** (fig) être en lice pour qch; **in ~ with** en accord avec, en conformité avec; **in a ~** aligné(e); **line up** vi s'aligner, se mettre en rang(s); (in queue) faire la queue ▷ vt aligner; (event) prévoir; (find) trouver; **to have sb/sth ~d up** avoir qn/qch en vue or de prévu(e)
linear ['lɪnɪəʳ] adj linéaire
linen ['lɪnɪn] n linge m (de corps or de maison); (cloth) lin m
liner ['laɪnəʳ] n (ship) paquebot m de ligne; (for bin) sac-poubelle m
line-up ['laɪnʌp] n (us: queue) file f; (also: **police** ~) parade f d'identification; (Sport) (composition f de l')équipe f
linger ['lɪŋgəʳ] vi s'attarder; traîner; (smell, tradition) persister
lingerie ['læʒəri:] n lingerie f
linguist ['lɪŋgwɪst] n linguiste m/f; **to be a good ~** être doué(e) pour les langues; **linguistic** adj linguistique
lining ['laɪnɪŋ] n doublure f; (of brakes) garniture f
link [lɪŋk] n (connection) lien m, rapport m; (Internet) lien; (of a chain) maillon m ▷ vt relier, lier, unir; **links** npl (Golf) (terrain m de) golf m; **link up** vt relier ▷ vi (people) se rejoindre; (companies etc) s'associer
lion ['laɪən] n lion m; **lioness** n lionne f
lip [lɪp] n lèvre f; (of cup etc) rebord m; **lipread** vi lire sur les lèvres; **lip salve** [-sælv] n pommade f pour les lèvres, pommade rosat; **lipstick** n rouge m à lèvres
liqueur [lɪˈkjuəʳ] n liqueur f
liquid ['lɪkwɪd] n liquide m ▷ adj liquide; **liquidizer** ['lɪkwɪdaɪzəʳ] n (BRIT Culin) mixer m
liquor ['lɪkəʳ] n spiritueux m, alcool m; **liquor store** (us) n magasin m de vins et spiritueux
Lisbon ['lɪzbən] n Lisbonne
lisp [lɪsp] n zézaiement m ▷ vi zézayer
list [lɪst] n liste f ▷ vt (write down) inscrire; (make list of) faire la liste de; (enumerate) énumérer
listen ['lɪsn] vi écouter; **to ~ to** écouter; **listener** n auditeur(-trice)
lit [lɪt] pt, pp of **light**
liter ['li:təʳ] n (us) = **litre**
literacy ['lɪtərəsɪ] n degré m d'alphabétisation, fait m de savoir lire et écrire
literal ['lɪtərl] adj littéral(e); **literally** adv littéralement; (really) réellement
literary ['lɪtərərɪ] adj littéraire
literate ['lɪtərət] adj qui sait lire et écrire; (educated) instruit(e)
literature ['lɪtrɪtʃəʳ] n littérature f; (brochures etc) copie f publicitaire, prospectus m
litre (us **liter**) ['li:təʳ] n litre m
litter ['lɪtəʳ] n (rubbish) détritus mpl; (dirtier) ordures fpl; (young animals) portée f; **litter bin** n (BRIT) poubelle f; **littered** adj: **littered with** (scattered) jonché(e) de
little ['lɪtl] adj (small) petit(e); (not much): **~ milk** peu de lait ▷ adv peu; **a ~** un peu (de); **a ~ milk** un peu de lait; **a ~ bit** un peu; **as ~ as possible**

le moins possible; **~ by ~** petit à petit,
peu à peu; **little finger** n auriculaire
m, petit doigt

live¹ [laɪv] adj (animal) vivant(e), en
vie; (wire) sous tension; (broadcast)
(transmis(e)) en direct; (unexploded)
non explosé(e)

live² [lɪv] vi vivre; (reside) vivre, habiter;
to ~ in London habiter (à) Londres;
where do you ~? où habitez-vous?; **live
together** vivre ensemble, cohabiter;
live up to vt fus se montrer à la
hauteur de

livelihood ['laɪvlɪhʊd] n moyens mpl
d'existence

lively ['laɪvlɪ] adj vif (vive), plein(e)
d'entrain; (place, book) vivant(e)

liven up ['laɪvn-] vt (room etc) égayer;
(discussion, evening) animer ▷ vi
s'animer

liver ['lɪvər] n foie m

lives [laɪvz] npl of **life**

livestock ['laɪvstɔk] n cheptel m,
bétail m

living ['lɪvɪŋ] adj vivant(e), en vie ▷ n:
to earn or **make a ~** gagner sa vie;
living room n salle f de séjour

lizard ['lɪzəd] n lézard m

load [ləʊd] n (weight) poids m; (thing
carried) chargement m, charge f;
(Elec, Tech) charge ▷ vt (also: **~ up**):
to ~ (with) (lorry, ship) charger (de);
(gun, camera) charger (avec); (Comput)
charger; **a ~ of, ~s of** (fig) un or des
tas de, des masses de; **to talk a ~
of rubbish** (inf) dire des bêtises;
loaded adj (dice) pipé(e); (question)
insidieux(-euse); (inf: rich) bourré(e)
de fric

loaf (pl **loaves**) [ləʊf, ləʊvz] n pain m,
miche f ▷ vi (also: **~ about, ~ around**)
fainéanter, traîner

loan [ləʊn] n prêt m ▷ vt prêter; **on ~**
prêté(e), en prêt

loathe [ləʊð] vt détester, avoir en
horreur

loaves [ləʊvz] npl of **loaf**

lobby ['lɔbɪ] n hall m, entrée f; (Pol)
groupe m de pression, lobby m ▷ vt
faire pression sur

lobster ['lɔbstər] n homard m

local ['ləʊkl] adj local(e) ▷ n (BRIT: pub)
pub m or café m du coin; **the locals** npl
les gens mpl du pays or du coin; **local
anaesthetic** n anesthésie locale;
local authority n collectivité locale,
municipalité f; **local government** n
administration locale or municipale;
locally ['ləʊkəlɪ] adv localement; dans
les environs or la région

locate [ləʊ'keɪt] vt (find) trouver,
repérer; (situate) situer; **to be ~d in** être
situé à or en

location [ləʊ'keɪʃən] n emplacement
m; **on ~** (Cine) en extérieur

  Be careful not to translate *location*
  by the French word *location*.

loch [lɔx] n lac m, loch m

lock [lɔk] n (of door, box) serrure f; (of
canal) écluse f; (of hair) mèche f, boucle f
▷ vt (with key) fermer à clé ▷ vi (door etc)
fermer à clé; (wheels) se bloquer; **lock
in** vt enfermer; **lock out** vt enfermer
dehors; (on purpose) mettre à la porte;
lock up vt (person) enfermer; (house)
fermer à clé ▷ vi tout fermer (à clé)

locker ['lɔkər] n casier m; (in station)
consigne f automatique; **locker-room**
(US) n (Sport) vestiaire m

locksmith ['lɔksmɪθ] n serrurier m

locomotive [ləʊkə'məʊtɪv] n
locomotive f

locum ['ləʊkəm] n (Med) suppléant(e)
de médecin etc

lodge [lɔdʒ] n pavillon m (de gardien);
(also: **hunting ~**) pavillon de chasse ▷ vi
(person): **to ~ with** être logé(e) chez,
être en pension chez; (bullet) se loger
▷ vt (appeal etc) présenter; déposer; **to
~ a complaint** porter plainte; **lodger**
n locataire m/f; (with room and meals)
pensionnaire m/f

lodging ['lɔdʒɪŋ] n logement m

loft [lɔft] n grenier m; (apartment)
grenier aménagé (en appartement)
(gén dans ancien entrepôt ou fabrique)

log [lɒg] *n* (*of wood*) bûche *f*; (*Naut*) livre *m or* journal *m* de bord; (*of car*) ≈ carte grise ▷ *vt* enregistrer; **log in, log on** *vi* (*Comput*) ouvrir une session, entrer dans le système; **log off, log out** *vi* (*Comput*) clore une session, sortir du système

logic ['lɒdʒɪk] *n* logique *f*; **logical** *adj* logique

logo ['ləugəu] *n* logo *m*

Loire [lwaː] *n*: **the (River) ~** la Loire

lollipop ['lɒlɪpɒp] *n* sucette *f*; **lollipop man/lady** (BRIT: *irreg*) *n* contractuel qui fait traverser la rue aux enfants

lolly ['lɒlɪ] *n* (*inf*: *ice*) esquimau *m*; (: *lollipop*) sucette *f*

London ['lʌndən] *n* Londres; **Londoner** *n* Londonien(ne)

lone [ləun] *adj* solitaire

loneliness ['ləunlɪnɪs] *n* solitude *f*, isolement *m*

lonely ['ləunlɪ] *adj* seul(e); (*childhood etc*) solitaire; (*place*) solitaire, isolé(e)

long [lɒŋ] *adj* long (longue) ▷ *adv* longtemps ▷ *vi*: **to ~ for sth/to do sth** avoir très envie de qch/de faire qch, attendre qch avec impatience/attendre avec impatience de faire qch; **how ~ is this river/course?** quelle est la longueur de ce fleuve/la durée de ce cours?; **6 metres ~** (long) de 6 mètres; **6 months ~** qui dure 6 mois, de 6 mois; **all night ~** toute la nuit; **he no ~er comes** il ne vient plus; **I can't stand it any ~er** je ne peux le supporter; **~ before** longtemps avant; **before ~** (+ *future*) avant peu, dans peu de temps; (+ *past*) peu de temps après; **don't be ~!** fais vite!, dépêche-toi!; **I shan't be ~** je n'en ai pas pour longtemps; **at ~ last** enfin; **so** *or* **as ~ as** à condition que + *sub*; **long-distance** *adj* (*race*) de fond; (*call*) interurbain(e); **long-haul** *adj* (*flight*) long-courrier; **longing** *n* désir *m*, envie *f*; (*nostalgia*) nostalgie *f* ▷ *adj* plein(e) d'envie *or* de nostalgie

longitude ['lɒŋgɪtjuːd] *n* longitude *f*

long: **long jump** *n* saut *m* en longueur;

long-life *adj* (*batteries etc*) longue durée *inv*; (*milk*) longue conservation; **long-sighted** *adj* (BRIT) presbyte; (*fig*) prévoyant(e); **long-standing** *adj* de longue date; **long-term** *adj* à long terme

loo [luː] *n* (BRIT *inf*) w.-c *mpl*, petit coin

look [luk] *vi* regarder; (*seem*) sembler, paraître, avoir l'air; (*building etc*): **to ~ south/on to the sea** donner au sud/sur la mer ▷ *n* regard *m*; (*appearance*) air *m*, allure *f*, aspect *m*; **looks** *npl* (*good looks*) physique *m*, beauté *f*; **to ~ like** ressembler à; **to have a ~** regarder; **to have a ~ at sth** jeter un coup d'œil à qch; **~ (here)!** (*annoyance*) écoutez!; **look after** *vt fus* s'occuper de; (*luggage etc*: *watch over*) garder, surveiller; **look around** *vi* regarder autour de soi; **look at** *vt fus* regarder; (*problem etc*) examiner; **look back** *vi*: **to ~ back at sth/sb** se retourner pour regarder qch/qn; **to ~ back on** (*event, period*) évoquer, repenser à; **look down on** *vt fus* (*fig*) regarder de haut, dédaigner; **look for** *vt fus* chercher; **we're ~ing for a hotel/restaurant** nous cherchons un hôtel/restaurant; **look forward to** *vt fus* attendre avec impatience; **~ing forward to hearing from you** (*in letter*) dans l'attente de vous lire; **look into** *vt fus* (*matter, possibility*) examiner, étudier; **look out** *vi* (*beware*): **to ~ out (for)** prendre garde (à), faire attention (à); **~ out!** attention!; **look out for** *vt fus* (*seek*) être à la recherche de; (*try to spot*) guetter; **look round** *vt fus* (*house, shop*) faire le tour de ▷ *vi* (*turn*) regarder derrière soi, se retourner; **look through** *vt fus* (*papers, book*) examiner; (: *briefly*) parcourir; **look up** *vi* lever les yeux; (*improve*) s'améliorer ▷ *vt* (*word*) chercher; **look up to** *vt fus* avoir du respect pour; **lookout** *n* (*tower etc*) poste *m* de guet; (*person*) guetteur *m*; **to be on the lookout (for)** guetter

loom [luːm] *vi* (*also*: **~ up**) surgir; (*event*) paraître imminent(e); (*threaten*) menacer

loony ['lu:nɪ] adj, n (inf) timbré(e), cinglé(e) m/f

loop [lu:p] n boucle f ▷ vt: **to ~ sth round sth** passer qch autour de qch; **loophole** n (fig) porte f de sortie, échappatoire f

loose [lu:s] adj (knot, screw) desserré(e); (clothes) vague, ample, lâche; (hair) dénoué(e), épars(e); (not firmly fixed) pas solide; (morals, discipline) relâché(e); (translation) approximatif(-ive) ▷ n: **to be on the ~** être en liberté; **~ connection** (Elec) mauvais contact; **to be at a ~ end** or (us) **at ~ ends** (fig) ne pas trop savoir quoi faire; **loosely** adv sans serrer; (imprecisely) approximativement; **loosen** vt desserrer, relâcher, défaire

loot [lu:t] n butin m ▷ vt piller

lop-sided ['lɔp'saɪdɪd] adj de travers, asymétrique

lord [lɔ:d] n seigneur m; **L~ Smith** lord Smith; **the L~** (Rel) le Seigneur; **my L~** (to noble) Monsieur le comte/le baron; (to judge) Monsieur le juge; (to bishop) Monseigneur; **good L~!** mon Dieu!; **Lords** npl (BRIT: Pol): **the (House of) Lords** (BRIT) la Chambre des Lords

lorry ['lɔrɪ] n (BRIT) camion m; **lorry driver** n (BRIT) camionneur m, routier m

lose (pt, pp lost) [lu:z, lɔst] vt perdre ▷ vi perdre; **I've lost my wallet/passport** j'ai perdu mon portefeuille/passeport; **to ~ (time)** (clock) retarder; **lose out** vi être perdant(e); **loser** n perdant(e)

loss [lɔs] n perte f; **to make a ~** enregistrer une perte; **to be at a ~** être perplexe or embarrassé(e)

lost [lɔst] pt, pp of **lose** ▷ adj perdu(e); **to get ~** vi se perdre; **I'm ~** je me suis perdu; **~ and found property** n (us) objets trouvés; **~ and found** n (us) (bureau m des) objets trouvés; **lost property** n (BRIT) objets trouvés; **lost property office** or **department** (bureau m des) objets trouvés

lot [lɔt] n (at auctions, set) lot m; (destiny) sort m, destinée f; **the ~** (everything) le tout; (everyone) tous mpl, toutes fpl; **a ~** beaucoup; **a ~ of** beaucoup de; **~s of** des tas de; **to draw ~s (for sth)** tirer (qch) au sort

lotion ['ləʊʃən] n lotion f

lottery ['lɔtərɪ] n loterie f

loud [laʊd] adj bruyant(e), sonore; (voice) fort(e); (condemnation etc) vigoureux(-euse); (gaudy) voyant(e), tapageur(-euse) ▷ adv (speak etc) fort; **out ~** tout haut; **loudly** adv fort, bruyamment; **loudspeaker** n haut-parleur m

lounge [laʊndʒ] n salon m; (of airport) salle f; (BRIT: also: **~ bar**) (salle de) café m or bar m ▷ vi (also: **~ about** or **around**) se prélasser, paresser

louse (pl **lice**) [laʊs, laɪs] n pou m

lousy ['laʊzɪ] (inf) adj (bad quality) infect(e), moche; **I feel ~** je suis mal fichu(e)

love [lʌv] n amour m ▷ vt aimer; (caringly, kindly) aimer beaucoup; **I ~ chocolate** j'adore le chocolat; **to ~ to do** aimer beaucoup or adorer faire; **"15 ~"** (Tennis) "15 à rien or zéro"; **to be/fall in ~ with** être/tomber amoureux(-euse) de; **to make ~** faire l'amour; **~ from Anne, ~, Anne** affectueusement, Anne; **I ~ you** je t'aime; **love affair** n liaison (amoureuse); **love life** n vie sentimentale

lovely ['lʌvlɪ] adj (pretty) ravissant(e); (friend, wife) charmant(e); (holiday, surprise) très agréable, merveilleux(-euse)

lover ['lʌvə*] n amant m; (person in love) amoureux(-euse); (amateur): **a ~ of** un(e) ami(e) de, un(e) amoureux(-euse) de

loving ['lʌvɪŋ] adj affectueux(-euse), tendre, aimant(e)

low [ləʊ] adj bas (basse); (quality) mauvais(e), inférieur(e) ▷ adv bas ▷ n (Meteorology) dépression f; **to feel ~** se sentir déprimé(e); **he's very ~** (*ill*) il est bien bas *or* très affaibli; **to turn (down) ~** *vt* baisser; **to be ~ on** (*supplies etc*) être à court de; **to reach a new** *or* **an all-time ~** tomber au niveau le plus bas; **low-alcohol** *adj* à faible teneur en alcool, peu alcoolisé(e); **low-calorie** *adj* hypocalorique

lower ['ləuə^r] *adj* inférieur(e) ▷ *vt* baisser; (*resistance*) diminuer; **to ~ o.s. to** s'abaisser à

low-fat ['ləu'fæt] *adj* maigre

loyal ['lɔɪəl] *adj* loyal(e), fidèle; **loyalty** *n* loyauté *f*, fidélité *f*; **loyalty card** *n* carte *f* de fidélité

L.P. *n abbr* = **long-playing record**

L-plates ['ɛlpleɪts] *npl* (BRIT) plaques *fpl* (obligatoires) d'apprenti conducteur

Lt *abbr* (= *lieutenant*) Lt.

Ltd *abbr* (*Comm: company: = limited*) ≈ S.A.

luck [lʌk] *n* chance *f*; **bad** ~ malchance *f*, malheur *m*; **good ~!** bonne chance!; **bad** *or* **hard** *or* **tough ~!** pas de chance!; **luckily** *adv* heureusement, par bonheur; **lucky** *adj* (*person*) qui a de la chance; (*coincidence*) heureux(-euse); (*number etc*) qui porte bonheur

lucrative ['lu:krətɪv] *adj* lucratif(-ive), rentable, qui rapporte

ludicrous ['lu:dɪkrəs] *adj* ridicule, absurde

luggage ['lʌgɪdʒ] *n* bagages *mpl*; **our ~ hasn't arrived** nos bagages ne sont pas arrivés; **could you send someone to collect our ~?** pourriez-vous envoyer quelqu'un chercher nos bagages?; **luggage rack** *n* (*in train*) porte-bagages *m inv*; (: *on car*) galerie *f*

lukewarm ['lu:kwɔ:m] *adj* tiède

lull [lʌl] *n* accalmie *f*; (*in conversation*) pause *f* ▷ *vt*: **to ~ sb to sleep** bercer qn pour qu'il s'endorme; **to be ~ed into a false sense of security** s'endormir dans une fausse sécurité

lullaby ['lʌləbaɪ] *n* berceuse *f*

lumber ['lʌmbə^r] *n* (*wood*) bois *m* de charpente; (*junk*) bric-à-brac *m inv* ▷ *vt* (BRIT inf): **to ~ sb with sth/sb** coller *or* refiler qch/qn à qn

luminous ['lu:mɪnəs] *adj* lumineux(-euse)

lump [lʌmp] *n* morceau *m*; (*in sauce*) grumeau *m*; (*swelling*) grosseur *f* ▷ *vt* (*also*: ~ **together**) réunir, mettre en tas; **lump sum** *n* somme globale *or* forfaitaire; **lumpy** *adj* (*sauce*) qui a des grumeaux; (*bed*) défoncé(e), peu confortable

lunatic ['lu:nətɪk] *n* fou (folle), dément(e) ▷ *adj* fou (folle), dément(e)

lunch [lʌntʃ] *n* déjeuner *m* ▷ *vi* déjeuner; **lunch break, lunch hour** *n* pause *f* de midi, heure *f* du déjeuner; **lunchtime** *n*: **it's lunchtime** c'est l'heure du déjeuner

lung [lʌŋ] *n* poumon *m*

lure [luə^r] *n* (*attraction*) attrait *m*, charme *m*; (*in hunting*) appât *m*, leurre *m* ▷ *vt* attirer *or* persuader par la ruse

lurk [lə:k] *vi* se tapir, se cacher

lush [lʌʃ] *adj* luxuriant(e)

lust [lʌst] *n* (*sexual*) désir (sexuel); (*Rel*) luxure *f*; (*fig*): ~ **for** soif *f* de

Luxembourg ['lʌksəmbə:g] *n* Luxembourg *m*

luxurious [lʌg'zjuəriəs] *adj* luxueux(-euse)

luxury ['lʌkʃərɪ] *n* luxe *m* ▷ *cpd* de luxe

Lycra® ['laɪkrə] *n* Lycra® *m*

lying ['laɪɪŋ] *n* mensonge(s) *m(pl)* ▷ *adj* (*statement, story*) mensonger(-ère), faux (fausse); (*person*) menteur(-euse)

Lyons ['ljɔ̃] *n* Lyon

lyrics ['lɪrɪks] *npl* (*of song*) paroles *fpl*

m. abbr (= metre) m; (= million) M;
(= mile) mi

M.A. n abbr (Scol) = **Master of Arts**

ma [mɑ:] (inf) n maman f

mac [mæk] n (BRIT) imper(méable m) m

macaroni [mækəˈrəʊnɪ] n
macaronis mpl

Macedonia [mæsɪˈdəʊnɪə]
n Macédoine f; **Macedonian**
[mæsɪˈdəʊnɪən] adj macédonien(ne)
▷ n Macédonien(ne); (Ling)
macédonien m

machine [məˈʃi:n] n machine f ▷ vt
(dress etc) coudre à la machine; (Tech)
usiner; **machine gun** n mitrailleuse f;
machinery n machinerie f, machines
fpl; (fig) mécanisme(s) m(pl); **machine
washable** adj (garment) lavable en
machine

macho [ˈmætʃəʊ] adj macho inv

mackerel [ˈmækrl] n (pl inv)
maquereau m

mackintosh [ˈmækɪntɔʃ] n (BRIT)
imperméable m

mad [mæd] adj fou (folle); (foolish)
insensé(e); (angry) furieux(-euse);
to be ~ (keen) about or **on sth** (inf)
être follement passionné de qch, être
fou de qch

Madagascar [mædəˈgæskəʳ] n
Madagascar m

madam [ˈmædəm] n madame f

mad cow disease n maladie f des
vaches folles

made [meɪd] pt, pp of **make**; **made-
to-measure** adj (BRIT) fait(e) sur
mesure; **made-up** [ˈmeɪdʌp] adj (story)
inventé(e), fabriqué(e)

madly [ˈmædlɪ] adv follement; **~ in love**
éperdument amoureux(-euse)

madman [ˈmædmən] (irreg) n fou m,
aliéné m

madness [ˈmædnɪs] n folie f

Madrid [məˈdrɪd] n Madrid

Mafia [ˈmæfɪə] n maf(f)ia f

mag [mæg] n abbr (BRIT inf: = magazine)
magazine m

magazine [mægəˈzi:n] n (Press)
magazine m, revue f; (Radio, TV)
magazine

maggot [ˈmægət] n ver m, asticot m

magic [ˈmædʒɪk] n magie f ▷ adj
magique; **magical** adj magique;
(experience, evening) merveilleux(-euse);
magician [məˈdʒɪʃən] n magicien(ne)

magistrate [ˈmædʒɪstreɪt] n
magistrat m; juge m

magnet [ˈmægnɪt] n aimant m;
magnetic [mægˈnɛtɪk] adj
magnétique

magnificent [mægˈnɪfɪsnt] adj
superbe, magnifique; (splendid:
robe, building) somptueux(-euse),
magnifique

magnify [ˈmægnɪfaɪ] vt grossir;
(sound) amplifier; **magnifying glass**
n loupe f

magpie [ˈmægpaɪ] n pie f

mahogany [məˈhɔgənɪ] n acajou m

maid [meɪd] n bonne f; (in hotel) femme
f de chambre; **old ~** (pej) vieille fille

maiden name n nom m de jeune fille

mail [meɪl] n poste f; (letters) courrier m ▷ vt envoyer (par la poste); **by ~** par la poste; **mailbox** n (US: also **mailbox**) boîte f aux lettres; **mailing list** n liste f d'adresses; **mailman** (irreg) n (US) facteur m; **mail-order** n vente f or achat m par correspondance

main [meɪn] adj principal(e) ▷ n (pipe) conduite principale, canalisation f; **the ~s** (Elec) le secteur; **the ~ thing** l'essentiel m; **in the ~** dans l'ensemble; **main course** n (Culin) plat m de résistance; **mainland** n continent m; **mainly** adv principalement, surtout; **main road** n grand axe, route nationale; **mainstream** n (fig) courant principal; **main street** n rue f principale

maintain [meɪnˈteɪn] vt entretenir; (continue) maintenir, préserver; (affirm) soutenir; **maintenance** [ˈmeɪntənəns] n entretien m; (Law: alimony) pension f alimentaire

maisonette [meɪzəˈnɛt] n (BRIT) appartement m en duplex

maize [meɪz] n (BRIT) maïs m

majesty [ˈmædʒɪstɪ] n majesté f; (title): **Your M~** Votre Majesté

major [ˈmeɪdʒər] n (Mil) commandant m ▷ adj (important) important(e); (most important) principal(e); (Mus) majeur(e) ▷ vi (US Scol): **to ~ (in)** se spécialiser (en)

Majorca [məˈjɔːkə] n Majorque f

majority [məˈdʒɔrɪtɪ] n majorité f

make [meɪk] vt (pt, pp made) faire; (manufacture) faire, fabriquer; (earn) gagner; (decision) prendre; (friend) se faire; (speech) faire, prononcer; (cause to be): **to ~ sb sad** etc rendre qn triste etc; (force): **to ~ sb do sth** obliger qn à faire qch, faire faire qch à qn; (equal): **2 and 2 ~ 4** 2 et 2 font 4 ▷ n (manufacture) fabrication f; (brand) marque f; **to ~ the bed** faire le lit; **to ~ a fool of sb** (ridicule) ridiculiser qn; (trick) avoir or duper qn; **to ~ a profit** faire un or des bénéfice(s); **to ~ a loss** essuyer une perte; **to ~ it** (in time etc) y arriver; (succeed) réussir;

what time do you ~ it? quelle heure avez-vous?; **I ~ it £249** d'après mes calculs ça fait 249 livres; **to be made of** être en; **to ~ do with** se contenter de; se débrouiller avec; **make off** vi filer; **make out** vt (write out: cheque) faire; (decipher) déchiffrer; (understand) comprendre; (see) distinguer; (claim, imply) prétendre, vouloir faire croire; **make up** vt (invent) inventer, imaginer; (constitute) constituer; (parcel, bed) faire ▷ vi se réconcilier; (with cosmetics) se maquiller, se farder; **to be made up of** se composer de; **make up for** vt fus compenser; (lost time) rattraper; **makeover** [ˈmeɪkəuvər] n (by beautician) soins mpl de maquillage; (change of image) changement m d'image; **maker** n fabricant m; (of film, programme) réalisateur(-trice); **makeshift** adj provisoire, improvisé(e); **make-up** n maquillage m

making [ˈmeɪkɪŋ] n (fig): **in the ~** en formation or gestation; **to have the ~s of** (actor, athlete) avoir l'étoffe de

malaria [məˈlɛərɪə] n malaria f, paludisme m

Malaysia [məˈleɪzɪə] n Malaisie f

male [meɪl] n (Biol, Elec) mâle m ▷ adj (sex, attitude) masculin(e); (animal) mâle; (child etc) du sexe masculin

malicious [məˈlɪʃəs] adj méchant(e), malveillant(e)

> Be careful not to translate **malicious** by the French word **malicieux**.

malignant [məˈlɪgnənt] adj (Med) malin(-igne)

mall [mɔːl] n (also: **shopping ~**) centre commercial

mallet [ˈmælɪt] n maillet m

malnutrition [mælnjuːˈtrɪʃən] n malnutrition f

malpractice [mælˈpræktɪs] n faute professionnelle; négligence f

malt [mɔːlt] n malt m ▷ cpd (whisky) pur malt

Malta ['mɔːltə] n Malte f; **Maltese** [mɔːl'tiːz] adj maltais(e) ▷ n (pl inv) Maltais(e)

mammal ['mæml] n mammifère m

mammoth ['mæməθ] n mammouth m ▷ adj géant(e), monstre

man (pl **men**) [mæn, mɛn] n homme m; (Sport) joueur m; (Chess) pièce f ▷ vt (Naut: ship) garnir d'hommes; (machine) assurer le fonctionnement de; (Mil: gun) servir; (: post) être de service à; **an old ~** un vieillard; **~ and wife** mari et femme

manage ['mænɪdʒ] vi se débrouiller; (succeed) y arriver, réussir ▷ vt (business) gérer; (team, operation) diriger; (control: ship) manier, manœuvrer; (: person) savoir s'y prendre avec; **to ~ to do** se débrouiller pour faire; (succeed) réussir à faire; **manageable** adj maniable; (task etc) faisable; (number) raisonnable; **management** n (running) administration f, direction f; (people in charge: of business, firm) dirigeants mpl, cadres mpl; (: of hotel, shop, theatre) direction; **manager** n (of business) directeur m; (of institution etc) administrateur m; (of department, unit) responsable m/f, chef m; (of hotel etc) gérant m; (Sport) manager m; (of artist) impresario m; **manageress** n directrice f; (of hotel etc) gérante f; **managerial** [mænɪ'dʒɪərɪəl] adj directorial(e); (skills) de cadre, de gestion; **managing director** n directeur général

mandarin ['mændərɪn] n (also: ~ **orange**) mandarine f

mandate ['mændeɪt] n mandat m

mandatory ['mændətərɪ] adj obligatoire

mane [meɪn] n crinière f

maneuver [mə'nuːvəʳ] (us) = **manoeuvre**

mangetout ['mɔnʒ'tuː] n mange-tout m inv

mango (pl **~es**) ['mæŋɡəu] n mangue f

man: **manhole** n trou m d'homme; **manhood** n (age) âge m d'homme;

(manliness) virilité f

mania ['meɪnɪə] n manie f; **maniac** ['meɪnɪæk] n maniaque m/f; (fig) fou (folle)

manic ['mænɪk] adj maniaque

manicure ['mænɪkjuəʳ] n manucure f

manifest ['mænɪfɛst] vt manifester ▷ adj manifeste, évident(e)

manifesto [mænɪ'fɛstəu] n (Pol) manifeste m

manipulate [mə'nɪpjuleɪt] vt manipuler; (system, situation) exploiter

man: **mankind** [mæn'kaɪnd] n humanité f, genre humain; **manly** adj viril(e); **man-made** adj artificiel(le); (fibre) synthétique

manner ['mænəʳ] n manière f, façon f; (behaviour) attitude f, comportement m; **manners** npl: **(good) ~s** (bonnes) manières; **bad ~s** mauvaises manières; **all ~ of** toutes sortes de

manoeuvre (us **maneuver**) [mə'nuːvəʳ] vt (move) manœuvrer; (manipulate: person) manipuler; (: situation) exploiter ▷ n manœuvre f

manpower ['mænpauəʳ] n main-d'œuvre f

mansion ['mænʃən] n château m, manoir m

manslaughter ['mænslɔːtəʳ] n homicide m involontaire

mantelpiece ['mæntlpiːs] n cheminée f

manual ['mænjuəl] adj manuel(le) ▷ n manuel m

manufacture [mænju'fæktʃəʳ] vt fabriquer ▷ n fabrication f; **manufacturer** n fabricant m

manure [mə'njuəʳ] n fumier m; (artificial) engrais m

manuscript ['mænjuskrɪpt] n manuscrit m

many ['mɛnɪ] adj beaucoup de, de nombreux(-euses) ▷ pron beaucoup, un grand nombre; **a great ~** un grand nombre (de); **~ a ...** bien des ..., plus d'un(e) ...

map [mæp] n carte f; (of town) plan

m; **can you show it to me on the ~?** pouvez-vous me l'indiquer sur la carte?; **map out** *vt* tracer; (*fig: task*) planifier

maple ['meɪpl] *n* érable *m*

Mar *abbr* = **March**

mar [mɑːʳ] *vt* gâcher, gâter

marathon ['mærəθən] *n* marathon *m*

marble ['mɑːbl] *n* marbre *m*; (*toy*) bille *f*

March [mɑːtʃ] *n* mars *m*

march [mɑːtʃ] *vi* marcher au pas; (*demonstrators*) défiler ▷ *n* marche *f*; (*demonstration*) manifestation *f*

mare [mɛəʳ] *n* jument *f*

margarine [mɑːdʒəˈriːn] *n* margarine *f*

margin ['mɑːdʒɪn] *n* marge *f*; **marginal** *adj* marginal(e); **marginal seat** (*Pol*) siège disputé; **marginally** *adv* très légèrement, sensiblement

marigold ['mærɪɡəuld] *n* souci *m*

marijuana [mærɪˈwɑːnə] *n* marijuana *f*

marina [məˈriːnə] *n* marina *f*

marinade *n* [mærɪˈneɪd] marinade *f*

marinate ['mærɪneɪt] *vt* (faire) mariner

marine [məˈriːn] *adj* marin(e) ▷ *n* fusilier marin; (*us*) marine *m*

marital ['mærɪtl] *adj* matrimonial(e); **marital status** *n* situation *f* de famille

maritime ['mærɪtaɪm] *adj* maritime

marjoram ['mɑːdʒərəm] *n* marjolaine *f*

mark [mɑːk] *n* marque *f*; (*of skid etc*) trace *f*; (*BRIT Scol*) note *f*; (*oven temperature*): **(gas) ~ 4** thermostat *m* 4 ▷ *vt* (*also Sport: player*) marquer; (*stain*) tacher; (*BRIT Scol*) corriger, noter; **to ~ time** marquer le pas; **marked** *adj* (*obvious*) marqué(e), net(te); **marker** *n* (*sign*) jalon *m*; (*bookmark*) signet *m*

market ['mɑːkɪt] *n* marché *m* ▷ *vt* (*Comm*) commercialiser; **marketing** *n* marketing *m*; **marketplace** *n* place *f* du marché; (*Comm*) marché *m*; **market research** *n* étude *f* de marché

marmalade ['mɑːməleɪd] *n* confiture *f* d'oranges

maroon [məˈruːn] *vt*: **to be ~ed** être

abandonné(e); (*fig*) être bloqué(e) ▷ *adj* (*colour*) bordeaux *inv*

marquee [mɑːˈkiː] *n* chapiteau *m*

marriage ['mærɪdʒ] *n* mariage *m*; **marriage certificate** *n* extrait *m* d'acte de mariage

married ['mærɪd] *adj* marié(e); (*life, love*) conjugal(e)

marrow ['mærəu] *n* (*of bone*) moelle *f*; (*vegetable*) courge *f*

marry ['mærɪ] *vt* épouser, se marier avec; (*subj: father, priest etc*) marier ▷ *vi* (*also:* **get married**) se marier

Mars [mɑːz] *n* (*planet*) Mars *f*

Marseilles [mɑːˈseɪ] *n* Marseille

marsh [mɑːʃ] *n* marais *m*, marécage *m*

marshal ['mɑːʃl] *n* maréchal *m*; (*us: fire, police*) ≈ capitaine *m*; (*for demonstration, meeting*) membre *m* du service d'ordre ▷ *vt* rassembler

martyr ['mɑːtəʳ] *n* martyr(e)

marvel ['mɑːvl] *n* merveille *f* ▷ *vi*: **to ~ (at)** s'émerveiller (de); **marvellous** (*us* **marvelous**) *adj* merveilleux(-euse)

Marxism ['mɑːksɪzəm] *n* marxisme *m*

Marxist ['mɑːksɪst] *adj, n* marxiste (*m/f*)

marzipan ['mɑːzɪpæn] *n* pâte *f* d'amandes

mascara [mæsˈkɑːrə] *n* mascara *m*

mascot ['mæskət] *n* mascotte *f*

masculine ['mæskjulɪn] *adj* masculin(e) ▷ *n* masculin *m*

mash [mæʃ] *vt* (*Culin*) faire une purée de; **mashed potato(es)** *n(pl)* purée *f* de pommes de terre

mask [mɑːsk] *n* masque *m* ▷ *vt* masquer

mason ['meɪsn] *n* (*also:* **stone~**) maçon *m*; (*also:* **free~**) franc-maçon *m*; **masonry** *n* maçonnerie *f*

mass [mæs] *n* multitude *f*, masse *f*; (*Physics*) masse; (*Rel*) messe *f* ▷ *cpd* (*communication*) de masse; (*unemployment*) massif(-ive) ▷ *vi* se masser; **masses** *npl*: **the ~es** les masses; **~es of** (*inf*) des tas de

massacre ['mæsəkəʳ] *n* massacre *m*

massage ['mæsɑːʒ] *n* massage *m*
▷ *vt* masser

massive ['mæsɪv] *adj* énorme,
massif(-ive)

mass media *npl* mass-media *mpl*

mass-produce ['mæsprə'djuːs] *vt*
fabriquer en série

mast [mɑːst] *n* mât *m*; (*Radio, TV*)
pylône *m*

master ['mɑːstə'] *n* maître *m*; (*in
secondary school*) professeur *m*; (*in
primary school*) instituteur *m*; (*title for
boys*): **M~ X** Monsieur X ▷ *vt* maîtriser;
(*learn*) apprendre à fond; **M~ of Arts/
Science (MA/MSc)** *n* ≈ titulaire *m/f*
d'une maîtrise (en lettres/science); **M~
of Arts/Science degree (MA/MSc)**
n ≈ maîtrise *f*; **mastermind** *n* esprit
supérieur ▷ *vt* diriger, être le cerveau
de; **masterpiece** *n* chef-d'œuvre *m*

masturbate ['mæstəbeɪt] *vi* se
masturber

mat [mæt] *n* petit tapis; (*also*: **door~**)
paillasson *m*; (*also*: **table~**) set *m* de
table ▷ *adj* = **matt**

match [mætʃ] *n* allumette *f*; (*game*)
match *m*, partie *f*; (*fig*) égal(e) ▷ *vt* (*also*:
~ up) assortir; (*go well with*) aller bien
avec, s'assortir à; (*equal*) égaler, valoir
▷ *vi* être assorti(e); **to be a good ~** être
bien assorti(e); **matchbox** *n* boîte *f*
d'allumettes; **matching** *adj* assorti(e)

mate [meɪt] *n* (*inf*) copain (copine);
(*animal*) partenaire *m/f*, mâle (femelle);
(*in merchant navy*) second *m* ▷ *vi*
s'accoupler

material [mə'tɪərɪəl] *n* (*substance*)
matière *f*, matériau *m*; (*cloth*) tissu *m*,
étoffe *f*; (*information, data*) données *fpl*
▷ *adj* matériel(le); (*relevant: evidence*)
pertinent(e); **materials** *npl* (*equipment*)
matériaux *mpl*

materialize [mə'tɪərɪəlaɪz] *vi* se
matérialiser, se réaliser

maternal [mə'tɜːnl] *adj* maternel(le)

maternity [mə'tɜːnɪtɪ] *n* maternité *f*;
maternity hospital *n* maternité *f*;
maternity leave *n* congé *m* de
maternité

math [mæθ] *n* (*US*: = *mathematics*)
maths *fpl*

mathematical [mæθə'mætɪkl] *adj*
mathématique

mathematician [mæθəmə'tɪʃən] *n*
mathématicien(ne)

mathematics [mæθə'mætɪks] *n*
mathématiques *fpl*

maths [mæθs] *n abbr* (*BRIT*:
= *mathematics*) maths *fpl*

matinée ['mætɪneɪ] *n* matinée *f*

matron ['meɪtrən] *n* (*in hospital*)
infirmière-chef *f*; (*in school*) infirmière *f*

matt [mæt] *adj* mat(e)

matter ['mætə'] *n* question *f*; (*Physics*)
matière *f*, substance *f*; (*Med: pus*) pus
m ▷ *vi* importer; **matters** *npl* (*affairs,
situation*) la situation; **it doesn't ~** cela
n'a pas d'importance; (*I don't mind*) cela
ne fait rien; **what's the ~?** qu'est-ce
qu'il y a?, qu'est-ce qui ne va pas?; **no ~
what** quoi qu'il arrive; **as a ~ of course**
tout naturellement; **as a ~ of fact** en
fait; **reading ~** (*BRIT*) de quoi lire, de
la lecture

mattress ['mætrɪs] *n* matelas *m*

mature [mə'tjuə'] *adj* mûr(e); (*cheese*)
fait(e); (*wine*) arrive(e) à maturité ▷ *vi*
mûrir; (*cheese, wine*) se faire; **mature
student** *n* étudiant(e) plus âgé(e) que la
moyenne; **maturity** *n* maturité *f*

maul [mɔːl] *vt* lacérer

mauve [məuv] *adj* mauve

max *abbr* = **maximum**

maximize ['mæksɪmaɪz] *vt* (*profits etc,
chances*) maximiser

maximum ['mæksɪməm] (*pl* **maxima**)
adj maximum ▷ *n* maximum *m*

May [meɪ] *n* mai *m*

may [meɪ] (*conditional* **might**) *vi*
(*indicating possibility*): **he ~ come** il se
peut qu'il vienne; (*be allowed to*): **~ I
smoke?** puis-je fumer?; (*wishes*): **~ God
bless you!** (que) Dieu vous bénisse!;
you ~ as well go vous feriez aussi
bien d'y aller

maybe ['meɪbiː] *adv* peut-être; **~**

he'll ... peut-être qu'il ...

May Day n le Premier mai

mayhem ['meɪhɛm] n grabuge m

mayonnaise [meɪə'neɪz] n
mayonnaise f

mayor [mɛəʳ] n maire m; **mayoress** n
(female mayor) maire m; (wife of mayor)
épouse f du maire

maze [meɪz] n labyrinthe m, dédale m

MD n abbr (Comm) = **managing director**

me [miː] pron me, m' + vowel or h mute;
(stressed, after prep) moi; **it's me** c'est
moi; **he heard me** il m'a entendu; **give
me a book** donnez-moi un livre; **it's for
me** c'est pour moi

meadow ['mɛdəu] n prairie f, pré m

meagre (US **meager**) ['miːgəʳ] adj
maigre

meal [miːl] n repas m; (flour) farine f;
mealtime n heure f du repas

mean [miːn] adj (with money) avare,
radin(e); (unkind) mesquin(e),
méchant(e); (shabby) misérable;
(average) moyen(ne) ⊳ vt (pt, pp **~t**)
(signify) signifier, vouloir dire; (refer to)
faire allusion à, parler de; (intend): **to
~ to do** avoir l'intention de faire ⊳ n
moyenne f; **means** npl (way, money)
moyens mpl; **by ~s of** (instrument) au
moyen de; **by all ~s** je vous en prie; **to
be ~t for** être destiné(e) à; **do you ~ it?**
vous êtes sérieux?; **what do you ~?** que
voulez-vous dire?

meaning ['miːnɪŋ] n signification
f, sens m; **meaningful** adj
significatif(-ive); (relationship) valable;
meaningless adj dénué(e) de sens

meant [mɛnt] pt, pp of **mean**

meantime ['miːntaɪm] adv (also: **in
the ~**) pendant ce temps

meanwhile ['miːnwaɪl] adv
= **meantime**

measles ['miːzlz] n rougeole f

measure ['mɛʒəʳ] vt, vi mesurer ⊳ n
mesure f; (ruler) règle (graduée)

measurements ['mɛʒəmənts] npl
mesures fpl; **chest/hip ~** tour m de
poitrine/hanches

meat [miːt] n viande f; **I don't eat ~** je
ne mange pas de viande; **cold ~s** (BRIT)
viandes froides; **meatball** n boulette
f de viande

Mecca ['mɛkə] n la Mecque

mechanic [mɪ'kænɪk] n mécanicien
m; **can you send a ~?** pouvez-vous
nous envoyer un mécanicien?;
mechanical adj mécanique

mechanism ['mɛkənɪzəm] n
mécanisme m

medal ['mɛdl] n médaille f; **medallist**
(US **medalist**) n (Sport) médaillé(e)

meddle ['mɛdl] vi: **to ~ in** se mêler de,
s'occuper de; **to ~ with** toucher à

media ['miːdɪə] npl media mpl ⊳ npl
of **medium**

mediaeval [mɛdɪ'iːvl] adj = **medieval**

mediate ['miːdɪeɪt] vi servir
d'intermédiaire

medical ['mɛdɪkl] adj médical(e) ⊳ n
(also: **~ examination**) visite médicale;
(private) examen médical; **medical
certificate** n certificat médical

medicated ['mɛdɪkeɪtɪd] adj
traitant(e), médicamenteux(-euse)

medication [mɛdɪ'keɪʃən] n (drugs etc)
médication f

medicine ['mɛdsɪn] n médecine f;
(drug) médicament m

medieval [mɛdɪ'iːvl] adj médiéval(e)

mediocre [miːdɪ'əukəʳ] adj médiocre

meditate ['mɛdɪteɪt] vi: **to ~ (on)**
méditer (sur)

meditation [mɛdɪ'teɪʃən] n
méditation f

Mediterranean [mɛdɪtə'reɪnɪən]
adj méditerranéen(ne); **the ~ (Sea)** la
(mer) Méditerranée

medium ['miːdɪəm] adj moyen(ne)
⊳ n (pl media: means) moyen m; (pl **~s**:
person) médium m; **the happy ~** le juste
milieu; **medium-sized** adj de taille
moyenne; **medium wave** n (Radio)
ondes moyennes, petites ondes

meek [miːk] adj doux (douce), humble

meet (pt, pp **met**) [miːt, mɛt] vt
rencontrer; (by arrangement) retrouver,

rejoindre; (for the first time) faire la connaissance de; (go and fetch): **I'll ~ you at the station** j'irai te chercher à la gare; (opponent, danger, problem) faire face à; (requirements) satisfaire à, répondre à ▷ vi (friends) se rencontrer; se retrouver; (in session) se réunir; (join: lines, roads) se joindre; **nice ~ing you** ravi d'avoir fait votre connaissance; **meet up** vi: **to ~ up with sb** rencontrer qn; **meet with** vt fus (difficulty) rencontrer; **to ~ with success** être couronné(e) de succès; **meeting** n (of group of people) réunion f; (between individuals) rendez-vous m; **she's at or in a meeting** (Comm) elle est en réunion; **meeting place** n lieu m de (la) réunion; (for appointment) lieu de rendez-vous

megabyte ['mɛgəbaɪt] n (Comput) méga-octet m

megaphone ['mɛgəfəʊn] n porte-voix m inv

megapixel ['mɛgəpɪksl] n mégapixel m

melancholy ['mɛlənkəlɪ] n mélancolie f ▷ adj mélancolique

melody ['mɛlədɪ] n mélodie f

melon ['mɛlən] n melon m

melt [mɛlt] vi fondre ▷ vt faire fondre

member ['mɛmbəʳ] n membre m; **Member of Congress** (US) n membre m du Congrès, ≈ député m; **Member of Parliament (MP)** n (BRIT) député m; **Member of the European Parliament (MEP)** n Eurodéputé m; **Member of the House of Representatives (MHR)** n (US) membre m de la Chambre des représentants; **Member of the Scottish Parliament (MSP)** n (BRIT) député m au Parlement écossais; **membership** n (becoming a member) adhésion f; admission f; (the members) membres mpl, adhérents mpl; **membership card** n carte f de membre

memento [mə'mɛntəʊ] n souvenir m

memo ['mɛməʊ] n note f (de service)

memorable ['mɛmərəbl] adj mémorable

memorandum (pl **memoranda**) [mɛmə'rændəm, -də] n note f (de service)

memorial [mɪ'mɔːrɪəl] n mémorial m ▷ adj commémoratif(-ive)

memorize ['mɛməraɪz] vt apprendre or retenir par cœur

memory ['mɛmərɪ] n (also Comput) mémoire f; (recollection) souvenir m; **in ~ of** à la mémoire de; **memory card** n (for digital camera) carte f mémoire

men [mɛn] npl of **man**

menace ['mɛnɪs] n menace f; (inf: nuisance) peste f, plaie f ▷ vt menacer

mend [mɛnd] vt réparer; (darn) raccommoder, repriser ▷ n: **on the ~** en voie de guérison; **to ~ one's ways** s'amender

meningitis [mɛnɪn'dʒaɪtɪs] n méningite f

menopause ['mɛnəʊpɔːz] n ménopause f

men's room (US) n: **the men's room** les toilettes fpl pour hommes

menstruation [mɛnstru'eɪʃən] n menstruation f

menswear ['mɛnzwɛəʳ] n vêtements mpl d'hommes

mental ['mɛntl] adj mental(e); **mental hospital** n hôpital m psychiatrique; **mentality** [mɛn'tælɪt] n mentalité f; **mentally** adv: **to be mentally handicapped** être handicapé(e) mental(e); **the mentally ill** les malades mentaux

menthol ['mɛnθɒl] n menthol m

mention ['mɛnʃən] n mention f ▷ vt mentionner, faire mention de; **don't ~ it!** je vous en prie, il n'y a pas de quoi!

menu ['mɛnjuː] n (set menu, Comput) menu m; (list of dishes) carte f; **could we see the ~?** est-ce qu'on peut voir la carte?

MEP n abbr = **Member of the European Parliament**

mercenary ['mɜːsɪnərɪ] adj (person) intéressé(e), mercenaire ▷ n mercenaire m

merchandise ['mə:tʃəndaɪz] n
marchandises fpl

merchant ['mə:tʃənt] n négociant
m, marchand m; **merchant bank** n
(BRIT) banque f d'affaires; **merchant
navy** (US **merchant marine**) n marine
marchande

merciless ['mə:sɪlɪs] adj impitoyable,
sans pitié

mercury ['mə:kjʊrɪ] n mercure m

mercy ['mə:sɪ] n pitié f, merci f; (Rel)
miséricorde f; **at the ~ of** à la merci de

mere [mɪər] adj simple; (chance) pur(e);
a ~ two hours seulement deux heures;
merely adv simplement, purement

merge [mə:dʒ] vt unir; (Comput)
fusionner, interclasser ▷ vi (colours,
shapes, sounds) se mêler; (roads) se
joindre; (Comm) fusionner; **merger** n
(Comm) fusion f

meringue [mə'ræŋ] n meringue f

merit ['mɛrɪt] n mérite m, valeur f ▷ vt
mériter

mermaid ['mə:meɪd] n sirène f

merry ['mɛrɪ] adj gai(e); **M~
Christmas!** joyeux Noël!; **merry-go-
round** n manège m

mesh [mɛʃ] n mailles fpl

mess [mɛs] n désordre m, fouillis m,
pagaille f; (muddle: of life) gâchis m;
(: of economy) pagaille f; (dirt) saleté f;
(Mil) mess m, cantine f; **to be (in) a**
~ être en désordre; **to be/get o.s. in a**
~ (fig) être/se mettre dans le pétrin;
mess about or **around** (inf) vi perdre
son temps; **mess up** vt (dirty) salir;
(spoil) gâcher; **mess with** (inf) vt fus
(challenge, confront) se frotter à; (interfere
with) toucher à

message ['mɛsɪdʒ] n message m; **can I**
leave a ~? est-ce que je peux laisser un
message?; **are there any ~s for me?**
est-ce que j'ai des messages?

messenger ['mɛsɪndʒər] n messager m

Messrs, Messrs. ['mɛsəz] abbr (on
letters: = messieurs) MM

messy ['mɛsɪ] adj (dirty) sale; (untidy)
en désordre

met [mɛt] pt, pp of **meet**

metabolism [mɛ'tæbəlɪzəm] n
métabolisme m

metal ['mɛtl] n métal m ▷ cpd en métal;
metallic [mɛ'tælɪk] adj métallique

metaphor ['mɛtəfər] n métaphore f

meteor ['mi:tɪər] n météore m;
meteorite ['mi:tɪəraɪt] n météorite
m or f

meteorology [mi:tɪə'rɔlədʒɪ] n
météorologie f

meter ['mi:tər] n (instrument) compteur
m; (also: **parking ~**) parc(o)mètre m; (US:
unit) = **metre** ▷ vt (US Post) affranchir
à la machine

method ['mɛθəd] n méthode f;
methodical [mɪ'θɔdɪkl] adj
méthodique

methylated spirit ['mɛθɪleɪtɪd-] n
(BRIT: also: **meths**) alcool m à brûler

meticulous [mɛ'tɪkjʊləs] adj
méticuleux(-euse)

metre (US **meter**) ['mi:tər] n mètre m

metric ['mɛtrɪk] adj métrique

metro ['mɛtrəʊ] n métro m

metropolitan [mɛtrə'pɔlɪtən] adj
métropolitain(e); **the M~ Police** (BRIT)
la police londonienne

Mexican ['mɛksɪkən] adj mexicain(e)
▷ n Mexicain(e)

Mexico ['mɛksɪkəʊ] n Mexique m

mg abbr (= milligram) mg

mice [maɪs] npl of **mouse**

micro... [maɪkrəʊ] prefix: **microchip**
n (Elec) puce f; **microphone** n
microphone m; **microscope** n
microscope m; **microwave** n (also:
microwave oven) four m à micro-
ondes

mid [mɪd] adj: **~ May** la mi-mai; **~
afternoon** le milieu de l'après-midi; **in
~ air** en plein ciel; **he's in his ~ thirties**
il a dans les trente-cinq ans; **midday**
n midi m

middle ['mɪdl] n milieu m; (waist)
ceinture f, taille f ▷ adj du milieu;
(average) moyen(ne); **in the ~ of the
night** au milieu de la nuit; **middle-**

aged adj d'un certain âge, ni vieux ni jeune; **Middle Ages** npl: **the Middle Ages** le moyen âge; **middle-class** adj bourgeois(e); **middle class(es)** n(pl): **the middle class(es)** ≈ les classes moyennes; **Middle East** n: **the Middle East** le Proche-Orient, le Moyen-Orient; **middle name** n second prénom; **middle school** n (US) école pour les enfants de 12 à 14 ans, ≈ collège m; (BRIT) école pour les enfants de 8 à 14 ans

midge [mɪdʒ] n moucheron m

midget ['mɪdʒɪt] n nain(e)

midnight ['mɪdnaɪt] n minuit m

midst [mɪdst] n: **in the ~ of** au milieu de

midsummer [mɪd'sʌmə^r] n milieu m de l'été

midway [mɪd'weɪ] adj, adv: **~ (between)** à mi-chemin (entre); **~ through ...** au milieu de ..., en plein(e) ...

midweek [mɪd'wiːk] adv au milieu de la semaine, en pleine semaine

midwife (pl **midwives**) ['mɪdwaɪf, -vz] n sage-femme f

midwinter [mɪd'wɪntə^r] n milieu m de l'hiver

might [maɪt] vb see **may** ▷ n puissance f, force f; **mighty** adj puissant(e)

migraine ['miːɡreɪn] n migraine f

migrant ['maɪɡrənt] n (bird, animal) migrateur m; (person) migrant(e) ▷ adj migrateur(-trice); migrant(e); (worker) saisonnier(-ière)

migrate [maɪ'ɡreɪt] vi migrer

migration [maɪ'ɡreɪʃən] n migration f

mike [maɪk] n abbr (= microphone) micro m

mild [maɪld] adj doux (douce); (reproach, infection) léger(-ère); (illness) bénin(-igne); (interest) modéré(e); (taste) peu relevé(e); **mildly** ['maɪldlɪ] adv doucement; légèrement; **to put it mildly** (inf) c'est le moins qu'on puisse dire

mile [maɪl] n mil(l)e m (= 1609 m); **mileage** n distance f en milles, ≈ kilométrage m; **mileometer**

[maɪ'lɔmɪtə^r] n compteur m kilométrique; **milestone** n borne f; (fig) jalon m

military ['mɪlɪtərɪ] adj militaire

militia [mɪ'lɪʃə] n milice f

milk [mɪlk] n lait m ▷ vt (cow) traire; (fig: person) dépouiller, plumer; (: situation) exploiter à fond; **milk chocolate** n chocolat m au lait; **milkman** (irreg) n laitier m; **milky** adj (drink) au lait; (colour) laiteux(-euse)

mill [mɪl] n moulin m; (factory) usine f, fabrique f; (spinning mill) filature f; (flour mill) minoterie f ▷ vt moudre, broyer ▷ vi (also: **~ about**) grouiller

millennium (pl **~s** or **millennia**) [mɪ'lɛnɪəm, -'lɛnɪə] n millénaire m

milli... ['mɪlɪ] prefix milli...; **milligram(me)** n milligramme m; **millilitre** (US **milliliter**) ['mɪlɪliːtə^r] n millilitre m; **millimetre** (US **millimeter**) n millimètre m

million ['mɪljən] n million m; **a ~ pounds** un million de livres sterling; **millionaire** [mɪljə'nɛə^r] n millionnaire m; **millionth** [-θ] num millionième

milometer [maɪ'lɔmɪtə^r] n = **mileometer**

mime [maɪm] n mime m ▷ vt, vi mimer

mimic ['mɪmɪk] n imitateur(-trice) ▷ vt, vi imiter, contrefaire

min. abbr (= minute(s)) mn.; (= minimum) min.

mince [mɪns] vt hacher ▷ n (BRIT Culin) viande hachée, hachis m; **mincemeat** n hachis de fruits secs utilisés en pâtisserie; (US) viande hachée, hachis m; **mince pie** n sorte de tarte aux fruits secs

mind [maɪnd] n esprit m ▷ vt (attend to, look after) s'occuper de; (be careful) faire attention à; (object to): **I don't ~ the noise** je ne crains pas le bruit, le bruit ne me dérange pas; **it is on my ~** cela me préoccupe; **to change one's ~** changer d'avis; **to my ~** à mon avis, selon moi; **to bear sth in ~** tenir compte de qch; **to have sb/sth**

in ~ avoir qn/qch en tête; **to make up one's ~** se décider; **do you ~ if ...?** est-ce que cela vous gêne si ...?; **I don't ~** cela ne me dérange pas; (*don't care*) ça m'est égal; **~ you, ...** remarquez, ...; **never ~** peu importe, ça ne fait rien; (*don't worry*) ne vous en faîtes pas; **"~ the step"** "attention à la marche"; **mindless** *adj* irréfléchi(e); (*violence, crime*) insensé(e); (*boring*) idiot(e)

mine¹ [maɪn] *pron* le (la) mien(ne), les miens (miennes); **a friend of ~** un de mes amis, un ami à moi; **this book is ~** ce livre est à moi

mine² [maɪn] *n* mine *f* ▷ *vt* (*coal*) extraire; (*ship, beach*) miner; **minefield** *n* champ *m* de mines; **miner** *n* mineur *m*

mineral ['mɪnərəl] *adj* minéral(e) ▷ *n* minéral *m*; **mineral water** *n* eau minérale

mingle ['mɪŋgl] *vi*: **to ~ with** se mêler à

miniature ['mɪnətʃər] *adj* (en) miniature ▷ *n* miniature *f*

minibar ['mɪnibɑːr] *n* minibar *m*

minibus ['mɪnibʌs] *n* minibus *m*

minicab ['mɪnikæb] (*BRIT*) taxi *m* indépendant

minimal ['mɪnɪml] *adj* minimal(e)

minimize ['mɪnɪmaɪz] *vt* (*reduce*) réduire au minimum; (*play down*) minimiser

minimum ['mɪnɪməm] *n* (*pl* minima) minimum *m* ▷ *adj* minimum

mining ['maɪnɪŋ] *n* exploitation minière

miniskirt ['mɪniskəːt] *n* mini-jupe *f*

minister ['mɪnɪstər] *n* (*BRIT Pol*) ministre *m*; (*Rel*) pasteur *m*

ministry ['mɪnɪstrɪ] *n* (*BRIT Pol*) ministère *m*; (*Rel*): **to go into the ~** devenir pasteur

minor ['maɪnər] *adj* petit(e), de peu d'importance; (*Mus, poet, problem*) mineur(e) ▷ *n* (*Law*) mineur(e)

minority [maɪ'nɔrɪtɪ] *n* minorité *f*

mint [mɪnt] *n* (*plant*) menthe *f*; (*sweet*) bonbon *m* à la menthe ▷ *vt* (*coins*)

battre; **the (Royal) M~**, **the (US) M~** ≈ l'hôtel *m* de la Monnaie; **in ~ condition** à l'état de neuf

minus ['maɪnəs] *n* (*also*: **~ sign**) signe *m* moins ▷ *prep* moins; **12 ~ 6 equals 6** 12 moins 6 égal 6; **~ 24° C** moins 24 °C

minute¹ *n* ['mɪnɪt] minute *f*; **minutes** *npl* (*of meeting*) procès-verbal *m*, compte rendu; **wait a ~!** (attendez) un instant!; **at the last ~** à la dernière minute

minute² *adj* [maɪ'njuːt] minuscule; (*detailed*) minutieux(-euse); **in ~ detail** par le menu

miracle ['mɪrəkl] *n* miracle *m*

miraculous [mɪ'rækjuləs] *adj* miraculeux(-euse)

mirage ['mɪrɑːʒ] *n* mirage *m*

mirror ['mɪrər] *n* miroir *m*, glace *f*; (*in car*) rétroviseur *m*

misbehave [mɪsbɪ'heɪv] *vi* mal se conduire

misc. *abbr* = **miscellaneous**

miscarriage ['mɪskærɪdʒ] *n* (*Med*) fausse couche; **~ of justice** erreur *f* judiciaire

miscellaneous [mɪsɪ'leɪnɪəs] *adj* (*items, expenses*) divers(es); (*selection*) varié(e)

mischief ['mɪstʃɪf] *n* (*naughtiness*) sottises *fpl*; (*playfulness*) espièglerie *f*; (*harm*) mal *m*, dommage *m*; (*maliciousness*) méchanceté *f*;

mischievous ['mɪstʃɪvəs] *adj* (*playful, naughty*) coquin(e), espiègle

misconception ['mɪskən'sɛpʃən] *n* idée fausse

misconduct [mɪs'kɔndʌkt] *n* inconduite *f*; **professional ~** faute professionnelle

miser ['maɪzər] *n* avare *m/f*

miserable ['mɪzərəbl] *adj* (*person, expression*) malheureux(-euse); (*conditions*) misérable; (*weather*) maussade; (*offer, donation*) minable; (*failure*) pitoyable

misery ['mɪzərɪ] *n* (*unhappiness*) tristesse *f*; (*pain*) souffrances *fpl*;

(*wretchedness*) misère *f*

misfortune [mɪsˈfɔːtʃən] *n* malchance *f*, malheur *m*

misgiving [mɪsˈgɪvɪŋ] *n* (*apprehension*) craintes *fpl*; **to have ~s about sth** avoir des doutes quant à qch

misguided [mɪsˈgaɪdɪd] *adj* malavisé(e)

mishap [ˈmɪshæp] *n* mésaventure *f*

misinterpret [mɪsɪnˈtəːprɪt] *vt* mal interpréter

misjudge [mɪsˈdʒʌdʒ] *vt* méjuger, se méprendre sur le compte de

mislay [mɪsˈleɪ] *vt* (*irreg: like* **lay**) égarer

mislead [mɪsˈliːd] *vt* (*irreg: like* **lead**) induire en erreur; **misleading** *adj* trompeur(-euse)

misplace [mɪsˈpleɪs] *vt* égarer; **to be ~d** (*trust etc*) être mal placé(e)

misprint [ˈmɪsprɪnt] *n* faute *f* d'impression

misrepresent [mɪsrɛprɪˈzɛnt] *vt* présenter sous un faux jour

Miss [mɪs] *n* Mademoiselle

miss [mɪs] *vt* (*fail to get, attend, see*) manquer, rater; (*regret the absence of*): **I ~ him/it** il/cela me manque ▷ *vi* manquer ▷ *n* (*shot*) coup manqué; **we ~ed our train** nous avons raté notre train; **you can't ~ it** vous ne pouvez pas vous tromper; **miss out** *vt* (*BRIT*) oublier; **miss out on** *vt fus* (*fun, party*) rater, manquer; (*chance, bargain*) laisser passer

missile [ˈmɪsaɪl] *n* (*Aviat*) missile *m*; (*object thrown*) projectile *m*

missing [ˈmɪsɪŋ] *adj* manquant(e); (*after escape, disaster: person*) disparu(e); **to go ~** disparaître; **~ in action** (*Mil*) porté(e) disparu(e)

mission [ˈmɪʃən] *n* mission *f*; **on a ~ to sb** en mission auprès de qn; **missionary** *n* missionnaire *m/f*

misspell [ˈmɪsˈspɛl] *vt* (*irreg: like* **spell**) mal orthographier

mist [mɪst] *n* brume *f* ▷ *vi* (*also: ~ over, ~ up*) devenir brumeux(-euse); (*BRIT: windows*) s'embuer

mistake [mɪsˈteɪk] *n* erreur *f*, faute *f* ▷ *vt* (*irreg: like* **take**) (*meaning*) mal comprendre; (*intentions*) se méprendre sur; **to ~ for** prendre pour; **by ~** par erreur, par inadvertance; **to make a ~** (*in writing*) faire une faute; (*in calculating etc*) faire une erreur; **there must be some ~** il doit y avoir une erreur, se tromper; **mistaken** *pp of* **mistake** ▷ *adj* (*idea etc*) erroné(e); **to be mistaken** faire erreur, se tromper

mister [ˈmɪstər] *n* (*inf*) Monsieur *m*; *see* **Mr**

mistletoe [ˈmɪsltəu] *n* gui *m*

mistook [mɪsˈtuk] *pt of* **mistake**

mistress [ˈmɪstrɪs] *n* maîtresse *f*; (*BRIT: in primary school*) institutrice *f*; (: *in secondary school*) professeur *m*

mistrust [mɪsˈtrʌst] *vt* se méfier de

misty [ˈmɪstɪ] *adj* brumeux(-euse); (*glasses, window*) embué(e)

misunderstand [mɪsʌndəˈstænd] *vt, vi* (*irreg: like* **stand**) mal comprendre; **misunderstanding** *n* méprise *f*, malentendu *m*; **there's been a misunderstanding** il y a eu un malentendu

misunderstood [mɪsʌndəˈstud] *pt, pp of* **misunderstand** ▷ *adj* (*person*) incompris(e)

misuse *n* (*mɪsˈjuːs*) mauvais emploi; (*of power*) abus *m* ▷ *vt* [mɪsˈjuːz] mal employer; abuser de

mitt(en) [ˈmɪt(n)] *n* moufle *f*; (*fingerless*) mitaine *f*

mix [mɪks] *vt* mélanger; (*sauce, drink etc*) préparer ▷ *vi* se mélanger; (*socialize*): **he doesn't ~ well** il est peu sociable ▷ *n* mélange *m*; **to ~ sth with sth** mélanger qch à qch; **cake ~** préparation *f* pour gâteau; **mix up** *vt* mélanger; (*confuse*) confondre; **to be ~ed up in sth** être mêlé(e) à qch ou impliqué(e) dans qch; **mixed** *adj* (*feelings, reactions*) contradictoire; (*school, marriage*) mixte; **mixed grill** *n* (*BRIT*) assortiment *m* de grillades; **mixed salad** *n* salade *f* de crudités; **mixed-up** *adj* (*person*) désorienté(e), embrouillé(e); **mixer**

n (for food) batteur *m*, mixeur *m*; *(drink)* boisson gazeuse *(servant à couper un alcool)*; *(person)*: **he is a good mixer** il est très sociable; **mixture** *n* assortiment *m*, mélange *m*; *(Med)* préparation *f*; **mix-up** *n*: **there was a mix-up** il y a eu confusion

ml *abbr (= millilitre(s))* ml

mm *abbr (= millimetre)* mm

moan [məun] *n* gémissement *m* ▷ *vi* gémir; *(inf: complain)*: **to ~ (about)** se plaindre (de)

moat [məut] *n* fossé *m*, douves *fpl*

mob [mɔb] *n* foule *f*; *(disorderly)* cohue *f* ▷ *vt* assaillir

mobile ['məubaɪl] *adj* mobile ▷ *n (Art)* mobile *m*; **mobile home** *n* caravane *f*; **mobile phone** *n* téléphone portatif

mobility [məu'bɪlɪtɪ] *n* mobilité *f*

mobilize ['məubɪlaɪz] *vt, vi* mobiliser

mock [mɔk] *vt* ridiculiser; *(laugh at)* se moquer de ▷ *adj* faux (fausse); **mocks** *npl (BRIT: Scol)* examens blancs; **mockery** *n* moquerie *f*, raillerie *f*

mod cons ['mɔd'kɔnz] *npl abbr (BRIT)* = **modern conveniences**; *see* **convenience**

mode [məud] *n* mode *m*; *(of transport)* moyen *m*

model ['mɔdl] *n* modèle *m*; *(person: for fashion)* mannequin *m*; *(: for artist)* modèle ▷ *vt (with clay etc)* modeler ▷ *vi* travailler comme mannequin ▷ *adj (railway: toy)* modèle réduit *inv*; *(child, factory)* modèle; **to ~ clothes** présenter des vêtements; **to ~ o.s. on** imiter

modem ['məudɛm] *n* modem *m*

moderate *adj* ['mɔdərət] modéré(e); *(amount, change)* peu important(e) ▷ *vb* ['mɔdəreɪt] ▷ *vi* se modérer, se calmer ▷ *vt* modérer; **moderation** [mɔdə'reɪʃən] *n* modération *f*, mesure *f*; **in ~** à dose raisonnable, pris(e) *or* pratiqué(e) modérément

modern ['mɔdən] *adj* moderne; **modernize** *vt* moderniser; **modern languages** *npl* langues vivantes

modest ['mɔdɪst] *adj* modeste;

modesty *n* modestie *f*

modification [mɔdɪfɪ'keɪʃən] *n* modification *f*

modify ['mɔdɪfaɪ] *vt* modifier

module ['mɔdjuːl] *n* module *m*

mohair ['məuhɛər] *n* mohair *m*

Mohammed [mə'hæmɛd] *n* Mahomet *m*

moist [mɔɪst] *adj* humide, moite; **moisture** ['mɔɪstʃər] *n* humidité *f*; *(on glass)* buée *f*; **moisturizer** ['mɔɪstʃəraɪzər] *n* crème hydratante

mold *etc* [məuld] *(US)* = **mould** *etc*

mole [məul] *n (animal, spy)* taupe *f*; *(spot)* grain *m* de beauté

molecule ['mɔlɪkjuːl] *n* molécule *f*

molest [məu'lɛst] *vt (assault sexually)* attenter à la pudeur de

molten ['məultən] *adj* fondu(e); *(rock)* en fusion

mom [mɔm] *n (US)* = **mum**

moment ['məumənt] *n* moment *m*, instant *m*; **at the ~** en ce moment; **momentarily** ['məuməntrɪlɪ] *adv* momentanément; *(US: soon)* bientôt; **momentary** *adj* momentané(e), passager(-ère); **momentous** [məu'mɛntəs] *adj* important(e), capital(e)

momentum [məu'mɛntəm] *n* élan *m*, vitesse acquise; *(fig)* dynamique *f*; **to gather ~** prendre de la vitesse; *(fig)* gagner du terrain

mommy ['mɔmɪ] *n (US: mother)* maman *f*

Mon *abbr (= Monday)* l.

Monaco ['mɔnəkəu] *n* Monaco *f*

monarch ['mɔnək] *n* monarque *m*; **monarchy** *n* monarchie *f*

monastery ['mɔnəstərɪ] *n* monastère *m*

Monday ['mʌndɪ] *n* lundi *m*

monetary ['mʌnɪtərɪ] *adj* monétaire

money ['mʌnɪ] *n* argent *m*; **to make ~** *(person)* gagner de l'argent; *(business)* rapporter; **money belt** *n* ceinture-portefeuille *f*; **money order** *n* mandat *m*

mongrel ['mʌŋgrəl] n (dog) bâtard m

monitor ['mɔnɪtəʳ] n (TV, Comput) écran m, moniteur m ▷ vt contrôler; (foreign station) être à l'écoute de; (progress) suivre de près

monk [mʌŋk] n moine m

monkey ['mʌŋkɪ] n singe m

monologue ['mɔnəlɔg] n monologue m

monopoly [mə'nɔpəlɪ] n monopole m

monosodium glutamate [mɔnə'səudɪəm 'glu:təmeɪt] n glutamate m de sodium

monotonous [mə'nɔtənəs] adj monotone

monsoon [mɔn'su:n] n mousson f

monster ['mɔnstəʳ] n monstre m

month [mʌnθ] n mois m; **monthly** adj mensuel(le) ▷ adv mensuellement

Montreal [mɔntrɪ'ɔ:l] n Montréal

monument ['mɔnjumənt] n monument m

mood [mu:d] n humeur f, disposition f; **to be in a good/bad ~** être de bonne/mauvaise humeur; **moody** adj (variable) d'humeur changeante, lunatique; (sullen) morose, maussade

moon [mu:n] n lune f; **moonlight** n clair m de lune

moor [muəʳ] n lande f ▷ vt (ship) amarrer ▷ vi mouiller

moose [mu:s] n (pl inv) élan m

mop [mɔp] n balai m à laver; (for dishes) lavette f à vaisselle ▷ vt éponger, essuyer; **~ of hair** tignasse f; **mop up** vt éponger

mope [məup] vi avoir le cafard, se morfondre

moped ['məupɛd] n cyclomoteur m

moral ['mɔrl] adj moral(e) ▷ n morale f; **morals** npl moralité f

morale [mɔ'rɑ:l] n moral m

morality [mə'rælɪtɪ] n moralité f

morbid ['mɔ:bɪd] adj morbide

 KEYWORD

more [mɔ:ʳ] adj **1** (greater in number etc) plus (de), davantage (de); **more people/work (than)** plus de gens/de travail (que)

2 (additional) encore (de); **do you want (some) more tea?** voulez-vous encore du thé?; **is there any more wine?** reste-t-il du vin?; **I have no** or **I don't have any more money** je n'ai plus d'argent; **it'll take a few more weeks** ça prendra encore quelques semaines ▷ pron plus, davantage; **more than 10** plus de 10; **it cost more than we expected** cela a coûté plus que prévu; **I want more** j'en veux plus or davantage; **is there any more?** est-ce qu'il en reste?; **there's no more** il n'y en a plus; **a little more** un peu plus; **many/much more** beaucoup plus, bien davantage ▷ adv plus; **more dangerous/easily (than)** plus dangereux/facilement (que); **more and more expensive** de plus en plus cher; **more or less** plus ou moins; **more than ever** plus que jamais; **once more** encore une fois, une fois de plus

moreover [mɔ:'rəuvəʳ] adv de plus

morgue [mɔ:g] n morgue f

morning ['mɔ:nɪŋ] n matin m; (as duration) matinée f ▷ cpd matinal(e); (paper) du matin; **in the ~** le matin; **7 o'clock in the ~** 7 heures du matin; **morning sickness** n nausées matinales

Moroccan [mə'rɔkən] adj marocain(e) ▷ n Marocain(e)

Morocco [mə'rɔkəu] n Maroc m

moron ['mɔ:rɔn] n idiot(e), minus m/f

morphine ['mɔ:fi:n] n morphine f

morris dancing ['mɔrɪs-] n (BRIT) danses folkloriques anglaises

● **MORRIS DANCING**
●
● Le **Morris dancing** est une
● danse folklorique anglaise
● traditionnellement réservée aux
● hommes. Habillés tout en blanc
● et portant des clochettes, ils

- exécutent différentes figures avec
- des mouchoirs et de longs bâtons.
- Cette danse est très populaire dans
- les fêtes de village.

Morse [mɔːs] n (also: **~ code**) morse m
mortal ['mɔːtl] adj, n mortel(le)
mortar ['mɔːtəʳ] n mortier m
mortgage ['mɔːɡɪdʒ] n hypothèque f;
(loan) prêt m (or crédit m) hypothécaire
▷ vt hypothéquer
mortician [mɔːˈtɪʃən] n (US)
entrepreneur m de pompes funèbres
mortified ['mɔːtɪfaɪd] adj mort(e)
de honte
mortuary ['mɔːtjuərɪ] n morgue f
mosaic [məuˈzeɪɪk] n mosaïque f
Moscow ['mɔskəu] n Moscou
Moslem ['mɔzləm] adj, n = **Muslim**
mosque [mɔsk] n mosquée f
mosquito (pl **~es**) [mɔsˈkiːtəu] n
moustique m
moss [mɔs] n mousse f
most [məust] adj (majority of) la plupart
de; (greatest amount of) le plus de ▷ pron
la plupart ▷ adv le plus; (very) très,
extrêmement; **the ~** le plus; **~ fish** la
plupart des poissons; **the ~ beautiful
woman in the world** la plus belle
femme du monde; **~ of** (with plural) la
plupart de; (with singular) la plus grande
partie de; **~ of them** la plupart d'entre
eux; **~ of the time** la plupart du temps;
I saw ~ (a lot but not all) j'en ai vu la
plupart; (more than anyone else) c'est
moi qui en ai vu le plus; **at the (very)
~** au plus; **to make the ~ of** profiter
au maximum de; **mostly** adv (chiefly)
surtout, principalement; (usually)
généralement
MOT n abbr (BRIT) = **Ministry of
Transport**; **the ~ (test)** visite technique
(annuelle) obligatoire des véhicules à
moteur
motel [məuˈtɛl] n motel m
moth [mɔθ] n papillon m de nuit; (in
clothes) mite f
mother ['mʌðəʳ] n mère f ▷ vt (pamper,

protect) dorloter; **motherhood** n
maternité f; **mother-in-law** n belle-
mère f; **mother-of-pearl** n nacre f;
Mother's Day n fête f des Mères;
mother-to-be n future maman;
mother tongue n langue maternelle
motif [məuˈtiːf] n motif m
motion ['məuʃən] n mouvement m;
(gesture) geste m; (at meeting) motion
f ▷ vt, vi: **to ~ (to) sb to do** faire signe à
qn de faire; **motionless** adj immobile,
sans mouvement; **motion picture**
n film m
motivate ['məutɪveɪt] vt motiver
motivation [məutɪˈveɪʃən] n
motivation f
motive ['məutɪv] n motif m, mobile m
motor ['məutəʳ] n moteur m; (BRIT inf:
vehicle) auto f; **motorbike** n moto f;
motorboat n bateau m à moteur;
motorcar n (BRIT) automobile f;
motorcycle n moto f; **motorcyclist**
n motocycliste m/f; **motoring** (BRIT)
n tourisme m automobile; **motorist**
n automobiliste m/f; **motor racing** n
(BRIT) course f automobile; **motorway**
n (BRIT) autoroute f
motto (pl **~es**) ['mɔtəu] n devise f
mould (US **mold**) [məuld] n moule
m; (mildew) moisissure f ▷ vt mouler,
modeler; (fig) façonner; **mouldy** adj
moisi(e); (smell) de moisi
mound [maund] n monticule m,
tertre m
mount [maunt] n (hill) mont m,
montagne f; (horse) monture f; (for
picture) carton m de montage ▷ vt
monter; (horse) monter à; (bike) monter
sur; (picture) monter sur carton ▷ vi
(inflation, tension) augmenter; **mount
up** vi s'élever, monter; (bills, problems,
savings) s'accumuler
mountain ['mauntɪn] n montagne
f ▷ cpd de (la) montagne; **mountain
bike** n VTT m, vélo m tout terrain;
mountaineer n alpiniste m/f;
mountaineering n alpinisme m;
mountainous adj montagneux(-euse)

mountain range n chaîne f de montagnes

mourn [mɔːn] vt pleurer ▷ vi: **to ~ for sb** pleurer qn; **to ~ for sth** se lamenter sur qch; **mourner** n parent(e) or ami(e) du défunt; personne f en deuil or venue rendre hommage au défunt; **mourning** n deuil m; **in mourning** en deuil

mouse (pl **mice**) [maus, maɪs] n (also Comput) souris f; **mouse mat** n (Comput) tapis m de souris

moussaka [muˈsɑːkə] n moussaka f

mousse [muːs] n mousse f

moustache (US **mustache**) [məsˈtɑːʃ] n moustache(s) f(pl)

mouth [mauθ, pl -ðz] n bouche f; (of dog, cat) gueule f; (of river) embouchure f; (of hole, cave) ouverture f; **mouthful** n bouchée f; **mouth organ** n harmonica m; **mouthpiece** n (of musical instrument) bec m, embouchure f; (spokesperson) porte-parole m inv; **mouthwash** n eau f dentifrice

move [muːv] n (movement) mouvement m; (in game) coup m; (: turn to play) tour m; (change of house) déménagement m; (change of job) changement m d'emploi ▷ vt déplacer, bouger; (emotionally) émouvoir; (Pol: resolution etc) proposer ▷ vi (gen) bouger, remuer; (traffic) circuler; (also: ~ house) déménager; (in game) jouer; **can you ~ your car, please?** pouvez-vous déplacer votre voiture, s'il vous plaît?; **to ~ sb to do sth** pousser or inciter qn à faire qch; **to get a ~ on** se dépêcher, se remuer; **move back** vi revenir, retourner; **move in** vi (to a house) emménager; (police, soldiers) intervenir; **move off** vi s'éloigner, s'en aller; **move on** vi se remettre en route; **move out** vi (of house) déménager; **move over** vi se pousser, se déplacer; **move up** vi avancer; (employee) avoir de l'avancement; (pupil) passer dans la classe supérieure; **movement** n mouvement m

movie [ˈmuːvɪ] n film m; **movies** npl: **the ~s** le cinéma; **movie theater** (US) n cinéma m

moving [ˈmuːvɪŋ] adj en mouvement; (touching) émouvant(e)

mow (pt **~ed**, pp **~ed** or **~n**) [məu, -d, -n] vt faucher; (lawn) tondre; **mower** n (also: **lawnmower**) tondeuse f à gazon

Mozambique [məuzəmˈbiːk] n Mozambique m

MP n abbr (BRIT) = **Member of Parliament**

MP3 n mp3 m; **MP3 player** n lecteur m mp3

mpg n abbr = miles per gallon (30 mpg = 9,4 l. aux 100 km)

m.p.h. abbr = miles per hour (60 mph = 96 km/h)

Mr (US **Mr.**) [ˈmɪstər] n: **Mr X** Monsieur X, M. X

Mrs (US **Mrs.**) [ˈmɪsɪz] n: **~ X** Madame X, Mme X

Ms (US **Ms.**) [mɪz] n (Miss or Mrs): **Ms X** Madame X, Mme X

MSP n abbr (= Member of the Scottish Parliament) député m au Parlement écossais

Mt abbr (Geo: = mount) Mt

much [mʌtʃ] adj beaucoup de ▷ adv, n or pron beaucoup; **we don't have ~ time** nous n'avons pas beaucoup de temps; **how ~ is it?** combien est-ce que ça coûte?; **it's not ~** ce n'est pas beaucoup; **too ~** trop (de); **so ~** tant (de); **I like it very/so ~** j'aime beaucoup/tellement ça; **as ~ as** autant de; **that's ~ better** c'est beaucoup mieux

muck [mʌk] n (mud) boue f; (dirt) ordures fpl; **muck up** vt (inf: ruin) gâcher, esquinter; (: dirty) salir; (: exam, interview) se planter à; **mucky** adj (dirty) boueux(-euse), sale

mucus [ˈmjuːkəs] n mucus m

mud [mʌd] n boue f

muddle [ˈmʌdl] n (mess) pagaille f, fouillis m; (mix-up) confusion f ▷ vt (also: ~ **up**) brouiller, embrouiller; **to get in a ~** (while explaining etc)

s'embrouiller
muddy ['mʌdɪ] adj boueux(-euse)
mudguard ['mʌdgɑːd] n garde-boue m inv
muesli ['mjuːzlɪ] n muesli m
muffin ['mʌfɪn] n (roll) petit pain rond et plat; (cake) petit gâteau au chocolat ou aux fruits
muffled ['mʌfld] adj étouffé(e), voilé(e)
muffler ['mʌflər] n (scarf) cache-nez m inv; (US Aut) silencieux m
mug [mʌg] n (cup) tasse f (sans soucoupe); (: for beer) chope f; (inf: face) bouille f; (: fool) poire f ▷ vt (assault) agresser; **mugger** ['mʌgər] n agresseur m; **mugging** n agression f
muggy ['mʌgɪ] adj lourd(e), moite
mule [mjuːl] n mule f
multicoloured (US **multicolored**) ['mʌltɪkʌləd] adj multicolore
multimedia ['mʌltɪ'miːdɪə] adj multimédia inv
multinational [mʌltɪ'næʃənl] n multinationale f ▷ adj multinational(e)
multiple ['mʌltɪpl] adj multiple ▷ n multiple m; **multiple choice (test)** n QCM m, questionnaire m à choix multiple; **multiple sclerosis** [-sklɪ'rəusɪs] n sclérose f en plaques
multiplex (cinema) ['mʌltɪplɛks-] n (cinéma m) multisalles m
multiplication [mʌltɪplɪ'keɪʃən] n multiplication f
multiply ['mʌltɪplaɪ] vt multiplier ▷ vi se multiplier
multistorey ['mʌltɪ'stɔːrɪ] adj (BRIT: building) à étages; (: car park) à étages or niveaux multiples
mum [mʌm] n (BRIT) maman f ▷ adj: **to keep ~** ne pas souffler mot
mumble ['mʌmbl] vt, vi marmotter, marmonner
mummy ['mʌmɪ] n (BRIT: mother) maman f; (embalmed) momie f
mumps [mʌmps] n oreillons mpl
munch [mʌntʃ] vt, vi mâcher
municipal [mjuː'nɪsɪpl] adj municipal(e)

mural ['mjuərl] n peinture murale
murder ['məːdər] n meurtre m, assassinat m ▷ vt assassiner; **murderer** n meurtrier m, assassin m
murky ['məːkɪ] adj sombre, ténébreux(-euse); (water) trouble
murmur ['məːmər] n murmure m ▷ vt, vi murmurer
muscle ['mʌsl] n muscle m; (fig) force f; **muscular** ['mʌskjulər] adj musculaire; (person, arm) musclé(e)
museum [mjuː'zɪəm] n musée m
mushroom ['mʌʃrum] n champignon m ▷ vi (fig) pousser comme un (or des) champignon(s)
music ['mjuːzɪk] n musique f; **musical** adj musical(e); (person) musicien(ne) ▷ n (show) comédie musicale; **musical instrument** n instrument m de musique; **musician** [mjuː'zɪʃən] n musicien(ne)
Muslim ['mʌzlɪm] adj, n musulman(e)
muslin ['mʌzlɪn] n mousseline f
mussel ['mʌsl] n moule f
must [mʌst] aux vb (obligation): **I ~ do it** je dois le faire, il faut que je le fasse; (probability): **he ~ be there by now** il doit y être maintenant, il y est probablement maintenant; (suggestion, invitation): **you ~ come and see me** il faut que vous veniez me voir ▷ n nécessité f, impératif m; **it's a ~** c'est indispensable; **I ~ have made a mistake** j'ai dû me tromper
mustache ['mʌstæʃ] n (US) = **moustache**
mustard ['mʌstəd] n moutarde f
mustn't ['mʌsnt] = **must not**
mute [mjuːt] adj, n muet(te)
mutilate ['mjuːtɪleɪt] vt mutiler
mutiny ['mjuːtɪnɪ] n mutinerie f ▷ vi se mutiner
mutter ['mʌtər] vt, vi marmonner, marmotter
mutton ['mʌtn] n mouton m
mutual ['mjuːtʃuəl] adj mutuel(le), réciproque; (benefit, interest) commun(e)

muzzle ['mʌzl] n museau m; (protective device) muselière f; (of gun) gueule f ▷ vt museler

my [maɪ] adj mon (ma), mes pl; **my house/car/gloves** ma maison/ma voiture/mes gants; **I've washed my hair/cut my finger** je me suis lavé les cheveux/coupé le doigt; **is this my pen or yours?** c'est mon stylo ou c'est le vôtre?

myself [maɪ'sɛlf] pron (reflexive) me; (emphatic) moi-même; (after prep) moi; see also **oneself**

mysterious [mɪs'tɪərɪəs] adj mystérieux(-euse)

mystery ['mɪstərɪ] n mystère m

mystical ['mɪstɪkl] adj mystique

mystify ['mɪstɪfaɪ] vt (deliberately) mystifier; (puzzle) ébahir

myth [mɪθ] n mythe m; **mythology** [mɪ'θɒlədʒɪ] n mythologie f

n/a abbr (= not applicable) n.a.

nag [næg] vt (scold) être toujours après, reprendre sans arrêt

nail [neɪl] n (human) ongle m; (metal) clou m ▷ vt clouer; **to ~ sth to sth** clouer qch à qch; **to ~ sb down to a date/price** contraindre qn à accepter or donner une date/un prix; **nailbrush** n brosse f à ongles; **nailfile** n lime f à ongles; **nail polish** n vernis m à ongles; **nail polish remover** n dissolvant m; **nail scissors** npl ciseaux mpl à ongles; **nail varnish** n (BRIT) = **nail polish**

naïve [naɪ'iːv] adj naïf(-ïve)

naked ['neɪkɪd] adj nu(e)

name [neɪm] n nom m; (reputation) réputation f ▷ vt nommer; (identify: accomplice etc) citer; (price, date) fixer, donner; **by ~** par son nom; de nom; **in the ~ of** au nom de; **what's your ~?** comment vous appelez-vous?, quel est votre nom?; **namely** adv à savoir

nanny ['nænɪ] n bonne f d'enfants

nap [næp] n (sleep) (petit) somme

napkin ['næpkɪn] n serviette f (de table)

nappy ['næpɪ] n (BRIT) couche f

narcotics [nɑːˈkɔtɪkz] npl (illegal drugs) stupéfiants mpl

narrative ['nærətɪv] n récit m ▷ adj narratif(-ive)

narrator [nəˈreɪtəʳ] n narrateur(-trice)

narrow ['nærəu] adj étroit(e); (fig) restreint(e), limité(e) ▷ vi (road) devenir plus étroit, se rétrécir; (gap, difference) se réduire; **to have a ~ escape** l'échapper belle; **narrow down** vt restreindre; **narrowly** adv: **he narrowly missed injury/the tree** il a failli se blesser/rentrer dans l'arbre; **he only narrowly missed the target** il a manqué la cible de peu or de justesse; **narrow-minded** adj à l'esprit étroit, borné(e); (attitude) borné(e)

nasal ['neɪzl] adj nasal(e)

nasty ['nɑːstɪ] adj (person: malicious) méchant(e); (: rude) très désagréable; (smell) dégoûtant(e); (wound, situation) mauvais(e), vilain(e)

nation ['neɪʃən] n nation f

national ['næʃənl] adj national(e) ▷ n (abroad) ressortissant(e); (when home) national(e); **national anthem** n hymne national; **national dress** n costume national; **National Health Service** n (BRIT) service national de santé, ≈ Sécurité Sociale; **National Insurance** n (BRIT) ≈ Sécurité Sociale; **nationalist** adj, n nationaliste m/f; **nationality** [næʃəˈnælɪtɪ] n nationalité f; **nationalize** vt nationaliser; **national park** n parc national; **National Trust** n (BRIT) ≈ Caisse f nationale des monuments historiques et des sites

● **NATIONAL TRUST**

● Le **National Trust** est un organisme
● indépendant, à but non lucratif,
● dont la mission est de protéger et
● de mettre en valeur les monuments

● et les sites britanniques en raison
● de leur intérêt historique ou de leur
● beauté naturelle.

nationwide ['neɪʃənwaɪd] adj s'étendant à l'ensemble du pays; (problem) à l'échelle du pays entier

native ['neɪtɪv] n habitant(e) du pays, autochtone m/f ▷ adj du pays, indigène; (country) natal(e); (language) maternel(le); (ability) inné(e); **Native American** n Indien(ne) d'Amérique ▷ adj amérindien(ne); **native speaker** n locuteur natif

NATO ['neɪtəu] n abbr (= North Atlantic Treaty Organization) OTAN f

natural ['nætʃrəl] adj naturel(le); **natural gas** n gaz naturel; **natural history** n histoire naturelle; **naturally** adv naturellement; **natural resources** npl ressources naturelles

nature ['neɪtʃəʳ] n nature f; **by ~** par tempérament, de nature; **nature reserve** n (BRIT) réserve naturelle

naughty ['nɔːtɪ] adj (child) vilain(e), pas sage

nausea ['nɔːsɪə] n nausée f

naval ['neɪvl] adj naval(e)

navel ['neɪvl] n nombril m

navigate ['nævɪgeɪt] vt (steer) diriger, piloter ▷ vi naviguer; (Aut) indiquer la route à suivre; **navigation** [nævɪˈgeɪʃən] n navigation f

navy ['neɪvɪ] n marine f

navy-blue ['neɪvɪ'bluː] adj bleu marine inv

Nazi ['nɑːtsɪ] n Nazi(e)

NB abbr (= nota bene) NB

near [nɪəʳ] adj proche ▷ adv près ▷ prep (also: ~ **to**) près de ▷ vt approcher de; **in the ~ future** dans un proche avenir; **nearby** [nɪəˈbaɪ] adj proche ▷ adv tout près, à proximité; **nearly** adv presque; **I nearly fell** j'ai failli tomber; **it's not nearly big enough** ce n'est vraiment pas assez grand, c'est loin d'être assez grand; **near-sighted** adj myope

neat [niːt] adj (person, work) soigné(e);

(*room etc*) bien tenu(e) *or* rangé(e);
(*solution, plan*) habile; (*spirits*) pur(e);
neatly *adv* avec soin *or* ordre; (*skilfully*)
habilement

necessarily ['nɛsɪsrɪlɪ] *adv*
nécessairement; **not ~** pas
nécessairement *or* forcément

necessary ['nɛsɪsrɪ] *adj* nécessaire; **if ~**
si besoin est, le cas échéant

necessity [nɪ'sɛsɪtɪ] *n* nécessité *f*;
chose nécessaire *or* essentielle

neck [nɛk] *n* cou *m*; (*of horse, garment*)
encolure *f*; (*of bottle*) goulot *m*; **~ and ~** à
égalité; **necklace** ['nɛklɪs] *n* collier *m*;
necktie ['nɛktaɪ] *n* (*esp us*) cravate *f*

nectarine ['nɛktərɪn] *n* brugnon *m*,
nectarine *f*

need [niːd] *n* besoin *m* ▷ *vt* avoir besoin
de; **to ~ to do** devoir faire; avoir besoin
de faire; **you don't ~ to go** vous n'avez
pas besoin *or* vous n'êtes pas obligé
de partir; **a signature is ~ed** il faut
une signature; **there's no ~ to do ....**
il n'y a pas lieu de faire ..., il n'est pas
nécessaire de faire ...

needle ['niːdl] *n* aiguille *f* ▷ *vt* (*inf*)
asticoter, tourmenter

needless ['niːdlɪs] *adj* inutile; **~ to
say, ...** inutile de dire que ...

needlework ['niːdlwəːk] *n* (*activity*)
travaux *mpl* d'aiguille; (*object*)
ouvrage *m*

needn't ['niːdnt] = **need not**

needy ['niːdɪ] *adj* nécessiteux(-euse)

negative ['nɛgətɪv] *n* (*Phot, Elec*)
négatif *m*; (*Ling*) terme *m* de négation
▷ *adj* négatif(-ive)

neglect [nɪ'glɛkt] *vt* négliger; (*garden*)
ne pas entretenir; (*duty*) manquer à
▷ *n* (*of person, duty, garden*) le fait de
négliger; **(state of) ~** abandon *m*; **to ~
to do sth** négliger *or* omettre de faire
qch; **to ~ one's appearance** se négliger

negotiate [nɪ'gəʊʃɪeɪt] *vi* négocier ▷ *vt*
négocier; (*obstacle*) franchir, négocier;
to ~ with sb for sth négocier avec qn
en vue d'obtenir qch

egotiation [nɪgəʊʃɪ'eɪʃən] *n*

négociation *f*, pourparlers *mpl*

negotiator [nɪ'gəʊʃɪeɪtəʳ] *n*
négociateur(-trice)

neighbour (*us* **neighbor** *etc*) ['neɪbəʳ]
n voisin(e); **neighbourhood** *n* (*place*)
quartier *m*; (*people*) voisinage *m*;
neighbouring *adj* voisin(e),
avoisinant(e)

neither ['naɪðəʳ] *adj, pron* aucun(e)
(des deux), ni l'un(e) ni l'autre ▷ *conj*:
~ do I moi non plus ▷ *adv*: **~ good nor
bad** ni bon ni mauvais; **~ of them** ni
l'un ni l'autre

neon ['niːɔn] *n* néon *m*

Nepal [nɪ'pɔːl] *n* Népal *m*

nephew ['nɛvjuː] *n* neveu *m*

nerve [nəːv] *n* nerf *m*; (*bravery*) sang-
froid *m*, courage *m*; (*cheek*) aplomb *m*,
toupet *m*; **nerves** *npl* (*nervousness*)
nervosité *f*; **he gets on my ~s** il
m'énerve

nervous ['nəːvəs] *adj* nerveux(-euse);
(*anxious*) inquiet(-ète), plein(e)
d'appréhension; (*timid*) intimidé(e);
nervous breakdown *n* dépression
nerveuse

nest [nɛst] *n* nid *m* ▷ *vi* (se) nicher,
faire son nid

Net [nɛt] *n* (*Comput*): **the ~** (*Internet*)
le Net

net [nɛt] *n* filet *m*; (*fabric*) tulle *f* ▷ *adj*
net(te) ▷ *vt* (*fish etc*) prendre au filet;
netball *n* netball *m*

Netherlands ['nɛðələndz] *npl*: **the ~**
les Pays-Bas *mpl*

nett [nɛt] *adj* = **net**

nettle ['nɛtl] *n* ortie *f*

network ['nɛtwəːk] *n* réseau *m*

neurotic [njuə'rɔtɪk] *adj* névrosé(e)

neuter ['njuːtəʳ] *adj* neutre ▷ *vt* (*cat etc*)
châtrer, couper

neutral ['njuːtrəl] *adj* neutre ▷ *n* (*Aut*)
point mort

never ['nɛvəʳ] *adv* (ne ...) jamais; **I ~
went** je n'y suis pas allé; **I've ~ been to
Spain** je ne suis jamais allé en Espagne;
~ again plus jamais; **~ in my life** jamais
de ma vie; *see also* **mind**; **never-ending**

adj interminable; **nevertheless** [nɛvəðə'lɛs] *adv* néanmoins, malgré tout

new [njuː] *adj* nouveau (nouvelle); (*brand new*) neuf (neuve); **New Age** *n* New Age *m*; **newborn** *adj* nouveau-né(e); **newcomer** ['njuːkʌməʳ] *n* nouveau venu (nouvelle venue); **newly** *adv* nouvellement, récemment

news [njuːz] *n* nouvelle(s) *f(pl)*; (*Radio, TV*) informations *fpl*, actualités *fpl*; **a piece of ~** une nouvelle; **news agency** *n* agence *f* de presse; **newsagent** *n* (*BRIT*) marchand *m* de journaux; **newscaster** *n* (*Radio, TV*) présentateur(-trice); **news dealer** *n* (*US*) marchand *m* de journaux; **newsletter** *n* bulletin *m*; **newspaper** *n* journal *m*; **newsreader** *n* = **newscaster**

newt [njuːt] *n* triton *m*

New Year *n* Nouvel An; **Happy ~!** Bonne Année!; **New Year's Day** *n* le jour de l'An; **New Year's Eve** *n* la Saint-Sylvestre

New York [-'jɔːk] *n* New York

New Zealand [-'ziːlənd] *n* Nouvelle-Zélande *f*; **New Zealander** *n* Néo-Zélandais(e)

next [nɛkst] *adj* (*in time*) prochain(e); (*seat, room*) voisin(e), d'à côté; (*meeting, bus stop*) suivant(e) ▷ *adv* la fois suivante; la prochaine fois; (*afterwards*) ensuite; **~ to** *prep* à côté de; **~ to nothing** presque rien; **~ time** *adv* la prochaine fois; **the ~ day** le lendemain, le jour suivant *or* d'après; **~ year** l'année prochaine; **~ please!** (*at doctor's etc*) au suivant!; **the week after ~** dans deux semaines; **next door** *adv* à côté ▷ *adj* (*neighbour*) d'à côté; **next-of-kin** *n* parent *m* le plus proche

NHS *n abbr* (*BRIT*) = **National Health Service**

nibble ['nɪbl] *vt* grignoter

nice [naɪs] *adj* (*holiday, trip, taste*) agréable; (*flat, picture*) joli(e); (*person*) gentil(le); (*distinction, point*) subtil(e);

nicely *adv* agréablement; joliment; gentiment; subtilement

niche [niːʃ] *n* (*Archit*) niche *f*

nick [nɪk] *n* (*indentation*) encoche *f*; (*wound*) entaille *f*; (*BRIT inf*): **in good ~** en bon état ▷ *vt* (*cut*): **to ~ o.s.** se couper; (*inf: steal*) faucher, piquer; **in the ~ of time** juste à temps

nickel ['nɪkl] *n* nickel *m*; (*US*) pièce *f* de 5 cents

nickname ['nɪkneɪm] *n* surnom *m* ▷ *vt* surnommer

nicotine ['nɪkətiːn] *n* nicotine *f*

niece [niːs] *n* nièce *f*

Nigeria [naɪ'dʒɪərɪə] *n* Nigéria *m or f*

night [naɪt] *n* nuit *f*; (*evening*) soir *m*; **at ~** la nuit; **by ~** de nuit; **last ~** (*evening*) hier soir; (*night-time*) la nuit dernière; **night club** *n* boîte *f* de nuit; **nightdress** *n* chemise *f* de nuit; **nightie** ['naɪtɪ] *n* chemise *f* de nuit; **nightlife** *n* vie *f* nocturne; **nightly** *adj* (*news*) du soir; (*by night*) nocturne ▷ *adv* (*every evening*) tous les soirs; (*every night*) toutes les nuits; **nightmare** *n* cauchemar *m*; **night school** *n* cours *mpl* du soir; **night shift** *n* équipe *f* de nuit; **night-time** *n* nuit *f*

nil [nɪl] *n* (*BRIT Sport*) zéro *m*

nine [naɪn] *num* neuf; **nineteen** *num* dix-neuf; **nineteenth** [naɪn'tiːnθ] *num* dix-neuvième; **ninetieth** ['naɪntɪɪθ] *num* quatre-vingt-dixième; **ninety** *num* quatre-vingt-dix

ninth [naɪnθ] *num* neuvième

nip [nɪp] *vt* pincer ▷ *vi* (*BRIT inf*): **to ~ out/down/up** sortir/descendre/monter en vitesse

nipple ['nɪpl] *n* (*Anat*) mamelon *m*, bout *m* du sein

nitrogen ['naɪtrədʒən] *n* azote *m*

 KEYWORD

no [nəʊ] (*pl* **noes**) *adv* (*opposite of "yes"*) non; **are you coming? — no (I'm not)** est-ce que vous venez? — non; **would you like some more? — no thank you**

vous en voulez encore? — non merci
▷ *adj* (*not any*) (ne …) pas de, (ne …)
aucun(e); **no money/books** je
n'ai pas d'argent/de livres; **no student
would have done it** aucun étudiant ne
l'aurait fait; **"no smoking"** "défense de
fumer"; **"no dogs"** "les chiens ne sont
pas admis"
▷ *n* non *m*

nobility [nəuˈbɪlɪtɪ] *n* noblesse *f*
noble [ˈnəubl] *adj* noble
nobody [ˈnəubədɪ] *pron* (ne …)
personne
nod [nɔd] *vi* faire un signe de (la) tête
(*affirmatif ou amical*); (*sleep*) somnoler
▷ *vt*: **to ~ one's head** faire un signe de
(la) tête; (*in agreement*) faire signe que
oui ▷ *n* signe *m* de (la) tête; **nod off** *vi*
s'assoupir
noise [nɔɪz] *n* bruit *m*; **I can't sleep for
the ~** je n'arrive pas à dormir à cause du
bruit; **noisy** *adj* bruyant(e)
nominal [ˈnɔmɪnl] *adj* (*rent, fee*)
symbolique; (*value*) nominal(e)
nominate [ˈnɔmɪneɪt] *vt* (*propose*)
proposer; (*appoint*) nommer;
nomination [nɔmɪˈneɪʃən] *n*
nomination *f*; **nominee** [nɔmɪˈniː] *n*
candidat agréé; personne nommée
none [nʌn] *pron* aucun(e); **~ of you**
aucun d'entre vous, personne parmi
vous; **I have ~ left** je n'en ai plus; **he's
~ the worse for it** il ne s'en porte pas
plus mal
nonetheless [ˈnʌnðəˈles] *adv*
néanmoins
non-fiction [nɔnˈfɪkʃən] *n* littérature *f*
non-romanesque
nonsense [ˈnɔnsəns] *n* absurdités *fpl*,
idioties *fpl*; **~!** ne dites pas d'idioties!
non: **non-smoker** *n* non-fumeur *m*;
non-smoking *adj* non-fumeur; **non-
stick** *adj* qui n'attache pas
noodles [ˈnuːdlz] *npl* nouilles *fpl*
noon [nuːn] *n* midi *m*
no-one [ˈnəuwʌn] *pron* = **nobody**
nor [nɔːʳ] *conj* = **neither** ▷ *adv see*

neither
norm [nɔːm] *n* norme *f*
normal [ˈnɔːml] *adj* normal(e);
normally *adv* normalement
Normandy [ˈnɔːməndɪ] *n* Normandie *f*
north [nɔːθ] *n* nord *m* ▷ *adj* nord *inv*;
(*wind*) du nord ▷ *adv* au *or* vers le nord;
North Africa *n* Afrique *f* du Nord;
North African *adj* nord-africain(e),
d'Afrique du Nord ▷ *n* Nord-Africain(e);
North America *n* Amérique *f* du Nord;
North American *n* Nord-Américain(e)
▷ *adj* nord-américain(e), d'Amérique
du Nord; **northbound** [ˈnɔːθbaund]
adj (*traffic*) en direction du nord;
(*carriageway*) nord *inv*; **north-east** *n*
nord-est *m*; **northeastern** *adj* (du)
nord-est *inv*; **northern** [ˈnɔːðən] *adj*
du nord, septentrional(e); **Northern
Ireland** *n* Irlande *f* du Nord; **North
Korea** *n* Corée *f* du Nord; **North
Pole** *n*: **the North Pole** le pôle Nord;
North Sea *n*: **the North Sea** la mer
du Nord; **north-west** *n* nord-ouest *m*;
northwestern [ˈnɔːθˈwestən] *adj* (du)
nord-ouest *inv*
Norway [ˈnɔːweɪ] *n* Norvège *f*;
Norwegian [nɔːˈwiːdʒən] *adj*
norvégien(ne) ▷ *n* Norvégien(ne);
(*Ling*) norvégien *m*
nose [nəuz] *n* nez *m*; (*of dog, cat*)
museau *m*; (*fig*) flair *m*; **nose about,
nose around** *vi* fouiner *or* fureter
(partout); **nosebleed** *n* saignement *m*
de nez; **nosey** *adj* (*inf*) curieux(-euse)
nostalgia [nɔsˈtældʒɪə] *n* nostalgie *f*
nostalgic [nɔsˈtældʒɪk] *adj*
nostalgique
nostril [ˈnɔstrɪl] *n* narine *f*; (*of horse*)
naseau *m*
nosy [ˈnəuzɪ] (*inf*) *adj* = **nosey**
not [nɔt] *adv* (ne …) pas; **he is ~
here** il n'est pas ici; **you must ~** or
mustn't do that tu ne dois pas faire
ça; **I hope ~** j'espère que non; **~ at
all** pas du tout; (*after thanks*) de rien;
it's too late, isn't it? c'est trop tard,
n'est-ce pas?; **~ yet/now** pas encore/

maintenant; *see also* **only**
notable ['nəutəbl] *adj* notable;
notably *adv* (*particularly*) en
particulier; (*markedly*) spécialement
notch [nɔtʃ] *n* encoche *f*
note [nəut] *n* note *f*; (*letter*) mot *m*;
(*banknote*) billet *m* ▷ *vt* (*also*: **~ down**)
noter; (*notice*) constater; **notebook**
n carnet *m*; (*for shorthand etc*) bloc-
notes *m*; **noted** ['nəutɪd] *adj* réputé(e);
notepad *n* bloc-notes *m*; **notepaper** *n*
papier *m* à lettres
nothing ['nʌθɪŋ] *n* rien *m*; **he does ~** il
ne fait rien; **~ new** rien de nouveau; **for
~** (*free*) pour rien, gratuitement; (*in vain*)
pour rien; **~ at all** rien du tout; **~ much**
pas grand-chose
notice ['nəutɪs] *n* (*announcement,
warning*) avis *m* ▷ *vt* remarquer,
s'apercevoir de; **advance ~** préavis *m*;
at short ~ dans un délai très court;
until further ~ jusqu'à nouvel ordre;
to give ~, **hand in one's ~** (*employee*)
donner sa démission, démissionner;
to take ~ of prêter attention à; **to
bring sth to sb's ~** porter qch à la
connaissance de qn; **noticeable** *adj*
visible
notice board *n* (*BRIT*) panneau *m*
d'affichage
notify ['nəutɪfaɪ] *vt*: **to ~ sb of sth**
avertir qn de qch
notion ['nəuʃən] *n* idée *f*; (*concept*)
notion *f*; **notions** *npl* (*US*: *haberdashery*)
mercerie *f*
notorious [nəu'tɔːrɪəs] *adj* notoire
(*souvent en mal*)
notwithstanding [nɔtwɪθ'stændɪŋ]
adv néanmoins ▷ *prep* en dépit de
nought [nɔːt] *n* zéro *m*
noun [naun] *n* nom *m*
nourish ['nʌrɪʃ] *vt* nourrir;
nourishment *n* nourriture *f*
Nov. *abbr* (= *November*) nov
novel ['nɔvl] *n* roman *m* ▷ *adj* nouveau
(nouvelle), original(e); **novelist** *n*
romancier *m*; **novelty** *n* nouveauté *f*
November [nəu'vɛmbər] *n*

novembre *m*
novice ['nɔvɪs] *n* novice *m/f*
now [nau] *adv* maintenant ▷ *conj*: **~
(that)** maintenant (que); **right ~** tout
de suite; **by ~** à l'heure qu'il est; **just ~**:
that's the fashion just ~ c'est la mode
en ce moment or maintenant; **~ and
then**, **~ and again** de temps en temps;
from ~ on dorénavant; **nowadays**
['nauədeɪz] *adv* de nos jours
nowhere ['nəuwɛər] *adv* (ne ...)
nulle part
nozzle ['nɔzl] *n* (*of hose*) jet *m*, lance *f*;
(*of vacuum cleaner*) suceur *m*
nr *abbr* (*BRIT*) = **near**
nuclear ['njuːklɪər] *adj* nucléaire
nucleus (*pl* **nuclei**) ['njuːklɪəs,
'njuːklɪaɪ] *n* noyau *m*
nude [njuːd] *adj* nu(e) ▷ *n* (*Art*) nu *m*; **in
the ~** (tout(e)) nu(e)
nudge [nʌdʒ] *vt* donner un (petit) coup
de coude à
nudist ['njuːdɪst] *n* nudiste *m/f*
nudity ['njuːdɪtɪ] *n* nudité *f*
nuisance ['njuːsns] *n*: **it's a ~** c'est
(très) ennuyeux or gênant; **he's a ~** il est
assommant or casse-pieds; **what a ~!**
quelle barbe!
numb [nʌm] *adj* engourdi(e); (*with fear*)
paralysé(e)
number ['nʌmbər] *n* nombre *m*;
(*numeral*) chiffre *m*; (*of house, car,
telephone, newspaper*) numéro *m* ▷ *vt*
numéroter; (*amount to*) compter; **a ~
of** un certain nombre de; **they were
seven in ~** ils étaient (au nombre de)
sept; **to be ~ed among** compter parmi;
number plate *n* (*BRIT Aut*) plaque *f*
minéralogique or d'immatriculation;
Number Ten *n* (*BRIT*: 10 *Downing Street*)
résidence du Premier ministre
numerical [njuː'mɛrɪkl] *adj*
numérique
numerous ['njuːmərəs] *adj*
nombreux(-euse)
nun [nʌn] *n* religieuse *f*, sœur *f*
nurse [nəːs] *n* infirmière *f*; (*also*: **~maid**)
bonne *f* d'enfants ▷ *vt* (*patient, cold*)

soigner

nursery ['nə:sərɪ] n (room) nursery f; (institution) crèche f, garderie f; (for plants) pépinière f; **nursery rhyme** n comptine f, chansonnette f pour enfants; **nursery school** n école maternelle; **nursery slope** n (BRIT Ski) piste f pour débutants

nursing ['nə:sɪŋ] n (profession) profession f d'infirmière; (care) soins mpl; **nursing home** n clinique f; (for convalescence) maison f de convalescence or de repos; (for old people) maison de retraite

nurture ['nə:tʃə'] vt élever

nut [nʌt] n (of metal) écrou m; (fruit: walnut) noix f; (: hazelnut) noisette f; (: peanut) cacahuète f (terme générique en anglais)

nutmeg ['nʌtmɛg] n (noix f) muscade f

nutrient ['nju:trɪənt] n substance nutritive

nutrition [nju:'trɪʃən] n nutrition f, alimentation f

nutritious [nju:'trɪʃəs] adj nutritif(-ive), nourrissant(e)

nuts [nʌts] (inf) adj dingue

NVQ n abbr (BRIT) = **National Vocational Qualification**

nylon ['naɪlɔn] n nylon m ▷ adj de or en nylon

O

oak [əuk] n chêne m ▷ cpd de or en (bois de) chêne

O.A.P. n abbr (BRIT) = **old age pensioner**

oar [ɔ:'] n aviron m, rame f

oasis (pl **oases**) [əu'eɪsɪs, əu'eɪsi:z] n oasis f

oath [əuθ] n serment m; (swear word) juron m; **on** (BRIT) or **under ~** sous serment; assermenté(e)

oatmeal ['əutmi:l] n flocons mpl d'avoine

oats [əuts] n avoine f

obedience [ə'bi:dɪəns] n obéissance f

obedient [ə'bi:dɪənt] adj obéissant(e)

obese [əu'bi:s] adj obèse

obesity [əu'bi:sɪtɪ] n obésité f

obey [ə'beɪ] vt obéir à; (instructions, regulations) se conformer à ▷ vi obéir

obituary [ə'bɪtjuərɪ] n nécrologie f

object n ['ɔbdʒɪkt] objet m; (purpose) but m, objet; (Ling) complément m d'objet ▷ vi [əb'dʒɛkt]: **to ~ to** (attitude) désapprouver; (proposal) protester contre, élever une objection contre; **I ~!** je proteste!; **he ~ed that ...** il a fait valoir ora objecté que ...; **money is no ~** l'argent n'est pas un problème; **objection** [əb'dʒɛkʃən] n objection f; **if you have no objection** si vous n'y voyez pas d'inconvénient; **objective** n objectif m ▷ adj objectif(-ive)

obligation [ɔblɪ'ɡeɪʃən] n obligation f, devoir m; (debt) dette f (de reconnaissance)

obligatory [ə'blɪɡətərɪ] adj obligatoire

oblige [ə'blaɪdʒ] vt (force): **to ~ sb to do** obliger ou forcer qn à faire; (do a favour) rendre service à, obliger; **to be ~d to sb for sth** être obligé(e) à qn de qch

oblique [ə'bliːk] adj oblique; (allusion) indirect(e)

obliterate [ə'blɪtəreɪt] vt effacer

oblivious [ə'blɪvɪəs] adj: **~ of** oublieux(-euse) de

oblong [ɔ'blɔŋ] adj oblong(ue) ▷ n rectangle m

obnoxious [əb'nɔkʃəs] adj odieux(-euse); (smell) nauséabond(e)

oboe ['əubəu] n hautbois m

obscene [əb'siːn] adj obscène

obscure [əb'skjuər] adj obscur(e) ▷ vt obscurcir; (hide: sun) cacher

observant [əb'zəːvnt] adj observateur(-trice)

observation [ɔbzə'veɪʃən] n observation f; (by police etc) surveillance f

observatory [əb'zəːvətrɪ] n observatoire m

observe [əb'zəːv] vt observer; (remark) faire observer ou remarquer; **observer** n observateur(-trice)

obsess [əb'sɛs] vt obséder; **obsession** [əb'sɛʃən] n obsession f; **obsessive** adj obsédant(e)

obsolete ['ɔbsəliːt] adj dépassé(e), périmé(e)

obstacle ['ɔbstəkl] n obstacle m

obstinate ['ɔbstɪnɪt] adj obstiné(e); (pain, cold) persistant(e)

obstruct [əb'strʌkt] vt (block) boucher obstruer; (hinder) entraver; **obstruction** [əb'strʌkʃən] n obstruction f; (to plan, progress) obstacle m

obtain [əb'teɪn] vt obtenir

obvious ['ɔbvɪəs] adj évident(e), manifeste; **obviously** adv manifestement; (of course): **obviously!** bien sûr!; **obviously not!** évidemment pas!, bien sûr que non!

occasion [ə'keɪʒən] n occasion f; (event) événement m; **occasional** adj pris(e) (or fait(e) etc) de temps en temps; (worker, spending) occasionnel(le); **occasionally** adv de temps en temps, quelquefois

occult [ɔ'kʌlt] adj occulte ▷ n: **the ~** le surnaturel

occupant ['ɔkjupənt] n occupant m

occupation [ɔkju'peɪʃən] n occupation f; (job) métier m, profession f

occupy ['ɔkjupaɪ] vt occuper; **to ~ o.s. with** or **by doing** s'occuper à faire

occur [ə'kəːr] vi se produire; (difficulty, opportunity) se présenter; (phenomenon, error) se rencontrer; **to ~ to sb** venir à l'esprit de qn; **occurrence** [ə'kʌrəns] n (existence) présence f, existence f; (event) cas m, fait m

ocean ['əuʃən] n océan m

o'clock [ə'klɔk] adv: **it is 5 o'clock** il est 5 heures

Oct. abbr (= October) oct

October [ɔk'təubər] n octobre m

octopus ['ɔktəpəs] n pieuvre f

odd [ɔd] adj (strange) bizarre, curieux(-euse); (number) impair(e); (not of a set) dépareillé(e); **60-~** 60 et quelques; **at ~ times** de temps en temps; **the ~ one out** l'exception f; **oddly** adv bizarrement, curieusement **odds** npl (in betting) cote f; **it makes no odds** cela n'a pas d'importance; **odds and ends** de petites choses; **at odds** en désaccord

odometer [ɔ'dɔmɪtər] n (us) odomètre m

dour (US **odor**) [ˈəudəʳ] n odeur f

○ **KEYWORD**

of [ɔv, əv] prep 1 (gen) de; **a friend of ours** un de nos amis; **a boy of 10** un garçon de 10 ans; **that was kind of you** c'était gentil de votre part
2 (expressing quantity, amount, dates etc) de; **a kilo of flour** un kilo de farine; **how much of this do you need?** combien vous en faut-il?; **there were three of them** (people) ils étaient 3; (objects) il y en avait 3; **three of us went** 3 d'entre nous y sont allé(e)s; **the 5th of July** le 5 juillet; **a quarter of 4** (US) 4 heures moins le quart
3 (from, out of) en, de; **a statue of marble** une statue de or en marbre; **made of wood** (fait) de or en bois

off [ɔf] adj, adv (engine) coupé(e); (light, TV) éteint(e); (tap) fermé(e); (BRIT: food) mauvais(e), avancé(e); (: milk) tourné(e); (absent) absent(e); (cancelled) annulé(e); (removed): **the lid was ~** le couvercle était retiré or n'était pas mis; (away): **to run/drive ~** partir en courant/en voiture ▷ prep de; **to be ~** (to leave) partir, s'en aller; **to be ~ sick** être absent pour cause de maladie; **a day ~** un jour de congé; **to have an ~ day** n'être pas en forme; **he had his coat ~** il avait enlevé son manteau; **10% ~** (Comm) 10% de rabais; **5 km ~ the road**) à 5 km (de la route); **~ the coast** au large de la côte; **it's a long way ~** c'est loin (d'ici); **I'm ~ meat** je ne mange plus de viande; je n'aime plus la viande; **on the ~** chance à tout hasard; **~ and on, on and ~** de temps à autre

offence (US **offense**) [əˈfɛns] n (crime) délit m, infraction f; **to take ~ at** se vexer de, s'offenser de

offend [əˈfɛnd] vt (person) offenser, blesser; **offender** n délinquant(e); (against regulations) contrevenant(e)

offense [əˈfɛns] n (US) = **offence**

offensive [əˈfɛnsɪv] adj offensant(e), choquant(e); (smell etc) très déplaisant(e); (weapon) offensif(-ive) ▷ n (Mil) offensive f

offer [ˈɔfəʳ] n offre f, proposition f ▷ vt offrir, proposer; **"on ~"** (Comm) "en promotion"

offhand [ɔfˈhænd] adj désinvolte ▷ adv spontanément

office [ˈɔfɪs] n (place) bureau m; (position) charge f, fonction f; **doctor's ~** (US) cabinet (médical); **to take ~** entrer en fonctions; **office block** (US **office building**) n immeuble m de bureaux; **office hours** npl heures fpl de bureau; (US Med) heures de consultation

officer [ˈɔfɪsəʳ] n (Mil etc) officier m; (also: **police ~**) agent m (de police); (of organization) membre m du bureau directeur

office worker n employé(e) de bureau

official [əˈfɪʃl] adj (authorized) officiel(le) ▷ n officiel m; (civil servant) fonctionnaire m/f; (of railways, post office, town hall) employé(e)

off: **off-licence** n (BRIT: shop) débit m de vins et de spiritueux; **off-line** adj (Comput) (en mode) autonome; (: switched off) non connecté(e); **off-peak** adj aux heures creuses; (electricity, ticket) au tarif heures creuses; **off-putting** adj (BRIT: remark) rébarbatif(-ive); (person) rebutant(e), peu engageant(e); **off-season** adj, adv hors-saison inv

offset [ˈɔfsɛt] vt (irreg: like **set**) (counteract) contrebalancer, compenser

offshore [ɔfˈʃɔːʳ] adj (breeze) de terre; (island) proche du littoral; (fishing) côtier(-ière)

offside [ˈɔfsaɪd] adj (Sport) hors jeu; (Aut: in Britain) de droite; (: in US, Europe) de gauche

offspring [ˈɔfsprɪŋ] n progéniture f

often [ˈɔfn] adv souvent; **how ~ do you go?** vous y allez tous les combien?; **every so ~** de temps en temps, de temps à autre

oh [əu] *excl* ô!, oh!, ah!
oil [ɔɪl] *n* huile *f*; (*petroleum*) pétrole
m; (*for central heating*) mazout *m* ▷ *vt*
(*machine*) graisser; **oil filter** *n* (*Aut*)
filtre *m* à huile; **oil painting** *n* peinture
f à l'huile; **oil refinery** *n* raffinerie *f*
de pétrole; **oil rig** *n* derrick *m*; (*at sea*)
plate-forme pétrolière; **oil slick** *n*
nappe *f* de mazout; **oil tanker** *n* (*ship*)
pétrolier *m*; (*truck*) camion-citerne *m*;
oil well *n* puits *m* de pétrole; **oily** *adj*
huileux(-euse); (*food*) gras(se)
ointment ['ɔɪntmənt] *n* onguent *m*
O.K., okay ['əu'keɪ] (*inf*) *excl* d'accord!
▷ *vt* approuver, donner son accord à
▷ *adj* (*not bad*) pas mal; **is it O.K.?, are
you O.K.?** ça va?
old [əuld] *adj* vieux (vieille); (*person*)
vieux, âgé(e); (*former*) ancien(ne), vieux;
how ~ are you? quel âge avez-vous?;
he's 10 years ~ il a 10 ans, il est âgé de
10 ans; **~er brother/sister** frère/sœur
aîné(e); **old age** *n* vieillesse *f*; **old-
age pension** *n* (*BRIT*) (pension *f* de)
retraite *f* (*de la sécurité sociale*); **old-age
pensioner** *n* (*BRIT*) retraité(e); **old-
fashioned** *adj* démodé(e); (*person*)
vieux jeu *inv*; **old people's home** *n* (*esp
BRIT*) maison *f* de retraite
olive ['ɔlɪv] *n* (*fruit*) olive *f*; (*tree*) olivier
m ▷ *adj* (*also*: **~-green**) (vert) olive *inv*;
olive oil *n* huile *f* d'olive
Olympic [əu'lɪmpɪk] *adj* olympique;
the ~ Games, the ~s les Jeux *mpl*
olympiques
omelet(te) ['ɔmlɪt] *n* omelette *f*
omen ['əumən] *n* présage *m*
ominous ['ɔmɪnəs] *adj* menaçant(e),
inquiétant(e); (*event*) de mauvais
augure
omit [əu'mɪt] *vt* omettre

 KEYWORD

on [ɔn] *prep* **1** (*indicating position*) sur; **on
the table** sur la table; **on the wall** sur le
or au mur; **on the left** à gauche
2 (*indicating means, method, condition*

etc): **on foot** à pied; **on the train/plane**
(*be*) dans le train/l'avion; (*go*) en
train/avion; **on the telephone/radio/**
television au téléphone/à la radio/à la
télévision; **to be on drugs** se droguer;
on holiday (*BRIT*), **on vacation** (*US*)
en vacances
3 (*referring to time*): **on Friday** vendredi;
on Fridays le vendredi; **on June 20th** le
20 juin; **a week on Friday** vendredi en
huit; **on arrival** à l'arrivée; **on seeing
this** en voyant cela
4 (*about, concerning*) sur, de; **a book on
Balzac/physics** un livre sur Balzac/de
physique
▷ *adv* **1** (*referring to dress*): **to have one's
coat on** avoir (mis) son manteau;
to put one's coat on mettre son
manteau; **what's she got on?** qu'est-ce
qu'elle porte?
2 (*referring to covering*): **screw the lid on
tightly** vissez bien le couvercle
3 (*further, continuously*): **to walk** *etc* **on**
continuer à marcher *etc*; **from that day
on** depuis ce jour
▷ *adj* **1** (*in operation: machine*) en
marche; (: *radio, TV, light*) allumé(e);
(: *tap, gas*) ouvert(e); (: *brakes*) mis(e);
is the meeting still on? (*not cancelled*)
est-ce que la réunion a bien lieu?; (*in
progress*) la réunion dure-t-elle encore?;
when is this film on? quand passe
ce film?
2 (*inf*): **that's not on!** (*not acceptable*)
cela ne se fait pas!; (*not possible*) pas
question!

once [wʌns] *adv* une fois; (*formerly*)
autrefois ▷ *conj* une fois que + *sub*; **~ he
had left/it was done** une fois qu'il fut
parti/ que ce fut terminé; **at ~** tout de
suite, immédiatement; (*simultaneously*)
à la fois; **all at ~** *adv* tout d'un coup; **~
a week** une fois par semaine; **~ more**
encore une fois; **~ and for all** une fois
pour toutes; **~ upon a time there
was …** il y avait une fois …, il était
une fois …

oncoming [ˈɒnkʌmɪŋ] *adj* (*traffic*) venant en sens inverse

KEYWORD

one [wʌn] *num* un(e); **one hundred and fifty** cent cinquante; **one by one** un(e) à or par un(e); **one day** un jour
▷ *adj* **1** (*sole*) seul(e), unique; **the one book which** l'unique or le seul livre qui; **the one man who** le seul (homme) qui **2** (*same*) même; **they came in the one car** ils sont venus dans la même voiture
▷ *pron* **1**: **this one** celui-ci (celle-ci); **that one** celui-là (celle-là); **I've already got one/a red one** j'en ai déjà un(e)/un(e) rouge; **which one do you want?** lequel voulez-vous?
2: **one another** l'un(e) l'autre; **to look at one another** se regarder
3 (*impersonal*) on; **one never knows** on ne sait jamais; **to cut one's finger** se couper le doigt; **one needs to eat** il faut manger

one-off [wʌnˈɒf] (*BRIT inf*) *n* exemplaire *m* unique
oneself [wʌnˈsɛlf] *pron* se; (*after prep, also emphatic*) soi-même; **to hurt ~** se faire mal; **to keep sth for ~** garder qch pour soi; **to talk to ~** se parler à soi-même; **by ~** tout seul
one: **one-shot** [wʌnˈʃɒt] (*US*) *n* = **one-off**; **one-sided** *adj* (*argument, decision*) unilatéral(e); **one-to-one** *adj* (*relationship*) univoque; **one-way** *adj* (*street, traffic*) à sens unique
ongoing [ˈɒnɡəʊɪŋ] *adj* en cours; (*relationship*) suivi(e)
onion [ˈʌnjən] *n* oignon *m*
on-line [ˈɒnlaɪn] *adj* (*Comput*) en ligne; (: *switched on*) connecté(e)
onlooker [ˈɒnlʊkə^r] *n* spectateur(-trice)
only [ˈəʊnlɪ] *adv* seulement ▷ *adj* seul(e), unique ▷ *conj* seulement, mais; **an ~ child** un enfant unique; **not ~ ... but also** non seulement ... mais aussi; **I**

~ took one j'en ai seulement pris un, je n'en ai pris qu'un
on-screen [ɒnˈskriːn] *adj* à l'écran
onset [ˈɒnsɛt] *n* début *m*; (*of winter, old age*) approche *f*
onto [ˈɒntʊ] *prep* = **on to**
onward(s) [ˈɒnwəd(z)] *adv* (*move*) en avant; **from that time ~** à partir de ce moment
oops [ups] *excl* houp!
ooze [uːz] *vi* suinter
opaque [əʊˈpeɪk] *adj* opaque
open [ˈəʊpn] *adj* ouvert(e); (*car*) découvert(e); (*road, view*) dégagé(e); (*meeting*) public(-ique); (*admiration*) manifeste ▷ *vt* ouvrir ▷ *vi* (*flower, eyes, door, debate*) s'ouvrir; (*shop, bank, museum*) ouvrir; (*book etc: commence*) commencer, débuter; **is it ~ to public?** est-ce ouvert au public?; **what time do you ~?** à quelle heure ouvrez-vous?; **in the ~ (air)** en plein air; **open up** *vt* ouvrir; (*blocked road*) dégager ▷ *vi* s'ouvrir; **open-air** *adj* en plein air; **opening** *n* ouverture *f*; (*opportunity*) occasion *f*; (*work*) débouché *m*; (*job*) poste vacant; **opening hours** *npl* heures *fpl* d'ouverture; **open learning** *n* enseignement universitaire à la carte, notamment par correspondance; (*distance learning*) télé-enseignement *m*; **openly** *adv* ouvertement; **open-minded** *adj* à l'esprit ouvert; **open-necked** *adj* à col ouvert; **open-plan** *adj* sans cloisons; **Open University** *n* (*BRIT*) cours universitaires par correspondance

● **OPEN UNIVERSITY**
●
● L'**Open University** a été fondée en
● 1969. L'enseignement comprend
● des cours (certaines plages horaires
● sont réservées à cet effet à la
● télévision et à la radio), des devoirs
● qui sont envoyés par l'étudiant à son
● directeur ou sa directrice d'études, et
● un séjour obligatoire en université
● d'été. Il faut préparer un certain

- nombre d'unités de valeur pendant
- une période de temps déterminée
- et obtenir la moyenne à un certain
- nombre d'entre elles pour recevoir le
- diplôme visé.

opera ['ɔpərə] n opéra m; **opera house** n opéra m; **opera singer** n chanteur(-euse) d'opéra
operate ['ɔpəreɪt] vt (machine) faire marcher, faire fonctionner ▷ vi fonctionner; **to ~ on sb (for)** (Med) opérer qn (de)
operating room n (US: Med) salle f d'opération
operating theatre n (BRIT: Med) salle f d'opération
operation [ɔpə'reɪʃən] n opération f; (of machine) fonctionnement m; **to have an ~ (for)** se faire opérer (de); **to be in ~** (machine) être en service; (system) être en vigueur; **operational** adj opérationnel(le); (ready for use) en état de marche
operative ['ɔpərətɪv] adj (measure) en vigueur ▷ n (in factory) ouvrier(-ière)
operator ['ɔpəreɪtər] n (of machine) opérateur(-trice); (Tel) téléphoniste m/f
opinion [ə'pɪnjən] n opinion f, avis m; **in my ~** à mon avis; **opinion poll** n sondage m d'opinion
opponent [ə'pəunənt] n adversaire m/f
opportunity [ɔpə'tju:nɪtɪ] n occasion f; **to take the ~ to do** or **of doing** profiter de l'occasion pour faire
oppose [ə'pəuz] vt s'opposer à; **to be ~d to sth** être opposé(e) à qch; **as ~d to** par opposition à
opposite ['ɔpəzɪt] adj opposé(e); (house etc) d'en face ▷ adv en face ▷ prep en face de ▷ n opposé m, contraire m; (of word) contraire
opposition [ɔpə'zɪʃən] n opposition f
oppress [ə'prɛs] vt opprimer
opt [ɔpt] vi: **to ~ for** opter pour; **to ~ to do** choisir de faire; **opt out** vi: **to ~ out of** choisir de ne pas participer à or de

ne pas faire
optician [ɔp'tɪʃən] n opticien(ne)
optimism ['ɔptɪmɪzəm] n optimisme m
optimist ['ɔptɪmɪst] n optimiste m/f; **optimistic** [ɔptɪ'mɪstɪk] adj optimiste
optimum ['ɔptɪməm] adj optimum
option ['ɔpʃən] n choix m, option f; (Scol) matière f à option; **optional** adj facultatif(-ive)
or [ɔːr] conj ou; (with negative): **he hasn't seen or heard anything** il n'a rien vu ni entendu; **or else** sinon; ou bien
oral ['ɔːrəl] adj oral(e) ▷ n oral m
orange ['ɔrɪndʒ] n (fruit) orange f ▷ adj orange inv; **orange juice** n jus m d'orange; **orange squash** n orangeade f
orbit ['ɔːbɪt] n orbite f ▷ vt graviter autour de
orchard ['ɔːtʃəd] n verger m
orchestra ['ɔːkɪstrə] n orchestre m; (US: seating) (fauteuils mpl d')orchestre
orchid ['ɔːkɪd] n orchidée f
ordeal [ɔː'diːl] n épreuve f
order ['ɔːdər] n ordre m; (Comm) commande f ▷ vt ordonner; (Comm) commander; **in ~** en ordre; (of document) en règle; **out of ~** (not in correct order) en désordre; (machine) hors service; (telephone) en dérangement; **a machine in working ~** une machine en état de marche; **in ~ to do/that** pour faire/que + sub; **could I ~ now, please?** je peux commander, s'il vous plaît?; **to be on ~** être en commande; **to ~ sb to do** ordonner à qn de faire; **order form** n bon m de commande; **orderly** n (Mil) ordonnance f; (Med) garçon m de salle ▷ adj (room) en ordre; (mind) méthodique; (person) qui a de l'ordre
ordinary ['ɔːdnrɪ] adj ordinaire, normal(e); (pej) ordinaire, quelconque; **out of the ~** exceptionnel(le)
ore [ɔːr] n minerai m
oregano [ɔrɪ'gɑːnəu] n origan m
organ ['ɔːgən] n organe m; (Mus) orgue m, orgues fpl; **organic** [ɔː'gænɪk] adj

organique; (*crops etc*) biologique,
naturel(le); **organism** *n* organisme *m*

rganization [ɔːɡənaɪˈzeɪʃən] *n*
organisation *f*

rganize [ˈɔːɡənaɪz] *vt* organiser;
organized [ˈɔːɡənaɪzd] *adj* (*planned*)
organisé(e); (*efficient*) bien organisé;
organizer *n* organisateur(-trice)

rgasm [ˈɔːɡæzəm] *n* orgasme *m*

rgy [ˈɔːdʒɪ] *n* orgie *f*

riental [ɔːrɪˈɛntl] *adj* oriental(e)

rientation [ɔːrɪɛnˈteɪʃən] *n* (*attitudes*)
tendance *f*; (*in job*) orientation *f*; (*of
building*) orientation, exposition *f*

rigin [ˈɒrɪdʒɪn] *n* origine *f*

riginal [əˈrɪdʒɪnl] *adj* original(e);
(*earliest*) originel(le) ▷ *n* original *m*;
originally *adv* (*at first*) à l'origine

riginate [əˈrɪdʒɪneɪt] *vi*: **to ~ from**
être originaire de; (*suggestion*) provenir
de; **to ~ in** (*custom*) prendre naissance
dans, avoir son origine dans

rkney [ˈɔːknɪ] *n* (*also*: **the ~s, the ~
Islands**) les Orcades *fpl*

rnament [ˈɔːnəmənt] *n* ornement *m*;
(*trinket*) bibelot *m*; **ornamental**
[ɔːnəˈmɛntl] *adj* décoratif(-ive),
(*garden*) d'agrément

rnate [ɔːˈneɪt] *adj* très orné(e)

rphan [ˈɔːfn] *n* orphelin(e)

rthodox [ˈɔːθədɔks] *adj* orthodoxe

rthopaedic (*US* **orthopedic**)
[ɔːθəˈpiːdɪk] *adj* orthopédique

steopath [ˈɒstɪəpæθ] *n* ostéopathe
m/f

strich [ˈɒstrɪtʃ] *n* autruche *f*

ther [ˈʌðər] *adj* autre ▷ *pron*: **the ~
(one)** l'autre; **~s** (*other people*) d'autres
▷ *adv*: **~ than** autrement que; à part;
the ~ day l'autre jour; **otherwise** *adv*,
conj autrement

ttawa [ˈɒtəwə] *n* Ottawa

ter [ˈɒtər] *n* loutre *f*

uch [autʃ] *excl* aïe!

ght (*pt* **~**) [ɔːt] *aux vb*: **I ~ to do it** je
devrais le faire, il faudrait que je le
fasse; **this ~ to have been corrected**
cela aurait dû être corrigé; **he ~ to win**

(*probability*) il devrait gagner

ounce [auns] *n* once *f* (28.35g; 16 in
a pound)

our [ˈauər] *adj* notre, nos *pl*; *see also* **my**;
ours *pron* le (la) nôtre, les nôtres; *see
also* **mine¹**; **ourselves** *pron pl* (*reflexive,
after preposition*) nous; (*emphatic*) nous-
mêmes; *see also* **oneself**

oust [aust] *vt* évincer

out [aut] *adv* dehors; (*published, not at
home etc*) sorti(e); (*light, fire*) éteint(e); **~
there** là-bas; **he's ~** (*absent*) il est sorti;
to be ~ in one's calculations s'être
trompé dans ses calculs; **to run/back
etc ~** sortir en courant/en reculant
etc; **~ loud** *adv* à haute voix; **~ of** *prep*
(*outside*) en dehors de; (*because of: anger
etc*) par; (*from among*): **10 ~ of 10** sur
10; (*without*): **~ of petrol** sans essence,
à court d'essence; **~ of order** (*machine*)
en panne; (*Tel: line*) en dérangement;
outback *n* (*in Australia*) intérieur *m*;
outbound *adj*: **outbound (from/for)**
en partance (de/pour); **outbreak**
n (*of violence*) éruption *f*, explosion
f; (*of disease*) de nombreux cas; **the
outbreak of war south of the border**
la guerre qui s'est déclarée au sud de
la frontière; **outburst** *n* explosion *f*,
accès *m*; **outcast** *n* exilé(e); (*socially*)
paria *m*; **outcome** *n* issue *f*, résultat *m*;
outcry *n* tollé (général); **outdated** *adj*
démodé(e); **outdoor** *adj* de or en plein
air; **outdoors** *adv* dehors; au grand air

outer [ˈautər] *adj* extérieur(e); **outer
space** *n* espace *m* cosmique

outfit [ˈautfɪt] *n* (*clothes*) tenue *f*

out: **outgoing** *adj* (*president, tenant*)
sortant(e); (*character*) ouvert(e),
extraverti(e); **outgoings** *npl* (*BRIT:
expenses*) dépenses *fpl*; **outhouse** *n*
appentis *m*, remise *f*

outing [ˈautɪŋ] *n* sortie *f*, excursion *f*

out: **outlaw** *n* hors-la-loi *m inv* ▷ *vt*
(*person*) mettre hors la loi; (*practice*)
proscrire; **outlay** *n* dépenses *fpl*;
(*investment*) mise *f* de fonds; **outlet**
n (*for liquid etc*) issue *f*, sortie *f*; (*for*

emotion) exutoire m; (also: **retail outlet**) point m de vente; (us: Elec) prise f de courant; **outline** n (shape) contour m; (summary) esquisse f, grandes lignes ▷ vt (fig: theory, plan) exposer à grands traits; **outlook** n perspective f; (point of view) attitude f; **outnumber** vt surpasser en nombre; **out-of-date** adj (passport, ticket) périmé(e); (theory, idea) dépassé(e); (custom) désuet(-ète); (clothes) démodé(e); **out-of-doors** adv = **outdoors**; **out-of-the-way** adj loin de tout; **out-of-town** adj (shopping centre etc) en périphérie; **outpatient** n malade m/f en consultation externe; **outpost** n avant-poste m; **output** n rendement m, production f; (Comput) sortie f ▷ vt (Comput) sortir

outrage ['autreɪdʒ] n (anger) indignation f; (violent act) atrocité f, acte m de violence; (scandal) scandale m ▷ vt outrager; **outrageous** [aut'reɪdʒəs] adj atroce; (scandalous) scandaleux(-euse)

outright adv [aut'raɪt] complètement; (deny, refuse) catégoriquement; (ask) carrément; (kill) sur le coup ▷ adj ['autraɪt] complet(-ète); catégorique

outset ['autsɛt] n début m

outside [aut'saɪd] n extérieur m ▷ adj extérieur(e) ▷ adv (au) dehors, à l'extérieur ▷ prep hors de, à l'extérieur de; (in front of) devant; **at the ~** (fig) au plus or maximum; **outside lane** n (Aut: in Britain) voie f de droite; (: in US, Europe) voie de gauche; **outside line** n (Tel) ligne extérieure; **outsider** n (stranger) étranger(-ère)

out: outsize adj énorme; (clothes) grande taille inv; **outskirts** npl faubourgs mpl; **outspoken** adj très franc (franche); **outstanding** adj remarquable, exceptionnel(le); (unfinished: work, business) en suspens, en souffrance; (debt) impayé(e); (problem) non réglé(e)

outward ['autwəd] adj (sign, appearances) extérieur(e); (journey)

(d')aller; **outwards** adv (esp BRIT) = **outward**

outweigh [aut'weɪ] vt l'emporter sur

oval ['əuvl] adj, n ovale m

ovary ['əuvərɪ] n ovaire m

oven ['ʌvn] n four m; **oven glove** n gar m de cuisine; **ovenproof** adj allant au four; **oven-ready** adj prêt(e) à cuire

over ['əuvər] adv (par-)dessus ▷ adj (or adv) (finished) fini(e), terminé(e); (too much) en plus ▷ prep sur; par-dessus; (above) au-dessus de; (on the other side of) de l'autre côté de; (more than) plus de; (during) pendant; (about, concerning) **they fell out ~ money/her** ils se sont brouillés pour des questions d'argent/ cause d'elle; **~ here** ici; **~ there** là-bas; **all ~** (everywhere) partout; **~ and ~ (again)** à plusieurs reprises; **~ and above** en plus de; **to ask sb ~** inviter qu (à passer); **to fall ~** tomber; **to turn sth ~** retourner qch

overall ['əuvərɔ:l] adj (length) total(e); (study, impression) d'ensemble ▷ n (BRIT) blouse f ▷ adv [əuvər'ɔ:l] dans l'ensemble, en général; **overalls** npl (boiler suit) bleus mpl (de travail)

overboard ['əuvəbɔ:d] adv (Naut) par-dessus bord

overcame [əuvə'keɪm] pt of **overcome**

overcast ['əuvəkɑ:st] adj couvert(e)

overcharge [əuvə'tʃɑ:dʒ] vt: **to ~ sb fo sth** faire payer qch trop cher à qn

overcoat ['əuvəkəut] n pardessus m

overcome [əuvə'kʌm] vt (irreg: like **come**) (defeat) triompher de; (difficulty) surmonter ▷ adj (emotionally boulversé(e); **~ with grief** accablé(e) de douleur

over: overcrowded adj bondé(e); (city country) surpeuplé(e); **overdo** vt (irreg like **do**) exagérer; (overcook) trop cuire; **to overdo it, to overdo things** (work too hard) en faire trop, se surmener; **overdone** [əuvə'dʌn] adj (vegetables, steak) trop cuit(e); **overdose** n dose excessive; **overdraft** n découvert m;

overdrawn adj (account) à découvert; **overdue** adj en retard; (bill) impayé(e); (change) qui tarde; **overestimate** vt surestimer

overflow vi [əuvə'fləu] déborder ▷ n [əuvə'fləu] (also: ~ **pipe**) tuyau m d'écoulement, trop-plein m

overgrown [əuvə'grəun] adj (garden) envahi(e) par la végétation

overhaul vt [əuvə'hɔːl] réviser ▷ n ['əuvəhɔːl] révision f

overhead adv [əuvə'hɛd] au-dessus ▷ adj, n ['əuvəhɛd] ▷ adj aérien(ne); (lighting) vertical(e) ▷ n (US) = **overheads**; **overhead projector** n rétroprojecteur m; **overheads** npl (BRIT) frais généraux

over: **overhear** vt (irreg: like **hear**) entendre (par hasard); **overheat** vi (engine) chauffer; **overland** adj, adv par voie de terre; **overlap** vi se chevaucher; **overleaf** adv au verso; **overload** vt surcharger; **overlook** vt (have view of) donner sur; (miss) oublier, négliger; (forgive) fermer les yeux sur

overnight adv [əuvə'naɪt] (happen) durant la nuit, (fig) soudain ▷ adj ['əuvənaɪt] d'une (or de) nuit; soudain(e); **to stay ~ (with sb)** passer la nuit (chez qn); **overnight bag** n nécessaire m de voyage

overpass ['əuvəpɑːs] n (US: for cars) pont autoroutier; (: for pedestrians) passerelle f, pont m

overpower [əuvə'pauə'] vt vaincre; (fig) accabler; **overpowering** adj irrésistible; (heat, stench) suffocant(e)

over: **overreact** [əuvəriː'ækt] vi réagir de façon excessive; **overrule** vt (decision) annuler; (claim) rejeter; (person) rejeter l'avis de; **overrun** vt (irreg: like **run**) (Mil: country etc) occuper; (time limit etc) dépasser le temps imparti

overseas [əuvə'siːz] adv outre-mer; (abroad) à l'étranger ▷ adj (trade) extérieur(e); (visitor) étranger(-ère)

oversee [əuvə'siː] vt (irreg: like **see**)

surveiller

overshadow [əuvə'ʃædəu] vt (fig) éclipser

oversight ['əuvəsaɪt] n omission f, oubli m

oversleep [əuvə'sliːp] vi (irreg: like **sleep**) se réveiller (trop) tard

overspend [əuvə'spɛnd] vi (irreg: like **spend**) dépenser de trop

overt [əu'vəːt] adj non dissimulé(e)

overtake [əuvə'teɪk] vt (irreg: like **take**) dépasser; (BRIT: Aut) dépasser, doubler

over: **overthrow** vt (irreg: like **throw**) (government) renverser; **overtime** n heures fpl supplémentaires

overtook [əuvə'tuk] pt of **overtake**

over: **overturn** vt renverser; (decision, plan) annuler ▷ vi se retourner; **overweight** adj (person) trop gros(se); **overwhelm** vt (subj: emotion) accabler, submerger; (enemy, opponent) écraser; **overwhelming** adj (victory, defeat) écrasant(e); (desire) irrésistible

ow [au] excl aïe!

owe [əu] vt devoir; **to ~ sb sth, to ~ sth to sb** devoir qch à qn; **how much do I ~ you?** combien est-ce que je vous dois?; **owing to** prep à cause de, en raison de

owl [aul] n hibou m

own [əun] vt posséder ▷ adj propre; **a room of my ~** une chambre à moi, ma propre chambre; **to get one's ~ back** prendre sa revanche; **on one's ~** tout(e) seul(e); **own up** vi avouer; **owner** n propriétaire m/f; **ownership** n possession f

ox (pl **oxen**) [ɔks, 'ɔksn] n bœuf m

Oxbridge ['ɔksbrɪdʒ] (BRIT) les universités d'Oxford et de Cambridge

oxen ['ɔksən] npl of **ox**

oxygen ['ɔksɪdʒən] n oxygène m

oyster ['ɔɪstə'] n huître f

oz. abbr = **ounce(s)**

ozone ['əuzəun] n ozone m; **ozone friendly** adj qui n'attaque pas or qui préserve la couche d'ozone; **ozone layer** n couche f d'ozone

P

p *abbr* (*BRIT*) = **penny**; **pence**

P.A. *n abbr* = **personal assistant**; **public address system**

p.a. *abbr* = **per annum**

pace [peɪs] *n* pas *m*; (*speed*) allure *f*; vitesse *f* ▷ *vi*: **to ~ up and down** faire les cent pas; **to keep ~ with** aller à la même vitesse que; (*events*) se tenir au courant de; **pacemaker** *n* (*Med*) stimulateur *m* cardiaque; (*Sport: also:* **pacesetter**) meneur(-euse) de train

Pacific [pə'sɪfɪk] *n*: **the ~ (Ocean)** le Pacifique, l'océan *m* Pacifique

pacifier ['pæsɪfaɪəʳ] *n* (*US: dummy*) tétine *f*

pack [pæk] *n* paquet *m*; (*of hounds*) meute *f*; (*of thieves, wolves etc*) bande *f*; (*of cards*) jeu *m*; (*US: of cigarettes*) paquet; (*back pack*) sac *m* à dos ▷ *vt* (*goods*) empaqueter, emballer; (*in suitcase etc*) emballer; (*box*) remplir; (*cram*) entasser ▷ *vi*: **to ~ (one's bags)** faire ses bagages; **pack in** (*BRIT inf*) ▷ *vi* (*machine*) tomber en panne ▷ *vt* (*boyfriend*) plaquer; **~ it in!** laisse tomber!; **pack off** *vt*: **to ~ sb off to** expédier qn à; **pack up** *vi* (*BRIT inf: machine*) tomber en panne; (: *person*) se tirer ▷ *vt* (*belongings*) ranger; (*goods, presents*) empaqueter, emballer

package ['pækɪdʒ] *n* paquet *m*; (*also:* **~ deal**: *agreement*) marché global; (: *purchase*) forfait *m*; (*Comput*) progiciel *m* ▷ *vt* (*goods*) conditionner; **package holiday** *n* (*BRIT*) vacances organisées; **package tour** *n* voyage organisé

packaging ['pækɪdʒɪŋ] *n* (*wrapping materials*) emballage *m*

packed [pækt] *adj* (*crowded*) bondé(e); **packed lunch** (*BRIT*) *n* repas froid

packet ['pækɪt] *n* paquet *m*

packing ['pækɪŋ] *n* emballage *m*

pact [pækt] *n* pacte *m*, traité *m*

pad [pæd] *n* bloc(-notes *m*) *m*; (*to prevent friction*) tampon *m* ▷ *vt* rembourrer; **padded** *adj* (*jacket*) matelassé(e); (*bra*) rembourré(e)

paddle ['pædl] *n* (*oar*) pagaie *f*; (*US: for table tennis*) raquette *f* de ping-pong ▷ *vi* (*with feet*) barboter, faire trempette ▷ *vt*: **to ~ a canoe** *etc* pagayer; **paddling pool** *n* petit bassin

paddock ['pædək] *n* enclos *m*; (*Racing*) paddock *m*

padlock ['pædlɔk] *n* cadenas *m*

paedophile (*US* **pedophile**) ['piːdəʊfaɪl] *n* pédophile *m*

page [peɪdʒ] *n* (*of book*) page *f*; (*also:* **~ boy**) groom *m*, chasseur *m*; (*at wedding*) garçon *m* d'honneur ▷ *vt* (*in hotel etc*) (faire) appeler

pager ['peɪdʒəʳ] *n* bip *m* (*inf*), Alphapage® *m*

paid [peɪd] *pt, pp of* **pay** ▷ *adj* (*work, official*) rémunéré(e); (*holiday*) payé(e); **to put ~ to** (*BRIT*) mettre fin à, mettre par terre

pain [peɪn] *n* douleur *f*; (*inf: nuisance*) plaie *f*; **to be in ~** souffrir, avoir mal; **to take ~s to do** se donner du mal pour faire; **painful** *adj* douloureux(-euse); (*difficult*) difficile, pénible; **painkiller**

n calmant *m*, analgésique *m*;
painstaking ['peɪnzteɪkɪŋ] *adj* (*person*) soigneux(-euse); (*work*) soigné(e)

paint [peɪnt] *n* peinture *f* ▷ *vt* peindre; **to ~ the door blue** peindre la porte en bleu; **paintbrush** *n* pinceau *m*; **painter** *n* peintre *m*; **painting** *n* peinture *f*; (*picture*) tableau *m*

pair [pɛəʳ] *n* (*of shoes, gloves etc*) paire *f*; (*of people*) couple *m*; **~ of scissors** (paire *f*) ciseaux *mpl*; **~ of trousers** pantalon *m*

pajamas [pə'dʒɑːməz] *npl* (*us*) pyjama(s) *m*(*pl*)

Pakistan [pɑːkɪ'stɑːn] *n* Pakistan *m*; **Pakistani** *adj* pakistanais(e) ▷ *n* Pakistanais(e)

pal [pæl] *n* (*inf*) copain (copine)

palace ['pæləs] *n* palais *m*

pale [peɪl] *adj* pâle; **~ blue** *adj* bleu pâle *inv*

Palestine ['pælɪstaɪn] *n* Palestine *f*; **Palestinian** [pælɪs'tɪnɪən] *adj* palestinien(ne) ▷ *n* Palestinien(ne)

palm [pɑːm] *n* (*Anat*) paume *f*; (*also*: **~ tree**) palmier *m* ▷ *vt*: **to ~ sth off on sb** (*inf*) refiler qch à qn

pamper ['pæmpəʳ] *vt* gâter, dorloter

pamphlet ['pæmflət] *n* brochure *f*

pan [pæn] *n* (*also*: **sauce~**) casserole *f*; (*also*: **frying ~**) poêle *f*

pancake ['pænkeɪk] *n* crêpe *f*

panda ['pændə] *n* panda *m*

pane [peɪn] *n* carreau *m* (de fenêtre), vitre *f*

panel ['pænl] *n* (*of wood, cloth etc*) panneau *m*; (*Radio, TV*) panel *m*, invités *mpl*; (*for interview, exams*) jury *m*

panhandler ['pænhændləʳ] *n* (*us inf*) mendiant(e)

panic ['pænɪk] *n* panique *f*, affolement *m* ▷ *vi* s'affoler, paniquer

panorama [pænə'rɑːmə] *n* panorama *m*

pansy ['pænzɪ] *n* (*Bot*) pensée *f*

pant [pænt] *vi* haleter

panther ['pænθəʳ] *n* panthère *f*

panties ['pæntɪz] *npl* slip *m*, culotte *f*

pantomime ['pæntəmaɪm] *n* (*BRIT*) spectacle *m* de Noël; *voir encadré*

● **PANTOMIME**
●
● Une **pantomime** (à ne pas confondre
● avec le mot tel qu'on l'utilise en
● français), que l'on appelle également
● de façon familière "panto", est un
● genre de farce où le personnage
● principal est souvent un jeune
● garçon et où il y a toujours une
● "dame", c'est-à-dire une vieille
● femme jouée par un homme, et
● un méchant. La plupart du temps,
● l'histoire est basée sur un conte de
● fées comme Cendrillon ou Le Chat
● botté, et le public est encouragé
● à participer en prévenant le héros
● d'un danger imminent. Ce genre de
● spectacle, qui s'adresse surtout aux
● enfants, vise également un public
● d'adultes au travers des nombreuses
● plaisanteries faisant allusion à des
● faits d'actualité.

pants [pænts] *n* (*BRIT*: *woman's*) culotte *f*, slip *m*; (: *man's*) slip, caleçon *m*; (*us*: *trousers*) pantalon *m*

pantyhose ['pæntɪhəʊz] (*us*) *npl* collant *m*

paper ['peɪpəʳ] *n* papier *m*; (*also*: **wall~**) papier peint; (*also*: **news~**) journal *m*; (*academic essay*) article *m*; (*exam*) épreuve écrite ▷ *adj* en ou de papier ▷ *vt* tapisser (de papier peint); **papers** *npl* (*also*: **identity ~s**) papiers *mpl* (d'identité); **paperback** *n* livre broché ou non relié; (*small*) livre *m* de poche; **paper bag** *n* sac *m* en papier; **paper clip** *n* trombone *m*; **paper shop** *n* (*BRIT*) marchand *m* de journaux; **paperwork** *n* papiers *mpl*; (*pej*) paperasserie *f*

paprika ['pæprɪkə] *n* paprika *m*

par [pɑːʳ] *n* pair *m*; (*Golf*) normale *f* du parcours; **on a ~ with** à égalité avec, au même niveau que

paracetamol [pærə'si:təmɔl] (BRIT) n
paracétamol m

parachute ['pærəʃu:t] n parachute m

parade [pə'reɪd] n défilé m ▷ vt (fig)
faire étalage de ▷ vi défiler

paradise ['pærədaɪs] n paradis m

paradox ['pærədɔks] n paradoxe m

paraffin ['pærəfɪn] n (BRIT): **~ (oil)**
pétrole (lampant)

paragraph ['pærəgrɑ:f] n
paragraphe m

parallel ['pærəlɛl] adj: **~ (with or to)**
parallèle (à); (fig) analogue (à) ▷ n (line)
parallèle f; (fig, Geo) parallèle m

paralysed ['pærəlaɪzd] adj paralysé(e)

paralysis (pl **paralyses**) [pə'rælɪsɪs,
-si:z] n paralysie f

paramedic [pærə'mɛdɪk] n auxiliaire
m/f médical m

paranoid ['pærənɔɪd] adj (Psych)
paranoïaque; (neurotic) paranoïde

parasite ['pærəsaɪt] n parasite m

parcel ['pɑ:sl] n paquet m, colis m ▷ vt
(also: **~ up**) empaqueter

pardon ['pɑ:dn] n pardon m; (Law)
grâce f ▷ vt pardonner à; (Law) gracier;
~! pardon!; **~ me!** (after burping etc)
excusez-moi!; **I beg your ~!** (I'm sorry)
pardon!, je suis désolé!; **(I beg your) ~?**,
(US) **~ me?** (what did you say?) pardon?

parent ['pɛərənt] n (father) père
m; (mother) mère f; **parents** npl
parents mpl; **parental** [pə'rɛntl] adj
parental(e), des parents

Paris ['pærɪs] n Paris

parish ['pærɪʃ] n paroisse f; (BRIT: civil)
≈ commune f

Parisian [pə'rɪzɪən] adj parisien(ne), de
Paris ▷ n Parisien(ne)

park [pɑ:k] n parc m, jardin public ▷ vt
garer ▷ vi se garer; **can I ~ here?** est-ce
que je peux me garer ici?

parking ['pɑ:kɪŋ] n stationnement
m; **"no ~"** "stationnement interdit";
parking lot n (US) parking m, parc m
de stationnement; **parking meter**
n parc(o)mètre m; **parking ticket**
n P.-V. m

▌ Be careful not to translate *parking*
by the French word *parking*.

parkway ['pɑ:kweɪ] n (US) route f
express (en site vert ou aménagé)

parliament ['pɑ:ləmənt] n
parlement m; **parliamentary**
[pɑ:lə'mɛntərɪ] adj parlementaire

Parmesan [pɑ:mɪ'zæn] n (also: **~
cheese**) Parmesan m

parole [pə'rəʊl] n: **on ~** en liberté
conditionnelle

parrot ['pærət] n perroquet m

parsley ['pɑ:slɪ] n persil m

parsnip ['pɑ:snɪp] n panais m

parson ['pɑ:sn] n ecclésiastique m;
(Church of England) pasteur m

part [pɑ:t] n partie f; (of machine) pièce
f; (Theat etc) rôle m; (of serial) épisode
m; (US: in hair) raie f ▷ adv = **partly** ▷ vt
séparer ▷ vi (people) se séparer; (crowd)
s'ouvrir; **to take ~ in** participer à,
prendre part à; **to take sb's ~** prendre
le parti de qn, prendre parti pour qn;
for my ~ en ce qui me concerne; **for
the most ~** en grande partie; dans la
plupart des cas; **in ~** en partie; **to take
sth in good/bad ~** prendre qch du
bon/mauvais côté; **part with** vt fus
(person) se séparer de; (possessions) se
défaire de

partial ['pɑ:ʃl] adj (incomplete)
partiel(le); **to be ~ to** aimer, avoir un
faible pour

participant [pɑ:'tɪsɪpənt] n (in
competition, campaign) participant(e)

participate [pɑ:'tɪsɪpeɪt] vi: **to ~ (in)**
participer (à), prendre part (à)

particle ['pɑ:tɪkl] n particule f; (of
dust) grain m

particular [pə'tɪkjʊlə^r] adj (specific)
particulier(-ière); (special) particulier,
spécial(e); (fussy) difficile, exigeant(e);
(careful) méticuleux(-euse); **in ~** en
particulier, surtout; **particularly** adv
particulièrement; (in particular) en
particulier; **particulars** npl détails mpl
(information) renseignements mpl

parting ['pɑ:tɪŋ] n séparation f; (BRIT:

in hair) raie f

partition [pɑːˈtɪʃən] *n (Pol)* partition f, division f; *(wall)* cloison f

partly [ˈpɑːtlɪ] *adv* en partie, partiellement

partner [ˈpɑːtnər] *n (Comm)* associé(e); *(Sport)* partenaire m/f; *(spouse)* conjoint(e); *(lover)* ami(e); *(at dance)* cavalier(-ière); **partnership** *n* association f

part of speech *n (Ling)* partie f du discours

partridge [ˈpɑːtrɪdʒ] *n* perdrix f

part-time [ˈpɑːtˈtaɪm] *adj, adv* à mi-temps, à temps partiel

party [ˈpɑːtɪ] *n (Pol)* parti m; *(celebration)* fête f; *(: formal)* réception f; *(: in evening)* soirée f; *(group)* groupe m; *(Law)* partie f

pass [pɑːs] *vt (time, object)* passer; *(place)* passer devant; *(friend)* croiser; *(exam)* être reçu(e) à, réussir; *(overtake)* dépasser; *(approve)* approuver, accepter ▷ *vi* passer; *(Scol)* être reçu(e) or admis(e), réussir ▷ *n (permit)* laissez-passer m inv; *(membership card)* carte f d'accès or d'abonnement; *(in mountains)* col m; *(Sport)* passe f; *(Scol: also:* **~ mark**): **to get a ~** être reçu(e) (sans mention); **to ~ sb sth** passer qch à qn; **could you ~ the salt/oil, please?** pouvez-vous me passer le sel/l'huile, s'il vous plaît?; **to make a ~ at sb** *(inf)* faire des avances à qn; **pass away** *vi* mourir; **pass by** *vi* passer ▷ *vt (ignore)* négliger; **pass on** *vt (hand on)*: **to ~ on (to)** transmettre (à); **pass out** *vi* s'évanouir; **pass over** *vt (ignore)* passer sous silence; **pass up** *vt (opportunity)* laisser passer; **passable** *adj (road)* praticable; *(work)* acceptable

Be careful not to translate *to pass an exam* by the French expression *passer un examen*.

passage [ˈpæsɪdʒ] *n (also:* **~way**) couloir m; *(gen, in book)* passage m; *(by boat)* traversée f

passenger [ˈpæsɪndʒər] *n* passager(-ère)

passer-by [pæsəˈbaɪ] *n* passant(e)

passing place *n (Aut)* aire f de croisement

passion [ˈpæʃən] *n* passion f; **passionate** *adj* passionné(e); **passion fruit** *n* fruit m de la passion

passive [ˈpæsɪv] *adj (also Ling)* passif(-ive)

passport [ˈpɑːspɔːt] *n* passeport m; **passport control** *n* contrôle m des passeports; **passport office** *n* bureau m de délivrance des passeports

password [ˈpɑːswəːd] *n* mot m de passe

past [pɑːst] *prep (in front of)* devant; *(further than)* au delà de, plus loin que; après; *(later than)* après ▷ *adv*: **to run ~** passer en courant ▷ *adj* passé(e); *(president etc)* ancien(ne) ▷ *n* passé m; **he's ~ forty** il a dépassé la quarantaine, il a plus de or passé quarante ans; **ten/quarter ~ eight** huit heures dix/un or et quart; **for the ~ few/3 days** depuis quelques/3 jours; ces derniers/3 derniers jours

pasta [ˈpæstə] *n* pâtes fpl

paste [peɪst] *n* pâte f; *(Culin: meat)* pâté m *(à tartiner)*; *(: tomato)* purée f, concentré m; *(glue)* colle f *(de pâte)* ▷ *vt* coller

pastel [ˈpæstl] *adj* pastel inv ▷ *n (Art: pencil)* crayon m) pastel m; *(: drawing)* (dessin m au) pastel; *(colour)* ton m pastel inv

pasteurized [ˈpæstəraɪzd] *adj* pasteurisé(e)

pastime [ˈpɑːstaɪm] *n* passe-temps m inv, distraction f

pastor [ˈpɑːstər] *n* pasteur m

past participle [-ˈpɑːtɪsɪpl] *n (Ling)* participe passé

pastry [ˈpeɪstrɪ] *n* pâte f; *(cake)* pâtisserie f

pasture [ˈpɑːstʃər] *n* pâturage m

pasty¹ *n* [ˈpæstɪ] petit pâté (en croûte)

pasty² [ˈpeɪstɪ] *adj (complexion)* terreux(-euse)

pat [pæt] *vt* donner une petite tape à; *(dog)* caresser

patch [pætʃ] n (of material) pièce f; (eye patch) cache m; (spot) tache f; (of land) parcelle f; (on tyre) rustine f ▷ vt (clothes) rapiécer; **a bad ~** (BRIT) une période difficile; **patchy** adj inégal(e); (incomplete) fragmentaire

pâté ['pæteɪ] n pâté m, terrine f

patent ['peɪtnt, US 'pætnt] n brevet m (d'invention) ▷ vt faire breveter ▷ adj patent(e), manifeste

paternal [pə'tə:nl] adj paternel(le)

paternity leave [pə'tə:nɪtɪ-] n congé m de paternité

path [pɑ:θ] n chemin m, sentier m; (in garden) allée f; (of missile) trajectoire f

pathetic [pə'θɛtɪk] adj (pitiful) pitoyable; (very bad) lamentable, minable

pathway ['pɑ:θweɪ] n chemin m, sentier m; (in garden) allée f

patience ['peɪʃns] n patience f; (BRIT: Cards) réussite f

patient ['peɪʃnt] n malade m/f; (of dentist etc) patient(e) ▷ adj patient(e)

patio ['pætɪəu] n patio m

patriotic [pætrɪ'ɔtɪk] adj patriotique; (person) patriote

patrol [pə'trəul] n patrouille f ▷ vt patrouiller dans; **patrol car** n voiture f de police

patron ['peɪtrən] n (in shop) client(e); (of charity) patron(ne); **~ of the arts** mécène m

patronizing ['pætrənaɪzɪŋ] adj condescendant(e)

pattern ['pætən] n (Sewing) patron m; (design) motif m; **patterned** adj à motifs

pause [pɔ:z] n pause f, arrêt m ▷ vi faire une pause, s'arrêter

pave [peɪv] vt paver, daller; **to ~ the way for** ouvrir la voie à

pavement ['peɪvmənt] n (BRIT) trottoir m; (US) chaussée f

pavilion [pə'vɪlɪən] n pavillon m; (Sport) stand m

paving ['peɪvɪŋ] n (material) pavé m, dalle f

paw [pɔ:] n patte f

pawn [pɔ:n] n (Chess, also fig) pion m ▷ vt mettre en gage; **pawnbroker** n prêteur m sur gages

pay [peɪ] n salaire m; (of manual worker) paie f ▷ vb (pt, pp **paid**) ▷ vt payer ▷ vi payer; (be profitable) être rentable; **can I ~ by credit card?** est-ce que je peux payer par carte de crédit?; **to ~ attention (to)** prêter attention (à); **to ~ sb a visit** rendre visite à qn; **to ~ one's respects to sb** présenter ses respects à qn; **pay back** vt rembourser; **pay for** vt fus payer; **pay in** vt verser; **pay off** vt (debts) régler, acquitter; (person) rembourser ▷ vi (scheme, decision) se révéler payant(e); **pay out** vt (money) payer, sortir de sa poche; **pay up** vt (amount) payer; **payable** adj payable; **to make a cheque payable to sb** établir un chèque à l'ordre de qn; **pay day** n jour m de paie; **pay envelope** n (US) paie f; **payment** n paiement m; (of bill) règlement m; (of deposit, cheque) versement m; **monthly payment** mensualité f; **payout** n (from insurance) dédommagement m; (in competition) prix m; **pay packet** n (BRIT) paie f; **pay phone** n cabine f téléphonique, téléphone public; **pay raise** n (US) = **pay rise**; **pay rise** n (BRIT) augmentation f (de salaire); **payroll** n registre m du personnel; **pay slip** n (BRIT) bulletin m de paie, feuille f de paie; **pay television** n chaînes fpl payantes

PC n abbr = **personal computer**; (BRIT) = **police constable** ▷ adj abbr = **politically correct**

p.c. abbr = **per cent**

PDA n abbr (= personal digital assistant) agenda m électronique

PE n abbr (= physical education) EPS f

pea [pi:] n (petit) pois

peace [pi:s] n paix f; (calm) calme m, tranquillité f; **peaceful** adj paisible, calme

peach [pi:tʃ] n pêche f

peacock ['pi:kɔk] n paon m
peak [pi:k] n (mountain) pic m, cime f; (of cap) visière f; (fig: highest level) maximum m; (: of career, fame) apogée m; **peak hours** npl heures fpl d'affluence or de pointe
peanut ['pi:nʌt] n arachide f, cacahuète f; **peanut butter** n beurre m de cacahuète
pear [pεəʳ] n poire f
pearl [pə:l] n perle f
peasant ['pεznt] n paysan(ne)
peat [pi:t] n tourbe f
pebble ['pεbl] n galet m, caillou m
peck [pεk] vt (also: ~ at) donner un coup de bec à; (food) picorer ▷ n coup m de bec; (kiss) bécot m; **peckish** adj (BRIT inf): **I feel peckish** je mangerais bien quelque chose, j'ai la dent
peculiar [pɪ'kju:lɪəʳ] adj (odd) étrange, bizarre, curieux(-euse); (particular) particulier(-ière); **~ to** particulier à
pedal ['pεdl] n pédale f ▷ vi pédaler
pedalo ['pεdələu] n pédalo m
pedestal ['pεdəstl] n piédestal m
pedestrian [pɪ'dεstrɪən] n piéton m; **pedestrian crossing** n (BRIT) passage clouté; **pedestrianized** adj: **a pedestrianized street** une rue piétonne; **pedestrian precinct** (US **pedestrian zone**) n (BRIT) zone piétonne
pedigree ['pεdɪgri:] n ascendance f; (of animal) pedigree m ▷ cpd (animal) de race
pedophile ['pi:dəufaɪl] (US) n = **paedophile**
pee [pi:] vi (inf) faire pipi, pisser
peek [pi:k] vi jeter un coup d'œil (furtif)
peel [pi:l] n pelure f, épluchure f; (of orange, lemon) écorce f ▷ vt peler, éplucher ▷ vi (paint etc) s'écailler; (wallpaper) se décoller; (skin) peler
peep [pi:p] n (BRIT: look) coup d'œil furtif; (sound) pépiement m ▷ vi (BRIT) jeter un coup d'œil (furtif)
peer [pɪəʳ] vi: **to ~ at** regarder attentivement, scruter ▷ n (noble) pair m; (equal) pair, égal(e)

peg [pεg] n (for coat etc) patère f; (BRIT: also: **clothes ~**) pince f à linge
pelican ['pεlɪkən] n pélican m; **pelican crossing** n (BRIT Aut) feu m à commande manuelle
pelt [pεlt] vt: **to ~ sb (with)** bombarder qn (de) ▷ vi (rain) tomber à seaux; (inf: run) courir à toutes jambes ▷ n peau f:
pelvis ['pεlvɪs] n bassin m
pen [pεn] n (for writing) stylo m; (for sheep) parc m
penalty ['pεnltɪ] n pénalité f; sanction f; (fine) amende f; (Sport) pénalisation f; (Football) penalty m; (Rugby) pénalité f
pence [pεns] npl of **penny**
pencil ['pεnsl] n crayon m; **pencil in** vt noter provisoirement; **pencil case** n trousse f (d'écolier); **pencil sharpener** n taille-crayon(s) m inv
pendant ['pεndnt] n pendentif m
pending ['pεndɪŋ] prep en attendant ▷ adj en suspens
penetrate ['pεnɪtreɪt] vt pénétrer dans; (enemy territory) entrer en
penfriend ['pεnfrεnd] n (BRIT) correspondant(e)
penguin ['pεŋgwɪn] n pingouin m
penicillin [pεnɪ'sɪlɪn] n pénicilline f
peninsula [pə'nɪnsjulə] n péninsule f
penis ['pi:nɪs] n pénis m, verge f
penitentiary [pεnɪ'tεnʃərɪ] n (US) prison f
penknife ['pεnnaɪf] n canif m
penniless ['pεnɪlɪs] adj sans le sou
penny (pl **pennies** or **pence**) ['pεnɪ, 'pεnɪz, pεns] n (BRIT) penny m; (US) cent m
penpal ['pεnpæl] n correspondant(e)
pension ['pεnʃən] n (from company) retraite f; **pensioner** n (BRIT) retraité(e)
pentagon ['pεntəgən] n: **the P~** (US Pol) le Pentagone
penthouse ['pεnthaus] n appartement m (de luxe) en attique
penultimate [pɪ'nʌltɪmət] adj pénultième, avant-dernier(-ière)
people ['pi:pl] npl gens mpl; personnes

fpl; (*inhabitants*) population *f*; (*Pol*)
peuple *m* ▷ *n* (*nation, race*) peuple *m*;
several ~ came plusieurs personnes
sont venues; **~ say that ...** on dit *or* les
gens disent que ...

pepper ['pɛpə^r] *n* poivre *m*; (*vegetable*)
poivron *m* ▷ *vt* (*Culin*) poivrer;
peppermint *n* (*sweet*) pastille *f* de
menthe

per [pə:^r] *prep* par; **~ hour** (*miles etc*) à
l'heure; (*fee*) (de) l'heure; **~ kilo** *etc* le kilo
etc; **~ day/person** par jour/personne; **~
annum** par an

perceive [pə'si:v] *vt* percevoir; (*notice*)
remarquer, s'apercevoir de

per cent *adv* pour cent

percentage [pə'sɛntɪdʒ] *n*
pourcentage *m*

perception [pə'sɛpʃən] *n* perception *f*;
(*insight*) sensibilité *f*

perch [pə:tʃ] *n* (*fish*) perche *f*; (*for bird*)
perchoir *m* ▷ *vi* (se) percher

percussion [pə'kʌʃən] *n* percussion *f*

perennial [pə'rɛnɪəl] *n* (*Bot*) (plante *f*)
vivace *f*, plante pluriannuelle

perfect ['pə:fɪkt] *adj* parfait(e) ▷ *n*
(*also*: **~ tense**) parfait *m* ▷ *vt* [pə'fɛkt]
(*technique, skill, work of art*) parfaire;
(*method, plan*) mettre au point;
perfection [pə'fɛkʃən] *n* perfection *f*;
perfectly ['pə:fɪktlɪ] *adv* parfaitement

perform [pə'fɔ:m] *vt* (*carry out*)
exécuter; (*concert etc*) jouer, donner ▷ *vi*
(*actor, musician*) jouer; **performance**
n représentation *f*, spectacle *m*; (*of an
artist*) interprétation *f*; (*Sport: of car,
engine*) performance *f*; (*of company,
economy*) résultats *mpl*; **performer** *n*
artiste *m/f*

perfume ['pə:fju:m] *n* parfum *m*

perhaps [pə'hæps] *adv* peut-être

perimeter [pə'rɪmɪtə^r] *n* périmètre *m*

period ['pɪərɪəd] *n* période *f*; (*History*)
époque *f*; (*Scol*) cours *m*; (*full stop*)
point *m*; (*Med*) règles *fpl* ▷ *adj* (*costume,
furniture*) d'époque; **periodical**
[pɪərɪ'ɔdɪkl] *n* périodique *m*;
periodically *adv* périodiquement

perish ['pɛrɪʃ] *vi* périr, mourir; (*decay*)
se détériorer

perjury ['pə:dʒərɪ] *n* (*Law: in court*) faux
témoignage; (*breach of oath*) parjure *m*

perk [pə:k] *n* (*inf*) avantage *m*, à-côté *m*

perm [pə:m] *n* (*for hair*) permanente *f*

permanent ['pə:mənənt] *adj*
permanent(e); **permanently** *adv*
de façon permanente; (*move abroad*)
définitivement; (*open, closed*)
en permanence; (*tired, unhappy*)
constamment

permission [pə'mɪʃən] *n* permission *f*,
autorisation *f*

permit *n* ['pə:mɪt] permis *m*

perplex [pə'plɛks] *vt* (*person*) rendre
perplexe

persecute ['pə:sɪkju:t] *vt* persécuter

persecution [pə:sɪ'kju:ʃən] *n*
persécution *f*

persevere [pə:sɪ'vɪə^r] *vi* persévérer

Persian ['pə:ʃən] *adj* persan(e); **the ~
Gulf** le golfe Persique

persist [pə'sɪst] *vi*: **to ~ (in doing)**
persister (à faire), s'obstiner (à faire);
persistent *adj* persistant(e), tenace

person ['pə:sn] *n* personne *f*;
in ~ en personne; **personal** *adj*
personnel(le); **personal assistant** *n*
secrétaire personnel(le); **personal
computer** *n* ordinateur individuel,
PC *m*; **personality** [pə:sə'nælɪtɪ]
n personnalité *f*; **personally** *adv*
personnellement; **to take sth
personally** se sentir visé(e) par
qch; **personal organizer** *n* agenda
(personnel) (*style Filofax®*); (*electronic*)
agenda électronique; **personal stereo**
n Walkman® *m*, baladeur *m*

personnel [pə:sə'nɛl] *n* personnel *m*

perspective [pə'spɛktɪv] *n*
perspective *f*

perspiration [pə:spɪ'reɪʃən] *n*
transpiration *f*

persuade [pə'sweɪd] *vt*: **to ~ sb to do
sth** persuader qn de faire qch, amener
or décider qn à faire qch

persuasion [pə'sweɪʒən] *n* persuasion

f; (*creed*) conviction f
persuasive [pə'sweɪsɪv] *adj*
persuasif(-ive)
perverse [pə'vəːs] *adj* pervers(e);
(*contrary*) entêté(e), contrariant(e)
pervert *n* ['pəːvəːt] perverti(e) ▷ *vt*
[pə'vəːt] pervertir; (*words*) déformer
pessimism ['pɛsɪmɪzəm] *n*
pessimisme *m*
pessimist ['pɛsɪmɪst] *n* pessimiste
m/f; **pessimistic** [pɛsɪ'mɪstɪk] *adj*
pessimiste
pest [pɛst] *n* animal *m* (*or* insecte *m*)
nuisible; (*fig*) fléau *m*
pester ['pɛstə'] *vt* importuner, harceler
pesticide ['pɛstɪsaɪd] *n* pesticide *m*
pet [pɛt] *n* animal familier ▷ *cpd*
(*favourite*) favori(e) ▷ *vt* (*stroke*)
caresser, câliner; **teacher's ~** chouchou
m du professeur; **~ hate** bête noire
petal ['pɛtl] *n* pétale *m*
petite [pə'tiːt] *adj* menu(e)
petition [pə'tɪʃən] *n* pétition f
petrified ['pɛtrɪfaɪd] *adj* (*fig*) mort(e)
de peur
petrol ['pɛtrəl] *n* (*BRIT*) essence f; **I've
run out of ~** je suis en panne d'essence

> Be careful not to translate *petrol* by
> the French word *pétrole*.

petroleum [pə'trəulɪəm] *n* pétrole *m*
petrol: **petrol pump** *n* (*BRIT*: *in car*,
at garage) pompe f à essence; **petrol
station** *n* (*BRIT*) station-service f;
petrol tank *n* (*BRIT*) réservoir *m*
d'essence
petticoat ['pɛtɪkəut] *n* jupon *m*
petty ['pɛtɪ] *adj* (*mean*) mesquin(e);
(*unimportant*) insignifiant(e), sans
importance
pew [pjuː] *n* banc *m* (d'église)
pewter ['pjuːtə'] *n* étain *m*
phantom ['fæntəm] *n* fantôme *m*
pharmacist ['fɑːməsɪst] *n*
pharmacien(ne)
pharmacy ['fɑːməsɪ] *n* pharmacie f
phase [feɪz] *n* phase f, période f; **phase
in** *vt* introduire progressivement;
phase out *vt* supprimer

progressivement
Ph.D. *abbr* = **Doctor of Philosophy**
pheasant ['fɛznt] *n* faisan *m*
phenomena [fə'nɔmɪnə] *npl of*
phenomenon
phenomenal [fɪ'nɔmɪnl] *adj*
phénoménal(e)
phenomenon (*pl* **phenomena**)
[fə'nɔmɪnən, -nə] *n* phénomène *m*
Philippines ['fɪlɪpiːnz] *npl* (*also*:
Philippine Islands): **the ~** les
Philippines fpl
philosopher [fɪ'lɔsəfə'] *n*
philosophe *m*
philosophical [fɪlə'sɔfɪkl] *adj*
philosophique
philosophy [fɪ'lɔsəfɪ] *n* philosophie f
phlegm [flɛm] *n* flegme *m*
phobia ['fəubjə] *n* phobie f
phone [fəun] *n* téléphone *m* ▷ *vt*
téléphoner à ▷ *vi* téléphoner; **to be
on the ~** avoir le téléphone; (*be calling*)
être au téléphone; **phone back** *vt*, *vi*
rappeler; **phone up** *vt* téléphoner à ▷ *vi*
téléphoner; **phone book** *n* annuaire *m*;
phone box (*US* **phone booth**) *n* cabine
f téléphonique; **phone call** *n* coup *m*
de fil *or* de téléphone; **phonecard** *n*
télécarte f; **phone number** *n* numéro
m de téléphone
phonetics [fə'nɛtɪks] *n* phonétique f
phoney ['fəunɪ] *adj* faux (fausse),
factice; (*person*) pas franc (franche)
photo ['fəutəu] *n* photo f; **photo album**
n album *m* de photos; **photocopier** *n*
copieur *m*; **photocopy** *n* photocopie f
▷ *vt* photocopier
photograph ['fəutəgræf] *n*
photographie f ▷ *vt* photographier;
photographer [fə'tɔgrəfə'] *n*
photographe *m/f*; **photography**
[fə'tɔgrəfɪ] *n* photographie f
phrase [freɪz] *n* expression f; (*Ling*)
locution f ▷ *vt* exprimer; **phrase
book** *n* recueil *m* d'expressions (pour
touristes)
physical ['fɪzɪkl] *adj* physique;
physical education *n* éducation

f physique; **physically** adv
physiquement
physician [fɪ'zɪʃən] n médecin m
physicist ['fɪzɪsɪst] n physicien(ne)
physics ['fɪzɪks] n physique f
physiotherapist [fɪzɪəʊ'θɛrəpɪst] n
kinésithérapeute m/f
physiotherapy [fɪzɪəʊ'θɛrəpɪ] n
kinésithérapie f
physique [fɪ'ziːk] n (appearance)
physique m; (health etc) constitution f
pianist ['piːənɪst] n pianiste m/f
piano [pɪ'ænəʊ] n piano m
pick [pɪk] n (tool: also: **~-axe**) pic m,
pioche f ▷ vt choisir; (gather) cueillir;
(remove) prendre; (lock) forcer; **take
your ~** faites votre choix; **the ~ of** le
(la) meilleur(e) de; **to ~ one's nose** se
mettre les doigts dans le nez; **to ~
one's teeth** se curer les dents; **to ~
a quarrel with sb** chercher noise à
qn; **pick on** vt fus (person) harceler;
pick out vt choisir; (distinguish)
distinguer; **pick up** vi (improve)
remonter, s'améliorer ▷ vt ramasser;
(collect) passer prendre; (Aut: give lift
to) prendre; (learn) apprendre; (Radio)
capter; **to ~ up speed** prendre de la
vitesse; **to ~ o.s. up** se relever
pickle ['pɪkl] n (also: **~s**: as condiment)
pickles mpl ▷ vt conserver dans du
vinaigre or dans de la saumure; **in a ~**
(fig) dans le pétrin
pickpocket ['pɪkpɔkɪt] n pickpocket m
pick-up ['pɪkʌp] n (also: **~ truck**)
pick-up m inv
picnic ['pɪknɪk] n pique-nique m ▷ vi
pique-niquer; **picnic area** n aire f de
pique-nique
picture ['pɪktʃə] n (also TV) image
f; (painting) peinture f, tableau m;
(photograph) photo(graphie) f;
(drawing) dessin m; (film) film m; (fig:
description) description f ▷ vt (imagine)
se représenter; **pictures** npl: **the ~s**
(BRIT) le cinéma; **to take a ~ of sb/sth**
prendre qn/qch en photo; **would you
take a ~ of us, please?** pourriez-vous

nous prendre en photo, s'il vous plaît?;
picture frame n cadre m; **picture
messaging** n picture messaging m,
messagerie f d'images
picturesque [pɪktʃə'rɛsk] adj
pittoresque
pie [paɪ] n tourte f; (of fruit) tarte f; (of
meat) pâté m en croûte
piece [piːs] n morceau m; (item): **a ~ of
furniture/advice** un meuble/conseil
▷ vt: **to ~ together** rassembler; **to take
to ~s** démonter
pie chart n graphique m à secteurs,
camembert m
pier [pɪə] n jetée f
pierce [pɪəs] vt percer, transpercer;
pierced adj (ears) percé(e)
pig [pɪg] n cochon m, porc m; (pej:
unkind person) mufle m; (: greedy person)
goinfre m
pigeon ['pɪdʒən] n pigeon m
piggy bank ['pɪgɪ-] n tirelire f
pigsty ['pɪgstaɪ] n porcherie f
pigtail ['pɪgteɪl] n natte f, tresse f
pike [paɪk] n (fish) brochet m
pilchard ['pɪltʃəd] n pilchard m (sorte
de sardine)
pile [paɪl] n (pillar, of books) pile f; (heap)
tas m; (of carpet) épaisseur f; **pile up** vi
(accumulate) s'entasser, s'accumuler
▷ vt (put in heap) empiler, entasser;
(accumulate) accumuler; **piles** npl
hémorroïdes fpl; **pile-up** n (Aut)
télescopage m, collision f en série
pilgrim ['pɪlgrɪm] n pèlerin m

● **PILGRIM FATHERS**
●
● Les "Pères pèlerins" sont un
● groupe de puritains qui quittèrent
● l'Angleterre en 1620 pour fuir les
● persécutions religieuses. Ayant
● traversé l'Atlantique à bord du
● "Mayflower", ils fondèrent New
● Plymouth en Nouvelle-Angleterre,
● dans ce qui est aujourd'hui le
● Massachusetts. Ces Pères pèlerins
● sont considérés comme les

● fondateurs des États-Unis, et l'on
● commémore chaque année, le jour
● de "Thanksgiving", la réussite de leur
● première récolte.

pilgrimage ['pɪlɡrɪmɪdʒ] n
pèlerinage m
pill [pɪl] n pilule f; **the ~** la pilule
pillar ['pɪləʳ] n pilier m
pillow ['pɪləu] n oreiller m; **pillowcase,
pillowslip** ~s taie f d'oreiller
pilot ['paɪlət] n pilote m ▷ cpd (scheme
etc) pilote, expérimental(e) ▷ vt piloter;
pilot light n veilleuse f
pimple ['pɪmpl] n bouton m
PIN n abbr (= personal identification
number) code m confidentiel
pin [pɪn] n épingle f; (Tech) cheville f ▷ vt
épingler; **~s and needles** fourmis fpl; **to
~ sb down** (fig) coincer qn; **to ~ sth on
sb** (fig) mettre qch sur le dos de qn
pinafore ['pɪnəfɔːʳ] n tablier m
pinch [pɪntʃ] n pincement m; (of salt
etc) pincée f ▷ vt pincer; (inf: steal)
piquer, chiper ▷ vi (shoe) serrer; **at a ~**
à la rigueur
pine [paɪn] n (also: **~ tree**) pin m ▷ vi: **to
~ for** aspirer à, désirer ardemment
pineapple ['paɪnæpl] n ananas m
ping [pɪŋ] n (noise) tintement m; **ping-
pong®** n ping-pong® m
pink [pɪŋk] adj rose ▷ n (colour) rose m
pinpoint ['pɪnpɔɪnt] vt indiquer (avec
précision)
pint [paɪnt] n pinte f (BRIT = 0.57 l; US =
0.47 l); (BRIT inf) ≈ demi m, ≈ pot m
pioneer [paɪə'nɪəʳ] n pionnier m
pious ['paɪəs] adj pieux(-euse)
pip [pɪp] n (seed) pépin m; **pips** npl: **the
~s** (BRIT: time signal on radio) le top
pipe [paɪp] n tuyau m, conduite f; (for
smoking) pipe f ▷ vt amener par tuyau;
pipeline n (for gas) gazoduc m, pipeline
m; (for oil) oléoduc m, pipeline; **piper** n
(flautist) joueur(-euse) de pipeau; (of
bagpipes) joueur(-euse) de cornemuse
pirate ['paɪərət] n pirate m ▷ vt (CD,
video, book) pirater

Pisces ['paɪsiːz] n les Poissons mpl
piss [pɪs] vi (inf!) pisser (!); **pissed** (inf!)
adj (BRIT: drunk) bourré(e); (US: angry)
furieux(-euse)
pistol ['pɪstl] n pistolet m
piston ['pɪstən] n piston m
pit [pɪt] n trou m, fosse f; (also: **coal ~**)
puits m de mine; (also: **orchestra ~**)
fosse d'orchestre; (US: fruit stone) noyau
m ▷ vt: **to ~ o.s.** or **one's wits against**
se mesurer à
pitch [pɪtʃ] n (BRIT Sport) terrain m; (Mus)
ton m; (fig: degree) degré m; (tar) poix
f ▷ vt (throw) lancer; (tent) dresser ▷ vi
(fall): **to ~ into/off** tomber dans/de;
pitch-black adj noir(e) comme poix
pitfall ['pɪtfɔːl] n piège m
pith [pɪθ] n (of orange etc) intérieur m
de l'écorce
pitiful ['pɪtɪful] adj (touching) pitoyable;
(contemptible) lamentable
pity ['pɪtɪ] n pitié f ▷ vt plaindre; **what a
~!** quel dommage!
pizza ['piːtsə] n pizza f
placard ['plækɑːd] n affiche f; (in march)
pancarte f
place [pleɪs] n endroit m, lieu m;
(proper position, job, rank, seat) place
f; (home): **at/to his ~** chez lui ▷ vt
(position) placer, mettre; (identify)
situer; reconnaître; **to take ~** avoir
lieu; **to change ~s with sb** changer
de place avec qn; **out of ~** (not suitable)
déplacé(e), inopportun(e); **in the first
~** d'abord, en premier; **place mat** n set
m de table; (in linen etc) napperon m;
placement n (during studies) stage m
placid ['plæsɪd] adj placide
plague [pleɪɡ] n (Med) peste f ▷ vt (fig)
tourmenter
plaice [pleɪs] n (pl inv) carrelet m
plain [pleɪn] adj (in one colour) uni(e);
(clear) clair(e), évident(e); (simple)
simple; (not handsome) quelconque,
ordinaire ▷ adv franchement,
carrément ▷ n plaine f; **plain
chocolate** n chocolat m à croquer;
plainly adv clairement; (frankly)

carrément, sans détours

plaintiff ['pleɪntɪf] n plaignant(e)

plait [plæt] n tresse f, natte f

plan [plæn] n plan m; (scheme) projet m ▷ vt (think in advance) projeter; (prepare) organiser ▷ vi faire des projets; **to ~ to do** projeter de faire

plane [pleɪn] n (Aviat) avion m; (also: **~ tree**) platane m; (tool) rabot m; (Art, Math etc) plan m; (fig) niveau m, plan ▷ vt (with tool) raboter

planet ['plænɪt] n planète f

plank [plæŋk] n planche f

planning ['plænɪŋ] n planification f; **family ~** planning familial

plant [plɑːnt] n plante f; (machinery) matériel m; (factory) usine f ▷ vt planter; (bomb) déposer, poser; (microphone, evidence) cacher

plantation [plæn'teɪʃən] n plantation f

plaque [plæk] n plaque f

plaster ['plɑːstəʳ] n plâtre m; (also: **~ of Paris**) plâtre à mouler; (BRIT: also: **sticking ~**) pansement adhésif ▷ vt plâtrer; (cover): **to ~ with** couvrir de; **plaster cast** n (Med) plâtre m; (model, statue) moule m

plastic ['plæstɪk] n plastique m ▷ adj (made of plastic) en plastique; **plastic bag** n sac m en plastique; **plastic surgery** n chirurgie f esthétique

plate [pleɪt] n (dish) assiette f; (sheet of metal, on door: Phot) plaque f; (in book) gravure f; (dental) dentier m

plateau (pl **~s** or **~x**) ['plætəʊ, -z] n plateau m

platform ['plætfɔːm] n (at meeting) tribune f; (stage) estrade f; (Rail) quai m; (Pol) plateforme f

platinum ['plætɪnəm] n platine m

platoon [plə'tuːn] n peloton m

platter ['plætəʳ] n plat m

plausible ['plɔːzɪbl] adj plausible; (person) convaincant(e)

play [pleɪ] n jeu m; (Theat) pièce f (de théâtre) ▷ vt (game) jouer à; (team, opponent) jouer contre; (instrument) jouer de; (part, piece of music, note) jouer; (CD etc) passer ▷ vi jouer; **to ~ safe** ne prendre aucun risque; **play back** vt repasser, réécouter; **play up** vi (cause trouble) faire des siennes; **player** n joueur(-euse); (Mus) musicien(ne); **playful** adj enjoué(e); **playground** n cour f de récréation; (in park) aire f de jeux; **playgroup** n garderie f; **playing card** n carte f à jouer; **playing field** n terrain m de sport; **playschool** n = **playgroup**; **playtime** n (Scol) récréation f; **playwright** n dramaturge m

plc abbr (BRIT: = public limited company) ≈ SARL f

plea [pliː] n (request) appel m; (Law) défense f

plead [pliːd] vt plaider; (give as excuse) invoquer ▷ vi (Law) plaider; (beg): **to ~ with sb (for sth)** implorer qn (d'accorder qch); **to ~ guilty/not guilty** plaider coupable/non coupable

pleasant ['plɛznt] adj agréable

please [pliːz] excl s'il te (or vous) plaît ▷ vt plaire à ▷ vi (think fit): **do as you ~** faites comme il vous plaira; **~ yourself!** (inf) (faites) comme vous voulez!; **pleased** adj: **pleased (with)** content(e) (de); **pleased to meet you** enchanté (de faire votre connaissance)

pleasure ['plɛʒəʳ] n plaisir m; **"it's a ~"** "je vous en prie"

pleat [pliːt] n pli m

pledge [plɛdʒ] n (promise) promesse f ▷ vt promettre

plentiful ['plɛntɪful] adj abondant(e), copieux(-euse)

plenty ['plɛntɪ] n: **~ of** beaucoup de; (sufficient) (bien) assez de

pliers ['plaɪəz] npl pinces fpl

plight [plaɪt] n situation f critique

plod [plɒd] vi avancer péniblement; (fig) peiner

plonk [plɒŋk] (inf) n (BRIT: wine) pinard m, piquette f ▷ vt: **to ~ sth down** poser brusquement qch

plot [plɒt] n complot m, conspiration f;

(of story, play) intrigue f; (of land) lot m
de terrain, lopin m ▷ vt (mark out) tracer
point par point; (Naut) pointer; (make
graph of) faire le graphique de; (conspire)
comploter ▷ vi comploter

plough (us **plow**) [plau] n charrue f
▷ vt (earth) labourer; **to ~ money into**
investir dans; **ploughman's lunch**
n (BRIT) assiette froide avec du pain, du
fromage et des pickles

plow [plau] (us) = **plough**

ploy [plɔɪ] n stratagème m

pluck [plʌk] vt (fruit) cueillir; (musical
instrument) pincer; (bird) plumer; **to ~
one's eyebrows** s'épiler les sourcils;
to ~ up courage prendre son courage
à deux mains

plug [plʌg] n (stopper) bouchon m,
bonde f; (Elec) prise f de courant; (Aut:
also: **spark(ing) ~**) bougie f ▷ vt (hole)
boucher; (inf: advertise) faire du battage
pour, matraquer; **plug in** vt (Elec)
brancher; **plughole** n (BRIT) trou m
(d'écoulement)

plum [plʌm] n (fruit) prune f

plumber ['plʌmər] n plombier m

plumbing ['plʌmɪŋ] n (trade)
plomberie f; (piping) tuyauterie f

plummet ['plʌmɪt] vi (person, object)
plonger; (sales, prices) dégringoler

plump [plʌmp] adj rondelet(te),
dodu(e), bien en chair; **plump for** vt fus
(inf: choose) se décider pour

plunge [plʌndʒ] n plongeon m; (fig)
chute f ▷ vt plonger ▷ vi (fall) tomber,
dégringoler; (dive) plonger; **to take the
~** se jeter à l'eau

pluperfect [pluːˈpəːfɪkt] n (Ling) plus-
que-parfait m

plural ['pluərl] adj pluriel(le) ▷ n
pluriel m

plus [plʌs] n (also: **~ sign**) signe m
plus; (advantage) atout m ▷ prep plus;
ten/twenty ~ plus de dix/vingt

ply [plaɪ] n (of wool) fil m ▷ vt (a
trade) exercer ▷ vi (ship) faire la
navette; **to ~ sb with drink** donner
continuellement à boire à qn; **plywood**

n contreplaqué m

P.M. n abbr (BRIT) = **prime minister**

p.m. adv abbr (= post meridiem) de
l'après-midi

PMS n abbr (= premenstrual syndrome)
syndrome prémenstruel

PMT n abbr (= premenstrual tension)
syndrome prémenstruel

pneumatic drill [njuːˈmætɪk-] n
marteau-piqueur m

pneumonia [njuːˈməʊnɪə] n
pneumonie f

poach [pəʊtʃ] vt (cook) pocher; (steal)
pêcher (or chasser) sans permis ▷ vi
braconner; **poached** adj (egg) poché(e)

P.O. Box n abbr = **post office box**

pocket ['pɔkɪt] n poche f ▷ vt
empocher; **to be (£5) out of ~**
(BRIT) en être de sa poche (pour 5
livres); **pocketbook** n (us: wallet)
portefeuille m; **pocket money** n
argent m de poche

pod [pɔd] n cosse f

podcast n podcast m

podiatrist [pɔˈdiːətrɪst] n (us)
pédicure m/f

podium ['pəʊdɪəm] n podium m

poem ['pəʊɪm] n poème m

poet ['pəʊɪt] n poète m; **poetic**
[pəʊˈetɪk] adj poétique; **poetry** n
poésie f

poignant ['pɔɪnjənt] adj poignant(e)

point [pɔɪnt] n point m; (tip) pointe f; (in
time) moment m; (in space) endroit m;
(subject, idea) point, sujet m; (purpose)
but m; (also: **decimal ~**): **2 ~ 3 (2.3)** 2
virgule 3 (2,3); (BRIT Elec: also: **power
~**) prise f (de courant) ▷ vt (show)
indiquer; (gun etc): **to ~ sth at** braquer
or diriger qch sur ▷ vi: **to ~ at** montrer
du doigt; **points** npl (Rail) aiguillage
m; **to make a ~ of doing sth** ne pas
manquer de faire qch; **to get/miss the
~** comprendre/ne pas comprendre;
to come to the ~ en venir au fait;
there's no ~ (in doing) cela ne sert à
rien (de faire), à quoi ça sert?; **to be on
the ~ of doing sth** être sur le point de

faire qch; **point out** vt (mention) faire remarquer, souligner; **point-blank** adv (fig) catégoriquement; (also: **at point-blank range**) à bout portant; **pointed** adj (shape) pointu(e); (remark) plein(e) de sous-entendus; **pointer** n (needle) aiguille f; (clue) indication f; (advice) tuyau m; **pointless** adj inutile, vain(e); **point of view** n point m de vue

poison ['pɔɪzn] n poison m ▷ vt empoisonner; **poisonous** adj (snake) venimeux(-euse); (substance, plant) vénéneux(-euse); (fumes) toxique

poke [pəuk] vt (jab with finger, stick etc) piquer; (put) pousser du doigt; (put): **to ~ sth in(to)** fourrer or enfoncer qch dans; **poke about** vi fureter; **poke out** vi (stick out) sortir

poker ['pəukə'] n tisonnier m; (Cards) poker m

Poland ['pəulənd] n Pologne f

polar ['pəulə'] adj polaire; **polar bear** n ours blanc

Pole [pəul] n Polonais(e)

pole [pəul] n (of wood) mât m, perche f; (Elec) poteau m; (Geo) pôle m; **pole bean** n (US) haricot m (à rames); **pole vault** n saut m à la perche

police [pə'li:s] npl police f ▷ vt maintenir l'ordre dans; **police car** n voiture f de police; **police constable** n (BRIT) agent m de police; **police force** n police f, forces fpl de l'ordre; **policeman** (irreg) n agent m de police, policier m; **police officer** n agent m de police; **police station** n commissariat m de police; **policewoman** (irreg) n femme-agent f

policy ['pɔlɪsɪ] n politique f; (also: **insurance ~**) police f (d'assurance)

polio ['pəulɪəu] n polio f

Polish ['pəulɪʃ] adj polonais(e) ▷ n (Ling) polonais m

polish ['pɔlɪʃ] n (for shoes) cirage m; (for floor) cire f, encaustique f; (for nails) vernis m; (shine) éclat m, poli m; (fig: refinement) raffinement m ▷ vt (put polish on: shoes, wood) cirer; (make

shiny) astiquer, faire briller; **polish off** vt (food) liquider; **polished** adj (fig) raffiné(e)

polite [pə'laɪt] adj poli(e); **politeness** n politesse f

political [pə'lɪtɪkl] adj politique; **politically** adv politiquement; **politically correct** politiquement correct(e)

politician [pɔlɪ'tɪʃən] n homme/ femme politique, politicien(ne)

politics ['pɔlɪtɪks] n politique f

poll [pəul] n scrutin m, vote m; (also: **opinion ~**) sondage m (d'opinion) ▷ vt (votes) obtenir

pollen ['pɔlən] n pollen m

polling station n (BRIT) bureau m de vote

pollute [pə'lu:t] vt polluer

pollution [pə'lu:ʃən] n pollution f

polo ['pəuləu] n polo m; **polo-neck** adj à col roulé ▷ n (sweater) pull m à col roulé; **polo shirt** n polo m

polyester [pɔlɪ'estə'] n polyester m

polystyrene [pɔlɪ'staɪri:n] n polystyrène m

polythene ['pɔlɪθi:n] n (BRIT) polyéthylène m; **polythene bag** n sac m en plastique

pomegranate ['pɔmɪgrænɪt] n grenade f

pompous ['pɔmpəs] adj pompeux(-euse)

pond [pɔnd] n étang m; (stagnant) mare f

ponder ['pɔndə'] vt considérer, peser

pony ['pəunɪ] n poney m; **ponytail** n queue f de cheval; **pony trekking** n (BRIT) randonnée f équestre or à cheval

poodle ['pu:dl] n caniche m

pool [pu:l] n (of rain) flaque f; (pond) mare f; (artificial) bassin m; (also: **swimming ~**) piscine f; (sth shared) fonds commun; (billiards) poule f ▷ vt mettre en commun; **pools** npl (football) ≈ loto sportif

poor [puə'] adj pauvre; (mediocre) médiocre, faible, mauvais(e) ▷ npl: **the ~** les pauvres mpl; **poorly** adv (badly) mal, médiocrement ▷ *adj* souffrant(e), malade

op [pɔp] *n* (*noise*) bruit sec; (*Mus*) musique *f* pop; (*inf: drink*) soda *m*; (*US inf: father*) papa *m* ▷ *vt* (*put*) fourrer, mettre (rapidement) ▷ *vi* éclater; (*cork*) sauter; **pop in** *vi* entrer en passant; **pop out** *vi* sortir; **popcorn** *n* pop-corn *m*

ope [pəup] *n* pape *m*

oplar ['pɔplə^r] *n* peuplier *m*

opper ['pɔpə^r] *n* (*BRIT*) bouton-pression *m*

oppy ['pɔpɪ] *n* (*wild*) coquelicot *m*; (*cultivated*) pavot *m*

opsicle® ['pɔpsɪkl] *n* (*US*) esquimau *m* (*glace*)

op star *n* pop star *f*

opular ['pɔpjulə^r] *adj* populaire; (*fashionable*) à la mode; **popularity** [pɔpju'lærɪtɪ] *n* popularité *f*

opulation [pɔpju'leɪʃən] *n* population *f*

op-up *adj* (*Comput: menu, window*) pop up *inv* ▷ *n* pop up *m inv*, fenêtre *f* pop up

orcelain ['pɔːslɪn] *n* porcelaine *f*

orch [pɔːtʃ] *n* porche *m*; (*US*) véranda *f*

ore [pɔː^r] *n* pore *m* ▷ *vi*: **to ~ over** s'absorber dans, être plongé(e) dans

ork [pɔːk] *n* porc *m*; **pork chop** *n* côte *f* de porc; **pork pie** *n* pâté *m* de porc en croûte

orn [pɔːn] *adj* (*inf*) porno ▷ *n* (*inf*) porno *m*; **pornographic** [pɔːnə'græfɪk] *adj* pornographique; **pornography** [pɔː'nɔgrəfɪ] *n* pornographie *f*

orridge ['pɔrɪdʒ] *n* porridge *m*

ort [pɔːt] *n* (*harbour*) port *m*; (*Naut: left side*) bâbord *m*; (*wine*) porto *m*; (*Comput*) port *m*, accès *m*; **~ of call** port d')escale *f*

ortable ['pɔːtəbl] *adj* portatif(-ive)

orter ['pɔːtə^r] *n* (*for luggage*) porteur *m*; (*doorkeeper*) gardien(ne); portier *m*

ortfolio [pɔːt'fəulɪəu] *n* portefeuille *n*; (*of artist*) portfolio *m*

ortion ['pɔːʃən] *n* portion *f*, part *f*

ortrait ['pɔːtreɪt] *n* portrait *m*

portray [pɔː'treɪ] *vt* faire le portrait de; (*in writing*) dépeindre, représenter; (*subj: actor*) jouer

Portugal ['pɔːtjugl] *n* Portugal *m*

Portuguese [pɔːtju'giːz] *adj* portugais(e) ▷ *n* (*pl inv*) Portugais(e); (*Ling*) portugais *m*

pose [pəuz] *n* pose *f* ▷ *vi* poser; (*pretend*): **to ~ as** se faire passer pour ▷ *vt* poser; (*problem*) créer

posh [pɔʃ] *adj* (*inf*) chic *inv*

position [pə'zɪʃən] *n* position *f*; (*job, situation*) situation *f* ▷ *vt* mettre en place *or* en position

positive ['pɔzɪtɪv] *adj* positif(-ive); (*certain*) sûr(e), certain(e); (*definite*) formel(le), catégorique; **positively** *adv* (*affirmatively, enthusiastically*) de façon positive; (*inf: really*) carrément

possess [pə'zɛs] *vt* posséder; **possession** [pə'zɛʃən] *n* possession *f*; **possessions** *npl* (*belongings*) affaires *fpl*; **possessive** *adj* possessif(-ive)

possibility [pɔsɪ'bɪlɪtɪ] *n* possibilité *f*; (*event*) éventualité *f*

possible ['pɔsɪbl] *adj* possible; **as big as ~** aussi gros que possible; **possibly** *adv* (*perhaps*) peut-être; **I cannot possibly come** il m'est impossible de venir

post [pəust] *n* (*BRIT: mail*) poste *f*; (*: letters, delivery*) courrier *m*; (*job, situation*) poste *m*; (*pole*) poteau *m* ▷ *vt* (*BRIT: send by post*) poster; (*: appoint*): **to ~ to** affecter à; **where can I ~ these cards?** où est-ce que je peux poster ces cartes postales?; **postage** *n* tarifs *mpl* d'affranchissement; **postal** *adj* postal(e); **postal order** *n* mandat(-poste *m*) *m*; **postbox** *n* (*BRIT*) boîte *f* aux lettres (*publique*); **postcard** *n* carte postale; **postcode** *n* (*BRIT*) code postal

poster ['pəustə^r] *n* affiche *f*

postgraduate ['pəust'grædjuət] *n* ≈ étudiant(e) de troisième cycle

postman ['pəustmən] (*BRIT: irreg*) *n*

facteur m

postmark ['pəustmɑ:k] n cachet m (de la poste)

post-mortem [pəust'mɔ:təm] n autopsie f

post office n (building) poste f; (organization): **the Post Office** les postes fpl

postpone [pəs'pəun] vt remettre (à plus tard), reculer

posture ['pɒstʃə'] n posture f; (fig) attitude f

postwoman [pəust'wumən] (BRIT: irreg) n factrice f

pot [pɒt] n (for cooking) marmite f; casserole f; (teapot) théière f; (for coffee) cafetière f; (for plants, jam) pot m; (inf: marijuana) herbe f ▷ vt (plant) mettre en pot; **to go to ~** (inf) aller à vau-l'eau

potato (pl ~**es**) [pə'teɪtəu] n pomme f de terre; **potato peeler** n épluche-légumes m

potent ['pəutnt] adj puissant(e); (drink) fort(e), très alcoolisé(e); (man) viril

potential [pə'tɛnʃl] adj potentiel(le) ▷ n potentiel m

pothole ['pɒthəul] n (in road) nid m de poule; (BRIT: underground) gouffre m, caverne f

pot plant n plante f d'appartement

potter ['pɒtə'] n potier m ▷ vi (BRIT): **to ~ around** or **about** bricoler; **pottery** n poterie f

potty ['pɒtɪ] n (child's) pot m

pouch [pautʃ] n (Zool) poche f; (for tobacco) blague f; (for money) bourse f

poultry ['pəultrɪ] n volaille f

pounce [pauns] vi: **to ~ (on)** bondir (sur), fondre (sur)

pound [paund] n livre f (weight = 453g, 16 ounces; money = 100 pence); (for dogs, cars) fourrière f ▷ vt (beat) bourrer de coups, marteler; (crush) piler, pulvériser ▷ vi (heart) battre violemment, taper; **pound sterling** n livre f sterling

pour [pɔ:'] vt verser ▷ vi couler à flots; (rain) pleuvoir à verse; **to ~ sb a drink** verser or servir à boire à qn; **pour in**

vi (people) affluer, se précipiter; (news, letters) arriver en masse; **pour out** vi (people) sortir en masse ▷ vt vider; (fig) déverser; (serve: a drink) verser; **pouring** adj: **pouring rain** pluie torrentielle

pout [paut] vi faire la moue

poverty ['pɒvətɪ] n pauvreté f, misère f

powder ['paudə'] n poudre f ▷ vt poudrer; **powdered milk** n lait m en poudre

power ['pauə'] n (strength, nation) puissance f, force f; (ability, Pol: of party, leader) pouvoir m; (of speech, thought) faculté f; (Elec) courant m; **to be in ~** être au pouvoir; **power cut** n (BRIT) coupure f de courant; **power failure** n panne f de courant; **powerful** adj puissant(e); (performance etc) très fort(e); **powerless** adj impuissant(e); **power point** n (BRIT) prise f de courant; **power station** n centrale f électrique

p.p. abbr (= per procurationem: by proxy) p.p.

PR n abbr = **public relations**

practical ['præktɪkl] adj pratique; **practical joke** n farce f; **practically** adv (almost) pratiquement

practice ['præktɪs] n pratique f; (of profession) exercice m; (at football etc) entraînement m; (business) cabinet m ▷ vt, vi (US) = **practise**; **in ~** (in reality) en pratique; **out of ~** rouillé(e)

practise (US **practice**) ['præktɪs] vt (work at: piano, backhand etc) s'exercer à, travailler; (train for: sport) s'entraîner à; (a sport, religion, method) pratiquer; (profession) exercer ▷ vi s'exercer, travailler; (train) s'entraîner; (lawyer, doctor) exercer; **practising** (US **practicing**) adj (Christian etc) pratiquant(e); (lawyer) en exercice

practitioner [præk'tɪʃənə'] n praticien(ne)

pragmatic [præg'mætɪk] adj pragmatique

prairie ['prɛərɪ] n savane f

praise [preɪz] n éloge(s) m(pl), louange(s) f(pl) ▷ vt louer, faire l'éloge de

pram [præm] n (BRIT) landau m, voiture f d'enfant

prank [præŋk] n farce f

prawn [prɔ:n] n crevette f (rose); **prawn cocktail** n cocktail m de crevettes

pray [preɪ] vi prier; **prayer** [prɛəʳ] n prière f

preach [pri:tʃ] vi prêcher; **preacher** n prédicateur m; (US: clergyman) pasteur m

precarious [prɪˈkɛərɪəs] adj précaire

precaution [prɪˈkɔ:ʃən] n précaution f

precede [prɪˈsi:d] vt, vi précéder; **precedent** [ˈprɛsɪdənt] n précédent m; **preceding** [prɪˈsi:dɪŋ] adj qui précède (or précédait)

precinct [ˈpri:sɪŋkt] n (US: district) circonscription f, arrondissement m; **pedestrian ~** (BRIT) zone piétonnière; **shopping ~** (BRIT) centre commercial

precious [ˈprɛʃəs] adj précieux(-euse)

precise [prɪˈsaɪs] adj précis(e); **precisely** adv précisément

precision [prɪˈsɪʒən] n précision f

predator [ˈprɛdətəʳ] n prédateur m, rapace m

predecessor [ˈpri:dɪsɛsəʳ] n prédécesseur m

predicament [prɪˈdɪkəmənt] n situation f difficile

predict [prɪˈdɪkt] vt prédire; **predictable** adj prévisible; **prediction** [prɪˈdɪkʃən] n prédiction f

predominantly [prɪˈdɔmɪnəntlɪ] adv en majeure partie; (especially) surtout

preface [ˈprɛfəs] n préface f

prefect [ˈpri:fɛkt] n (BRIT: in school) élève chargé de certaines fonctions de discipline

prefer [prɪˈfə:ʳ] vt préférer; **preferable** [ˈprɛfrəbl] adj préférable; **preferably** [ˈprɛfrəblɪ] adv de préférence; **preference** [ˈprɛfrəns] n préférence f

prefix [ˈpri:fɪks] n préfixe m

pregnancy [ˈprɛgnənsɪ] n grossesse f

pregnant [ˈprɛgnənt] adj enceinte adj f; (animal) pleine

prehistoric [ˈpri:hɪsˈtɔrɪk] adj préhistorique

prejudice [ˈprɛdʒudɪs] n préjugé m; **prejudiced** adj (person) plein(e) de préjugés; (in a matter) partial(e)

preliminary [prɪˈlɪmɪnərɪ] adj préliminaire

prelude [ˈprɛlju:d] n prélude m

premature [ˈprɛmətʃuəʳ] adj prématuré(e)

premier [ˈprɛmɪəʳ] adj premier(-ière), principal(e) ▷ n (Pol: Prime Minister) premier ministre; (Pol: President) chef m de l'État

premiere [ˈprɛmɪɛəʳ] n première f

Premier League n première division

premises [ˈprɛmɪsɪz] npl locaux mpl; **on the ~** sur les lieux; sur place

premium [ˈpri:mɪəm] n prime f; **to be at a ~** (fig: housing etc) être très demandé(e), être rarissime

premonition [prɛməˈnɪʃən] n prémonition f

preoccupied [pri:ˈɔkjupaɪd] adj préoccupé(e)

prepaid [pri:ˈpeɪd] adj payé(e) d'avance

preparation [prɛpəˈreɪʃən] n préparation f; **preparations** npl (for trip, war) préparatifs mpl

preparatory school n école primaire privée; (US) lycée privé

prepare [prɪˈpɛəʳ] vt préparer ▷ vi: **to ~ for** se préparer à

prepared [prɪˈpɛəd] adj: **~ for** préparé(e) à; **~ to** prêt(e) à

preposition [prɛpəˈzɪʃən] n préposition f

prep school n = **preparatory school**

prerequisite [pri:ˈrɛkwɪzɪt] n condition f préalable

preschool [ˈpri:ˈsku:l] adj préscolaire; (child) d'âge préscolaire

prescribe [prɪˈskraɪb] vt prescrire

prescription [prɪˈskrɪpʃən] n (Med) ordonnance f; (: medicine) médicament m (obtenu sur ordonnance); **could you write me a ~?** pouvez-vous me faire une ordonnance?

presence [ˈprɛzns] n présence f; **in**

sb's ~ en présence de qn; **~ of mind** présence d'esprit

present ['prɛznt] *adj* présent(e); (*current*) présent, actuel(le) ▷ *n* cadeau *m*; (*actuality*) présent *m* ▷ *vt* [prɪ'zɛnt] présenter; (*prize, medal*) remettre; (*give*): **to ~ sb with sth** offrir qch à qn; **at ~** en ce moment; **to give sb a ~** offrir un cadeau à qn; **presentable** [prɪ'zɛntəbl] *adj* présentable; **presentation** [prɛzn'teɪʃən] *n* présentation *f*; (*ceremony*) remise *f* du cadeau (*or* de la médaille *etc*); **present-day** *adj* contemporain(e), actuel(le); **presenter** [prɪ'zɛntə*r*] *n* (*BRIT Radio, TV*) présentateur(-trice); **presently** *adv* (*soon*) tout à l'heure, bientôt; (*with verb in past*) peu après; (*at present*) en ce moment; **present participle** [-'pɑːtɪsɪpl] *n* participe *m* présent

preservation [prɛzə'veɪʃən] *n* préservation *f*, conservation *f*

preservative [prɪ'zə:vətɪv] *n* agent *m* de conservation

preserve [prɪ'zə:v] *vt* (*keep safe*) préserver, protéger; (*maintain*) conserver, garder; (*food*) mettre en conserve ▷ *n* (*for game, fish*) réserve *f*; (*often pl: jam*) confiture *f*

preside [prɪ'zaɪd] *vi* présider

president ['prɛzɪdənt] *n* président(e); **presidential** [prɛzɪ'dɛnʃl] *adj* présidentiel(le)

press [prɛs] *n* (*tool, machine, newspapers*) presse *f*; (*for wine*) pressoir *m* ▷ *vt* (*push*) appuyer sur; (*squeeze*) presser, serrer; (*clothes: iron*) repasser; (*insist*): **to ~ sth on sb** presser qn d'accepter qch; (*urge, entreat*): **to ~ sb to do** *or* **into doing sth** pousser qn à faire qch ▷ *vi* appuyer; **we are ~ed for time** le temps nous manque; **to ~ for sth** faire pression pour obtenir qch; **press conference** *n* conférence *f* de presse; **pressing** *adj* urgent(e), pressant(e); **press stud** *n* (*BRIT*) bouton-pression *m*; **press-up** *n* (*BRIT*) traction *f*

pressure ['prɛʃə*r*] *n* pression *f*; (*stress*) tension *f*; **to put ~ on sb (to do sth)** faire pression sur qn (pour qu'il fasse qch); **pressure cooker** *n* cocotte-minute *f*; **pressure group** *n* groupe *m* de pression

prestige [prɛs'tiːʒ] *n* prestige *m*

prestigious [prɛs'tɪdʒəs] *adj* prestigieux(-euse)

presumably [prɪ'zjuːməblɪ] *adv* vraisemblablement

presume [prɪ'zjuːm] *vt* présumer, supposer

pretence (*US* **pretense**) [prɪ'tɛns] *n* (*claim*) prétention *f*; **under false ~s** sous des prétextes fallacieux

pretend [prɪ'tɛnd] *vt* (*feign*) feindre, simuler ▷ *vi* (*feign*) faire semblant

pretense [prɪ'tɛns] *n* (*US*) = **pretence**

pretentious [prɪ'tɛnʃəs] *adj* prétentieux(-euse)

pretext ['priːtɛkst] *n* prétexte *m*

pretty ['prɪtɪ] *adj* joli(e) ▷ *adv* assez

prevail [prɪ'veɪl] *vi* (*win*) l'emporter, prévaloir; (*be usual*) avoir cours; **prevailing** *adj* (*widespread*) courant(e), répandu(e); (*wind*) dominant(e)

prevalent ['prɛvələnt] *adj* répandu(e), courant(e)

prevent [prɪ'vɛnt] *vt*: **to ~ (from doing)** empêcher (de faire); **prevention** [prɪ'vɛnʃən] *n* prévention *f*; **preventive** *adj* préventif(-ive)

preview ['priːvjuː] *n* (*of film*) avant-première *f*

previous ['priːvɪəs] *adj* (*last*) précédent(e); (*earlier*) antérieur(e); **previously** *adv* précédemment, auparavant

prey [preɪ] *n* proie *f* ▷ *vi*: **to ~ on** s'attaquer à; **it was ~ing on his mind** ça le rongeait *or* minait

price [praɪs] *n* prix *m* ▷ *vt* (*goods*) fixer le prix de; **priceless** *adj* sans prix, inestimable; **price list** *n* tarif *m*

prick [prɪk] *n* (*sting*) piqûre *f* ▷ *vt* piquer; **to ~ up one's ears** dresser *or* tendre l'oreille

prickly ['prɪklɪ] *adj* piquant(e),

épineux(-euse); (*fig: person*) irritable

pride [praɪd] n fierté f; (*pej*) orgueil m ▷ vt: **to ~ o.s. on** se flatter de; s'enorgueillir de

priest [priːst] n prêtre m

primarily ['praɪmərɪlɪ] adv principalement, essentiellement

primary ['praɪmərɪ] adj primaire; (*first in importance*) premier(-ière), primordial(e) ▷ n (*US: election*) (élection f) primaire f; **primary school** n (*BRIT*) école f primaire

prime [praɪm] adj primordial(e), fondamental(e); (*excellent*) excellent(e) ▷ vt (*fig*) mettre au courant ▷ n: **in the ~ of life** dans la fleur de l'âge; **Prime Minister** n Premier ministre

primitive ['prɪmɪtɪv] adj primitif(-ive)

primrose ['prɪmrəuz] n primevère f

prince [prɪns] n prince m

princess [prɪn'sɛs] n princesse f

principal ['prɪnsɪpl] adj principal(e) ▷ n (*head teacher*) directeur m, principal m; **principally** adv principalement

principle ['prɪnsɪpl] n principe m; **in ~** en principe; **on ~** par principe

print [prɪnt] n (*mark*) empreinte f; (*letters*) caractères mpl; (*fabric*) imprimé m; (*Art*) gravure f, estampe f; (*Phot*) épreuve f ▷ vt imprimer; (*publish*) publier; (*write in capitals*) écrire en majuscules; **out of ~** épuisé(e); **print out** vt (*Comput*) imprimer; **printer** n (*machine*) imprimante f; (*person*) imprimeur m; **printout** n (*Comput*) sortie f imprimante

prior ['praɪər] adj antérieur(e), précédent(e); (*more important*) prioritaire ▷ adv: **~ to doing** avant de faire

priority [praɪ'ɔrɪtɪ] n priorité f; **to have or take ~ over sth/sb** avoir la priorité sur qch/qn

prison ['prɪzn] n prison f ▷ cpd pénitentiaire; **prisoner** n prisonnier(-ière); **prisoner of war** n prisonnier(-ière) de guerre

pristine ['prɪstiːn] adj virginal(e)

privacy ['prɪvəsɪ] n intimité f, solitude f

private ['praɪvɪt] adj (*not public*) privé(e); (*personal*) personnel(le); (*house, car, lesson*) particulier(-ière); (*quiet: place*) tranquille ▷ n soldat m de deuxième classe; **"~"** (*on envelope*) "personnelle"; (*on door*) "privé"; **in ~** en privé; **privately** adv en privé; (*within oneself*) intérieurement; **private property** n propriété privée; **private school** n école privée

privatize ['praɪvɪtaɪz] vt privatiser

privilege ['prɪvɪlɪdʒ] n privilège m

prize [praɪz] n prix m ▷ adj (*example, idiot*) parfait(e); (*bull, novel*) primé(e) ▷ vt priser, faire grand cas de; **prize-giving** n distribution f des prix; **prizewinner** n gagnant(e)

pro [prəu] n (*inf: Sport*) professionnel(le) ▷ prep pro ...; **pros** npl: **the ~s and cons** le pour et le contre

probability [prɔbə'bɪlɪtɪ] n probabilité f; **in all ~** très probablement

probable ['prɔbəbl] adj probable

probably ['prɔbəblɪ] adv probablement

probation [prə'beɪʃən] n: **on ~** (*employee*) à l'essai; (*Law*) en liberté surveillée

probe [prəub] n (*Med, Space*) sonde f; (*enquiry*) enquête f, investigation f ▷ vt sonder, explorer

problem ['prɔbləm] n problème m

procedure [prə'siːdʒər] n (*Admin, Law*) procédure f; (*method*) marche f à suivre, façon f de procéder

proceed [prə'siːd] vi (*go forward*) avancer; (*act*) procéder; (*continue*): **to ~ (with)** continuer, poursuivre; **to ~ to do** se mettre à faire; **proceedings** npl (*measures*) mesures fpl; (*Law: against sb*) poursuites fpl; (*meeting*) réunion f, séance f; (*records*) compte rendu; actes mpl; **proceeds** ['prəusiːdz] npl produit m, recette f

process ['prəusɛs] n processus m; (*method*) procédé m ▷ vt traiter

procession [prə'sɛʃən] n défilé m,

cortège m; **funeral ~** (on foot) cortège funèbre; (in cars) convoi m mortuaire

proclaim [prə'kleɪm] vt déclarer, proclamer

prod [prɒd] vt pousser

produce n ['prɒdjuːs] (Agr) produits mpl ▷ vt [prə'djuːs] produire; (show) présenter; (cause) provoquer, causer; (Theat) monter, mettre en scène; (TV: programme) réaliser; (: play, film) mettre en scène; (Radio: programme) réaliser; (: play) mettre en ondes; **producer** n (Theat) metteur m en scène; (Agr, Comm, Cine) producteur m; (TV: of programme) réalisateur m; (: of play, film) metteur en scène; (Radio: of programme) réalisateur m; (: of play) metteur en ondes

product ['prɒdʌkt] n produit m; **production** [prə'dʌkʃən] n production f; (Theat) mise f en scène; **productive** [prə'dʌktɪv] adj productif(-ive); **productivity** [prɒdʌk'tɪvɪtɪ] n productivité f

Prof. [prɒf] abbr (= professor) Prof

profession [prə'fɛʃən] n profession f; **professional** n professionnel(le) ▷ adj professionnel(le); (work) de professionnel

professor [prə'fɛsə^r] n professeur m (titulaire d'une chaire); (US: teacher) professeur m

profile ['prəʊfaɪl] n profil m

profit ['prɒfɪt] n (from trading) bénéfice m; (advantage) profit m ▷ vi: **to ~ (by** or **from)** profiter (de); **profitable** adj lucratif(-ive), rentable

profound [prə'faʊnd] adj profond(e)

programme (US **program**) ['prəʊgræm] n (Comput: also BRIT: **program**) programme m; (Radio, TV) émission f ▷ vt programmer; **programmer** (US **programer**) n programmeur(-euse); **programming** (US **programing**) n programmation f

progress n ['prəʊgrɛs] progrès m(pl) ▷ vi [prə'grɛs] progresser, avancer; **in ~** en cours; **progressive** [prə'grɛsɪv] adj progressif(-ive); (person) progressiste

prohibit [prə'hɪbɪt] vt interdire, défendre

project n ['prɒdʒɛkt] (plan) projet m, plan m; (venture) opération f, entreprise f; (Scol: research) étude f, dossier m ▷ vb [prə'dʒɛkt] ▷ vt projeter ▷ vi (stick out) faire saillie, s'avancer; **projection** [prə'dʒɛkʃən] n projection f; (overhang) saillie f; **projector** [prə'dʒɛktə^r] n projecteur m

prolific [prə'lɪfɪk] adj prolifique

prolong [prə'lɒŋ] vt prolonger

prom [prɒm] n abbr = **promenade** (US: ball) bal m d'étudiants; **the P~s** série de concerts de musique classique; voir encadré

● **PROM**
●
● En Grande-Bretagne, un **promenade**
● **concert** ou **prom** est un concert
● de musique classique, ainsi appelé
● car, à l'origine, le public restait
● debout et se promenait au lieu de
● rester assis. De nos jours, une partie
● du public reste debout, mais il y a
● également des places assises (plus
● chères). Les **Proms** les plus connus
● sont les Proms londoniens. La
● dernière séance (the "Last Night of
● the Proms") est un grand événement
● médiatique où se jouent des airs
● traditionnels et patriotiques. Aux
● États-Unis et au Canada, le **prom**
● ou **promenade** est un bal organisé
● par le lycée.

promenade [prɒmə'nɑːd] n (by sea) esplanade f, promenade f

prominent ['prɒmɪnənt] adj (standing out) proéminent(e); (important) important(e)

promiscuous [prə'mɪskjuəs] adj (sexually) de mœurs légères

promise ['prɒmɪs] n promesse f ▷ vt, vi promettre; **promising** adj prometteur(-euse)

promote [prə'məʊt] vt promouvoir; (new product) lancer; **promotion**

[prə'məuʃən] n promotion f

prompt [prɔmpt] adj rapide ▷ n (Comput) message m (de guidage) ▷ vt (cause) entraîner, provoquer; (Theat) souffler (son rôle or ses répliques) à; **at 8 o'clock ~** à 8 heures précises; **to ~ sb to do** inciter or pousser qn à faire; **promptly** adv (quickly) rapidement, sans délai; (on time) ponctuellement

prone [prəun] adj (lying) couché(e) (face contre terre); (liable): **~ to** enclin(e) à

prong [prɔŋ] n (of fork) dent f

pronoun ['prəunaun] n pronom m

pronounce [prə'nauns] vt prononcer; **how do you ~ it?** comment est-ce que ça se prononce?

pronunciation [prənʌnsɪ'eɪʃən] n prononciation f

proof [pru:f] n preuve f ▷ adj: **~ against** à l'épreuve de

prop [prɔp] n support m, étai m; (fig) soutien m ▷ vt (also: **~ up**) étayer, soutenir; **props** npl accessoires mpl

propaganda [prɔpə'gændə] n propagande f

propeller [prə'pɛlər] n hélice f

proper ['prɔpər] adj (suited, right) approprié(e), bon (bonne); (seemly) correct(e), convenable; (authentic) vrai(e), véritable; (referring to place): **the village ~** le village proprement dit; **properly** adv correctement, convenablement; **proper noun** n nom m propre

property ['prɔpətɪ] n (possessions) biens mpl; (house etc) propriété f; (land) terres fpl, domaine m

prophecy ['prɔfɪsɪ] n prophétie f

prophet ['prɔfɪt] n prophète m

proportion [prə'pɔ:ʃən] n proportion f; (share) part f, partie f; **proportions** npl (size) dimensions fpl; **proportional, proportionate** adj proportionnel(le)

proposal [prə'pəuzl] n proposition f, offre f; (plan) projet m; (of marriage) demande f en mariage

propose [prə'pəuz] vt proposer, suggérer ▷ vi faire sa demande en

mariage; **to ~ to do** avoir l'intention de faire

proposition [prɔpə'zɪʃən] n proposition f

proprietor [prə'praɪətər] n propriétaire m/f

prose [prəuz] n prose f; (Scol: translation) thème m

prosecute ['prɔsɪkju:t] vt poursuivre; **prosecution** [prɔsɪ'kju:ʃən] n poursuites fpl judiciaires; (accusing side: in criminal case) accusation f; (: in civil case) la partie plaignante; **prosecutor** n (lawyer) procureur m; (also: **public prosecutor**) ministère public; (us: plaintiff) plaignant(e)

prospect n ['prɔspɛkt] perspective f; (hope) espoir m, chances fpl ▷ vt, vi [prə'spɛkt] prospecter; **prospects** npl (for work etc) possibilités fpl d'avenir, débouchés mpl; **prospective** [prə'spɛktɪv] adj (possible) éventuel(le); (future) futur(e)

prospectus [prə'spɛktəs] n prospectus m

prosper ['prɔspər] vi prospérer; **prosperity** [prɔ'spɛrɪtɪ] n prospérité f; **prosperous** adj prospère

prostitute ['prɔstɪtju:t] n prostituée f; **male ~** prostitué m

protect [prə'tɛkt] vt protéger; **protection** [prə'tɛkʃən] n protection f; **protective** adj protecteur(-trice); (clothing) de protection

protein ['prəuti:n] n protéine f

protest n ['prəutɛst] protestation f ▷ vb [prə'tɛst] ▷ vi: **to ~ against/about** protester contre/à propos de; **to ~ (that)** protester que

Protestant ['prɔtɪstənt] adj, n protestant(e)

protester, protestor [prə'tɛstər] n (in demonstration) manifestant m

protractor [prə'træktər] n (Geom) rapporteur m

proud [praud] adj fier(-ère); (pej) orgueilleux(-euse)

prove [pru:v] vt prouver, démontrer

▷ vi: **to ~ correct** etc s'avérer juste etc; **to ~ o.s.** montrer ce dont on est capable

proverb ['prɒvɜːb] n proverbe m

provide [prə'vaɪd] vt fournir; **to ~ sb with sth** fournir qch à qn; **provide for** vt fus (person) subvenir aux besoins de; (future event) prévoir; **provided** conj: **provided (that)** à condition que + sub; **providing** [prə'vaɪdɪŋ] conj à condition que + sub

province ['prɒvɪns] n province f; (fig) domaine m; **provincial** [prə'vɪnʃəl] adj provincial(e)

provision [prə'vɪʒən] n (supplying) fourniture f; approvisionnement m; (stipulation) disposition f; **provisions** npl (food) provisions fpl; **provisional** adj provisoire

provocative [prə'vɒkətɪv] adj provocateur(-trice), provocant(e)

provoke [prə'vəuk] vt provoquer

prowl [praul] vi (also: ~ about, ~ around) rôder

proximity [prɒk'sɪmɪtɪ] n proximité f

proxy ['prɒksɪ] n: **by ~** par procuration

prudent ['pruːdnt] adj prudent(e)

prune [pruːn] n pruneau m ▷ vt élaguer

pry [praɪ] vi: **to ~ into** fourrer son nez dans

PS n abbr (= postscript) PS m

pseudonym ['sjuːdənɪm] n pseudonyme m

PSHE n abbr (BRIT: Scol: = personal, social and health education) cours d'éducation personnelle, sanitaire et sociale préparant à la vie adulte

psychiatric [saɪkɪ'ætrɪk] adj psychiatrique

psychiatrist [saɪ'kaɪətrɪst] n psychiatre m/f

psychic ['saɪkɪk] adj (also: ~al) (méta)psychique; (person) doué(e) de télépathie or d'un sixième sens

psychoanalysis (pl -ses) [saɪkəuə'nælɪsɪs, -siːz] n psychanalyse f

psychological [saɪkə'lɒdʒɪkl] adj psychologique

psychologist [saɪ'kɒlədʒɪst] n psychologue m/f

psychology [saɪ'kɒlədʒɪ] n psychologie f

psychotherapy [saɪkəu'θɛrəpɪ] n psychothérapie f

pt abbr = pint(s); point(s)

PTO abbr (= please turn over) TSVP

pub [pʌb] n abbr (= public house) pub m

puberty ['pjuːbətɪ] n puberté f

public ['pʌblɪk] adj public(-ique) ▷ n public m; **in ~** en public; **to make ~** rendre public

publication [pʌblɪ'keɪʃən] n publication f

public: public company n société f anonyme; **public convenience** n (BRIT) toilettes fpl; **public holiday** n (BRIT) jour férié; **public house** n (BRIT) pub m

publicity [pʌb'lɪsɪtɪ] n publicité f

publicize ['pʌblɪsaɪz] vt (make known) faire connaître, rendre public; (advertise) faire de la publicité pour

public: public limited company n ≈ société f anonyme (SA) (cotée en Bourse); **publicly** adv publiquement, en public; **public opinion** n opinion publique; **public relations** n or npl relations publiques (RP); **public school** n (BRIT) école privée; (US) école publique; **public transport** n (US **public transportation**) n transports mpl en commun

publish ['pʌblɪʃ] vt publier; **publisher** n éditeur m; **publishing** n (industry) édition f

pub lunch n repas m de bistrot

pudding ['pudɪŋ] n (BRIT: dessert) dessert m, entremets m; (sweet dish) pudding m, gâteau m

puddle ['pʌdl] n flaque f d'eau

puff [pʌf] n bouffée f ▷ vt (also: ~ out: sails, cheeks) gonfler ▷ vi (pant) haleter; **puff pastry** (US **puff paste**) n pâte feuilletée

pull [pul] n (tug): **to give sth a ~** tirer sur qch ▷ vt tirer; (trigger) presser;

(strain: muscle, tendon) se claquer
▷ vi tirer; **to ~ to pieces** mettre en
morceaux; **to ~ one's punches** (also
fig) ménager son adversaire; **to ~ one's
weight** y mettre du sien; **to ~ o.s.
together** se ressaisir; **to ~ sb's leg** (fig)
faire marcher qn; **pull apart** vt (break)
mettre en pièces, démantibuler; **pull
away** vi (vehicle: move off) partir; (draw
back) s'éloigner; **pull back** vt (lever etc)
tirer sur; (curtains) ouvrir ▷ vi (refrain)
s'abstenir; (Mil: withdraw) se retirer;
pull down vt baisser, abaisser; (house)
démolir; **pull in** vi (Aut) se ranger; (Rail)
entrer en gare; **pull off** vt enlever,
ôter; (deal etc) conclure; **pull out** vi
démarrer, partir; (Aut: come out of line)
déboîter ▷ vt (from bag, pocket) sortir;
(remove) arracher; **pull over** vi (Aut) se
ranger; **pull up** vi (stop) s'arrêter ▷ vt
remonter; (uproot) déraciner, arracher
pulley ['pulɪ] n poulie f
pullover ['puləʊvər] n pull-over m,
tricot m
pulp [pʌlp] n (of fruit) pulpe f; (for paper)
pâte f à papier
pulpit ['pulpɪt] n chaire f
pulse [pʌls] n (of blood) pouls m; (of
heart) battement m; **pulses** npl (Culin)
légumineuses fpl
puma ['pju:mə] n puma m
pump [pʌmp] n pompe f; (shoe)
escarpin m ▷ vt pomper; **pump up**
vt gonfler
pumpkin ['pʌmpkɪn] n potiron m,
citrouille f
pun [pʌn] n jeu m de mots, calembour m
punch [pʌntʃ] n (blow) coup m de poing;
(tool) poinçon m; (drink) punch m ▷ vt
(make a hole in) poinçonner, perforer;
(hit): **to ~ sb/sth** donner un coup de
poing à qn/sur qch; **punch-up** n (BRIT
inf) bagarre f
punctual ['pʌŋktjuəl] adj ponctuel(le)
punctuation [pʌŋktju'eɪʃən] n
ponctuation f
puncture ['pʌŋktʃər] n (BRIT) crevaison
f ▷ vt crever

punish ['pʌnɪʃ] vt punir; **punishment** n
punition f, châtiment m
punk [pʌŋk] n (person: also: ~ **rocker**)
punk m/f; (music: also: ~ **rock**) le punk;
(us inf: hoodlum) voyou m
pup [pʌp] n chiot m
pupil ['pju:pl] n élève m/f; (of eye)
pupille f
puppet ['pʌpɪt] n marionnette f,
pantin m
puppy ['pʌpɪ] n chiot m, petit chien
purchase ['pə:tʃɪs] n achat m ▷ vt
acheter
pure [pjuər] adj pur(e); **purely** adv
purement
purify ['pjuərɪfaɪ] vt purifier, épurer
purity ['pjuərɪtɪ] n pureté f
purple ['pə:pl] adj violet(te); (face)
cramoisi(e)
purpose ['pə:pəs] n intention f, but m;
on ~ exprès
purr [pə:r] vi ronronner
purse [pə:s] n (BRIT: for money) porte-
monnaie m inv; (us: handbag) sac m (à
main) ▷ vt serrer, pincer
pursue [pə'sju:] vt poursuivre
pursuit [pə'sju:t] n poursuite f;
(occupation) occupation f, activité f
pus [pʌs] n pus m
push [puʃ] n poussée f ▷ vt pousser;
(button) appuyer sur; (fig: product)
mettre en avant, faire de la publicité
pour ▷ vi pousser; **to ~ for** (better
pay, conditions) réclamer; **push in**
vi s'introduire de force; **push off** vi
(inf) filer, ficher le camp; **push on** vi
(continue) continuer; **push over** vt
renverser; **push through** vi (in crowd)
se frayer un chemin; **pushchair** n
(BRIT) poussette f; **pusher** n (also: **drug
pusher**) revendeur(-euse) (de drogue),
ravitailleur(-euse) (en drogue); **push-
up** n (US) traction f
pussy(-cat) ['pusɪ-] n (inf) minet m
put (pt, pp ~) [put] vt mettre; (place)
poser, placer; (say) dire, exprimer; (a
question) poser; (case, view) exposer,
présenter; (estimate) estimer; **put**

aside vt mettre de côté; **put away** vt (store) ranger; **put back** vt (replace) remettre, replacer; (postpone) remettre; **put by** vt (money) mettre de côté, économiser; **put down** vt (parcel etc) poser, déposer; (in writing) mettre par écrit, inscrire; (suppress: revolt etc) réprimer, écraser; (attribute) attribuer; (animal) abattre; (cat, dog) faire piquer; **put forward** vt (ideas) avancer, proposer; **put in** vt (complaint) soumettre; (time, effort) consacrer; **put off** vt (postpone) remettre à plus tard, ajourner; (discourage) dissuader; **put on** vt (clothes, lipstick, CD) mettre; (play etc) allumer; (play etc) monter; (weight) prendre; (assume: accent, manner) prendre; **put out** vt (take outside) mettre dehors; (one's hand) tendre; (light etc) éteindre; (person: inconvenience) déranger, gêner; **put through** vt (Tel: caller) mettre en communication; (: call) passer; (plan) faire accepter; **put together** vt mettre ensemble; (assemble: furniture) monter, assembler; (meal) préparer; **put up** vt (raise) lever, relever, remonter; (hang) accrocher; (build) construire, ériger; (increase) augmenter; (accommodate) loger; **put up with** vt fus supporter

putt [pʌt] n putt m; **putting green** n green m

puzzle ['pʌzl] n énigme f, mystère m; (game) jeu m, casse-tête m; (jigsaw) puzzle m; (also: **crossword ~**) mots croisés ▷ vt intriguer, rendre perplexe ▷ vi: **to ~ over** chercher à comprendre; **puzzled** adj perplexe; **puzzling** adj déconcertant(e), inexplicable

pyjamas [pɪ'dʒɑ:məz] npl (BRIT) pyjama m

pylon ['paɪlən] n pylône m

pyramid ['pɪrəmɪd] n pyramide f

Pyrenees [pɪrə'ni:z] npl Pyrénées fpl

q

quack [kwæk] n (of duck) coin-coin m inv; (pej: doctor) charlatan m

quadruple [kwɔ'dru:pl] vt, vi quadrupler

quail [kweɪl] n (Zool) caille f ▷ vi: **to ~ at** or **before** reculer devant

quaint [kweɪnt] adj bizarre; (old-fashioned) désuet(-ète); (picturesque) au charme vieillot, pittoresque

quake [kweɪk] vi trembler ▷ n abbr = **earthquake**

qualification [kwɔlɪfɪ'keɪʃən] n (often pl: degree etc) diplôme m; (training) qualification(s) f(pl); (ability) compétence(s) f(pl); (limitation) réserve f, restriction f

qualified ['kwɔlɪfaɪd] adj (trained) qualifié(e); (professionally) diplômé(e); (fit, competent) compétent(e), qualifié(e); (limited) conditionnel(le)

qualify ['kwɔlɪfaɪ] vt qualifier; (modify) atténuer, nuancer ▷ vi: **to ~ (as)** obtenir son diplôme (de); **to ~ (for)** remplir les conditions requises (pour),

quality [ˈkwɔlɪtɪ] n qualité f
qualm [kwɑːm] n doute m; scrupule m
quantify [ˈkwɔntɪfaɪ] vt quantifier
quantity [ˈkwɔntɪtɪ] n quantité f
quarantine [ˈkwɔrntiːn] n quarantaine f
quarrel [ˈkwɔrl] n querelle f, dispute f ▷ vi se disputer, se quereller
quarry [ˈkwɔrɪ] n (for stone) carrière f; (animal) proie f, gibier m
quart [kwɔːt] n ≈ litre m
quarter [ˈkwɔːtəʳ] n quart m; (of year) trimestre m; (district) quartier m; (US, CANADA: 25 cents) (pièce f de) vingt-cinq cents mpl ▷ vt partager en quartiers or en quatre; (Mil) caserner, cantonner; **quarters** npl logement m; (Mil) quartiers mpl, cantonnement m; **a ~ of an hour** un quart d'heure; **quarter final** n quart m de finale; **quarterly** adj trimestriel(le) ▷ adv tous les trois mois
quartet(te) [kwɔːˈtɛt] n quatuor m; (jazz players) quartette m
quartz [kwɔːts] n quartz m
quay [kiː] n (also: **~side**) quai m
queasy [ˈkwiːzɪ] adj: **to feel ~** avoir mal au cœur
Quebec [kwɪˈbɛk] n (city) Québec; (province) Québec m
queen [kwiːn] n (gen) reine f; (Cards etc) dame f
queer [kwɪəʳ] adj étrange, curieux(-euse); (suspicious) louche ▷ n (inf: highly offensive) homosexuel m
quench [kwɛntʃ] vt: **to ~ one's thirst** se désaltérer
query [ˈkwɪərɪ] n question f ▷ vt (disagree with, dispute) mettre en doute, questionner
quest [kwɛst] n recherche f, quête f
question [ˈkwɛstʃən] n question f ▷ vt (person) interroger; (plan, idea) mettre en question or en doute; **beyond ~** sans aucun doute; **out of the ~** hors de question; **questionable** adj discutable; **question mark** n point m d'interrogation; **questionnaire**

[kwɛstʃəˈnɛəʳ] n questionnaire m
queue [kjuː] (BRIT) n queue f, file f ▷ vi (also: **~ up**) faire la queue
quiche [kiːʃ] n quiche f
quick [kwɪk] adj rapide; (mind) vif (vive); (agile) agile, vif (vive) ▷ n: **cut to the ~** (fig) touché(e) au vif; **be ~!** dépêche-toi!; **quickly** adv (fast) vite, rapidement; (immediately) tout de suite
quid [kwɪd] n (pl inv: BRIT inf) livre f
quiet [ˈkwaɪət] adj tranquille, calme; (voice) bas(se); (ceremony, colour) discret(-ète) ▷ n tranquillité f, calme m; (silence) silence m; **quietly** adv tranquillement; (silently) silencieusement; (discreetly) discrètement
quilt [kwɪlt] n édredon m; (continental quilt) couette f
quirky [ˈkwɜːkɪ] adj singulier(-ère)
quit [kwɪt] (pt, pp **~** or **~ted**) vt quitter ▷ vi (give up) abandonner, renoncer; (resign) démissionner
quite [kwaɪt] adv (rather) assez, plutôt; (entirely) complètement, tout à fait; **~ a few of them** un assez grand nombre d'entre eux; **that's not ~ right** ce n'est pas tout à fait juste; **~ (so)!** exactement!
quits [kwɪts] adj: **~ (with)** quitte (envers); **let's call it ~** restons-en là
quiver [ˈkwɪvəʳ] vi trembler, frémir
quiz [kwɪz] n (on TV) jeu-concours m (télévisé); (in magazine etc) test m de connaissances ▷ vt interroger
quota [ˈkwəutə] n quota m
quotation [kwəuˈteɪʃən] n citation f; (estimate) devis m; **quotation marks** npl guillemets mpl
quote [kwəut] n citation f; (estimate) devis m ▷ vt (sentence, author) citer; (price) donner, soumettre ▷ vi: **to ~ from** citer; **quotes** npl (inverted commas) guillemets mpl

r

Rabat [rə'bɑːt] *n* Rabat
rabbi ['ræbaɪ] *n* rabbin *m*
rabbit ['ræbɪt] *n* lapin *m*
rabies ['reɪbiːz] *n* rage *f*
RAC *n abbr* (BRIT: = Royal Automobile Club) ≈ ACF *m*
rac(c)oon [rə'kuːn] *n* raton *m* laveur
race [reɪs] *n* (*species*) race *f*; (*competition, rush*) course *f* ▷ *vt* (*person*) faire la course avec ▷ *vi* (*compete*) faire la course, courir; (*pulse*) battre très vite; **race car** *n* (US) = **racing car**; **racecourse** *n* champ *m* de courses; **racehorse** *n* cheval *m* de course; **racetrack** *n* piste *f*
racial ['reɪʃl] *adj* racial(e)
racing ['reɪsɪŋ] *n* courses *fpl*; **racing car** *n* (BRIT) voiture *f* de course; **racing driver** *n* (BRIT) pilote *m* de course
racism ['reɪsɪzəm] *n* racisme *m*; **racist** ['reɪsɪst] *adj, n* raciste *m/f*
rack [ræk] *n* (*for guns, tools*) râtelier *m*; (*for clothes*) portant *m*; (*for bottles*) casier *m*; (*also:* **luggage ~**) filet *m* à bagages; (*also:* **roof ~**) galerie *f*; (*also:* **dish ~**) égouttoir *m* ▷ *vt* tourmenter; **to ~ one's brains** se creuser la cervelle
racket ['rækɪt] *n* (*for tennis*) raquette *f*; (*noise*) tapage *m*, vacarme *m*; (*swindle*) escroquerie *f*
racquet ['rækɪt] *n* raquette *f*
radar ['reɪdɑːʳ] *n* radar *m*
radiation [reɪdɪ'eɪʃən] *n* rayonnement *m*; (*radioactive*) radiation *f*
radiator ['reɪdɪeɪtəʳ] *n* radiateur *m*
radical ['rædɪkl] *adj* radical(e)
radio ['reɪdɪəu] *n* radio *f* ▷ *vt* (*person*) appeler par radio; **on the ~** à la radio; **radioactive** *adj* radioactif(-ive); **radio station** *n* station *f* de radio
radish ['rædɪʃ] *n* radis *m*
RAF *n abbr* (BRIT) = **Royal Air Force**
raffle ['ræfl] *n* tombola *f*
raft [rɑːft] *n* (*craft: also:* **life ~**) radeau *m*; (*logs*) train *m* de flottage
rag [ræg] *n* chiffon *m*; (*pej: newspaper*) feuille *f*, torchon *m*; (*for charity*) attractions organisées par les étudiants au profit d'œuvres de charité; **rags** *npl* haillons *mpl*
rage [reɪdʒ] *n* (*fury*) rage *f*, fureur *f* ▷ *vi* (*person*) être fou (folle) de rage; (*storm*) faire rage, être déchaîné(e); **it's all the ~** cela fait fureur
ragged ['rægɪd] *adj* (*edge*) inégal(e), qui accroche; (*clothes*) en loques; (*appearance*) déguenillé(e)
raid [reɪd] *n* (*Mil*) raid *m*; (*criminal*) hold-up *m inv*; (*by police*) descente *f*, rafle *f* ▷ *vt* faire un raid sur *or* une descente dans *or* un hold-up dans
rail [reɪl] *n* (*on stair*) rampe *f*; (*on bridge, balcony*) balustrade *f*; (*of ship*) bastingage *m*; (*for train*) rail *m*; **railcard** *n* (BRIT) carte *f* de chemin de fer; **railing(s)** *n(pl)* grille *f*; **railway** (US **railroad**) *n* chemin *m* de fer; (*track*) voie *f* ferrée; **railway line** *n* (BRIT) ligne *f* de chemin de fer; (*track*) voie ferrée; **railway station** *n* (BRIT) gare *f*
rain [reɪn] *n* pluie *f* ▷ *vi* pleuvoir; **in the ~** sous la pluie; **it's ~ing** il pleut;

rainbow n arc-en-ciel m; **raincoat** n impermeable m; **raindrop** n goutte f de pluie; **rainfall** n chute f de pluie; (measurement) hauteur f des précipitations; **rainforest** n forêt tropicale; **rainy** adj pluvieux(-euse)

raise [reɪz] n augmentation f ▷ vt (lift) lever; hausser; (increase) augmenter; (morale) remonter; (standards) améliorer; (a protest, doubt) provoquer, causer; (a question) soulever; (cattle, family) élever; (crop) faire pousser; (army, funds) rassembler; (loan) obtenir; **to ~ one's voice** élever la voix

raisin ['reɪzn] n raisin sec

rake [reɪk] n (tool) râteau m; (person) débauché m ▷ vt (garden) ratisser

rally ['rælɪ] n (Pol etc) meeting m, rassemblement m; (Aut) rallye m; (Tennis) échange m ▷ vt rassembler, rallier; (support) ▷ vi (sick person) aller mieux; (Stock Exchange) reprendre

RAM [ræm] n abbr (Comput: = random access memory) mémoire vive

ram [ræm] n bélier m ▷ vt (push) enfoncer; (crash into: vehicle) emboutir; (: lamppost etc) percuter

Ramadan [ræmə'dæn] n Ramadan m

ramble ['ræmbl] n randonnée f ▷ vi (walk) se promener, faire une randonnée; (pej: also: **~ on**) discourir, pérorer; **rambler** n promeneur(-euse), randonneur(-euse); **rambling** adj (speech) décousu(e); (house) plein(e) de coins et de recoins; (Bot) grimpant(e)

ramp [ræmp] n (incline) rampe f; (Aut) dénivellation f; (in garage) pont m; **on/off ~** (us Aut) bretelle f d'accès

rampage [ræm'peɪdʒ] n: **to be on the ~** se déchaîner

ran [ræn] pt of **run**

ranch [rɑːntʃ] n ranch m

random ['rændəm] adj fait(e) or établi(e) au hasard; (Comput, Math) aléatoire ▷ n: **at ~** au hasard

rang [ræŋ] pt of **ring**

range [reɪndʒ] n (of mountains) chaîne f; (of missile, voice) portée f; (of products) choix m, gamme f; (also: **shooting ~**) champ m de tir; (also: **kitchen ~**) fourneau m (de cuisine) ▷ vt (place) mettre en rang, placer ▷ vi: **to ~ over** couvrir; **to ~ from ... to** aller de ... à

ranger ['reɪndʒəʳ] n garde m forestier

rank [ræŋk] n rang m; (Mil) grade m; (BRIT: also: **taxi ~**) station f de taxis ▷ vi: **to ~ among** compter or se classer parmi ▷ adj (smell) nauséabond(e); **the ~ and file** (fig) la masse, la base

ransom ['rænsəm] n rançon f; **to hold sb to ~** (fig) exercer un chantage sur qn

rant [rænt] vi fulminer

rap [ræp] n (music) rap m ▷ vt (door) frapper sur or à; (table etc) taper sur

rape [reɪp] n viol m; (Bot) colza m ▷ vt violer

rapid ['ræpɪd] adj rapide; **rapidly** adv rapidement; **rapids** npl (Geo) rapides mpl

rapist ['reɪpɪst] n auteur m d'un viol

rapport [ræ'pɔːᵗ] n entente f

rare [rɛəʳ] adj rare; (Culin: steak) saignant(e); **rarely** adv rarement

rash [ræʃ] adj imprudent(e), irréfléchi(e) ▷ n (Med) rougeur f, éruption f; (of events) série f (noire)

rasher ['ræʃəʳ] n fine tranche (de lard)

raspberry ['rɑːzbərɪ] n framboise f

rat [ræt] n rat m

rate [reɪt] n (ratio) taux m, pourcentage m; (speed) vitesse f, rythme m; (price) tarif m ▷ vt (price) évaluer, estimer; (people) classer; **rates** npl (BRIT: property tax) impôts locaux; **to ~ sb/sth as** considérer qn/qch comme

rather ['rɑːðəʳ] adv (somewhat) assez, plutôt; (to some extent) un peu; **it's ~ expensive** c'est assez cher; (too much) c'est un peu cher; **there's ~ a lot** il y en a beaucoup; **I would** or **I'd ~ go** j'aimerais mieux or je préférerais partir; **or ~** (more accurately) ou plutôt

rating ['reɪtɪŋ] n (assessment) évaluation f; (score) classement m; (Finance) cote f; **ratings** npl (Radio) indice(s) m(pl) d'écoute; (TV) Audimat®

ratio ['reɪʃɪəu] n proportion f; **in the ~ of 100 to 1** dans la proportion de 100 contre 1

ration ['ræʃən] n ration f ▷ vt rationner; **rations** npl (food) vivres mpl

rational ['ræʃənl] adj raisonnable, sensé(e); (solution, reasoning) logique; (Med: person) lucide

rat race n foire f d'empoigne

rattle ['rætl] n (of door, window) battement m; (of coins, chain) cliquetis m; (of train, engine) bruit m de ferraille; (for baby) hochet m ▷ vi cliqueter; (car, bus): **to ~ along** rouler en faisant un bruit de ferraille ▷ vt agiter (bruyamment); (inf: disconcert) décontenancer

rave [reɪv] vi (in anger) s'emporter; (with enthusiasm) s'extasier; (Med) délirer ▷ n (inf: party) rave f, soirée f techno

raven ['reɪvən] n grand corbeau

ravine [rə'viːn] n ravin m

raw [rɔː] adj (uncooked) cru(e); (not processed) brut(e); (sore) à vif, irrité(e); (inexperienced) inexpérimenté(e); **~ materials** matières premières

ray [reɪ] n rayon m; **~ of hope** lueur f d'espoir

razor ['reɪzər] n rasoir m; **razor blade** n lame f de rasoir

Rd abbr = **road**

RE n abbr (BRIT) = **religious education**

re [riː] prep concernant

reach [riːtʃ] n portée f, atteinte f; (of river etc) étendue f ▷ vt atteindre, arriver à; (conclusion, decision) parvenir à ▷ vi s'étendre; **out of/within ~** (object) hors de/à portée; **reach out** vt tendre ▷ vi: **to ~ out (for)** allonger le bras (pour prendre)

react [riː'ækt] vi réagir; **reaction** [riː'ækʃən] n réaction f; **reactor** [riː'æktər] n réacteur m

read (pt, pp **~**) [riːd, rɛd] vi lire ▷ vt lire; (understand) comprendre, interpréter; (study) étudier; (meter) relever; (subj: instrument etc) indiquer, marquer; **read out** vt lire à haute voix; **reader** n

lecteur(-trice)

readily ['rɛdɪlɪ] adv volontiers, avec empressement; (easily) facilement

reading ['riːdɪŋ] n lecture f; (understanding) interprétation f; (on instrument) indications fpl

ready ['rɛdɪ] adj prêt(e); (willing) prêt, disposé(e); (available) disponible ▷ n: **at the ~** (Mil) prêt à faire feu; **when will my photos be ~?** quand est-ce que mes photos seront prêtes?; **to get ~** (as vi) se préparer; (as vt) préparer; **ready-cooked** adj précuit(e); **ready-made** adj tout(e) faite(e)

real [rɪəl] adj (world, life) réel(le); (genuine) véritable; (proper) vrai(e) ▷ adv (US inf: very) vraiment; **real ale** n bière traditionnelle; **real estate** n biens fonciers or immobiliers; **realistic** [rɪə'lɪstɪk] adj réaliste; **reality** [riː'ælɪtɪ] n réalité f

reality TV n téléréalité f

realization [rɪəlaɪ'zeɪʃən] n (awareness) prise f de conscience; (fulfilment: also: of asset) réalisation f

realize ['rɪəlaɪz] vt (understand) se rendre compte de, prendre conscience de; (a project, Comm: asset) réaliser

really ['rɪəlɪ] adv vraiment; **~?** vraiment?, c'est vrai?

realm [rɛlm] n royaume m; (fig) domaine m

realtor ['rɪəltɔːr] n (US) agent immobilier

reappear [riːə'pɪər] vi réapparaître, reparaître

rear [rɪər] adj de derrière, arrière inv; (Aut: wheel etc) arrière ▷ vt (cattle, family) élever ▷ vi (also: **~ up**: animal) se cabrer

rearrange [riːə'reɪndʒ] vt réarranger

rear: **rear-view mirror** n (Aut) rétroviseur m; **rear-wheel drive** n (Aut) traction f arrière

reason ['riːzn] n raison f ▷ vi: **to ~ with sb** raisonner qn, faire entendre raison à qn; **it stands to ~ that** il va sans dire que; **reasonable** adj raisonnable;

(*not bad*) acceptable; **reasonably** *adv*
(*behave*) raisonnablement; (*fairly*) assez;
reasoning *n* raisonnement *m*

reassurance [riːəˈʃuərəns] *n* (*factual*)
assurance *f*, garantie *f*; (*emotional*)
réconfort *m*

reassure [riːəˈʃuəʳ] *vt* rassurer

rebate [ˈriːbeɪt] *n* (*on tax etc*)
dégrèvement *m*

rebel *n* [ˈrɛbl] rebelle *m/f* ▷ *vi* [rɪˈbɛl]
se rebeller, se révolter; **rebellion**
[rɪˈbɛljən] *n* rébellion *f*, révolte *f*;
rebellious [rɪˈbɛljəs] *adj* rebelle

rebuild [riːˈbɪld] *vt* (*irreg: like* **build**)
reconstruire

recall *vt* [rɪˈkɔːl] rappeler; (*remember*)
se rappeler, se souvenir de ▷ *n* [ˈriːkɔl]
rappel *m*; (*ability to remember*) mémoire *f*

rec'd *abbr of* **received**

receipt [rɪˈsiːt] *n* (*document*) reçu *m*;
(*for parcel etc*) accusé *m* de réception;
(*act of receiving*) réception *f*; **receipts**
npl (*Comm*) recettes *fpl*; **can I have a
~, please?** je peux avoir un reçu, s'il
vous plaît?

receive [rɪˈsiːv] *vt* recevoir; (*guest*)
recevoir, accueillir; **receiver** *n* (*Tel*)
récepteur *m*, combiné *m*; (*Radio*)
récepteur; (*of stolen goods*) receleur
m; (*for bankruptcies*) administrateur *m*
judiciaire

recent [ˈriːsnt] *adj* récent(e); **recently**
adv récemment

reception [rɪˈsɛpʃən] *n* réception
f; (*welcome*) accueil *m*, réception;
reception desk *n* réception *f*;
receptionist *n* réceptionniste *m/f*

recession [rɪˈsɛʃən] *n* (*Econ*) récession *f*

recharge [riːˈtʃɑːdʒ] *vt* (*battery*)
recharger

recipe [ˈrɛsɪpɪ] *n* recette *f*

recipient [rɪˈsɪpɪənt] *n* (*of payment*)
bénéficiaire *m/f*; (*of letter*) destinataire
m/f

recital [rɪˈsaɪtl] *n* récital *m*

recite [rɪˈsaɪt] *vt* (*poem*) réciter

reckless [ˈrɛkləs] *adj* (*driver
etc*) imprudent(e); (*spender etc*)

insouciant(e)

reckon [ˈrɛkən] *vt* (*count*) calculer,
compter; (*consider*) considérer, estimer;
(*think*): **I ~ (that) ...** je pense (que) ...,
j'estime (que) ...

reclaim [rɪˈkleɪm] *vt* (*land: from sea*)
assécher; (*demand back*) réclamer (le
remboursement *or* la restitution de);
(*waste materials*) récupérer

recline [rɪˈklaɪn] *vi* être allongé(e) *or*
étendu(e)

recognition [rɛkəgˈnɪʃən] *n*
reconnaissance *f*; **transformed
beyond ~** méconnaissable

recognize [ˈrɛkəgnaɪz] *vt*: **to ~ (by/as)**
reconnaître (à/comme étant)

recollection [rɛkəˈlɛkʃən] *n*
souvenir *m*

recommend [rɛkəˈmɛnd] *vt*
recommander; **can you ~ a good
restaurant?** pouvez-vous me
conseiller un bon restaurant?;
recommendation [rɛkəmɛnˈdeɪʃən] *n*
recommandation *f*

reconcile [ˈrɛkənsaɪl] *vt* (*two people*)
réconcilier; (*two facts*) concilier,
accorder; **to ~ o.s.** se résigner à

reconsider [riːkənˈsɪdəʳ] *vt*
reconsidérer

reconstruct [riːkənˈstrʌkt] *vt*
(*building*) reconstruire; (*crime, system*)
reconstituer

record *n* [ˈrɛkɔːd] rapport *m*, récit
m; (*of meeting etc*) procès-verbal *m*;
(*register*) registre *m*; (*file*) dossier *m*;
(*Comput*) article *m*; (*also:* **police ~**)
casier *m* judiciaire; (*Mus: disc*) disque
m; (*Sport*) record *m* ▷ *adj* record *inv* ▷ *vt*
[rɪˈkɔːd] (*set down*) noter; (*Mus: song
etc*) enregistrer; **public ~s** archives
fpl; **in ~ time** dans un temps record;
recorded delivery *n* (*BRIT Post*): **to
send sth recorded delivery** ≈ envoyer
qch en recommandé; **recorder** *n*
(*Mus*) flûte *f* à bec; **recording** *n* (*Mus*)
enregistrement *m*; **record player** *n*
tourne-disque *m*

recount [rɪˈkaunt] *vt* raconter

recover [rɪ'kʌvə'] vt récupérer ▷ vi
(from illness) se rétablir; (from shock) se
remettre; **recovery** n récupération
f; rétablissement m; (Econ)
redressement m

recreate [ri:krɪ'eɪt] vt recréer

recreation [rɛkrɪ'eɪʃən] n (leisure)
récréation f, détente f; **recreational
drug** n drogue récréative;
recreational vehicle n (US) camping-
car m

recruit [rɪ'kru:t] n recrue f
▷ vt recruter; **recruitment** n
recrutement m

rectangle ['rɛktæŋgl] n rectangle m;
rectangular [rɛk'tæŋgjulə'] adj
rectangulaire

rectify ['rɛktɪfaɪ] vt (error) rectifier,
corriger

rector ['rɛktə'] n (Rel) pasteur m

recur [rɪ'kə:'] vi se reproduire; (idea,
opportunity) se retrouver; (symptoms)
réapparaître; **recurring** adj (problem)
périodique, fréquent(e); (Math)
périodique

recyclable [ri:'saɪkləbl] adj recyclable

recycle [ri:'saɪkl] vt, vi recycler

recycling [ri:'saɪklɪŋ] n recyclage m

red [rɛd] n rouge m; (Pol: pej) rouge m/f
▷ adj rouge; (hair) roux (rousse); **in the
~** (account) à découvert; (business) en
déficit; **Red Cross** n Croix-Rouge f;
redcurrant n groseille f (rouge)

redeem [rɪ'di:m] vt (debt) rembourser;
(sth in pawn) dégager; (fig, also Rel)
racheter

red: **red-haired** adj roux (rousse);
redhead n roux (rousse); **red-hot** adj
chauffé(e) au rouge, brûlant(e); **red
light** n: **to go through a red light** (Aut)
brûler un feu rouge; **red-light district**
n quartier mal famé

red meat n viande f rouge

reduce [rɪ'dju:s] vt réduire; (lower)
abaisser; **"~ speed now"** (Aut)
"ralentir"; **to ~ sb to tears** faire pleurer
qn; **reduced** adj réduit(e); **"greatly
reduced prices"** "gros rabais"; **at a
reduced price** (goods) au rabais; (ticket
etc) à prix réduit; **reduction** [rɪ'dʌkʃən]
n réduction f; (of price) baisse f;
(discount) rabais m; réduction; **is there
a reduction for children/students?** y
a-t-il une réduction pour les enfants/
les étudiants?

redundancy [rɪ'dʌndənsɪ] n (BRIT)
licenciement m, mise f au chômage

redundant [rɪ'dʌndnt] adj (BRIT:
worker) licencié(e), mis(e) au chômage;
(detail, object) superflu(e); **to be made
~** (worker) être licencié, être mis au
chômage

reed [ri:d] n (Bot) roseau m

reef [ri:f] n (at sea) récif m, écueil m

reel [ri:l] n bobine f; (Fishing) moulinet
m; (Cine) bande f; (dance) quadrille
écossais ▷ vi (sway) chanceler

ref [rɛf] n abbr (inf: = referee) arbitre m

refectory [rɪ'fɛktərɪ] n réfectoire m

refer [rɪ'fə:'] vt: **to ~ sb to** (inquirer,
patient) adresser qn à; (reader: to text)
renvoyer qn à ▷ vi: **to ~ to** (allude to)
parler de, faire allusion à; (consult) se
reporter à; (apply to) s'appliquer à

referee [rɛfə'ri:] n arbitre m; (BRIT:
for job application) répondant(e) ▷ vt
arbitrer

reference ['rɛfrəns] n référence f,
renvoi m; (mention) allusion f, mention
f; (for job application: letter) références;
lettre f de recommandation; **with ~
to** en ce qui concerne; (Comm: in letter)
me référant à; **reference number** n
(Comm) numéro m de référence

refill vt [ri:'fɪl] remplir à nouveau; (pen,
lighter etc) recharger ▷ n ['ri:fɪl] (for pen
etc) recharge f

refine [rɪ'faɪn] vt (sugar, oil) raffiner;
(taste) affiner; (idea, theory) peaufiner;
refined adj (person, taste) raffiné(e);
refinery n raffinerie f

reflect [rɪ'flɛkt] vt (light, image)
réfléchir, refléter ▷ vi (think) réfléchir,
méditer; **it ~s badly on him** cela le
discrédite; **it ~s well on him** c'est tout
à son honneur; **reflection** [rɪ'flɛkʃən]

n réflexion *f*; (*image*) reflet *m*; **on reflection** réflexion faite

reflex ['riːflɛks] *adj*, *n* réflexe (*m*)

reform [rɪ'fɔːm] *n* réforme *f* ▷ *vt* réformer

refrain [rɪ'freɪn] *vi*: **to ~ from doing** s'abstenir de faire ▷ *n* refrain *m*

refresh [rɪ'frɛʃ] *vt* rafraîchir; (*subj: food, sleep etc*) redonner des forces à; **refreshing** *adj* (*drink*) rafraîchissant(e); (*sleep*) réparateur(-trice); **refreshments** *npl* rafraîchissements *mpl*

refrigerator [rɪ'frɪdʒəreɪtəʳ] *n* réfrigérateur *m*, frigidaire *m*

refuel [riː'fjuəl] *vi* se ravitailler en carburant

refuge ['rɛfjuːdʒ] *n* refuge *m*; **to take ~ in** se réfugier dans; **refugee** [rɛfju'dʒiː] *n* réfugié(e)

refund *n* ['riːfʌnd] remboursement *m* ▷ *vt* [rɪ'fʌnd] rembourser

refurbish [riː'fəːbɪʃ] *vt* remettre à neuf

refusal [rɪ'fjuːzəl] *n* refus *m*; **to have first ~ on sth** avoir droit de préemption sur qch

refuse[1] ['rɛfjuːs] *n* ordures *fpl*, détritus *mpl*

refuse[2] [rɪ'fjuːz] *vt*, *vi* refuser; **to ~ to do sth** refuser de faire qch

regain [rɪ'geɪn] *vt* (*lost ground*) regagner; (*strength*) retrouver

regard [rɪ'gɑːd] *n* respect *m*, estime *f*, considération *f* ▷ *vt* considérer; **to give one's ~s to** faire ses amitiés à; **"with kindest ~s"** "bien amicalement"; **as ~s, with ~ to** en ce qui concerne; **regarding** *prep* en ce qui concerne; **regardless** *adv* quand même; **regardless of** sans se soucier de

regenerate [rɪ'dʒɛnəreɪt] *vt* régénérer ▷ *vi* se régénérer

reggae ['rɛgeɪ] *n* reggae *m*

regiment ['rɛdʒɪmənt] *n* régiment *m*

region ['riːdʒən] *n* région *f*; **in the ~ of** (*fig*) aux alentours de; **regional** *adj* régional(e)

register ['rɛdʒɪstəʳ] *n* registre *m*;

(*also*: **electoral ~**) liste électorale ▷ *vt* enregistrer, inscrire; (*birth*) déclarer; (*vehicle*) immatriculer; (*letter*) envoyer en recommandé; (*subj: instrument*) marquer ▷ *vi* s'inscrire; (*at hotel*) signer le registre; (*make impression*) être (bien) compris(e); **registered** *adj* (BRIT: *letter*) recommandé(e)

registered trademark *n* marque déposée

registrar ['rɛdʒɪstrɑːʳ] *n* officier *m* de l'état civil

registration [rɛdʒɪs'treɪʃən] *n* (*act*) enregistrement *m*; (*of student*) inscription *f*; (BRIT Aut: also: **~ number**) numéro *m* d'immatriculation

registry office ['rɛdʒɪstrɪ-] *n* (BRIT) bureau *m* de l'état civil; **to get married in a ~** ≈ se marier à la mairie

regret [rɪ'grɛt] *n* regret *m* ▷ *vt* regretter; **regrettable** *adj* regrettable, fâcheux(-euse)

regular ['rɛgjuləʳ] *adj* régulier(-ière); (*usual*) habituel(le), normal(e); (*soldier*) de métier; (Comm: *size*) ordinaire ▷ *n* (*client etc*) habitué(e); **regularly** *adv* régulièrement

regulate ['rɛgjuleɪt] *vt* régler; **regulation** [rɛgju'leɪʃən] *n* (*rule*) règlement *m*; (*adjustment*) réglage *m*

rehabilitation ['riːəbɪlɪ'teɪʃən] *n* (*of offender*) réhabilitation *f*; (*of addict*) réadaptation *f*

rehearsal [rɪ'həːsəl] *n* répétition *f*

rehearse [rɪ'həːs] *vt* répéter

reign [reɪn] *n* règne *m* ▷ *vi* régner

reimburse [riːɪm'bəːs] *vt* rembourser

rein [reɪn] *n* (*for horse*) rêne *f*

reincarnation [riːɪnkɑː'neɪʃən] *n* réincarnation *f*

reindeer ['reɪndɪəʳ] *n* (*pl inv*) renne *m*

reinforce [riːɪn'fɔːs] *vt* renforcer; **reinforcements** *npl* (Mil) renfort(s) *m(pl)*

reinstate [riːɪn'steɪt] *vt* rétablir, réintégrer

reject *n* ['riːdʒɛkt] (Comm) article *m* de rebut ▷ *vt* [rɪ'dʒɛkt] refuser; (*idea*) rejeter; **rejection** [rɪ'dʒɛkʃən] n rejet m, refus m

rejoice [rɪ'dʒɔɪs] vi: **to ~ (at** or **over)** se réjouir (de)

relate [rɪ'leɪt] vt (tell) raconter; (connect) établir un rapport entre ▷ vi: **to ~ to** (connect) se rapporter à; **to ~ to sb** (interact) entretenir des rapports avec qn; **related** adj apparenté(e); **related to** (subject) lié(e) à; **relating to** prep concernant

relation [rɪ'leɪʃən] n (person) parent(e); (link) rapport m, lien m; **relations** npl (relatives) famille f; **relationship** n rapport m, lien m; (personal ties) relations fpl, rapports; (also: **family relationship**) lien de parenté; (affair) liaison f

relative ['rɛlətɪv] n parent(e) ▷ adj relatif(-ive); (respective) respectif(-ive); **relatively** adv relativement

relax [rɪ'læks] vi se relâcher; (muscle) se relâcher; (person: unwind) se détendre ▷ vt relâcher; (mind, person) détendre; **relaxation** [riːlæk'seɪʃən] n relâchement m; (of mind) détente f; (recreation) détente, délassement m; **relaxed** adj relâché(e); détendu(e); **relaxing** adj délassant(e)

relay ['riːleɪ] n (Sport) course f de relais ▷ vt (message) retransmettre, relayer

release [rɪ'liːs] n (from prison, obligation) libération f; (of gas etc) émission f; (of film etc) sortie f; (new recording) disque m ▷ vt (prisoner) libérer; (book, film) sortir; (report, news) rendre public, publier; (gas etc) émettre, dégager; (free: from wreckage etc) dégager; (Tech: catch, spring etc) déclencher; (let go: person, animal) relâcher; (: hand, object) lâcher; (: grip, brake) desserrer

relegate ['rɛləgeɪt] vt reléguer; (BRIT Sport): **to be ~d** descendre dans une division inférieure

relent [rɪ'lɛnt] vi se laisser fléchir; **relentless** adj implacable; (non-stop) continuel(le)

relevant ['rɛləvənt] adj (question) pertinent(e); (corresponding) approprié(e); (fact) significatif(-ive); (information) utile

reliable [rɪ'laɪəbl] adj (person, firm) sérieux(-euse), fiable; (method, machine) fiable; (news, information) sûr(e)

relic ['rɛlɪk] n (Rel) relique f; (of the past) vestige m

relief [rɪ'liːf] n (from pain, anxiety) soulagement m; (help, supplies) secours m(pl); (Art, Geo) relief m

relieve [rɪ'liːv] vt (pain, patient) soulager; (fear, worry) dissiper; (bring help) secourir; (take over from: gen) relayer; (: guard) relever; **to ~ sb of sth** débarrasser qn de qch; **to ~ o.s.** (euphemism) se soulager, faire ses besoins; **relieved** adj soulagé(e)

religion [rɪ'lɪdʒən] n religion f

religious [rɪ'lɪdʒəs] adj religieux(-euse); (book) de piété; **religious education** n instruction religieuse

relish ['rɛlɪʃ] n (Culin) condiment m; (enjoyment) délectation f ▷ vt (food etc) savourer; **to ~ doing** se délecter à faire

relocate [riːləʊ'keɪt] vt (business) transférer ▷ vi se transférer, s'installer or s'établir ailleurs

reluctance [rɪ'lʌktəns] n répugnance f

reluctant [rɪ'lʌktənt] adj peu disposé(e), qui hésite; **reluctantly** adv à contrecœur, sans enthousiasme

rely on [rɪ'laɪ-] vt fus (be dependent on) dépendre de; (trust) compter sur

remain [rɪ'meɪn] vi rester; **remainder** n reste m; (Comm) fin f de série; **remaining** adj qui reste; **remains** npl restes mpl

remand [rɪ'mɑːnd] n: **on ~** en détention préventive ▷ vt: **to be ~ed in custody** être placé(e) en détention préventive

remark [rɪ'mɑːk] n remarque f, observation f ▷ vt (faire) remarquer, dire; **remarkable** adj remarquable

remarry [riː'mærɪ] vi se remarier

remedy ['rɛmədɪ] n: **~ (for)** remède m

(contre or à) ▷ vt remédier à

remember [rɪ'mɛmbər] vt se rappeler, se souvenir de; (send greetings): **~ me to him** saluez-le de ma part; **Remembrance Day** [rɪ'mɛmbrəns-] n (BRIT) ≈ (le jour de) l'Armistice m, ≈ le 11 novembre

- **REMEMBRANCE DAY**

- **Remembrance Day** ou
- **Remembrance Sunday** est le
- dimanche le plus proche du 11
- novembre, jour où la Première
- Guerre mondiale a officiellement
- pris fin. Il rend hommage aux
- victimes des deux guerres
- mondiales. À cette occasion, on
- observe deux minutes de silence
- à 11h, heure de la signature de
- l'armistice avec l'Allemagne en
- 1918; certaines membres de la
- famille royale et du gouvernement
- déposent des gerbes de coquelicots
- au cénotaphe de Whitehall, et des
- couronnes sont placées sur les
- monuments aux morts dans toute
- la Grande-Bretagne; par ailleurs,
- les gens portent des coquelicots
- artificiels fabriqués et vendus
- par des membres de la légion
- britannique blessés au combat, au
- profit des blessés de guerre et de
- leur famille.

remind [rɪ'maɪnd] vt: **to ~ sb of sth** rappeler qch à qn; **to ~ sb to do** penser à qn à faire, rappeler à qn qu'il doit faire; **reminder** n (Comm: letter) rappel m; (note etc) pense-bête m; (souvenir) souvenir m

reminiscent [rɛmɪ'nɪsnt] adj: **~ of** qui rappelle, qui fait penser à

remnant ['rɛmnənt] n reste m, restant m; (of cloth) coupon m

remorse [rɪ'mɔːs] n remords m

remote [rɪ'məut] adj éloigné(e), lointain(e); (person) distant(e);

(possibility) vague; **remote control** n télécommande f; **remotely** adv au loin; (slightly) très vaguement

removal [rɪ'muːvəl] n (taking away) enlèvement m; suppression f; (BRIT: from house) déménagement m; (from office: dismissal) renvoi m; (of stain) nettoyage m; (Med) ablation f; **removal man** (irreg) n (BRIT) déménageur m; **removal van** n (BRIT) camion m de déménagement

remove [rɪ'muːv] vt enlever, retirer; (employee) renvoyer; (stain) faire partir; (abuse) supprimer; (doubt) chasser

Renaissance [rɪ'neɪsãs] n: **the ~** la Renaissance

rename [riː'neɪm] vt rebaptiser

render ['rɛndər] vt rendre

rendezvous ['rɔndɪvuː] n rendez-vous m inv

renew [rɪ'njuː] vt renouveler; (negotiations) reprendre; (acquaintance) renouer

renovate ['rɛnəveɪt] vt rénover; (work of art) restaurer

renowned [rɪ'naund] adj renommé(e)

rent [rɛnt] pt, pp of **rend** ▷ n loyer m ▷ vt louer; **rental** n (for television, car) (prix m de) location f

reorganize [riː'ɔːgənaɪz] vt réorganiser

rep [rɛp] n abbr (Comm) = **representative**

repair [rɪ'pɛər] n réparation f ▷ vt réparer; **in good/bad ~** en bon/mauvais état; **where can I get this ~ed?** où est-ce que je peux faire réparer ceci?; **repair kit** n trousse f de réparations

repay [riː'peɪ] vt (irreg: like **pay**) (money, creditor) rembourser; (sb's efforts) récompenser; **repayment** n remboursement m

repeat [rɪ'piːt] n (Radio, TV) reprise f ▷ vt répéter; (promise, attack, also Comm: order) renouveler; (Scol: a class) redoubler ▷ vi répéter; **can you ~ that, please?** pouvez-vous répéter,

s'il vous plaît?; **repeatedly** adv
souvent, à plusieurs reprises; **repeat
prescription** n (BRIT): **I'd like a repeat
prescription** je voudrais renouveler
mon ordonnance

repellent [rɪ'pɛlənt] adj repoussant(e)
▷ n: **insect ~** insectifuge m

repercussions [riːpə'kʌʃənz] npl
répercussions fpl

repetition [rɛpɪ'tɪʃən] n répétition f

repetitive [rɪ'pɛtɪtɪv] adj (movement,
work) répétitif(-ive); (speech) plein(e)
de redites

replace [rɪ'pleɪs] vt (put back)
remettre, replacer; (take the place
of) remplacer; **replacement** n
(substitution) remplacement m; (person)
remplaçant(e)

replay ['riːpleɪ] n (of match) match
rejoué; (of tape, film) répétition f

replica ['rɛplɪkə] n réplique f, copie
exacte

reply [rɪ'plaɪ] n réponse f ▷ vi répondre

report [rɪ'pɔːt] n rapport m; (Press
etc) reportage m; (BRIT: also: **school
~**) bulletin m (scolaire); (of gun)
détonation f ▷ vt rapporter, faire un
compte rendu de; (Press etc) faire un
reportage sur; (notify: accident) signaler;
(: culprit) dénoncer ▷ vi (make a report)
faire un rapport; **I'd like to ~ a theft**
je voudrais signaler un vol; (present
o.s.): **to ~ (to sb)** se présenter (chez
qn); **report card** n (US, SCOTTISH)
bulletin m (scolaire); **reportedly** adv:
she is reportedly living in Spain elle
habiterait en Espagne; **he reportedly
told them to ...** il leur aurait dit de ...;
reporter n reporter m

represent [rɛprɪ'zɛnt] vt représenter;
(view, belief) présenter, expliquer;
(describe): **to ~ sth as** présenter or
décrire qch comme; **representation**
[rɛprɪzɛn'teɪʃən] n représentation f;
representative n représentant(e); (US
Pol) député m ▷ adj représentatif(-ive),
caractéristique

repress [rɪ'prɛs] vt réprimer;

repression [rɪ'prɛʃən] n répression f

reprimand ['rɛprɪmɑːnd] n
réprimande f ▷ vt réprimander

reproduce [riːprə'djuːs] vt reproduire
▷ vi se reproduire; **reproduction**
[riːprə'dʌkʃən] n reproduction f

reptile ['rɛptaɪl] n reptile m

republic [rɪ'pʌblɪk] n république f;
republican adj, n républicain(e)

reputable ['rɛpjutəbl] adj de bonne
réputation; (occupation) honorable

reputation [rɛpju'teɪʃən] n
réputation f

request [rɪ'kwɛst] n demande f;
(formal) requête f ▷ vt: **to ~ (of or from
sb)** demander (à qn); **request stop** n
(BRIT: for bus) arrêt facultatif

require [rɪ'kwaɪə^r] vt (need: subj: person)
avoir besoin de; (: thing, situation)
nécessiter, demander; (want) exiger;
(order): **to ~ sb to do sth/sth of sb**
exiger que qn fasse qch/qch de qn;
requirement n (need) exigence f;
besoin m; (condition) condition f
(requise)

resat [riː'sæt] pt, pp of **resit**

rescue ['rɛskjuː] n (from accident)
sauvetage m; (help) secours mpl ▷ vt
sauver

research [rɪ'səːtʃ] n recherche(s) f(pl)
▷ vt faire des recherches sur

resemblance [rɪ'zɛmbləns] n
ressemblance f

resemble [rɪ'zɛmbl] vt ressembler à

resent [rɪ'zɛnt] vt être contrarié(e)
par; **resentful** adj irrité(e), plein(e)
de ressentiment; **resentment** n
ressentiment m

reservation [rɛzə'veɪʃən] n (booking)
réservation f; **to make a ~ (in an
hotel/a restaurant/on a plane)**
réserver or retenir une chambre/une
table/une place; **reservation desk** n
(US: in hotel) réception f

reserve [rɪ'zəːv] n réserve f; (Sport)
remplaçant(e) ▷ vt (seats etc) réserver,
retenir; **reserved** adj réservé(e)

reservoir ['rɛzəvwɑː^r] n réservoir m

reshuffle [riː'ʃʌfl] n: **Cabinet ~** (Pol) remaniement ministériel

residence ['rezidəns] n résidence f; **residence permit** n (BRIT) permis m de séjour

resident ['rezidənt] n (of country) résident(e); (of area, house) habitant(e); (in hotel) pensionnaire ▷ adj résidant(e); **residential** [rezi'dɛnʃəl] adj de résidence; (area) résidentiel(le); (course) avec hébergement sur place

residue ['rezidjuː] n reste m; (Chem, Physics) résidu m

resign [ri'zain] vt (one's post) se démettre de ▷ vi démissionner; **to ~ o.s. to** (endure) se résigner à; **resignation** [rezig'neiʃən] n (from post) démission f; (state of mind) résignation f

resin ['rezin] n résine f

resist [ri'zist] vt résister à; **resistance** n résistance f

resit (BRIT) vt [riː'sit] (pt, pp **resat**) (exam) repasser ▷ n ['riː'sit] deuxième session f (d'un examen)

resolution [rezə'luːʃən] n résolution f

resolve [ri'zɔlv] n résolution f ▷ vt (decide): **to ~ to do** résoudre or décider de faire; (problem) résoudre

resort [ri'zɔːt] n (seaside town) station f balnéaire; (for skiing) station de ski; (recourse) recours m ▷ vi: **to ~ to** avoir recours à; **in the last ~** en dernier ressort

resource [ri'sɔːs] n ressource f; **resourceful** adj ingénieux(-euse), débrouillard(e)

respect [ris'pɛkt] n respect m ▷ vt respecter; **respectable** adj respectable; (quite good: result etc) honorable; **respectful** adj respectueux(-euse); **respective** adj respectif(-ive); **respectively** adv respectivement

respite ['respait] n répit m

respond [ris'pɔnd] vi répondre; (react) réagir; **response** [ris'pɔns] n réponse f; (reaction) réaction f

responsibility [rispɔnsi'biliti] n

responsabilité f

responsible [ris'pɔnsibl] adj (liable): **~ (for)** responsable (de); (person) digne de confiance; (job) qui comporte des responsabilités; **responsibly** adv avec sérieux

responsive [ris'pɔnsiv] adj (student, audience) réceptif(-ive); (brakes, steering) sensible

rest [rest] n repos m; (stop) arrêt m, pause f; (Mus) silence m; (support) support m, appui m; (remainder) reste m, restant m ▷ vi se reposer; (be supported): **to ~ on** appuyer or reposer sur ▷ vt (lean): **to ~ sth on/against** appuyer qch sur/contre; **the ~ of them** les autres

restaurant ['restərɔ̃] n restaurant m; **restaurant car** n (BRIT Rail) wagon-restaurant m

restless ['restlis] adj agité(e)

restoration [restə'reiʃən] n (of building) restauration f; (of stolen goods) restitution f

restore [ri'stɔː'] vt (building) restaurer; (sth stolen) restituer; (peace, health) rétablir; (to a former state) ramener à

restrain [ris'trein] vt (feeling) contenir; (person): **to ~ (from doing)** retenir (de faire); **restraint** n (restriction) contrainte f; (moderation) retenue f; (of style) sobriété f

restrict [ris'trikt] vt restreindre, limiter; **restriction** [ris'trikʃən] n restriction f, limitation f

rest room n (US) toilettes fpl

restructure [riː'strʌktʃə'] vt restructurer

result [ri'zʌlt] n résultat m ▷ vi: **to ~ in** aboutir à, se terminer par; **as a ~ of** à la suite de

resume [ri'zjuːm] vt (work, journey) reprendre ▷ vi (work etc) reprendre

résumé ['reizjuːmei] n (summary) résumé m; (US: curriculum vitae) curriculum vitae m inv

resuscitate [ri'sʌsiteit] vt (Med) réanimer

retail ['ri:teɪl] *adj* de or au détail ▷ *adv* au détail; **retailer** *n* détaillant(e)

retain [rɪ'teɪn] *vt* (*keep*) garder, conserver

retaliation [rɪtælɪ'eɪʃən] *n* représailles *fpl*, vengeance *f*

retarded [rɪ'tɑːdɪd] *adj* retardé(e)

retire [rɪ'taɪəʳ] *vi* (*give up work*) prendre sa retraite; (*withdraw*) se retirer, partir; (*go to bed*) (aller) se coucher; **retired** *adj* (*person*) retraité(e); **retirement** *n* retraite *f*

retort [rɪ'tɔːt] *vi* riposter

retreat [rɪ'triːt] *n* retraite *f* ▷ *vi* battre en retraite

retrieve [rɪ'triːv] *vt* (*sth lost*) récupérer; (*situation, honour*) sauver; (*error, loss*) réparer; (*Comput*) rechercher

retrospect ['rɛtrəspɛkt] *n*: **in ~** rétrospectivement, après coup; **retrospective** [rɛtrə'spɛktɪv] *adj* rétrospectif(-ive); (*law*) rétroactif(-ive) ▷ *n* (*Art*) rétrospective *f*

return [rɪ'tɜːn] *n* (*going or coming back*) retour *m*; (*of sth stolen etc*) restitution *f*; (*Finance: from land, shares*) rapport *m* ▷ *cpd* (*journey*) de retour; (*BRIT: ticket*) aller et retour; (*match*) retour ▷ *vi* (*person etc: come back*) revenir; (: *go back*) retourner ▷ *vt* rendre; (*bring back*) rapporter; (*send back*) renvoyer; (*put back*) remettre; (*Pol: candidate*) élire; **returns** *npl* (*Comm*) recettes *fpl*; (*Finance*) bénéfices *mpl*; **many happy ~s (of the day)!** bon anniversaire!; **by ~ (of post)** par retour (du courrier); **in ~ (for)** en échange (de); **a ~ (ticket) for ...** un billet aller et retour pour ...; **return ticket** *n* (*esp BRIT*) billet *m* aller-retour

reunion [riː'juːnɪən] *n* réunion *f*

reunite [riːjuː'naɪt] *vt* réunir

revamp [riː'væmp] *vt* (*house*) retaper; (*firm*) réorganiser

reveal [rɪ'viːl] *vt* (*make known*) révéler; (*display*) laisser voir; **revealing** *adj* révélateur(-trice); (*dress*) au décolleté généreux or suggestif

revel ['rɛvl] *vi*: **to ~ in sth/in doing** se

délecter de qch/à faire

revelation [rɛvə'leɪʃən] *n* révélation *f*

revenge [rɪ'vɛndʒ] *n* vengeance *f*; (*in game etc*) revanche *f* ▷ *vt* venger; **to take ~ (on)** se venger (sur)

revenue ['rɛvənjuː] *n* revenu *m*

Reverend ['rɛvərənd] *adj* (*in titles*): **the ~ John Smith** (*Anglican*) le révérend John Smith; (*Catholic*) l'abbé (John) Smith; (*Protestant*) le pasteur (John) Smith

reversal [rɪ'vɜːsl] *n* (*of opinion*) revirement *m*; (*of order*) renversement *m*; (*of direction*) changement *m*

reverse [rɪ'vɜːs] *n* contraire *m*, opposé *m*; (*back*) dos *m*, envers *m*; (*of paper*) verso *m*; (*of coin*) revers *m*; (*Aut: also*: **~ gear**) marche arrière *f* ▷ *adj* (*order, direction*) opposé(e), inverse ▷ *vt* (*order, position*) changer, inverser; (*direction, policy*) changer complètement de; (*decision*) annuler; (*roles*) renverser ▷ *vi* (*BRIT Aut*) faire marche arrière; **reverse-charge call** *n* (*BRIT Tel*) communication *f* en PCV; **reversing lights** *npl* (*BRIT Aut*) feux *mpl* de marche arrière or de recul

revert [rɪ'vɜːt] *vi*: **to ~ to** revenir à, retourner à

review [rɪ'vjuː] *n* revue *f*; (*of book, film*) critique *f*; (*of situation, policy*) examen *m*, bilan *m*; (*US: examination*) examen *m* ▷ *vt* passer en revue; faire la critique de; examiner

revise [rɪ'vaɪz] *vt* réviser, modifier; (*manuscript*) revoir, corriger ▷ *vi* (*study*) réviser; **revision** [rɪ'vɪʒən] *n* révision *f*

revival [rɪ'vaɪvəl] *n* reprise *f*; (*recovery*) rétablissement *m*; (*of faith*) renouveau *m*

revive [rɪ'vaɪv] *vt* (*person*) ranimer; (*custom*) rétablir; (*economy*) relancer; (*hope, courage*) faire renaître; (*play, fashion*) reprendre ▷ *vi* (*person*) reprendre connaissance; (: *from ill health*) se rétablir; (*hope etc*) renaître; (*activity*) reprendre

revolt [rɪ'vəult] *n* révolte *f* ▷ *vi* se

révolter, se rebeller ▷ *vt* révolter,
dégoûter; **revolting** *adj* dégoûtant(e)
revolution [rɛvə'luːʃən] *n* révolution
f; (*of wheel etc*) tour *m*, révolution;
revolutionary *adj, n* révolutionnaire
(*m/f*)
revolve [rɪ'vɔlv] *vi* tourner
revolver [rɪ'vɔlvə*] *n* revolver *m*
reward [rɪ'wɔːd] *n* récompense *f* ▷ *vt*:
to ~ (for) récompenser (de); **rewarding**
adj (*fig*) qui (en) vaut la peine,
gratifiant(e)
rewind [riː'waɪnd] *vt* (*irreg: like* **wind**)
(*tape*) réembobiner
rewritable [riː'raɪtəbl] *adj* (*CD, DVD*)
réinscriptible
rewrite [riː'raɪt] *vt* (*pt* **rewrote**, *pp*
rewritten) *vt* récrire
rheumatism ['ruːmətɪzəm] *n*
rhumatisme *m*
Rhine [raɪn] *n*: **the (River) ~** le Rhin
rhinoceros [raɪ'nɔsərəs] *n*
rhinocéros *m*
Rhône [rəun] *n*: **the (River) ~** le Rhône
rhubarb ['ruːbɑːb] *n* rhubarbe *f*
rhyme [raɪm] *n* rime *f*; (*verse*) vers *mpl*
rhythm ['rɪðm] *n* rythme *m*
rib [rɪb] *n* (*Anat*) côte *f*
ribbon ['rɪbən] *n* ruban *m*; **in ~s** (*torn*)
en lambeaux
rice [raɪs] *n* riz *m*; **rice pudding** *n* riz
m au lait
rich [rɪtʃ] *adj* riche; (*gift, clothes*)
somptueux(-euse); **to be ~ in sth** être
riche en qch
rid [rɪd] (*pt, pp* ~) *vt*: **to ~ sb of**
débarrasser qn de; **to get ~ of** se
débarrasser de
riddle ['rɪdl] *n* (*puzzle*) énigme *f* ▷ *vt*: **to
be ~d with** être criblé(e) de; (*fig*) être
en proie à
ride [raɪd] *n* promenade *f*, tour *m*;
(*distance covered*) trajet *m* ▷ *vb* (*pt* **rode**,
pp **ridden**) ▷ *vi* (*as sport*) monter (à
cheval), faire du cheval; (*go somewhere:
on horse, bicycle*) aller (à cheval ou
bicyclette *etc*); (*travel: on bicycle, motor
cycle, bus*) rouler ▷ *vt* (*a horse*) monter;

(*distance*) parcourir, faire; **to ~ a horse/
bicycle** monter à cheval/à bicyclette;
to take sb for a ~ (*fig*) faire marcher qn;
(*cheat*) rouler qn; **rider** *n* cavalier(-ière)
(*in race*) jockey *m*; (*on bicycle*) cycliste
m/f; (*on motorcycle*) motocycliste *m/f*
ridge [rɪdʒ] *n* (*of hill*) faîte *m*; (*of roof,
mountain*) arête *f*; (*on object*) strie *f*
ridicule ['rɪdɪkjuːl] *n* ridicule *m*;
dérision *f* ▷ *vt* ridiculiser, tourner en
dérision; **ridiculous** [rɪ'dɪkjuləs] *adj*
ridicule
riding ['raɪdɪŋ] *n* équitation *f*;
riding school *n* manège *m*, école *f*
d'équitation
rife [raɪf] *adj* répandu(e); **~ with**
abondant(e) en
rifle ['raɪfl] *n* fusil *m* (à canon rayé) ▷ *vt*
vider, dévaliser
rift [rɪft] *n* fente *f*, fissure *f*; (*fig:
disagreement*) désaccord *m*
rig [rɪg] *n* (*also:* **oil ~**: *on land*) derrick *m*;
(: *at sea*) plate-forme pétrolière ▷ *vt*
(*election etc*) truquer
right [raɪt] *adj* (*true*) juste, exact(e);
(*correct*) bon (bonne); (*suitable*)
approprié(e), convenable; (*just*) juste,
équitable; (*morally good*) bien *inv*; (*not
left*) droit(e) ▷ *n* (*moral good*) bien *m*;
(*title, claim*) droit *m*; (*not left*) droite
f ▷ *adv* (*answer*) correctement; (*treat*)
bien, comme il faut; (*not on the left*) à
droite ▷ *vt* redresser ▷ *excl* bon!; **do
you have the ~ time?** avez-vous l'heure
juste ou exacte?; **to be ~** (*person*) avoir
raison; (*answer*) être juste ou correct(e);
by ~s en toute justice; **on the ~** à
droite; **to be in the ~** avoir raison; **~ in
the middle** en plein milieu; **~ away**
immédiatement; **right angle** *n* (*Math*)
angle droit; **rightful** *adj* (*heir*) légitime;
right-hand *adj*: **the right-hand side**
la droite; **right-hand drive** *n* (*BRIT*)
conduite *f* à droite; (*vehicle*) véhicule
m avec la conduite à droite; **right-
handed** *adj* (*person*) droitier(-ière);
rightly *adv* bien, correctement; (*with
reason*) à juste titre; **right of way** *n*

(*on path etc*) droit *m* de passage; (*Aut*) priorité *f*; **right-wing** *adj* (*Pol*) de droite

rigid ['rɪdʒɪd] *adj* rigide; (*principle, control*) strict(e)

rigorous ['rɪgərəs] *adj* rigoureux(-euse)

rim [rɪm] *n* bord *m*; (*of spectacles*) monture *f*; (*of wheel*) jante *f*

rind [raɪnd] *n* (*of bacon*) couenne *f*; (*of lemon etc*) écorce *f*, zeste *m*; (*of cheese*) croûte *f*

ring [rɪŋ] *n* anneau *m*; (*on finger*) bague *f*; (*also:* **wedding ~**) alliance *f*; (*of people, objects*) cercle *m*; (*of spies*) réseau *m*; (*of smoke etc*) rond *m*; (*arena*) piste *f*, arène *f*; (*for boxing*) ring *m*; (*sound of bell*) sonnerie *f* ▷ *vb* (*pt* **rang**, *pp* **rung**) ▷ *vi* (*telephone, bell*) sonner; (*person: by telephone*) téléphoner; (*ears*) bourdonner; (*also:* **~ out**: *voice, words*) retentir ▷ *vt* (*BRIT Tel: also:* **~ up**) téléphoner à, appeler; **to ~ the bell** sonner; **to give sb a ~** (*Tel*) passer un coup de téléphone *or* de fil à qn; **ring back** *vt, vi* (*BRIT Tel*) rappeler; **ring off** *vi* (*BRIT Tel*) raccrocher; **ring up** (*BRIT*) ▷ *vt* (*Tel*) téléphoner à, appeler; **ringing tone** *n* (*BRIT Tel*) tonalité *f* d'appel; **ringleader** *n* (*of gang*) chef *m*, meneur *m*; **ring road** *n* (*BRIT*) rocade *f*; (*motorway*) périphérique *m*; **ringtone** *n* (*on mobile*) sonnerie *f* (*de téléphone portable*)

rink [rɪŋk] *n* (*also:* **ice ~**) patinoire *f*

rinse [rɪns] *n* rinçage *m* ▷ *vt* rincer

riot ['raɪət] *n* émeute *f*, bagarres *fpl* ▷ *vi* (*demonstrators*) manifester avec violence; (*population*) se soulever, se révolter; **to run ~** se déchaîner

rip [rɪp] *n* déchirure *f* ▷ *vt* déchirer ▷ *vi* se déchirer; **rip off** *vt* (*inf: cheat*) arnaquer; **rip up** *vt* déchirer

ripe [raɪp] *adj* (*fruit*) mûr(e); (*cheese*) fait(e)

rip-off ['rɪpɔf] *n* (*inf*): **it's a ~!** c'est du vol manifeste!, c'est de l'arnaque!

ripple ['rɪpl] *n* ride *f*, ondulation *f*; (*of applause, laughter*) cascade *f* ▷ *vi* se rider, onduler

rise [raɪz] *n* (*slope*) côte *f*, pente *f*; (*hill*) élévation *f*; (*increase: in wages:* BRIT) augmentation *f*; (: *in prices, temperature*) hausse *f*, augmentation; (*fig: to power etc*) ascension *f* ▷ *vi* (*pt* **rose**, *pp* **~n**) s'élever, monter; (*prices, numbers*) augmenter, monter; (*waters, river*) monter; (*sun, wind, person: from chair, bed*) se lever; (*also:* **~ up**: *tower, building*) s'élever; (: *rebel*) se révolter; (*in rank*) s'élever; **to give ~ to** donner lieu à; **to ~ to the occasion** se montrer à la hauteur; **risen** ['rɪzn] *pp of* **rise**; **rising** *adj* (*increasing: number, prices*) en hausse; (*tide*) montant(e); (*sun, moon*) levant(e)

risk [rɪsk] *n* risque *m* ▷ *vt* risquer; **to take** *or* **run the ~ of doing** courir le risque de faire; **at ~** en danger; **at one's own ~** à ses risques et périls; **risky** *adj* risqué(e)

rite [raɪt] *n* rite *m*; **the last ~s** les derniers sacrements

ritual ['rɪtjuəl] *adj* rituel(le) ▷ *n* rituel *m*

rival ['raɪvl] *n* rival(e); (*in business*) concurrent(e) ▷ *adj* rival(e); qui fait concurrence ▷ *vt* (*match*) égaler; **rivalry** *n* rivalité *f*; (*in business*) concurrence *f*

river ['rɪvə*r*] *n* rivière *f*; (*major: also fig*) fleuve *m* ▷ *cpd* (*port, traffic*) fluvial(e); **up/down ~** en amont/aval; **riverbank** *n* rive *f*, berge *f*

rivet ['rɪvɪt] *n* rivet *m* ▷ *vt* (*fig*) river, fixer

Riviera [rɪvɪˈɛərə] *n*: **the (French) ~** la Côte d'Azur

road [rəud] *n* route *f*; (*in town*) rue *f*; (*fig*) chemin, voie *f* ▷ *cpd* (*accident*) de la route; **major/minor ~** route principale *or* à priorité/voie secondaire; **which ~ do I take for...?** quelle route dois-je prendre pour aller à...?; **roadblock** *n* barrage routier; **road map** *n* carte routière; **road rage** *n comportement très agressif de certains usagers de la route*; **road safety** *n* sécurité routière; **roadside** *n* bord *m* de la route, bas-côté m; **roadsign** n panneau m de signalisation; **road tax** n (BRIT Aut) taxe f sur les automobiles; **roadworks** npl travaux mpl (de réfection des routes)

roam [rəum] vi errer, vagabonder

roar [rɔːʳ] n rugissement m; (of crowd) hurlements mpl; (of vehicle, thunder, storm) grondement m ▷ vi rugir; hurler; gronder; **to ~ with laughter** rire à gorge déployée; **to do a ~ing trade** faire des affaires en or

roast [rəust] n rôti m ▷ vt (meat) (faire) rôtir; (coffee) griller, torréfier; **roast beef** n rôti de bœuf, rosbif m

rob [rɒb] vt (person) voler; (bank) dévaliser; **to ~ sb of sth** voler or dérober qch à qn; (fig: deprive) priver qn de qch; **robber** n bandit m, voleur m; **robbery** n vol m

robe [rəub] n (for ceremony etc) robe f; (also: **bath~**) peignoir m; (US: rug) couverture f ▷ vt revêtir (d'une robe)

robin ['rɒbɪn] n rouge-gorge m

robot ['rəubɒt] n robot m

robust [rəu'bʌst] adj robuste; (material, appetite) solide

rock [rɒk] n (substance) roche f, roc m; (boulder) rocher m, roche; (US: small stone) caillou m; (BRIT: sweet) ≈ sucre m d'orge ▷ vt (swing gently: cradle) balancer; (: child) bercer; (shake) ébranler, secouer ▷ vi se balancer, être ébranlé(e) or secoué(e); **on the ~s** (drink) avec des glaçons; (marriage etc) en train de craquer; **rock and roll** n rock (and roll) m, rock'n'roll m; **rock climbing** n varappe f

rocket ['rɒkɪt] n fusée f; (Mil) fusée, roquette f; (Culin) roquette

rocking chair ['rɒkɪŋ-] n fauteuil m à bascule

rocky ['rɒkɪ] adj (hill) rocheux(-euse); (path) rocailleux(-euse)

rod [rɒd] n (metallic) tringle f; (Tech) tige f; (wooden) baguette f; (also: **fishing ~**) canne f à pêche

rode [rəud] pt of **ride**

rodent ['rəudnt] n rongeur m

rogue [rəug] n coquin(e)

role [rəul] n rôle m; **role-model** n modèle m à émuler

roll [rəul] n rouleau m; (of banknotes) liasse f; (also: **bread ~**) petit pain; (register) liste f; (sound: of drums etc) roulement m ▷ vt rouler; (also: **~ up**: string) enrouler; (also: **~ out**: pastry) étendre au rouleau, abaisser ▷ vi rouler; **roll over** vi se retourner; **roll up** vi (inf: arrive) arriver, s'amener ▷ vt (carpet, cloth, map) rouler; (sleeves) retrousser; **roller** n rouleau m; (wheel) roulette f; (for road) rouleau compresseur; (for hair) bigoudi m; **roller coaster** n montagnes fpl russes; **roller skates** npl patins mpl à roulettes; **roller-skating** n patin m à roulettes; **to go roller-skating** faire du patin à roulettes; **rolling pin** n rouleau m à pâtisserie

ROM [rɒm] n abbr (Comput: = read-only memory) mémoire morte, ROM f

Roman ['rəumən] adj romain(e) ▷ n Romain(e); **Roman Catholic** adj, n catholique (m/f)

romance [rə'mæns] n (love affair) idylle f; (charm) poésie f; (novel) roman m à l'eau de rose

Romania etc [rəu'meɪnɪə] = **Rumania** etc

Roman numeral n chiffre romain

romantic [rə'mæntɪk] adj romantique; (novel, attachment) sentimental(e)

Rome [rəum] n Rome

roof [ruːf] n toit m; (of tunnel, cave) plafond m ▷ vt couvrir (d'un toit); **the ~ of the mouth** la voûte du palais; **roof rack** n (Aut) galerie f

rook [ruk] n (bird) freux m; (Chess) tour f

room [ruːm] n (in house) pièce f; (also: **bed~**) chambre f (à coucher); (in school etc) salle f; (space) place f; **roommate** n camarade m/f de chambre; **room service** n service m des chambres (dans un hôtel); **roomy** adj spacieux(-euse);

(garment) ample

rooster ['ru:stə^r] n coq m

root [ru:t] n (Bot, Math) racine f; (fig: of problem) origine f, fond m ▷ vi (plant) s'enraciner

rope [rəup] n corde f; (Naut) cordage m ▷ vt (tie up or together) attacher; (climbers: also: ~ **together**) encorder; (area: also: ~ **off**) interdire l'accès de; (: divide off) séparer; **to know the ~s** (fig) être au courant, connaître les ficelles

rose [rəuz] pt of **rise** ▷ n rose f; (also: **~bush**) rosier m

rosé ['rəuzeɪ] n rosé m

rosemary ['rəuzmərɪ] n romarin m

rosy ['rəuzɪ] adj rose; **a ~ future** un bel avenir

rot [rɔt] n (decay) pourriture f; (fig: pej: nonsense) idioties fpl, balivernes fpl ▷ vt, vi pourrir

rota ['rəutə] n liste f, tableau m de service

rotate [rəu'teɪt] vt (revolve) faire tourner; (change round: crops) alterner; (: jobs) faire à tour de rôle ▷ vi (revolve) tourner

rotten ['rɔtn] adj (decayed) pourri(e); (dishonest) corrompu(e); (inf: bad) mauvais(e), moche; **to feel ~** (ill) être mal fichu(e)

rough [rʌf] adj (cloth, skin) rêche, rugueux(-euse); (terrain) accidenté(e); (path) rocailleux(-euse); (voice) rauque, rude; (person, manner: coarse) rude, fruste; (: violent) brutal(e); (district, weather) mauvais(e); (sea) houleux(-euse); (plan) ébauché(e); (guess) approximatif(-ive) ▷ n (Golf) rough m ▷ vt: **to ~ it** vivre à la dure; **to sleep ~** (BRIT) coucher à la dure; **roughly** adv (handle) rudement, brutalement; (speak) avec brusquerie; (make) grossièrement; (approximately) à peu près, en gros

roulette [ru:'lɛt] n roulette f

round [raund] adj rond(e) ▷ n rond m, cercle m; (BRIT: of toast) tranche f; (duty: of policeman, milkman etc)

tournée f; (: of doctor) visites fpl; (game: of cards, in competition) partie f; (Boxing) round m; (of talks) série f ▷ vt (corner) tourner ▷ prep autour de ▷ adv: **right ~, all ~** tout autour; ~ **of ammunition** cartouche f; ~ **of applause** applaudissements mpl; ~ **of drinks** tournée f; ~ **of sandwiches** (BRIT) sandwich m; **the long way ~** (par) le chemin le plus long; **all (the) year ~** toute l'année; **it's just ~ the corner** (fig) c'est tout près; **to go ~ to sb's (house)** aller chez qn; **go ~ the back** passez par derrière; **enough to go ~** assez pour tout le monde; **she arrived ~ (about) noon** (BRIT) elle est arrivée vers midi; ~ **the clock** 24 heures sur 24; **round off** vt (speech etc) terminer; **round up** vt rassembler; (criminals) effectuer une rafle de; (prices) arrondir (au chiffre supérieur); **roundabout** n (BRIT Aut) rond-point m (à sens giratoire); (at fair) manège m (de chevaux de bois) ▷ adj (route, means) détourné(e); **round trip** n (voyage m) aller et retour m; **roundup** n rassemblement m; (of criminals) rafle f

rouse [rauz] vt (wake up) réveiller; (stir up) susciter, provoquer; (interest) éveiller; (suspicions) susciter, éveiller

route [ru:t] n itinéraire m; (of bus) parcours m; (of trade, shipping) route f

routine [ru:'ti:n] adj (work) ordinaire, courant(e); (procedure) d'usage ▷ n (habits) habitudes fpl; (pej) train-train m; (Theat) numéro m

row¹ [rəu] n (line) rangée f; (of people, seats, Knitting) rang m; (behind one another: of cars, people) file f ▷ vi (in boat) ramer; (as sport) faire de l'aviron ▷ vt (boat) faire aller à la rame or à l'aviron; **in a ~** (fig) d'affilée

row² [rau] n (noise) vacarme m; (dispute) dispute f, querelle f; (scolding) réprimande f, savon m ▷ vi (also: **to have a ~**) se disputer, se quereller

rowboat ['rəubəut] n (US) canot m (à rames)

rowing ['rəʊɪŋ] n canotage m; (as sport) aviron m; **rowing boat** n (BRIT) canot m (à rames)

royal ['rɔɪəl] adj royal(e); **royalty** n (royal persons) (membres mpl de la) famille royale; (payment: to author) droits mpl d'auteur; (: to inventor) royalties fpl

rpm abbr (= revolutions per minute) t/mn (= tours/minute)

R.S.V.P. abbr (= répondez s'il vous plaît) RSVP

Rt. Hon. abbr (BRIT: = Right Honourable) titre donné aux députés de la Chambre des communes

rub [rʌb] n: **to give sth a ~** donner un coup de chiffon or de torchon à qch ▷ vt frotter; (person) frictionner; (hands) se frotter; **to ~ sb up** (BRIT) or **to ~ sb** (US) **the wrong way** prendre qn à rebrousse-poil; **rub in** vt (ointment) faire pénétrer; **rub off** vi partir; **rub out** vt effacer

rubber ['rʌbər] n caoutchouc m; (BRIT: eraser) gomme f (à effacer); **rubber band** n élastique m; **rubber gloves** npl gants mpl en caoutchouc

rubbish ['rʌbɪʃ] n (from household) ordures fpl; (fig: pej) choses fpl sans valeur; camelote f; (nonsense) bêtises fpl, idioties fpl; **rubbish bin** n (BRIT) boîte fà ordures, poubelle f; **rubbish dump** n (BRIT: in town) décharge publique, dépotoir m

rubble ['rʌbl] n décombres mpl; (smaller) gravats mpl; (Constr) blocage m

ruby ['ruːbɪ] n rubis m

rucksack ['rʌksæk] n sac m à dos

rudder ['rʌdər] n gouvernail m

rude [ruːd] adj (impolite: person) impoli(e); (: word, manners) grossier(-ière); (shocking) indécent(e), inconvenant(e)

ruffle ['rʌfl] vt (hair) ébouriffer; (clothes) chiffonner; (fig: person): **to get ~d** s'énerver

rug [rʌg] n petit tapis; (BRIT: blanket) couverture f

rugby ['rʌgbɪ] n (also: **~ football**) rugby m

rugged ['rʌgɪd] adj (landscape) accidenté(e); (features, character) rude

ruin ['ruːɪn] n ruine f ▷ vt ruiner; (spoil: clothes) abîmer; (: event) gâcher; **ruins** npl (of building) ruine(s)

rule [ruːl] n règle f; (regulation) règlement m; (government) autorité f, gouvernement m ▷ vt (country) gouverner; (person) dominer; (decide) décider ▷ vi commander; (Law): **as a ~** normalement, en règle générale; **rule out** vt exclure; **ruler** n (sovereign) souverain(e); (leader) chef m (d'État); (for measuring) règle f; **ruling** adj (party) au pouvoir; (class) dirigeant(e) ▷ n (Law) décision f

rum [rʌm] n rhum m

Rumania [ruːˈmeɪnɪə] n Roumanie f; **Rumanian** adj roumain(e) ▷ n Roumain(e); (Ling) roumain m

rumble ['rʌmbl] n grondement m; (of stomach, pipe) gargouillement m ▷ vi gronder; (stomach, pipe) gargouiller

rumour (US **rumor**) ['ruːmər] n rumeur f, bruit m (qui court) ▷ vt: **it is ~ed that** le bruit court que

rump steak n romsteck m

run [rʌn] n (race) course f; (outing) tour m or promenade f (en voiture); (distance travelled) parcours m, trajet m; (series) suite f, série f; (Theat) série de représentations; (Ski) piste f; (Cricket, Baseball) point m; (in tights, stockings) maille filée, échelle f ▷ vb (pt **ran**, pp **~**) ▷ vt (business) diriger; (competition, course) organiser; (hotel, house) tenir; (race) participer à; (Comput: program) exécuter; (to pass: hand, finger): **to ~ sth over** promener or passer qch sur; (water, bath) faire couler; (Press: feature) publier ▷ vi courir; (pass: road etc) passer; (work: machine, factory) marcher; (bus, train) circuler; (continue: play) se jouer, être à l'affiche; (: contract) être valide or en vigueur; (flow: river, bath, nose) couler; (colours, washing) déteindre; (in election) être candidat, se présenter; **at a ~** au pas de course; **to go for a ~** aller courir or faire un peu de course à pied; (in car) faire un tour or une promenade (en voiture); **there was a ~ on** (meat, tickets) les gens se sont rués sur; **in the long ~** à la longue; **on the ~** en fuite; **I'll ~ you to the station** je vais vous emmener or conduire à la gare; **to ~ a risk** courir un risque; **run after** vt fus (to catch up) courir après; (chase) poursuivre; **run away** vi s'enfuir; **run down** vt (Aut: knock over) renverser; (BRIT: reduce: production) réduire progressivement; (: factory/shop) réduire progressivement la production/ l'activité de; (criticize) critiquer, dénigrer; **to be ~ down** (tired) être fatigué(e) or à plat; **run into** vt fus (meet: person) rencontrer par hasard; (: trouble) se heurter à; (collide with) heurter; **run off** vi s'enfuir ▷ vt (water) laisser s'écouler; (copies) tirer; **run out** vi (person) sortir en courant; (liquid) couler; (lease) expirer; (money) être épuisé(e); **run out of** vt fus se trouver à court de; **run over** vt (Aut) écraser ▷ vt fus (revise) revoir, reprendre; **run through** vt fus (recap) reprendre, revoir; (play) répéter; **run up** vi; **to ~ up against** (difficulties) se heurter à; **runaway** adj (horse) emballé(e); (truck) fou (folle); (person) fugitif(-ive); (child) fugueur(-euse)

rung [rʌŋ] pp of **ring** ▷ n (of ladder) barreau m

runner ['rʌnə'] n (in race: person) coureur(-euse); (: horse) partant m; (on sledge) patin m; (for drawer etc) coulisseau m; **runner bean** n (BRIT) haricot m (à rames); **runner-up** n second(e)

running ['rʌnɪŋ] n (in race etc) course f; (of business, organization) direction f, gestion f ▷ adj (water) courant(e); (commentary) suivi(e); **6 days ~** 6 jours de suite; **to be in/out of the ~ for sth**

être/ne pas être sur les rangs pour qch

runny ['rʌnɪ] adj qui coule

run-up ['rʌnʌp] n (BRIT): **~ to sth** période f précédant qch

runway ['rʌnweɪ] n (Aviat) piste f (d'envol or d'atterrissage)

rupture ['rʌptʃə'] n (Med) hernie f

rural ['ruərl] adj rural(e)

rush [rʌʃ] n (of crowd, Comm: sudden demand) ruée f; (hurry) hâte f; (of anger, joy) accès m; (current) flot m; (Bot) jonc m ▷ vt (hurry) transporter or envoyer d'urgence ▷ vi se précipiter; **to ~ sth off** (do quickly) faire qch à la hâte; **rush hour** n heures fpl de pointe or d'affluence

Russia ['rʌʃə] n Russie f; **Russian** adj russe ▷ n Russe m/f; (Ling) russe m

rust [rʌst] n rouille f ▷ vi rouiller

rusty ['rʌstɪ] adj rouillé(e)

ruthless ['ruːθlɪs] adj sans pitié, impitoyable

RV n abbr (US) = **recreational vehicle**

rye [raɪ] n seigle m

S

Sabbath ['sæbəθ] n (Jewish) sabbat m;
(Christian) dimanche m
sabotage ['sæbətɑːʒ] n sabotage m
▷ vt saboter
saccharin(e) ['sækərɪn] n saccharine f
sachet ['sæʃeɪ] n sachet m
sack [sæk] n (bag) sac m ▷ vt (dismiss)
renvoyer, mettre à la porte; (plunder)
piller, mettre à sac; **to get the ~** être
renvoyé(e) or mis(e) à la porte
sacred ['seɪkrɪd] adj sacré(e)
sacrifice ['sækrɪfaɪs] n sacrifice m
▷ vt sacrifier
sad [sæd] adj (unhappy) triste;
(deplorable) triste, fâcheux(-euse); (inf:
pathetic: thing) triste, lamentable;
(: person) minable
saddle ['sædl] n selle f ▷ vt (horse)
seller; **to be ~d with sth** (inf) avoir qch
sur les bras
sadistic [sə'dɪstɪk] adj sadique
sadly ['sædlɪ] adv tristement;
(unfortunately) malheureusement;
(seriously) fort

sadness ['sædnɪs] n tristesse f
s.a.e. n abbr (BRIT: = stamped addressed
envelope) enveloppe affranchie pour la
réponse
safari [sə'fɑːrɪ] n safari m
safe [seɪf] adj (out of danger) hors de
danger, en sécurité; (not dangerous)
sans danger; (cautious) prudent(e);
(sure: bet etc) assuré(e) ▷ n coffre-fort
m; **could you put this in the ~, please?**
pourriez-vous mettre ceci dans le
coffre-fort?; **~ and sound** sain(e) et
sauf (sauve); **(just) to be on the ~ side**
pour plus de sûreté, par précaution;
safely adv (assume, say) sans risque
d'erreur; (drive, arrive) sans accident;
safe sex n rapports sexuels protégés
safety ['seɪftɪ] n sécurité f; **safety belt**
n ceinture f de sécurité; **safety pin** n
épingle f de sûreté or de nourrice
saffron ['sæfrən] n safran m
sag [sæg] vi s'affaisser, fléchir; (hem,
breasts) pendre
sage [seɪdʒ] n (herb) sauge f; (person)
sage m
Sagittarius [sædʒɪ'tɛərɪəs] n le
Sagittaire
Sahara [sə'hɑːrə] n: **the ~ (Desert)** le
(désert du) Sahara m
said [sɛd] pt, pp of **say**
sail [seɪl] n (on boat) voile f; (trip): **to
go for a ~** faire un tour en bateau ▷ vt
(boat) manœuvrer, piloter ▷ vi (travel:
ship) avancer, naviguer; (set off) partir,
prendre la mer; (Sport) faire de la voile;
they ~ed into Le Havre ils sont entrés
dans le port du Havre; **sailboat** n (US)
bateau m à voiles, voilier m; **sailing** n
(Sport) voile f; **to go sailing** faire de la
voile; **sailing boat** n bateau m à voiles,
voilier m; **sailor** n marin m, matelot m
saint [seɪnt] n saint(e)
sake [seɪk] n: **for the ~ of** (out of concern
for) pour (l'amour de), dans l'intérêt de;
(out of consideration for) par égard pour
salad ['sæləd] n salade f; **salad cream**
n (BRIT) (sorte f de) mayonnaise f; **salad
dressing** n vinaigrette f

salami [sə'lɑ:mɪ] n salami m
salary ['sælərɪ] n salaire m, traitement m
sale [seɪl] n vente f; (at reduced prices) soldes mpl; **sales** npl (total amount sold) chiffre m de ventes; **"for ~"** "à vendre"; **on ~** en vente; **sales assistant** (US **sales clerk**) n vendeur(-euse); **salesman** (irreg) n (in shop) vendeur m; **salesperson** (irreg) n (in shop) vendeur(-euse); **sales rep** n (Comm) représentant(e) m/f; **saleswoman** (irreg) n (in shop) vendeuse f
saline ['seɪlaɪn] adj salin(e)
saliva [sə'laɪvə] n salive f
salmon ['sæmən] n (pl inv) saumon m
salon ['sælɔn] n salon m
saloon [sə'lu:n] n (US) bar m; (BRIT Aut) berline f; (ship's lounge) salon m
salt [sɔ:lt] n sel m ▷ vt saler; **saltwater** adj (fish etc) (d'eau) de mer; **salty** adj salé(e)
salute [sə'lu:t] n salut m; (of guns) salve f ▷ vt saluer
salvage ['sælvɪdʒ] n (saving) sauvetage m; (things saved) biens sauvés or récupérés ▷ vt sauver, récupérer
Salvation Army [sæl'veɪʃən-] n Armée f du Salut
same [seɪm] adj même ▷ pron: **the ~** le (la) même, les mêmes; **the ~ book as** le même livre que; **at the ~ time** en même temps; (yet) néanmoins; **all** or **just the ~** tout de même, quand même; **to do the ~** faire de même, en faire autant; **to do the ~ as sb** faire comme qn; **and the ~ to you!** et à vous de même!; (after insult) toi-même!
sample ['sɑ:mpl] n échantillon m; (Med) prélèvement m ▷ vt (food, wine) goûter
sanction ['sæŋkʃən] n approbation f, sanction f ▷ vt cautionner, sanctionner; **sanctions** npl (Pol) sanctions
sanctuary ['sæŋktjuərɪ] n (holy place) sanctuaire m; (refuge) asile m; (for wildlife) réserve f

sand [sænd] n sable m ▷ vt (also: **~ down**: wood etc) poncer
sandal ['sændl] n sandale f
sand: **sandbox** n (US: for children) tas m de sable; **sandcastle** n château m de sable; **sand dune** n dune f de sable; **sandpaper** n papier m de verre; **sandpit** n (BRIT: for children) tas m de sable; **sands** npl plage f (de sable); **sandstone** ['sændstəun] n grès m
sandwich ['sændwɪtʃ] n sandwich m ▷ vt (also: **~ in**) intercaler; **~ed between** pris en sandwich entre; **cheese/ham ~** sandwich au fromage/jambon
sandy ['sændɪ] adj sablonneux(-euse); (colour) sable inv, blond roux inv
sane [seɪn] adj (person) sain(e) d'esprit; (outlook) sensé(e), sain(e)
sang [sæŋ] pt of **sing**
sanitary towel (US **sanitary napkin**) ['sænɪtərɪ-] n serviette f hygiénique
sanity ['sænɪtɪ] n santé mentale; (common sense) bon sens
sank [sæŋk] pt of **sink**
Santa Claus [sæntə'klɔ:z] n le Père Noël
sap [sæp] n (of plants) sève f ▷ vt (strength) saper, miner
sapphire ['sæfaɪə'] n saphir m
sarcasm ['sɑ:kæzm] n sarcasme m, raillerie f
sarcastic [sɑ:'kæstɪk] adj sarcastique
sardine [sɑ:'di:n] n sardine f
SASE n abbr (US: = self-addressed stamped envelope) enveloppe affranchie pour la réponse
sat [sæt] pt, pp of **sit**
Sat. abbr (= Saturday) sa
satchel ['sætʃl] n cartable m
satellite ['sætəlaɪt] n satellite m; **satellite dish** n antenne f parabolique; **satellite television** n télévision f par satellite
satin ['sætɪn] n satin m ▷ adj en or de satin, satiné(e)
satire ['sætaɪə'] n satire f
satisfaction [sætɪs'fækʃən] n satisfaction f

satisfactory [sætɪsˈfæktərɪ] *adj*
satisfaisant(e)

satisfied [ˈsætɪsfaɪd] *adj* satisfait(e);
to be ~ with sth être satisfait de qch

satisfy [ˈsætɪsfaɪ] *vt* satisfaire,
contenter; (*convince*) convaincre,
persuader

Saturday [ˈsætədɪ] *n* samedi *m*

sauce [sɔːs] *n* sauce *f*; **saucepan** *n*
casserole *f*

saucer [ˈsɔːsəʳ] *n* soucoupe *f*

Saudi Arabia [ˈsaʊdɪ-] *n* Arabie *f*
Saoudite

sauna [ˈsɔːnə] *n* sauna *m*

sausage [ˈsɔsɪdʒ] *n* saucisse *f*; (*salami
etc*) saucisson *m*; **sausage roll** *n*
friand *m*

sautéed [ˈsəʊteɪd] *adj* sauté(e)

savage [ˈsævɪdʒ] *adj* (*cruel, fierce*)
brutal(e), féroce; (*primitive*)
primitif(-ive), sauvage ▷ *n* sauvage *m/f*
▷ *vt* attaquer férocement

save [seɪv] *vt* (*person, belongings*) sauver;
(*money*) mettre de côté, économiser;
(*time*) (faire) gagner; (*keep*) garder;
(*Comput*) sauvegarder; (*Sport*: *stop*)
arrêter; (*avoid*: *trouble*) éviter ▷ *vi* (*also*:
~ up) mettre de l'argent de côté ▷ *n*
(*Sport*) arrêt *m* (du ballon) ▷ *prep* sauf, à
l'exception de

savings [ˈseɪvɪŋz] *npl* économies *fpl*;
savings account *n* compte *m*
d'épargne; **savings and loan
association** (*us*) *n* ≈ société *f* de crédit
immobilier

savoury (*us* **savory**) [ˈseɪvərɪ] *adj*
savoureux(-euse); (*dish*: *not sweet*)
salé(e)

saw [sɔː] *pt of* **see** ▷ *n* (*tool*) scie *f* ▷ *vt*
(*pt* **~ed**, *pp* **~ed** *or* **~n**) scier; **sawdust**
n sciure *f*

sawn [sɔːn] *pp of* **saw**

saxophone [ˈsæksəfəʊn] *n*
saxophone *m*

say [seɪ] *n*: **to have one's ~** dire ce qu'on
a à dire ▷ *vt* (*pt, pp* **said**) dire; **to have
a ~** avoir voix au chapitre; **could you ~
that again?** pourriez-vous répéter ce

que vous venez de dire?; **to ~ yes/no**
dire oui/non; **my watch ~s 3 o'clock**
ma montre indique 3 heures, il est 3
heures à ma montre; **that is to ~** c'est-
à-dire, cela va sans dire, cela va de soi;
saying *n* dicton *m*, proverbe *m*

scab [skæb] *n* croûte *f*; (*pej*) jaune *m*

scaffolding [ˈskæfəldɪŋ] *n*
échafaudage *m*

scald [skɔːld] *n* brûlure *f* ▷ *vt*
ébouillanter

scale [skeɪl] *n* (*of fish*) écaille *f*; (*Mus*)
gamme *f*; (*of ruler, thermometer etc*)
graduation *f*, échelle (graduée); (*of
salaries, fees etc*) barème *m*; (*of map,
also size, extent*) échelle ▷ *vt* (*mountain*)
escalader; **scales** *npl* balance *f*; (*larger*)
bascule *f*; (*also*: **bathroom ~s**) pèse-
personne *m inv*; **~ of charges** tableau *m*
des tarifs; **on a large ~** sur une grande
échelle, en grand

scallion [ˈskæljən] *n* (*us*: *salad onion*)
ciboule *f*

scallop [ˈskɒləp] *n* coquille *f* Saint-
Jacques; (*Sewing*) feston *m*

scalp [skælp] *n* cuir chevelu ▷ *vt*
scalper

scalpel [ˈskælpl] *n* scalpel *m*

scam [skæm] *n* (*inf*) arnaque *f*

scampi [ˈskæmpɪ] *npl* langoustines
(frites), scampi *mpl*

scan [skæn] *vt* (*examine*) scruter,
examiner; (*glance at quickly*) parcourir;
(*TV, Radar*) balayer ▷ *n* (*Med*)
scanographie *f*

scandal [ˈskændl] *n* scandale *m*;
(*gossip*) ragots *mpl*

Scandinavia [skændɪˈneɪvɪə] *n*
Scandinavie *f*; **Scandinavian** *adj*
scandinave ▷ *n* Scandinave *m/f*

scanner [ˈskænəʳ] *n* (*Radar, Med*)
scanner *m*, scanographe *m*; (*Comput*)
scanner, numériseur *m*

scapegoat [ˈskeɪpgəʊt] *n* bouc *m*
émissaire

scar [skɑːʳ] *n* cicatrice *f* ▷ *vt* laisser une
cicatrice *or* une marque à

scarce [skɛəs] *adj* rare, peu

abondant(e); **to make o.s. ~** (inf)
se sauver; **scarcely** adv à peine,
presque pas
scare [skɛə^r] n peur f, panique f ▷ vt
effrayer, faire peur à; **to ~ sb stiff** faire
une peur bleue à qn; **bomb ~** alerte f à
la bombe; **scarecrow** n épouvantail m;
scared adj: **to be scared** avoir peur
scarf (pl **scarves**) [ska:f, ska:vz] n (long)
écharpe f; (square) foulard m
scarlet ['ska:lɪt] adj écarlate
scarves [ska:vz] npl of **scarf**
scary ['skɛərɪ] adj (inf) effrayant(e);
(film) qui fait peur
scatter ['skætə^r] vt éparpiller,
répandre; (crowd) disperser ▷ vi se
disperser
scenario [sɪ'nɑ:rɪəu] n scénario m
scene [si:n] n (Theat, fig etc) scène f; (of
crime, accident) lieu(x) m(pl), endroit m;
(sight, view) spectacle m, vue f; **scenery**
n (Theat) décor(s) m(pl); (landscape)
paysage m; **scenic** adj offrant de beaux
paysages or panoramas
scent [sɛnt] n parfum m, odeur f; (fig:
track) piste f
sceptical (us **skeptical**) ['skɛptɪkl] adj
sceptique
schedule ['ʃɛdju:l, us 'skɛdju:l] n
programme m, plan m; (of trains) horaire
m; (of prices etc) barème m, tarif m ▷ vt
prévoir; **on ~** à l'heure (prévue); à la
date prévue; **to be ahead of/behind ~**
avoir de l'avance/du retard; **scheduled
flight** n vol régulier
scheme [ski:m] n plan m, projet
m; (plot) complot m, combine f;
(arrangement) arrangement m,
classification f; (pension scheme
etc) régime m ▷ vt, vi comploter,
manigancer
schizophrenic [skɪtsə'frɛnɪk] adj
schizophrène
scholar ['skɔlə^r] n érudit(e); (pupil)
boursier(-ère); **scholarship** n
érudition f; (grant) bourse f (d'études)
school [sku:l] n (gen) école f; (secondary
school) collège m, lycée m; (in university)

faculté f; (us: university) université
f ▷ cpd scolaire; **schoolbook** n livre
m scolaire or de classe; **schoolboy**
n écolier m; (at secondary school)
collégien m, lycéen m; **schoolchildren**
npl écoliers mpl; (at secondary school)
collégiens mpl, lycéens mpl; **schoolgirl**
n écolière f; (at secondary school)
collégienne f, lycéenne f; **schooling** n
instruction f, études fpl; **schoolteacher**
n (primary) instituteur(-trice);
(secondary) professeur m
science ['saɪəns] n science f; **science
fiction** n science-fiction f; **scientific**
[saɪən'tɪfɪk] adj scientifique; **scientist**
n scientifique m/f; (eminent) savant m
sci-fi ['saɪfaɪ] n abbr (inf: = science
fiction) SF f
scissors ['sɪzəz] npl ciseaux mpl; **a pair
of ~** une paire de ciseaux
scold [skəuld] vt gronder
scone [skɔn] n sorte de petit pain rond
au lait
scoop [sku:p] n pelle f (à main); (for ice
cream) boule f à glace; (Press) reportage
exclusif or à sensation
scooter ['sku:tə^r] n (motor cycle) scooter
m; (toy) trottinette f
scope [skəup] n (capacity: of plan,
undertaking) portée f, envergure f; (: of
person) compétence f, capacités fpl;
(opportunity) possibilités fpl
scorching ['skɔ:tʃɪŋ] adj torride,
brûlant(e)
score [skɔ:^r] n score m, décompte m
des points; (Mus) partition f ▷ vt (goal,
point) marquer; (success) remporter;
(cut: leather, wood, card) entailler, inciser
▷ vi marquer des points; (Football)
marquer un but; (keep score) compter
les points; **on that ~** sur ce chapitre,
à cet égard; **a ~ of** (twenty) vingt; **~s of**
(fig) des tas de; **to ~ 6 out of 10** obtenir
6 sur 10; **score out** vt rayer, barrer,
biffer; **scoreboard** n tableau m; **scorer**
n (Football) auteur m du but; buteur m;
(keeping score) marqueur m
scorn [skɔ:n] n mépris m, dédain m

Scorpio ['skɔːpɪəu] n le Scorpion

scorpion ['skɔːpɪən] n scorpion m

Scot [skɔt] n Écossais(e)

Scotch [skɔtʃ] n whisky m, scotch m

Scotch tape® (US) n scotch® m, ruban adhésif

Scotland ['skɔtlənd] n Écosse f

Scots [skɔts] adj écossais(e); **Scotsman** (irreg) n Écossais m; **Scotswoman** (irreg) n Écossaise f; **Scottish** ['skɔtɪʃ] adj écossais(e); **Scottish Parliament** n Parlement écossais

scout [skaut] n (Mil) éclaireur m; (also: **boy ~**) scout m; **girl ~** (US) guide f

scowl [skaul] vi se renfrogner, avoir l'air maussade; **to ~ at** regarder de travers

scramble ['skræmbl] n (rush) bousculade f, ruée f ▷ vi grimper/ descendre tant bien que mal; **to ~ for** se bousculer or se disputer pour (avoir); **to go scrambling** (Sport) faire du trial; **scrambled eggs** npl œufs brouillés

scrap [skræp] n bout m, morceau m; (fight) bagarre f; (also: **~ iron**) ferraille f ▷ vt jeter, mettre au rebut; (fig) abandonner, laisser tomber ▷ vi se bagarrer; **scraps** npl (waste) déchets mpl; **scrapbook** n album m

scrape [skreip] vt, vi gratter, racler ▷ n: **to get into a ~** s'attirer des ennuis; **scrape through** vi (exam etc) réussir de justesse

scrap paper n papier m brouillon

scratch [skrætʃ] n égratignure f, rayure f; (on paint) éraflure f; (from claw) coup m de griffe ▷ vt (rub) (se) gratter; (paint etc) érafler; (with claw, nail) griffer ▷ vi (se) gratter; **to be up to ~** être à la hauteur; **scratch card** n carte f à gratter

scream [skriːm] n cri perçant, hurlement m ▷ vi crier, hurler

screen [skriːn] n écran m; (in room) paravent m; (fig) écran, rideau m ▷ vt masquer, cacher; (from the wind etc) abriter, protéger; (film) projeter; (candidates etc) filtrer; **screening** n (of film) projection f; (Med) test m (or tests) de dépistage; **screenplay** n scénario m; **screen saver** n (Comput) économiseur m d'écran

screw [skruː] n vis f ▷ vt (also: **~ in**) visser; **screw up** vt (paper etc) froisser; **to ~ up one's eyes** se plisser les yeux; **screwdriver** n tournevis m

scribble ['skrɪbl] n gribouillage m ▷ vt gribouiller, griffonner

script [skrɪpt] n (Cine etc) scénario m, texte m; (writing) (écriture f) script m

scroll [skrəul] n rouleau m ▷ vt (Comput) faire défiler (sur l'écran)

scrub [skrʌb] n (land) broussailles fpl ▷ vt (floor) nettoyer à la brosse; (pan) récurer; (washing) frotter

scruffy ['skrʌfɪ] adj débraillé(e)

scrum(mage) ['skrʌm(ɪdʒ)] n mêlée f

scrutiny ['skruːtɪnɪ] n examen minutieux

scuba diving ['skuːbə-] n plongée sous-marine (autonome)

sculptor ['skʌlptər] n sculpteur m

sculpture ['skʌlptʃər] n sculpture f

scum [skʌm] n écume f, mousse f; (pej: people) rebut m, lie f

scurry ['skʌrɪ] vi filer à toute allure; **to ~ off** détaler, se sauver

sea [siː] n mer f ▷ cpd marin(e), de (la) mer, maritime; **by** or **beside the ~** (holiday, town) au bord de la mer; **by ~** par mer, en bateau; **out to ~** au large; **(out) at ~** en mer; **to be all at ~** (fig) nager complètement; **seafood** n fruits mpl de mer; **sea front** n bord m de mer; **seagull** n mouette f

seal [siːl] n (animal) phoque m; (stamp) sceau m, cachet m ▷ vt sceller; (envelope) coller; (: with seal) cacheter; **seal off** vt (forbid entry to) interdire l'accès de

sea level n niveau m de la mer

seam [siːm] n couture f; (of coal) veine f, filon m

search [səːtʃ] n (for person, thing, Comput) recherche(s) f(pl); (of drawer, pockets) fouille f; (Law: at sb's home) perquisition f ▷ vt fouiller; (examine)

examiner minutieusement; scruter
▷ vi: **to ~ for** chercher; **in ~ of** à la
recherche de; **search engine** n
(*Comput*) moteur m de recherche;
search party n expédition f de secours
sea: **seashore** n rivage m, plage f,
bord m de (la) mer; **seasick** adj: **to be
seasick** avoir le mal de mer; **seaside**
n bord m de mer; **seaside resort** n
station f balnéaire
season ['si:zn] n saison f ▷ vt
assaisonner, relever; **to be in/out of ~**
être/ne pas être de saison; **seasonal**
adj saisonnier(-ière); **seasoning** n
assaisonnement m; **season ticket** n
carte f d'abonnement
seat [si:t] n siège m; (*in bus, train:
place*) place f; (*buttocks*) postérieur m;
(*of trousers*) fond m ▷ vt faire asseoir,
placer; (*have room for*) avoir des places
assises pour, pouvoir accueillir; **I'd like
to book two ~s** je voudrais réserver
deux places; **to be ~ed** être assis; **seat
belt** n ceinture f de sécurité; **seating** n
sièges fpl, places assises
sea: **sea water** n eau f de mer; **seaweed**
n algues fpl
sec. abbr (= second) sec
secluded [sɪ'klu:dɪd] adj retiré(e),
à l'écart
second ['sɛkənd] num deuxième,
second(e) ▷ adv (*in race etc*) en seconde
position ▷ n (*unit of time*) seconde f;
(*Aut: also:* **~ gear**) seconde; (*Comm:
imperfect*) article m de second choix;
(*BRIT Scol*) ≈ licence f avec mention ▷ vt
(*motion*) appuyer; **seconds** npl (*inf: food*)
rab m (*inf*); **secondary** adj secondaire;
secondary school n collège m; lycée m;
second-class adj de deuxième classe;
(*Rail*) de seconde (classe); (*Post*) au
tarif réduit; (*pej*) de qualité inférieure
▷ adv (*Rail*) en seconde; (*Post*) au tarif
réduit; **secondhand** adj d'occasion;
(*information*) de seconde main;
secondly adv deuxièmement; **second-
rate** adj de deuxième ordre, de qualité
inférieure; **second thoughts** npl: **to**

have second thoughts changer d'avis;
on second thoughts or **thought** (*us*)
à la réflexion
secrecy ['si:krəsɪ] n secret m
secret ['si:krɪt] adj secret(-ète)
▷ n secret m; **in ~** en secret,
secrètement, en cachette
secretary ['sɛkrətrɪ] n secrétaire m/f;
S~ of State (for) (*Brit Pol*) ministre
m (de)
secretive ['si:krətɪv] adj réservé(e);
(*pej*) cachottier(-ière), dissimulé(e)
secret service n services secrets
sect [sɛkt] n secte f
section ['sɛkʃən] n section f; (*Comm*)
rayon m; (*of document*) section, article
m, paragraphe m; (*cut*) coupe f
sector ['sɛktəʳ] n secteur m
secular ['sɛkjʊləʳ] adj laïque
secure [sɪ'kjʊəʳ] adj (*free from anxiety*)
sans inquiétude, sécurisé(e); (*firmly
fixed*) solide, bien attaché(e) (or
fermé(e) etc); (*in safe place*) en lieu sûr,
en sûreté ▷ vt (*fix*) fixer, attacher; (*get*)
obtenir, se procurer
security [sɪ'kjʊərɪtɪ] n sécurité f,
mesures fpl de sécurité; (*for loan*)
caution f, garantie f; **securities** npl
(*Stock Exchange*) valeurs fpl, titres mpl;
security guard n garde chargé
de la sécurité; (*transporting money*)
convoyeur m de fonds
sedan [sə'dæn] n (*us Aut*) berline f
sedate [sɪ'deɪt] adj calme; posé(e) ▷ vt
donner des sédatifs à
sedative ['sɛdɪtɪv] n calmant m,
sédatif m
seduce [sɪ'dju:s] vt séduire; **seductive**
[sɪ'dʌktɪv] adj séduisant(e);
(*smile*) séducteur(-trice); (*fig: offer*)
alléchant(e)
see [si:] vb (*pt* **saw**, *pp* **~n**) ▷ vt (*gen*)
voir; (*accompany*): **to ~ sb to the
door** reconduire or raccompagner qn
jusqu'à la porte ▷ vi voir; **to ~ that**
(*ensure*) veiller à ce que + sub, faire en
sorte que + sub, s'assurer que; **~ you
soon/later/tomorrow!** à bientôt/plu

tard/demain!; **see off** vt accompagner (à la gare or à l'aéroport etc); **see out** vt (take to door) raccompagner à la porte; **see through** vt mener à bonne fin ▷ vt fus voir clair dans; **see to** vt fus s'occuper de, se charger de

eed [si:d] n graine f; (fig) germe m; (Tennis etc) tête f de série; **to go to ~** (plant) monter en graine; (fig) se laisser aller

eeing ['si:ɪŋ] conj: **~ (that)** vu que, étant donné que

eek (pt, pp **sought**) [si:k, sɔ:t] vt chercher, rechercher

eem [si:m] vi sembler, paraître; **there ~s to be ...** il semble qu'il y a ..., on dirait qu'il y a ...; **seemingly** adv apparemment

een [si:n] pp of **see**

eesaw ['si:sɔ:] n (jeu m de) bascule f

egment ['sɛgmənt] n segment m; (of orange) quartier m

egregate ['sɛgrɪgeɪt] vt séparer, isoler

eine [seɪn] n: **the (River) ~** la Seine

eize [si:z] vt (grasp) saisir, attraper; (take possession of) s'emparer de; (opportunity) saisir

eizure ['si:ʒər] n (Med) crise f, attaque f; (of power) prise f

eldom ['sɛldəm] adv rarement

elect [sɪ'lɛkt] adj choisi(e), d'élite; (hotel, restaurant, club) chic inv, sélect inv ▷ vt sélectionner, choisir; **selection** n sélection f, choix m; **selective** adj sélectif(-ive); (school) à recrutement sélectif

elf [self] n (pl **selves**): **the ~** le moi inv ▷ prefix auto-; **self-assured** adj sûr(e) de soi, plein(e) d'assurance; **self-catering** adj (BRIT: flat) avec cuisine, où l'on peut faire sa cuisine; (: holiday) en appartement (or chalet etc) loué; **self-centred** (US **self-centered**) adj égocentrique; **self-confidence** n confiance f en soi; **self-confident** adj sûr(e) de soi, plein(e) d'assurance; **self-conscious** adj timide, qui manque d'assurance; **self-contained**

adj (BRIT: flat) avec entrée particulière, indépendant(e); **self-control** n maîtrise f de soi; **self-defence** (US **self-defense**) n autodéfense f; (Law) légitime défense f; **self-drive** adj (BRIT): **self-drive car** voiture f de location; **self-employed** adj qui travaille à son compte; **self-esteem** n amour-propre m; **self-indulgent** adj qui ne se refuse rien; **self-interest** n intérêt personnel; **selfish** adj égoïste; **self-pity** n apitoiement m sur soi-même; **self-raising** [sɛlf'reɪzɪŋ] (US **self-rising** [sɛlf'raɪzɪŋ]) adj: **self-raising flour** farine f pour gâteaux (avec levure incorporée); **self-respect** n respect m de soi, amour-propre m; **self-service** adj, n libre-service (m), self-service (m)

sell (pt, pp **sold**) [sɛl, səuld] vt vendre ▷ vi se vendre; **to ~ at** or **for 10 euros** se vendre 10 euros; **sell off** vt liquider; **sell out** vi: **to ~ out (of sth)** (use up stock) vendre tout son stock (de qch); **sell-by date** n date f limite de vente; **seller** n vendeur(-euse), marchand(e)

Sellotape® ['sɛləuteɪp] n (BRIT) scotch® m

selves [sɛlvz] npl of **self**

semester [sɪ'mɛstər] n (esp US) semestre m

semi... ['sɛmɪ] prefix semi-, demi-; à demi, à moitié; **semicircle** n demi-cercle m; **semidetached (house)** n (BRIT) maison jumelée or jumelle; **semi-final** n demi-finale f

seminar ['sɛmɪnɑːr] n séminaire m

semi-skimmed ['sɛmɪ'skɪmd] adj demi-écrémé(e)

senate ['sɛnɪt] n sénat m; (US): **the S~** le Sénat; **senator** n sénateur m

send (pt, pp **sent**) [sɛnd, sɛnt] vt envoyer; **send back** vt renvoyer; **send for** vt fus (by post) se faire envoyer, commander par correspondance; **send in** vt (report, application, resignation) remettre; **send off** vt (goods) envoyer, expédier; (BRIT Sport: player) expulser or renvoyer du terrain; **send on** vt

(BRIT: *letter*) faire suivre; (*luggage etc: in advance*) (faire) expédier à l'avance; **send out** vt (*invitation*) envoyer (par la poste); (*emit: light, heat, signal*) émettre; **send up** vt (*person, price*) faire monter; (BRIT: *parody*) mettre en boîte, parodier; **sender** n expéditeur(-trice); **send-off** n: **a good send-off** des adieux chaleureux

senile ['siːnaɪl] *adj* sénile

senior ['siːnɪəʳ] *adj* (*high-ranking*) de haut niveau; (*of higher rank*): **to be ~ to sb** être le supérieur de qn; **senior citizen** n personne f du troisième âge; **senior high school** n (US) ≈ lycée m

sensation [sɛnˈseɪʃən] n sensation f; **sensational** adj qui fait sensation; (*marvellous*) sensationnel(le)

sense [sɛns] n sens m; (*feeling*) sentiment m; (*meaning*) sens, signification f; (*wisdom*) bon sens ▷ vt sentir, pressentir; **it makes ~** c'est logique; **senseless** adj insensé(e), stupide; (*unconscious*) sans connaissance; **sense of humour** (US **sense of humor**) n sens m de l'humour

sensible ['sɛnsɪbl] *adj* sensé(e), raisonnable; (*shoes etc*) pratique

▌ Be careful not to translate *sensible* by the French word *sensible*.

sensitive ['sɛnsɪtɪv] *adj*: **~ (to)** sensible (à)

sensual ['sɛnsjuəl] *adj* sensuel(le)

sensuous ['sɛnsjuəs] *adj* voluptueux(-euse), sensuel(le)

sent [sɛnt] *pt, pp of* **send**

sentence ['sɛntns] n (Ling) phrase f; (Law: judgment) condamnation f, sentence f; (: punishment) peine f ▷ vt: **to ~ sb to death/to 5 years** condamner qn à mort/à 5 ans

sentiment ['sɛntɪmənt] n sentiment m; (opinion) opinion f, avis m; **sentimental** [sɛntɪˈmɛntl] *adj* sentimental(e)

Sep. abbr (= September) septembre

separate adj ['sɛprɪt] séparé(e); (organization) indépendant(e); (day,

occasion, issue) différent(e) ▷ vb ['sɛpəreɪt] ▷ vt séparer; (distinguish) distinguer ▷ vi se séparer; **separately** adv séparément; **separates** npl (clothes) coordonnés mpl; **separation** [sɛpəˈreɪʃən] n séparation f

September [sɛpˈtɛmbəʳ] n septembre m

septic ['sɛptɪk] *adj* (wound) infecté(e); **septic tank** n fosse f septique

sequel ['siːkwl] n conséquence f, séquelles fpl; (of story) suite f

sequence ['siːkwəns] n ordre m, suite f; (in film) séquence f; (dance) numéro m

sequin ['siːkwɪn] n paillette f

Serb [səːb] *adj, n* = **Serbian**

Serbia ['səːbɪə] n Serbie f

Serbian ['səːbɪən] *adj* serbe ▷ n Serbe m/f; (Ling) serbe m

sergeant ['sɑːdʒənt] n sergent m; (Police) brigadier m

serial ['sɪərɪəl] n feuilleton m; **serial killer** n meurtrier m tuant en série; **serial number** n numéro m de série

series ['sɪəriːz] n série f; (Publishing) collection f

serious ['sɪərɪəs] *adj* sérieux(-euse); (accident etc) grave; **seriously** adv sérieusement; (hurt) gravement

sermon ['səːmən] n sermon m

servant ['səːvənt] n domestique m/f; (fig) serviteur (servante)

serve [səːv] vt (employer etc) servir, être au service de; (purpose) servir à; (customer, food, meal) servir; (subj: train) desservir; (apprenticeship) faire, accomplir; (prison term) faire; purger ▷ vi (Tennis) servir; (be useful): **to ~ as/for/to do** servir de/à/à faire ▷ vt (Tennis) service m; **it ~s him right** c'est bien fait pour lui; **server** n (Comput) serveur m

service ['səːvɪs] n (gen) service m; (Aut) révision f; (Rel) office m ▷ vt (car etc) réviser; **services** npl (Econ: tertiary sector) (secteur m) tertiaire m, secteur des services; (BRIT: on motorway) station-service f; (Mil): **the**

S~s npl les forces armées; **to be of ~ to sb**, **to do sb a ~** rendre service à qn; **~ included/not included** service compris/non compris; **service area** n (on motorway) aire f de services; **service charge** n (BRIT) service m; **serviceman** (irreg) n militaire m; **service station** n station-service f

erviette [sə:vɪˈɛt] n (BRIT) serviette f (de table)

ession [ˈsɛʃən] n (sitting) séance f; **to be in ~** siéger, être en session or en séance

et [sɛt] n série f, assortiment m; (of tools etc) jeu m; (Radio, TV) poste m; (Tennis) set m; (group of people) cercle m, milieu m; (Cine) plateau m; (Theat: stage) scène f; (: scenery) décor m; (Math) ensemble m; (Hairdressing) mise f en plis ▷ adj (fixed) fixe, déterminé(e); (ready) prêt(e) ▷ vb (pt, pp ~) ▷ vt (place) mettre, poser, placer; (fix, establish) fixer; (: record) établir; (assign: task, homework) donner; (exam) composer; (adjust) régler; (decide: rules etc) fixer, choisir ▷ vi (sun) se coucher; (jam, jelly, concrete) prendre; (bone) se ressouder; **to be ~ on doing** être résolu(e) à faire; **to ~ to music** mettre en musique; **to ~ on fire** mettre le feu à; **to ~ free** libérer; **to ~ sth going** déclencher qch; **to ~ sail** partir, prendre la mer; **set aside** vt mettre de côté; (time) garder; **set down** vt (subj: bus, train) déposer; **set in** vi (infection, bad weather) s'installer; (complications) survenir, surgir; **set off** vi se mettre en route, partir ▷ vt (bomb) faire exploser; (cause to start) déclencher; (show up well) mettre en valeur, faire valoir; **set out** vi: **to ~ out (from)** partir (de) ▷ vt (arrange) disposer; (state) présenter; exposer; **to ~ out to do** entreprendre de faire; avoir pour but or intention de faire; **set up** vt (organization) fonder, créer; **setback** n (hitch) revers m, contretemps m; **set menu** n menu m

ettee [sɛˈtiː] n canapé m

tting [ˈsɛtɪŋ] n cadre m; (of jewel)

monture f; (position: of controls) réglage m

settle [ˈsɛtl] vt (argument, matter, account) régler; (problem) résoudre; (Med: calm) calmer ▷ vi (bird, dust etc) se poser; **to ~ for sth** accepter qch, se contenter de qch; **to ~ on sth** opter or se décider pour qch; **settle down** vi (get comfortable) s'installer; (become calmer) se calmer; se ranger; (live quietly) se fixer; **settle in** vi s'installer; **settle up** vi: **to ~ up with sb** régler (ce que l'on doit à) qn; **settlement** n (payment) règlement m; (agreement) accord m; (village etc) village m, hameau m

setup [ˈsɛtʌp] n (arrangement) manière f dont les choses sont organisées; (situation) situation f, allure f des choses

seven [ˈsɛvn] num sept; **seventeen** num dix-sept; **seventeenth** [sɛvnˈtiːnθ] num dix-septième; **seventh** num septième; **seventieth** [ˈsɛvntɪɪθ] num soixante-dixième; **seventy** num soixante-dix

sever [ˈsɛvəʳ] vt couper, trancher; (relations) rompre

several [ˈsɛvərl] adj, pron plusieurs pl; **~ of us** plusieurs d'entre nous

severe [sɪˈvɪəʳ] adj (stern) sévère, strict(e); (serious) grave, sérieux(-euse); (plain) sévère, austère

sew (pt **~ed**, pp **~n**) [səu, səud, səun] vt, vi coudre

sewage [ˈsuːɪdʒ] n vidange(s) f(pl)

sewer [ˈsuːəʳ] n égout m

sewing [ˈsəuɪŋ] n couture f; (item(s)) ouvrage m; **sewing machine** n machine f à coudre

sewn [səun] pp of **sew**

sex [sɛks] n sexe m; **to have ~ with** avoir des rapports (sexuels) avec; **sexism** [ˈsɛksɪzəm] n sexisme m; **sexist** adj sexiste; **sexual** [ˈsɛksjuəl] adj sexuel(le); **sexual intercourse** n rapports sexuels; **sexuality** [sɛksjuˈælɪtɪ] n sexualité f; **sexy** adj sexy inv

shabby [ˈʃæbɪ] adj miteux(-euse);

(*behaviour*) mesquin(e), méprisable

shack [ʃæk] n cabane f, hutte f

shade [ʃeɪd] n ombre f; (*for lamp*) abat-jour m inv; (*of colour*) nuance f, ton m; (*us: window shade*) store m; (*small quantity*): **a ~ of** un soupçon de ▷ vt abriter du soleil, ombrager; **shades** npl (*us: sunglasses*) lunettes fpl de soleil; **in the ~** à l'ombre; **a ~ smaller** un tout petit peu plus petit

shadow [ʃædəu] n ombre f ▷ vt (*follow*) filer; **shadow cabinet** n (*BRIT Pol*) cabinet parallèle formé par le parti qui n'est pas au pouvoir

shady [ʃeɪdɪ] adj ombragé(e); (*fig: dishonest*) louche, véreux(-euse)

shaft [ʃɑːft] n (*of arrow, spear*) hampe f; (*Aut, Tech*) arbre m; (*of mine*) puits m; (*of lift*) cage f; (*of light*) rayon m, trait m

shake [ʃeɪk] vb (*pt* **shook**, *pp* **~n**) ▷ vt secouer; (*bottle, cocktail*) agiter; (*house, confidence*) ébranler ▷ vi trembler; **to ~ one's head** (*in refusal etc*) dire or faire non de la tête; (*in dismay*) secouer la tête; **to ~ hands with sb** serrer la main à qn; **shake off** vt secouer; (*pursuer*) se débarrasser de; **shake up** vt secouer; **shaky** adj (*hand, voice*) tremblant(e); (*building*) branlant(e), peu solide

shall [ʃæl] aux vb: **I ~ go** j'irai; **~ I open the door?** j'ouvre la porte?; **I'll get the coffee, ~ I?** je vais chercher le café, d'accord?

shallow [ʃæləu] adj peu profond(e); (*fig*) superficiel(le), qui manque de profondeur

sham [ʃæm] n frime f

shambles [ʃæmblz] n confusion f, pagaïe f, fouillis m

shame [ʃeɪm] n honte f ▷ vt faire honte à; **it is a ~ (that/to do)** c'est dommage (que + sub/de faire); **what a ~!** quel dommage!; **shameful** adj honteux(-euse), scandaleux(-euse); **shameless** adj éhonté(e), effronté(e)

shampoo [ʃæm'puː] n shampooing m ▷ vt faire un shampooing à

shandy [ʃændɪ] n bière panachée

shan't [ʃɑːnt] = **shall not**

shape [ʃeɪp] n forme f ▷ vt façonner, modeler; (*sb's ideas, character*) former; (*sb's life*) déterminer ▷ vi (*also*: **~ up**: *events*) prendre tournure; (*: person*) faire des progrès, s'en sortir; **to take ~** prendre forme or tournure

share [ʃɛəʳ] n part f; (*Comm*) action f ▷ vt partager; (*have in common*) avoir en commun; **to ~ out (among** or **between)** partager (entre); **shareholder** n (*BRIT*) actionnaire m/f

shark [ʃɑːk] n requin m

sharp [ʃɑːp] adj (*razor, knife*) tranchant(e), bien aiguisé(e); (*point, voice*) aigu(ë); (*nose, chin*) pointu(e); (*outline, increase*) net(te); (*cold, pain*) vif (vive); (*taste*) piquant(e), âcre; (*Mus*) dièse; (*person: quick-witted*) vif (vive), éveillé(e); (*: unscrupulous*) malhonnête ▷ n (*Mus*) dièse m ▷ adv: **at 2 o'clock ~** à 2 heures pile or tapantes; **sharpen** vt aiguiser; (*pencil*) tailler; (*fig*) aviver; **sharpener** n (*also*: **pencil sharpener**) taille-crayon(s) m inv; **sharply** adv (*turn, stop*) brusquement; (*stand out*) nettement; (*criticize, retort*) sèchement, vertement

shatter [ʃætəʳ] vt briser; (*fig: upset*) bouleverser; (*: ruin*) briser, ruiner ▷ vi voler en éclats, se briser; **shattered** adj (*overwhelmed, grief-stricken*) bouleversé(e); (*inf: exhausted*) éreinté(e)

shave [ʃeɪv] vt raser ▷ vi se raser ▷ n: **to have a ~** se raser; **shaver** n (*also*: **electric shaver**) rasoir m électrique

shaving cream n crème f à raser

shaving foam n mousse f à raser

shavings [ʃeɪvɪŋz] npl (*of wood etc*) copeaux mpl

shawl [ʃɔːl] n châle m

she [ʃiː] pron elle

sheath [ʃiːθ] n gaine f, fourreau m, étui m; (*contraceptive*) préservatif m

shed [ʃed] n remise f, resserre f ▷ vt (*pt, pp* **~**) (*leaves, fur etc*) perdre; (*tears*) verser, répandre; (*workers*) congédier

she'd [ʃiːd] = **she had**; **she would**

sheep [ʃi:p] n (pl inv) mouton m;
sheepdog n chien m de berger;
sheepskin n peau f de mouton

sheer [ʃɪəʳ] adj (utter) pur(e), pur et
simple; (steep) à pic, abrupt(e); (almost
transparent) extrêmement fin(e) ▷ adv à
pic, abruptement

sheet [ʃi:t] n (on bed) drap m; (of paper)
feuille f; (of glass, metal etc) feuille,
plaque f

sheik(h) [ʃeɪk] n cheik m

shelf (pl **shelves**) [ʃɛlf, ʃɛlvz] n étagère
f, rayon m

shell [ʃɛl] n (on beach) coquillage m; (of
egg, nut etc) coquille f; (explosive) obus
m; (of building) carcasse f ▷ vt (peas)
écosser; (Mil) bombarder (d'obus)

she'll [ʃi:l] = **she will**; **she shall**

shellfish [ʃɛlfɪʃ] n (pl inv: crab etc)
crustacé m; (: scallop etc) coquillage m
▷ npl (as food) fruits mpl de mer

shelter [ʃɛltəʳ] n abri m, refuge m
▷ vt abriter, protéger; (give lodging to)
donner asile à ▷ vi s'abriter, se mettre
à l'abri; **sheltered** adj (life) retiré(e), à
l'abri des soucis; (spot) abrité(e)

shelves [ʃɛlvz] npl of **shelf**

shelving [ʃɛlvɪŋ] n (shelves)
rayonnage(s) m(pl)

shepherd [ʃɛpəd] n berger m ▷ vt
(guide) guider, escorter; **shepherd's pie**
n ≈ hachis m Parmentier

sheriff [ʃɛrɪf] (US) n shérif m

sherry [ʃɛrɪ] n xérès m, sherry m

she's [ʃi:z] = **she is**; **she has**

Shetland [ʃɛtlənd] n (also: **the ~s, the
~ Isles** or **Islands**) les îles fpl Shetland

shield [ʃi:ld] n bouclier m; (protection)
écran m de protection ▷ vt: **to ~ (from)**
protéger (de or contre)

shift [ʃɪft] n (change) changement m;
(work period) période f de travail; (of
workers) équipe f, poste m ▷ vt déplacer,
changer de place; (remove) enlever ▷ vi
changer de place, bouger

shin [ʃɪn] n tibia m

shine [ʃaɪn] n éclat m, brillant m ▷ vb
(pt, pp **shone**) ▷ vi briller ▷ vt (torch): **to**

~ on braquer sur; (polish: pt, pp **~d**) faire
briller or reluire

shingles [ʃɪŋglz] n (Med) zona m

shiny [ʃaɪnɪ] adj brillant(e)

ship [ʃɪp] n bateau m; (large) navire
m ▷ vt transporter (par mer); (send)
expédier (par mer); **shipment** n
cargaison f; **shipping** n (ships)
navires mpl; (traffic) navigation f; (the
industry) industrie navale; (transport)
transport m; **shipwreck** n épave
f; (event) naufrage m ▷ vt: **to be
shipwrecked** faire naufrage; **shipyard**
n chantier naval

shirt [ʃə:t] n chemise f; (woman's)
chemisier m; **in ~ sleeves** en bras de
chemise

shit [ʃɪt] excl (inf!) merde (!)

shiver [ʃɪvəʳ] n frisson m ▷ vi frissonner

shock [ʃɔk] n choc m; (Elec) secousse
f, décharge f; (Med) commotion
f, choc ▷ vt (scandalize) choquer,
scandaliser; (upset) bouleverser;
shocking adj (outrageous) choquant(e),
scandaleux(-euse); (awful)
épouvantable

shoe [ʃu:] n chaussure f, soulier m;
(also: **horse~**) fer m à cheval ▷ vt (pt, pp
shod) (horse) ferrer; **shoelace** n lacet
m (de soulier); **shoe polish** n cirage m;
shoeshop n magasin m de chaussures

shone [ʃɔn] pt, pp of **shine**

shook [ʃuk] pt of **shake**

shoot [ʃu:t] n (on branch, seedling)
pousse f ▷ vb (pt, pp **shot**) ▷ vt (game:
hunt) chasser; (: aim at) tirer; (: kill)
abattre; (person) blesser/tuer d'un
coup de fusil (or de revolver); (execute)
fusiller; (arrow) tirer; (gun) tirer un
coup de; (Cine) tourner ▷ vi (with gun,
bow): **to ~ (at)** tirer (sur); (Football)
shooter, tirer; **shoot down** vt (plane)
abattre; **shoot up** vi (fig: prices etc)
monter en flèche; **shooting** n (shots)
coups mpl de feu; (attack) fusillade f;
(murder) homicide m (à l'aide d'une arme
à feu); (Hunting) chasse f

shop [ʃɔp] n magasin m; (workshop)

atelier m ▷ vi (also: **go ~ping**) faire ses courses or ses achats; **shop assistant** n (BRIT) vendeur(-euse); **shopkeeper** n marchand(e), commerçant(e); **shoplifting** n vol m à l'étalage; **shopping** n (goods) achats mpl, provisions fpl; **shopping bag** n sac m (à provisions); **shopping centre** (US **shopping center**) n centre commercial; **shopping mall** n centre commercial; **shopping trolley** n (BRIT) Caddie® m; **shop window** n vitrine f

shore [ʃɔːʳ] n (of sea, lake) rivage m, rive f ▷ vt: **to ~ (up)** étayer; **on ~** à terre

short [ʃɔːt] adj (not long) court(e); (soon finished) court, bref (brève); (person, step) petit(e); (curt) brusque, sec (sèche); (insufficient) insuffisant(e) ▷ n (also: **~ film**) court métrage; (Elec) court-circuit m; **to be ~ of sth** être à court de or manquer de qch; **in ~** bref; en bref; **~ of doing** à moins de faire; **everything ~ of** tout sauf; **it is ~ for** c'est l'abréviation or le diminutif de; **to cut ~** (speech, visit) abréger, écourter; **to fall ~ of** ne pas être à la hauteur de; **to run ~ of** arriver à court de, venir à manquer de; **to stop ~** s'arrêter net; **to stop ~ of** ne pas aller jusqu'à; **shortage** n manque m, pénurie f; **shortbread** n ≈ sablé m; **shortcoming** n défaut m; **short(crust) pastry** n (BRIT) pâte brisée; **shortcut** n raccourci m; **shorten** vt raccourcir; (text, visit) abréger; **shortfall** n déficit m; **shorthand** n (BRIT) sténo(graphie) f; **shortlist** n (BRIT: for job) liste f des candidats sélectionnés; **short-lived** adj de courte durée; **shortly** adv bientôt, sous peu; **shorts** npl: **(a pair of) shorts** un short; **short-sighted** adj (BRIT) myope; (fig) qui manque de clairvoyance; **short-sleeved** adj à manches courtes; **short story** n nouvelle f; **short-tempered** adj qui s'emporte facilement; **short-term** adj (effect) à court terme

shot [ʃɔt] pt, pp of **shoot** ▷ n coup m

(de feu); (try) coup, essai m; (injection) piqûre f; (Phot) photo f; **to be a good/poor ~** (person) tirer bien/mal; **like a ~** comme une flèche; (very readily) sans hésiter; **shotgun** n fusil m de chasse

should [ʃud] aux vb: **I ~ go now** je devrais partir maintenant; **he ~ be there now** il devrait être arrivé maintenant; **I ~ go if I were you** si j'étais vous j'irais; **I ~ like to** j'aimerais bien, volontiers

shoulder ['ʃəʊldəʳ] n épaule f ▷ vt (fig) endosser, se charger de; **shoulder blade** n omoplate f

shouldn't ['ʃudnt] = **should not**

shout [ʃaut] n cri m ▷ vt crier ▷ vi crier, pousser des cris

shove [ʃʌv] vt pousser; (inf: put): **to ~ sth in** fourrer or ficher qch dans ▷ n poussée f

shovel ['ʃʌvl] n pelle f ▷ vt pelleter, enlever (or enfourner) à la pelle

show [ʃəu] n (of emotion) manifestation f, démonstration f; (semblance) semblant m, apparence f; (exhibition) exposition f, salon m; (Theat, TV) spectacle m; (Cine) séance f ▷ vb (pt **~ed**, pp **~n**) ▷ vt montrer; (film) passer; (courage etc) faire preuve de, manifester; (exhibit) exposer ▷ vi se voir, être visible; **can you ~ me where it is, please?** pouvez-vous me montrer où c'est?; **to be on ~** être exposé(e); **it's just for ~** c'est juste pour l'effet; **show in** vt faire entrer; **show off** vi (pej) crâner ▷ vt (display) faire valoir; (pej) faire étalage de; **show out** vt reconduire à la porte; **show up** vi (stand out) ressortir; (inf: turn up) se montrer ▷ vt (unmask) démasquer, dénoncer; (flaw) faire ressortir; **show business** n le monde du spectacle

shower ['ʃauəʳ] n (for washing) douche f; (rain) averse f; (of stones etc) pluie f, grêle f; (US: party) réunion organisée pour la remise de cadeaux ▷ vi prendre une douche, se doucher ▷ vt: **to ~ sb with** (gifts etc) combler qn de; **to have**

or **take a ~** prendre une douche, se
doucher; **shower cap** n bonnet m de
douche; **shower gel** n gel m douche
showing ['ʃəʊɪŋ] n (of film) projection f
show jumping [-dʒʌmpɪŋ] n
concours m hippique
shown [ʃəʊn] pp of **show**
show: **show-off** n (inf: person)
crâneur(-euse), m'as-tu-vu(e);
showroom n magasin m or salle f
d'exposition
shrank [ʃræŋk] pt of **shrink**
shred [ʃrɛd] n (gen pl) lambeau m, petit
morceau; (fig: of truth, evidence) parcelle
f ▷ vt mettre en lambeaux, déchirer;
(documents) détruire; (Culin: grate) râper;
(: lettuce etc) couper en lanières
shrewd [ʃruːd] adj astucieux(-euse),
perspicace; (business person) habile
shriek [ʃriːk] n cri perçant or aigu,
hurlement m ▷ vt, vi hurler, crier
shrimp [ʃrɪmp] n crevette grise
shrine [ʃraɪn] n (place) lieu m de
pèlerinage
shrink (pt **shrank**, pp **shrunk**) [ʃrɪŋk,
ʃræŋk, ʃrʌŋk] vi rétrécir; (fig) diminuer;
(also: **~ away**) reculer ▷ vt (wool) (faire)
rétrécir ▷ n (inf: pej) psychanalyste m/f;
to ~ from (doing) sth reculer devant
(la pensée de faire) qch
shrivel ['ʃrɪvl] (also: **~ up**) vt ratatiner,
flétrir ▷ vi se ratatiner, se flétrir
shroud [ʃraud] n linceul m ▷ vt: **~ed in
mystery** enveloppé(e) de mystère
Shrove Tuesday ['ʃrəʊv-] n (le)
Mardi gras
shrub [ʃrʌb] n arbuste m
shrug [ʃrʌg] n haussement m d'épaules
▷ vt, vi: **to ~ (one's shoulders)** hausser
les épaules; **shrug off** vt faire fi de
shrunk [ʃrʌŋk] pp of **shrink**
shudder ['ʃʌdər] n frisson m,
frémissement m ▷ vi frissonner, frémir
shuffle ['ʃʌfl] vt (cards) battre; **to ~
(one's feet)** traîner les pieds
shun [ʃʌn] vt éviter, fuir
shut (pt, pp **~**) [ʃʌt] vt fermer ▷ vi
(se) fermer; **shut down** vt fermer

définitivement ▷ vi fermer
définitivement; **shut up** vi (inf: keep
quiet) se taire ▷ vt (close) fermer;
(silence) faire taire; **shutter** n volet m;
(Phot) obturateur m
shuttle ['ʃʌtl] n navette f; (also: **~
service**) (service m de) navette f;
shuttlecock n volant m (de badminton)
shy [ʃaɪ] adj timide
siblings ['sɪblɪŋz] npl (formal) frères et
sœurs mpl (de mêmes parents)
Sicily ['sɪsɪlɪ] n Sicile f
sick [sɪk] adj (ill) malade; (BRIT:
vomiting): **to be ~** vomir; (humour)
noir(e), macabre; **to feel ~** avoir envie
de vomir, avoir mal au cœur; **to be ~
of** (fig) en avoir assez de; **sickening**
adj (fig) écœurant(e), révoltant(e),
répugnant(e); **sick leave** n congé m
de maladie; **sickly** adj maladif(-ive),
souffreteux(-euse); (causing nausea)
écœurant(e); **sickness** n maladie f;
(vomiting) vomissement(s) m(pl)
side [saɪd] n côté m; (of lake, road) bord
m; (of mountain) versant m; (fig: aspect)
côté, aspect m; (team: Sport) équipe
f; (TV: channel) chaîne f ▷ adj (door,
entrance) latéral(e) ▷ vi: **to ~ with sb**
prendre le parti de qn, se ranger du
côté de qn; **by the ~ of** au bord de; **~
by ~** côte à côte; **to rock from ~ to ~**
se balancer; **to take ~s (with)** prendre
parti (pour); **sideboard** n buffet m;
sideboards (BRIT), **sideburns** npl
(whiskers) pattes fpl; **side effect** n
effet m secondaire; **sidelight** n (Aut)
veilleuse f; **sideline** n (Sport) (ligne f de)
touche f; (fig) activité f secondaire; **side
order** n garniture f; **side road** n petite
route, route transversale; **side street** n
rue transversale; **sidetrack** vt (fig) faire
dévier de son sujet; **sidewalk** n (US)
trottoir m; **sideways** adv de côté
siege [siːdʒ] n siège m
sieve [sɪv] n tamis m, passoire f ▷ vt
tamiser, passer (au tamis)
sift [sɪft] vt passer au tamis or au crible;
(fig) passer au crible

sigh [saɪ] n soupir m ▷ vi soupirer, pousser un soupir

sight [saɪt] n (faculty) vue f; (spectacle) spectacle m; (on gun) mire f ▷ vt apercevoir; **in ~** visible; (fig) en vue; **out of ~** hors de vue; **sightseeing** n tourisme m; **to go sightseeing** faire du tourisme

sign [saɪn] n (gen) signe m; (with hand etc) signe, geste m; (notice) panneau m, écriteau m; (also: **road~**) panneau de signalisation ▷ vt signer; **where do I ~?** où dois-je signer?; **sign for** vt fus (item) signer le reçu pour; **sign in** vi signer le registre (en arrivant); **sign on** vi (BRIT: as unemployed) s'inscrire au chômage; (enrol) s'inscrire ▷ vt (employee) embaucher; **sign over** vt: **to ~ sth over to sb** céder qch par écrit à qn; **sign up** vi (Mil) s'engager; (for course) s'inscrire

signal ['sɪɡnl] n signal m ▷ vi (Aut) mettre son clignotant ▷ vt (person) faire signe à; (message) communiquer par signaux

signature ['sɪɡnətʃə'] n signature f

significance [sɪɡ'nɪfɪkəns] n signification f; importance f

significant [sɪɡ'nɪfɪkənt] adj significatif(-ive); (important) important(e), considérable

signify ['sɪɡnɪfaɪ] vt signifier

sign language n langage m par signes

signpost ['saɪnpəust] n poteau indicateur

Sikh [siːk] adj, n Sikh m/f

silence ['saɪləns] n silence m ▷ vt faire taire, réduire au silence

silent ['saɪlnt] adj silencieux(-euse); (film) muet(te); **to keep** or **remain ~** garder le silence, ne rien dire

silhouette [sɪluːˈɛt] n silhouette f

silicon chip ['sɪlɪkən-] n puce f électronique

silk [sɪlk] n soie f ▷ cpd de or en soie

silly ['sɪlɪ] adj stupide, sot(te), bête

silver ['sɪlvə'] n argent m; (money) monnaie f (en pièces d'argent); (also: **~ware**) argenterie f ▷ adj (made of silver) d'argent, en argent; (in colour) argenté(e); **silver-plated** adj plaqué(e) argent

similar ['sɪmɪlə'] adj: **~ (to)** semblable (à); **similarity** [sɪmɪˈlærɪtɪ] n ressemblance f, similarité f; **similarly** adv de la même façon, de même

simmer ['sɪmə'] vi cuire à feu doux, mijoter

simple ['sɪmpl] adj simple; **simplicity** [sɪmˈplɪsɪtɪ] n simplicité f; **simplify** ['sɪmplɪfaɪ] vt simplifier; **simply** adv simplement; (without fuss) avec simplicité; (absolutely) absolument

simulate ['sɪmjuleɪt] vt simuler, feindre

simultaneous [sɪməl'teɪnɪəs] adj simultané(e); **simultaneously** adv simultanément

sin [sɪn] n péché m ▷ vi pécher

since [sɪns] adv, prep depuis ▷ conj (time) depuis que; (because) puisque, étant donné que, comme; **~ then**, **ever ~** depuis ce moment-là

sincere [sɪnˈsɪə'] adj sincère; **sincerely** adv sincèrement; **Yours sincerely** (at end of letter) veuillez agréer, Monsieur (or Madame) l'expression de mes sentiments distingués or les meilleurs

sing (pt **sang**, pp **sung**) [sɪŋ, sæŋ, sʌŋ] vt, vi chanter

Singapore [sɪŋɡəˈpɔː'] n Singapour m

singer ['sɪŋə'] n chanteur(-euse)

singing ['sɪŋɪŋ] n (of person, bird) chant m

single ['sɪŋɡl] adj seul(e), unique; (unmarried) célibataire; (not double) simple ▷ n (BRIT: also: **~ ticket**) aller m (simple); (record) 45 tours m; **singles** npl (Tennis) simple m; **every ~ day** chaque jour sans exception; **single out** vt choisir; (distinguish) distinguer; **single bed** n lit m d'une personne or à une place; **single file** n: **in single file** en file indienne; **single-handed** adv tout(e) seul(e), sans (aucune) aide; **single-minded** adj résolu(e), tenace; **single parent** n parent unique (or

célibataire); **single-parent family**
famille monoparentale; **single room** *n*
chambre f à un lit *or* pour une personne

singular ['sɪŋgjʊlə^r] *adj*
singulier(-ière); (*odd*) singulier,
étrange; (*outstanding*) remarquable;
(*Ling*) (au) singulier, du singulier ▷ *n*
(*Ling*) singulier *m*

sinister ['sɪnɪstə^r] *adj* sinistre

sink [sɪŋk] *n* évier *m*; (*washbasin*)
lavabo *m* ▷ *vb* (*pt* **sank**, *pp* **sunk**) ▷ *vt*
(*ship*) (faire) couler, faire sombrer;
(*foundations*) creuser ▷ *vi* couler,
sombrer; (*ground etc*) s'affaisser; **to ~
into sth** (*chair*) s'enfoncer dans qch;
sink in *vi* (*explanation*) rentrer (*inf*),
être compris

sinus ['saɪnəs] *n* (*Anat*) sinus *m inv*

sip [sɪp] *n* petite gorgée ▷ *vt* boire à
petites gorgées

sir [sə^r] *n* monsieur *m*; **S~ John Smith** sir
John Smith; **yes ~** oui Monsieur

siren ['saɪərn] *n* sirène f

sirloin ['sə:lɔɪn] *n* (*also*: **~ steak**)
aloyau *m*

sister ['sɪstə^r] *n* sœur f; (*nun*) religieuse
f, (bonne) sœur; (*BRIT: nurse*) infirmière f
en chef; **sister-in-law** *n* belle-sœur f

sit (*pt*, *pp* **sat**) [sɪt, sæt] *vi* s'asseoir; (*be
sitting*) être assis(e); (*assembly*) être en
séance, siéger; (*for painter*) poser ▷ *vt*
(*exam*) passer, se présenter à; **sit back**
vi (*in seat*) bien s'installer, se carrer; **sit
down** *vi* s'asseoir; **sit on** *vt fus* (*jury,
committee*) faire partie de; **sit up** *vi*
s'asseoir; (*straight*) se redresser; (*not go
to bed*) rester debout, ne pas se coucher

itcom ['sɪtkɔm] *n abbr* (*TV*: = *situation
comedy*) sitcom f, comédie f de situation

ite [saɪt] *n* emplacement *m*, site *m*;
(*also*: **building ~**) chantier *m* ▷ *vt* placer

itting ['sɪtɪŋ] *n* (*of assembly etc*) séance
f; (*in canteen*) service *m*; **sitting room**
n salon *m*

ituated ['sɪtjueɪtɪd] *adj* situé(e)

ituation [sɪtju'eɪʃən] *n* situation f;
"~s vacant/wanted" (*BRIT*) "offres/
demandes d'emploi"

six [sɪks] *num* six; **sixteen** *num* seize;
sixteenth [sɪks'ti:nθ] *num* seizième;
sixth ['sɪksθ] *num* sixième; **sixth form**
n (*BRIT*) ≈ classes fpl de première et
de terminale; **sixth-form college** *n*
lycée n'ayant que des classes de première
et de terminale; **sixtieth** ['sɪkstɪɪθ] *num*
soixantième; **sixty** *num* soixante

size [saɪz] *n* dimensions fpl; (*of person*)
taille f; (*of clothing*) taille; (*of shoes*)
pointure f; (*of problem*) ampleur f; (*glue*)
colle f; **sizeable** *adj* assez grand(e);
(*amount, problem, majority*) assez
important(e)

sizzle ['sɪzl] *vi* grésiller

skate [skeɪt] *n* patin *m*; (*fish: pl inv*)
raie f ▷ *vi* patiner; **skateboard** *n*
skateboard *m*, planche f à roulettes;
skateboarding *n* skateboard *m*;
skater *n* patineur(-euse); **skating** *n*
patinage *m*; **skating rink** *n* patinoire f

skeleton ['skɛlɪtn] *n* squelette *m*;
(*outline*) schéma *m*

skeptical ['skɛptɪkl] (*US*) = **sceptical**

sketch [skɛtʃ] *n* (*drawing*) croquis
m, esquisse f; (*outline plan*) aperçu
m; (*Theat*) sketch *m*, saynète f ▷ *vt*
esquisser, faire un croquis *or* une
esquisse de; (*plan etc*) esquisser

skewer ['skjuːə^r] *n* brochette f

ski [skiː] *n* ski *m* ▷ *vi* skier, faire du ski;
ski boot *n* chaussure f de ski

skid [skɪd] *n* dérapage *m* ▷ *vi* déraper

ski: skier *n* skieur(-euse); **skiing** *n* ski *m*;
to go skiing (aller) faire du ski

skilful (*US* **skillful**) ['skɪlful] *adj* habile,
adroit(e)

ski lift *n* remonte-pente *m inv*

skill [skɪl] *n* (*ability*) habileté f,
adresse f, talent *m*; (*requiring training*)
compétences fpl; **skilled** *adj* habile,
adroit(e); (*worker*) qualifié(e)

skim [skɪm] *vt* (*soup*) écumer; (*glide
over*) raser, effleurer ▷ *vi*: **to ~ through**
(*fig*) parcourir; **skimmed milk** (*US* **skim
milk**) *n* lait écrémé

skin [skɪn] *n* peau f ▷ *vt* (*fruit etc*)
éplucher; (*animal*) écorcher; **skinhead**

n skinhead *m*; **skinny** *adj* maigre, maigrichon(ne)

skip [skɪp] *n* petit bond *or* saut; (BRIT: *container*) benne *f* ▷ *vi* gambader, sautiller; (*with rope*) sauter à la corde ▷ *vt* (*pass over*) sauter

ski: **ski pass** *n* forfait-skieur(s) *m*; **ski pole** *n* bâton *m* de ski

skipper ['skɪpə^r] *n* (*Naut, Sport*) capitaine *m*; (*in race*) skipper *m*

skipping rope ['skɪpɪŋ-] (US **skip rope**) *n* (BRIT) corde *f* à sauter

skirt [skə:t] *n* jupe *f* ▷ *vt* longer, contourner

skirting board ['skə:tɪŋ-] *n* (BRIT) plinthe *f*

ski slope *n* piste *f* de ski

ski suit *n* combinaison *f* de ski

skull [skʌl] *n* crâne *m*

skunk [skʌŋk] *n* mouffette *f*

sky [skaɪ] *n* ciel *m*; **skyscraper** *n* gratte-ciel *m inv*

slab [slæb] *n* (*of stone*) dalle *f*; (*of meat, cheese*) tranche épaisse

slack [slæk] *adj* (*loose*) lâche, desserré(e); (*slow*) stagnant(e); (*careless*) négligent(e), peu sérieux(-euse) *or* consciencieux(-euse); **slacks** *npl* pantalon *m*

slain [sleɪn] *pp of* **slay**

slam [slæm] *vt* (*door*) (faire) claquer; (*throw*) jeter violemment, flanquer; (*inf: criticize*) éreinter, démolir ▷ *vi* claquer

slander ['slɑ:ndə^r] *n* calomnie *f*; (*Law*) diffamation *f*

slang [slæŋ] *n* argot *m*

slant [slɑ:nt] *n* inclinaison *f*; (*fig*) angle *m*, point *m* de vue

slap [slæp] *n* claque *f*, gifle *f*; (*on the back*) tape *f* ▷ *vt* donner une claque *or* une gifle (*or* une tape) à; **to ~ on** (*paint*) appliquer rapidement ▷ *adv* (*directly*) tout droit, en plein

slash [slæʃ] *vt* entailler, taillader; (*fig: prices*) casser

slate [sleɪt] *n* ardoise *f* ▷ *vt* (*fig: criticize*) éreinter, démolir

slaughter ['slɔ:tə^r] *n* carnage *m*, massacre *m*; (*of animals*) abattage *m* ▷ *vt* (*animal*) abattre; (*people*) massacrer; **slaughterhouse** *n* abattoir *m*

Slav [slɑ:v] *adj* slave

slave [sleɪv] *n* esclave *m/f* ▷ *vi* (*also:* **~ away**) trimer, travailler comme un forçat; **slavery** *n* esclavage *m*

slay (*pt* **slew**, *pp* **slain**) [sleɪ, slu:, sleɪn] *vt* (*literary*) tuer

sleazy ['sli:zɪ] *adj* miteux(-euse), minable

sled [slɛd] (US) = **sledge**

sledge [slɛdʒ] *n* luge *f*

sleek [sli:k] *adj* (*hair, fur*) brillant(e), luisant(e); (*car, boat*) aux lignes pures *or* élégantes

sleep [sli:p] *n* sommeil *m* ▷ *vi* (*pt, pp* **slept**) dormir; **to go to ~** s'endormir; **sleep in** *vi* (*oversleep*) se réveiller trop tard; (*on purpose*) faire la grasse matinée; **sleep together** *vi* (*have sex*) coucher ensemble; **sleeper** *n* (*person*) dormeur(-euse); (BRIT Rail: on track) traverse *f*; (: *train*) train-couchettes *m*; (: *berth*) couchette *f*; **sleeping bag** *n* sac *m* de couchage; **sleeping car** *n* wagon-lits *m*, voiture-lits *f*; **sleeping pill** *n* somnifère *m*; **sleepover** *n* nuit *f* chez un copain *or* une copine; **we're having a sleepover at Jo's** nous allons passer la nuit chez Jo; **sleepwalk** *vi* marcher en dormant; **sleepy** *adj* (*fig*) endormi(e)

sleet [sli:t] *n* neige fondue

sleeve [sli:v] *n* manche *f*; (*of record*) pochette *f*; **sleeveless** *adj* (*garment*) sans manches

sleigh [sleɪ] *n* traîneau *m*

slender ['slɛndə^r] *adj* svelte, mince; (*fig*) faible, ténu(e)

slept [slɛpt] *pt, pp of* **sleep**

slew [slu:] *pt of* **slay**

slice [slaɪs] *n* tranche *f*; (*round*) rondelle *f*; (*utensil*) spatule *f*; (*also:* **fish ~**) pelle *f* à poisson ▷ *vt* couper en tranches (*or* en rondelles)

slick [slɪk] *adj* (*skilful*) bien ficelé(e);

(*salesperson*) qui a du bagout ▷ *n* (*also*: **oil ~**) nappe *f* de pétrole, marée noire

slide [slaɪd] *n* (*in playground*) toboggan *m*; (*Phot*) diapositive *f*; (BRIT: *also*: **hair ~**) barrette *f*; (*in prices*) chute *f*, baisse *f* ▷ *vb* (*pt, pp* **slid**) ▷ *vt* (*faire*) glisser ▷ *vi* glisser; **sliding** *adj* (*door*) coulissant(e)

slight [slaɪt] *adj* (*slim*) mince, menu(e); (*frail*) frêle; (*trivial*) faible, insignifiant(e); (*small*) petit(e), léger(-ère) *before n* ▷ *n* offense *f*, affront *m* ▷ *vt* (*offend*) blesser, offenser; **not in the ~est** pas le moins du monde, pas du tout; **slightly** *adv* légèrement, un peu

slim [slɪm] *adj* mince ▷ *vi* maigrir; (*diet*) suivre un régime amaigrissant; **slimming** *n* amaigrissement *m* ▷ *adj* (*diet, pills*) amaigrissant(e), pour maigrir; (*food*) qui ne fait pas grossir

slimy ['slaɪmɪ] *adj* visqueux(-euse), gluant(e)

sling [slɪŋ] *n* (*Med*) écharpe *f*; (*for baby*) porte-bébé *m*; (*weapon*) fronde *f*, lance-pierre *m* ▷ *vt* (*pt, pp* **slung**) lancer, jeter

slip [slɪp] *n* faux pas; (*mistake*) erreur *f*, bévue *f*; (*underskirt*) combinaison *f*; (*of paper*) petite feuille, fiche *f* ▷ *vt* (*slide*) glisser ▷ *vi* (*slide*) glisser; (*move smoothly*): **to ~ into/out of** se glisser or se faufiler dans/hors de; (*decline*) baisser; **to ~ sth on/off** enfiler/enlever qch; **to give sb the ~** fausser compagnie à qn; **a ~ of the tongue** un lapsus; **slip up** *vi* faire une erreur, gaffer

slipped disc [slɪpt-] *n* déplacement *m* de vertèbre

slipper ['slɪpər] *n* pantoufle *f*

slippery ['slɪpərɪ] *adj* glissant(e)

slip road *n* (BRIT: *to motorway*) bretelle *f* d'accès

slit [slɪt] *n* fente *f*; (*cut*) incision *f* ▷ *vt* (*pt, pp* **~**) fendre; couper, inciser

slog [slɒg] *n* (BRIT: *effort*) gros effort; (: *work*) tâche fastidieuse ▷ *vi* travailler très dur

slogan ['sləʊgən] *n* slogan *m*

slope [sləʊp] *n* pente *f*, côte *f*; (*side of mountain*) versant *m*; (*slant*) inclinaison *f* ▷ *vi*: **to ~ down** être or descendre en pente; **to ~ up** monter; **sloping** *adj* en pente, incliné(e); (*handwriting*) penché(e)

sloppy ['slɒpɪ] *adj* (*work*) peu soigné(e), bâclé(e); (*appearance*) négligé(e), débraillé(e)

slot [slɒt] *n* fente *f* ▷ *vt*: **to ~ sth into** encastrer or insérer qch dans; **slot machine** *n* (BRIT: *vending machine*) distributeur *m* (automatique), machine *f* à sous; (*for gambling*) appareil *m* or machine à sous

Slovakia [sləʊ'vækɪə] *n* Slovaquie *f*

Slovene [sləʊ'viːn] *adj* slovène ▷ *n* Slovène *m/f*; (*Ling*) slovène *m*

Slovenia [sləʊ'viːnɪə] *n* Slovénie *f*; **Slovenian** *adj, n* = **Slovene**

slow [sləʊ] *adj* lent(e); (*watch*): **to be ~** retarder ▷ *adv* lentement ▷ *vt, vi* ralentir; **"~"** (*road sign*) "ralentir"; **slow down** *vi* ralentir; **slowly** *adv* lentement; **slow motion** *n*: **in slow motion** au ralenti

slug [slʌg] *n* limace *f*; (*bullet*) balle *f*; **sluggish** *adj* (*person*) mou (molle), lent(e); (*stream, engine, trading*) lent(e)

slum [slʌm] *n* (*house*) taudis *m*; **slums** *npl* (*area*) quartiers *mpl* pauvres

slump [slʌmp] *n* baisse soudaine, effondrement *m*; (*Econ*) crise *f* ▷ *vi* s'effondrer, s'affaisser

slung [slʌŋ] *pt, pp* of **sling**

slur [sləːr] *n* (*smear*): **~ (on)** atteinte *f* (à); insinuation *f* (contre) ▷ *vt* mal articuler

slush [slʌʃ] *n* neige fondue

sly [slaɪ] *adj* (*person*) rusé(e); (*smile, expression, remark*) sournois(e)

smack [smæk] *n* (*slap*) tape *f*; (*on face*) gifle *f* ▷ *vt* donner une tape à; (*on face*) gifler; (*on bottom*) donner la fessée à ▷ *vi*: **to ~ of** avoir des relents de, sentir

small [smɔːl] *adj* petit(e); **small ads** *npl* (BRIT) petites annonces; **small change** *n* petite or menue monnaie

smart [smɑːt] *adj* élégant(e), chic

inv; (*clever*) intelligent(e); (*quick*) vif (vive), prompt(e) ▷ *vi* faire mal, brûler; **smartcard** *n* carte f à puce

smash [smæʃ] *n* (*also*: **~-up**) collision f, accident *m*; (*Mus*) succès foudroyant ▷ *vt* casser, briser, fracasser; (*opponent*) écraser; (*Sport: record*) pulvériser ▷ *vi* se briser, se fracasser; s'écraser; **smashing** *adj* (*inf*) formidable

smear [smɪəʳ] *n* (*stain*) tache f; (*mark*) trace f; (*Med*) frottis *m* ▷ *vt* enduire; (*make dirty*) salir; **smear test** *n* (BRIT Med) frottis *m*

smell [smɛl] *n* odeur f; (*sense*) odorat *m* ▷ *vb* (*pt, pp* **smelt** *or* **~ed**) ▷ *vt* sentir ▷ *vi* (*pej*) sentir mauvais; **smelly** *adj* qui sent mauvais, malodorant(e)

smelt [smɛlt] *pt, pp of* **smell**

smile [smaɪl] *n* sourire *m* ▷ *vi* sourire

smirk [smə:k] *n* petit sourire suffisant *or* affecté

smog [smɔg] *n* brouillard mêlé de fumée

smoke [sməuk] *n* fumée f ▷ *vt, vi* fumer; **do you mind if I ~?** ça ne vous dérange pas que je fume?; **smoke alarm** *n* détecteur *m* de fumée; **smoked** *adj* (*bacon, glass*) fumé(e); **smoker** *n* (*person*) fumeur(-euse); (*Rail*) wagon *m* fumeurs; **smoking** *n*: **"no smoking"** (*sign*) "défense de fumer"; **smoky** *adj* enfumé(e); (*taste*) fumé(e)

smooth [smu:ð] *adj* lisse; (*sauce*) onctueux(-euse); (*flavour, whisky*) moelleux(-euse); (*movement*) régulier(-ière), sans à-coups *or* heurts; (*flight*) sans secousses; (*pej: person*) doucereux(-euse), mielleux(-euse) ▷ *vt* (*also*: **~ out**) lisser, défroisser; (*creases, difficulties*) faire disparaître

smother ['smʌðəʳ] *vt* étouffer

SMS *n abbr* (= *short message service*) SMS *m*; **SMS message** *n* message *m* SMS

smudge [smʌdʒ] *n* tache f, bavure f ▷ *vt* salir, maculer

smug [smʌg] *adj* suffisant(e), content(e) de soi

smuggle ['smʌgl] *vt* passer en contrebande *or* en fraude; **smuggling** *n* contrebande f

snack [snæk] *n* casse-croûte *m* inv; **snack bar** *n* snack(-bar) *m*

snag [snæg] *n* inconvénient *m*, difficulté f

snail [sneɪl] *n* escargot *m*

snake [sneɪk] *n* serpent *m*

snap [snæp] *n* (*sound*) claquement *m*, bruit sec; (*photograph*) photo f, instantané *m* ▷ *adj* subit(e), fait(e) sans réfléchir ▷ *vt* (*fingers*) faire claquer; (*break*) casser net ▷ *vi* se casser net *or* avec un bruit sec; (*speak sharply*) parler d'un ton brusque; **to ~ open/shut** s'ouvrir/se refermer brusquement; **snap at** *vt fus* (*subj: dog*) essayer de mordre; **snap up** *vt* sauter sur, saisir; **snapshot** *n* photo f, instantané *m*

snarl [snɑ:l] *vi* gronder

snatch [snætʃ] *n* (*small amount*) ▷ *vt* saisir (*d'un geste vif*); (*steal*) voler; **to ~ some sleep** arriver à dormir un peu

sneak [sni:k] (*US: pt* **snuck**) *vi*: **to ~ in/out** entrer/sortir furtivement *or* à la dérobée ▷ *n* (*inf: pej: informer*) faux jeton; **to ~ up on sb** s'approcher de qn sans faire de bruit; **sneakers** *npl* tennis *mpl*, baskets *fpl*

sneer [snɪəʳ] *vi* ricaner; **to ~ at sb/sth** se moquer de qn/qch avec mépris

sneeze [sni:z] *vi* éternuer

sniff [snɪf] *vi* renifler ▷ *vt* renifler, flairer; (*glue, drug*) sniffer, respirer

snigger ['snɪgəʳ] *vi* ricaner

snip [snɪp] *n* (*cut*) entaille f; (BRIT: *inf: bargain*) (bonne) occasion *or* affaire f ▷ *vt* couper

sniper ['snaɪpəʳ] *n* (*marksman*) tireur embusqué

snob [snɔb] *n* snob *m/f*

snooker ['snu:kəʳ] *n* sorte de jeu de billard

snoop [snu:p] *vi*: **to ~ about** fureter

snooze [snu:z] *n* petit somme ▷ *vi* faire un petit somme

snore [snɔ:ʳ] *vi* ronfler ▷ *n*

ronflement m

snorkel ['snɔːkl] n (of swimmer) tuba m

snort [snɔːt] n grognement m ▷ vi grogner; (horse) renâcler

snow [snəu] n neige f ▷ vi neiger; **snowball** n boule f de neige; **snowdrift** n congère f; **snowman** (irreg) n bonhomme m de neige; **snowplough** (US **snowplow**) n chasse-neige m inv; **snowstorm** n tempête f de neige

snub [snʌb] vt repousser, snober ▷ n rebuffade f

snug [snʌg] adj douillet(te), confortable; (person) bien au chaud

○ **KEYWORD**

so [səu] adv **1** (thus, likewise) ainsi, de cette façon; **if so** si oui; **so do** or **have I** moi aussi; **it's 5 o'clock - so it is!** il est 5 heures - en effet! or c'est vrai!; **I hope/think so** je l'espère/le crois; **so far** jusqu'ici, jusqu'à maintenant; (in past) jusque-là

2 (in comparisons etc: to such a degree) si, tellement; **so big (that)** si or tellement grand (que); **she's not so clever as her brother** elle n'est pas aussi intelligente que son frère

3: **so much** adj, adv tant (de); **I've got so much work** j'ai tant de travail; **I love you so much** je vous aime tant; **so many** tant (de)

4 (phrases): **10 or so** à peu près or environ 10; **so long!** (inf: goodbye) au revoir!, à un de ces jours!; **so (what)?** (inf) (bon) et alors?, et après?

▷ conj **1** (expressing purpose): **so as to do** pour faire, afin de faire; **so (that)** pour que or afin que + sub

2 (expressing result) donc, par conséquent; **so that** si bien que, de (telle) sorte que; **so that's the reason!** c'est donc (pour) ça!; **so you see, I could have gone** alors tu vois, j'aurais pu y aller

soak [səuk] vt faire or laisser tremper; (drench) tremper ▷ vi tremper; **soak up** vt absorber; **soaking** adj (also: **soaking wet**) trempé(e)

so-and-so ['səuənsəu] n (somebody) un(e) tel(le)

soap [səup] n savon m; **soap opera** n feuilleton télévisé (quotidienneté réaliste ou embellie); **soap powder** n lessive f, détergent m

soar [sɔː] vi monter (en flèche), s'élancer; (building) s'élancer

sob [sɔb] n sanglot m ▷ vi sangloter

sober ['səubər] adj qui n'est pas (or plus) ivre; (serious) sérieux(-euse), sensé(e); (colour, style) sobre, discret(-ète); **sober up** vi se dégriser

so-called ['səu'kɔːld] adj soi-disant inv

soccer ['sɔkər] n football m

sociable ['səuʃəbl] adj sociable

social ['səuʃl] adj social(e); (sociable) sociable ▷ n (petite) fête; **socialism** n socialisme m; **socialist** adj, n socialiste (m/f); **socialize** vi: **to socialize with** (meet often) fréquenter; (get to know) lier connaissance or parler avec; **social life** n vie sociale; **socially** adv socialement, en société; **social security** n aide sociale; **social services** npl services sociaux; **social work** n assistance sociale; **social worker** n assistant(e) sociale(e)

society [sə'saɪətɪ] n société f; (club) société, association f; (also: **high ~**) (haute) société, grand monde

sociology [səusɪ'ɔlədʒɪ] n sociologie f

sock [sɔk] n chaussette f

socket ['sɔkɪt] n cavité f; (Elec: also: **wall ~**) prise f de courant

soda ['səudə] n (Chem) soude f; (also: **~ water**) eau f de Seltz; (US: also: **~ pop**) soda m

sodium ['səudɪəm] n sodium m

sofa ['səufə] n sofa m, canapé m; **sofa bed** n canapé-lit m

soft [sɔft] adj (not rough) doux (douce); (not hard) doux, mou (molle); (not loud) doux, léger(-ère); (kind) doux, gentil(le); **soft drink** n boisson non alcoolisée;

soft drugs npl drogues douces; **soften** ['sɔfn] vt (r)amollir; (fig) adoucir ▷ vi se ramollir; (fig) s'adoucir; **softly** adv doucement; (touch) légèrement; (kiss) tendrement; **software** n (Comput) logiciel m, software m

soggy ['sɔgɪ] adj (clothes) trempé(e); (ground) détrempé(e)

soil [sɔɪl] n (earth) sol m, terre f ▷ vt salir; (fig) souiller

solar ['səʊlə'] adj solaire; **solar power** n énergie f solaire; **solar system** n système m solaire

sold [səʊld] pt, pp of **sell**

soldier ['səʊldʒə'] n soldat m, militaire m

sold out adj (Comm) épuisé(e)

sole [səʊl] n (of foot) plante f; (of shoe) semelle f; (fish: pl inv) sole f ▷ adj seul(e), unique; **solely** adv seulement, uniquement

solemn ['sɔləm] adj solennel(le); (person) sérieux(-euse), grave

solicitor [sə'lɪsɪtə'] n (BRIT: for wills etc) ≈ notaire m; (: in court) ≈ avocat m

solid ['sɔlɪd] adj (not liquid) solide; (not hollow: mass) compact(e); (: metal, rock, wood) massif(-ive) ▷ n solide m

solitary ['sɔlɪtərɪ] adj solitaire

solitude ['sɔlɪtjuːd] n solitude f

solo ['səʊləʊ] n solo m ▷ adv (fly) en solitaire; **soloist** n soliste m/f

soluble ['sɔljʊbl] adj soluble

solution [sə'luːʃən] n solution f

solve [sɔlv] vt résoudre

solvent ['sɔlvənt] adj (Comm) solvable ▷ n (Chem) (dis)solvant m

sombre (US **somber**) ['sɔmbə'] adj sombre, morne

 KEYWORD

some [sʌm] adj **1** (a certain amount or number of): **some tea/water/ice cream** du thé/de l'eau/de la glace; **some children/apples** des enfants/pommes; **I've got some money but not much** j'ai de l'argent mais pas beaucoup

2 (certain: in contrasts): **some people say that ...** il y a des gens qui disent que ...; **some films were excellent, but most were mediocre** certains films étaient excellents, mais la plupart étaient médiocres

3 (unspecified): **some woman was asking for you** il y avait une dame qui vous demandait; **he was asking for some book (or other)** il demandait un livre quelconque; **some day** un de ces jours; **some day next week** un jour la semaine prochaine

▷ pron **1** (a certain number) quelques-un(e)s, certain(e)s; **I've got some** (books etc) j'en ai (quelques-uns); **some (of them) have been sold** certains ont été vendus

2 (a certain amount) un peu; **I've got some** (money, milk) j'en ai (un peu); **would you like some?** est-ce que vous en voulez?, en voulez-vous?; **could I have some of that cheese?** pourrais-je avoir un peu de ce fromage?; **I've read some of the book** j'ai lu une partie du livre

▷ adv: **some 10 people** quelque 10 personnes, 10 personnes environ; **somebody** ['sʌmbədɪ] pron = **someone**; **somehow** adv d'une façon ou d'une autre; (for some reason) pour une raison ou une autre; **someone** pron quelqu'un; **someplace** adv (US) = **somewhere**; **something** pron quelque chose m; **something interesting** quelque chose d'intéressant; **something to do** quelque chose à faire; **sometime** adv (in future) un de ces jours, un jour ou l'autre; (in past): **sometime last month** au cours du mois dernier; **sometimes** adv quelquefois, parfois; **somewhat** adv quelque peu, un peu; **somewhere** adv quelque part; **somewhere else** ailleurs, autre part

son [sʌn] n fils m

song [sɔŋ] n chanson f; (of bird) chant m
son-in-law ['sʌnɪnlɔ:] n gendre m, beau-fils m
soon [su:n] adv bientôt; (early) tôt; **~ afterwards** peu après; see also **as**; **sooner** adv (time) plus tôt; (preference): **I would do that** j'aimerais autant or je préférerais faire ça; **sooner or later** tôt ou tard
soothe [su:ð] vt calmer, apaiser
sophisticated [sə'fɪstɪkeɪtɪd] adj raffiné(e), sophistiqué(e); (machinery) hautement perfectionné(e), très complexe
sophomore ['sɔfəmɔ:ʳ] n (us) étudiant(e) de seconde année
soprano [sə'prɑ:nəu] n (singer) soprano m/f
sorbet ['sɔ:beɪ] n sorbet m
sordid ['sɔ:dɪd] adj sordide
sore [sɔ:ʳ] adj (painful) douloureux(-euse), sensible ▷ n plaie f
sorrow ['sɔrəu] n peine f, chagrin m
sorry ['sɔrɪ] adj désolé(e); (condition, excuse, tale) triste, déplorable; **~!** pardon!, excusez-moi!; **~?** pardon?; **to feel ~ for sb** plaindre qn
sort [sɔ:t] n genre m, espèce f, sorte f; (make: of coffee, car etc) marque f ▷ vt (also: **~ out**: select which to keep) trier; (classify) classer; (tidy) ranger; **sort out** vt (problem) résoudre, régler
SOS n SOS m
so-so ['səusəu] adv comme ci comme ça
sought [sɔ:t] pt, pp of **seek**
soul [səul] n âme f
sound [saund] adj (healthy) en bonne santé, sain(e); (safe, not damaged) solide, en bon état; (reliable, not superficial) sérieux(-euse), solide; (sensible) sensé(e) ▷ adv: **~ asleep** profondément endormi(e) ▷ n (noise, volume) son m; (louder) bruit m; (Geo) détroit m, bras m de mer ▷ vt (alarm) sonner ▷ vi sonner, retentir; (fig: seem) sembler (être); **to ~ like** ressembler à; **sound bite** n phrase toute faite (pour

être citée dans les médias); **soundtrack** n (of film) bande f sonore
soup [su:p] n soupe f, potage m
sour ['sauəʳ] adj aigre; **it's ~ grapes** c'est du dépit
source [sɔ:s] n source f
south [sauθ] n sud m ▷ adj sud inv; (wind) du sud ▷ adv au sud, vers le sud; **South Africa** n Afrique f du Sud; **South African** adj sud-africain(e) ▷ n Sud-Africain(e); **South America** n Amérique f du Sud; **South American** adj sud-américain(e) ▷ n Sud-Américain(e); **southbound** adj en direction du sud; (carriageway) sud inv; **south-east** n sud-est m; **southeastern** [sauθ'i:stən] adj du or au sud-est; **southern** ['sʌðən] adj (du) sud; méridional(e); **South Korea** n Corée f du Sud; **South of France** n: **the South of France** le Sud de la France, le Midi; **South Pole** n Pôle m Sud; **southward(s)** adv vers le sud; **south-west** n sud-ouest m; **southwestern** [sauθ'westən] adj du or au sud-ouest
souvenir [su:və'nɪəʳ] n souvenir m (objet)
sovereign ['sɔvrɪn] adj, n souverain(e)
sow¹ [səu] (pt **~ed**, pp **~n**) vt semer
sow² n [sau] truie f
soya ['sɔɪə] (us **soy** [sɔɪ]) n: **~ bean** graine f de soja; **~ sauce** sauce f au soja
spa [spɑ:] n (town) station thermale; (us: also: **health ~**) établissement m de cure de rajeunissement
space [speɪs] n (gen) espace m; (room) place f, espace; (length of time) laps m de temps ▷ cpd spatial(e) ▷ vt (also: **~ out**) espacer; **spacecraft** n engin or vaisseau spatial; **spaceship** n = **spacecraft**
spacious ['speɪʃəs] adj spacieux(-euse), grand(e)
spade [speɪd] n (tool) bêche f, pelle f; (child's) pelle; **spades** npl (Cards) pique m
spaghetti [spə'gɛtɪ] n spaghetti mpl
Spain [speɪn] n Espagne f

spam [spæm] n (Comput) spam m

span [spæn] n (of bird, plane) envergure f; (of arch) portée f; (in time) espace m de temps, durée f ▷ vt enjamber, franchir; (fig) couvrir, embrasser

Spaniard ['spænjəd] n Espagnol(e)

Spanish ['spænɪʃ] adj espagnol(e), d'Espagne ▷ n (Ling) espagnol m; **the Spanish** npl les Espagnols

spank [spæŋk] vt donner une fessée à

spanner ['spænə'] n (BRIT) clé f (de mécanicien)

spare [spɛə'] adj de réserve, de rechange; (surplus) de or en trop, de reste ▷ n (part) pièce f de rechange, pièce détachée ▷ vt (do without) se passer de; (afford to give) donner, accorder, passer; (not hurt) épargner; **to ~** (surplus) en surplus, de trop; **spare part** n pièce f de rechange, pièce détachée; **spare room** n chambre f d'ami; **spare time** n moments mpl de loisir; **spare tyre** n (US **spare tire**) n (Aut) pneu m de rechange; **spare wheel** n (Aut) roue f de secours

spark [spɑːk] n étincelle f; **spark(ing) plug** n bougie f

sparkle ['spɑːkl] n scintillement m, étincellement m, éclat m ▷ vi étinceler, scintiller

sparkling ['spɑːklɪŋ] adj (wine) mousseux(-euse), pétillant(e); (water) pétillant(e), gazeux(-euse)

sparrow ['spærəu] n moineau m

sparse [spɑːs] adj clairsemé(e)

spasm ['spæzəm] n (Med) spasme m

spat [spæt] pt, pp of **spit**

spate [speɪt] n (fig): **~ of** avalanche f or torrent m de

spatula ['spætjulə] n spatule f

speak (pt **spoke**, pp **spoken**) [spiːk, spəuk, 'spəukn] vt (language) parler; (truth) dire ▷ vi parler; (make a speech) prendre la parole; **to ~ to sb/of** or **about sth** parler à qn/de qch; **I don't ~ French** je ne parle pas français; **do you ~ English?** parlez-vous anglais?; **can I ~ to ...?** est-ce que je peux parler

à ...?; **speaker** n (in public) orateur m; (also: **loudspeaker**) haut-parleur m; (for stereo etc) baffle m, enceinte f; (Pol): **the Speaker** (BRIT) le président de la Chambre des communes or des représentants; (US) le président de la Chambre

spear [spɪə'] n lance f ▷ vt transpercer

special ['spɛʃl] adj spécial(e); **special delivery** n (Post): **by special delivery** en express; **special effects** npl (Cine) effets spéciaux; **specialist** n spécialiste m/f; **speciality** [spɛʃɪ'ælɪtɪ] n (BRIT) spécialité f; **specialize** vi: **to specialize (in)** se spécialiser (dans); **specially** adv spécialement, particulièrement; **special needs** npl (BRIT) difficultés fpl d'apprentissage scolaire; **special offer** n (Comm) réclame f; **special school** n (BRIT) établissement m d'enseignement spécialisé; **specialty** n (US) = **speciality**

species ['spiːʃiːz] n (pl inv) espèce f

specific [spə'sɪfɪk] adj (not vague) précis(e), explicite; (particular) particulier(-ière); **specifically** adv explicitement, précisément; (intend, ask, design) expressément, spécialement

specify ['spɛsɪfaɪ] vt spécifier, préciser

specimen ['spɛsɪmən] n spécimen m, échantillon m; (Med: of blood) prélèvement m; (: of urine) échantillon m

speck [spɛk] n petite tache, petit point m; (particle) grain m

spectacle ['spɛktəkl] n spectacle m; **spectacles** npl (BRIT) lunettes fpl; **spectacular** [spɛk'tækjulə'] adj spectaculaire

spectator [spɛk'teɪtə'] n spectateur(-trice)

spectrum (pl **spectra**) ['spɛktrəm, -rə] n spectre m; (fig) gamme f

speculate ['spɛkjuleɪt] vi spéculer; (try to guess): **to ~ about** s'interroger sur

sped [spɛd] pt, pp of **speed**

speech [spiːtʃ] n (faculty) parole f; (talk) discours m, allocution f; (manner of speaking) façon f de parler, langage m;

(*enunciation*) élocution *f*; **speechless**
adj muet(te)

speed [spiːd] *n* vitesse *f*; (*promptness*)
rapidité *f* ▷ *vi* (*pt, pp* **sped**: *Aut: exceed
speed limit*) faire un excès de vitesse; **at
full** *or* **top ~** à toute vitesse *or* allure;
speed up (*pt, pp* **~ed up**) *vi* aller plus
vite, accélérer *vt* accélérer;
speedboat *n* vedette *f*, hors-bord *m
inv*; **speeding** *n* (*Aut*) excès *m* de
vitesse; **speed limit** *n* limitation *f* de
vitesse, vitesse maximale permise;
speedometer [spɪˈdɔmɪtə*r*] *n*
compteur *m* (de vitesse); **speedy** *adj*
rapide, prompt(e)

spell [spɛl] *n* (*also*: **magic ~**) sortilège
m, charme *m*; (*period of time*) (courte)
période *f* (*Aut*) monter en flèche ▷ *vt* (*in
writing*) écrire, orthographier; (*aloud*)
épeler; (*fig*) signifier; **to cast a ~ on
sb** jeter un sort à qn; **he can't ~** il fait
des fautes d'orthographe; **spell out** *vt*
(*explain*): **to ~ sth out for sb** expliquer
qch clairement à qn; **spellchecker**
[ˈspɛltʃɛkə*r*] *n* (*Comput*) correcteur
m or vérificateur *m* orthographique;
spelling *n* orthographe *f*

spelt [spɛlt] *pt, pp of* **spell**

spend (*pt, pp* **spent**) [spɛnd, spɛnt] *vt*
(*money*) dépenser; (*time, life*) passer;
(*devote*) consacrer; **spending** *n*:
government spending les dépenses
publiques

spent [spɛnt] *pt, pp of* **spend** ▷ *adj*
(*cartridge, bullets*) vide

sperm [spəːm] *n* spermatozoïde *m*;
(*semen*) sperme *m*

sphere [sfɪə*r*] *n* sphère *f*; (*fig*) sphère,
domaine *m*

spice [spaɪs] *n* épice *f* ▷ *vt* épicer

spicy [ˈspaɪsɪ] *adj* épicé(e), relevé(e);
(*fig*) piquant(e)

spider [ˈspaɪdə*r*] *n* araignée *f*

spike [spaɪk] *n* pointe *f*; (*Bot*) épi *m*

spill (*pt, pp* **spilt** *or* **~ed**) [spɪl, -t, -d] *vt*
renverser; répandre ▷ *vi* se répandre;
spill over *vi* déborder

spin [spɪn] *n* (*revolution of wheel*) tour

m; (*Aviat*) (chute *f* en) vrille *f*; (*trip in
car*) petit tour, balade *f*; (*on ball*) effet *m*
▷ *vb* (*pt, pp* **spun**) ▷ *vt* (*wool etc*) filer;
(*wheel*) faire tourner ▷ *vi* (*turn*) tourner,
tournoyer

spinach [ˈspɪnɪtʃ] *n* épinards *mpl*

spinal [ˈspaɪnl] *adj* vertébral(e),
spinal(e)

spinal cord *n* moelle épinière

spin doctor *n* (*inf*) personne employée
*pour présenter un parti politique sous un
jour favorable*

spin-dryer [spɪnˈdraɪə*r*] *n* (BRIT)
essoreuse *f*

spine [spaɪn] *n* colonne vertébrale;
(*thorn*) épine *f*, piquant *m*

spiral [ˈspaɪərl] *n* spirale *f* ▷ *vi* (*fig: prices
etc*) monter en flèche

spire [ˈspaɪə*r*] *n* flèche *f*, aiguille *f*

spirit [ˈspɪrɪt] *n* (*soul*) esprit *m*, âme
f; (*ghost*) esprit, revenant *m*; (*mood*)
esprit, état m d'esprit; (*courage*)
courage *m*, énergie *f*; **spirits** *npl* (*drink*)
spiritueux *mpl*, alcool *m*; **in good ~s** de
bonne humeur

spiritual [ˈspɪrɪtjuəl] *adj* spirituel(le);
(*religious*) religieux(-euse)

spit [spɪt] *n* (*for roasting*) broche *f*;
(*spittle*) crachat *m*; (*saliva*) salive *f* ▷ *vi*
(*pt, pp* **spat**) cracher; (*sound*) crépiter;
(*rain*) crachiner

spite [spaɪt] *n* rancune *f*, dépit *m* ▷ *vt*
contrarier, vexer; **in ~ of** en dépit de,
malgré; **spiteful** *adj* malveillant(e),
rancunier(-ière)

splash [splæʃ] *n* (*sound*) plouf *m*; (*of
colour*) tache *f* ▷ *vt* éclabousser ▷ *vi*
(*also*: **~ about**) barboter, patauger;
splash out *vi* (BRIT) faire une folie

splendid [ˈsplɛndɪd] *adj* splendide,
superbe, magnifique

splinter [ˈsplɪntə*r*] *n* (*wood*) écharde
f; (*metal*) éclat *m* ▷ *vi* (*wood*) se fendre;
(*glass*) se briser

split [splɪt] *n* fente *f*, déchirure *f*; (*fig:
Pol*) scission *f* ▷ *vb* (*pt, pp* **~**) ▷ *vt* fendre,
déchirer; (*party*) diviser; (*work, profits*)
partager, répartir ▷ *vi* (*break*) se fendre,

se briser; (*divide*) se diviser; **split up** vi
(*couple*) se séparer, rompre; (*meeting*)
se disperser

spoil (*pt, pp* **~ed** *or* **~t**) [spɔɪl, -d, -t] vt
(*damage*) abîmer; (*mar*) gâcher; (*child*)
gâter

spoilt [spɔɪlt] *pt, pp of* **spoil** ▷ *adj* (*child*)
gâté(e); (*ballot paper*) nul(le)

spoke [spəʊk] *pt of* **speak** ▷ *n* rayon *m*

spoken ['spəʊkn] *pp of* **speak**

spokesman ['spəʊksmən] (*irreg*) *n*
porte-parole *m inv*

spokesperson ['spəʊkspɜːsn] *n*
porte-parole *m inv*

spokeswoman ['spəʊkswʊmən]
(*irreg*) *n* porte-parole *m inv*

sponge [spʌndʒ] *n* éponge *f*; (*Culin:
also:* **~ cake**) ≈ biscuit *m* de Savoie
▷ *vt* éponger ▷ *vi*: **to ~ off** *or* **on** vivre
aux crochets de; **sponge bag** *n* (BRIT)
trousse *f* de toilette

sponsor ['spɒnsə^r] *n* (*Radio, TV, Sport*)
sponsor *m*; (*for application*) parrain *m*,
marraine *f*; (BRIT: *for fund-raising event*)
donateur(-trice) ▷ *vt* sponsoriser,
parrainer, faire un don à; **sponsorship**
n sponsoring *m*, parrainage *m*; dons *mpl*

spontaneous [spɒn'teɪnɪəs] *adj*
spontané(e)

spooky ['spuːkɪ] *adj* (*inf*) qui donne la
chair de poule

spoon [spuːn] *n* cuiller *f*; **spoonful** *n*
cuillerée *f*

sport [spɔːt] *n* sport *m*; (*person*) chic
type *m*/chic fille *f* ▷ *vt* (*wear*) arborer;
sport jacket *n* (US) = **sports jacket**;
sports car *n* voiture *f* de sport;
sports centre *n* (BRIT) centre sportif;
sports jacket *n* (BRIT) veste *f* de sport;
sportsman (*irreg*) *n* sportif *m*; **sports
utility vehicle** *n* véhicule *m* de loisirs
(*de type SUV*); **sportswear** *n* vêtements
mpl de sport; **sportswoman** (*irreg*) *n*
sportive *f*; **sporty** *adj* sportif(-ive)

spot [spɒt] *n* tache *f*; (*dot: on pattern*)
pois *m*; (*pimple*) bouton *m*; (*place*)
endroit *m*, coin *m*; (*small amount*): **a ~
of** un peu de ▷ *vt* (*notice*) apercevoir,

repérer; **on the ~** sur place, sur les lieux;
(*immediately*) sur le champ; **spotless** *adj*
immaculé(e); **spotlight** *n* projecteur
m; (*Aut*) phare *m* auxiliaire

spouse [spaʊz] *n* époux (épouse)

sprain [spreɪn] *n* entorse *f*, foulure
f ▷ *vt*: **to ~ one's ankle** se fouler *or* se
tordre la cheville

sprang [spræŋ] *pt of* **spring**

sprawl [sprɔːl] *vi* s'étaler

spray [spreɪ] *n* jet *m* (en fines
gouttelettes); (*from sea*) embruns
mpl; (*aerosol*) vaporisateur *m*, bombe
f; (*for garden*) pulvérisateur *m*; (*of
flowers*) petit bouquet ▷ *vt* vaporiser,
pulvériser; (*crops*) traiter

spread [sprɛd] *n* (*distribution*)
répartition *f*; (*Culin*) pâte *f* à tartiner;
(*inf: meal*) festin *m* ▷ *vb* (*pt, pp* **~**) ▷ *vt*
(*paste, contents*) étendre, étaler; (*rumour,
disease*) répandre, propager; (*wealth*)
répartir ▷ *vi* s'étendre; se répandre; se
propager; (*stain*) s'étaler; **spread out**
vi (*people*) se disperser; **spreadsheet** *n*
(*Comput*) tableur *m*

spree [spriː]: *n*: **to go on a ~** faire la fête

spring [sprɪŋ] *n* (*season*) printemps
m; (*leap*) bond *m*, saut *m*; (*coiled metal*)
ressort *m*; (*of water*) source *f* ▷ *vb* (*pt*
sprang, *pp* **sprung**) ▷ *vi* bondir, sauter;
spring up *vi* (*problem*) se présenter,
surgir; (*plant, buildings*) surgir de terre;
spring onion *n* (BRIT) ciboule *f*, cive *f*

sprinkle ['sprɪŋkl] *vt*: **to ~ water** *etc*
on, **~ with water** *etc* asperger d'eau
etc; **to ~ sugar** *etc* **on,** **~ with sugar** *etc*
saupoudrer de sucre *etc*

sprint [sprɪnt] *n* sprint *m* ▷ *vi* courir à
toute vitesse; (*Sport*) sprinter

sprung [sprʌŋ] *pp of* **spring**

spun [spʌn] *pt, pp of* **spin**

spur [spɜː^r] *n* éperon *m*; (*fig*) aiguillon
m ▷ *vt* (*also:* **~ on**) éperonner;
aiguillonner; **on the ~ of the moment**
sous l'impulsion du moment

spurt [spɜːt] *n* jet *m*; (*of blood*)
jaillissement *m*; (*of energy*) regain *m*,
sursaut *m* ▷ *vi* jaillir, gicler

spy [spaɪ] n espion(ne) ▷ vi: **to ~ on** espionner, épier ▷ vt (see) apercevoir

sq. abbr = **square**

squabble ['skwɒbl] vi se chamailler

squad [skwɒd] n (Mil, Police) escouade f, groupe m; (Football) contingent m

squadron ['skwɒdrn] n (Mil) escadron m; (Aviat, Naut) escadrille f

squander ['skwɒndəʳ] vt gaspiller, dilapider

square [skwɛəʳ] n carré m; (in town) place f ▷ adj carré(e) ▷ vt (arrange) régler; arranger; (Math) élever au carré; (reconcile) concilier; **all ~** quitte; à égalité; **a ~ meal** un repas convenable; **2 metres ~** (de) 2 mètres sur 2; **1 ~ metre** 1 mètre carré; **square root** n racine carrée

squash [skwɒʃ] n (BRIT: drink): **lemon/ orange ~** citronnade f/orangeade f; (Sport) squash m; (US: vegetable) courge f ▷ vt écraser

squat [skwɒt] adj petit(e) et épais(se), ramassé(e) ▷ vi (also: **~ down**) s'accroupir; **squatter** n squatter m

squeak [skwiːk] vi (hinge, wheel) grincer; (mouse) pousser un petit cri

squeal [skwiːl] vi pousser un or des cri(s) aigu(s) or perçant(s); (brakes) grincer

squeeze [skwiːz] n pression f ▷ vt presser; (hand, arm) serrer

squid [skwɪd] n calmar m

squint [skwɪnt] vi loucher

squirm [skwəːm] vi se tortiller

squirrel ['skwɪrəl] n écureuil m

squirt [skwəːt] vi jaillir, gicler ▷ vt faire gicler

Sr abbr = **senior**

Sri Lanka [srɪ'læŋkə] n Sri Lanka m

St abbr = **saint**; **street**

stab [stæb] n (with knife etc) coup m (de couteau etc); (of pain) lancée f; (inf: try): **to have a ~ at (doing) sth** s'essayer à (faire) qch ▷ vt poignarder

stability [stə'bɪlɪtɪ] n stabilité f

stable ['steɪbl] n écurie f ▷ adj stable

stack [stæk] n tas m, pile f ▷ vt empiler, entasser

stadium ['steɪdɪəm] n stade m

staff [stɑːf] n (work force) personnel m; (BRIT Scol: also: **teaching ~**) professeurs mpl, enseignants mpl, personnel enseignant ▷ vt pourvoir en personnel

stag [stæg] n cerf m

stage [steɪdʒ] n scène f; (platform) estrade f; (point) étape f, stade m; (profession): **the ~** le théâtre ▷ vt (play) monter, mettre en scène; (demonstration) organiser; **in ~s** par étapes, par degrés

⬛ Be careful not to translate *stage* by the French word *stage*.

stagger ['stægəʳ] vi chanceler, tituber ▷ vt (person: amaze) stupéfier; (hours, holidays) étaler, échelonner; **staggering** adj (amazing) stupéfiant(e), renversant(e)

stagnant ['stægnənt] adj stagnant(e)

stag night, stag party n enterrement m de vie de garçon

stain [steɪn] n tache f; (colouring) colorant m ▷ vt tacher; (wood) teindre; **stained glass** n (decorative) verre coloré; (in church) vitraux mpl; **stainless steel** n inox m, acier m inoxydable

staircase ['stɛəkeɪs] n = **stairway**

stairs [stɛəz] npl escalier m

stairway ['stɛəweɪ] n escalier m

stake [steɪk] n pieu m, poteau m; (Comm: interest) intérêts mpl; (Betting) enjeu m ▷ vt risquer, jouer; (also: **~ out**: area) marquer, délimiter; **to be at ~** être en jeu

stale [steɪl] adj (bread) rassis(e); (food) pas frais (fraîche); (beer) éventé(e); (smell) de renfermé; (air) confiné(e)

stalk [stɔːk] n tige f ▷ vt traquer

stall [stɔːl] n (BRIT: in street, market etc) éventaire m, étal m; (in stable) stalle f ▷ vt (Aut) caler; (fig: delay) retarder ▷ vi (Aut) caler; (fig) essayer de gagner du temps; **stalls** npl (BRIT: in cinema, theatre) orchestre m

stamina ['stæmɪnə] n vigueur f, endurance f

stammer ['stæmə^r] n bégaiement m
▷ vi bégayer
stamp [stæmp] n timbre m; (also:
rubber ~) tampon m; (mark, also fig)
empreinte f; (on document) cachet
m ▷ vi (also: **~ one's foot**) taper du
pied ▷ vt (letter) timbrer; (with rubber
stamp) tamponner; **stamp out** vt (fire)
piétiner; (crime) éradiquer; (opposition)
éliminer; **stamped addressed
envelope** n (BRIT) enveloppe
affranchie pour la réponse
stampede [stæm'pi:d] n ruée f; (of
cattle) débandade f
stance [stæns] n position f
stand [stænd] n (position) position f;
(for taxis) station f (de taxis); (Comm)
étalage m, stand m; (Sport: also: **~s**)
tribune f; (also: **music ~**) pupitre m
▷ vb (pt, pp **stood**) ▷ vi être or se tenir
(debout); (rise) se lever, se mettre
debout; (be placed) se trouver; (remain:
offer etc) rester valable ▷ vt (place)
mettre, poser; (tolerate, withstand)
supporter; (treat, invite) offrir, payer;
to make a ~ prendre position; **to ~
for parliament** (BRIT) se présenter
aux élections (comme candidat à la
députation); **I can't ~ him** je ne peux
pas le voir; **stand back** vi (move back)
reculer, s'écarter; **stand by** vi (be ready)
se tenir prêt(e) ▷ vt fus (opinion) s'en
tenir à; (person) ne pas abandonner,
soutenir; **stand down** vi (withdraw)
se retirer; **stand for** vt fus (signify)
représenter, signifier; (tolerate)
supporter, tolérer; **stand in for** vt fus
remplacer; **stand out** vi (be prominent)
ressortir; **stand up** vi (rise) se lever,
se mettre debout; **stand up for** vt fus
défendre; **stand up to** vt fus tenir tête
à, résister à
standard ['stændəd] n (norm) norme
f, étalon m; (level) niveau m (voulu);
(criterion) critère m; (flag) étendard m
▷ adj (size etc) ordinaire, normal(e);
(model, feature) standard inv; (practice)
courant(e); (text) de base; **standards**

npl (morals) morale f, principes mpl;
standard of living n niveau m de vie
stand-by ticket n (Aviat) billet m
stand-by
standing ['stændɪŋ] adj debout
inv; (permanent) permanent(e) ▷ n
réputation f, rang m, standing m; **of
many years' ~** qui dure or existe depuis
longtemps; **standing order** n (BRIT:
at bank) virement m automatique,
prélèvement m bancaire
stand: **standpoint** n point m de vue;
standstill n: **at a standstill** à l'arrêt;
(fig) au point mort; **to come to a
standstill** s'immobiliser, s'arrêter
stank [stæŋk] pt of **stink**
staple ['steɪpl] n (for papers) agrafe f
▷ adj (food, crop, industry etc) de base
principal(e) ▷ vt agrafer
star [stɑː^r] n étoile f; (celebrity) vedette f
▷ vt (Cine) avoir pour vedette; **stars** npl:
the ~s (Astrology) l'horoscope m
starboard ['stɑːbəd] n tribord m
starch [stɑːtʃ] n amidon m; (in food)
fécule f
stardom ['stɑːdəm] n célébrité f
stare [stɛə^r] n regard m fixe ▷ vi: **to ~ at**
regarder fixement
stark [stɑːk] adj (bleak) désolé(e),
morne ▷ adv: **~ naked** complètement
nu(e)
start [stɑːt] n commencement m,
début m; (of race) départ m; (sudden
movement) sursaut m; (advantage)
avance f, avantage m ▷ vt commencer;
(cause: fight) déclencher; (rumour)
donner naissance à; (fashion) lancer;
(found: business, newspaper) lancer, créer
(engine) mettre en marche ▷ vi (begin)
commencer; (begin journey) partir, se
mettre en route; (jump) sursauter;
when does the film ~? à quelle heure
est-ce que le film commence?; **to ~
doing** or **to do sth** se mettre à faire qch
start off vi commencer; (leave) partir;
start out vi (begin) commencer; (set
out) partir; **start up** vi commencer;
(car) démarrer ▷ vt (fight) déclencher;

(business) créer; (car) mettre en marche; **starter** n (Aut) démarreur m; (Sport: official) starter m; (BRIT Culin) entrée f; **starting point** n point m de départ

startle ['stɑːtl] vt faire sursauter; donner un choc à; **startling** adj surprenant(e), saisissant(e)

starvation [stɑːˈveɪʃən] n faim f, famine f

starve [stɑːv] vi mourir de faim ▷ vt laisser mourir de faim

state [steɪt] n état m; (Pol) État ▷ vt (declare) déclarer, affirmer; (specify) indiquer, spécifier; **States** npl: the **S~s** les États-Unis; **to be in a ~** être dans tous ses états; **stately home** n manoir m or château m (ouvert au public); **statement** n déclaration f; (Law) déposition f; **state school** n école publique; **statesman** (irreg) n homme m d'État

static ['stætɪk] n (Radio) parasites mpl; (also: **~ electricity**) électricité f statique ▷ adj statique

station ['steɪʃən] n gare f; (also: **police ~**) poste m or commissariat m (de police) ▷ vt placer, poster

stationary ['steɪʃnərɪ] adj à l'arrêt, immobile

stationer's (shop) n (BRIT) papeterie f

stationery ['steɪʃnərɪ] n papier m à lettres, petit matériel de bureau

station wagon n (US) break m

statistic [stəˈtɪstɪk] n statistique f; **statistics** n (science) statistique f

statue ['stætjuː] n statue f

stature ['stætʃər] n stature f; (fig) envergure f

status ['steɪtəs] n position f, situation f; (prestige) prestige m; (Admin, official position) statut m; **status quo** [-ˈkwəʊ] n: **the status quo** le statu quo

statutory ['stætjutrɪ] adj statutaire, prévu(e) par un article de loi

staunch [stɔːntʃ] adj sûr(e), loyal(e)

stay [steɪ] n (period of time) séjour m ▷ vi rester; (reside) loger; (spend some time)

séjourner; **to ~ put** ne pas bouger; **to ~ the night** passer la nuit; **stay away** vi (from person, building) ne pas s'approcher; (from event) ne pas venir; **stay behind** vi rester en arrière; **stay in** vi (at home) rester à la maison; **stay on** vi rester; **stay out** vi (of house) ne pas rentrer; (strikers) rester en grève; **stay up** vi (at night) ne pas se coucher

steadily ['stedɪlɪ] adv (regularly) progressivement; (firmly) fermement; (walk) d'un pas ferme; (fixedly: look) sans détourner les yeux

steady ['stedɪ] adj stable, solide, ferme; (regular) constant(e), régulier(-ière); (person) calme, pondéré(e) ▷ vt assurer, stabiliser; (nerves) calmer; **a ~ boyfriend** un petit ami

steak [steɪk] n (meat) bifteck m, steak m; (fish, pork) tranche f

steal (pt **stole**, pp **stolen**) [stiːl, stəʊl, 'stəʊln] vt, vi voler; (move) se faufiler, se déplacer furtivement; **my wallet has been stolen** on m'a volé mon portefeuille

steam [stiːm] n vapeur f ▷ vt (Culin) cuire à la vapeur ▷ vi fumer; **steam up** vi (window) se couvrir de buée; **to get ~ed up about sth** (fig: inf) s'exciter à propos de qch; **steamy** adj humide; (window) embué(e); (sexy) torride

steel [stiːl] n acier m ▷ cpd d'acier

steep [stiːp] adj raide, escarpé(e); (price) très élevé(e), excessif(-ive) ▷ vt (faire) tremper

steeple ['stiːpl] n clocher m

steer [stɪər] vt diriger; (boat) gouverner; (lead: person) guider, conduire ▷ vi tenir le gouvernail; **steering** n (Aut) conduite f; **steering wheel** n volant m

stem [stem] n (of plant) tige f; (of glass) pied m ▷ vt contenir, endiguer; (attack, spread of disease) juguler

step [step] n pas m; (stair) marche f; (action) mesure f, disposition f ▷ vi: **to ~ forward/back** faire un pas en avant/arrière, avancer/reculer; **steps** npl (BRIT) = **stepladder**; **to be in/out of**

~ (with) (fig) aller dans le sens (de)/être déphasé(e) (par rapport à); **step down** vi (fig) se retirer, se désister; **step in** vi (fig) intervenir; **step up** vt (production, sales) augmenter; (campaign, efforts) intensifier; **stepbrother** n demi-frère m; **stepchild** (pl **~ren**) n beau-fils m, belle-fille f; **stepdaughter** n belle-fille f; **stepfather** n beau-père m; **stepladder** n (BRIT) escabeau m; **stepmother** n belle-mère f; **stepsister** n demi-sœur f; **stepson** n beau-fils m

stereo ['stɛrɪəu] n (sound) stéréo f; (hi-fi) chaîne f stéréo ▷ adj (also: **~phonic**) stéréo(phonique)

stereotype ['stɪərɪətaɪp] n stéréotype m ▷ vt stéréotyper

sterile ['stɛraɪl] adj stérile; **sterilize** ['stɛrɪlaɪz] vt stériliser

sterling ['stə:lɪŋ] adj (silver) de bon aloi, fin(e) ▷ n (currency) livre f sterling inv

stern [stə:n] adj sévère ▷ n (Naut) arrière m, poupe f

steroid ['stɪərɔɪd] n stéroïde m

stew [stju:] n ragoût m ▷ vt, vi cuire à la casserole

steward ['stju:əd] n (Aviat, Naut, Rail) steward m; **stewardess** n hôtesse f

stick [stɪk] n bâton m; (for walking) canne f; (of chalk etc) morceau m ▷ vb (pt, pp **stuck**) ▷ vt (glue) coller; (thrust): **to ~ sth into** piquer or planter or enfoncer qch dans; (inf: put) mettre, fourrer; (: tolerate) supporter ▷ vi (adhere) tenir, coller; (remain) rester; (get jammed: door, lift) se bloquer; **stick out** vi dépasser, sortir; **stick up** vi dépasser, sortir; **stick up for** vt fus défendre; **sticker** n auto-collant m; **sticking plaster** n sparadrap m, pansement adhésif; **stick insect** n phasme m; **stick shift** n (US Aut) levier m de vitesses

sticky ['stɪkɪ] adj poisseux(-euse); (label) adhésif(-ive); (fig: situation) délicat(e)

stiff [stɪf] adj (gen) raide, rigide; (door, brush) dur(e); (difficult) difficile, ardu(e); (cold) froid(e), distant(e); (strong, high) fort(e), élevé(e) ▷ adv: **to be bored/scared/frozen ~** s'ennuyer à mourir/être mort(e) de peur/froid

stifling ['staɪflɪŋ] adj (heat) suffocant(e)

stigma ['stɪgmə] n stigmate m

stiletto [stɪ'lɛtəu] n (BRIT: also: **~ heel**) talon m aiguille

still [stɪl] adj immobile ▷ adv (up to this time) encore, toujours; (even) encore; (nonetheless) quand même, tout de même

stimulate ['stɪmjuleɪt] vt stimuler

stimulus (pl **stimuli**) ['stɪmjuləs, 'stɪmjulaɪ] n stimulant m; (Biol, Psych) stimulus m

sting [stɪŋ] n piqûre f; (organ) dard m ▷ vt, vi (pt, pp **stung**) piquer

stink [stɪŋk] n puanteur f ▷ vi (pt **stank**, pp **stunk**) puer, empester

stir [stə:ʳ] n agitation f, sensation f ▷ vt remuer ▷ vi remuer, bouger; **stir up** vt (trouble) fomenter, provoquer; **stir-fry** vt faire sauter ▷ n: **vegetable stir-fry** légumes sautés à la poêle

stitch [stɪtʃ] n (Sewing) point m; (Knitting) maille f; (Med) point de suture; (pain) point de côté ▷ vt coudre, piquer; (Med) suturer

stock [stɔk] n réserve f, provision f; (Comm) stock m; (Agr) cheptel m, bétail m; (Culin) bouillon m; (Finance) valeurs fpl, titres mpl; (descent, origin) souche f ▷ adj (fig: reply etc) classique ▷ vt (have in stock) avoir, vendre; **in ~** en stock, en magasin; **out of ~** épuisé(e); **to take ~** (fig) faire le point; **~s and shares** valeurs, titres; **stockbroker** ['stɔkbrəukəʳ] n agent m de change; **stock cube** n (BRIT Culin) bouillon-cube m; **stock exchange** n Bourse f (des valeurs); **stockholder** ['stɔkhəuldəʳ] n (US) actionnaire m/f

stocking ['stɔkɪŋ] n bas m

stock market n Bourse f, marché financier

stole [stəul] pt of **steal** ▷ n étole f

stolen ['stəuln] pp of **steal**

stomach ['stʌmək] n estomac m; (abdomen) ventre m ▷ vt supporter, digérer; **stomachache** n mal m à l'estomac or au ventre

stone [stəun] n pierre f; (pebble) caillou m, galet m; (in fruit) noyau m; (Med) calcul m; (BRIT: weight) = 6.348 kg; 14 pounds ▷ cpd de or en pierre ▷ vt (person) lancer des pierres sur, lapider; (fruit) dénoyauter

stood [stud] pt, pp of **stand**

stool [stu:l] n tabouret m

stoop [stu:p] vi (also: **have a ~**) être voûté(e); (also: **~ down**: bend) se baisser, se courber

stop [stɔp] n arrêt m; (in punctuation) point m ▷ vt arrêter; (break off) interrompre; (also: **put a ~ to**) mettre fin à; (prevent) empêcher ▷ vi s'arrêter; (rain, noise etc) cesser, s'arrêter; **to ~ doing sth** cesser or arrêter de faire qch; **to ~ sb (from) doing sth** empêcher qn de faire qch; **~ it!** arrête!; **stop by** vi s'arrêter (au passage); **stop off** vi faire une courte halte; **stopover** n halte f; (Aviat) escale f; **stoppage** n (strike) arrêt m de travail; (obstruction) obstruction f

storage ['stɔːrɪdʒ] n emmagasinage m

store [stɔːʳ] n (stock) provision f, réserve f; (depot) entrepôt m; (BRIT: large shop) grand magasin; (US: shop) magasin m ▷ vt emmagasiner; (information) enregistrer; **stores** npl (food) provisions f; **who knows what is in ~ for us?** qui sait ce que l'avenir nous réserve or ce qui nous attend?; **storekeeper** n (US) commerçant(e)

storey (US **story**) ['stɔːrɪ] n étage m

storm [stɔːm] n tempête f; (thunderstorm) orage m ▷ vi (fig) fulminer ▷ vt prendre d'assaut; **stormy** adj orageux(-euse)

story ['stɔːrɪ] n histoire f; (Press: article) article m; (US) = **storey**

stout [staut] adj (strong) solide; (fat) gros(se), corpulent(e) ▷ n bière brune

stove [stəuv] n (for cooking) fourneau m;

(: small) réchaud m; (for heating) poêle m

straight [streɪt] adj droit(e); (hair) raide; (frank) honnête, franc (franche); (simple) simple ▷ adv (tout) droit; (drink) sec, sans eau; **to put** or **get ~** mettre en ordre, mettre de l'ordre dans; (fig) mettre au clair; **~ away**, **~ off** (at once) tout de suite; **straighten** vt ajuster; (bed) arranger; **straighten out** vt (fig) débrouiller; **straighten up** (stand up) se redresser; **straightforward** adj simple; (frank) honnête, direct(e)

strain [streɪn] n (Tech) tension f; pression f; (physical) effort m; (mental) tension (nerveuse); (Med) entorse f; (breed: of plants) variété f; (: of animals) race f ▷ vt (fig: resources etc) mettre à rude épreuve, grever; (hurt: back etc) se faire mal à; (vegetables) égoutter; **strains** npl (Mus) accords mpl, accents mpl; **strained** adj (muscle) froissé(e); (laugh etc) forcé(e), contraint(e); (relations) tendu(e); **strainer** n passoire f

strait [streɪt] n (Geo) détroit m; **straits** npl: **to be in dire ~s** (fig) avoir de sérieux ennuis

strand [strænd] n (of thread) fil m, brin m; (of rope) toron m; (of hair) mèche f ▷ vt (boat) échouer; **stranded** adj en rade, en plan

strange [streɪndʒ] adj (not known) inconnu(e); (odd) étrange, bizarre; **strangely** adv étrangement, bizarrement; see also **enough**; **stranger** n (unknown) inconnu(e); (from somewhere else) étranger(-ère)

strangle ['stræŋgl] vt étrangler

strap [stræp] n lanière f, courroie f, sangle f; (of slip, dress) bretelle f

strategic [strə'ti:dʒɪk] adj stratégique

strategy ['strætɪdʒɪ] n stratégie f

straw [strɔː] n paille f; **that's the last ~!** ça c'est le comble!

strawberry ['strɔːbərɪ] n fraise f

stray [streɪ] adj (animal) perdu(e), errant(e); (scattered) isolé(e) ▷ vi s'égarer; **~ bullet** balle perdue

streak [striːk] n bande f, filet m; (in hair) raie f ▷ vt zébrer, strier

stream [striːm] n (brook) ruisseau m; (current) courant m, flot m; (of people) défilé ininterrompu, flot ▷ vt (Scol) répartir par niveau ▷ vi ruisseler; **to ~ in/out** entrer/sortir à flots

street [striːt] n rue f; **streetcar** n (US) tramway m; **street light** n réverbère m; **street map, street plan** n plan m des rues

strength [strɛŋθ] n force f; (of girder, knot etc) solidité f; **strengthen** vt renforcer; (muscle) fortifier; (building, Econ) consolider

strenuous ['strɛnjuəs] adj vigoureux(-euse), énergique; (tiring) ardu(e), fatigant(e)

stress [strɛs] n (force, pressure) pression f; (mental strain) tension (nerveuse), stress m; (accent) accent m; (emphasis) insistance f ▷ vt insister sur, souligner; (syllable) accentuer; **stressed** adj (tense) stressé(e); (syllable) accentué(e); **stressful** adj (job) stressant(e)

stretch [strɛtʃ] n (of sand etc) étendue f ▷ vi s'étirer; (extend): **to ~ to or as far as** s'étendre jusqu'à ▷ vt tendre, étirer; (fig) pousser (au maximum); **at a ~** d'affilée; **stretch out** vi s'étendre ▷ vt (arm etc) allonger, tendre; (to spread) étendre

stretcher ['strɛtʃəʳ] n brancard m, civière f

strict [strɪkt] adj strict(e); **strictly** adv strictement

stride [straɪd] n grand pas, enjambée f ▷ vi (pt **strode**, pp **stridden**) marcher à grands pas

strike [straɪk] n grève f; (of oil etc) découverte f; (attack) raid m ▷ vb (pt, pp **struck**) ▷ vt frapper; (oil etc) trouver, découvrir; (make: agreement, deal) conclure ▷ vi faire grève; (attack) attaquer; (clock) sonner; **to go on or come out on ~** se mettre en grève, faire grève; **to ~ a match** frotter une allumette; **striker** n gréviste

m/f; (Sport) buteur m; **striking** adj frappant(e), saisissant(e); (attractive) éblouissant(e)

string [strɪŋ] n ficelle f, fil m; (row: of beads) rang m; (Mus) corde f ▷ vt (pt, pp **strung**): **to ~ out** échelonner; **to ~ together** enchaîner; **the strings** npl (Mus) les instruments mpl à cordes; **to pull ~s** (fig) faire jouer le piston

strip [strɪp] n bande f; (Sport) tenue f ▷ vt (undress) déshabiller; (paint) décaper; (fig) dégarnir, dépouiller; (also: **~ down**: machine) démonter ▷ vi se déshabiller; **strip off** vt (paint etc) décaper ▷ vi (person) se déshabiller

stripe [straɪp] n raie f, rayure f; (Mil) galon m; **striped** adj rayé(e), à rayures

stripper ['strɪpəʳ] n strip-teaseuse f

strip-search ['strɪpsəːtʃ] vt: **to ~ sb** fouiller qn (en le faisant se déshabiller)

strive (pt **strove**, pp **~n**) [straɪv, strəuv, 'strɪvn] vi: **to ~ to do/for sth** s'efforcer de faire/d'obtenir qch

strode [strəud] pt of **stride**

stroke [strəuk] n coup m; (Med) attaque f; (Swimming: style) (sorte f de) nage f ▷ vt caresser; **at a ~** d'un (seul) coup

stroll [strəul] n petite promenade ▷ vi flâner, se promener nonchalamment; **stroller** n (US: for child) poussette f

strong [strɔŋ] adj (gen) fort(e); (healthy) vigoureux(-euse); (heart, nerves) solide; **they are 50 ~** ils sont au nombre de 50; **stronghold** n forteresse f, fort m; (fig) bastion m; **strongly** adv fortement, avec force; vigoureusement; solidement

strove [strəuv] pt of **strive**

struck [strʌk] pt, pp of **strike**

structure ['strʌktʃəʳ] n structure f; (building) construction f

struggle ['strʌgl] n lutte f ▷ vi lutter, se battre

strung [strʌŋ] pt, pp of **string**

stub [stʌb] n (of cigarette) bout m, mégot m; (of ticket etc) talon m ▷ vt: **to ~ one's toe (on sth)** se heurter le doigt de pied (contre qch); **stub out** vt écraser

stubble ['stʌbl] n chaume m; (on chin) barbe f de plusieurs jours

stubborn ['stʌbən] adj têtu(e), obstiné(e), opiniâtre

stuck [stʌk] pt, pp of **stick** ▷ adj (jammed) bloqué(e), coincé(e)

stud [stʌd] n (on boots etc) clou m; (collar stud) bouton m de col; (earring) petite boucle d'oreille; (of horses: also: **~ farm**) écurie f, haras m; (also: **~ horse**) étalon m ▷ vt (fig): **~ded with** parsemé(e) or criblé(e) de

student ['stju:dənt] n étudiant(e) ▷ adj (life) estudiantin(e), étudiant(e), d'étudiant; (residence, restaurant) universitaire; (loan, movement) étudiant; **student driver** n (US) (conducteur(-trice)) débutant(e); **students' union** n (BRIT: association) ≈ union f des étudiants; (: building) ≈ foyer m des étudiants

studio ['stju:dɪəu] n studio m, atelier m; (TV etc) studio; **studio flat** (US **studio apartment**) n studio m

study ['stʌdɪ] n étude f; (room) bureau m ▷ vt étudier; (examine) examiner ▷ vi étudier, faire ses études

stuff [stʌf] n (gen) chose(s) f(pl), truc m; (belongings) affaires fpl, trucs; (substance) substance f ▷ vt rembourrer; (Culin) farcir; (inf: push) fourrer; **stuffing** n bourre f, rembourrage m; (Culin) farce f; **stuffy** adj (room) mal ventilé(e) or aéré(e); (ideas) vieux jeu inv

stumble ['stʌmbl] vi trébucher; **to ~ across** or **on** (fig) tomber sur

stump [stʌmp] n souche f; (of limb) moignon m ▷ vt: **to be ~ed** sécher, ne pas savoir que répondre

stun [stʌn] vt (blow) étourdir; (news) abasourdir, stupéfier

stung [stʌŋ] pt, pp of **sting**

stunk [stʌŋk] pp of **stink**

stunned [stʌnd] adj assommé(e); (fig) sidéré(e)

stunning ['stʌnɪŋ] adj (beautiful) étourdissant(e); (news etc) stupéfiant(e)

stunt [stʌnt] n (in film) cascade f, acrobatie f; (publicity) truc m publicitaire ▷ vt retarder, arrêter

stupid ['stju:pɪd] adj stupide, bête; **stupidity** [stju:'pɪdɪtɪ] n stupidité f, bêtise f

sturdy ['stə:dɪ] adj (person, plant) robuste, vigoureux(-euse); (object) solide

stutter ['stʌtər] n bégaiement m ▷ vi bégayer

style [staɪl] n style m; (distinction) allure f, cachet m, style; (design) modèle m; **stylish** adj élégant(e), chic inv; **stylist** n (hair stylist) coiffeur(-euse)

sub... [sʌb] prefix sub..., sous-; **subconscious** adj subconscient(e)

subdued [səb'dju:d] adj (light) tamisé(e); (person) qui a perdu de son entrain

subject n ['sʌbdʒɪkt] sujet m; (Scol) matière f ▷ vt [səb'dʒɛkt]: **to ~ to** soumettre à; **to be ~ to** (law) être soumis(e) à; **subjective** [səb'dʒɛktɪv] adj subjectif(-ive); **subject matter** n (content) contenu m

subjunctive [səb'dʒʌŋktɪv] n subjonctif m

submarine [sʌbmə'ri:n] n sous-marin m

submission [səb'mɪʃən] n soumission f

submit [səb'mɪt] vt soumettre ▷ vi se soumettre

subordinate [sə'bɔ:dɪnət] adj (junior) subalterne; (Grammar) subordonné(e) ▷ n subordonné(e)

subscribe [səb'skraɪb] vi cotiser; **to ~ to** (opinion, fund) souscrire à; (newspaper) s'abonner à; être abonné(e) à

subscription [səb'skrɪpʃən] n (to magazine etc) abonnement m

subsequent ['sʌbsɪkwənt] adj ultérieur(e), suivant(e); **subsequently** adv par la suite

subside [səb'saɪd] vi (land) s'affaisser;

(flood) baisser; (wind, feelings) tomber

subsidiary [səbˈsɪdɪərɪ] adj subsidiaire; accessoire; (BRIT Scol: subject) complémentaire ▷ n filiale f

subsidize [ˈsʌbsɪdaɪz] vt subventionner

subsidy [ˈsʌbsɪdɪ] n subvention f

substance [ˈsʌbstəns] n substance f

substantial [səbˈstænʃl] adj substantiel(le); (fig) important(e)

substitute [ˈsʌbstɪtjuːt] n (person) remplaçant(e); (thing) succédané m ▷ vt: **to ~ sth/sb for** substituer qch/qn à, remplacer par qch/qn; **substitution** n substitution f

subtitles [ˈsʌbtaɪtlz] npl (Cine) sous-titres mpl

subtle [ˈsʌtl] adj subtil(e)

subtract [səbˈtrækt] vt soustraire, retrancher

suburb [ˈsʌbəːb] n faubourg m; **the ~s** la banlieue; **suburban** [səˈbəːbən] adj de banlieue, suburbain(e)

subway [ˈsʌbweɪ] n (BRIT: underpass) passage souterrain; (US: railway) métro m

succeed [səkˈsiːd] vi réussir ▷ vt succéder à; **to ~ in doing** réussir à faire

success [səkˈsɛs] n succès m; réussite f; **successful** adj (business) prospère, qui réussit; (attempt) couronné(e) de succès; **to be successful (in doing)** réussir (à faire); **successfully** adv avec succès

succession [səkˈsɛʃən] n succession f

successive [səkˈsɛsɪv] adj successif(-ive)

successor [səkˈsɛsəʳ] n successeur m

succumb [səˈkʌm] vi succomber

such [sʌtʃ] adj tel (telle); (of that kind): **~ a book** un livre de ce genre or pareil, un tel livre; (so much): **~ courage** un tel courage ▷ adv si; **~ a long trip** un si long voyage; **~ a lot of** tellement or tant de; **~ as** (like) tel (telle) que, comme; **as ~** adv en tant que tel (telle), à proprement parler; **such-and-such** adj tel ou tel (telle ou telle)

suck [sʌk] vt sucer; (breast, bottle) téter

Sudan [suˈdɑːn] n Soudan m

sudden [ˈsʌdn] adj soudain(e), subit(e); **all of a ~** soudain, tout à coup; **suddenly** adv brusquement, tout à coup, soudain

sue [suː] vt poursuivre en justice, intenter un procès à

suede [sweɪd] n daim m, cuir suédé

suffer [ˈsʌfəʳ] vt souffrir, subir; (bear) tolérer, supporter, subir ▷ vi souffrir; **to ~ from** (illness) souffrir de, avoir; **suffering** n souffrance(s) f(pl)

suffice [səˈfaɪs] vi suffire

sufficient [səˈfɪʃənt] adj suffisant(e)

suffocate [ˈsʌfəkeɪt] vi suffoquer; étouffer

sugar [ˈʃugəʳ] n sucre m ▷ vt sucrer

suggest [səˈdʒɛst] vt suggérer, proposer; (indicate) sembler indiquer; **suggestion** [səˈdʒɛstʃən] n suggestion f

suicide [ˈsuɪsaɪd] n suicide m; **~ bombing** attentat m suicide; see also **commit**; **suicide bomber** n kamikaze m/f

suit [suːt] n (man's) costume m, complet m; (woman's) tailleur m, ensemble m; (Cards) couleur f; (lawsuit) procès m ▷ vt (subj: clothes, hairstyle) aller à; (be convenient for) convenir à; (adapt): **to ~ sth to** adapter or approprier qch à; **well ~ed** (couple) faits l'un pour l'autre, très bien assortis; **suitable** adj qui convient; approprié(e), adéquat(e); **suitcase** n valise f

suite [swiːt] n (of rooms, also Mus) suite f; (furniture): **bedroom/dining room ~** (ensemble m de) chambre f à coucher/ salle f à manger; **a three-piece ~** un salon (canapé et deux fauteuils)

sulfur [ˈsʌlfəʳ] (US) n = **sulphur**

sulk [sʌlk] vi bouder

sulphur (US **sulfur**) [ˈsʌlfəʳ] n soufre m

sultana [sʌlˈtɑːnə] n (fruit) raisin (sec) de Smyrne

sum [sʌm] n somme f; (Scol etc) calcul m; **sum up** vt résumer ▷ vi résumer

summarize ['sʌməraɪz] vt résumer

summary ['sʌmərɪ] n résumé m

summer ['sʌmə^r] n été m ▷ cpd d'été, estival(e); **in (the) ~** en été, pendant l'été; **summer holidays** npl grandes vacances; **summertime** n (season) été m

summit ['sʌmɪt] n sommet m; (also: **~ conference**) (conférence f au) sommet m

summon ['sʌmən] vt appeler, convoquer; **to ~ a witness** citer or assigner un témoin

Sun. abbr (= Sunday) dim

sun [sʌn] n soleil m; **sunbathe** vi prendre un bain de soleil; **sunbed** n lit pliant; (with sun lamp) lit à ultra-violets; **sunblock** n écran m total; **sunburn** n coup m de soleil; **sunburned, sunburnt** adj bronzé(e), hâlé(e); (painfully) brûlé(e) par le soleil

Sunday ['sʌndɪ] n dimanche m

sunflower ['sʌnflauə^r] n tournesol m

sung [sʌŋ] pp of **sing**

sunglasses ['sʌnglɑːsɪz] npl lunettes fpl de soleil

sunk [sʌŋk] pp of **sink**

sun: **sunlight** n (lumière f du) soleil m; **sun lounger** n chaise longue; **sunny** adj ensoleillé(e); **it is sunny** il fait (du) soleil, il y a du soleil; **sunrise** n lever m du soleil; **sun roof** n (Aut) toit ouvrant; **sunscreen** n crème f solaire; **sunset** n coucher m du soleil; **sunshade** n (over table) parasol m; **sunshine** n (lumière f du) soleil m; **sunstroke** n insolation f, coup m de soleil; **suntan** n bronzage m; **suntan lotion** n lotion f or lait m solaire; **suntan oil** n huile f solaire

super ['suːpə^r] adj (inf) formidable

superb [suː'pəːb] adj superbe, magnifique

superficial [suːpə'fɪʃəl] adj superficiel(le)

superintendent [suːpərɪn'tɛndənt] n directeur(-trice); (Police) ≈ commissaire m

superior [suː'pɪərɪə^r] adj supérieur(e); (smug) condescendant(e), méprisant(e) ▷ n supérieur(e)

superlative [suː'pəːlətɪv] n (Ling) superlatif m

supermarket ['suːpəmɑːkɪt] n supermarché m

supernatural [suːpə'nætʃərəl] adj surnaturel(le) ▷ n: **the ~** le surnaturel

superpower ['suːpəpauə^r] n (Pol) superpuissance f

superstition [suːpə'stɪʃən] n superstition f

superstitious [suːpə'stɪʃəs] adj superstitieux(-euse)

superstore ['suːpəstɔː^r] n (BRIT) hypermarché m, grande surface

supervise ['suːpəvaɪz] vt (children etc) surveiller; (organization, work) diriger; **supervision** [suːpə'vɪʒən] n surveillance f; (monitoring) contrôle m; (management) direction f; **supervisor** n surveillant(e); (in shop) chef m de rayon

supper ['sʌpə^r] n dîner m; (late) souper m

supple ['sʌpl] adj souple

supplement n ['sʌplɪmənt] supplément m ▷ vt [sʌplɪ'mɛnt] ajouter à, compléter

supplier [sə'plaɪə^r] n fournisseur m

supply [sə'plaɪ] vt (provide) fournir; (equip): **to ~ (with)** approvisionner or ravitailler (en); fournir (en) ▷ n provision f, réserve f; (supplying) approvisionnement m; **supplies** npl (food) vivres mpl; (Mil) subsistances fpl

support [sə'pɔːt] n (moral, financial etc) soutien m, appui m; (Tech) support m, soutien ▷ vt soutenir, supporter; (financially) subvenir aux besoins de; (uphold) être pour, être partisan de, appuyer; (Sport: team) être pour; **supporter** n (Pol etc) partisan(e); (Sport) supporter m

suppose [sə'pəuz] vt, vi supposer; imaginer; **to be ~d to do/be** être censé(e) faire/être; **supposedly** [sə'pəuzɪdlɪ] adv soi-disant; **supposing** conj si, à supposer que + sub

suppress [sə'prɛs] *vt* (*revolt, feeling*) réprimer; (*information*) (*gen*) faire disparaître; (*scandal, yawn*) étouffer

supreme [su'priːm] *adj* suprême

surcharge ['səːtʃɑːdʒ] *n* surcharge *f*

sure [ʃuəʳ] *adj* sûr(e); (*definite, convinced*) sûr, certain(e); **~!** (*of course*) bien sûr!; **~ enough** effectivement; **to make ~ of sth/that** s'assurer de qch/que, vérifier qch/que; **surely** *adv* sûrement; certainement

surf [səːf] *n* (*waves*) ressac *m* ▷ *vt*: **to ~ the Net** surfer sur Internet, surfer sur le net

surface ['səːfɪs] *n* surface *f* ▷ *vt* (*road*) poser un revêtement sur ▷ *vi* remonter à la surface; (*fig*) faire surface; **by ~ mail** par voie de terre; (*by sea*) par voie maritime

surfboard ['səːfbɔːd] *n* planche *f* de surf

surfer ['səːfəʳ] *n* (*in sea*) surfeur(-euse); **web** *or* **net ~** internaute *m/f*

surfing ['səːfɪŋ] *n* surf *m*

surge [səːdʒ] *n* (*of emotion*) vague *f* ▷ *vi* déferler

surgeon ['səːdʒən] *n* chirurgien *m*

surgery ['səːdʒərɪ] *n* chirurgie *f*; (*BRIT: room*) cabinet *m* (de consultation); (*also*: **~ hours**) heures *fpl* de consultation

surname ['səːneɪm] *n* nom *m* de famille

surpass [səː'pɑːs] *vt* surpasser, dépasser

surplus ['səːpləs] *n* surplus *m*, excédent *m* ▷ *adj* en surplus, de trop; (*Comm*) excédentaire

surprise [sə'praɪz] *n* (*gen*) surprise *f*; (*astonishment*) étonnement *m* ▷ *vt* surprendre, étonner; **surprised** *adj* (*look, smile*) surpris(e), étonné(e); **to be surprised** être surpris; **surprising** *adj* surprenant(e), étonnant(e); **surprisingly** *adv* (*easy, helpful*) étonnamment, étrangement; **(somewhat) surprisingly, he agreed** curieusement, il a accepté

surrender [sə'rɛndəʳ] *n* reddition *f*, capitulation *f* ▷ *vi* se rendre, capituler

surround [sə'raund] *vt* entourer; (*Mil etc*) encercler; **surrounding** *adj* environnant(e); **surroundings** *npl* environs *mpl*, alentours *mpl*

surveillance [səː'veɪləns] *n* surveillance *f*

survey *n* ['səːveɪ] enquête *f*, étude *f*; (*in house buying etc*) inspection *f*, (rapport *m* d')expertise *f*; (*of land*) levé *m* ▷ *vt* [səː'veɪ] (*situation*) passer en revue; (*examine carefully*) inspecter; (*building*) expertiser; (*land*) faire le levé de; (*look at*) embrasser du regard; **surveyor** *n* (*of building*) expert *m*; (*of land*) (arpenteur *m*) géomètre *m*

survival [sə'vaɪvl] *n* survie *f*

survive [sə'vaɪv] *vi* survivre; (*custom etc*) subsister ▷ *vt* (*accident etc*) survivre à, réchapper de; (*person*) survivre à; **survivor** *n* survivant(e)

suspect *adj, n* ['sʌspɛkt] suspect(e) ▷ *vt* [səs'pɛkt] soupçonner, suspecter

suspend [səs'pɛnd] *vt* suspendre; **suspended sentence** *n* (*Law*) condamnation *f* avec sursis; **suspenders** *npl* (*BRIT*) jarretelles *fpl*; (*US*) bretelles *fpl*

suspense [səs'pɛns] *n* attente *f*, incertitude *f*; (*in film etc*) suspense *m*; **to keep sb in ~** tenir qn en suspens, laisser qn dans l'incertitude

suspension [səs'pɛnʃən] *n* (*gen, Aut*) suspension *f*; (*of driving licence*) retrait *m* provisoire; **suspension bridge** *n* pont suspendu

suspicion [səs'pɪʃən] *n* soupçon(s) *m*(*pl*); **suspicious** *adj* (*suspecting*) soupçonneux(-euse), méfiant(e); (*causing suspicion*) suspect(e)

sustain [səs'teɪn] *vt* soutenir; (*subj: food*) nourrir, donner des forces à; (*damage*) subir; (*injury*) recevoir

SUV *n abbr* (*esp US*: = *sports utility vehicle*) SUV *m*, véhicule *m* de loisirs

swallow ['swɔləu] *n* (*bird*) hirondelle *f* ▷ *vt* avaler; (*fig*: *story*) gober

swam [swæm] *pt of* **swim**

swamp [swɔmp] *n* marais *m*, marécage *m* ▷ *vt* submerger

swan [swɔn] *n* cygne *m*

swap [swɔp] *n* échange *m*, troc *m* ▷ *vt*: **to ~ (for)** échanger (contre), troquer (contre)

swarm [swɔ:m] *n* essaim *m* ▷ *vi* (*bees*) essaimer; (*people*) grouiller; **to be ~ing with** grouiller de

sway [sweɪ] *vi* se balancer, osciller ▷ *vt* (*influence*) influencer

swear [swɛəʳ] (*pt* **swore**, *pp* **sworn**) *vt*, *vi* jurer; **swear in** *vt* assermenter; **swearword** *n* gros mot, juron *m*

sweat [swɛt] *n* sueur *f*, transpiration *f* ▷ *vi* suer

sweater ['swɛtəʳ] *n* tricot *m*, pull *m*

sweatshirt ['swɛtʃə:t] *n* sweat-shirt *m*

sweaty ['swɛtɪ] *adj* en sueur, moite *or* mouillé(e) de sueur

Swede [swi:d] *n* Suédois(e)

swede [swi:d] *n* (*BRIT*) rutabaga *m*

Sweden ['swi:dn] *n* Suède *f*; **Swedish** ['swi:dɪʃ] *adj* suédois(e) ▷ *n* (*Ling*) suédois *m*

sweep [swi:p] *n* (*curve*) grande courbe; (*also*: **chimney ~**) ramoneur *m* ▷ *vb* (*pt*, *pp* **swept**) ▷ *vt* balayer; (*subj*: *current*) emporter

sweet [swi:t] *n* (*BRIT*: *pudding*) dessert *m*; (*candy*) bonbon *m* ▷ *adj* doux (douce); (*not savoury*) sucré(e); (*kind*) gentil(le); (*baby*) mignon(ne); **sweetcorn** *n* maïs doux; **sweetener** ['swi:tnəʳ] *n* (*Culin*) édulcorant *m*; **sweetheart** *n* amoureux(-euse); **sweetshop** *n* (*BRIT*) confiserie *f*

swell [swɛl] *n* (*of sea*) houle *f* ▷ *adj* (*US*: *inf*: *excellent*) chouette ▷ *vb* (*pt* **~ed**, *pp* **swollen** *or* **~ed**) ▷ *vt* (*increase*) grossir, augmenter ▷ *vi* (*increase*) grossir, augmenter; (*sound*) s'enfler; (*Med*: *also*: **~ up**) enfler; **swelling** *n* (*Med*) enflure *f*; (*: lump*) grosseur *f*

swept [swɛpt] *pt*, *pp of* **sweep**

swerve [swə:v] *vi* (*to avoid obstacle*) faire une embardée *or* un écart; (*off the road*) dévier

swift [swɪft] *n* (*bird*) martinet *m* ▷ *adj* rapide, prompt(e)

swim [swɪm] *n*: **to go for a ~** aller nager *or* se baigner ▷ *vb* (*pt* **swam**, *pp* **swum**) ▷ *vi* nager; (*Sport*) faire de la natation; (*fig*: *head, room*) tourner ▷ *vt* traverser (à la nage); **to ~ a length** nager une longueur; **swimmer** *n* nageur(-euse); **swimming** *n* nage *f*, natation *f*; **swimming costume** *n* (*BRIT*) maillot *m* (de bain); **swimming pool** *n* piscine *f*; **swimming trunks** *npl* maillot *m* de bain; **swimsuit** *n* maillot *m* (de bain)

swing [swɪŋ] *n* (*in playground*) balançoire *f*; (*movement*) balancement *m*, oscillations *fpl*; (*change in opinion etc*) revirement *m* ▷ *vb* (*pt*, *pp* **swung**) ▷ *vt* balancer, faire osciller; (*also*: **~ round**) tourner, faire virer ▷ *vi* se balancer, osciller; (*also*: **~ round**) virer, tourner; **to be in full ~** battre son plein

swipe card [swaɪp-] *n* carte *f* magnétique

swirl [swə:l] *vi* tourbillonner, tournoyer

Swiss [swɪs] *adj* suisse ▷ *n* (*pl inv*) Suisse(-esse)

switch [swɪtʃ] *n* (*for light, radio etc*) bouton *m*; (*change*) changement *m*, revirement *m* ▷ *vt* (*change*) changer; **switch off** *vt* éteindre; (*engine, machine*) arrêter; **could you ~ off the light?** pouvez-vous éteindre la lumière?; **switch on** *vt* allumer; (*engine, machine*) mettre en marche; **switchboard** *n* (*Tel*) standard *m*

Switzerland ['swɪtsələnd] *n* Suisse *f*

swivel ['swɪvl] *vi* (*also*: **~ round**) pivoter, tourner

swollen ['swəulən] *pp of* **swell**

swoop [swu:p] *n* (*by police etc*) rafle *f*, descente *f* ▷ *vi* (*bird*: *also*: **~ down**) descendre en piqué, piquer

swop [swɔp] *n*, *vt* = **swap**

sword [sɔ:d] *n* épée *f*; **swordfish** *n* espadon *m*

swore [swɔ:ʳ] *pt of* **swear**

sworn [swɔ:n] *pp of* **swear** ▷ *adj*

(*statement, evidence*) donné(e) sous
serment; (*enemy*) juré(e)
swum [swʌm] *pp of* **swim**
swung [swʌŋ] *pt, pp of* **swing**
syllable ['sɪləbl] *n* syllabe *f*
syllabus ['sɪləbəs] *n* programme *m*
symbol ['sɪmbl] *n* symbole *m*;
  symbolic(al) [sɪm'bɔlɪk(l)] *adj*
  symbolique
symmetrical [sɪ'mɛtrɪkl] *adj*
  symétrique
symmetry ['sɪmɪtrɪ] *n* symétrie *f*
sympathetic [sɪmpə'θɛtɪk] *adj*
  (*showing pity*) compatissant(e);
  (*understanding*) bienveillant(e),
  compréhensif(-ive); **~ towards** bien
  disposé(e) envers

  > Be careful not to translate
  > *sympathetic* by the French word
  > *sympathique*.

sympathize ['sɪmpəθaɪz] *vi*: **to ~
  with sb** plaindre qn; (*in grief*) s'associer
  à la douleur de qn; **to ~ with sth**
  comprendre qch
sympathy ['sɪmpəθɪ] *n* (*pity*)
  compassion *f*
symphony ['sɪmfənɪ] *n* symphonie *f*
symptom ['sɪmptəm] *n* symptôme
  m; indice *m*
synagogue ['sɪnəgɔg] *n* synagogue *f*
syndicate ['sɪndɪkɪt] *n* syndicat *m*,
  coopérative *f*; (*Press*) agence *f* de presse
syndrome ['sɪndrəum] *n* syndrome *m*
synonym ['sɪnənɪm] *n* synonyme *m*
synthetic [sɪn'θɛtɪk] *adj* synthétique
Syria ['sɪrɪə] *n* Syrie *f*
syringe [sɪ'rɪndʒ] *n* seringue *f*
syrup ['sɪrəp] *n* sirop *m*; (*BRIT: also:*
  golden ~) mélasse raffinée
system ['sɪstəm] *n* système *m*;
  (*Anat*) organisme *m*; **systematic**
  [sɪstə'mætɪk] *adj* systématique;
  méthodique; **systems analyst** *n*
  analyste-programmeur *m/f*

ta [tɑː] *excl* (*BRIT inf*) merci!
tab [tæb] *n* (*label*) étiquette *f*; (*on drinks
  can etc*) languette *f*; **to keep ~s on** (*fig*)
  surveiller
table ['teɪbl] *n* table *f* ▷ *vt* (*BRIT: motion
  etc*) présenter; **a ~ for 4, please** une
  table pour 4, s'il vous plaît; **to lay** *or*
  set the ~ mettre le couvert *or* la table;
  tablecloth *n* nappe *f*; **table d'hôte**
  [tɑːbl'dəut] *adj* (*meal*) à prix fixe; **table
  lamp** *n* lampe décorative *or* de table;
  tablemat *n* (*for plate*) napperon *m*,
  set *m*; (*for hot dish*) dessous-de-plat *m*
  inv; **tablespoon** *n* cuiller *f* de service;
  (*also*: **tablespoonful**: *as measurement*)
  cuillerée *f* à soupe
tablet ['tæblɪt] *n* (*Med*) comprimé *m*; (*of
  stone*) plaque *f*
table tennis *n* ping-pong *m*, tennis
  m de table
tabloid ['tæblɔɪd] *n* (*newspaper*)
  quotidien *m* populaire
taboo [tə'buː] *adj, n* tabou (*m*)
tack [tæk] *n* (*nail*) petit clou; (*fig*)

direction f ▷ vt (nail) clouer; (sew) bâtir ▷ vi (Naut) tirer un or des bord(s); **to ~ sth on to (the end of) sth** (of letter, book) rajouter qch à la fin de qch

tackle ['tækl] n matériel m, équipement m; (for lifting) appareil m de levage; (Football, Rugby) plaquage m ▷ vt (difficulty, animal, burglar) s'attaquer à; (person: challenge) s'expliquer avec; (Football, Rugby) plaquer

tacky ['tækɪ] adj collant(e); (paint) pas sec (sèche); (pej: poor-quality) minable; (: showing bad taste) ringard(e)

tact [tækt] n tact m; **tactful** adj plein(e) de tact

tactics ['tæktɪks] npl tactique f

tactless ['tæktlɪs] adj qui manque de tact

tadpole ['tædpəul] n têtard m

taffy ['tæfɪ] n (US) (bonbon m au) caramel m

tag [tæg] n étiquette f

tail [teɪl] n queue f; (of shirt) pan m ▷ vt (follow) suivre, filer; **tails** npl (suit) habit m; see also **head**

tailor ['teɪləʳ] n tailleur m (artisan)

Taiwan ['taɪ'wɑːn] n Taïwan (no article); **Taiwanese** [taɪwə'niːz] adj taïwanais(e) ▷ n inv Taïwanais(e)

take [teɪk] vb (pt took, pp ~n) ▷ vt prendre; (gain: prize) remporter; (require: effort, courage) demander; (tolerate) accepter, supporter; (hold: passengers etc) contenir; (accompany) emmener, accompagner; (bring, carry) apporter, emporter; (exam) passer, se présenter à; **to ~ sth from** (drawer etc) prendre qch dans; (person) prendre qch à; **I ~ it that** je suppose que; **to be ~n ill** tomber malade; **it won't ~ long** ça ne prendra pas longtemps; **I was quite ~n with her/it** elle/cela m'a beaucoup plu; **take after** vt fus ressembler à; **take apart** vt démonter; **take away** vt (carry off) emporter; (remove) enlever; (subtract) soustraire; **take back** vt (return) rendre, rapporter; (one's words) retirer; **take down** vt (building) démolir; (letter etc) prendre, écrire; **take in** vt (deceive) tromper, rouler; (understand) comprendre, saisir; (include) couvrir, inclure; (lodger) prendre; (dress, waistband) reprendre; **take off** vi (Aviat) décoller ▷ vt (remove) enlever; **take on** vt (work) accepter, se charger de; (employee) prendre, embaucher; (opponent) accepter de se battre contre; **take out** vt sortir; (remove) enlever; (invite) sortir avec; **to ~ sth out of** (out of drawer etc) prendre qch dans; **to ~ sb out to a restaurant** emmener qn au restaurant; **take over** vt (business) reprendre ▷ vi: **to ~ over from sb** prendre la relève de qn; **take up** vt (one's story) reprendre; (dress) raccourcir; (occupy: time, space) prendre, occuper; (engage in: hobby etc) se mettre à; (accept: offer, challenge) accepter; **takeaway** (BRIT) adj (food) à emporter ▷ n (shop, restaurant) ≈ magasin m qui vend des plats à emporter; **taken** pp of **take**; **is this seat taken?** la place est prise?; **takeoff** n (Aviat) décollage m; **takeout** adj, n (US) = **takeaway**; **takeover** n (Comm) rachat m; **takings** npl (Comm) recette f

talc [tælk] n (also: **~um powder**) talc m

tale [teɪl] n (story) conte m, histoire f; (account) récit m; **to tell ~s** (fig) rapporter

talent ['tælnt] n talent m, don m; **talented** adj doué(e), plein(e) de talent

talk [tɔːk] n (a speech) causerie f, exposé m; (conversation) discussion f; (interview) entretien m; (gossip) racontars mpl (pej) ▷ vi parler; (chatter) bavarder; **talks** npl (Pol etc) entretiens mpl; **to ~ about** parler de; **to ~ sb out of/into doing** persuader qn de ne pas faire/de faire; **to ~ shop** parler métier or affaires; **talk over** vt discuter (de); **talk show** n (TV, Radio) émission-débat f

tall [tɔːl] adj (person) grand(e); (building, tree) haut(e); **to be 6 feet ~** ≈ mesurer 1 mètre 80

tambourine [tæmbə'riːn] n

tambourin m

tame [teɪm] adj apprivoisé(e); (fig: story, style) insipide

tamper ['tæmpə'] vi: **to ~ with** toucher à (en cachette ou sans permission)

tampon ['tæmpən] n tampon m hygiénique or périodique

tan [tæn] n (also: **sun~**) bronzage m ▷ vt, vi bronzer, brunir ▷ adj (colour) marron clair inv

tandem ['tændəm] n tandem m

tangerine [tændʒə'riːn] n mandarine f

tangle ['tæŋgl] n enchevêtrement m; **to get in(to) a ~** s'emmêler

tank [tæŋk] n réservoir m; (for fish) aquarium m; (Mil) char m d'assaut, tank m

tanker ['tæŋkə'] n (ship) pétrolier m, tanker m; (truck) camion-citerne m

tanned [tænd] adj bronzé(e)

tantrum ['tæntrəm] n accès m de colère

Tanzania [tænzə'nɪə] n Tanzanie f

tap [tæp] n (on sink etc) robinet m; (gentle blow) petite tape ▷ vt frapper or taper légèrement; (resources) exploiter, utiliser; (telephone) mettre sur écoute; **on ~** (fig: resources) disponible; **tap dancing** n claquettes fpl

tape [teɪp] n (for tying) ruban m; (also: **magnetic ~**) bande f (magnétique); (cassette) cassette f; (sticky) Scotch® m ▷ vt (record) enregistrer (au magnétoscope or sur cassette); (stick) coller avec du Scotch®; **tape measure** n mètre m à ruban; **tape recorder** n magnétophone m

tapestry ['tæpɪstrɪ] n tapisserie f

tar [tɑː] n goudron m

target ['tɑːgɪt] n cible f; (fig: objective) objectif m

tariff ['tærɪf] n (Comm) tarif m; (taxes) tarif douanier

tarmac ['tɑːmæk] n (BRIT: on road) macadam m; (Aviat) aire f d'envol

tarpaulin [tɑː'pɔːlɪn] n bâche goudronnée

tarragon ['tærəgən] n estragon m

tart [tɑːt] n (Culin) tarte f; (BRIT inf: pej: prostitute) poule f ▷ adj (flavour) âpre, aigrelet(te)

tartan ['tɑːtn] n tartan m ▷ adj écossais(e)

tartar(e) sauce n sauce f tartare

task [tɑːsk] n tâche f; **to take to ~** prendre à partie

taste [teɪst] n goût m; (fig: glimpse, idea) idée f, aperçu m ▷ vt goûter ▷ vi: **to ~ of** (fish etc) avoir le or un goût de; **you can ~ the garlic (in it)** on sent bien l'ail; **to have a ~ of sth** goûter (à) qch; **can I have a ~?** je peux goûter?; **to be in good/bad** or **poor ~** être de bon/mauvais goût; **tasteful** adj de bon goût; **tasteless** adj (food) insipide; (remark) de mauvais goût; **tasty** adj savoureux(-euse), délicieux(-euse)

tatters ['tætəz] npl: **in ~** (also: **tattered**) en lambeaux

tattoo [tə'tuː] n tatouage m; (spectacle) parade f militaire ▷ vt tatouer

taught [tɔːt] pt, pp de **teach**

taunt [tɔːnt] n raillerie f ▷ vt railler

Taurus ['tɔːrəs] n le Taureau

taut [tɔːt] adj tendu(e)

tax [tæks] n (on goods etc) taxe f; (on income) impôts mpl, contributions fpl ▷ vt taxer; imposer; (fig: patience etc) mettre à l'épreuve; **tax disc** n (BRIT Aut) vignette f (automobile); **tax-free** adj exempt(e) d'impôts

taxi ['tæksɪ] n taxi m ▷ vi (Aviat) rouler (lentement) au sol; **can you call me a ~, please?** pouvez-vous m'appeler un taxi, s'il vous plaît?; **taxi driver** n chauffeur m de taxi; **taxi rank** (BRIT), **taxi stand** n station f de taxis

tax payer [-peɪə'] n contribuable m/f

tax return n déclaration f d'impôts or de revenus =

TB n abbr = **tuberculosis**

tea [tiː] n thé m; (BRIT: snack: for children) goûter m; **high ~** (BRIT) collation combinant goûter et dîner; **tea bag** n sachet m de thé; **tea break** n (BRIT) pause-thé f

teach (pt, pp **taught**) [tiːtʃ, tɔːt] vt: **to**

~ sb sth, **to ~ sth to sb** apprendre qch à qn; (*in school etc*) enseigner qch à qn ▷ vi enseigner; **teacher** n (*in secondary school*) professeur m; (*in primary school*) instituteur(-trice); **teaching** n enseignement m

tea: **tea cloth** n (BRIT) torchon m; **teacup** n tasse f à thé

tea leaves npl feuilles fpl de thé

team [tiːm] n équipe f; (*of animals*) attelage m; **team up** vi: **to ~ up (with)** faire équipe (avec)

teapot ['tiːpɔt] n théière f

tear¹ [tɪəʳ] n larme f; **in ~s** en larmes

tear² [tɛəʳ] déchirure f ▷ vb (*pt* **tore**, *pp* **torn**) ▷ vt déchirer ▷ vi se déchirer; **tear apart** vt (*also fig*) déchirer; **tear down** vt (*building, statue*) démolir; (*poster, flag*) arracher; **tear off** vt (*sheet of paper etc*) arracher; (*one's clothes*) enlever à toute vitesse; **tear up** vt (*sheet of paper etc*) déchirer, mettre en morceaux or pièces

tearful ['tɪəful] adj larmoyant(e)

tear gas ['tɪə-] n gaz m lacrymogène

tearoom ['tiːruːm] n salon m de thé

tease [tiːz] vt taquiner; (*unkindly*) tourmenter

tea: **teaspoon** n petite cuiller; (*also*: **teaspoonful**: *as measurement*) ≈ cuillerée f à café; **teatime** n l'heure f du thé; **tea towel** n (BRIT) torchon m (à vaisselle)

technical ['tɛknɪkl] adj technique

technician [tɛk'nɪʃən] n technicien(ne)

technique [tɛk'niːk] n technique f

technology [tɛk'nɔlədʒɪ] n technologie f

teddy (bear) ['tɛdɪ-] n ours m (en peluche)

tedious ['tiːdɪəs] adj fastidieux(-euse)

tee [tiː] n (*Golf*) tee m

teen [tiːn] adj = **teenage** ▷ n (US) = **teenager**

teenage ['tiːneɪdʒ] adj (*fashions etc*) pour jeunes, pour adolescents; (*child*) qui est adolescent(e); **teenager** n

adolescent(e)

teens [tiːnz] npl: **to be in one's ~** être adolescent(e)

teeth [tiːθ] npl of **tooth**

teetotal ['tiː'təutl] adj (*person*) qui ne boit jamais d'alcool

telecommunications ['tɛlɪkəmjuːnɪ'keɪʃənz] n télécommunications fpl

telegram ['tɛlɪgræm] n télégramme m

telegraph pole ['tɛlɪgrɑːf-] n poteau m télégraphique

telephone ['tɛlɪfəun] n téléphone m ▷ vt (*person*) téléphoner à; (*message*) téléphoner; **to be on the ~** (*be speaking*) être au téléphone; **telephone book** n = **telephone directory**; **telephone booth** (BRIT), **telephone box** n cabine f téléphonique; **telephone call** n appel m téléphonique; **telephone directory** n annuaire m (du téléphone); **telephone number** n numéro m de téléphone

telesales ['tɛlɪseɪlz] npl télévente f

telescope ['tɛlɪskəup] n télescope m

televise ['tɛlɪvaɪz] vt téléviser

television ['tɛlɪvɪʒən] n télévision f; **on ~** à la télévision; **television programme** n émission f de télévision

tell (*pt*, *pp* **told**) [tɛl, təuld] vt dire; (*relate: story*) raconter; (*distinguish*): **to ~ sth from** distinguer qch de ▷ vi (*talk*): **to ~ of** parler de; (*have effect*) se faire sentir, se voir; **to ~ sb to do** dire à qn de faire; **to ~ the time** (*know how to*) savoir lire l'heure; **tell off** vt réprimander, gronder; **teller** n (*in bank*) caissier(-ière)

telly ['tɛlɪ] n abbr (BRIT inf: = television) télé f

temp [tɛmp] n (BRIT = temporary worker) intérimaire m/f ▷ vi travailler comme intérimaire

temper ['tɛmpəʳ] n (*nature*) caractère m; (*mood*) humeur f; (*fit of anger*) colère f ▷ vt (*moderate*) tempérer, adoucir; **to be in a ~** être en colère; **to lose one's ~** se mettre en colère

temperament ['tɛmprəmənt]
n (*nature*) tempérament *m*;
temperamental [tɛmprə'mɛntl] *adj*
capricieux(-euse)
temperature ['tɛmprətʃəʳ] *n*
température *f*; **to have** *or* **run a ~** avoir
de la fièvre
temple ['tɛmpl] *n* (*building*) temple *m*;
(*Anat*) tempe *f*
temporary ['tɛmpərərɪ] *adj*
temporaire, provisoire; (*job, worker*)
temporaire
tempt [tɛmpt] *vt* tenter; **to ~ sb into
doing** induire qn à faire; **temptation** *n*
tentation *f*; **tempting** *adj* tentant(e);
(*food*) appétissant(e)
ten [tɛn] *num* dix
tenant ['tɛnənt] *n* locataire *m/f*
tend [tɛnd] *vt* s'occuper de ▷ *vi*: **to ~ to
do** avoir tendance à faire; **tendency**
['tɛndənsɪ] *n* tendance *f*
tender ['tɛndəʳ] *adj* tendre; (*delicate*)
délicat(e); (*sore*) sensible ▷ *n* (*Comm*:
offer) soumission *f*; (*money*): **legal ~**
cours légal ▷ *vt* offrir
tendon ['tɛndən] *n* tendon *m*
tenner ['tɛnəʳ] *n* (*BRIT inf*) billet *m* de
dix livres
tennis ['tɛnɪs] *n* tennis *m*; **tennis ball**
n balle *f* de tennis; **tennis court**
n (court *m* de) tennis *m*; **tennis match**
n match *m* de tennis; **tennis player** *n*
joueur(-euse) de tennis; **tennis racket**
n raquette *f* de tennis
tenor ['tɛnəʳ] *n* (*Mus*) ténor *m*
tenpin bowling ['tɛnpɪn-] *n* (*BRIT*)
bowling *m* (à 10 quilles)
tense [tɛns] *adj* tendu(e) ▷ *n* (*Ling*)
temps *m*
tension ['tɛnʃən] *n* tension *f*
tent [tɛnt] *n* tente *f*
tentative ['tɛntətɪv] *adj* timide,
hésitant(e); (*conclusion*) provisoire
tenth [tɛnθ] *num* dixième
tent: **tent peg** *n* piquet *m* de tente; **tent
pole** *n* montant *m* de tente
tepid ['tɛpɪd] *adj* tiède
term [tə:m] *n* terme *m*; (*Scol*) trimestre

m ▷ *vt* appeler; **terms** *npl* (*conditions*)
conditions *fpl*; (*Comm*) tarif *m*; **in the
short/long ~** à court/long terme; **to
come to ~s with** (*problem*) faire face à;
to be on good ~s with bien s'entendre
avec, être en bons termes avec
terminal ['tə:mɪnl] *adj* (*disease*) dans sa
phase terminale; (*patient*) incurable ▷ *n*
(*Elec*) borne *f*; (*for oil, ore etc, also Comput*)
terminal *m*; (*also*: **air ~**) aérogare *f*;
(*BRIT*: *also*: **coach ~**) gare routière
terminate ['tə:mɪneɪt] *vt* mettre fin à;
(*pregnancy*) interrompre
termini ['tə:mɪnaɪ] *npl of* **terminus**
terminology [tə:mɪ'nɔlədʒɪ] *n*
terminologie *f*
terminus (*pl* **termini**) ['tə:mɪnəs,
'tə:mɪnaɪ] *n* terminus *m* inv
terrace ['tɛrəs] *n* terrasse *f*; (*BRIT*: *row of
houses*) rangée *f* de maisons (*attenantes
les unes aux autres*); **the ~s** (*BRIT Sport*)
les gradins *mpl*; **terraced** *adj* (*garden*)
en terrasses; (*in a row*: *house, cottage etc*)
attenant(e) aux maisons voisines
terrain [tɛ'reɪn] *n* terrain *m* (*sol*)
terrestrial [tɪ'rɛstrɪəl] *adj* terrestre
terrible ['tɛrɪbl] *adj* terrible, atroce;
(*weather, work*) affreux(-euse),
épouvantable; **terribly** *adv*
terriblement; (*very badly*) affreusement
mal
terrier ['tɛrɪəʳ] *n* terrier *m* (*chien*)
terrific [tə'rɪfɪk] *adj* (*very
great*) fantastique, incroyable,
terrible; (*wonderful*) formidable,
sensationnel(le)
terrified ['tɛrɪfaɪd] *adj* terrifié(e); **to be
~ of sth** avoir très peur de qch
terrify ['tɛrɪfaɪ] *vt* terrifier; **terrifying**
adj terrifiant(e)
territorial [tɛrɪ'tɔ:rɪəl] *adj*
territorial(e)
territory ['tɛrɪtərɪ] *n* territoire *m*
terror ['tɛrəʳ] *n* terreur *f*; **terrorism** *n*
terrorisme *m*; **terrorist** *n* terroriste
m/f; **terrorist attack** *n* attentat *m*
terroriste
test [tɛst] *n* (*trial, check*) essai *m*; (*: of*

courage etc) épreuve f; (*Med*) examen m; (*Chem*) analyse f; (*Scol*) interrogation f de contrôle; (*also*: **driving ~**) (examen du) permis m de conduire ▷ vt essayer; mettre à l'épreuve; examiner; analyser; faire subir une interrogation (de contrôle) à

testicle ['tɛstɪkl] n testicule m

testify ['tɛstɪfaɪ] vi (*Law*) témoigner, déposer; **to ~ to sth** (*Law*) attester qch

testimony ['tɛstɪmənɪ] n (*Law*) témoignage m, déposition f

test: **test match** n (*Cricket, Rugby*) match international; **test tube** n éprouvette f

tetanus ['tɛtənəs] n tétanos m

text [tɛkst] n texte m; (*on mobile phone*) texto m, SMS m inv ▷ vt (*inf*) envoyer un texto or SMS à; **textbook** n manuel m

textile ['tɛkstaɪl] n textile m

text message n texto m, SMS m inv

text messaging ['-'mɛsɪdʒɪŋ] n messagerie textuelle

texture ['tɛkstʃə^r] n texture f; (*of skin, paper etc*) grain m

Thai [taɪ] adj thaïlandais(e) ▷ n Thaïlandais(e)

Thailand ['taɪlænd] n Thaïlande f

Thames [tɛmz] n: **the (River) ~** la Tamise

than [ðæn, ðən] conj que; (*with numerals*): **more ~ 10/once** plus de 10/d'une fois; **I have more/less ~ you** j'en ai plus/moins que toi; **she has more apples ~ pears** elle a plus de pommes que de poires; **it is better to phone ~ to write** il vaut mieux téléphoner (plutôt) qu'écrire; **she is older ~ you think** elle est plus âgée que tu le crois

thank [θæŋk] vt remercier, dire merci à; **thanks** npl remerciements mpl ▷ excl merci!; **~ you (very much)** merci (beaucoup); **~ God** Dieu merci; **~s to** prep grâce à; **thankfully** adv (*fortunately*) heureusement; **Thanksgiving (Day)** n jour m d'action de grâce; *voir encadré*

- **THANKSGIVING (DAY)**
-
- **Thanksgiving (Day)** est un
- jour de congé aux États-Unis,
- le quatrième jeudi du mois de
- novembre, commémorant la bonne
- récolte que les Pèlerins venus de
- Grande-Bretagne ont eue en 1621;
- traditionnellement, c'était un jour
- où l'on remerciait Dieu et où l'on
- organisait un grand festin. Une
- fête semblable, mais qui n'a aucun
- rapport avec les Pères Pèlerins, a
- lieu au Canada le deuxième lundi
- d'octobre.

O **KEYWORD**

that [ðæt] adj (*demonstrative: pl* **those**) ce, cet + *vowel or h mute*, cette f; **that man/woman/book** cet homme/cette femme/ce livre; (*not this one*) cet homme-là/cette femme-là/ce livre-là; **that one** celui-là (celle-là)
▷ pron **1** (*demonstrative: pl* **those**) ce; (*not this one*) cela, ça; (*that one*) celui (celle); **who's that?** qui est-ce?; **what's that?** qu'est-ce que c'est?; **is that you?** c'est toi?; **I prefer this to that** je préfère ceci à cela or ça; **that's what he said** c'est or voilà ce qu'il a dit; **will you eat all that?** est-ce que tu vas manger tout ça?; **that is (to say)** c'est-à-dire, à savoir
2 (*relative: subject*) qui; (: *object*) que; (: *after prep*) lequel (laquelle), lesquels (lesquelles) pl; **the book that I read** le livre que j'ai lu; **the books that are in the library** les livres qui sont dans la bibliothèque; **all that I have** tout ce que j'ai; **the box that I put it in** la boîte dans laquelle je l'ai mis; **the people that I spoke to** les gens auxquels or à qui j'ai parlé
3 (*relative: of time*) où; **the day that he came** le jour où il est venu
▷ conj que; **he thought that I was ill** il pensait que j'étais malade

▷ *adv* (*demonstrative*): **I don't like it that much** ça ne me plaît pas tant que ça; **I didn't know it was that bad** je ne savais pas que c'était si *or* aussi mauvais; **it's about that high** c'est à peu près de cette hauteur

thatched [θætʃt] *adj* (*roof*) de chaume; **~ cottage** chaumière *f*
thaw [θɔː] *n* dégel *m* ▷ *vi* (*ice*) fondre; (*food*) dégeler ▷ *vt* (*food*) (faire) dégeler

○ **KEYWORD**

the [ðiː, ðə] *def art* **1** (*gen*) le, la *f*, l' + *vowel or h mute*, les *pl* (NB: *à* + *le(s)* = **au(x)**; *de* + *le* = **du**; *de* + *les* = **des**); **the boy/girl/ink** le garçon/la fille/l'encre; **the children** les enfants; **the history of the world** l'histoire du monde; **give it to the postman** donne-le au facteur; **to play the piano/flute** jouer du piano/de la flûte
2 (+ *adj to form n*) le, la *f*, l' + *vowel or h mute*, les *pl*; **the rich and the poor** les riches et les pauvres; **to attempt the impossible** tenter l'impossible
3 (*in titles*): **Elizabeth the First** Elisabeth première; **Peter the Great** Pierre le Grand
4 (*in comparisons*): **the more he works, the more he earns** plus il travaille, plus il gagne de l'argent

theatre (*us* **theater**) ['θɪətə^r] *n* théâtre *m*; (*Med*: *also*: **operating ~**) salle *f* d'opération
theft [θɛft] *n* vol *m* (*larcin*)
their [ðɛə^r] *adj* leur, leurs *pl*; *see also* **my**; **theirs** *pron* le (la) leur, les leurs; *see also* **mine**¹
them [ðɛm, ðəm] *pron* (*direct*) les; (*indirect*) leur; (*stressed, after prep*) eux (elles); **give me a few of ~** donnez m'en quelques uns (*or* quelques unes); *see also* **me**
theme [θiːm] *n* thème *m*; **theme park** *n* parc *m* à thème

themselves [ðəm'sɛlvz] *pl pron* (*reflexive*) se; (*emphatic, after prep*) eux-mêmes (elles-mêmes); **between ~** entre eux (elles); *see also* **oneself**
then [ðɛn] *adv* (*at that time*) alors, à ce moment-là; (*next*) puis, ensuite; (*and also*) et puis ▷ *conj* (*therefore*) alors, dans ce cas ▷ *adj*: **the ~ president** le président d'alors *or* de l'époque; **by ~** (*past*) à ce moment-là; (*future*) d'ici là; **from ~ on** dès lors; **until ~** jusqu'à ce moment-là, jusque-là
theology [θɪ'ɒlədʒɪ] *n* théologie *f*
theory ['θɪərɪ] *n* théorie *f*
therapist ['θɛrəpɪst] *n* thérapeute *m/f*
therapy ['θɛrəpɪ] *n* thérapie *f*

○ **KEYWORD**

there [ðɛə^r] *adv* **1**: **there is, there are** il y a; **there are 3 of them** (*people, things*) il y en a 3; **there is no-one here/no bread left** il n'y a personne/il n'y a plus de pain; **there has been an accident** il y a eu un accident
2 (*referring to place*) là, là-bas; **it's there** c'est là(-bas); **in/on/up/down there** là-dedans/là-dessus/là-haut/en bas; **he went there on Friday** il y est allé vendredi; **I want that book there** je veux ce livre-là; **there he is!** le voilà!
3: **there, there** (*esp to child*) allons, allons

there: **thereabouts** *adv* (*place*) par là, près de là; (*amount*) environ, à peu près; **thereafter** *adv* par la suite; **thereby** *adv* ainsi; **therefore** *adv* donc, par conséquent
there's ['ðɛəz] = **there is**; **there has**
thermal ['θəːml] *adj* thermique; **~ underwear** sous-vêtements *mpl* en Thermolactyl®
thermometer [θə'mɒmɪtə^r] *n* thermomètre *m*
thermostat ['θəːməustæt] *n* thermostat *m*
these [ðiːz] *pl pron* ceux-ci (celles-ci) ▷ *pl adj* ces; (*not those*): **~ books** ces

livres-ci

thesis (pl **theses**) ['θi:sɪs, 'θi:si:z] n
thèse f

they [ðeɪ] pl pron ils (elles); (stressed)
eux (elles); **~ say that …** (it is said
that) on dit que …; **they'd=they had**;
they would; **they'll=they shall**;
they will; **they're=they are**; **they've
=they have**

thick [θɪk] adj épais(se); (stupid) bête,
borné(e) ▷ n: **in the ~ of** au beau milieu
de, en plein cœur de; **it's 20 cm ~** ça a
20 cm d'épaisseur; **thicken** vi s'épaissir
▷ vt (sauce etc) épaissir; **thickness** n
épaisseur f

thief (pl **thieves**) [θi:f, θi:vz] n
voleur(-euse)

thigh [θaɪ] n cuisse f

thin [θɪn] adj mince; (skinny) maigre;
(soup) peu épais(se); (hair, crowd)
clairsemé(e) ▷ vt (also: **~ down**: sauce,
paint) délayer

thing [θɪŋ] n chose f; (object) objet
m; (contraption) truc m; **things** npl
(belongings) affaires fpl; **the ~ is …** c'est
que …; **the best ~ would be to** le mieux
serait de; **how are ~s?** comment ça va?;
to have a ~ about (be obsessed by) être
obsédé(e) par; (hate) détester; **poor ~!**
le (or la) pauvre!

think (pt, pp **thought**) [θɪŋk, θɔ:t] vi
penser, réfléchir ▷ vt penser, croire;
(imagine) s'imaginer; **what did you ~
of them?** qu'avez-vous pensé d'eux?;
to ~ about sth/sb penser à qch/qn;
I'll ~ about it je vais y réfléchir; **to ~ of
doing** avoir l'idée de faire; **I ~ so/not** je
crois or pense que oui/non; **to ~ well
of** avoir une haute opinion de; **think
over** vt bien réfléchir à; **think up** vt
inventer, trouver

third [θə:d] num troisième ▷ n (fraction)
tiers m; (Aut) troisième (vitesse) f; (BRIT
Scol: degree) ≈ licence f avec mention
passable; **thirdly** adv troisièmement;
third party insurance n (BRIT)
assurance f au tiers; **Third World** n: **the
Third World** le Tiers-Monde

thirst [θə:st] n soif f; **thirsty** adj qui a
soif, assoiffé(e); (work) qui donne soif;
to be thirsty avoir soif

thirteen [θə:'ti:n] num treize;
thirteenth [-'ti:nθ] num treizième

thirtieth ['θə:tɪɪθ] num trentième

thirty ['θə:tɪ] num trente

KEYWORD

this [ðɪs] adj (demonstrative: pl **these**)
ce, cet + vowel or h mute, cette f; **this
man/woman/book** cet homme/cette
femme/ce livre; (not that) cet homme-
ci/cette femme-ci/ce livre-ci; **this one**
celui-ci (celle-ci)
▷ pron (demonstrative: pl **these**) ce;
(not that one) celui-ci (celle-ci), ceci;
who's this? qui est-ce?; **what's this?**
qu'est-ce que c'est?; **I prefer this
to that** je préfère ceci à cela; **this is
where I live** c'est ici que j'habite; **this
is what he said** voici ce qu'il a dit; **this
is Mr Brown** (in introductions) je vous
présente Mr Brown; (in photo) c'est Mr
Brown; (on telephone) ici Mr Brown
▷ adv (demonstrative): **it was about this
big** c'était à peu près de cette grandeur
or grand comme ça; **I didn't know
it was this bad** je ne savais pas que
c'était si or aussi mauvais

thistle ['θɪsl] n chardon m

thorn [θɔ:n] n épine f

thorough ['θʌrə] adj (search)
minutieux(-euse); (knowledge,
research) approfondi(e); (work,
person) consciencieux(-euse);
(cleaning) à fond; **thoroughly** adv
(search) minutieusement; (study)
en profondeur; (clean) à fond; (very)
tout à fait

those [ðəuz] pl pron ceux-là (celles-là)
▷ pl adj ces; (not these): **~ books** ces
livres-là

though [ðəu] conj bien que + sub,
quoique + sub ▷ adv pourtant

thought [θɔ:t] pt, pp of **think** ▷ n

pensée f; (idea) idée f; (opinion) avis m;
thoughtful adj (deep in thought)
pensif(-ive); (serious) réfléchie(e);
(considerate) prévenant(e); **thoughtless**
adj qui manque de considération
thousand ['θaʊzənd] num mille; **one**
~ mille; **two** ~ deux mille; **~s of** des
milliers de; **thousandth** num millième
thrash [θræʃ] vt rouer de coups; (as
punishment) donner une correction à;
(inf: defeat) battre à plate(s) couture(s)
thread [θrɛd] n fil m; (of screw) pas m,
filetage m ▷ vt (needle) enfiler
threat [θrɛt] n menace f; **threaten** vi
(storm) menacer ▷ vt: **to threaten sb**
with sth/to do menacer qn de qch/de
faire; **threatening** adj menaçant(e)
three [θriː] num trois; **three-**
dimensional adj à trois dimensions;
three-piece suite n salon m (canapé
et deux fauteuils); **three-quarters** npl
trois-quarts mpl; **three-quarters full**
aux trois-quarts plein
threshold ['θrɛʃhəʊld] n seuil m
threw [θruː] pt of **throw**
thrill [θrɪl] n (excitement) émotion f,
sensation forte; (shudder) frisson m
▷ vt (audience) électriser; **thrilled** adj:
thrilled (with) ravi(e) de; **thriller**
n film m (or roman m or pièce f) à
suspense; **thrilling** adj (book, play
etc) saisissant(e); (news, discovery)
excitant(e)
thriving ['θraɪvɪŋ] adj (business,
community) prospère
throat [θrəʊt] n gorge f; **to have a sore**
~ avoir mal à la gorge
throb [θrɒb] vi (heart) palpiter; (engine)
vibrer; **my head is ~bing** j'ai des
élancements dans la tête
throne [θrəʊn] n trône m
through [θruː] prep (from) pendant,
durant; (by means of) par, par
l'intermédiaire de; (owing to) à cause
de ▷ adj (ticket, train, passage) direct(e)
▷ adv à travers; **from Monday ~**
Friday (us) de lundi à vendredi; **to put**
sb ~ to sb (Tel) passer qn à qn; **to be**

~ (brit: Tel) avoir la communication;
(esp us: have finished) avoir fini; **"no ~**
traffic" (us) "passage interdit"; **"no ~**
road" (brit) "impasse"; **throughout**
prep (place) partout dans; (time) durant
tout(e) le (la) ▷ adv partout
throw [θrəʊ] n jet m; (Sport) lancer
m ▷ vt (pt **threw**, pp **~n**) lancer, jeter;
(Sport) lancer; (rider) désarçonner; (fig)
décontenancer; **to ~ a party** donner
une réception; **throw away** vt jeter;
(money) gaspiller; **throw in** vt (Sport:
ball) remettre en jeu; (include) ajouter;
throw off vt se débarrasser de; **throw**
out vt jeter; (reject) rejeter; (person)
mettre à la porte; **throw up** vi vomir
thru [θruː] (us) = **through**
thrush [θrʌʃ] n (Zool) grive f
thrust [θrʌst] vt (pt, pp ~) pousser
brusquement; (push in) enfoncer
thud [θʌd] n bruit sourd
thug [θʌɡ] n voyou m
thumb [θʌm] n (Anat) pouce m ▷ vt: **to**
~ **a lift** faire de l'auto-stop, arrêter une
voiture; **thumbtack** n (us) punaise
f (clou)
thump [θʌmp] n grand coup m; (sound)
bruit sourd ▷ vt cogner sur ▷ vi cogner
frapper
thunder ['θʌndəʳ] n tonnerre m ▷ vi
tonner; (train etc): **to ~ past** passer dan
un grondement or un bruit de tonnerre
thunderstorm n orage m
Thur(s) abbr (= Thursday) jeu
Thursday ['θəːzdɪ] n jeudi m
thus [ðʌs] adv ainsi
thwart [θwɔːt] vt contrecarrer
thyme [taɪm] n thym m
Tibet [tɪ'bɛt] n Tibet m
tick [tɪk] n (sound: of clock) tic-tac m;
(mark) coche f; (Zool) tique f; (brit
inf): **in a ~** dans un instant ▷ vi faire
tic-tac ▷ vt (item on list) cocher; **tick**
off vt (item on list) cocher; (person)
réprimander, attraper
ticket ['tɪkɪt] n billet m; (for bus, tube)
ticket m; (in shop: on goods) étiquette
f; (for library) carte f; (also: **parking** ~)

contravention f, p.-v. m; **ticket barrier** n (BRIT: Rail) portillon m automatique; **ticket collector** n contrôleur(-euse); **ticket inspector** n contrôleur(-euse); **ticket machine** n billetterie f automatique; **ticket office** n guichet m, bureau m de vente des billets

tickle ['tɪkl] vi chatouiller ▷ vt chatouiller; **ticklish** adj (person) chatouilleux(-euse); (problem) épineux(-euse)

tide [taɪd] n marée f; (fig: of events) cours m

tidy ['taɪdɪ] adj (room) bien rangé(e); (dress, work) net (nette), soigné(e); (person) ordonné(e), qui a de l'ordre ▷ vt (also: ~ up) ranger

tie [taɪ] n (string etc) cordon m; (BRIT: also: **neck~**) cravate f; (fig: link) lien m; (Sport: draw) égalité f de points; match nul ▷ vt (parcel) attacher; (ribbon) nouer ▷ vi (Sport) faire match nul; finir à égalité de points; **to ~ sth in a bow** faire un nœud à or avec qch; **to ~ a knot in sth** faire un nœud à qch; **tie down** vt (fig); **to ~ sb down to** contraindre qn à accepter; **to feel ~d down** (by relationship) se sentir coincé(e); **tie up** vt (parcel) ficeler; (dog, boat) attacher; (prisoner) ligoter; (arrangements) conclure; **to be ~d up** (busy) être pris(e) or occupé(e)

tier [tɪəʳ] n gradin m; (of cake) étage m

tiger ['taɪgəʳ] n tigre m

tight [taɪt] adj (rope) tendu(e), raide; (clothes) étroit(e), très juste; (budget, programme, bend) serré(e); (control) strict(e), sévère; (inf: drunk) ivre, rond(e) ▷ adv (squeeze) très fort; (shut) à bloc, hermétiquement; **hold ~!** accrochez-vous bien!; **tighten** vt (rope) tendre; (screw) resserrer; (control) renforcer ▷ vi se tendre; se resserrer; **tightly** adv (grasp) bien, très fort; **tights** npl (BRIT) collant m

tile [taɪl] n (on roof) tuile f; (on wall or floor) carreau m

till [tɪl] n caisse (enregistreuse) f ▷ prep, conj = **until**

tilt [tɪlt] vt pencher, incliner ▷ vi pencher, être incliné(e)

timber ['tɪmbəʳ] n (material) bois m de construction

time [taɪm] n temps m; (epoch: often pl) époque f, temps; (by clock) heure f; (moment) moment m; (occasion, also Math) fois f; (Mus) mesure f ▷ vt (race) chronométrer; (programme) minuter; (visit) fixer; (remark etc) choisir le moment de; **a long ~** un long moment, longtemps; **four at a ~** quatre à la fois; **for the ~ being** pour le moment; **from ~ to ~** de temps en temps; **at ~s** parfois; **in ~** (soon enough) à temps; (after some time) avec le temps, à la longue; (Mus) en mesure; **in a week's ~** dans une semaine; **in no ~** en un rien de temps; **any ~** n'importe quand; **on ~** à l'heure; **5 ~s 5** 5 fois 5; **what ~ is it?** quelle heure est-il?; **what ~ is the museum/shop open?** à quelle heure ouvre le musée/magasin?; **to have a good ~** bien s'amuser; **time limit** n limite f de temps, délai m; **timely** adj opportun(e); **timer** n (in kitchen) compte-minutes m inv; (Tech) minuteur m; **time-share** n maison f/appartement m en multipropriété; **timetable** n (Rail) (indicateur m) horaire m; (Scol) emploi m du temps; **time zone** n fuseau m horaire

timid ['tɪmɪd] adj timide; (easily scared) peureux(-euse)

timing ['taɪmɪŋ] n (Sport) chronométrage m; **the ~ of his resignation** le moment choisi pour sa démission

tin [tɪn] n étain m; (also: ~ **plate**) fer-blanc m; (BRIT: can) boîte f (de conserve); (: for baking) moule m (à gâteau); (for storage) boîte f; **tinfoil** n papier m d'étain or d'aluminium

tingle ['tɪŋgl] vi picoter; (person) avoir des picotements

tinker ['tɪŋkəʳ]; **tinker with** vt fus bricoler, rafistoler

tinned [tɪnd] *adj* (BRIT: *food*) en boîte, en conserve

tin opener [-'əupnə^r] *n* (BRIT) ouvre-boîte(s) *m*

tinsel ['tɪnsl] *n* guirlandes *fpl* de Noël (*argentées*)

tint [tɪnt] *n* teinte *f*; (*for hair*) shampooing colorant; **tinted** *adj* (*hair*) teint(e); (*spectacles, glass*) teinté(e)

tiny ['taɪnɪ] *adj* minuscule

tip [tɪp] *n* (*end*) bout *m*; (*gratuity*) pourboire *m*; (BRIT: *for rubbish*) décharge *f*; (*advice*) tuyau *m* ▷ *vt* (*waiter*) donner un pourboire à; (*tilt*) incliner; (*overturn: also*: **~ over**) renverser; (*empty: also*: **~ out**) déverser; **how much should I ~?** combien de pourboire est-ce qu'il faut laisser?; **tip off** *vt* prévenir, avertir

tiptoe ['tɪptəu] *n*: **on ~** sur la pointe des pieds

tire ['taɪə^r] *n* (US) = **tyre** ▷ *vt* fatiguer ▷ *vi* se fatiguer; **tired** *adj* fatigué(e); **to be tired of** en avoir assez de, être las (lasse) de; **tire pressure** (US) = **tyre pressure**; **tiring** *adj* fatigant(e)

tissue ['tɪʃuː] *n* tissu *m*; (*paper handkerchief*) mouchoir *m* en papier, kleenex® *m*; **tissue paper** *n* papier *m* de soie

tit [tɪt] *n* (*bird*) mésange *f*; **to give ~ for tat** rendre coup pour coup

title ['taɪtl] *n* titre *m*

T-junction ['tiː'dʒʌŋkʃən] *n* croisement *m* en T

TM *n abbr* = **trademark**

 KEYWORD

to [tuː, tə] *prep* **1** (*direction*) à; (*towards*) vers; envers; **to go to France/Portugal/London/school** aller en France/au Portugal/à Londres/à l'école; **to go to Claude's/the doctor's** aller chez Claude/le docteur; **the road to Edinburgh** la route d'Édimbourg **2** (*as far as*) (jusqu')à; **to count to 10** compter jusqu'à 10; **from 40 to 50**

people de 40 à 50 personnes

3 (*with expressions of time*): **a quarter to 5** 5 heures moins le quart; **it's twenty to 3** il est 3 heures moins vingt

4 (*for, of*) de; **the key to the front door** la clé de la porte d'entrée; **a letter to his wife** une lettre (adressée) à sa femme

5 (*expressing indirect object*) à; **to give sth to sb** donner qch à qn; **to talk to sb** parler à qn; **to be a danger to sb** être dangereux(-euse) pour qn

6 (*in relation to*) à; **3 goals to 2** 3 (buts) à 2; **30 miles to the gallon** ≈ 9,4 litres aux cent (km)

7 (*purpose, result*): **to come to sb's aid** venir au secours de qn, porter secours à qn; **to sentence sb to death** condamner qn à mort; **to my surprise** à ma grande surprise

▷ *with vb* **1** (*simple infinitive*): **to go/eat** aller/manger

2 (*following another vb*): **to want/try/start to do** vouloir/essayer de/commencer à faire

3 (*with vb omitted*): **I don't want to** je ne veux pas

4 (*purpose, result*) pour; **I did it to help you** je l'ai fait pour vous aider

5 (*equivalent to relative clause*): **I have things to do** j'ai des choses à faire; **the main thing is to try** l'important est d'essayer

6 (*after adjective etc*): **ready to go** prêt(e) à partir; **too old/young to ...** trop vieux/jeune pour ...

▷ *adv*: **push/pull the door to** tirez/poussez la porte

toad [təud] *n* crapaud *m*; **toadstool** *n* champignon (vénéneux)

toast [təust] *n* (Culin) pain grillé, toast *m*; (*drink, speech*) toast ▷ *vt* (Culin) faire griller; (*drink to*) porter un toast à; **toaster** *n* grille-pain *m inv*

tobacco [tə'bækəu] *n* tabac *m*

toboggan [tə'bɔgən] *n* toboggan *m*; (*child's*) luge *f*

today [təˈdeɪ] adv, n (also fig) aujourd'hui (m)

toddler [ˈtɒdlər] n enfant m/f qui commence à marcher, bambin m

toe [təʊ] n doigt m de pied, orteil m; (of shoe) bout m ▷ vt: **to ~ the line** (fig) obéir, se conformer; **toenail** n ongle m de l'orteil

toffee [ˈtɒfɪ] n caramel m

together [təˈgɛðər] adv ensemble; (at same time) en même temps; **~ with** prep avec

toilet [ˈtɔɪlət] n (BRIT: lavatory) toilettes fpl, cabinets mpl; **to go to the ~** aller aux toilettes; **where's the ~?** où sont les toilettes?; **toilet bag** n (BRIT) nécessaire m de toilette; **toilet paper** n papier m hygiénique; **toiletries** npl articles mpl de toilette; **toilet roll** n rouleau m de papier hygiénique

token [ˈtəʊkən] n (sign) marque f, témoignage m; (metal disc) jeton m ▷ adj (fee, strike) symbolique; **book/record ~** (BRIT) chèque-livre/-disque m

Tokyo [ˈtəʊkjəʊ] n Tokyo

told [təʊld] pt, pp of **tell**

tolerant [ˈtɒlərnt] adj: **~ (of)** tolérant(e) (à l'égard de)

tolerate [ˈtɒləreɪt] vt supporter

toll [təʊl] n (tax, charge) péage m ▷ vi (bell) sonner; **the accident ~ on the roads** le nombre des victimes de la route; **toll call** n (US Tel) appel m (à) longue distance; **toll-free** adj (US) gratuit(e) ▷ adv gratuitement

tomato [təˈmɑːtəʊ] (pl **-es**) n tomate f; **tomato sauce** n sauce f tomate

tomb [tuːm] n tombe f; **tombstone** n pierre tombale

tomorrow [təˈmɒrəʊ] adv, n (also fig) demain (m); **the day after ~** après-demain; **a week ~** demain en huit; **~ morning** demain matin

ton [tʌn] n tonne f (BRIT: = 1016 kg; US = 907 kg; metric = 1000 kg); **~s of** (inf) des tas de

tone [təʊn] n ton m; (of radio, BRIT Tel) tonalité f ▷ vi (also: **~ in**) s'harmoniser;

tone down vt (colour, criticism) adoucir

tongs [tɒŋz] npl pinces fp (for coal) pincettes fpl; (for hair) fer m à friser

tongue [tʌŋ] n langue f; **~ in cheek** adv ironiquement

tonic [ˈtɒnɪk] n (Med) tonique m; (also: **~ water**) Schweppes® m

tonight [təˈnaɪt] adv, n cette nuit; (this evening) ce soir

tonne [tʌn] n (BRIT: metric ton) tonne f

tonsil [ˈtɒnsl] n amygdale f; **tonsillitis** [tɒnsɪˈlaɪtɪs] n: **to have tonsillitis** avoir une angine or une amygdalite

too [tuː] adv (excessively) trop; (also) aussi; **~ much** (as adv) trop; (as adj) trop de; **~ many** adj trop de

took [tʊk] pt of **take**

tool [tuːl] n outil m; **tool box** n boîte f à outils; **tool kit** n trousse f à outils

tooth (pl **teeth**) [tuːθ, tiːθ] n (Anat, Tech) dent f; **to brush one's teeth** se laver les dents; **toothache** n mal m de dents; **to have toothache** avoir mal aux dents; **toothbrush** n brosse f à dents; **toothpaste** n (pâte f) dentifrice m; **toothpick** n cure-dent m

top [tɒp] n (of mountain, head) sommet m; (of page, ladder) haut m; (of box, cupboard, table) dessus m; (lid: of box, jar) couvercle m; (: of bottle) bouchon m; (toy) toupie f; (Dress: blouse etc) haut m; (: of pyjamas) veste f ▷ adj du haut; (in rank) premier(-ière); (best) meilleur(e) ▷ vt (exceed) dépasser; (be first in) être en tête de; **from ~ to bottom** de fond en comble; **on ~ of** sur; (in addition to) en plus de; **over the ~** (inf: behaviour etc) qui dépasse les limites; **top up** (US **top off**) vt (bottle) remplir; (salary) compléter; **to ~ up one's mobile (phone)** recharger son compte; **top floor** n dernier étage; **top hat** n haut-de-forme m

topic [ˈtɒpɪk] n sujet m, thème m; **topical** adj d'actualité

topless [ˈtɒplɪs] adj (bather etc) aux seins nus

topping [ˈtɒpɪŋ] n (Culin) couche de

crème, fromage etc qui recouvre un plat

topple ['tɔpl] *vt* renverser, faire tomber ▷ *vi* basculer; tomber

top-up ['tɔpʌp] *n* (*for mobile phone*) recharge *f*, minutes *fpl*; **top-up card** *n* (*for mobile phone*) recharge *f*

torch [tɔːtʃ] *n* torche *f*; (BRIT: *electric*) lampe *f* de poche

tore [tɔːʳ] *pt of* **tear²**

torment *n* ['tɔːment] tourment *m* ▷ *vt* [tɔːˈment] tourmenter; (*fig: annoy*) agacer

torn [tɔːn] *pp of* **tear²**

tornado [tɔːˈneɪdəu] (*pl* **~es**) *n* tornade *f*

torpedo [tɔːˈpiːdəu] (*pl* **~es**) *n* torpille *f*

torrent ['tɔrnt] *n* torrent *m*; **torrential** [tɔˈrenʃl] torrentiel(le)

tortoise ['tɔːtəs] *n* tortue *f*

torture ['tɔːtʃəʳ] *n* torture *f* ▷ *vt* torturer

Tory ['tɔːrɪ] *adj, n* (BRIT Pol) tory *m/f*, conservateur(-trice)

toss [tɔs] *vt* lancer, jeter; (BRIT: *pancake*) faire sauter; (*head*) rejeter en arrière ▷ *vi*: **to ~ up for sth** (BRIT) jouer qch à pile ou face; **to ~ a coin** jouer à pile ou face; **to ~ and turn** (*in bed*) se tourner et se retourner

total ['təutl] *adj* total(e) ▷ *n* total *m* ▷ *vt* (*add up*) faire le total de, additionner; (*amount to*) s'élever à

totalitarian [təutælɪˈtɛərɪən] *adj* totalitaire

totally ['təutəlɪ] *adv* totalement

touch [tʌtʃ] *n* contact *m*, toucher *m*; (*sense, skill: of pianist etc*) toucher *m* ▷ *vt* (*gen*) toucher; (*tamper with*) toucher à; **a ~ of** (*fig*) un petit peu de; une touche de; **to get in ~ with** prendre contact avec; **to lose ~** (*friends*) se perdre de vue; **touch down** *vi* (Aviat) atterrir; (*on sea*) amerrir; **touchdown** *n* (Aviat) atterrissage *m*; (*on sea*) amerrissage *m*; (US Football) essai *m*; **touched** *adj* (*moved*) touché(e); **touching** *adj* touchant(e), attendrissant(e); **touchline** *n* (Sport) (ligne *f* de) touche

f; **touch-sensitive** *adj* (*keypad*) à effleurement; (*screen*) tactile

tough [tʌf] *adj* dur(e); (*resistant*) résistant(e), solide; (*meat*) dur, coriace; (*firm*) inflexible; (*task, problem, situation*) difficile

tour ['tuəʳ] *n* voyage *m*; (*also:* **package ~**) voyage organisé; (*of town, museum*) tour *m*, visite *f*; (*by band*) tournée *f* ▷ *vt* visiter; **tour guide** *n* (*person*) guide *m/f*

tourism ['tuərɪzm] *n* tourisme *m*

tourist ['tuərɪst] *n* touriste *m/f* ▷ *cpd* touristique; **tourist office** *n* syndicat *m* d'initiative

tournament ['tuənəmənt] *n* tournoi *m*

tour operator *n* (BRIT) organisateur *m* de voyages, tour-opérateur *m*

tow [təu] *vt* remorquer; (*caravan, trailer*) tracter; **"on ~",** (US) **"in ~"** (Aut) "véhicule en remorque"; **tow away** *vt* (*subj: police*) emmener à la fourrière; (: *breakdown service*) remorquer

towel ['tauəl] *n* serviette *f* (de toilette); **towelling** *n* (*fabric*) tissu-éponge *m*

tower ['tauəʳ] *n* tour *f*; **tower block** *n* (BRIT) tour *f* (d'habitation)

town [taun] *n* ville *f*; **to go to ~** aller en ville; (*fig*) y mettre le paquet; **town centre** *n* (BRIT) centre *m* de la ville, centre-ville *m*; **town hall** *n* ≈ mairie *f*

tow truck *n* (US) dépanneuse *f*

toxic ['tɔksɪk] *adj* toxique

toy [tɔɪ] *n* jouet *m*; **toy with** *vt fus* jouer avec; (*idea*) caresser; **toyshop** *n* magasin *m* de jouets

trace [treɪs] *n* trace *f* ▷ *vt* (*draw*) tracer, dessiner; (*follow*) suivre la trace de; (*locate*) retrouver

tracing paper ['treɪsɪŋ-] *n* papier-calque *m*

track [træk] *n* (*mark*) trace *f*; (*path: gen*) chemin *m*, piste *f*; (: *of bullet etc*) trajectoire *f*; (: *of suspect, animal*) piste *f*; (Rail) voie ferrée, rails *mpl*; (*on tape,*

Comput, Sport) piste; (*on CD*) piste *f*; (*on record*) plage *f* ▷ *vt* suivre la trace or la piste de; **to keep ~ of** suivre; **track down** *vt* (*prey*) trouver et capturer; (*sth lost*) finir par retrouver; **tracksuit** *n* survêtement *m*

tractor ['træktəʳ] *n* tracteur *m*

trade [treɪd] *n* commerce *m*; (*skill, job*) métier *m* ▷ *vi* faire du commerce ▷ *vt* (*exchange*): **to ~ sth (for sth)** échanger qch (contre qch); **to ~ with/in** faire du commerce avec/le commerce de; **trade in** *vt* (*old car etc*) faire reprendre; **trademark** *n* marque *f* de fabrique; **trader** *n* commerçant(e), négociant(e); **tradesman** (*irreg*) *n* (*shopkeeper*) commerçant *m*; **trade union** *n* syndicat *m*

trading ['treɪdɪŋ] *n* affaires *fpl*, commerce *m*

tradition [trəˈdɪʃən] *n* tradition *f*; **traditional** *adj* traditionnel(le)

traffic ['træfɪk] *n* trafic *m*; (*cars*) circulation *f* ▷ *vi*: **to ~ in** (*pej: liquor, drugs*) faire le trafic de; **traffic circle** *n* (*US*) rond-point *m*; **traffic island** *n* refuge *m* (pour piétons); **traffic jam** *n* embouteillage *m*; **traffic lights** *npl* feux *mpl* (de signalisation); **traffic warden** *n* contractuel(le)

tragedy ['trædʒədɪ] *n* tragédie *f*

tragic ['trædʒɪk] *adj* tragique

trail [treɪl] *n* (*tracks*) trace *f*, piste *f*; (*path*) chemin *m*, piste; (*of smoke etc*) traînée *f* ▷ *vt* (*drag*) traîner, tirer; (*follow*) suivre ▷ *vi* traîner; (*in game, contest*) être en retard; **trailer** *n* (*Aut*) remorque *f*; (*US*) caravane *f*; (*Cine*) bande-annonce *f*

train [treɪn] *n* train *m*; (*in underground*) rame *f*; (*of dress*) traîne *f*; (*BRIT: series*): **~ of events** série *f* d'événements ▷ *vt* (*apprentice, doctor etc*) former; (*Sport*) entraîner; (*dog*) dresser; (*memory*) exercer; (*point: gun etc*): **to ~ sth on** braquer qch sur ▷ *vi* recevoir sa formation; (*Sport*) s'entraîner; **one's ~ of thought** le fil de sa pensée; **what**

time does the ~ from Paris get in? à quelle heure arrive le train de Paris?; **is this the ~ for ...?** c'est bien le train pour...?; **trainee** [treɪˈniː] *n* stagiaire *m/f*; (*in trade*) apprenti(e); **trainer** *n* (*Sport*) entraîneur(-euse); (*of dogs etc*) dresseur(-euse); **trainers** *npl* (*shoes*) chaussures *fpl* de sport; **training** *n* formation *f*; (*Sport*) entraînement *m*; (*of dog etc*) dressage *m*; **in training** (*Sport*) à l'entraînement; (*fit*) en forme; **training course** *n* cours *m* de formation professionnelle; **training shoes** *npl* chaussures *fpl* de sport

trait [treɪt] *n* trait *m* (de caractère)

traitor ['treɪtəʳ] *n* traître *m*

tram [træm] *n* (*BRIT: also: ~car*) tram(way) *m*

tramp [træmp] *n* (*person*) vagabond(e), clochard(e); (*inf: pej: woman*): **to be a ~** être coureuse

trample ['træmpl] *vt*: **to ~ (underfoot)** piétiner

trampoline ['træmpəliːn] *n* trampoline *m*

tranquil ['træŋkwɪl] *adj* tranquille; **tranquillizer** (*US* **tranquilizer**) *n* (*Med*) tranquillisant *m*

transaction [trænˈzækʃən] *n* transaction *f*

transatlantic ['trænzətˈlæntɪk] *adj* transatlantique

transcript ['trænskrɪpt] *n* transcription *f* (*texte*)

transfer *n* ['trænsfəʳ] (*gen, also Sport*) transfert *m*; (*Pol: of power*) passation *f*; (*of money*) virement *m*; (*picture, design*) décalcomanie *f*; (*: stick-on*) autocollant *m* ▷ *vt* [trænsˈfəːʳ] transférer; passer; virer; **to ~ the charges** (*BRIT Tel*) téléphoner en P.C.V.

transform [trænsˈfɔːm] *vt* transformer; **transformation** *n* transformation *f*

transfusion [trænsˈfjuːʒən] *n* transfusion *f*

transit ['trænzɪt] *n*: **in ~** en transit

transition [trænˈzɪʃən] *n* transition *f*

transitive ['trænzɪtɪv] *adj* (*Ling*)
transitif(-ive)

translate [trænz'leɪt] *vt*: **to ~
(from/into)** traduire (du/en); **can
you ~ this for me?** pouvez-vous
me traduire ceci?; **translation**
[trænz'leɪʃən] *n* traduction *f*; (*Scol: as
opposed to prose*) version *f*; **translator** *n*
traducteur(-trice)

transmission [trænz'mɪʃən] *n*
transmission *f*

transmit [trænz'mɪt] *vt* transmettre;
(*Radio, TV*) émettre; **transmitter** *n*
émetteur *m*

transparent [træns'pærnt] *adj*
transparent(e)

transplant [ˈtrænsplɑːnt] (*Med*)
transplantation *f*

transport *n* ['trænspɔːt] transport
m ▷ *vt* [træns'pɔːt] transporter;
transportation [trænspɔː'teɪʃən] *n*
(*moyen m de*) transport *m*

transvestite [trænz'vɛstaɪt] *n*
travesti(e)

trap [træp] *n* (*snare, trick*) piège *m*;
(*carriage*) cabriolet *m* ▷ *vt* prendre au
piège; (*confine*) coincer

trash [træʃ] *n* (*pej: goods*) camelote *f*;
(*: nonsense*) sottises *fpl*; (*us: rubbish*)
ordures *fpl*; **trash can** *n* (*us*) poubelle *f*

trauma ['trɔːmə] *n* traumatisme *m*;
traumatic [trɔː'mætɪk] *adj*
traumatisant(e)

travel ['trævl] *n* voyage(s) *m(pl)* ▷ *vi*
voyager; (*news, sound*) se propager
▷ *vt* (*distance*) parcourir; **travel
agency** *n* agence *f* de voyages;
travel agent *n* agent *m* de voyages;
travel insurance *n* assurance-
voyage *f*; **traveller** (*us* **traveler**) *n*
voyageur(-euse); **traveller's cheque**
(*us* **traveler's check**) *n* chèque *m* de
voyage; **travelling** (*us* **traveling**) *n*
voyage(s) *m(pl)*; **travel-sick** *adj*: **to get
travel-sick** avoir le mal de la route (*or*
de mer *or* de l'air); **travel sickness** *n*
mal *m* de la route (*or* de mer *or* de l'air)

tray [treɪ] *n* (*for carrying*) plateau *m*; (*on
desk*) corbeille *f*

treacherous ['trɛtʃərəs] *adj*
traître(sse); (*ground, tide*) dont il faut
se méfier

treacle ['triːkl] *n* mélasse *f*

tread [trɛd] *n* (*step*) pas *m*; (*sound*) bruit
m de pas; (*of tyre*) chape *f*, bande *f* de
roulement ▷ *vi* (*pt* **trod**, *pp* **trodden**)
marcher; **tread on** *vt fus* marcher sur

treasure ['trɛʒə*ʳ*] *n* trésor *m* ▷ *vt*
(*value*) tenir beaucoup à; **treasurer** *n*
trésorier(-ière)

treasury ['trɛʒərɪ] *n*: **the T~**, (*us*) **the
T~ Department** ≈ le ministère des
Finances

treat [triːt] *n* petit cadeau, petite
surprise ▷ *vt* traiter; **to ~ sb to
sth** offrir qch à qn; **treatment** *n*
traitement *m*

treaty ['triːtɪ] *n* traité *m*

treble ['trɛbl] *adj* triple ▷ *vt, vi* tripler

tree [triː] *n* arbre *m*

trek [trɛk] *n* (*long walk*) randonnée *f*;
(*tiring walk*) longue marche, trotte *f*

tremble ['trɛmbl] *vi* trembler

tremendous [trɪ'mɛndəs] *adj*
(*enormous*) énorme; (*excellent*)
formidable, fantastique

trench [trɛntʃ] *n* tranchée *f*

trend [trɛnd] *n* (*tendency*) tendance *f*; (*of
events*) cours *m*; (*fashion*) mode *f*; **trendy**
adj (*idea, person*) dans le vent; (*clothes*)
dernier cri *inv*

trespass ['trɛspəs] *vi*: **to ~ on**
s'introduire sans permission dans;
"no ~ing" "propriété privée", "défense
d'entrer"

trial ['traɪəl] *n* (*Law*) procès *m*, jugement
m; (*test: of machine etc*) essai *m*; **trials**
npl (*unpleasant experiences*) épreuves *fpl*;
trial period *n* période *f* d'essai

triangle ['traɪæŋgl] *n* (*Math, Mus*)
triangle *m*

triangular [traɪ'æŋgjulə*ʳ*] *adj*
triangulaire

tribe [traɪb] *n* tribu *f*

tribunal [traɪ'bjuːnl] *n* tribunal *m*

tribute ['trɪbjuːt] *n* tribut *m*, hommage

m; **to pay ~ to** rendre hommage à
trick [trɪk] n (magic) tour m; (joke, prank)
tour, farce f; (skill, knack) astuce f; (Cards)
levée f ▷ vt attraper, rouler; **to play a ~
on sb** jouer un tour à qn; **that should
do the ~** (fam) ça devrait faire l'affaire
trickle ['trɪkl] n (of water etc) filet m ▷ vi
couler en un filet or goutte à goutte
tricky ['trɪkɪ] adj difficile, délicat(e)
tricycle ['traɪsɪkl] n tricycle m
trifle ['traɪfl] n bagatelle f; (Culin)
≈ diplomate m ▷ adv: **a ~ long** un
peu long
trigger ['trɪgəʳ] n (of gun) gâchette f
trim [trɪm] adj (house, garden) bien
tenu(e); (figure) svelte ▷ n (haircut etc)
légère coupe; (on car) garnitures fpl
▷ vt (cut) couper légèrement;
(decorate): **to ~ (with)** décorer (de);
(Naut: a sail) gréer
trio ['triːəu] n trio m
trip [trɪp] n voyage m; (excursion)
excursion f; (stumble) faux pas ▷ vi
faire un faux pas, trébucher; **trip up** vi
trébucher ▷ vt faire un croc-en-jambe à
triple ['trɪpl] adj triple
triplets ['trɪplɪts] npl triplés(-ées)
tripod ['traɪpɔd] n trépied m
triumph ['traɪʌmf] n triomphe
m ▷ vi: **to ~ (over)** triompher (de);
triumphant [traɪ'ʌmfənt] adj
triomphant(e)
trivial ['trɪvɪəl] adj insignifiant(e);
(commonplace) banal(e)
trod [trɔd] pt of **tread**
trodden ['trɔdn] pp of **tread**
trolley ['trɔlɪ] n chariot m
trombone [trɔm'bəun] n trombone m
troop [truːp] n bande f, groupe m;
troops npl (Mil) troupes fpl; (: men)
hommes mpl, soldats mpl
trophy ['trəufɪ] n trophée m
tropical ['trɔpɪkl] adj tropical(e)
trot [trɔt] n trot m ▷ vi trotter; **on the ~**
(BRIT: fig) d'affilée
trouble ['trʌbl] n difficulté(s) f(pl),
problème(s) m(pl); (worry) ennuis mpl,
soucis mpl; (bother, effort) peine f; (Pol)

conflit(s) m(pl), troubles mpl; (Med):
stomach etc **~** troubles gastriques etc
▷ vt (disturb) déranger, gêner; (worry)
inquiéter ▷ vi: **to ~ to do** prendre la
peine de faire; **troubles** npl (Pol etc)
troubles; (personal) ennuis, soucis;
to be in ~ avoir des ennuis; (ship,
climber etc) être en difficulté; **to have
~ doing sth** avoir du mal à faire qch;
it's no ~! je vous en prie!; **the ~ is ...**
le problème, c'est que ...; **what's the
~?** qu'est-ce qui ne va pas?; **troubled**
adj (person) inquiet(-ète); (times, life)
agité(e); **troublemaker** n élément
perturbateur, fauteur m de troubles;
troublesome adj (child) fatigant(e),
difficile; (cough) gênant(e)
trough [trɔf] n (also: **drinking ~**)
abreuvoir m; (also: **feeding ~**) auge f;
(depression) creux m
trousers ['trauzəz] npl pantalon m;
short ~ (BRIT) culottes courtes
trout [traut] n (pl inv) truite f
trowel ['trauəl] n truelle f; (garden tool)
déplantoir m
truant ['truənt] n: **to play ~** (BRIT) faire
l'école buissonnière
truce [truːs] n trêve f
truck [trʌk] n camion m; (Rail) wagon
m à plate-forme; **truck driver** n
camionneur m
true [truː] adj vrai(e); (accurate) exact(e);
(genuine) vrai, véritable; (faithful) fidèle;
to come ~ se réaliser
truly ['truːlɪ] adv vraiment, réellement;
(truthfully) sans mentir; **yours ~** (in
letter) je vous prie d'agréer, Monsieur
(or Madame etc), l'expression de mes
sentiments respectueux
trumpet ['trʌmpɪt] n trompette f
trunk [trʌŋk] n (of tree, person) tronc
m; (of elephant) trompe f; (case) malle
f; (US Aut) coffre m; **trunks** npl (also:
swimming ~s) maillot m or slip m
de bain
trust [trʌst] n confiance f;
(responsibility): **to place sth in sb's
~** confier la responsabilité de qch à

qn; (*Law*) fidéicommis *m* ▷ *vt* (*rely on*) avoir confiance en; (*entrust*): **to ~ sth to sb** confier qch à qn; (*hope*): **to ~ (that)** espérer (que); **to take sth on ~** accepter qch les yeux fermés; **trusted** *adj* en qui l'on a confiance; **trustworthy** *adj* digne de confiance

truth [truːθ, (*pl*) truːðz] *n* vérité *f*; **truthful** *adj* (*person*) qui dit la vérité; (*answer*) sincère

try [traɪ] *n* essai *m*, tentative *f*; (*Rugby*) essai *f* ▷ *vt* (*attempt*) essayer, tenter; (*test: sth new: also: ~ out*) essayer, tester; (*Law: person*) juger; (*strain*) éprouver ▷ *vi* essayer; **to ~ to do** essayer de faire; (*seek*) chercher à faire; **try on** *vt* (*clothes*) essayer; **trying** *adj* pénible

T-shirt ['tiːʃəːt] *n* tee-shirt *m*

tub [tʌb] *n* cuve *f*, tentative *f*; (*for washing clothes*) baquet *m*; (*bath*) baignoire *f*

tube [tjuːb] *n* tube *m*; (BRIT: *underground*) métro *m*; (*for tyre*) chambre *f* à air

tuberculosis [tjubəːkjuˈləʊsɪs] *n* tuberculose *f*

tube station *n* (BRIT) station *f* de métro

tuck [tʌk] *vt* (*put*) mettre; **tuck away** *vt* cacher, ranger; (*money*) mettre de côté; (*building*): **to be ~ed away** être caché(e); **tuck in** *vt* rentrer; (*child*) border ▷ *vi* (*eat*) manger de bon appétit; attaquer le repas; **tuck shop** *n* (BRIT Scol) boutique *f* à provisions

Tue(s) *abbr* (= *Tuesday*) ma

Tuesday ['tjuːzdɪ] *n* mardi *m*

tug [tʌg] *n* (*ship*) remorqueur *m* ▷ *vt* tirer (sur)

tuition [tjuːˈɪʃən] *n* (BRIT: *lessons*) leçons *fpl*; (: *private*) cours particuliers; (US: *fees*) frais *mpl* de scolarité

tulip ['tjuːlɪp] *n* tulipe *f*

tumble ['tʌmbl] *n* (*fall*) chute *f*, culbute *f* ▷ *vi* tomber, dégringoler; **to ~ to sth** (*inf*) réaliser qch; **tumble dryer** *n* (BRIT) séchoir *m* (à linge) à air chaud

tumbler ['tʌmblər] *n* verre (droit), gobelet *m*

tummy ['tʌmɪ] *n* (*inf*) ventre *m*

tumour (US **tumor**) ['tjuːmər] *n* tumeur *f*

tuna ['tjuːnə] *n* (*pl inv: also: ~ fish*) thon *m*

tune [tjuːn] *n* (*melody*) air *m* ▷ *vt* (*Mus*) accorder; (*Radio, TV, Aut*) régler, mettre au point; **to be in/out of ~** (*instrument*) être accordé/désaccordé; (*singer*) chanter juste/faux; **tune in** *vi* (*Radio, TV*): **to ~ in (to)** se mettre à l'écoute (de); **tune up** *vi* (*musician*) accorder son instrument

tunic ['tjuːnɪk] *n* tunique *f*

Tunis ['tjuːnɪs] *n* Tunis

Tunisia [tjuːˈnɪzɪə] *n* Tunisie *f*

Tunisian [tjuːˈnɪzɪən] *adj* tunisien(ne) ▷ *n* Tunisien(ne)

tunnel ['tʌnl] *n* tunnel *m*; (*in mine*) galerie *f* ▷ *vi* creuser un tunnel (or une galerie)

turbulence ['təːbjuləns] *n* (*Aviat*) turbulence *f*

turf [təːf] *n* gazon *m*; (*clod*) motte *f* (de gazon) ▷ *vt* gazonner

Turk [təːk] *n* Turc (Turque)

Turkey ['təːkɪ] *n* Turquie *f*

turkey ['təːkɪ] *n* dindon *m*, dinde *f*

Turkish ['təːkɪʃ] *adj* turc (turque) ▷ *n* (*Ling*) turc *m*

turmoil ['təːmɔɪl] *n* trouble *m*, bouleversement *m*

turn [təːn] *n* tour *m*; (*in road*) tournant *m*; (*tendency: of mind, events*) tournure *f*; (*performance*) numéro *m*; (*Med*) crise *f*, attaque *f* ▷ *vt* tourner; (*collar, steak*) retourner; (*change*): **to ~ sth into** changer qch en; (*age*) atteindre ▷ *vi* (*object, wind, milk*) tourner; (*person: look back*) se (re)tourner; (*reverse direction*) faire demi-tour; (*become*) devenir; **to ~ into** se changer en, se transformer en; **a good ~** un service; **it gave me quite a ~** ça m'a fait un coup; **"no left ~"** (*Aut*) "défense de tourner à gauche"; **~ left/right at the next junction** tournez à gauche/ droite au prochain carrefour; **it's your ~** c'est (à) votre tour; **in ~** à son tour;

à tour de rôle; **to take ~s** se relayer;
turn around vi (*person*) se retourner
▷ vt (*object*) tourner; **turn away** vi se
détourner, tourner la tête ▷ vt (*reject:
person*) renvoyer; (: *business*) refuser;
TV [tiː'viː] n abbr (= *television*) télé f, TV f
turn back vi revenir, faire demi-tour;
turn down vt (*refuse*) rejeter, refuser;
(*reduce*) baisser; (*fold*) rabattre; **turn
in** vi (*inf: go to bed*) aller se coucher
▷ vt (*fold*) rentrer; **turn off** vi (*from
road*) tourner ▷ vt (*light, radio etc*)
éteindre; (*tap*) fermer; (*engine*) arrêter;
I can't ~ the heating off je n'arrive
pas à éteindre le chauffage; **turn on**
vt (*light, radio etc*) allumer; (*tap*) ouvrir;
(*engine*) mettre en marche; **I can't ~ the
heating on** je n'arrive pas à allumer
le chauffage; **turn out** vt (*light, gas*)
éteindre; (*produce*) produire ▷ vi (*voters,
troops*) se présenter; **to ~ out to be ...**
s'avérer ..., se révéler ...; **turn over**
vi (*person*) se retourner ▷ vt (*object*)
retourner; (*page*) tourner; **turn round**
vi faire demi-tour; (*rotate*) tourner;
turn to vt fus: **to ~ to sb** s'adresser à
qn; **turn up** vi (*person*) arriver,
se pointer (*inf*); (*lost object*) être
retrouvé(e) ▷ vt (*collar*) remonter;
(*radio, heater*) mettre plus fort;
turning n (*in road*) tournant m;
turning point n (*fig*) tournant m,
moment décisif
turnip ['təːnɪp] n navet m
turn: **turnout** n (*of voters*) taux m de
participation; **turnover** n (*Comm:
amount of money*) chiffre m d'affaires;
(: *of goods*) roulement m; (*of staff*)
renouvellement m, changement m;
turnstile n tourniquet m (*d'entrée*);
turn-up n (*BRIT: on trousers*) revers m
turquoise ['təːkwɔɪz] n (*stone*)
turquoise f ▷ adj turquoise inv
turtle ['təːtl] n tortue marine;
turtleneck (sweater) n pullover m à
col montant
tusk [tʌsk] n défense f (*d'éléphant*)
tutor ['tjuːtəʳ] n (*BRIT Scol: in college*)
directeur(-trice) d'études; (*private*

teacher) précepteur(-trice); **tutorial**
[tjuː'tɔːrɪəl] n (*Scol*) (séance f de)
travaux mpl pratiques
tuxedo [tʌk'siːdəu] n (*US*) smoking m
TV [tiː'viː] n abbr (= *television*) télé f, TV f
tweed [twiːd] n tweed m
tweezers ['twiːzəz] npl pince f à épiler
twelfth [twelfθ] num douzième
twelve [twelv] num douze; **at ~
(o'clock)** à midi; (*midnight*) à minuit
twentieth ['twentɪɪθ] num vingtième
twenty ['twentɪ] num vingt
twice [twaɪs] adv deux fois; **~ as much**
deux fois plus
twig [twɪg] n brindille f ▷ vt, vi (*inf*)
piger
twilight ['twaɪlaɪt] n crépuscule m
twin [twɪn] adj, n jumeau(-elle) ▷ vt
jumeler; **twin(-bedded) room** n
chambre f à deux lits; **twin beds** npl lits
mpl jumeaux
twinkle ['twɪŋkl] vi scintiller; (*eyes*)
pétiller
twist [twɪst] n torsion f, tour m; (*in
wire, flex*) tortillon m; (*bend: in road*)
tournant m; (*in story*) coup m de théâtre
▷ vt tordre; (*weave*) entortiller; (*roll
around*) enrouler; (*fig*) déformer ▷ vi
(*road, river*) serpenter; **to ~ one's
ankle/wrist** (*Med*) se tordre la
cheville/le poignet
twit [twɪt] n (*inf*) crétin(e)
twitch [twɪtʃ] n (*pull*) coup sec, saccade
f; (*nervous*) tic m ▷ vi se convulser;
avoir un tic
two [tuː] num deux; **to put ~ and ~
together** (*fig*) faire le rapprochement
type [taɪp] n (*category*) genre m, espèce
f; (*model*) modèle m; (*example*) type m;
(*Typ*) type, caractère m ▷ vt (*letter etc*)
taper (à la machine); **typewriter** n
machine f à écrire
typhoid ['taɪfɔɪd] n typhoïde f
typhoon [taɪ'fuːn] n typhon m
typical ['tɪpɪkl] adj typique,
caractéristique; **typically** adv (*as usual*)
comme d'habitude; (*characteristically*)
typiquement

typing ['taɪpɪŋ] n dactylo(graphie) f
typist ['taɪpɪst] n dactylo m/f
tyre (us **tire**) ['taɪər] n pneu m; **I've got a flat ~** j'ai un pneu crevé; **tyre pressure** n (BRIT) pression f (de gonflage)

UFO ['juːfəu] n abbr (= unidentified flying object) ovni m
Uganda [juːˈgændə] n Ouganda m
ugly ['ʌglɪ] adj laid(e), vilain(e); (fig) répugnant(e)
UHT adj abbr = **ultra-heat treated**; **~ milk** lait m UHT or longue conservation
UK n abbr = **United Kingdom**
ulcer ['ʌlsər] n ulcère m; **mouth ~** aphte f
ultimate ['ʌltɪmət] adj ultime, final(e); (authority) suprême; **ultimately** adv (at last) en fin de compte; (fundamentally) finalement; (eventually) par la suite
ultimatum (pl **~s** or **ultimata**) [ʌltɪˈmeɪtəm, -tə] n ultimatum m
ultrasound ['ʌltrəsaund] n (Med) ultrason m
ultraviolet ['ʌltrəˈvaɪəlɪt] adj ultraviolet(te)
umbrella [ʌmˈbrɛlə] n parapluie m; (for sun) parasol m
umpire ['ʌmpaɪər] n arbitre m; (Tennis) juge m de chaise

UN *n abbr* = **United Nations**

unable [ʌnˈeɪbl] *adj*: **to be ~ to** ne (pas) pouvoir, être dans l'impossibilité de; (*not capable*) être incapable de

unacceptable [ʌnəkˈsɛptəbl] *adj* (*behaviour*) inadmissible; (*price, proposal*) inacceptable

unanimous [juːˈnænɪməs] *adj* unanime

unarmed [ʌnˈɑːmd] *adj* (*person*) non armé(e); (*combat*) sans armes

unattended [ʌnəˈtɛndɪd] *adj* (*car, child, luggage*) sans surveillance

unattractive [ʌnəˈtræktɪv] *adj* peu attrayant(e); (*character*) peu sympathique

unavailable [ʌnəˈveɪləbl] *adj* (*article, room, book*) (qui n'est) pas disponible; (*person*) (qui n'est) pas libre

unavoidable [ʌnəˈvɔɪdəbl] *adj* inévitable

unaware [ʌnəˈwɛər] *adj*: **to be ~ of** ignorer, ne pas savoir, être inconscient(e) de; **unawares** *adv* à l'improviste, au dépourvu

unbearable [ʌnˈbɛərəbl] *adj* insupportable

unbeatable [ʌnˈbiːtəbl] *adj* imbattable

unbelievable [ʌnbɪˈliːvəbl] *adj* incroyable

unborn [ʌnˈbɔːn] *adj* à naître

unbutton [ʌnˈbʌtn] *vt* déboutonner

uncalled-for [ʌnˈkɔːldfɔːr] *adj* déplacé(e), injustifié(e)

uncanny [ʌnˈkænɪ] *adj* étrange, troublant(e)

uncertain [ʌnˈsəːtn] *adj* incertain(e); (*hesitant*) hésitant(e); **uncertainty** *n* incertitude *f*, doutes *mpl*

unchanged [ʌnˈtʃeɪndʒd] *adj* inchangé(e)

uncle [ˈʌŋkl] *n* oncle *m*

unclear [ʌnˈklɪər] *adj* (qui n'est) pas clair(e) or évident(e); **I'm still ~ about what I'm supposed to do** je ne sais pas encore exactement ce que je dois faire

uncomfortable [ʌnˈkʌmfətəbl] *adj* inconfortable, peu confortable; (*uneasy*) mal à l'aise, gêné(e); (*situation*) désagréable

uncommon [ʌnˈkɔmən] *adj* rare, singulier(-ière), peu commun(e)

unconditional [ʌnkənˈdɪʃənl] *adj* sans conditions

unconscious [ʌnˈkɔnʃəs] *adj* sans connaissance, évanoui(e); (*unaware*): **~ of** inconscient(e) (de) ▷ *n*: **the ~** l'inconscient *m*

uncontrollable [ʌnkənˈtrəuləbl] *adj* (*child, dog*) indiscipliné(e); (*temper, laughter*) irrépressible

unconventional [ʌnkənˈvɛnʃənl] *adj* peu conventionnel(le)

uncover [ʌnˈkʌvər] *vt* découvrir

undecided [ʌndɪˈsaɪdɪd] *adj* indécis(e), irrésolu(e)

undeniable [ʌndɪˈnaɪəbl] *adj* indéniable, incontestable

under [ˈʌndər] *prep* sous; (*less than*) (de) moins de; au-dessous de; (*according to*) selon, en vertu de ▷ *adv* au-dessous; en dessous; **~ there** là-dessous; **~ the circumstances** étant donné les circonstances; **~ repair** en (cours de) réparation; **undercover** *adj* secret(-ète), clandestin(e); **underdone** *adj* (*Culin*) saignant(e); (: *pej*) pas assez cuit(e); **underestimate** *vt* sous-estimer, mésestimer; **undergo** *vt* (*irreg: like* **go**) subir; (*treatment*) suivre; **undergraduate** *n* étudiant(e) (qui prépare la licence); **underground** *adj* souterrain(e); (*fig*) clandestin(e) ▷ *n* (*BRIT: railway*) métro *m*; (*Pol*) clandestinité *f*; **undergrowth** *n* broussailles *fpl*, sous-bois *m*; **underline** *vt* souligner; **undermine** *vt* saper, miner; **underneath** [ʌndəˈniːθ] *adv* (en) dessous ▷ *prep* sous, au-dessous de; **underpants** *npl* caleçon *m*, slip *m*; **underpass** *n* (*BRIT: for pedestrians*) passage souterrain; (: *for cars*) passage inférieur;

underprivileged adj défavorisé(e); **underscore** vt souligner; **undershirt** n (US) tricot m de corps; **underskirt** n (BRIT) jupon m

understand [ʌndə'stænd] vt, vi (irreg: like **stand**) comprendre; **I don't ~** je ne comprends pas; **understandable** adj compréhensible; **understanding** adj compréhensif(-ive) ▷ n compréhension f; (agreement) accord m

understatement [ˈʌndəsteɪtmənt] n: **that's an ~** c'est (bien) peu dire, le terme est faible

understood [ʌndə'stud] pt, pp of **understand** ▷ adj entendu(e); (implied) sous-entendu(e)

undertake [ʌndə'teɪk] vt (irreg: like **take**) (job, task) entreprendre; (duty) se charger de; **to ~ to do sth** s'engager à faire qch

undertaker [ˈʌndəteɪkəʳ] n (BRIT) entrepreneur m des pompes funèbres, croque-mort m

undertaking [ˈʌndəteɪkɪŋ] n entreprise f; (promise) promesse f

under: **underwater** adv sous l'eau ▷ adj sous-marin(e); **underway** adj: **to be underway** (meeting, investigation) être en cours; **underwear** n sous-vêtements mpl; (women's only) dessous mpl; **underwent** pt of **undergo**; **underworld** n (of crime) milieu m, pègre f

undesirable [ʌndɪ'zaɪərəbl] adj peu souhaitable; (person, effect) indésirable

undisputed [ˈʌndɪs'pju:tɪd] adj incontesté(e)

undo [ʌn'du:] vt (irreg: like **do**) défaire

undone [ʌn'dʌn] pp of **undo** ▷ adj: **to come ~** se défaire

undoubtedly [ʌn'dautɪdlɪ] adv sans aucun doute

undress [ʌn'drɛs] vi se déshabiller

unearth [ʌn'ə:θ] vt déterrer; (fig) dénicher

uneasy [ʌn'i:zɪ] adj mal à l'aise, gêné(e); (worried) inquiet(-ète); (feeling) désagréable; (peace, truce) fragile

unemployed [ʌnɪm'plɔɪd] adj sans travail, au chômage ▷ n: **the ~** les chômeurs mpl

unemployment [ʌnɪm'plɔɪmənt] n chômage m; **unemployment benefit** (US **unemployment compensation**) n allocation f de chômage

unequal [ʌn'i:kwəl] adj inégal(e)

uneven [ʌn'i:vn] adj inégal(e); (quality, work) irrégulier(-ière)

unexpected [ʌnɪk'spɛktɪd] adj inattendu(e), imprévu(e); **unexpectedly** adv (succeed) contre toute attente; (arrive) à l'improviste

unfair [ʌn'fɛəʳ] adj: **~ (to)** injuste (envers)

unfaithful [ʌn'feɪθful] adj infidèle

unfamiliar [ʌnfə'mɪlɪəʳ] adj étrange, inconnu(e); **to be ~ with sth** mal connaître qch

unfashionable [ʌn'fæʃnəbl] adj (clothes) démodé(e); (place) peu chic inv

unfasten [ʌn'fɑ:sn] vt défaire; (belt, necklace) détacher; (open) ouvrir

unfavourable (US **unfavorable**) [ʌn'feɪvrəbl] adj défavorable

unfinished [ʌn'fɪnɪʃt] adj inachevé(e)

unfit [ʌn'fɪt] adj (physically: ill) en mauvaise santé; (: out of condition) pas en forme; (incompetent): **~ (for)** impropre (à); (work, service) inapte (à)

unfold [ʌn'fəuld] vt déplier ▷ vi se dérouler

unforgettable [ʌnfə'gɛtəbl] adj inoubliable

unfortunate [ʌn'fɔ:tʃnət] adj malheureux(-euse); (event, remark) malencontreux(-euse); **unfortunately** adv malheureusement

unfriendly [ʌn'frɛndlɪ] adj peu aimable, froid(e)

unfurnished [ʌn'fə:nɪʃt] adj non meublé(e)

unhappiness [ʌn'hæpɪnɪs] n tristesse f, peine f

unhappy [ʌn'hæpɪ] adj triste, malheureux(-euse); (unfortunate: remark etc) malheureux(-euse); (not *pleased*): **~ with** mécontent(e) de, peu satisfait(e) de

unhealthy [ʌnˈhɛlθɪ] *adj* (*gen*) malsain(e); (*person*) maladif(-ive)

unheard-of [ʌnˈhəːdɒv] *adj* inouï(e), sans précédent

unhelpful [ʌnˈhɛlpful] *adj* (*person*) peu serviable; (*advice*) peu utile

unhurt [ʌnˈhəːt] *adj* indemne, sain(e) et sauf (sauve)

unidentified [ʌnaɪˈdɛntɪfaɪd] *adj* non identifié(e); *see also* **UFO**

uniform [ˈjuːnɪfɔːm] *n* uniforme *m* ▷ *adj* uniforme

unify [ˈjuːnɪfaɪ] *vt* unifier

unimportant [ʌnɪmˈpɔːtənt] *adj* sans importance

uninhabited [ʌnɪnˈhæbɪtɪd] *adj* inhabité(e)

unintentional [ʌnɪnˈtɛnʃənəl] *adj* involontaire

union [ˈjuːnjən] *n* union *f*; (*also*: **trade ~**) syndicat *m* ▷ *cpd* du syndicat, syndical(e); **Union Jack** *n* drapeau du *Royaume-Uni*

unique [juːˈniːk] *adj* unique

unisex [ˈjuːnɪsɛks] *adj* unisexe

unit [ˈjuːnɪt] *n* unité *f*; (*section: of furniture etc*) élément *m*, bloc *m*; (*team, squad*) groupe *m*, service *m*; **kitchen ~** élément de cuisine

unite [juːˈnaɪt] *vt* unir ▷ *vi* s'unir; **united** *adj* uni(e); (*country, party*) unifié(e); (*efforts*) conjugué(e); **United Kingdom** *n* Royaume-Uni *m* (R.U.); **United Nations (Organization)** *n* (Organisation *f* des) Nations unies (ONU); **United States (of America)** *n* États-Unis *mpl*

unity [ˈjuːnɪtɪ] *n* unité *f*

universal [juːnɪˈvəːsl] *adj* universel(le)

universe [ˈjuːnɪvəːs] *n* univers *m*

university [juːnɪˈvəːsɪtɪ] *n* université *f* ▷ *cpd* (*student, professor*) d'université; (*education, year, degree*) universitaire

unjust [ʌnˈdʒʌst] *adj* injuste

unkind [ʌnˈkaɪnd] *adj* peu gentil(le), méchant(e)

unknown [ʌnˈnəun] *adj* inconnu(e)

unlawful [ʌnˈlɔːful] *adj* illégal(e)

unleaded [ʌnˈlɛdɪd] *n* (*also*: **~ petrol**) essence *f* sans plomb

unleash [ʌnˈliːʃ] *vt* (*fig*) déchaîner, déclencher

unless [ʌnˈlɛs] *conj*: **~ he leaves** à moins qu'il (ne) parte; **~ otherwise stated** sauf indication contraire

unlike [ʌnˈlaɪk] *adj* dissemblable, différent(e) ▷ *prep* à la différence de, contrairement à

unlikely [ʌnˈlaɪklɪ] *adj* (*result, event*) improbable; (*explanation*) invraisemblable

unlimited [ʌnˈlɪmɪtɪd] *adj* illimité(e)

unlisted [ˈʌnˈlɪstɪd] *adj* (*us Tel*) sur la liste rouge

unload [ʌnˈləud] *vt* décharger

unlock [ʌnˈlɔk] *vt* ouvrir

unlucky [ʌnˈlʌkɪ] *adj* (*person*) malchanceux(-euse); (*object, number*) qui porte malheur; **to be ~** (*person*) ne pas avoir de chance

unmarried [ʌnˈmærɪd] *adj* célibataire

unmistak(e)able [ʌnmɪsˈteɪkəbl] *adj* indubitable; qu'on ne peut pas ne pas reconnaître

unnatural [ʌnˈnætʃrəl] *adj* non naturel(le); (*perversion*) contre nature

unnecessary [ʌnˈnɛsəsərɪ] *adj* inutile, superflu(e)

UNO [ˈjuːnəu] *n abbr* = **United Nations Organization**

unofficial [ʌnəˈfɪʃl] *adj* (*news*) officieux(-euse), non officiel(le); (*strike*) ≈ sauvage

unpack [ʌnˈpæk] *vi* défaire sa valise ▷ *vt* (*suitcase*) défaire; (*belongings*) déballer

unpaid [ʌnˈpeɪd] *adj* (*bill*) impayé(e); (*holiday*) non-payé(e), sans salaire; (*work*) non rétribué(e)

unpleasant [ʌnˈplɛznt] *adj* déplaisant(e), désagréable

unplug [ʌnˈplʌg] *vt* débrancher

unpopular [ʌnˈpɔpjuləʳ] *adj* impopulaire

unprecedented [ʌn'prɛsɪdəntɪd] *adj* sans précédent

unpredictable [ʌnprɪ'dɪktəbl] *adj* imprévisible

unprotected ['ʌnprə'tɛktɪd] *adj* (*sex*) non protégé(e)

unqualified [ʌn'kwɔlɪfaɪd] *adj* (*teacher*) non diplômé(e), sans titres; (*success*) sans réserve, total(e); (*disaster*) total(e)

unravel [ʌn'rævl] *vt* démêler

unreal [ʌn'rɪəl] *adj* irréel(le); (*extraordinary*) incroyable

unrealistic ['ʌnrɪə'lɪstɪk] *adj* (*idea*) irréaliste; (*estimate*) peu réaliste

unreasonable [ʌn'ri:znəbl] *adj* qui n'est pas raisonnable

unrelated [ʌnrɪ'leɪtɪd] *adj* sans rapport; (*people*) sans lien de parenté

unreliable [ʌnrɪ'laɪəbl] *adj* sur qui (*or quoi*) on ne peut pas compter, peu fiable

unrest [ʌn'rɛst] *n* agitation *f*, troubles *mpl*

unroll [ʌn'rəul] *vt* dérouler

unruly [ʌn'ru:lɪ] *adj* indiscipliné(e)

unsafe [ʌn'seɪf] *adj* (*in danger*) en danger; (*journey, car*) dangereux(-euse)

unsatisfactory ['ʌnsætɪs'fæktərɪ] *adj* peu satisfaisant(e)

unscrew [ʌn'skru:] *vt* dévisser

unsettled [ʌn'sɛtld] *adj* (*restless*) perturbé(e); (*unpredictable*) instable; incertain(e); (*not finalized*) non résolu(e)

unsettling [ʌn'sɛtlɪŋ] *adj* qui a un effet perturbateur

unsightly [ʌn'saɪtlɪ] *adj* disgracieux(-euse), laid(e)

unskilled [ʌn'skɪld] *adj*: **~ worker** manœuvre *m*

unspoiled ['ʌn'spɔɪld], **unspoilt** ['ʌn'spɔɪlt] *adj* (*place*) non dégradé(e)

unstable [ʌn'steɪbl] *adj* instable

unsteady [ʌn'stɛdɪ] *adj* mal assuré(e), chancelant(e), instable

unsuccessful [ʌnsək'sɛsful] *adj* (*attempt*) infructueux(-euse); (*writer, proposal*) qui n'a pas de succès; **to be**

~ (*in attempting sth*) ne pas réussir; ne pas avoir de succès; (*application*) ne pas être retenu(e)

unsuitable [ʌn'su:təbl] *adj* qui ne convient pas, peu approprié(e); (*time*) inopportun(e)

unsure [ʌn'ʃuər] *adj* pas sûr(e); **to be ~ of o.s.** ne pas être sûr de soi, manquer de confiance en soi

untidy [ʌn'taɪdɪ] *adj* (*room*) en désordre; (*appearance, person*) débraillé(e); (*person: in character*) sans ordre, désordonné; (*work*) peu soigné(e)

untie [ʌn'taɪ] *vt* (*knot, parcel*) défaire; (*prisoner, dog*) détacher

until [ən'tɪl] *prep* jusqu'à; (*after negative*) avant ▷ *conj* jusqu'à ce que + *sub*; (*in past, after negative*) avant que + *sub*; **~ he comes** jusqu'à ce qu'il vienne, jusqu'à son arrivée; **~ now** jusqu'à présent, jusqu'ici; **~ then** jusque-là

untrue [ʌn'tru:] *adj* (*statement*) faux (fausse)

unused[1] [ʌn'ju:zd] *adj* (*new*) neuf (neuve)

unused[2] [ʌn'ju:st] *adj*: **to be ~ to sth/ to doing sth** ne pas avoir l'habitude de qch/de faire qch

unusual [ʌn'ju:ʒuəl] *adj* insolite, exceptionnel(le), rare; **unusually** *adv* exceptionnellement, particulièrement

unveil [ʌn'veɪl] *vt* dévoiler

unwanted [ʌn'wɔntɪd] *adj* (*child, pregnancy*) non désiré(e); (*clothes etc*) à donner

unwell [ʌn'wɛl] *adj* souffrant(e); **to feel ~** ne pas se sentir bien

unwilling [ʌn'wɪlɪŋ] *adj*: **to be ~ to do** ne pas vouloir faire

unwind [ʌn'waɪnd] *vb* (*irreg: like* **wind**) ▷ *vt* dérouler ▷ *vi* (*relax*) se détendre

unwise [ʌn'waɪz] *adj* imprudent(e), peu judicieux(-euse)

unwittingly [ʌn'wɪtɪŋlɪ] *adv* involontairement

unwrap [ʌn'ræp] *vt* défaire; ouvrir

unzip [ʌn'zɪp] *vt* ouvrir (la fermeture

éclair de); (*Comput*) dézipper

O KEYWORD

up [ʌp] *prep*: **he went up the stairs/the hill** il a monté l'escalier/la colline; **the cat was up a tree** le chat était dans un arbre; **they live further up the street** ils habitent plus haut dans la rue; **go up that road and turn left** remontez la rue et tournez à gauche
▷ *adv* **1** en haut; en l'air; (*upwards, higher*): **up in the sky/the mountains** (là-haut) dans le ciel/les montagnes; **put it a bit higher up** mettez-le un peu plus haut; **to stand up** (*get up*) se lever, se mettre debout; (*be standing*) être debout; **up there** là-haut; **up above** au-dessus
2: **to be up** (*out of bed*) être levé(e); (*prices*) avoir augmenté or monté; (*finished*): **when the year was up** à la fin de l'année
3: **up to** (*as far as*) jusqu'à; **up to now** jusqu'à présent
4: **to be up to** (*depending on*): **it's up to you** c'est à vous de décider; (*equal to*): **he's not up to it** (*job, task etc*) il n'en est pas capable; (*inf: be doing*): **what is he up to?** qu'est-ce qu'il peut bien faire?
▷ *n*: **ups and downs** hauts et bas *mpl*

up-and-coming [ʌpənd'kʌmɪŋ] *adj* plein(e) d'avenir or de promesses
upbringing ['ʌpbrɪŋɪŋ] *n* éducation *f*
update [ʌp'deɪt] *vt* mettre à jour
upfront [ʌp'frʌnt] *adj* (*open*) franc (franche) ▷ *adv* (*pay*) d'avance; **to be ~ about sth** ne rien cacher de qch
upgrade [ʌp'greɪd] *vt* (*person*) promouvoir; (*job*) revaloriser; (*property, equipment*) moderniser
upheaval [ʌp'hiːvl] *n* bouleversement *m*; (*in room*) branle-bas *m*; (*event*) crise *f*
uphill [ʌp'hɪl] *adj* qui monte; (*fig: task*) difficile, pénible ▷ *adv* (*face, look*) en amont, vers l'amont; **to go ~** monter
upholstery [ʌp'həulstəri] *n*

rembourrage *m*; (*cover*) tissu *m* d'ameublement; (*of car*) garniture *f*
upmarket [ʌp'maːkɪt] *adj* (*product*) haut de gamme *inv*; (*area*) chic *inv*
upon [ə'pɔn] *prep* sur
upper ['ʌpə'] *adj* supérieur(e); du dessus ▷ *n* (*of shoe*) empeigne *f*; **upper-class** *adj* de la haute société, aristocratique; (*district*) élégant(e), huppé(e); (*accent, attitude*) caractéristique des classes supérieures
upright ['ʌpraɪt] *adj* droit(e); (*fig*) droit, honnête
uprising ['ʌpraɪzɪŋ] *n* soulèvement *m*, insurrection *f*
uproar ['ʌprɔː'] *n* tumulte *m*, vacarme *m*; (*protests*) protestations *fpl*
upset *n* ['ʌpset] dérangement *m*
▷ *vt* (*irreg: like* **set** [ʌp'set]) (*glass etc*) renverser; (*plan*) déranger; (*person: offend*) contrarier; (*: grieve*) faire de la peine à; bouleverser ▷ *adj* [ʌp'set] contrarié(e); peiné(e); **to have a stomach ~** (*BRIT*) avoir une indigestion
upside down ['ʌpsaɪd-] *adv* à l'envers; **to turn sth ~** (*fig: place*) mettre sens dessus dessous
upstairs [ʌp'stɛəz] *adv* en haut ▷ *adj* (*room*) du dessus, d'en haut ▷ *n*: **the ~** l'étage *m*
up-to-date [ʌptə'deɪt] *adj* moderne; (*information*) très récent(e)
uptown ['ʌptaun] (*US*) *adv* (*live*) dans les quartiers chics; (*go*) vers les quartiers chics ▷ *adj* des quartiers chics
upward ['ʌpwəd] *adj* ascendant(e); vers le haut; **upward(s)** *adv* vers le haut; (*more than*): **upward(s) of** plus de
uranium [juə'reɪnɪəm] *n* uranium *m*
Uranus [juə'reɪnəs] *n* Uranus *f*
urban ['əːbən] *adj* urbain(e)
urge [əːdʒ] *n* besoin (impératif), envie (pressante) ▷ *vt* (*person*): **to ~ sb to do** exhorter qn à faire, pousser qn à faire, recommander vivement à qn de faire
urgency ['əːdʒənsɪ] *n* urgence *f*; (*of tone*) insistance *f*

urgent [ˈəːdʒənt] *adj* urgent(e); (*plea, tone*) pressant(e)

urinal [ˈjuərɪnl] *n* (BRIT: *place*) urinoir *m*

urinate [ˈjuərɪneɪt] *vi* uriner

urine [ˈjuərɪn] *n* urine *f*

URL *abbr* (= *uniform resource locator*) URL *f*

US *n abbr* = **United States**

us [ʌs] *pron* nous; *see also* **me**

USA *n abbr* = **United States of America**

use *n* [juːs] emploi *m*, utilisation *f*; (*usefulness*) utilité *f* ▷ *vt* [juːz] se servir de, utiliser, employer; **in ~** en usage; **out of ~** hors d'usage; **to be of ~** servir, être utile; **it's no ~** ça ne sert à rien; **to have the ~ of** avoir l'usage de; **she ~d to do it** elle le faisait (autrefois), elle avait coutume de le faire; **to be ~d to** avoir l'habitude de, être habitué(e) à; **use up** *vt* finir, épuiser; (*food*) consommer; **used** [juːzd] *adj* (*car*) d'occasion; **useful** *adj* utile; **useless** *adj* inutile; (*inf: person*) nul(le); **user** *n* utilisateur(-trice), usager *m*; **user-friendly** *adj* convivial(e), facile d'emploi

usual [ˈjuːʒuəl] *adj* habituel(le); **as ~** comme d'habitude; **usually** *adv* d'habitude, d'ordinaire

utensil [juːˈtɛnsl] *n* ustensile *m*; **kitchen ~s** batterie *f* de cuisine

utility [juːˈtɪlɪtɪ] *n* utilité *f*; (*also:* **public ~**) service public

utilize [ˈjuːtɪlaɪz] *vt* utiliser; (*make good use of*) exploiter

utmost [ˈʌtməust] *adj* extrême, le (la) plus grand(e) ▷ *n*: **to do one's ~** faire tout son possible

utter [ˈʌtəʳ] *adj* total(e), complet(-ète) ▷ *vt* prononcer, proférer; (*sounds*) émettre; **utterly** *adv* complètement, totalement

U-turn [ˈjuːˈtəːn] *n* demi-tour *m*; (*fig*) volte-face *f inv*

v. *abbr* = **verse** (= *vide*) v.; (= *versus*) c.; (= *volt*) V

vacancy [ˈveɪkənsɪ] *n* (BRIT: *job*) poste vacant; (*room*) chambre *f* disponible; **"no vacancies"** "complet"

vacant [ˈveɪkənt] *adj* (*post*) vacant(e); (*seat etc*) libre, disponible; (*expression*) distrait(e)

vacate [vəˈkeɪt] *vt* quitter

vacation [vəˈkeɪʃən] *n* (*esp US*) vacances *fpl*; **on ~** en vacances; **vacationer** (US **vacationist**) *n* vacancier(-ière)

vaccination [væksɪˈneɪʃən] *n* vaccination *f*

vaccine [ˈvæksiːn] *n* vaccin *m*

vacuum [ˈvækjum] *n* vide *m*; **vacuum cleaner** *n* aspirateur *m*

vagina [vəˈdʒaɪnə] *n* vagin *m*

vague [veɪg] *adj* vague, imprécis(e); (*blurred: photo, memory*) flou(e)

vain [veɪn] *adj* (*useless*) vain(e); (*conceited*) vaniteux(-euse); **in ~** en vain

Valentine's Day [ˈvæləntaɪnz-] *n*

Saint-Valentin f
valid ['vælɪd] adj (document) valide,
valable; (excuse) valable
valley ['vælɪ] n vallée f
valuable ['væljuəbl] adj (jewel)
de grande valeur; (time, help)
précieux(-euse); **valuables** npl objets
mpl de valeur
value ['vælju:] n valeur f ▷ vt (fix
price) évaluer, expertiser; (appreciate)
apprécier; **values** npl (principles)
valeurs fpl
valve [vælv] n (in machine) soupape f;
(on tyre) valve f; (Med) valve, valvule f
vampire ['væmpaɪər] n vampire m
van [væn] n (Aut) camionnette f
vandal ['vændl] n vandale m/f;
vandalism n vandalisme m; **vandalize**
vt saccager
vanilla [və'nɪlə] n vanille f
vanish ['vænɪʃ] vi disparaître
vanity ['vænɪtɪ] n vanité f
vapour (US **vapor**) ['veɪpər] n vapeur f;
(on window) buée f
variable ['vɛərɪəbl] adj variable; (mood)
changeant(e)
variant ['vɛərɪənt] n variante f
variation [vɛərɪ'eɪʃən] n variation f; (in
opinion) changement m
varied ['vɛərɪd] adj varié(e), divers(e)
variety [və'raɪətɪ] n variété f; (quantity)
nombre m, quantité f
various ['vɛərɪəs] adj divers(e),
différent(e); (several) divers, plusieurs
varnish ['vɑːnɪʃ] n vernis m ▷ vt vernir
vary ['vɛərɪ] vt, vi varier, changer
vase [vɑːz] n vase m
Vaseline® ['væsɪliːn] n vaseline f
vast [vɑːst] adj vaste, immense;
(amount, success) énorme
VAT [væt] n abbr (BRIT: = value added
tax) TVA f
vault [vɔːlt] n (of roof) voûte f; (tomb)
caveau m; (in bank) salle f des coffres;
chambre forte ▷ vt (also: **~ over**) sauter
(d'un bond)
VCR n abbr = **video cassette recorder**
VDU n abbr = **visual display unit**

veal [viːl] n veau m
veer [vɪər] vi tourner; (car, ship) virer
vegan ['viːgən] n végétalien(ne)
vegetable ['vɛdʒtəbl] n légume m ▷ adj
végétal(e)
vegetarian [vɛdʒɪ'tɛərɪən] adj,
n végétarien(ne); **do you have
any ~ dishes?** avez-vous des plats
végétariens?
vegetation [vɛdʒɪ'teɪʃən] n
végétation f
vehicle ['viːɪkl] n véhicule m
veil [veɪl] n voile m
vein [veɪn] n veine f; (on leaf) nervure f
Velcro® ['vɛlkrəu] n velcro® m
velvet ['vɛlvɪt] n velours m
vending machine ['vɛndɪŋ-] n
distributeur m automatique
vendor ['vɛndər] n vendeur(-euse);
street ~ marchand ambulant
Venetian blind [vɪ'niːʃən-] n store
vénitien
vengeance ['vɛndʒəns] n vengeance f;
with a ~ (fig) vraiment, pour de bon
venison ['vɛnɪsn] n venaison f
venom ['vɛnəm] n venin m
vent [vɛnt] n conduit m d'aération;
(in dress, jacket) fente f ▷ vt (fig: one's
feelings) donner libre cours à
ventilation [vɛntɪ'leɪʃən] n
ventilation f, aération f
venture ['vɛntʃər] n entreprise f ▷ vt
risquer, hasarder ▷ vi s'aventurer, se
risquer; **a business ~** une entreprise
commerciale
venue ['vɛnjuː] n lieu m
Venus ['viːnəs] n (planet) Vénus f
verb [vəːb] n verbe m; **verbal** adj
verbal(e)
verdict ['vəːdɪkt] n verdict m
verge [vəːdʒ] n bord m; **"soft ~s"** (BRIT)
"accotements non stabilisés"; **on the ~
of doing** sur le point de faire
verify ['vɛrɪfaɪ] vt vérifier
versatile ['vəːsətaɪl] adj polyvalent(e)
verse [vəːs] n vers mpl; (stanza) strophe
f; (in Bible) verset m
version ['vəːʃən] n version f

versus ['vəːsəs] *prep* contre

vertical ['vəːtɪkl] *adj* vertical(e)

very ['vɛrɪ] *adv* très ▷ *adj*: **the ~ book which** le livre même que; **the ~ last** le tout dernier; **at the ~ least** au moins; **~ much** beaucoup

vessel ['vɛsl] *n* (*Anat, Naut*) vaisseau *m*; (*container*) récipient *m*; *see also* **blood**

vest [vɛst] *n* (BRIT: *underwear*) tricot *m* de corps; (US: *waistcoat*) gilet *m*

vet [vɛt] *n abbr* (BRIT: = *veterinary surgeon*) vétérinaire *m/f*; (US: = *veteran*) ancien(ne) combattant(e) ▷ *vt* examiner minutieusement

veteran ['vɛtərn] *n* vétéran *m*; (*also*: **war ~**) ancien combattant

veterinary surgeon ['vɛtrɪnərɪ-] (BRIT) (US **veterinarian** [vɛtrɪ'nɛərɪən]) *n* vétérinaire *m/f*

veto ['viːtəu] *n* (*pl* **~es**) veto *m* ▷ *vt* opposer son veto à

via ['vaɪə] *prep* par, via

viable ['vaɪəbl] *adj* viable

vibrate [vaɪ'breɪt] *vi*: **to ~ (with)** vibrer (de)

vibration [vaɪ'breɪʃən] *n* vibration *f*

vicar ['vɪkər] *n* pasteur *m* (*de l'Église anglicane*)

vice [vaɪs] *n* (*evil*) vice *m*; (*Tech*) étau *m*; **vice-chairman** *n* vice-président *m*

vice versa ['vaɪsɪ'vəːsə] *adv* vice versa

vicinity [vɪ'sɪnɪtɪ] *n* environs *mpl*, alentours *mpl*

vicious ['vɪʃəs] *adj* (*remark*) cruel(le), méchant(e); (*blow*) brutal(e); (*dog*) méchant(e), dangereux(-euse); **a ~ circle** un cercle vicieux

victim ['vɪktɪm] *n* victime *f*

victor ['vɪktər] *n* vainqueur *m*

Victorian [vɪk'tɔːrɪən] *adj* victorien(ne)

victorious [vɪk'tɔːrɪəs] *adj* victorieux(-euse)

victory ['vɪktərɪ] *n* victoire *f*

video ['vɪdɪəu] *n* (*video film*) vidéo *f*; (*also*: **~ cassette**) vidéocassette *f*; (*also*: **~ cassette recorder**) magnétoscope *m* ▷ *vt* (*with recorder*) enregistrer;

(*with camera*) filmer; **video camera** *n* caméra *f* vidéo *inv*; **video (cassette) recorder** *n* magnétoscope *m*; **video game** *n* jeu *m* vidéo *inv*; **video shop** *n* vidéoclub *m*; **video tape** *n* bande *f* vidéo *inv*; (*cassette*) vidéocassette *f*

vie [vaɪ] *vi*: **to ~ with** lutter avec, rivaliser avec

Vienna [vɪ'ɛnə] *n* Vienne

Vietnam, Viet Nam ['vjɛt'næm] *n* Viêt-nam *or* Vietnam *m*; **Vietnamese** [vjɛtnə'miːz] *adj* vietnamien(ne) ▷ *n* (*pl inv*) Vietnamien(ne)

view [vjuː] *n* vue *f*; (*opinion*) avis *m*, vue ▷ *vt* voir, regarder; (*situation*) considérer; (*house*) visiter; **on ~** (*in museum etc*) exposé(e); **in full ~ of sb** sous les yeux de qn; **in my ~** à mon avis; **in ~ of the fact that** étant donné que; **viewer** *n* (*TV*) téléspectateur(-trice); **viewpoint** *n* point *m* de vue

vigilant ['vɪdʒɪlənt] *adj* vigilant(e)

vigorous ['vɪgərəs] *adj* vigoureux(-euse)

vile [vaɪl] *adj* (*action*) vil(e); (*smell, food*) abominable; (*temper*) massacrant(e)

villa ['vɪlə] *n* villa *f*

village ['vɪlɪdʒ] *n* village *m*; **villager** *n* villageois(e)

villain ['vɪlən] *n* (*scoundrel*) scélérat *m*; (BRIT: *criminal*) bandit *m*; (*in novel etc*) traître *m*

vinaigrette [vɪneɪ'grɛt] *n* vinaigrette *f*

vine [vaɪn] *n* vigne *f*

vinegar ['vɪnɪgər] *n* vinaigre *m*

vineyard ['vɪnjɑːd] *n* vignoble *m*

vintage ['vɪntɪdʒ] *n* (*year*) année *f*, millésime *m* ▷ *cpd* (*car*) d'époque; (*wine*) de grand cru

vinyl ['vaɪnl] *n* vinyle *m*

viola [vɪ'əulə] *n* alto *m*

violate ['vaɪəleɪt] *vt* violer

violation [vaɪə'leɪʃən] *n* violation *f*; **in ~ of** (*rule, law*) en infraction à, en violation de

violence ['vaɪələns] *n* violence *f*

violent ['vaɪələnt] *adj* violent(e)

violet ['vaɪələt] *adj* (*colour*) violet(te)

▷ n (plant) violette f

violin [vaɪə'lɪn] n violon m

VIP n abbr (= very important person) VIP m

virgin ['və:dʒɪn] n vierge f

Virgo ['və:gəu] n la Vierge

virtual ['və:tjuəl] adj (Comput, Physics) virtuel(le); (in effect): **it's a ~ impossibility** c'est quasiment impossible; **virtually** adv (almost) pratiquement; **virtual reality** n (Comput) réalité virtuelle

virtue ['və:tju:] n vertu f; (advantage) mérite m, avantage m; **by ~ of** en vertu or raison de

virus ['vaɪərəs] n (Med, Comput) virus m

visa ['vɪːzə] n visa m

vise [vaɪs] n (US Tech) = **vice**

visibility [vɪzɪ'bɪlɪtɪ] n visibilité f

visible ['vɪzəbl] adj visible

vision ['vɪʒən] n (sight) vue f, vision f; (foresight, in dream) vision f

visit ['vɪzɪt] n visite f; (stay) séjour m ▷ vt (person: us: also: **~ with**) rendre visite à; (place) visiter; **visiting hours** npl heures fpl de visite; **visitor** n visiteur(-euse); (to one's house) invité(e); **visitor centre** (us **visitor center**) n hall m or centre m d'accueil

visual ['vɪzjuəl] adj visuel(le); **visualize** vt se représenter

vital ['vaɪtl] adj vital(e); **of ~ importance (to sb/sth)** d'une importance capitale (pour qn/qch)

vitality [vaɪ'tælɪtɪ] n vitalité f

vitamin ['vɪtəmɪn] n vitamine f

vivid ['vɪvɪd] adj (account) frappant(e), vivant(e); (light, imagination) vif (vive)

V-neck ['viːnɛk] n décolleté m en V

vocabulary [vəu'kæbjulərɪ] n vocabulaire m

vocal ['vəukl] adj vocal(e); (articulate) qui n'hésite pas à s'exprimer, qui sait faire entendre ses opinions

vocational [vəu'keɪʃənl] adj professionnel(le)

vodka ['vɔdkə] n vodka f

vogue [vəug] n: **to be in ~** être en vogue or à la mode

voice [vɔɪs] n voix f ▷ vt (opinion) exprimer, formuler; **voice mail** n (system) messagerie f vocale; (device) boîte f vocale

void [vɔɪd] n vide m ▷ adj (invalid) nul(le); (empty): **~ of** vide de, dépourvu(e) de

volatile ['vɔlətaɪl] adj volatil(e); (fig: person) versatile; (: situation) explosif(-ive)

volcano (pl **~es**) [vɔl'keɪnəu] n volcan m

volleyball ['vɔlɪbɔːl] n volley(-ball) m

volt [vəult] n volt m; **voltage** n tension f, voltage m

volume ['vɔljuːm] n volume m; (of tank) capacité f

voluntarily ['vɔləntrɪlɪ] adv volontairement

voluntary ['vɔləntərɪ] adj volontaire; (unpaid) bénévole

volunteer [vɔlən'tɪəʳ] n volontaire m/f ▷ vt (information) donner spontanément ▷ vi (Mil) s'engager comme volontaire; **to ~ to do** se proposer pour faire

vomit ['vɔmɪt] n vomissure f ▷ vt, vi vomir

vote [vəut] n vote m, suffrage m; (votes cast) voix f, vote; (franchise) droit m de vote ▷ vt (chairman) élire; (propose): **to ~ that** proposer que + sub ▷ vi voter; **~ of thanks** discours m de remerciement; **voter** n électeur(-trice); **voting** n scrutin m, vote m

voucher ['vautʃəʳ] n (for meal, petrol, gift) bon m

vow [vau] n vœu m, serment m ▷ vi jurer

vowel ['vauəl] n voyelle f

voyage ['vɔɪɪdʒ] n voyage m par mer, traversée f

vulgar ['vʌlgəʳ] adj vulgaire

vulnerable ['vʌlnərəbl] adj vulnérable

vulture ['vʌltʃəʳ] n vautour m

waddle ['wɔdl] *vi* se dandiner
wade [weid] *vi*: **to ~ through** marcher
dans, patauger dans; (*fig: book*) venir
à bout de
wafer ['weifə*r*] *n* (*Culin*) gaufrette *f*
waffle ['wɔfl] *n* (*Culin*) gaufre *f* ▷ *vi*
parler pour ne rien dire; faire du
remplissage
wag [wæg] *vt* agiter, remuer ▷ *vi*
remuer
wage [weidʒ] *n* (*also*: **~s**) salaire *m*, paye
f ▷ *vt*: **to ~ war** faire la guerre
wag(g)on ['wægən] *n* (*horse-drawn*)
chariot *m*; (*BRIT Rail*) wagon *m* (de
marchandises)
wail [weil] *n* gémissement *m*; (*of siren*)
hurlement *m* ▷ *vi* gémir; (*siren*) hurler
waist [weist] *n* taille *f*, ceinture *f*;
waistcoat (*BRIT*) gilet *m*
wait [weit] *n* attente *f* ▷ *vi* attendre;
to ~ for sb/sth attendre qn/qch; **to
keep sb ~ing** faire attendre qn; **~ for
me, please** attendez-moi, s'il vous
plaît; **I can't ~ to ...** (*fig*) je meurs

d'envie de ...; **to lie in ~ for** guetter;
wait on *vt fus* servir; **waiter** *n* garçon
m (de café), serveur *m*; **waiting list**
n liste *f* d'attente; **waiting room** *n*
salle *f* d'attente; **waitress** ['weitris] *n*
serveuse *f*
waive [weiv] *vt* renoncer à,
abandonner
wake [weik] *vb* (*pt* **woke** *or* **~d**, *pp*
woken *or* **~d**) ▷ *vt* (*also*: **~ up**) réveiller
▷ *vi* (*also*: **~ up**) se réveiller ▷ *n* (*for
dead person*) veillée *f* mortuaire; (*Naut*)
sillage *m*
Wales [weilz] *n* pays *m* de Galles; **the
Prince of ~** le prince de Galles
walk [wɔ:k] *n* promenade *f*; (*short*) petit
tour; (*gait*) démarche *f*; (*path*) chemin
m; (*in park etc*) allée *f* ▷ *vi* marcher;
(*for pleasure, exercise*) se promener ▷ *vt*
(*distance*) faire à pied; (*dog*) promener;
10 minutes' ~ from à 10 minutes de
marche de; **to go for a ~** se promener;
faire un tour; **from all ~s of life** de
toutes conditions sociales; **walk out**
vi (*go out*) sortir; (*as protest*) partir
(en signe de protestation); (*strike*) se
mettre en grève; **to ~ out on sb** quitter
qn; **walker** *n* (*person*) marcheur(-euse);
walkie-talkie ['wɔ:ki'tɔ:ki] *n* talkie-
walkie *m*; **walking** *n* marche *f* à pied;
walking shoes *npl* chaussures *fpl*
de marche; **walking stick** *n* canne *f*;
Walkman® *n* Walkman® *m*; **walkway**
n promenade *f*, cheminement piéton
wall [wɔ:l] *n* mur *m*; (*of tunnel, cave*)
paroi *f*
wallet ['wɔlit] *n* portefeuille *m*; **I can't
find my ~** je ne retrouve plus mon
portefeuille
wallpaper ['wɔ:lpeipə*r*] *n* papier peint
▷ *vt* tapisser
walnut ['wɔ:lnʌt] *n* noix *f*; (*tree, wood*)
noyer *m*
walrus (*pl* **~** *or* **~es**) ['wɔ:lrəs] *n* morse *m*
waltz [wɔ:lts] *n* valse *f* ▷ *vi* valser
wand [wɔnd] *n* (*also*: **magic ~**)
baguette *f* (magique)
wander ['wɔndə*r*] *vi* (*person*) errer, aller

sans but; (*thoughts*) vagabonder ▷ *vt* errer dans

want [wɒnt] *vt* vouloir; (*need*) avoir besoin de ▷ *n*: **for ~ of** par manque de, faute de; **to ~ to do** vouloir faire; **to ~ sb to do** vouloir que qn fasse; **wanted** *adj* (*criminal*) recherché(e) par la police; **"cook wanted"** "on recherche un cuisinier"

war [wɔːʳ] *n* guerre *f*; **to make ~ (on)** faire la guerre (à)

ward [wɔːd] *n* (*in hospital*) salle *f*; (*Pol*) section électorale; (*Law: child: also*: **~ of court**) pupille *m/f*

warden ['wɔːdn] *n* (*BRIT: of institution*) directeur(-trice); (*of park, game reserve*) gardien(ne); (*BRIT: also*: **traffic ~**) contractuel(le)

wardrobe ['wɔːdrəub] *n* (*cupboard*) armoire *f*; (*clothes*) garde-robe *f*

warehouse ['wɛəhaus] *n* entrepôt *m*

warfare ['wɔːfɛəʳ] *n* guerre *f*

warhead ['wɔːhɛd] *n* (*Mil*) ogive *f*

warm [wɔːm] *adj* chaud(e); (*person, thanks, welcome, applause*) chaleureux(-euse); **it's ~** il fait chaud; **I'm ~** j'ai chaud; **warm up** *vi* (*person, room*) se réchauffer; (*athlete, discussion*) s'échauffer ▷ *vt* (*food*) (faire) réchauffer; (*water*) (faire) chauffer; (*engine*) faire chauffer; **warmly** *adv* (*dress*) chaudement; (*thank, welcome*) chaleureusement; **warmth** *n* chaleur *f*

warn [wɔːn] *vt* avertir, prévenir; **to ~ sb (not) to do** conseiller à qn de (ne pas) faire; **warning** *n* avertissement *m*; (*notice*) avis *m*; **warning light** *n* avertisseur lumineux

warrant ['wɒrnt] *n* (*guarantee*) garantie *f*; (*Law: to arrest*) mandat *m* d'arrêt; (*: to search*) mandat de perquisition ▷ *vt* (*justify, merit*) justifier

warranty ['wɒrəntɪ] *n* garantie *f*

warrior ['wɒrɪəʳ] *n* guerrier(-ière)

Warsaw ['wɔːsɔː] *n* Varsovie

warship ['wɔːʃɪp] *n* navire *m* de guerre

wart [wɔːt] *n* verrue *f*

wartime ['wɔːtaɪm] *n*: **in ~** en temps de guerre

wary ['wɛərɪ] *adj* prudent(e)

was [wɒz] *pt of* **be**

wash [wɒʃ] *vt* laver ▷ *vi* se laver; (*sea*): **to ~ over/against sth** inonder/baigner qch ▷ *n* (*clothes*) lessive *f*; (*washing programme*) lavage *m*; (*of ship*) sillage *m*; **to have a ~** se laver, faire sa toilette; **wash up** *vi* (*BRIT*) faire la vaisselle; (*US: have a wash*) se débarbouiller; **washbasin** *n* lavabo *m*; **wash cloth** *n* (*US*) gant *m* de toilette; **washer** *n* (*Tech*) rondelle *f*, joint *m*; **washing** *n* (*BRIT: linen etc: dirty*) linge *m*; (*: clean*) lessive *f*; **washing line** *n* (*BRIT*) corde *f* à linge; **washing machine** *n* machine *f* à laver; **washing powder** *n* (*BRIT*) lessive *f* (en poudre)

Washington ['wɒʃɪŋtən] *n* Washington *m*

wash: **washing-up** *n* (*BRIT*) vaisselle *f*; **washing-up liquid** *n* (*BRIT*) produit *m* pour la vaisselle; **washroom** *n* (*US*) toilettes *fpl*

wasn't ['wɒznt] = **was not**

wasp [wɒsp] *n* guêpe *f*

waste [weɪst] *n* gaspillage *m*; (*of time*) perte *f*; (*rubbish*) déchets *mpl*; (*also*: **household ~**) ordures *fpl* ▷ *adj* (*land, ground: in city*) à l'abandon; (*leftover*): **~ material** déchets *mpl* ▷ *vt* gaspiller; (*time, opportunity*) perdre; **waste ground** *n* (*BRIT*) terrain *m* vague; **wastepaper basket** *n* corbeille *f* à papier

watch [wɒtʃ] *n* montre *f*; (*act of watching*) surveillance *f*; (*guard: Mil*) sentinelle *f*; (*: Naut*) homme *m* de quart; (*Naut: spell of duty*) quart *m* ▷ *vt* (*look at*) observer; (*: match, programme*) regarder; (*spy on, guard*) surveiller; (*be careful of*) faire attention à ▷ *vi* regarder; (*keep guard*) monter la garde; **to keep ~** faire le guet; **watch out** *vi* faire attention; **watchdog** *n* chien *m* de garde; (*fig*) gardien(ne); **watch strap** *n* bracelet *m* de montre

water ['wɔːtəʳ] *n* eau *f* ▷ *vt* (*plant, garden*) arroser ▷ *vi* (*eyes*) larmoyer; **in**

British ~s dans les eaux territoriales Britanniques; **to make sb's mouth ~** mettre l'eau à la bouche de qn; **water down** vt (milk etc) couper avec de l'eau; (fig: story) édulcorer; **watercolour** (us **watercolor**) n aquarelle f; **watercress** n cresson m (de fontaine); **waterfall** n chute f d'eau; **watering can** n arrosoir m; **watermelon** n pastèque f; **waterproof** adj imperméable; **water-skiing** n ski m nautique

watt [wɔt] n watt m

wave [weɪv] n vague f; (of hand) geste m, signe m; (Radio) onde f; (in hair) ondulation f; (fig: of enthusiasm, strikes etc) vague f ▷ vi faire signe de la main; (flag) flotter au vent; (grass) ondoyer ▷ vt (handkerchief) agiter; (stick) brandir; **wavelength** n longueur f d'ondes

waver [ˈweɪvəʳ] vi vaciller; (voice) trembler; (person) hésiter

wavy [ˈweɪvɪ] adj (hair, surface) ondulé(e); (line) onduleux(-euse)

wax [wæks] n cire f; (for skis) fart m ▷ vt cirer; (car) lustrer; (skis) farter ▷ vi (moon) croître

way [weɪ] n chemin m, voie f; (distance) distance f; (direction) chemin, direction f; (manner) façon f, manière f; (habit) habitude f, façon; **which ~? — this ~/that ~** par où ou de quel côté? — par ici/par là; **to lose one's ~** perdre son chemin; **on the ~ (to)** en route (pour); **to be on one's ~** être en route; **to be in the ~** bloquer le passage; (fig) gêner; **it's a long ~ away** c'est loin d'ici; **to go out of one's ~ to do** (fig) se donner beaucoup de mal pour faire; **to be under ~** (work, project) être en cours; **in a ~** dans un sens; **by the ~** à propos; **"~ in"** (BRIT) "entrée"; **"~ out"** (BRIT) "sortie"; **the ~ back** le chemin du retour; **"give ~"** (BRIT Aut) "cédez la priorité"; **no ~!** (inf) pas question!

W.C. n abbr (BRIT: = water closet) w.-c. mpl, waters mpl

we [wiː] pl pron nous

weak [wiːk] adj faible; (health) fragile; (beam etc) peu solide; (tea, coffee) léger(-ère); **weaken** vi faiblir ▷ vt affaiblir; **weakness** n faiblesse f; (fault) point m faible

wealth [wɛlθ] n (money, resources) richesse(s) f(pl); (of details) profusion f; **wealthy** adj riche

weapon [ˈwɛpən] n arme f; **~s of mass destruction** armes fpl de destruction massive

wear [wɛəʳ] n (use) usage m; (deterioration through use) usure f ▷ vb (pt **wore**, pp **worn**) ▷ vt (clothes) porter; (put on) mettre; (damage: through use) user ▷ vi (last) faire de l'usage; (rub etc through) s'user; **sports/baby~** vêtements mpl de sport/pour bébés; **evening ~** tenue f de soirée; **wear off** vi disparaître; **wear out** vt user; (person, strength) épuiser

weary [ˈwɪərɪ] adj (tired) épuisé(e); (dispirited) las (lasse); abattu(e) ▷ vi: **to ~ of** se lasser de

weasel [ˈwiːzl] n (Zool) belette f

weather [ˈwɛðəʳ] n temps m ▷ vt (storm: lit, fig) essuyer; (crisis) survivre à; **under the ~** (fig: ill) mal fichu(e); **weather forecast** n prévisions fpl météorologiques, météo f

weave (pt **wove**, pp **woven**) [wiːv, wəuv, ˈwəuvn] vt (cloth) tisser; (basket) tresser

web [wɛb] n (of spider) toile f; (on duck's foot) palmure f; (fig) tissu m; (Comput): **the (World-Wide) W~** le Web; **web page** n (Comput) page f Web; **website** n (Comput) site m web

wed [wɛd] (pt, pp **~ded**) vt épouser ▷ vi se marier

Wed abbr (= Wednesday) me

we'd [wiːd] = **we had**; **we would**

wedding [ˈwɛdɪŋ] n mariage m; **wedding anniversary** n anniversaire m de mariage; **silver/golden wedding anniversary** noces fpl d'argent/d'or; **wedding day** n jour m du mariage; **wedding dress** n robe f de mariée;

wedding ring n alliance f

wedge [wɛdʒ] n (of wood etc) coin m; (under door etc) cale f; (of cake) part f ▷ vt (fix) caler; (push) enfoncer, coincer

Wednesday ['wɛdnzdɪ] n mercredi m

wee [wiː] adj (SCOTTISH) petit(e); tout(e) petit(e)

weed [wiːd] n mauvaise herbe ▷ vt désherber; **weedkiller** n désherbant m

week [wiːk] n semaine f; **a ~ today/on Tuesday** aujourd'hui/mardi en huit; **weekday** n jour m de semaine; (Comm) jour ouvrable; **weekend** n week-end m; **weekly** adv une fois par semaine, chaque semaine ▷ adj, n hebdomadaire (m)

weep [wiːp] (pt, pp wept) vi (person) pleurer

weigh [weɪ] vt, vi peser; **to ~ anchor** lever l'ancre; **weigh up** vt examiner

weight [weɪt] n poids m; **to put on/ lose ~** grossir/maigrir; **weightlifting** n haltérophilie f

weir [wɪəʳ] n barrage m

weird [wɪəd] adj bizarre; (eerie) surnaturel(le)

welcome ['wɛlkəm] adj bienvenu(e) ▷ n accueil m ▷ vt accueillir; (also: **bid ~**) souhaiter la bienvenue à; (be glad of) se réjouir de; **you're ~!** (after thanks) de rien, il n'y a pas de quoi

weld [wɛld] vt souder

welfare ['wɛlfɛəʳ] n (wellbeing) bien-être m; (social aid) assistance sociale; **welfare state** n État-providence m

well [wɛl] n puits m ▷ adv bien ▷ adj: **to be ~** aller bien ▷ excl eh bien!; (relief also) bon!; (resignation) enfin!; **~ done!** bravo!; **get ~ soon!** remets-toi vite!; **to do ~** bien réussir; (business) prospérer; **as ~** (in addition) aussi, également; **as ~ as** aussi bien que or de; en plus de

we'll [wiːl] = **we will**; **we shall**

well: **well-behaved** adj sage, obéissant(e); **well-built** adj (person) bien bâti(e); **well-dressed** adj bien habillé(e), bien vêtu(e)

well-groomed [-'gruːmd] adj très soigné(e)

wellies ['wɛlɪz] (inf) npl (BRIT) = **wellingtons**

wellingtons ['wɛlɪŋtənz] npl (also: **wellington boots**) bottes fpl en caoutchouc

well: **well-known** adj (person) bien connu(e); **well-off** adj aisé(e), assez riche; **well-paid** [wɛl'peɪd] adj bien payé(e)

Welsh [wɛlʃ] adj gallois(e) ▷ n (Ling) gallois m; **the Welsh** npl (people) les Gallois; **Welshman** (irreg) n Gallois m; **Welshwoman** (irreg) n Galloise f

went [wɛnt] pt of **go**

wept [wɛpt] pt, pp of **weep**

were [wəːʳ] pt of **be**

we're [wɪəʳ] = **we are**

weren't [wəːnt] = **were not**

west [wɛst] n ouest m ▷ adj (wind) d'ouest; (side) ouest inv ▷ adv à or vers l'ouest; **the W~** l'Occident m, l'Ouest; **westbound** ['wɛstbaʊnd] adj en direction de l'ouest; (carriageway) ouest inv; **western** adj occidental(e), de or à l'ouest ▷ n (Cine) western m; **West Indian** adj antillais(e) ▷ n Antillais(e)

West Indies [-'ɪndɪz] npl Antilles fpl

wet [wɛt] adj mouillé(e); (damp) humide; (soaked: also: **~ through**) trempé(e); (rainy) pluvieux(-euse); **to get ~** se mouiller; **"~ paint"** "attention peinture fraîche"; **wetsuit** n combinaison f de plongée

we've [wiːv] = **we have**

whack [wæk] vt donner un grand coup à

whale [weɪl] n (Zool) baleine f

wharf (pl **wharves**) [wɔːf, wɔːvz] n quai m

 KEYWORD

what [wɔt] adj **1** (in questions) quel(le); **what size is he?** quelle taille fait-il?; **what colour is it?** de quelle couleur est-ce?; **what books do you need?**

quels livres vous faut-il?
2 (in exclamations): **what a mess!** quel
désordre!; **what a fool I am!** que je
suis bête!
▷ pron **1** (interrogative) que; de/à/en
etc quoi; **what are you doing?** que
faites-vous?, qu'est-ce que vous faites?;
what is happening? qu'est-ce qui se
passe?, que se passe-t-il?; **what are
you talking about?** de quoi parlez-
vous?; **what are you thinking about?**
à quoi pensez-vous?; **what is it called?**
comment est-ce que ça s'appelle?;
what about me? et moi?; **what about
doing ...?** et si on faisait ...?
2 (relative: subject) ce qui; (: direct object)
ce que; (: indirect object) ce à quoi, ce
dont; **I saw what you did/was on the
table** j'ai vu ce que vous avez fait/ce
qui était sur la table; **tell me what
you remember** dites-moi ce dont
vous vous souvenez; **what I want is
a cup of tea** ce que je veux, c'est une
tasse de thé
▷ excl (disbelieving) quoi!, comment!

whatever [wɔtˈɛvəʳ] adj: **take ~ book
you prefer** prenez le livre que vous
préférez, peu importe lequel; **~ book
you take** quel que soit le livre que
vous preniez ▷ pron: **do ~ is
necessary** faites (tout) ce qui est
nécessaire; **~ happens** quoi qu'il
arrive; **no reason ~ or whatsoever**
pas la moindre raison; **nothing ~ or
whatsoever** rien du tout
whatsoever [wɔtsəuˈɛvəʳ] adj see
whatever
wheat [wiːt] n blé m, froment m
wheel [wiːl] n roue f; (Aut: also:
steering ~) volant m; (Naut)
gouvernail m ▷ vt (pram etc) pousser,
rouler ▷ vi (birds) tournoyer; (also:
~ round: person) se retourner, faire
volte-face; **wheelbarrow** n brouette f;
wheelchair n fauteuil roulant;
wheel clamp n (Aut) sabot m (de
Denver)

wheeze [wiːz] vi respirer bruyamment

when [wɛn] adv quand; **when did he
go?** quand est-ce qu'il est parti?
▷ conj **1** (at, during, after the time that)
quand, lorsque; **she was reading
when I came in** elle lisait quand or
lorsque je suis entré
2 (on, at which): **on the day when I met
him** le jour où je l'ai rencontré
3 (whereas) alors que; **I thought I was
wrong when in fact I was right** j'ai
cru que j'avais tort alors qu'en fait
j'avais raison

whenever [wɛnˈɛvəʳ] adv quand donc
▷ conj quand; (every time that) chaque
fois que
where [wɛəʳ] adv, conj où; **this is ~**
c'est là que; **whereabouts** adv où
donc ▷ n: **nobody knows his
whereabouts** personne ne sait où
il se trouve; **whereas** conj alors que;
whereby adv (formal) par lequel (or
laquelle etc); **wherever** adv où donc
▷ conj où que + sub; **sit wherever
you like** asseyez-vous (là) où vous
voulez
whether [ˈwɛðəʳ] conj si; **I don't know
~ to accept or not** je ne sais pas si je
dois accepter ou non; **it's doubtful ~** il
est peu probable que + sub; **~ you go or
not** que vous y alliez ou non

which [wɪtʃ] adj **1** (interrogative: direct,
indirect) quel(le); **which picture do
you want?** quel tableau voulez-vous?;
which one? lequel (laquelle)?
2: **in which case** auquel cas; **we got
there at 8pm, by which time the
cinema was full** quand nous
sommes arrivés à 20h, le cinéma
était complet
▷ pron **1** (interrogative) lequel (laquelle),

lesquels (lesquelles) pl; **I don't mind which** peu importe lequel; **which (of these) are yours?** lesquels sont à vous?; **tell me which you want** dites-moi lesquels or ceux que vous voulez

2 (relative: subject) qui; (: object) que; sur/vers etc lequel (laquelle) (NB: à + lequel = **auquel**; de + lequel = **duquel**); **the apple which you ate/which is on the table** la pomme que vous avez mangée/qui est sur la table; **the chair on which you are sitting** la chaise sur laquelle vous êtes assis; **the book of which you spoke** le livre dont vous avez parlé; **he said he knew, which is true/I was afraid of** il a dit qu'il le savait, ce qui est vrai/ce que je craignais; **after which** après quoi

whichever [wɪtʃˈɛvəʳ] adj: **take ~ book you prefer** prenez le livre que vous préférez, peu importe lequel; **~ book you take** quel que soit le livre que vous preniez

while [waɪl] n moment m ▷ conj pendant que; (as long as) tant que; (as, whereas) alors que; (though) bien que + sub, quoique + sub; **for a ~** pendant quelque temps; **in a ~** dans un moment

whilst [waɪlst] conj = **while**

whim [wɪm] n caprice m

whine [waɪn] n gémissement m; (of engine, siren) plainte stridente ▷ vi gémir, geindre, pleurnicher; (dog, engine, siren) gémir

whip [wɪp] n fouet m; (for riding) cravache f; (Pol: person) chef m de file (assurant la discipline dans son groupe parlementaire) ▷ vt fouetter; (snatch) enlever (or sortir) brusquement; **whipped cream** n crème fouettée

whirl [wəːl] vi tourbillonner; (dancers) tournoyer ▷ vt faire tourbillonner; faire tournoyer

whisk [wɪsk] n (Culin) fouet m ▷ vt

(eggs) fouetter, battre; **to ~ sb away** or **off** emmener qn rapidement

whiskers [ˈwɪskəz] npl (of animal) moustaches fpl; (of man) favoris mpl

whisky (IRISH, US **whiskey**) [ˈwɪskɪ] n whisky m

whisper [ˈwɪspəʳ] n chuchotement m ▷ vt, vi chuchoter

whistle [ˈwɪsl] n (sound) sifflement m; (object) sifflet m ▷ vi siffler ▷ vt siffler, siffloter

white [waɪt] adj blanc (blanche); (with fear) blême ▷ n blanc m; (person) blanc (blanche); **White House** n (US): **the White House** la Maison-Blanche; **whitewash** n (paint) lait m de chaux ▷ vt blanchir à la chaux; (fig) blanchir

whiting [ˈwaɪtɪŋ] n (pl inv: fish) merlan m

Whitsun [ˈwɪtsn] n la Pentecôte

whittle [ˈwɪtl] vt: **to ~ away**, **to ~ down** (costs) réduire, rogner

whizz [wɪz] vi aller (or passer) à toute vitesse

who [huː] pron qui

whoever [huːˈɛvəʳ] pron: **~ finds it** celui (celle) qui le trouve (, qui que ce soit), quiconque le trouve; **ask ~ you like** demandez à qui vous voulez; **~ he marries** qui que ce soit or quelle que soit la personne qu'il épouse; **~ told you that?** qui a bien pu vous dire ça?, qui donc vous a dit ça?

whole [həʊl] adj (complete) entier(-ière), tout(e); (not broken) intact(e), complet(-ète) ▷ n (all): **the ~ of** la totalité de, tout(e) le (la); (entire unit) tout m; **the ~ of the town** la ville tout entière; **on the ~**, **as a ~** dans l'ensemble; **wholefood(s)** n(pl) aliments complets; **wholeheartedly** [həʊlˈhɑːtɪdlɪ] adv sans réserve; **to agree wholeheartedly** être entièrement d'accord; **wholemeal** adj (BRIT: flour, bread) complet(-ète); **wholesale** n (vente f en) gros m ▷ adj (price) de gros; (destruction) systématique; **wholewheat**

adj = **wholemeal**; **wholly** *adv*
entièrement, tout à fait

whom [hu:m] *pron* **1** (*interrogative*) qui;
whom did you see? qui avez-vous vu?;
to whom did you give it? à qui l'avez-vous donné?
2 (*relative*) que; à/de *etc* qui; **the man whom I saw/to whom I spoke** l'homme que j'ai vu/à qui j'ai parlé

whore [hɔːʳ] *n* (*inf: pej*) putain *f*

KEYWORD

whose [hu:z] *adj* **1** (*possessive: interrogative*): **whose book is this?**, **whose is this book?** à qui est ce livre?; **whose pencil have you taken?** à qui est le crayon que vous avez pris?, c'est le crayon de qui que vous avez pris?; **whose daughter are you?** de qui êtes-vous la fille?
2 (*possessive: relative*): **the man whose son you rescued** l'homme dont *or* de qui vous avez sauvé le fils; **the girl whose sister you were speaking to** la fille à la sœur de qui *or* de laquelle vous parliez; **the woman whose car was stolen** la femme dont la voiture a été volée
▷ *pron* à qui; **whose is this?** à qui est ceci?; **I know whose it is** je sais à qui c'est

KEYWORD

why [waɪ] *adv* pourquoi; **why not?** pourquoi pas?
▷ *conj*: **I wonder why he said that** je me demande pourquoi il a dit ça; **that's not why I'm here** ce n'est pas pour ça que je suis là; **the reason why** la raison pour laquelle
▷ *excl* eh bien!, tiens!; **why, it's**

you! tiens, c'est vous!; **why, that's impossible!** voyons, c'est impossible!

wicked ['wɪkɪd] *adj* méchant(e); (*mischievous: grin, look*) espiègle, malicieux(-euse); (*crime*) pervers(e); (*inf: very good*) génial(e) (*inf*)

wicket ['wɪkɪt] *n* (*Cricket: stumps*) guichet *m*; (: *grass area*) espace compris entre les deux guichets

wide [waɪd] *adj* large; (*area, knowledge*) vaste, très étendu(e); (*choice*) grand(e)
▷ *adv*: **to open ~** ouvrir tout grand; **to shoot ~** tirer à côté; **it is 3 metres ~** cela fait 3 mètres de large; **widely** *adv* (*different*) radicalement; (*spaced*) sur une grande étendue; (*believed*) généralement; (*travel*) beaucoup; **widen** *vt* élargir ▷ *vi* s'élargir; **wide open** *adj* grand(e) ouvert(e); **widespread** *adj* (*belief etc*) très répandu(e)

widow ['wɪdəu] *n* veuve *f*; **widower** *n* veuf *m*

width [wɪdθ] *n* largeur *f*

wield [wi:ld] *vt* (*sword*) manier; (*power*) exercer

wife (*pl* **wives**) [waɪf, waɪvz] *n* femme *f*, épouse *f*

wig [wɪg] *n* perruque *f*

wild [waɪld] *adj* sauvage; (*sea*) déchaîné(e); (*idea, life*) fou (folle); (*behaviour*) déchaîné(e), extravagant(e); (*inf: angry*) hors de soi, furieux(-euse)
▷ *n*: **the ~** la nature; **wilderness** ['wɪldənɪs] *n* désert *m*, région *f* sauvage; **wildlife** *n* faune *f* (et flore *f*); **wildly** *adv* (*behave*) de manière déchaînée; (*applaud*) frénétiquement; (*hit, guess*) au hasard; (*happy*) follement

KEYWORD

will [wɪl] *aux vb* **1** (*forming future tense*): **I will finish it tomorrow** je le finirai demain; **I will have finished it by tomorrow** je l'aurai fini d'ici demain; **will you do it? - yes I will/no I won't** le

ferez-vous? - oui/non
2 (*in conjectures, predictions*): **he will** or
he'll be there by now il doit être arrivé
à l'heure qu'il est; **that will be the
postman** ça doit être le facteur
3 (*in commands, requests, offers*): **will
you be quiet!** voulez-vous bien vous
taire!; **will you help me?** est-ce que
vous pouvez m'aider?; **will you have a
cup of tea?** voulez-vous une tasse de
thé?; **I won't put up with it!** je ne le
tolérerai pas!
▷ *vt* (*pt, pp* **willed**): **to will sb to do**
souhaiter ardemment que qn fasse;
he willed himself to go on par un
suprême effort de volonté, il continua
▷ *n* volonté *f*; (*document*) testament *m*;
against one's will à contre-cœur

willing ['wɪlɪŋ] *adj* de bonne volonté,
serviable; **he's ~ to do it** il est disposé
à le faire, il veut bien le faire; **willingly**
adv volontiers
willow ['wɪləu] *n* saule *m*
willpower ['wɪl'pauə'] *n* volonté *f*
wilt [wɪlt] *vi* dépérir
win [wɪn] *n* (*in sports etc*) victoire *f* ▷ *vb*
(*pt, pp* **won**) ▷ *vt* (*battle, money*) gagner;
(*prize, contract*) remporter; (*popularity*)
acquérir ▷ *vi* gagner; **win over** *vt*
convaincre
wince [wɪns] *vi* tressaillir
wind¹ [wɪnd] *n* (*also Med*) vent *m*;
(*breath*) souffle *m* ▷ *vt* (*take breath away*)
couper le souffle à; **the ~(s)** (*Mus*) les
instruments *mpl* à vent
wind² (*pt, pp* **wound**) [waɪnd, waund]
vt enrouler; (*wrap*) envelopper;
(*clock, toy*) remonter ▷ *vi* (*road, river*)
serpenter; **wind down** *vt* (*car window*)
baisser; (*fig: production, business*) réduire
progressivement; **wind up** *vt* (*clock*)
remonter; (*debate*) terminer, clôturer
windfall ['wɪndfɔ:l] *n* coup *m* de
chance
winding ['waɪndɪŋ] *adj* (*road*)
sinueux(-euse); (*staircase*) tournant(e)
windmill ['wɪndmɪl] *n* moulin *m* à vent

window ['wɪndəu] *n* fenêtre *f*; (*in
car, train: also: ~pane*) vitre *f*; (*in
shop etc*) vitrine *f*; **window box** *n*
jardinière *f*; **window cleaner** *n* (*person*)
laveur(-euse) de vitres; **window pane**
n vitre *f*, carreau *m*; **window seat** *n* (*in
vehicle*) place *f* côté fenêtre; **windowsill**
n (*inside*) appui *m* de la fenêtre; (*outside*)
rebord *m* de la fenêtre
windscreen ['wɪndskri:n] *n* pare-
brise *m inv*; **windscreen wiper** *n*
essuie-glace *m inv*
windshield ['wɪndʃi:ld] (*US*) *n*
= **windscreen**
windsurfing ['wɪndsə:fɪŋ] *n* planche
f à voile
windy ['wɪndɪ] *adj* (*day*) de vent,
venteux(-euse); (*place, weather*)
venteux; **it's ~** il y a du vent
wine [waɪn] *n* vin *m*; **wine bar** *n* bar *m*
à vin; **wine glass** *n* verre *m* à vin; **wine
list** *n* carte *f* des vins; **wine tasting** *n*
dégustation *f* (de vins)
wing [wɪŋ] *n* aile *f*; **wings** *npl* (*Theat*)
coulisses *fpl*; **wing mirror** *n* (*BRIT*)
rétroviseur latéral
wink [wɪŋk] *n* clin *m* d'œil ▷ *vi* faire un
clin d'œil; (*blink*) cligner des yeux
winner ['wɪnə'] *n* gagnant(e)
winning ['wɪnɪŋ] *adj* (*team*)
gagnant(e); (*goal*) décisif(-ive);
(*charming*) charmeur(-euse)
winter ['wɪntə'] *n* hiver *m* ▷ *vi*
hiverner; **in ~** en hiver; **winter sports**
npl sports *mpl* d'hiver; **wintertime**
n hiver *m*
wipe [waɪp] *n*: **to give sth a ~** donner
un coup de torchon/de chiffon/
d'éponge à qch ▷ *vt* essuyer; (*erase:
tape*) effacer; **to ~ one's nose** se
moucher; **wipe out** *vt* (*debt*) éteindre,
amortir; (*memory*) effacer; (*destroy*)
anéantir; **wipe up** *vt* essuyer
wire ['waɪə'] *n* fil *m* (de fer); (*Elec*) fil
électrique; (*Tel*) télégramme *m* ▷ *vt*
(*house*) faire l'installation électrique
de; (*also: ~ up*) brancher; (*person: send
telegram to*) télégraphier à

wiring ['waɪərɪŋ] *n* (*Elec*) installation *f* électrique

wisdom ['wɪzdəm] *n* sagesse *f*; (*of action*) prudence *f*; **wisdom tooth** *n* dent *f* de sagesse

wise [waɪz] *adj* sage, prudent(e); (*remark*) judicieux(-euse)

wish [wɪʃ] *n* (*desire*) désir *m*; (*specific desire*) souhait *m*, vœu *m* ▷ *vt* souhaiter, désirer, vouloir; **best ~es** (*on birthday etc*) meilleurs vœux; **with best ~es** (*in letter*) bien amicalement; **to ~ sb goodbye** dire au revoir à qn; **he ~ed me well** il m'a souhaité bonne chance; **to ~ to do/sb to do** désirer or vouloir faire/que qn fasse; **to ~ for** souhaiter

wistful ['wɪstful] *adj* mélancolique

wit [wɪt] *n* (*also*: **~s**: *intelligence*) intelligence *f*, esprit *m*; (*presence of mind*) présence *f* d'esprit; (*wittiness*) esprit; (*person*) homme/femme d'esprit

witch [wɪtʃ] *n* sorcière *f*

○ **KEYWORD**

with [wɪð, wɪθ] *prep* **1** (*in the company of*) avec; (*at the home of*) chez; **we stayed with friends** nous avons logé chez des amis; **I'll be with you in a minute** je suis à vous dans un instant

2 (*descriptive*): **a room with a view** une chambre avec vue; **the man with the grey hat/blue eyes** l'homme au chapeau gris/aux yeux bleus

3 (*indicating manner, means, cause*): **with tears in her eyes** les larmes aux yeux; **to walk with a stick** marcher avec une canne; **red with anger** rouge de colère; **to shake with fear** trembler de peur; **to fill sth with water** remplir qch d'eau

4 (*in phrases*): **I'm with you** (*I understand*) je vous suis; **to be with it** (*inf*: *up-to-date*) être dans le vent

withdraw [wɪθ'drɔː] *vt* (*irreg*: *like* **draw**) retirer ▷ *vi* se retirer; **withdrawal** *n* retrait *m*; (*Med*) état *m* de manque;

withdrawn *pp of* **withdraw** ▷ *adj* (*person*) renfermé(e)

withdrew [wɪθ'druː] *pt of* **withdraw**

wither ['wɪðəʳ] *vi* se faner

withhold [wɪθ'həuld] *vt* (*irreg*: *like* **hold**) (*money*) retenir; (*decision*) remettre; (*permission*): **to ~ (from)** (*permission*) refuser (à); (*information*): **to ~ (from)** cacher (à)

within [wɪð'ɪn] *prep* à l'intérieur de ▷ *adv* à l'intérieur; **~ his reach** à sa portée; **~ sight of** en vue de; **~ a mile of** à moins d'un mille de; **~ the week** avant la fin de la semaine

without [wɪð'aut] *prep* sans; **~ a coat** sans manteau; **~ speaking** sans parler; **to go** *or* **do ~ sth** se passer de qch

withstand [wɪθ'stænd] *vt* (*irreg*: *like* **stand**) résister à

witness ['wɪtnɪs] *n* (*person*) témoin *m* ▷ *vt* (*event*) être témoin de; (*document*) attester l'authenticité de; **to bear ~ to sth** témoigner de qch

witty ['wɪtɪ] *adj* spirituel(le), plein(e) d'esprit

wives [waɪvz] *npl of* **wife**

wizard ['wɪzəd] *n* magicien *m*

wk *abbr* = **week**

wobble ['wɔbl] *vi* trembler; (*chair*) branler

woe [wəu] *n* malheur *m*

woke [wəuk] *pt of* **wake**

woken ['wəukn] *pp of* **wake**

wolf (*pl* **wolves**) [wulf, wulvz] *n* loup *m*

woman (*pl* **women**) ['wumən, 'wɪmɪn] *n* femme *f* ▷ *cpd*: **~ doctor** femme *f* médecin; **~ teacher** professeur *m* femme

womb [wuːm] *n* (*Anat*) utérus *m*

women ['wɪmɪn] *npl of* **woman**

won [wʌn] *pt*, *pp of* **win**

wonder ['wʌndəʳ] *n* merveille *f*, miracle *m*; (*feeling*) émerveillement *m* ▷ *vi*: **to ~ whether/why** se demander si/pourquoi; **to ~ at** (*surprise*) s'étonner de; (*admiration*) s'émerveiller de; **to ~ about** songer à; **it's no ~ that** il n'est pas étonnant que + *sub*; **wonderful** *adj*

merveilleux(-euse)
won't [wəʊnt] = **will not**
wood [wʊd] n (timber, forest) bois m;
wooden adj en bois; (fig: actor) raide;
(: performance) qui manque de naturel;
woodwind n: **the woodwind** (Mus) les
bois mpl; **woodwork** n menuiserie f
wool [wʊl] n laine f; **to pull the ~ over
sb's eyes** (fig) en faire accroire à qn;
woollen (us **woolen**) adj de or en laine;
woolly (us **wooly**) adj laineux(-euse);
(fig: ideas) confus(e)
word [wəːd] n mot m; (spoken) mot,
parole f; (promise) parole; (news)
nouvelles fpl ▷ vt rédiger, formuler; **in
other ~s** en d'autres termes; **to have
a ~ with sb** toucher un mot à qn; **to
break/keep one's ~** manquer à sa
parole/tenir (sa) parole; **wording** n
termes mpl, langage m; (of document)
libellé m; **word processing** n
traitement m de texte; **word processor**
n machine f de traitement de texte
wore [wɔːʳ] pt of **wear**
work [wəːk] n travail m; (Art, Literature)
œuvre f ▷ vi travailler; (mechanism)
marcher, fonctionner; (plan etc)
marcher; (medicine) agir ▷ vt (clay,
wood etc) travailler; (mine etc) exploiter;
(machine) faire marcher or fonctionner;
(miracles etc) faire; **works** n (BRIT:
factory) usine f; **how does this ~?**
comment est-ce que ça marche?; **the
TV isn't ~ing** la télévision est en
panne or ne marche pas; **to be out of
~** être au chômage or sans emploi; **to
~ loose** se défaire, se desserrer; **work
out** vi (plans etc) marcher; (Sport)
s'entraîner ▷ vt (problem) résoudre;
(plan) élaborer; **it ~s out at £100** ça fait
100 livres; **worker** n travailleur(-euse),
ouvrier(-ière); **work experience** n
stage m; **workforce** n main-d'œuvre f;
working class n classe ouvrière ▷ adj:
working-class ouvrier(-ière), de la
classe ouvrière; **working week** n
semaine f de travail; **workman** (irreg)
n ouvrier m; **work of art** n œuvre

f d'art; **workout** n (Sport) séance
f d'entraînement; **work permit** n
permis m de travail; **workplace** n lieu
m de travail; **worksheet** n (Scol) feuille
f d'exercices; **workshop** n atelier m;
work station n poste m de travail;
work surface n plan m de travail;
worktop n plan m de travail
world [wəːld] n monde m ▷ cpd
(champion) du monde; (power, war)
mondial(e); **to think the ~ of sb** (fig)
ne jurer que par qn; **World Cup** n:
the World Cup (Football) la Coupe du
monde; **world-wide** adj universel(le);
World-Wide Web n: **the World-Wide
Web** le Web
worm [wəːm] n (also: **earth~**) ver m
worn [wɔːn] pp of **wear** ▷ adj usé(e);
worn-out adj (object) complètement
usé(e); (person) épuisé(e)
worried ['wʌrɪd] adj inquiet(-ète); **to
be ~ about sth** être inquiet au sujet
de qch
worry ['wʌrɪ] n souci m ▷ vt inquiéter
▷ vi s'inquiéter, se faire du souci;
worrying adj inquiétant(e)
worse [wəːs] adj pire, plus mauvais(e)
▷ adv plus mal ▷ n pire m; **to get
~** (condition, situation) empirer,
se dégrader; **a change for the ~**
une détérioration; **worsen** vt, vi
empirer; **worse off** adj moins à l'aise
financièrement; (fig): **you'll be worse
off this way** ça ira moins bien de
cette façon
worship ['wəːʃɪp] n culte m ▷ vt (God)
rendre un culte à; (person) adorer
worst [wəːst] adj le (la) pire, le (la) plus
mauvais(e) ▷ adv le plus mal ▷ n pire
m; **at ~** au pis aller
worth [wəːθ] n valeur f ▷ adj: **to be ~**
valoir; **it's ~ it** cela en vaut la peine,
ça vaut la peine; **it is ~ one's while
(to do)** ça vaut le coup (inf) (de faire);
worthless adj qui ne vaut rien;
worthwhile adj (activity) qui en vaut la
peine; (cause) louable
worthy ['wəːðɪ] adj (person) digne;

(*motive*) louable; **~ of** digne de

○ KEYWORD

would [wud] *aux vb* **1** (*conditional tense*): **if you asked him he would do it** si vous le lui demandiez, il le ferait; **if you had asked him he would have done it** si vous le lui aviez demandé, il l'aurait fait

2 (*in offers, invitations, requests*): **would you like a biscuit?** voulez-vous un biscuit?; **would you close the door please?** voulez-vous fermer la porte, s'il vous plaît?

3 (*in indirect speech*): **I said I would do it** j'ai dit que je le ferais

4 (*emphatic*): **it WOULD have to snow today!** naturellement il neige aujourd'hui! *or* il fallait qu'il neige aujourd'hui!

5 (*insistence*): **she wouldn't do it** elle n'a pas voulu *or* elle a refusé de le faire

6 (*conjecture*): **it would have been midnight** il devait être minuit; **it would seem so** on dirait bien

7 (*indicating habit*): **he would go there on Mondays** il y allait le lundi

wouldn't ['wudnt] = **would not**
wound¹ [wu:nd] *n* blessure *f* ▷ *vt* blesser
wound² [waund] *pt, pp of* **wind**
wove [wəuv] *pt of* **weave**
woven ['wəuvn] *pp of* **weave**
wrap [ræp] *vt* (*also*: **~ up**) envelopper; (*parcel*) emballer; (*wind*) enrouler; **wrapper** *n* (*on chocolate etc*) papier *m*; (*BRIT: of book*) couverture *f*; **wrapping** *n* (*of sweet, chocolate*) papier *m*; (*of parcel*) emballage *m*; **wrapping paper** *n* papier *m* d'emballage; (*for gift*) papier cadeau
wreath [ri:θ, *pl* ri:ðz] *n* couronne *f*
wreck [rɛk] *n* (*sea disaster*) naufrage *m*; (*ship*) épave *f*; (*vehicle*) véhicule accidenté; (*pej: person*) loque (humaine) ▷ *vt* démolir; (*fig*) briser,

ruiner; **wreckage** *n* débris *mpl*; (*of building*) décombres *mpl*; (*of ship*) naufrage *m*
wren [rɛn] *n* (*Zool*) troglodyte *m*
wrench [rɛntʃ] *n* (*Tech*) clé *f* (à écrous); (*tug*) violent mouvement de torsion; (*fig*) déchirement *m* ▷ *vt* tirer violemment sur, tordre; **to ~ sth from** arracher qch (violemment) à *or* de
wrestle ['rɛsl] *vi*: **to ~ (with sb)** lutter (avec qn); **wrestler** *n* lutteur(-euse); **wrestling** *n* lutte *f*; (*also*: **all-in wrestling**: *BRIT*) catch *m*
wretched ['rɛtʃɪd] *adj* misérable
wriggle ['rɪgl] *vi* (*also*: **~ about**) tortiller
wring (*pt, pp* **wrung**) [rɪŋ, rʌŋ] *vt* tordre; (*wet clothes*) essorer; (*fig*): **to ~ sth out of** arracher qch à
wrinkle ['rɪŋkl] *n* (*on skin*) ride *f*; (*on paper etc*) pli *m* ▷ *vt* rider, plisser ▷ *vi* se plisser
wrist [rɪst] *n* poignet *m*
write (*pt* **wrote**, *pp* **written**) [raɪt, rəut, 'rɪtn] *vt, vi* écrire; (*prescription*) rédiger; **write down** *vt* noter; (*put in writing*) mettre par écrit; **write off** *vt* (*debt*) passer aux profits et pertes; (*project*) mettre une croix sur; (*smash up: car etc*) démolir complètement; **write out** *vt* écrire; (*copy*) recopier; **write-off** *n* perte totale; **the car is a write-off** la voiture est bonne pour la casse; **writer** *n* auteur *m*, écrivain *m*
writing ['raɪtɪŋ] *n* écriture *f*; (*of author*) œuvres *fpl*; **in ~** par écrit; **writing paper** *n* papier *m* à lettres
written ['rɪtn] *pp of* **write**
wrong [rɒŋ] *adj* (*incorrect*) faux (fausse); (*incorrectly chosen: number, road etc*) mauvais(e); (*not suitable*) qui ne convient pas; (*wicked*) mal; (*unfair*) injuste ▷ *adv* mal ▷ *n* tort *m* ▷ *vt* faire du tort à, léser; **you are ~ to do it** tu as tort de le faire; **you are ~ about that**, **you've got it ~** tu te trompes; **what's ~?** qu'est-ce qui ne va pas?; **what's ~ with the car?** qu'est-ce qu'elle a, la

voiture?; **to go ~** (*person*) se tromper; (*plan*) mal tourner; (*machine*) se détraquer; **I took a ~ turning** je me suis trompé de route; **wrongly** *adv* à tort; (*answer, do, count*) mal, incorrectement; **wrong number** *n* (*Tel*): **you have the wrong number** vous vous êtes trompé de numéro

wrote [rəut] *pt of* **write**

wrung [rʌŋ] *pt, pp of* **wring**

WWW *n abbr* = **World-Wide Web**; **the ~** le Web

XL *abbr* (= *extra large*) XL

Xmas ['ɛksməs] *n abbr* = **Christmas**

X-ray ['ɛksreɪ] *n* (*ray*) rayon *m* X; (*photograph*) radio(graphie) *f* ▷ *vt* radiographier

xylophone ['zaɪləfəun] *n* xylophone *m*

yacht [jɔt] n voilier m; (motor, luxury yacht) yacht m; **yachting** n yachting m, navigation f de plaisance

yard [jɑːd] n (of house etc) cour f; (us: garden) jardin m; (measure) yard m (= 914 mm; 3 feet); **yard sale** n (us) brocante f (dans son propre jardin)

yarn [jɑːn] n fil m; (tale) longue histoire

yawn [jɔːn] n bâillement m ▷ vi bâiller

yd. abbr = **yard(s)**

yeah [jɛə] adv (inf) ouais

year [jɪəʳ] n an m, année f; (Scol etc) année; **to be 8 ~s old** avoir 8 ans; **an eight-~-old child** un enfant de huit ans; **yearly** adj annuel(le) ▷ adv annuellement; **twice yearly** deux fois par an

yearn [jəːn] vi: **to ~ for sth/to do** aspirer à qch/à faire

yeast [jiːst] n levure f

yell [jɛl] n hurlement m, cri m ▷ vi hurler

yellow [ˈjɛləu] adj, n jaune (m); **Yellow Pages®** npl (Tel) pages fpl jaunes

yes [jɛs] adv oui; (answering negative question) si ▷ n oui m; **to say ~ (to)** dire oui (à)

yesterday [ˈjɛstədɪ] adv, n hier (m); **~ morning/evening** hier matin/soir; **all day ~** toute la journée d'hier

yet [jɛt] adv encore; (in questions) déjà ▷ conj pourtant, néanmoins; **it is not finished ~** ce n'est pas encore fini or toujours pas fini; **have you eaten ~?** vous avez déjà mangé?; **the best ~** le meilleur jusqu'ici or jusque-là; **as ~** jusqu'ici, encore

yew [juː] n if m

Yiddish [ˈjɪdɪʃ] n yiddish m

yield [jiːld] n production f, rendement m; (Finance) rapport m ▷ vt produire, rendre, rapporter; (surrender) céder ▷ vi céder; (us Aut) céder la priorité

yob(bo) [ˈjɔb(əu)] n (BRIT inf) loubar(d) m

yoga [ˈjəugə] n yoga m

yog(h)ourt n = **yog(h)urt**

yog(h)urt [ˈjɔgət] n yaourt m

yolk [jəuk] n jaune m (d'œuf)

 KEYWORD

you [juː] pron **1** (subject) tu; (polite form) vous; (plural) vous; **you are very kind** vous êtes très gentil; **you French enjoy your food** vous autres Français, vous aimez bien manger; **you and I will go** toi et moi or vous et moi, nous irons; **there you are!** vous voilà!
2 (object: direct, indirect) te, t' + vowel; vous; **I know you** je te or vous connais; **I gave it to you** je te l'ai donné, je vous l'ai donné
3 (stressed) toi; vous; **I told YOU to do it** c'est à toi or vous que j'ai dit de le faire
4 (after prep, in comparisons) toi; vous; **it's for you** c'est pour toi or vous; **she's younger than you** elle est plus jeune que toi or vous
5 (impersonal: one) on; **fresh air does you good** l'air frais fait du bien; **you**

never know on ne sait jamais; **you can't do that!** ça ne se fait pas!

you'd [juːd] = **you had**; **you would**

you'll [juːl] = **you will**; **you shall**

young [jʌŋ] *adj* jeune ▷ *npl* (*of animal*) petits *mpl*; (*people*): **the ~** les jeunes, la jeunesse; **my ~er brother** mon frère cadet; **youngster** *n* jeune *m/f*; (*child*) enfant *m/f*

your [jɔːʳ] *adj* ton (ta), tes *pl*; (*polite form, pl*) votre, vos *pl*; *see also* **my**

you're [juəʳ] = **you are**

yours [jɔːz] *pron* le (la) tien(ne), les tiens (tiennes), (*polite form, pl*) le (la) vôtre, les vôtres; **is it ~?** c'est à toi (*or* à vous)?; **a friend of ~** un(e) de tes (*or* de vos) amis; *see also* **faithfully**; **mine¹**; **sincerely**

yourself [jɔːˈsɛlf] *pron* (*reflexive*) te; (: *polite form*) vous; (*after prep*) toi; vous; (*emphatic*) toi-même; vous-même; *see also* **oneself**; **yourselves** *pl pron* vous; (*emphatic*) vous-mêmes; *see also* **oneself**

youth [juːθ] *n* jeunesse *f*; (*young man*) (*pl* **~s**) jeune homme *m*; **youth club** *n* centre *m* de jeunes; **youthful** *adj* jeune; (*enthusiasm etc*) juvénile; **youth hostel** *n* auberge *f* de jeunesse

you've [juːv] = **you have**

Yugoslav [ˈjuːgəuslɑːv] *adj* yougoslave ▷ *n* Yougoslave *m/f*

Yugoslavia [juːgəuˈslɑːvɪə] *n* (*Hist*) Yougoslavie *f*

Z

zeal [ziːl] *n* (*revolutionary etc*) ferveur *f*; (*keenness*) ardeur *f*, zèle *m*

zebra [ˈziːbrə] *n* zèbre *m*; **zebra crossing** *n* (BRIT) passage clouté *or* pour piétons

zero [ˈzɪərəu] *n* zéro *m*

zest [zɛst] *n* entrain *m*, élan *m*; (*of lemon etc*) zeste *m*

zigzag [ˈzɪgzæg] *n* zigzag *m* ▷ *vi* zigzaguer, faire des zigzags

Zimbabwe [zɪmˈbɑːbwɪ] *n* Zimbabwe *m*

zinc [zɪŋk] *n* zinc *m*

zip [zɪp] *n* (*also*: **~ fastener**) fermeture *f* éclair® *or* à glissière ▷ *vt* (*file*) zipper; (*also*: **~ up**) fermer (avec une fermeture éclair®); **zip code** *n* (US) code postal; **zip file** *n* (*Comput*) fichier *m* zip *inv*; **zipper** *n* (US) = **zip**

zit [zɪt] (*inf*) *n* bouton *m*

zodiac [ˈzəudɪæk] *n* zodiaque *m*

zone [zəun] *n* zone *f*

zoo [zuː] *n* zoo *m*

zoology [zuːˈɔlədʒɪ] *n* zoologie *f*

zoom [zuːm] *vi*: **to ~ past** passer en
trombe; **zoom lens** *n* zoom *m*
zucchini [zuːˈkiːnɪ] *n(pl)* (*US*)
courgette(s) *f(pl)*

VERB TABLES

Introduction

The **Verb Tables** in the following section contain 29 tables of French verbs (some regular and some irregular) in alphabetical order. Each table shows you the following forms: **Present**, **Perfect**, **Future**, **Subjunctive**, **Imperfect**, **Conditional**, **Imperative** and the **Present** and **Past Participles**.

In order to help you use the verbs shown in Verb Tables correctly, there are also a number of example phrases at the bottom of each page to show the verb as it is used in context.

In French there are both **regular** verbs (their forms follow the normal rules) and **irregular** verbs (their forms do not follow the normal rules). The regular verbs in these tables are:

donner (regular -er verb, Verb Table 11)
finir (regular -ir verb, Verb Table 16)
attendre (regular -re verb, Verb Table 3)

The irregular verbs are shown in full.

For a further list of French irregular verb forms see pages xv–xvi.

▶ aller (to go)

PRESENT

je	vais
tu	vas
il/elle/on	va
nous	allons
vous	allez
ils/elles	vont

PRESENT SUBJUNCTIVE

j'	aille
tu	ailles
il/elle/on	aille
nous	allions
vous	alliez
ils/elles	aillent

PERFECT

je	suis allé(e)
tu	es allé(e)
il/elle/on	est allé(e)
nous	sommes allé(e)s
vous	êtes allé(e)(s)
ils/elles	sont allé(e)s

IMPERFECT

j'	allais
tu	allais
il/elle/on	allait
nous	allions
vous	alliez
ils/elles	allaient

FUTURE

j'	irai
tu	iras
il/elle/on	ira
nous	irons
vous	irez
ils/elles	iront

CONDITIONAL

j'	irais
tu	irais
il/elle/on	irait
nous	irions
vous	iriez
ils/elles	iraient

IMPERATIVE

va / allons / allez

PAST PARTICIPLE

allé

PRESENT PARTICIPLE

allant

EXAMPLE PHRASES

*Vous **allez** au cinéma?* Are you going to the cinema?
*Je **suis allé** à Londres.* I went to London.
*Est-ce que tu **es** déjà **allé** en Allemagne?* Have you ever been to Germany?

---

je/j' = I   **tu** = you   **il** = he/it   **elle** = she/it   **on** = we/one   **nous** = we   **vous** = you   **ils/elles** = they

▶ **attendre** (to wait)

PRESENT

j'	attends
tu	attends
il/elle/on	attend
nous	attendons
vous	attendez
ils/elles	attendent

PRESENT SUBJUNCTIVE

j'	attende
tu	attendes
il/elle/on	attende
nous	attendions
vous	attendiez
ils/elles	attendent

PERFECT

j'	ai attendu
tu	as attendu
il/elle/on	a attendu
nous	avons attendu
vous	avez attendu
ils/elles	ont attendu

IMPERFECT

j'	attendais
tu	attendais
il/elle/on	attendait
nous	attendions
vous	attendiez
ils/elles	attendaient

FUTURE

j'	attendrai
tu	attendras
il/elle/on	attendra
nous	attendrons
vous	attendrez
ils/elles	attendront

CONDITIONAL

j'	attendrais
tu	attendrais
il/elle/on	attendrait
nous	attendrions
vous	attendriez
ils/elles	attendraient

IMPERATIVE

attends / attendons / attendez

PAST PARTICIPLE

attendu

PRESENT PARTICIPLE

attendant

EXAMPLE PHRASES

Attends-*moi!* Wait for me!
*Tu **attends** depuis longtemps?* Have you been waiting long?
*Je l'**ai attendu** à la poste.* I waited for him at the post office.
*Je **m'attends** à ce qu'il soit en retard.* I expect he'll be late.

---

je/j' = I **tu** = you **il** = he/it **elle** = she/it **on** = we/one **nous** = we **vous** = you **ils/elles** = they

▶ **avoir** (to have)

PRESENT

j'	ai
tu	as
il/elle/on	a
nous	avons
vous	avez
ils/elles	ont

PRESENT SUBJUNCTIVE

j'	aie
tu	aies
il/elle/on	ait
nous	ayons
vous	ayez
ils/elles	aient

PERFECT

j'	ai eu
tu	as eu
il/elle/on	a eu
nous	avons eu
vous	avez eu
ils/elles	ont eu

IMPERFECT

j'	avais
tu	avais
il/elle/on	avait
nous	avions
vous	aviez
ils/elles	avaient

FUTURE

j'	aurai
tu	auras
il/elle/on	aura
nous	aurons
vous	aurez
ils/elles	auront

CONDITIONAL

j'	aurais
tu	aurais
il/elle/on	aurait
nous	aurions
vous	auriez
ils/elles	auraient

IMPERATIVE

aie / ayons / ayez

PAST PARTICIPLE

eu

PRESENT PARTICIPLE

ayant

EXAMPLE PHRASES

Il **a** les yeux bleus. He's got blue eyes.
Quel âge **as**-tu? How old are you?
Il **a eu** un accident. He's had an accident.
J'**avais** faim. I was hungry.
Il y **a** beaucoup de monde. There are lots of people.

---

je/j' = I　**tu** = you　**il** = he/it　**elle** = she/it　**on** = we/one　**nous** = we　**vous** = you　**ils/elles** = they

▶ **boire** (to drink)

PRESENT

je	bois
tu	bois
il/elle/on	boit
nous	buvons
vous	buvez
ils/elles	boivent

PRESENT SUBJUNCTIVE

je	boive
tu	boives
il/elle/on	boive
nous	buvions
vous	buviez
ils/elles	boivent

PERFECT

j'	ai bu
tu	as bu
il/elle/on	a bu
nous	avons bu
vous	avez bu
ils/elles	ont bu

IMPERFECT

je	buvais
tu	buvais
il/elle/on	buvait
nous	buvions
vous	buviez
ils/elles	buvaient

FUTURE

je	boirai
tu	boiras
il/elle/on	boira
nous	boirons
vous	boirez
ils/elles	boiront

CONDITIONAL

je	boirais
tu	boirais
il/elle/on	boirait
nous	boirions
vous	boiriez
ils/elles	boiraient

IMPERATIVE

bois / buvons / buvez

PAST PARTICIPLE

bu

PRESENT PARTICIPLE

buvant

EXAMPLE PHRASES

*Qu'est-ce que tu veux **boire**?* What would you like to drink?
*Il ne **boit** jamais d'alcool.* He never drinks alcohol.
*J'**ai bu** un litre d'eau.* I drank a litre of water.

je/j' = I **tu** = you **il** = he/it **elle** = she/it **on** = we/one **nous** = we **vous** = you **ils/elles** = they

▶ connaître (to know)

PRESENT

je	connais
tu	connais
il/elle/on	connaît
nous	connaissons
vous	connaissez
ils/elles	connaissent

PRESENT SUBJUNCTIVE

je	connaisse
tu	connaisses
il/elle/on	connaisse
nous	connaissions
vous	connaissiez
ils/elles	connaissent

PERFECT

j'	ai connu
tu	as connu
il/elle/on	a connu
nous	avons connu
vous	avez connu
ils/elles	ont connu

IMPERFECT

je	connaissais
tu	connaissais
il/elle/on	connaissait
nous	connaissions
vous	connaissiez
ils/elles	connaissaient

FUTURE

je	connaîtrai
tu	connaîtras
il/elle/on	connaîtra
nous	connaîtrons
vous	connaîtrez
ils/elles	connaîtront

CONDITIONAL

je	connaîtrais
tu	connaîtrais
il/elle/on	connaîtrait
nous	connaîtrions
vous	connaîtriez
ils/elles	connaîtraient

IMPERATIVE

connais / connaissons / connaissez

PAST PARTICIPLE

connu

PRESENT PARTICIPLE

connaissant

EXAMPLE PHRASES

*Je ne **connais** pas du tout cette région.* I don't know the area at all.
*Vous **connaissez** M Amiot?* Do you know Mr Amiot?
*Il n'a pas **connu** son grand-père.* He never knew his granddad.
*Ils **se sont connus** à Rouen.* They first met in Rouen.

---

je/j' = I **tu** = you **il** = he/it **elle** = she/it **on** = we/one **nous** = we **vous** = you **ils/elles** = they

▶ **courir** (to run)

PRESENT

je	cours
tu	cours
il/elle/on	court
nous	courons
vous	courez
ils/elles	courent

PRESENT SUBJUNCTIVE

je	coure
tu	coures
il/elle/on	coure
nous	courions
vous	couriez
ils/elles	courent

PERFECT

j'	ai couru
tu	as couru
il/elle/on	a couru
nous	avons couru
vous	avez couru
ils/elles	ont couru

IMPERFECT

je	courais
tu	courais
il/elle/on	courait
nous	courions
vous	couriez
ils/elles	couraient

FUTURE

je	courrai
tu	courras
il/elle/on	courra
nous	courrons
vous	courrez
ils/elles	courront

CONDITIONAL

je	courrais
tu	courrais
il/elle/on	courrait
nous	courrions
vous	courriez
ils/elles	courraient

IMPERATIVE

cours / courons / courez

PAST PARTICIPLE

couru

PRESENT PARTICIPLE

courant

EXAMPLE PHRASES

*Je ne **cours** pas très vite.* I can't run very fast.
*Elle est sortie en **courant**.* She ran out.
*Ne **courez** pas dans le couloir.* Don't run in the corridor.
*J'**ai couru** jusqu'à l'école.* I ran all the way to school.

---

je/j' = I **tu** = you **il** = he/it **elle** = she/it **on** = we/one **nous** = we **vous** = you **ils/elles** = they

▶ **croire** (to believe)

PRESENT

je	crois
tu	crois
il/elle/on	croit
nous	croyons
vous	croyez
ils/elles	croient

PRESENT SUBJUNCTIVE

je	croie
tu	croies
il/elle/on	croie
nous	croyions
vous	croyiez
ils/elles	croient

PERFECT

j'	ai cru
tu	as cru
il/elle/on	a cru
nous	avons cru
vous	avez cru
ils/elles	ont cru

IMPERFECT

je	croyais
tu	croyais
il/elle/on	croyait
nous	croyions
vous	croyiez
ils/elles	croyaient

FUTURE

je	croirai
tu	croiras
il/elle/on	croira
nous	croirons
vous	croirez
ils/elles	croiront

CONDITIONAL

je	croirais
tu	croirais
il/elle/on	croirait
nous	croirions
vous	croiriez
ils/elles	croiraient

IMPERATIVE

crois / croyons / croyez

PAST PARTICIPLE

cru

PRESENT PARTICIPLE

croyant

EXAMPLE PHRASES

*Je ne te **crois** pas.* I don't believe you.
*J'**ai cru** que tu n'allais pas venir.* I thought you weren't going to come.
*Elle **croyait** encore au père Noël.* She still believed in Santa.

---

je/j' = I **tu** = you **il** = he/it **elle** = she/it **on** = we/one **nous** = we **vous** = you **ils/elles** = they

▶ **devoir** (to have to; to owe)

PRESENT

je	dois
tu	dois
il/elle/on	doit
nous	devons
vous	devez
ils/elles	doivent

PRESENT SUBJUNCTIVE

je	doive
tu	doives
il/elle/on	doive
nous	devions
vous	deviez
ils/elles	doivent

PERFECT

j'	ai dû
tu	as dû
il/elle/on	a dû
nous	avons dû
vous	avez dû
ils/elles	ont dû

IMPERFECT

je	devais
tu	devais
il/elle/on	devait
nous	devions
vous	deviez
ils/elles	devaient

FUTURE

je	devrai
tu	devras
il/elle/on	devra
nous	devrons
vous	devrez
ils/elles	devront

CONDITIONAL

je	devrais
tu	devrais
il/elle/on	devrait
nous	devrions
vous	devriez
ils/elles	devraient

IMPERATIVE

dois / devons / devez

PAST PARTICIPLE

dû (**NB**: due, dus, dues)

PRESENT PARTICIPLE

devant

EXAMPLE PHRASES

*Je **dois** aller faire les courses ce matin.* I have to do the shopping this morning.
*À quelle heure est-ce que tu **dois** partir?* What time do you have to leave?
*Il **a dû** faire ses devoirs hier soir.* He had to do his homework last night.
*Il **devait** prendre le train pour aller travailler.* He had to go to work by train.

je/j' = I   **tu** = you   **il** = he/it   **elle** = she/it   **on** = we/one   **nous** = we   **vous** = you   **ils/elles** = they

▶ **dire** (to say)

PRESENT

je	dis
tu	dis
il/elle/on	dit
nous	disons
vous	dites
ils/elles	disent

PRESENT SUBJUNCTIVE

je	dise
tu	dises
il/elle/on	dise
nous	disions
vous	disiez
ils/elles	disent

PERFECT

j'	ai dit
tu	as dit
il/elle/on	a dit
nous	avons dit
vous	avez dit
ils/elles	ont dit

IMPERFECT

je	disais
tu	disais
il/elle/on	disait
nous	disions
vous	disiez
ils/elles	disaient

FUTURE

je	dirai
tu	diras
il/elle/on	dira
nous	dirons
vous	direz
ils/elles	diront

CONDITIONAL

je	dirais
tu	dirais
il/elle/on	dirait
nous	dirions
vous	diriez
ils/elles	diraient

IMPERATIVE

dis / disons / dites

PAST PARTICIPLE

dit

PRESENT PARTICIPLE

disant

EXAMPLE PHRASES

*Qu'est-ce qu'elle **dit**?* What is she saying?
*"Bonjour!", **a-t-il dit**.* "Hello!" he said.
*Ils m'**ont dit** que le film était nul.* They told me that the film was rubbish.
*Comment ça **se dit** en anglais?* How do you say that in English?

---

je/j' = I **tu** = you **il** = he/it **elle** = she/it **on** = we/one **nous** = we **vous** = you **ils/elles** = they

▶ **donner** (to give)

PRESENT

je	donne
tu	donnes
il/elle/on	donne
nous	donnons
vous	donnez
ils/elles	donnent

PRESENT SUBJUNCTIVE

je	donne
tu	donnes
il/elle/on	donne
nous	donnions
vous	donniez
ils/elles	donnent

PERFECT

j'	ai donné
tu	as donné
il/elle/on	a donné
nous	avons donné
vous	avez donné
ils/elles	ont donné

IMPERFECT

je	donnais
tu	donnais
il/elle/on	donnait
nous	donnions
vous	donniez
ils/elles	donnaient

FUTURE

je	donnerai
tu	donneras
il/elle/on	donnera
nous	donnerons
vous	donnerez
ils/elles	donneront

CONDITIONAL

je	donnerais
tu	donnerais
il/elle/on	donnerait
nous	donnerions
vous	donneriez
ils/elles	donneraient

IMPERATIVE

donne / donnons / donnez

PAST PARTICIPLE

donné

PRESENT PARTICIPLE

donnant

EXAMPLE PHRASES

Donne-*moi la main.* Give me your hand.
*Est-ce que je t'**ai donné** mon adresse?* Did I give you my address?
*L'appartement **donne** sur la place.* The flat overlooks the square.

---

je/j' = I **tu** = you **il** = he/it **elle** = she/it **on** = we/one **nous** = we **vous** = you **ils/elles** = they

▶ **écrire** (to write)

PRESENT

j'	écris
tu	écris
il/elle/on	écrit
nous	écrivons
vous	écrivez
ils/elles	écrivent

PRESENT SUBJUNCTIVE

j'	écrive
tu	écrives
il/elle/on	écrive
nous	écrivions
vous	écriviez
ils/elles	écrivent

PERFECT

j'	ai écrit
tu	as écrit
il/elle/on	a écrit
nous	avons écrit
vous	avez écrit
ils/elles	ont écrit

IMPERFECT

j'	écrivais
tu	écrivais
il/elle/on	écrivait
nous	écrivions
vous	écriviez
ils/elles	écrivaient

FUTURE

j'	écrirai
tu	écriras
il/elle/on	écrira
nous	écrirons
vous	écrirez
ils/elles	écriront

CONDITIONAL

j'	écrirais
tu	écrirais
il/elle/on	écrirait
nous	écririons
vous	écririez
ils/elles	écriraient

IMPERATIVE

écris / écrivons / écrivez

PAST PARTICIPLE

écrit

PRESENT PARTICIPLE

écrivant

EXAMPLE PHRASES

*Tu **as écrit** à ta correspondante récemment?* Have you written to your penfriend lately?
*Elle **écrit** des romans.* She writes novels.
*Comment ça **s'écrit**, "brouillard"?* How do you spell "brouillard"?

je/j' = I **tu** = you **il** = he/it **elle** = she/it **on** = we/one **nous** = we **vous** = you **ils/elles** = they

▶ être (to be)

PRESENT		PRESENT SUBJUNCTIVE	
je	suis	je	sois
tu	es	tu	sois
il/elle/on	est	il/elle/on	soit
nous	sommes	nous	soyons
vous	êtes	vous	soyez
ils/elles	sont	ils/elles	soient

PERFECT		IMPERFECT	
j'	ai été	j'	étais
tu	as été	tu	étais
il/elle/on	a été	il/elle/on	était
nous	avons été	nous	étions
vous	avez été	vous	étiez
ils/elles	ont été	ils/elles	étaient

FUTURE		CONDITIONAL	
je	serai	je	serais
tu	seras	tu	serais
il/elle/on	sera	il/elle/on	serait
nous	serons	nous	serions
vous	serez	vous	seriez
ils/elles	seront	ils/elles	seraient

IMPERATIVE

sois / soyons / soyez

PAST PARTICIPLE

été

PRESENT PARTICIPLE

étant

EXAMPLE PHRASES

*Mon père **est** professeur.* My father's a teacher.
*Quelle heure **est**-il? – Il **est** dix heures.* What time is it? – It's 10 o'clock.
*Ils ne **sont** pas encore arrivés.* They haven't arrived yet.

---

je/j' = I **tu** = you **il** = he/it **elle** = she/it **on** = we/one **nous** = we **vous** = you **ils/elles** = they

▶ **faire** (to do; to make)

PRESENT

je	fais
tu	fais
il/elle/on	fait
nous	faisons
vous	faites
ils/elles	font

PRESENT SUBJUNCTIVE

je	fasse
tu	fasses
il/elle/on	fasse
nous	fassions
vous	fassiez
ils/elles	fassent

PERFECT

j'	ai fait
tu	as fait
il/elle/on	a fait
nous	avons fait
vous	avez fait
ils/elles	ont fait

IMPERFECT

je	faisais
tu	faisais
il/elle/on	faisait
nous	faisions
vous	faisiez
ils/elles	faisaient

FUTURE

je	ferai
tu	feras
il/elle/on	fera
nous	ferons
vous	ferez
ils/elles	feront

CONDITIONAL

je	ferais
tu	ferais
il/elle/on	ferait
nous	ferions
vous	feriez
ils/elles	feraient

IMPERATIVE

fais / faisons / faites

PAST PARTICIPLE

fait

PRESENT PARTICIPLE

faisant

EXAMPLE PHRASES

*Qu'est-ce que tu **fais**?* What are you doing?
*Qu'est-ce qu'il **a fait**?* What has he done? *or* What did he do?
*J'**ai fait** un gâteau.* I've made a cake *or* I made a cake.
*Il **s'est fait** couper les cheveux.* He's had his hair cut.

---

je/j' = I **tu** = you **il** = he/it **elle** = she/it **on** = we/one **nous** = we **vous** = you **ils/elles** = they

▶ **falloir** (to be necessary)

PRESENT

   il   faut

PRESENT SUBJUNCTIVE

   il   faille

PERFECT

   il a fallu

IMPERFECT

   il   fallait

FUTURE

   il faudra

CONDITIONAL

   il   faudrait

IMPERATIVE

not used

PAST PARTICIPLE

   fallu

PRESENT PARTICIPLE

not used

EXAMPLE PHRASES

*Il **faut** se dépêcher!* We have to hurry up!
*Il me **fallait** de l'argent.* I needed money.
*Il **faudra** que tu sois là à 8 heures.* You'll have to be there at 8.

---

je/j' = I **tu** = you **il** = he/it **elle** = she/it **on** = we/one **nous** = we **vous** = you **ils/elles** = they

▶ **finir** (to finish)

PRESENT

je	finis
tu	finis
il/elle/on	finit
nous	finissons
vous	finissez
ils/elles	finissent

PRESENT SUBJUNCTIVE

je	finisse
tu	finisses
il/elle/on	finisse
nous	finissions
vous	finissiez
ils/elles	finissent

PERFECT

j'	ai fini
tu	as fini
il/elle/on	a fini
nous	avons fini
vous	avez fini
ils/elles	ont fini

IMPERFECT

je	finissais
tu	finissais
il/elle/on	finissait
nous	finissions
vous	finissiez
ils/elles	finissaient

FUTURE

je	finirai
tu	finiras
il/elle/on	finira
nous	finirons
vous	finirez
ils/elles	finiront

CONDITIONAL

je	finirais
tu	finirais
il/elle/on	finirait
nous	finirions
vous	finiriez
ils/elles	finiraient

IMPERATIVE

finis / finissons / finissez

PAST PARTICIPLE

fini

PRESENT PARTICIPLE

finissant

EXAMPLE PHRASES

***Finis** ta soupe!* Finish your soup!
*J'ai **fini**!* I've finished!
*Je **finirai** mes devoirs demain.* I'll finish my homework tomorrow.

▶ **se laver** (to wash oneself)

PRESENT

je	me lave
tu	te laves
il/elle/on	se lave
nous	nous lavons
vous	vous lavez
ils/elles	se lavent

PRESENT SUBJUNCTIVE

je	me lave
tu	te laves
il/elle/on	se lave
nous	nous lavions
vous	vous laviez
ils/elles	se lavent

PERFECT

je	me suis lavé(e)
tu	t'es lavé(e)
il/elle/on	s'est lavé(e)
nous	nous sommes lavé(e)s
vous	vous êtes lavé(e)(s)
ils/elles	se sont lavé(e)s

IMPERFECT

je	me lavais
tu	te lavais
il/elle/on	se lavait
nous	nous lavions
vous	vous laviez
ils/elles	se lavient

FUTURE

je	me laverai
tu	te laveras
il/elle/on	se lavera
nous	nous laverons
vous	vous laverez
ils/elles	se laveront

CONDITIONAL

je	me laverais
tu	te laverais
il/elle/on	se laverait
nous	nous laverions
vous	vous laveriez
ils/elles	se laveraient

IMPERATIVE

lave-toi / lavons-nous / lavez-vous

PAST PARTICIPLE

lavé(e)

PRESENT PARTICIPLE

se lavant

EXAMPLE PHRASES

Lave-toi vite, tu vas être en retard. Have a quick wash, you're going to be late.
Lavez-vous les mains avant de vous mettre à table. Wash your hands before you sit at the table.
Nous nous sommes **lavé** les dents puis nous sommes allés nous coucher. We cleaned our teeth and went to bed.

---

je/j′ = I **tu** = you **il** = he/it **elle** = she/it **on** = we/one **nous** = we **vous** = you **ils/elles** = they

▶ **mettre** (to put)

PRESENT		PRESENT SUBJUNCTIVE	
je	mets	je	mette
tu	mets	tu	mettes
il/elle/on	met	il/elle/on	mette
nous	mettons	nous	mettions
vous	mettez	vous	mettiez
ils/elles	mettent	ils/elles	mettent

PERFECT		IMPERFECT	
j'	ai mis	je	mettais
tu	as mis	tu	mettais
il/elle/on	a mis	il/elle/on	mettait
nous	avons mis	nous	mettions
vous	avez mis	vous	mettiez
ils/elles	ont mis	ils/elles	mettaient

FUTURE		CONDITIONAL	
je	mettrai	je	mettrais
tu	mettras	tu	mettrais
il/elle/on	mettra	il/elle/on	mettrait
nous	mettrons	nous	mettrions
vous	mettrez	vous	mettriez
ils/elles	mettront	ils/elles	mettraient

IMPERATIVE

mets / mettons / mettez

PRESENT PARTICIPLE

mettant

PAST PARTICIPLE

mis

EXAMPLE PHRASES

Mets ton manteau! Put your coat on!
Où est-ce que tu as mis les clés? Where have you put the keys?
J'ai mis le livre sur la table. I put the book on the table.
Elle s'est mise à pleurer. She started crying.

je/j' = I **tu** = you **il** = he/it **elle** = she/it **on** = we/one **nous** = we **vous** = you **ils/elles** = they

▶ **mourir** (to die)

PRESENT

je	meurs
tu	meurs
il/elle/on	meurt
nous	mourons
vous	mourez
ils/elles	meurent

PRESENT SUBJUNCTIVE

je	meure
tu	meures
il/elle/on	meure
nous	mourions
vous	mouriez
ils/elles	meurent

PERFECT

je	suis mort(e)
tu	es mort(e)
il/elle/on	est mort(e)
nous	sommes mort(e)s
vous	êtes mort(e)(s)
ils/elles	sont mort(e)s

IMPERFECT

je	mourais
tu	mourais
il/elle/on	mourait
nous	mourions
vous	mouriez
ils/elles	mouraient

FUTURE

je	mourrai
tu	mourras
il/elle/on	mourra
nous	mourrons
vous	mourrez
ils/elles	mourront

CONDITIONAL

je	mourrais
tu	mourrais
il/elle/on	mourrait
nous	mourrions
vous	mourriez
ils/elles	mourraient

IMPERATIVE

meurs / mourons / mourez

PAST PARTICIPLE

mort

PRESENT PARTICIPLE

mourant

EXAMPLE PHRASES

*Elle **est morte** en 1998*. She died in 1998.
*Ils **sont morts***. They're dead.
*On **meurt** de froid ici!* We're freezing to death in here!

---

je/j' = I **tu** = you **il** = he/it **elle** = she/it **on** = we/one **nous** = we **vous** = you **ils/elles** = they

▶ naître (to be born)

PRESENT

je	nais
tu	nais
il/elle/on	naît
nous	naissons
vous	naissez
ils/elles	naissent

PRESENT SUBJUNCTIVE

je	naisse
tu	naisses
il/elle/on	naisse
nous	naissions
vous	naissiez
ils/elles	naissent

PERFECT

je	suis né(e)
tu	es né(e)
il/elle/on	est né(e)
nous	sommes né(e)s
vous	êtes né(e)(s)
ils/elles	sont né(e)s

IMPERFECT

je	naissais
tu	naissais
il/elle/on	naissait
nous	naissions
vous	naissiez
ils/elles	naissaient

FUTURE

je	naîtrai
tu	naîtras
il/elle/on	naîtra
nous	naîtrons
vous	naîtrez
ils/elles	naîtront

CONDITIONAL

je	naîtrais
tu	naîtrais
il/elle/on	naîtrait
nous	naîtrions
vous	naîtriez
ils/elles	naîtraient

IMPERATIVE

nais / naissons / naissez

PAST PARTICIPLE

né

PRESENT PARTICIPLE

naissant

EXAMPLE PHRASES

*Je **suis née** le 12 février.* I was born on 12 February.
*Le bébé de Delphine **naîtra** en mars.* Delphine is going to have a baby in March.
*Quand est-ce que tu **es né**?* When were you born?

---

je/j' = I   **tu** = you   **il** = he/it   **elle** = she/it   **on** = we/one   **nous** = we   **vous** = you   **ils/elles** = they

▶ **ouvrir** (to open)

PRESENT

j'	ouvre
tu	ouvres
il/elle/on	ouvre
nous	ouvrons
vous	ouvrez
ils/elles	ouvrent

PRESENT SUBJUNCTIVE

j'	ouvre
tu	ouvres
il/elle/on	ouvre
nous	ouvrions
vous	ouvriez
ils/elles	ouvrent

PERFECT

j'	ai ouvert
tu	as ouvert
il/elle/on	a ouvert
nous	avons ouvert
vous	avez ouvert
ils/elles	ont ouvert

IMPERFECT

j'	ouvrais
tu	ouvrais
il/elle/on	ouvrait
nous	ouvrions
vous	ouvriez
ils/elles	ouvraient

FUTURE

j'	ouvrirai
tu	ouvriras
il/elle/on	ouvrira
nous	ouvrirons
vous	ouvrirez
ils/elles	ouvriront

CONDITIONAL

j'	ouvrirais
tu	ouvrirais
il/elle/on	ouvrirait
nous	ouvririons
vous	ouvririez
ils/elles	ouvriraient

IMPERATIVE

ouvre / ouvrons / ouvrez

PAST PARTICIPLE

ouvert

PRESENT PARTICIPLE

ouvrant

EXAMPLE PHRASES

*Elle **a ouvert** la porte.* She opened the door.
*Est-ce que tu pourrais **ouvrir** la fenêtre?* Could you open the window?
*Je me suis coupé en **ouvrant** une boîte de conserve.* I cut myself opening a tin.
*La porte **s'est ouverte**.* The door opened.

---

je/j' = I **tu** = you **il** = he/it **elle** = she/it **on** = we/one **nous** = we **vous** = you **ils/elles** = they

▶ **pouvoir** (to be able)

PRESENT

je	peux
tu	peux
il/elle/on	peut
nous	pouvons
vous	pouvez
ils/elles	peuvent

PRESENT SUBJUNCTIVE

je	puisse
tu	puisses
il/elle/on	puisse
nous	puissions
vous	puissiez
ils/elles	puissent

PERFECT

j'	ai pu
tu	as pu
il/elle/on	a pu
nous	avons pu
vous	avez pu
ils/elles	ont pu

IMPERFECT

je	pouvais
tu	pouvais
il/elle/on	pouvait
nous	pouvions
vous	pouviez
ils/elles	pouvaient

FUTURE

je	pourrai
tu	pourras
il/elle/on	pourra
nous	pourrons
vous	pourrez
ils/elles	pourront

CONDITIONAL

je	pourrais
tu	pourrais
il/elle/on	pourrait
nous	pourrions
vous	pourriez
ils/elles	pourraient

IMPERATIVE

not used

PAST PARTICIPLE

pu

PRESENT PARTICIPLE

pouvant

EXAMPLE PHRASES

*Je **peux** t'aider, si tu veux.* I can help you if you like.
*J'ai fait tout ce que j'**ai pu**.* I did all I could.
*Je ne **pourrai** pas venir samedi.* I won't be able to come on Saturday.

---

je/j' = I   **tu** = you   **il** = he/it   **elle** = she/it   **on** = we/one   **nous** = we   **vous** = you   **ils/elles** = they

▶ **prendre** (to take)

PRESENT

je	prends
tu	prends
il/elle/on	prend
nous	prenons
vous	prenez
ils/elles	prennent

PRESENT SUBJUNCTIVE

je	prenne
tu	prennes
il/elle/on	prenne
nous	prenions
vous	preniez
ils/elles	prennent

PERFECT

j'	ai pris
tu	as pris
il/elle/on	a pris
nous	avons pris
vous	avez pris
ils/elles	ont pris

IMPERFECT

je	prenais
tu	prenais
il/elle/on	prenait
nous	prenions
vous	preniez
ils/elles	prenaient

FUTURE

je	prendrai
tu	prendras
il/elle/on	prendra
nous	prendrons
vous	prendrez
ils/elles	prendront

CONDITIONAL

je	prendrais
tu	prendrais
il/elle/on	prendrait
nous	prendrions
vous	prendriez
ils/elles	prendraient

IMPERATIVE

prends / prenons / prenez

PAST PARTICIPLE

pris

PRESENT PARTICIPLE

prenant

EXAMPLE PHRASES

*J'**ai pris** plein de photos.* I took lots of pictures.
*N'oublie pas de **prendre** ton passeport.* Don't forget to take your passport.
*Il **prendra** le train de 8h20.* He'll take the 8.20 train.
*Pour qui est-ce qu'il **se prend**?* Who does he think he is?

je/j' = I **tu** = you **il** = he/it **elle** = she/it **on** = we/one **nous** = we **vous** = you **ils/elles** = they

▶ **savoir** (to know)

PRESENT

je	sais
tu	sais
il/elle/on	sait
nous	savons
vous	savez
ils/elles	savent

PRESENT SUBJUNCTIVE

je	sache
tu	saches
il/elle/on	sache
nous	sachions
vous	sachiez
ils/elles	sachent

PERFECT

j'	ai su
tu	as su
il/elle/on	a su
nous	avons su
vous	avez su
ils/elles	ont su

IMPERFECT

je	savais
tu	savais
il/elle/on	savait
nous	savions
vous	saviez
ils/elles	savaient

FUTURE

je	saurai
tu	sauras
il/elle/on	saura
nous	saurons
vous	saurez
ils/elles	sauront

CONDITIONAL

je	saurais
tu	saurais
il/elle/on	saurait
nous	saurions
vous	sauriez
ils/elles	sauraient

IMPERATIVE

sache / sachons / sachez

PAST PARTICIPLE

su

PRESENT PARTICIPLE

sachant

EXAMPLE PHRASES

*Tu **sais** ce que tu vas faire l'année prochaine?* Do you know what you're doing next year?
*Je ne **sais** pas.* I don't know.
*Elle ne **sait** pas nager.* She can't swim.
*Tu **savais** que son père était pakistanais?* Did you know her father was Pakistani?

---

je/j' = I **tu** = you **il** = he/it **elle** = she/it **on** = we/one **nous** = we **vous** = you **ils/elles** = they

▶ **sortir** (to go out)

PRESENT

je	sors
tu	sors
il/elle/on	sort
nous	sortons
vous	sortez
ils/elles	sortent

PRESENT SUBJUNCTIVE

je	sorte
tu	sortes
il/elle/on	sorte
nous	sortions
vous	sortiez
ils/elles	sortent

PERFECT

je	suis sorti(e)
tu	es sorti(e)
il/elle/on	est sorti(e)
nous	sommes sorti(e)s
vous	êtes sorti(e)(s)
ils/elles	sont sorti(e)s

IMPERFECT

je	sortais
tu	sortais
il/elle/on	sortait
nous	sortions
vous	sortiez
ils/elles	sortaient

FUTURE

je	sortirai
tu	sortiras
il/elle/on	sortira
nous	sortirons
vous	sortirez
ils/elles	sortiront

CONDITIONAL

je	sortirais
tu	sortirais
il/elle/on	sortirait
nous	sortirions
vous	sortiriez
ils/elles	sortiraient

IMPERATIVE

sors / sortons / sortez

PAST PARTICIPLE

sorti

PRESENT PARTICIPLE

sortant

EXAMPLE PHRASES

*Je ne **suis** pas **sortie** ce week-end.* I didn't go out this weekend.
*Aurélie **sort** avec Bruno.* Aurélie is going out with Bruno.
*Elle **est sortie** de l'hôpital hier.* She came out of hospital yesterday.
*Je n'**ai** pas **sorti** le chien parce qu'il pleuvait.* I didn't take the dog out for a walk because it was raining.

[i] Note that **sortir** takes **avoir** in the perfect tense when it is used with a

je/j' = I **tu** = you **il** = he/it **elle** = she/it **on** = we/one **nous** = we **vous** = you **ils/elles** = they

▶ **tenir** (to hold)

PRESENT		PRESENT SUBJUNCTIVE	
je	tiens	je	tienne
tu	tiens	tu	tiennes
il/elle/on	tient	il/elle/on	tienne
nous	tenons	nous	tenions
vous	tenez	vous	teniez
ils/elles	tiennent	ils/elles	tiennent

PERFECT		IMPERFECT	
j'	ai tenu	je	tenais
tu	as tenu	tu	tenais
il/elle/on	a tenu	il/elle/on	tenait
nous	avons tenu	nous	tenions
vous	avez tenu	vous	teniez
ils/elles	ont tenu	ils/elles	tenaient

FUTURE		CONDITIONAL	
je	tiendrai	je	tiendrais
tu	tiendras	tu	tiendrais
il/elle/on	tiendra	il/elle/on	tiendrait
nous	tiendrons	nous	tiendrions
vous	tiendrez	vous	tiendriez
ils/elles	tiendront	ils/elles	tiendraient

IMPERATIVE

tiens / tenons / tenez

PAST PARTICIPLE

tenu

PRESENT PARTICIPLE

tenant

EXAMPLE PHRASES

Tiens-*moi la main*. Hold my hand.
Elle **tenait** *beaucoup à son chat*. She was really attached to her cat.
Tiens, *prends mon stylo*. Here, have my pen.
Tiens-toi *droit!* Sit up straight!

▶ **venir** (to come)

PRESENT

je	viens
tu	viens
il/elle/on	vient
nous	venons
vous	venez
ils/elles	viennent

PRESENT SUBJUNCTIVE

je	vienne
tu	viennes
il/elle/on	vienne
nous	venions
vous	veniez
ils/elles	viennent

PERFECT

je	suis venu(e)
tu	es venu(e)
il/elle/on	est venu(e)
nous	sommes venu(e)s
vous	êtes venu(e)(s)
ils/elles	sont venu(e)s

IMPERFECT

je	venais
tu	venais
il/elle/on	venait
nous	venions
vous	veniez
ils/elles	venaient

FUTURE

je	viendrai
tu	viendras
il/elle/on	viendra
nous	viendrons
vous	viendrez
ils/elles	viendront

CONDITIONAL

je	viendrais
tu	viendrais
il/elle/on	viendrait
nous	viendrions
vous	viendriez
ils/elles	viendraient

IMPERATIVE

viens / venons / venez

PAST PARTICIPLE

venu

PRESENT PARTICIPLE

venant

EXAMPLE PHRASES

*Elle ne **viendra** pas cette année.* She won't be coming this year.
*Fatou et Malik **viennent** du Sénégal.* Fatou and Malik come from Senegal.
*Je **viens** de manger.* I've just eaten.

---

je/j' = I   **tu** = you   **il** = he/it   **elle** = she/it   **on** = we/one   **nous** = we   **vous** = you   **ils/elles** = they

▶ **vivre** (to live)

PRESENT		PRESENT SUBJUNCTIVE	
je	vis	je	vive
tu	vis	tu	vives
il/elle/on	vit	il/elle/on	vive
nous	vivons	nous	vivions
vous	vivez	vous	viviez
ils/elles	vivent	ils/elles	vivent

PERFECT		IMPERFECT	
j'	ai vécu	je	vivais
tu	as vécu	tu	vivais
il/elle/on	a vécu	il/elle/on	vivait
nous	avons vécu	nous	vivions
vous	avez vécu	vous	viviez
ils/elles	ont vécu	ils/elles	vivaient

FUTURE		CONDITIONAL	
je	vivrai	je	vivrais
tu	vivras	tu	vivrais
il/elle/on	vivra	il/elle/on	vivrait
nous	vivrons	nous	vivrions
vous	vivrez	vous	vivriez
ils/elles	vivront	ils/elles	vivraient

IMPERATIVE

vis / vivons / vivez

PAST PARTICIPLE

vécu

PRESENT PARTICIPLE

vivant

EXAMPLE PHRASES

*Ma sœur **vit** en Espagne.* My sister lives in Spain.
*Il **a vécu** dix ans à Lyon.* He lived in Lyons for 10 years.
*Les gorilles **vivent** surtout dans la forêt.* Gorillas mostly live in the forest.

▶ **voir** (to see)

PRESENT

je	vois
tu	vois
il/elle/on	voit
nous	voyons
vous	voyez
ils/elles	voient

PRESENT SUBJUNCTIVE

je	voie
tu	voies
il/elle/on	voie
nous	voyions
vous	voyiez
ils/elles	voient

PERFECT

j'	ai vu
tu	as vu
il/elle/on	a vu
nous	avons vu
vous	avez vu
ils/elles	ont vu

IMPERFECT

je	voyais
tu	voyais
il/elle/on	voyait
nous	voyions
vous	voyiez
ils/elles	voyaient

FUTURE

je	verrai
tu	verras
il/elle/on	verra
nous	verrons
vous	verrez
ils/elles	verront

CONDITIONAL

je	verrais
tu	verrais
il/elle/on	verrait
nous	verrions
vous	verriez
ils/elles	verraient

IMPERATIVE

vois / voyons / voyez

PAST PARTICIPLE

vu

PRESENT PARTICIPLE

voyant

EXAMPLE PHRASES

*Venez me **voir** quand vous serez à Paris.* Come and see me when you're in Paris.
*Je ne **vois** rien sans mes lunettes.* I can't see anything without my glasses.
*Est-ce que tu l'**as vu**?* Did you see him? or Have you seen him?
*Est-ce que cette tache **se voit**?* Does that stain show?

---

je/j' = I **tu** = you **il** = he/it **elle** = she/it **on** = we/one **nous** = we **vous** = you **ils/elles** = they

▶ **vouloir** (to want)

PRESENT

je	veux
tu	veux
il/elle/on	veut
nous	voulons
vous	voulez
ils/elles	veulent

PRESENT SUBJUNCTIVE

je	veuille
tu	veuilles
il/elle/on	veuille
nous	voulions
vous	vouliez
ils/elles	veuillent

PERFECT

j'	ai voulu
tu	as voulu
il/elle/on	a voulu
nous	avons voulu
vous	avez voulu
ils/elles	ont voulu

IMPERFECT

je	voulais
tu	voulais
il/elle/on	voulait
nous	voulions
vous	vouliez
ils/elles	voulaient

FUTURE

je	voudrai
tu	voudras
il/elle/on	voudra
nous	voudrons
vous	voudrez
ils/elles	voudront

CONDITIONAL

je	voudrais
tu	voudrais
il/elle/on	voudrait
nous	voudrions
vous	voudriez
ils/elles	voudraient

IMPERATIVE

veuille / veuillons / veuillez

PAST PARTICIPLE

voulu

PRESENT PARTICIPLE

voulant

EXAMPLE PHRASES

*Elle **veut** un vélo pour Noël.* She wants a bike for Christmas.
*Ils **voulaient** aller au cinéma.* They wanted to go to the cinema.
*Tu **voudrais** une tasse de thé?* Would you like a cup of tea?

---

je/j' = I   **tu** = you   **il** = he/it   **elle** = she/it   **on** = we/one   **nous** = we   **vous** = you   **ils/elles** = they